2010 TAX LEGISLATION

Tax Relief, Unemployment Insurance Reauthorization, and Job Creation Act of 2010 RIC Modernization Act of 2010 and Other Recent Tax Acts

Law, Explanation and Analysis

CCH Editorial Staff Publication

®.CCH

a Wolters Kluwer business

This publication is designed to provide accurate and authoritative information in regard to the subject matter covered. It is sold with the understanding that the publisher is not engaged in rendering legal, accounting, or other professional service. If legal advice or other expert assistance is required, the services of a competent professional person should be sought.

ISBN 978-0-8080-2611-2

4025 W. Peterson Ave.
Chicago, IL 60646-6085
1 800 248 3248
www.CCHGroup.com

No claim is made to original government works; however, within this Product or Publication, the following are subject to CCH's copyright: (1) the gathering, compilation, and arrangement of such government materials; (2) the magnetic translation and digital conversion of data, if applicable; (3) the historical, statutory and other notes and references; and (4) the commentary and other materials.

Printed in the United States of America

Tax Relief and RIC Modernization Tax Acts of 2010

With just weeks before the scheduled sunset of numerous taxpayer-friendly tax rates and incentives, generally referred to as the "Bush Tax Cuts," Congress passed the Tax Relief, Unemployment Insurance Reauthorization, and Job Creation Act of 2010 (Tax Relief Act of 2010) (P.L. 111-312), which extends these popular provisions for two years. In addition to the extension of the "Bush Tax Cuts," the new law extends many other tax provisions that expired at the end of 2009, business incentives and energy-related tax provisions in what has become an annual endeavor. In all, the Tax Relief Act of 2010 carries a price tag in excess of $850 billion and impacts hundreds of Internal Revenue Code provisions.

The Tax Relief Act of 2010 extends lower marginal individual income tax rates, marriage penalty relief, lower capital gains tax rates, as well as more that 50 other tax benefits put into place pursuant to the Economic Growth and Tax Relief Reconciliation Act of 2001 (EGTRRA) and the Jobs and Growth Tax Relief Reconciliation Act of 2003 (JGTRRA). In order to comply with budget requirements, the provisions in EGTRRA were subject to a sunset provision. Pursuant to the sunset provision, the changes made by EGTRRA would no longer apply after December 31, 2010. The provisions contained in JGTRRA were subject to similar sunset rules.

When EGTRRA and JGTRRA were enacted with these sunset provisions, few members of Congress expected those sunsets to ever take place. Heading into the 2010 mid-term elections, however, it appeared that was exactly what was going to happen. An extension of these provisions was far from guaranteed. However, facing a sluggish economy and job market, Congress and the White House reached a compromise to prevent what was termed as a tax increase for Americans. Despite an initial backlash from lawmakers in both parties, the Senate passed the Tax Relief Act of 2010 on December 15, 2010. The House subsequently passed the measure on December 16, 2010. President Obama signed the legislation into law on December 17, 2010.

The new law temporarily extends all the Bush tax cuts for two years, reinstates the estate and gift tax (although at higher rates and with higher exclusion amounts than if the sunset had occurred), and extends many other expired tax benefits. In exchange for an extension of tax cuts for all Americans, the Tax Relief Act of 2010 also includes an extension of unemployment insurance benefits and a one-year payroll tax cut. In addition, the new law:

1. Extends the deduction for elementary and secondary school teacher expenses;
2. Extends the deduction for state and local general sales taxes;
3. Extends the deduction for qualified tuition and related expenses;
4. Reinstates the research and development credit;
5. Extends the credit for energy-efficient appliances;
6. Extends the alternatives fuels credit; and
7. More!

While the new law gives taxpayers some certainty in tax planning for the next two years, the provisions are temporary. The Tax Relief Act of 2010 punts the ultimate fate of the Bush-era tax cuts to 2012, a presidential election year.

Regulated Investment Company Modernization Act of 2010

On December 15, Congress passed the Regulated Investment Company Modernization Act of 2010 (H.R. 4337). The legislation simplifies the rules that apply to mutual funds and ensures that small investor groups are treated equally with direct individual investors. The measure has been presented to President Obama for signature and is expected to become law.

About this Work

Since 1913, CCH has provided tax professionals with the most comprehensive, ongoing, practical and timely analysis of the federal tax law. In the spirit of this tradition, CCH is providing practitioners with a single integrated law and explanation of the tax provisions impacted by Tax Relief, Unemployment Insurance Reauthorization, and Job Creation Act of 2010, Regulated Investment Company Modernization Act of 2010 and other recently passed federal tax legislation. As always, CCH Tax and Accounting remains dedicated to responding to the needs of tax professionals in helping them quickly understand and work with these impending law changes.

December 2010

Contributors

Stephen R. Baker, J.D., M.B.T.
LECG
New York, New York

Jeff Bryant, J.D., Ph.D.
Wichita State University
Wichita, Kansas

Carol A. Cantrell, CPA, J.D., CAP®
Briggs & Veselka Co.
Bellaire, Texas

Baruch Cohen, CPA
Deloitte Tax LLP
New York, New York

Dale S. Collinson, J.D.
KPMG LLP
Washington, D.C.

Jasper L. Cummings, Jr., J.D., LL.M.
Alston + Bird LLP
Raleigh, North Carolina

John Everett, Ph.D., CPA
Virginia Commonwealth University
Richmond Virginia

Deanna Flores, J.D.
KPMG
Washington, D.C.

Kristen Garry, J.D., LLM
Shearman & Sterling LLP
Washington, D.C.

Martin R. Goodman, LLB
Schlesinger, Gannon & Lazetera LLP
New York, New York

Michael J. Grace, J.D., CPA
Milbank, Tweed, Hadley & McCloy LLP
Washington, D.C.

Cherie Hennig, Ph.D., CPA
Florida International University
Miami Beach, Florida

Daniel S. Hoops, J.D., LL.M.
Walsh College
Troy, Michigan

**Robert S. Keebler, CPA, MST, AEP
(Distinguished)**
Keebler & Associates, LLP
Green Bay, Wisconsin

Sidney Kess, CPA, J.D., LL.M.
New York, New York

Paul C. Lau, CPA, CMA, CFM
Blackman Kallick
Chicago, Illinois

Gary Maydew, Ph.D., CPA
Iowa State University, Retired
Ames, Iowa

Peter J. Melcher, MBA, J.D., LL.M.
Keebler & Associates, LLP
Green Bay, Wisconsin

Martin Miller, J.D., LL.M.
Miller & Miller, LLP
New York, New York

Paul Murphy, J.D., LL.M.
Deloitte Tax LLP
Boston, Massachusetts

Vincent O'Brien, CPA
Vincent J. O'Brien, CPA, PC
Lynbrook, New York

Sanford J. Schlesinger, J.D.
Schlesinger Gannon & Lazetera LLP
New York, New York

William A. Raabe, Ph.D., CPA
Ohio State University
Bexley, Ohio

Mark R. Solomon, J.D., LL.M.
Walsh College
Troy, Michigan

Michael Schlesinger, J.D., LL.M.
Schlesinger and Sussman
New York, New York

Sandy Soltis, CPA, CFP
Blackman Kallick
Chicago, Illinois

CCH appreciates the contributions of our expert authors for their insight and practical analysis of the new law. The analysis provided by these experts is not intended as or written for use by any taxpayer to avoid penalties. The analysis is not intended as legal advice. Taxpayers should seek advice based on their own particular circumstances from an independent tax advisor.

CCH Tax and Accounting Publishing
EDITORIAL STAFF

¶1 Features of This Publication

This publication is your complete guide to the tax provisions of the *Tax Relief, Unemployment Insurance Reauthorization, and Job Creation Act of 2010* (P.L. 111-312), *Regulated Investment Company Modernization Act of 2010* (H.R. 4337), and the tax provisions of other recently passed legislation.

The core portion of this publication contains the CCH Explanations of this Act. The explanations outline all of the impending tax law changes and what they mean for you and your clients. The explanations also feature practical guidance, examples, planning opportunities and strategies, as well as pitfalls to be avoided.

The publication also contains numerous other features designed to help you locate and understand the changes made by the Act. These features include cross references to related materials, detailed effective dates, and numerous finding tables and indexes. A more detailed description of these features appears below.

HIGHLIGHTS

Highlights are quick summaries of the major tax provisions impacted by the Tax Relief, Unemployment Insurance Reauthorization, and Job Creation Act of 2010 (P.L. 111-312) and Regulated Investment Company Modernization Act of 2010 (H.R. 4337). The Highlights are arranged by taxpayer type and area of interest, such as tax credits and deductions for individuals and businesses, and reporting requirements. At the end of each summary is a paragraph reference to the more detailed CCH Explanation on that topic, giving you an easy way to find the portions of the publication that are of most interest to you. *Highlights begin at ¶5.*

EXPLANATION OF THE SUNSET OF EGTRRA AND JGTRRA

The first chapter of the publication, *The Sunset of EGTRRA and JGTRRA*, explains the EGTRRA and JGTRRA sunset provisions, and how the sunset provisions of these Acts is impacted by the Tax Relief, Unemployment Insurance Reauthorization, and Job Creation Act of 2010. *Explanation of the Sunset of EGTRRA and JGTRRA begins at ¶105.*

TAXPAYERS AFFECTED

The second chapter of the publication, *Taxpayers Affected*, contains a detailed look at how the Tax Relief, Unemployment Insurance Reauthorization, and Job Creation Act of 2010 (P.L. 111-312), affects specific categories of taxpayers. This chapter provides a quick reference for readers who want to know the impact that the laws will have on their clients. *Taxpayers Affected begins at ¶205.*

CCH EXPLANATIONS

CCH Explanations are designed to give you a complete, accessible understanding of the new law. Explanations are arranged by subject for ease of use. There are two main finding devices you can use to locate explanations on a given topic. These are:

- A detailed table of contents at the beginning of the publication listing all of the CCH Explanations of the sunset provisions;
- A table of contents preceding each chapter.

Each CCH Explanation contains special features to aid in your complete understanding of the tax law. These include:

- A summary at the beginning of each explanation providing a brief overview of the impacted provisions;
- A background or prior law discussion that puts the law changes into perspective;
- Editorial aids, including examples, cautions, planning notes, elections, comments, compliance tips, and key rates and figures, that highlight the impact of the sunset provisions;
- Charts and examples illustrating the ramifications of specific law changes;
- Captions at the end of each explanation identifying the Code sections added, amended or repealed, as well as the Act sections containing the changes;
- Cross references to the law and committee report paragraphs related to the explanation;
- A line highlighting the effective date of each law change, marked by an arrow symbol; and
- References at the end of the discussion to related information in the Standard Federal Tax Reporter, Tax Research Consultant and Practical Tax explanations.

The CCH Explanations begin at ¶305.

AMENDED CODE PROVISIONS

Changes to the Internal Revenue Code made by the *Tax Relief, Unemployment Insurance Reauthorization, and Job Creation Act of 2010* (P.L. 111-312), *Regulated Investment Company Modernization Act of 2010* (H.R. 4337), and the tax provisions of other recent legislation appear under the heading "Code Sections Added, Amended or Repealed." Deleted Code material or the text of the Code Section prior to amendment appears in the amendment notes following each amended Code provision. *The text of the Code begins at ¶5001.*

Sections of the Act that do not amend the Internal Revenue Code, appear in full text following "Code Sections Added, Amended or Repealed." *The text of these provisions appears in Act Section order beginning at ¶7005.*

COMMITTEE REPORTS

The Joint Committee on Taxation (JCT), Technical Explanation of the Revenue Provisions Contained in the "Tax Relief, Unemployment Insurance Reauthorization, and Job Creation Act of 2010" (JCX-55-10), explains the intent of Congress regarding the provisions of the Tax Relief, Unemployment Insurance Reauthorization, and Job Creation Act of 2010 (P.L. 111-312). There was no conference report issued for the Tax Relief, Unemployment Insurance Reauthorization, and Job Creation Act of 2010 (P.L. 111-312). The relevant portions of the Technical Explanation from the JCT are included in this section to aid the reader's understanding, but may not be cited as the official House, Senate or Conference Committee Report accompanying the Tax Relief, Unemployment Insurance Reauthorization, and Job Creation Act of 2010 (P.L. 111-312). At the end of each section, references are provided to the corresponding CCH explanations and the Internal Revenue Code provisions. *The pertinent sections of the Technical Explanation relating to the Tax Relief, Unemployment Insurance Reauthorization, and Job Creation Act of 2010 (P.L. 111-312) appear in Act Section order beginning at ¶10,001.*

The Joint Committee on Taxation, Technical Explanation of H.R. 4337, the "Regulated Investment Company Modernization Act of 2010" for Consideration on the Floor of the House of Representatives, September 28, 2010, (JCX-49-10), is reproduced to aid the reader's understanding of the Regulated Investment Company Modernization Act of 2010 (H.R. 4337). It may not be cited as the official Conference Committee Report accompanying the Act. *The pertinent sections of the Technical Explanation relating to the Regulated Investment Company Modernization Act of 2010 appear in Act Section order beginning at ¶15,010.*

EFFECTIVE DATES

A table listing the major effective dates provides a reference bridge between Code Sections and Act Sections. The table also indicates the retroactive or prospective nature of the law. *The effective dates table for the provisions of the Tax Relief, Unemployment Insurance Reauthorization, and Job Creation Act of 2010 (P.L. 111-312) begins at ¶20,001. The effective dates table for the provisions of the Regulated Investment Company Modernization Act of 2010 (H.R. 4337) begins at ¶20,005*

SPECIAL FINDING DEVICES

Other special tables and finding devices in this book include:

- A table cross-referencing Code Sections to the CCH Explanations (*see* ¶25,001);

- A table showing all Code Sections added, amended or repealed (*see* ¶25,005);

- A table showing provisions of other acts that were amended (*see* ¶25,010); and

- A table of Act Sections not amending the Internal Revenue Code (*see* ¶25,015);

- An Act Section table amending Code Section table (*see* ¶25,020); and

CLIENT LETTERS

Sample client letters allow you to quickly communicate the changes made by the *Tax Relief, Unemployment Insurance Reauthorization, and Job Creation Act of 2010* (P.L. 111-312) to clients and customers (*see* ¶27,001).

¶2 Table of Contents

¶1   Features of This Publication
¶5   Highlights

EXPLANATION

¶105   Chapter 1   The Sunset of EGTRRA and JGTRRA
¶205   Chapter 2   Taxpayers Affected
¶305   Chapter 3   Individual Tax Relief
¶405   Chapter 4   Capital Gains, Dividends, and Investment
¶502   Chapter 5   Business Deductions and Credits
¶603   Chapter 6   Corporations, Trusts, and Other Provisions
¶705   Chapter 7   Estate, Gift, and Generation-Skipping Taxes
¶803   Chapter 8   Regulated Investment Companies (RICs)

LAW

¶5001   Code Sections Added, Amended or Repealed
¶7005   Act Sections Not Amending Code Sections

COMMITTEE REPORTS

¶10,001   Tax Relief, Unemployment Insurance Reauthorization, and Job Creation Act of 2010
¶15,001   Regulated Investment Company Modernization Act of 2010

SPECIAL TABLES

Effective Dates Table
¶20,001   Tax Relief, Unemployment Insurance Reauthorization, and Job Creation Act of 2010
¶20,005   Regulated Investment Company Modernization Act of 2010
Other Tables
¶25,001   Code Section to Explanation Table
¶25,005   Code Sections Added, Amended or Repealed
¶25,010   Table of Amendments to Other Acts
¶25,015   Table of Act Sections Not Amending Internal Revenue Code Sections
¶25,020   Act Sections Amending Code Sections

APPENDICES

¶27,001   Client Letters

¶3 Detailed Table of Contents

CHAPTER 1. THE SUNSET OF EGTRRA AND JGTRRA

¶105   Overview

CHAPTER 2. TAXPAYERS AFFECTED

THE TAX RELIEF, UNEMPLOYMENT INSURANCE REAUTHORIZATION, AND JOB CREATION ACT OF 2010

¶205   Overview

¶208   Effect on Individuals Generally

¶210   Effect on Joint Filers

¶211   Effect on Homeowners

¶212   Effect on Lower-Income Taxpayers

¶214   Effect on High-Income Taxpayers

¶215   Effect on Exempt Organizations

¶216   Effect on Investors

¶217   Effect on Tax-Exempt Bond Investors

¶218   Effect on Parents

¶220   Effect on Students

¶222   Effect on Businesses Generally

¶224   Effect on Corporations

¶226   Effect on S Corporations

¶228   Effect on Foreign Corporations

¶230   Effect on International Business

¶232   Effect on Partnerships and LLCs

¶236   Effect on Personal Holding Companies

¶240   Effect on Small Business

¶245   Effect on Businesses in Puerto Rico

¶250   Effect on Regulated Investment Companies

¶255   Effect on Estates Generally

¶260   Effect on Trusts

¶265   Effect on Commuters

¶267   Effect on Film and Television Industry

¶270   Effect on Government Entities

CHAPTER 3. INDIVIDUAL TAX RELIEF

INCOME AND PAYROLL TAXES

¶305   Individual, Estate and Trust Tax Rates

¶310   15-Percent Tax Rate Bracket for Joint Filers

¶312   Payroll Tax Cut

DEDUCTIONS

¶315   Standard Deduction for Joint Filers

¶320   Overall Limitation on Itemized Deductions for Higher-Income Individuals

¶325   Phaseout of Personal Exemptions

¶326   Deduction of State and Local General Sales Taxes

¶327   Teachers' Classroom Expense Deduction

¶328   Mortgage Insurance Premiums

EDUCATION INCENTIVES

¶330   Coverdell Education Savings Accounts

¶335   Educational Assistance Programs

¶340   Federal Scholarships With Obligatory Service Requirements

¶345   Student Loan Interest Deduction

¶350   Deduction for Qualified Tuition and Related Expenses

CHARITABLE CONTRIBUTIONS

¶352   Qualified Charitable Distributions from IRAs

¶353   Charitable Contribution of Real Property for Conservation Purposes Enhanced Deduction

TAX CREDITS

¶355   Earned Income Tax Credit

¶356   Increase in Earned Income Tax Credit

¶360   Child Tax Credit

¶365   Child and Dependent Care Credit

¶370   Adoption Credit and Adoption Assistance Programs

¶371   American Opportunity Credit

¶372   Residential Energy Property Credit

¶373   Health Insurance Premium Assistance Credit

ALTERNATIVE MINIMUM TAX AND OTHER PROVISIONS

¶375   Alternative Minimum Tax Exemption Amount

¶376   Use of Nonrefundable Personal Credits Against AMT Liability

¶380   Limitation on Qualified Transportation Fringe Benefits

¶382   Refund Offsets for Unemployment Compensation Debts

¶3

¶384 Disregard of Tax Refunds for Determining Government Assistance Eligibility

¶386 Estate Tax Treatment of Stock in Regulated Investment Companies

¶388 Indian Money Account Litigation Settlement

CHAPTER 4. CAPITAL GAINS, DIVIDENDS, AND INVESTMENT

CAPITAL GAINS

¶405 Maximum Capital Gains Rates

¶410 Five-Year Holding Period for Capital Assets

¶415 Tax Preference Items: Excluded Gain on Sale of Small Business Stock

¶418 Exclusion of Gain from Sale of Qualified Small Business Stock

DIVIDENDS

¶420 Qualified Dividends Received by Individuals, Estates, and Trusts

¶425 Pass-Through Treatment of Qualified Dividend Income

¶430 Tax Treatment of Regulated Investment Company Dividends Paid to Foreign Persons

COMMUNITY ASSISTANCE

¶440 Empowerment Zone Tax Benefits

¶445 District of Columbia Enterprise Zone Tax Incentives

¶450 GO Zone Tax Incentives

TAX-EXEMPT BONDS

¶455 School Construction Bonds

¶460 Exempt Facility Bonds

¶465 Qualified Zone Academy Bonds

¶470 New York Liberty Bonds

CHAPTER 5. BUSINESS DEDUCTIONS AND CREDITS

DEDUCTIONS AND EXPENSING

¶502 Additional Depreciation Allowance (Bonus Depreciation)

¶504 Election to Claim Accelerated AMT Credit in Lieu of Bonus Depreciation

¶506 Section 179 Expensing of Depreciable Assets

¶508 15-Year Straight-Line Cost Recovery for Qualified Leasehold Improvements, Qualified Restaurant Property, and Qualified Retail Improvements

¶510 Seven-Year Recovery Period for Motorsports Entertainment Complexes

¶512 Accelerated Depreciation for Business Property on Indian Reservations

¶514 Special Expensing Rules for Certain Film and Television Productions

¶516 Election to Expense Advanced Mine Safety Equipment

¶518 Expensing of Brownfields Environmental Remediation Costs

TAX CREDITS

¶520   Credit for Increasing Research Activities

¶522   Credit for Employer-Provided Child Care Facilities and Services

¶524   Work Opportunity Credit

¶526   Employer Wage Credit for Activated Military Reservists

¶528   New Markets Tax Credit

¶530   Indian Employment Tax Credit

¶532   Railroad Track Maintenance Credit

¶534   Mine Rescue Team Training Credit

¶536   American Samoa Economic Development Credit

ENERGY

¶538   Credit for New Energy Efficient Homes

¶540   Grants for Investment in Specified Energy Property in Lieu of Tax Credits

¶542   Energy Efficient Appliance Credit for Manufacturers

¶544   Incentives for Biodiesel, Renewable Diesel, and Alternative Fuels

¶546   Incentives for Alcohol Fuels

¶548   Alternative Fuel Vehicle Refueling Property Credit

¶550   Refined Coal Production Facilities Credit

¶552   Percentage Depletion for Marginal Oil and Gas Production

¶554   Gain Rule on Sales or Dispositions to Implementing FERC or State Electric Restructuring Policy

CHARITABLE CONTRIBUTIONS

¶557   Basis Adjustment to Stock of an S Corporation Making Charitable Contributions

¶560   Enhanced Deduction for Charitable Contributions of Food Inventory Enhanced Deduction

¶563   Enhanced Deduction for Corporate Charitable Contributions of Book Inventory

¶566   Enhanced Deduction for Corporate Charitable Contributions of Computers

CHAPTER 6. CORPORATIONS, TRUSTS, AND OTHER PROVISIONS

CORPORATIONS, TRUSTS, AND OTHER PROVISIONS

¶603   Accumulated Earnings Tax

¶606   Personal Holding Company Tax Rate

¶609   Collapsible Corporations

¶612   Treatment and Information Requirements of Alaska Native Settlement Trusts

¶615   Modification of Tax Treatment of Payments to Controlling Exempt Organizations

FOREIGN AND OTHER PROVISIONS

¶620   Look-Through Rule for FIRPTA Distributions

¶623   Subpart F Exceptions for Active Financing Income

¶626   Subpart F Exceptions for Insurance Income

¶629   Look-Through Rule for Related Controlled Foreign Corporation Payments

¶632   Code Sec. 199 Deduction for Production Activities in Puerto Rico

¶635   Cover Over of Rum Excise Tax

¶638   Aviation Excise Taxes

CHAPTER 7. ESTATE, GIFT, AND GENERATION-SKIPPING TAXES

TRANSFER TAXES

¶705   Sunset Extended; Transfer Taxes Reinstated

¶710   Transfer Tax Rates Lowered

¶715   Transfer Tax Exclusion and Exemption Amounts Increased

¶718   Deceased Spouse's Unused Applicable Exclusion Amount to be Portable

¶720   Qualified Family-Owned Business Interest Deduction

¶725   State Death Tax Credit

¶730   State Death Tax Deduction

¶735   Estate Tax Exclusion for Qualified Conservation Easements

BASIS RULES AND REPORTING REQUIREMENTS

¶740   Stepped-Up Basis for Property Acquired from a Decedent

¶745   Reporting and Penalty Provisions

¶750   Income Tax Exclusion for Sale of Principal Residence

¶755   Treatment of Appreciated Property Upon Distribution

¶760   Miscellaneous Amendments to Incorporate Carryover Basis Rules Repealed

GENERATION-SKIPPING TRUSTS

¶765   Deemed and Retroactive Allocations of GST Exemption

¶770   Severing of Trusts

¶775   Modification of Valuation Rules

¶780   Late Elections and Substantial Compliance

INSTALLMENT PAYMENTS

¶785   Allowable Number of Members for Closely Held Business

¶790   Election for Installment Payment of Estate Tax With Respect to Lending and Finance Businesses

¶795   Estate Tax Installment Payments and Stock of Holding Companies

CHAPTER 8. REGULATED INVESTMENT COMPANIES (RICs)

CAPITAL LOSS CARRYOVER

¶803   RIC Capital Loss Carryover

GROSS INCOME AND ASSET TESTS

¶806   RIC Asset and Gross Income Tests

DIVIDENDS AND OTHER DISTRIBUTIONS

¶809   RIC Dividend Distributions

¶812   Earnings and Profits of RICs

¶815   Pass-Through of Exempt-Interest Dividends and Foreign Tax Credits

¶818   Dividends Paid by RICs After Close of Tax Year

¶821   Return of Capital Distributions of RICs

¶824   Redemptions of Stock of RICs

¶827   Preferential Dividends of Publicly Offered RICs

¶830   Elective Deferral of Certain Late-Year Losses of RICs

¶833   Holding Period Requirement For Certain Regularly Declared Exempt-Interest Dividends

OTHER PROVISIONS

¶836   Excise Tax on RIC Distributions

¶839   Assessable Penalty with Respect to Tax Liability of RICs

¶842   Sale Load Basis Deferral Rule

¶5 Highlights

INDIVIDUAL TAX RELIEF

¶305 **Individual, estate and trust tax rates.** Lower income tax rates applicable to individuals, estates and trusts are extended for two years. Thus, through 2012, the 10-percent tax rate continues to apply to the first taxable portion of an individual's income, and the 15%, 25%, 28%, 33% and 35% tax rates continue to apply to individuals, estates and trusts.

¶310, ¶315 **Marriage penalty relief.** Reductions of the marriage penalty in tax rates and the standard deduction are extended for two years. Thus, for joint filers and surviving spouses in 2011 and 2012, the 15% tax bracket and the standard deduction are both twice as large as they are for single filers.

¶312 **Payroll tax holiday.** For 2011, the employee's portion of the old age, survivors, and disability insurance (OASDI) tax and the railroad retirement tax, as well as the OASDI component of the self-employment tax, are all reduced by two percentage points.

¶320 **Cap on itemized deductions.** The repeal of the limit on itemized deductions for higher-income taxpayers is extended for two years, through 2012.

¶325 **Personal exemption phaseout.** The elimination of the phaseout of personal exemptions for higher-income taxpayers is extended for two years, through 2012.

¶326 **Sales taxes.** The election to claim an itemized deduction for state and local sales taxes in lieu of state and local income taxes is extended for two years, though 2012.

¶327 **Teachers' expenses.** The above-the-line deduction for eligible educator expenses, which expired at the end of 2009, is extended for two years, through 2011.

¶328 **Mortgage insurance.** The deduction for qualified mortgage insurance premiums is extended for one year, through 2011.

¶330 **Coverdell education savings accounts.** Enhancements to Coverdell education savings accounts, including increased contribution limits and an expanded definition of qualified education expenses, are extended for two years, through 2012..

¶335   **Excludable educational assistance.** An employee's exclusion from gross income and from wages of up to $5,250 in annual employer-provided education expenses is extended for two years, through 2012.

¶340   **Federal health scholarships.** The exclusion from gross income for certain federal and military medical scholarships that include obligatory service requirements is extended for two years, through 2012.

¶345   **Student loan interest.** Expansions of the student loan interest deduction are extended for two years. Thus, for 2011 and 2012, the deduction is not limited to interest paid during the first 60 months of repayment, and higher deduction phaseouts apply.

¶350   **Tuition and fees.** The above-the-line deduction for qualified tuition and related expenses, which expired at the end of 2009, is extended for two years, through 2011.

¶352   **Charitable IRA distributions.** The exclusion from gross income of qualified charitable IRA distributions, which expired at the end of 2009, is extended for two years, through 2011.

¶353   **Charitable conservation contributions.** The enhanced deduction for charitable contributions of real property for conservation purposes, which expired at the end of 2009, is extended for two years, through 2011.

¶355, ¶356   **Earned income tax credit.** Several modifications of the earned income credit are extended for two years. Thus, for 2011 and 2012, the phaseout and earned-income rules remain more generous, the credit is not reduced by AMT liability, and the tiebreaker rules and relationship tests are simplified. In addition, the maximum credit and phaseout ranges are increased for taxpayers with at least three qualifying children, and the marriage penalty in the phaseout of the credit is reduced.

¶360   **Child tax credit.** Expansions of the child tax credit are extended for two years. Thus, for 2011 and 2012, the credit remains $1,000 per qualifying child, a greater portion of the credit is refundable, and the credit is not reduced by AMT liability.

¶365   **Child and dependent care credit.** Increased credit percentages and expense limits for the child and dependent care credit are extended for two years, through 2012.

¶370   **Adoption credit and excludable assistance.** The increases in the maximum adoption credit and excludable employer-provided adoption assistance are extended for two years, through 2012.

¶371   **American Opportunity credit.** The expanded version of the Hope scholarship credit, known as the American Opportunity credit, is extended for two years, through 2012.

¶372   **Residential energy property credit.** The residential energy property credit is modified and extended for one year, through 2011.

¶373   **Health insurance credit.** For tax years beginning after 2013, the maximum repayment of advance premium assistance payments that exceed the allowable health insurance premium assistance credit is increased.

¶375, ¶376   **Alternative minimum tax.** A new AMT patch applies for 2010 and 2011, with increased exemption amounts. The expanded use of nonrefundable personal tax credits against an individual's AMT liability, which expired at the end of 2009, is also extended for two years, through 2011.

¶380   **Transportation fringe benefits.** An employee's increased exclusion for employer-provided transit passes and van pool benefits, which expired at the end of 2009, is extended for two years, through 2011.

¶382   **Refund offsets.** For purposes of refund offsets to collect unemployment compensation debts, the definition of covered unemployment compensation debt is expanded, and the 10-year lookback period and state residency requirements are eliminated.

¶384   **Federal assistance.** In determining whether an individual is eligible for federal assistance or federally-financed state assistance, federal tax refunds and advance payments of refundable credits received through 2012 are not taken into account as income or resources.

¶386   **Nonresident alien's RIC stock.** Rules allowing the exclusion of some stock in a regulated investment company (RIC) from a nonresident alien's gross estate are extended for two years, through 2012.

¶388   **Indian lawsuit settlement payments.** Indians can exclude from gross income amounts received in settlement of the class action lawsuit over federal mismanagement of Indian trust accounts.

CAPITAL GAINS, DIVIDENDS AND INVESTMENT

¶405, ¶410   **Capital gains tax rates.** The reductions in maximum capital gains tax rates for noncorporate taxpayers are extended for two years. Thus, for 2011 and 2012, the rate is zero for taxpayers in the 10% and 15% tax brackets, and 15% for other noncorporate taxpayers. The restoration of the special rates for five-year property is postponed until 2013.

¶415, ¶418   **Small business stock.** The reduction in the amount of certain gain on small-business stock that is treated as an alternative minimum tax (AMT) preference item is extended for two years, through 2012. The 100% exclusion of a noncorporate taxpayer's gain on the sale or exchange of qualified small business stock is extended for one year, through 2011.

¶420, ¶425   **Dividend tax rate.** The taxation of noncorporate taxpayers' dividends (including those received through mutual funds, REITs and other pass-through entities) as capital gain, rather than ordinary income, is extended for two years, through 2012.

¶430   **RIC dividends.** Special rules for certain regulated investment company (RIC) dividends paid to foreign persons, which expired at the end of 2009, are extended for two years. Thus, for 2010 and 2011, a RIC's interest-related or short-term capital gain dividends paid to nonresident aliens and foreign corporations are exempt from the 30% withholding tax.

¶440   **Empowerment zones.** Tax benefits for empowerment zones, which generally expired at the end of 2009, are extended for two years, through 2011.

¶445   **D.C. tax benefits.** The District of Columbia enterprise zone provisions and the D.C. homebuyer credit, which expired at the end of 2009, are extended for two years, through 2011.

¶450   **GO Zone tax benefits.** Several special tax benefits for the Gulf Opportunity (GO) Zone, including the rehabilitation credit, low-income housing credit, tax-exempt financing, and bonus depreciation, are extended.

¶455, ¶460   **School bonds.** The increase in the amount of public schools bonds that small governmental units may issue without being subject to arbitrage rebate requirements, and the treatment of public school bonds as exempt facility bonds, are both extended for two years, through 2012.

¶465   **QZABs.** The qualified zone academy bond (QZAB) program is extended for one year, through 2011, and the refundable credit for QZABs is repealed for obligations issued under the 2011 limitation.

¶470   **New York Liberty Bonds.** The authorization of $8 billion in tax-exempt bonds to finance construction and renovation in the New York Liberty Zone, which expired at the end of 2009, is extended for two years, through 2011.

BUSINESS DEDUCTIONS AND CREDITS

¶502, ¶504   **Bonus depreciation.** The additional depreciation allowance is extended for two years to apply to qualifying property placed in service before 2013, and the bonus depreciation allowance rate is increased to 100 percent for certain qualified property acquired and placed in service before 2012. These placed-in-service deadlines are extended for one year for property with longer production periods and certain noncommercial aircraft. Corporations may elect an accelerated AMT tax credit in lieu of this extended bonus depreciation allowance.

¶506   **Code Sec. 179 expensing.** For tax years beginning in 2012, the dollar limit for the Code Sec. 179 expense election is increased to $125,000, and the investment limit is increased to $500,000. Rules applicable to off-the-shelf computer software and election methods are also extended for one year, through 2012.

¶508   **Leasehold, retail and restaurant properties.** The 15-year recovery period for qualified leasehold improvement property, qualified restaurant property and qualified retail improvement property, which expired at the end of 2009, is extended for two years, through 2011.

¶510   **Motorsports entertainment complexes.** The seven-year recovery period for motorsports entertainment complexes, which expired at the end of 2009, is extended for two years, through 2011.

¶512   **Indian reservation property.** Accelerated depreciation periods for qualified Indian reservation property, which expired at the end of 2009, are extended for two years, through 2011.

¶514   **Film and television productions.** Special expensing rules for qualified film and television productions, which expired at the end of 2009, are extended for two years, through 2011.

¶516, ¶534   **Mine safety.** The election to expense 50% of the cost of advanced mine safety equipment, and the credit for qualified mine rescue training team expenses, which both expired at the end of 2009, are extended for two years, through 2011.

¶518   **Brownfield remediation costs.** The election to deduct environmental remediation costs, which expired at the end of 2009, is extended for two years, through 2011.

¶520   **R&D credit.** The research and development credit, which expired at the end of 2009, is extended for two years, through 2011.

¶522   **Employer-provided child care.** The credit for an employer's qualified expenses for employee child care is extended for two years, through 2012.

¶524   **Work opportunity credit.** The work opportunity credit is extended for four months, through December 31, 2011.

¶526   **Employer's differential wage credit.** The employer's credit for small businesses that pay differential wage payments to employees on military duty, which expired at the end of 2009, is extended for two years.

¶528   **New markets credit.** The new markets tax credit, which expired at the end of 2009, is extended for two years, through 2011.

¶530   **Indian employment credit.** The Indian employment tax credit, which expired at the end of 2009, is extended for two years, through 2011.

¶532   **Railroad track maintenance credit.** The railroad track maintenance credit is extended for two years, through 2012.

¶536   **American Samoa.** The credit for qualifying possessions corporations that are existing claimants operating in American Samoa, which expired at the end of 2009, is extended for two years, through 2011.

¶538   **New energy efficient homes.** The builder's credit for the construction or manufacture of new energy efficient homes, which expired at the end of 2009, is extended for two years, through 2011.

¶540   **Grants in lieu of energy credits.** The authority of the Secretary of the Treasury to issue grants in lieu of the renewable electricity production credit and the energy credit is extended for one year, through 2011.

¶542   **Energy-efficient appliances.** The manufacturer's credit for energy efficient dishwashers, clothes washers and refrigerators is modified and extended for one year, through 2011.

¶5

¶544 **Biodiesel, renewable diesel and alternative fuels.** Several tax benefits for diesel and alternative fuels that expired in 2009 are extended for two years, through 2011.

¶546 **Alcohol fuels.** The income tax credit, excise tax credit, and outlay payment provisions for alcohol fuels and alcohol fuel mixtures are extended for one year, through 2011.

¶548 **Alternative fuel vehicle refueling property.** The alternative fuel vehicle refueling property credit is extended for one year, through 2011.

¶550 **Refined coal production facilities.** The credit for refined coal facilities, which expired at the end of 2009, is extended for two years, through 2011.

¶552 **Percentage depletion for marginal wells.** The suspension of the percentage depletion limitation for oil and gas produced from marginal properties is extended for two years, through 2012.

¶554 **Dispositions to implement electric restructuring.** The special gain recognition rule for qualifying electric transmission transactions that implement Federal Energy Regulatory Commission or state electric restructuring policy, which expired at the end of 2009, is extended for two years, through 2011.

¶557 **S corporation charitable donations.** Rules that reduce a shareholder's basis in S corporation stock in accordance with the corporation's charitable donations, which expired at the end of 2009, are extended for two years, through 2011.

¶560, ¶563, ¶566 **Food, book and computer donations.** The enhanced deduction for charitable contributions of food inventory, and for corporate contributions of book inventory and computers, which all expired at the end of 2009, are extended for two years, through 2011.

CORPORATIONS, TRUSTS AND OTHER PROVISIONS

¶603 **Accumulated earnings tax rate.** The reduction in the tax rate on corporate accumulated earnings to 15% is extended for two years, through 2012.

¶606 **Personal holding company tax rate.** The reduction in the tax rate on personal holding companies to 15% is extended for two years, through 2012.

¶609   **Collapsible corporations.** The repeal of the collapsible corporation rules is extended for two years. Thus, for 2011 and 2012, shareholders' gain on collapsible corporation stock, as well as certain corporate distributions, is treated as capital gain, rather than ordinary income.

¶612   **Alaska Native Settlement Trusts.** Several special rules for calculating, taxing and reporting the income of Alaska Settlement Trusts and their beneficiaries are extended for two years, through 2012.

¶615   **Exempt organizations.** The exclusion from unrelated business income for an exempt organization's qualifying payments received from a controlled entity, which expired at the end of 2009, are extended for two years, through 2011.

¶620   **FIRPTA distributions.** For purposes of the Foreign Investment in Real Property Tax Act (FIRPTA), the expansion of qualified investment entities to include companies that are both regulated investment companies and U.S. real property holding companies, which expired at the end of 2009, are extended for two years, through 2011.

¶623, ¶626   **Subpart F exceptions.** Rules that treat active financing income and certain insurance and insurance investment income as exempt from subpart F, which expired at the end of 2009, are extended for two years, through 2011.

¶629   **Payments to related CFC.** Look-through treatment for certain payments that a controlled foreign corporation (CFC) receives from a related corporation, which expired at the end of 2009, is extended for two years, through 2011.

¶632   **DPAD and Puerto Rico.** For purposes of the domestic production activities deduction (DPAD), the treatment of Puerto Rico as part of the United States in determining domestic production gross receipts, which expired at the end of 2009, is extended for two years, through 2011.

¶635   **Rum excise tax.** The temporary increase in the cover over amount for certain rum imports, which expired at the end of 2009, is extended for two years, through 2011.

ESTATE, GIFT, AND GENERATION-SKIPPING TAXES

¶705   **Estate and GST taxes.** For decedents dying and generating-skipping transfers (GSTs) made during 2010, 2011 and 2012, modified federal estate and generation-skipping transfer (GST) taxes are reinstated, as outlined below.

¶710   **Transfer tax rates.** New transfer tax rates apply for decedents dying and GSTs made after 2009 and before 2013. The maximum tax rate is generally reduced to 35%, though the tax rate for GSTs in 2010 is zero. Gift tax rates are the same as estate tax rates. The reinstatement of the surtax on certain estates and gifts that exceed $10 million is postponed until 2013.

¶715, ¶718   **Transfer tax exclusion and exemption amounts.** The applicable exclusion amount increases to $5 million for estates of decedents dying and GSTs made after 2009 and before 2013, and for gifts made after 2010 and before 2013. An estate can allow the surviving spouse's estate to utilize the unused portion of the decedent's applicable exclusion amount.

¶720   **QFOBIs.** The reinstatement of the qualified family-owned business interest (QFOBI) deduction is postponed until 2013.

¶725, ¶730   **State death taxes.** The treatment of estate, inheritance, legacy, and succession taxes paid to any state or the District of Columbia as a tax deduction, rather than a tax credit, is extended for two years, through 2012.

¶735   **Qualified conservation easements.** The easing of location requirements for an estate's excludable qualified conservation easement is extended for two years, through 2012.

¶740, ¶745,   **Property acquired from decedent.** Generally, property received
¶760   from decedents dying after 2009 gets a stepped up (or down) basis, but the estate of a decedent dying in 2010 can elect to apply the modified carryover basis rules instead. Reporting requirements and penalties are adjusted accordingly. Several provisions related to the modified carryover basis rules are repealed..

¶750   **Decedent's principal residence.** Gain on the sale of a decedent's principal residence is excludable by heirs, estates and qualified revocable trusts only if the decedent dies in 2010, and the estate elects to apply the modified carryover basis rules.

¶755   **Distributions of appreciated property.** The general limitation on the recognition of gain on appreciated carryover basis property in satisfaction of a pecuniary bequest apply only if the decedent dies in 2010, and the estate elects to apply the modified carryover basis rules.

¶765, ¶770,   **GST rules.** Several GST rules are extended for two years, through
¶775, ¶780   2012, including those governing deemed and retroactive allocations, qualified severance of a trust, clarification of valuation rules applicable to the inclusion ratio, and relief from late GST allocations and elections.

¶785, ¶790, ¶795   **Estate tax payments.** Rules expanding eligibility for making deferred and installment estate tax payments are extended for two years, through 2012.

REGULATED INVESTMENT COMPANIES (RICS)

¶803   **Capital loss carryovers.** Capital loss carryover rules applicable to individuals are generally extended to RICs.

¶806   **RIC status** Certain companies that fail the asset value or gross income test can retain their status as RICs.

¶809   **Dividend distributions.** Modified rules for RIC dividend distributions and other pass-through items replace written notice to shareholders with formal reporting, and revise the allocation method for excess distributions.

¶812, ¶718   **Earnings and profits.** The rules for the taxable income treatment of a RIC's net capital loss apply for purposes of determining both current and accumulated earnings and profits (E&P). Disallowed expense deductions related to tax-exempt interest are allowed in calculating current, but not accumulated, E&P.

¶815   **Pass-through of dividends and credits.** An upper-tier RIC that is a qualified fund of funds may pass through exempt-interest dividends and foreign tax credits to its shareholders, even if it does not satisfy the 50-percent asset test.

¶818, ¶730   **Spillover dividends.** The timing rules for when a RIC must declare and distribute spillover dividends are modified.

¶821   **Return-of-capital distributions.** If a portion of a non-calendar year RIC's distributions constitute return of capital or capital gain, current E&P is allocated first to the distributions that occur before January 1.

¶824   **Redemptions.** Certain stock redemptions by publicly offered RICs are treated as exchanges, and losses on certain redemptions by fund-of-funds RICs are allowed.

¶827   **Preferential dividends.** Publicly offered RICs are exempt from the preferential dividend rule of Code Sec. 562(c).

¶830   **Loss deferral.** For purposes of determining taxable income, net capital gain, net short-term capital gain, and E&P, a RIC can elect to defer qualified late-year losses to the first day of the next tax year.

¶833   **RIC stock dispositions.** Certain losses on the sale or exchange of RIC stock are allowed even if the shareholder received an exempt-interest dividend

¶836   **Excise taxes.** Excise taxes applicable to RICs are modified in several respects, including permitted shareholders of exempt RICs, "push" rules, the coordination of distributions with estimated tax payments, and the required distributions of capital gain net income.

¶839   **Penalty on deficiency dividends.** The assessable penalty imposed on a RIC that claims a deficiency dividend deduction is repealed.

¶842   **Sale load basis deferral.** The sale load basis deferral rule for the acquisition of RIC stock is limited to cases where the taxpayer acquires stock in the same or a different RIC during the January following the calendar year the original stock was disposed of.

¶5

The Sunset of EGTRRA and JGTRRA

On May 26, 2001, Congress passed the Economic Growth and Tax Relief Reconciliation Act of 2001 (EGTRRA). Hailed as the largest tax cut since 1981, the Act included cuts in marginal income tax rates, marriage penalty relief, the phase-out and ultimate repeal of the estate tax. Although the rate breaks and estate tax repeal seemed straightforward enough, the unprecedented myriad of phase-in rules and effective dates added another layer of complexity to an already obtuse tax code.

To further complicate matters, each provision in EGTRRA is subject to a sunset provision. Specifically, Act Section 901 provides:

SEC. 901. SUNSET OF PROVISIONS OF ACT.

(a) In General.--All provisions of, and amendments made by, this Act shall not apply--

(1) to taxable, plan, or limitation years beginning after December 31, 2010, or

(2) in the case of title V, to estates of decedents dying, gifts made, or generation skipping transfers, after December 31, 2010.

(b) Application of Certain Laws.--The Internal Revenue Code of 1986 and the Employee Retirement Income Security Act of 1974 shall be applied and administered to years, estates, gifts, and transfers described in subsection (a) as if the provisions and amendments described in subsection (a) had never been enacted.

The Committee Report (S. Rep. No. 107-30) explained that the sunset provision was necessary to comply with Section 313 of the Congressional Budget Act of 1974 (2 U.S.C. 644). Section 313, which was permanently incorporated into the Budget Act in 1990, is commonly referred to as the "Byrd rule" and was named after its principal sponsor, Senator Robert C. Byrd.

The Byrd rule generally permits Senators to raise a point of order on the Senate floor against "extraneous" provisions contained in a reconciliation bill. If the point of order is sustained by the presiding officer (and not overturned if the ruling is appealed by any Senator), the offending provision is stricken unless 3/5 of the Senate membership vote to waive the rule with respect to that provision (i.e., 60 Senators if no seats are vacant).

One of the six types of extraneous provisions is a provision that would increase net outlays or decrease revenues for a fiscal year beyond those covered by the reconciliation measure. The sunset language in EGTRRA prevented any provision in the Act from violating this particular rule and becoming subject to a "point of order."

On May 28, 2003, the Jobs and Growth Tax Relief Reconciliation Act of 2003 (JGTRRA) was signed into law. JGTRRA accelerated many of the tax cuts set in motion under EGTRRA. However, like EGTRRA, the provisions contained in JGTRRA were subject to sunset rules. In fact, JGTRRA contained two sunset rules.

Provisions in Title I of JGTRRA are generally subject to the sunset in EGTRRA and will not apply to tax years beginning after December 31, 2010. Provisions in Title III of JGTRRA are subject to a separate sunset under which such provisions will not apply to tax years beginning after December 31, 2008.

Specifically, Act Section 107 of the Jobs and Growth Tax Relief Reconciliation Act of 2003 provides:

SEC. 107. APPLICATION OF EGTRRA SUNSET TO THIS TITLE.

Each amendment made by this title [Title I] shall be subject to title IX of the Economic Growth and Tax Relief Reconciliation Act of 2001 to the same extent and in the same manner as the provision of such Act to which such amendment relates.

Specifically, Act Section 303 of the Jobs and Growth Tax Relief Reconciliation Act of 2003 provides:

SEC. 303. SUNSET OF TITLE.

All provisions of, and amendments made by, this title [Title III] shall not apply to taxable years beginning after December 31, 2008, and the Internal Revenue Code of 1986 shall be applied and administered to such years as if such provisions and amendments had never been enacted.

The Tax Increase Prevention and Reconciliation Act of 2005 (TIPRA), which was signed into law on May 17, 2006, extended the sunset date applicable to JGTRRA, Title III. Pursuant to TIPRA, the provisions and amendments of Title III of JGTRRA will not apply to tax years beginning after December 31, 2010.

The Tax Relief, Unemployment Insurance Reauthorization, and Job Creation Act of 2010 (Tax Relief Act of 2010), passed by the Senate on December 15, 2010, and by the House on December 16, 2010, generally extended the sunset date applicable to Act Section 901 of EGTRRA (a separate sunset provision applied to adoption benefits) and Act Section 303 of JGTRRA, for two years, though December 31, 2012.

For all in EGTRRA and JGTRRA that is subject to the extended sunset at the end of 2012, it is also important to remember that since EGTRRA and JGTRRA were passed, many of those provisions have been made permanent or extended by other legislation. A number of provisions in EGTRRA and JGTRRA were scheduled to expire even before the sunset. Most of these have been extended by other legislation, some of the provisions, such as AMT relief and the above-the-line deduction for tuition and fees, joined the list of the regularly expiring provisions that Congress deals with every year.

Provisions from EGTRRA involving contribution and benefit limits for IRAs, defined contribution plans, and defined benefit plans; catch-up contributions; rollover provisions; deemed IRA provisions; qualified retirement planning services; the start-up credit; the saver's credit; ESOP rules; and top-heavy rules were all permanently extended by the Pension Protection Act of 2006. Provisions from the EGTRRA involving qualified tuition and 529 plans were also permanently extended by the Pension Protection Act of 2006. The EGTRRA exclusion for restitution payments to victims of Nazi persecution has been made permanent by other legislation. The sunset of enhancements to the adoption credit and the exclusion for employer-provided adoption assistance is now scheduled for 2012 rather than 2011, thanks to a provision in the 2010 health care reform legislation. Other provisions, such as those involving extended filing deadlines for Presidentially-declared disasters, have also been made obsolete by subsequent legislation.

In relation to those provisions not made permanent by other legislation, the extension enacted under the Tax Relief Act of 2010 gives taxpayers some certainty in tax planning for the next two years, especially concerning the individual income tax rates, capital gains and dividend tax rates and the estate tax. However, the provisions are temporary and the new law punts the ultimate fate of numerous tax cuts and incentives to 2012, a presidential election year.

For a detailed analysis of the Tax Relief Act of 2010, the tax provisions impacted by the EGTRRA and JGTRRA sunset provisions, and other recently enacted legislation, see the following chapters in this publication.

> **State Tax Consequences:** Many of the provisions of EGTRRA and JGTRRA that have been extended, as well other provisions, by the Tax Relief Act will affect 2010 state income tax returns. In addition, because the provisions that were due to "sunset" are effective as of the dates of the original legislation, previous tax years may be affected for state purposes.
>
> For example, the provisions related to tax rates (including special rates for capital gains and dividends), alternative minimum tax exemption amounts, and phase-out amounts for high-income taxpayers will not affect the states as they generally either do not impose a special rate or set their own rates and amounts. Also, the extension of many credits will not affect the states as the states do not directly incorporate federal credits. However, extension of the research credit could affect states that only allow their research credit as long as the federal credit exists. Because the federal credit expired after 2009, its extension through 2011 could affect such states.
>
> However, many provisions, including those extending the deductions for state and local sales tax, teacher expenses, mortgage insurance premiums, tuition and fees, and student loan interest will not be adopted by most states, if at all, until their next legislative sessions. Provisions extending the enhanced contribution deductions for food and book inventories, and computer equipment, as well as those allowing tax-free distributions from IRAs for charitable purposes and contributions of capital gain real property made for charitable purposes may also have an impact on the states. Therefore, adjustments will be required on the 2010 state income tax returns. Presumably, if a state incorporates these changes retroactively, taxpayers will be able to file amended 2010 returns.
>
> Some of the "extenders," such as the exclusion for employer-provided educational assistance, are not set to expire until after 2010 and have been extended through 2012. Presumably, most states will conform to these extensions by the time they go into effect.

Taxpayers Affected

THE TAX RELIEF, UNEMPLOYMENT INSURANCE REAUTHORIZATION, AND JOB CREATION ACT OF 2010

¶205   Overview

¶208   Effect on Individuals Generally

¶210   Effect on Joint Filers

¶211   Effect on Homeowners

¶212   Effect on Lower-Income Taxpayers

¶214   Effect on High-Income Taxpayers

¶215   Effect on Exempt Organizations

¶216   Effect on Investors

¶217   Effect on Tax-Exempt Bond Investors

¶218   Effect on Parents

¶220   Effect on Students

¶222   Effect on Businesses Generally

¶224   Effect on Corporations

¶226   Effect on S Corporations

¶228   Effect on Foreign Corporations

¶230   Effect on International Business

¶232   Effect on Partnerships and LLCs

¶236   Effect on Personal Holding Companies

¶240   Effect on Small Business

¶245   Effect on Businesses in Puerto Rico

¶250   Effect on Regulated Investment Companies

¶255   Effect on Estates Generally

¶260   Effect on Trusts

¶265   Effect on Commuters

¶267   Effect on Film and Television Industry

¶270   Effect on Government Entities

The Tax Relief, Unemployment Insurance Reauthorization, and Job Creation Act of 2010

¶205 Overview

Just as the enactment of EGTRRA and JGTRRA provided tax relief for most taxpayers, the sunset of those tax acts at the end of 2010 would have resulted in tax increases for most taxpayers. The Tax Relief, Unemployment Insurance Reauthorization, and Job Creation Act of 2010 has extended many of the provisions for two additional years, so that they expire at the end of 2012. This will give taxpayers some certainty in tax planning for the next two years. The new law includes tax rate reductions, an AMT patch, bonus depreciation, across-the-board payroll tax cut, business and energy incentives, estate tax relief, and more.

The broadest impact will come from the extension of the lower marginal rates enacted in EGTRRA. The extension of the lower capital gain and dividend rates from JGTRRA will also have a significant impact on investors. The Act also provides for a one-year payroll tax cut. Other key individually focused provisions that are extended include marriage penalty relief, relief from the phase out of exemptions and itemized deductions, increased credits with respect to children, education tax breaks, and alternative minimum tax relief.

Although the focus of EGTRRA and JGTRRA was on individual tax relief, they also had a significant effect of business. By maintaining the relative tax rates of individuals and corporations, the relative attractiveness of the corporate form as compared to the passthrough form of operation is not affected. Similarly, by maintaining the tax rates and capital gains and dividends rates, the relative merits of corporations paying dividends as compared to compensation is not affected. The new law also includes 100-percent bonus depreciation through 2011 and 50-percent bonus depreciation for 2012.

EGTRRA has led to a decade long problem in determining how to conduct estate planning, with gradual increases in exemption amounts, gradual decreases in estate tax rates, and a repeal of the estate tax in 2010 combined with modified carryover basis. Now, the legislation provides a return of the estate tax with high exemption amounts and low tax rates. In addition, the Act includes provisions on portability for a surviving spouse, and a stepped-up basis regime.

¶208 Effect on Individuals Generally

Individual income tax rates.—The individual income tax rates will remain at 10, 15, 25, 28, 33 and 35 percent through 2012 (¶305).

Employee payroll tax rates.—The employee OASDI (old age, survivors, and disability insurance) tax rate under the FICA tax is reduced by two percentage points to 4.2 percent for one year (2011). Similarly, the OASDI tax rate under the self-employment tax is reduced by two percentage points to 10.4 percent for tax years of individuals that begin in 2011 (¶312).

Teacher expenses.—The deduction for certain expenses of elementary and secondary school teachers is extended for two years so that it is available for tax years beginning before January 1, 2012 (¶327).

Deduction of state and local general sales taxes.—The election to deduct state and local sales taxes in lieu of state and local income taxes is extended for two years (through December 31, 2011) (¶326).

¶210 Effect on Joint Filers

Standard deduction.—A marriage penalty relief provision is enacted through 2012. Tax on a two-income earner married couple will typically exceed the sum of the taxes that would be imposed if each spouse filed a separate return as a single person. The basic standard deduction for married taxpayers filing a joint return is twice the basic standard deduction for unmarried individuals filing a single return (¶315).

15-percent income tax bracket.—The 15-percent tax bracket for joint filers will be the combined 15-percent tax brackets of two single filers through 2012 (¶310).

¶211 Effect on Homeowners

Home energy credits.—The energy efficient home credit is extended to homes that are purchased prior to January 1, 2012 (¶538). Also, the credit for energy efficient appliances is extended for one year, for appliances manufactured in 2011(¶542).

Mortgage insurance premiums.—The deduction for private mortgage insurance premiums is extended for one year (only with respect to contracts entered into after December 31, 2006). Thus, the deduction applies to amounts paid or accrued in 2011 (¶328).

¶212 Effect on Lower-Income Taxpayers

Earned Income Tax Credit.—Certain EITC provisions adopted by EGTRRA are extended for two years, through 2012. These include: (1) a simplified definition of earned income; (2) a simplified relationship test; (3) use of adjusted gross income instead of modified AGI; (4) a simplified tie-breaking rule; (5) additional math error authority for the IRS; (6) a repeal of the prior-law provision that reduced an individual's EITC by the amount of his alternative minimum tax liability; and (7) increases in the beginning and ending points of the credit phaseout for married taxpayers by $5,000. The EITC rate of 45 percent for three or more qualifying children is extended for two years, through 2012 (¶¶355 and 356).

Low-income housing credit rules for buildings in Gulf Opportunity Zones.—The placed-in-service deadline is extended for one year, to December 31, 2011. The new law also extends for two additional years the increase in the rehabilitation credit from 20 to 26 percent, and from 10 to 13 percent, respectively, with respect to any certified historic structure or qualified rehabilitated building located in the Gulf Opportunity

Zone. Thus, the increase applies for qualified rehabilitation expenditures with respect to such buildings or structures incurred before January 1, 2012 (¶450).

¶214 Effect on High-Income Taxpayers

Itemized deduction phaseout.—The overall limitation on itemized deductions does not apply for two additional years. In 2013, higher income taxpayers become limited in their ability deduct their itemized deductions (¶320).

Personal exemption phaseout.—The personal exemption phaseout for high-income taxpayers does not apply until 2013. Higher income taxpayers will not be required to reduce the amount of their personal exemptions when their adjusted gross income exceeds certain threshold levels (¶325).

Alternative minimum tax.—EGTRRA created relief from the alternative minimum tax for the greater numbers of taxpayers who would be caught by the AMT as a result of the relief from the regular tax provided for in EGTRRA. The relief was temporary and has been extended from time to time by other legislation. The relief expired at the end of 2009. The Tax Relief Act of 2010 extended the relief for 2010 and 2011. The alternative minimum tax exemption amounts in 2010 for individuals is $47,450 for single taxpayers, $72,450 for married taxpayers filing jointly and surviving spouses, and $36,225 for married taxpayers filing separately. The exemption amounts for corporations and estates or trusts remains unchanged (¶375).

¶215 Effect on Exempt Organizations

Conservation purposes.—The special rule regarding contributions of capital gain real property for conservation purposes is extended for two years for contributions made in tax years beginning before January 1, 2012 (¶353).

Tax-free distributions from individual retirement plans.—The exclusion for qualified charitable distributions from IRAs is extended to distributions made in tax years beginning after December 31, 2009, and before January 1, 2012. There is a special rule permitting taxpayers to elect to have qualified charitable distributions made in January 2011 treated as having been made on December 31, 2010 (¶352).

Food inventory.—The enhanced charitable deduction for contributions of food inventory is extended to contributions made before January 1, 2012 (¶560).

Book inventories to public schools.—The enhanced charitable deduction for contributions of book inventories to public schools is extended to contributions made before January 1, 2012 (¶563).

Computer equipment for educational purposes.—The enhanced charitable deduction for corporate contributions of computer technology and equipment for educational purposes is extended to contributions made before January 1, 2012 (¶566).

Payments to controlling organization.—A favorable provision of the Pension Protection Act of 2006 (P.L. 109-280) dealing with the treatment of payments to controlling organizations is extended to payments received or accrued before January 1, 2012 (¶615).

S corporation basis adjustment.—The basis adjustment to stock of S corporations making charitable contributions of property is extended for two years to contributions made in tax years beginning before January 1, 2012 (¶557).

¶216 Effect on Investors

Capital gains rates holding periods.—Investors who sell assets before 2013 will generally incur a lower rate of tax than they will if they sell the same assets in 2013. The maximum capital gains rate in 2013 becomes 20 percent. The maximum rate through 2012 for capital assets held longer than one year is 15 percent. The lowest rate on capital gains in 2013 will jump from 0 to 10 percent (¶405).

Special rates for assets held longer than five years.—The maximum rate of tax on the adjusted net capital gain of an individual is 15 percent. Any adjusted net capital gain which otherwise would be taxed at a 10- or 15-percent rate is taxed at a zero rate. These rates apply for purposes of both the regular tax and the AMT. In 2013, any gain from the sale or exchange of property held more than five years that would otherwise have been taxed at the 10-percent capital gain rate is taxed at an eight-percent rate. Any gain from the sale or exchange of property held more than five years and the holding period for which began after December 31, 2000, that would otherwise have been taxed at a 20-percent rate is taxed at an 18-percent rate (¶410).

Tax rate on dividends.—Qualified dividends received by a shareholder are taxed at capital gain tax rates through 2012. Thus, qualified dividends received by individuals, trusts or estates will be taxed at a maximum rate of 15 percent (¶420).

Qualified small business stock.—A greater percentage of the excluded gain on the sale of qualified small business stock will be treated as an AMT preference item (¶415).

New markets tax credit.—The new markets tax credit is extended for two years, through 2011, permitting up to $3.5 billion in qualified equity investments for each of the 2010 and 2011 calendar years. The carryover period for unused new markets tax credits is also extended for two years, though 2016 (¶528).

¶217 Effect on Tax-Exempt Bond Investors

Qualified zone academy bonds.—The qualified zone academy bond program is extended for one year. The new law authorizes issuance of up to $400 million of qualified zone academy bonds for 2011 (¶465).

New York Liberty Zone bonds.—The new law extends authority to issue Liberty Zone bonds for two years (through December 31, 2011) (¶470).

Gulf Opportunity Zone bonds.—The authority to issue Gulf Opportunity Zone bonds is extended for one year (through December 31, 2011) (¶450).

School construction bonds.—The additional amount of governmental bonds for public schools that small governmental units may issue without being subject to the arbitrage rebate requirement will remain at $10 million for two more years, until

December 31, 2012. In 2013, the arbitrage rebate requirement will decrease from $10 million to $5 million (¶455).

Exempt facility bonds.—Bonds used to provide qualified public educational facilities will be treated as exempt facility bonds under Code Sec. 142(a)(13) for two additional years until December 31, 2012 (¶460).

¶218 Effect on Parents

Child tax credit.—The child tax credit remains at $1,000 through 2012. The refundable component of the credit is not subject to a reduction for any alternative minimum tax. The supplemental child credit structured under the earned income credit is restored for eligible lower income taxpayers who have at least one child. The portion of the refundable credit does not constitute income and is not treated as resources for purposes of determining eligibility under federal or state programs. The earned income threshold of $3,000 is extended two years. Also, indexation for inflation of the $3,000 earnings threshold is stopped for that period (¶360).

Child and dependent care credit.—The child and dependent care expense credits are extended two years, through 2012. Thus, 35 percent of qualifying dependent care expenses that allow an individual to be gainfully employed are allowed. Individuals with one qualifying child or dependent may claim a maximum credit of $1,050, while individuals with two or more qualifying children may claim a maximum credit of $2,100. These amounts are reduced for individuals whose adjusted gross incomes exceed $15,000 (¶365).

Adoption credit and employer assistance exclusion.—The dollar limitation for the adoption credit and income exclusion for employer-paid or employer-reimbursed adoption expenses through a qualified adoption assistance program is extended one year. For 2012 the maximum benefit is $12,170 (indexed for inflation after 2010) (¶370).

¶220 Effect on Students

NHSC and Armed Forces Scholarships.—Amounts received by degree candidates at qualified educational organizations from the NHSC Scholarship Program or the Armed Forces Scholarship Program for tuition, fees, books, supplies, and equipment required in the student's course of instruction are not included in the recipient's gross income through 2012 (¶340).

Education IRAs.—The maximum annual contribution that can be made to a Coverdell Education Savings Account (ESA), and the threshold amount for imposing a six-percent excise tax on excess contributions made to a Coverdell account remains at $2,000 through 2012. Qualified education expenses include costs incurred for elementary or secondary school attendance (¶330).

American Opportunity Tax credit.—The temporary modifications to the Hope credit, that are known as the American Opportunity Tax Credit, including the rules governing the treatment of the U.S. possessions, are extended for two years (through

2012). Thus, the modified credit rate is 100 percent on the first $2,000 of qualified tuition and related expenses, and 25 percent on the next $2,000 of qualified tuition and related expenses (¶371).

Student loan interest deduction.—The deduction for student loan interest is allowed only with respect to interest paid on a qualified education loan during the first 60 months in which interest payments are required is extended two years. In 2013, the maximum allowable annual deduction is phased out for taxpayers whose modified adjusted gross incomes exceed exceeds $40,000 ($60,000 for joint returns), and phases out to zero once modified adjusted gross income exceeds $55,000 ($75,000 for joint returns), adjusted for inflation since 2002 (¶345).

Deduction for qualified tuition and related expenses.—EGTRRA created the above-the-line deduction for qualified tuition and related expenses on a temporary basis that has been extended from time to time by other legislation. The provision is extended for two years so that it is generally available for tax years beginning before January 1, 2012 (¶350).

¶222 Effect on Businesses Generally

Education assistance programs.—The exclusion for employer-provided education assistance programs remains through 2012 (¶335).

Child care facilities and services.—The tax credit for qualified expenses incurred by an employer in providing child care for employees is extended two years through 2012 (¶522).

Bonus depreciation.—Additional first-year depreciation to equal 100 percent of the cost of qualified property placed in service after September 8, 2010, and before January 1, 2012 (before January 1, 2013, for certain longer-lived and transportation property), and for a 50-percent first-year additional depreciation deduction for qualified property placed in service after December 31, 2011, and before January 1, 2013, is provided (¶502).

Biodiesel and renewable diesel.—The income tax credit, excise tax credit, and payment provisions for biodiesel and renewable diesel are extended for two additional years (through December 31, 2011) (¶544).

Work opportunity credit.—The work opportunity tax credit is extended for four months (for individuals who begin work for an employer after August 31, 2011, before January 1, 2012) (¶524).

Research credit.—The 20-percent research credit for incremental increases in qualified research is extended for two years, through December 31, 2011 (¶520).

Indian employment credit.—The tax credit for Indian employment is extended for two years, through December 31, 2011 (¶530).

15-year straight-line cost recovery.—Current depreciation rules for qualified leasehold improvement property, qualified restaurant property, and qualified retail improvement property are extended for two years to apply to property placed in service on or before December 31, 2011 (¶508).

Environmental remediation costs.—The expensing of environmental remediation costs is extended for two years to include expenditures paid or incurred before January 1, 2012 (¶518).

Empowerment zone tax incentives.—The period for which the designation of an empowerment zone is in effect is extended for two years, through December 31, 2011, thus extending the empowerment zone tax incentives, including the wage credit, accelerated depreciation deductions on qualifying equipment, tax-exempt bond financing, and deferral of capital gains tax on sale of qualified assets sold and replaced. Also, the legislation extends for two years, through December 31, 2016, the period for which the percentage exclusion for qualified small business stock (of a corporation which is a qualified business entity) acquired on or before February 17, 2009, is 60 percent. Gain attributable to periods after December 31, 2016, for qualified small business stock acquired on or before February 17, 2009, or after December 31, 2011, is subject to the general rule which provides for a percentage exclusion of 50 percent (¶440).

¶224 Effect on Corporations

Dividend rates.—The increase in the dividend rate that could affect the relative attractiveness of paying dividends as compared to other forms of payouts is now delayed to 2013 (¶420).

Election to accelerate AMT credit.—A corporation may elect to forgo bonus depreciation on "round 2 extension property" and claim unused AMT credits from tax years beginning before January 1, 2006 (¶504).

Accumulated earnings tax.—A corporation's accumulated earnings tax rate of 15 percent is extended two years through 2012 (¶603).

Collapsible corporations.—The complicated collapsible corporation rules are extended through 2012 (¶609).

¶226 Effect on S Corporations

Basis adjustment.—The basis adjustment to stock of S corporations making charitable contributions of property is extended for two years to contributions made in tax years beginning before January 1, 2012 (¶557).

¶228 Effect on Foreign Corporations

The dividend rate reduction.—The dividend rate reduction for qualified dividends received from a qualified foreign corporation is extended through 2012 (¶420).

Look-through treatment of payments between related controlled foreign corporations.—The application of the look-through rule (dividends, interest (including factoring income that is treated as equivalent to interest under Code Sec. 954(c)(1)(E)), rents, and royalties received by one CFC from a related CFC are not treated as foreign personal holding company income to the extent attributable or properly allocable to income of the payor that is neither subpart F income nor treated as ECI), is extended for two years to tax years of foreign corporations beginning before January 1, 2012, and for tax years of U.S. shareholders with or within which such tax years of such foreign corporations (¶629).

¶230 Effect on International Business

Subpart F active financing income.—The legislation extends for two years (for tax years beginning before 2012) the present-law temporary exceptions from subpart F foreign personal holding company income, foreign base company services income, and insurance income for certain income that is derived in the active conduct of a banking, financing, or similar business, or in the conduct of an insurance business (¶¶623 and 626).

¶232 Effect on Partnerships and LLCs

Qualified dividend income.—The treatment of qualified dividend income passed through a partnership as qualified dividend income is extended for two years, through 2012 (¶425).

¶236 Effect on Personal Holding Companies

Personal holding company tax rate.—The personal holding company tax rate of 15 percent is extended through 2012 (¶606).

¶240 Effect on Small Business

Qualified small business stock.—A greater percentage of the excluded gain on the sale of qualified small business stock will be treated as an AMT preference item (¶415). Also, the temporary exclusion of 100 percent of gain on certain small business stock is extended one year (¶418).

Small business expensing.—Increased small business expensing for qualifying property is temporarily extended to 2012 (¶506).

Installment payments available for closely held business.—For purposes of the rules governing qualification for installment payment of estate tax, the maximum allowable number of partners or shareholders in a closely held business owned by a decedent at the time of his or her death remains at 45 for the estates of decedents dying after December 31, 2010 and before January 1, 2013 (¶785).

¶245 Effect on Businesses in Puerto Rico

Domestic production activities.—The Code Sec. 199 domestic production activities deduction with respect to income attributable to domestic production activities in Puerto Rico has been extended for two years (¶632).

Rum excise taxes.—The legislation suspends for two years the $10.50 per proof gallon limitation on the amount of excise taxes on rum covered over to Puerto Rico and the Virgin Islands. The cover over limitation of $13.25 per proof gallon is extended for rum brought into the United States after December 31, 2009, and before January 1, 2012. After December 31, 2011, the cover over amount reverts to $10.50 per proof gallon (¶635).

¶250 Effect on Regulated Investment Companies

Look-through of certain regulated investment company stock.—The estate tax look-through rule for RIC stock applies to estates of decedents dying before January 1, 2012 (¶386).

Dividends and certain assets of mutual funds.—The legislation extends the rules exempting from gross basis tax and from withholding tax the interest-related dividends and short-term capital gain dividends received from a RIC, to dividends with respect to tax years of a RIC beginning before January 1, 2012 (¶430).

Mutual fund qualified investments.—The inclusion of a RIC within the definition of a "qualified investment entity" under Code Sec. 897 is extended through December 31, 2011, for those situations in which that inclusion would otherwise have expired at the end of 2009 (¶620).

¶255 Effect on Estates Generally

Estate, gift and generation-skipping transfer taxes.—The estate tax and generation-skipping transfer tax is reinstated for 2010. The estate tax applicable exclusion amount is $5 million, is indexed for inflation for decedents dying in calendar years after 2011, and the maximum estate tax rate is 35 percent. For gifts made in 2010, the applicable exclusion amount for gift tax purposes is $1 million, and the gift tax rate is 35 percent. For gifts made after December 31, 2010, the gift tax is reunified with the estate tax, with an applicable exclusion amount of $5 million and a top estate and gift tax rate of 35 percent. Any applicable exclusion amount that remains unused as of the death of a spouse who dies after December 31, 2010 (the "deceased spousal unused exclusion amount"), generally is available for use by the surviving spouse as an addition to such surviving spouse's applicable exclusion amount (¶¶705, 715, 718).

Transfer tax exclusion and exemption amounts.—The generation skipping transfer tax exemption for decedents dying or gifts made after December 31, 2009, is equal to the applicable exclusion amount for estate tax purposes (for example, $5 million for 2010). Therefore, up to $5 million in generation skipping transfer tax exemption may be allocated to a trust created or funded during 2010, depending upon the amount of such exemption used by the taxpayer before 2010. Although the generation skipping transfer tax is applicable in 2010, the generation skipping transfer tax rate for transfers made during 2010 is zero percent. The generation skipping transfer tax rate for transfers made after 2010 is equal to the highest estate and gift tax rate in effect for such year (35 percent for 2011 and 2012) (¶710).

Stepped up basis/carryover basis.—The modified carryover basis rules that, under EGTRRA, would apply for purposes of determining basis in property acquired from a decedent who dies in 2010, is repealed. Therefore, a recipient of property acquired from a decedent who dies after December 31, 2009, generally will receive fair market value basis (i.e., "stepped up" basis) under the basis rules applicable to assets acquired from decedents who died in 2009 (¶¶740, 755, 760).

Reporting and penalty provisions.—Reporting and penalty provisions associated with the carryover basis rules will not apply after to decedents dying after December 31, 2009 (¶745).

Qualified family-owned business interest deduction.—The estate tax qualified family-owned business deduction is available to the estates of decedents dying after December 31, 2012 (¶720).

State death tax deduction.—The state death tax deduction is allowed for taxes paid for decedents dying after December 31, 2009 (¶¶725, 730).

Exclusion for sale of a principal residence.—The exclusion for sale of a principal residence by a decedent's estate, heir or qualified revocable trust applies in 2010 if an election is made (¶750).

Exclusion for qualified conservation easements.—The distance requirements for the estate tax exclusion of a qualified conservation easement and the language clarifying the proper date to use is extended two years, through 2012 (¶735).

Installment payments available for closely held business.—For purposes of the rules governing qualification for installment payment of estate tax, the maximum allowable number of partners or shareholders in a closely held business owned by a decedent at the time of his or her death remains at 45 for the estates of decedents dying after December 31, 2010 and before January 1, 2013 (¶785).

Installment payments available for lending and finance businesses.—The rule that permits a decedent's estate to pay estate tax in installments with respect to interests attributable to businesses that are engaged in lending and finance activities is extended to apply to the estates of decedents dying before January 1, 2013 (¶790)

Look-through of certain regulated investment company stock.—The estate tax look-through rule for RIC stock applies to estates of decedents dying before January 1, 2012 (¶386).

¶260 Effect on Trusts

Generation-skipping trusts.—The deemed and retroactive GST allocation provisions (¶765), the qualified severance provision (¶770), the valuation rules with respect to the determination of the inclusion ratio for GST tax purposes (¶775), and the provisions providing relief from late GST allocations and elections, as well as the provision pertaining to substantial compliance (¶780), will remain in force through December 31, 2012.

Alaska Native Settlement Trusts.—The special income tax treatment for Alaska Native Settlement Trusts and their beneficiaries is extended for two years (¶612).

Dividend rates.—The lower dividend rates applicable to qualified dividends received by trusts is extended two years, through December 31, 2012 (¶420).

¶265 Effect on Commuters

Fringe transportation benefits.—The parity for exclusion from income for employer-provided mass transit and parking benefits is extended for one year (through December 31, 2011) (¶380).

¶267 Effect on Film and Television Industry

Expensing film and television production.—The legislation provides for an extension of the expensing rules for qualified film and television productions for two years, to qualified film and television productions commencing prior to January 1, 2012 (¶514).

¶270 Effect on Government Entities

State death tax credit/deduction.—The state death tax credit is now scheduled to return in 2013 and replace the state death tax deduction (¶¶725, 730).

School construction bonds.—The expanded limit of the amount of governmental bonds for public schools enacted under EGTRRA is scheduled to sunset (¶455).

Exempt facilities bonds.—The ability to use exempt facilities bonds for elementary and secondary schools under public-private partnership agreements with state or local educational agencies is extended through 2012 (¶460).

Individual Tax Relief

INCOME AND PAYROLL TAXES

¶305   Individual, Estate and Trust Tax Rates
¶310   15-Percent Tax Rate Bracket for Joint Filers
¶312   Payroll Tax Cut

DEDUCTIONS

¶315   Standard Deduction for Joint Filers
¶320   Overall Limitation on Itemized Deductions for Higher-Income Individuals
¶325   Phaseout of Personal Exemptions
¶326   Deduction of State and Local General Sales Taxes
¶327   Teachers' Classroom Expense Deduction
¶328   Mortgage Insurance Premiums

EDUCATION INCENTIVES

¶330   Coverdell Education Savings Accounts
¶335   Educational Assistance Programs
¶340   Federal Scholarships With Obligatory Service Requirements
¶345   Student Loan Interest Deduction
¶350   Deduction for Qualified Tuition and Related Expenses

CHARITABLE CONTRIBUTIONS

¶352   Qualified Charitable Distributions from IRAs
¶353   Charitable Contribution of Real Property for Conservation Purposes Enhanced Deduction

TAX CREDITS

¶355   Earned Income Tax Credit
¶356   Increase in Earned Income Tax Credit
¶360   Child Tax Credit

¶365   Child and Dependent Care Credit

¶370   Adoption Credit and Adoption Assistance Programs

¶371   American Opportunity Credit

¶372   Residential Energy Property Credit

¶373   Health Insurance Premium Assistance Credit

ALTERNATIVE MINIMUM TAX AND OTHER PROVISIONS

¶375   Alternative Minimum Tax Exemption Amount

¶376   Use of Nonrefundable Personal Credits Against AMT Liability

¶380   Limitation on Qualified Transportation Fringe Benefits

¶382   Refund Offsets for Unemployment Compensation Debts

¶384   Disregard of Tax Refunds for Determining Government Assistance Eligibility

¶386   Estate Tax Treatment of Stock in Regulated Investment Companies

¶388   Indian Money Account Litigation Settlement

INCOME AND PAYROLL TAXES

¶305 Individual, Estate and Trust Tax Rates

SUMMARY OF NEW LAW

Lower income tax rates applicable to individuals, estates and trusts are extended to apply to tax years beginning in 2011 and 2012. Thus, for tax years beginning in 2011 and 2012, the 10 percent tax rate continues to apply for lower-income individuals and the 15, 25, 28, 33 and 35 percent tax rates for individuals, estates and trusts continue to apply.

BACKGROUND

The Economic Growth and Tax Relief Reconciliation Act of 2001 (EGTRRA) (P.L. 107-16) amended the tax rates under Code Sec. 1 applicable to all individual taxpayers, estates and trusts, for tax years beginning after December 31, 2000 (Code Sec. 1(i)).

Under a progressive tax system, higher amounts of income are taxed at progressively higher rates. Beginning in 2001, new rates applied to individuals, estates and trusts on a phased-in basis. The higher tax rates in existence prior to 2001 in excess of the lowest rate (15 percent) were scheduled for a phased-in reduction between 2001 and 2006 as follows (Code Sec. 1(i)(2)):

¶305

BACKGROUND

- Tax rates for 2001 — 15 percent, 27.5 percent, 30.5 percent, 35.5 percent and 39.1 percent;

- Tax rates for 2002 and 2003 — 15 percent, 27 percent, 30 percent, 35 percent and 38.6 percent;

- Tax rates for 2004 and 2005 — 15 percent, 26 percent, 29 percent, 34 percent, and 37.6 percent; and

- Tax rates for 2006 through 2010 — 15 percent, 25 percent, 28 percent, 33 percent, and 35 percent.

Additionally, a portion of an individual's income historically taxed at 15 percent was subject to a new tax rate of 10 percent (Code Sec. 1(i)(1)(A)). For tax years 2001 through 2007, this 10 percent rate was scheduled to apply to the first $6,000 of income for single filers and married taxpayers filing separately, the first $12,000 for joint filers and the first $10,000 for heads of households. For the 2008 tax year, these amounts were scheduled to increase so that the 10 percent rate applied to the first $7,000 of income for single filers and married taxpayers filing separately and the first $14,000 for joint filers. For heads of households, the amount remained at $10,000 (Code Sec. 1(i)(1)(B)). In tax years after 2008, all 10 percent income bracket amounts, including for heads of households, were to be adjusted for inflation (Code Sec. 1(i)(1)(C)).

The Jobs and Growth Tax Relief Reconciliation Act of 2003 (JGTRRA) (P.L. 108-27) accelerated the phase-in of these rate reductions. The fully phased-in amounts, originally scheduled to first take effect in 2006, were accelerated to take effect in 2003. As a result, for tax years 2003 through 2010, six tax rates apply for individuals; 10, 15, 25, 28, 33 and 35 percent (Code Sec. 1(i)(2)). Five tax rates (15, 25, 28, 33 and 35 percent) apply for estates and trusts in tax years 2003 through 2010.

The 10 percent rate applicable only to individuals, not to estates and trusts, was expanded by JGTRRA to accelerate the increased income bracket amounts (originally scheduled to apply in tax years beginning in 2008) to tax years beginning in 2003 and 2004, with adjustments for inflation to apply in 2004 in addition to tax years beginning after 2008 (Code Sec. 1(i)(1)(B)(i); (C)). These changes do not apply to heads of households.

The Working Families Tax Relief Act of 2004 (WFTRA) (P.L. 108-311) further accelerated the increased 10 percent income bracket amounts to tax years beginning in 2005, 2006 and 2007 (Code Sec. 1(i)(1)(B)(i)). The end result is that the increased income amounts in the 10 percent bracket apply to all individuals for tax years beginning after 2002 and the income brackets are adjusted for inflation in all tax years beginning after 2003. The increased bracket amounts do not apply to heads of households.

In 2010, the applicable tax rate schedules for single filers, married taxpayers filing separately, joint filers, heads of households, estates and trusts, after application of the EGTRRA, JGTRRA and WFTRA changes, are as follows (Rev. Proc. 2009-50, I.R.B. 2009-45, 617):

BACKGROUND

SINGLE TAXPAYERS
FOR TAX YEARS BEGINNING IN 2010

If taxable income is:		The tax is:	of the amount
Over—	but not over—		over—
$0	$8,375	10 %	$0
8,375	34,000	$837.50 + 15%	8,375
34,000	82,400	4,681.25 + 25%	34,000
82,400	171,850	16,781.25 + 28%	82,400
171,850	373,650	41,827.25 + 33%	171,850
373,650	. . . . .	108,421.25 + 35%	373,650

MARRIED INDIVIDUALS FILING SEPARATE RETURNS
FOR TAX YEARS BEGINNING IN 2010

If taxable income is:		The tax is:	of the amount
Over—	but not over—		over—
$0	$8,375	10 %	$0
8,375	34,000	$837.50 + 15%	8,375
34,000	68,650	4,681.25 + 25%	34,000
68,650	104,625	13,343.75 + 28%	68,650
104,625	186,825	23,416.75 + 33%	104,625
186,825	. . . . .	50,542.75 + 35%	186,825

MARRIED INDIVIDUALS FILING JOINT RETURNS AND SURVIVING SPOUSES
FOR TAX YEARS BEGINNING IN 2010

If taxable income is:		The tax is:	of the amount
Over—	but not over—		over—
$0	$16,750	10 %	$0
16,750	68,000	$1,675 + 15%	16,750
68,000	137,300	9,362.50 + 25%	68,000
137,300	209,250	26,687.50 + 28%	137,300
209,250	373,650	46,833.50 + 33%	209,250
373,650	. . . . .	101,085.50 + 35%	373,650

¶305

BACKGROUND

HEADS OF HOUSEHOLD
FOR TAX YEARS BEGINNING IN 2010

| If taxable income is: | | The tax is: | |
Over—	but not over—		of the amount over—
$0	$11,950	10 %	$0
11,950	45,550	$1,195 + 15%	11,950
45,550	117,650	6,235 + 25%	45,550
117,650	190,550	24,260 + 28%	117,650
190,550	373,650	44,672 + 33%	190,550
373,650	. . . . .	105,095 + 35%	373,650

ESTATES AND TRUSTS
FOR TAX YEARS BEGINNING IN 2010

| If taxable income is: | | The tax is: | |
Over—	but not over—		of the amount over—
$0	2,300	15 %	$0
2,300	5,350	$345 + 25%	2,300
5,350	8,200	1,107.50 + 28%	5,350
8,200	11,200	1,905.50 + 33%	8,200
11,200	. . . . .	2,895.50 + 35%	11,200

Sunset provision. Under the sunset provision of EGTRRA, amendments made by the Act will not apply to tax years beginning after December 31, 2010 (Act Sec. 901 of P.L. 107-16). Under provisions of both the Jobs Growth and Tax Relief Reconciliation Act of 2003 (JGTRRA) (P.L. 108-27) and the Working Families Tax Relief Act of 2004 (WFTRA) (P.L. 108-311) certain amendments made by JGTRRA and WFTRA are subject to the sunset provision of EGTRRA and will not apply to tax years beginning after December 31, 2010 (Act Sec. 901 of P.L. 107-16; Act Sec. 107 of P.L. 108-27; Act Sec. 105 of P.L. 108-311). With the reversion of applicable rates to pre-2001 levels, the following rate brackets would apply in 2011, as projected by CCH.

SINGLE TAXPAYERS
FOR TAX YEARS BEGINNING IN 2011 WITH SUNSET OF EGTRRA RATES

| If taxable income is: | | The tax is: | |
Over—	but not over—		of the amount over—
$0	$34,500	15 %	$0
34,500	83,600	5,175 + 28%	34,500
83,600	174,400	18,923 + 31%	83,600
174,400	379,150	47,071 + 36%	174,400
379,150	. . . . .	120,781 + 39.6%	379,150

¶305

BACKGROUND

MARRIED INDIVIDUALS FILING SEPARATE RETURNS
FOR TAX YEARS BEGINNING IN 2011 WITH SUNSET OF EGTRRA RATES

If taxable income is:		The tax is:	of the amount
Over—	but not over—		over—
$0	$28,825	15 %	$0
28,825	69,675	4,323.75 + 28%	28,825
69,675	106,150	15,761.75 + 31%	69,675
106,150	189,575	27,069 + 36%	106,150
189,575	. . . . .	57,102 + 39.6%	189,575

MARRIED INDIVIDUALS FILING JOINT RETURNS AND SURVIVING SPOUSES
FOR TAX YEARS BEGINNING IN 2011 WITH SUNSET OF EGTRRA RATES

If taxable income is:		The tax is:	of the amount
Over—	but not over—		over—
$0	$57,650	15 %	$0
57,650	139,350	8,647.50 + 28%	57,650
139,350	212,300	31,523.50 + 31%	139,350
212,300	379,150	54,138 + 36%	212,300
379,150	. . . . .	114,204 + 39.6%	379,150

HEADS OF HOUSEHOLDS
FOR TAX YEARS BEGINNING IN 2011 WITH SUNSET OF EGTRRA RATES

If taxable income is:		The tax is:	of the amount
Over—	but not over—		over—
$0	$46,250	15 %	$0
46,250	119,400	6,937.50 + 28%	46,250
119,400	193,350	27,419.50 + 31%	119,400
193,350	379,150	50,344 + 36%	193,350
379,150	. . . . .	117,232 + 39.6%	379,150

¶305

BACKGROUND

ESTATES AND TRUSTS
FOR TAX YEARS BEGINNING IN 2011 WITH SUNSET OF EGTRRA RATES

| If taxable income is: | | The tax is: | |
Over—	but not over—		of the amount over—
$0	2,300	15 %	$0
2,300	5,450	$345 + 28%	2,300
5,450	8,300	1,227 + 31%	5,450
8,300	11,350	2,110.50 + 36%	8,300
11,350	. . . . .	3,208.50 + 39.6%	11,350

NEW LAW EXPLAINED

Reduced tax rates for individuals, estates and trusts extended.—In tax years beginning in 2011 and 2012, the lower rates of tax imposed by Code Sec. 1 will continue to apply as the sunset date provided in the Economic Growth and Tax Relief Reconciliation Act of 2001 (P.L. 107-16) is extended to December 31, 2012 (Act. Sec 901 of the P.L. 107-16, as amended by the Tax Relief, Unemployment Insurance Reauthorization, and Job Creation Act of 2010 (P.L. 111-312)). This includes the extension of the 10 percent tax rate for lower individual incomes and the rates in excess of the 15 percent rate. For tax years beginning on or before December 31, 2012, the six rate brackets below will apply to individuals. Note that the 10 percent bracket does not apply to estates and trusts:

- 10 percent,
- 15 percent,
- 25 percent,
- 28 percent,
- 33 percent, and
- 35 percent (Code Sec. 1(a), (b), (c), (d) and (e)).

NEW LAW EXPLAINED

Key Rates and Figures: The estimated tax rate schedules for 2011, as projected by CCH, are as follows:

SINGLE TAXPAYERS
FOR TAX YEARS BEGINNING IN 2011 WITH EXTENSION OF EGTRRA RATES

| If taxable income is: | | The tax is: | |
Over—	but not over—		of the amount over—
$0	$8,500	10 %	$0
$8,500	$34,500	$850 + 15 %	8,500
34,500	83,600	4,750 + 25%	34,500
83,600	174,400	17,025 + 28%	83,600
174,400	379,150	42,449 + 33%	174,400
379,150	. . . . .	110,016.50 + 35%	379,150

MARRIED INDIVIDUALS FILING SEPARATE RETURNS
FOR TAX YEARS BEGINNING IN 2011 WITH EXTENSION OF EGTRRA RATES

| If taxable income is: | | The tax is: | |
Over—	but not over—		of the amount over—
$0	$8,500	10 %	$0
$8,500	$34,500	$850 + 15 %	$8,500
34,500	69,675	4,750 + 25%	34,500
69,675	106,150	13,543.75 + 28%	69,675
106,150	189,575	23,476.75 + 33%	106,150
189,575	. . . . .	51,337 + 35%	189,575

MARRIED INDIVIDUALS FILING JOINT RETURNS AND SURVIVING SPOUSES
FOR TAX YEARS BEGINNING IN 2011 WITH EXTENSION OF EGTRRA RATES

| If taxable income is: | | The tax is: | |
Over—	but not over—		of the amount over—
$0	$17,000	10 %	$0
$17,000	$69,000	$1,700 + 15 %	$17,000
69,000	139,350	9,500 + 25%	69,000
139,350	212,300	27,087.50 +28%	139,350
212,300	379,150	47,513.50 + 33%	212,300
379,150	. . . . .	102,574 + 35%	379,150

¶305

NEW LAW EXPLAINED

HEADS OF HOUSEHOLDS
FOR TAX YEARS BEGINNING IN 2011 WITH EXTENSION OF EGTRRA RATES

If taxable income is: Over—	but not over—	The tax is:	of the amount over—
$0	$12,150	10 %	$0
$12,150	$46,250	$1,215 + 15 %	$12,150
46,250	119,400	6,330 + 25%	46,250
119,400	193,350	24,617 + 28%	119,400
193,350	379,150	45,323 + 33%	193,350
379,150	. . . . .	106,637 + 35%	379,150

ESTATES AND TRUSTS
FOR TAX YEARS BEGINNING IN 2011 WITH EXTENSION OF EGTRRA RATES

If taxable income is: Over—	but not over—	The tax is:	of the amount over—
$0	2,300	15 %	$0
2,300	5,450	$345 + 25%	2,300
5,450	8,300	1,132.50 + 28%	5,450
8,300	11,350	1,930.50 + 33%	8,300
11,350	. . . . .	2,937 + 35%	11,350

Comment: The 2011 schedules for married individuals filing separate returns and joint filers and surviving spouses also reflect the extension of marriage penalty relief. See ¶310 for a complete discussion.

The extension of tax rates, including the 10 percent tax rate bracket significantly decreases the amount of taxes paid by all taxpayers when compared to the tax liability resulting from the sunset of the EGTRRA rates and reversion to pre-2001 rates. Further, taxpayers with lower incomes experience proportionally disparate benefits due to the extension of the 10 percent bracket.

> **Example 1:** Andy and Sue, married taxpayers filing joint returns, have taxable income of $170,000 in 2011. Using the schedules above, they will pay $35,669.50 in taxes in 2011 with the lower rates extended as opposed to $41,025 with the pre-2001 rates in place, a decrease of more than 13 percent.

> **Example 2:** Fred and Wilma, married taxpayers filing joint returns, have taxable income of $30,000 in 2011. Using the schedules above, they will pay $3,650 in

¶305

NEW LAW EXPLAINED

> taxes in 2011 with the lower rates extended as opposed to $4,500 with the pre-2001 rates in place, a decrease of almost 19 percent.

> **Example 3:** Homer and Marge, married taxpayers filing joint returns, have taxable income of $16,750 in 2011. Using the schedules above, they will pay $1,675 in taxes in 2011 with the lower rates extended as opposed to $2,512.50 with the pre-2001 rates in place, a decrease of 33 percent.

Rates sunset in 2013. The lower rates are scheduled to sunset, and therefore no longer apply, to tax years beginning after December 31, 2012 (Act. Sec 901 of P.L. 107-16, as amended by the Tax Relief Act of 2010). For tax years beginning after December 31, 2012, the following pre-2001 rates will once again apply:

- 15 percent,
- 28 percent,
- 31 percent,
- 36 percent, and
- 39.6 percent (Code Sec. 1(a), (b), (c), (d) and (e)), prior to amendment by P.L. 107-16.

> **Planning Note:** Since the tax rates will be higher in 2013 than the rates applicable in 2012, acceleration of compensation and bonuses into 2012 will be advantageous for taxpayers where applicable. Those working on projects subject to a bonus payment upon completion should strive to complete these projects in 2012. Because deductions are less valuable at lower tax rates, however, payments that result in deductible expenses should be postponed until 2013, when possible.

> **Planning Note:** The increase in tax rates for 2013 may impact any retirement savings or deferred compensation plan distributions. Where these types of plans provide for periodic distributions that are subject to tax, taxpayers should consider the feasibility of accelerating such distributions to 2012.

Other changes. Other provisions of Code Sec. 1 relating to rates of tax on capital gains and dividends were also subject to the EGTRRA sunset provision. For a discussion of these rates, see ¶405 and ¶420, respectively. Also, the lower accumulated earnings tax rate under Code Sec. 531 and the personal holding company tax rate under Code Sec. 541 are both subject to the EGTRRA sunset provision. For a discussion of these two special taxes, see ¶435 and ¶440, respectively.

> **Practical Analysis:** According to *Vincent O'Brien*, President of Vincent J. O'Brien, CPA, PC, Lynbrook, New York, the extension of the lower ordinary income tax rates for individuals (Code Sec. 1) for the 2011 and 2012 tax years will keep the maximum tax rate for ordinary income at 35 percent (instead of the 39.6 percent rate that would

NEW LAW EXPLAINED

have applied under the original expiration date of The Economic Growth and Tax Relief Reconciliation Act of 2001 (EGTRRA) (P.L. 107-16).

This will benefit higher-income taxpayers who converted traditional IRAs into Roth IRAs during 2010 and who will recognize one-half of the income from the conversion in 2011 and the other half of the income in 2012. These taxpayers will receive both the benefit of deferring the payment of the tax due and the benefit of the 35 percent bracket for both years. Under the original expiration date of EGTRRA, such taxpayers would have been subject to a higher tax on the income deferred into 2011 and 2012.

▶ **Effective date.** The provision applies to tax years beginning after December 31, 2000 (Act Sec. 101(a)(2) of the Tax Relief, Unemployment Insurance Reauthorization, and Job Creation Act of 2010 (P.L. 111-312)); Act Sec. 101(d)(1) of the Economic Growth and Tax Relief Reconciliation Act of 2001 (EGTRRA) (P.L. 107-16)). The provision does not apply to tax years beginning after December 31, 2012 (Act Sec. 101(a)(1) of the Tax Relief Act of 2010; Act Sec. 901 of EGTRRA). See ¶105 for a specific discussion of the sunset provision of EGTRRA and how it is applied.

Law source: Law at ¶5005, ¶7010, and ¶7015. Committee Report at ¶10,010.

— Act Sec. 101(a)(1) of the Tax Relief, Unemployment Insurance Reauthorization, and Job Creation Act of 2010 (P.L. 111-312), amending Act Sec. 901 of the Economic Growth and Tax Relief Reconciliation Act of 2001 (EGTRRA) (P.L. 107-16).

Reporter references: For further information, consult the following CCH reporters.

— Standard Federal Tax Reporter, ¶3270.01

— Tax Research Consultant, FILEIND: 15,054.05

— Practical Tax Explanation, § 1,015

¶310 15-Percent Tax Rate Bracket for Joint Filers

SUMMARY OF NEW LAW

The 15-percent tax bracket for joint filers (and surviving spouses) remains twice the size of the corresponding rate bracket for single filers for tax years 2011 and 2012.

BACKGROUND

A marriage penalty exists when the tax on the combined income of a married couple exceeds the sum of the taxes that would be imposed if each spouse filed a separate return as a single person. This occurs most often when both spouses have income. If one spouse does not work or has a small amount of income, a marriage bonus may occur—that is, the couple may pay less tax by filing a joint return than they would have if each spouse filed his or her own return. Although many factors can contribute

BACKGROUND

to a marriage penalty, the two most significant factors are the disparity in the size of a married and single person's standard deduction and the income levels at which the various tax brackets are applied.

The Economic Growth and Tax Relief Reconciliation Act of 2001 (EGTRRA) (P.L. 107-16) included provisions that addressed these two issues. First, EGTRRA included a provision that would increase the size of the standard deduction for joint filers to twice the size (i.e., 200 percent) of the standard deduction for a single filer. The EGTRRA increase to the standard deduction for married couples filing jointly is discussed at ¶315.

EGTRRA also provided a phased-in increase in the top end of the 15-percent tax bracket for married taxpayers filing jointly (and surviving spouses), which would gradually increase the size of the 15-percent bracket for joint filers until it reached twice the size of the 15-percent bracket for single filers (Code Sec. 1(f)(8), as added by P.L. 107-16). The phase-in period, which was scheduled to start in 2005 and be completed in 2008, would eventually cause the amount of taxable income that falls within a joint filer's 15-percent tax bracket to be exactly twice the amount (i.e., 200 percent) of the taxable income that falls within the 15-percent tax bracket of a single filer. For 2005, the applicable percentage was scheduled to be 180; for 2006, the applicable percentage was scheduled to be 187; and for 2007, the applicable percentage was scheduled to be 193. The marriage penalty relief was to be fully phased in at 200 percent for 2008 through 2010 (Code Sec. 1(f)(8)).

Additionally, EGTRRA added a new 10-percent bracket with an income range for joint filers equal to twice the amount for individuals (Code Sec. 1(i)(1)). However, relief from the disparity between the single and joint tax brackets was limited to the 10-percent and 15-percent brackets. Limits to joint filer brackets for tax rates above 15 percent were not increased to twice the amount of corresponding limits for single filers.

The Jobs and Growth Tax Relief Reconciliation Act of 2003 (JGTRRA) (P.L. 108-27) accelerated the EGTRRA increases, making the size of the 15-percent tax bracket for joint filers equal to twice the size of a single person's tax bracket for the 2003 and 2004 tax years. Beginning in 2005, the size of the 15-percent tax bracket for joint filers was to be determined in accordance with the phase-in schedule enacted by EGTRRA, as amended by JGTRRA.

The Working Families Tax Relief Act of 2004 (P.L. 108-311) eliminated the phase-in schedule that was to have applied to the tax years 2005 through 2008. As a result, the size of the 15-percent rate bracket for joint returns was increased to twice the size of the corresponding rate bracket for single returns for tax years 2005 through 2007. Therefore, the size of the 15-percent rate bracket for joint returns was twice the size of the corresponding rate bracket for single returns for tax years 2003 through 2010.

Sunset provision. Under the sunset provision of EGTRRA, amendments made by the Act will not apply to tax years beginning after December 31, 2010 (Act Sec. 901 of P.L. 107-16).

¶310

NEW LAW EXPLAINED

Marriage penalty relief in 15-percent tax bracket extended.—The increase in the size of the 15-percent tax bracket for joint filers (and surviving spouses) to twice the size of the corresponding rate bracket for single filers is extended for two years. As a result, the size of the 15-percent rate bracket for joint returns will remain twice the size of the corresponding rate bracket for single returns, for tax years 2011 and 2012 (Code Sec. 1(f)(8), Act Sec. 901 of the Economic Growth and Tax Relief Reconciliation Act of 2001 (EGTRRA) (P.L. 107-16), as amended by the Tax Relief, Unemployment Insurance Reauthorization, and Job Creation Act of 2010 (P.L. 111-312)).

If the EGTRRA sunset takes effect at the end of 2012, the increase in the size of the 15-percent tax bracket for joint filers will not apply to tax years beginning after December 31, 2012, and the taxable income levels for joint filers in the 15-percent tax bracket will revert to the statutory dollar amount (adjusted annually for inflation). As a result of the sunset, the 15-percent tax bracket for joint filers will be less than the combined 15-percent tax brackets of two single filers and married taxpayers may have more of their taxable income pushed into a higher marginal tax bracket than their unmarried counterparts.

> **Planning Note:** Married taxpayers who may face higher tax liabilities as a result of this change may need to adjust their tax withholding or be prepared to make larger estimated tax payments beginning in 2013.

▶ **Effective date.** The provision is effective for tax years beginning after December 31, 2002 (Act Sec. 101(a)(2) of the Tax Relief, Unemployment Insurance Reauthorization, and Job Creation Act of 2010 (P.L. 111-312)); Act Sec. 102(c) of the Jobs and Growth Tax Reconciliation Act of 2003 (JGTRRA) (P.L. 108-27); Act Sec. 302(c) of the Economic Growth and Tax Relief Reconciliation Act of 2001 (EGTRRA) (P.L. 107-16)). The provision shall not apply to tax years beginning after December 31, 2012 (Act Sec. 101(a)(1) of the Tax Relief Act of 2010; Act Sec. 901 of EGTRRA). See ¶105 for a specific discussion of the sunset provision of EGTRRA and how it is applied.

Law source: Law at ¶5005 and ¶7010. Committee Report at ¶10,040.

— Act Sec. 101(a)(1) of the Tax Relief, Unemployment Insurance Reauthorization, and Job Creation Act of 2010 (P.L. 111-312), amending Act Sec. 901 of the Economic Growth and Tax Relief Reconciliation Act of 2001 (EGTRRA) (P.L. 107-16);

— Act Sec. 101(a)(2), providing the effective date.

Reporter references: For further information, consult the following CCH reporters.

— Standard Federal Tax Reporter, ¶3270.01

— Tax Research Consultant, FILEIND: 3,210

— Practical Tax Explanation, § 1,015

¶310

¶312 Payroll Tax Cut

SUMMARY OF NEW LAW

The employee's portion of the old age, survivors, and disability insurance (OASDI) tax rate under the payroll tax is reduced by two percentage points to 4.2 percent for 2011. Similarly, the OASDI portion of the self-employment tax is reduced by two percentage points to 10.4 percent for 2011. A similar reduction applies to the railroad retirement tax.

BACKGROUND

Under the Federal Insurance Contributions Act (FICA), an employer is required to withhold social security taxes (including hospital insurance tax) from wages paid to an employee during the year and must also match the tax withheld from the employee's wages. For 2010, the combined tax rate is 7.65 percent, which consists of a 6.2 percent component for old-age, survivors, and disability insurance (OASDI) and a 1.45 percent component for hospital insurance (Medicare). The OASDI rate applies only to wages paid up to the OASDI wage base, which is $106,800 in 2010 and 2011. There is no cap on wages subject to the Medicare tax (Code Secs. 3101, 3111 and 3121(a)).

Generally, the term "wages" includes all remuneration (other than fees paid to a public official) for services performed by an employee for an employer, including the cash value of all remuneration (including benefits) paid in any medium other than cash (Code Sec. 3401(a)). Salaries, fees, bonuses, commissions on sales or on insurance premiums, taxable fringe benefits, pensions and retirement pay (unless taxed as an annuity) are, if paid as compensation for services, subject to withholding (Reg. §31.3401(a)-1(a)(2)).

The Railroad Retirement System has two main components. Tier I is financed by taxes on employers and employees equal to the Social Security payroll tax and provides benefits that are about the same as those under Social Security. Covered workers and their employers pay the Tier 1 tax instead of the Social Security payroll tax. Tier II is the equivalent of a private pension plan, with employers and employees contributing a certain percentage of pay toward to system to finance benefits. The federal government collects the Tier II payroll contribution and pays out the benefits.

The Self-Employment Contributions Act (SECA) applies to the self-employment income of self-employed individuals (Code Sec. 1401). The combined rate of tax on self-employment income is 15.3 percent: a 12.4 percent component for OASDI and a 2.9 percent component for Medicare. For 2010 and 2011, the OASDI maximum wage base is $106,800. There is no cap for the Medicare component. If wages subject to social security or railroad retirement tax are received during the tax year by a person who also has self-employment income, the maximum is reduced by the amount of wages on which these taxes were paid (Code Sec. 1402(b)). If net earnings from self-employment are less than $400, no self-employment tax is payable.

BACKGROUND

The tax is based on "self-employment income", which is defined as net earnings from self-employment (Code Sec. 1402(b)). In order to determine self-employment tax liability, a self-employed individual is entitled to deduct from net self-employment earnings an amount equal to one half of the combined OASDI (12.4 percent) and HI (2.9 percent) rates multiplied by net earnings from self-employment (Code Sec. 1402(a)(12)). This reduced amount of self-employment income is then multiplied by the self-employment tax rate (15.3 percent) to arrive at the amount of self-employment tax imposed. In order to figure income tax liability, a self-employed individual is entitled to deduct one half of his self-employment tax liability in arriving at adjusted gross income (Code Sec. 164(f)).

The Making Work Pay credit allows a credit against income tax in an amount equal to the lesser of 6.2 percent of the individual's earned income or $400 ($800 for married couples filing jointly), subject to income limitations (Code Sec. 36A). The credit is phased out for single taxpayers with a modified adjusted gross income that exceeds $75,000 ($150,000 for joint filers) and is scheduled to expire after 2010.

NEW LAW EXPLAINED

Payroll and self-employment taxes temporarily reduced.—For 2011, the rate of the old age, survivors, and disability insurance (OASDI) tax on self-employment income under Code Sec. 1401(a) is reduced by two percent, to 10.4 percent. The rate of the employee's OASDI portion of the payroll tax under Code Sec. 3101(a) is also reduced by two percent, to 4.2 percent. The employer's share of OASDI remains at 6.2 percent. The 4.2 rate also applies for purposes of determining the applicable percentage under Code Sec. 3201(a) (railroad retirement tax) and Code Sec. 3211(a)(1) (tax on employee representatives) (Act Sec. 601(a) of the Tax Relief, Unemployment Insurance Reauthorization, and Job Creation Act of 2010 (P.L. 111-312)).

The rate reduction is not taken into account in determining the Code Sec. 1402(a)(12) self-employment income deduction allowed for determining the amount of the net earnings from self-employment for the tax year (Act Sec. 601(b)(1) of the Tax Relief Act of 2010). Thus, the deduction for 2011 remains at 7.65 percent of self-employment income. For any tax year that begins in 2011, the self-employment tax liability deduction under Code Sec. 164(f) equals the sum of:

- 59.6 percent of the applicable OASDI taxes, plus
- 50 percent of the applicable Medicare taxes (Act Sec. 601(b)(2) of the Tax Relief Act of 2010).

  Comment: As a result of the two-percent reduction in the OASDI tax rate, the deductible percent of the OASDI tax requires modification to compute the deduction for self-employment taxes under Code Sec. 164(f). According to the Joint Committee on Taxation, *Technical Explanation of the Revenue Provisions Contained in the "Tax Relief, Unemployment Insurance Reauthorization, and Job Creation Act of 2010"* (JCX-55-10), December 10, 2010: "The new percentage is necessary to continue to allow the self-employed taxpayer to deduct the full amount of the employer portion of SECA taxes. The employer OASDI tax rate

¶312

NEW LAW EXPLAINED

remains at 6.2 percent, while the employee portion falls to 4.2 percent. Thus, the employer share of total OASDI taxes is 6.2 divided by 10.4, or 59.6 percent of the OASDI portion of SECA taxes."

The two-percent reductions in the OASDI portions of the payroll and self-employment taxes apply during the *payroll tax holiday period*, which is calendar year 2011 (Act Sec. 601(c) of the Tax Relief Act of 2010). The Secretary of the Treasury is to notify employers of the payroll tax holiday period in any manner deemed appropriate (Act Sec. 601(d) of the Tax Relief Act of 2010).

Compliance Tip: The IRS has issued the 2011 Percentage Method Tables for Income Tax Withholding, based on the passage of the Tax Relief Act of 2010 (Notice 1036, Rev. December 2010). Employers should implement the 2011 withholding tables as soon as possible, but not later than January 31, 2011.

Amounts equal to the reduction in revenues to the Treasury resulting from the two-percent payroll tax deduction are to be transferred to the Federal Old-Age and Survivors Trust Fund and the Federal Disability Insurance Trust Fund, and to the Social Security Equivalent Benefit Account. Such amounts are to be transferred from the General Fund of the United States Treasury at such times and in such a manner as to replicate, to the extent possible, the transfers that would have occurred to the Trust Funds and Benefit Account had the payroll tax reduction provision not been enacted (Act Sec. 601(e) of the Tax Relief Act of 2010).

The payroll tax reduction is not to be applied for purposes of any federal law other than the provisions of the Internal Revenue Code (Act Sec. 601(e)(3) of the Tax Relief Act of 2010).

Comment: The Tax Relief Act of 2010 does not renew the Making Work Pay credit under Code Sec. 36A. Under that provision, a single taxpayer making $6,450 would get the full $400 credit amount. Under the two-percent payroll tax deduction, an employee would need to make $20,000 to receive a $400 reduction in taxes. However, unlike the Making Work Pay credit, the two percent OASDI reduction is available to all wage earners, with no phase-out limit irrespective of income level. Thus, individuals earning at or above the OASDI cap of $106,800 would receive a $2,136 tax benefit in 2011.

▶ **Effective date.** No specific effective date is provided by the Act. The provision is, therefore, considered effective on December 17, 2010, the date of enactment.

Law source: Law at ¶7040. Committee Report at ¶10,160.

— Act Sec. 601 of the Tax Relief, Unemployment Insurance Reauthorization, and Job Creation Act of 2010 (P.L. 111-312).

Reporter references: For further information, consult the following CCH reporters.

— Standard Federal Tax Reporter, ¶32,543.01, ¶32,543.01

— Tax Research Consultant, PAYROLL: 9,052 and INDIV: 63,050

— Practical Tax Explanation, § 22,205.10 and § 23,105

¶312

DEDUCTIONS

¶315 Standard Deduction for Joint Filers

SUMMARY OF NEW LAW

The standard deduction for joint filers (and surviving spouses) remains twice the inflation-adjusted amount of the standard deduction applicable to single taxpayers and married taxpayers filing separately, for tax years 2011 and 2012.

BACKGROUND

A marriage penalty exists when the tax on the combined income of a married couple exceeds the sum of the taxes that would be imposed if each spouse filed a separate return as a single person. This situation exists most often when both spouses have income. If one spouse does not work or has a small amount of income a marriage bonus may occur, that is, the couple pays less tax by filing a joint return than they would have if each spouse filed his or her own return. Although many factors can contribute to a marriage penalty, the two most significant factors are the disparity in the size of a married and single person's standard deduction and the income levels at which the various tax brackets are applied.

The Economic Growth and Tax Relief Reconciliation Act of 2001 (EGTRRA) (P.L. 107-16) eliminated the marriage penalty, by among other things, increasing the size of the 15-percent tax bracket (see ¶310) and increasing the standard deduction, for married couples filing jointly (and surviving spouses).

The Economic Growth and Tax Relief Reconciliation Act of 2001 (EGTRRA) (P.L. 107-16) phased in the increase in the standard deduction for joint filers, to 200 percent of the basic standard deduction for single taxpayers and married taxpayers filing separately, beginning in 2005 through 2008, with full phase in accomplished in 2009 and 2010. EGTRRA eliminated the distinct standard deduction for married taxpayers who file separate returns (Code Sec. 63(c)(2), (c)(4) and (c)(7)). EGTRRA also eliminated a special rounding rule under which inflation adjustments to the basic standard deduction for married taxpayers who file separate returns were rounded down to the next lowest increment of $25, rather than $50 (Code Sec. 1(f)(6)(B)). The EGTRRA changes expire at the end of 2010 (Act Sec. 901 of P.L. 107-16).

The timing and other details of these basic EGTRRA changes were subsequently modified as follows:

- The Job Creation and Worker Assistance Tax Act of 2002 (P.L. 107-147) restored the distinct standard deduction for married taxpayers who file separate returns, but made it equal to half the deduction for joint filers. A rounding rule was added, under which the standard deduction for joint filers (and surviving spouses) was rounded down to the next lowest multiple of $50. These changes were made via technical amendments that were treated as if they were enacted as part of EGTRRA (Act Sec. 411 of P.L. 107-147).

BACKGROUND

- The Jobs and Growth Tax Relief Reconciliation Act of 2003 (JGTRRA) (P.L. 108-27) accelerated the full increase in the standard deduction for joint filers to 2003 and 2004. The effective date of the EGTRRA amendments and consequently the technical corrections made by P.L. 107-147 was accelerated to apply to tax years beginning after 2002. The EGTRRA sunset applies to these changes (Act Sec. 107 of P.L. 108-27).

- The Working Families Tax Relief Act of 2004 (P.L. 108-311) eliminated the original phase-in of the increase in the standard deduction for joint filers, and accelerated the full increase to 2005. It also eliminated the distinct standard deduction for married taxpayers who file separate returns, and instead applied the same standard deduction to them and to single taxpayers (Code Sec. 63(c)(2)). The EGTRRA sunset applies to these changes (Act Sec. 105 of P.L. 108-311).

As a result of all of these changes, for tax years beginning in 2003 through 2010, the standard deduction for married taxpayers who file joint returns is equal to twice the standard deduction for single taxpayers and married taxpayers who file separate returns (Code Sec. 63(c)).

Sunset provision. Under a sunset provision of EGTRRA, amendments made by the Act will not apply to tax years beginning after December 31, 2010 (Act Sec. 901 of P.L. 107-16).

NEW LAW EXPLAINED

Marriage penalty relief in standard deduction extended.—Relief from the marriage penalty in the standard deduction for married taxpayers filing joint returns (and surviving spouses) is extended for two years. Thus, the standard deduction for these taxpayers remains twice the inflation-adjusted amount of the standard deduction for single taxpayers and married taxpayers filing separately, for tax years 2011 and 2012 (Code Sec. 63(c)(2) and (4); Act Sec. 901 of the Economic Growth and Tax Relief Reconciliation Act of 2001 (EGTRRA) (P.L. 107-16), as amended by the Tax Relief, Unemployment Insurance Reauthorization, and Job Creation Act of 2010 (P.L. 111-312)).

> **Comment:** The IRS has already announced several inflation adjustments for 2011, but it has not yet announced the standard deduction amounts. CCH projects that for 2011, the standard deduction for a married couple filing jointly (and surviving spouses) will be $11,600 and the standard deduction for single taxpayers and married taxpayers filing separately will be $5,800.

Additionally, the special $25 rounding rule for determining the inflation adjusted amount of the basic standard deduction for married persons filing separate returns, will not apply to tax years 2011 and 2012 (Code Sec. 1(f)(6)(B); Act Sec. 901 of EGTRRA, as amended by the Tax Relief Act of 2010).

If the sunset provision of EGTRRA takes effect in 2013:

- the basic standard deduction for married taxpayers who file a joint return will no longer be 200 percent of the amount allowed for unmarried taxpayers; instead, it will be $5,000 (adjusted annually for inflation); and

¶315

NEW LAW EXPLAINED

- married taxpayers who file separate returns will have a standard deduction of $2,500 (adjusted annually for inflation) while the basic standard deduction for single filers will remain at $3,000 (adjusted annually for inflation).

> **Planning Note:** These decreases in the standard deduction will increase the number of married taxpayers who should consider itemizing deductions, since their basic standard deductions will more likely be less than their itemized deductions.

Additionally, if the EGTRRA sunset takes effect in 2013, the special rounding rule for determining the inflation adjusted amount of the basic standard deduction for married persons filing separately will apply and the inflation adjusted amount will be rounded down to the next lowest $25 increment instead of the next lowest $50 increment).

> **Comment:** This rounding down to the next lowest $25 increment is appropriate for the standard deduction for separate filers because that deduction is split in half for each spouse that files separately (Omnibus Budget Reconciliation Act of 1989 (P.L. 101-239), Conference Committee Report). However, the $25-rounding rule will not apply if the married taxpayer is claimed as another taxpayer's dependent, or to the married taxpayer's additional standard deduction for old age or blindness.

▶ **Effective date.** The provision is effective for tax years beginning after December 31, 2002 (Act Sec. 101(a)(2) of the Tax Relief, Unemployment Insurance Reauthorization, and Job Creation Act of 2010 (P.L. 111-312); Act Sec. 103(b) of the Jobs and Growth Tax Reconciliation Act of 2003 (JGTRRA) (P.L. 108-27); Act Sec. 301 of the Economic Growth and Tax Relief Reconciliation Act of 2001 (EGTRRA) (P.L. 107-16)). The provision will not apply to tax years beginning after December 31, 2012 (Act Sec. 101(a)(1) of the Tax Relief Act of 2010; Act Sec. 901 of EGTRRA). See ¶105 for a specific discussion of the sunset provision of EGTRRA and how it is applied.

Law source: Law at ¶5005, ¶5185, and ¶7010. Committee Report at ¶10,040.

— Act Sec. 101(a)(1) of the Tax Relief, Unemployment Insurance Reauthorization, and Job Creation Act of 2010 (P.L. 111-312), amending Act Sec. 901 of the Economic Growth and Tax Relief Reconciliation Act of 2001 (EGTRRA) (P.L. 107-16).

— Act Sec. 101(a)(2), providing the effective date.

Reporter references: For further information, consult the following CCH reporters.

— Standard Federal Tax Reporter, ¶6023.01

— Tax Research Consultant, FILEIND: 12,102

— Practical Tax Explanation, § 1,010.15

¶320 Overall Limitation on Itemized Deductions for Higher-Income Individuals

SUMMARY OF NEW LAW

The repeal of the limitation of itemized deductions for higher-income individuals is extended for two years. As a result, the itemized deduction phaseout for affected individuals will not apply to tax years beginning in 2011 and 2012, and higher-income taxpayers will not be required to reduce the amount of their itemized deductions when their adjusted gross income exceeds certain threshold amounts.

BACKGROUND

The Economic Growth and Tax Relief Reconciliation Act of 2001 (EGTRRA) (P.L. 107-16) repealed the limitation on itemized deductions for higher-income individuals (ofter referred to as the "Pease limitation" after its originator, Congressman Donald J. Pease). The repeal was phased in over a five-year period beginning in 2006 and ending with the total repeal of the limitation in 2010 (Code Sec. 68(f) and (g)).

Under the Pease limitation, individuals whose adjusted gross income (AGI) exceeded a specified threshold amount were required to reduce the amount of their otherwise allowable itemized deductions (Code Sec. 68). Specifically, itemized deductions that would otherwise be allowable were reduced by the lesser of (1) three percent of AGI that exceeded the threshold amount of $100,000 ($50,000 for a married individual filing separately), adjusted for inflation, or (2) 80 percent of the total amount of otherwise allowable itemized deductions (Code Sec. 68(a)).

> **Comment:** For example, for tax years beginning in 2009, the inflation-adjusted threshold amount of AGI, above which the amount of otherwise allowable itemized deductions was reduced, was $166,800 for married individuals filing jointly, single individuals, and heads of households, and $83,400 for married individuals filing separately.

Under Code Sec. 68, as amended by EGTRRA, for tax years beginning after December 31, 2005, and before January 1, 2010, the limitation on itemized deductions was reduced every two years. Thus, for tax years beginning in 2006 and 2007, the limitation was reduced by one-third, and, for tax years beginning in 2008 and 2009, the limitation was reduced by two-thirds (Code Sec. 68(f)). For tax years beginning after December 31, 2009, the limitation on itemized deductions no longer applies (Code Sec. 68(g)).

Sunset provision. Under the sunset provision of EGTRRA, amendments made by EGTRRA will not apply to tax years beginning after December 31, 2010 (Act Sec. 901 of P.L. 107-16).

¶315

NEW LAW EXPLAINED

Repeal of limitation on itemized deductions for higher-income individuals extended.—The repeal of the limitation on the amount of allowable itemized deductions for higher-income individuals (Code Sec. 68) is extended for two years. Thus, the limitation will not apply to tax years beginning in 2011 and 2012. The repeal of the limitation is now scheduled to expire, under the sunset provision of EGTRRA, for tax years beginning after December 31, 2012 (Act Sec. 901 of the Economic Growth and Tax Relief Reconciliation Act of 2001 (EGTRRA) (P.L. 107-16), as amended by the Tax Relief, Unemployment Insurance Reauthorization, and Job Creation Act of 2010 (P.L. 111-312)).

Tax years beginning after 2012. As it now stands, for tax years beginning after December 31, 2012, the amount of otherwise allowable itemized deductions will be reduced for higher-income taxpayers whose AGI exceeds the threshold amount (Code Sec. 68(b)). The threshold amount, $100,000 for most taxpayers and $50,000 for married taxpayers filing separate returns, was set by statute when Code Sec. 68 was originally enacted in 1991, and is adjusted annually for inflation.

Under the itemized deduction (Pease) limitation, taxpayers with AGI over the threshold amount will need to reduce their otherwise allowable itemized deductions by the lesser of:

- three percent of the amount of the taxpayer's AGI in excess of $100,000, as adjusted for inflation ($50,000, as adjusted for inflation, for a married individual filing separately), or

- 80 percent of the itemized deductions otherwise allowable for the tax year (Code Sec. 68(a)).

> **Comment:** The Pease limitation is restricted to higher-income individuals; it does not apply to estates and trusts (Code Sec. 68(e)).

For purposes of the 80-percent limitation, itemized deductions will not include the deduction relating to medical expenses (Code Sec. 213), investment interest expenses (Code Sec. 163(d)), casualty or theft losses (Code Sec. 165(c)), or allowable wagering losses (Code Sec. 165(d)) (Code Sec. 68(c)). Also, in computing the reduction of itemized deductions, all other limitations on itemized deductions, such as the two-percent floor for miscellaneous itemized deductions and, for tax years beginning after 2012 (see below), the 10- or 7.5-percent floor for medical expense deductions, will be applied first and then the otherwise allowable total amount of itemized deductions will be reduced (Code Sec. 68(d)).

Example: For the 2013 tax year, Freddie and Fannie Smith, who are married and file a joint return, have deductible unreimbursed employee business expenses in excess of the two-percent-of-AGI floor, state and local income and real estate taxes, and charitable contributions, totaling $15,000. They also have deductible unreimbursed medical expenses in excess of the 10 percent-of-AGI floor of $2,000. Their AGI is $220,000, and, for purposes of this example only, assume an

---

¶315

NEW LAW EXPLAINED

inflation-adjusted threshold amount of $169,550 applies to married taxpayers filing jointly in 2013.

Since their AGI of $220,000 exceeds the projected inflation-adjusted threshold amount of $169,550, the amount of their otherwise allowable itemized deductions of $17,000 must be reduced. The first possible reduction is three percent of the excess of AGI over the inflation-adjusted threshold amount, or $1,514 (($220,000 − $169,550) × three percent). The second possible reduction is 80 percent of the amount of itemized deductions (excluding medical expenses) or $12,000 (.8 × $15,000). The lesser of the two amounts is $1,514, which is the applicable reduction of their itemized deductions. The Smiths must reduce their otherwise allowable itemized deductions to $15,486 ($17,000 − $1,514).

Comment: Effective for tax years beginning after December 31, 2012, the threshold to claim an itemized deduction for unreimbursed medical expenses is increased from 7.5 percent of AGI to 10 percent of AGI for regular tax purposes (Code Sec. 213(a), as amended by the Patient Protection and Affordable Care Act (PPACA) (P.L. 111-148)). Taxpayers (or their spouses) who are age 65 and older before the close of the tax year are exempt from the increased threshold and continue to be eligible to claim the medical expense deduction if their medical expenses exceed 7.5 percent of AGI. This temporary waiver applies to tax years beginning after December 31, 2012, and ending before January 1, 2017 (Code Sec. 213(f), as added by PPACA).

Planning Note: Higher-income individuals who anticipate being close to the threshold amounts of AGI for the 2013 tax year should look to shift their projected itemized deductions for 2013 to 2012, where possible, by accelerating payment of deductible expenses if they are on the cash method. For example, individuals who planned on making charitable contributions in 2013 might want to make those contributions in 2012. Since the itemized deduction limitation does not apply in 2012, affected individuals would not lose a portion of the amount of itemized deductions due to the reinstatement of the Pease limitation in 2013.

Further, for purposes of determining the tax treatment of state income tax refunds and other similar payments, the tax benefit rule (Code Sec. 111) will continue to apply (Senate Committee Report for the Omnibus Budget Reconciliation Act of 1990 (P.L. 101-508)). Thus, for example, if an amount is received in 2014 as a refund or recovery of an itemized deduction that was subject to the Pease limitation rules in 2013, the refund or recovery is included in gross income in the year received (2014). The amount that is includible equals the difference between the prior year's itemized deductions (subject to the overall deduction limitation) and the deductions that would have been claimed if the proper amount of tax had been paid and no recovery made (Rev. Rul. 93-75, 1993-2 CB 63).

For purposes of the alternative minimum tax, itemized deductions that are otherwise allowed in computing alternative minimum taxable income (AMTI) will not be reduced (Code Sec. 56(b)(1)(F)). In other words, the amount of itemized deductions

NEW LAW EXPLAINED

that are cut back for regular income tax purposes are not cut back in calculating AMTI.

Practical Analysis: According to *Daniel S. Hoops*, Walsh College, Troy, Michigan, the limitation on the amount of allowable itemized deductions for high-income individuals (Code Sec. 68) is extended through December 31, 2012 under the Tax Relief, Unemployment Insurance Reauthorization and Job Creation Act of 2010 (2010 Tax Relief Act).

Until enactment of the 2010 Tax Relief Act, individuals who met a threshold AGI amount were scheduled to have to reduce their, otherwise allowable, itemized deductions. The extension of this tax relief provides those covered taxpayers a benefit beyond December 31, 2010 in having to project what year-end expenditures they should pay before being subject to the cutback under the Economic Growth and Tax Relief Reconciliation Act of 2001. Many affected taxpayers may not have planned or saved sufficient funds to cover these expenditures before January 1, 2011.

For example, if the taxpayer owed state income taxes for 2010, those amounts may not have been due until 2011. If the taxpayer planned and saved for this liability in advance, paying that amount before December 31, 2010 would have been advisable; if the taxpayer had not planned or saved, he or she would have been detrimentally impacted by the scheduled cutback. The same detriment would have been felt if the taxpayer received his or her 2011 real estate taxes at the end of 2010, but was unable to pay the amount upon receipt in 2010. The 2010 Tax Relief Act also eliminates the cutback of several miscellaneous itemized deductions that are subject to the two percent AGI floor.

Charitable organizations are probably the biggest beneficiaries of the 2010 Tax Relief Act as many taxpayers covered by the AGI limitation may also have been the larger or more likely charitable donors. As a direct result of the overall itemized deduction limitation that was scheduled to take place on December 31, 2010, many donors revised their planned giving to off set the deduction limitations. With additional funds to donate (and without the loss or limitation on the amount that may be taken as a charitable deduction), taxpayers that were subject to the cutback are more likely to continue with their planned giving activities. Taxpayers now have two years to forecast and re-plan their itemized expenses in anticipation of the sunset of the AGI limitation.

▶ **Effective date.** The provision is effective for tax years beginning after December 31, 2005 (Act Sec. 101(a)(2) of the Tax Relief, Unemployment Insurance Reauthorization, and Job Creation Act of 2010 (P.L. 111-312)); Act Sec. 103(b) of the Economic Growth and Tax Relief Reconciliation Act of 2001 (EGTRRA) (P.L. 107-16)). The provision shall not apply to tax years beginning after December 31, 2012 (Act Sec. 101(a)(1) of the Tax Relief Act of 2010; Act Sec. 901 of EGTRRA). See ¶105 for a specific discussion of the sunset provision of EGTRRA and how it is applied.

NEW LAW EXPLAINED

Law source: Law at ¶5190 and ¶7010. Committee Report at ¶10,020.

— Act Sec. 101(a)(1) of the Tax Relief, Unemployment Insurance Reauthorization, and Job Creation Act of 2010 (P.L. 111-312), amending Act Sec. 901 of the Economic Growth and Tax Relief Reconciliation Act of 2001 (EGTRRA) (P.L. 107-16);

— Act Sec. 101(a)(2), providing the effective date.

Reporter references: For further information, consult the following CCH reporters.

— Standard Federal Tax Reporter, ¶6081.01

— Tax Research Consultant, FILEIND: 12,056

— Practical Tax Explanation, §7,015

¶325 Phaseout of Personal Exemptions

SUMMARY OF NEW LAW

The repeal of the phaseout of personal exemptions for high-income taxpayers is extended for two years, through December 31, 2012. Thus, the personal exemption phaseout for high-income taxpayers will not apply to tax years beginning in 2011 and 2012, and higher-income taxpayers will not be required to reduce the amount of their personal exemptions when their adjusted gross income exceeds certain threshold levels.

BACKGROUND

The Economic Growth and Tax Relief Reconciliation Act of 2001 (EGTRRA) (P.L. 107-16) added Code Sec. 151(d)(3)(E) and (F), which provided for a repeal of the personal exemption phaseout (often referred to as PEP) for high-income taxpayers.

Exemptions, along with itemized deductions or the standard deduction, are subtracted from an individual's adjusted gross income (AGI) to arrive at taxable income (Code Sec. 151(a)). An individual is entitled to one personal exemption plus an exemption for his or her spouse if filing a joint return (Code Sec. 151(b)). An exemption is also allowed for each qualified dependent (Code Sec. 151(c)). The number of the taxpayer's exemptions is multiplied by the exemption amount to determine how much is subtracted from the taxpayer's AGI in computing taxable income. The exemption amount is adjusted annually for inflation (Code Sec. 151(d)(4)).

The exemption amount is phased out for taxpayers whose AGI is greater than certain threshold amounts that are indexed for inflation (Code Sec. 151(d)(3)(A)). The original threshold amounts in 1991 were $150,000 for married taxpayers filing joint returns or surviving spouses, $125,000 for heads of households, $100,000 for single taxpayers, and $75,000 for married taxpayers filing separate returns (Code Sec. 151(d)(3)(C)).

BACKGROUND

Under the phaseout, the exemption amount is reduced by two percent for each $2,500 (or fraction thereof) by which the taxpayer's AGI exceeds the applicable threshold amount. For a married person filing a separate return, however, the reduction is two percent for each $1,250 (or fraction thereof) by which the taxpayer's AGI exceeds the applicable threshold amount (Code Sec. 151(d)(3)(B)).

Under EGTRRA, the personal exemption phaseout was gradually eliminated during a four-year period beginning in 2006, leading to full elimination in 2010. The exemption amount was reduced by one-third for tax years beginning in 2006 and 2007 and by two-thirds for tax years beginning in 2008 and 2009 (Code Sec. 151(d)(3)(E)). Thus, two computations were required for the reduction years. After the reduction in the exemption amount was determined, the taxpayer was required to take this amount and multiply it by two-thirds for tax years beginning in 2006 and 2007 or by one-third for tax years beginning in 2008 and 2009. This resulting fractional amount of the limitation was the amount by which the taxpayer's otherwise allowable exemption amount was reduced.

For tax years beginning after December 31, 2009, the phaseout of the personal exemption amount for high-income taxpayers no longer applies (Code Sec. 151(d)(3)(F)). Thus, in 2010, such taxpayers are no longer required to reduce the amount of their exemptions when their adjusted gross income exceeds certain threshold amounts.

Sunset provision. Under the sunset provision of EGTRRA, amendments made by the Act will not apply to tax years beginning after December 31, 2010 (Act Sec. 901 of P.L. 107-16).

NEW LAW EXPLAINED

Repeal of personal exemption phaseout extended.—The repeal of the personal exemption phaseout for high-income taxpayers will continue to apply to tax years beginning in 2011 and 2012 (Code Sec. 151(d)(3)(E) and (F); Act Sec. 901 of the Economic Growth and Tax Relief Reconciliation Act of 2001 (EGTRRA) (P.L. 107-16), as amended by the Tax Relief, Unemployment Insurance Reauthorization, and Job Creation Act of 2010 (P.L. 111-312)).

When the phaseout of the personal exemption returns for tax years beginning in 2013 (after the EGTRRA sunset occurs at the end of 2012), the deduction for personal exemptions will be reduced or even eliminated for certain high income taxpayers. If a taxpayer's adjusted gross income (AGI) exceeds the appropriate threshold amount (based on filing status), the exemption amount will be reduced by two percent for each $2,500 or fraction thereof by which the AGI exceeds the threshold amount. In the case of a married individual filing separately, the exemption reduction will be reduced by two percent for each $1,250 or fraction thereof by which AGI exceeds the threshold amount. The deduction for personal exemptions will be fully eliminated when AGI exceeds the threshold amount by more than $122,500 ($61,250 in the case of a married individual filing separately). It takes 50 two-percent reductions to achieve a 100-percent reduction. Because 49 two-percent reductions would result from an excess of $122,500 (49 × $2,500

NEW LAW EXPLAINED

= \$122,500), any excess above that amount would be a fraction of a \$2,500 amount and create the fiftieth two-percent reduction.

> **Comment:** For alternative minimum tax (AMT) purposes, there is no deduction for, or in lieu of, personal exemptions (Code Sec. 56(b)(1)(E)). Only the amount of personal exemptions actually deducted in calculating taxable income is added back to determine alternative minimum taxable income. Thus, for tax years beginning after December 31, 2012, if a taxpayer's deduction for personal exemptions is reduced under the reinstituted phaseout provisions of Code Sec. 151(d)(3), only the reduced amount would be deducted for AMT purposes.

Practical Analysis: William A Raabe, Ohio State University, and Capital University Law School, Columbus, Ohio, John O. Everett, Virginia Commonwealth University, Richmond Virginia, and Cherie J. Hennig, University of North Carolina, Wilmington observe the repeal of the personal exemption phaseout for an additional two years is welcomed news to taxpayers and tax professionals. The annoying part of the phaseout rules is not the computations (which are easily handled by tax software); rather, it is the backdoor approach to taxing individuals by taking away deductions as the taxpayer's adjusted gross income increases. Congress "discovered" this approach in 1984, when the "bubbles" in the corporate tax rate structure (*i.e.*, the 39 percent and 38 percent rates) were created to eliminate the benefits of paying tax at the lower rates of 15 percent and 25 percent. Applying these backdoor tax increases to individuals was inevitable, especially since the rules affected only high-income taxpayers (and precious few voters).

The effects of the phaseouts of the exemption and itemized deductions can generate significant revenue for the government. The Joint Committee on Taxation estimates the revenue cost of the extension of the repeal to be approximately \$20 billion. And on an individual level, the repeal can create dizzying marginal tax rates on additional income. For example, assume that a 35 percent-rate taxpayer with four exemptions has \$100 additional income that causes adjusted gross income to "round up" to the next \$2,500 increment in the exemption phaseout computations. If the 2013 exemption amount is \$3,700 for each exemption, then this means that the taxpayer is losing an additional \$296 of exemption deductions (\$3,700 × 4 x .02) and \$3 of itemized deductions (\$100 × 3). Thus, the \$100 of additional income suddenly becomes \$399 of additional taxable income, generating \$140 marginal income taxes (\$399 × .35), and a 140 percent marginal tax rate. Of course, the same would be true with \$1 additional dollar of income, if it adds another \$2,500 increment; that would be a 1,400 percent marginal tax rate!

▶ **Effective date.** The provision is effective for tax years beginning after December 31, 2005 (Act Sec. 101(a)(2) of the Tax Relief, Unemployment Insurance Reauthorization, and Job Creation Act of 2010 (P.L. 111-312)); Act Sec. 102(b) of the Economic Growth and Tax Relief Reconciliation Act of 2001 (EGTRRA) (P.L. 107-16)). The provision shall not apply to tax years beginning after December 31, 2012 (Act Sec. 101(a)(1) of the Tax Relief Act of 2010; Act Sec. 901 of EGTRRA). See ¶105 for a specific discussion of the sunset provision of EGTRRA and how it is applied.

¶325

NEW LAW EXPLAINED

Law source: Law at ¶5250 and ¶7010. Committee Report at ¶10,020.

— Act Sec. 101(a)(1) of the Tax Relief, Unemployment Insurance Reauthorization, and Job Creation Act of 2010 (P.L. 111-312), amending Act Sec. 901 of the Economic Growth and Tax Relief Reconciliation Act of 2001 (EGTRRA) (P.L. 107-16);

— Act Sec. 101(a)(2), providing the effective date.

Reporter references: For further information, consult the following CCH reporters.

— Standard Federal Tax Reporter, ¶8005.01

— Tax Research Consultant, FILEIND: 6,052

— Practical Tax Explanation, § 1,205

¶326 Deduction of State and Local General Sales Taxes

SUMMARY OF NEW LAW

The election to claim an itemized deduction for State and local *general sales* taxes in lieu of State and local *income* taxes is extended two years and may be claimed for tax years beginning in 2010 and 2011.

BACKGROUND

In determining regular income tax liability (but not alternative minimum tax liability), an individual is generally permitted to claim itemized deductions for State and local taxes including income taxes, real property taxes, personal property taxes and qualified motor vehicle taxes (Code Sec. 164(a)). In lieu of claiming a deduction for State and local *income* taxes, the taxpayer may elect to claim State and local *general sales* taxes as an itemized deduction (Code Sec. 164(b)(5)). The election is available for tax years beginning after 2003 and before 2010. However, a taxpayer who makes the election to claim State and local general sales taxes may not claim a separate deduction for qualified motor vehicle taxes, which include State and local sales and excise taxes on a qualified motor vehicle purchased after February 17, 2009, and before January 1, 2010 (Code Sec. 164(b)(6)(F)).

The amount of the deduction a taxpayer may claim for State and local general sales taxes is either:

- the actual amount of general State and local sales taxes paid or accrued during the tax year; or

- the amount prescribed in IRS tables taking into account the taxpayer's State of residence, filing status, adjusted gross income (AGI), number of dependents, and the rates of State and local general sales taxes, as well as any general sales taxes

BACKGROUND

paid by the taxpayer on the purchase of a motor vehicle, boat, or other items specified by the IRS.

Compliance Pointer: Taxpayers choosing to deduct the actual amount of general sales taxes should keep receipts to substantiate taxes paid during the year, which are reported on Form 1040, Schedule A, Itemized Deductions. Taxpayers choosing to deduct the amount prescribed by the IRS can figure the deduction using the sales tax tables and worksheet provided in the Instructions to Schedule A of Form 1040. Alternatively, taxpayers can use the Sales Tax Deduction Calculator provided on the IRS website.

For purposes of the deduction, "general sales tax" is broadly defined and includes any tax imposed at one rate on the retail sales of a broad range of classes of items (Code Sec. 164(b)(5)(B)). In the case of food, clothing, medical supplies and motor vehicles, if the applicable sales tax rate for some or all items is lower than the general sales tax rate it is not a factor in determining whether the tax is imposed at one rate, and if the tax does not apply to some or all items, the taxes are still considered a "general sales tax" for the broad range of classes of items (Code Sec. 164(b)(5)(C)). A special rule for motor vehicles provides that if the sales tax rate for motor vehicles exceeds the general sales tax rate, then only the amount of the general sales tax rate is allowed as a deduction. Any excess motor vehicle sales taxes are disregarded (Code Sec. 164(b)(5)(F)). In addition, compensating use taxes are treated as general sales taxes, provided a deduction for sales tax is allowed for similar items sold at retail in the taxing jurisdiction (Code Sec. 164(b)(5)(E)).

NEW LAW EXPLAINED

Deduction of State and local general sales taxes extended.—The election to deduct State and local *general sales* taxes as an itemized deduction in lieu of State and local *income* taxes is extended to apply to tax years beginning before January 1, 2012 (Code Sec. 164(b)(5)(I), as amended by the Tax Relief, Unemployment Insurance Reauthorization, and Job Creation Act of 2010 (P.L. 111-312)). Thus, an individual may elect to claim an itemized deduction for State and local general sales taxes for the tax years 2010 and 2011.

Comment: A taxpayer who makes the election to claim State and local general sales taxes in 2010 may not claim a separate deduction for qualified motor vehicle taxes under Code Sec. 164(a)(6), which include State and local sales and excise taxes paid on the purchase of a qualified motor vehicle purchased after February 17, 2009, and before January 1, 2010. A taxpayer who purchased the vehicle during the appropriate time period in 2009, but paid some of the sales or excise taxes for that purchase in 2010, may claim an itemized deduction in 2010 for qualified motor vehicle taxes, but only if he or she does not make the election under Code Sec. 164(b)(5) to claim State and local general sales taxes in lieu of State and local income taxes for that year Code Sec. 164(b)(6)(F).

Planning Note: The election to deduct State and local general sales taxes is available to all individual taxpayers, although it is primarily designed to benefit residents of states without State and local income taxes. Residents in States and

NEW LAW EXPLAINED

localities in which the sales tax exceeds the highest individual income tax rate may also benefit from the election. While the amount of a deduction of State and a local general sales taxes will usually be less than a deduction of State and local income taxes, if the taxpayer bought big ticket items during the year this may cause the sales tax deduction to be more, whether using actual receipts or the IRS-provided tables in computing the deduction.

State Tax Consequences: The extension of the deduction for State and local general sales taxes does not impact states such as California, Illinois, and Oregon that have decoupled from the deduction, or states such as Connecticut, Michigan, or West Virginia that do not allow federal itemized deductions. For states like Maryland and Ohio that allow the deduction, whether they adopt this amendment will depend on their Code conformity dates. Those states that update their Internal Revenue Code conformity dates annually will most likely conform during their next legislative sessions.

▶ **Effective date.** The provision applies to tax years beginning after December 31, 2009 (Act Sec. 722(b) of the Tax Relief, Unemployment Insurance Reauthorization, and Job Creation Act of 2010 (P.L. 111-312)).

Law source: Law at ¶5260. Committee Reports at ¶10,290.

— Act Sec. 722(a) of the Tax Relief, Unemployment Insurance Reauthorization, and Job Creation Act of 2010 (P.L. 111-312), amending Code Sec. 164(b)(5)(I);

— Act Sec. 722(b) providing the effective date.

Reporter references: For further information, consult the following CCH reporters.

— Standard Federal Tax Reporter, ¶9502.0385

— Tax Research Consultant, INDIV: 45,110

— Practical Tax Explanations, §7,330

¶327 Teachers' Classroom Expense Deduction

SUMMARY OF NEW LAW

The above-the-line deduction for eligible educator expenses has been extended two years so that it is available for tax years beginning in 2010 and 2011.

BACKGROUND

Generally, a taxpayer may deduct ordinary and necessary business expenses paid during the tax year. However, unreimbursed employee business expenses of an individual are only deductible as miscellaneous itemized deductions to the extent they exceed two percent of the taxpayer's adjusted gross income (AGI). Nonetheless, for tax years beginning in 2002 through 2009, eligible educators are allowed an above-the-line deduction in determining AGI of up to $250 for qualified expenses

BACKGROUND

paid or incurred during the year, rather than as a miscellaneous itemized deduction (Code Sec. 62(a)(2)(D)). In the case of married taxpayers filing a joint return, if both spouses are eligible, the maximum deduction is $500 but neither spouse can deduct more than $250 of his or her qualified expenses.

A taxpayer is an eligible educator for purposes of the deduction if, for at least 900 hours during a school year, the individual was a kindergarten through grade 12 teacher, instructor, counselor, principal, or aide in a school that provides elementary or secondary education as determined under state law. Qualified expenses include ordinary and necessary business expenses paid out-of-pocket by the teacher for books, supplies, equipment (including computer equipment, software and services), and other materials used in the classroom. Expenses for home-schooling and nonathletic supplies for courses in health or physical education do not qualify. In addition, qualified expenses must be reduced by: (1) any reimbursements the taxpayer received for the expenses that are not reported on his or her Form W-2; (2) any expenses that are paid with tax-free interest on U.S. savings bonds; and (3) any expenses used in determining any amount excluded from gross income from a distribution from a qualified tuition program (also known as a qualified tuition plan or 529 plan) or a Coverdell education savings account (ESA).

NEW LAW EXPLAINED

Teacher expense deduction extended.—The above-the-line deduction for eligible educators for up to $250 of qualified expenses paid during the year ($500 for joint filers), has been extended to tax years beginning in 2010 and 2011 (Code Sec. 62(a)(2)(D), as amended by the Tax Relief, Unemployment Insurance Reauthorization, and Job Creation Act of 2010 (P.L. 111-312)).

> **State Tax Consequences:** The extension of the teacher classroom expense deduction through the 2011 tax year will not impact those states such as California, Minnesota, or Wisconsin that have specifically decoupled from the deduction. Other states that use federal AGI as the starting point for computing the state tax liability will conform to the extension provided they incorporate the Internal Revenue Code as currently amended or enact annual conformity update legislation.

▶ **Effective date.** The provision applies to tax years beginning after December 31, 2009 (Act Sec. 721(b) of the Tax Relief, Unemployment Insurance Reauthorization, and Job Creation Act of 2010 (P.L. 111-312)).

Law source: Law at ¶5180. Committee Report at ¶10,280.

— Act Sec. 721(a) of the Tax Relief, Unemployment Insurance Reauthorization, and Job Creation Act of 2010 (P.L. 111-312), amending Code Sec. 62(a)(2)(D);

— Act Sec. 721(b), providing the effective date.

Reporter references: For further information, consult the following CCH reporters.

— Standard Federal Tax Reporter, ¶6005.029

— Tax Research Consultant, INDIV: 36,364

— Practical Tax Explanation, §5,325

¶327

¶328 Mortgage Insurance Premiums

SUMMARY OF NEW LAW

The deduction for mortgage insurance premiums is extended through December 31, 2011.

BACKGROUND

Generally, individuals may not deduct any interest paid or accrued during the tax year that is considered personal interest (Code Sec. 163(h)(1)). However, this restriction does not apply to certain types of interest, such as qualified residence interest (Code Sec. 163(h)(2)(D)). Qualified residence interest includes interest on home acquisition indebtedness of up to $1 million ($500,000 for married individuals filing separately) and interest on home equity indebtedness of up to $100,000 ($50,000 for married individuals filing separately) (Code Sec. 163(h)(3)(A)-(C)).

Usually, in the case of a home acquisition loan, an individual who cannot pay the entire downpayment amount may be required to purchase mortgage insurance. Premiums paid or accrued for qualified mortgage insurance in connection with acquisition indebtedness for a qualified residence are treated as qualified residence interest, and therefore deductible (Code Sec. 163(h)(4)(E)(i)).

For this purpose, qualified mortgage insurance includes mortgage insurance provided by the Veterans Administration, the Federal Housing Administration, or the Rural Housing Administration, and private mortgage insurance defined under Act Sec. 2 of the Homeowners Protection Act of 1998 (12 U.S.C. Sec. 4901), as in effect on December 20, 2006 (Code Sec. 163(h)(4)(E)). A qualified residence includes the taxpayer's principal residence or a second home selected by the taxpayer for purposes of the qualified residence interest rules. If the second home is not rented out, it qualifies regardless of whether the taxpayer uses it during the year. If the second home is rented out, it qualifies only if it is used during the tax year by the taxpayer for personal purposes for the greater of 14 days or 10 percent of the number of days during the year the home is rented at fair market value (Code Secs. 121 and 163(h)(4)(A)).

The treatment of mortgage insurance premiums as deductible interest does not apply with respect to mortgage insurance contracts issued prior to January 1, 2007 (Code Sec. 163(h)(3)(E)(iii)). Nor does it apply to premiums paid or accrued after December 31, 2010, or properly allocable to any period after December 31, 2010 (Code Sec. 163(h)(3)(E)(iv)).

The deduction for mortgage insurance premiums is also subject to a phaseout. For every $1,000 ($500 in the case of a married individual filing separately), or a fraction thereof, by which the taxpayer's adjusted gross income exceeds $100,000 ($50,000 in the case of a married individual filing separately), the amount of mortgage insurance

BACKGROUND

premiums treated as interest is reduced by 10 percent (Code Sec. 163(h)(3)(E)(iii)). Restrictions on deductibility also apply with respect to prepaid qualified mortgage insurance (Code Sec. 163(h)(4)(F)).

NEW LAW EXPLAINED

Deduction for mortgage insurance premiums extended.—The treatment of qualified mortgage insurance premiums as deductible qualified residence interest is extended for amounts paid or accrued in 2011, and not properly allocable to a period after 2011 (Code Sec. 163(h)(3)(E)(iv), as amended by the Tax Relief, Unemployment Insurance Reauthorization, and Job Creation Act of 2010 (P.L. 111-312)). Thus, absent subsequent extension, taxpayers will not be able to deduct mortgage insurance premiums that are paid or accrued after December 31, 2011, or properly allocable to any period after December 31, 2011. The requirement that the premiums be paid pursuant to a mortgage insurance contract issued on or after January 1, 2007, remains unchanged.

► **Effective date.** The provision applies to amounts paid or accrued after December 31, 2010 (Act Sec. 759(b) of the Tax Relief, Unemployment Insurance Reauthorization, and Job Creation Act of 2010 (P.L. 111-312)).

Law source: Law at ¶5255. Committee Report at ¶10,650.

— Act Sec. 759(a) of the Tax Relief, Unemployment Insurance Reauthorization, and Job Creation Act of 2010 (P.L. 111-312), amending Code Sec. 163(h)(3)(E)(iv);

— Act Sec. 759(b), providing the effective date.

Reporter references: For further information, consult the following CCH reporters.

— Standard Federal Tax Reporter, ¶9402.026

— Tax Research Consultant, REAL: 6,060

— Practical Tax Explanation, §18,520

EDUCATION INCENTIVES

¶330   Coverdell Education Savings Accounts

SUMMARY OF NEW LAW

The increased annual contribution limits under Code Sec. 530 for Coverdell education savings accounts and certain corresponding rules and provisions regarding such accounts are extended to tax years beginning in 2011 and 2012.

¶330

BACKGROUND

The Economic Growth and Tax Relief Reconciliation Act of 2001 (EGTRRA) (P.L. 107-16) amended Code Sec. 530 by increasing the maximum annual contribution that can be made to an education individual retirement account (education IRA) from $500 to $2,000, and correspondingly increasing the threshold amount for imposing the six-percent excise tax on excess contributions made to an education IRA from $500 to $2,000. In addition, to improve the attractiveness and operation of education IRAs, a series of additional modifications were enacted. Education individual retirement accounts were subsequently renamed Coverdell education savings accounts by P.L. 107-22.

A Coverdell education savings accounts is a trust or custodial account established exclusively for the purpose of paying the qualified educational expenses of an individual named beneficiary. Earnings on the accumulated contributions in a Coverdell account are generally not taxable until they are withdrawn, but such distributions are excludable from the gross income of the distributee/beneficiary to the extent they are used for qualified educational expenses; amounts distributed in excess of qualified educational expenses in the year of distribution are includible in the gross income of the distributee and are also generally subject to an additional 10 percent tax. Any amounts remaining in a Coverdell education savings account after a designated beneficiary's qualified higher education expenses have been paid may either be rolled over into another Coverdell education savings account for another beneficiary in the same family (see "Rollovers", below), or may be distributed to the original beneficiary who must then include the earnings component of the distribution in income and pay a 10-percent penalty

Contribution limits. The maximum contribution limit applies to annual contributions to a Coverdell education savings account, but a phaseout limitation applies for individual contributors. The amount that a taxpayer is permitted to contribute to a Coverdell education savings account is limited if the taxpayer's modified adjusted gross income (AGI) exceeds certain threshold amounts; the modified AGI amounts used to determine the contribution limit phaseout range for married taxpayers filing jointly is twice the amounts applicable for single filers. This doubling of the modified AGI amounts in the phaseout range was established to avoid situations in which a married couple could contribute less to a Coverdell education savings account than was possible if the couple divorced and contributed separately. Corporations and other entities are permitted to make contributions to Coverdell accounts, and no such phaseout or income limitation applies to such contributions.

The annual contribution limit cannot be circumvented by multiple Coverdell education savings accounts. The same mechanism that discourages taxpayers from circumventing the annual limit on traditional IRAs applies to annual contributions greater than the annual limit on Coverdell education savings account contributions. Specifically, Code Sec. 4973 imposes a six-percent excise tax on excess contributions. In addition, any contributions to a qualified tuition program (QTP, also known as a qualified tuition plan or 529 plan) for the benefit of the same beneficiary covered by the Coverdell education savings account are treated as excess contributions to the Coverdell education savings account.

BACKGROUND

The 10-percent penalty tax, as well as the six-percent excise tax on excess contributions, will not be imposed on corrective withdrawals of excess contributions if such distributions are made before the first day of the sixth month following the tax year of the contribution. If the beneficiary does not have to file a return, then the distribution must be made by the 15th day of the fourth month of the tax year following the tax year in which the contribution was made. The distribution must be accompanied by any net earnings on the excess contribution.

Although an additional 10-percent tax is generally imposed on excess distributions from a Coverdell education savings account that are includible in income, the 10-percent additional tax will not apply to a distribution from a Coverdell education savings account that is includible in the beneficiary's income because the taxpayer elected to claim a HOPE scholarship credit or lifetime learning credit with respect to the beneficiary (Code Sec. 530(d)(4)(B)(v)). Coordination rules are provided that allow a student to take advantage of the Coverdell education savings account provisions, as well as the HOPE and lifetime learning credits under Code Sec. 25A and the qualified tuition program under Code Sec. 529 in the same tax year.

Rollovers. Amounts held in a Coverdell education savings account may be distributed and put into a Coverdell education savings account for a member of the beneficiary's family. Such distributions will not be included in the distributee's gross income provided the rollover occurs within 60 days of the distribution. Similarly, any change in the beneficiary of a Coverdell education savings account does not constitute a distribution for gross income purposes if the new beneficiary is a member of the family of the original beneficiary. A "member of the family" for this purpose includes ancestors, descendants, brothers, sisters, nephews, nieces, first cousins, certain in-laws and the spouses of these relatives. Stepparents, stepsiblings and stepchildren are also considered members of the family.

The new beneficiary following a rollover to another Coverdell education savings account or a change in beneficiary must be under age 30 as of the date of such distribution or change of beneficiary. Similarly, any balance remaining in a Coverdell education savings account (formerly known as an education IRA) must be distributed within 30 days after a beneficiary reaches age 30. The 30-year age limit is extended in the case of special needs individuals who, due to a physical, mental, or emotional condition (including learning disability), require additional time to complete their education.

Qualified education expenses. Tuition, fees, books, supplies, and equipment required for the enrollment or attendance of a designated beneficiary at an eligible educational institution fall under the definition of "qualified higher education expenses." The term also includes room and board to the extent of the minimum room and board allowance applicable to the student as determined by the institution in calculating costs of attendance for federal financial aid programs. For students residing in housing owned and operated by an eligible educational institution, if the actual room and board expenses charged by an eligible institution exceed that allowed under 20 U.S.C. 1087ll, the allowance is the actual amount charged to the student by the institution for room and board.

¶330

BACKGROUND

Qualified education expenses also include elementary or secondary school expenses incurred while the beneficiary is in attendance or enrolled at an elementary or secondary school (i.e., kindergarten through grade 12, as defined by state law). The school may be either a public, private or religious school. Like expenses for qualified higher education, elementary and secondary education expenses include expenses for tuition, fees, books, supplies and equipment, but the differ in that they include expenses for (1) academic tutoring, (2) the purchase of computer technology or equipment, or internet access and related services, and (3) expenses for room and board, uniforms, transportation and supplementary items and services, such as extended day programs, as required or provided by the school.

Sunset provision. Under the sunset provision of EGTRRA, amendments made by the Act will not apply to tax years beginning after December 31, 2010 (Act Sec. 901 of P.L. 107-16).

NEW LAW EXPLAINED

Coverdell ESA increased contribution limits and other enhancements extended.—The increased annual contribution limits for Coverdell education savings accounts (ESAs) and certain corresponding rules and provisions regarding such accounts are extended two years, to tax years beginning in 2011 and 2012. Barring further extension of the Coverdell enhancements, the enhancements will sunset for tax years beginning after December 31, 2012 (Code Sec. 530; Act Sec. 901 of the Economic Growth and Tax Relief Reconciliation Act of 2001 (EGTRRA) (P.L. 107-16), as amended by the Tax Relief, Unemployment Insurance Reauthorization, and Job Creation Act of 2010 (P.L. 111-312)).

Maximum annual contribution reduced in 2013. If the changes made by EGTRRA sunset, the maximum annual contribution that can be made to a Coverdell ESA will be reduced from $2,000 to $500, for tax years beginning after December 31, 2012 (Code Sec. 530(b)(1)(A)(iii)). The threshold amount for imposing the six-percent excise tax on excess contributions made to a Coverdell ESA will be correspondingly decreased from $2,000 to $500 (Code Sec. 4973(e)(1)(A)).

> **Planning Note:** Since 1981, the cost of attending a two or four-year colleges has consistently risen faster than the rate of inflation. Families with many children should mitigate the low $500 annual contribution limit by funding their older children's Coverdell ESAs as much as possible (including the full $2,000 for 2010, 2011 and 2012, if possible), then rolling over unused portions of the accounts for the use of the younger children. With the reduction in the contribution limit, this tax planning strategy could be even more important.

Marriage penalty reinstated after 2012. The provision which specified that the modified adjusted gross income (AGI) threshold phaseout amount for joint filers is double ($190,000) the threshold amount for single taxpayers ($95,000) will not apply to tax years beginning after December 31, 2012 if the EGTRRA changes sunset (Code Sec. 530(c)(1)). This doubling of the modified AGI amounts in the phaseout range was established to avoid situations in which a married couple could contribute less to a

¶330

NEW LAW EXPLAINED

Coverdell education savings account than was possible if the couple divorced and contributed separately. Thus the annual contribution limit will be phased out for joint filers with modified AGI at or greater than $150,000 (rather than $190,000) and less than $160,000 (rather than $200,000). For other filers, the modified AGI phaseout amounts will remain at or greater than $95,000 and less than $110,000. Taxpayers with modified AGI at or above the $160,000 or $110,000 phaseout limits will not be allowed to make contributions to an education IRA on behalf of any other individual.

When the modified AGI threshold is met, the $500 maximum annual contribution will be reduced by an amount that bears the same ratio to $500 as the amount by which the contributor's modified AGI for the tax year exceeds $150,000 (for joint filers, $95,000 for all others), bears to $10,000 (for joint filers, or $15,000 for other taxpayers).

Example: Travis Finn, a single (widowed) parent, has modified AGI for the tax year of $104,000. Under the contribution phaseout provision, his annual contribution to the Coverdell ESA established for his son will be limited to $200. To arrive at this amount, Finn must:

- determine the excess of his modified AGI of $104,000 over $95,000 ($104,000 − $95,000 = $9,000);
- determine the ratio that the excess amount of $9,000 bears to $15,000 ($9,000 ÷ $15,000 = .6);
- determine the reduction amount by multiplying the maximum amount of $500 by .6 ($500 × .6 = $300); and, finally
- subtract the reduction amount of $300 from the maximum amount of $500 to arrive at his annual contribution limit of $200 ($500 − $300 = $200).

Another contributor (Finn's mother) who does not file a joint return and has modified AGI of $95,000 or less may contribute up to $300 to Finn's son's Coverdell ESA for the year. If Finn remarries and files a joint return, any contribution by Finn and his new spouse will begin phasing out at modified AGI of $150,000.

Clarification that employers are not subject to contribution limits. EGTRRA amended the language of Code Sec. 530(c)(1) to clarify that the limitation regarding the maximum contribution amount per contributor to a Coverdell account only applied to individual contributors. While the bill merely changed the language of Code Sec. 530(c)(1) to limit its application to individuals, the committee report specifically stated that the "bill clarifies that corporations and other entities (including tax-exempt organizations) are permitted to make contributions to education IRAs, regardless of the income of the corporation or entity during the year of the contribution." If the EGTRRA changes sunset, this clarifying amendment will not apply in tax years beginning after December 31, 2012.

Qualified education expenses after 2012. Qualified education expenses will no longer include expenses incurred while the beneficiary is in attendance or enrolled at an

NEW LAW EXPLAINED

elementary or secondary school (i.e., kindergarten through grade 12, as defined by state law) for tax years beginning after December 31, 2012 if the EGTRRA changes sunset (Code Sec. 530(b)(4)). This means that after that date expenses cannot be paid tax-free from a Coverdell ESA for expenses such as: (1) tuition, fees, academic tutoring, special need services, books, supplies, computer equipment (including related software and services), and other equipment incurred in connection with the enrollment or attendance of the beneficiary at a public, private, or religious school providing elementary or secondary education (kindergarten through grade 12) as determined under State law, or (2) room and board, uniforms, transportation, and supplementary items or services (including extended day programs) required or provided by such a school in connection with such enrollment or attendance of the beneficiary.

Special needs children. The exception contained in Code Sec. 530(b)(1) that permits contributions to a Coverdell ESA to continue even after the date when a beneficiary reaches age 18 for certain special needs individuals who, due to a physical, mental, or emotional condition (including learning disability), require additional time to complete their education will no longer be available for tax years beginning after December 31, 2012 if the EGTRRA changes sunset (Code Sec. 530(b)(1)).

Similarly, the special needs beneficiary exceptions to: (1) the 30-year age limit used to determine when the remaining balances in an education IRA must be distributed, and (2) whether rollover contributions can be received and beneficiaries changed, will also no longer apply to tax years beginning after December 31, 2012 if the EGTRRA changes sunset (Code Sec. 530(b)(1)).

Time for making or returning contributions. Contributions to a Coverdell ESA will apply against the annual contribution limit for the year in which the contribution is made, for tax years beginning after December 31, 2012 if the EGTRRA changes sunset. The provision within Code Sec. 530(b)(1) permitting an individual to make a contribution to a Coverdell account by the return due date (not including extensions) for the tax year of the contribution and have that contribution deemed to be made on the last day of the preceding tax year will not apply for tax years beginning after December 31, 2012 if the EGTRRA changes sunset (Code Sec. 530(b)(5)).

Although an additional 10-percent tax is generally imposed on excess distributions from a Coverdell ESA, an exception is provided for timely distributions of excess contributions. In tax years beginning after December 31, 2012, if the EGTRRA changes sunset, the distribution of excess contribution amounts must be made (returned) by the due date (including extensions) for filing the beneficiary's tax return for the tax year in which the contribution was made and be accompanied by the amount of income attributable to the excess contribution (Code Sec. 530(d)(4)(C)). In tax years beginning on or before December 31, 2012, the distribution of excess contribution amounts must be made (returned) before the first day of the sixth month of the tax year following the tax year in which the contribution was made, and be accompanied by the amount of income attributable to the excess contribution (Code Sec. 530(d)(4)(C)).

Coordination rules for education credits and qualified tuition programs. The coordination rules that allow a student to take advantage of the Coverdell ESA provi-

NEW LAW EXPLAINED

sions, as well as the education credits under Code Sec. 25A (HOPE and lifetime learning credits) and the qualified tuition program under Code Sec. 529 in the same tax year, will also expire if the EGTRRA changes sunset. In tax years beginning after December 31, 2012, if the EGTRRA changes sunset, if a beneficiary claims an exclusion under the Coverdell ESA provisions, that beneficiary may not claim either the HOPE credit nor the lifetime learning credit for the same tax year. A beneficiary will be required to waive the tax-free treatment for distributions from a Coverdell ESA in order for the education credits to be claimed during the same tax year (Code Sec. 530(d)(2)(D)). Correspondingly, an election of the HOPE or lifetime learning credits will not be effective for any individual for whom a distribution from a Coverdell account is excluded from gross income under Code Sec. 530(d)(2) for the same tax year (Code Sec. 25A(e)(2)). The six-percent excise tax will also be reinstated for contributions made during the same tax year to both a beneficiary's education IRA and qualified tuition plan (Code Sec. 4973(e)(1)).

Practical Analysis: *Jeffrey Bryant*, Wichita State University, Wichita, Kansas, observes that the tax advantages of the Coverdell Education Savings Account (CESA), or education IRA, were enhanced in several respects by EGTRRA. The enhanced advantages will continue for at least two more years.

Contributions. The maximum annual contribution remains at the increased level of $2,000 during that time. Consequently, the prudent approach is to contribute to CESAs in both years for as many family members as possible. AGI limits restrict high income individuals from contributing to a CESA, but these restrictions are minor nuisances. Anyone can fund the account. No relationship connection is required. Corporations, partnerships, and trusts can be used to make contributions, and these entities are allowed to contribute regardless of the income level of the entity. Child beneficiaries can contribute to their own CESAs. A withdrawal from a UGMA custodial account for a beneficiary is a permissible source of funding. Contributions are not deductible, so there is no tax planning opportunity associated with choosing a particular contributor. Contributions should be maximized in terms of amount and number of beneficiaries while the $2,000 window remains open. At some point, various accounts may be consolidated for the benefit of someone whose need exceeds the other beneficiaries. There is a ceiling on the amount which can be contributed to a CESA in any year. No limit exists on the account balances that can be rolled over to a replacement beneficiary during any year.

Distributions. The primary risk associated with tax incentives of this type is that beneficiaries do not derive the intended benefit until the year in which funds are withdrawn and used for qualified education expenses. The very situation we are now experiencing with these arrangements exposes the nature of the risk. The tax status of certain distributions from a CESA is known only for two more years. Taking advantage of the intended tax benefit depends upon the continued application of existing rules in future years when funds are distributed to a beneficiary. A unique and valuable feature of CESAs is the ability to pay elementary and secondary school expenses with tax free distributions. This ability is scheduled to expire again on December 31, 2012. Parents planning to use CESA distributions for the middle or

¶330

NEW LAW EXPLAINED

high school education of their children will have to set aside money for the next two years and only hope that in fact the funds can be used for their intended tax-advantaged purpose several years from now. Taking the risk is probably a reasonable choice. The reason is that CESAs are easily transferred between beneficiaries. A CESA beneficiary can be changed or the balance rolled over tax free, as long as the new beneficiary is related to the previous one. The relationship list is fairly comprehensive, including siblings and children of the existing beneficiary. As a result, handing down a CESA through an unlimited number of generations is possible. A rollover must be completed before the current beneficiary reaches age 30. The replacement beneficiary can be any related party under the age of 30. Although a contribution is not permitted for a beneficiary 18 years or older, rollovers can be made to any beneficiary who has not yet reached age 30. If nothing else, CESAs can serve as a backup education payment source. Income accumulates in the account tax free, and the custodian has complete control over investments. The earnings portion of amounts withdrawn and not used to pay qualified education expenses represents gross income to the beneficiary and is usually subject to a 10-percent penalty, but there is no danger that the balance will lapse from non-use. Pass them across and down the generations until someone is unable to get a scholarship or use another education incentive. At that point, hopefully the account balance will have grown substantially, and hopefully the extant law will favorably treat the use of any withdrawals.

Practical Analysis: William A. Raabe, Ohio State University, and Capital University Law School, Columbus Ohio, John O. Everett, Virginia Commonwealth University, Richmond Virginia, and Cherie J. Hennig, University of North Carolina, Wilmington observe that the Coverdell education savings account (CESA) can be an important means by which funds can be accumulated for certain education costs of a student under age 18. Inclusion in the 2010 Tax Relief Act represents an important tax and savings incentive for the US middle class. The 2010 Tax Relief Act generally retains and extends the CESA provisions as they existed for 2010, through the end of 2012.

The CESA often is referred to as the "education IRA," but the Code no longer uses that term. A CESA may be structured as a trust or custodial account, under state law.

Contributions to a CESA are not deductible, but the earnings on the funds in the account are excluded from gross income, and withdrawals are not subject to Federal income tax to the student beneficiary if the funds then are used for tuition and related costs. Excluded Coverdell withdrawals cannot be used in computing any other education deduction or credit, e.g., the American Opportunity credit.

Qualifying education expenses include only tuition, fees, books, supplies, tutoring and special-needs services, and related equipment. Room and board can qualify for a student who carries at least one-half of a full-time load, as defined by the school.

If the withdrawal for the tax year exceeds qualifying education costs, the distribution is allocated pro rata as (1) income exclusion, (2) nontaxable return of the nondeductible contributions, and (3) gross income. Any gross income that is recognized for this reason also is subject to a ten percent penalty tax.

¶330

NEW LAW EXPLAINED

CESA balances can be rolled over tax-free from one student beneficiary to another, as long as the "new" beneficiary is under age 30 and a family member of the original beneficiary. A CESA balance usually is deemed to be distributed when the beneficiary reaches age 30, or upon the beneficiary's earlier death.

The CESA is a student-level account. The beneficiary must be a living individual. Any number of donors can contribute to the account during the tax year, but a ceiling limitation is applied to the aggregate contribution every year. Excess contributions are subject to a six percent excise tax.

The annual contribution to a CESA is limited to $2,000. The annual contribution maximum would have reverted to $500 (the pre-EGTRRA amount) without the provisions of the 2010 Tax Relief Act. These amounts also are used in computing the excise tax on excess contributions. The $500 maximum is scheduled to return for 2013.

A CESA contribution is phased out when the donor's income exceeds certain limits. Under the Tax Relief Act, the income limitations are as follows. Note that the limits for joint filers are exactly twice those for single filers—this eliminates a marriage penalty that existed under earlier versions of the law, *i.e.*, comparing the contributions of a married couple with divorced or unmarried individuals (*See* Table 1).

Table 1		*Modified AGI*
	Phase-Out Under Tax Relief Act	*Phase-Out Under Prior Law*
Joint Returns	190,000 – 220,000	150,000 – 160,000
Other Individual Returns	95,000 – 110,000	95,000 – 110,000

In general, then, nondeductible CESA contributions of up to $36,000 can be made on behalf of a student, *i.e.*, annual contributions from birth through age 18. The tax treatment of CESA funds parallels those of the Roth IRA, although with different income limitations and withdrawal penalties.

Because of the contribution and income limitations, and the relatively low maximum amount of the annual contribution, the CESA often is not as attractive as a 529 plan or other tax-advantaged education vehicles—the large tuition and other costs of education far exceed the amounts that can be accumulated in a CESA, even assuming a successful, aggressive investment strategy. These disadvantages become greater if the $500 annual pre-EGTRRA contribution maximum returns as scheduled in 2013. And many successful individuals will not be able to make any CESA contribution because of the income phase-outs, amounts that are not indexed for inflation. But CESAs still represent an important tax incentive for many middle-class taxpayers, and for family members (say grandparents with lower incomes) who wish to support a student's education.

CESA withdrawals may be made to cover elementary and secondary school costs, under favorable EGTRRA rules. This feature of the CESA is attractive relative to most other education incentives, which are targeted to college- and graduate-level, as well as continuing professional education. After 2012, though, CESA withdrawals cannot be used for elementary and secondary school expenses, i.e., this CESA advantage is scheduled to expire.

¶330

NEW LAW EXPLAINED

Tax Relief Act committee report language clarifies that CESA contributions can be made by corporations and other entities (e.g., a partnership or foundation), and that no income phase-out applies to such transfers. This allows for a broader base of contributors, including perhaps a matching plan as part of a compensation package for the donor. Such language does not appear to exist for 529 plans, so this represents another advantage of the CESA.

The age-30 rules as to deemed distributions are extended by the Tax Relief Act for students with special needs, e.g., a physical or learning disability. Similarly, contributions to a CESA can be made after the student reaches age 18. Both of these extensions (unlimited as to the beneficiary's age) recognize that certain students need more time than others to complete an education. The provisions are scheduled to expire, though, after 2012.

Other restrictive rules are scheduled to return in tax year 2013. For instance, under the 2010 Tax Relief Act, CESA contributions can be made up to the unextended due date of the contributor's tax return (say April 15 of the following year). And excess contributions can be withdrawn by June 1 of the following year without incurring the six percent excise tax. After 2012, both of these dates are reset to be the end of the tax year of the contribution (e.g., December 31, not April 15). The income deferral advantages of the CESA suggest that contributions should be made early in the tax year and not at its end anyway, but the rules scheduled for 2013 surely will reduce the likelihood that a CESA contribution will be made.

Coordination of the CESA withdrawals with the use of other education incentives also is scheduled to become more restrictive in 2013. EGTRRA and other rules allow for a tax-free CESA withdrawal to be claimed in the same year as a lifetime learning or other credit is claimed for the student, although with respect to different expenses. The Tax Relief Act extends those rules, but stricter rules return in 2013, whereunder an education credit or a CESA exclusion can be claimed, but not both, with respect to a specific student. The extension by the Tax Relief Act broadens the number of donors who can support a student's education costs, and it increases the amount of funds that a student can use in a single tax year for his/her education—both of these results support the middle class family in a way that pre-EGTRRA law did not.

▶ **Effective date.** The provision is effective for tax years beginning after December 31, 2001 (Act Sec. 101(a)(2) of the Tax Relief, Unemployment Insurance Reauthorization, and Job Creation Act of 2010 (P.L. 111-312); Act Sec. 401(h) of the Economic Growth and Tax Relief Reconciliation Act of 2001 (EGTRRA) (P.L. 107-16)). The provision shall not apply to tax years beginning after December 31, 2012 (Act Sec. 101(a)(1) of the Tax Relief Act of 2010; Act Sec. 901 of EGTRRA). See ¶105 for a specific discussion of the sunset provision of EGTRRA and how it is applied.

Law source: Law at ¶5380 and ¶7010. Committee Report at ¶10,050.

— Act Sec. 101(a)(1) of the Tax Relief, Unemployment Insurance Reauthorization, and Job Creation Act of 2010 (P.L. 111-312), amending Act Sec. 901 of the Economic Growth and Tax Relief Reconciliation Act of 2001 (EGTRRA) (P.L. 107-16);

— Act Sec. 101(a)(2), providing the effective date.

¶330

NEW LAW EXPLAINED

Reporter references: For further information, consult the following CCH reporters.

— Standard Federal Tax Reporter, ¶22,955.01

— Tax Research Consultant, INDIV: 60,202 and PLANIND: 3,064.10

— Practical Tax Explanation, § 1,810.05

¶335 Educational Assistance Programs

SUMMARY OF NEW LAW

The exclusion from gross income and from wages of up to $5,250 in annual employer-provided education expenses is extended through December 31, 2012.

BACKGROUND

The Internal Revenue Code has long allowed employees to exclude some educational assistance they receive from their employers (Code Sec. 127) and, by reference, to exclude the same amounts from their wages for purposes of employment taxes (Code Sec. 3121(a)(18)). Before 2002, however, these exclusions were enacted on a temporary basis, and often had to be extended retroactively.

The Economic Growth and Tax Relief Reconciliation Act of 2001 (EGTRRA) (P.L. 107-16) provides employees with a permanent exclusion from gross income for income tax purposes, and from wages for employment tax purposes, of up to $5,250 in annual educational assistance provided under an employer's nondiscriminatory educational assistance plan (Code Sec. 127, as amended by P.L. 107-16; Code Sec. 3121(a)(18)). Like most changes made by EGTRRA, these "permanent" exclusions apply only through 2010.

> **Comment:** Employer-provided educational benefits can also be excludable from income and wages as working condition fringe benefits under Code Sec. 132.

A qualified educational assistance program must be a separate written plan to provide qualified educational assistance for the exclusive benefit of the employer's employees. The program can benefit all employees, including those who are retired, disabled, laid-off, or on military leave, as well as officers, shareholders, self-employed individuals and highly compensated employees. However, the program cannot discriminate in favor of highly compensated employees, and assistance for individuals who own more than five percent of the employer (and their spouses and dependents) cannot exceed five percent of the employer's total annual educational assistance during the tax year. If an employee works for more than one employer, the $5,250 cap on the exclusion applies to the aggregate amount of educational assistance benefits received from all employers (Code Sec. 127(b)).

Excludable educational assistance consists of the employer's payment of expenses incurred by or on behalf of an employee for education, or the employer's direct provision of education to an employee. Assistance includes, but is not limited to,

BACKGROUND

tuition, fees, and similar payments, as well as books, supplies, and equipment for both graduate and undergraduate courses. Educational assistance does not include (1) tools or supplies that may be retained by the employee after completion of a course, (2) meals, lodging, or transportation, or (3) any education involving sports, games, or hobbies (Code Sec. 127(c), as amended by P.L. 107-16).

> **Comment:** The pre-EGTRRA temporary version of the exclusion did not apply to graduate courses.

Sunset provision. Under the sunset provision of EGTRRA, amendments made by the Act will not apply to tax years beginning after December 31, 2010 (Act Sec. 901 of P.L. 107-16).

NEW LAW EXPLAINED

Employer-provided educational assistance exclusion extended.—The exclusion from gross income for income tax purposes (Code Sec. 127) and from wages for employment tax purposes (Code Sec. 3121(a)(18)) of up to $5,250 annually in educational assistance provided by an employer to an employee is extended to apply to tax years beginning in 2011 and 2012 (Act Sec. 901 of the Economic Growth and Tax Relief Extension Act of 2001 (EGTRRA) (P.L. 107-16), as amended by Tax Relief, Unemployment Insurance Reauthorization, and Job Creation Act of 2010 (P.L. 111-312)).

If the EGTRRA changes are allowed to sunset, employees' incomes and wages for tax years beginning after 2012 will include all employer-provided educational assistance that:

- pays for graduate education expenses, or

- does not qualify as a working condition fringe benefit. An employer's educational assistance qualifies as a working condition fringe benefit only if the educational expenses would qualify as an employee business expense if they were paid by the employee (Code Sec. 132(d)). This effectively limits the exclusion to assistance for education related to the employee's current job (Reg. § 1.162-5).

> **Practical Analysis:** *Jasper L. Cummings, Jr.*, Alston & Bird LLP, Raleigh, N.C., observes that for two more years employees will be able to rely on the statutory exclusion in Code Sec. 127 for up to $5,250 in employer-paid assistance under a qualifying educational assistance program.
>
> *Impact on Employers.* The employer can continue not to include in the employee's Form W-2 any educational expense reimbursements paid to or for the benefit of employees even though (1) such payments do not qualify as a working condition fringe benefit under Code Sec. 132, which generally includes job-related educational expenses that the employee could deduct, as discussed below, and (2) the employer does not handle those payments under an "accountable plan" (generally meaning that the employee must provide proper documentation to the employer). If the plan for the payments is an "accountable plan," the employer does not need to reflect the

NEW LAW EXPLAINED

payments on the employee's Form W-2. If the plan is a "nonaccountable plan," the employer does reflect the payments on the W-2 and the employee must include and attempt to deduct the payments unless they qualify for the Code Sec. 127 allowance. In any event, the employer will be allowed a deduction for such payments that are compensatory as to the employee.

Impact on Employees. Such benefits received by employees will continue through 2012 to be excludable from gross income even though they do not qualify as working condition fringe benefits under Code Sec. 132, and are not paid under an accountable plan. If the benefits are not subject to Code Sec. 127 and are paid under a nonaccountable plan, the employee may be allowed a business expense deduction for the cost of the education if the education is not needed to meet minimum requirements for his employment, is not part of a study program that can qualify him for a new trade or business, and either is required by the current employer or maintains and improves the skills needed for his current job. However, the deduction will be subject to the two-percent-of-adjusted-gross-income floor on miscellaneous itemized deductions, and in any event the employee must itemize deductions to claim such a deduction above the two percent floor.

▶ **Effective date.** The provision applies to expenses relating to courses beginning after December 31, 2001 (Act Sec. 101(a)(2) of the Tax Relief, Unemployment Insurance Reauthorization, and Job Creation Act of 2010 (P.L. 111-312)); Act Sec. 411(d) of the Economic Growth and Tax Relief Reconciliation Act of 2001 (EGTRRA) (P.L. 107-16)). The provision shall not apply to tax years beginning after December 31, 2012 (Act Sec. 101(a)(1) of the Tax Relief Act of 2010; Act Sec. 901 of EGTRRA). See ¶105 for a specific discussion of the sunset provision of EGTRRA and how it is applied.

Law source: Law at ¶5210, and ¶7010. Committee Report at ¶10,050.

— Act Sec. 101(a)(1) of the Tax Relief, Unemployment Insurance Reauthorization, and Job Creation Act of 2010 (P.L. 111-312), amending Act Sec. 901 of the Economic Growth and Tax Relief Reconciliation Act of 2001 (EGTRRA) (P.L. 107-16);

— Act Sec. 101(a)(2), providing the effective date.

Reporter references: For further information, consult the following CCH reporters.

— Standard Federal Tax Reporter, ¶7353.01

— Tax Research Consultant, COMPEN: 36,550 and PLANIND: 3,352.01

— Practical Tax Explanation, § 20,101

¶340 Federal Scholarships With Obligatory Service Requirements

SUMMARY OF NEW LAW

The exclusion from gross income under Code Sec. 117 for scholarships with obligatory service requirements received by degree candidates at qualified educational

SUMMARY OF NEW LAW

organizations from the National Health Service Corps Scholarship Program or the F. Edward Hebert Armed Forces Health Professions Scholarship and Financial Assistance Program is extended through 2012.

BACKGROUND

The Economic Growth and Tax Relief Reconciliation Act of 2001 (EGTRRA) (P.L. 107-16) amended Code Sec. 117(c) to allow recipients of scholarships from the National Health Service Corps Scholarship Program (NHSC) or the F. Edward Hebert Armed Forces Health Professions Scholarship and Financial Assistance Program (Armed Forces Scholarship Program) to exclude their scholarship distributions from gross income even if the scholarship required as a quid pro quo the performance of specified services.

General rule. Under Code Sec. 117(a), any amount received as a "qualified scholarship" by an individual who is a candidate for a degree at a qualified educational organization is excluded from gross income. A qualified educational organization is a university, college, or other educational institution that has a regular faculty and curriculum and normally has a regularly enrolled body of students at the place its educational activities are conducted (Code Sec. 170(b)(1)(A)(ii)). A "qualified scholarship" includes amounts received for the payment of tuition, fees, books, supplies, and equipment required in the student's course of instruction at the qualified educational organization (Code Sec. 117(b)). For most scholarship recipients, any portion of a scholarship amount that represents payment for teaching, research, or other services by the student required as a condition for receiving the scholarship is includable in gross income (Code Sec. 117(c)).

Special rule for certain federal scholarships. The limit on the exclusion for amounts that represent payment for services does not apply to scholarship distributions from the NHSC or the Armed Forces Scholarship Program. Recipients of these scholarships are required to serve in either an underserved community or an Army hospital. Nonetheless, scholarship amounts from the NHSC or the Armed Forces Scholarship Program received in tax years beginning after December 31, 2001, are excluded from gross income as an exception to the general rule (Code Sec. 117(c)(2)).

Sunset provision. Under the sunset provision of EGTRRA, the exclusion from gross income is scheduled to expire for tax years beginning after December 31, 2010 (Act Sec. 901 of P.L. 107-16).

NEW LAW EXPLAINED

Federal scholarships with obligatory service requirements exclusion extended.—The exclusion from gross income for scholarships with obligatory service requirements received by degree candidates at qualified educational organizations from the National Health Service Corps Scholarship Program or the F. Edward Hebert Armed Forces Health Professions Scholarship and Financial Assistance Program is extended to December 31, 2012. Thus, amounts received by degree candidates at

¶340

NEW LAW EXPLAINED

qualified educational organizations from these programs is excluded from gross income for tax years 2011 and 2012 (Code Sec. 117(c); Act Sec. 901 of the Economic Growth and Tax Relief Reconciliation Act of 2001 (EGTRRA) (P.L. 107-16), as amended by the Tax Relief, Unemployment Insurance Reauthorization, and Job Creation Act of 2010 (P.L. 111-312)).

If the EGTRRA changes sunset, amounts received by degree candidates who are recipients of these federal scholarships will be taxed on amounts received for services performed as a condition for receiving the scholarship, for tax years beginning after December 31, 2012.

> **Comment:** The primary impetus for the special exclusion for the applicable federal scholarships was that after tax withholding the scholarship recipients were not taking home enough of the distribution to cover basic expenses. Thus, there was fear that qualified candidates would not participate in the programs and communities with underresourced medical services would suffer. Scholarship recipients will likely fact similar cost issues in 2013 when the provisions of EGTRRA sunset.

▶ **Effective date.** The amendments made to this provision apply to tax years beginning after December 31, 2001 (Act Sec. 101(a)(2) of the Tax Relief, Unemployment Insurance Reauthorization, and Jobs Creation Act of 2010 (P.L. 111-312)); Act Sec. 413(b) of the Economic Growth and Tax Relief Reconciliation Act of 2001 (EGTRRA) (P.L. 107-16)). The provision shall not apply to tax years beginning after December 31, 2012 (Act Sec. 101(a)(1) of the Tax Relief Act of 2010; Act Sec. 901 of EGTRRA). See ¶105 for a specific discussion of the sunset provision of EGTRRA and how it is applied.

Law source: Law at ¶5200, and ¶7010. Committttee Report at ¶10,050.

— Act Sec. 101(a)(1) of the Tax Relief, Unemployment Insurance Reauthorization, and Jobs Creation Act of 2010 (P.L. 111-312), amending Act Sec. 901 of the Economic Growth and Tax Relief Reconciliation Act of 2001 (EGTRRA) (P.L. 107-16);

— Act Sec. 101(a)(2), providing the effective date.

Reporter references: For further information, consult the following CCH reporters.

— Standard Federal Tax Reporter, ¶7183.01

— Tax Research Consultant, INDIV: 60,060.15 and PLANIND: 3,352.05

— Practical Tax Explanation, § 3,905.10

¶345 Student Loan Interest Deduction

SUMMARY OF NEW LAW

The increase in the modified adjusted gross income (AGI) phaseout ranges for eligibility for the student loan interest deduction under Code Sec. 221(b) that was scheduled to expire after 2010 has been extended for two years. In addition, the 60-month limitation as to the number of months during which interest paid on a

SUMMARY OF NEW LAW

student loan is deductible under Code Sec. 221(d) and the restriction that makes voluntary payments of interest nondeductible remain repealed for two more years.

BACKGROUND

The Economic Growth and Tax Relief Reconciliation Act of 2001 (EGTRRA) (P.L. 107-16) increased the modified adjusted gross income (AGI) phaseout ranges for eligibility for the student loan interest deduction for tax years ending after December 31, 2001. An eligible taxpayer can deduct qualified interest on a qualified loan for an eligible student's qualified educational expenses at an eligible institution. The $2,500 maximum student loan interest deduction begins to phase out for taxpayers whose modified AGI exceeds $50,000 ($100,000 for joint returns), and phases out to zero at modified AGI of $65,000 ($130,000 for joint returns). The phaseout thresholds are adjusted each year for inflation in increments of $5,000. For tax years beginning in 2010 (Rev. Proc. 2009-50, I.R.B. 2009-45, 617), the $2,500 maximum deduction for interest paid on qualified education loans is reduced when modified AGI exceeds $60,000 ($120,000 for joint returns), and is completely eliminated when modified AGI is $75,000 or more ($150,000 or more for joint returns).

EGTRRA also repealed the 60-month limitation as to the number of months during which interest paid on a student loan is deductible, as well as the restriction that makes voluntary payments of interest nondeductible.

Sunset provision. Under the sunset provision of EGTRRA, amendments made by the Act will not apply to tax years beginning after December 31, 2010 (Act Sec. 901 of P.L. 107-16).

NEW LAW EXPLAINED

Increased AGI phaseout ranges for student loan interest deduction extended.— The increase in the modified adjusted gross income (AGI) phaseout ranges for eligibility for the student loan interest deduction (Code Sec. 221(b)) has been extended for two years through 2012. The 60-month limitation as to the number of months during which interest paid on a student loan is deductible and the restriction that makes voluntary payments of interest nondeductible remain repealed for two more years through 2012 ((Act Sec. 901 of the Economic Growth and Tax Relief Reconciliation Act of 2001 (EGTRRA) (P.L. 107-16), as amended by the Tax Relief, Unemployment Insurance Reauthorization, and Job Creation Act of 2010 (P.L. 111-312)).

If the EGTRRA changes sunset, for tax years beginning after December 31, 2012, the deduction begins to phase out for taxpayers whose modified AGI exceeds $40,000 ($60,000 for joint returns), and phases out to zero at a modified AGI of $55,000 ($75,000 for joint returns) (Code Sec. 221(b)). Additionally, for tax years beginning after December 31, 2012, education loan interest will be deductible only if paid during the first 60 months, whether or not consecutive, that interest payments are required. The 60-month period is determined by treating any loan and all of its refinancings as one loan (Code

NEW LAW EXPLAINED

Sec. 221(d)). This means that a taxpayer will not be able to obtain a longer period of deductions by consolidating loans and changing payment schedules.

Example: Jason obtains a qualified education loan to pay for an undergraduate degree at an eligible educational institution. After graduation, Jason is required to make interest payments on the loan beginning in January 2013. Jason makes the required interest payments for 15 months. In April 2014, Jason borrows money from another lender to be used exclusively to repay the first qualified education loan. The new loan requires interest payments to start immediately. At the time Jason is required to make interest payments on the new loan there are forty-five months remaining of the original 60-month period.

Comment: The reinstatement of the 60-month limitation in 2013 will prevent those college graduates who may take many years to pay their college debts from deducting the interest payments for the full term of their loan.

Compliance Tip: The reinstatement of the 60-month limitation may bring back the complexity and administrative burdens regarding information reporting requirements for taxpayers, lenders, and loan servicing agencies, as well as for the IRS.

Practical Analysis: Gary L. Maydew, Ph.D, CPA, retired accounting professor at Iowa State University, observes that the two year extension of the increased AGI phaseout range and the two-year repeal of the 60-month limitation will be moderately helpful to holders of student loans. However, the restrictions set to begin in 2013 will hurt recent graduates at a time in which tuition is still rising rapidly and good-paying jobs are hard to find. Resumption of the 60-month limitation is more damaging than the drop down of the AGI phaseout range for those students who borrowed in their name, because many recent graduates will not be significantly above the modified AGI phaseout.

Practical Analysis: William A Raabe, Ohio State University, and Capital University Law School, Columbus, Ohio, John O. Everett, Virginia Commonwealth University, Richmond Virginia, and Cherie J. Hennig, University of North Carolina, Wilmington observe that the Code allows a deduction for only a few types of interest paid by an individual, but the deduction allowed for AGI concerning interest paid on qualifying student loans is an important incentive for middle-class taxpayers in their quest for higher education. The 2010 Tax Relief Act extends through 2012 the EGTRRA deduction of up to $2,500 per year per student.

The Code Sec. 221 deduction can be claimed by all individuals, not just those who itemize deductions. This is an important distinction for those college graduates who, early in their career, attempt to pay down student loans so as to better qualify for a home mortgage or other long-term business financing. One who does not own a

---

¶345

NEW LAW EXPLAINED

principal residence is not likely to itemize deductions, so if the Code Sec. 221 amount were allowed (like most other personal interest deductions) only as a deduction from AGI, its benefit would be lost for most taxpayers.

The deduction for student loan interest is allowed if the loan proceeds were used within 90 days for the higher education expenses of a degree-seeking student who carries at least a half-time load of courses. The deduction cannot be claimed by an individual who is the dependent of another, or on a Married-Separate return.

One's student loan interest deduction is phased out when the borrower's income exceeds certain limits. Under the 2010 Tax Relief Act, the income limitations are as follows through 2012. Note that the limits for joint filers are exactly twice those for single filers—this eliminates a marriage penalty that existed under earlier versions of the law, *i.e.*, comparing the payments of a married couple with divorced or unmarried individuals (*See* Table 1).

Table 1

	Modified AGI	
	Phase-Out Under 2010 Tax Relief Act	*Phase-Out Under Prior Law*
Joint Returns	120,000 – 150,000	60,000 – 75,000
Other Individual Returns	60,000 – 75,000	40,000 – 55,000

Under the 2010 Tax Relief Act, the phase-out amounts are indexed for inflation. The pre-EGTRRA limits are scheduled to return in 2013. The deduction phase-outs already are lower than the phase-outs that apply to other education provisions, and the sunset of the 2010 Tax Relief Act amounts will trigger the loss or reduction of the deduction to many taxpayers beginning in 2013.

Pre-EGTRRA rules included other restrictions. The Code Sec. 221 deduction could be claimed for no more than sixty months on the individual's Forms 1040. The sixty month period begins with the date of the first required payment against the loan balance, but the rule does not require that the sixty months of payments be consecutive, *e.g.*, payments could be suspended by a return to school, a lack of funds, or a military engagement.

Any voluntary interest payments (say to prepay against the amount due) were not deductible under pre-EGTRRA law. EGTRRA and the 2010 Tax Relief Act waived these restrictions, but both of them are scheduled to return in 2013.

Both of these rules seem arbitrary and counter to the support of middle-class efforts to acquire education, especially given that many students acquire sizable loan balances that, even in the best of circumstances, would require more than five years to pay off. The rules become especially difficult to enforce when (as often is the case) the student carries more than one loan, and refinances or consolidates them during the repayment period. But the restrictions remain in the Code and would seem to be a costly result for most taxpayers after 2012, such that only some of the interest payments made under a reasonable amortization schedule would actually be deductible.

▶ **Effective date.** The amendments eliminating the 60-month payback period shall apply with respect to any loan interest paid after December 31, 2001, in tax years ending after such date. The amendments increasing the phaseout limits shall apply to tax years ending after

NEW LAW EXPLAINED

December 31, 2001 (Act Sec. 101(a)(2) of the Tax Relief, Unemployment Insurance Reauthorization, and Job Creation Act of 2010 (P.L. 111-312)); Act Sec. 412(a)(3) and 412(b)(3) of the Economic Growth and Tax Relief Reconciliation Act of 2001 (EGTRRA) (P.L. 107-16)). See ¶105 for a specific discussion of the sunset provision of EGTRRA and how it is applied.

Law source: Law at ¶5305, ¶5780, and ¶7010. Committee Report at ¶10,050.

— Act Sec. 101(a)(1) of the Tax Relief, Unemployment Insurance Reauthorization, and Job Creation Act of 2010 (P.L. 111-312), amending Act Sec. 901 of the Economic Growth and Tax Relief Reconciliation Act of 2001 (EGTRRA) (P.L. 107-16);

— Act Sec. 101(a)(2), providing the effective date.

Reporter references: For further information, consult the following CCH reporters.

— Standard Federal Tax Reporter, ¶12,695.01

— Tax Research Consultant, INDIV: 60,054.15 and PLANIND: 3,354.05

— Practical Tax Explanation, §5,901

¶350   Deduction for Qualified Tuition and Related Expenses

SUMMARY OF NEW LAW

The above-the-line deduction for qualified tuition and related expenses is extended for two years through December 31, 2011.

BACKGROUND

The Economic Growth and Tax Relief Reconciliation Act of 2001 (EGTRRA) (P.L. 107-16) added an above-the-line deduction for qualified tuition and related expenses as new Code Sec. 222 (P.L. 107-16, redesignating former Code Sec. 222 (Cross-references) as Code Sec. 223. Code Sec. 223 was later redesignated as Code Sec. 224 by P.L. 108-473).

"Qualified tuition and related expenses" are defined as tuition and fees required for the enrollment or attendance of the taxpayer, the taxpayer's spouse, or any dependent that the taxpayer is entitled to deduct under a dependency exemption at an eligible educational institution for courses of instruction. Special rules apply for individuals claimed as dependents by another taxpayer, married individuals filing separately, and nonresident aliens. Generally, any accredited public, nonprofit, or proprietary post-secondary institution is an eligible educational institution. This definition is the same as that for Hope Scholarship and lifetime learning credits under Code Sec. 25A (Code Sec. 222(d)(1)).

Taxpayers may not use the deduction for qualified tuition and related expenses to claim a double benefit. If a qualified tuition and related expense is deductible under

BACKGROUND

any other provision, it is not deductible under Code Sec. 222 (Code Sec. 222(c)(1)). Further, the taxpayer must reduce the total amount of qualified tuition and related expenses by the amount excluded for: (1) interest on U.S. savings bonds used to pay for higher education (Code Sec. 135); (2) distributions from a qualified tuition program (or qualified tuition plan (QTP) or 529 plan) (Code Sec. 529(c)(1)); or (3) distributions from a Coverdell education savings account (formerly, an education IRA) (Code Sec. 530(d)(2)). Finally, in determining the amount to exclude from qualified tuition and related expenses for distributions from a qualified tuition plan, the amount excluded does not include the portion of that distribution that represents a return on contributions to the plan (Code Sec. 222(c)(2)(B)).

Originally, the deduction was available to individual taxpayers for payments made in tax years beginning after December 31, 2001 and before January 1, 2006 (Code Sec. 222, as added by P.L. 107-16). The deduction applied to qualifying tuition and related expenses paid by the taxpayer during the tax year. However, the amount of this deduction was limited by several factors: (1) the taxpayer's adjusted gross income (AGI) and (2) the tax year in which the deduction was claimed. In 2002 and 2003, the deduction was limited to $3,000 and was only available to taxpayers with an adjusted gross income not exceeding $65,000 ($130,000 for joint filers) for the year (Code Sec. 222(a)). Code Sec. 222(b)(2)(B) provided for an increase in the amount of the deduction, placing the limit at $4,000 for taxpayers with an adjusted gross income not exceeding $65,000 ($130,000 for joint filers), for tax years beginning in 2004 and 2005. It also provided a deduction of $2,000 for taxpayers whose adjusted gross income for the tax year exceeded $65,000 ($130,000 for joint filers) but did not exceed $80,000 ($160,000 for joint filers). The deduction under Code Sec. 222 was not available to taxpayers with adjusted gross incomes above $80,000 ($160,000 for joint filers).

The American Jobs Creation Act of 2004 (P.L. 108-357) amended Code Sec. 222 by changing the factors considered in determining the taxpayer's adjusted gross income, specifying that for purposes of this deduction, adjusted gross income would be determined without regard to the exclusions contained in Code Sec. 199 (income attributable to domestic production activities) (Code Sec. 222(b)(2)(C)(i)). This change was effective for tax years beginning after December 31, 2004.

While the dollar limitations were unaltered, the Tax Relief and Health Care Act of 2006 (P.L. 109-432) extended the availability of the deduction for qualifying tuition and related expenses paid during 2006 and 2007, making it applicable to tax years beginning after December 31, 2005 (Code Sec. 222(b)(2)(B) and (e)).

Finally, the Tax Extenders and Alternative Minimum Tax Relief Act of 2008 (P.L. 110-343) extended the availability of the deduction once again for qualifying tuition and related expenses paid during 2008 and 2009. Since the deduction was not extended any further, it terminated on December 31, 2009, and is not available in tax years beginning after December 31, 2009 (Code Sec. 222(e)).

NEW LAW EXPLAINED

Higher education deduction extended.—The above-the-line deduction for qualified tuition and related expenses is extended for two years through December 31, 2011

NEW LAW EXPLAINED

(Code Sec. 222(e), as amended by the Tax Relief, Unemployment Insurance Reauthorization, and Job Creation Act of 2010 (P.L. 111-312)). Act Sec. 901 of the Economic Growth and Tax Relief Reconciliation Act of 2001 (EGTRRA) (P.L. 107-16), the sunset provision, has no practical effect on the deduction for qualified tuition and related expenses under Code Sec. 222 since the deduction expired on December 31, 2009, one year before the EGTRRA sunset provision takes effect. Therefore, the sunset provision of EGTRRA along with its extension through December 31, 2012 (Act Sec. 101(a) of the Tax Relief Act of 2010) has no impact on this deduction.

State Tax Consequences: The extension of the above-the-line deduction for qualified tuition and related expenses will have no impact on states such as California, Iowa and Maine that have decoupled from this federal provision or states such as Mississippi or New Jersey that do not allow an adjustment for such expenses. For other states, whether an adjustment is required will depend on the state's Internal Revenue Code conformity date. Those states that update their Code conformity dates annually will most likely conform during their next legislative sessions

Practical Analysis: William A Raabe, Ohio State University, and Capital University Law School, Columbus, Ohio, John O. Everett, Virginia Commonwealth University, Richmond Virginia, and Cherie J. Hennig, University of North Carolina, Wilmington observe that the Code allows a deduction for AGI for higher education tuition and related expenses. Unlike most other education provisions, the Code Sec. 222 deduction does not have requirements as to the prior skills of the student, or to the student's employment status.

The Code Sec. 222 deduction can be claimed by all individuals, not just those who itemize deductions. This is an important distinction for those college students who have not yet entered the work force on a full-time basis. One who does not own a principal residence is not likely to itemize deductions, so if the Code Sec. 222 amount were allowed (like most other personal education deductions) only as a deduction from AGI, and then perhaps subject to the two percent of AGI floor, its benefit would be lost for most taxpayers.

A Code Sec. 222 deduction is allowed only for tuition and other required costs of college attendance. Activity fees, books, room and board, and supplies generally do not qualify for the deduction. The deduction can be claimed by the payor with respect to the costs of the taxpayer, spouse, and dependents. Costs that qualify for the deduction cannot be "used twice" on the same tax return, e.g., the deduction is reduced by the amount of other educational assistance received from the school or other sources, by the application of educational savings bonds or Coverdell withdrawals, and by 529 plan payments.

The Code Sec. 222 deduction was created by the EGTRRA, so it was scheduled to expire after 2009. The 2010 Tax Relief Act extends the deduction through 2011. The deduction is scheduled to expire in full after 2011. The deduction is determined by the taxpayer's modified AGI and filing status. One's deduction equals the lesser of the qualifying amount paid in the tax year or the corresponding amount in Table 1,

NEW LAW EXPLAINED

below. The current limitations are summarized as follows—they are not indexed for inflation. Note that the limits for joint filers are exactly twice those for single filers—this eliminates a possible marriage penalty, *i.e.*, comparing the payments of a married couple with divorced or unmarried individuals. The deduction is not allowed on a Married-Separate return.

Table 1. Filing Status	Modified AGI	Maximum Deduction
Married	$0 – 130,000	$4,000
Single/Head of Household	$0 – 65,000	4,000
Married	$130,000 – 160,000	2,000
Single/Head of Household	$65,000 – 80,000	2,000
Married	$160,000 +	0
Single/Head of Household	$80,000 +	0

The Code Sec. 222 deduction is an important component of Congress' support for middle-class higher education. The deduction acts as a direct rebate of tuition and other costs. The income limitations are reasonable but not overly generous, and the reduction in the maximum deduction amount is steep at the margin, *e.g.*, an additional dollar of MAGI might reduce the deduction amount by $2,000.

In coordinating the Code Sec. 222 deduction with the American Opportunity or other credits, the deduction is more likely to be attractive when the taxpayer's marginal tax rate is higher, or when other incentives reach their maximum amounts. Education credits are non-refundable, so the use of an education deduction for AGI may have other positive effects on the Form 1040, *i.e.*, in reducing AGI and modified AGI for other purposes.

The Code Sec. 222 deduction for tuition and other costs of higher education provides important support for middle-class taxpayers seeking to improve their knowledge and skills. The deduction is costly to the Treasury, however, so it is not likely to be made a permanent part of the tax law in the near future. Extension of the deduction for two more years is critical to the cash flow planning of many taxpayers, but note that the deduction is scheduled to expire at the end of 2011, not 2012 like most of the other 2010 Tax Relief Act provisions.

▶ **Effective date.** The provision applies to tax years beginning after December 31, 2009 (Act Sec. 724(b) of the Tax Relief, Unemployment Insurance Reauthorization, and Job Creation Act of 2010 (P.L. 111-312)).

Law source: Law at ¶5310. Committee Report at ¶10,310.

— Act Sec. 724(a) of the Tax Relief, Unemployment Insurance Reauthorization, and Job Creation Act of 2010 (P.L. 111-312), amending Code Sec. 222(e);

— Act Sec. 724(b), providing the effective date.

Reporter references: For further information, consult the following CCH reporters.

— Standard Federal Tax Reporter, ¶12,772.01

— Tax Research Consultant, INDIV: 60,064

— Practical Tax Explanation, §5,201

CHARITABLE CONTRIBUTIONS

¶352 Qualified Charitable Distributions from IRAs

SUMMARY OF NEW LAW

The exclusion from gross income of qualified charitable distributions received from IRAs by individuals aged 70½ or older has been extended two years to apply to distributions made in 2010 and 2011.

BACKGROUND

Generally, a taxpayer must include in gross income distributions made from a traditional or Roth individual retirement account (IRA) to the extent they represent a return of nondeductible contributions to the account and the distribution is not rolled over into another qualified retirement plan or IRA. In the case of Roth IRAs, a distribution may also be excluded from gross income if it meets a five-year holding period and is made after the taxpayer reaches age 59½, due to his or her death or disability, or for qualified first-time homebuyer expenses. Distributions from both a traditional or Roth IRA before the taxpayer reaches age 59½ may be subject to an additional 10-percent tax, unless an exception applies. A traditional IRA must generally begin required minimum distributions (RMDs) by the April 1 of the calendar year following the year in which the IRA owner attains age 70½.

For tax years beginning in 2006 through 2009, a taxpayer may exclude from gross income a qualified charitable distribution made during the year that would otherwise be taxable. A qualified charitable distribution is a distribution from the IRA made directly by the trustee to a charitable organization on or after the date the taxpayer has attained age 70½ (Code Sec. 408(d)(8)). The amount of the distribution is limited to the amount of the distribution that would otherwise be included in gross income. However, the total amount of qualified charitable distributions from all of the taxpayer's IRAs cannot exceed $100,000 for the tax year ($100,000 for each spouse on a joint return). A qualified charitable distribution also counts toward satisfying a taxpayer's RMDs from a traditional IRA.

If the taxpayer's IRA includes nondeductible contributions, the qualified charitable distribution is first considered to be paid out of otherwise taxable income. However, a special ordering rule applies to separate taxable distributions from nontaxable IRA distributions for charitable distribution purposes. Under the rule, a distribution is treated first as income up to the aggregate amount that would otherwise be includible in the owner's gross income if all amounts in all the owner's IRAs were distributed during the tax year, and all such plans were treated as one contract for purposes of determining the aggregate amount includible as gross income.

Qualified charitable distributions are not taken into account for purposes of determining the IRA owner's charitable deduction. However, the entire distribution must otherwise have been allowed as a charitable deduction (disregarding the percentage limitations) to be excluded from gross income. Thus, if the contribution would be

BACKGROUND

reduced for any reason (e.g., a benefit received in exchange or substantiation problems), the exclusion is not available for any part of the qualified charitable distribution.

NEW LAW EXPLAINED

Tax treatment of qualified charitable distributions from IRAs extended.—The exclusion from gross income for qualified charitable distributions of up to $100,000 received from traditional or Roth IRAs is extended to apply to distributions made in tax years beginning in 2010 and 2011 (Code Sec. 408(d)(8)(F), as amended by the Tax Relief, Unemployment Insurance Reauthorization, and Job Creation Act of 2010 (P.L. 111-312)). A special rule permits a taxpayer to elect to have a qualified charitable distribution made in January 2011 treated as having been made on December 31, 2010 (Act Sec. 725(b)(2) of the Tax Relief Act of 2010). If a taxpayer makes the election as prescribed by the IRS, then the distribution made in January 2011 counts toward: (1) the taxpayer's $100,000 exclusion limitation for the 2010 calendar year; *and* (2) the taxpayer's required minimum distribution (RMD) for the 2010 calendar year.

> **Comment:** The special rule allowing a taxpayer to elect to treat a qualified charitable distribution in January 2011 as having been made in 2010 was most likely put in place given that the legislation extending the rule for qualified charitable distributions occurred so late during the 2010 year. Thus, the rule is meant to give taxpayers time to arrange to have qualified charitable distributions made for the calendar year.

▶ **Effective date.** The provision applies to distributions made in tax years beginning after December 31, 2009 (Act Sec. 725(b)(1) of the Tax Relief, Unemployment Insurance Reauthorization, and Job Creation Act of 2010 (P.L. 111-312)).

Law source: Law at ¶5355 and ¶7060. Committee Report at ¶10,320.

— Act Sec. 725(a) of the Tax Relief, Unemployment Insurance Reauthorization, and Job Creation Act of 2010 (P.L. 111-312), amending Code Sec. 408(d)(8)(F);

— Act Sec. 725(b), providing the effective date.

Reporter references: For further information, consult the following CCH reporters.

— Standard Federal Tax Reporter, ¶18,922.0326

— Tax Research Consultant, RETIRE: 66,514

— Practical Tax Explanation, §25,450.35

¶353 Charitable Contribution of Real Property for Conservation Purposes Enhanced Deduction

SUMMARY OF NEW LAW

The enhanced deduction for charitable contributions of real property for conservation purposes has been extended for two years, through December 31, 2011.

BACKGROUND

The Code contains several rules to encourage taxpayers to donate appreciated capital gain real property to qualified charities for conservation purposes. Specific provisions also encourage both corporate and individual farmers and ranchers to make "qualified conservation contributions." Specifically, the deduction percentage limits are significantly raised and enhanced carry forward rules apply for charitable contributions of property for conservation purposes made in tax years beginning after December 31, 2005, and before January 1, 2010.

Qualified conservation contributions. Although a charitable deduction is not usually allowed for a contribution of a partial interest in real property, an exception is made for a donation of property that is considered a "qualified conservation contribution" (Code Sec. 170(f)(3)(B)(iii)). A qualified conservation contribution is a contribution of a qualified real property interest to a qualified organization, exclusively for conservation purposes (Code Sec. 170(h)(1)(C)). The contribution may consist of all of the owner's interests in the property or a remainder interest, provided however that the property must be subject to a perpetual easement or restrictive covenant that prevents the development of the property, safeguarding its natural character or historic significance (Code Sec. 170(h)(2) and 170(h)(4)).

Limitations on deductions. The amount of a deduction for charitable contributions of appreciated capital gain real property is limited to a percentage of the donor's contribution base. The limitation is generally either 20 percent or 30 percent depending on the type of charitable organization receiving the donation (Code Sec. 170(b)(1)). However, the Pension Protection Act of 2006 (P.L. 109-280) increased the deduction limitation to 50 percent for qualified conservation contributions (Code Sec. 170(b)(1)(E)(i)).

Individual farmers and ranchers. If an individual is a "qualified farmer or rancher" for the tax year in which a charitable contribution of appreciated capital gain real property is made, the individual's contribution base for that year is raised from 50 percent to 100 percent (Code Sec. 170(b)(1)(E)(iv)(I)). A "qualified farmer or rancher" is an individual whose gross income from the trade or business of farming is greater than 50 percent of the taxpayer's gross income for the tax year (Code Sec. 170(b)(1)(E)(v)). The property donated must be subject to a restriction that ensures it will remain available for agriculture or livestock production (Code Sec. 170(b)(1)(E)(iv)(II)).

Corporations. A corporation's charitable contribution deduction for the tax year generally may not exceed 10 percent of its taxable income. However, a corporation

BACKGROUND

that is a qualified farmer or rancher during the contribution year is allowed to deduct qualified conservation contributions to the extent that the aggregate of such contributions is not more than the excess of the corporation's taxable income over the amount of allowable charitable deductions for the tax year (which cannot exceed 10 percent of its taxable income) (Code Sec. 170(b)(2)(B)(i)(I) and (II)).

The enhanced charitable deduction for contributions of property for conservation purposes does not apply to contributions made during any tax year beginning after December 31, 2009.

NEW LAW EXPLAINED

Enhanced deduction for charitable contributions of real property for conservation purposes extended.—The enhanced deduction for charitable contributions of real property for conservation purposes ("qualified conservation contributions") has been extended for two years and applies to contributions made through December 31, 2011 (Code Sec. 170(b)(1)(E)(vi) and 170(b)(2)(B)(iii), as amended by the Tax Relief, Unemployment Insurance Reauthorization, and Job Creation Act of 2010 (P.L. 111-312)).

> **State Tax Consequences:** The extension of the enhanced charitable contribution deduction for contributions of real property donated for conservation purposes does not impact states such as California and Pennsylvania that have specifically decoupled from this provision or states such as Connecticut or Illinois that do not allow itemized deductions. Similarly, states that do not allow a charitable contribution deduction such as Indiana and New Jersey will also not be impacted. For those states that do allow a charitable deduction and that recognize these enhanced deductions, whether the state will recognize the extension depends upon the state's Internal Revenue Code conformity date. Those states that update their Code conformity dates annually will most likely conform during their next legislative sessions.

▶ **Effective date.** This provision applies to contributions made in tax years beginning after December 31, 2009 (Act Sec. 723(c) of the Tax Relief, Unemployment Insurance Reauthorization, and Job Creation Act of 2010 (P.L. 111-312)).

Law source: Law at ¶5270. Committee Report at ¶10,300.

— Act Sec. 723(a) of the Tax Relief, Unemployment Insurance Reauthorization, and Job Creation Act of 2010 (P.L. 111-312), amending Code Sec. 170(b)(1)(E)(vi);

— Act Sec. 723(b), amending Code Sec. 170(b)(2)(B)(iii);

— Act Sec. 723(c), providing the effective date.

Reporter references: For further information, consult the following CCH reporters.

— Standard Federal Tax Reporter, ¶11,670.033, ¶11,670.034, ¶11,680.033, ¶11,710.01

— Tax Research Consultant, INDIV: 51,256.20, INDIV: 51,364, CCORP: 9,350

— Practical Tax Explanation, §7,565.30

¶353

TAX CREDITS

¶355 Earned Income Tax Credit

SUMMARY OF NEW LAW

Several modifications of the earned income tax credit are extended for two years, through December 31, 2012. The phaseout rule is applied by multiplying the phaseout percentage by a taxpayer's adjusted gross income, the credit is not reduced by AMT liability and tiebreaker rules and relationship tests are simplified.

BACKGROUND

The earned income credit (EIC) is available to lower-income individuals who earn income by working during the tax year. The credit is calculated as a percentage of the taxpayer's earned income, up to a cut-off amount referred to as the "earned income amount". The credit percentage is highest for individuals with two or more qualifying children (three or more, for 2009 and 2010) and lowest for individuals with no qualifying children. The credit can be claimed against both regular income tax and alternative minimum tax liability, and it is refundable. The credit is completely phased out for higher-income individuals.

Amount of earned income credit. The EIC is determined by multiplying an individual's earned income not in excess of the applicable "earned income amount," by the appropriate "credit percentage" (Code Sec. 32(a)(1)). Three sets of credit percentages (four sets, for tax years beginning in 2009 and 2010) are provided, depending on the number of "qualifying children" that a taxpayer claims (Code Sec. 32(b)).

The credit so computed is subject to phaseout. Specifically, the credit may not exceed the excess of:

- the credit percentage of the earned income amount (i.e., the maximum possible credit for a taxpayer), over

- the "phaseout percentage" of adjusted gross income (earned income, if greater) in excess of the "phaseout amount" (Code Sec. 32(a)(2)).

The credit percentage and phaseout percentage used in calculating the EIC are listed in the following chart (Code Sec. 32(b)(1)). For tax years beginning in 2009 and 2010, the credit percentage for taxpayers with three or more qualifying children is temporarily increased from 40 percent to 45 percent (Code Sec. 32(b)(3)(A)).

Tax Year Beginning	Number of Qualifying Children	Credit Percentage	Phaseout Percentage
After 1995	One	34.00	15.98
	Two or more	40.00	21.06
	None	7.65	7.65

BACKGROUND

Tax Year Beginning	Number of Qualifying Children	Credit Percentage	Phaseout Percentage
In 2009 or 2010 only	One	34.00	15.98
	Two	40.00	21.06
	Three or more	45.00	21.06
	None	7.65	7.65

The earned income amount and the phaseout amount used in calculating the EIC are based on the number of qualifying children claimed by the taxpayer (Code Sec. 32(b)(2)).

For tax years beginning in 2010, the earned income amount, the phaseout ranges, and the maximum credit for individuals (*other than joint filers*) are as follows (Rev. Proc. 2009-50, § 3.06(1), 2009-45 I.R.B. 617):

Number of Qualifying Children	Maximum Credit	Earned Income Amount	Threshold Phaseout Amount	Completed Phaseout Amount
1	$3,050	$8,970	$16,450	$35,535
2	$5,036	$12,590	$16,450	$40,363
3 or more	$5,666	$12,590	$16,450	$43,352
None	$457	$5,980	$7,480	$13,460

The inflation-adjusted figures for *joint filers* in 2010 are as follows (Rev. Proc. 2009-50, § 3.06(1), 2009-45 I.R.B. 617):

Number of Qualifying Children	Maximum Credit	Earned Income Amount	Threshold Phaseout Amount	Completed Phaseout Amount
1	$3,050	$8,970	$21,460	$40,545
2	$5,036	$12,590	$21,460	$45,373
3 or more	$5,666	$12,590	$21,460	$48,362
None	$457	$5,980	$12,490	$18,470

For *2010*, the maximum credit is as follows:

One qualifying child: $3,050 (34 percent of $8,970). The maximum credit is reduced by 15.98 percent of adjusted gross income (or earned income, if greater) over $16,450 ($21,460 if married filing jointly (MFJ)). The credit is completely phased out if AGI (or earned income if greater) is $35,535 or greater ($40,545 or greater if MFJ).

Two qualifying children: $5,036 (40 percent of $12,590). The maximum credit is reduced by 21.06 percent of adjusted gross income (or earned income, if greater) over $16,450 ($21,460 if MFJ). The credit is completely phased out if AGI (or earned income if greater) is $40,363 or greater ($45,373 or greater if MFJ).

Three or more qualifying children: $5,666 (45 percent of $12,590). The maximum credit is reduced by 21.06 percent of adjusted gross income (or earned income, if greater) over $16,450 ($21,460 if MFJ). The credit is completely phased out if AGI (or earned income if greater) is $43,352 or greater ($48,362 or greater if MFJ).

No qualifying children: $457 (7.65 percent of $5,980). The maximum credit is reduced by 7.65 percent of adjusted gross income (or earned income, if greater) over $7,480

BACKGROUND

($12,490 if MFJ). The credit is completely phased out if AGI (or earned income if greater) is $13,460 or greater ($18,470 or greater if MFJ) (Code Sec. 32(b)(3); Rev. Proc. 2009-50, § 3.06(1), 2009-45 I.R.B. 617).

Increase in phaseout amount for joint filers. In the case of taxpayers filing a joint return, the *phaseout amounts* are increased by $1,000 in tax years beginning in 2002, 2003, and 2004, $2,000 in tax years beginning in 2005, 2006, and 2007, and $3,000 in tax years beginning after 2007 (Code Sec. 32(b)(2)(B)). However, for tax years beginning in 2009 and 2010, the phaseout amounts are increased by $5,000 for joint filers rather than $3,000. This $5,000 amount is adjusted for inflation for tax years beginning in 2010 (Code Sec. 32(b)(3)(B)). The phaseout ranges listed for joint filers in the chart above reflect the required $5,000 increase in the phaseout amount.

Treatment of wages, salaries, tips, and other employee compensation as earned income. Wages, salaries, tips, and other employee compensation are treated as earned income for purposes of the EIC only to the extent included in a taxpayer's gross income for the tax year (Code Sec. 32(c)(2)(A)(i)).

Earned income credit may be claimed by taxpayers subject to alternative minimum tax. A taxpayer who must pay the alternative minimum tax may claim the EIC against the sum of the taxpayer's regular and alternative minimum tax liabilities.

Authority to deny earned income credit claims based on information from DHSS child support database. In order to reduce the number of erroneous claims due to taxpayers claiming the EIC for children who do not meet the EIC residency requirements, the IRS has the authority to deny questionable claims filed by parents who, according to the Department of Health and Human Services Federal Case Registry of Child Support Orders database, do not have custody of the claimed child (Code Sec. 6213(g)(2)(M)).

Definition of a qualifying child. For purposes of the EIC, a qualifying child is defined by reference to the definition of a qualifying child that is used to determine entitlement to a dependency exemption (i.e., by reference to the definition contained in Code Sec. 152(c)) but with the following modifications:

- the requirement in Code Sec. 152(c)(1)(D) that the child may not provide more than one-half of his or her own support is disregarded (Code Sec. 32(c)(3)(A));
- the rule in Code Sec. 152(e) for determining the qualifying child of divorced parents does not apply (Code Sec. 32(c)(3)(A));
- a qualifying child does not include a married individual unless the taxpayer may claim a dependency exemption for that individual (Code Sec. 32(c)(3)(B)); and
- the qualifying child's principal place of abode must be in the United States (Code Sec. 32(c)(3)(C)).

   Comment: Prior to enactment of the Working Families Tax Relief Act of 2004 (P.L. 108-311), the definition of a qualifying child for purposes of determining dependency exemptions (Code Sec. 151), head-of-household filing status (Code Sec. 2(b)), whether a taxpayer could claim the child credit (Code Sec. 24), dependent care credit (Code Sec. 21), and EIC (Code Sec. 32) was separately stated in each of the corresponding Code provisions. In the case of the EIC, a

¶355

BACKGROUND

detailed definition of a qualifying child was provided in Code Sec. 32(c)(3). These separate definitions of a qualifying child were replaced with a uniform definition by way of a cross reference to the definition of a qualifying child provided for the exemption for dependents in Code Sec. 152(c), as amended by P.L. 108-311.

The tie-breaker rule provided in Code Sec. 152(c)(4) for determining which taxpayer may treat an individual as a qualifying child if two or more taxpayers otherwise meet the requirements for claiming the individual as a qualifying child also applies for purposes of the EIC (Code Sec. 32(c)(3)).

> **Comment:** The tie-breaker rule was made part of the uniform definition of a qualifying child by the Working Families Tax Relief Act of 2004 (P.L. 108-311). Prior to enactment of P.L. 108-311, the tie-breaker rule for the EIC was separately stated in Code Sec. 32(c)(1)(C).

Sunset provision. Under the sunset provision of EGTRRA, amendments made by the Act will not apply to tax years beginning after December 31, 2010 (Act Sec. 901 of P.L. 107-16).

NEW LAW EXPLAINED

EGTRRA changes to earned income tax credit extended.—The following changes to the earned income credit (EIC) made by the Economic Growth and Tax Relief Reconciliation Act of 2001 (EGTRRA) (P.L. 107-16) will apply to tax years beginning in 2011 and 2012 (Act Sec. 901 of EGTRRA, as amended by the Tax Relief, Unemployment Insurance Reauthorization, and Job Creation Act of 2010 (P.L. 111-312)):

- The EIC phaseout rule will be applied by multiplying the phaseout percentage by a taxpayer's adjusted gross income (Code Sec. 32(a)(2)(B));
- The requirement that wages, salaries, tips, and other employee compensation are treated as earned income only if included in gross income applies (Code Sec. 32(c)(2)(A)(i));
- The EIC will not be reduced by alternative minimum tax liability;
- The IRS may deny the EIC on the basis of custody information obtained from the Department of Health and Human Services' child support database (Code Sec. 6213(g)(2)(M)); and
- A simplified tie-breaking rule and definition of a qualified child apply.

The following changes to the earned income credit (EIC) will take effect in tax years beginning after December 31, 2012, provided the EGTRRA changes sunset after the two year extension of the EGTRRA sunset provision (Act Sec. 901 of EGTRRA, as amended by the Tax Relief, Unemployment Insurance Reauthorization, and Job Creation Act of 2010 (P.L. 111-312)):

- The EIC phaseout rule will be applied by multiplying the phaseout percentage by a taxpayer's modified adjusted gross income rather than adjusted gross income (Code Sec. 32(a)(2)(A), as amended by P.L. 107-16);

NEW LAW EXPLAINED

- The $3,000 increase in the phaseout amount for joint filers expires (Code Sec. 32(b)(2)(B), as added by P.L. 107-16);
- The requirement that wages, salaries, tips, and other employee compensation are treated as earned income only if included in gross income expires (Code Sec. 32(c)(2)(A)(i), as amended by P.L. 107-16);
- The EIC will be reduced by alternative minimum tax liability (Code Sec. 32(h), prior to repeal by P.L. 107-16);
- The IRS may no longer deny the EIC on the basis of custody information obtained from the Department of Health and Human Services' child support database (Code Sec. 6213(g)(2)(M), as added by P.L. 107-16); and
- A simplified tie-breaking rule and definition of a qualified child will be replaced with more complicated pre-EGTRRA rules.

Earned income credit phaseout to be determined by reference to modified adjusted gross income rather than adjusted gross income. The amount of the EIC cannot exceed the credit percentage of the earned income amount over the phaseout percentage of so much of the *modified adjusted gross income* (or, if greater, the earned income) of the taxpayer for the tax year as exceeds the phaseout amount, effective for tax years beginning after December 31, 2012, provided the EGTRRA changes sunset after the two year extension of the EGTRAA sunset provision (Code Sec. 32(a)(2)(B), as amended by P.L. 107-16; Act Sec. 901 of P.L. 107-16).

> **Comment:** Prior to EGTRRA, the phaseout percentage was applied to *modified* adjusted gross income in excess of the phaseout amount. EGTRRA simplified the phaseout rule by applying the phaseout percentage to adjusted gross income. After the extended sunset of the EGTRRA provision, the phaseout percentage will once again be applied to a taxpayer's modified adjusted gross income (earned income, if greater) in excess of the phaseout amount.

Effective for tax years beginning after December 31, 2012, the definition of modified adjusted gross income will be contained in Code Sec. 32(c)(5). Modified adjusted gross income is equal to a taxpayer's adjusted gross income determined without regard to:

- net capital losses (to the extent that they do not exceed the amount under Code Sec. 1211(b)(1) which limits an individual's annual capital loss deduction to $3,000);
- net losses from trusts and estates;
- net losses relating to nonbusiness rents and royalties; and
- 75 percent of net losses from trades or businesses (excluding trades or businesses that consist of the performance of services by the individual as an employee), computed separately for: (a) sole proprietorships other than farming; (b) sole proprietorships engaged in farming; and (c) other trades or businesses (Code Sec. 32(c)(5)(B), prior to being stricken by P.L. 107-16).

NEW LAW EXPLAINED

In addition, modified adjusted gross income is increased by:

- tax-exempt interest and

- nontaxable distributions from pensions, annuities, and IRAs (unless these distributions are rolled over into similar tax-favored vehicles) (Code Sec. 32(c)(5)(C), prior to being stricken by P.L. 107-16).

> **Comment:** The elimination of the use of modified adjusted gross income and replacement with the use of adjusted gross income by EGTRRA was a simplification measure intended to reduce the number of calculations needed to compute the credit.

EIC phaseout tables to be determined by reference to modified adjusted gross income. The pre-EGTRRA rule which required the IRS to issue EIC tables in income brackets of no greater than fifty dollars that reflect the phaseout based on *modified* adjusted gross income is reinstated as the result of the extended sunset effective for tax years beginning after December 31, 2012 (Code Sec. 32(f)(2)(B), prior to amendment by P.L. 107-16). Under the current post-EGTRRA rules, these tables reflect a phaseout based on adjusted gross income (Code Sec. 32(f)(2)(B), as amended by P.L. 107-16).

Increase in "phaseout amount" for joint filers to be eliminated. The provision added by EGTRRA which increases the phaseout amount of an eligible individual and an eligible individual's spouse who file a joint return by $1,000 in the case of tax years beginning in 2002, 2003, and 2004, by $2,000 in the case of tax years beginning in 2005, 2006, and 2007, and by $3,000 in the case of tax years beginning after 2007 (Code Sec. 32(b)(2)(B), as added by P.L. 107-16), will no longer apply in tax years beginning after December 31, 2012 if the EGTRRA changes sunset after the two year extension of the EGTRRA sunset provision (Act Sec. 901 of P.L. 107-16). Accordingly, the phaseout amount for a joint filer will be the same as any other type of filer, namely, $11,610 for an eligible individual with one or more qualifying children and $5,280 for an eligible individual with no qualifying children (Code Sec. 32(b)(2)(A)).

> **Comment:** In the case of a tax year beginning in 2009 and 2010, the phaseout amount for joint filers was temporarily increased from $3,000 to $5,000 (Code Sec. 32(b)(3), as added by the American Recovery and Reinvestment Tax Act of 2009 (P.L. 111-5)). The new law extends the $5,000 increase an additional two years through 2012. See ¶356. Since the extended sunset of Code Sec. 32(b)(2)(B) is effective for tax years beginning after December 31, 2012, this temporary increase in the phaseout amount for joint filers is unaffected by the EGTRRA sunset provision.

> **Comment:** The temporary increase for 2009 and 2010 in the credit percentage for taxpayers with three or more qualifying children from 40 percent to 45 percent is extended through 2012 by the new law. For tax years beginning after 2012, the credit percentage will return to 40 percent without regard to the EGTRRA sunset provision. See ¶356. (Code Sec. 32(b)(3)(A)).

> **Comment:** The increase in the phaseout amount by EGTRRA for joint filers was intended to address the fact that a married couple filing jointly receives a smaller earned income credit than the combined amount that they would receive if they were not married filing jointly. The expiration of the increase in the phaseout

¶355

NEW LAW EXPLAINED

amount for joint filers will reinstate this earned income credit "marriage penalty."

Comment: EGTRRA also provides for an inflation adjustment to the $3,000 increase in the phaseout amount (Code Sec. 32(j)(1)(B)), as amended by P.L. 111-5). This inflation adjustment provision will also sunset effective for tax years beginning after December 31, 2012.

Earned income taken into account in computing the earned income credit will no longer need to be included in gross income. Prior to the enactment of EGTRRA, earned income included wages, salaries, tips, and other employee compensation whether or not such amounts were included in a taxpayer's gross income for the tax year (Code Sec. 32(c)(2)(A)(i), prior to amendment by P.L. 107-16). Pursuant to EGTRRA such amounts are treated as earned income only if includible in a taxpayer's gross income for the tax year (Code Sec. 32(c)(2)(A)(i), as amended by P.L. 107-16). If the EGTRRA changes sunset after the two year extension of the EGTRRA sunset provision, effective for tax years beginning after December 31, 2012, the gross income inclusion requirement will no longer apply.

Comment: The addition of the gross income requirement was added by EGTRRA primarily to simplify the computation of the earned income credit. Furthermore, since the IRS does not have ready access to information regarding some types of nontaxable earned income (such amounts are not always reported on Form W-2) a compliance problem was deemed to exist. The following are examples of nontaxable compensation (earned income) which may be taken into account in computing the earned income tax credit if the sunset provision takes effect:

- elective deferrals under a cash or deferred arrangement or Code Sec. 403(b) annuity (Code Sec. 402(g));

- employer contributions for non-taxable fringe benefits, including contributions for accident and health insurance (Code Sec. 106), dependent care (Code Sec. 129), adoption assistance (Code Sec. 137), educational assistance (Code Sec. 127), and miscellaneous fringe benefits (Code Sec. 132);

- salary reduction contributions under a cafeteria plan (Code Sec. 125);

- meals and lodging provided for the convenience of the employer (Code Sec. 119); and

- housing allowance or rental value of a parsonage for the clergy (Code Sec. 107) (Senate Report accompanying P.L. 107-16 (S. Rep. No. 107-30))

Earned income credit will need to be reduced by taxpayers subject to the alternative minimum tax. Prior to enactment of EGTRRA, the EIC was reduced by the amount (if any) of a taxpayer's alternative minimum tax liability (Code Sec. 32(h), prior to repeal by P.L. 107-16). If the EGTRRA changes sunset after the two year extension of the EGTRRA sunset provision, Code Sec. 32(h) will be reinstated effective for tax years beginning after December 31, 2012 and the EIC must once again be reduced by a taxpayer's alternative minimum tax liability.

NEW LAW EXPLAINED

Authority to deny earned income credit claims based on custody information from DHSS child support database will expire. In order to reduce the number of erroneous claims due to taxpayers claiming the EIC for children who do not meet the residency (principle place of abode) requirements for qualifying child status, EGTRRA authorized the IRS to deny questionable claims filed by parents who, according to the Department of Health and Human Services Federal Case Registry of Child Support Orders database, do not have custody of the claimed child (Code Sec. 6213(g)(2)(M), as added by P.L. 107-16). This power was granted as part of the IRS's authority to summarily assess deficiencies attributable to mathematical or clerical errors without issuing a notice of deficiency (Code Sec. 6213(b)(1)). If the EGTRRA changes sunset after the two year extension of the EGTRRA sunset provision, this authority will expire, effective for tax years beginning after December 31, 2012.

> **Comment:** The most common earned income tax credit error involves taxpayers claiming children who do not meet the residency requirement. The Department of Health and Human Services' Federal Case Registry of Child Support Orders, a Federal database containing state information on child support payments, assists the IRS in identifying erroneous earned income credit claims by noncustodial parents.

Definition of a qualifying child. Prior to the enactment of EGTRRA, the qualifying child residency test for the EIC was applied to a brother, sister, stepbrother, or stepsister of a taxpayer (or a descendent of any such relative) and a foster child of a taxpayer by requiring that such an individual must have the same principal place of abode as the taxpayer for the *entire* tax year. A son, daughter, stepson, stepdaughter, or a descendant of any such individual, however, only needed to live with the taxpayer more than one-half of the tax year (Code Sec. 32(c)(3)(B), prior to amendment by P.L. 107-16).

EGTRRA simplified the residency rule by making the more-than-one-half year requirement applicable to all individuals (Code Sec. 32(c)(3)(B), as amended by P.L. 107-16).

EGTRRA also modified a tie-breaker rule for determining the taxpayer who would be allowed to claim an individual as a qualifying child when two or more taxpayers were eligible to claim the same individual as a qualifying child (Code Sec. 32(c)(1)(C), as amended by P.L. 107-16).

Prior to the EGTRRA , the taxpayer with the highest modified adjusted gross income for the tax year was entitled to claim the qualifying child (Code Sec. 32(c)(1)(C), prior to amendment by P.L. 107-16). As modified by EGTRRA, the tie-breaker rule provided that if one of the competing taxpayers was the parent, the parent claimed the individual as a qualifying child and that if neither of the competing taxpayers was a parent, the taxpayer with the highest adjusted gross income claimed the individual as a qualifying child (Code Sec. 32(c)(1)(C)(i), as amended by P.L. 107-16). If the competing taxpayers were both parents of the child and did not file a joint return, the parent with whom the child resided the longest period during the tax year claimed the child as a qualifying child. If the child lived with both parents the same amount of time, the parent with the highest adjusted gross income claimed the child as a qualifying child (Code Sec. 32(c)(1)(C)(ii), as amended by P.L. 107-16).

NEW LAW EXPLAINED

As a result of the two year extension of the EGTRRA sunset provision, these pre-EGTRAA rules would not be reinstated until tax years beginning after December 31, 2012.

Treatment of combat zone compensation as earned income unaffected by EGTRRA. The EGTRRA sunset provision will not impact the rule which allows military personnel to elect to treat combat compensation which is excludible from gross income under Code Sec. 112 as earned income for purposes of the EIC (Code Sec. 32(c)(2)(b)(vi)). Although the combat compensation election, as enacted by the Working Families Tax Relief Act (P.L. 108-311), was made subject to the EGTRRA sunset rule (Act Sec. 105 of P.L. 108-311), subsequent legislation, which made the election permanent, specifically removed the provision from the scope of the EGTRRA sunset rule (Act Sec. 102(c) of the Heroes Earnings Assistance and Relief Tax Act of 2008 (P.L. 110-245)).

▶ **Effective date.** The provisions are generally effective for tax years beginning after December 31, 2001 (Act Sec. 101(a)(2) of the Tax Relief, Unemployment Insurance Reauthorization, and Job Creation Act of 2010 (P.L. 111-312)); Act Sec. 303(i)(1) of the Economic Growth and Tax Relief Reconciliation Act of 2001 (EGTRRA) (P.L. 108-27)). The provision granting mathematical error authority to the IRS to deny EIC claims based on the federal child support order database is effective on January 1, 2004 (Act Sec. 101(a)(2) of the Tax Relief Act of 2010; Act Sec. 303(i)(2) of EGTRRA). The provisions shall not apply to tax years beginning after December 31, 2012 (Act Sec. 101(a)(1) of the Tax Relief Act of 2010; Act Sec. 901 of EGTRRA). See ¶105 for a specific discussion of the sunset provision of EGTRRA and how it is applied.

Law source: Law at ¶5075, ¶5795, and ¶7010. Committee Report at ¶10,040 and ¶10,110.

— Act Sec. 101(a)(1) of the Tax Relief, Unemployment Insurance Reauthorization, and Job Creation Act of 2010 (P.L. 111-312), amending Act Sec. 901 of the Economic Growth and Tax Relief Reconciliation Act of 2001 (EGTRRA) P.L. 107-16;

— Act Sec. 101(a)(2), providing the effective date.

Reporter references: For further information, consult the following CCH reporters.

— Standard Federal Tax Reporter, ¶4082.01

— Tax Research Consultant, INDIV: 57,250

— Practical Tax Explanation, § 12,601

¶356 Increase in Earned Income Tax Credit

SUMMARY OF NEW LAW

The increased maximum amount of the earned income tax credit and broader AGI phaseout ranges for taxpayers with three or more qualifying children, provided for tax years beginning in 2009 and 2010, are extended to apply to tax years beginning in 2011 and 2012. Increased phaseout amounts for joint filers, regardless of the number of qualifying children, are also extended to apply to tax years beginning in 2011 and 2012.

¶356

BACKGROUND

A refundable earned income credit is available to certain low-income individuals (Code Sec. 32). The amount of credit varies depending on the number of the taxpayer's qualifying children, the amount of a taxpayer's adjusted gross income and earned income, and whether or not a joint return is filed (Code Sec. 32(b)). The credit amount is determined by multiplying an individual's earned income that does not exceed a maximum amount (called the earned income amount) by the applicable credit percentage (Code Sec. 32(a)(1)). The credit is subject to phaseout if a taxpayer has adjusted gross income (or, if greater, earned income) in excess of a phaseout amount based on the number of a taxpayer's qualifying child (Code Sec. 32(a)(2)). The credit reduction attributable to the phaseout is determined by multiplying the applicable phaseout percentage by the excess of the amount of the individual's adjusted gross income (AGI) (or earned income, if greater) over the phaseout amount. The earned income amount and the phaseout amount are adjusted annually for inflation (Code Sec. 32(j)).

The applicable credit percentage is generally 7.65 percent for taxpayers with no qualifying child, 34 percent for taxpayers with one qualifying child, and 40 percent for taxpayers with two or more qualifying children (Code Sec. 32(b)(1)(A)). However, for tax years beginning in 2009 and 2010 only, pursuant to the American Recovery and Reinvestment Tax Act of 2009 (P.L. 111-5), the applicable credit percentage for taxpayers with three or more qualifying children is 45 percent (rather than 40 percent) (Code Sec. 32(b)(3)(A), as added by the 2009 Recovery Act).

The threshold amount at which the phaseout of the earned income credit begins for taxpayers whose filing status is married filing jointly increases by $3,000 generally for tax years beginning in 2008 and thereafter (Code Sec. 32(b)(2)(B)). The $3,000 amount is adjusted for inflation (Code Sec. 32(j)). However, for tax years beginning in 2009 and 2010 only, the phaseout amount is increased by $5,000 for joint filers, pursuant to the 2009 Recovery Act. This $5,000 amount is adjusted for inflation for tax years beginning in 2010 (Code Sec. 32(b)(3)(B), as added by the 2009 Recovery Act). Consequently, for joint filers, regardless of the number of qualifying children, the AGI phaseout amounts are increased for those tax years.

For a discussion of the earned income tax credit and the sunset provision of the Economic Growth and Tax Relief Reconciliation Act of 2001 (P.L. 107-16), see ¶355.

NEW LAW EXPLAINED

Increase in earned income tax credit extended.—The credit percentage of 45 percent for taxpayers with three or more qualifying children and the $5,000 phaseout amount increase for joint filers have been extended to tax years beginning in 2011 and 2012 (Code Sec. 32(b)(3), as amended by the Tax Relief, Unemployment Insurance Reauthorization, and Job Creation Act of 2010 (P.L. 111-312)). Thus, for tax years beginning in 2011 and 2012, the applicable credit percentage for taxpayers with three or more qualifying children is 45 percent. Also, the phaseout amount is increased by $5,000 for joint filers, regardless of the number of qualifying children (Code Sec. 32(b)(3), as amended by the Tax Relief Act of 2010).

NEW LAW EXPLAINED

Comment: Under Code Sec. 32(b)(3)(B)(ii), as added by the American Recovery and Reinvestment Tax Act of 2009 (P.L. 111-5), this $5,000 amount is adjusted for inflation for tax years beginning in 2010. As adjusted for inflation, the 2010 increase is $5,010. Although the Tax Relief Act of 2010 did not amend the language in Code Sec. 32(b)(3)(B)(ii), presumably this was an oversight and the intention was for this inflation adjustment to apply for tax years beginning in 2011 and 2012, in addition to those beginning in 2010.

Comment: A credit percentage of 45 percent, instead of 40 percent, for taxpayers with three or more qualifying children yields not only a higher maximum credit amount but also a broader AGI phaseout range for those taxpayers, even if they do not file a joint return. For example, the maximum credit amount is $630 higher for these taxpayers in 2010 with a credit percentage of 45 percent, rather than 40 percent ($5,666 maximum rather than $5,036 maximum), and the end point of the AGI (or, if greater, earned income) phaseout in 2010 is $2,989 higher ($43,352 rather than $40,363 for those whose filing status is single, surviving spouse, or head of household; $48,362 rather than $45,373 for those whose filing status is married filing jointly).

As a result of the $5,000 phaseout amount increase for joint filers, the credit begins to phase out at AGI (or, if greater, earned income) above $21,460 in 2010 for joint filers with one qualifying child and $12,490 for joint filers with no qualifying children, compared to $16,450 and $7,480, respectively, for those whose filing status is single, surviving spouse, or head of household. For married taxpayers filing jointly with two or more qualifying children the credit begins to phaseout at $21,460 ($16,450 for other taxpayers). The end points of the phaseout are also higher in 2010 for joint filers: $40,545, rather than $35,535, for taxpayers with one qualifying child; $45,373, rather than $40,363, for those with two qualifying children; $48,362, rather than $43,352, for those with three or more qualifying children; and $18,470, rather than $13,460, for those with no qualifying children. Prior to the $5,000 increase for joint filers added in 2009, a similar increase for joint filers of up to $3,000, adjusted for inflation, had applied pursuant to changes made by the Economic Growth and Tax Relief Reconciliation Act of 2010 (EGTRRA) (P.L. 107-16) (see ¶355).

▶ **Effective date.** The provision applies to tax years beginning after December 31, 2010 (Act Sec. 103(d) of the Tax Relief, Unemployment Insurance Reauthorization, and Job Creation Act of 2010 (P.L. 111-312)).

Law source: Law at ¶5075. Committee Report at ¶10,040 and ¶10,110.

— Act Sec. 103(c) of the Tax Relief, Unemployment Insurance Reauthorization, and Job Creation Act of 2010 (P.L. 111-312), amending Code Sec. 32(b)(3);

— Act Sec. 103(d), providing the effective date.

¶356

NEW LAW EXPLAINED

Reporter references: For further information, consult the following CCH reporters.

— Standard Federal Tax Reporter, ¶4082.01

— Tax Research Consultant, INDIV: 57,250

— Practical Tax Explanation, § 12,601

¶360 Child Tax Credit

SUMMARY OF NEW LAW

The $1,000 child tax credit amount per qualifying child, the earned income refundable component, the repeal of the AMT offset against the additional child credit for families with three or more children, the repeal of the supplemental child credit under the earned income credit, and the offset of the nonrefundable component of the child tax credit against regular tax and AMT liability have been extended two years, through December 31, 2012.

BACKGROUND

The Economic Growth and Tax Relief Reconciliation Act of 2001 (EGTRRA) (P.L. 107-16) amended Code Sec. 24 to increase the child tax credit amount per qualifying child, allow the nonrefundable component of the credit to offset both regular tax and AMT, add a refundable component in addition to that applicable to families with three or more children, and repeal the alternative minimum tax (AMT) offset against the additional credit for families with three or more children. The supplemental child tax credit under Code Sec. 32 was also repealed by P.L. 107-16.

Amount of credit. Taxpayers who have dependent children under age 17 at the close of a calendar year are eligible for a child tax credit that is $1,000 per qualifying child for tax years 2003-2010 (Code Sec. 24(a)).

Tax liability limitation. For tax year 2010, the nonrefundable child tax credit is limited to the excess of the sum of the taxpayer's regular tax (defined under Code Sec. 26(b)) plus AMT liabilities over the sum of the taxpayer's other nonrefundable personal credits (other than the child tax credit, the American Opportunity credit (modified Hope credit), the retirement savings contributions credit, the residential alternative energy credit, the credit for certain plug-in electric vehicles, the alternative motor vehicle credit, and the new qualified plug-in electric drive motor vehicle credit) and his or her foreign tax credit (Code Sec. 24(b)(3)).

Refundability. For tax years beginning in 2009 and 2010, the child tax credit may be refundable to the extent of 15 percent of the taxpayer's earned income in excess of $3,000 (Code Sec. 24(d)(1) and (4)). For purposes of this refundable component, earned income includes combat zone pay although such pay is otherwise excluded from gross income (Code Sec. 24(d)(1)). Taxpayers with three or more children must calculate the refundable portion of the credit using the excess of their social security

BACKGROUND

taxes (*i.e.*, the taxpayer's share of FICA taxes and one-half of self-employment taxes) over the earned income credit, instead of the 15 percent amount, if it results in a greater refundable credit (Code Sec. 24(d)(1)). The nonrefundable child tax credit allowable under Code Sec. 24(a), without regard to the tax liability limitation, must be reduced by the amount of any refundable component (Code Sec. 24(d)(1)).

The refundable credit amount will reduce the nonrefundable credit otherwise allowable (*i.e.*, converting some or all of the nonrefundable credit into a refundable credit), and the refundable credit is not taken into account in applying the tax liability limitation on nonrefundable personal credits (Code Sec. 24(d)(1)). These rules apply regardless of whether the refundable credit is computed under the 15 percent of earned income method or the additional credit for families with three or more children method.

Example: Joe and Paula Hart have two children and earned income of $25,000 in 2010. They have no other income and no alternative minimum tax liability. They are not entitled to any nonrefundable personal credits other than the chid tax credit. Since they file jointly, they are entitled to a standard deduction of $11,400. They are also entitled to a personal exemption of $3,650 for each family member, or $14,600. They have no taxable income after the standard deduction and exemptions are applied, therefore, their tax liability is $0. Their allowable nonrefundable child tax credit is equal to $2,000 ($1,000 per child). However, the nonrefundable credit is limited to the amount of tax liability, or $0.

The refundable credit is equal to the lesser of either the unclaimed portion of the nonrefundable credit amount, $2,000 ($2,000 – $0), or 15 percent of the Harts' earned income that exceeds $3,000, $3,300 (($25,000 – $3,000) × .15). Their total refundable credit amount is $2,000. Joe and Paula receive 100 percent of their otherwise allowable child tax credit in 2010.

If the Hart's earned income remains at $25,000 in 2011, they will have no tax liability against which to offset the nonrefundable child tax credit; there will be no refundable component of the child tax credit applicable to them if the EGTRRA sunset provision (see below) applies, and, therefore, they will receive no child tax credit.

Any payment made to a taxpayer as a refundable child tax credit is not to be treated as income, nor taken into account as resources for the month of receipt or the following month, for purposes of determining a taxpayer's eligibility for any benefits, assistance or supportive services having income limitations on eligibility under any federal program or federally financed program (Act Sec. 203 of EGTRRA).

AMT offset against additional child credit for families with three or more children. In 2010, a taxpayer's AMT does not reduce the amount of the refundable child credit for families with three or more children (Code Sec. 24(d)). Prior to the enactment of P.L. 107-16, the only refundable component of the child tax credit was the "additional child credit for families with three or more children," but this refundable amount was to become subject to a reduction equal to the amount of the taxpayer's AMT that did not

BACKGROUND

result in a reduction of the earned income credit pursuant to Code Sec. 32(h), for tax years beginning after December 31, 2001 (Code Sec. 24(d)(2), prior to being stricken by P.L. 107-16). This AMT offset applicable to the "additional child credit for families with three or more children" was repealed by EGTRRA prior to going into effect.

Supplemental child credit. In 2010, there is no supplemental child credit under the earned income credit regime for qualified children under Code Sec. 24. Prior to the enactment of P.L. 107-16, there was a refundable child tax credit structured under the earned income credit ("supplemental child credit") for taxpayer's who qualified for the child tax credit pursuant to Code Sec. 24 (Code Sec. 32(n), prior to being stricken by P.L. 107-16). This supplemental child credit was repealed by EGTRRA.

Sunset provision. Under the EGTRRA sunset provision, amendments made by the Act will not apply to tax years beginning after December 31, 2010 (Act Sec. 901 of P.L. 107-16).

NEW LAW EXPLAINED

Child tax credit enhancements extended—The $1,000 child tax credit amount (Code Sec. 24(a), as amended by the Economic Growth and Tax Relief Reconciliation Act of 2001 (EGTRRA) (P.L. 107-16)), the offset of the nonrefundable child tax credit against regular tax and AMT (Code Sec. 24(b)(3), as added by P.L. 107-16), and the addition of the earned income refundable component (Code Sec. 24(d)(1)(B), as amended by P.L. 107-16) are extended for two years, through 2012 (Act Sec. 901 of P.L. 107-16, as amended by the Tax Relief, Unemployment Insurance Reauthorization, and Job Creation Act of 2010 (P.L. 111-312)). In addition, the repeal of the AMT offset applicable to the "additional child credit for families with three or more children," (Code Sec. 24(d)(2), stricken by P.L. 107-16), and the repeal of the "supplemental child credit" under the earned income credit rules (Code Sec. 32(n), stricken by P.L. 107-16) are also extended for two years, through 2012 (Act Sec. 901 of P.L. 107-16, as amended by the Tax Relief Act of 2010).

Amount of credit. In 2011 and 2012, the child tax credit amount is $1,000 per qualifying child (Code Sec. 24(a)). For tax years beginning after December 31, 2012, taxpayers who have dependent children under age 17 at the close of a calendar year will only be eligible for a $500 child tax credit per qualifying child. A dependent child is a child for whom the taxpayer is allowed a personal exemption that he or she claims on the return upon which the child tax credit is claimed.

> **Comment:** Taxpayers who are eligible for the child tax credit in 2013 must adjust their withholding, or increase the amount of their estimated tax payments, to account for a lower child tax credit amount per qualifying child. In addition, the smaller credit amount will phase out more quickly when modified adjusted gross income (AGI) exceeds the income threshold amounts that have never been adjusted for inflation. The credit is reduced by $50 for each $1,000, or fraction thereof, of modified AGI above the threshold amounts. This should also be taken

¶360

NEW LAW EXPLAINED

into consideration when adjusting withholding or increasing estimated tax payments.

Example: John and Peggy have one child and modified AGI of $115,000 in 2012. They file a joint return and claim the child tax credit. Their $1,000 credit is subject to reduction ($50 for each $1,000 of modified AGI in excess of $110,000), therefore, their child tax credit in 2012 is $750, a twenty-five percent reduction of the full credit amount. When joint filers have modified AGI of $130,000, the total $1,000 child tax credit is phased out in 2012, if there is only one qualifying child.

If the facts are the same, but the tax year is 2013 when the credit is $500 per qualifying child, their child tax credit would be $250, a fifty percent reduction of the full credit amount. When joint filers have modified AGI of $120,000, the total $500 child tax credit is phased out in 2013, if there is only one qualifying child.

Tax liability limitation. In tax years 2010 and 2011, the nonrefundable child tax credit can be offset against regular tax (reduced by any foreign tax credit) and AMT liabilities (Code Sec. 26(a)(2), as amended by the Tax Relief Act of 2010). See ¶ 376. In tax year 2012, the nonrefundable child tax credit is limited to the excess of the sum of the taxpayer's regular tax (as defined under Code Sec. 26(b)) plus AMT liabilities over the sum of the taxpayer's other nonrefundable personal credits (other than the child tax credit, the American Opportunity credit (modified Hope credit), the retirement savings contributions credit, the residential alternative energy credit, the credit for certain plug-in electric vehicles, the alternative motor vehicle credit, and the new qualified plug-in electric drive motor vehicle credit) and his or her foreign tax credit (Code Sec. 24(b)(3)). The tax liability rule in Code Sec. 26(a)(2) does not apply in 2012.

For tax years beginning after December 31, 2012, the general tax liability limitation rule under Code Sec. 26(a)(1) applies to the nonrefundable portion of the child tax credit. Specifically, the general limitation rule requires that the total amount of the nonrefundable personal credits may not exceed the excess of the taxpayer's regular tax liability for the tax year over the taxpayer's tentative minimum tax liability (Code Sec. 26(a)(1)). The tax liability limitation rule in Code Sec. 24(b)(3) is scheduled to sunset after December 31, 2012, as does the language in Code Sec. 26(a)(1) excepting the child tax credit from the application of this general tax liability limitation rule.

Refundability. For tax years beginning in 2011 and 2012, the child tax credit may be refundable to the extent of 15 percent of the taxpayer's earned income in excess of $3,000 (Code Sec. 24(d)(1); Code Sec. 24(d)(4), as amended by the Tax Relief Act of 2010). Taxpayers with three or more children must calculate the refundable portion of the credit using the excess of their social security taxes over the earned income credit, instead of the 15 percent amount, if it results in a greater refundable credit (Code Sec. 24(d)(1)).

¶360

NEW LAW EXPLAINED

In 2011 and 2012, the threshold requirements for the 15 percent of earned income refundable component of the child tax credit are:

- a total tax liability (regular plus alternative minimum), minus nonrefundable credits previously taken, of less than the taxpayer's allowable child tax credit ($1,000 per qualifying child); and

- earned income in excess of $3,000.

> **Comment:** Prior to 2008, eligibility for the 15 percent refundable component of the child tax credit required that an individual have earned income *in excess* of $10,000, as adjusted for inflation. In 2008, an individual was required to have earned income in excess of $8,500 to be eligible for the 15 percent refundable component of the child tax credit. In 2009 and 2010, the income threshold was lowered to $3,000 and the Tax Relief Act of 2010 has now extended the $3,000 income threshold to 2011 and 2012.

Example: In 2011, Pam and Jim Allen have two children and earned income of $25,000. They have no other income, no alternative minimum tax liability, and are not entitled to any nonrefundable personal credits other than the child tax credit. The CCH 2011 projected inflation-adjusted standard deduction for married taxpayers is $11,600 and the personal exemption is $3,700. As joint filers, Pam and Jim are entitled to a standard deduction of $11,600, and a personal exemption of $3,700 for each family member, for a total of $26,400. This results in no taxable income and no tax liability. Their allowable nonrefundable child tax credit is equal to $2,000 ($1,000 per child). However, the nonrefundable credit is limited to the amount of tax liability, which in this case is 0.

The refundable credit is equal to the lesser of either the unclaimed portion of the nonrefundable credit amount, $2,000 ($2,000 − $0), or 15 percent of the Allens' earned income in excess of $3,000, $3,300 (($25,000 − $3,000) × .15). Therefore, the total refundable credit amount is $2,000. Pam and Jim get the full benefit of the child tax credit ($0 nonrefundable and $2,000 refundable).

Absent the amendment keeping the earned income threshold at $3,000, the 2011 earned income threshold would have been $10,000, as adjusted for inflation. This would have reduced Pam and Jim's refundable child tax credit to less than the full child tax credit in 2011.

> **Comment:** By keeping the earned income threshold at $3,000 for computing the earned income refundable child tax credit, more low-income taxpayers will continue to be eligible for the refundable child tax credit.

For tax years beginning after December 31, 2012, the child tax credit is refundable only for families with three or more children ("additional child credit for families with three or more children") and only to the extent of the smaller of:

- the amount of the child tax credit determined under Code Sec. 24(a) (without regard to the tax liability limitation under Code Sec. 26(a) or this refundable component); or

NEW LAW EXPLAINED

- the amount by which the taxpayer's social security taxes for the tax year exceed the taxpayer's allowed earned income credit (determined without regard to the supplemental child credit of Code Sec. 32(n)) for the tax year (Code Sec. 24(d)(1)).

   Comment: The amount of the refundable "additional child credit for families with three or more children" reduces the amount of the nonrefundable child tax credit otherwise allowable under Code Sec. 24(a), without regard to the tax liability limitation for nonrefundable personal credits under Code Sec. 26(a). In effect, some or all of the nonrefundable credit is converted into a refundable credit.

   Caution: For tax years beginning after December 31, 2012, the amount of the refundable "additional child credit for families with three or more children" may be subject to reduction, if the taxpayer has AMT liability. This AMT offset is discussed, below.

For purposes of determining the eligibility of any individual for benefits or assistance (or the amount or extent of benefits or assistance) under any federal program or any state or local program financed in whole or in part with federal funds, any payment made to a taxpayer as a refundable child tax credit in 2010, 2011 and 2012 will not be taken into account as income, nor taken into account as resources, for a period of 12 months from receipt by the taxpayer (Code Sec. 6409, as added by the Tax Relief Act of 2010). See ¶384 for further discussion.

AMT offset against additional child credit for families with three or more children. In 2011 and 2012, there is no AMT offset applicable to the additional child credit for families with three or more children. The AMT offset was repealed by EGTRRA and the repeal has been extended through 2012. However, for tax years beginning after December 31, 2012, a taxpayer's AMT liability that does not result in a reduction of the earned income credit pursuant to Code Sec. 32(h) will reduce the amount of any refundable "additional child credit for families with three or more children" (Code Sec. 24(d)(2)).

Supplemental child credit. In 2011 and 2012, there is no supplemental child credit under the earned income rules of Code Sec. 32. This credit was repealed by EGTRRA and the repeal has been extended through 2012. For tax years beginning after December 31, 2012, however, part or all of the child credit may be treated as a refundable "supplemental child credit" if the taxpayer is entitled to the earned income credit (EIC)). The supplemental child credit is structured as part of the EIC without the eligibility restrictions or phaseout rules otherwise applicable to the EIC.

The supplemental child credit equals the lesser of:

- the amount by which the taxpayer's total nonrefundable personal credits (as limited by the tax liability limitation of Code Sec. 26(a)) are increased by reason of the child tax credit, or
- the excess of taxpayer's total tax credits, including the EIC, over the sum of the taxpayer's regular income tax liability plus the employee share of FICA (and one-half any SECA tax liability) (Code Sec. 32(n)).

The supplemental child credit may not exceed the amount of the nonrefundable child credit allowed under Code Sec. 24 determined without regard to the tax liability

NEW LAW EXPLAINED

limitation. The nonrefundable portion of the child credit otherwise allowable under Code Sec. 24 is reduced by the amount of the supplemental child credit claimed under Code Sec. 32(n).

▶ **Effective date.** The provisions are generally effective for tax years beginning after December 31, 2000 (Act Sec. 101(a)(2) of the Tax Relief, Unemployment Insurance Reauthorization, and Job Creation Act of 2010 (P.L. 111-312)); Act Sec. 201(a) of the Economic Growth and Tax Relief Reconciliation Act of 2001 (EGTRRA) (P.L. 107-16)). The Code Sec. 24 tax liability limitation and the earned income refundable component are effective for tax years beginning after December 31, 2001 (Act Sec. 101(a)(2) of the Tax Relief Act of 2010; Act Secs. 201(b), 201(c)(1), 202(f)(2)(B) and 618(b)(2)(A) of EGTRRA). The provisions will not apply to tax years beginning after December 31, 2012 (Act Sec. 101(a)(1) of the Tax Relief Act of 2010; Act Sec. 901 of EGTRRA). See ¶105 for a specific discussion of the sunset provision of EGTRRA and how it is applied. The threshold earned income provision applies to tax years beginning after December 31, 2010 (Act Sec. 103(d) of the Tax Relief Act of 2010).

Law source: Law at ¶5025, ¶5050, ¶5075, ¶5475, ¶5580, ¶5825, ¶7010, and ¶7015. Committee Report at ¶10,030, ¶10,040, ¶10,110, and ¶10,120.

— Act Sec. 101(a)(1) of the Tax Relief, Unemployment Insurance Reauthorization, and Job Creation Act of 2010 (P.L. 111-312), amending Act Sec. 901 of the Economic Growth and Tax Relief Reconciliation Act of 2001 (EGTRRA) (P.L. 107-16);

— Act Sec. 103(b) of the Tax Relief Act of 2010, amending Code Sec. 24(d)(4);

— Act Sec. 101(a)(2) and 103(d), providing the effective date.

Reporter references: For further information, consult the following CCH reporters.

— Standard Federal Tax Reporter, ¶3770.01 and ¶3770.03

— Tax Research Consultant, INDIV: 57,454, INDIV: 57,454.10 and PLANIND: 3,054

— Practical Tax Explanation, § 12,101 and § 12,120.15

¶365 Child and Dependent Care Credit

SUMMARY OF NEW LAW

The increased amounts and higher limits provided for the child and dependent care expense credit by the Economic Growth and Tax Relief Reconciliation Act of 2001 (EGTRRA) (P.L. 107-16) are extended for two years, through December 31, 2012. Thus, the amount of the credit allowed will continue to be 35 percent of qualifying child or dependent care expenses. The maximum amount of qualifying expenses to which the credit may be applied will be $3,000 for individuals with one qualifying child or dependent (for a maximum credit of $1,050), or $6,000 for individuals with two or more qualifying children or dependents (for a maximum credit of $2,100). For taxpayers with adjusted gross income (AGI) between $15,000 and $43,000, the 35-percent credit rate is reduced by one percentage point for each $2,000 of AGI until the credit percentage is 20 percent for taxpayers with AGI of $43,000.

BACKGROUND

The Economic Growth and Tax Relief Reconciliation Act of 2001 (EGTRRA) (P.L. 107-16) expanded the child and dependent care credit allowed under Code Sec. 21. Under the amended provision, a taxpayer can claim a nonrefundable credit for a portion of qualifying child or dependent care expenses paid by the taxpayer in order to be gainfully employed. Taxpayers with adjusted gross income of $15,000 or less are allowed a credit equal to 35 percent of employment-related expenses. (Under pre-EGTRRA law, taxpayers with adjusted gross income of $10,000 or less could claim a credit equal to 30 percent of employment-related expenses). The credit is reduced by one percentage point for each $2,000 of adjusted gross income, or fraction thereof, above $15,000 through $43,000 ($10,000 through $28,000 under pre-EGTRRA law). Taxpayers with adjusted gross income over $43,000 ($28,000) are allowed a credit equal to 20 percent of employment-related expenses (Code Sec. 21(a)). The maximum amount of employment-related expenses to which the credit may be applied is $3,000 ($2,400 under pre-EGTRRA law) if there is one qualifying individual or $6,000 ($4,800 under pre-EGTRRA law) if there are two or more qualifying individuals (Code Sec. 21(c)).

For married taxpayers, the expenses taken into account in calculating the credit may not exceed the earned income of the spouse who earns the lesser amount. Thus, a married person with a nonworking spouse cannot take the credit, unless the non-working spouse is incapable of self-care or is a full-time student. If the nonworking spouse is incapable of self-care or is a student, that person is deemed to have earned income for each month of disability or school attendance of $250 if there is one qualifying child or dependent, or $500 if there are two or more children or dependents ($200 and $400, respectively, under pre-EGTRRA law) (Code Sec. 21(d)(2)).

To be eligible for the dependent care credit, the taxpayer must maintain a household for one or more of the following qualifying individuals: a dependent under the age of 13 for whom a dependency exemption may be claimed, a dependent who is physically or mentally incapable of taking care of himself or herself, or the taxpayer's spouse, if the spouse is physically or mentally incapable of taking care of himself or herself (Code Sec. 21(a)(1)). To be a qualifying individual for purposes of the dependent care credit, a disabled dependent or spouse of the taxpayer will have to have the same principal place of abode as the taxpayer for more than one-half of the tax year (Code Sec. 21(b)(1)). Moreover, an individual will not be treated as having the same principal place of abode as the taxpayer if, at any time during the tax year, the relationship between the individual and the taxpayer is in violation of local law (Code Sec. 21(e)(1)).

A taxpayer's dependent is someone who is a qualifying child or a qualifying relative. A qualifying relative is: (1) a person who has the same principal abode as the taxpayer and is a member of the taxpayer's household, or who is a relative such as a parent, stepparent, sibling, stepsibling, aunt, uncle, in-law, child, or grandchild, (2) for whom the taxpayer provides over one-half of the person's support for the year, (3) who is not a qualifying child of another taxpayer, and (4) whose gross income is less than the exemption amount (Code Sec. 152(d)).

¶365

BACKGROUND

The dependent care credit is also available for expenses incurred to care for an individual if the individual would qualify as the taxpayer's dependent but for one or more of the following reasons:

- the taxpayer or spouse was claimed as a dependent on another person's return (and thus was not eligible to claim dependency exemptions);

- the individual receiving care could not be claimed as a dependent because he or she was married and filed a joint return; or

- the individual receiving care could not be claimed as a dependent because his or her gross income equaled or exceeded the exemption amount (Code Sec. 21(b)(1)(B)).

NEW LAW EXPLAINED

Increased credit percentages and expense limits for child and dependent care credit extended.—The increased credit percentages and higher income limits for the child and dependent care expense credit are extended for two years, through December 31, 2012. Thus, taxpayers with adjusted gross income of $15,000 or less are allowed a credit equal to 35 percent of employment-related expenses. The credit is reduced by one percentage point for each $2,000 of adjusted gross income, or fraction thereof, above $15,000 through $43,000. Taxpayers with adjusted gross income over $43,000 ($28,000) are allowed a credit equal to 20 percent of employment-related expenses. The maximum amount of employment-related expenses to which the credit may be applied is $3,000 if there is one qualifying individual or $6,000 if there are two or more qualifying individuals. For married taxpayers, the expenses taken into account in calculating the credit may not exceed the earned income of the spouse who earns the lesser amount. Thus, a married person with a nonworking spouse cannot take the credit, unless the nonworking spouse is incapable of self-care or is a full-time student. If the nonworking spouse is incapable of self-care or is a student, that person is deemed to have earned income for each month of disability or school attendance of $250 if there is one qualifying child or dependent, or $500 if there are two or more children or dependents (Code Sec. 21; Act Sec. 901 of the Economic Growth and Tax Relief Reconciliation Act of 2001 (EGTRRA) (P.L. 107-16)), as amended by the Tax Relief, Unemployment Reauthorization, and Job Creation Act of 2010 (P.L. 111-312). For tax years beginning after December 31, 2012, the lower, pre-EGTRRA amounts and limits will apply.

▶ **Effective date.** The provision is effective for tax years beginning after December 31, 2002 (Act Sec. 101(a)(2) of the Tax Relief, Unemployment Insurance Reauthorization, and Job Creation Act of 2010 (P.L. 111-312); Act Sec. 204(c) of the Economic Growth and Tax Relief Reconciliation Act of 2001 (EGTRRA) (P.L. 107-16)). The provision shall not apply to tax years beginning after December 31, 2012 (Act Sec. 101(a)(1) of the Tax Relief Act of 2010; Act Sec. 901 of EGTRRA). See ¶105 for a specific discussion of the sunset provision of EGTRRA and how it is applied.

NEW LAW EXPLAINED

Law source: Law at ¶5015 and ¶7010. Committee Report at ¶10,060.

— Act Sec. 101(a)(1) of the Tax Relief, Unemployment Insurance Reauthorization, and Job Creation Act of 2010 (P.L. 111-312), amending Act Sec. 901 of the Economic Growth and Tax Relief Reconciliation Act of 2001 (EGTRRA) (P.L. 107-16);

— Act Sec. 101(a)(2), providing the effective date.

Reporter references: For further information, consult the following CCH reporters.

— Standard Federal Tax Reporter, ¶3507.01

— Tax Research Consultant, INDIV: 57,058.05 and PLANIND: 3,056

— Practical Tax Explanation, § 12,201

¶370 Adoption Credit and Adoption Assistance Programs

SUMMARY OF NEW LAW

The adoption credit and income exclusion for employer-provided adoption assistance will revert after December 31, 2011, to rules in effect for tax years before 2010. The dollar limitation in 2012 will therefore be $12,170 (adjusted for inflation after 2010) and the credit will no longer be refundable. Also, changes made to the credit and exclusion in 2001 are extended and are now scheduled to expire for tax years beginning after December 31, 2012. Thus, for 2013 and later tax years, the amount of the credit and the exclusion reverts back to $5,000 (or $6,000 in the case of a special needs child).

BACKGROUND

Two related tax provisions can assist families who adopt children: a nonrefundable tax credit and an income exclusion for employer-paid or employer-reimbursed adoption expenses through a qualified adoption assistance program (Code Secs. 36C and 137). A qualified adoption assistance program is a separate, written plan by an employer, for the exclusive benefit of its employees, which provides adoption assistance. The plan must meet requirements similar to those that apply to educational assistance programs under Code Sec. 127(b) regarding eligibility, principal sharehold-ers or owners, funding, and notification of employees. Both the tax credit and the exclusion may apply to the same adoption, but not for the same expenses. In addition, a taxpayer may not claim the tax credit or the exclusion for any expense for which another deduction or credit is allowed. Further, no credit is allowed for any expense to the extent the taxpayer receives funds under any federal, State, or local program.

For tax years before 2010, the credit and income exclusion apply to the first $10,000, adjusted for inflation. For 2010, the credit and income exclusion were increased by

BACKGROUND

$1,000, so that they apply to the first $13,170 of qualified adoption expenses for each eligible child (including a special needs child, see below). For 2010, the amount of the credit and exclusion phases out ratably for taxpayers with modified adjusted gross income (AGI) between $182,520 and $222,520. Modified AGI for this purpose is the taxpayer's AGI plus any amount of foreign earned income and foreign housing expenses otherwise excluded from income, any income from U.S. possessions otherwise excluded from income, and all employer payments and reimbursements for adoption expenses whether or not they are taxable to the employee.

Qualified expenses are taken into account for purposes of the credit in the tax year following the tax year they are paid or incurred. However, expenses paid or incurred in the tax year when the adoption becomes final may be taken into account in that tax year. Qualified adoption expenses include reasonable and necessary adoption fees, court costs, attorney fees, and other expenses that are directly related to, and the principal purpose of which is, the legal adoption by the taxpayer of an eligible child. All reasonable and necessary expenses required by a State as a condition of adoption are qualified adoption expenses. For example, expenses may include the cost of construction, renovations, alterations or purchases specifically required by the State to meet the needs of the child. However, the increase in the basis of the property that would result from such an expenditure must be reduced by the amount of the credit or exclusion. Qualified adoption expenses may not be incurred in violation of State or federal law or be reimbursed under an employer or other program. Expenses incurred in carrying out a surrogate parenting arrangement or in adopting a spouse's child do not qualify for the credit. Qualified adoption expenses do not include expenses for a child who is not a citizen or resident of the United States unless the adoption is finalized. Any expense paid or incurred before the tax year in which a foreign adoption becomes final is treated as if it were paid or incurred in the year the adoption becomes final.

An eligible child for purposes of the adoption credit and exclusion is an individual who has not attained the age of 18 as of the time of the adoption or who is physically or mentally incapable of caring for himself or herself. The credit or exclusion is also allowed for the adoption of a special needs child, regardless of actual expenses incurred by the parents. A child with special needs is one whom a State has determined both cannot and should not be returned home to his parents and cannot be placed with adoptive parents without providing some adoption assistance. In either case, the child must be a citizen or resident of the United States (Code Sec. 36C(d)(3)).

For tax years before 2010, the adoption credit, like all nonrefundable personal tax credits, can offset alternative minimum tax (AMT) liability (Code Sec. 26(a)(2)). For tax years beginning in 2010, the Patient Protection and Affordable Care Act of 2010 (P.L. 111-148) converted the nonrefundable adoption credit, previously allowed under former Code Sec. 23, into a refundable credit available under Code Sec. 36C (as redesignated by P.L. 111-148). Consequently, as of 2010, the adoption credit is no longer a nonrefundable personal credit listed in Code Sec. 26(a)(1) and subject to the general tax liability limitation rule.

NEW LAW EXPLAINED

Sunset provision. Under the sunset provision of EGTRRA, amendments made by the Act will not apply to tax years beginning after December 31, 2010 (Act Sec. 901 of P.L. 107-16). However, in the case of the adoption credit and adoption assistance program under Code Secs. 36C and 137, the sunset provision was modified by the Patient Protection Act of 2010 (PPACA) (P.L. 111-148) to apply for tax years beginning after December 31, 2011.

Sunset of adoption credit and adoption assistance program modified, delayed.— The sunset provided by the Patient Protection and Affordable Care Act of 2010 (PPACA) (P.L. 111-148) is modified to provide that after December 31, 2011, the adoption credit and exclusion for employer-provided adoption assistance will revert to the rules in place before the enactment of that Act (Act. Sec. 10909(c) of the PPACA , as amended by Act. Sec. 101(b) of the Tax Relief, Unemployment Reauthorization, and Job Creation Act of 2010 (P.L. 111-312)). Thus, the maximum amount of the credit and exemption will decrease to $12,170, adjusted for inflation after 2010, and the credit will no longer be refundable. In addition, the law under which the credit is allowed will return to Code Sec. 23, rather than its current designation under Code Sec. 36C.

The sunset provided by Economic Growth and Tax Relief Reconciliation Act of 2001 (EGTRRA) (P.L. 107-16), which would have reduced the amount of credit and exclusion allowable to previous levels, is also extended, so that now these pre-EGTRRA rules will apply for tax years beginning after December 31, 2012 (Act Sec. 901 of EGTRRA, as amended by Act Sec. 101(a) of the Tax Relief Act of 2010. Under the sunset provisions of EGTRRA, the provisions and amendments to the qualified adoption assistance provisions of Code Sec. 23 and 137 made by EGTRRA would not apply to tax years beginning after December 31, 2010. The PPACA had already delayed the EGTRRA sunset provision relative to these adoption provisions to apply to tax years beginning after December 31, 2011 (Act Sec. 10909(c) of PPACA, prior to amendment by Act. Sec. 101(b) of the Tax Relief Act of 2010).

The December 31, 2011, sunset provided by PPACA is effective for only one year because, for tax years beginning after December 31, 2012, the delayed sunset of the applicable EGTRRA adoption provisions will be effective. Thereafter, the amount of the credit and the exclusion will be limited to $5,000, or $6,000 in the case of a special needs child. Also, the credit phaseout range will revert to the pre-EGTRRA levels (i.e., a ratable phaseout between modified adjusted gross income between $75,000 and $115,000). Finally, the adoption credit will be allowed only to the extent the individual's regular income tax liability exceeds the individual's tentative minimum tax, determined without regard to the minimum foreign tax credit.

▶ **Effective date.** The provision is effective for tax years beginning after December 31, 2005 (Act Sec. 101(a)(2) of the Tax Relief, Unemployment Insurance Reauthorization, and Job Creation Act of 2010 (P.L. 111-312)); Act Sec. 202(g) of the Economic Growth and Tax Relief Reconciliation Act of 2001 (EGTRRA) (P.L. 107-16)). The provision shall not apply to tax years beginning after December 31, 2012 (Act Sec. 101(a)(1) of the Tax Relief Act of 2010; Act Sec. 901 of EGTRRA). See ¶105 for a specific discussion of the sunset provision

¶370

NEW LAW EXPLAINED

of EGTRRA and how it is applied. The $13,170 dollar limit on the amount of the adoption credit and income exclusion and the refundable nature of the credit apply to tax years beginning after December 31, 2009 (Act Sec. 10909(d) of the Patient Protection and Affordable Care Act of 2010 (P.L. 111-148). The provision will not apply to tax years beginning after December 31, 2011 (Act Sec. 101(b) of the Tax Relief Act of 2010).

Law source: Law at ¶5083, ¶5225, and ¶7010. Committee Report at ¶10,060 and ¶10,120.

— Act Sec. 101(a) of the Tax Relief, Unemployment Insurance Reauthorization, and Job Creation Act of 2010 (P.L. 111-312), amending Act Sec. 901 of the Economic Growth and Tax Relief Reconciliation Act of 2001 (EGTRRA) (P.L. 107-16);

— Act Sec. 101(b) providing the effective date.

Reporter references: For further information, consult the following CCH reporters.

— Standard Federal Tax Reporter, ¶4199.01 and ¶7625.01

— Tax Research Consultant, INDIV: 57,350, COMPEN: 36,650 and PLANIND: 3,060

— Practical Tax Explanation, § 12,301 and § 20,201

¶371 American Opportunity Credit

SUMMARY OF NEW LAW

The American Opportunity credit (modified Hope credit) is extended to apply to tax years 2011 and 2012, including the $2,500 maximum credit per eligible student, the higher income phaseout ranges of $80,000 - $90,000 for single filers ($160,000 - $180,000 for joint filers), the eligibility extension to the first four years of post-secondary education, the inclusion of text books and course materials as eligible expenses, and the 40 percent refundable credit component.

BACKGROUND

The Hope scholarship credit generally allows individual taxpayers to claim a nonrefundable credit against federal income taxes for tuition and related expenses paid for the first two years of post-secondary education for each eligible student. In tax years beginning before 2009, the Hope credit was limited to 100 percent of the first $1,000 of tuition and related expenses, and 50 percent of the next $1,000 of such expenses (Code Sec. 25A(b)(1) and (4), prior to amendment by the American Recovery and Reinvestment Tax Act of 2009 (P.L. 111-5)). The $1,000 amount was adjusted annually for inflation (Code Sec. 25A(h)(1), prior to amendment by P.L. 111-5).

> **Comment:** Prior to the P.L. 111-5 amendment, the maximum Hope Scholarship Credit, as adjusted for inflation for 2009, would have been $1,800 (Rev. Proc. 2008-66, I.R.B. 2008-45, 1107).

For tax years beginning prior to 2009, the credit could only be claimed for the first two years of post-secondary education, and qualified tuition and related expenses

BACKGROUND

did not include text books and other course materials (Code Sec. 25A(b)(2)(C) and (f)(1), prior to amendment by P.L. 111-5). The Hope credit was phased out ratably for taxpayers with modified adjusted gross income (AGI) between $40,000 and $50,000 ($80,000 and $100,000 for joint filers) (Code Sec. 25A(d), prior to amendment by P.L. 111-5). The modified AGI amounts were subject to annual adjustments for inflation (Code Sec. 25A(h)(2), prior to amendment by P.L. 111-5).

> **Comment:** For 2009, the inflation adjusted phase-out range would have been $50,000 to $60,000 for single taxpayers and $100,000 to $120,000 for joint filers (Rev. Proc. 2008-66, I.R.B. 2008-45, 1107).

Effective for tax years beginning in 2009 or 2010, the Hope scholarship credit was modified to allow a higher credit amount that can be claimed by a broader spectrum of taxpayers. The modifications are entitled the American Opportunity credit (Code Sec. 25A(i), as added by P.L. 111-5). The credit is increased to the sum of 100 percent of the first $2,000 of qualified tuition and related expenses and 25 percent of the next $2,000, for a total maximum credit of $2,500 per eligible student per year in 2009 and 2010 (Code Sec. 25A(i)(1), as added by P.L. 111-5). The credit is expanded to apply to the first four years of a student's post-secondary education for tax years 2009 and 2010 (Code Sec. 25A(i)(2), as added by P.L. 111-5).

The modified AGI phase-out limits for taxpayers claiming the credit in 2009 and 2010 are increased to between $80,000 and $90,000 for single filers ($160,000 - $180,000 for joint filers). The credit is ratably reduced by the amount bearing the same ratio to the credit as the excess of the taxpayer's modified AGI over $80,000 bears to $10,000. These amounts double to $160,000 and $20,000 for joint filers (Code Sec. 25A(i)(4), as added by P.L. 111-5).

> **Example:** Opie was a full-time student in 2010 at a university with tuition and related expenses of $10,000. Opie's unmarried father, Andy, paid for Opie's tuition at the college and wishes to claim the American Opportunity credit on behalf of Opie. Andy's modified AGI as a small-town sheriff for 2010 was $82,000. The ratio of the excess of Andy's AGI over $80,000, $2,000, to $10,000 is 1/5 ($2,000/$10,000 = 1/5). The $2,500 American Opportunity credit claimed by Andy is reduced by 1/5, so Andy can only claim a $2,000 credit ($2,500-(1/5 × $2,500) = $2,000).

The American Opportunity credit retains most Hope credit qualification requirements and definitions in 2009 and 2010, such as the half-time enrollment requirement and the definitions of an eligible student and an eligible educational institution. While the Hope credit applied to qualified tuition and related expenses prior to 2009, the American Opportunity credit can be claimed for tuition, fees and course materials in 2009 and 2010 (Code Sec. 25A(i) (3), as added by P.L. 111-5). This allows claimants of the credit to include the cost of books and other required course materials in the determination of the credit amount in 2009 and 2010.

Forty percent of a taxpayer's otherwise allowable American Opportunity credit is refundable in 2009 and 2010. However, if the taxpayer claiming the credit is a child who

¶371

BACKGROUND

has unearned income subject to the "kiddie tax" under Code Sec. 1(g), none of the credit is refundable (Code Sec. 25A(i)(6), as added by P.L. 111-5). The nonrefundable portion of the credit may be offset against both regular tax (reduced by any foreign tax credit) and alternative minimum tax (AMT) liabilities in 2009 pursuant to Code Sec. 26(a)(2) because the application of this tax liability limitation rule was amended by P.L. 111-5 to apply to tax years beginning in 2009. In 2010, when the tax liability limitation rule of Code Sec. 26(a)(2) does not apply, the nonrefundable portion of the American Opportunity credit can be offset against the excess of the sum of the regular tax plus AMT liabilities over the sum of the other nonrefundable credits allowable (other than the American Opportunity, adoption, residential alternative energy and plug-in electric vehicle credits) and the foreign tax credit (Code Sec. 25A(i)(5), as added by P.L. 111-5).

> **Example:** In 2009, Sue and Tim McComb have two children and taxable income of $13,100. Their regular tax is $1,310 and they have alternative minimum tax of $100. They paid $5,000 in college tuition for their son Jim in 2009. Jim has no unearned income in 2009. Their otherwise allowable credit is $2,500 ($2,000 × 1 + $2,000 × .25). Forty percent of $2,500 (.40 × $2,500 = $1,000) is refundable and the remaining $1,500 is nonrefundable, but limited to the total of their regular and alternative minimum tax liabilities, or $1,410. The McCombs are entitled to a Hope credit of $2,410, $1,000 refundable and $1,410 nonrefundable. Under prior law, they would have only been entitled to a $1,410 nonrefundable credit, but due to the addition of the refundable component to the credit, they can now claim a credit of $2,410 ($1,410 + $1,000).

Any reference in Code Secs. 24, 25, 25A, 25B, 26, 904 or 1400C to the increased Hope credit (American Opportunity credit) is treated as a reference to the amount of the education credits under Code Sec. 25A(a) attributable to the Hope Scholarship Credit (Code Sec. 25A(i)(5), flush language, as added by P.L. 111-5).

The refundable portion of the American Opportunity credit is generally available to bona fide residents of U.S. possessions, but cannot be claimed by those residents in the U.S. (Act Sec. 1004(c)(2) of P.L. 111-5). A bona fide resident of a possession with a mirror code tax system (Commonwealth of the Northern Mariana Islands, Guam, and the Virgin Islands) may claim the refundable portion of the credit in the possession in which the individual is a resident. The Secretary of the Treasury is required to provide payment for the amount of loss incurred by that possession due to the refundable portion of the American Opportunity credit, based upon information provided by the possession (Act Sec. 1004(c)(1)(A) of P.L. 111-5). A mirror code tax system exists if the income tax liability of the residents of the possession is determined by reference to the income tax laws of the U.S. as if the possession were the U.S. (Act Sec. 1004(c)(3)(B) of P.L. 111-5). A bona fide resident of a possession that does not have a mirror code tax system (Commonwealth of Puerto Rico and American Samoa) can also claim the refundable portion of the credit in the possession, but only if the possession establishes a plan for permitting the claim under internal law (Act Sec. 1004(c)(1)(B) of P.L. 111-5; Conference Committee Report for American Recovery and Reinvestment Act of 2009).

BACKGROUND

The Secretary of the Treasury is also required to provide a payment to non-mirror code tax system possessions equaling the aggregate benefits provided to residents of the possession due to the application of the refundable portion of the credit, but only if the possession has a plan in effect to promptly distribute such payments to residents of the possession (Act Sec. 1004(c)(1)(B) of P.L. 111-5).

NEW LAW EXPLAINED

Hope credit increase and expansion extended.—The modifications to the Hope Scholarship Credit, including an increased credit amount, increased income phaseout ranges, extension to four years of college, expansion of qualifying expenses to include books and course materials, and the allowance of a refund for a portion of the credit (collectively titled the American Opportunity credit) are extended to apply to tax years beginning in 2011 and 2012 (Code Sec. 25A(i), as amended by the Tax Relief, Unemployment Insurance Reauthorization, and Job Creation Act of 2010 (P.L. 111-312)).

> **Comment:** The Tax Relief Act of 2010 also amends Code Sec. 26(a)(2) to apply to tax years beginning in 2010 and 2011 (see ¶375). Therefore, the nonrefundable portion of the credit may be offset against both regular tax (reduced by any foreign tax credit) and alternative minimum tax (AMT) liabilities in 2010 and 2011. In 2012, when the tax liability limitation rule of Code Sec. 26(a)(2) does not apply, the nonrefundable portion of the American Opportunity credit can be offset against the excess of the sum of the regular tax plus AMT liabilities over the sum of the other nonrefundable credits allowable (other than the American Opportunity, residential alternative energy and plug-in electric vehicle credits) and the foreign tax credit (Code Sec. 25A(i)(5)).

The extension of the credit to 2011 and 2012 also applies to the refundable portion of the credit as it applies to bona fide residents of U.S. possessions (Act Sec. 1004(c)(1) of the American Recovery and Reinvestment Tax Act of 2009 (P.L. 111-5), as amended by the Tax Relief Act of 2010).

▶ **Effective date.** The provision applies to tax years beginning after December 31, 2010 (Act Sec. 103(d) of the Tax Relief, Unemployment Insurance Reauthorization, and Job Creation Act of 2010 (P.L. 111-312)).

Law source: Law at ¶5035 and ¶7017. Committee Report at ¶10,090 and ¶10,120.

— Act Sec. 103(a)(1) of the Tax Relief, Unemployment Insurance Reauthorization, and Job Creation Act of 2010 (P.L. 111-312), amending Code Sec. 25A(i);

— Act Sec. 103(a)(2), amending Act Sec. 1004(c)(1) of the American Recovery and Reinvestment Tax Act of 2009 (P.L. 111-5);

— Act Sec. 103(d), providing the effective date.

Reporter references: For further information, consult the following CCH reporters.

— Standard Federal Tax Reporter, ¶3830.01, ¶3830.034

— Tax Research Consultant, INDIV: 60,152

— Practical Tax Explanation, § 12,405

¶371

¶372 Residential Energy Property Credit

SUMMARY OF NEW LAW

The residential energy property credit is extended for one year, through 2011. The credit amount is reduced to $500 and no more than $200 of the credit amount can be attributed to exterior windows and skylights. Additional limitations apply and minimum energy standards are modified.

BACKGROUND

Individuals who own a dwelling unit in the United States and use it as their principal residence are eligible for a nonrefundable personal credit equal to 30 percent of the amount paid or incurred for nonbusiness energy property installed in or on the dwelling unit and originally placed in service by the individual in 2009 and 2010 (Code Sec. 25C(a), (c)(1), (d)(1) and (g)). The aggregate amount of the credit allowed for a taxpayer cannot exceed $1,500 for tax years beginning in 2009 and 2010 (Code Sec. 25C(b)). Vacation homes and rental dwelling units do not qualify for the credit.

Nonbusiness energy property includes *qualified energy efficiency improvements* (building envelope components) and *residential energy property expenditures* (Code Sec. 25C(a)). There must be a reasonable expectation that the qualified energy efficiency improvements (exterior doors and windows, insulation, and certain metal and asphalt roofs) will remain in use for at least 5 years (Code Sec. 25C(c)(1)(C)). Residential energy property expenditures (certain heat pumps, furnaces, central air conditioners, water heaters, stoves using biomass fuel) include labor costs (Code Sec. 25C(d)(1)).

> **Comment:** In tax years 2006 and 2007, a tax credit of up to $500 over both years was available to individuals for nonbusiness energy property installed in or on the dwelling unit and originally placed in service by the individual in those years. The credit was equal to:
>
> - 10 percent of the cost of qualified energy efficiency improvements (building envelope components), plus
>
> - the residential energy property expenditures (heat pumps, furnaces, central air conditioners and water heaters).
>
> No more than $200 of the credit could be based on expenditures for windows. The credit amount was also limited to: $50 for an advanced main air circulating fan; $150 for any qualified natural gas, propane, or oil furnace or hot water boiler; and $300 for any item of energy-efficient building property meeting minimum energy standards (electric heat pump water heater, electric heat pump, geothermal heat pump, central air conditioner, and natural gas, propane, or oil water heater). The credit terminated for tax years beginning in 2008.

The American Recovery and Reinvestment Act of 2009 (P.L. 111-5), enacted on February 17, 2009, modified the minimum energy standards for certain qualified energy efficiency improvements (insulation, exterior windows, and exterior doors)

BACKGROUND

and certain residential energy property expenditures (qualified natural gas furnace, qualified propane furnace, qualified oil furnace, qualified natural gas hot water boiler, qualified propane hot water boiler, qualified oil hot water boiler, electric heat pump, natural gas, propane, or oil water heater) placed in service after February 17, 2009.

Qualified energy efficiency improvements. Building envelope components include:

- any insulation material or system specifically designed to reduce the heat loss or gain of a dwelling unit when installed in or on the dwelling unit;
- exterior windows (including skylights);
- exterior doors; and
- any metal roof with appropriate pigmented coatings specifically and primarily designed to reduce the heat gain of the dwelling (and after October 3, 2008, any asphalt roof with cooling granules designed to reduce heat gain) (Code Sec. 25C(c)(2)).

Building envelope components, other than roofs, placed in service on or before February 17, 2009, must meet the criteria set forth in the 2000 International Energy Conservation Code (IECC), as in effect on August 8, 2005 (Code Sec. 25C(c)(1)). For property placed in service after February 17, 2009, insulation materials must meet the criteria established by the 2009 IECC, as in effect (with any supplements) on February 17, 2009, and exterior windows, skylights and doors must have a U-factor and a solar heat gain coefficient (SHGC) of 0.30 or less (Code Sec. 25C(c)(2)(A) and (c)(4)). The Energy Star Program requirements in effect at purchase control in the case of metal roofs coated with heat-reduction pigment or asphalt roofs with cooling granules.

Residential energy property expenditures. Costs, including labor, incurred by an individual for qualified energy property installed on or in connection with the individual's principal United States residence and originally placed in service by the individual are residential energy property expenditures (Code Sec. 25C(d)(1)). Qualified energy property includes:

- a qualified natural gas furnace, a qualified propane furnace, a qualified oil furnace, a qualified natural gas hot water boiler, a qualified propane hot water boiler, or a qualified oil hot water boiler;
- an advanced main air circulating fan; and
- energy-efficient building property (Code Sec. 25C(d)(2)).

For property placed in service on or before February 17, 2009, an annual fuel utilization efficiency (AFUE) rate of at least 95 for a qualified natural gas, propane, or oil furnace or hot water boiler was required. After February 17, 2009, an AFUE rate of 90 applies to a qualified natural gas hot water boiler, a qualified propane hot water boiler, a qualified oil hot water boiler, or a qualified oil furnace, and an AFUE rate of 95 continues to apply to any qualified natural gas or qualified propane furnace (Code Sec. 25C(d)(4)).

An advanced main air circulating fan is a fan that is used in a natural gas, propane, or oil furnace that has an annual electricity use of no more than two percent of the total annual energy use of the furnace (Code Sec. 25C(d)(5)).

¶372

BACKGROUND

Energy-efficient building property includes:

- an electric heat pump water heater yielding an energy factor of at least 2.0 in the standard Department of Energy test procedure;

- an electric heat pump achieving the highest efficiency tier of the Consortium for Energy Efficiency (as in effect on January 1, 2009) after February 17, 2009; on or before February 17, 2009, with a heating seasonal performance factor (HSPF) of at least 9, a seasonal energy efficiency ratio (SEER) of at least 15, and an energy efficiency ratio (EER) of at least 13;

- a central air conditioner achieving the highest efficiency tier of the Consortium for Energy Efficiency (as in effect on January 1, 2009) after February 17, 2009; on or before February 17, 2009, achieving the highest efficiency tier of the Consortium for Energy Efficiency (as in effect on January 1, 2006)

- a natural gas, propane, or oil water heater with either an energy factor of at least .82 or a thermal efficiency of at least 90 percent after February 17, 2009; on or before February 17, 2009, with an energy factor of at least .80 or a thermal efficiency of at least 90 percent; and

- a biomass fueled stove used to heat the taxpayer's United States residence, or to heat water used in the residence, having a thermal efficiency rating of at least 75 percent, as measured using a lower heating value (Code Sec. 25C(d)(3)).

> **Comment:** In 2006 and 2007, any expenditures made with funds obtained from subsidized energy financing were ineligible for the credit. Subsidized energy financing included any financing provided under a federal, state, or local program with the principal purpose of providing subsidized financing for projects designed to conserve or produce energy. This prohibition was removed for tax years 2009 and 2010.

NEW LAW EXPLAINED

Residential energy property credit modified and extended.—The residential energy property credit is extended with respect to qualifying property placed in service in 2011 (Code Sec. 25C(g)(2), as amended by the Tax Relief, Unemployment Insurance Reauthorization, and Job Creation Act of 2010 (P.L. 111-312)).

Amount of credit. Effective for property placed in service after December 31, 2010, an individual is entitled to a credit against tax in an amount equal to:

- 10 percent of the amount paid or incurred for qualified energy efficiency improvements (building envelope components) installed during the tax year, and

- the amount of residential energy property expenditures paid or incurred during the tax year (Code Sec. 25C(a), as amended by the Tax Relief Act of 2010).

The maximum credit allowable is $500 over the lifetime of the taxpayer. The $500 amount must be reduced by the aggregate amount of previously allowed credits the taxpayer received in 2006, 2007, 2009 and 2010 (Code Sec. 25C(b)(1), as amended by the Tax Relief Act of 2010).

NEW LAW EXPLAINED

> **Comment:** The maximum aggregate credit for 2006 and 2007 was $500 and $1,500 for 2009 and 2010.

Credit limits. The maximum amount of the residential energy property credit that may be allocated to exterior windows and skylights is $200. This $200 amount must be reduced by the aggregate amount of previously allowed credits for windows and skylights that the taxpayer received in 2006, 2007, 2009 and 2010 (Code Sec. 25C(b)(2), as amended by the Tax Relief Act of 2010).

With regard to residential energy property expenditures, the following credit dollar limitations apply to property placed in service in 2011:

- $50 for any advanced main air circulating fan;
- $150 for any qualified natural gas, propane, or oil furnace or hot water boiler;
- $300 for any item of energy-efficient building property (Code Sec. 25C(b)(3), as amended by the Tax Relief Act of 2010).

Minimum energy standards. In 2011, insulation materials and systems specifically and primarily designed to reduce the heat loss or gain of a dwelling when installed in or on the dwelling must meet the prescriptive criteria for the insulation materials and systems as established by the 2009 International Energy Conservation Code (IECC), as such code including supplements is in effect on February 17, 2009, in order to be qualified energy efficiency improvements (Code Sec. 25C(c)(1) and (c)(2)(A), as amended by the Tax Relief Act of 2010). Exterior windows, skylights and exterior doors are qualified energy efficiency improvements if they meet the Energy Star Program requirements in 2011 (Code Sec. 25C(c)(1), as amended, and (c)(4), as stricken, by the Tax Relief Act of 2010).

A stove that uses the burning of biomass fuel to heat a dwelling unit located in the United States and used as a residence by the taxpayer, or to heat water for use in the dwelling, must have a thermal efficiency rating of at least 75 percent to qualify as energy-efficient building property in 2011 (Code Sec. 25C(d)(3)(E), as amended by the Tax Relief Act of 2010).

> **Comment:** There is no longer a requirement that the thermal efficiency rating for biomass stoves be measured using a lower heating value.

In order to satisfy the definition for a qualified natural gas, qualified propane, or qualified oil furnace or qualified hot water boiler, the natural gas, propane, or oil furnace or hot water boiler must achieve an annual fuel utilization efficiency (AFUE) rate of not less than 95 in 2011 (Code Sec. 25C(d)(4), as amended by the Tax Relief Act of 2010).

> **Comment:** The reduced AFUE rate of 90 that applies after February 17, 2009, has now been returned to the AFUE rate of 95 that was applicable on or before February 17, 2009.

Subsidized energy financing. Any expenditures made with funds obtained from subsidized energy financing are ineligible for the credit (Code Sec. 25C(e)(3), as added by the Tax Relief Act of 2010). Subsidized energy financing is defined under Code Sec. 48(a)(4)(C) and includes any financing provided under a federal, state, or

NEW LAW EXPLAINED

local program with the principal purpose of providing subsidized financing for projects designed to conserve or produce energy.

> **Comment:** There has been no change to the general requirements for the non-business energy property credit. The qualified energy efficiency improvements (building envelope components) and qualified energy property must be installed in or on a United States dwelling unit owned by the taxpayer and used as his or her principal residence. The property must originally be placed in service by the taxpayer in 2011. There must be a reasonable expectation that the qualified energy efficiency improvements (exterior doors and windows, skylights, insulation, and certain metal and asphalt roofs) will remain in use for at least 5 years. If less than 80 percent of otherwise eligible property is for nonbusiness use, then only the percentage of the costs properly allocated to nonbusiness uses can be taken into account in calculating the credit.

▶ **Effective date.** The provisions apply to property placed in service after December 31, 2010 (Act Sec. 710(c) of the Tax Relief, Unemployment Insurance Reauthorization, and Job Creation Act of 2010 (P.L. 111-312)).

Law source: Law at ¶5040. Committee Report at ¶10,260.

— Act Sec. 710(a) of the Tax Relief, Unemployment Insurance Reauthorization, and Job Creation Act of 2010 (P.L. 111-312), amending Code Sec. 25C(g)(2);

— Act Sec. 710(b)(1), amending Code Sec. 25C(a) and (b);

— Act Sec. 710(b)(2)(A), amending Code Sec. 25C(c)(1);

— Act Sec. 710(b)(2)(B), amending Code Sec. 25C(d)(3)(E);

— Act Sec. 710(b)(2)(C), amending Code Sec. 25C(d)(2)(A)(ii) and (d)(4);

— Act Sec. 710(b)(2)(D), amending Code Sec. 25C(c)(1) and striking (c)(4);

— Act Sec. 710(b)(2)(E), amending Code Sec. 25C(c)(2)(A);

— Act Sec. 710(b)(3), adding Code Sec. 25C(e)(3);

— Act Sec. 710(c), providing the effective date.

Reporter references: For further information, consult the following CCH reporters.

— Standard Federal Tax Reporter, ¶3843.021, ¶3843.025 and ¶3843.03

— Tax Research Consultant, INDIV: 57,804, INDIV: 57,806 and INDIV: 57,808

— Practical Tax Explanation, § 13,205, § 13,210 and § 13,215

¶373 Health Insurance Premium Assistance Credit

SUMMARY OF NEW LAW

For tax years beginning after 2013, if advance premium assistance payments exceed the allowable health insurance premium assistance credit, the maximum repayment is increased to between $600 and $3,500 for joint filers (or half those amounts for

SUMMARY OF NEW LAW

single taxpayers) with household incomes of less than 500 percent of the poverty line for the tax year.

BACKGROUND

As part of health care reform, by January 1, 2014, each state must establish an American Health Benefit Exchange and Small Business Health Options Program (SHOP Exchange) to provide qualified individuals and qualified small business employers access to qualified health plans pursuant to the Patient Protection and Affordable Care Act (P.L. 111-148). The Exchanges will have four levels of essential benefits coverage available to participants: "bronze," "silver," "gold," and "platinum" levels. The bronze level plans must provide benefits that are actuarially equivalent to 60 percent of the full actuarial value of the benefits provided under the plan. The percentage increases to 70 percent for silver level plans, 80 percent for gold level plans, and 90 percent for platinum level plans.

In 2014, certain individuals who purchase qualified health care coverage through an American Health Benefit Exchange are entitled to a refundable income tax credit equal to the premium assistance credit amount (Code Sec. 36B(a)). The health insurance premium assistance credit applies to qualified individuals who have household income between 100 percent and 400 percent of the federal poverty line (Code Sec. 36B(c)(1)(A)). A qualified individual must be seeking to enroll in a qualified health plan in the individual market offered through an Exchange, and must reside in the state that established the Exchange (Act Sec. 1312(f)(1)(A) of P.L. 111-148). The refundable premium assistance credit can limit the out-of-pocket expense for an individual who purchases coverage within the Exchange (Code Sec. 36B(a) and (b)(3)(B)).

In order to reduce the premiums payable by individuals eligible for the premium assistance credit, P.L. 111-148 provides for advance determination of credit eligibility and advance payments of qualified health plan premiums by the Secretary of the Treasury to the health plan issuers. The premium assistance credit must be reduced, but not below zero, by the amount of any advance payment of the credit (Code Sec. 36B(f)(1)).

If the advance payments for a tax year exceed the premium assistance credit allowed, the excess is an increase to the tax imposed for the tax year (Code Sec. 36B(f)(2)(A)). For any taxpayer whose household income is less than 400 percent of the federal poverty line for the family size involved, the increase in tax is limited to $400 ($250 for unmarried taxpayers) (Code Sec. 36B(f)(2)(B)(i)). The $400 and $250 limitations on the tax increase are subject to cost of living adjustments after 2014, rounded to the next lowest multiple of $50 if the adjustment is not a multiple of $50 (Code Sec. 36B(f)(2)(B)(ii)).

¶373

NEW LAW EXPLAINED

Tax increase limits raised when advance credit payments exceed allowable credit.—For taxpayers with household income of less than 500 percent of the poverty line for the family size involved, the increase in reportable tax that results when advance premium assistance payments exceed the allowable credit, is limited according to the following table:

If the household income (expressed as a percent of poverty line) is:	The applicable dollar amount is:
Less than 200%	$600
At least 200% but less than 250%	$1,000
At least 250% but less than 300%	$1,500
At least 300% but less than 350%	$2,000
At least 350% but less than 400%	$2,500
At least 400% but less than 450%	$3,000
At least 450% but less than 500%	$3,500

One-half of the amounts shown in the table apply to unmarried taxpayers other than surviving spouses and heads of households (Code Sec. 36B(f)(2)(B)(i), as amended by the Medicare and Medicaid Extenders Act of 2010 (P.L. 111-309)). The amounts in the table are subject to cost-of-living adjustments for calendar years beginning after 2014, rounded to the next lowest multiple of $50 if the adjustment is not a multiple of $50 (Code Sec. 36B(f)(2)(B)(ii), as amended by the Medicare and Medicaid Extenders Act of 2010).

> **Comment:** For joint filers, the maximum tax increase ranges from $600 to $3,500, up from the original maximum of $400. The maximum tax increase for unmarried taxpayers ranges from $300 to $1,750, up from the $250 original maximum. According to a Press Release from the United States Senate Committee on Finance, these increases are intended to pay for Medicare changes, including extensions of several provisions that were scheduled to expire, and a one-year delay in reductions to physician reimbursements.

▶ **Effective date.** The provisions apply to tax years beginning after December 31, 2013 (Act Sec. 208(c) of the Medicare and Medicaid Extenders Act of 2010 (P.L. 111-309)).

Law source: Law at ¶5080.

— Act Sec. 208(a) of the Medicare and Medicaid Extenders Act of 2010 (P.L. 111-309), amending Code Sec. 36B(f)(2)(B);

— Act Sec. 208(b), amending Code Sec. 36B(f)(2)(B)(ii);

— Act Sec. 208(c), providing the effective date.

Reporter references: For further information, consult the following CCH reporters.

— Standard Federal Tax Reporter, ¶4197.027

— Tax Research Consultant, INDIV: 58,150

— Practical Tax Explanation, § 42,015.20

ALTERNATIVE MINIMUM TAX AND OTHER PROVISIONS

¶375 Alternative Minimum Tax Exemption Amount

SUMMARY OF NEW LAW

The alternative minimum tax (AMT) exemption amounts for individuals have been increased for tax years beginning in 2010 and 2011.

BACKGROUND

In addition to all other tax liabilities, an individual is subject to the AMT to the extent that his or her tentative minimum tax exceeds the amount of regular income tax owed (Code Sec. 55). An individual's tentative minimum tax is generally equal to the sum of: (1) 26 percent of the first $175,000 of the taxpayer's alternative minimum taxable income (AMTI) ($87,500 for a married taxpayer filing a separate return); and (2) 28 percent of the taxpayer's remaining AMTI (Code Sec. 55(b)(1)(A)). AMTI is the individual's regular taxable income recomputed with certain adjustments and increased by certain tax preferences (Code Sec. 56).

A specified amount of AMTI is exempt from AMT based on the taxpayer's filing status and the tax year involved (Code Sec. 55(d)(1)). The number of individuals affected by the AMT, however, continues to grow each year as the exemption amounts are not indexed for inflation. The Economic Growth and Tax Relief Reconciliation Act of 2001 (EGTRRA) (P.L. 107-16) provided higher exemption amounts for individuals subject to AMT for tax years beginning in 2001 and 2004. The exemption amounts have been periodically extended and enhanced by subsequent legislation.

For example, for tax years beginning in 2009, the exemption amounts were increased to: (1) $46,700 for unmarried individuals, (2) $70,950 for married couples filing a joint return and surviving spouses, and (3) $35,475 for married couples filing separate returns (Code Sec. 55(d)(1), as amended by the American Recovery and Reinvestment Tax Act of 2009 (P.L. 111-5)). Without the legislative patches, the exemption amounts would have automatically reverted to the amounts that applied prior to the enactment of EGTRRA. For this reason, the exemption amounts for tax years beginning after 2009 are scheduled to revert to: (1) $33,750 for unmarried individuals, (2) $45,000 for married taxpayers filing a joint return and surviving spouses, and (3) $22,500 for married taxpayers filing separate returns. These are the same as the amounts that were in place for tax years beginning before 2001.

> **Comment:** The exemption amounts for corporations and estates or trusts have remained unchanged during this period. The exemption amount is $40,000 for a corporation and $22,500 for an estate or trust.

BACKGROUND

The AMT exemption amount is phased out by 25 percent of the amount by which the individual's AMTI exceeds: (1) $112,500 in the case of unmarried individuals, (2) $150,000 in the case of married individuals filing a joint return and surviving spouses, and (3) $75,000 in the case of married individuals filing a separate return (Code Sec. 55(d)(3)). Although the base amounts for the exemption phaseout computations were unchanged by EGTRRA, the computations are affected by the amount of the exemption. Thus, the increased exemption amounts also increased the maximum amount of AMTI a person can have before the exemption amount is phased out.

Married taxpayers filing separately. A married taxpayer filing separately must increase AMTI for purposes of calculating the exemption phaseout by the lesser of: (1) 25 percent of the excess of AMTI (as determined before this adjustment) over the minimum amount of such income (as so determined) for which the married filing separately exemption amount is zero, or (2) the married filing separately exemption amount (Code Sec. 55(d)(3)).

> **Comment:** The purpose of this provision is to equate the tax liabilities of married taxpayers filing separately with married taxpayers filing jointly.

Sunset provision. Under the sunset provision of EGTRRA, amendments made by the Act are scheduled not to apply to tax years beginning after December 31, 2010 (Act. Sec. 901 of P.L. 107-16).

NEW LAW EXPLAINED

Increase in AMT exemption amounts.—The alternative minimum tax (AMT) exemption amounts for individuals have been increased for tax years beginning in 2010 and 2011 (Code Sec. 55(d)(1), as amended by the Tax Relief, Unemployment Insurance Reauthorization, and Job Creation Act of 2010 (P.L. 111-312)).

For tax years beginning in 2010, the AMT exemption amounts for individuals have increased to:

- $47,450 for unmarried individuals,
- $72,450 for married taxpayers filing jointly and surviving spouses, and
- $36,225 for married taxpayers filing separately.

For tax years beginning in 2011, the AMT exemption amounts for individuals have increased to:

- $48,450 for unmarried individuals,
- $74,450 for married taxpayers filing jointly and surviving spouses, and
- $37,225 for married taxpayers filing separately.

The $40,000 exemption amount for corporations and the $22,500 exemption amount for estates or trusts remain unchanged (Code Sec. 55(d)(1)(D) and (d)(2)).

> **Caution:** Absent another legislative change, the AMT exemption amounts for individuals for tax years beginning after 2011 are scheduled to revert to the amounts that applied prior to the 2001 tax year. Thus, the exemption amounts

¶375

NEW LAW EXPLAINED

would be: (1) $33,750 for unmarried individuals, (2) $45,000 for married taxpayers filing a joint return and surviving spouses, and (3) $22,500 for married taxpayers filing separate returns.

This decrease in the AMT exemption amounts for tax years beginning after 2011 occurs by operation of Code Sec. 55(d)(1). Before enactment of the Tax Relief Act of 2010, it would have occurred for tax years beginning after 2010 by operation of the sunset provision of the Economic Growth and Tax Relief Reconciliation Act of 2001 (EGTRRA) (Act Sec. 901 of P.L. 107-16), but the sunset has been repealed with respect to EGTRRA's AMT provisions (Act Sec. 201(c) of the Tax Relief Act of 2010).

AMT exemption phaseout. Although the AMT exemption amounts for individuals have increased for 2010 and 2011, the threshold levels for calculating the exemption phaseout remain unchanged. Thus, the exemption amount for tax years beginning in 2010 and 2011 is still reduced by 25 percent for each $1 of alternative minimum taxable income (AMTI) in excess of: (1) $112,500 in the case of unmarried individuals, (2) $150,000 in the case of married individuals filing a joint return and surviving spouses, and (3) $75,000 in the case of married individuals filing separate returns (Code Sec. 55(d)(3)). However, because the calculation of the phaseout amount is affected by the amount of AMTI exempted, an increase in the exemption amount will also increase the maximum amount of AMTI a person can have before the exemption amount is phased out.

In 2010, the increased exemption amounts are completely phased out when AMTI reaches:

- $302,300 for unmarried taxpayers (up from $299,300 in 2009),
- $439,800 for married taxpayers filing joint returns (up from $433,800 in 2009), and
- $219,900 for married taxpayers filing a separate return (up from $216,900 in 2009).

Similarly, in 2011, the exemption amounts are completely phased out when AMTI reaches:

- $306,300 for unmarried taxpayers,
- $447,800 for married taxpayers filing joint returns, and
- $223,900 for married taxpayers filing a separate return.

Married individuals filing separately. Married taxpayer filing separately must continue to increase AMTI for purposes of calculating the exemption phaseout in 2010 and 2011 by the lesser of: (1) 25 percent of the excess of AMTI (as determined before this adjustment) over the minimum amount of such income (as so determined) for which the married filing separately exemption amount is zero, or (2) the married filing separately exemption amount (Code Sec. 55(d)(3)).

Comment: Prior to the enactment of EGTRRA, a married taxpayer filing separately would have been required to increase his or her AMTI for purposes of calculating the exemption phaseout by the lesser of: (1) 25 percent of the excess of AMTI (determined without regard to this adjustment) over $165,000 or (2) the $22,500 exemption amount. The law would have reverted to these specific dollar limits under the EGTRRA sunset. However, the EGTRRA sunset has been

NEW LAW EXPLAINED

repealed for AMT purposes and the amount added to AMTI by a married taxpayer filing separately is determined by reference to the exemption amount for the year.

Practical Analysis: William A Raabe, Ohio State University, and Capital University Law School, Columbus, Ohio, John O. Everett, Virginia Commonwealth University, Richmond Virginia, and Cherie J. Hennig, University of North Carolina, Wilmington observe with the two-year patch of the AMT exemption, the exemption amounts for the years 2009 through 2011 are scheduled to be as shown Table 1.

Table 1	2009	2010	2011	2012
Exemption Amounts	$70,950 (MJ)	$72,450 (MJ)	$74.450 (MJ)	$45,000 (MJ)
	$46,700 (S)	$47,450 (S)	$48,450 (S)	$33,750 (S)
	$35,475 (MS)	$36,225 (MS)	$37,225 (MS)	$22,500 (MS)

Most likely, Congress will once again act before 2012 to "kick the can further down the road" with higher exemption amounts for 2012, rather than have the amounts revert to 2001 levels ($45,000 (MJ), $33,750 (S), $22,500 (MS)). It appears that the AMT exemption amount has been added to the list of extenders that tax professionals live and die by each year, awaiting a reprieve from Congress (often in retroactive form, to add to the frustration). Congress seems to lack the conviction to make such changes permanent, as the long-term revenue cost would be staggering.

The increased AMT exemptions for 2010 and 2011 also raise the levels of alternative minimum taxable income (AMTI) necessary to completely phase out the exemption amount, although the beginning of this phaseout remains the same (e.g., $150,000 for MJ, $112,500 for S, and $75,000 MS). Taxpayers and tax professionals alike should consider this phaseout range when considering additional income or deductions for taxpayers already in an AMT situation near year-end.

For example, consider a married taxpayer who near the end of the year 2010 desires to accelerate $50,000 income into a year that the AMT already applies, rationalizing that paying the 28 percent AMT rate this year is better than paying a 35 percent regular tax rate next year. Assume the taxpayer's alternative minimum taxable income (AMTI) before AMT exemption is $300,000. Recall from the previous discussion that the exemption phaseout for a married taxpayer in 2010 is $.25 for each dollar of AMTI over $150,000. Since the AMT exemption of $72,450 is not phased out until AMTI reaches $439,800, the additional $50,000 of gross income actually increases AMTI by 125% of that amount, or $62,500. This is because the $50,000 additional AMTI also decreases the exemption deduction by $12,500 ($50,000 × .25). This is the same as paying 125 percent of the normal AMT rate on the $50,000 additional income, i.e., the normal 28 percent AMT rate becomes 35 percent on the $50,000 marginal income ($62,500 × .28 = $50,000 × .35 = $17,500).

▶ **Effective date.** The provision applies to tax years beginning after December 31, 2009 (Act Sec. 201(b) of the Tax Relief, Unemployment Insurance Reauthorization, and Job Creation Act of 2010 (P.L. 111-312)).

¶375

NEW LAW EXPLAINED

Law source: Law at ¶5170 and ¶7020. Committee Report at ¶10,120.

— Act Sec. 201(a) of the Tax Relief, Unemployment Insurance Reauthorization, and Job Creation Act of 2010 (P.L. 111-312), amending Code Sec. 55(d);

— Act Sec. 201(c), repealing the sunset provision of the Economic Growth and Tax Relief Reconciliation Act of 2001 (EGTRRA) (P.L. 107-16) with respect to EGTRRA changes to Code Sec. 55(d);

— Act Sec. 201(b), providing the effective date.

Reporter references: For further information, consult the following CCH reporters.

— Standard Federal Tax Reporter, ¶5101.01

— Tax Research Consultant, FILEIND: 30,400

— Practical Tax Explanation, §15,001

¶376 Use of Nonrefundable Personal Credits Against AMT Liability

SUMMARY OF NEW LAW

The use of nonrefundable personal tax credits against an individual's regular tax and alternative minimum tax (AMT) liability is extended to tax years beginning in 2010 and 2011.

BACKGROUND

An alternative minimum tax (AMT) is imposed on an individual taxpayer to the extent his or her tentative minimum tax liability exceeds his or her regular income tax liability (Code Sec. 55(a)). An individual's tentative minimum tax is the sum of: (1) 26 percent of the first $175,000 ($87,500 for married individuals filing separately) of the taxpayer's alternative minimum taxable income (AMTI) in excess of an exemption amount; and (2) 28 percent of any remaining AMTI in excess of the exemption amount (Code Sec. 55(b)(1)(A)). AMTI is the individual's regular taxable income recomputed with certain adjustments and increased by certain tax preferences (Code Sec. 56).

Pre-2010 tax years. For tax years beginning before 2010, all nonrefundable personal tax credits available to an individual may be claimed to the extent of the full amount of the taxpayer's combined regular tax and AMT liability. The taxpayer's regular tax liability, however, must first be reduced by the amount of any applicable foreign or U.S. possession tax credit (Code Sec. 26(a)(2)).

The nonrefundable personal tax credits include: the dependent care credit, the credit for the elderly and disabled, the adoption credit (in tax years before 2010), the child tax credit, the credit for interest on certain home mortgages, the Hope Scholarship and Lifetime Learning credits (including the American Opportunity tax credit), the

BACKGROUND

retirement savings contributions credit, the credit for certain nonbusiness energy property, the credit for residential energy efficient property, the plug-in electric drive motor vehicle credit, the new qualified plug-in electric drive motor vehicle credit, the alternative motor vehicle credit, and the District of Columbia first-time homebuyer credit.

2010 tax years. For tax years beginning in 2010, only specified nonrefundable personal credits are fully allowed against the taxpayer's combined regular tax and AMT liability (Code Sec. 26(a)(1)). These credits are:

- the child tax credit (Code Sec. 24);

- the American Opportunity tax credit (Code Sec. 25A(i));

- the retirement savings contributions credit (Code Sec. 25B);

- the credit for residential energy efficient property (Code Sec. 25D);

- the credit for small plug-in electric vehicles (Code Sec. 30);

- the alternative motor vehicle credit (Code Sec. 30B), and

- the credit for new plug-in electric drive motor vehicles (Code Sec. 30D).

Special limitation rules apply to the credits listed above that operate in addition to the Code Sec. 26 limitation. Specifically, a special limitation rule applies to the child tax credit (Code Secs. 24(b)(3)), the American Opportunity tax credit (Code Sec. 25A(i)(5)), the retirement savings contributions credit (Code Sec. 25B(g)), the credit for residential energy efficient property (Code Sec. 25D(c)), the credit for small plug-in electric vehicles (Code Sec. 30(c)(2)(B)), the alternative motor vehicle credit (Code Sec. 30B(g)(2)), and the credit for new plug-in electric drive motor vehicles (Code Sec. 30D(c)(2)(B)).

Other nonrefundable personal credits are allowed only to the extent the taxpayer's regular tax liability exceeds the taxpayer's tentative minimum tax (determined without regard to the AMT foreign tax credit) (Code Sec. 26(a)(1)). These would include the dependent care credit, the credit for the elderly and disabled, the credit for interest on certain home mortgages, the Lifetime Learning credit, the credit for certain nonbusiness energy property, and the District of Columbia first-time homebuyer credit.

Post-2010 tax years. Without further legislative action, for tax years beginning after 2010, all nonrefundable credits other than the credit for residential energy efficient property, the credit for small plug-in electric vehicles, the alternative motor vehicle credit, and the credit for new plug-in electric drive motor vehicles will be allowed only to the extent the taxpayer's regular tax liability exceeds the taxpayer's tentative minimum tax (determined without regard to the AMT foreign tax credit) due to application of the sunset of the Economic Growth and Tax Relief and Reconciliation Act of 2009 (EGTRRA) (P.L. 107-16) (Code Sec. 26(a)(1); Act Sec. 901 of P.L. 107-16). The special limitation rules for each credit will continue apply. The American Opportunity tax credit is scheduled to expire after 2010.

NEW LAW EXPLAINED

Nonrefundable personal credits allowed against regular tax and AMT liability for 2010, 2011 tax years.—For tax years beginning in 2010 and 2011, all nonrefundable personal tax credits are allowed to the full extent of the taxpayer's regular tax and AMT liability. For this purpose, the regular tax liability is first reduced by the amount of any applicable foreign tax credit (Code Sec. 26(a)(2), as amended by the Tax Relief, Unemployment Insurance Reauthorization, and Job Creation Act of 2010 (P.L. 111-312)).

2012 tax years. Without further legislative action, for tax years beginning in 2012, only the following nonrefundable personal credits will be allowed against AMT liability because they are specifically set forth in Code Sec. 26(a)(1), but the special limitation rules for each credit also apply:

- the child tax credit (Code Sec. 24);
- the American Opportunity tax credit (Code Sec. 25A(i));
- the retirement savings contributions credit (Code Sec. 25B);
- the credit for residential energy efficient property (Code Sec. 25D);
- the credit for small plug-in electric vehicles (Code Sec. 30);
- the alternative motor vehicle credit (Code Sec. 30B), and
- the credit for new plug-in electric drive motor vehicles (Code Sec. 30D).

> **Comment:** The Joint Committee on Taxation notes that, beginning in 2012, the adoption credit is a nonrefundable credit and treated for AMT purposes in the same manner as the child tax credit (Joint Committee on Taxation, *Technical Explanation of the Revenue Provisions Contained in the "Tax Relief, Unemployment Insurance Reauthorization, and Job Creation Act of 2010"* (JCX-55-10), December 10, 2010).

Other nonrefundable personal credits will be allowed only to the extent the taxpayer's regular tax liability exceeds the taxpayer's tentative minimum tax (determined without regard to the AMT foreign tax credit) (Code Sec. 26(a)(1)).

> **Caution:** For tax years beginning after 2012, it is unclear how the Code Sec. 26(a)(1) limitation will be applied. Without further legislative action, it appears that, for tax years beginning after 2012, all nonrefundable credits other than the credit for residential energy efficient property, the credit for small plug-in electric vehicles, the alternative motor vehicle credit, and the credit for new plug-in electric drive motor vehicles will be allowed only to the extent the taxpayer's regular tax liability exceeds the taxpayer's tentative minimum tax (determined without regard to the AMT foreign tax credit) due to application of the sunset of EGTRRA (Code Sec. 26(a)(1); Act Sec. 901 of the Economic Growth and Tax Relief and Reconciliation Act of 2009 (EGTRRA) (P.L. 107-17, as amended by Act Sec. 101 of the Tax Relief Act of 2010). The special limitation rules for each of the above credits will apply. The child tax credit (see ¶360) and the adoption credit (see ¶370) may not apply after 2012 due to the extended EGTRRA sunset, and the American Opportunity tax credit is scheduled to expire after 2012 (see ¶371).

¶376

NEW LAW EXPLAINED

▶ **Effective date.** The provision is effective for tax years beginning after December 31, 2009 (Act Sec. 202(b) of the Tax Relief, Unemployment Insurance Reauthorization, and Job Creation Act of 2010 (P.L. 111-312)).

Law source: Law at ¶5050. Committee Report at ¶10,120.

— Act Sec. 202(a) of the Tax Relief, Unemployment Insurance Reauthorization, and Job Creation Act of 2010 (P.L. 111-312), amending Code Sec. 26(a)(2);

— Act Sec. 202(b), providing the effective date.

Reporter references: For further information, consult the following CCH reporters.

— Standard Federal Tax Reporter, ¶3851.021

— Tax Research Consultant, INDIV: 57,200

— Practical Tax Explanation, §15,515.10

¶380 Limitation on Qualified Transportation Fringe Benefits

SUMMARY OF NEW LAW

The temporary increase to the limitation on the amount employees may exclude for transit passes and van pool benefits provided by an employer is extended through 2011, and equals the limitation on the exclusion for qualified parking.

BACKGROUND

The costs of commuting to and from work are not deductible as a business expense or an expense incurred in the production of income. Instead, they are nondeductible personal expenses (Reg. §§1.162-2(e), 1.212-1(f) and 1.262-1(b)(5)). However, transportation fringe benefits are sometimes provided by employers to their employees in addition to cash compensation. Although compensation for services is generally taxable, qualified transportation fringe benefits provided by an employer to an employee are excluded from an employee's gross income for income tax purposes and from wages for payroll tax purposes (Code Secs. 132(a)(5), 3121(a)(20), 3306(b)(16), and 3401(a)(19)). The exclusion is limited to employees, including only common law employees and statutory employees, such as corporate officers, at the time the benefit is provided (Reg. §1.132-9). If a fringe benefit is not specifically excluded, it is treated as taxable income.

Qualified transportation fringe benefits include—

- transportation in a commuter highway vehicle (i.e., "van pooling"),
- transit passes,
- qualified parking, and
- qualified bicycle commuting reimbursement (Code Sec. 132(f)(1)).

BACKGROUND

An employer can generally provide an employee with any combination of these benefits simultaneously, but a qualified bicycle commuting reimbursement cannot be given in any month in which any of the other qualified transportation fringe benefit are given (Code Sec. 132(f)(5)(F)(iii)(II)). A qualified transportation fringe generally includes a cash reimbursement by the employer for these types of benefits (Code Sec. 132(f)(3)).

To be excluded, transportation in a commuter highway vehicle (i.e., "van pooling") must be provided by an employer in connection with travel between the employee's residence and place of employment. A "commuter highway vehicle" is any highway vehicle that can seat at least six adults (excluding the driver), and at least 80 percent of its mileage use must be reasonably expected to be for (1) transporting employees in connection with travel between their residences and their place of employment, and (2) trips during which the number of employees transported is at least one-half of the vehicle's adult seating capacity (excluding the driver) (Code Sec. 132(f)(5)(B) and (D)).

A "transit pass" is a pass, token, fare card, voucher or similar item (including an item exchangeable for fare media) that entitles a person to transportation (including transportation at a reduced price) on public or private mass transit facilities, or provided by a person in the business of transporting persons for compensation or hire in a vehicle which meets the requirements of a commuter highway vehicle. The IRS does not require any substantiation if an employer distributes transit passes. Unless the employer chooses to require it, employees receiving passes need not certify that they will use the passes for commuting (Code Sec. 132(f)(5)(A); Reg. § 1.132-9).

"Qualified parking" is parking provided to an employee on or near the employer's business premises or a location from which the employee commutes to work (including commuting by carpool, commuter highway vehicle, mass transit facilities, or transportation provided by a person in the business of transporting persons for compensation or hire). It does not include parking on or near property used by the employee for residential purposes (Code Sec. 132(f)(5)(C); Reg. § 1.132-9).

A "qualified bicycle commuting reimbursement" is any employer reimbursement during the 15-month period beginning on the first day of the calendar year, for reasonable expenses that the employee incurs for a bicycle purchase, improvements, repair and storage, if the bicycle is regularly used for travel between the employee's residence and place of employment (Code Sec. 132(f)(5)(D)).

Limitations on exclusion. Generally, the excludible amount for qualified transportation fringes is limited to $100 per month total for a transit pass and qualified van pooling, and $175 per month for qualified parking; these amounts are adjusted for inflation (Code Sec. 132(f)(2) and (6)). However, effective for any month beginning on or after February 17, 2009, and before January 1, 2011, the monthly exclusion for transit passes and van pool benefits is increased to match the exclusion amount for qualified parking (Code Sec. 132(f)(2), flush language). For tax years beginning in 2010, the inflation-adjusted exclusion amount for these three qualified transportation fringes is $230 per month (Rev. Proc. 2009-50, I.R.B. 2009-45, 617)). After 2010, the inflation-adjusted monthly exclusion amount for transit passes and van pool benefits will again be lower than that for qualified parking.

BACKGROUND

The exclusion for a qualified bicycle reimbursement is limited to $20 times the number of months during which the employee regularly uses the bicycle for a substantial portion of the travel between his residence and place of employment, and does not receive any of the other qualified transportation fringe benefits (Code Sec. 132(f)(2)(C), (F)(ii) and (iii)).

NEW LAW EXPLAINED

Parity for exclusion limitation on van pool benefits, transit passes and qualified parking extended.—The temporary increase to the monthly exclusion amount for van pool benefits and transit passes provided by an employer to an employee, so that these two qualified transportation fringes match the monthly exclusion amount for qualified parking, is extended and applies through 2011 (Code Sec. 132(f)(2), as amended by the Tax Relief, Unemployment Insurance Reauthorization, and Job Creation Act of 2010 (P.L. 111-312)). The increased exclusion amount will not apply to any month beginning on or after January 1, 2012.

> **State Tax Consequences:** The extension of the provision requiring parity among employer-provided transit benefits from March 2009 through the end of 2011 (formerly, 2010) should not have much of an affect on states that adopted the original provision. These states will most likely adopt the extension during their next legislative sessions.

> **Comment:** According to RideFinders, a regional rideshare program, commuters who drive alone may experience an expensive, frustrating workday commute that increases traffic congestion and air pollution. Van pool riders lower their commuting stress by not driving, which reduces traffic congestion and improves the region's air quality (http://www.ridefinders.org/Vanpool/benefits.aspx). Additionally, public transportation can make a significant contribution toward job creation, reducing our dependence on foreign oil, and becoming carbon efficient. According to the American Public Transportation Association, public transportation use in America saves 4.2 billion gallons of fuel and 37 million metric tons of carbon dioxide emissions per year while supporting two million jobs (http://www.apta.com).

▶ **Effective date.** The amendment applies to months after December 31, 2010 (Act Sec. 727(b) of the Tax Relief, Unemployment Insurance Reauthorization, and Job Creation Act of 2010 (P.L. 111-312)).

Law source: Law at ¶5215. Committee Report at ¶10,340.

— Act Sec. 727(a) of the Tax Relief, Unemployment Insurance Reauthorization, and Job Creation Act of 2010 (P.L. 111-312), amending Code Sec. 132(f)(2);

— Act Sec. 727(b), providing the effective date.

Reporter references: For further information, consult the following CCH reporters.

— Standard Federal Tax Reporter, ¶7438.054

— Tax Research Consultant, COMPEN: 36,350 and PAYROLL: 3,200

— Practical Tax Explanation, §21,125.05

¶382 Refund Offsets for Unemployment Compensation Debts

SUMMARY OF NEW LAW

For purposes of refund offsets to collect unemployment compensation debts, the definition of covered unemployment compensation debt has been modified to include past-due debts for erroneous payment of unemployment due to failure to report earnings, as well as erroneous payments due to fraud. Additionally, the 10-year lookback period for covered unemployment debts and the limitation permitting offsets only against residents of the state seeking the offset have been eliminated. The changes apply to refunds payable under Code Sec. 6402 on or after December 8, 2010.

BACKGROUND

Within the applicable period of limitations, the IRS may credit any overpayment of tax, including interest on such overpayment, against any outstanding liability for any tax, interest, additional amount, addition to tax, or assessable penalty, owed by the person making the overpayment. Any remaining balance will be refunded to the person making the overpayment (Code Sec. 6402; Reg. § 301.6402-1). In addition to the IRS's authority to claim the overpayment in satisfaction of outstanding tax liabilities, a taxpayer's refund is subject to offset to collect certain other debts, including past-due child support, debts owed to federal agencies; and past due, legally enforceable State income tax debts.

For refunds payable on or after September 30, 2008, the IRS may also offset an overpayment of federal taxes to collect covered unemployment compensation debts. Upon receiving notice from a State that a named person owes a covered unemployment compensation debt to that State, the Secretary of the Treasury is required to offset any overpayment of federal taxes by that person by the amount of the covered employment compensation debt, and pay the amount of the offset to the State (Code Sec. 6402(f)(1), as added by the SSI Extension for Elderly and Disabled Refugees Act (P.L. 110-328). A covered unemployment compensation debt is defined as:

- a past-due debt for erroneous payment of unemployment compensation due to fraud which has become final under the law of a State certified by the Secretary of Labor pursuant to Code Sec. 3304 and which remains uncollected for not more than 10 years;

- contributions due to the unemployment fund of a State for which the State has determined the person to be liable due to fraud and which remain uncollected for not more than 10 years; and

- any penalties and interest assessed on such debt (Code Sec. 6402(f)(5), as added by P.L. 110-328).

Offsets to collect covered unemployment compensation debts are only permitted against residents of the State seeking the offset. An offset of an overpayment will only

¶380

BACKGROUND

be allowed if the taxpayer who makes the overpayment has shown on the federal return for the year of the overpayment an address within the State seeking the offset (Code Sec. 6402(f)(3), as added by P.L. 110-328).

Prior to pursuing a refund offset to collect a covered unemployment compensation debt, a State is required to notify by certified mail with return receipt the person owing the debt that the State proposes to take action to collect the covered unemployment compensation debt by offset. The State must provide the person at least 60 days to present evidence that all or part of the liability is not legally enforceable or due to fraud. The State must consider any evidence presented and determine that an amount of the debt is legally enforceable and due to fraud (Code Sec. 6402(f)(4), as added by P.L. 110-328).

The authority to collect covered unemployment compensation debts does not apply to refunds payable after the date which is 10 years after September 30, 2008, the date of enactment of the SSI Extension for Elderly and Disabled Refugees Act (Code Sec. 6402(f)(8), as added by P.L. 110-328).

NEW LAW EXPLAINED

Authority to offset refunds to collect unemployment compensation debts modified.—For purposes of refund offsets to collect unemployment compensation debts on or after December 8, 2010, the definition of covered unemployment compensation debt is modified to include past-due debts of an individual for erroneous payment of unemployment due to failure to report earnings, as well as those due to fraud (Code Sec. 6402(f)(4)(A), as redesignated and amended by the Claims Resolution Act of 2010 (P.L. 111-291)). Thus, a covered unemployment compensation debt includes a past-due debt for erroneous payment of unemployment compensation due to a person's failure to report earnings which has become final under the law of a State certified by the Secretary of Labor pursuant to Code Sec. 3304.

Additionally, a covered unemployment compensation debt includes contributions due to a State's unemployment fund for which the State has determined the person to be liable, regardless of whether the liability is due to fraud. In either case, a covered unemployment compensation debt can include a debt that remains uncollected for more than 10 years (Code Sec. 6402(f)(4)(B), as redesignated and amended by the 2010 Claims Resolution Act).

For refunds payable on or after December 8, 2010, the limitation permitting an offset only against a resident of the State seeking the offset is eliminated (Act Sec. 801(a)(2) of the 2010 Claims Resolution Act, striking former Code Sec. 6402(f)(3)). Thus, an offset of an overpayment to collect a covered unemployment compensation debt will be allowed even if the taxpayer's federal tax return showing the overpayment lists an address outside of the State seeking the offset.

Additionally, the State seeking the offset is no longer required to give notice by certified mail with return receipt that it intends to pursue a refund offset to collect a covered unemployment compensation debt (Code Sec. 6402(f)(3), as redesignated and amended

NEW LAW EXPLAINED

by the 2010 Claims Resolution Act). However, prior to pursuing a refund offset a State is still required to notify the person owing the debt of the proposed action, and the State must provide the person at least 60 days to present evidence that all or part of the liability is not legally enforceable or is not a covered unemployment compensation debt. The State must consider any evidence presented and determine that an amount of the debt is legally enforceable and is a covered unemployment compensation debt. Further, the State must also satisfy any other conditions that the Secretary may prescribe to ensure that the State's determination is valid and that the State has made reasonable efforts to obtain payment of the debt (Code Sec. 6402(f)(3), as redesignated and amended by the 2010 Claims Resolution Act, and amended by the Tax Relief, Unemployment Insurance Reauthorization, and Job Creation Act of 2010 (P.L. 111-312)).

> **Comment:** Act Sec. 801(a)(3)(C) of the 2010 Claims Resolution Act, as enacted, required a State seeking an offset to determine that an amount the debt at issue is legally enforceable and **is not** a covered unemployment compensation debt. A technical amendment in the Tax Relief Act of 2010 clarifies that the State is required to determine that the debt is legally enforceable and **is** a covered unemployment compensation debt.

The termination provision which would have eliminated the authority to collect covered unemployment compensation debts as offsets against refunds payable after the date which is 10 years after September 30, 2008, the date of enactment of the SSI Extension for Elderly and Disabled Refugees Act (P.L. 110-238), has been stricken (Act Sec. 801(a)(2) of the Claims Resolution Act of 2010, striking former Code Sec. 6402(f)(8)). Therefore, absent further legislative changes, the authority to collect such debts will continue indefinitely.

▶   **Effective date.** The amendments apply to refunds payable under Code Sec. 6402 on or after December 8, 2010, the date of enactment (Act Sec. 801(b) of the Claims Resolution Act of 2010 (P.L. 111-291) and Act Sec. 503(b) of the Tax Relief, Unemployment Insurance Reauthorization, and Job Creation Act of 2010 (P.L. 111-312)).

Law source: Law at ¶5800.

— Act Sec. 801(a)(1) and (2) of the Claims Resolution Act of 2010 (P.L. 111-291), striking Code Sec. 6402(f)(3) and (8), and redesignating Code Sec. 6402(f)(4) through (7) as Code Sec. 6402(f)(3) through (6), respectively;

— Act Sec. 801(a)(3) and (4) of the Claims Resolution Act of 2010, amending Code Sec. 6402(f)(3) and (4), as redesignated;

— Act Sec. 503(a) of the Tax Relief, Unemployment Insurance Reauthorization, and Job Creation Act of 2010 (P.L. 111-312), amending Code Sec. 6402(f)(3)(C), as amended by the Claims Resolution Act of 2010;

— Act Sec. 801(b) of the Claims Resolution Act of 2010 and Act Sec. 503(b) of the Tax Relief Act of 2010, providing the effective date.

Reporter references: For further information, consult the following CCH reporters.

— Standard Federal Tax Reporter, ¶38,530.047

— Tax Research Consultant, IRS: 33,304.20

— Practical Tax Explanation, §40,015.05

¶384 Disregard of Tax Refunds for Determining Government Assistance Eligibility

SUMMARY OF NEW LAW

Federal tax refunds and advance payments of refundable credits are not taken into account as income, or as resources for a 12-month period after receipt, in determining an individual's eligibility for federal assistance or federally-financed State assistance. This treatment applies to amounts received in 2010, 2011 and 2012.

BACKGROUND

Individuals who seek government assistance are generally required to reveal to the assistance provider certain information about their income and assets. This allows the assistance provider to determine a particular person's eligibility for specific benefits sought, to better assure that government benefits are provided to individuals of the most limited means.

For example, the Supplemental Security Income program (SSI), which pays monthly benefits to people with limited income and resources who are disabled, blind, or age 65 or older, requires SSI applicants to provide details on the types of income they receive, as well as the resources they own. Certain types of income do not count for purposes of determining a person's eligibility for SSI, including income tax refunds. Similarly, certain resources do not count or are given special treatment in determining SSI eligibility. For example, earned income tax credit payments and child tax credit payments are not counted for nine months. (For more information, see http://www.ssa.gov/ssi/text-understanding-ssi.htm.)

Under the federal tax law, several refundable credits that qualifying individuals may receive are expressly not taken into account for purposes of determining an individual's eligibility for benefits or assistance under government programs. The Internal Revenue Code specifically provides that for purposes of the United States Housing Act of 1937, title V of the Housing Act of 1949, section 101 of the Housing and Urban Development Act of 1965, sections 221(d)(3), 235, and 236 of the National Housing Act, and the Food and Nutrition Act of 2008 (i.e., the food stamp program), any earned income tax credit (EITC) refund made to an individual or his or her spouse, and any advance EITC payment made to that individual or spouse by an employer under Code Sec. 3507, cannot be treated as income and cannot be taken into account in determining resources for the month of its receipt and the following month (Code Sec. 32(l)).

Any payment made to an individual pursuant to the child tax credit under Code Sec. 24 also cannot be taken into account as income and cannot not be taken into account as resources for the month of receipt and the following month, for purposes of determining the individual's eligibility (or that of any other individual) for benefits or assistance, or the amount or extent of benefits or assistance, under any federal program, or under any State or local program financed in whole or in part with

BACKGROUND

federal funds (Act Sec. 203 of the Economic Growth and Tax Relief Reconciliation Act of 2001 (EGTRRA) (P.L. 107-16)).

Restrictions similar to that affecting the child tax credit similarly limit the treatment of any credit or refund made to a person pursuant to the Making Work Pay Credit under Code Sec. 36A (Act Sec. 1001(c) of the American Recovery and Reinvestment Tax Act of 2009 (P.L. 111-5)), and the $250 credit for government retirees available for 2009 (Act Sec. 2202 of the Assistance for Unemployed Workers and Struggling Families Act (P.L. 111-5)). These credits or refunds cannot not be taken into account as resources for the month of receipt and the following two months.

NEW LAW EXPLAINED

Federal tax refunds disregarded for means-tested assistance programs.—Effective for amounts received after December 31, 2009, any federal tax refund, or advance payment with respect to a refundable federal tax credit, made to any individual cannot be taken into account as income, or as resources for a period of 12 months from receipt, for purposes of determining the individual's eligibility (or that of any other individual) for benefits or assistance, or for the amount or extent of benefits or assistance, under—

- any federal program, or
- any State or local program financed in whole or in part with federal funds (Code Sec. 6409(a), as added by the Tax Relief, Unemployment Insurance Reauthorization, and Job Creation Act of 2010 (P.L. 111-312)).

This treatment will not apply to any amount received after December 31, 2012 (Code Sec. 6409(b), as added by the Tax Relief Act of 2010).

> **Comment:** The new provision expressly applies "[n]otwithstanding any other provision of law." This would appear to mean that the provision overrides similar provisions in federal and state statutes and regulations regarding the treatment of federal tax refunds and refundable credits as they affect an individual's eligibility for government benefits and assistance.

> **Comment:** For tax years beginning after December 31, 2010, eligible individuals will no longer be able to request an advance payment of the earned income tax credit (Code Sec. 3507, repealed by the Education Jobs and Medicaid Assistance Act of 2010 (P.L. 111-226)).

▶ **Effective date.** This provision applies to amounts received after December 31, 2009 (Act Sec. 728(c) of the Tax Relief, Unemployment Insurance Reauthorization, and Job Creation Act of 2010 (P.L. 111-312)).

Law source: Law at ¶5805. Committee Report at ¶10,350.

— Act Sec. 728(a) of the Tax Relief, Unemployment Insurance Reauthorization, and Job Creation Act of 2010 (P.L. 111-312), adding Code Sec. 6409;

— Act Sec. 728(c), providing the effective date.

¶380

NEW LAW EXPLAINED

Reporter references: For further information, consult the following CCH reporters.

— Standard Federal Tax Reporter, ¶3770.03, ¶4082.05, ¶38,490.01
— Tax Research Consultant, INDIV: 57,264.05, INDIV: 57,454.10, IRS: 33,000
— Practical Tax Explanation, § 12,120.15, § 12,601, § 40,001

¶386 Estate Tax Treatment of Stock in Regulated Investment Companies

SUMMARY OF NEW LAW

The exclusion of a portion of the stock in a regulated investment company (RIC) from the gross estate of a nonresident alien, is extended for two years.

BACKGROUND

The value of the gross estate of a nonresident decedent who was not a citizen of the United States includes only the portion of the gross estate located in the United States (Code Sec. 2103). A portion of stock in a regulated investment company (RIC), commonly known as a mutual fund, that is owned by a nonresident, non-U.S. citizen, is treated as property located outside of the United States and is not includible in the estate of the person for federal estate tax purposes (Code Sec. 2105(d)(1)). The exempt amount is the proportion of the RIC's assets that were "qualifying assets" in relation to the total assets of the RIC. Qualifying assets are assets that, if owned directly by the decedent, would have been:

- bank deposits that are exempt from income tax;

- portfolio debt obligations;

- certain original issue discount (OID) obligations;

- debt obligations of a U.S. corporation that are treated as giving rise to foreign source income; and

- other property not within the United States (Code Sec. 2105(d)(2)).

The provision relating to stock in a RIC applies to the estates of nonresident noncitizens dying after December 31, 2004, and before January 1, 2010 (Code Sec. 2105(d)(3)).

NEW LAW EXPLAINED

Favorable estate tax treatment of RIC stock extended.—The favorable estate tax treatment afforded a portion of stock in a regulated investment company (RIC) that is owned by a nonresident, non-U.S. citizen, is extended for two years. Specifically, stock

NEW LAW EXPLAINED

of a RIC is not deemed property located within the United States in the proportion that the assets held by the RIC are debt obligations, deposits, or other property that would be treated as situated outside the United States if held directly by the estate. With the two-year extension, the provision now applies to the estates of nonresident, non-U.S. citizens, dying after December 31, 2004, and before January 1, 2012 (Code Sec. 2105(d)(3), as amended by the Tax Relief, Unemployment Insurance Reauthorization, and Job Creation Act of 2010 (P.L. 111-312)).

▶ **Effective date.** This provision applies to the estates of decedents dying after December 31, 2009 (Act Sec. 726(b) of the Tax Relief, Unemployment Insurance Reauthorization, and Job Creation Act of 2010 (P.L. 111-312)).

Law source: Law at ¶10,330. Committee Report at ¶10,330.

— Act Sec. 726(a) of the Tax Relief, Unemployment Insurance Reauthorization, and Job Creation Act of 2010 (P.L. 111-312), amending Code Sec. 2105(d)(3);

— Act Sec. 726(b), providing the effective date.

Reporter references: For further information, consult the following CCH reporters.

— Tax Research Consultant, ESTGIFT: 60,150

— Practical Tax Explanation, § 35,005.10

— Federal Estate and Gift Tax Reporter, ¶7975.11

¶388 Indian Money Account Litigation Settlement

SUMMARY OF NEW LAW

Amounts received by an Native American Indian individual as part of the approved settlement of a class action lawsuit filed against the Federal government for mismanagement of individual Indian trust accounts and trusts are excluded from the individual's gross income.

BACKGROUND

Gross income of a taxpayer includes items of income from any source and in any form (Code Sec. 61(a); Reg. § 1.61-1(a)). Thus, such common items as wages, tips, profit earned by a business, interest from savings and other bank accounts, dividends, and profit from the sale or exchange of property are generally treated as gross income, unless different treatment is specifically provided in the Code or regulations (Reg. § 1.61-1(b)). For example, a taxpayer may exclude from gross income amounts received as damages in a suit or settlement for personal injuries or sickness (Code Sec. 104(a)(2)).

The Code and regulations do not exempt a Native American Indian from the payment of income taxes. However, certain types of income received by an individ-

BACKGROUND

ual member of an Indian tribe may be excluded from gross income. For example, income derived from protected fishing activities (fishing rights-related activities) is exempt from federal and state income taxation, as well Social Security and unemployment compensation insurance taxes (Code Sec. 7873). Similarly, income derived directly from allotted and restricted Indian lands held by the United States as trustee under Sec. 5 of the General Allotment Act of 1887 (24 Stat. 388) is exempt from taxation (Rev. Rul. 67-284). This includes rentals (including crop rentals), royalties, proceeds of sales of the natural resources on the land, income from the sale of crops grown on the land, and income from the use of the land for grazing purposes.

NEW LAW EXPLAINED

Settlement payments excluded from gross income.—A proposed settlement has been approved in a class action lawsuit filed against the Federal government for mismanagement of individual Indian trust accounts and trusts (Act Sec. 101(c) of the Claims Resolution Act of 2010 (P.L. 111-291)). The individual Indian trust accounts relate to land, oil, natural gas, mineral, timber, grazing, water and other resources and rights on or under individual Indian lands.

Under the terms of the settlement, amounts received by an individual Indian as a lump sum or periodic payment as a result of the settlement and paid through the appropriate trust funds will not be included in the individual's gross income (Act Sec. 101(f) of the 2010 Claims Resolution Act). In addition, any payment received will not be taken into consideration for purposes of applying any provision of the Code that takes into account excludible income in computing adjusted gross income (AGI) or modified adjusted gross income (AGI).

> **Comment:** For purposes of determining eligibility under any Federal assisted program, the amounts received will not be treated as income for the month during which the amounts were received or as a resource during the one-year period beginning on the date of receipt.

▶ **Effective date.** No effective date is provided by the Act. The provision, therefore, is considered effective on December 8, 2010, the date of enactment.

Law source: Committee Report at ¶10,960.

— Act Sec. 101(f) of the Claims Resolution Act of 2010 (P.L. 111-291).

Reporter references: For further information, consult the following CCH reporters.

— Standard Federal Tax Reporter, ¶5504.01

— Tax Research Consultant, INDIV: 33,050

— Practical Tax Explanation, §3,001

¶388

Capital Gains, Dividends, and Investment

4

CAPITAL GAINS

¶405   Maximum Capital Gains Rates

¶410   Five-Year Holding Period for Capital Assets

¶415   Tax Preference Items: Excluded Gain on Sale of Small Business Stock

¶418   Exclusion of Gain from Sale of Qualified Small Business Stock

DIVIDENDS

¶420   Qualified Dividends Received by Individuals, Estates and Trusts

¶425   Pass-Through Treatment of Qualified Dividend Income

¶430   Tax Treatment of Regulated Investment Company Dividends Paid to Foreign Persons

COMMUNITY ASSISTANCE

¶440   Empowerment Zone Tax Benefits

¶445   District of Columbia Enterprise Zone Tax Incentives

¶450   GO Zone Tax Incentives

TAX-EXEMPT BONDS

¶455   School Construction Bonds

¶460   Exempt Facility Bonds

¶465   Qualified Zone Academy Bonds

¶470   New York Liberty Bonds

CAPITAL GAINS

¶405 Maximum Capital Gains Rates

SUMMARY OF NEW LAW

The reduced maximum capital gains rate of 15 percent on adjusted net capital gain of noncorporate taxpayers (for regular tax and AMT purposes), and the zero percent capital gains rate on adjusted net capital gain of noncorporate taxpayers in the 10-percent or 15-percent income tax bracket, which were scheduled to expire for tax years beginning after December 31, 2010, under the sunset provisions of JGTRRA, have been extended to apply to tax years 2011 and 2012.

BACKGROUND

For tax years ending on or after May 6, 2003, the Jobs and Growth Tax Relief Reconciliation Act of 2003 (JGTRRA) (P.L. 108-27) reduced the maximum tax rate on the adjusted net capital gain of noncorporate taxpayers from 20 percent to 15 percent. The 15-percent rate applies to that portion of adjusted net capital gain that, were it *non-capital* gain, would be taxed at an income tax rate of at least 25 percent. Similarly, for tax years ending on or after May 6, 2003, JGTRRA reduced the tax rate on the adjusted net capital gain of noncorporate taxpayers from 10 percent to five percent to that portion of adjusted net capital gain that, were it *non-capital* gain, would be taxed at an income tax rate of rate below 25 percent (that is, at the 10-or 15-percent rate). Under JGTRRA, as amended by the Tax Increase Prevention and Reconciliation Act of 2005 (P.L. 109-222), the five-percent tax rate was reduced to zero for tax years 2008 through 2010.

> **Comment:** Adjusted net capital gain is net capital gain from capital assets held for more than one year *other than* collectibles gain and unrecaptured Code Sec. 1250 gain, which carry their own rates (Code Sec. 1(h)(3)).

> **Comment:** JGTRRA did not institute an overall reduction in maximum long-term capital gain rates. For example, it left unchanged the 28-percent rate imposed on net long-term gain from collectibles and net gain from small business stock, as well as the maximum 25-percent rate on unrecaptured Code Sec. 1250 gain.

Prior to JGTRRA, which ushered in the rate reduction on adjusted net capital gain, capital gains on the sale or exchange of assets got a break from the 20-percent or 10-percent rate if the assets were held more than five years. Specifically, the 20-percent tax rate was reduced to 18 percent for qualified five-year gain. And the 10-percent rate (which applied to adjusted net capital gain that would otherwise have fallen into a tax bracket below 25 percent) was reduced to eight percent. But for tax years ending on or after May 6, 2003, the lower rates for qualified five-year gain are not applicable (see ¶410).

BACKGROUND

Comment: Since JGTRRA lowered the general maximum capital gains tax rate to 15 percent (five percent for taxpayers in the 10-percent and 15-percent income tax brackets), it was not necessary to have special rules for five-year property.

Dividend income. Under JGTRRA, the tax rate on dividend income is the same as the tax rate on adjusted net capital gains (see ¶420). Thus, under JGTRRA, the maximum tax rate on qualified dividends is 15 percent for tax years beginning on or before December 31, 2010. The rate for dividends that would otherwise fall into the 10-percent or 15-percent income tax bracket is zero (Code Sec. 1(h)(11)).

Alternative minimum tax. For noncorporate taxpayers, the maximum tax rates on adjusted net capital gain of 15 percent and zero percent are the same for the alternative minimum tax (AMT) as for the regular income tax (Code Sec. 55(b)(3)(B) and (C)).

Comment: The amount of the AMT on adjusted net capital gain may, however, differ from the amount under the regular income tax because, for example, of a difference in the basis for regular tax and AMT purposes.

Withholding by domestic partnerships, estates and trusts. Under Code Sec. 1445(e)(1), if a domestic partnership, trust, or estate disposes of a U.S. real property interest and any partner, beneficiary, or substantial owner of the entity is a foreign person, the partnership or fiduciary must withhold tax with respect to that foreign person. The amount that must be withheld is 35 percent of any amount over which the partnership or fiduciary has custody.

Under JGTRRA, for amounts paid after May 28, 2003, the IRS may, by regulation, reduce the amount of income tax required to be withheld on a foreign person's gain from the disposition of an interest in U.S. real property to 15 percent (rather than the 35 percent specified by the Internal Revenue Code) (Code Sec. 1445(e)(1)).

Nonqualified withdrawals of construction funds established under the Merchant Marine Act. Under JGTRRA, the maximum tax rate imposed on individuals who make nonqualified withdrawals from the capital gain account of a capital construction fund established under the Merchant Marine Act is 15 percent (Code Sec. 7518(g)(6)(A) and Act Sec. 607(h)(6)(A) of the Merchant Marine Act of 1936).

Comment: Prior to JGTRRA, the applicable tax rate imposed on individuals who made nonqualified withdrawals from the capital gain account of a capital construction fund established under the Merchant Marine Act was 20 percent.

Sunset provision. Under a sunset provision of JGTRRA, certain amendments made by the Act will not apply to tax years beginning after December 31, 2010 (Act. Sec. 303 of P.L. 108-27, as amended by Act Sec. 102 of P.L. 109-222).

NEW LAW EXPLAINED

Reduced rates for capital gain extended.—The reduced maximum capital gains rate of 15 percent on adjusted net capital gain of noncorporate taxpayers (for regular tax and AMT purposes) and the zero percent capital gains rate on adjusted net capital gain of noncorporate taxpayers in the 10-percent or 15-percent income tax bracket (Code Sec. 1(h)(1)(B) and Code Sec. 55(b)(3)(C)), have been extended for two years and will apply

¶405

NEW LAW EXPLAINED

to the 2011 and 2012 tax years (Act Sec. 102(a) of the Tax Relief, Unemployment Insurance Reauthorization, and Job Creation Act of 2010 (P.L. 111-312)). Thus, for tax years beginning in 2013, the maximum rate on adjusted net capital gain of noncorporate taxpayers will generally return to 20 percent, and to 10 percent for taxpayers in the 15-percent income tax bracket.

A separate change will apply to the tax rate on dividend income. The capital gain tax rates on qualified dividends received by individuals, trusts, or estates will not apply to tax years beginning after December 31, 2012 (Act Sec. 303 of P.L. 108-27, as amended by Act Sec. 102 of P.L. 109-222 and Act. Sec. 102(a) of the Tax Relief Act of 2010). Therefore, for tax years beginning in 2013, such dividends will be taxed at the applicable ordinary income tax rates (see ¶ 420).

> **Planning Note:** In light of the increased rates on adjusted net capital gain in 2013, parents may start to steer clear of having their child hold assets directly in his or her own name. Instead, parents may shift to other tax-favored savings vehicles, such as Code Sec. 529 plans and Coverdell Education Savings Accounts.

> **Planning Note:** The higher capital gains rates should be carefully considered when planning employee compensation in the form of stock for services, employee stock options, and in particular, incentive stock options.

Qualified five-year gain. Under the sunset provisions of JGTRRA and the Tax Relief Act of 2010, the special tax rate break for assets held for more than five years will not be reinstated for two years. Thus, for tax years beginning after December 31, 2012, an 18-percent rate will be imposed on five-year gain that otherwise would be taxed at the 20-percent maximum rate. Similarly, the 10-percent rate will be reduced to eight percent for five-year gain for taxpayers in the 15-percent income tax bracket (Code Sec. 1(h)(2) and (h)(9), repealed by Act Sec. 301 of JGTRRA, P.L. 108-27) (see ¶410).

Withholding by domestic partnerships, estates and trusts. Under the sunset provision of JGTRRA and the extension by the Tax Relief Act of 2010, for amounts paid after December 31, 2012, the IRS may, by regulation, reduce the amount of income tax required to be withheld on a foreign person's gain from the disposition of an interest in U.S. real property to 20 percent (rather than the 15-percent lower limit prior to the sunset provision taking effect) (Code Sec. 1445(e)(1)).

Nonqualified withdrawals of construction funds established under the Merchant Marine Act. Under the sunset provision of JGTRRA and the extension by the Tax Relief Act of 2010, the maximum tax rate imposed on individuals who make nonqualified withdrawals from the capital gain account of a capital construction fund established under the Merchant Marine Act will return to 20 percent in 2012 (up from 15 percent prior to the extended sunset provision taking place) (Code Sec. 7518(g)(6)(A)).

> **Practical Analysis:** According to Vincent O'Brien, President of Vincent J. O'Brien, CPA, PC, Lynbrook, New York, the extension of the lower capital gains rate for individuals (Code Sec. 1) for the 2011 and 2012 tax years will maintain the 15 percent rate that generally applies to long-term capital gains, instead of the 20

¶405

NEW LAW EXPLAINED

percent rate that generally would have applied under the original expiration date of The Jobs and Growth Tax Relief Reconciliation Act of 2003 (JGTRRA) (P.L. 108-27). (Special rates apply to gains from the sale of depreciable realty, collectibles, and Code Sec. 1202 small business stock.)

Those who have entered into installment sales prior to January 1, 2011 will benefit from this extension, since they are subject to whatever capital gain rate is in effect on the date on which they collect proceeds and recognize gains from those installment sales. Even if the capital gain rate in effect on the date of the sale differs, it is the rate in effect at the time of collection that determines the amount of tax due.

For this reason, such taxpayers would have been subject to a higher rate on gains recognized from collections of installment sales during 2011 and 2012.

Practical Analysis: Jasper L. Cummings, Jr., Alston & Bird LLP, Raleigh, N.C., observes that the reduced rates for long-term capital gains and dividends are now scheduled to expire as a result of the 2010 Act at the end of 2012 rather than at the end of 2010. Beginning on January 1, 2013, individual taxpayers will face somewhat higher rates on long-term capital gains recognized and substantially higher rates on dividends received (taxed as ordinary income). The differential for capital gains is not huge but sufficient to require planning if the gross amounts involved are large enough.

Obviously the acceleration of recognition of gains and receipt of dividends into the pre-2013 period is desirable if possible. This may require identifying capital assets as such, determining a long-term holding period, and insuring the occurrence of a sale or exchange or receipt of a dividend before 2013. However, planning over the next two years can be done in a relatively leisurely manner compared with planning to recognize gains or dividends within 2010, which would have been desirable if the sunset had not been extended. Many footfaults can occur in trying to effect transactions at year end. The payment of a dividend requires payment by the corporation out of earnings and profits, of which some C corporations are short as a result of recent economic problems. S corporations need not be concerned with their own dividends, but to the extent they receive dividends or can earn capital gains, they similarly must plan for passthrough gains and dividends to benefit their shareholders.

Shareholders considering a sale of their stock (or other capital assets) to accelerate gain recognition must consider the offsetting benefits of holding onto stock or other capital assets until death, in order to afford heirs the tax-free basis step-up at death, now that the estate tax and the basis step-up at death have also been reinstated temporarily. But if the taxpayer has capital losses that it has not been able to deduct due to the unavailability of capital gains, the rate increase on capital gains will make the capital losses more valuable after 2012. That is, offsetting a loss against a gain that would be taxed at 15 percent is not as useful as offsetting it against the gain that would be taxed at 20 percent.

As to dividends, the increased rate (the ordinary income rate) may affect corporate behavior after 2010 in issuing dividends and offering stock redemption plans, but likely not much. Studies have shown that the reduction of the rates earlier did not

¶405

NEW LAW EXPLAINED

necessarily spur a great increase in dividends, although it is thought that the presence of foreign shareholders may have spurred the use of redemption plans. The foreign shareholders will not be taxed at all on a capital gain in a U.S. asset, and generally non–*pro rata* stock redemptions produce capital gain to the shareholders as opposed to dividends.

Practical Analysis: Michael J. Grace, Milbank, Tweed, Hadley & McCloy LLP, Washington, D.C., observes that Code Secs. 1(h)(1) (regular tax) and 55(b)(3) (alternative minimum tax) subject adjusted net capital gains of noncorporate taxpayers to a maximum income tax rate of 15 percent. These provisions had been scheduled to sunset for tax years beginning after December 31, 2010, under Section 303 of the Jobs and Growth Tax Reconciliation Act of 2003 (JGTRRA) (P.L. 108-27), as amended by Section 102 of the Tax Increase Prevention and Reconciliation Act of 2005 (TIPRA) (P.L. 109-222). However, Section 102 of the Tax Relief, Unemployment Insurance Reauthorization, and Job Creation Act of 2010 (2010 Tax Relief Act) has extended the preferential rates for an additional two years. Now, the maximum tax rate of 15 percent on net capital gains is scheduled to sunset for tax years beginning after December 31, 2012. Because individuals generally use the calendar year as their taxable years, these preferential rates will continue to apply essentially for tax years 2011 and 2012. Beginning in 2013, absent intervening legislation, applicable rates will revert to those predating JGTRRA. Thus, noncorporate taxpayers beginning in 2013 will be subject to tax on net capital gains at a maximum rate of 20 percent (18 percent for qualified five-year gain).

Importance of Planning for Two Separate Time Periods. In view of the 2010 Tax Relief Act's having temporarily extended the maximum rate of 15 percent, individuals in planning for the taxation of capital gains should think in terms of two separate periods of time: (i) 2011-2012 and (ii) after 2012. Planning should address various issues including forms of holding investments and timing of selling decisions. Planning for capital gains should consider factors besides taxes including economic and investment objectives.

Continuing Long-Term Uncertainty. The political posturing that delayed until late December 2010 the agreement to extend the maximum 15 percent rate had prompted some taxpayers to take actions earlier in the year that some in hindsight may regret. Anticipating that tax rates on capital gains might increase after 2010, some taxpayers sold and locked in gains on investments that absent tax considerations they would have retained. Those types of choices highlight the risks of trying to predict future tax rates. Taxpayers in the wake of the 2010 Tax Relief Act now run the risk that the rates scheduled to take effect after 2012 may be further postponed or changed. Subject to these risks, tax advisers and taxpayers might consider the following planning ideas for the indicated tax years.

Taxable Years Through 2012

Forms of Holding Investments. Through the end of 2012, individuals when possible should continue to make choices that JGTRRA suggested. They should consider holding in taxable accounts investments on which they anticipate recognizing capital

¶405

NEW LAW EXPLAINED

gains by the end of 2012. Capital gains recognized through 2012 and not sheltered by capital losses will be subject to a maximum tax rate of 15 percent. Beginning in 2013 those same gains are scheduled to be taxable at rates up to 20 percent.

Timing of Selling Decisions. During 2011 and 2012 individuals should consider accelerating and recognizing capital gains that they do not anticipate sheltering with capital losses. Unsheltered capital gains will be subject to tax at a maximum rate of 15 percent compared to the rate of 20 percent scheduled to take effect in 2013. Additionally, beginning in 2013 upper-income individuals are scheduled to be subject to increased Medicare taxes on net investment income including capital gains. During these years individuals also should consider postponing transactions that would harvest capital losses. After 2012, absent Congressional action, recognized losses will have a comparatively higher value because they will be able to offset recognized capital gains otherwise taxable at increased rates.

Disposition Planning Under Federal Estate Tax Election (2010). The temporary extension of preferential income tax rates on net capital gains may influence a testamentary transferee's planning for disposing of property inherited from a decedent who died in 2010. The Economic Growth and Tax Relief Reconciliation Act (EGTRRA) repealed the federal estate tax for decedents dying during 2010. The 2010 Tax Relief Act amends and reinstates the federal estate tax for estates of decedents dying after 2009. However, estates of individuals who died during 2010 may elect to apply in lieu of the reinstated rules the estate tax under EGTRRA. See Section 301 of the 2010 Tax Relief Act and Temporary Estate Tax Relief. Under EGTRRA no estate tax is imposed for 2010, but transferees take a modified carryover basis in property acquired from a decedent. This basis equals the lesser of the decedent's adjusted basis or the property's fair market value on the date of the decedent's death. In general, and subject to special rules and exceptions, an executor under EGTRRA may increase the basis in transferred assets by a total of $1.3 million applicable to all transferred property plus particular categories of a decedent's tax losses, if any. The 2010 Tax Relief Act reinstates the federal estate tax at a maximum rate of 35 percent of a taxable estate's value exceeding an applicable exclusion amount of $5 million. However, transferees of property from decedents take a basis in transferred property equaling its fair market value upon either the date of the decedent's death or an alternate valuation date. If, for example, a transferred property's fair market value on the selected date exceeds the decedent's basis in the property, then the transferee obtains a "stepped up" basis. An executor's choice between the available estate tax regimes for 2010 may affect as follows a transferee's planning for disposing of inherited property. Assume that the estate of a decedent who died in 2010 elects to apply the federal estate tax under EGTRRA. The estate thus is not subject to federal estate tax, but a transferee of property from the estate takes a modified carryover basis in the property. Assume also that were the estate instead subject to the estate tax as amended and reinstated by the 2010 Tax Relief Act, the transferee would have taken a stepped-up basis in the transferred property exceeding the modified carryover basis. The transferee thus can anticipate recognizing a higher capital gain (or a smaller capital loss) upon eventually selling the transferred property compared to the transferee having enjoyed a stepped-up basis. Assume also that the transferee does not anticipate

NEW LAW EXPLAINED

having capital losses to shelter capital gain upon selling the inherited property. The transferee might consider selling the carryover basis property before 2013 when the tax rates on net capital gains are scheduled to increase.

Coordination with Investment Interest Limitation. Under Code Sec. 1(h)(2), net capital gain eligible for the maximum rate of 15 percent will continue not to include gains that a taxpayer elects to treat as investment income under Code Sec. 163(d)(4)(B)(iii). Net investment income measures the amount of investment interest expense a noncorporate taxpayer currently may deduct. Capital gains that a taxpayer elects to treat as investment income will continue to be taxable at generally applicable marginal rates.

Taxable Years After 2012

Forms of Holding Investments. Starting in 2013, individuals should consider holding in tax-deferred accounts such as 401(k)s and IRAs positions that they may have held in taxable accounts based on JGTRRA. The higher the rate at which recognized (and unsheltered) capital gains would have been taxed had the sold property been held in a taxable account, the higher the value of tax deferral. The Code, however, limits the amounts that individuals annually may contribute to tax-deferred accounts. Additionally, the Code narrowly restricts opportunities to transfer an existing investment to a tax-deferred account without recognizing taxable gain. In choosing forms of holding investments, individuals also should consider the rates at which amounts they eventually withdraw from a tax-deferred account may be taxed. Amounts eventually withdrawn from a tax-deferred account may end up being taxed at rates exceeding the rates at which capital gains earlier recognized in a taxable account would have been taxed. Nevertheless, if the investor does not plan to start withdrawing funds anytime soon, then the present value of the projected tax on amounts eventually withdrawn from a tax deferred account may prove attractive. Starting in 2013, scheduled increases in Medicare taxes on taxable investment income including capital gains also may make tax-deferred accounts more attractive.

Timing of Selling Decisions. Starting in 2013, individuals should consider postponing events that would require them to recognize capital gains until either the individual has sufficient capital losses to shelter the gains or Congress, seeking to stimulate the economy out of a future recession, again reduces tax rates on capital gains. Individuals should harvest capital losses as needed in order to shelter capital gains otherwise taxable at the increased rates scheduled to apply beginning in 2013.

Coordination with Investment Interest Limitation. Under Code Sec. 1(h)(2), net capital gain eligible for the maximum rate of 20 percent will continue not to include gains that a taxpayer elects to treat as investment income under Code Sec. 163(d)(4)(B)(iii). Net investment income measures the amount of investment interest expense a noncorporate taxpayer currently may deduct. Code Sec. 1(h)(2) predates EGTRRA and JGTRRA. Consequently, the rule will survive their scheduled sunsetting, and capital gains that a taxpayer elects to treat as investment income will continue to be taxable at generally applicable marginal rates.

Importance of Maintaining Parity in Rates Between Dividends and Capital Gains. Even if a future Congress does not act further to extend JGTRRA's rates beyond 2012, it is urged that the Code continue to tax at the same rates noncorporate

¶405

NEW LAW EXPLAINED

taxpayers' dividends and capital gains. For example, if after 2012 capital gains become taxable at 20 percent as scheduled, then the Code should be amended also to tax dividends at 20 percent. Otherwise, dividends beginning in 2013 will become taxable at the marginal rates applicable to ordinary income. For many if not most individuals, that marginal rate will exceed 20 percent. During 2010, one or more bills were introduced in Congress to preserve the parity in rates advocated here. The 2010 Act's temporarily extending JGTRRA's preferential rates on capital gains and dividends rendered such action unnecessary for now. However, the issue will resurface as 2013 approaches. Economically, dividends and capital gains represent merely different ways of earning a return on an investment. Taxing dividends and capital gains at different rates would distort their economic equivalence. From a tax perspective, dividends and capital gains differ primarily in that in measuring recognizable capital gain a taxpayer offsets adjusted basis in the sold property. It would seem counterintuitive to tax income net of a basis offset (capital gains) at a lower rate than the rate on income not similarly offset (dividends). The tax rate on dividends also should be constrained in order to mitigate the sting of corporate double taxation. Some argue that dividends received and interest received should be taxable at the same rates. Otherwise, the argument goes, the Code artificially favors one form of corporate financing over the other. When, however, one considers all the tax consequences of a corporation's paying a dividend compared to paying interest, the argument fails to withstand scrutiny. Corporations in determining their taxable income may not deduct dividends they pay their shareholders. By contrast, corporations subject to applicable limitations can deduct interest paid to debt holders. In order to mitigate the consequences of this distinction, the rate at which dividends received are subject to tax should be kept meaningfully lower than the rates applicable to interest received.

Practical Analysis: Mark R. Solomon, Walsh College, Troy, Michigan, notes that Sections 101 and 102 of the Tax Relief, Unemployment Insurance Reauthorization, and Jobs Creation Act of 2010 (2010 Tax Relief Act) have extended until December 31, 2012, the tax relief provisions of the Economic Growth and Tax Reconciliation Act of 2001 (EGTRRA) and the Jobs and Growth Tax Reconciliation Act of 2003 (JGTRRA) (P.L. 108-27). Among other things, this extension has the effect of maintaining the status quo as to capital gains.

Code Sections 1(h)(1)(B) and 55(b)(3)(C), providing for reduced capital gains rates for individuals of zero and 15 percent, have been extended through December 31, 2012. For taxpayers with net capital gains in 2011 or 2012, this is a most favorable development. Thus, it is business as usual for capital gains. Taxpayers should carefully time their capital gains and losses and their capital loss carryforwards. Caution should be exercised in 2012, as the favorable capital gains rates are set to expire at the end of that year. However, careful tax planning may be able to reduce the adverse effects of the new rates scheduled to appear in 2013 (if Congress does not extend the current favorable rates). Taxpayers could, for example, sell their capital gains items in 2012 and delay the sale of capital loss items until after 2012 when they could be used to offset higher-taxed post-2012 capital gains. Starting in

NEW LAW EXPLAINED

2013 taxpayers should also consider delaying capital gains until they qualify for the 8 or 18 percent rates that are then scheduled to apply to investments held for at least five years (as opposed to the rates of 10 or 20 percent). Another possibility is for taxpayers holding relatively short term installment notes or obligations to trigger reporting of an installment sale capital gain in 2012 by perhaps factoring the note or obligation or taking some other action that will accelerate the unreported gain. Taxpayers should also note that with the increase in capital gain rates starting in 2013, there is an increased premium on making charitable contributions of appreciated capital assets, rather than of cash. Taxpayers subject to the investment interest limitation of Code Sec. 163(j) are perhaps a little more likely in 2013 to consider electing (on Form 4952) to include their capital gains as investment income to achieve a larger investment interest deduction at a cost of paying a 28 percent capital gains tax instead of the 20 percent capital gains tax scheduled to go into effect after 2012.

Aging or ill taxpayers should give increased consideration to holding investments until death when their heirs will get a step-up in basis, now that the 2010 Tax Relief Act has fully restored the step-up in basis at death rules, thus potentially avoiding a life-time tax at whatever capital gain rates apply in the year of death. Taxpayers are cautioned not to let the tax-tail wag the economic-dog. All of the above tax reduction techniques involve economic risk as well as time value of money consequences that should be carefully weighed and evaluated. Taxpayers are also cautioned that the 2010 Tax Relief Act does not reduce the capital gains rates on collectibles (28 percent) or on unrecaptured Code Sec. 1250 gain (25 percent).

▶ **Effective date.** These provisions generally apply to tax years ending on or after May 6, 2003 (Act Sec. 102(b) of the Tax Relief, Unemployment Insurance Reauthorization, and Job Creation Act of 2010 (P.L. 111-312)). However, the provision concerning the 15-percent withholding rate on certain payments made by domestic partnerships, estates, and trusts to foreign persons applies to amounts paid after May 28, 2003 (Act Sec. 301(d)(2) of the Jobs and Growth Tax Relief Reconciliation Act of 2003 (P.L. 108-27)).

Law source: Law at ¶5005, ¶5170, ¶5595, ¶5855, and ¶7015. Committee Report at ¶10,080.

— Act Sec. 102(a) of the Tax Relief, Unemployment Insurance Reauthorization, and Job Creation Act of 2010 (P.L. 111-312), amending Act Sec. 303 of the Jobs and Growth Relief Reconciliation Act of 2003 (P.L. 109-27);

— Act Sec. 102(b), providing the effective date.

Reporter references: For further information, consult the following CCH reporters.

— Standard Federal Tax Reporter, ¶3285.01

— Tax Research Consultant, SALES: 15,200, FILEIND: 15,054.15 and PLANIND: 12,208.40

— Practical Tax Explanation, § 16,525.10

¶405

¶410 Five-Year Holding Period for Capital Assets

SUMMARY OF NEW LAW

Gains from the disposition of certain property held by individuals for more than five years will continue to be taxed in a manner similar to other long-term capital gains, without special treatment, effective for tax years beginning in 2011 and 2012. The maximum rate applicable to long-term capital gain from sales of such five-year property will remain at 15 percent (zero percent for individuals with taxable income in the 10- or 15-percent tax brackets) during that period. This treatment will not apply for tax years beginning after December 31, 2012.

BACKGROUND

The Jobs and Growth Tax Relief Reconciliation Act of 2003 (JGTRRA) (P.L. 108-27) removed special lower capital gain tax rates that were available for "qualified five-year gain" of individuals, estates and trusts (Code Sec. 1(h)(2) and (9)). The lower rates — eight percent for taxpayers in a 10-percent or 15-percent income tax bracket, and 18 percent for taxpayers in higher brackets — applied to capital gain on assets held for more than five years. Additionally, these stricken provisions no longer applied in computing the alternative minimum tax liability of a noncorporate taxpayer (Code Sec. 55(b)(3)).

JGTRRA also lowered the maximum capital gain tax rates on "other" capital gain (i.e., gain that is not collectible gain, gain on qualified small business stock equal to the exclusion under Code Sec. 1202, or unrecaptured Code Sec. 1250 gain). The 20-percent capital gain tax rate was reduced to 15 percent, and the 10-percent capital gain tax rate for taxpayers in the 15- or 10-percent income tax brackets was reduced to five percent (zero percent for these taxpayers after 2007) (Code Sec. 1(h)(1)). Thus, it was unnecessary to have special rules for qualified five-year property with tax rates (18 percent, eight percent) that were higher than JGTRRA's new lower capital gain rates (15 percent, five percent). Further, the JGTRRA capital gain rates generally apply to assets held under the normal holding period rules, which means that a capital gain is "long term" if the capital asset is held for more than one year (see Code Secs. 1(h) and 1222(3)).

Sunset provision. Under a sunset provision of JGTRRA, certain amendments made by the Act will not apply to tax years beginning after December 31, 2010 (Act Sec. 303 of the Jobs and Growth Tax Relief Reconciliation Act of 2003 (P.L. 108-27), as amended by Act Sec. 102 of the Tax Increase Prevention and Reconciliation Act of 2005 (P.L. 109-222)).

NEW LAW EXPLAINED

Return of reduced capital gain rate for qualified five-year gain delayed two years.—The sunset provision of the Jobs and Growth Tax Relief Reconciliation Act of 2003 (JGTRRA) has been extended for two years (Act Sec. 303 of the Jobs and Growth

NEW LAW EXPLAINED

Tax Relief Reconciliation Act of 2003 (P.L. 108-27), as amended by Act Sec. 102 of the Tax Increase Prevention and Reconciliation Act of 2005 (P.L. 109-222), and by Act Sec. 102 of the Tax Relief, Unemployment Insurance Reauthorization, and Job Creation Act of 2010 (P.L. 111-312)). Accordingly, there will be no special capital gain treatment in 2011 or 2012 for property held for more than five years. The maximum rate applicable to long-term capital gain under current law will remain at 15 percent (zero percent for individuals with taxable income in the 10- or 15-percent tax brackets) for tax years beginning after December 31, 2010, and before January 1, 2013 (Code Sec. 1(h)(1)). The reduced rates under current law apply to individuals, estates, and trusts for sales of capital assets that are held for more than 12 months, and apply for both regular income tax and alternative minimum tax (AMT) purposes (see ¶ 405).

Treatment of qualified five-year gain after 2012, generally. Lower capital gain rates for qualified five-year gain of individuals, estates, and trusts (Code Sec. 1(h)(2) and (9), prior to being stricken by P.L. 108-27) will apply for tax years beginning after December 31, 2012, under the sunset provision of JGTRRA as extended by the Tax Relief Act of 2010 (Act Sec. 303 of P.L. 108-27, as amended by Act Sec. 102 of P.L. 109-222, and by Act Sec. 102 of the Tax Relief Act of 2010). Thus, long-term capital gain on the sale or exchange of property held more than five years will generally be taxed at 18 percent. The capital gain rate for such property will be eight percent for taxpayers in the 15-percent income tax bracket.

> **Comment:** The sunset provision of the Economic Growth and Tax Relief Reconciliation Act of 2001 (EGTRRA) (P.L. 107-16) will eliminate the 10-percent income tax bracket (for ordinary income), thereby making the 15-percent income tax bracket the lowest bracket after 2012 (see ¶305). Additionally, the JGTRRA sunset provision will restore the maximum capital gain tax rate to 20 percent (10 percent for taxpayers in the 15-percent income tax bracket) (see ¶405).

"Qualified five-year gain" in tax years beginning after December 31, 2012 is the aggregate amount of long-term capital gain that would be computed for the tax year if only gain from the sale or exchange of property held by the taxpayer for more than five years is taken into account. Gain from collectibles, unrecaptured Code Sec. 1250 gain, and gain from the sale of qualified small business stock under Code Sec. 1202 is not taken into account and, accordingly, is not eligible for the lower capital gain rates that apply to qualified five-year gain (Code Sec. 1(h)(9), prior to being stricken by P.L. 108-27).

Rate calculation. The special eight-percent capital gain rate for qualified five-year gain in tax years beginning after December 31, 2012 will apply to the amount of adjusted net capital gain that otherwise would be taxed at the 10-percent capital gain rate under Code Sec. 1(h)(1)(B) (see ¶405), but not in excess of total qualified five-year gain. The 10-percent rate will apply to the remainder of any adjusted net capital gain that is subject to the 10-percent capital gain rate (Code Sec. 1(h)(2)(A), prior to being stricken by P.L. 108-27).

> **Comment:** The 10-percent capital gain rate, when reinstated under the JGTRRA extended sunset in tax years beginning after December 31, 2012 (see ¶405), will apply to the amount of a taxpayer's adjusted net capital gain that would fall

NEW LAW EXPLAINED

within the 15-percent income tax bracket if the taxpayer's taxable income were computed without including adjusted net capital gain in taxable income. For example, if the 15-percent income tax bracket applies to the first $36,900 of a taxpayer's taxable income and the taxpayer's taxable income without regard to adjusted net capital gain is $36,000, the 10-percent capital gain rate applies to the first $900 of the taxpayer's adjusted net capital gain and the remainder of the taxpayer's adjusted net capital gain is subject to a 20-percent capital gain rate (Code Sec. 1(h)(1)(B) and (C), prior to amendment by P.L. 108-27). Adjusted net capital gain is net capital gain reduced by any unrecaptured section 1250 gain (to which a 25-percent rate applies) and any 28-percent rate gain (the rate imposed on collectibles gain and section 1202 gain) (Code Sec. 1(h)(4), prior to redesignation as Code Sec. 1(h)(3) by P.L. 108-27).

The special 18-percent capital gain rate for qualified five-year gain will apply to the amount of adjusted net capital gain that would be taxed at the 20-percent capital gain rate under Code Sec. 1(h)(1)(C) (see ¶405), but not in excess of the lesser of:

- the excess of qualified five-year gain over the amount of qualified five-year gain that is taxed at the eight-percent rate; or

- the amount of qualified five-year gain determined by taking into account only property with a holding period that begins after December 31, 2000 (Code Sec. 1(h)(2)(B), prior to being stricken by P.L. 108-27).

The 20-percent rate will apply to the remainder of the gain (Code Sec. 1(h)(2)(B), prior to being stricken by P.L. 108-27).

Example 1: In 2013, John Dough has an adjusted net capital gain of $10,000 which includes a $5,000 capital gain that is qualified five-year gain under Code Sec. 1(h)(9). Without regard to the reduced capital gain rates for qualified five-year gain, assume that $3,000 of the adjusted net capital gain is subject to a 10-percent capital gain rate under Code Sec. 1(h)(1)(B) and $7,000 is subject to a 20-percent capital gain rate under Code Sec. 1(h)(1)(C). In this scenario, under Code Sec. 1(h)(2), John Dough will pay an 8-percent tax on $3,000 of the adjusted net capital gain that is qualified five-year gain, an 18-percent tax on $2,000 adjusted net capital gain that is qualified five-year gain, and a 20-percent tax on the remaining $5,000 of adjusted net capital gain ($10,000 − $2,000 − $3,000).

Holding period. The 18-percent capital gain rate for qualified five-year gain in tax years beginning after December 31, 2012, will be available if the holding period of the asset begins after December 31, 2000. In other words, the asset must generally be acquired after December 31, 2000. For purposes of determining when this holding period begins, the holding period of property acquired by the exercise of an option, or of some other right or obligation to acquire property, includes the period that the option, right or obligation was held (Code Sec. 1(h)(2)(B), prior to being stricken by P.L. 108-27).

NEW LAW EXPLAINED

The holding period for the eight-percent capital gain rate for qualified five-year gain will not be required to begin after December 31, 2000 (see Code Sec. 1(h)(2)(A), prior to being stricken by P.L. 108-27).

Example 2: On January 2, 2001, Jane Smith purchases 10 shares of stock in Azor Inc. If she sells the stock at a gain after December 31, 2012, the long-term capital gain is subject to an 18-percent capital gain tax rate if she is in the 28-percent income tax bracket in the year of the sale.

Example 3: James Anderson acquires company stock on January 1, 2003 pursuant to the exercise of an option that was granted on December 2, 1997. If James sells the stock at a gain after December 31, 2012, the gain will not qualify for the 18-percent rate if he is in the 28-percent income tax bracket in the year of the sale, because the holding period is deemed to have begun before December 31, 2000.

Example 4: On December 3, 2000, Bob Bailey purchases 100 shares of stock. If he sells the stock at a gain after December 31, 2012, the gain will be taxed at eight-percent if he is in the 15-percent tax bracket at the time of the sale.

Example 5: Same facts as in Example 4 above, but Bob is in a higher tax bracket at the time of sale. His gain is subject to tax at the 20-percent rate; the 18-percent rate for qualified five-year property is not available because Bob's holding period did not begin after December 31, 2000.

Planning Note: The revival of the special lower rates for property held more than five years in tax years beginning after 2012, along with increases in the capital gain tax rates, present several planning considerations to the taxpayer wishing to dispose of a capital asset (including a section 1231 asset) at a gain. Since tax rates in 2012 may be lower than those in 2013, there may be an incentive to accelerate gains into 2012, and defer losses until 2013 when they can offset income taxed at a higher rate (see ¶405).

For the higher-income taxpayer (i.e., above the 15-percent income tax bracket)—

- The current-law 15-percent capital gain tax rate will apply if the taxpayer has held the capital asset for more than one year, but only if he sells the asset by no later than December 31, 2012.

- The 18-percent capital gain tax rate for qualified five-year gain will apply if the taxpayer acquired the capital asset in 2001 or later, has held the asset for more than five years, and sells it after December 31, 2012. Note that the holding period of property acquired by the exercise of an option or some

¶410

NEW LAW EXPLAINED

other right or obligation to acquire property includes the period that the option, right or obligation was held.

- The 20-percent capital gain tax rate will apply if the taxpayer has acquired the capital asset in 2001 or later, sells the asset after December 31, 2012, and—

  — has held the asset for more than one year but not more than five years; or

  — has held the asset for more than five years, but has acquired the asset by exercising an option, right or obligation to acquire property and the taxpayer has held the option, right or obligation since before January 1, 2001.

For the lower-income taxpayer (i.e., in the 10-percent or 15-percent income tax bracket for 2010, 2011 or 2012; in the 15-percent income tax bracket for 2013 and later)—

- The zero-percent capital gain tax rate will apply if the taxpayer has held the capital asset for more than one year, but only if he sells the asset by no later than December 31, 2012.

- The eight-percent capital gain tax rate for qualified five-year gain will apply if the taxpayer has held the capital asset for more than five years and sells it after December 31, 2012. The eight-percent rate for qualified five-year gain will apply even if the taxpayer's holding period began before 2001.

- The 10-percent capital gain rate will apply if the taxpayer has held the capital asset for more than one year but not more than five years and sells it after December 31, 2012.

Comment: Higher-income taxpayers who held certain assets before January 1, 2001, and who still hold those assets and dispose of them at a gain after December 31, 2012, can take advantage of the 18-percent rate for qualified five-year gain instead of the 20-percent rate if they made a "deemed sale election" regarding those assets on their 2001 income tax returns. The Taxpayer Relief Act of 1997 (P.L. 105-34), which added the special rules for qualified five-year gain, allowed higher-income noncorporate taxpayers to make a special irrevocable election to treat pre-January 1, 2001, property as being acquired on January 1, 2001, thereby resetting the start of the holding period in order to make the property eligible for the five-year holding period rule. This treatment applied to readily tradable stock and to any other capital asset or property used in a trade or business (i.e., section 1231 property). Generally, the taxpayer must have elected to treat the asset as if it were sold on January 1, 2001 (January 2, 2001, for stock) at its fair market value (closing market price for stock), then reacquired on the same day at the same price. Gain from the deemed sale was required to be recognized, but loss was not (Act Sec. 311(e) of the Taxpayer Relief Act of 1997 (P.L. 105-34)).

Alternative minimum tax. A noncorporate taxpayer's tentative minimum tax for alternative minimum tax purposes will be limited by the taxpayer's net capital gain in tax years beginning after December 31, 2012 (see ¶405). In calculating the tax-

NEW LAW EXPLAINED

payer's tentative minimum tax, rules similar to those for determining the reduced capital gain rates for qualified five-year property will apply for purposes of determining the 10-percent and 20-percent capital gain tax amounts (Code Sec. 55(b)(3), prior to amendment by P.L. 108-27).

Practical Analysis: Gary L. Maydew, Ph.D, CPA, retired accounting professor at Iowa State University, observes that the reinstatement in the year 2013 of the reduced capital gains rate for property held more than five years will require careful tax planning. Taxpayers holding capital gain property at the end of the year 2012 will want to consider selling before the end of the year to gain the 15 percent (zero percent for taxpayers in the 10 or 15-percent brackets). The so-called "lock-in effect" will apply to taxpayers who retain capital assets retained after 2012, *i.e.*, taxpayers will have an incentive to wait five years so as to achieve the 18-percent rate (eight percent for those in the 15-percent bracket). Otherwise, taxpayers would pay at 20-percent and 10-percent rates.

Practical Analysis: William A Raabe, Ohio State University, and Capital University Law School, Columbus, Ohio, John O. Everett, Virginia Commonwealth University, Richmond Virginia, and Cherie J. Hennig, University of North Carolina, Wilmington observe that the return of the 18 percent maximum tax rate on qualified five-year properties is consistent with one of the most persuasive arguments for lower capital gains rates: minimize the telescoping of appreciation in value of property into one year for tax purposes. Given that the property has been held for more than five years, Congress believes that such accretion in value should not be taxed in the same manner as other income. Thus, the 20 percent rate applicable in 2013 to long-term gains will be reduced to 18 percent, and the 10 percent rate (applicable to taxpayers in the lowest 15 percent bracket after 2010) will be reduced to 8 percent.

These special rates do not apply to properties that otherwise qualify for either the 25 percent tax rate (unrecaptured Code Sec. 1250 income) or the 28 percent rate (collectibles and Code Sec. 1202 gain). There is one additional restriction on qualifying five-year properties for purposes of the 18 percent rate; the property must have a holding period that begins after December 31, 2000. This restriction does not apply to 8 percent gain; the lower rate applies to all qualifying five-year properties, even if the holding period begins after December 31, 2000.

The return of the 18 percent rate for qualified five-year properties raises an interesting question that tax professionals should remember to ask taxpayers who engage in capital asset transactions after 2012 that involve capital assets acquired prior to 2001. Specifically, did the taxpayer make a "deemed sale election" in 2001? Recall that the Taxpayer Relief Act of 1997 (P.L. 105-34) allowed non-corporate taxpayers to elect to report a "deemed sale" of readily tradable stock held on January 1, 2001, and pay tax on the hypothetical gain on the 2001 tax return. In effect, the Code treated the taxpayer as if such stock was repurchased on January 1, 2001 (for the hypothetical sales price), allowing the stock to qualify for the lower 18 percent rate when held for more than five years after the January 1, 2001 date. If the taxpayer did

NEW LAW EXPLAINED

indeed make that election, then any gain will be taxed at 18 percent, rather than 20 percent, and the holding period would begin on January 1, 2001.

Would Congress consider bringing this election back as a short-term revenue raiser, by requiring that the holding period begin anew after the hypothetical sale for the "replacement stock" that would qualify for the 18 percent rate? Evidence suggests that the 2001 election provided a noticeable boost in federal tax revenues, and there is a precedent for such short-term actions; witness the temporary elimination of the $100,000 limit on conversions of traditional IRAs into Roth IRAs in 2010. Interestingly, a simple breakeven analysis of the election back in 2001 revealed that the price of the stock would have to almost triple in certain cases to justify such an election when the taxpayer has to wait more than five years to dispose of the replacement stock. (John O. Everett, Roxanne Spindle, and Thomas Turman, *Using Breakeven Formulas to Analyze Tax Planning Strategies*, THE CPA JOURNAL (June, 2003), at. 56-59.)

▶ **Effective date.** The provision is effective for tax years ending on or after May 6, 2003 (Act Sec. 102(b) of the Tax Relief, Unemployment Insurance Reauthorization, and Job Creation Act of 2010 (P.L. 111-312)); Act Sec. 301 of the Jobs and Growth Tax Relief Reconciliation Act of 2003 (JGTRRA) (P.L. 108-27)). The provision shall not apply to tax years beginning after December 31, 2012 (Act Sec. 102(a) of the Tax Relief Act of 2010; Act Sec. 303 of JGTRRA). See ¶105 for a specific discussion of the sunset provision of JGTRRA and how it is applied.

Law source: Law at ¶5005, ¶5170, and ¶7015. Committee Report at ¶10,080.

— Act Sec. 102(a) of the Tax Relief, Unemployment Insurance Reauthorization, and Job Creation Act of 2010 (P.L. 111-312), amending Act Sec. 303 of the Jobs and Growth Tax Relief Reconciliation Act of 2003 (P.L. 108-27), as amended by Act Sec. 102 of the Tax Increase Prevention and Reconciliation Act of 2005 (P.L. 109-222);

— Act Sec. 102(b), providing the effective date.

Reporter references: For further information, consult the following CCH reporters.

— Standard Federal Tax Reporter, ¶3285.01 and ¶3285.03

— Tax Research Consultant, SALES: 15,400

— Practical Tax Explanation, § 16,525.10

¶415 Tax Preference Items: Excluded Gain on Sale of Small Business Stock

SUMMARY OF NEW LAW

The amount of excluded gain on qualified small business stock held for more than five years that is treated as an alternative minimum tax (AMT) preference item will remain unchanged for the two tax years beginning after December 31, 2010. Thus, for dispositions before January 1, 2013, seven percent of the excluded gain will be a tax

SUMMARY OF NEW LAW

preference item. The amount of excluded gain will be increased for tax years beginning after December 31, 2012: generally, 42 percent of the excluded gain will be a tax preference item, and for stock having a holding period that began after December 31, 2000, the tax preference will be 28 percent of the excluded gain.

BACKGROUND

The Jobs and Growth Tax Relief Reconciliation Act of 2003 (JGTRRA) (P.L. 108-27) amended Code Sec. 57(a)(7) to provide that seven percent (rather than 42 percent) of the gain excluded from gross income on the sale or exchange of certain small business stock under Code Sec. 1202 is treated as a tax preference item for purposes of the alternative minimum tax (AMT). A separate preference amount for stock on which the holding period began after December 31, 2000, was stricken.

The AMT regime recaptures certain tax savings by requiring high income individuals or corporations to modify their regular taxable income and take into account certain preference items and adjustments. Tax preference items (TPIs), which include portions of deductions or exclusions from income, are added back to the taxpayer's taxable income in computing the alternative minimum taxable income (AMTI), which is the basis on which the taxpayers compute their tentative minimum tax (Code Secs. 55 and 57).

Noncorporate investors may exclude up to 50 percent of the gain they realize on the sale or exchange of small business stock that was issued after August 10, 1993, and that they have held for more than five years. The exclusion is 75 percent for stock acquired after February 17, 2009, and on or before September 27, 2010. Further, the exclusion is 100 percent for stock acquired after September 27, 2010, and before January 1, 2011; for stock acquired during this period, none of the excluded gain on such stock is considered an AMT preference (Code Sec. 1202(a) and (b)). Generally, to qualify as "small business stock," the stock must be issued by a C corporation, at least 80 percent of the corporation's assets must be invested in assets used in the active conduct of a business, and the corporation's aggregate assets at the time the stock is issued must not exceed $50 million (Code Sec. 1202(c) and (d)).

Sunset provision. Under a sunset provision of JGTRRA, certain amendments made by the Act will not apply to tax years beginning after December 31, 2010 (Act Sec. 303 of the Jobs and Growth Tax Relief Reconciliation Act of 2003 (P.L. 108-27), as amended by Act Sec. 102 of the Tax Increase Prevention and Reconciliation Act of 2005 (P.L. 109-222)).

NEW LAW EXPLAINED

Extension of lower AMT preference percentage for gain on sale of certain small business stock.—The sunset provision of the Jobs and Growth Tax Relief Reconciliation Act of 2003 (JGTRRA) has been extended for two years (Act Sec. 303 of the Jobs and Growth Tax Relief Reconciliation Act of 2003 (P.L. 108-27), as amended by Act Sec. 102 of the Tax Increase Prevention and Reconciliation Act of 2005 (P.L. 109-222), and by

¶415

NEW LAW EXPLAINED

Act Sec. 102 of the Tax Relief, Unemployment Insurance Reauthorization, and Job Creation Act of 2010 (P.L. 111-312)). Accordingly, for tax years beginning in 2011 and 2012, Code Sec. 57(a)(7) continues to provide that seven percent (not 42 percent) of the gain excluded from gross income on the sale or exchange of certain small business stock under Code Sec. 1202 is treated as a tax preference item for purposes of the alternative minimum tax (AMT), and the separate preference amount for stock on which the holding period began after December 31, 2000, continues to be stricken.

After 2012, higher percentages of the excluded gain on the disposition of Code Sec. 1202 qualified small business stock will be treated as alternative minimum tax (AMT) preference items (Code Sec. 57(a)(7), prior to amendment by P.L. 108-27), for sales and exchanges in tax years beginning after December 31, 2012, under the JGTRRA sunset provision (Act Sec. 303 of P.L. 108-27, as amended by Act Sec. 102 of P.L. 109-222, and by Act Sec. 102 of P.L. 111-312). After the sunset, the amount of the preference item will be increased to 42 percent of the excluded gain. In addition, a separate preference amount for small business stock on which the holding period began after December 31, 2000, will be restored. For such stock, 28 percent of the excluded gain will be a tax preference item (Code Sec. 57(a)(7), prior to amendment by P.L. 108-27).

After December 31, 2012, in determining whether the holding period begins after December 31, 2000, the holding period of property acquired by the exercise of an option, or of some other right or obligation to acquire property, will include the period that the option, right, or obligation was held (Code Secs. 1(h)(2)(B) and 57(a)(7), prior to amendment by P.L. 108-27). In other words, the holding period of qualified small business stock acquired after December 31, 2000, by the exercise of an option granted before that date will *not* begin after December 31, 2000 (see ¶ 410).

Planning Note: The revival of the higher percentages of excluded gain that are included as AMT tax preference items (TPIs) in tax years beginning after December 31, 2012 provides a number of planning considerations to the taxpayer wishing to dispose of appreciated Code Sec. 1202 small business stock (for this discussion, a calendar-year taxpayer is assumed)—

- The seven-percent TPI treatment applies to Code Sec. 1202 stock acquired on or before December 30, 2007, if the stock is disposed of by December 31, 2012. (Generally, the holding period is computed by excluding the day the taxpayer acquired the property, but including the day the taxpayer disposed of the property (see Rev. Rul. 66-7, 1966-1 CB 188).) Thus, 3.5 percent (50 percent exclusion × seven percent) of the investor's total realized gain from the disposition will be used in the calculation of alternative minimum taxable income (AMTI).

- The seven-percent TPI treatment will *not* apply to Code Sec. 1202 stock for which the 75-percent gain exclusion is allowed under Code Sec. 1202(a)(3), because the more-than-five-years holding requirement for the stock means that the earliest disposition date falls beyond December 31, 2012, which is the latest disposition date for seven-percent TPI treatment. For the 75-percent exclusion to apply, stock acquired on February 18, 2009 (the earliest acquisition date for the 75-percent exclusion) can be sold no earlier than February 20,

NEW LAW EXPLAINED

2014, and stock acquired by September 27, 2010 (the latest acquisition date for the 75-percent exclusion) can be sold no earlier than September 28, 2015. Such stock will be subject to 28-percent TPI treatment.

- The 28-percent TPI treatment will apply to Code Sec. 1202 stock disposed of after December 31, 2012, if the stock's holding period began after December 31, 2000. Generally, 14 percent (50 percent exclusion × 28 percent) of the investor's total realized gain from the disposition will be used in the AMTI computation. If the stock qualifies for the 75-percent gain exclusion under Code Sec. 1202(a)(3), then 21 percent (75 percent exclusion × 28 percent) of the realized gain will be used in the AMTI computation. If the stock qualifies for the 100-percent gain exclusion under Code Sec. 1202(a)(4), then none of the excluded gain on such stock is considered an AMT preference.

- The 42-percent TPI treatment will apply to Code Sec. 1202 stock disposed of after December 31, 2012, if the stock's holding period began before January 1, 2001. Thus, 21 percent (50 percent exclusion × 42 percent) of the investor's total realized gain from the disposition will be used in the AMTI computation. Because the acquisition date of such stock falls outside the acquisition period for the 75-percent gain exclusion (February 18, 2009, through September 27, 2010), the larger exclusion percentage does not apply.

- For Code Sec. 1202 stock acquired after September 27, 2010, and before January 1, 2012, Code Sec. 57(a)(7) does not apply (see ¶418). Thus, no AMT (or federal income tax) will be imposed on gain from the sale or exchange of such stock that is acquired during that period and held for more than five years.

Practical Analysis: Mark R. Solomon, Walsh College, Troy, Michigan, observes that Section 760 of the Tax Relief, Unemployment Insurance Reauthorization, and Jobs Creation Act of 2010 (2010 Tax Relief Act) extends those provisions of the Creating Small Business Jobs Act of 2010 (P.L. 111-240) which provided for the complete exclusion of gain from the sale of qualified small business stock for noncorporate shareholders of C corporation stock that was acquired after September 27, 2010, and before December 31, 2010, and which is held for at least five years. Such qualified stock also escapes treatment as a tax preference item. Under the 2010 Tax Relief Act, stock acquired after September 27, 2010, and before December 31, 2011, if otherwise qualified, will be eligible for this highly favorable treatment. The purpose of this extension appears to be to encourage capital investment and thus applies only to stock acquired directly from the corporation for cash, property, or the performance of services.

This extended ability to qualify for the previously little-utilized (although its use was never optional) exclusion under Code Sec. 1202(a)(4) provides a greater, but still narrow, window of opportunity for a small business which chooses to operate in C corporation form to escape the double taxation inherent in C corporations. In the past the principal means of escaping two tiers of taxation were (1) to avoid corporate level taxation by making an S election, (2) to avoid corporate level taxation by paying out

¶415

NEW LAW EXPLAINED

the earnings of the corporation to the owners as deductible compensation or rent (to the extent reasonable), and (3) to avoid shareholder level taxation by dying and leaving the stock to the survivors with a stepped-up basis (now fully allowed by Section 301(a) and (c) of the 2010 Tax Relief Act). To these, a fourth technique continues to be available for those acquiring qualified stock after September 27, 2010, and before 2012—namely, avoiding shareholder level taxation by taking advantage of the 100 percent exclusion available under Code Sec. 1202, assuming all other requirements are met.

Taxpayers should note that Code Sec. 1202 applies not only to sales of stock, but also to transactions that are treated as sales or exchanges. Thus, liquidations under Code Sec. 331, redemptions under Code Secs. 302(a) and 303 (to the extent there is taxable gain), and distributions under Code Sec. 301(c)(3) (after earnings and profits and adjusted basis have both been exhausted) appear to be eligible for the Code Sec. 1202 exclusion.

Taxpayers who are thinking of starting a new business in C corporation form before January 1, 2012, would be well-advised to complete the incorporation and issue stock before the end of 2011. Of concern will be the question of whether additional assets contributed after 2011 without the issuance of additional stock will partially affect the eligibility of the stock issued before January 1, 2012, or whether the IRS will take the position that there is constructive receipt of additional stock not eligible for the 100 percent exclusion.

▶ **Effective date.** The provision is effective for dispositions on or after May 6, 2003 (Act Sec. 102(b) of the Tax Relief, Unemployment Insurance Reauthorization, and Job Creation Act of 2010 (P.L. 111-312)); Act Sec. 301(d)(3) of the Jobs and Growth Tax Relief Reconciliation Act of 2003 (JGTRRA) (P.L. 108-27)). The provision shall not apply to tax years beginning after December 31, 2012 (Act Sec. 102(a) of the Tax Relief Act of 2010; Act Sec. 303 of JGTRRA). See ¶105 for a specific discussion of the sunset provision of JGTRRA and how it is applied.

Law source: Law at ¶5175 and ¶7015. Committee Report at ¶10,080.

— Act Sec. 102(a) of the Tax Relief, Unemployment Insurance Reauthorization, and Job Creation Act of 2010 (P.L. 111-312), amending Act Sec. 303 of the Jobs and Growth Tax Relief Reconciliation Act of 2003 (P.L. 108-27), as amended by Act Sec. 102 of the Tax Increase Prevention and Reconciliation Act of 2005 (P.L. 109-222);

— Act Sec. 102(b), providing the effective date.

Reporter references: For further information, consult the following CCH reporters.

— Standard Federal Tax Reporter, ¶5307.01

— Tax Research Consultant, FILEIND: 30,256

— Practical Tax Explanation, § 15,305

¶418 Exclusion of Gain from Sale of Qualified Small Business Stock

SUMMARY OF NEW LAW

A noncorporate taxpayer may now exclude 100 percent of gain on the sale or exchange of qualified small business stock held for more than five years for stock acquired after September 27, 2010, and before January 1, 2012—a one-year extension of the 100-percent exclusion.

BACKGROUND

To encourage investment in small businesses and specialized small business investment companies (SSBICs), Code Sec. 1202(a) allows a taxpayer (other than a corporation) to exclude from gross income 50 percent of the gain realized from the sale or exchange of qualified small business stock held for more than five years. The amount of the exclusion is 60 percent in the case of the sale or exchange of qualified small business stock issued by a corporation in an empowerment zone. The 60-percent exclusion, however, does not apply to gain attributable to periods after December 31, 2014.

The 50-percent exclusion is increased to a 75-percent exclusion of gain from the sale or exchange of qualified small business stock acquired after February 17, 2009, and before September 27, 2010. And for stock acquired after September 27, 2010, and before January 1, 2011, the percentage of gain from the sale or exchange of qualified small business stock that may be excluded from gross income by a noncorporate taxpayer is increased to 100 percent.

Eligible gain from the disposition of qualified stock of any single issuer is subject to a cumulative limit for any given tax year equal to the greater of: (1) 10 times the taxpayer's adjusted basis in all qualified stock disposed of during the tax year; or (2) $10 million ($5 million for married taxpayers filing separately), reduced by the total amount of eligible gain taken in prior tax years (Code Sec. 1202(b)).

NEW LAW EXPLAINED

Comment: Gain excluded under the small business stock provision is not used in computing the taxpayer's long-term capital gain or loss, and it is not investment income for purposes of the investment interest limitation. As a result, the taxable portion of the gain is taxed at a maximum rate of 28 percent (Code Sec. 1(h)). In addition, seven percent of the excluded gain is an alternative minimum tax (AMT) preference item (Code Sec. 57(a)(7)).

To be eligible for the exclusion, the small business stock must be acquired by the individual at its original issue (directly or through an underwriter), for money, property other than stock, or as compensation for services provided to the corporation (Code Sec. 1202(c)). Stock acquired through the conversion of stock (such as preferred stock) that was qualified stock in the taxpayer's hands is also

NEW LAW EXPLAINED

qualified stock in the taxpayer's hands (Code Sec. 1202(f)). However, small business stock does not include stock that has been the subject of certain redemptions that are more than de minimis (Code Sec. 1202(c)(3)). A taxpayer who acquires qualified stock by gift or inheritance is treated as having acquired that stock in the same manner as the transferor and adds the transferor's holding period to his or her own (Code Sec. 1202(h)). A partnership may distribute qualified stock to its partners so long as the partner held the partnership interest when the stock was acquired, and only to the extent that partner's share in the partnership has not increased since the stock was acquired.

The issuing corporation must be a domestic C corporation (other than a mutual fund, cooperative, or other similar "pass-though" corporation). Both before and immediately after the qualified stock's issuance, the qualified small business corporation must have had aggregate gross assets that did not exceed $50 million (Code Sec. 1202(d)). In addition, during substantially all of the taxpayer's holding period, at least 80 percent of the value of the corporation's assets must be used in the active conduct of one or more qualified trades or businesses (Code Sec. 1202(e)).

Increased exclusion of gain from qualified small business stock sales extended.— The 100-percent exclusion of gain from the sale or exchange of qualified small business stock by a noncorporate taxpayer is extended one year. Therefore, the 100-percent exclusion now applies to qualified small business stock acquired after September 27, 2010, and before January 1, 2012, and held for more than five years (Code Sec. 1202(a)(4), as amended by the Tax Relief, Unemployment Insurance Reauthorization, and Job Creation Act of 2010 (P.L. 111-312)). In addition, none of the excluded gain on such stock will be considered an alternative minimum tax (AMT) preference. Thus, no federal income tax or AMT will be imposed on gain from the sale or exchange of qualified small business stock that is acquired after September 27, 2010, and before January 1, 2012, and that is held for more than five years. Also, the rules applicable to empowerment zone businesses under Code Sec. 1202(a)(2), including that which normally grants an enhanced 60-percent exclusion of gain, will not apply to such stock.

Caution: Because of the various changes to the percentage of the exclusion, a taxpayer must be aware not only of meeting the five year holding requirement, but also of the date the qualified small business stock was acquired. For example, if a taxpayer acquired qualified small business stock after February 17, 2009, then only 75 percent of the gain will be subject to tax if the stock is sold or exchanged more than five years later. If a taxpayer acquired qualified small business stock on February 17, 2009, then only 50 percent of the gain will be subject to tax if the stock is sold or exchanged after February 17, 2014. If the taxpayer acquired the stock after September 27, 2010 and before January 1, 2012, then no tax will be imposed on the gain if the stock is sold or exchanged more than five years later.

State Tax Consequences: The extension through 2011 of the increase in the 100 percent exclusion from income on the gain from the sale of small business stock issued after September 27, 2010, will affect states that either did not adopt the

¶418

NEW LAW EXPLAINED

original exclusion (such as Wisconsin), decoupled from the increased percentage from 50 percent to 75 percent (such as Hawaii), or did adopt the exclusion, but because of their Code conformity dates, do not adopt the increase for 2010 or 2011 (such as Indiana and Oregon). In such states the amount required to be added back will be increased. States that are out of conformity may conform for 2011 or for both years during their next legislative sessions.

▶ **Effective date.** The provision applies to stock acquired after December 31, 2010 (Act Sec. 760(b) of the Tax Relief, Unemployment Insurance Reauthorization, and Job Creation Act of 2010 (P.L. 111-312)).

Law source: Law at ¶5510. Committee Report at ¶10,660.

— Act Sec. 760a) of the Tax Relief, Unemployment Insurance Reauthorization, and Job Creation Act of 2010 (P.L. 111-312), amending Code Sec. 1202(a)(4);

— Act Sec. 760(b), providing the effective date.

Reporter references: For further information, consult the following CCH reporters.

— Standard Federal Tax Reporter, ¶30,375.01

— Tax Research Consultant, SALES:15,302.05

— Practical Tax Explanation, §16,605.05

DIVIDENDS

¶420 Qualified Dividends Received by Individuals, Estates and Trusts

SUMMARY OF NEW LAW

The taxation of qualified dividends received by individuals, trusts or estates at capital gain rates is extended for two years, through December 31, 2012.

BACKGROUND

The Jobs and Growth Tax Relief Reconciliation Act of 2003 (JGTRRA) (P.L. 108-27) reduced the federal tax rates for qualified dividends received by individuals, estates or trusts, by providing that such dividends will be taxed at capital gain rates for tax years beginning after December 31, 2002 (Code Sec. 1(h)(11)). The top federal tax rate for qualified dividends is 15 percent (five percent for those whose income falls in the 10- or 15-percent rate brackets). A zero-percent rate applies to taxpayers in the 10- or 15-percent brackets for tax years beginning after 2007 (Code Sec. 1(h)(1)(B) and (C)).

Comment: The reduced dividend rates apply for both regular income tax and alternative minimum tax purposes.

¶420

BACKGROUND

Qualified dividends. The reduced dividend rates apply only to qualified dividends, which include dividends received during the tax year from a domestic corporation or a qualified foreign corporation (Code Sec. 1(h)(11)(B)(i)).

> **Comment:** Code Sec. 316 defines a dividend as a distribution made by a corporation with respect to its stock out of the corporation's current or accumulated earnings and profits. Thus, any amounts paid by a corporation that are unrelated to stock holdings (such as salaries, payments to creditors, etc.) are not dividends and do not qualify for the reduced tax rates. In addition, a corporate distribution made with respect to a corporation's stock that exceeds the corporation's current or accumulated earnings and profits (or where the corporation does not have current or accumulated earnings and profits) is not treated as a dividend, but as a return of capital that reduces the shareholder's basis (with any excess treated as capital gain) (Code Sec. 301).

> **Comment:** Excessive salaries paid to employee-shareholders may be recharacterized by the IRS as constructive dividends. Under the reduced rates for dividends, employee-shareholders may actually prefer dividend treatment over salaries taxed at ordinary income rates. Dividends also have the advantage of being free of employment taxes, which benefits both the employee-shareholder and the corporation. Because a corporation takes a deduction for salaries paid, dividends would be preferable in situations in which the corporation does not need the salary deduction because its taxable income is fully offset by other deductions.

In order for a dividend to qualify for the lower capital gain rates, the underlying stock must have been held for at least 61 days during the 121-day period beginning 60 days before the ex-dividend date (Code Sec. 1(h)(11)(B)(iii)(I)).

The ex-dividend date is the date following the record date on which the corporation finalizes the list of shareholders who will receive the dividend. Thus, a stock bought on the last day before the ex-dividend date (i.e., the latest purchase date for collecting a dividend) could still meet the holding period test for that dividend since there would have been 61 days left in the 121-day period. A stock sold on the ex-dividend date (i.e., the earliest selling date after entitlement to a dividend) can also meet the test since that is the 61st day in the period. As long as the taxpayer holds the stock for at least 61 continuous days, the holding period test will be met for any dividend received (unless another restriction applies, such as a diminished risk of loss).

A similar holding period applies for preferred stock dividends attributable to a more-than-366-day period (dividends paid on cumulative preferred stock). This holding period is at least 91 days during a 181-day period beginning 90 days before the ex-dividend date.

> **Practice Tip:** For purposes of counting the number of days, the day of disposition, but not the day of acquisition, is included (Code Sec. 246(c)(3)).

> **Example:** The ex-dividend date for Omega Corp. is February 28, 2009. On January 20, 2009, Joe Rowley purchases 10,000 shares of Omega for $260,000.

BACKGROUND

On March 6, 2009, having held the shares long enough to avoid the wash sale rules, Rowley sells the 10,000 shares of Omega for $258,000. Rowley receives the dividend of $.19 per share ($1,900). Rowley's economic loss is $100. Assuming this is his only transaction, he can use the capital loss from the stock sale to offset $2,000 of other income, for a potential tax savings of $700 (35% × $2,000). If the special dividend tax rate applied, Rowley's liability on the $1,900 dividend would be $285 (at 15 percent), meaning that his economic loss of $100 produced a tax savings of $415 ($700 – $285). However, since he did not hold the shares for more than 61 days during the period from December 30 to April 28 (60 days before and after the February 28, 2009 ex-dividend date), Rowley's regular tax rate will apply (35 percent). His $665 ($1,900 × 35%) liability on the dividend, combined with the $700 saved by the capital loss, means that in this situation his $100 economic loss produces net tax savings of only $35. The holding period rule prevents the taxpayer from using price drops due to dividends to generate capital loss to offset ordinary income while paying tax on the dividend at a lower rate.

Corporate stock dividends passed through to partners by a partnership or held by a common trust fund are eligible for the reduced rate, assuming the distribution would otherwise be classified as qualified dividend income (Code Secs. 584(c) and 702(a)(5)). Such qualified dividends are reported by the partners as a separately stated item, and participants in the common trust fund report their proportionate share of qualified dividends received by the fund.

Dividends received from a mutual fund or other regulated investment company (RIC) or from a real estate investment trust (REIT) may also qualify for the reduced rates, subject to certain limitations (Code Secs. 854 and 857). See ¶ 425 for discussion of dividends received by RICs and REITs. Proceeds from a disposition, other than a redemption, of Code Sec. 306 stock that was received as a nontaxable stock dividend may also be eligible for the reduced dividend tax rate (Code Sec. 306(a)(1)(D)).

Compliance Note: Taxpayers must report qualified dividends shown in Box 1b of Form 1099-DIV on Line 9b of Form 1040, U.S. Individual Income Tax Return, and Line 22 of Schedule D, Capital Gains and Losses (if Schedule D is filed). However, certain dividends reported in Box 1b of Form 1099-DIV may not be qualified dividends. Taxpayers must use the Qualified Dividends and Capital Gain Tax Worksheet, or the Schedule D Tax Worksheet (if Schedule D is filed), both provided in the instructions to Form 1040, to compute their tax liability.

Dividends ineligible for the reduced tax rates. Certain dividends do not qualify for the capital gain rates. These include dividends paid by:

- credit unions;
- mutual insurance companies;
- farmers' cooperatives;
- tax-exempt cemetery companies;
- nonprofit voluntary employee benefit associations (VEBAs);

¶420

BACKGROUND

- any corporation exempt from federal tax under Code Sec. 501 or 521 in the tax year in which the dividend is paid or in the preceding tax year;
- any mutual savings bank, savings and loan, domestic building and loan, cooperative bank, or other type of bank eligible for the dividends paid deduction under Code Sec. 591 (Code Sec. 1(h)(11)(B)(ii)).

> **Comment:** Credit union "dividends" paid on savings accounts, certificates of deposits, and other savings vehicles are taxed as interest at ordinary tax rates and are not eligible for the reduced dividend tax rates.

Dividends paid on employer securities owned by an employee stock ownership plan (ESOP) also do not qualify to the extent the dividends are deductible under Code Sec. 404(k) (Code Sec. 1(h)(11)(B)(ii)).

> **Comment:** Dividends from investments in tax-deferred retirement vehicles such as regular IRAs, 401(k)s and deferred annuities are taxed at ordinary income rates, not at capital gain rates.

Qualified dividends of noncorporate taxpayers are generally excluded from investment income, unless the taxpayer makes an election to include all or a portion of the qualified dividend in investment income under Code Sec. 163(d)(4)(B) (Code Sec. 1(h)(11)(D)(i)). In such a case, the dividend amount included as investment income is not eligible for the lower capital gain rates.

> **Comment:** This election is available in the case where the taxpayer purchases dividend-paying stock with borrowed funds, the interest on which qualifies as investment interest expense. The election can be advantageous since investment expenses are deductible only to the extent of investment income by noncorporate taxpayers. Any excess expenses may be carried forward to the next tax year but would otherwise go to waste. By electing to treat qualified dividend income as investment income to the extent of this excess investment expense, that dividend income can effectively be transformed into totally tax free income.

> **Compliance Tip:** A taxpayer must specifically elect to include a qualified dividend in investment income. If no election is made, the IRS will assume that the reduced dividend rate is to apply and the dividend is excluded in calculating the maximum permissible investment interest deduction. The election must be made on or before the due date (including extensions) of the income tax return for the tax year in which the qualified dividend income is received. The election is made on Form 4952, Investment Interest Expense Deduction. The election is revocable only with the IRS's consent (Reg. § 1.163(d)-1).

A dividend also does not qualify for the reduced tax rates to the extent that the taxpayer is obligated to make related payments with respect to positions in substantially similar or related property (Code Sec. 1(h)(11)(B)(iii)(II)). The related payments can be pursuant to a short sale or other arrangement.

> **Comment:** This restriction is similar to the restriction imposed on corporations claiming the dividends received deduction (Code Sec. 246(c)(1)(B)). It addresses situations in which taxpayers do not retain, or do not genuinely own, the dividends they receive. The restriction applies regardless of how long the taxpayer has owned the dividend-paying stock (Reg. § 1.246-3(c)(3)).

¶420

BACKGROUND

> **Example:** Joe Black purchases 100 shares of Microco on January 10, 1987. On February 10, 2010, Black short sells 25 shares of Microco and remains in the position on February 28, 2010, when the stock goes ex-dividend. Assuming Black receives a $100 dividend and is obligated to pay $25 to the lender for the sales that were sold short, only $75 of the dividend is eligible for the reduced dividend rate.

Comment: The IRS regulations illustrate the rule with an example in which identical company shares are held in offsetting positions. It is not clear to what extent positions in different company stocks will be considered substantially similar or related. Positions in different issuers in unrelated industries have been held not to be substantially similar (Duke Energy Corp., 2000-1 USTC ¶50,143). However, the IRS has also ruled that groups of preferred shares in unrelated industry stocks were substantially similar property (IRS Letter Ruling 9128050 (April 4, 1991)).

Extraordinary dividends. A special rule applies in the case of extraordinary dividends. If a noncorporate taxpayer eligible for the reduced dividend rates receives with respect to any stock qualified dividend income from one or more dividends that are extraordinary dividends, then any loss on the sale or exchange of that stock is treated as a long-term capital loss to the extent of such dividends (Code Sec. 1(h)(11)(D)(ii)).

An extraordinary dividend is a dividend that exceeds five percent of the taxpayer's adjusted basis in preferred stock and 10 percent of a taxpayer's adjusted basis in all other types of stock. Certain aggregation rules apply in determining whether the threshold percentage limitations are met. Thus, all dividends that are received by a taxpayer with respect to any share of stock and that have ex-dividend dates within the same period of 85 consecutive days are treated as one dividend. In addition, all dividends that are received by a taxpayer with respect to any share of stock and that have ex-dividend dates within the same one-year period are treated as extraordinary dividends if the total of these dividends exceeds 20 percent of the taxpayer's adjusted basis in the stock (Code Sec. 1059(c)).

Comment: The holding period of the stock on which the extraordinary dividend is paid is not taken into account in determining whether a taxpayer is subject to the extraordinary dividend rule or whether the loss on the stock (to the extent of the extraordinary dividends) is long-term capital loss. Also, the long-term capital loss characterization rule affects taxpayers with both short-term capital gain and long-term capital gain from other transactions in excess of the loss generated by the extraordinary dividend transaction. The characterization makes no difference to a taxpayer having no capital gains, capital gain not in excess of the dividend transaction loss, or only capital losses.

> **Example:** Joe Black purchases and sells 100 shares of Smallco at a $10,000 loss during 2009 and also receives a $10,000 extraordinary dividend from the

¶420

BACKGROUND

> company during the year. He also incurs $10,000 in net long-term capital gain and $10,000 in short-term capital gain in other unrelated transactions. He must use his $10,000 Smallco loss to offset the net long-term capital gain, leaving $10,000 of short-term capital gain to be taxed at ordinary income tax rates. Without the extraordinary dividend rule, Joe could characterize the loss as short-term and use it to offset his short-term capital gain, allowing his net $10,000 gain to be taxed at the preferable long-term capital gain rates.

There is an alternative provision for determining whether a dividend is extraordinary. It permits the taxpayer to elect to substitute for the adjusted basis the fair market value of the share of stock on the day before the ex-dividend date, provided that the fair market value can be established to the satisfaction of the IRS (Code Sec. 1059(c)(4)). This election can prevent a basis reduction for stock that has appreciated significantly since it was acquired.

Dividends paid by foreign corporations. Dividends paid by foreign corporations may also enjoy the reduced dividend tax rates. In addition to meeting the minimum holding period requirement, the dividend must be paid by a qualified foreign corporation. A qualified foreign corporation is any foreign corporation:

- that is incorporated in a U.S. possession; or
- that is eligible for benefits under a comprehensive income tax treaty with the United States that includes an exchange of information program (Code Sec. 1(h)(11)(C)(i)).

> **Comment:** To be eligible for treaty benefits, a foreign corporation must be a resident as defined by the relevant treaty and meet other treaty requirements. However, the mere fact that a corporation is organized in a country with which the United States has a comprehensive treaty is not sufficient (Notice 2003-79, 2003-2 CB 1206).

> The IRS has provided a list of income tax treaties between the Unites States and various countries that have been identified as comprehensive income tax treaties including an information exchange program. The IRS has also identified several U.S. income tax treaties that do not meet these requirements. In particular, the income tax treaties with Bermuda and The Netherlands Antilles are not comprehensive tax treaties, and the income tax treaty with the USSR, which currently applies to certain former Soviet Republics, does not include an information program. The IRS intends to update the list as appropriate and any changes will apply only to dividends paid after the date the revised list is published (Notice 2006-101, 2006-2 CB 930).

A foreign corporation that does not meet either of the above two tests may still be treated as a qualified foreign corporation with respect to any dividend paid on its stock that is readily tradeable on an established U.S. securities market (Code Sec. 1(h)(11)(C)(ii)).

> **Comment:** Stock is considered readily tradeable on an established U.S. securities market if it is listed on a national securities exchange that is registered under section 6 of the Securities Exchange Act of 1934 (15 USC 78f), or the NASDAQ

¶420

BACKGROUND

Stock Market. Registered national exchanges include the American Stock Exchange, Boston Stock Exchange, Cincinnati Stock Exchange, Chicago Stock Exchange, NYSE, Philadelphia Stock Exchange and the Pacific Exchange, Inc. (Notice 2003-71, 2003-2 CB 922, and Notice 2004-71, 2004-2 CB 793). The IRS is considering the treatment of dividends paid from stock that does not meet this definition, such as stock listed on the OTC Bulletin Board, as well as the inclusion of certain other requirements.

A foreign corporation is not treated as a qualified foreign corporation if, for the year in which the dividend was paid or for the preceding tax year, it is a passive foreign investment company (PFIC) (Code Sec. 1(h)(11)(C)(iii)). A foreign corporation qualifies as a PFIC if at least 50 percent of its assets on average produce passive income or are held for the production of passive income, or at least 75 percent of the gross income of the corporation for the tax year is passive income (Code Sec. 1297).

Compliance Note: The IRS has issued guidance for persons required to make returns and provide statements under Code Sec. 6042 (such as Form 1099-DIV) regarding distributions made with respect to securities issued by a foreign corporation, and for individuals receiving such statements. The guidance identifies certain determinations that must be made in order to make a decision as to whether a distribution with respect to a security issued by a foreign corporation is eligible for the reduced dividend tax rates, and provides simplified procedures for information reporting regarding such a distribution. The IRS has indicated that it intends to issue regulations that would require a foreign corporation to certify that it is a qualified foreign corporation by filing an annual information return. It has also admitted that more detailed information reporting procedures may be necessary, but that such procedures are currently under study. The guidance initially applied to tax years 2003 and 2004, but has been subsequently extended to apply to all succeeding years (Notice 2003-79, 2003-2 CB 1206, extended by Notice 2004-71, 2004-2 CB 793; Notice 2006-3, 2006-1 CB 306).

Foreign tax credit adjustments. A taxpayer with qualified dividend income that is subject to the reduced dividend rates must make certain adjustments in computing the foreign tax credit (Code Sec. 1(h)(11)(C)(iv)).

These adjustments are similar to the adjustments for capital gains in computing the credit. The maximum credit is roughly equal to the percentage of U.S. tax that equals the taxpayer's foreign source taxable income as a percentage of worldwide taxable income (Code Sec. 904(a)). In computing the foreign income part of the equation, capital gain is subject to special rules. The overall effect is to reduce capital gain by taxes saved due to special rates and to require domestic source net capital loss to be taken into account in determining foreign source capital gain (Code Sec. 904(b)(2)(B)). The capital gain reduction rules are invoked in any year there is a capital rate gain differential. These capital gain adjustments in computing the foreign tax credit also apply to qualified dividend income.

According to the formula prescribed under Code Sec. 904(b)(2)(B), foreign source taxable income and worldwide taxable income are both reduced by the rate differential portion of any dividend income before calculating the proportions that make up the credit limitation. The rate differential portion for capital gain is defined as the

¶420

BACKGROUND

excess of: (i) the highest applicable tax rate, less the maximum preferential capital gain rate under Code Sec. 1(h)(11), over (ii) the highest applicable individual tax rate (Code Sec. 904(b)(3)(E)).

> **Practice Note:** Applying this formula to qualified dividends at the current rates would mean that the rate differential would be .5714 (35-percent maximum individual rate, less the 15-percent maximum rate for qualified dividends, divided by the highest individual rate of 35 percent). Thus, for example, a person with $10,000 in foreign dividend income would have a rate differential adjustment of $5,714, meaning that only $4,286 would be included in foreign source taxable income for purposes of claiming the foreign tax credit.

Qualifying noncorporate taxpayers may elect not to apply the rate differential adjustments for any tax year (Reg. § 1.904(b)-1(e)). The taxpayer must not be subject to alternative minimum tax for the tax year of the election. The highest rate for the taxpayer's income, excluding net capital gain and qualified dividend income, cannot exceed the highest rate of tax in effect under Code Sec. 1(h) for the tax year. In addition, the taxpayer's net capital gain from foreign sources, plus the amount of the taxpayer's qualified dividend income from foreign sources, must be less than $20,000 (Reg. § 1.904(b)-1(b)(3)).

Unrecaptured section 1250 gain. Qualified dividends are excluded from calculations of the net capital gain limit on the amount of gain taxed at the 25-percent rate (Code Sec. 1(h)(1)(D)(i)). Gain attributable to prior depreciation claimed on real property is taxed at a 25-percent rate, and is referred to as "unrecaptured section 1250 gain." Recapture occurs to prevent a taxpayer from obtaining favorable capital gain treatment on gain attributable to depreciation deductions that were used to offset ordinary income taxed at a higher rate.

In general, unrecaptured section 1250 gain is the amount of depreciation claimed on section 1250 property that is not recaptured as ordinary income. Since MACRS real property is not subject to ordinary income recapture, all depreciation on such property, to the extent of gain, is potentially characterized as unrecaptured section 1250 gain taxed at the 25 percent rate. The maximum amount subject to the 25-percent rate is the taxpayer's net capital gain.

> **Comment:** Section 1250 net capital gain is the excess of net long-term capital gain over net short-term capital loss, increased by qualified dividend income.

Under the formula for computing the tax on unrecaptured section 1250 gain, a tax rate of 25 percent is imposed on the excess of:

- the unrecaptured section 1250 gain (or, if less, net capital gain, determined without regard to qualified dividends), over
- the excess of the sum of the amount subject to tax at ordinary income rates, plus the net capital gain determined without regard to qualified dividends, over taxable income (Code Sec. 1(h)(1)(D)).

Adjusted net capital gain. Qualified dividends are included in the computation of adjusted net capital gain, which is the sum of: (i) the net capital gain, determined without regard to any qualified dividends, reduced by the sum of (a) any unrecaptured section 1250 gain, and (b) any 28-percent rate gain, plus (ii) any qualified

BACKGROUND

dividends (Code Sec. 1(h)(3)). See ¶405 for discussion of capital gain rates and computation.

Alternative minimum tax. The lower dividend rates of 15 and five percent (zero percent for taxpayers in the 10- or 15-percent bracket for tax years after 2007) are also used in computing an individual's liability for the alternative minimum tax (AMT) (Code Sec. 55(b)(3)(C)). AMT rules ensure that at least a minimum amount of income tax is paid by high-income taxpayers with large amounts of deductions.

An individual's AMT for a tax year is the excess of the individual's tentative minimum tax over the regular tax (Code Sec. 55(a)). Generally, the maximum rate of tax, including the AMT, on the net capital gain of an individual is 15 percent; five percent to the extent the taxpayer's taxable income is taxed at a rate below 25 percent (currently equivalent to the 10- and 15-percent brackets) (Code Sec. 55(b)(3)). Since qualified dividends are included in net capital gain for purposes of computing the tax, the dividends also qualify for the reduced AMT rate. See ¶405 for discussion of the treatment of capital gains for AMT purposes.

Sunset provision. Under a sunset provision of JGTRRA, certain amendments made by the Act will not apply to tax years beginning after December 31, 2010 (Act Sec. 303 of P.L. 108-27, as amended by Act Sec. 102 of the Tax Increase Prevention and Reconciliation Act of 2005 (TIPRA) (P.L. 109-222)).

NEW LAW EXPLAINED

Reduced rates for dividends extended for two years.—The reduced rates for qualified dividends received by individuals, trusts or estates under Code Secs. 1(h)(11) are extended for two years, through December 31, 2012. Thus, qualified dividends will continue to be taxed at capital gains rates in tax years beginning on or before December 31, 2012 (Act Sec. 102(a) of the Tax Relief, Unemployment Insurance Reauthorization, and Job Creation Act of 2010 (P.L. 111-312)).

> **Comment:** Because the current long-term capital gain rates are also extended through December 31, 2012 (see ¶405), the top federal tax rate for qualified dividends in 2011 and 2012 will be 15 percent (zero percent for those taxpayers whose income falls in the 10- or 15-percent rate brackets) (Code Sec. 1(h)(1)(B) and (C)).

Since qualified dividends will be taxed as net capital gain in 2011 and 2012, such dividends will continue to be included in the computation of the adjusted net capital gain under Code Sec. 1(h)(3), and taxpayers will make capital gain adjustments under Code Sec. 904(b)(2)(B) for dividend income in computing the foreign tax credit for such tax years. Qualified dividends also will be excluded from net capital gain in computing the tax on unrecaptured section 1250 gain, as provided in Code Sec. 1(h)(1)(D)(i).

In addition, proceeds from a disposition, other than a redemption, of Code Sec. 306 stock that was received as a nontaxable stock dividend will continue to be taxed as qualified dividends, pursuant to Code Sec. 306(a)(1)(D), in 2011 and 2012. Also, the general exclusion of qualified dividends received by a noncorporate taxpayer from

¶420

NEW LAW EXPLAINED

investment income and their inclusion only at the taxpayer's election (Code Sec. 163(d)(4)(B)) will still apply for tax years beginning before 2013. Moreover, dividends passed through to partners by a partnership or held by a common trust fund will be eligible for the reduced dividend rates in 2011 and 2012, assuming the distribution would otherwise be classified as qualified dividend income (Code Secs. 584(c) and 702(a)(5)).

Under the sunset provision of the Jobs and Growth Tax Relief Reconciliation Act of 2003 (JGTRRA) (P.L. 108-27), qualified dividends will be taxed at the applicable ordinary income tax rates in tax years beginning after December 31, 2012 (Act Sec. 303 of P.L. 108-27, as amended by Act Sec. 102 of the Tax Relief Act of 2010). Thus, for such tax years, taxpayers will not have to make capital gain adjustments under Code Sec. 904(b)(2)(B) for dividend income in computing the foreign tax credit, and dividends will not be included in the computation of the adjusted net capital gain under Code Sec. 1(h)(3). Also, since dividends will no longer be taxed at capital gain rates after 2012, the exclusion of qualified dividends from net capital gain in computing the tax on unrecaptured section 1250 gain will be inapplicable for such periods.

In addition, once the JGTRRA sunset takes effect in 2013, proceeds received upon the disposition of Code Sec. 306 stock will be taxed as ordinary income, and the general exclusion of qualified dividends of noncorporate taxpayers from investment income will not apply. Since there will be no dividends qualifying for lower capital gain rates after 2012, no such dividends will be reported as a separately stated item by partners and the rule providing that the proportionate share of each common trust fund participant in a qualified dividend received by the fund is treated as received by the participant will not apply to tax years beginning after 2012.

> **Comment:** Under the sunset provision of the Economic Growth and Tax Relief Reconciliation Act of 2001 (EGTRRA) (Act Sec. 901 of EGTRRA (P.L. 107-16), as amended by Act Sec. 101(a) of the Tax Relief Act of 2010), the individual ordinary income tax rates will rise for tax years beginning after December 31, 2012, with the top marginal rate rising from 35 percent to 39.6 percent (see ¶305). The maximum rate on long-term capital gains will also rise from 15 percent to 20 percent (see ¶405). Since qualified dividends will no longer enjoy capital gains treatment and will be subject to the ordinary income tax rates for those years, individuals will see a significant jump in the dividend tax rates, especially those individuals in the highest income tax brackets as the top tax rate on qualified dividends will rise from 15 percent to 39.6 percent.

> Beginning in 2013, dividends received by high-income individuals may be subject to a further tax increase as such individuals will also have to pay an additional Medicare tax of 3.8 percent on the lesser of their net investment income (which includes interest, dividends, capital gains, and certain types of business income) or the amount of modified adjusted gross income in excess of $200,000 ($250,000 in the case of joint filers and surviving spouses, and $125,000 in the case of a married taxpayer filing separately) (Code Sec. 1411, as added by the Health Care and Education Reconciliation Act of 2010 (P.L. 111-152)). The change in the effective rates on dividends and capital gains will also result in an increase in the alternative minimum tax (AMT) paid by individuals.

¶420

NEW LAW EXPLAINED

Planning Note: To allow shareholders to take advantage of the low dividend tax rates before they expire, corporations may plan to increase the amount of dividend distributions in 2011 and 2012. If a corporation does not have enough cash to distribute, it may consider distributing notes to its shareholders, instead. In such cases, the fair market value of the notes will be treated as a dividend.

When the high ordinary income tax rates on dividends kick in, corporations may consider buying back or redeeming stock from their shareholders, which may result in more preferable capital gain treatment to the shareholders. However, the Code Sec. 302 rules should be carefully considered to avoid dividend treatment of any distribution in redemption. Corporations may also try to reduce their earnings and profits since corporate distributions are taxed as dividends to the shareholders only to the extent of the corporation's earnings and profits.

In addition, individual investors may consider shifting from stock investments to investments in state and local bonds as the tax-exempt interest on such bonds may be more attractive than the highly taxed dividend income. Debt financing may also be more favorable than equity financing in light of the increase in the dividend tax rates and the deductibility of interest payments on debt.

Practical Analysis: According to Vincent O'Brien, President of Vincent J. O'Brien, CPA, PC, Lynbrook, New York, the extension of the lower rate on qualified dividends for individuals (Code Sec. 1) for the 2011 and 2012 tax year will stay at the same maximum rate as long-term capital gains (generally 15 percent). Without this extension, such dividends would have been taxed as ordinary income, under the original expiration date of The Jobs and Growth Tax Relief Reconciliation Act of 2003 (JGTRRA) (P.L. 108-27).

This will benefit the shareholders of certain S corporations. If an S corporation was a C corporation prior to making an S election, it may have undistributed profits from its period as a C corporation. These undistributed profits are referred to as accumulated earnings and profits ("AE&P"). Distributions of AE&P are treated as taxable dividends to a shareholder, even after the company has become an S corporation. That is, AE&P retains its taxable-dividend character, even after the company is no longer a C corporation. Unless otherwise elected, an S corporation distribution is first treated as coming from its earnings from its period of operation as an S corporation. Such distributions are tax-free to the extent of basis. S corporations with AE&P must carefully keep track of earnings during the period as an S corporation, by using the accumulated adjustments account ("AAA") on Schedule M-2 of Form 1120S.

However, once the company has exhausted its S corporation earnings, any additional distributions will come from AE&P and create a taxable dividend for the shareholders. Due to the extension of the lower tax rate for qualified dividends, if such dividends are paid prior to January 1, 2013, they will generally be taxed at a maximum rate of 15 percent. Without the extension, they would have been taxed as ordinary income.

If a shareholder owns an S corporation with AE&P, and the shareholder will have the need to withdraw a large amount of funds from the S corporation in the foreseeable

¶420

NEW LAW EXPLAINED

future, the shareholder should consider making the withdrawal before 2013, while the tax rates on dividends are relatively low. Eliminating the AE&P also eliminates the chance that the S corporation will be subject to the excess passive income tax, which can also cause the S corporation to lose its S status after three consecutive years of being subject to the tax.

An S corporation can elect to treat a distribution as coming from AE&P before S corporation earnings. Furthermore, if an S corporation is illiquid and is unable to pay such a distribution, the S corporation can elect to have a deemed distribution, where the shareholder is treated as receiving a dividend and immediately contributing it back to the capital of the company. All shareholders must consent to these elections.

Practical Analysis: According to Daniel S. Hoops, Walsh College, Troy, Michigan, the capital gain rates on qualified dividends received by individuals, trusts or estates (Code Sec. 1(h)) is extended for two years under the Tax Relief, Unemployment Insurance Reauthorization and Job Creation Act of 2010 (2010 Tax Relief Act).

Continuing after December 31, 2010, individual taxpayers that were subject to the ordinary income tax rates on qualified dividends under the expiration of the Jobs and Growth Tax Relief Reconciliation Act of 2003 (JGTRRA) should be relieved that this change has been delayed. The extension of the favorable capital gains rates should also, indirectly, affect the behavior of some corporations.

From a shareholder perspective, continuing the favorable capital gains rates goes beyond paying tax at a higher rate. Individuals, estates and trusts may include their qualified dividends in calculating adjusted net capital gains and any unrecaptured gains under Code Sec. 1250. Individuals with net capital losses may continue to apply qualified dividends against those losses in calculating the $3,000 ($1,500 for married individuals) limitation for deducting net capital losses against ordinary income.

For many individual shareholders, they will be less inclined to make any drastic investment decisions before the end of 2010. There may have been individuals willing to take an immediate capital gain on shares of dividend-paying stock or replacing those shares with investments that would not generate additional ordinary income tax. This type of investment behavior would have had a detrimental effect on many publicly traded corporations.

In addition to individual investors, the investment strategies of fiduciaries are also given a two-year reprieve under the 2010 Tax Relief Act. Investments will not be scrutinized by the amount of tax generated by the assets owned by estates and trusts if dividends are received, but taxed at the preferential capital gains rate. Without the extension, for example, a trustee's investment plan could be challenged, or even considered imprudent, if the trustee continued to retain stocks generating income that would be taxed at a much higher rate, as opposed to holding municipal bonds which pay a lower yield but are tax free. Trustees will also be relieved that they will not be called upon to consider the ordinary income tax rates of their trust and beneficiaries when making discretionary distributions of dividends and capital gains. For example, under the JGTRRA sunset, a dividend distribution may have

¶420

NEW LAW EXPLAINED

placed one income beneficiary (and not another) into a higher bracket, whereas a distribution of a capital gain to the one income beneficiary and dividends to the other would not affect either of the beneficiaries' tax rates.

Corporate operations should also be stabilized with the continuation of the capital gains rate on dividends. Until the enactment of the 2010 Tax Relief Act, many corporations were presumably racing to declare dividends to beat the expiration of the rate change. In addition, the 2010 Tax Relief Act does not compel corporations to completely reduce their current and accumulated earnings and profits by year-end with increased borrowing or additional business expenditures from corporate earnings in profits to minimize the dividend treatment of distributions to shareholders.

The motivation of a corporation to make distributions to its individual shareholders is not as great with the ordinary income tax rate on dividends being deferred until December 31, 2012. Stock redemptions, as opposed to cash dividends, are also not a tax motivated option for individual shareholders under the 2010 Tax Relief Act because capital gains treatment is available for both dividends and redemptions.

Although the retention of corporate income was an option that many individual shareholders may have preferred if the favorable tax rates on dividends expired, the Internal Revenue Code does not share that same philosophy. As a result of the 2010 Tax Relief Act, corporations will be less likely to please their individual shareholders with retained income and face punitive taxation.

Under Code Secs. 541-547, the Personal Holding Company ("PHC") tax is a punitive tax on the passive income or income derived from certain personal services of corporations that meet the definition of a PHC. The PHC tax is levied upon the undistributed PHC income at a flat 15 percent rate; it is in addition to the corporation's regular income tax. For corporations that meet the definition of a PHC, this tax is easily avoided when the corporation makes a distribution of its PHC income, i.e., pays dividends. The motivation to retain PHC income is not a wise decision and with the capital gains rate on dividends retained, individual shareholders will, most likely, not pressure directors to retain income and subject the corporation to the additional 15 percent PHC tax.

Without the extension of the capital gains rate on dividends, corporations also ran the risk of accumulating their earnings to such an extent that they would be subject to the 15-percent accumulated earnings tax ("AET") under Code Secs. 531 through 537. Shareholder loans or expenditures that benefit shareholders personally may have become more common without the tax relief and thereby susceptible to the AET. Investments in assets without a reasonable connection to the corporation's business could also have become more likely and subjected the corporate income to the AET.

Unlike the PHC tax, which is assessed mechanically (*e.g.*, stock ownership, percentage of passive and operating income) the 15-percent AET is levied on undistributed earnings of the corporation that exceed its "reasonable needs". The IRS would have to make a determination that the corporation had a tax avoidance purpose in not distributing its earnings. This is a more difficult assessment to make considering the AET is based on the facts and circumstances of each business decision. Proving a tax avoidance motivation requires a subjective analysis of the corporation's activities; in other words, the corporation would need to be audited and "caught" before the

NEW LAW EXPLAINED

tax rates they may reduce their yields after 2012. Corporations making these types of timing decisions generally would be closely held. Corporations whose stock is held by large numbers of individuals and/or institutions are less likely to change the timing or the rate of dividends based on recipients' tax rates. Widely held corporations tend to experience pressure to increase dividends over time or at least to maintain them regardless of tax rates.

Taxable Years After 2012

Forms of Holding Investments. Starting in 2013, scheduled rate increases on dividends will for some investments render tax-deferred accounts relatively more attractive than taxable accounts. The anticipated increase in rates also may render relatively more attractive, compared to taxable investments, tax-exempt investments such as municipal bonds. The higher the yield on a prospective investment, the higher the value of holding the investment in a tax-deferred account. The Code, however, limits the amounts that individuals annually may contribute to tax-deferred accounts. Additionally, the Code narrowly restricts opportunities to transfer an existing investment from a taxable account to a tax-deferred account without recognizing taxable gain. In choosing forms of holding investments, individuals also should consider the rates at which amounts they eventually withdraw from a tax-deferred account may be taxed. Amounts eventually withdrawn from a tax-deferred account may end up being taxed at rates exceeding the rates at which dividends earlier realized in a taxable account would have been taxed. Nevertheless, if the investor does not plan to start withdrawing funds anytime soon, then the present value of the projected tax on amounts eventually withdrawn from a tax deferred account may prove attractive. Starting in 2013, scheduled increases in Medicare taxes on taxable investment income including dividends also may make tax-deferred accounts more attractive.

Holding Period in Dividend Stock. If Code Sec. 1(h)(11) sunsets as scheduled, then the disappearing rules will include those cross-referencing Code Sec. 246(c) that require a minimum holding period for qualified dividends. Thus, starting in 2013, the rate at which dividends received are taxed no longer will depend on whether those holding periods have been satisfied.

Coordination with Investment Interest Limitation. If Code Sec. 1(h)(11) sunsets as scheduled, then also disappearing will be the rule excluding from qualified dividend income those dividends a taxpayer elects to treat as investment income under Code Sec. 163(d). Presumably, as under the law predating JGTRRA, dividends will be included in investment income without a taxpayer's having so to elect. However, the Code will continue to require taxpayers to elect whether to treat capital gains as investment income.

Timing of Selling Decisions. Starting in 2013, increased rates on dividends will diminish the attractiveness of continuing to hold significantly yielding equities in taxable accounts. Beginning in 2013, upper-income individuals also are scheduled to be subject to increased Medicare taxes on net investment income including dividends. Under an alternative point of view, one may decide to continue holding such investments with the hope that Congress eventually again will reduce tax rates on dividends received.

NEW LAW EXPLAINED

Corporate Financing Decisions. Beginning in 2013, corporations that may have decided under the rates applicable through 2012 to issue additional stock rather than additional debt may decide differently once the rates revert to levels predating JGTRRA. Absent intervening legislation, dividends received and interest received will be subject to tax at the same rates. Corporations in determining their taxable income cannot deduct dividends they pay their shareholders. By contrast, corporations subject to applicable limitations may deduct interest paid on their debt. The higher the rates on dividends received, the more the entity-level deduction for interest paid may influence some corporations to raise needed capital by issuing new debt rather than new stock.

Dividend Yields on Corporate Stock. Reacting to higher rates on dividends received, some corporations may reduce the rates at which they pay dividends. Instead of paying out cash, they may choose to retain it. Corporations that react to higher dividend rates in this way generally would be closely held. Widely held corporations tend to experience pressure to increase dividends over time or at least to maintain them regardless of tax rates.

Importance of Continuing Parity in Rates Between Dividends and Capital Gains. Even if a future Congress does not act further to extend JGTRRA's rates beyond 2012, it is urged that the Code continue to tax at the same rates noncorporate taxpayers' dividends and capital gains. For example, if after 2012 capital gains become taxable at 20 percent as scheduled, then the Code should be amended also to tax dividends at 20 percent. Otherwise, dividends beginning in 2013 will become taxable at the marginal rates applicable to ordinary income. For many if not most individuals, that marginal rate will exceed 20 percent. During 2010, one or more bills were introduced in Congress to preserve the parity in rates advocated here. The 2010 Act's temporarily extending JGTRRA's preferential rates on capital gains and dividends rendered such action unnecessary for now. However, the issue will resurface as 2013 approaches. Economically, dividends and capital gains represent merely different ways of earning a return on an investment. Taxing dividends and capital gains at different rates would distort their economic equivalence. From a tax perspective, dividends and capital gains differ primarily in that in measuring recognizable capital gain a taxpayer offsets adjusted basis in the sold property. It would seem counterintuitive to tax income net of a basis offset (capital gains) at a lower rate than the rate on income not similarly offset (dividends). The tax rate on dividends also should be constrained in order to mitigate the sting of corporate double taxation. Some argue that dividends received and interest received should be taxable at the same rates. Otherwise, the argument goes, the Code artificially favors one form of corporate financing over the other. When, however, one considers all the tax consequences of a corporation's paying a dividend compared to paying interest, the argument fails to withstand scrutiny. Corporations in determining their taxable income may not deduct dividends they pay their shareholders. By contrast, corporations subject to applicable limitations can deduct interest paid to debtholders. In order to mitigate the consequences of this distinction, the rate at which dividends received are subject to tax should be kept meaningfully lower than the rates applicable to interest received.

Practical Analysis: Mark R. Solomon, Walsh College, Troy, Michigan, notes that Sections 101 and 102 of the Tax Relief, Unemployment Insurance Reauthorization, and Jobs Creation Act of 2010 (2010 Tax Relief Act) have extended until December 31, 2012, the tax relief provisions of the Economic Growth and Tax Reconciliation Act of 2001 (EGTRRA) and the Jobs and Growth Tax Reconciliation Act of 2003 (JGTRRA) (P.L. 108-27). Among other things, this extension has the effect of maintaining the status quo as to dividends.

While the extension of favorable dividend rates for qualified dividend income as defined in Code Sec. 1(h)(1) is unlikely to affect the dividend behavior of publicly-traded corporations, which are under heavy pressure from institutional investors (for example, pension plans) to pay dividends, whatever the rate, closely-held corporations will continue to experience less need to pay dividends in order to avoid the accumulated earnings tax under Code Sec. 531 or the personal holding tax under Code Sec. 541. However, reasonable compensation questions are likely to continue to appear at audit, as revenue agents are likely to continue to be interested in paid, but non-deductible excessive compensation (treated as dividends and thus a source of double taxation). Advisors to newly-formed closely-held businesses will thus continue to have reason to recommend the use of limited liability companies or S corporations, absent compelling business or tax reasons for the use of C corporations. Advisors are cautioned that the favorable treatment of qualified dividends is scheduled to sunset at the end of 2012. Because 2012 is an election year, it is difficult to predict whether favorable dividend treatment will be extended, made permanent, or expire. Thus, before recommending the use of C corporations to clients based on the low rate of dividend double taxation, advisors should further note that it is much more difficult taxwise to convert a C corporation to an LLC than the other way around.

▶ **Effective date.** The provision applies to tax years beginning after December 31, 2002 (Act Sec. 102(b) of the Tax Relief, Unemployment Insurance Reauthorization, and Job Creation Act of 2010 (P.L. 111-312)); Act Sec. 302(f)(1) of the Jobs and Growth Tax Relief Reconciliation Act of 2003 (JGTRRA) (P.L. 108-27)). The provision shall not apply to tax years beginning after December 31, 2012 (Act Sec. 102(a) of the Tax Relief Act of 2010; Act Sec. 303 of JGTRRA). See ¶105 for a specific discussion of the sunset provision of JGTRRA and how it is applied.

Law source: Law at ¶5005, ¶5255, ¶5325, ¶5335, ¶5400, ¶5420, and ¶7015. Committee Report at ¶10,080.

— Act Sec. 102(a) of the the Tax Relief, Unemployment Insurance Reauthorization, and Job Creation Act of 2010 (P.L. 111-312), amending Act Sec. 303 of the Jobs and Growth Tax Relief Reconciliation Act of 2003 (JGTRRA) (P.L. 108-27);

— Act Sec. 102(b), providing the effective date.

Reporter references: For further information, consult the following CCH reporters.

— Standard Federal Tax Reporter, ¶3285.01

— Tax Research Consultant, FILEIND: 15,054.15, CCORP: 6,062, SALES: 15,202.55 and PLANIND: 12,202

— Practical Tax Explanation, §3,030.05, §7,414.15, §13,245.10 and §26,230

¶420

¶425 Pass-Through Treatment of Qualified Dividend Income

SUMMARY OF NEW LAW

The reduced rates applicable to qualified dividend income passed through a mutual fund (Code Sec. 854(b)(1)(B)), real estate investment trust (Code Sec. 857(c)), or other pass-through entity as qualified dividend income in the hands of recipients is extended two years and is now scheduled to expire for tax years beginning after December 31, 2012. This change corresponds to the general two-year extension for taxing qualified dividend income at capital gains rates.

BACKGROUND

The Jobs and Growth Tax Relief Reconciliation Act of 2003 (JGTRRA) (P.L. 108-27) reduced the federal tax rates for qualified dividends received by individuals, estates or trusts, by providing that such dividends will be taxed at capital gain rates for tax years beginning after December 31, 2002 (see ¶420) (Code Sec. 1(h)(11)). The top federal tax rate for qualified dividends is 15 percent (five percent for those whose income falls in the 10- or 15-percent rate brackets). A zero-percent rate applies to taxpayers in the 10-percent or 15-percent income tax brackets for tax years beginning after 2007 (Code Sec. 1(h)(1)(B) and (C)).

JGTRRA (as amended by the Tax Increase Prevention and Reconciliation Act of 2005 (TIPRA) (P.L. 109-222)) provides that qualified dividend income passed through to investors through certain entities are treated as qualified dividend income in the hands of recipients for this purpose. These entities include:

- regulated investment companies (RICs), commonly known as mutual funds;
- real estate investment trusts (REITs);
- partnerships and S corporations;
- estates and revocable trusts treated as part of an estate; and
- common trust funds (Act Sec. 302(f) of JGTRRA, as amended by Act Sec. 402(a)(6) of the Working Families Tax Relief Act of 2004 (2004 Tax Relief Act) (P.L. 108-311)).

The pass-through provisions are effective for tax years beginning after December 31, 2002. Dividends received by the pass-through entity on or before that date are not treated as qualified dividend income (Act Sec. 302(f) of JGTRRA, as amended by the 2004 Tax Relief Act).

Qualified dividend income paid by mutual funds. A shareholder in a mutual fund can treat qualified dividend income passed through the fund as qualified dividend income subject to capital gains rates. For this purpose, the mutual fund can designate dividends paid to its shareholders as qualified dividend income if less than 95 percent of its income is derived from qualified dividend income (Code Sec. 854(b)(1)(B)). However, the aggregate amount designated as qualified dividend income may not exceed the sum of:

BACKGROUND

- the qualified dividend income of the mutual fund for the tax year; and
- the amount of any earnings and profits distributed for the tax year accumulated in a tax year in which the mutual fund rules did not apply (Code Sec. 854(b)(1)(C)).

Qualified dividend income paid by REITs. A portion of a REIT's distribution may be classified as qualified dividend income if it is either:

- attributable to income that was subject to corporate tax at the REIT level; or
- a corporate dividend received as investment income by the REIT (and was qualified dividend income when it was received by the REIT).

The amount of dividends paid by a REIT that will qualify for the reduced rate may not exceed the amount of aggregate qualifying dividends received by the REIT, and the aggregate amount of qualifying dividends received by the REIT must be less than 95 percent of its gross income (Code Sec. 857(c), as amended by JGTRRA, the 2004 Tax Relief Act, and TIPRA). The most that can be designated as qualified dividend income is the sum of:

- the qualified dividend income of the REIT for the tax year;
- the excess of the REIT's taxable income, over the taxes payable by the REIT for that preceding tax year; and
- the amount of earnings and profits distributed by the REIT during the preceding tax year that were accumulated in a tax year to which the REIT rules did not apply (Code Sec. 857(c)(2)(B)).

Qualified dividend income paid by partnerships, S corporations, estates, and trusts. Partnerships, S corporations, estates, revocable trusts treated as part of an estate, or common trust fund can pass through dividends received to their partners, shareholders and beneficiaries as dividends qualifying for the lower tax rates, to the extent that the dividends are otherwise qualified. Each partner in a partnership takes into account separately the partner's distributive share of the partnership's qualified dividend income (Code Sec. 702(a)(5)), and each participant in a common trust fund includes in taxable income its proportionate share of the amount of qualified dividend income received by the trust (Code Sec. 584(c)).

Sunset provision. Under a sunset provision of JGTRRA, certain amendments (including the amendments related to qualified dividend income) made by that act will not apply to tax years beginning after December 31, 2010 (Act Sec. 303 of JGTRRA, as amended by TIPRA).

NEW LAW EXPLAINED

Sunset for pass-through of qualified dividend income extended.—The treatment of qualified dividend income passed through a regulated investment company (mutual fund) (Code Sec. 854(b)(1)(B)), real estate investment trust (REIT) (Code Sec. 857(c)), or other pass-through entity as qualified dividend income in the hands of recipients is extended two years. Under the Tax Relief, Unemployment Insurance Reauthorization, and Job Creation Act of 2010 (P.L. 111-312), this treatment will expire for tax years

NEW LAW EXPLAINED

beginning after December 31, 2012. This change corresponds to the general two-year extension for taxing qualified dividend income at capital gains rates (see ¶ 420).

> **Comment:** If the lower rates are allowed to expire after 2012, dividends passed through a mutual fund, REIT, and other pass-through entities will be taxed at ordinary income tax rates for dividend income distributed on or after January 1, 2013, even if the dividends were received by the pass-through entity before that date.

> **Comment:** The top rate on ordinary income after 2012 is scheduled to be as high as 39.6 percent, but the top capital gains rate will still be tempting 20 percent (18 percent for five-year property) (see ¶ 305, ¶ 405 and ¶ 410).

> **Comment:** Taxing corporate dividends at capital gains rates has not had much impact on REIT investors because REIT distributions mostly consist of rent (taxable at ordinary rates), capital gain dividends (already tax-favored), and the return of capital based on depreciation which is not currently taxed at all (and ultimately taxed at capital gains rates). Because REITs are capital gain generators, they should do well if and when the lower rates for capital gains are allowed to expire.

▶ **Effective date.** The provision is effective for tax years beginning after December 31, 2002 (Act Sec. 102(b) of the Tax Relief, Unemployment Insurance Reauthorization, and Job Creation Act of 2010 (P.L. 111-312)); Act Sec. 302(f) of the Jobs and Growth Tax Relief Reconciliation Act of 2003 (JGTRRA) (P.L. 108-27), as amended by Act Sec. 402(a)(6) of the Working Families Tax Relief Act of 2004 (P.L. 108-311)). The provision shall not apply to tax years beginning after December 31, 2012 (Act Sec. 102(a) of the Tax Relief Act of 2010; Act Sec. 303 of JGTRRA). See ¶ 105 for a specific discussion of the sunset provision of JGTRRA and how it is applied.

Law source: Law at ¶5005, ¶5325, ¶5335, ¶5345, ¶5365, ¶5385, ¶5390, ¶5400, ¶5420, ¶5445, ¶5535, ¶5540, and ¶7015. Committee Report at ¶10,080

— Act Sec. 102(a) of the Tax Relief, Unemployment Insurance Reauthorization, and Job Creation Act of 2010 (P.L. 111-312), amending Act Sec. 303 of the Jobs and Growth Tax Relief Reconciliation Act of 2003 (P.L. 108-27);

— Act Sec. 102(b), providing the effective date.

Reporter references: For further information, consult the following CCH reporters.

— Standard Federal Tax Reporter, ¶3,285.01, ¶26,465.01, ¶26,533.04

— Tax Research Consultant, RIC: 3,400 and RIC: 6,150

— Practical Tax Explanation, § 19,205.15

¶425

¶430 Tax Treatment of Regulated Investment Company Dividends Paid to Foreign Persons

SUMMARY OF NEW LAW

The exemption from the 30-percent tax, collected through withholding, on regulated investment company (RIC) dividends, designated as either interest-related or short-term capital gain dividends, is extended for two years, through 2011.

BACKGROUND

A regulated investment company (RIC), commonly known as a mutual fund, is a domestic corporation or common trust fund that invests in stocks and securities. RICs must satisfy a number of complex tests relating to income, assets, and other matters (Code Secs. 851 and 852). A RIC passes through the character of its long-term capital gains to its shareholders, by designating a dividend paid as a capital gain dividend to the extent that the RIC has net capital gain available. Shareholders treat these dividends as long-term capital gains (Code Sec. 852(b)(3)).

Generally, U.S. source income received by a nonresident alien or foreign corporation that is not "effectively connected with a U.S. trade or business" is subject to a flat 30-percent tax, collected through withholding (or, if applicable, a lower treaty tax rate) (Code Secs. 871(a) and 881). U.S. source net income that is "effectively connected" to a trade or business is subject to the regular graduated tax rates (Code Secs. 871(b) and 882).

The following items received by a nonresident alien or foreign corporation are exempt from the 30-percent tax:

- interest on certain bank deposits (Code Secs. 871(i)(2)(A) and 881(d));

- original issue discount on obligations that mature within 183 days from the original issue date (Code Sec. 871(g)); and

- interest paid on portfolio obligations (Code Secs. 871(h) and 881(c)).

Foreign persons are generally not subject to tax on gain realized when they dispose of stock or securities issued by a U.S. entity, unless the gain is effectively connected with the conduct of a U.S. trade or business. This exception does not apply, however, in the case of a nonresident alien who is present in the United States for 183 or more aggregated days in a tax year (Code Sec. 871(a)(2)).

A RIC may elect not to withhold tax on a distribution to a foreign person that represents a capital gain dividend or an exempt-interest dividend under the RIC rules (Code Sec. 852(b)(3)(C) and (b)(5); Reg. § 1.1441-3(c)(2)(i)(D)).

Interest-related dividend. For dividends with respect to tax years of RICs beginning after December 31, 2004, but before January 1, 2010, a RIC can designate all or a portion of a dividend paid to a nonresident alien or foreign corporation as an interest-related dividend. The RIC must designate the dividend as an interest-related dividend by written notice mailed to its shareholders no later than 60 days after the

BACKGROUND

close of its tax year. As a result of the designation, and with some exceptions, the dividend is exempt from the 30-percent tax, collected through withholding. The provision applies to amounts that would be exempt if paid to a nonresident alien or foreign corporation directly (Code Secs. 871(k)(1)(C), 881(e)(1), 1441(c)(12) and 1442(a)). An interest-related dividend is limited to the RIC's qualified net interest income. Qualified interest income is the sum of the RIC's U.S. source income with respect to:

- bank deposit interest described in Code Sec. 871(i)(2)(A);
- short-term original issue discount that is currently exempt from tax under Code Sec. 871(g);
- any interest (including amounts recognized as ordinary income in respect of original issue discount, market discount, or acquisition discount, and any other such amounts that may be prescribed by regulations) on an obligation that is in registered form (unless the interest was earned on an obligation issued by a corporation or partnership in which the RIC is a 10-percent shareholder or is contingent interest not treated as portfolio interest under Code Sec. 871(h)(4)); and
- any interest-related dividend from another RIC (Code Sec. 871(k)(1)(E)).

If the exemption is inapplicable because the interest is on certain debt of the RIC dividend recipient or any corporation or partnership for which the recipient is a 10-percent shareholder, the RIC remains exempt from its withholding obligation unless it knows the dividend is subject to the exception (Code Secs. 871(k)(1)(B)(i) and 1441(c)(12)(B)). A similar rule applies in the case of dividends received by controlled foreign corporations where the interest is attributable to a related person (Code Secs. 881(e)(1)(B)(ii) and 1442(a)).

Short-term capital gain dividend. For dividends with respect to tax years of a RIC beginning after December 31, 2004, but before January 1, 2010, a RIC can designate all or a portion of a dividend paid to a nonresident alien or foreign corporation as a short-term capital gain dividend. The RIC must designate the dividend as a short-term capital gain dividend by written notice mailed to its shareholders no later than 60 days after the close of its tax year. As a result of the designation, the short-term capital gain dividend is exempt from the 30-percent tax, collected through withholding (Code Secs. 871(k)(2)(C), 881(e)(2), 1441(c)(12) and 1442(a)). This exemption does not apply when the nonresident alien is present in the United States for 183 days or more during the tax year (Code Sec. 871(k)(2)(B)). If the exemption is inapplicable, the RIC, nevertheless, remains exempt from its withholding obligation, unless it knows that the dividend recipient has been present in the United States for such period (Code Sec. 1441(c)(12)(B)).

The amount designated as a short-term capital gain dividend cannot exceed the qualified short-term capital gain for the tax year. The amount qualified to be designated as a short-term capital gain dividend for the RIC's tax year is equal to the excess of the RIC's net short-term capital gain over its net long-term capital loss. Short-term capital gain includes short-term capital gain dividends from another RIC. Net short-term capital gain is determined without regard to any net capital loss or net short-term capital loss attributable to transactions occurring after October 31 of the

BACKGROUND

tax year. The loss is treated as arising on the first day of the next tax year. To the extent provided in regulations, this rule will apply for purposes of computing the RIC's taxable income (Code Sec. 871(k)(2)(D)).

NEW LAW EXPLAINED

Favorable tax treatment of RIC dividends paid to foreign persons extended.—The provision that allows a regulated investment company (RIC) to designate dividends paid to nonresident aliens or foreign corporations as interest-related dividends or short-term capital gain dividends is extended for two years. Dividends that are so designated are generally exempt from the 30-percent tax collected through withholding. Specifically, interest-related dividends and short-term capital gain dividends include dividends with respect to a tax year of a RIC beginning after December 31, 2004, and before January 1, 2012 (Code Sec. 871(k)(1)(C) and (2)(C), as amended by the Tax Relief, Unemployment Insurance Reauthorization, and Job Creation Act of 2010 (P.L. 111-312)).

State Tax Consequences: States such as Arizona and Ohio that exempt regulated investment companies from taxation will not be impacted by the extension of the RIC provisions. Nor will states such as Michigan or New Jersey that treat RICs as taxable entities. For those states that follow the federal treatment of RICs, whether the state will conform to the extension is dependent on the state's Internal Revenue Code conformity date.

Comment: The requirements by which a RIC may designate a dividend as an interest-related dividend or a short-term capital gain dividend by giving written notice to shareholders within 60 days after the close of the RIC's tax year has been replaced with new requirements that such dividends be reported by the RIC in written statements to its shareholders. For a discussion of the new requirements, see ¶809.

▶ **Effective date.** The amendments made by this provision apply to tax years beginning after December 31, 2009 (Act Sec. 748(b) of the Tax Relief, Unemployment Insurance Reauthorization, and Job Creation Act of 2010 (P.L. 111-312)).

Law source: Law at ¶5465. Committee Report at ¶10,530.

— Act Sec. 748(a) of the Tax Relief, Unemployment Insurance Reauthorization, and Job Creation Act of 2010 (P.L. 111-312), amending Code Sec. 871(k)(1)(C) and (2)(C);

— Act Sec. 748(b), providing the effective date.

Reporter references: For further information, consult the following CCH reporters.

— Standard Federal Tax Reporter, ¶27,343.0444 and ¶27,484.0255

— Tax Research Consultant, INTL: 33,150

— Practical Tax Explanation, §37,010.15

COMMUNITY ASSISTANCE

¶440 Empowerment Zone Tax Benefits

SUMMARY OF NEW LAW

The tax benefits available to certain businesses and employers operating in financially distressed "Empowerment Zones" have been extended two years, and the procedure for designating the period of empowerment zone status has been revised.

BACKGROUND

Since 1994, numerous economically depressed areas of the country have been designated as "empowerment zones" entitling certain businesses operating in these zones to a series of tax benefits that, generally, expire at the end of 2009 (Code Sec. 1391(d)(1)(A)(i)). These tax breaks include the following:

Tax-exempt bonds for empowerment zones. Qualifying businesses operating in empowerment zones are able to obtain tax-exempt bond financing through the end of 2009 if 95 percent of the proceeds are used for certain business facilities operating in the applicable empowerment zone (Code Secs. 1391(d)(1)(A)(i) and 1394).

Empowerment zone employment credit. Through the end of 2009, empowerment zone employers are entitled to a 20-percent credit against income tax for the first $15,000 of qualified wages (i.e., a maximum credit of $3,000) paid to full or part-time employees who are residents of the empowerment zones and who perform substantially all their employment services within the zone in the employer's trade or business (Code Secs. 1391(d)(1)(A)(i) and 1396).

Increase in Code Sec. 179 expensing. Businesses operating in an empowerment zone are entitled to deduct an increased amount of the cost of certain tangible depreciable property placed in service before January 1, 2010, which is used in an empowerment zone trade or business and placed in service during the tax year (Code Secs. 1391(d)(1)(A)(i) and 1397A).

Empowerment zone gain rollover. Through the end of 2009, certain taxpayers can elect to roll over, or defer the recognition of, capital gain realized from the sale or exchange of qualified empowerment zone assets which are held for more than one year if the taxpayer uses the proceeds to purchase other qualifying empowerment zone assets in the same zone within 60 days of the initial sale (Code Secs. 1391(d)(1)(A)(i) and 1397B).

Additional gain exclusion for sale of qualified small business stock. Noncorporate taxpayers who sell stock of certain small businesses operating in an empowerment zone are entitled to exclude up to 60 percent of the gain from the sale. This gain exclusion provision is slated to expire at the end of 2014 (Code Sec. 1202(a)(2)).

¶440

The Secretaries of Housing and Urban Development and Agriculture designate empowerment zones and enterprise communities from areas nominated by state and local governments. The designation period for empowerment zone status must end no later than December 31, 2009 (Code Sec. 1391(d)(1)(A)(i)). Earlier termination dates are permitted if the state or local government designated an earlier date in its nomination application (Code Sec. 1391(d)(1)(B)), or the appropriate federal authority revokes the designation (Code Sec. 1391(d)(1)(C)).

A round of nine empowerment zones were authorized to be designated by the appropriate authorities before January 1, 2002. The default designation period for those empowerment zones began on January 1, 2002, and ended on December 31, 2009, unless an earlier termination date was identified in the nomination application or the designation was revoked (Code Sec. 1391(h)(2)).

Expiration date for empowerment zone tax benefits extended.—The Tax Relief, Unemployment Insurance Reauthorization, and Job Creation Act of 2010 (P.L. 111-312) extends the expiration date for the empowerment zone tax benefits for two years. As a result, the empowerment zone tax benefits are generally extended through the end of 2011, and gain exclusion under Code Sec. 1202 is extended through 2016.

The specific changes are as follows:

- **Additional gain exclusion for sale of qualified small business stock.** Taxpayers may apply the gain exclusion provisions of Code Sec. 1202 to gain attributable to transactions occurring through December 31, 2016 (Code Sec. 1202(a)(2)(C), as amended by the Tax Relief Act of 2010).

- **Tax-exempt bonds for empowerment zones.** Qualifying businesses operating in empowerment zones are able to obtain tax-exempt bond financing under the provisions of Code Sec. 1394 through the end of 2011 (Code Sec. 1391(d)(1)(A)(i), as amended by the Tax Relief Act of 2010).

- **Empowerment zone employment credit.** Employers in empowerment zones may take the 20-percent credit against income tax for qualified wages paid to eligible employees in empowerment zones under Code Sec. 1396 through the end of 2011 (Code Sec. 1391(d)(1)(A)(i), as amended by the Tax Relief Act of 2010).

- **Increase in Code Sec. 179 expensing.** The increased Code Sec. 179 expensing available to eligible businesses operating in an empowerment zone under Code Sec. 1397A is extended through the end of 2011 (Code Sec. 1391(d)(1)(A)(i), as amended by the Tax Relief Act of 2010).

- **Empowerment zone gain rollover.** The ability to elect to roll over, or defer the recognition of, capital gain realized from the sale or exchange of qualified empowerment zone assets which are held for more than one year where the taxpayer uses the proceeds to purchase other qualifying empowerment zone assets in the same zone within 60 days of the initial sale under Code Sec. 1397B is extended through the end of 2011 (Code Sec. 1391(d)(1)(A)(i), as amended by the Tax Relief Act of 2010).

NEW LAW EXPLAINED

Period of designation. In the case of a designation of an empowerment zone the nomination for which included a termination date contemporaneous with the date specified in Code Sec. 1391(d)(1)(A)(i) as in effect before being amended by the Tax Relief Act of 2010, the rule that the state or local government can adopt an earlier termination date for the designation period (Code Sec. 1391(d)(1)(B)) does not apply, if (after December 17, 2010, the date of the enactment of the Tax Relief Act of 2010) the entity which made the nomination amends the nomination to provide for a new termination date in such manner as the Secretary of the Treasury may provide (Act Sec. 753(c) of the Tax Relief Act of 2010).

> **Comment:** Under this rule, if the state or local government that made the nomination does not amend its nomination application, the designation period will be extended to December 31, 2011.

In addition, the default period for designation of additional empowerment zones of January 1, 2002, to December 31, 2009, no longer applies (Code Sec. 1391(h)(2), as amended by the Tax Relief Act of 2010). Accordingly, the designation period for such zones ends December 31, 2011 (Code Sec. 1391(d)(1)(A)(i), as amended by the Tax Relief Act of 2010) under the general designation period rules of Code Sec. 1391(d)(1).

▶ **Effective date.** The provision shall apply to periods after December 31, 2009 (Act Sec. 753(d) of the Tax Relief, Unemployment Insurance Reauthorization, and Job Creation Act of 2010 (P.L. 111-312)).

Law source: Law at ¶5510, ¶5560, and ¶7065. Committee Report at ¶10,580.

— Act Sec. 753(a)(1) of the Tax Relief, Unemployment Insurance Reauthorization, and Job Creation Act of 2010 (P.L. 111-312), amending Code Sec. 1391(d)(1)(A)(i);

— Act Sec. 753(a)(2), amending Code Sec. 1391(h)(2);

— Act Sec. 753(b), amending Code Sec. 1202(a)(2)(C);

— Act Sec. 753(c);

— Act Sec. 753(d), providing the effective date.

Reporter references: For further information, consult the following CCH reporters.

— Standard Federal Tax Reporter, ¶30,375.01, ¶32,386.01, ¶32,386.023, ¶32,392.01, ¶32,394.01, ¶32,398.01, ¶32,398B.01

— Tax Research Consultant, BUSEXP: 57,054, BUSEXP: 57,056, BUSEXP: 57,108

— Practical Tax Explanation, §9,815.05, §10,001, §13,810, §16,601

¶445 District of Columbia Enterprise Zone Tax Incentives

SUMMARY OF NEW LAW

The District of Columbia enterprise zone provisions and the D.C. homebuyer credit are extended for two years.

BACKGROUND

Since 1998, numerous economically depressed census tracts within the District of Columbia have been designated as the "District of Columbia Enterprise Zone" ("D.C. Zone") entitling certain businesses and individuals operating in these zones to a series of tax benefits that, generally, expire at the end of 2009. These tax breaks include the following:

Tax-exempt D.C. Zone bonds. Qualifying businesses operating in the D.C. Zone are able to obtain tax-exempt bond financing through the end of 2009, if 95 percent of the proceeds are used for certain business facilities operating in the D.C. Zone (Code Secs. 1394 and 1400A).

D.C. Zone employment credit. Through the end of 2009, D.C. Zone employers are entitled to a 20-percent credit against income tax for the first $15,000 of qualified wages (i.e., a maximum credit of $3,000 with respect to each qualified employee) paid to full- or part-time employees who are residents of the empowerment zones and who perform substantially all their employment services within the zone in the employer's trade or business (Code Secs. 1400(c), 1400(f) and 1396).

Zero-percent capital gains rate. A zero-percent capital gains rate applies to qualified capital gains from the sale or exchange of D.C. Zone assets purchased and held for more than five years such, as D.C. Zone business stock, D.C. Zone partnership interests, and D.C. Zone business property (Code Sec. 1400B). Eligible property must be acquired before January 1, 2010, and the gain must be recognized before December 31, 2014. With respect to business property (and any land on which the property is located) that is substantially improved by the taxpayer before January 1, 2010, the original use of the property need not commence with the taxpayer in order to be treated as D.C. Zone business property.

Increase in Code Sec. 179 expensing. Businesses operating in the D.C. Zone are entitled to deduct an increased amount of the cost of certain tangible depreciable property placed in service through the end of 2009 in the D.C. Zone (Code Secs. 1397A, 1397C and 1400(e)).

First-time homebuyer credit. For property purchased after August 4, 1997, and before January 1, 2010, a first-time homebuyer of a principal residence in the District of Columbia is entitled to a tax credit of up to $5,000 of the purchase price of the residence (Code Sec. 1400C(a) and 1400C(i)).

NEW LAW EXPLAINED

Expiration date for District of Columbia tax benefits extended.—The Tax Relief, Unemployment Insurance Reauthorization, and Job Creation Act of 2010 (P.L. 111-312) extends the expiration date for the District of Columbia enterprise zone ("D.C. Zone") tax benefits for two years. As detailed below, these tax benefits are generally extended through the end of 2011. However, the zero-percent capital gains rate under Code Sec. 1400B is extended through 2016.

NEW LAW EXPLAINED

The specific changes are as follows:

- **Tax-exempt D.C. Zone bonds.** Qualifying businesses operating in empowerment zones are able to obtain tax-exempt bond financing under the provisions of Code Sec. 1394 through the end of 2011 (Code Sec. 1400A(b), as amended by the Tax Relief Act of 2010).

- **D.C. Zone employment credit.** Employers in the D.C. Zone may take the 20-percent credit against income tax for qualified wages paid to eligible employees in empowerment zones under Code Sec. 1396 (Code Sec. 1400(d)) through the end of 2011 (Code Sec. 1400(f), as amended by the Tax Relief Act of 2010).

- **Zero-percent capital gains rate.** Taxpayers are eligible for a zero-percent capital gains rates for qualified capital gains from the sale or exchange of D.C. Zone assets held more than five years, so long as the qualified gain is recognized before December 31, 2016 (Code Secs. 1400B(e)(2) and (g)(2), as amended by the Tax Relief Act of 2010). With respect to business property (and any land on which the property is located) that is substantially improved by the taxpayer before January 1, 2012, the original use of the property need not commence with the taxpayer in order to be treated as D.C. Zone business property (Code Sec. 1400B(b), as amended by the Tax Relief Act of 2010).

- **Increase in Code Sec. 179 expensing.** The increased Code Sec. 179 expensing available to eligible businesses operating in the D.C. Zone is extended through the end of 2011 (Code Sec. 1400(f), as amended by the Tax Relief Act of 2010).

- **First-time homebuyer credit.** For property purchased after August 4, 1997, and before January 1, 2012, a first-time homebuyer of a principal residence in the District of Columbia is entitled to a tax credit of up to $5,000 of the purchase price of the residence through the end of 2011 (Code Sec. 1400C(i), as amended by the Tax Relief Act of 2010).

▶ **Effective date.** The amendments extending the date that qualifying businesses can issue tax-exempt bonds shall apply to bonds issued after December 31, 2009 (Act Sec. 754(e)(2) of the Tax Relief, Unemployment Insurance Reauthorization, and Job Creation Act of 2010 (P.L. 111-312)). The amendments extending the D.C. Zone employment credit and extending the allowance for increased Code Sec. 179 expensing shall apply to periods after December 31, 2009 (Act Sec. 754(e)(1) of the Tax Relief Act of 2010). The amendments extending the purchase date for property eligible for the zero-percent capital gains rate shall apply to property acquired or substantially improved after December 31, 2009 (Act Sec. 754(e)(3) of the Tax Relief Act of 2010). The amendments extending the eligible purchase date for property to qualify under the first time homebuyer's credit applies to homes purchased after December 31, 2009 (Act Sec. 754(e)(4) of the Tax Relief Act of 2010).

Law source: Law at ¶5565, ¶5570, ¶5575, and ¶5580. Committee Report at ¶10,600.

— Act Sec. 754(a) of the Tax Relief, Unemployment Insurance Reauthorization, and Job Creation Act of 2010 (P.L. 111-312), amending Code Sec. 1400(f);

— Act Sec. 754(b), amending Code Sec. 1400A(b);

— Act Sec. 754(c)(1), amending Code Sec. 1400B(b)(2)(A)(i), (b)(3)(A), (b)(4)(A)(i), (b)(4)(B)(i)(I);

— Act Sec. 754(c)(2), amending Code Sec. 1400B(e)(2) and (g)(2);

NEW LAW EXPLAINED

— Act Sec. 754(d), amending Code Sec. 1400C(i);

— Act Sec. 754(e), providing the effective dates.

Reporter references: For further information, consult the following CCH reporters.

— Standard Federal Tax Reporter, ¶32,423.01, ¶32,425.01, ¶32,427.01 and ¶32,429.01

— Tax Research Consultant, BUSEXP: 57,056.30

— Practical Tax Explanation, §§ 13,005 and 16,525.05.

¶450 GO Zone Tax Incentives

SUMMARY OF NEW LAW

The following tax benefits available for victims of the 2005 Gulf storms have been extended: rehabilitation credit, low-income housing credit, tax-exempt financing, and bonus depreciation.

BACKGROUND

Numerous tax benefits were created for the victims of the Gulf coast storms of 2005. Among these include:

- **Rehabilitation credit.** A two-tier tax credit is provided for certain rehabilitation expenditures. A 20-percent credit is available for qualified rehabilitation expenditures of certified historic structures. A credit of 10 percent of qualified rehabilitation expenditures is available for a substantial rehabilitation of a building for which depreciation is allowable that was placed in service before 1936 (Code Sec. 47). These percentages are increased from 20 to 26 percent for any certified historic structure, and from 10 to 13 percent for qualified rehabilitated building, provided the structure or building is located in the Gulf Opportunity Zone (GO Zone). The increased credit is applicable to qualified rehabilitation expenditures that are paid or incurred on or after August 28, 2005, and before January 1, 2010 (Code Sec. 1400N(h)).

- **Low-income housing credit.** The low-income housing credit is a general business credit (Code Sec. 38(b)(5)) that may be claimed for the cost of building qualified buildings and for the expenses of rehabilitating existing structures. The purpose is to provide an incentive for the provision of rental housing for tenants with incomes below specified levels. The amount of the credit is equal to the applicable percentage of the qualified basis of each qualified low-income building, subject to certain limitations (Code Sec. 42). A modified version of the credit was extended to victims of the Gulf storms (Code Sec. 1400N(c)). The Small Business and Work Opportunity Tax Act of 2007 (P.L. 110-28) extends the time for making low-income housing credit allocations by temporarily repealing the general allocation timing rule under Code Sec. 42(h)(1)(B). Accordingly, owners of qualified buildings may

BACKGROUND

carry over a credit installment for the 2006, 2007, and 2008 tax years if the building is located in one of the applicable zones, receives an allocation in 2006, 2007, or 2008, and is placed in service before January 1, 2011 (Code Sec. 1400N(c)(5)).

- **Tax-exempt bond financing.** Tax-exempt bonds (GO Zone bonds) can be authorized prior to January 1, 2011, for the purpose of financing the construction and repair of real estate and infrastructure in the Gulf Opportunity Zone (Code Sec. 1400N(a)). Qualified GO Zone bonds are treated as exempt facility bonds or as qualified mortgage bonds. Proceeds from the GO Zone bonds can be used for repairs and construction of both residential and nonresidential real property, as well as for public utility projects. With certain modifications, the same tax-exempt bond financing provisions apply for reconstruction and repairs in certain Midwestern and Hurricane Ike disaster areas (Act Secs. 702, 704 of the Heartland Disaster Tax Relief Act of 2008, Subtitle A of Title VII of the Tax Extenders and Alternative Minimum Tax Relief Act of 2008 (Division C of P.L. 110-343)); Notice 2010-10, I.R.B. 2010-3, 299).

- **Bonus depreciation.** Taxpayers may claim an additional first-year depreciation allowance equal to 50 percent of the adjusted basis of qualified Gulf Opportunity Zone property acquired on or after August 28, 2005, and placed in service on or before December 31, 2007. The placed-in-service deadline is December 31, 2008, in the case of nonresidential real property and residential rental property. The December 31, 2008, deadline is extended to December 31, 2010, if such property is located in any county or parish in which one or more hurricanes that occurred during 2005 damaged more than 60 percent of occupied housing units (Code Sec. 1400N(d)(6)). If the December 31, 2010, placed-in-service deadline applies, only progress expenditures paid or incurred prior to January 1, 2010, actually qualify for the bonus deduction (Code Sec. 1400N(d)(6)(D)).

NEW LAW EXPLAINED

Extension of benefits for victims of Gulf Storms.—The Tax Relief, Unemployment Insurance Reauthorization, and Job Creation Act of 2010 (P.L. 111-312) extends the tax benefits available to victims of the 2005 Gulf storms.

Rehabilitation credit. The 13-and 26-percent rehabilitation tax credit for qualified expenditures on, respectively, qualifying rehabilitated buildings and certified historic structures in the "Gulf Opportunity" Zone, has been extended for two years, until December 31, 2011 (Code Sec. 1400N(h), as amended by the Tax Relief Act of 2010).

> **Compliance Pointer:** The rehabilitation credit may be claimed on Form 3468, Investment Credit.

Low-income housing credit. The temporary repeal of the general allocation timing rule for qualifying buildings under Code Sec. 42(h)(1)(B) is extended to 2012. Accordingly, owners of qualified buildings may carry over a credit installment for the 2006, 2007, and 2008 tax years if the building is located in one of the applicable zones, receives an allocation in 2006, 2007, or 2008, and is placed in service before January 1, 2013 (Code Sec. 1400N(c)(5), as amended by the 2010 American Jobs Act).

¶450

NEW LAW EXPLAINED

Tax-exempt bond financing. Special tax-exempt bond financing to help rebuild in the Gulf Opportunity Zone, and in the Midwestern and Hurricane Ike disaster areas is extended through 2011 (Code Sec. 1400N(a)(2)(D), (7)(C), and Act Secs. 702(d)(1) and 704(a) of the Heartland Disaster Act of 2008, Subtitle A of Title VII of the Tax Extenders and Alternative Minimum Tax Relief Act of 2008 (Division C of P.L. 110-343), as amended by the Tax Relief Act of 2010).

Bonus depreciation. The December 31, 2010, placed-in-service deadline for nonresidential real property and residential rental property is extended one year to December 31, 2011 (Code Sec. 1400N(d)(6)(B), as amended by the Tax Relief Act of 2010). The deadline for which progress expenditures must be paid or incurred is extended two years to January 1, 2012 (Code Sec. 1400N(d)(6)(D), as amended by the Tax Relief Act of 2010).

▶ **Effective date.** The provision extending the rehabilitation credit shall apply to amounts paid or incurred after December 31, 2009 (Act Sec. 762(b) of the Tax Relief, Unemployment Insurance Reauthorization, and Job Creation Act of 2010 (P.L. 111-312)). The provisions extending the low-income housing credit, and tax-exempt bond financing are effective on December 17, 2010, the date of enactment. The provision extending bonus depreciation shall apply to property placed in service after December 31, 2009 (Act Sec. 765(b) of the Tax Relief Act of 2010).

Law source: Law at ¶5590. Committee Report at ¶10,680, ¶10,690, ¶10,700, and ¶10,710.

— Act Sec. 762(a) of the Tax Relief, Unemployment Insurance Reauthorization, and Job Creation Act of 2010 P.L. 111-312), amending Code Sec. 1400N(h);

— Act Sec. 763 amending Code Sec. 1400N(c)(5);

— Act Sec. 764 amending Code Sec. 1400N(a), and Act Secs. 702(d)(1) and 704(a) of the Heartland Disaster Act of 2008

— Act Sec. 765, amending Code Sec. 1400N(d); and

— Act Secs. 762(b) and 765(b), providing the effective dates.

Reporter references: For further information, consult the following CCH reporters.

— Standard Federal Tax Reporter, ¶32,487.0211, ¶32,487.0315, ¶32,487.041, ¶32,487.042

— Tax Research Consultant BUSEXP: 57,300, BUSEXP: 57,302.05, BUSEXP: 57,304.05, BUSEXP: 57,306.10 , DEPR: 3,650, REAL: 3,056.05, SALES: 51,222

— Practical Tax Explanation, § 10,030.10, § 10,030.15, § 10,030.35, § 10,030.55, § 10,040.40

TAX-EXEMPT BONDS

¶455 School Construction Bonds

SUMMARY OF NEW LAW

The additional amount of bonds for public schools that small governmental units may issue under Code Sec. 148 without being subject to arbitrage rebate requirements

SUMMARY OF NEW LAW

is scheduled to expire for tax years beginning after December 31, 2010, under the sunset provision of EGTRRA (Act Sec. 901(a)(1) of P.L. 107-16). The scheduled expiration for this additional amount has been extended two years to December 31, 2012.

BACKGROUND

The Economic Growth and Tax Relief Reconciliation Act of 2001 (EGTRRA) (P.L. 107-16) increased, from $5 million to $10 million, the additional amount of governmental bonds for public schools that small governmental units may issue without being subject to the arbitrage rebate requirement (Code Sec. 148(f)(4)(D)(vii)).

Generally, income of state and local governments that is derived from the exercise of an essential governmental function is tax exempt. However, to prevent these tax-exempt entities from issuing more tax-exempt bonds than is necessary for the activity being financed, arbitrage restrictions limit the ability to profit from investment of tax-exempt bond proceeds. In general, arbitrage profits may be earned only during specified periods (for example, defined temporary periods) before funds are needed for the purpose of borrowing or on specified types of investments (for example, reasonably required reserve or replacement funds). Subject to limited exceptions, investment profits that are earned during these periods or on such investments must be rebated to the government.

A small issuer exception to the arbitrage rebate requirement is provided in Code Sec. 148(f)(4)(D). This exception applies only to bonds issued by governmental units with general taxing powers, as defined in the regulations (Reg. § 1.148-8(b)). For purposes of this small issuer exception, bonds issued by a subordinate entity are treated as also being issued by each entity to which it is subordinate (Reg. § 1.148-8(c)(2)).

The dollar limit of the "small issuer" exception is raised for tax-exempt bonds issued that are used to finance public school capital expenditures (Code Sec. 148(f)(4)(D)(vii)). A $5 million per calendar year limit on the amount of such tax-exempt bonds that can be issued under the small issuer exception is increased by up to an additional $5 million, equal to the aggregate face amount of the bonds issued that is attributable to financing the construction of public school facilities. Small issuers benefit from the exception to arbitrage rebate if they issue no more than $10 million in governmental bonds per calendar year and no more than $5 million of the bonds is used to finance expenditures other than for public school capital expenditures. Thus, under EGTRRA, small governmental units may issue up to $15 million of governmental bonds in a calendar year provided that at least $10 million of the bonds are used to finance public school construction expenditures.

Sunset provision. Under the sunset provision of EGTRRA, amendments made by the Act will not apply to tax years beginning after December 31, 2010 (Act Sec. 901 of P.L. 107-16).

¶455

NEW LAW EXPLAINED

Small governmental unit exception extended.—The additional amount of governmental bonds for public schools that small governmental units may issue without being subject to the arbitrage rebate requirement will remain at $10 million for two more years (Act Sec. 101(a)(1) of the Tax Relief, Unemployment Insurance Reauthorization, and Job Creation Act of 2010 (P.L. 111-312)). Thus, these governmental units may issue up to $10 million of governmental bonds in a calendar year until December 31, 2012 (Code Sec. 148(f)(4)(D)(vii)). In 2013, the arbitrage rebate requirement will decrease from $10 million to $5 million.

> **Comment:** The policy underlying the arbitrage rebate exception for bonds of small governmental units is to reduce complexity for these entities as they do not often have in-house financial staff to engage in the expenditure and investment tracking necessary for rebate compliance. The exception is further justified by the limited potential for arbitrage profits at small issuance levels and the limitation of the provision to governmental bonds, which typically require voter approval before issuance.

> **Planning Pointer:** While governmental units may try to issue bonds with the higher cap before December 31, 2012, issuing these bonds may be limited without voter approval.

▶ **Effective date.** The provision applies to obligations issued in calendar years beginning after December 31, 2001 (Act Sec. 101(a)(2) of the Tax Relief, Unemployment Insurance Reauthorization, and Job Creation Act of 2010 (P.L. 111-312)); Act Sec. 421(b) of the Economic Growth and Tax Relief Reconciliation of 2001 (EGTRRA) (P.L. 107-16)). The provision shall not apply to tax years beginning after December 31, 2012 (Act Sec. 101(a)(1) of the Tax Relief Act of 2010; Act Sec. 901 of EGTRRA). See ¶105 for a specific discussion of the sunset provision of EGTRRA and how it is applied.

Law source: Law at ¶5245 and ¶7010. Committee Report at ¶10,050.

— Act Sec. 101(a)(1) of the Tax Relief, Unemployment Insurance Reauthorization, and Job Creation Act of 2010 (P.L. 111-312);

— Act Sec. 101(a)(2), providing the effective date.

Reporter references: For further information, consult the following CCH reporters.

— Standard Federal Tax Reporter, ¶7889.01 and ¶7889.044

— Tax Research Consultant, SALES: 51,556

¶460 Exempt Facility Bonds

SUMMARY OF NEW LAW

The treatment of bonds used to provide qualified educational facilities (*i.e.* public schools) as exempt facility bonds is scheduled to expire for tax years beginning after December 31, 2010, under the sunset provision of EGTRRA (Act Sec. 901(a)(1) of P.L. 107-16). The expiration of such treatment has been extended for two years to December 31, 2012.

BACKGROUND

The Economic Growth and Tax Relief Reconciliation Act of 2001 (EGTRRA) (P.L. 107-16) added exempt facility bond treatment for bonds issued to provide qualified public educational facilities (Code Sec. 142(a)(13)). Without such treatment, interest earned on private activity bonds used to finance public school construction would be taxable under Code Sec. 103. Private activities for which tax-exempt bonds may be issued include elementary and secondary public school facilities which are owned by private, for-profit corporations pursuant to public-private partnership agreements with a state or local educational agency (Code Sec. 142(k)(1)).

A "qualified public educational facility" includes any school facility that is part of an elementary or secondary public school and is owned by a private, for-profit corporation pursuant to a public-private partnership agreement with a state or local educational agency (Code Sec. 142(k)(1)). The term "elementary school" means a nonprofit institutional day or residential school, including a public elementary charter school, that provides elementary education, as determined under state law. The term "secondary school" means a nonprofit institutional day or residential school, including a public secondary charter school that provides secondary education, as determined under state law, but not beyond grade 12 (Code Sec. 142(k)(4); see 20 U.S.C. § 8801).

A "school facility" is broadly defined to include school buildings, related facilities and land, such as athletic stadiums or fields used for school events and depreciable personal property used in the facility (Code Sec. 142(k)(3)). The school facility must be operated by a public educational agency as part of a system of public schools (Code Sec. 142(k)(1)(A)).

A "public-private partnership agreement" is an arrangement under which a private for-profit corporation agrees to construct, rehabilitate, refurbish, or equip a school facility. The agreement must also provide that, at the end of the contract term, ownership of the school facility will be transferred to the public school agency for no additional consideration. The term of the agreement cannot exceed the term of the bond issue used to provide the school facility (Code Sec. 142(k)(2)).

Issuance of these bonds is subject to separate annual volume limits. The volume limit applicable to each state equals the greater of $10 per state resident or $5 million (Code Sec. 142(k)(5)(A)). As with other private activity bond volume limits, states are permitted to decide how to allocate the bond amounts among state and local government agencies (Code Sec. 142(k)(5)(B)). Bond volume that is unused for any calendar year may be carried forward for up to three years under rules similar to the carryforward rules for private activity bond volume limits under Code Sec. 146(f), so long as the carryforward amount is used only to issue exempt facility bonds for qualified public educational facility projects (Code Sec. 142(k)(5)(B)(ii)).

Comment: Interest earned on state and local bonds is generally excluded from gross income under Code Sec. 103. However, interest on state and local bonds that are considered "private activity bonds" under Code Sec 141(a) is included in gross income, unless the bonds are "qualified bonds" as defined under Code Sec. 141(e) (Code Sec. 103(b)(1)). Exempt facility bonds are qualified bonds under Code Sec. 141(e)(1)(A) and therefore, the interest earned on exempt facility bonds issued for qualified public educational facilities is tax exempt.

¶460

BACKGROUND

Sunset provision. Under the sunset provision of EGTRRA, amendments made by the Act will not apply to tax years beginning after December 31, 2010 (Act Sec. 901 of P.L. 107-16).

NEW LAW EXPLAINED

Treatment of qualified public educational facility bonds as exempt facility bonds extended for two years.—Bonds used to provide "qualified public educational facilities" will be treated as exempt facility bonds under Code Sec. 142(a)(13) for two additional years until December 31, 2012 (Act Sec. 101(a)(1) of the Tax Relief, Unemployment Insurance Reauthorization, and Job Creation Act of 2010 (P.L. 111-312)). Thus, private activities for which tax-exempt bonds may be issued continue to include elementary or secondary public school facilities which are owned by private, for-profit corporations pursuant to public-private partnership agreements until December 31, 2012.

> **Gray Area:** It is possible that after December 31, 2012, investors holding bonds for qualified public school facilities, that were issued prior to January 1, 2013, will have to pay tax on the interest earned on those bonds, as private activity bonds under Code Sec. 103(b)(1). Under the sunset provision of EGTRRA, extended by the Tax Relief Act of 2010, Code Sec. 142(a)(13) does not apply after December 31, 2012, which could mean that state and local bonds for public school facilities, issued prior to January 1, 2013, would not be considered "qualified" under Code Sec. 141(e)(1)(A) and, therefore, would not be tax-exempt. If that is the case, then the interest would be includable in investors' gross income under Code Sec. 103(b)(1).

> On the other hand, the IRS may treat interest on bonds issued for qualified public school facilities as tax-exempt, so long as the bonds were issued prior to January 1, 2013, despite the technical result of the sunset provision which, in effect, removes Code Sec. 142(a)(13). If the IRS does not provide guidance on this matter prior to the 2012 filing season, concerned investors should consider seeking advance counsel from the IRS on this issue.

> **Planning Note:** Tax credit bonds remain an unexplored territory for most investors. In order to be a competitive option, the credit rate as set by the IRS should yield a return greater than the prevailing municipal bond rate and at least equal to the after-tax rate for corporate bonds of similar maturity and risk. The relatively small volume of tax credit bonds available means there is less incentive for bond analysts to evaluate them ("Tax Credit Bonds: A Brief Explanation," CRS Report for Congress, August 20, 2008). School construction bonds may nevertheless be attractive to some investors for their social benefit.

▶ **Effective date.** The provision applies to bonds issued after December 31, 2001 (Act Sec. 101(a)(2) of the Tax Relief, Unemployment Insurance Reauthorization, and Job Creation Act of 2010 (P.L. 111-312)); Act Sec. 422(f) of the Economic Growth and Tax Relief Reconciliation Act of 2001 (EGTRRA) (P.L. 107-16)). The provision does not apply to tax years beginning after December 31, 2012 (Act Sec. 101(a)(1) of the Tax Relief Act of 2010;

NEW LAW EXPLAINED

Act Sec. 901 of EGTRRA). See ¶105 for a specific discussion of the sunset provision of EGTRRA and how it is applied.

Law source: Law at ¶5230, ¶5235, ¶5240, and ¶7010. Committee Report at ¶10,050.

— Act Sec. 101(a)(1) of the Tax Relief, Unemployment Insurance Reauthorization, and Job Creation Act of 2010 (P.L. 111-312), amending Act Sec. 901 of the Economic Growth and Tax Relief Reconciliation Act of 2001 (EGTRRA) (P.L. 107-16);

— Act Sec. 101(a)(2), providing the effective date.

Reporter references: For further information, consult the following CCH reporters.

— Standard Federal Tax Reporter, ¶7752.01

— Tax Research Consultant, SALES: 51,218

¶465 Qualified Zone Academy Bonds

SUMMARY OF NEW LAW

The qualified zone academy bond (QZAB) program has been extended for an additional year. State and local governments are authorized to issue up to $400 million of qualified zone academy bonds for 2011. The refundable credit for QZABs is repealed for obligations issued under the 2011 limitation or any carryforward of such an allocation.

BACKGROUND

As an alternative to traditional tax-exempt bonds, state and local governments have been given the authority to issue qualified zone academy bonds (QZABs) on an annual basis, with a $400 million limit in 2008 and a $1.4 billion limit in 2009 and 2010. The annual bond cap is allocated each year to the states according to their respective populations of individuals below the poverty line. Each state in turn allocates the credit authority to qualified zone academies within the state (Code Sec. 54E(c)).

QZABs were the first tax credit bonds, introduced under the Taxpayer Relief Act of 1997 (P.L. 105-34). Under this program, qualified zone academies, through their state and local governments, use the bond proceeds for school renovations, equipment, teacher training, and course materials.

A "qualified zone academy bond" is any bond issued as part of an issue if: (1) 100 percent of the available project proceeds of the issue are to be used for a qualified purpose with respect to a qualified zone academy established by an eligible local education agency; (2) the bond is issued by the state or a local government within the jurisdiction of which the academy is located; and (3) the issuer designates the bond as a QZAB, certifies that it has written assurances of the required private contributions

¶465

BACKGROUND

with respect to the academy, and certifies that it has the written approval of the eligible local education agency for the bond issuance (Code Sec. 54E(a)).

In general, a "qualified zone academy" is any public school (or academic program within a public school) that: (1) provides education and training below the college level; (2) operates a special academic program in cooperation with businesses to enhance the academic curriculum and increase graduation and employment rates; and (3) is either located in an empowerment zone or enterprise community or it is reasonably expected that at least 35 percent of the students at the school will be eligible for free or reduced-cost lunches under the school lunch program established under the National School Lunch Act (Code Sec. 54E(d)(1)). A QZAB is a form of tax credit bond which offers the holder a federal tax credit instead of interest.

For bonds issued after March 18, 2010, issuers of specified tax credit bonds may elect to receive the credit that would otherwise be payable to purchasers of the specified tax credit bonds (Code Sec. 6431(f)(1)). "Specified tax credit bonds" for purposes of this election are new clean renewable energy bonds under Code Sec. 54C, qualified energy conservation bonds under Code Sec. 54D, qualified zone academy bonds under Code Sec. 54E, and qualified school construction bonds under Code Sec. 54F (Code Sec. 6431(f)(3)).

NEW LAW EXPLAINED

Qualified zone academy bond program extended.—The authority of state and local governments to issue qualified zone academy bonds (QZABs) has been extended for one additional year. The new law allows $400 million of QZAB issuing authority to state and local governments in 2011, which can be used to finance renovations, equipment purchases, developing course material, and training teachers and personnel at a qualified zone academy (Code Sec. 54E(c)(1), as amended by the Tax Relief, Unemployment Insurance Reauthorization, and Job Creation Act of 2010 (P.L. 111-312))

The refundable credit for QZABs is repealed for obligations issued under the 2011 limitation or any carryforward of such an allocation (Code Sec. 6431(f)(3)(A)(iii), as amended by the Tax Relief Act of 2010). The provision has no effect on bonds issued with the limitation carried forward from 2009 or 2010 (Joint Committee on Taxation, *Technical Explanation of the Revenue Provisions Contained in the "Tax Relief, Unemployment Insurance Reauthorization, and Job Creation Act of 2010"* (JCX-55-10), December 10, 2010).

▶ **Effective date.** The provision applies to obligations issued after December 31, 2010 (Act Sec. 758(c) of the Tax Relief, Unemployment Insurance Reauthorization, and Job Creation Act of 2010 (P.L. 111-312)).

Law source: Law at ¶5165 and ¶5830. Committee Report at ¶10,640.

— Act Sec. 758(a) of the Tax Relief, Unemployment Insurance Reauthorization, and Job Creation Act of 2010 (P.L. 111-312), amending Code Sec. 54E(c)(1);

— Act Sec. 758(b), amending Code Sec. 6431(f)(3)(A)(iii);

— Act Sec. 758(c), providing the effective date.

NEW LAW EXPLAINED

Reporter references: For further information, consult the following CCH reporters.

— Standard Federal Tax Reporter, ¶4916.01 and ¶38,933.021

— Tax Research Consultant, BUSEXP: 55,802 and BUSEXP: 55,810

— Practical Tax Explanation, § 14,510.25

¶470 New York Liberty Bonds

SUMMARY OF NEW LAW

The authorization of $8 billion in tax-exempt bonds to finance construction and renovation of real estate and infrastructure in the New York Liberty Zone has been extended for two years.

BACKGROUND

The area of New York City south of Canal Street was substantially damaged in the September 11, 2001 terrorist attacks. Many businesses operating in the area of the World Trade Center experienced economic hardships as a result of the attack. In response, Congress created a new "Liberty Zone" in New York City with an accompanying series of tax breaks for businesses operating in the area. These tax breaks include authorization of $8 billion in "qualified New York Liberty Bonds," which are tax-exempt bonds issued over 2002-2009 to finance construction and renovation of real estate and infrastructure in the Liberty Zone (Code Secs. 1400L(d)).

NEW LAW EXPLAINED

The expiration date for authorization of New York Liberty Bonds is extended.— The Tax Relief, Unemployment Insurance Reauthorization, and Job Creation Act of 2010 (P.L. 111-312) extends the date for issuing qualified New York Liberty Bonds. Bonds that otherwise qualify may be issued before January 1, 2012 (Code Sec. 1400L(d)(2)(D), as amended by the Tax Relief Act of 2010).

▶ **Effective date.** This amendment shall apply to bonds issued after December 31, 2009 (Act Sec. 761(b) of the Tax Relief, Unemployment Insurance Reauthorization, and Job Creation Act of 2010 (P.L. 111-312)).

Law source: Law at ¶5585. Committee Report at ¶10,670.

— Act Sec. 761(a) of the Tax Relief, Unemployment Insurance Reauthorization, and Job Creation Act of 2010 (P.L. 111-312), amending Code Sec. 1400L(d)(2)(D);

— Act Sec. 761(b), providing the effective date.

Reporter references: For further information, consult the following CCH reporters.

— Standard Federal Tax Reporter, ¶32,477.01 and ¶32,477.037.

— Tax Research Consultant, BUSEXP: 57,254

— Practical Tax Explanation, § 10,001

Business Deductions and Credits

5

DEDUCTIONS AND EXPENSING

¶502   Additional Depreciation Allowance (Bonus Depreciation)

¶504   Election to Claim Accelerated AMT Credit in Lieu of Bonus Depreciation

¶506   Section 179 Expensing of Depreciable Assets

¶508   15-Year Straight-Line Cost Recovery for Qualified Leasehold Improvements, Qualified Restaurant Property, and Qualified Retail Improvements

¶510   Seven-Year Recovery Period for Motorsports Entertainment Complexes

¶512   Accelerated Depreciation for Business Property on Indian Reservations

¶514   Special Expensing Rules for Certain Film and Television Productions

¶516   Election to Expense Advanced Mine Safety Equipment

¶518   Expensing of Brownfields Environmental Remediation Costs

TAX CREDITS

¶520   Credit for Increasing Research Activities

¶522   Credit for Employer-Provided Child Care Facilities and Services

¶524   Work Opportunity Credit

¶526   Employer Wage Credit for Activated Military Reservists

¶528   New Markets Tax Credit

¶530   Indian Employment Tax Credit

¶532   Railroad Track Maintenance Credit

¶534   Mine Rescue Team Training Credit

¶536   American Samoa Economic Development Credit

ENERGY

¶538   Credit for New Energy Efficient Homes

¶540   Grants for Investment in Specified Energy Property in Lieu of Tax Credits

¶542   Energy Efficient Appliance Credit for Manufacturers

¶544   Incentives for Biodiesel, Renewable Diesel, and Alternative Fuels

¶546   Incentives for Alcohol Fuels

¶548   Alternative Fuel Vehicle Refueling Property Credit

¶550   Refined Coal Production Facilities Credit

¶552   Percentage Depletion for Marginal Oil and Gas Production

¶554   Gain Rule for Sales or Dispositions Implementing FERC or State Electric Restructuring Policy

CHARITABLE CONTRIBUTIONS

¶557   Basis Adjustment to Stock of an S Corporation Making Charitable Contributions

¶560   Enhanced Deduction for Charitable Contributions of Food Inventory

¶563   Enhanced Deduction for Corporate Charitable Contributions of Book Inventory

¶566   Enhanced Deduction for Corporate Charitable Contributions of Computers

DEDUCTIONS AND EXPENSING

¶502   Additional Depreciation Allowance (Bonus Depreciation)

SUMMARY OF NEW LAW

The additional depreciation allowance (bonus depreciation) is extended for two years to apply to qualifying property acquired after December 31, 2007, and placed in service before January 1, 2013 (or before January 1, 2014, in the case of property with a longer production period and certain noncommercial aircraft). The bonus depreciation allowance rate is increased from 50 percent to 100 percent for qualified property acquired after September 8, 2010, and before January 1, 2012, and placed in service before January 1, 2012 (or before January 1, 2013, for longer period production property and certain noncommercial aircraft).

BACKGROUND

A 50-percent bonus depreciation deduction is allowed for the first year in which qualifying MACRS property is placed in service. The property must be acquired after

BACKGROUND

December 31, 2007, and placed in service before January 1, 2011 (Code Sec. 168(k)). No written binding contract for the acquisition of the property may be in effect prior to January 1, 2008. Property acquired after December 31, 2007, pursuant to a written binding contract entered into after December 31, 2007, and before January 1, 2011, and placed in service before January 1, 2011, however, may qualify for bonus depreciation (Code Sec. 168(k)(2)(A)(iii)).

There is no limit on the total amount of bonus depreciation that may be claimed in any given tax year. The amount of the bonus depreciation deduction is not affected by a short tax year. The bonus depreciation deduction is allowed in full for alternative minimum tax (AMT) purposes. In addition, the regular depreciation deductions claimed on property on which bonus depreciation is claimed are also allowed in full for AMT purposes (Code Sec. 168(k)(2)(G)).

A taxpayer may elect out of the bonus depreciation allowance for any class of property for the tax year (Code Sec. 168(k)(2)(D)(iii)).

Qualifying property. The bonus depreciation allowance is only available for new property (i.e., property the original use of which begins with the taxpayer after December 31, 2007) depreciable under MACRS that (i) has a recovery period of 20 years or less, (ii) is MACRS water utility property, (iii) is computer software depreciable over three years under Code Sec. 167(f), or (iv) is qualified leasehold improvement property (Code Sec. 168(k)(2)(A)(i)).

Property that must be depreciated using the MACRS alternative depreciation system (ADS) does not qualify. However, if the taxpayer elects to depreciate property under ADS, the property may qualify. Listed property (Code Sec. 280F), such as a passenger automobile, which is used 50 percent or less for business, does not qualify for bonus depreciation because such property must be depreciated using ADS (Code Sec. 168(k)(2)(D)).

Property is not qualifying property unless it is acquired by a taxpayer after December 31, 2007, and before January 1, 2012 (or pursuant to a written binding contract entered into after December 31, 2007, and before January 1, 2012), and placed in service before January 1, 2012 (or before January 1, 2013, in the case of property with a longer production period and certain noncommercial aircraft) (Code Sec. 168(k)(2)(A)(ii), (iii) and (iv)).

Property with a longer production period. The placed-in-service deadline is extended one year (through December 31, 2011) for property with a longer production period (Code Sec. 168(k)(2)(A)(iii)). Thus, property with a longer production period qualifies for bonus depreciation if it is not acquired pursuant to a binding contract that was entered into before January 1, 2008, or after December 31, 2010, and the property is placed in service before January 1, 2012. Property with a longer production period is property which:

- is subject to the Code Sec. 263A uniform capitalization rules;
- has a production period greater than one year and a cost exceeding $1 million; and
- has an MACRS recovery period of at least 10 years, or is used in the trade or business of transporting persons or property for hire, such as commercial aircraft (i.e., "transportation property") (Code Sec. 168(k)(2)(A)(iv)).

BACKGROUND

Only pre-January 1, 2011, manufacturing, construction or production costs ("progress expenditures") are taken into account in computing the bonus depreciation deduction for property with a longer production period (Code Sec. 168(k)(2)(B)(ii)).

Noncommercial aircraft. The extended placed-in-service deadline (i.e., prior to January 1, 2012) also applies to certain noncommercial aircraft acquired by purchase. Progress expenditures made in 2011 on noncommercial aircraft placed in service before January 1, 2012, are eligible for bonus depreciation (Code Sec. 168(k)(2)(A)(iv) and (C)).

Self-constructed property. If a taxpayer manufactures, constructs, or produces property for the taxpayer's own use, the requirement that the property be acquired after December 31, 2007, and placed in service before January 1, 2011, is deemed satisfied if the taxpayer begins manufacturing, constructing, or producing the property after December 31, 2007, and before January 1, 2011 (Code Sec. 168(k)(2)(E)(i)). The property, however, still needs to be placed in service before January 1, 2011 (unless the one-year extension for property with a longer production period, discussed above, applies).

Luxury car depreciation caps. Assuming that the election out of bonus depreciation is not made, the first-year Code Sec. 280F depreciation cap for passenger automobiles that qualify for bonus depreciation is increased by $8,000 in the case of vehicles acquired and placed in service after December 31, 2007 (Code Sec. 168(k)(2)(F)).

NEW LAW EXPLAINED

Bonus depreciation extended to property placed in service before January 1, 2013; rate increased to 100 percent for certain pre-2012 property.—The Code Sec. 168(k) 50-percent bonus depreciation allowance is extended two additional years to apply to qualifying property acquired by a taxpayer after December 31, 2007, and before January 1, 2013 (or pursuant to a written binding contract entered into after December 31, 2007, and before January 1, 2013), and placed in service before January 1, 2013 (or before January 1, 2014, in the case of property with a longer production period and certain noncommercial aircraft) (Code Sec. 168(k)(2), as amended by the Tax Relief, Unemployment Insurance Reauthorization, and Job Creation Act of 2010 (P.L. 111-312)). The bonus depreciation rate is increased from 50 percent to 100 percent in the case of qualifying property acquired after September 8, 2010, and before January 1, 2012, and placed in service before January 1, 2012 (or before January 1, 2013, in the cases of property with a longer production period and certain noncommercial aircraft) (Code Sec. 168(k)(5), as added by the Tax Relief Act of 2010).

> **Comment:** Bonus depreciation, at either the 50-percent rate or the 100-percent rate, may not be claimed on property acquired pursuant to a written binding contract that was in effect before January 1, 2008. Accordingly, a property may be eligible for the 100-percent rate even if it is subject to a contract entered into before September 9, 2010, as long as the contract is entered into after December 31, 2007 (Joint Committee on Taxation, *Technical Explanation of the Revenue*

NEW LAW EXPLAINED

Provisions Contained in the "Tax Relief, Unemployment Insurance Reauthorization, and Job Creation Act of 2010" (JCX-55-10), December 10, 2010).

> **Example 1:** A taxpayer enters into a written binding contract on September 1, 2010, for the purchase of a machine. The machine is acquired after September 8, 2010, and placed in service before January 1, 2012. The machine will qualify for bonus depreciation at the 100-percent rate even though a binding contract was in effect prior to September 9, 2010, because the binding contract was entered into after December 31, 2007. If the machine had been placed in service in 2012, the 50-percent rate would apply.

Comment: The new law does not contain a provision that would allow a taxpayer to elect the standard 50-percent rate for property which qualifies for the 100-percent rate. However, as under existing law, a taxpayer may make an election out of bonus depreciation under Code Sec. 168(k)(2)(D)(iii) with respect to any class of property placed in service during the tax year. The election applies to all property in the property class that is placed in service in the tax year of the election. For example, if the machine in Example 1, above, is MACRS five-year property, the taxpayer may elect not to claim bonus depreciation on all five-year property placed in service during 2011, assuming that the taxpayer uses a calendar tax year. If the machine in the preceding example had been placed in service in 2010, an election out would apply to all five-year property placed in service in 2010, whether it qualified for the 100-percent rate or the 50-percent rate.

Place-in-service deadline for property with a longer production period further extended one-year. The otherwise applicable placed-in-service deadline (December 31, 2012, for 50-percent rate property and December 31, 2011, for 100-percent rate property) is extended an additional year for property with a longer production period (Code Sec. 168(k)(2)(A)(iv), as amended by the Tax Relief Act of 2010). Thus, property with a longer production period will qualify for bonus depreciation if it is acquired after December 31, 2007, and before January 1, 2013, and placed in service before January 1, 2014. The 100-percent rate applies to property with a longer production period if it is acquired after September 8, 2010, and before January 1, 2012, and placed in service before January 1, 2013 (Code Sec. 168(k)(2)(A)(iv), as amended by the Tax Relief Act of 2010; Code Sec. 168(k)(5), as added by the Tax Relief Act of 2010).

Progress expenditures. Although the placed-in-service deadline for 50-percent bonus depreciation property with a longer production period is extended one-year through December 31, 2013, only pre-January 1, 2013, progress expenditures are taken into account in computing the bonus depreciation allowance. Thus, progress expenditures that increase the adjusted basis of such property during 2013 do not qualify for bonus depreciation (Code Sec. 168(k)(2)(B)(ii), as amended by the Tax Relief Act of 2010).

¶502

NEW LAW EXPLAINED

Example 2: A taxpayer enters into a contract for the purchase of a new commercial passenger plane (i.e., property with a longer production period) on February 1, 2009. The plane is delivered and placed in service on November 1, 2013. The plane qualifies for bonus depreciation at the 50-percent rate because it was acquired pursuant to a contract entered into after December 31, 2007, and before January 1, 2013, and was placed in service before January 1, 2014. However, progress expenditures attributable to 2013 construction do not qualify for the bonus deduction.

Comment: Property with a longer production period is subject to the progress expenditures rule only if it qualifies for bonus depreciation (i.e., it is "qualified property") *solely* by reason of the extended placed-in-service date that applies to property with a longer production period (Code Sec. 168(k)(2)(B)(ii)). Since long-production property that qualifies for the 100-percent bonus depreciation would also qualify for the bonus depreciation at the 50-percent rate without regard to the extended December 31, 2012 placed-in service deadline for 100-percent rate property, it appears that the progress expenditures rule does not apply to such 100-percent rate property. It may be necessary for the IRS to clarify this issue.

Example 3: A taxpayer enters into a contract for the purchase of a new commercial passenger plane (i.e., property with a longer production period) on November 1, 2010. The plane is delivered and placed in service on December 1, 2012. Under the new law, long-production property qualifies for a 100-percent bonus depreciation if it is acquired after September 8, 2010, and placed in service before January 1, 2013. The progress expenditures rule of Code Sec. 168(k)(2)(b)(ii), which generally prohibits a taxpayer from claiming bonus depreciation on progress expenditures during the one-year deadline extension period, should not apply because the 2012 expenditures would have qualified for bonus depreciation at a 50-percent rate without regard to any extension period for long-production property.

Noncommercial aircraft. In addition to property with a longer production period, the placed-in-service deadline for noncommercial aircraft described in Code Sec. 168(k)(2)(C) is extended for an additional year. Such noncommercial aircraft must be acquired after December 31, 2007, and before January 1, 2013, and placed in service before January 1, 2014, in order to qualify for bonus depreciation at the 50-percent rate (Code Sec. 168(k)(2)(A)(iv), as amended by the Tax Relief Act of 2010). However, the 100-percent rate will apply if the noncommercial aircraft was acquired after September 8, 2010, and before January 1, 2012, and placed in service before January 1, 2013 (Code Sec. 168(k)(5), as added by the Tax Relief Act of 2010).

Comment: The progress expenditures rule, which limits the bonus depreciation deduction for property with a longer production period to pre-January 1, 2013, adjusted basis, does not apply to qualifying noncommercial aircraft (Code Sec.

NEW LAW EXPLAINED

168(k)(2)(B)(iv)). Thus, the entire adjusted basis of a qualifying noncommercial aircraft placed in service before January 1, 2014, qualifies for bonus depreciation.

> **Example 4:** A taxpayer enters into a binding contract for the purchase of a new noncommercial passenger plane on February 1, 2011. The plane is delivered and placed in service on September 1, 2013. The plane qualifies for bonus depreciation at the 50-percent rate because it was acquired pursuant to a contract entered into after December 31, 2007, and before January 1, 2013, and was placed in service before the extended December 31, 2013 deadline for 50-percent rate property that is a noncommercial passenger plane. Progress expenditures attributable to 2013 construction will qualify for the bonus deduction because the rule that disqualifies 2013 progress expenditures does not apply to noncommercial aircraft.

> **Example 5:** A taxpayer enters into a binding contract for the purchase of a new noncommercial passenger plane on February 1, 2010. The plane is delivered and placed in service on September 1, 2012. The plane qualifies for bonus depreciation at the 100-percent rate because it was acquired pursuant to a contract entered into after December 31, 2007, and before January 1, 2012, and was placed in service before the December 31, 2012 deadline for 100-percent rate property that is a noncommercial passenger plane. Progress expenditures attributable to 2012 construction will qualify for bonus depreciation.

Self-constructed property. If a taxpayer manufactures, constructs, or produces property for the taxpayer's own use, the requirement that the property be acquired after December 31, 2007, and placed in service before January 1, 2013, is deemed satisfied if the taxpayer begins manufacturing, constructing, or producing the property after December 31, 2007, and before January 1, 2013 (Code Sec. 168(k)(2)(E)(i), as amended by the Tax Relief Act of 2010). The property, however, still needs to be placed into service before January 1, 2013 (or before January 1, 2014, in the case of property with a longer production period). The applicable bonus depreciation rate is 50-percent unless the 100-percent rate applies because the manufacturing, construction, or production begins after September 8, 2010, and the property is placed in service before January 1, 2012 (or before January 1, 2013, in the case of longer period production property).

Conforming amendments to provisions incorporating self-constructed property rule. Code Sec. 168(l) provides a separate 50-percent bonus depreciation allowance for cellulosic biofuel plant property placed in service on or before January 1, 2013. Code Sec. 168(l)(5) incorporates the bonus depreciation rule for self-constructed property by cross reference to Code Sec. 168(k)(2)(E) but by substituting the acquisition and placed-in-service deadlines that apply to cellulosic biofuel plant property. A conforming amendment is made to Code Sec. 168(l)(5) to take into account the extended placed-in-service deadlines that appear in the text of Code Sec. 168(k)(2)(E) (Code Sec. 168(l)(5),

¶502

NEW LAW EXPLAINED

as amended by the Tax Relief Act of 2010). This conforming amendment has no effect on any other aspect of the existing rules for cellulosic biofuel plant property.

Similar nonsubstantive conforming amendments relating to the self-constructed property rule are made to the Code provisions that provide a 50-percent bonus depreciation allowance for qualified disaster assistance property (Code Sec. 168(n)(2)(C), as amended by the Tax Relief Act of 2010), a bonus depreciation allowance for property placed in service in the Gulf Opportunity Zone (i.e., GO-Zone bonus depreciation) (Code Sec. 1400N(d)(3)(B), as amended by the Tax Relief Act of 2010), and a bonus depreciation allowance for New York Liberty Zone property (Code Sec. 1400L(b)(2), as amended by the Tax Relief Act of 2010).

Luxury car depreciation cap. The $8,000 increase in the first-year depreciation cap for vehicles on which bonus depreciation is claimed remains unchanged and continues to apply to vehicles placed in service in 2011 and 2012 for which bonus depreciation is claimed (Code Sec. 168(k)(2)(F)).

> **Comment:** Taking into account the $8,000 increase, the first-year depreciation limit on luxury automobiles first put into use during the 2010 tax year for business and investment purposes if bonus depreciation is claimed is $11,060 for passenger automobiles, other than trucks and vans, and $11,160 for trucks and vans. If the vehicle does not qualify for bonus depreciation (e.g., a used vehicle is purchased or an election out of bonus depreciation is made), the first year cap is $3,060 for passenger automobiles, other than trucks and vans, and $3,160 for qualifying trucks and vans (Rev. Proc. 2010-18, I.R.B. 2010-9, 427). The depreciation caps for 2011 and 2012 have not been announced yet.

> **Comment:** Even though the bonus depreciation rate has doubled under the new law from 50 percent to 100 percent for vehicles acquired after September 8, 2010, and placed in service before January 1, 2012, the applicable first-year depreciation cap for such vehicles continues to be increased only by $8,000.

> **Caution:** If a taxpayer claims a 100-percent bonus depreciation deduction on a vehicle acquired after September 8, 2010, and placed in service before January 1, 2012, any cost in excess of the applicable first-year cap can only be deducted after the end of the vehicle's recovery period at a specified annual rate. In the case of a vehicle placed in service in 2010, the specified rate is $1,775 for cars and $1,885 for trucks and vans (Rev. Proc. 2010-18, I.R.B. 2010-9, 427).

Example 6: A car costing $35,000 that is subject to the luxury car limitations is placed in service in November 2010 and used 100 percent for business purposes. The 100-percent bonus depreciation rate applies. However, because the first-year luxury car cap for the vehicle is $11,060, the bonus deduction that may be claimed is limited to $11,060. The $23,940 excess ($35,000 − $11,060) may only be recovered at the rate of $1,775 per year beginning in 2016, which is the first year after the end of the vehicle's depreciation period. No regular depreciation deductions are allowed after the first year of the vehicle's regular depreciation period because the vehicle's basis for computing depreciation deductions is

---

NEW LAW EXPLAINED

reduced by the entire amount of the bonus depreciation allowed without regard to the first-year cap.

Comment: By making an election out of bonus depreciation on a vehicle that is eligible for a 100-percent bonus depreciation, a taxpayer will generally be able to claim substantially more depreciation over the entire recovery period of the vehicle. Assuming that the first-year caps in each year of the vehicle's recovery period are greater than the depreciation deduction computed without regard to the first-year caps, the taxpayer will claim aggregate depreciation equal to the sum of the applicable depreciation caps. If an election out of bonus depreciation is not made, then the taxpayer's aggregate depreciation deductions during the regular recovery period are limited to the first-year cap that applies when bonus depreciation is claimed.

Example 7: A car costing $35,000 that is subject to the luxury car limitations is placed in service in November 2010 and used 100 percent for business purposes. An election out of bonus depreciation is made. The car is depreciated using the MACRS General Depreciation System by applying the 200-percent declining balance method and half-year convention (most cars are depreciated in this manner). The caps for a vehicle placed in service in 2010 for which bonus depreciation is not claimed are $3,060 in the first year, $4,900 for the second year, $2,950 for the third year, $1,775 for the fourth year, $1,775 for the fifth year, and $1,775 for the sixth year. Because the regular depreciation deductions computed for each year in the vehicle's depreciation period will exceed the applicable cap for each year in the depreciation period, the total depreciation deductions that the taxpayer may claim during the vehicle's depreciation period are limited to $16,235, the sum of the applicable caps. The $18,765 excess ($35,000 − $16,235) may be deducted at the rate of $1,775 per year beginning in 2017 assuming 100-percent business use continues in each post-recovery year. If an election had not been made out of bonus depreciation, the taxpayer's aggregate depreciation deduction during the recovery period would have been limited to $11,060, as illustrated in Example 6, above.

Comment: The election out of bonus depreciation is not made for individual assets. It is made on a property class basis. Automobiles are five-year property. Accordingly, a taxpayer would need to make an election out of bonus depreciation for all five-year property placed in service during the tax year in order to avoid any adverse consequence of claiming 100-percent bonus depreciation on a vehicle.

CCH Comment: Sport Utility Vehicles (SUVs) and pickup trucks with a gross vehicle weight rating (GVWR) in excess of 6,000 pounds are exempt from the luxury car depreciation caps. However, no more than $25,000 of the cost of an SUV with a GVWR in excess of 6,000 pounds or a pickup truck in excess of 6,000 pounds GVWR with a bed length of less than six feet may be expensed under

NEW LAW EXPLAINED

Code Sec. 179. This $25,000 limitation does not apply to bonus depreciation. Thus, the entire cost of a new heavy SUV or new heavy short-bed pickup truck may be expensed as a bonus depreciation deduction if the 100 percent rate applies. If a 50 percent bonus rate applies, a taxpayer may expense up to $25,000 of the cost under Code Sec. 179, claim a 50% bonus deduction on the cost as reduced by the section 179 allowance, and then claim a regular first-year depreciation deduction equal to 20 percent of the cost as reduced by the section 179 deduction and 50% bonus allowance, assuming the 200 percent declining balance method and half-year convention are used to depreciate the vehicle.

Comment: The corporate election to claim a credit for unused pre-2006 AMT and research credits in lieu of bonus depreciation (Code Sec. 168(k)(4)) has been extended to apply to bonus depreciation that is allowed solely by reason of the Tax Relief Act of 2010 with respect to property placed in service in 2011 and 2012 (and 2013 for property with a long production period and certain noncommercial aircraft). However, only unused AMT credits may be claimed. See ¶504.

Alternative minimum tax. The new law does not change the rule that the bonus deduction, as well as regular depreciation deductions on bonus depreciation property, are allowed in full for AMT tax purposes (i.e., this rule continues to apply to bonus depreciation claimed on property placed in service in 2011 and 2012) (Code Sec. 168(k)(2)(G)).

State Tax Consequences: The increase of 50 percent bonus depreciation to 100 percent for qualified investments made on or after September 8, 2010, and on or before December 31, 2012 (2013 for certain property), and the extension of 50 percent bonus depreciation available for qualified property placed in service before 2013 (2014 for certain property), would affect only those states that have not decoupled from Code Sec. 168(k) and that have Code conformity dates that would not include the extension of the provision. For those states like Delaware, Idaho, and Louisiana, the extension will not apply unless or until they update their conformity dates. However states that allow bonus depreciation and that conform to the Code annually (including Virginia) will most likely conform to the extension during their next legislative sessions. However, it should be noted that more states have been decoupling from bonus depreciation to alleviate further state revenue shortfalls. The majority of states have decoupled from federal bonus depreciation and they will not be affected by the extension.

In addition, the extension of the following provisions, may require adjustments in those states that have previously adopted them, but that have Code conformity dates that do not adopt the extension: 15-year straight-line cost recovery for qualified leasehold improvements, restaurant buildings and improvements and retail improvements (¶508); seven-year recovery period for motor sports entertainment complexes (¶510); accelerated depreciation for business property on Indian reservations (¶512); and first year bonus depreciation for property placed in service in a Gulf Opportunity Zone.

▶ **Effective date.** The provision applies to property placed in service after December 31, 2010, in tax years ending after such date (Act Sec. 401(e)(1) of the Tax Relief, Unemployment Insurance Reauthorization, and Job Creation Act of 2010 (P.L. 111-312)). However,

¶502

NEW LAW EXPLAINED

the rule in Code Sec. 168(k)(5) providing for the temporary 100-percent bonus depreciation applies to property placed in service after September 8, 2010, in tax years ending after such date (Act Sec. 401(e)(2) of the Tax Relief Act of 2010)

Law source: Law at ¶5265, ¶5585, and ¶5590. Committee Report at ¶10,140.

— Act Sec. 401(a) of the Tax Relief, Unemployment Insurance Reauthorization, and Job Creation Act of 2010 (P.L. 111-312), amending Code Sec. 168(k)(2);

— Act Sec. 401(b), adding Code Sec. 168(k)(5);

— Act Sec. 401(d), amending Code Secs. 168(k) (heading), 168(k)(2)(B)(ii), 168(l)(5), 168(n)(2)(C), 1400L(b)(2)(D), and 1400N(d)(3)(B);

— Act Sec. 401(e), providing the effective date.

Reporter references: For further information, consult the following CCH reporters.

— Standard Federal Tax Reporter, ¶11,279.058

— Tax Research Consultant, DEPR: 3,600

— Practical Tax Explanation, § 11,225

¶504 Election to Claim Accelerated AMT Credit in Lieu of Bonus Depreciation

SUMMARY OF NEW LAW

A corporation may elect to accelerate the AMT tax credit by forgoing bonus depreciation on round 2 extension property, which is property eligible for bonus depreciation solely by reason of the new extension of the bonus depreciation provision to property acquired after December 31, 2007, and before January 1, 2013, and placed in service before January 1, 2013 (or January 1, 2014, in the case of property with a longer production period and certain noncommercial aircraft).

BACKGROUND

The Housing Assistance Tax Act of 2008 (P.L. 110-289) allowed a corporation to make an election in its first tax year ending after March 31, 2008, to forgo the bonus depreciation deduction on "eligible qualified property" and instead claim a refundable credit (in each tax year that eligible qualified property was placed in service) for a portion of (1) its unused general business credit carryforward attributable to research credits from tax years that began before January 1, 2006 (determined by using the ordering rules of Code Sec. 38(d)), and/or (2) its unused alternative minimum tax (AMT) liability credit attributable to tax years that began before January 1, 2006 (Code Sec. 168(k)(4); Rev. Proc. 2009-33, I.R.B. 2009-29, 150, modifying Rev. Proc. 2009-16, I.R.B. 2009-6, 449, and Rev. Proc. 2008-65, I.R.B. 2008-44, 1082).

If this election was made, depreciation on eligible qualified property is computed without claiming bonus depreciation and by using the MACRS straight-line method

BACKGROUND

(Code Sec. 168(k)(4)(A)). Thus, the entire basis of eligible qualified property, including the 50 percent of basis which would have been recovered as bonus depreciation in a single year, is recovered through straight-line depreciation deductions over the applicable MACRS recovery period for the property.

Eligible qualified property defined. Eligible qualified property is property that is acquired after March 31, 2008, and placed in service before January 1, 2010 (or before January 1, 2011, for longer-period production property and certain noncommercial aircraft) and that is eligible for the bonus depreciation deduction under Code Sec. 168(k). No binding purchase contract may be in effect before April 1, 2008 (Code Sec. 168(k)(4)(D)). In the case of eligible qualified property with a longer production period that is entitled to an extended December 31, 2010 placed-in-service deadline, only the portion of the property's basis that is attributable to manufacture, construction, or production after March 31, 2008, and before January 1, 2010, is taken into account under the Code Sec. 168(k)(2)(B)(ii) progress expenditures rule (Code Sec. 168k)(4)(D)(iii)). Thus, no credit may be claimed with respect to 2010 progress expenditures if the eligible qualified property is longer-period production property that is placed in service in 2010.

Additional election to exclude extension property. The American Recovery and Reinvestment Act of 2009 (P.L. 111-5) provided for an additional election that a corporation could make to exclude certain "extension property" if the corporation has made the accelerated credit election in its first tax year ending after March 31, 2008 (Code Sec. 168(k)(4)(H)(i)). Extension property is property that qualifies for bonus depreciation only by reason of the one-year extension of the bonus depreciation provision by P.L. 111-5 (i.e., the provision that made bonus depreciation available to qualifying property placed in service in 2009 (in 2010 for property with a longer production period and certain noncommercial aircraft) (Code Sec. 168(k)(4)(H)(iii)). Thus, if this additional election was made, the corporation could claim bonus depreciation on the extension property and the extension property was not taken into account in determining the accelerated AMT and/or research credit.

First-time election to apply provision to extension property. A corporation that did not make the accelerated credit election for its first tax year ending after March 31, 2008, was allowed to make an election to apply the provision to its first tax year ending after December 31, 2008, and all subsequent tax years. The election, however, only applied to eligible qualified property that was extension property (Code Sec. 168(k)(4)(H)(ii)).

Credit computation. The total amount of the unused research and AMT credits that may be claimed for any tax year is generally equal to the bonus depreciation amount for that tax year. The bonus depreciation amount is equal to 20 percent of the difference between:

- the aggregate bonus depreciation and regular depreciation that would be allowed on eligible qualified property placed in service during the tax year if bonus depreciation was claimed, and

BACKGROUND

- the aggregate depreciation that would be allowed on the eligible qualified property placed in service during the tax year if no bonus depreciation was claimed (Code Sec. 168(k)(4)(C)(i)).

The bonus depreciation amount for any tax year may not exceed the "maximum increase amount" reduced (but not below zero) by the sum of the bonus depreciation amounts for all preceding tax years (Code Sec. 168(k)(4)(C)(ii)). The bonus depreciation amount, as limited by this rule, is referred to as the "maximum amount."

The maximum increase amount is the lesser of: (1) $30 million, or (2) six percent of the sum of the "business credit increase amount" (i.e., unused research credits from tax years beginning before 2006) and the "AMT credit increase amount" (i.e., unused AMT credits from tax years beginning before 2006) (Code Sec. 168(k)(4)(C)(iii); Rev. Proc. 2008-65, Section 5.03).

If a corporation does not make the election described above to exclude extension property, a separate bonus depreciation amount, maximum amount, and maximum increase amount are computed and applied to eligible qualified property which is extension property and to eligible qualified property which is not extension property (Code Sec. 168(k)(4)(H)(i)(II)). This separate computation means that a corporation may claim a maximum $30 million of credits with respect to property that is not extension property and a maximum $30 million of credits with respect to property that is extension property (Rev. Proc. 2009-33, Section 5.02).

To claim a tax credit for an unused research credit from a tax year beginning before January 1, 2006, a corporation increases the Code Sec. 38(c) tax liability limitation for the tax year by the bonus depreciation amount for the tax year, as computed above (Code Sec. 168(k)(4)(A)(iii) and (B)). The bonus depreciation amount allocated to the Code Sec. 38(c) tax liability limitation, however, may not exceed the corporation's pre-2006 research credit carryforwards, reduced by any amount allocated to the Code Sec. 38(c) tax liability limitation under this provision in earlier tax years. The bonus depreciation amount may be allocated between the Code Sec. 38(c) tax liability limitation for the general business credit and the Code Sec. 53(c) tax liability limitation for the AMT credit. The amount allocated to the AMT liability limitation may not exceed the pre-2006 AMT credits, reduced by any bonus depreciation amount allocated to the Code Sec. 53(c) tax liability limitation in previous tax years (Code Sec. 168(k)(4)(E)(ii)).

> **Example:** QPEX is a calendar-year corporation that placed extension property costing $10,000 in service in June 2009. Assume that QPEX had an NOL in 2009. As a result, its Code Sec. 38(c) tax liability limitation was $0 and it was not entitled to claim any general business credit. If QPEX made the election for its first tax year ending after March 31, 2008, and did not make the election to exclude extension property, it first computes the bonus depreciation and regular depreciation on the MACRS extension property. Bonus depreciation is $50,000 ($100,000 × 50%). Regular depreciation is $5,000 (($100,000 − $50,000) × 10% first-year table percentage for 10-year property). The sum of these amounts ($55,000) is reduced to $45,000 by the $10,000 depreciation that could be

BACKGROUND

claimed in 2009 on the property if the bonus deduction was not claimed ($100,000 × 10% first year percentage for 10-year property = $10,000). Assume that QPEX has $200,000 in unused pre-2006 research credits and no unused AMT credits. The bonus depreciation amount is equal to the lesser of: (1) $9,000 ($45,000 × 20%); (2) $12,000 (6% of the sum of QPEX's unused pre-2006 research and AMT credits ($200,000 × 6% = $12,000); or (3) $30 million. Since $9,000 is less than $12,000 ($200,000 ×6%), the bonus depreciation amount is $9,000. In this situation QPEX could increase its Code Sec. 38(c) tax liability limitation by $9,000 and claim a refundable $9,000 research credit.

NEW LAW EXPLAINED

Election to accelerate AMT credit in lieu of bonus depreciation provided for round 2 extension property.—A corporation may elect to forgo bonus depreciation on "round 2 extension property" and claim unused AMT credits from tax years beginning before January 1, 2006 (Code Sec. 168(k)(4)(I), as added by the Tax Relief, Unemployment Insurance Reauthorization, and Job Creation Act of 2010 (P.L. 111-312)).

> **Comment:** A corporation may not claim unused pre-2006 research credits by forgoing bonus depreciation on round 2 extension property. The new law only allows a corporation to increase the minimum tax credit limitation by the bonus depreciation amount computed with respect to round 2 extension property and claim pre-2006 AMT credits that may remain after reduction by accelerated AMT credits that were claimed by reason of a prior election to forgo bonus depreciation.

> **Comment:** As explained below, a corporation which previously made an election to forgo bonus depreciation must forgo bonus depreciation on round 2 extension property unless it makes an election out of the provision. On the other hand, a corporation which did not make a prior election to forgo bonus depreciation can make an election to forgo bonus depreciation on round 2 extension property only.

Round 2 extension property defined. Round 2 extension property is property which is eligible qualified property (as defined in Code Sec. 168(k)(4)(D), as amended by the Tax Relief Act of 2010 (see **Eligible qualified property**, below) solely by reason of the two-year extension of the bonus depreciation allowance by the Tax Relief Act of 2010 to property acquired after December 31, 2007, and placed in service in 2011 or 2012, and, in the case of longer-period production property and certain noncommercial aircraft, to property placed in service in 2013 (Code Sec. 168(k)(4)(I)(iv), as added by the Tax Relief Act of 2010). The new two-year extension of the bonus depreciation is discussed in detail at ¶502.

> **Comment:** Property placed in service during 2010, which qualifies for bonus depreciation, is never considered round 2 extension property.

¶504

NEW LAW EXPLAINED

Example 1: A corporation with a fiscal year beginning October 1, 2010, and ending September 30, 2011, acquires and places in service in November 2010, $1,000,000 of equipment that qualifies for bonus deprecation under the rules in effect prior to the two-year extension of the bonus depreciation by the new law. This property is not round 2 extension property.

Comment: Since the bonus depreciation amount, maximum amount, and maximum increase amounts are computed separately for round 2 extension property, a corporation may claim a maximum $30 million credit with respect to round 2 extension property (i.e., property placed in service in 2011 and 2012 which qualifies for bonus depreciation). As indicated in the *Background* section, above, separate bonus depreciation amounts, maximum amounts, and maximum increase amounts are computed and applied to eligible qualified property which is extension property and to eligible qualified property which is not extension property (Code Sec. 168(k)(4)(H)(i)(II)). Accordingly, a corporation can claim a maximum $30 million of credits with respect to property that is not extension property and a maximum $30 million of credits with respect to property that is extension property (Rev. Proc. 2009-33, Section 5.02). Taking into account property which is not extension property, extension property, and round 2 extension property, a corporation may claim up to $90 million in credits.

Eligible qualified property. Eligible qualified property is property that is acquired after March 31, 2008, and before January 1, 2013, and placed in service before January 1, 2013 (before January 1, 2014 for longer-period production property and certain noncommercial aircraft) and that is eligible for the bonus depreciation deduction. No binding written purchase contract may be in effect before April 1, 2008 (Code Sec. 168(k)(2)(A) and (4)(D), as amended by the Tax Relief Act of 2010).

Comment: Since this definition of eligible qualified property only applies to property placed in service after December 31, 2010 (Act Sec. 401(e)(1) of the Tax Relief Act of 2010), property placed in service before January 1, 2011, is not eligible qualified property unless it was eligible qualified property under the prior law. Under the prior-law definition, property placed in service in 2010 is generally not eligible qualified property. See *Background* discussion.

Comment: Property with a longer production period and certain noncommercial aircraft that are placed in service in 2011 may qualify for bonus depreciation without regard to the two-year extension of bonus depreciation by the new law. See ¶502. Since such property qualifies for bonus depreciation without regard to the new law, it is not considered round 2 extension property.

Example 2: A calendar tax year corporation enters into a contract in November 2009 for the construction of a noncommercial aircraft that qualifies for an extended December 31, 2011 placed-in-service deadline under the rules in effect prior to enactment of the new law. The plane is placed in service in 2011. The plane would have qualified for bonus depreciation even if the bonus deprecia-

NEW LAW EXPLAINED

> tion provision had not been extended for two years by the new law. Therefore, it is not round 2 extension property.

> **Example 3:** Assume the same facts as in Example 2, above, except that the plane is placed in service in 2013. The plane qualifies for bonus depreciation solely by reason of the extension of the placed-in-service deadline through 2013 by the new law for property with a longer production period and noncommercial aircraft. Therefore, the plane is round 2 extension property.

Eligible qualified property with a longer production period. In the case of eligible qualified property with a longer production period that is entitled to an extended December 31, 2013 placed-in-service deadline, only the portion of the property's basis that is attributable to manufacture, construction, or production (1) after March 31, 2008, and before January 1, 2010, and (2) after December 31, 2010, and before January 1, 2013, is taken into account under the Code Sec. 168(k)(2)(B)(ii) progress expenditures rule in computing the credit (Code Sec. 168(k)(4)(D)(iii), as amended by the Tax Relief Act of 2010).

> **Example 4:** Construction on a passenger plane, which qualifies as property with a longer production period, begins on January 1, 2009. Although round 2 extension property must generally be placed in service by December 31, 2012, an extended December 31, 2013 deadline applies because the plane is property with a longer production period. If the plane is placed in service in 2013, and the election to forgo bonus depreciation applies to round 2 extension property, no portion of the 2010 or 2013 progress expenditures are taken into account in computing the accelerated AMT credit.

Election rules for corporations previously electing to forgo bonus depreciation. If a corporation previously made an election under Code Sec. 168(k)(4)(A) to forgo bonus depreciation for its first tax year beginning after March 31, 2008, or made an election to forgo bonus depreciation with respect to extension property under Code Sec. 168(k)(4)(H)(ii) for its first tax year ending after December 31, 2008, the election to forgo bonus depreciation will apply to round 2 extension property, unless the corporation makes an election not to forgo bonus depreciation on round 2 extension property (Code Sec. 168(k)(4)(I)(ii), as added by the Tax Relief Act of 2010).

> **Caution:** A corporation with a prior election in effect will be required to forgo bonus depreciation on all round 2 extension property even if it has no available pre-2006 AMT credits to claim *unless* an election is made not to forgo bonus depreciation on round 2 extension property. The manner of making the election is not provided in the new law. **It is possible that** the IRS may consider the election made if a corporation simply claims bonus depreciation on round 2

¶504

NEW LAW EXPLAINED

property on its income tax return. **However, the IRS will need to address this point.**

If the election to forgo bonus depreciation applies to round 2 extension property, the bonus depreciation amount, maximum amount, and maximum increase amount are computed separately for eligible qualified property which is round 2 extension property. These computations are not combined with any amounts computed for eligible qualified property which is not round 2 extension property and which is subject to a prior election (Code Sec. 168(k)(4)(I)(ii), as added by the Tax Relief Act of 2010).

Election rules for corporations with no previous election to forgo bonus depreciation. If a corporation did not previously make an election under Code Sec. 168(k)(4)(A) to forgo bonus depreciation in its first tax year beginning after March 31, 2008, and did not make an election to forgo bonus depreciation with respect to extension property under Code Sec. 168(k)(4)(H)(ii) for its first tax year ending after December 31, 2008, the corporation may make an election to forgo bonus depreciation in its first tax year ending after December 31, 2010, and each subsequent tax year. However, if the election is made, it only applies to round 2 extension property (Code Sec. 168(k)(4)(I)(iii), as added by the Tax Relief Act of 2010).

▶ **Effective date.** The provisions apply to property placed in service after December 31, 2010, in tax years ending after such date (Act Sec. 401(e)(1) of the Tax Relief, Unemployment Insurance Reauthorization, and Job Creation Act of 2010 (P.L. 111-312)).

Law source: Law at ¶5265. Committee Report at ¶10,140.

— Act Sec. 401(c)(1) of the Tax Relief, Unemployment Insurance Reauthorization, and Job Creation Act of 2010 (P.L. 111-312), amending Code Sec. 168(k)(4)(D)(iii);

— Act Sec. 401(c)(2), adding Code Sec. 168(k)(4)(I);

— Act Sec. 401(d)(3), amending Code Sec. 168(k)(4)(D);

— Act Sec. 401(e)(1), providing the effective date.

Reporter references: For further information, consult the following CCH reporters.

— Standard Federal Tax Reporter, ¶11,279.0583

— Tax Research Consultant, DEPR: 3,606

— Practical Tax Explanation, § 11,225.25

¶506 Section 179 Expensing of Depreciable Assets

SUMMARY OF NEW LAW

The Code Sec. 179 dollar limit for tax years beginning in 2012 is increased from $25,000 to $125,000. The investment limit for 2012 is increased from $200,000 to $500,000. The rule allowing off-the-shelf computer software to be expensed is extended for one year to apply to software placed in service in tax years beginning after 2002 and before 2013. The rule allowing taxpayers to make, change, or revoke a Code

SUMMARY OF NEW LAW

Sec. 179 election on a timely-filed amended return is extended for one year to apply to elections for tax years beginning after 2002 and before 2013.

BACKGROUND

An expense deduction is provided for taxpayers (other than estates, trusts or certain noncorporate lessors) who elect to treat the cost of qualifying property, called section 179 property, as an expense rather than a capital expenditure (Code Sec. 179).

Section 179 property is generally defined as new or used depreciable tangible section 1245 property that is purchased for use in the active conduct of a trade or business (Code Sec. 179(d)(1)). For tax years beginning in 2010 and 2011, a taxpayer may elect to treat qualified real property as section 179 property. Qualified real property generally consists of qualified leasehold improvements as defined in Code Sec. 168(e)(6), qualified restaurant property as defined in Code Sec. 168(e)(7), and qualified retail improvement property as defined in Code Sec. 168(e)(8) (Code Sec. 179(f)).

Dollar limitation. A dollar limit is placed on the maximum cost of section 179 property a taxpayer may expense during the tax year before applying the "investment" and "taxable income" limitations. For tax years beginning in 2008 and 2009, the dollar limitation is $250,000 (Code Sec. 179(b)(1)(A)). For tax years beginning in 2010 and 2011, dollar limitation is $500,000 (Code Sec. 179(b)(1)(B)). The limit is reduced to $25,000 for tax years beginning after 2011.

A taxpayer that elects to treat qualified real property as section 179 property in a tax year beginning in 2010 or 2011 may only expense up to $250,000 of its cost. The elected amount is applied toward the $500,000 annual dollar limitation that applies to those years (Code Sec. 179(f)(3)).

Investment limitation. The annual dollar limitation is reduced dollar for dollar by the portion of the cost of section 179 property placed in service during the tax year that is in excess of an investment limitation. The investment limitation is $800,000 for tax years beginning in 2008 and 2009, $2 million for tax years beginning in 2010 and 2011, and $200,000 for tax years beginning after 2011 (Code Sec. 179(b)(2)).

Taxable income limitation. The Code Sec. 179 deduction is limited to the taxpayer's taxable income derived from the active conduct of any trade or business during the tax year, computed without taking into account any Code Sec. 179 deduction, deduction for self-employment taxes, net operating loss carryback or carryover, or deductions suspended under any provision (Code Sec. 179(b)(3); Reg. § 1.179-2(c)(1)). Any amount disallowed by this limitation may be carried forward and deducted in subsequent tax years, subject to the maximum dollar and investment limitations, or, if lower, the taxable income limitation in effect for the carryover year (Code Sec. 179(b)(3)(B)).

However, a Code Sec. 179 deduction on qualified real property that is disallowed by reason of the taxable income limitation may not be carried forward to a tax year that begins after 2011. Any amount that cannot be carried forward is recovered through depreciation deductions (Code Sec. 179(f)(4)).

¶506

BACKGROUND

Off-the-shelf computer software. Code Sec. 179 expensing is allowed for off-the-shelf computer software placed in service in tax years beginning after 2002 and before 2012 (Code Sec. 179(d)(1)(A)(ii)). Off-the-shelf computer software for this purpose is defined by reference to Code Sec. 197(e)(3)(A)(i) and (B) and to mean any program designed to cause a computer to perform a desired function that (i) is readily available for purchase by the general public, (ii) is subject to a non-exclusive license, and (iii) has not been substantially modified. Software does not include any database or similar item unless it is in the public domain and is incidental to the operation of otherwise qualifying software.

> **Comment:** Computer software that is not amortized under Code Sec. 197 may be amortized over three years using the straight-line method whether or not it is off-the-shelf software (Code Sec. 167(f)(1)(A)).

Making, changing, or revoking the Code Sec. 179 election. A taxpayer makes a Code Sec. 179 election for a tax year on its return for that year or on an amended return filed by the due date of the original return, including extensions. The election must specify the items of section 179 property to which the election applies and the portion of the cost of each item that the taxpayer elects to expense (Code Sec. 179(c)(1); Reg. § 1.179-5(a)). For tax years beginning in 2003 through 2011, a taxpayer may make, revoke, or change a Code Sec. 179 election or a specification contained in the election without the IRS consent on an amended return filed during the period prescribed for filing the amended return (generally, three years from the filing of the original return) (Code Sec. 179(c)(2); Reg. § 1.179-5(c)). For tax years beginning after 2011, an election not made on an original return must be made on an amended return filed by the due date of the original return (including extensions). A revocation of an election or change of an election specification can only be made with the IRS consent (Reg. § 1.179-5(a)).

NEW LAW EXPLAINED

Code Sec. 179 deduction limitations increased for 2012; computer software deduction and election revocation extended through 2012.—The Code Sec. 179 dollar limitation for tax years beginning in 2012 is increased to $125,000, subject to inflation adjustment. For tax years beginning after 2012, the dollar limit is $25,000 (Code Sec. 179(b)(1), as amended by the Tax Relief, Unemployment Insurance Reauthorization, and Job Creation Act of 2010 (P.L. 111-312)). For tax years beginning in 2012, the investment limitation is $500,000, subject to inflation adjustment. For tax years beginning after 2012, the investment limitation is $200,000 (Code Sec. 172(b)(2), as amended by the Tax Relief Act of 2010).

> **Comment:** The entire cost of most new depreciable section 1245 property acquired after September 8, 2010, and placed in service before January 1, 2012, can be claimed as a 100-percent bonus depreciation deduction under Code Sec. 168(k)(5), as added by the Tax Relief Act of 2010. The 100-percent bonus depreciation deduction is also referred to as the "100-percent expensing deduction." A Code Sec. 168(k) 50-percent bonus depreciation deduction applies to

NEW LAW EXPLAINED

other qualifying property acquired after December 31, 2007, and placed in service before January 1, 2013. See ¶502.

Comment: A taxpayer will receive the greatest benefit from Code Sec. 179 by expensing property that does not qualify for bonus depreciation (e.g., used property) and property with a long MACRS depreciation period. For example, given the choice between expensing an item of MACRS five-year property and an item of MACRS 15-year property, the 15-year property should be expensed since it takes 10 additional tax years to recover its cost through annual depreciation deductions.

Comment: Without regard to the inflation adjustment, the Code Sec. 179 deduction is completely phased out in a tax year that begins in 2012 on account of the investment limitation if the taxpayer places more than $625,000 of section 179 property in service ($625,000 – $500,000 = $125,000).

State Tax Consequences: The $125,000 dollar limit and the $500,000 investment limit for tax years beginning in 2012 will not impact states, including California, Florida, Indiana, New Jersey, and Wisconsin that have decoupled from the federal expensing allowance and limitation amounts. For states like Connecticut, Illinois, Massachusetts, Michigan, and Pennsylvania that adopt the federal allowance and limitation amounts, whether they adopt this amendment will depend on their Code conformity dates. Those states that update their Code conformity dates annually will most likely conform during their next legislative sessions. However, it should be noted that more states have been decoupling from the increased expense allowances and limitations to alleviate further state revenue shortfalls.

Inflation adjustment. The dollar and investment limitations for a tax year that begins in 2012 ($125,000 and $500,000, respectively) will be adjusted for inflation (Code Sec. 179(b)(6), as added by the Tax Relief Act of 2010). Thus, the actual dollar and investment limitation that applies to a tax year that begins in 2012 will be slightly higher than the $125,000 and $500,000 figures.

The inflation adjustment is equal to the limit amount (i.e., $125,000 or $500,000) multiplied by the cost-of-living adjustment for the calendar year in which the tax year begins. The cost of living adjustment is equal to the percentage by which the consumer price index for calendar year 2011 exceeds the consumer price index for calendar year 2006 (Code Sec. 179(b)(6)(A), as added by the Tax Relief Act of 2010).

If the $125,000 dollar limitation as increased by the inflation adjustment is not a multiple of $1,000, the dollar limitation is rounded to the nearest multiple of $1,000 (Code Sec. 179(b)(6)(B)(i), as added by the Tax Relief Act of 2010). If the $500,000 investment limit as increased by the inflation adjustment is not a multiple of $10,000, the investment limitation is rounded to the nearest multiple of $10,0000 (Code Sec. 179(b)(6)(B)(ii), as added by the Tax Relief Act of 2010).

Comment: The $25,000 dollar limit and $200,000 investment limit that apply to tax years beginning after 2012 are not adjusted for inflation.

Off-the-shelf computer software. The Code Sec. 179 expense deduction for off-the-shelf computer software is extended an additional year to apply to software placed in

NEW LAW EXPLAINED

service in tax years beginning after 2002 and before 2013 (Code Sec. 179(d)(1)(A)(ii), as amended by the Tax Relief Act of 2010).

> **Comment:** The new law does not extend the rule which allows a taxpayer to expense qualified real property (Code Sec. 179(f)). The election to expense qualified real property continues to apply only to qualified real property placed in service in a tax year that begins in 2010 or 2011. See the *Background* section, above.

Revocation of election. The temporary rule which allows a taxpayer to revoke a Code Sec. 179 expense election without IRS consent is extended an additional year to apply to elections and election specifications with respect to any tax year beginning after 2002 and before 2013 (Code Sec. 179(c)(2), as amended by the Tax Relief Act of 2010).

▶ **Effective date.** The provision applies to tax years beginning after December 31, 2011 (Act Sec. 402(f) of the Tax Relief, Unemployment Insurance Reauthorization, and Job Creation Act of 2010 (P.L. 111-312)).

Law source: Law at ¶5275. Committee Report at ¶10,150.

— Act Sec. 402(a) of the Tax Relief, Unemployment Insurance Reauthorization, and Job Creation Act of 2010 (P.L. 111-312), amending Code Sec. 179(b)(1);

— Act Sec. 402(b), amending Code Sec. 179(b)(2);

— Act Sec. 402(c), adding Code Sec. 179(b)(6);

— Act Sec. 402(d), amending Code Sec. 179(d)(1)(A)(ii);

— Act Sec. 402(e), amending Code Sec. 179(c)(2);

— Act Sec. 402(f), providing the effective date.

Reporter references: For further information, consult the following CCH reporters.

— Standard Federal Tax Reporter, ¶12,126.01

— Tax Research Consultant, DEPR: 12,000

— Practical Tax Explanation, §9,801

¶508 15-Year Straight-Line Cost Recovery for Qualified Leasehold Improvements, Qualified Restaurant Property, and Qualified Retail Improvements

SUMMARY OF NEW LAW

The 15-year recovery period for qualified leasehold improvement property, qualified restaurant property and qualified retail improvement property is extended to apply to property placed in service before January 1, 2012.

BACKGROUND

The American Jobs Creation Act of 2004 (P.L. 108-357) created a 15-year recovery period under the Modified Adjusted Cost Recovery System (MACRS) for qualified leasehold improvement property and qualified restaurant property placed in service after October 22, 2004, and before January 1, 2006, using the straight-line method and the half-year convention (unless the mid-quarter convention applies) (Code Sec. 168(e)(3)(E)(iv)). The Tax Relief and Health Care Act of 2006 (P.L. 109-432) extended allowance of the 15-year recovery period to apply to qualified leasehold improvement property placed in service before January 1, 2008. The Tax Extenders and Alternative Minimum Tax Relief Act of 2008 (P.L. 110-343) (2008 Extenders and AMT Act) extended this provision further to apply to qualified leasehold improvement property placed in service before January 1, 2010. In addition, the 2008 Extenders and AMT Act created a 15-year recovery period for qualified retail property. If the MACRS alternative depreciation system (ADS) is elected or otherwise applies, the recovery period for nonresidential real property is 39 years, and depreciation is computed using the straight-line method and half-year or mid-quarter convention (Code Sec. 168(g)(3)(B)).

Leasehold improvement. For purposes of this provision, a leasehold improvement is generally considered a structural component of a building and depreciated over 39 years using the straight-line method beginning in the month the improvement was placed in service. To be eligible for the 15-year recovery period, "qualified leasehold improvement property" is any improvement to an interior portion of *nonresidential real property* if the following requirements are satisfied:

- The improvement is made under, or pursuant to, a lease by the lessee, lessor or any sublessee of the interior portion.
- The improvement is section 1250 property (i.e., a structural component and not section 1245 personal property that is eligible for a shortened recovery period under the cost segregation rules).
- The lease is not between related persons.
- The interior portion of the building is to be occupied exclusively by the lessee or any sublessee of that interior portion.
- The improvement is placed in service more than three years after the date the building was first placed in service by any person (Code Sec. 168(k)(3); Reg. § 1.168(k)-1(c)).

Expenditures for the following are not qualified leasehold improvement property:

- the enlargement (as defined in Reg. § 1.48-12(c)(10)) of the building;
- elevators and escalators;
- structural components (as defined in Reg. § 1.48-1(e)(2)) that benefit a common area; and
- internal structural framework (as defined in Reg. § 1.48-12(b)(3)(i)(D)).

Restaurant property. For property placed in service after October 22, 2004, and before January 1, 2009, qualified restaurant property is any section 1250 property which is an improvement to a building if the improvement is placed in service more

¶508

BACKGROUND

than three years after the date the building was first placed in service and more than 50 percent of the building's square footage is devoted to preparation of and seating for on-premises consumption of prepared meals (Code Sec. 168(e)(7)). The three-year period is measured from the date that the building was originally placed in service, whether or not it was originally placed in service by the taxpayer. For example, improvements to a restaurant building that is at least three years old at the time the taxpayer buys the building may qualify.

For property placed in service after December 31, 2008, and before January 1, 2010, qualified restaurant property also includes a building (or improvements thereto), if more than 50 percent of the building's square footage is devoted to preparation of, and seating for on-premises consumption of, prepared meals. In other words, for property placed in service between these dates, qualified restaurant property includes a new building and improvements made to an existing building. The three-year waiting period has been eliminated.

The provision only applies to improvements to a restaurant building. Improvements that are not part of or attached to the restaurant building, for example, a detached sign supported on a concrete foundation, sidewalk, or depreciable landscaping, would generally constitute separately depreciable land improvements that also have a 15-year recovery period but are depreciated using the 150-percent declining balance method. Other unattached improvements may qualify for a shorter recovery period if not considered a land improvement

Qualified retail improvement property. The following requirements must be met in order to meet the definition of a qualified retail improvement (Code Sec. 168(e)(8)(A) and (E)):

- The property must be an improvement to an interior portion of a building that is nonresidential real property.

- The interior portion of the building must be open to the general public and used in the retail trade or business of selling tangible personal property to the general public.

- The improvement must be placed in service more than three years after the building was first placed in service.

- The improvement must be placed in service after December 31, 2008, and before January 1, 2010 (i.e., it must be placed in service during the 2009 calendar year).

The following improvements are specifically disqualified from the definition of qualified retail improvement property (Code Sec. 168(e)(8)(D)):

- elevators and escalators;

- internal structural framework of a building;

- structural components that benefit a common area; and

- improvements relating to the enlargement of a building.

15-year recovery period extended.—The 15-year recovery period for qualified leasehold improvement property, qualified restaurant property (including restaurant buildings), and qualified retail improvement property is extended for two years and now applies to property placed in service before January 1, 2012 (Code Sec. 168(e)(3)(E), as amended by the Tax Relief, Unemployment Insurance Reauthorization, and Job Creation Act of 2010 (P.L. 111-312)).

> **Comment:** The current law rule that an improvement to qualified leasehold improvement property or qualified retail improvement property must be placed in service more than three years after the related building was placed in service continues to apply (Code Sec. 168(e)(8)(A) and (k)(3)(A)(iii)).

> **Comment:** Under current law, a taxpayer that places qualified leasehold improvement property, qualified restaurant property (including buildings), or qualified retail improvement property in service in a tax year that begins in 2010 or 2011 may elect to treat such property as section 179 property and expense under Code Sec. 179 up to $250,000 of the cost of the property (Code Sec. 179(f)). The new law makes some nonsubstantive changes to Code Sec. 179(f) to reflect the extension of the 15-year recovery period to these types of property to tax years beginning in 2010 and 2011 (Code Sec. 179(f)(2), as amended by the Tax Relief Act of 2010).

> **Comment:** The new law makes no change to the rules that qualified restaurant property placed in service after 2008 and retail improvement property do not qualify for bonus depreciation (Code Sec. 168(e)(7)(B) and (e)(8)(D)). Qualified leasehold improvement property, however, does qualify for bonus depreciation (Code Sec. 168(k)(3)).

A 15-year qualified retail improvement will generally qualify as a 15-year qualified leasehold improvement if the improvement is placed in service by a lessor or lessee (or sublessee) pursuant to or under the terms of a lease with an unrelated person. Similarly, a 15-year qualified restaurant improvement may qualify as a 15-year qualified leasehold improvement. Since bonus depreciation does not apply to qualified restaurant property placed in service after 2008 or qualified retail improvement property, a taxpayer will generally want to identify its treatment of dual status property as a qualified leasehold improvement in order to claim the bonus deduction.

A proposed technical correction, which was never enacted, would have retroactively clarified that building improvements that qualify as both qualified leasehold improvement property and qualified retail improvement property or qualified restaurant property qualify for bonus depreciation even if the taxpayer treats the property as a qualified retail improvement or restaurant improvement (Act Sec. 4(b) of the Tax Technical Corrections Act of 2009, proposing a retroactive amendment to Code Sec. 168(e)(8)(D)). However, even though this technical correction was never enacted, footnotes 27 and 29 in the Joint Committee Report to the Tax Relief Act of 2010 state that property that satisfies the definition of both qualified leasehold improvement property and qualified restaurant property or qualified retail improvement property is eligible for bonus depreciation. This seems to imply that the IRS will interpret the law as if the technical

NEW LAW EXPLAINED

correction had been enacted (Joint Committee on Taxation, *Technical Explanation of the Revenue Provisions Contained in the "Tax Relief, Unemployment Insurance Reauthorization, and Job Creation Act of 2010"* (JCX-55-10), December 10, 2010).

Comment: Qualified leasehold, retail, and restaurant property does not lose its status as section 1250 property by reason of its status as MACRS 15-year property. Thus, any section 179 allowance or bonus deduction is subject to recapture as ordinary income to the extent the section 179 deduction or bonus allowance claimed is in excess of the straight-line depreciation that would have been allowed on such amounts. Recapture is limited to the gain recognized upon a disposition. No recapture is required if the property is disposed after the end of its 15-year recovery period.

Comment: The Joint Committee states that for purposes of qualifying for the 15-year recovery period for retail improvement property, it is generally intended businesses defined as a store retailer under the current North American Industry Classification System (industry sub-sectors 441 through 453) qualify while those in other industry classes do not qualify. This information does not appear to have been previously provided to taxpayers. Applying this standard, businesses primarily engaged in providing services, such as professional services, health services, and entertainment services will not qualify. Examples of qualifying businesses are grocery, hardware, convenience, and clothing stores (Joint Committee on Taxation, *Technical Explanation of the Revenue Provisions Contained in the "Tax Relief, Unemployment Insurance Reauthorization, and Job Creation Act of 2010"* (JCX-55-10), December 10, 2010).

▶ **Effective date.** The provision applies to property placed in service after December 31, 2009 (Act Sec. 737(c) of the Tax Relief, Unemployment Insurance Reauthorization, and Job Creation Act of 2010 (P.L. 111-312)).

Law source: Law at ¶5265 and ¶5275. Committee Report at ¶10,420.

— Act Sec. 737(a) of the Tax Relief, Unemployment Insurance Reauthorization, and Job Creation Act of 2010 (P.L. 111-312), amending Code Sec. 168(e)(3)(E);

— Act Sec. 737(b)(1), amending Code Sec. 168(e)(7)(A)(i);

— Act Sec. 737(b)(2), striking Code Sec. 168(e)(8)(E);

— Act Sec. 737(b)(3), amending Code Sec. 179(f)(2);

— Act Sec. 737(c), providing the effective date.

Reporter references: For further information, consult the following CCH reporters.

— Standard Federal Tax Reporter, ¶11,279.023, ¶11,279.0311, ¶11,279.0312 and ¶11,279.05

— Tax Research Consultant, DEPR: 3,156.25 and DEPR: 6052

— Practical Tax Explanation, § 11,210, § 11,215 and § 11,230

¶508

¶510 Seven-Year Recovery Period for Motorsports Entertainment Complexes

SUMMARY OF NEW LAW

The seven-year recovery period for motorsports entertainment complexes is extended to apply to property placed in service on or before December 31, 2011.

BACKGROUND

Under the modified accelerated cost recovery system (MACRS), most types of property associated with theme parks and/or amusement parks are depreciated over a seven-year period (Code Sec. 168(e)(1)). For depreciation purposes, Rev. Proc. 87-56, 1987-2 CB 674, as clarified and modified by Rev. Proc. 88-22, 1988-1 CB 785, provides that theme parks and amusement parks fall within Asset Class 80.0 and have a class life of 12.5 years. Historically, racing track facilities were treated by the IRS the same as theme or amusement parks and, thus, were depreciated over a seven-year period. The American Jobs Creation Act of 2004 (P.L. 108-357) (2004 Jobs Act) codified this treatment by adding motorsports entertainment complexes (and their related ancillary and support facilities) placed in service after October 22, 2004, to the list of "seven-year property" types (Code Sec. 168(e)(3)(C)(ii)). Under current law, the seven-year recovery period for a motorsports entertainment complex and related ancillary and support facilities applies to property placed in service before January 1, 2010 (Code Sec. 168(i)(15)(D), as amended by the Tax Extenders and Alternative Minimum Tax Relief Act of 2008 (P.L. 110-343)).

Motorsports entertainment complex. A "motorsports entertainment complex" is a racing track facility that is permanently situated on land, hosts at least one racing event for cars of any type, trucks, or motorcycles during the 36-month period following the first day of the month in which it is placed in service, and is open to the public for an admission fee (Code Sec. 168(i)(15)(A)). Other related facilities owned by the taxpayer who owns the complex and provided for the benefit of patrons of the complex also fall within the definition of a motorsports entertainment complex, such as:

- ancillary facilities and land improvements in support of the complex's activities, including parking lots, sidewalks, waterways, bridges, fences, and landscaping;

- support facilities, including food and beverage retailing, souvenir vending, and other nonlodging accommodations; and

- appurtenances associated with the facilities and related attractions and amusements, including ticket booths, race track surfaces, suites and hospitality facilities, grandstands and viewing structures, props, walls, facilities that support entertainment services delivery, other special purpose structures, facades, shop interiors, and buildings (Code Sec. 168(i)(15)(B)).

"Motorsports entertainment complex" does *not* include any transportation equipment, administrative services assets, warehouses, administrative buildings, hotels, or

¶510

BACKGROUND

motels (Code Sec. 168(i)(15)(C)). In addition, motorsports facilities placed in service after October 22, 2004, are *not* treated as theme and amusement facilities classified as Asset Class 80.0 in Rev. Proc. 87-56 (Act Sec. 704(c)(2) of the 2004 Jobs Act).

NEW LAW EXPLAINED

Seven-year depreciation period for motorsports entertainment complexes extended.—The seven-year recovery period for motorsports entertainment complexes is extended for one year, to apply to property placed in service on or before December 31, 2011 (Code Sec. 168(i)(15)(D), as amended by the Tax Relief, Unemployment Insurance Reauthorization, and Job Creation Act of 2010 (P.L. 111-312)).

▶ **Effective date.** The provision applies to property placed in service after December 31, 2009 (Act Sec. 738(b) of the Tax Relief, Unemployment Insurance Reauthorization, and Job Creation Act of 2010 (P.L. 111-312)).

Law source: Law at ¶5265. Committee Report at ¶10,430.

— Act Sec. 738(a) of the Tax Relief, Unemployment Insurance Reauthorization, and Job Creation Act of 2010 (P.L. 111-312), amending Code Sec. 168(i)(15)(D);

— Act Sec. 738(b), providing the effective date.

Reporter references: For further information, consult the following CCH reporters.

— Standard Federal Tax Reporter, ¶11,279.01 and ¶11,279.0314

— Tax Research Consultant, DEPR: 3,156.152

— Practical Tax Explanation, §11,110.20

¶512 Accelerated Depreciation for Business Property on Indian Reservations

SUMMARY OF NEW LAW

The incentives pertaining to depreciation of qualified Indian reservation property are extended to apply to property placed in service on or before December 31, 2011.

BACKGROUND

Special Modified Accelerated Cost Recovery System (MACRS) recovery periods that permit faster write-offs are provided for "qualified Indian reservation property" that is placed in service after December 31, 1993, and on or before December 31, 2010 (Code Sec. 168(j), as amended by Act Sec. 315(a) of the Tax Extenders and Alternative Minimum Tax Relief Act of 2008 (P.L. 110-343)). The regular tax depreciation deduction claimed on qualified Indian reservation property is allowed for alternative minimum tax (AMT) purposes (Code Sec. 168(j)(3)). Although the recovery periods

BACKGROUND

are shortened for Indian reservation property, no change is made to the depreciation method or convention that would otherwise apply.

The following chart shows the shortened recovery periods.

Property Class	Recovery Period
3-year property	2 years
5-year property	3 years
7-year property	4 years
10-year property	6 years
15-year property	9 years
20-year property	12 years
Nonresidential real property	22 years

> **Comment:** The recovery period for MACRS 27.5-year residential rental property used on an Indian reservation is not shortened.

Qualified Indian reservation property is MACRS 3-, 5-, 7-, 10-, 15-, and 20-year property and nonresidential real property that is:

- used predominantly in the active conduct of a trade or business within an Indian reservation;

- not used or located outside an Indian reservation on a regular basis;

- not acquired (directly or indirectly) from a related person (as defined by Code Sec. 465(b)(3)(C)); and

- not used for certain gaming purposes.

NEW LAW EXPLAINED

Incentives provided for qualified Indian reservation property extended.—The allowance of shortened recovery periods for qualified Indian reservation property is extended for one year to property placed in service before January 1, 2011. Depreciation deductions taken with reference to the shortened periods will also be allowed for purposes of calculating the taxpayer's alternative minimum tax (AMT) (Code Sec. 168(j)(8), as amended by the Tax Relief, Unemployment Insurance Reauthorization, and Job Creation Act of 2010 (P.L. 111-312)).

▶ **Effective date.** The provision applies to property placed in service after December 31, 2009 (Act Sec. 739(b) of the Tax Relief, Unemployment Insurance Reauthorization, and Job Creation Act of 2010 (P.L. 111-312)).

Law source: Law at ¶5265. Committee Report at ¶10,440.

— Act Sec. 739(a) of the Tax Relief, Unemployment Insurance Reauthorization, and Job Creation Act of 2010 (P.L. 111-312), amending Code Sec. 168(j)(8);

— Act Sec. 739(b), providing the effective date.

¶512

NEW LAW EXPLAINED

Reporter references: For further information, consult the following CCH reporters.
— Standard Federal Tax Reporter, ¶11,279.031
— Tax Research Consultant, DEPR: 3,156.55
— Practical Tax Explanation, § 11,120

¶514 Special Expensing Rules for Certain Film and Television Productions

SUMMARY OF NEW LAW

The special expensing provision for qualified film and television productions is extended for two years, to apply to qualified film and television productions commencing in 2010 and 2011.

BACKGROUND

A taxpayer may elect to deduct the production costs of a qualifying film or television production that commences after October 22, 2004, and before January 1, 2010 (Code Sec. 181). The owner of the production makes the election and claims the deduction. The election is usually made in the first tax year that production costs are paid or incurred. The production costs are then deducted in each tax year that such costs are paid or incurred.

To qualify for the election on productions that commence after October 22, 2004, and before January 1, 2008, the aggregate production cost may not exceed $15 million ($20 million for films produced in certain low-income or distressed communities). In addition, 75 percent of the compensation paid with respect to the production must be for services performed in the United States. The deduction is recaptured if the production ceases to be a qualifying production either before or after it is placed in service.

To qualify for the election on productions that commence after December 31, 2007, and before January 1, 2010, the first $15 million ($20 million for productions in low income communities or distressed area or isolated area of distress) of an otherwise qualified film or television production may be treated as an expense in cases where the aggregate cost of the production exceeds the dollar limitation (Code Sec. 181(a)(2)(A)). The cost of the production in excess of the dollar limitation must be capitalized and recovered under the taxpayer's method of accounting for the recovery of such property.

NEW LAW EXPLAINED

Special rules for expensing qualified film and television productions extended.— The special expensing provision for qualified film and television productions is extended for two years, to apply to qualified film and television productions commencing

NEW LAW EXPLAINED

before January 1, 2012 (Code Sec. 181(f), as amended by the Tax Relief, Unemployment Insurance Reauthorization, and Job Creation Act of 2010 (P.L. 111-312)).

> **State Tax Consequences:** For states such as California, Hawaii, and Indiana, which have decoupled from the federal election to expense qualifying film and television production expenses, the extension of the deduction will have no impact. For other states, whether an adjustment is required will depend on the state's Internal Revenue Code conformity date. States that incorporate the Internal Revenue Code as currently in effect will incorporate the amendment, whereas those states, such as Kentucky, that have not updated their Internal Revenue Code reference in years, will require an adjustment. Those states that update their Code conformity dates annually will most likely conform during their next legislative sessions. Taxpayers in states that will require an adjustment must also adjust the amount of depreciation claimed for such property.

▶ **Effective date.** The provision applies to qualified film and television productions commencing after December 31, 2009 (Act Sec. 744(b) of the Tax Relief, Unemployment Insurance Reauthorization, and Job Creation Act of 2010 (P.L. 111-312)).

Law source: Law at ¶5285. Committee Report at ¶10,490.

— Act Sec. 744(a) of the Tax Relief, Unemployment Insurance Reauthorization, and Job Creation Act of 2010 (P.L. 111-312), amending Code Sec. 181(f);

— Act Sec. 744(b), providing the effective date.

Reporter references: For further information, consult the following CCH reporters.

— Standard Federal Tax Reporter, ¶12,146.01

— Tax Research Consultant, DEPR: 12,300

— Practical Tax Explanation, § 10,235

¶516 Election to Expense Advanced Mine Safety Equipment

SUMMARY OF NEW LAW

The election to expense 50 percent of the cost of advanced mine safety equipment is extended for two years, for property placed in service in 2010 and 2011.

BACKGROUND

In order to encourage mining companies to invest in safety equipment that goes above and beyond current safety requirements, a taxpayer may elect to immediately expense 50 percent of the cost of qualified mine safety equipment in the year the equipment is placed into service (Code Sec. 179E). Qualified advanced mine safety equipment is defined as advanced mine safety equipment property for use in any underground mine located in the United States the original use of which commences

BACKGROUND

with the taxpayer. Used property does not qualify even if its first use at a mine is by the taxpayer.

Advanced mine safety equipment property includes:

- communications technology enabling miners to remain in constant contact with an individual who is not in the mine;
- electronic tracking devices that enable an individual above ground to locate miners in the mine at all times;
- self-contained self-rescue emergency breathing apparatuses carried by miners;
- additional oxygen supplies stored in the mine; and
- comprehensive atmospheric monitoring equipment to measure levels of carbon monoxide, methane, and oxygen in the mine and which can detect smoke.

The election is made on the taxpayer's tax return and must specify the equipment to which the election applies. The election may only be revoked with IRS consent. The amount expensed is not capitalized and the election applies to new property placed in service after December 20, 2006, and before January 1, 2010 (Code Sec. 179E(g)). The cost of any mine safety equipment which is expensed under Code Sec. 179 may not be taken into account in computing the 50-percent deduction for advance mine safety equipment.

NEW LAW EXPLAINED

Election to expense advanced mine safety equipment extended.—The election to expense 50 percent of the cost of advanced mine safety equipment is extended for two years to new property placed in service on or before December 31, 2011 (Code Sec. 179E(g), as amended by the Tax Relief, Unemployment Insurance Reauthorization, and Job Creation Act of 2010 (P.L. 111-312)).

State Tax Consequences: With the exception of California, which has specifically decoupled from the current expense deduction for mine safety equipment, the impact of the extension for this deduction will depend on a state's Internal Revenue Code (IRC) conformity date. Those states that annually update their Internal Revenue Code conformity date will likely conform during their next legislative session. Conversely, corporations operating in a state that does not update its Code conformity date may have to make an addition adjustment as well as modifying the amount of the depreciation deduction claimed.

▶ **Effective date.** The provision applies to property placed in service after December 31, 2009 (Act Sec. 743(b) of the Tax Relief, Unemployment Insurance Reauthorization, and Job Creation Act of 2010 (P.L. 111-312)).

Law source: Law at ¶5280. Committee Report at ¶10,480.

- Act Sec. 743(a) of the Tax Relief, Unemployment Insurance Reauthorization, and Job Creation Act of 2010 (P.L. 111-312), amending Code Sec. 179E(g);
- Act Sec. 743(b), providing the effective date.

¶516

NEW LAW EXPLAINED

Reporter references: For further information, consult the following CCH reporters.

— Standard Federal Tax Reporter, ¶ 12,139D.01

— Tax Research Consultant, BUSEXP: 19,000

— Practical Tax Explanation, § 10,255

¶518 Expensing of Brownfields Environmental Remediation Costs

SUMMARY OF NEW LAW

The election to deduct environmental remediation costs is extended and may be taken for qualifying expenses paid or incurred before January 1, 2012.

BACKGROUND

For both regular and alternative minimum tax (AMT) purposes, a taxpayer may elect to deduct qualifying environmental remediation expenses, rather than charging them to a capital account (Code Sec. 198). The election is available for amounts paid or incurred after December 31, 2007, in connection with a disaster declared after that date and occurring before January 1, 2010. Qualified environmental remediation expenses are expenses paid or incurred in connection with a trade or business (or business-related property) that would otherwise be chargeable to a capital account and are for the abatement or control of hazardous substances at a "qualified contaminated site" (a so-called "brownfield") (Code Sec. 198(b)). Deductions for environmental remediation expenses are subject to recapture as ordinary income upon a sale or other disposition of the property (Code Sec. 198(e)).

A "qualified contaminated site," or "brownfield," is any urban or rural property that is held for use in a trade or business, for the production of income, or as inventory, and which is certified by the appropriate State environmental agency as an area at or on which there has been a release, threat of release, or disposal of a hazardous substance. However, sites that are identified on the national priorities list under the Comprehensive Environmental Response, Compensation, and Liability Act of 1980 (CERCLA) cannot qualify as targeted areas.

Hazardous substances are defined by reference to sections 101(14) and 102 of CERCLA, subject to additional exclusions applicable to asbestos and similar substances within buildings, certain naturally occurring substances, and certain other substances released into drinking water supplies due to deterioration through ordinary use. The term "hazardous substance" also includes any petroleum product, as defined in Code Sec. 4612(a)(3), which includes crude oil, crude oil condensates, and natural gasoline.

NEW LAW EXPLAINED

Election to deduct environmental remediation costs extended.—The election to deduct environmental remediation costs is extended for two years and may be taken for qualifying expenditures paid or incurred before January 1, 2012 (Code Sec. 198(h), as amended by of the Tax Relief, Unemployment Insurance Reauthorization, and Job Creation Act of 2010 (P.L. 111-312)).

> **State Tax Consequences:** For states such as California and Texas, which have decoupled from the federal election to expense environmental remediation costs, the extension of the deduction will have no impact. For other states, whether an adjustment is required will depend on the state's Internal Revenue Code conformity date. States that incorporate the Code as currently in effect will incorporate the amendment, whereas those states, such as New Hampshire, Kentucky, and Wisconsin, that have not updated Code reference in years, will require an adjustment. Those states that update their Code conformity dates annually will most likely conform during their next legislative sessions. Taxpayers in states that will require an adjustment must also adjust the amount of depreciation claimed for such property.

▶ **Effective date.** The provision applies to expenditures paid or incurred after December 31, 2009 (Act Sec. 745(b) of the Tax Relief, Unemployment Insurance Reauthorization, and Job Creation Act of 2010 (P.L. 111-312)).

Law source: Law at ¶5290. Committee Report at ¶10,500.

— Act Sec. 745(a) of the Tax Relief, Unemployment Insurance Reauthorization, and Job Creation Act of 2010 (P.L. 111-312), amending Code Sec. 198(h);

— Act Sec. 745(b), providing the effective date.

Reporter references: For further information, consult the following CCH reporters.

— Standard Federal Tax Reporter, ¶12,465.01

— Tax Research Consultant, BUSEXP: 18,756

— Practical Tax Explanation, §10,230

TAX CREDITS

¶520 Credit for Increasing Research Activities

SUMMARY OF NEW LAW

The research credit is extended for two years, through December 31, 2011.

BACKGROUND

In order to encourage businesses to increase their spending on research and development of new technologies, products, and services, a research credit is available under

BACKGROUND

Code Sec. 41. The research credit consists of the sum of three separately calculated components:

- 20 percent of the excess of qualified research expenses for the current tax year over a base period amount (Code Sec. 41(a)(1));
- 20 percent of the basic research payments to universities and other qualified organizations (available only to C corporations) (Code Sec. 41(a)(2)); and
- 20 percent of the amounts paid or incurred by a taxpayer in carrying on any trade or business to an energy research consortium for qualified energy research (Code Sec. 41(a)(3)).

The credit applies to amounts paid or incurred—

- before July 1, 1995, and
- after June 30, 1996, and before January 1, 2010 (Code Sec. 41(h)(1)).

The component credit for energy research consortium payments, however, applies only to amounts paid or incurred after August 8, 2005.

The calculation of the clinical testing expenses on certain drugs for rare diseases and conditions, commonly known as the orphan drug credit under Code Sec. 45C, is linked to the research credit. In particular, the qualified clinical testing expenses for which the orphan drug credit is allowed are generally determined by reference to the qualified research expenses for which the research credit is allowed, subject to certain modifications. In determining the expenses qualifying for the orphan credit, the research credit is deemed to remain in effect for periods after June 30, 1995, and before July 1, 1996, and periods after December 31, 2009 (Code Sec. 45C(b)(1)).

When it was first enacted in 1981, the research credit was to terminate after four-and-a-half years. It has been subject, however, to several extensions over the years, and was even allowed to expire at one point without the extension being made retroactive to the prior termination date. The latest extension was in 2008, for a period of two years. Manufacturing associations continue to lobby to make the credit permanent. In making long-term plans for research projects, they would like to be certain that the tax incentive will be available.

NEW LAW EXPLAINED

Research credit extended.—The credit for increasing research activities (the research credit) has been extended for two years, through December 31, 2011 (Code Sec. 41(h)(1)(B), as amended by the Tax Relief, Unemployment Insurance Reauthorization, and Job Creation Act of 2010 (P.L. 111-312)). For purposes of the orphan drug credit, the research credit is deemed to remain in effect for periods after December 31, 2011 (Code Sec. 45C(b)(1)(D), as amended by the Tax Relief Act of 2010).

> **State Tax Consequences:** While states do not generally incorporate or follow the majority of federal credits, many states offer a research credit that is either based on or follows the federal research credit. Whether the extension of the federal credit will impact one of these states is dependent upon whether the state

NEW LAW EXPLAINED

bases its eligibility on receipt of the federal credit and/or the state's Internal Revenue Code conformity date.

▶ **Effective date.** The provision applies to amounts paid or incurred after December 31, 2009 (Act Sec. 731(c) of the Tax Relief, Unemployment Insurance Reauthorization, and Job Creation Act of 2010 (P.L. 111-312)).

Law source: Law at ¶5100 and ¶5115. Committee Report at ¶10,360 and ¶10,370.

— Act Sec. 731(a) of the Tax Relief, Unemployment Insurance Reauthorization, and Job Creation Act of 2010 (P.L. 111-312), amending Code Sec. 41(h)(1)(B);

— Act Sec. 731(b), amending Code Sec. 45C(b)(1)(D);

— Act Sec. 731(c), providing the effective date.

Reporter references: For further information, consult the following CCH reporters.

— Standard Federal Tax Reporter, ¶4362.01 and ¶4475.01

— Tax Research Consultant, BUSEXP: 54,150 and BUSEXP: 54,456

— Practical Tax Explanation, § 13,901, § 14,405

¶522 Credit for Employer-Provided Child Care Facilities and Services

SUMMARY OF NEW LAW

The income tax credit for qualified expenses incurred by an employer in providing child care for employees has been extended for two years and is not scheduled to expire until tax years beginning after December 31, 2012.

BACKGROUND

The Economic Growth and Tax Relief Reconciliation Act of 2001 (EGTRRA) (P.L. 107-16) added an income tax credit for employers who provide certain child care assistance to their employees, starting with tax years beginning after December 31, 2001 (Code Sec. 45F). The amount of the credit for a given tax year is the sum of 25 percent of the qualified child care expenditures and 10 percent of the qualified child care resource and referral expenditures incurred by the taxpayer for the tax year (Code Sec. 45F(a)). The maximum amount of the employer-provided child care credit allowable in any given tax year is $150,000 (Code Sec. 45F(b)).

Compliance Tip: Most employers use Form 8882, Credit for Employer-Provided Childcare Facilities and Services, to determine the Code Sec. 45F credit. The credit amount from Form 8882 is then reported by partnerships and S corporations on Schedule K and by others on Form 3800, General Business Credit.

Qualified child care expenditures. Qualified child care expenditures are any amounts paid or incurred:

BACKGROUND

- to acquire, construct, rehabilitate or expand property that is to be used as a qualified child care facility of the taxpayer;
- for the operating costs of a qualified child care facility, including the costs related to the training of employees, scholarship programs, and providing increased compensation for employees with high levels of child care training; or
- under a contract with a qualified child care facility to provide child care services to the taxpayer's employees.

With respect to any acquisition, construction, rehabilitation, or expansion of any property for a child care facility, the property must qualify for a depreciation deduction (or amortization) and must not be the principal residence of the taxpayer or employee of the taxpayer (Code Sec. 45F(c)(1)(A)). Qualified child care expenditures may not exceed the fair market value of such care (Code Sec. 45F(c)(1)(B)).

A qualified child care facility is a facility the principal use of which is to provide child care assistance and that also meets the requirements of all applicable laws and regulations of the state and local government in which it is located, including the licensing requirements applicable to a child care facility (Code Sec. 45F(c)(2)). A facility will not be treated as a qualified child care facility for purposes of the taxpayer claiming the employer-provided child care credit, unless:

- enrollment is open to the taxpayer's employees during the tax year;
- in the event that the facility is the taxpayer's principal trade or business, at least 30 percent of the enrollees at the facility are the dependents of the taxpayer's employees; and
- the use of the child care facility does not discriminate in favor of highly-compensated employees within the meaning of Code Sec. 414(q) (Code Sec. 45F(c)(2)(B)).

If a credit is determined under Code Sec. 45F, the amount of the credit will be used to reduce the taxpayer's basis in the qualified child care facility (Code Sec. 45F(f)(1)(A)).

Qualified child care resource and referral expenditures. Qualified child care resource and referral expenditures are expenses paid or incurred by the taxpayer under a contract to provide child care resource and referral services to the taxpayer's employees (Code Sec. 45F(c)(3)(A)). The provision of the child care resource and referral services cannot discriminate in favor of highly-compensated employees within the meaning of Code Sec. 414(q) (Code Sec. 45F(c)(3)(B)).

Recapture of credit. If a recapture event occurs by the close of the tax year with respect to a qualified child care facility of the taxpayer, then the tax liability of that tax year must be increased by an amount equal to the applicable recapture percentage multiplied by the aggregate decrease in the general business credit (Code Sec. 38) as if all previously allowed employer-provided child care credits with respect to the employer's child care facility had been zero (Code Sec. 45F(d)). A recapture event is defined for this purpose as either: (1) termination of the operation of the facility as a qualified child care facility, or (2) a change of ownership of a qualified child care facility, unless prior to acquisition, the purchaser agrees in writing to assume the seller's recapture liability (Code Sec. 45F(d)(3)(B)). A casualty loss will not trigger a

BACKGROUND

recapture event as long as the qualified child care facility is replaced within a reasonable time period, as determined by the IRS (Code Sec. 45F(d)(4)(C)). The applicable recapture percentage ranges from 100 percent to zero percent depending on how long the child care facility has been in service (Code Sec. 45F(d)(2)).

Sunset provision. Under the sunset provision of EGTRRA, amendments made by the Act will not apply to tax years beginning after December 31, 2010 (Act Sec. 901 of P.L. 107-16).

NEW LAW EXPLAINED

Employer-provided child care credit extended.—The income tax credit for qualified expenses incurred by an employer in providing child care for employees (Code Sec. 45F) has been extended for two years. Thus, employers can continue to count on this important tax incentive to provide child care benefits to their employees for tax years beginning in 2011 and 2012. The credit is scheduled to expire and cannot be claimed for tax years beginning after December 31, 2012, under the sunset provision of the Economic Growth and Tax Relief Reconciliation Act of 2001 (EGTRRA) (P.L. 107-16) (Act Sec. 901 of P.L. 107-16, as amended by Act Sec. 101(a)(1) of the Tax Relief, Unemployment Insurance Reauthorization, and Job Creation Act of 2010 (P.L. 111-312)).

> **Comment:** Since the extension of the employer-provided child care credit is only temporary, employers who do not currently provide a child care benefit will have to consider carefully whether to implement this benefit. Further extension of the credit is not certain, so the costs of providing child care for employees may be too much of an economic burden for employers to bear if the credit ends up expiring for tax years beginning after 2012.

> **Caution:** Employers that have claimed or expect to claim the employer-provided child care credit with respect to a child care facility should be careful not to cease operating the facility or to sell the facility too soon in expectation of the sunset of the credit for tax years beginning after 2012. First, the credit may be extended again in the next two years. Second, taking such an action before the close of the 2012 tax year could trigger recapture of the credit and possibly a much higher tax liability than was anticipated (Code Sec. 45F(d), as added by P.L. 107-16).

▶ **Effective date.** The provision is effective for tax years beginning after December 31, 2001 (Act Sec. 101(a)(2) of the Tax Relief, Unemployment Insurance Reauthorization, and Job Creation Act of 2010 (P.L. 111-312); Act Sec. 205(c) of the Economic Growth and Tax Relief Reconciliation Act of 2001 (EGTRRA) (P.L. 107-16)). The provision will not apply to tax years beginning after December 31, 2012 (Act Sec. 101(a)(1) of the Tax Relief Act of 2010; Act Sec. 901 of EGTRRA). See ¶105 for a specific discussion of the sunset provision of EGTRRA and how it is applied.

Law source: Law at ¶5085, ¶5125, ¶5495, and ¶7010. Committee Report at ¶10,060.

— Act Sec. 101(a)(1) of the Tax Relief, Unemployment Insurance Reauthorization, and Job Creation Act of 2010 (P.L. 111-312), amending Act Sec. 901 of the Economic Growth and Tax Relief Reconciliation Act of 2001 (EGTRRA) (P.L. 107-16);

— Act Sec. 101(a)(2), providing the effective date.

¶522

NEW LAW EXPLAINED

Reporter references: For further information, consult the following CCH reporters.

— Standard Federal Tax Reporter, ¶4494.01 and ¶4494.06

— Tax Research Consultant, BUSEXP: 55,000

— Practical Tax Explanation, §14,015

¶524 Work Opportunity Credit

SUMMARY OF NEW LAW

The work opportunity credit is extended through December 31, 2011.

BACKGROUND

The work opportunity tax credit provides an elective credit to employers that hire individuals from targeted groups (Code Sec. 51). These groups include:

- qualified individuals in families receiving certain government benefits, including Title IV-A social security benefits (aid for dependent children) or food stamps,
- qualified individuals who receive supplemental social security income or long-term family assistance;
- veterans who are members of families receiving food stamps or who have service-connected disabilities;
- designated community residents;
- high-risk youths age 18 through 24 who live in empowerment zones, enterprise communities, or renewal communities;
- vocational rehabilitation referrals certified to have physical or mental disabilities;
- qualified summer youth employees who live in empowerment zones, enterprise communities, or renewal communities;
- ex-felons hired no more than one year after the later of their conviction or release from prison;
- unemployed veterans who begin work for the employer in 2009 or 2010; and
- disconnected youth who begin work for the employer in 2009 or 2010 (Code Sec. 51(d)).

The amount of the credit is generally 40 percent of the qualified worker's first-year wages up to $6,000 ($3,000 for summer youths and $12,000 for qualified veterans) (Code Sec. 51(b)). For long-term family aid recipients, the credit is equal to 40 percent of the first $10,000 in qualified first year wages and 50 percent of the first $10,000 of qualified second-year wages (Code Sec. 51(e)).

The work opportunity credit is part of the general business credit and may be carried back and forward accordingly (Code Sec. 38(b)(2)). The credit terminates with respect

BACKGROUND

to wages paid to persons who begin work for the employer after August 31, 2011 (Code Sec. 51(c)(4)(B)).

NEW LAW EXPLAINED

Four-month extension of work opportunity credit.—The work opportunity credit is extended through December 31, 2011 (Code Sec. 51(c)(4)(B)), as amended by the Tax Relief, Unemployment Insurance Reauthorization, and Job Creation Act of 2010 (P.L. 111-312)). Thus, the credit applies with respect to wages paid to persons who begin work for the employer before January 1, 2012.

> **Comment:** The credit for unemployed veterans and disconnected youths remains limited to those who begin work for the employer during 2009 and 2010.

▶ **Effective date.** The provision applies to individuals who begin work for the employer after December 17, 2010, the date of the enactment (Act Sec. 757(b) of the Tax Relief, Unemployment Insurance Reauthorization, and Job Creation Act of 2010 (P.L. 111-312)).

Law source: Law at ¶5155. Committee Report at ¶10,630.

— Act Sec. 757(a) of the Tax Relief, Unemployment Insurance Reauthorization, and Job Creation Act of 2010 (P.L. 111-312), amending Code Sec. 51(c)(4)(B);

— Act Sec. 757(b), providing the effective date.

Reporter references: For further information, consult the following CCH reporters.

— Standard Federal Tax Reporter, ¶4803.01

— Tax Research Consultant, BUSEXP: 54,250

— Practical Tax Explanation, § 13,805.10

¶526 Employer Wage Credit for Activated Military Reservists

SUMMARY OF NEW LAW

Small businesses with fewer than 50 employees can claim a credit equal to 20 percent of qualified differential wages paid to qualified workers called up for active military duty through 2011.

BACKGROUND

When members of the National Guard or Reserves are called up to active military duty, their civilian jobs and salaries are placed on hiatus and they begin receiving military pay. If a member's civilian salary was higher, the civilian employer might voluntarily provide military differential pay in an amount equal to the difference between the member's civilian pay and military pay.

BACKGROUND

Eligible small businesses can qualify for a temporary 20-percent tax credit for differential wage payments made to qualified employees before 2010 (Code Sec. 45P, as added by the Heroes Earnings Assistance and Relief Tax Act of 2008 (P.L. 110-245)). Qualified payments (i) must be made by a small business employer to a qualified employee with respect to any period during which the employee is performing service in the uniformed services while on active duty for a period of more than 30 days; (ii) must represent all or a portion of the wages that the employee would have received from the employer for performing services for the employer; and (iii) must not exceed $20,000 per year (Code Sec. 45P(b)(1)).

An eligible small business employer must employ, on average, fewer than 50 employees on business days during the tax year, and provide eligible differential wage payments to every qualified employee under a written plan (Code Sec. 45P(b)(3)). A qualified employee must be employed by the small business employer during the 91-day period immediately preceding the period for which the for differential wage payment is made (Code Sec. 45P(b)(2)).

The credit reduces the employer's compensation deduction and any other credits otherwise allowable with respect to compensation paid (Code Secs. 280C(a) and 45P(c); Notice 2010-15, 2010-6 I.R.B. 390). The differential wages credit is part of the Code Sec. 38 general business credit, and is also restricted for certain types of taxpayers under rules similar to those that govern the Code Sec. 52 work opportunity credit.

The temporary credit applies to differential wage payments made after June 17, 2008, and before January 1, 2010. The credit does not apply to payments made after December 31, 2009 (Code Sec. 45P(f)).

NEW LAW EXPLAINED

Credit for employer's differential wage payments to military personnel extended for two years.—An eligible small business employer can claim a tax credit for up to 20 percent of the military differential wage payments it makes to activated military reservists during the tax year through December 31, 2011 (Code Sec. 45P(f), as amended by the Tax Relief, Unemployment Insurance Reauthorization, and Job Creation Act of 2010 (P.L. 111-312)).

▶ **Effective date.** The provision applies to payments made after December 31, 2009 (Act Sec. 736(b) of the Tax Relief, Unemployment Insurance Reauthorization, and Job Creation Act of 2010 (P.L. 111-312)).

Law source: Law at ¶5150. Committee Report at ¶10,410.

— Act Sec.736(a) of the Tax Relief, Unemployment Insurance Reauthorization, and Job Creation Act of 2010 (P.L. 111-312), amending Code Sec. 45P(f);

— Act Sec. 736(b), providing the effective date.

Reporter references: For further information, consult the following CCH reporters.

— Standard Federal Tax Reporter, ¶4500ZF.01

— Tax Research Consultant, BUSEXP: 55,500

— Practical Tax Explanation, § 14,020

¶528 New Markets Tax Credit

SUMMARY OF NEW LAW

The new markets tax credit is extended for two years, through December 31, 2011. The carryover period for unused new markets tax credits is also extended for two years, through December 31, 2016.

BACKGROUND

Among the incentives offered to encourage taxpayers to invest in, or make loans to, small businesses located in low-income communities is the new markets tax credit (Code Sec. 45D). The new markets tax credit provides a credit for qualified equity investments made to acquire stock in a corporation, or a capital interest in a partnership, that is a qualified community development entity (CDE). The credit allowable to the investor is (1) a five-percent credit for the first three years from the date that the equity interest was purchased from the CDE, and (2) a six-percent credit for each of the following four years (Code Sec. 45D(a)(2)). The credit is determined by applying the applicable percentage (five or six) to the amount paid to the CDE for the investment at its original issue (Code Sec. 45D(a)(1)). The credit is subject to recapture in certain circumstances (Code Sec. 45D(g)).

There is a national limitation with respect to the new markets tax credit. The maximum annual amount of qualified equity investments was capped at $2 billion for calendar years 2004 and 2005. In 2006 and 2007 the cap was $3.5 billion. For calendar years 2008 and 2009, the maximum amount was increased to $5 billion for each year (Code Sec. 45D(f)(1)(E) and (F)). The additional amount for 2008 must be allocated in accordance with Code Sec. 45D(f)(2) to qualified CDEs that submitted an allocation application for calendar year 2008 and either (1) did not receive an allocation for that year, or (2) received an allocation for that year in an amount less than the amount requested in the application (Act Sec. 1403(b) of the American Recovery and Reinvestment Tax Act of 2009 (P.L. 111-5)).

The Secretary of the Treasury is authorized to allocate the amounts among qualified CDEs, giving preference (in part) to any entity with a record of successfully providing capital or technical assistance to disadvantaged businesses or communities (Code Sec. 45D(f)(2)). If the new markets tax credit limitation for any calendar year exceeds the aggregate amount allocated for the year, the limitation for the succeeding calendar year will be increased by the amount of such excess. However no amount may be carried to any calendar year after 2014 (Code Sec. 45D(f)(3)).

A qualified CDE includes any domestic corporation or partnership: (1) whose primary mission is serving or providing investment capital for low-income communities or persons; (2) that maintains accountability to the residents of low-income communities by their representation on any governing board of or any advisory board to the CDE; and (3) that is certified by the Secretary of the Treasury as being a qualified

BACKGROUND

CDE (Code Sec. 45D(c)). A qualified equity investment means stock (other than nonqualified preferred stock) in a corporation or a capital interest in a partnership that is acquired directly from a CDE for cash. Substantially all of the investment proceeds must be used by the CDE to make qualified low-income community investments (Code Sec. 45D(b)(1)).

For purposes of Code Sec. 45D, the term "low-income community" means any population census tract with either (1) a poverty rate of at least 20 percent or (2) median family income that does not exceed 80 percent of the greater of statewide median family income or the metropolitan area median family income (or in the case of a non-metropolitan census tract, does not exceed 80 percent of statewide median family income) (Code Sec. 45D(e)(1)). A modification is made for census tracts within high migration rural counties (Code Sec. 45D(e)(5)).

The American Recovery and Reinvestment Tax Act of 2009 (P.L. 111-5) extended the new markets tax credit through 2009. As a result, up to $5 billion in qualified equity investments could be allocated among qualified CDEs for that calendar year (Code Sec. 45D(f)(1)(F)).

NEW LAW EXPLAINED

New markets tax credit extended.—The new markets tax credit is extended two years, through December 31, 2011, permitting up to $3.5 billion in qualified equity investments for each of the calendar years 2010 and 2011 (Code Sec. 45D(f)(1)(G), as added by the Tax Relief, Unemployment Insurance Reauthorization, and Job Creation Act of 2010 (P.L. 111-312)). Further, the year to which excess credits can be carried forward has been extended two years, to 2016 (Code Sec. 45D(f)(3), as amended by the Tax Relief Act of 2010). Thus, if the new markets tax credit limitation for a calendar year exceeds the aggregate amount allocated for that year, the limitation for the succeeding calendar year will be increased by the amount of such excess. However, no amount may be carried to any calendar year after 2016.

> **Comment:** The $3.5 billion in qualified equity investments for each of calendar years 2010 and 2011 is a decrease from the $5 billion allocated to each of the calendar years 2008 and 2009.

▶ **Effective date.** The provision applies to calendar years beginning after 2009 (Act Sec. 733(c) of the Tax Relief, Unemployment Insurance Reauthorization, and Job Creation Act of 2010 (P.L. 111-312)).

Law source: Law at ¶5120. Committee Report at ¶10,380.

— Act Sec. 733(a) of the Tax Relief, Unemployment Insurance Reauthorization, and Job Creation Act of 2010 Tax Extenders Act of 2009 (P.L. 111-312), amending Code Sec. 45D(f)(1);

— Act Sec. 733(b), amending Code Sec. 45D(f)(3);

— Act Sec. 733(c), providing the effective date.

Mine rescue training team credit extended.—The mine rescue team training credit is extended for two years. The credit now terminates for tax years beginning after December 31, 2011 (Code Sec. 45N(e), as amended by the Tax Relief, Unemployment Insurance Reauthorization, and Job Creation Act of 2010 (P.L. 111-312)).

▶ **Effective date.** The provision applies to tax years beginning after December 31, 2009 (Act Sec. 735(b) of the Tax Relief, Unemployment Insurance Reauthorization, and Job Creation Act of 2010 (P.L. 111-312)).

Law source: Law at ¶5145. Committee Report at ¶10,400.

— Act Sec.735(a) of the Tax Relief, Unemployment Insurance Reauthorization, and Job Creation Act of 2010 (P.L. 111-312), amending Code Sec. 45N(e);

— Act Sec. 735(b), providing the effective date.

Reporter references: For further information, consult the following CCH reporters.

— Standard Federal Tax Reporter, ¶4251.01 and ¶4500V.01

— Tax Research Consultant, BUSEXP: 55,450

— Practical Tax Explanation, § 14,435

¶536 American Samoa Economic Development Credit

SUMMARY OF NEW LAW

The temporary credit for qualifying possessions corporations that are existing claimants operating in American Samoa has been extended for two additional years or until January 1, 2012.

BACKGROUND

Certain domestic corporations with a substantial portion of business operations in Puerto Rico and the U.S. possessions are eligible for a tax credit under Code Sec. 936. This credit offsets the U.S. tax imposed on taxable non-U.S.-source income from:

• the active conduct of a trade or business within a U.S. possession;

• the sale or exchange of substantially all of the assets used by the taxpayer in such a trade or business; or

• qualified possessions investment.

For purposes of the credit, U.S. possessions include, among other places, American Samoa. U.S. corporations with activities in Puerto Rico are also eligible for the Code Sec. 30A economic activity credit, which is calculated under the rules set forth in Code Sec. 936. The Code Sec. 936 credit expired for tax years beginning after December 31, 2005, with some exceptions (Code Sec. 936(j)).

BACKGROUND

A U.S. corporation, in order to qualify for the possession tax credit, must satisfy two gross income tests:

- 80 percent or more of its gross income for the three-year period immediately preceding the close of the tax year must be from sources within a U.S. possession, and

- 75 percent or more of the corporation's gross income during the same period must be from the active conduct of a trade or business within a U.S. possession (Code Sec. 936(a)(2)).

The general rules for determining the source of the income apply. The possession tax credit is available only to a corporation that qualifies as an existing credit claimant. A determination as to whether that corporation is an existing credit claimant is made separately for each possession.

Existing credit claimant. An existing credit claimant is a corporation that was actively conducting a trade or business within a possession on October 13, 1995, and elected the benefits of the possession tax credit for its tax year that included October 13, 1995 (Code Sec. 936(j)(9)). Although a corporation can also qualify as an existing credit claimant if it acquires all of an existing credit claimant's trade or business, status as an existing claimant is lost if a substantial new line of business is added (Code Sec. 936(j)(9)(B)).

Economic activity-based limitation. The possession tax credit is computed separately for each possession with respect to which the corporation is an existing credit claimant. For tax years beginning after December 13, 1993, the credit is subject to either an economic activity-based limit or an income-based limit (Code Sec. 936(a)(4)). Under the economic activity-based limit, the amount of the credit for the tax year may not exceed an amount equal to the sum of:

- 60 percent of the possession corporation's "qualified possession wages" and "allocable employee fringe benefit expenses";

- 15 percent of the depreciation deductions allowable for the tax year under Code Sec. 167 with respect to short-life qualified tangible property (three-year or five-year property to which Code Sec. 168 applies);

- 40 percent of the depreciation deductions allowable for the tax year under Code Sec. 167 with respect to medium-life qualified tangible property (seven-year or 10-year property to which Code Sec. 168 applies);

- 65 percent of the depreciation deductions allowable for the tax year under Code Sec. 167 with respect to long-life qualified tangible property (property that is not described in (2) or (3) above and to which Code Sec. 168 applies); and

- in certain cases, a portion of the taxpayer's possession income taxes (Code Sec. 30A(d)).

Income based limitation/reduced credit election. As an alternative to the economic activity limitation, a possession corporation may elect to apply a limit equal to the applicable percentage of the credit that would otherwise be allowed with respect to possession business income; currently, that applicable percentage is 40 percent (Code Sec. 936(a)(4)(B)(ii)).

BACKGROUND

Repeal and transition rules. The Code Sec. 936 possession tax credit is not available to new claimants for any tax year beginning after 1995. The credit is phased out for existing credit claimants over a period that includes tax years beginning before 2008 (Act Sec. 119 of the Tax Relief and Health Care Act of 2006 (P.L. 109-432)). The amount of the credit available during the phase-out period is generally reduced according to special limitation rules. The special limitation rules do not apply, however, to existing credit claimants for income from activities in Guam, American Samoa, and the Northern Mariana Islands.

American Samoa economic development credit. A U.S. corporation that was an existing credit claimant with respect to American Samoa, and that elected the application of Code Sec. 936 for its last tax year beginning before January 1, 2006, is allowed a credit for two years. The credit applies to the first two tax years of a qualifying corporation that begin after December 31, 2005, and before January 1, 2008 (Act Sec. 119(d) of the 2006 Tax Relief Act). This credit was extended for two additional years by the Emergency Economic Stabilization Act of 2008 (P.L. 110-343). This allowed the credit to be claimed by a qualifying corporation with tax years beginning before January 1, 2010.

This temporary credit is not part of the Code, but is computed based on the rules in Code Sec. 936 and the economic-based limitation rules described above; any term used in the provision that is also used in Code Sec. 30A or 936 has the same meaning given to such term by Code Sec. 30A or 936 (Act Sec. 119(c) of the 2006 Tax Relief Act).

Accordingly, the amount of the credit is equal to the sum of the amounts used in computing the corporation's economic activity-based limitation with respect to American Samoa, except that no credit is allowed for the amount of any American Samoa income taxes. Thus, the amount of the credit for any qualifying corporation equals the sum of:

- 60 percent of the corporation's qualified American Samoa wages and allocable employee fringe benefit expenses; plus
- the sum of the following depreciation allowances:
  - 15 percent of the corporation's depreciation allowances with respect to short-life qualified American Samoa tangible property (three-year or five-year property to which Code Sec. 168 applies), plus
  - 40 percent of the corporation's depreciation allowances with respect to medium-life qualified American Samoa tangible property (seven-year or 10-year property to which Code Sec. 168 applies), plus
  - 65 percent of the corporation's depreciation allowances with respect to long-life qualified American Samoa tangible property (property that is not described in (a) or (b) above and to which Code Sec. 168 applies).

Foreign tax credit allowed. The rule in Code Sec. 936(c) that denies a credit or deduction for any possessions or foreign tax paid with respect to taxable income taken into account in computing the Code Sec. 936 credit does not apply with respect to this temporary credit (Act Sec. 119(b)(3) of the 2006 Tax Relief Act).

Economic development credit for American Samoa extended.—The economic development credit for a U.S. corporation that is an existing credit claimant with respect to American Samoa, and that elected the application of Code Sec. 936 for its last tax year beginning before January 1, 2006, has been extended for two additional tax years. Thus, when the new extension is combined with both the temporary credit that was previously allowed (Act Sec. 119(d) of the Tax Relief and Health Care Act of 2006 (P.L. 109-432)) and the extension for two additional years (Act Sec. 309(a), Division C, of the Emergency Economic Stabilization Act of 2008 (P.L. 110-343)), the credit now applies to the first six tax years of a qualifying corporation that begin after December 31, 2005, and before January 1, 2012 (Act Sec. 756(a), of the Tax Relief, Unemployment Insurance Reauthorization, and Job Creation Act of 2010 (P.L. 111-312)).

▶ **Effective date.** The provision applies to tax years beginning after December 31, 2009 (Act Sec. 756(b), of the Tax Relief, Unemployment Insurance Reauthorization, and Job Creation Act of 2010 (P.L. 111-312)).

Law source: Law at ¶7070. Committee Report at ¶10,620.

— Act Sec. 756(a) of the Tax Relief, Unemployment Insurance Reauthorization, and Job Creation Act of 2010 (P.L. 111-312), amending Act Sec. 119(d), Division A, of the Tax Relief and Health Care Act of 2006 (P.L. 109-432);

— Act Sec. 756(b), providing the effective date.

Reporter references: For further information, consult the following CCH reporters.

— Standard Federal Tax Reporter, ¶4059.01, ¶28,394.01, and ¶28,394.032

— Tax Research Consultant, INTL: 27,070.20

— Practical Tax Explanation, § 13,435

ENERGY

¶538 Credit for New Energy Efficient Homes

SUMMARY OF NEW LAW

The credit available to eligible contractors for the construction or manufacture of a new energy efficient home is extended through December 31, 2011.

BACKGROUND

To help encourage the construction of more energy efficient homes, an eligible contractor may claim, as part of the general business credit, a tax credit of $1,000 or $2,000 for the construction or manufacture of a new energy efficient home that meets the qualifying criteria (Code Secs. 38(b)(23) and 45L(a)). An "eligible contractor" is a

BACKGROUND

person who constructed a qualified new energy efficient home or, with respect to manufactured homes, the producer of that home (Code Sec. 45L(b)(1)).

In order to be considered a qualified new energy efficient home, the dwelling must be located in the United States, must meet specified energy saving requirements, must be purchased or acquired by a person from the eligible contractor during 2006, 2007, 2008, or 2009 for use as a residence during the tax year, and construction of the home must be substantially completed after August 8, 2005. Further, a qualified new energy efficient home must receive a written certification that describes its energy-saving features including the energy efficient building envelope components used in its construction and energy efficient heating or cooling equipment that has been installed (Code Sec. 45L(c) and (d)).

The applicable amount of the credit depends on the energy savings realized by the home. The maximum credit is $2,000 for homes and manufactured homes that meet rigorous energy-saving requirements; alternatively, manufactured homes that meet a less demanding test may qualify for a $1,000 credit. The taxpayer's basis in the property is reduced by the amount of any new energy efficient home credit allowed with respect to that property (Code Sec. 45L(e)). Expenditures taken into account under the rehabilitation and energy components of the investment tax credit are not taken into account under the energy efficient home credit (Code Sec. 45L(f)). The credit, which was extended for one year by the Emergency Economic Stabilization Act of 2008 (P.L. 110-343), does not apply to any qualified new energy efficient home acquired after December 31, 2009 (Code Sec. 45L(g)).

NEW LAW EXPLAINED

Credit for new energy efficient homes extended.—The credit available to eligible contractors for the construction or manufacture of new energy efficient homes is extended for two years. Accordingly, the credit applies to qualified new energy efficient homes that are acquired before January 1, 2012 (Code Sec. 45L(g), as amended by the Tax Relief, Unemployment Insurance Reauthorization, and Job Creation Act of 2010 (P.L. 111-312)).

▶ **Effective date.** The provision applies to homes acquired after December 31, 2009 (Act Sec. 703(b) of the Tax Relief, Unemployment Insurance Reauthorization, and Job Creation Act of 2010 (P.L. 111-312)).

Law source: Law at ¶5135. Committee Report at ¶10,190.

— Act Sec. 703(a) of the Tax Relief, Unemployment Insurance Reauthorization, and Job Creation Act of 2010 (P.L. 111-312), amending Code Sec. 45L(g);

— Act Sec. 703(b), providing the effective date.

Reporter references: For further information, consult the following CCH reporters.

— Standard Federal Tax Reporter, ¶4500L.01

— Tax Research Consultant, BUSEXP: 55,352

— Practical Tax Explanation, § 14,315

¶540 Grants for Investment in Specified Energy Property in Lieu of Tax Credits

SUMMARY OF NEW LAW

The authority of the Secretary of the Treasury to issue grants, in lieu of the renewable electricity production credit and the energy credit, to each person who places specified energy property in service has been extended for one year through 2011.

BACKGROUND

The Secretary of the Treasury is authorized to provide a grant to each person who places into service, generally in 2009 or 2010, an electricity production facility otherwise eligible for the Code Sec. 45 renewable electricity production credit or qualifying property otherwise eligible for the Code Sec. 48 energy credit (Act Sec. 1603(a) of the American Recovery and Reinvestment Act of 2009 (P.L. 111-5)). The amount of the grant is based on a percentage of the basis of the property placed into service (Act Sec. 1603(b) of the 2009 Recovery Act). If the grant is paid, no renewable electricity credit or energy credit may be claimed with respect to the grant eligible property (Code Sec. 48(d)(1)).

Eligible energy property. The following property is eligible for the grant unless depreciation, or amortization in lieu of depreciation, is not allowable with respect to the property:

- certain qualified property, including a wind facility, closed-loop biomass facility, open-loop biomass facility, geothermal or solar energy facility, landfill gas facility, trash facility, qualified hydropower facility, marine and hydrokinetic renewable energy facility (Code Secs. 45(d) and 48(a)(5)(D);
- qualified fuel cell property (Code Sec. 48(c)(1));
- solar property (Code Sec. 48(a)(3)(A)(i) or (ii));
- qualified small wind energy property (Code Sec. 48(c)(4));
- geothermal property (Code Sec. 48(a)(3)(A)(iii));
- qualified microturbine property (Code Sec. 48(c)(2));
- combined heat and power system property (Code Sec. 48(c)(3)); and
- geothermal heat pump property (Code Sec. 48(a)(3)(A)(vii)) (Act Sec. 1603(d) of the 2009 Recovery Act).

The property must be placed in service during 2009 or 2010, or placed in service after 2010 and before the credit termination date for such property, if construction of the property began during 2009 or 2010 (Act Sec. 1603(a) of the 2009 Recovery Act). The credit termination date for a wind facility is January 1, 2013; for a closed-loop biomass facility, open-loop biomass facility, geothermal or solar energy facility, landfill gas facility, trash facility, qualified hydropower facility, marine and hydrokinetic renewable energy facility is January 1, 2014; and for specified property other-

¶540

BACKGROUND

wise eligible for the Code Sec. 48 energy credit is January 17, 2017 (Act Sec. 1603(e) of the 2009 Recovery Act).

Amount of grant. The amount of the grant will be an applicable percentage of the basis of the specified energy property placed into service (Act Sec. 1603(b)(1) of the 2009 Recovery Act). The applicable percentage is 30 percent for qualified facilities, qualified fuel cell property, solar property, and qualified small wind energy property (Act Sec. 1603(b)(2) of the 2009 Recovery Act). For any other property, the applicable percentage is 10 percent. However, in the case of qualified fuel cell property, qualified microturbine property, and combined heat and power system property, the amount of the grant cannot exceed the credit limitation established, respectively, with respect to such property under Code Sec. 48 (Act Sec. 1603(b)(3) of the 2009 Recovery Act).

The amount of the grant received is not includible in the gross income of the taxpayer, but is taken into account for determining the basis of the specified energy property (Code Sec. 48(d)(3), as added by the 2009 Recovery Act). The basis of the specified property for which the grant is made must be reduced by 50 percent of the amount of the grant under rules similar to those that apply for the investment tax credit under Code Sec. 50. In addition, if the specified property is disposed of by the grant recipient or ceases to be a specified property within five years of being placed in service, some or all of the grant will be subject to recapture (Act Sec. 1603(f) of the 2009 Recovery Act).

Ineligible grant recipients. No grant may be awarded to any:

- federal, state or local government (or any political subdivision, agency or instrumentality thereof);

- Code Sec. 501(c)(3) tax-exempt entity;

- qualified issuer of clean renewable energy bonds;

- partnership or other pass-through entity partner (or holder of an equity or profits interest) described in any of the preceding items (Act Sec. 1603(g) of the 2009 Recovery Act).

Grant applications. Applications for the grant must be received by the Secretary of the Treasury before October 1, 2011 (Act Sec. 1603(j) of the 2009 Recovery Act).

NEW LAW EXPLAINED

Extension of grants for investment in energy property.—The authority of the Secretary of the Treasury to issue grants, in lieu of the Code Sec. 45 renewable electricity production credit and the Code Sec. 48 energy credit, to each person who places specified energy property in service has been extended for one year. In order to be eligible for the grant, the specified energy property must be:

- placed in service during 2009, 2010 or 2011, or

- placed in service after 2011 and before the credit termination date for such property, if construction of the property began during 2009, 2010 or 2011 (Act Sec. 1603(a) of

¶540

NEW LAW EXPLAINED

the American Recovery and Reinvestment Act of 2009 (P.L. 111-5), as amended by the Tax Relief, Unemployment Insurance Reauthorization, and Job Creation Act of 2010 (P.L. 111-312)).

> **Comment:** Although the placed in service date for the specified energy property has been extended for one year, the credit termination date for this purpose did not change. Thus, the credit termination date for a wind facility remains January 1, 2013; for a closed-loop biomass facility, open-loop biomass facility, geothermal or solar energy facility, landfill gas facility, trash facility, qualified hydropower facility, marine and hydrokinetic renewable energy facility remains January 1, 2014; and for specified property otherwise eligible for the Code Sec. 48 energy credit remains January 17, 2017 (Act Sec. 1603(e) of P.L. 111-5).

Grant applications. The time for submitting applications for the grant has also been extended for one year. Applications for the grant must be received by the Secretary of the Treasury before October 1, 2012 (Act Sec. 1603(j) of the 2009 Recovery Act, as amended by the Tax Relief Act of 2010).

▶ **Effective date.** No specific effective date is provided by the Act. The provision is, therefore, considered effective on December 17, 2010, the date of enactment.

Law source: Law at ¶7055. Committee Report at ¶10,230.

— Act Sec. 707(a) of the Tax Relief, Unemployment Insurance Reauthorization, and Job Creation Act of 2010 (P.L. 111-312), amending Act Sec. 1603(a) of the American Recovery and Reinvestment Act of 2009 (P.L. 111-5).

— Act Sec. 707(b), amending Act Sec. 1603(j) of the 2009 Recovery Act.

Reporter references: For further information, consult the following CCH reporters.

— Standard Federal Tax Reporter, ¶4671.045

— Tax Research Consultant, BUSEXP: 54,558

— Practical Tax Explanation, § 14,215

¶542 Energy Efficient Appliance Credit for Manufacturers

SUMMARY OF NEW LAW

The credit for manufacturers of energy efficient dishwashers, clothes washers and refrigerators will be allowed for an additional year. Thus, the credit can be claimed for qualifying appliances manufactured in 2011, with modifications to the credit amount and efficiency requirements for the appliances and to the limitations on the credit.

BACKGROUND

Manufacturers of energy efficient dishwashers, clothes washers and refrigerators are allowed a credit for appliances produced before 2011 (Code Sec. 45M). The amount of the credit varies based on the type of appliance, the year of manufacture and the efficiency of the appliance. The total credit amount is equal to the sum of the credit amount for each type of energy efficient appliance. The credit amount for each type of appliance is computed by multiplying the eligible production for that type of appliance by the applicable amount for that type of appliance (Code Sec. 45M(a)). The credit is part of the general business credit.

Dishwashers. Manufactured dishwashers are eligible for either a $45 or $75 applicable amount based on their efficiency and the year of manufacture.

- In order to be eligible for the $45 applicable amount, the dishwasher must be manufactured during calendar year 2008 or 2009 and must not use more than 324 kilowatt hours per year and 5.8 gallons of water per normal dishwasher cycle.

- In order to be eligible for the $75 applicable amount, the dishwasher must be manufactured during calendar year 2008, 2009 or 2010 and must not use more than 307 kilowatt hours per year and 5.0 gallons of water per normal dishwasher cycle (5.5 gallons of water for dishwashers designed for greater than 12 place settings) (Code Sec. 45M(b)(1)).

Clothes washers. Manufactured clothes washers are eligible for an applicable amount that varies based on their efficiency, whether or not they are residential or commercial, and the year of manufacture.

- In order to be eligible for the $75 applicable amount, a residential top-loading clothes washer must be manufactured during calendar year 2008 and must meet or exceed a 1.72 modified energy factor and not exceed a 8.0 water consumption factor.

- In order to be eligible for the $125 applicable amount, a residential top-loading clothes washer must be manufactured during calendar year 2008 or 2009 and must meet or exceed a 1.8 modified energy factor and not exceed a 7.5 water consumption factor.

- In order to be eligible for the $150 applicable amount, a residential or commercial clothes washer must be manufactured during calendar year 2008, 2009, or 2010 and must meet or exceed a 2.0 modified energy factor and not exceed a 6.0 water consumption factor.

- In order to be eligible for the $250 applicable amount, a residential or commercial clothes washer must be manufactured during calendar year 2008, 2009, or 2010 and must meet or exceed a 2.2 modified energy factor and not exceed a 4.5 water consumption factor (Code Sec. 45M(b)(2)).

The modified energy factor is established by the Department of Energy for compliance with the federal energy conservation standard (Code Sec. 45M(f)(6)). The water consumption factor is the quotient of the total weighted per-cycle water consumption divided by the cubic foot (or liter) capacity of the clothes washer (Code Sec. 45M(f)(10)).

¶542

BACKGROUND

Refrigerators. Manufactured refrigerators are eligible for an applicable amount that ranges from $50 to $200 based on their efficiency and the year of manufacture.

- In order to be eligible for the $50 applicable amount, the refrigerator must be manufactured during calendar year 2008 and consume at least 20 percent but not more than 22.9 percent less kilowatt hours per year than the 2001 energy conservation standards.

- In order to be eligible for the $75 applicable amount, the refrigerator must be manufactured during calendar year 2008 or 2009, and consume at least 23 percent but not more than 24.9 percent less kilowatt hours per year than the 2001 energy conservation standards.

- In order to be eligible for the $100 applicable amount, the refrigerator must be manufactured during calendar year 2008, 2009 or 2010, and consume at least 25 percent but not more than 29.9 percent less kilowatt hours per year than the 2001 energy conservation standards.

- In order to be eligible for the $200 applicable amount, the refrigerator must be manufactured during calendar year 2008, 2009 or 2010, and consume at least 30 percent less energy than the 2001 energy conservation standards (Code Sec. 45M(b)(3)).

The 2001 energy conservation standard against which a refrigerator's efficiency is measured is the energy standard set forth by the Department of Energy and effective July 1, 2001 (Code Sec. 45M(f)(8)).

Limitations on credit. Two limitations apply to the energy efficient appliance credit. The aggregate credit allowed with respect to a taxpayer for any tax year is limited to $75 million. The $75 million amount is reduced by the amount of the credit allowed to the taxpayer or any predecessor of the taxpayer for all prior tax years beginning after December 31, 2007 (Code Sec. 45M(e)(1)). However, credits for the most energy efficient refrigerators and clothes washers do not count against the $75 million limit (Code Sec. 45M(e)(2)).

The second limitation on the energy efficient appliance credit is based on the taxpayer's gross receipts. The credit allowed with respect to a taxpayer for the tax year cannot exceed two percent of the taxpayer's average annual gross receipts for the three tax years preceding the tax year in which the credit is determined (Code Sec. 45M(e)(3)). For this purpose, a taxpayer's gross receipts are determined according to the rules in Code Sec. 448(c)(2) and (3) (Code Sec. 45M(e)(4)).

NEW LAW EXPLAINED

Energy efficient appliance production credit modified and extended.—The credit for manufacturers of energy efficient dishwashers, clothes washers and refrigerators will be allowed for an additional year. Thus, the credit can be claimed for qualifying appliances manufactured in 2011, with modifications to the applicable amount and efficiency requirements. In addition, the limitations on the credit have also been modified (Code Sec. 45M, as amended by the Tax Relief, Unemployment Insurance Reauthorization, and Job Creation Act of 2010 (P.L. 111-312)).

¶542

NEW LAW EXPLAINED

Dishwashers. Dishwashers manufactured in calendar year 2011 will be eligible for a $25, $50 or $75 applicable amount based on their efficiency as follows:

- The applicable amount will be $25 for dishwashers manufactured in calendar year 2011 that use no more than 307 kilowatt hours of electricity per year and 5.0 gallons of water per normal dishwasher cycle (5.5 gallons of water for dishwashers designed for greater than 12 place settings) (Code Sec. 45M(b)(1)(C), as added by the Tax Relief Act of 2010).

- The applicable amount will be $50 for dishwashers manufactured in calendar year 2011 that use no more than 295 kilowatt hours of electricity per year and 4.25 gallons of water per normal dishwasher cycle (4.75 gallons of water for dishwashers designed for greater than 12 place settings) (Code Sec. 45M(b)(1)(D), as added by the Tax Relief Act of 2010).

- The applicable amount will be $75 for dishwashers manufactured in calendar year 2011 that use no more than 280 kilowatt hours of electricity per year and 4.0 gallons of water per normal dishwasher cycle (4.5 gallons of water for dishwashers designed for greater than 12 place settings) (Code Sec. 45M(b)(1)(E), as added by the Tax Relief Act of 2010).

Clothes washers. Clothes washers manufactured in calendar year 2011 will be eligible for a $175 or $225 applicable amount based on their efficiency and type of machine as follows:

- The applicable amount will be $175 for top-loading clothes washers manufactured in calendar year 2011 that meet or exceed a 2.2 modified energy factor and do not exceed 4.5 water consumption factor (Code Sec. 45M(b)(2)(E), as added by the Tax Relief Act of 2010).

- The applicable amount will be $225 for top-loading clothes washers manufactured in calendar year 2011 that meet or exceed a 2.4 modified energy factor and do not exceed 4.2 water consumption factor (Code Sec. 45M(b)(2)(F)(i), as added by the Tax Relief Act of 2010).

- The applicable amount will be $225 for front-loading clothes washers manufactured in calendar year 2011 that meet or exceed a 2.8 modified energy factor and do not exceed 3.5 water consumption factor (Code Sec. 45M(b)(2)(F)(ii), as added by the Tax Relief Act of 2010).

Refrigerators. Refrigerators manufactured in calendar year 2011 will be eligible for a $150 or $200 applicable amount based on their efficiency as follows:

- The applicable amount will be $150 for refrigerators manufactured in calendar year 2011 that consume at least 30 percent less energy than the 2001 energy conservation standards (Code Sec. 45M(b)(3)(E), as added by the Tax Relief Act of 2010).

- The applicable amount will be $200 for refrigerators manufactured in calendar year 2011 that consume at least 35 percent less energy than the 2001 energy conservation standards (Code Sec. 45M(b)(3)(F), as added by the Tax Relief Act of 2010).

¶542

NEW LAW EXPLAINED

Limitations on credit. Effective for tax years beginning after December 31, 2010, the limitations on the energy efficient appliance credit will be adjusted. The aggregate credit allowed with respect to a taxpayer for any tax year beginning after 2010 will be limited to $25 million, reduced by the amount of the credit allowed to the taxpayer or any predecessor of the taxpayer for all prior tax years beginning after December 31, 2010 (Code Sec. 45M(e)(1), as amended by the Tax Relief Act of 2010). Credits for the most energy efficient refrigerators and clothes washers will not count against the $25 million limit (Code Sec. 45M(e)(2), as amended by the Tax Relief Act of 2010).

> **Comment:** Credits claimed in tax years beginning on or before December 31, 2010, will not reduce the $25 million limitation. For example, in the case of a producer with a fiscal-year beginning July 1, 2011, credits attributable to production in 2011 that occurs before July 1, 2011, count against the former $75 million limitation. However, all 2011 production is subject to the efficiency standards (and credit amounts) established under the new law for the 2011 calendar year.

The most energy efficient refrigerators and clothes washers are: (1) refrigerators eligible for the $200 applicable amount (consuming at least 35 percent less energy than the 2001 energy conservation standards) (Code Sec. 45M(b)(3)(F), as added by the Tax Relief Act of 2010), and (2) clothes washers eligible for the $225 applicable amount (top-loading clothes washers that meet or exceed a 2.4 modified energy factor and do not exceed 4.2 water consumption factor and front-loading clothes washers that meet or exceed a 2.8 modified energy factor and do not exceed 3.5 water consumption factor) (Code Sec. 45M(b)(2)(F), as added by the Tax Relief Act of 2010).

The gross receipts limitation on the energy efficient appliance credit has also been modified for tax years beginning after December 31, 2010. The credit allowed with respect to a taxpayer for the tax year cannot exceed four percent of the taxpayer's average annual gross receipts for the three tax years preceding the tax year in which the credit is determined (Code Sec. 45M(e)(3), as amended by the Tax Relief Act of 2010). A two-percent gross receipts limitation currently applies.

▶ **Effective date.** The amendments made to the applicable amount for dishwashers, clothes washers and refrigerators apply to appliances produced after December 31, 2010 (Act Sec. 709(e)(1) of the Tax Relief, Unemployment Insurance Reauthorization, and Job Creation Act of 2010 (P.L. 111-312)). The amendments made to the limitations on the credit apply to tax years beginning after December 31, 2010 (Act Sec. 709(e)(1) of the Tax Relief Act of 2010).

Law source: Law at ¶5140. Committee Report at ¶10,250.

— Act Sec. 709(a) of the Tax Relief, Unemployment Insurance Reauthorization, and Job Creation Act of 2010 (P.L. 111-312), amending Code Sec. 45M(b)(1);

— Act Sec. 709(b), amending Code Sec. 45M(b)(2);

— Act Sec. 709(c), amending Code Sec. 45M(b)(3);

— Act Sec. 709(d), amending Code Sec. 45M(e)(1), (2) and (3);

— Act Sec. 709(e), providing the effective dates.

NEW LAW EXPLAINED

definition of liquid fuel derived from biomass now excludes "any fuel (including lignin, wood residues, or spent pulping liquors) derived from the production of paper or pulp" (Code Sec. 6426(d)(2)(G), as amended by the Tax Relief Act of 2010). Thus, while the alternative fuel incentive provisions have been extended for liquid fuel derived from biomass, those incentives no longer apply to black liquor.

Special rule for retroactive claims. In light of the retroactive nature of these provisions, a special rule addresses claims for excise credits and outlay payments for periods occurring during 2010. The IRS is directed to issue guidance within 30 days of enactment providing for a one-time submission of claims covering periods during 2010. Under the guidance, there will be a 180-day window, beginning no later than 30 days after the guidance is issued, during which to submit such claims. The IRS is directed to pay claims for 2010 within 60 days of receipt. If the IRS does not pay a claim within 60 days, the claim will be paid with interest (Act Secs. 701(c) and 704(c) of the Tax Relief Act of 2010).

▶ **Effective date.** The provisions apply to fuel sold or used after December 31, 2009 (Act Secs. 701(d) and 704(d) of the Tax Relief, Unemployment Insurance Reauthorization, and Job Creation Act of 2010 (P.L. 111-312)).

Law source: Law at ¶5095, ¶5810, ¶5815, ¶7045, and ¶7050. Committee Report at ¶10,170 and ¶10,200.

— Act Sec. 701(a) of the Tax Relief, Unemployment Insurance Reauthorization, and Job Creation Act of 2010 (P.L. 111-312), amending Code Sec. 40A(g);

— Act Sec. 701(b), amending Code Secs. 6426(c)(6) and 6427(e)(6)(B);

— Act Sec. 704(a), amending Code Secs. 6426(d)(5), 6426(e)(3) and 6427(e)(6)(C);

— Act Sec. 704(b), amending Code Sec. 6426(d)(2);

— Act Secs. 701(c) and 704(c);

— Act Secs. 701(d) and 704(d), providing the effective dates.

Reporter references: For further information, consult the following CCH reporters.

— Standard Federal Tax Reporter, ¶4320.01 and ¶6431.01

— Tax Research Consultant, EXCISE: 3,110.10 and EXCISE: 24,374

— Practical Tax Explanation, §51,010.25

— Federal Excise Tax Reporter, ¶2325, ¶49,250 and ¶49,685.095

¶546 Incentives for Alcohol Fuels

SUMMARY OF NEW LAW

The income tax credit, excise tax credit, and outlay payment provisions for alcohol fuels and alcohol fuel mixtures have been extended for an additional year, through December 31, 2011.

BACKGROUND

To promote the production of alcohol fuels, Code Secs. 40, 6426 and 6427(e) provide per-gallon incentives for the sale, use and production of alcohol fuel and alcohol fuel mixtures.

Code Sec. 40 provides a nonrefundable income tax credit, called the alcohol fuels credit. That credit is the sum of the alcohol fuel mixture credit, the alcohol credit, the small ethanol producer credit, and the cellulosic biofuel producer credit.

"Alcohol" means any alcohol that is not derived from petroleum, natural gas, or coal (including peat). The term includes methanol and ethanol not derived from those natural resources, as well as the alcohol equivalent of ethyl tertiary butyl ether or other ethers produced from alcohol (Code Secs. 40(d)(1) and 6426(b)(4)). In practice, however, most fuel alcohol is ethanol produced from corn. While the term "alcohol" generally excludes alcohol with a proof of less than 190 (determined without regard to added denaturants), for purposes of the Code Sec. 40 credit, the term includes alcohol with a proof of at least 150 (Notice 2005-4, 2005-1 CB 289; Reg. § 48.4081-(6)(b)(1)).

For fuel sold or used after December 31, 2008, the volume of alcohol includes the volume of any denaturant (including gasoline) which is added under any formula approved by the IRS to the extent the denaturants do not exceed two percent of the volume of the alcohol (Code Sec. 40(d)(4), as amended by the Heartland, Habitat, Harvest and Horticulture Act of 2008 (P.L. 110-246)).

An "alcohol fuel mixture" is any mixture of alcohol and a taxable fuel that is sold by the producer to any person for use as a fuel, or is used as a fuel by the producer (Code Sec. 40(b)(1)(B)).

The alcohol *mixture* credit is 60 cents per gallon on methanol used by the taxpayer in the production of a qualified mixture (Code Sec. 40(b)(1)). This rate applies to methanol that is at least 190 proof. A 45 cents per gallon rate applies to methanol between 150 and 190 proof, and no credit is allowed for methanol under 150 proof (Code Sec. 40(b)(3) and (d)(3)(A)).

The alcohol credit is 60 cents per gallon on alcohol (generally methanol) that is not in a mixture with gas or a special fuel (other than any denaturant). Similar to the alcohol mixture credit, this rate is also subject to reduction for lower-proof alcohol (Code Sec. 40(b)(3) and (d)(3)(B)).

For ethanol blenders (as opposed to methanol), the alcohol mixture credit and the alcohol credit are reduced for ethanol that is sold or used in tax years beginning after 1990. The credit for 190 or greater proof ethanol is 45 cents per gallon in calendar years 2009 and 2010. For ethanol at least 150 proof and less than 190 proof, the credit is 33.33 cents per gallon in calendar years 2009 and 2010 (Code Sec. 40(h)).

An eligible small ethanol producer may claim the small ethanol producer credit of 10 cents per gallon on production of up to 15 million gallons per year of ethanol (Code Sec. 40(b)(4)). An eligible small ethanol producer is a producer that has a production capacity of up to 60 million gallons of alcohol per year (Code Sec. 40(g)(1)).

A $1.01 per gallon nonrefundable income tax credit for the production of qualified cellulosic biofuel is the fourth component of the alcohol fuels credit under Code Sec.

¶546

BACKGROUND

40. If the cellulosic biofuel is alcohol, whether ethanol or methanol, the $1.01 per gallon credit is reduced by any applicable alcohol mixture credit amount under Code Sec. 40(b)(1). In addition, if the cellulosic biofuel is ethanol, the credit is reduced by any applicable small ethanol producer credit amount under Code Sec. 40(b)(4) (Code Sec. 40(b)(6)(B); Form 6478, Alcohol and Cellulosic Biofuel Fuels Credit).

Income tax credit v. excise tax credit or payment. While alcohol fuel mixtures may qualify for the Code Sec. 40 income tax credit, taxpayers most often claim a Code Sec. 6426 excise tax credit or a payment under Code Sec. 6427 for these mixtures. This is because the alcohol fuel mixture credit must first be taken to reduce excise tax liability for gasoline, diesel fuel or kerosene. Any excess credit may then be taken as a payment or an income tax credit (Joint Committee on Taxation, *Technical Explanation of the Revenue Provisions Contained in the "Tax Relief, Unemployment Insurance Reauthorization, and Job Creation Act"* (JCX-55-10), December 10, 2010).

The excise tax credit rates for alcohol fuel mixtures conform with the income tax credit rates. Thus, the per-gallon rate for ethanol of 190 proof or better is 45 cents, and the per-gallon rate for methanol is 60 cents (Code Sec. 6426(b)(2)). In addition, as with the income tax credit, the volume of alcohol includes the volume of any denaturant (including gasoline) which is added under any formula approved by the IRS to the extent the denaturants do not exceed two percent of the volume of the alcohol (Code Sec. 6426(b)(5)).

To the extent that the alcohol fuel mixture credit (along with several other credits) exceeds a taxpayer's Code Sec. 4081 liability for any quarter, a payment under Code Sec. 6427(e) is available to the producer of the mixture. If a person receives a payment under Code Sec. 6427(e) for an alcohol fuel mixture that is eligible for a Code Sec. 6426 credit, the amount of the payment will constitute an excessive amount under Code Sec. 6206, and the amount (as well as a penalty under Code Sec. 6675) may be assessed against the person. Similarly, if a person claims an income tax credit for a fuel mixture that qualifies for a Code Sec. 6426 credit, the rules relating to assessing an underpayment of income tax liability apply (Notice 2005-4, 2005-1 CB 289).

Effective dates. The incentives for alcohol fuel discussed above generally do not apply after December 31, 2010. The incentive for cellulosic biofuel, however, is available until December 31, 2012. Note, however, that the income tax credit for alcohol fuels will not apply for any period *before* January 1, 2011, during which the Highway Trust Fund financing rates of tax under Code Sec. 4081(a)(2)(A) are 4.3 cents per gallon (Code Sec. 40(e)(1)).

Duties on ethanol. The Harmonized Tariff Schedule of the United States imposes a cumulative general duty of 14.27 cents per liter (about 54 cents per gallon) on imports of ethyl alcohol, and any mixture containing ethyl alcohol, that is used as a fuel or to produce a mixture to be used as a fuel, that enter into the United States prior to January 1, 2011 (Heading 9901.00.50). In addition, the Harmonized Tariff Schedule imposes a general duty of 5.99 cents per liter on imports of ethyl tertiary-butyl ether, and any mixture containing ethyl tertiary-butyl ether, that enter into the United States prior to January 1, 2011 (Heading 9901.00.52) (Joint Committee on Taxation, *Technical Explanation of the Revenue Provisions Contained in the "Tax Relief, Unemployment Insurance Reauthorization, and Job Creation Act"* (JCX-55-10), December 10, 2010).

¶546

Incentives for alcohol fuel extended.—The income tax credit, excise tax credit, and outlay payment provisions for alcohol fuels (except the cellulosic biofuel producer credit) and alcohol fuel mixtures have been extended for an additional year, through December 31, 2011 (Code Secs. 40(e)(1)(A), 6426(b)(6), and 6427(e)(6)(A), as amended by the Tax Relief, Unemployment Insurance Reauthorization, and Job Creation Act of 2010 (P.L. 111-312)).

Note, however, that the income tax credit for alcohol fuels will not apply for any period before January 1, 2012, during which the Highway Trust Fund financing rates of tax under Code Sec. 4081(a)(2)(A) are 4.3 cents per gallon (Code Sec. 40(e)(1)(B), as amended by the Tax Relief Act of 2010).

> **Comment:** Currently, the Highway Trust Fund financing rates for gasoline (other than aviation gasoline), diesel fuel and kerosene are scheduled to decrease to 4.3 cents per gallon on October 1, 2011 (Code Sec. 4081(d)(1)).

The reduced income tax credit rates for ethanol blenders are also extended through 2011 (Code Sec. 40(h), as amended by the Tax Relief Act of 2010).

> **Comment:** The reduced excise tax credit rate for at least 190 proof ethanol fuel mixtures remains at 45 cents without the need for an extension (Code Sec. 6426(b)(2)(A)(ii)).

Finally, the duties on ethanol and ethyl tertiary-butyl ether imposed by the Harmonized Tariff Schedule of the United States have been extended for an additional year, through December 31, 2011 (Act Sec. 708(d) of the Tax Relief Act of 2010).

▶ **Effective date.** The extension of the income tax credit for alcohol fuels (including mixtures) and the excise tax credit for alcohol fuel mixtures applies to periods after December 31, 2010 (Act Sec. 708(a)(3) and (b)(2) of the Tax Relief, Unemployment Insurance Reauthorization, and Job Creation Act of 2010 (P.L. 111-312)). The extension of the outlay payment provision for alcohol fuel mixtures applies to sales and uses after December 31, 2010 (Act Sec. 708(c)(2) of the Tax Relief Act of 2010). The extension of additional duties on ethanol takes effect on January 1, 2011 (Act Sec. 708(d)(2) of the Tax Relief Act of 2010).

Law source: Law at ¶5090, ¶5810, and ¶5815. Committee Report at ¶10,240.

— Act Sec. 708(a)(1) of the Tax Relief, Unemployment Insurance Reauthorization, and Job Creation Act of 2010 (P.L. 111-312), amending Code Sec. 40(e)(1);

— Act Sec. 708(a)(2), amending Code Sec. 40(h);

— Act Sec. 708(b)(1), amending Code Sec. 6426(b)(6);

— Act Sec. 708(c)(1), amending Code Sec. 6427(e)(6)(A);

— Act Sec. 708(d), amending the Harmonized Tariff Schedule of the United States;

— Act Sec. 708(a)(3), (b)(2), (c)(2), and (d)(2), providing the effective dates.

Reporter references: For further information, consult the following CCH reporters.

— Standard Federal Tax Reporter, ¶4304.01

— Tax Research Consultant, BUSEXP: 54,106, EXCISE: 3,106.15, EXCISE: 6,104.05, EXCISE: 24,310 and EXCISE: 24,374

— Federal Excise Tax Reporter, ¶2215.01, ¶49,250.02 and ¶49,685.095

¶546

¶548 Alternative Fuel Vehicle Refueling Property Credit

SUMMARY OF NEW LAW

The alternative fuel vehicle refueling property credit is extended to apply to refueling property (other than property relating to hydrogen) placed in service through December 31, 2011.

BACKGROUND

A credit for the installation of alternative fuel (clean-fuel) vehicle property used in a trade or business, or installed at the taxpayer's residence, applies to property placed in service after December 31, 2005 (Code Sec. 30C, as added by the Energy Tax Incentive Act of 2005 (P.L. 109-58)). A taxpayer may elect not to claim a credit under this provision (Code Sec. 30C(e)(4)), however the tax basis of any property for which the credit is claimed is reduced by the portion of the property's cost that is taken into account in computing the credit (Code Sec. 30C(e)(1)). This credit replaced the Code Sec. 179A deduction for clean-fuel vehicle refueling property, which is unavailable for property placed in service after December 31, 2005.

Amount of credit allowed. A taxpayer will be allowed a tax credit of up to 30 percent of the cost of "qualified alternative fuel vehicle refueling property," that is placed in service during the tax year (Code Sec. 30C(a)). In addition to the 30-percent limit, there is a yearly cap on the dollar amount of the credit. For commercial (retail) taxpayers (that is, taxpayers for whom the property would be subject to a depreciation deduction), the maximum yearly credit is $30,000. However, taxpayers who install qualified vehicle refueling property at their principal residence will be limited to a $1,000 yearly credit (Code Sec. 30C(b)). The Joint Committee on Taxation, Description and Technical Explanation of the Energy Tax Incentives Act of 2005 (JCX-60-05) indicates that a taxpayer may carry forward unused credits for 20 years.

Qualified alternative fuel vehicle refueling property defined. To qualify for the credit, the property (which cannot include a building or its structural components) must:

- be of a character that would be subject to the depreciation deduction;

- be property originally used by the taxpayer;

- be at the site at which the vehicle is refueled (if the property is for the storage or dispensing of alternative fuels into the fuel tank of a vehicle propelled by the fuel); *or*

- be located at the point where the vehicles are recharged (if the property is for recharging electrically-propelled vehicles) (Code Sec. 30C(c)(1)).

BACKGROUND

The above rules also apply to refueling property installed at a residence, except that the property does not have to be of a type that qualifies for the depreciation deduction (Code Sec. 30C(c)(2)).

In order to qualify for the credit, the fuels to be stored or dispensed must be:

- at least 85 percent in volume consist of one or more of the following: ethanol, natural gas, compressed natural gas, liquefied natural gas, liquefied petroleum gas, or hydrogen (Code Sec. 30C(c)(1)(A)); *or*

- electricity (if the property is for recharging electrically-propelled vehicles placed in service before January 1, 2011) (Code Sec. 30C(c)(2)(C)); *or*

- any mixture of biodiesel and diesel fuel (determined without regard to any use of kerosene) containing at least 20 percent of biodiesel (Code Sec. 30C(c)(1)(B)).

No alternative fuel vehicle refueling property credit will be allowed for property that is used predominately outside the United States (Code Sec. 30C(e)(3)).

Coordination with other credits. The business portion of the credit for alternative fuel vehicle refueling property (that is, the portion relating to property of a character subject to depreciation) is treated as a portion of the general business credit under Code Sec. 38 (Code Sec. 30C(d)(1)). The remaining portion of the credit (that is, the credit related to residential or nonbusiness property) is allowable to the extent of the excess of the regular tax (reduced by the nonrefundable credits of subpart A, the foreign tax credit (Code Sec. 27), the electric vehicle credit (Code Sec. 30), and the credit for alternate motor vehicles (Code Sec. 30B)) over the alternative minimum tax for the tax year (Code Sec. 30C(d)(2)).

Termination of the credit. Generally, no credit for qualified alternative fuel vehicle refueling property will be available for property placed in service after December 31, 2010 (Act Sec. 1342(c) of the Energy Act (P.L. 109-58) as amended by Act Sec. 207 of the Emergency Economic Stabilization Act of 2008 (P.L. 110-343)). However, for qualified refueling property relating to hydrogen, the credit will not apply to property placed in service after December 31, 2014 (Code Sec. 30C(g)).

NEW LAW EXPLAINED

Alternative fuel vehicle refueling property credit extended.—The alternative fuel vehicle refueling property credit is extended to apply to refueling property (other than property relating to hydrogen) placed in service through December 31, 2011 (Code Sec. 30C(g)(2), as amended by the Tax Relief, Unemployment Insurance Reauthorization, and Job Creation Act of 2010 (P.L. 111-312)).

> **Caution:** The extension of the alternative fuel vehicle refueling property credit does not apply to property relating to refueling hydrogen. The alternative fuel vehicle refueling property credit continues to apply to refueling hydrogen property placed in service through December 31, 2014.

> **Compliance Tip:** The alternative fuel vehicle refueling property credit is claimed on Form 8911, Alternative Fuel Vehicle Refueling Property Credit.

¶548

NEW LAW EXPLAINED

▶ **Effective date.** The provision applies to property placed in service after December 31, 2010 (Act Sec. 711(b) of the Tax Relief, Unemployment Insurance Reauthorization, and Job Creation Act of 2010 (P.L. 111-312)).

Law source: Law at ¶5065. Committee Report at ¶10,270.

— Act Sec. 711(a) of the Tax Relief, Unemployment Insurance Reauthorization, and Job Creation Act of 2010 (P.L. 111-312), amending Code Sec. 30C(g)(2);

— Act Sec. 711(b), providing the effective date.

Reporter references: For further information, consult the following CCH reporters.

— Standard Federal Tax Reporter, ¶4059K.021 and ¶4059K.05

— Tax Research Consultant, INDIV: 57,750

— Practical Tax Explanation, § 12,910 and § 14,310

¶550 Refined Coal Production Facilities Credit

SUMMARY OF NEW LAW

The placed-in-service date for a refined coal facility has been extended to facilities placed in service before January 1, 2012.

BACKGROUND

As part of the general business credit, a nonrefundable credit is available for the domestic production of electricity from certain renewable sources (Code Sec. 45(a)). To be eligible for the refined coal credit, a refined coal production facility must be placed in service after October 22, 2004, and before January 1, 2010. A refined coal production facility with respect to a facility producing steel industry fuel is any facility (or any modification to a facility) which is placed in service before January 1, 2010 (Code Sec. 45(d)(8)). The credit amount for refined coal will begin to phase out when the reference price for the current year exceeds the reference price for 2002 times the inflation rate times 1.7 and will completely phase out when the current reference price exceeds the reference price for 2002 times the inflation rate times 1.7 by $8.75 (Notice 2010-37, 2010-18 I.R.B. 645).

The credit for refined coal production may not be claimed if production from the facility was eligible for the nonconventional fuel source credit during any tax year under Code Sec. 45K (or Code Sec. 29, prior to being redesignated as Code Sec. 45K by the Energy Tax Incentives Act of 2005 (P.L. 109-58)) (Code Sec. 45(e)(9)(B)).

Refined coal, other than steel industry fuel, is fuel that meets the following requirements:

● It must be a liquid, gaseous, or solid fuel (including feedstock coal mixed with an additive or additives) produced from coal (including lignite) or high carbon fly ash, including such fuel used as a feedstock.

BACKGROUND

- It must be sold by the taxpayer-producer to an unrelated person with the reasonable expectation that it will be used to produce steam.
- It must be certified by the taxpayer as resulting (when used in the production of steam) in a qualified emission reduction (Code Sec. 45(c)(7)(A); Notice 2010-54, 2010-40 IRB 403).

The credit only applies to United States production and is claimed on Form 8835 (Renewable Electricity, Refined Coal, and Indian Coal Production Credit). The certification statement must be attached to the tax return on which the credit is claimed and include the statements, information, and declaration described in Section 6.05 of Notice 2010-54. Coal means anthracite, bituminous coal, subbituminous coal, and lignite. Coal includes waste coal that is a by-product of the preceding types of coal. The credit is claimed without regard to whether the producer owns, leases, or merely operates the refined coal production facility (Notice 2010-54, 2010-40 I.R.B. 403).

NEW LAW EXPLAINED

Placed-in-service deadline extended two years for refined coal facilities not producing steel industry fuel.—A facility that produces refined coal is now treated as a qualifying refined coal facility if placed in service before January 1, 2012 (Code Sec. 45(d)(8)(B), as amended by the Tax Relief, Unemployment Insurance Reauthorization, and Job Creation Act of 2010 (P.L. 111-312)). However, this extension does not apply to facilities that produce steel industry fuel (Code Sec. 45(d)(8)(A)).

▶ **Effective date.** The provision applies to facilities placed in service after December 31, 2009 (Act Sec. 702(b) of the Tax Relief, Unemployment Insurance Reauthorization, and Job Creation Act of 2010 (P.L. 111-312)).

Law source: Law at ¶5105. Committee Report at ¶10,180.

— Act Sec. 702(a) of the Tax Relief, Unemployment Insurance Reauthorization, and Job Creation Act of 2010 (P.L. 111-312), amending Code Sec. 45(d)(8)(B);

— Act Sec. 702(b), providing the effective date.

Reporter references: For further information, consult the following CCH reporters.

— Standard Federal Tax Reporter, ¶4415.04

— Tax Research Consultant, BUSEXP: 54,550 and BUSEXP: 54,554

— Practical Tax Explanation, § 14,215

¶552 Percentage Depletion for Marginal Oil and Gas Production

SUMMARY OF NEW LAW

The suspension of the percentage depletion limitation for oil and gas produced from marginal properties is extended for two years, through 2011.

¶552

BACKGROUND

Depletion allowances are among the many tax benefits available to owners and operators of mineral resources. Generally, taxpayers must use whichever depletion method (cost or percentage) produces the largest deduction (Reg. §1.611-1(a)(1)). However, an independent producer or royalty owner can generally use percentage depletion with respect to oil and gas wells, even if the taxpayer's cost depletion deduction would be larger (Code Sec. 613A).

This percentage depletion allowance is generally limited to the first 1,000 barrels of average daily production of domestic crude oil or the equivalent amount of natural gas (six million cubic feet). In addition, percentage depletion is generally limited to 65 percent of the taxpayer's taxable income from the property for the year (Code Sec. 613(a)). However, for production from marginal oil and gas wells, the production limit is relaxed (Code Sec. 613A(c)(6)). In addition:

- the maximum percentage depletion allowance is generally increased to 100 percent of the taxpayer's taxable income from the property, computed without the depletion allowance and the Code Sec. 199 domestic production activities deduction (Code Sec. 613(a)(c)(6)(A)); and

- for tax years beginning after 1997 and before 2010, this 100-percent-income limitation applies only during 2008 (Code Sec. 613A(c)(6)(H)). Thus, there is no income limitation on the percentage depletion allowance with respect to oil and gas production from marginal wells for tax years 1998 through 2007, and 2009.

NEW LAW EXPLAINED

Suspension of net-income limit on percentage depletion extended.—The temporary suspension of the taxable income limit on the percentage depletion allowance for oil and gas produced from marginal wells is extended to include tax years beginning after December 31, 2009, and before January 1, 2012 (Code Sec. 613A(c)(6)(H)(ii), as amended by the Tax Relief, Unemployment Insurance Reauthorization, and Job Creation Act of 2010 (P.L. 111-312)). Thus, for tax years beginning after 1997 and before 2012, the depletion allowance for independent operators and royalty owners with respect to oil and gas production from marginal wells is limited to 100 percent of the taxpayer's taxable income from the property only for tax years beginning during 2008.

> **State Tax Consequences:** The extension of the suspension of the taxable income limit to for the depletion of qualified marginal oil and gas wells will not impact states such as California that have specifically decoupled from the suspension provision, states such as Maryland and Oregon that do not allow the percentage depletion method, or states such as Arkansas that do not place limitations on the percentage depletion method. For states like Indiana, Virginia and Wisconsin that adopt the federal allowance and limitation amounts, whether they adopt this amendment will depend on their Code conformity dates. Those states that update their Code conformity dates annually will most likely conform during their next legislative sessions.

NEW LAW EXPLAINED

▶ **Effective date.** The provision applies to tax years beginning after December 31, 2009 (Act Sec. 706(b) of the Tax Relief, Unemployment Insurance Reauthorization, and Job Creation Act of 2010 (P.L. 111-312)).

Law source: Law at ¶5405. Committee Report at ¶10,220.

— Act Sec. 706(a) of the Tax Relief, Unemployment Insurance Reauthorization, and Job Creation Act of 2010 (P.L. 111-312), amending Code Sec. 613A(c)(6)(H)(ii);

— Act Sec. 706(b), providing the effective date.

Reporter references: For further information, consult the following CCH reporters.

— Standard Federal Tax Reporter, ¶23,988.044

— Tax Research Consultant, FARM: 15,216.10

— Practical Tax Explanation, § 11,625.10

¶554 Gain Rule for Sales or Dispositions Implementing FERC or State Electric Restructuring Policy

SUMMARY OF NEW LAW

The special gain recognition rule for qualifying electric transmission transactions that implement Federal Energy Regulatory Commission (FERC) or state electric restructuring policy is extended for two years to apply to sales or dispositions by qualified electric utilities occurring prior to January 1, 2012.

BACKGROUND

A special gain recognition rule applies to sales or dispositions of qualifying electric transmission property that are made to implement Federal Energy Regulatory Commission (FERC) or state electric restructuring policy (Code Sec. 451(i)). A taxpayer can elect to recognize qualified gain from a qualifying electric transmission transaction over an eight-year period to the extent that the amount realized from the sale is used to purchase exempt utility property within the applicable period (Code Sec. 451(i)(1)(B)). Qualified gain is immediately recognized beginning in the tax year of the transaction to the extent the amount realized from the transaction exceeds:

- the cost of exempt utility property that is purchased by the taxpayer during the four-year period beginning on the date of the transaction reduced, but not below zero, by

- any portion of the cost previously taken into account under these rules (Code Sec. 451(i)(1)(A)).

Exempt utility property is property used in the trade or business of generating, transmitting, distributing, or selling electricity, or producing, transmitting, distribut-

BACKGROUND

ing, or selling natural gas. Exempt utility property does not include any property that is located outside the United States (Code Sec. 451(i)(5)).

Qualified gain is:

- any ordinary income derived from a qualifying electric transmission transaction that would be required to be recognized under Code Secs. 1245 or 1250, and

- any income from a transaction in excess of the amount, above, which is required to be included in gross income for the tax year (Code Sec. 451(i)(2)).

Qualifying electric transmission transaction. A qualifying electric transmission transaction is any sale or other disposition to an independent transmission company of: (1) property used in the trade or business of providing electric transmission services; or (2) an ownership interest in a corporation or partnership whose principal trade or business consists of providing such services. The sale or disposition must be made before January 1, 2008 (Code Sec. 451(i)(3)).

An independent transmission company is:

(1) an independent transmission provider approved by the FERC;

(2) a person: (a) who the FERC determines is not a "market participant," and (b) whose transmission facilities to which the election applies are under the operational control of a FERC-approved independent transmission provider within a specified time frame; or

(3) in the case of facilities subject to the jurisdiction of the Public Utility Commission of Texas, a person approved by that commission as consistent with Texas state law regarding an independent transmission organization, or a political subdivision or affiliate whose transmission facilities are under the operational control of that person (Code Sec. 451(i)(4)).

In the case of item (2) above, the transmission facilities must be under the control of the independent transmission provider before the close of the period specified in the FERC authorization of the transaction (Code Sec. 451(i)(4)(B)(ii)). In any event, control must be exercised no later than December 31, 2007 (Code Sec. 451(i)(4)(B)(ii)).

The Emergency Economic Stabilization Act of 2008 (P.L.110-343) provided for a two-year extension of deferral treatment for sales or other dispositions of electric transmission property to independent transmission companies to transactions occurring before January 1, 2010, for sales or dispositions by qualified electric utilities (Code Sec. 451(i)(3), as amended by the Emergency Economic Act of 2008).

A qualified electric utility is a person that, as of the date of the qualifying electric transmission transaction, is vertically integrated. Vertically integrated means that it is both:

- a transmitting utility (as defined in section 3(23) of the Federal Power Act (16 U.S.C. §796(23))) with respect to the transmission facilities to which the deferral election applies, and

- an electric utility (as defined in section 3(22) of the Federal Power Act (16 U.S.C. §796(22))) (Code Sec. 451(i)(6), as added by the Emergency Economic Act of 2008).

¶554

BACKGROUND

In determining whether a sale or disposition is a qualifying electric transmission transaction, the period for transfer of operational control to an independent transmission provider authorized by FERC was extended from December 31, 2007, to the date which is four years after the close of the tax year in which the transaction occurs (Code Sec. 451(i)(4)(B)(ii), as amended by the Emergency Economic Act of 2008).

NEW LAW EXPLAINED

Tax deferral extended for qualified electric utilities.—Deferral treatment for sales or other dispositions of electric transmission property to independent transmission companies is extended for two years, to transactions occurring before January 1, 2012, for sales or dispositions by qualified electric utilities (Code Sec. 451(i)(3), as amended by the Tax Relief, Unemployment Insurance Reauthorization, and Jobs Creation Act of 2010 (P.L. 111-312)).

▶   **Effective date.** The provision applies to dispositions after December 31, 2009 (Act Sec. 705(b) of the Tax Relief, Unemployment Insurance Reauthorization, and Jobs Creation Act of 2010 (P.L. 111-312)).

Law source: Law at ¶5360. Committee Report at ¶10,210.

— Act Sec. 705(a) of the Tax Relief, Unemployment Insurance Reauthorization, and Jobs Creation Act of 2010 (P.L. 111-312), amending Code Sec. 451(i)(3);

— Act Sec. 705(b), providing the effective date.

Reporter references: For further information, consult the following CCH reporters.

— Standard Federal Tax Reporter, ¶21,030.022 and ¶21,030.06

— Tax Research Consultant, SALES: 21,056

CHARITABLE CONTRIBUTIONS

¶557   Basis Adjustment to Stock of an S Corporation Making Charitable Contributions

SUMMARY OF NEW LAW

The rule providing that a shareholder's basis in the stock of an S corporation making a charitable contribution of property is reduced by the shareholder's pro rata share of the adjusted basis of the contributed property is extended for two years to apply to contributions made in tax years beginning before January 1, 2012.

BACKGROUND

If an S corporation contributes money or other property to a charity, each shareholder takes into account the shareholder's pro rata share of the contribution in determining its own income tax liability (Code Sec. 1366(a)(1)(A)). The shareholder's basis in the stock of the S corporation is reduced by the amount of the charitable contribution that flows through to the shareholder (Code Sec. 1367(a)(2)(B)).

In the case of charitable contributions made in tax years beginning before January 1, 2006, and after December 31, 2009, the amount of the reduction of a shareholder's basis in the stock of an S corporation by reason of the S corporation's charitable contribution of property is equal to the shareholder's pro rata share of the fair market value of the contributed property. For charitable contributions made in tax years beginning after December 31, 2005, and before January 1, 2010, the stock basis reduction rule is modified to provide that the shareholder's basis in the stock of an S corporation making charitable contribution of property is reduced by the shareholder's pro rata share of the adjusted basis of the contributed property (Code Sec. 1367(a)(2)).

NEW LAW EXPLAINED

Modified rule for basis reduction in stock of S corporation making charitable contribution of property extended.—The rule providing that the amount of the reduction of a shareholder's basis in the stock of an S corporation by reason of the corporation's charitable contribution of property is equal to the shareholder's pro rata share of the adjusted basis of the contributed property is extended for two years to apply to contributions made in tax years beginning before January 1, 2012 (Code Sec. 1367(a)(2), as amended by the Tax Relief, Unemployment Insurance Reauthorization, and Job Creation Act of 2010 (P.L. 111-312)).

> **Comment:** Rev. Rul. 2008-16, I.R.B. 2008-11, 585, provides that the amount of the charitable contribution deduction a shareholder is entitled to claim may not exceed the sum of (1) the shareholder's pro rata share of the fair market value of the contributed property over the property's adjusted tax basis, and (2) the amount of the Code Sec. 1366(d) loss limitation that is allocable to the property's adjusted basis under Reg. § 1.1366-2(a)(4). Pursuant to Code Sec. 1367(a)(2)(B), the shareholder's basis in the corporate stock was reduced to zero to reflect the reduction in basis attributable to the capital loss and the reduction in basis attributable to the charitable contribution deduction. Pursuant to Code Sec. 1366(d)(2), the disallowed portion of the charitable contribution and the capital loss is treated as incurred by the corporation in the following tax year with respect to the shareholder.

> **State Tax Consequences:** States such as Michigan, New Hampshire, and Tennessee, which treat S corporations as any other taxable entity would not be impacted by the extension of the favorable basis treatment given to shareholders of S corporations that make charitable donations. For other states that do follow the federal treatment of S corporations, whether a state will be impacted will depend on the state's Internal Revenue Code conformity date.

NEW LAW EXPLAINED

▶ **Effective date.** The provision applies to contributions made in tax years beginning after December 31, 2009 (Act Sec. 752(b) of the Tax Relief, Unemployment Insurance Reauthorization, and Job Creation Act of 2010 (P.L. 111-312)).

Law source: Law at ¶5555. Committee Report at ¶10,570.

— Act Sec. 752(a) of the Tax Relief, Unemployment Insurance Reauthorization, and Job Creation Act of 2010 (P.L. 111-312), amending Code Sec. 1367(a)(2);

— Act Sec. 752(b), providing the effective date.

Reporter references: For further information, consult the following CCH reporters.

— Standard Federal Tax Reporter, ¶32,101.01

— Tax Research Consultant, SCORP: 410.05

— Practical Tax Explanation, §28,615

¶560 Enhanced Deduction for Charitable Contributions of Food Inventory

SUMMARY OF NEW LAW

The enhanced deduction for charitable contributions of food inventory from corporate and noncorporate taxpayers is extended for two years, through December 31, 2011.

BACKGROUND

Generally, charitable contributions of capital gain property are deductible to the extent of the fair market value of the property on the date of contribution. However, for both individuals and corporations, the amount of the deduction for a charitable contribution of ordinary income property, such as inventory, is usually limited to the donor's basis in the donated property (Code Sec. 170(e)).

Under an exception to this general rule, C corporations can claim an enhanced deduction for inventory that is contributed to a qualified charity or private operating foundation. The amount of the enhanced deduction equals the lesser of (1) the donated item's basis plus one-half of the item's appreciation, or (2) two times the donated item's basis. A corporation's charitable contribution deduction for a year is limited to 10 percent of the corporation's taxable income, computed with certain adjustments (Code Sec. 170(b)(2)). A corporation can carry over charitable contributions that exceed 10 percent of its taxable income for a five-year period (Code Sec. 170(d)(2)).

In response to the hurricane disasters along the Gulf coast in 2005, legislation modified the rules relating to the enhanced deductions for donations of inventory to a qualified charity or private operating foundation. Noncorporate, as well as corporate, taxpayers can claim an enhanced deduction for contributions of food inventory

BACKGROUND

made on or after August 28, 2005, and before January 1, 2010 (Code Sec. 170(e)(3)(C)). The food inventory must consist of items fit for human consumption and contributed to a qualified charity or private operating foundation for use in the care of the ill, the needy, or infants. The amount of the enhanced deduction for donated food inventory equals the lesser of (1) the donated item's basis plus one-half of the item's appreciation, or (2) two times the donated item's basis. For a taxpayer other than a C corporation, the total deduction for donations of food inventory during the tax year is limited to a maximum of 10 percent of the taxpayer's net income from all sole proprietorships, S corporations, or partnerships (or other non C corporation) from which the contributions are made.

The enhanced charitable deduction for contributions of food inventory does not apply to contributions made during any tax year beginning after December 31, 2009.

NEW LAW EXPLAINED

Enhanced deduction extended for charitable contributions of food inventory.— The enhanced deduction for charitable contributions of food inventory from any trade or business of a corporate or noncorporate taxpayer is extended for two years and applies to contributions made through December 31, 2011 (Code Sec. 170(e)(3)(C)(iv), as amended by the Tax Relief, Unemployment Insurance Reauthorization, and Job Creation Act of 2010 (P.L. 111-312)).

> **State Tax Consequences:** The extension of the enhanced charitable contribution deduction for contributions of food inventory does not impact states such as California and Pennsylvania that have specifically decoupled from this provision or states such as Connecticut or Illinois that do not allow itemized deductions. Similarly, states that do not allow a charitable contribution deduction such as Indiana and New Jersey will also not be impacted. For those states that do allow a charitable deduction and that recognize these enhanced deductions, whether the state will recognize the extension depends upon the state's Internal Revenue Code conformity date. Those states that update their Code conformity dates annually will most likely conform during their next legislative sessions.

▶ **Effective date.** The provision applies to contributions made after December 31, 2009 (Act Sec. 740(b) of the Tax Relief, Unemployment Insurance Reauthorization, and Job Creation Act of 2010 (P.L. 111-312)).

Law source: Law at ¶5270. Committee Report at ¶10,450.

— Act Sec. 740(a) of the Tax Relief, Unemployment Insurance Reauthorization, and Job Creation Act of 2010 (P.L. 111-312), amending Code Sec. 170(e)(3)(C)(iv);

— Act Sec. 740(b), providing the effective date.

Reporter references: For further information, consult the following CCH reporters.

— Standard Federal Tax Reporter, ¶11,620.059 and ¶11,680.031

— Tax Research Consultant, INDIV: 51,152.15 and CCORP: 9,354

— Practical Tax Explanation, §7,575.25

¶563 Enhanced Deduction for Corporate Charitable Contributions of Book Inventory

SUMMARY OF NEW LAW

The enhanced deduction for corporate charitable contributions of book inventory to public schools is extended for two years, through December 31, 2011.

BACKGROUND

Generally, charitable contributions of capital gain property are deductible to the extend of the fair market value of the property on the date of contribution. However, for both individuals and corporations, the amount of the deduction for a charitable contribution of ordinary income property, such as inventory, is usually limited to the donor's basis in the donated property (Code Sec. 170(e)). Under an exception to this general rule, C corporations can claim an enhanced deduction for inventory that is contributed to a qualified charity or private operating foundation. The amount of the enhanced deduction equals the lesser of (1) the donated item's basis plus one-half of the item's appreciation, or (2) two times the donated item's basis.

In response to the hurricane disasters along the Gulf coast in 2005, legislation modified the rules relating to the enhanced deductions for donations of inventory to a qualified charity or private operating foundation. C corporations that make qualified book contributions on or after August 28, 2005, and before January 1, 2010, are eligible for an enhanced deduction equal to the lesser of (1) the donated inventory item's basis plus one-half of the item's appreciation, or (2) two times the donated inventory item's basis.

A qualified book contribution is a charitable contribution of books to a public school that provides elementary or secondary education (kindergarten through grade 12) and maintains a regular faculty and curriculum with a regularly enrolled student body. In addition, the donee educational institution is required to certify in writing that: (1) the books are suitable in terms of currency, content, and quality for use in the school's educational programs, and (2) the school actually uses the books in its educational programs.

The enhanced charitable deduction for corporate contributions of books to public schools or public libraries does not apply to contributions made during any tax year beginning after December 31, 2009.

NEW LAW EXPLAINED

Enhanced deduction extended for corporate charitable contributions of book inventory.—The enhanced deduction for corporate charitable contributions of book inventory to public schools is extended for two years and applies to contributions made through December 31, 2011 (Code Sec. 170(e)(3)(D)(iv), as amended by the Tax Relief, Unemployment Insurance Reauthorization, and Job Creation Act of 2010 (P.L. 111-312)).

¶563

NEW LAW EXPLAINED

> **State Tax Consequences:** The extension of the enhanced charitable contribution deduction for contributions of book inventory does not impact states such as California that decouple from the deduction. Similarly these amendments would not impact jurisdictions such as Alaska and the District of Columbia that do not recognize the federal charitable contributions deduction for corporate tax returns. Whether other states that incorporate the federal charitable contributions deduction will be impacted depends on the state's Internal Revenue Code conformity date. Those states that update their Code conformity dates annually will most likely conform during their next legislative sessions.

▶ **Effective date.** The provision applies to contributions made after December 31, 2009 (Act. Sec. 741(b) of the Tax Relief, Unemployment Insurance Reauthorization, and Job Creation Act of 2010 (P.L. 111-312)).

Law source: Law at ¶5270. Committee Report at ¶10,460.

— Act Sec. 741(a) of the Unemployment Insurance Reauthorization, and Job Creation Act of 2010 (P.L. 111-312), amending Code Sec. 170(e)(3)(D)(iv);

— Act Sec. 741(b), providing the effective date.

Reporter references: For further information, consult the following CCH reporters.

— Standard Federal Tax Reporter, ¶11,620.059, ¶11,660.027, and ¶11,680.031

— Tax Research Consultant, CCORP: 9,354

— Practical Tax Explanation, §7,575.30

¶566 Enhanced Deduction for Corporate Charitable Contributions of Computers

SUMMARY OF NEW LAW

The enhanced deduction for charitable contributions of computer technology or equipment by corporations is extended for two years, through December 31, 2011.

BACKGROUND

Generally, the amount of a deduction for the donation of property is limited to the donor's basis in the property (Code Sec. 170(e)). Under an exception to this general rule, certain corporations can claim an enhanced deduction for "qualified contributions" (Code Sec. 170(e)(3)). A qualified contribution is the donation of certain inventory and other specified property to a qualified charity or private foundation for use in the care of the ill, the needy or infants.

Corporations that make qualified contributions of computer technology and equipment to specific types of recipients ("qualified computer contributions") may claim an enhanced deduction equal to the corporation's basis in the donated property plus one-half of the ordinary income that would have been realized if the property had

BACKGROUND

been sold. However, the enhanced deduction may not exceed twice the corporation's basis in the property (Code Sec. 170(e)(6)).

Qualified computer contributions include donations of computers and peripheral equipment, computer software, and fiber optic cable related to computer use, to be used within the United States for educational purposes. In order to qualify for the enhanced deduction, donations can only be made to certain recipients, including:

- an educational organization that normally maintains a regular faculty and curriculum and has regularly enrolled students in attendance at the place where its educational activities are regularly conducted;

- a tax-exempt entity that is organized primarily for purposes of supporting elementary and secondary education;

- a private foundation that, within 30 days after receipt of the contribution, contributes the property to an eligible donee described in (1) or (2) above, and notifies the donor of the contribution; or

- a public library, as defined in the Library Services and Technology Act (20 U.S.C. §9122(2)(A)).

The enhanced charitable deduction for contributions of computer technology and/or equipment to schools or public libraries does not apply to contributions made during any tax year beginning after December 31, 2009.

NEW LAW EXPLAINED

Enhanced deduction extended for corporate charitable contributions of computers.—The enhanced deduction for charitable contributions of computer technology or equipment ("qualified computer contributions") by a corporation is extended for two years, and applies to contributions made during tax years beginning prior to January 1, 2012 (Code Sec. 170(e)(6)(G), as amended by the Tax Relief, Unemployment Insurance Reauthorization, and Job Creation Act of 2010 (P.L. 111-312)). C corporations can continue to benefit from increased deductions for qualified computer contributions, equal to the corporation's basis in the donated property plus one-half of the ordinary income that would have been realized if the property had been sold. However, the enhanced deduction may not exceed twice the corporation's basis in the property (Code Sec. 170(e)(6)(A)).

State Tax Consequences: The extension of the enhanced charitable contribution deduction for contributions of computer equipment does not impact states such as California and Pennsylvania that have specifically decoupled from this provision or states such as Connecticut or Illinois that do not allow itemized deductions. Similarly, states that do not allow a charitable contribution deduction such as Indiana and New Jersey will also not be impacted. For those states that do allow a charitable deduction and that recognize these enhanced deductions, whether the state will recognize the extension depends upon the state's Internal Revenue Code conformity date. Those states that update their Code conformity dates annually will most likely conform during their next legislative sessions.

¶566

NEW LAW EXPLAINED

▶ **Effective date.** The provision applies to contributions made in tax years beginning after December 31, 2009 (Act Sec. 742(b) of the Tax Relief, Unemployment Insurance Reauthorization, and Job Creation Act of 2010 (P.L. 111-312)).

Law source: Law at ¶5270. Committee Report at ¶10,470.

— Act Sec. 742(a) of the Tax Relief, Unemployment Insurance Reauthorization, and Job Creation Act of 2010 (P.L. 111-312), amending Code Sec. 170(e)(6)(G);

— Act Sec. 742(b), providing the effective date.

Reporter references: For further information, consult the following CCH reporters.

— Standard Federal Tax Reporter, ¶11,680.037

— Tax Research Consultant, CCORP: 9,358

— Practical Tax Explanation, §7,575.25

NEW LAW EXPLAINED

as royalty income. Further, Code Sec. 543(a)(1) treats income from the use of secret processes, trade brands and other intangible property as PHC income, royalty income, regardless of the source, shareholder(s) of the corporation or from an unrelated third party. The obvious solution to avoid these situations is to operate the corporation as an S corporation. Likewise, S corporate status avoids taxation in the classic situations, namely when the C corporation has five or fewer shareholders owning more than 50 percent in value of the corporation's outstanding stock and 60 percent or more of the corporation's AGI comes from dividends, interest, royalties, etc.

▶ **Effective date.** With respect to the amendments made to the Economic Growth and Tax Relief Reconciliation Act of 2001 (EGTRRA) (P.L. 107-16), the provision is effective for tax years beginning after December 31, 2000 (Act Sec. 101(b) of the Tax Relief, Unemployment Insurance Reauthorization, and Job Creation Act of 2010 (P.L. 111-312); Act. Sec. 101(d)(1) of EGTRRA). With respect to the amendments made to the Jobs and Growth Tax Relief Reconciliation Act of 2003 (JGTRRA) (P.L. 108-27), the provision is effective for tax years beginning after December 31, 2002 (Act. Sec. 102(b) of the Tax Relief Act of 2010; Act Sec. 302(f)(1) of JGTRRA). The provision shall not apply to tax years beginning after December 31, 2012 (Act Secs. 101(a) and 102(a) of the Tax Relief Act of 2010; Act Sec. 901 of EGTRRA; Act Sec. 303 of JGTRRA). See ¶105 for a specific discussion of the sunset provisions of EGTRRA and JGTRRA and how they are applied.

Law source: Law at ¶5390, ¶7010, and ¶7015. Committee Report at ¶10,080.

— Act Sec.101(a) of the Tax Relief, Unemployment Insurance Reauthorization, and Job Creation Act of 2010 (P.L. 111-312), amending Act Sec. 901 of the Economic Growth and Tax Relief Reconciliation Act of 2001 (EGTRRA) (P.L. 107-16);

— Act Sec.102(a), amending Act Sec. 303 of the Jobs and Growth Tax Relief Reconciliation Act of 2003 (JGTRRA) (P.L. 108-27);

— Act Secs. 101(a) and 102(b), providing the effective dates.

Reporter references: For further information, consult the following CCH reporters.

— Standard Federal Tax Reporter, ¶23,154.01

— Tax Research Consultant, CCORP: 36,000, CCORP: 36,250 and STAGES: 9,114

— Practical Tax Explanation, §27,001

¶609 Collapsible Corporations

SUMMARY OF NEW LAW

The repeal of the collapsible corporation rules of Code Sec. 341 has been extended for two years, through December 31, 2012. Thus, in tax years beginning in 2011 and 2012, shareholders of collapsible corporations will continue to report as capital gain, rather than ordinary income, any gain realized on sales or exchanges of their stock or on certain distributions that would normally result in capital gain treatment.

BACKGROUND

The Jobs and Growth Tax Relief Reconciliation Act of 2003 (JGTRRA) (P.L. 108-27) repealed the collapsible corporation rules of Code Sec. 341, effective for tax years beginning after December 31, 2002. These rules were intended to prevent shareholders of collapsible corporations from obtaining favorable long-term capital gain treatment for income that would otherwise be taxable as ordinary income.

Normally, gain on the sale or exchange of a corporation stock or gain on complete or partial liquidation distributions under Code Sec. 302(e) constitutes capital gain. Capital gain treatment also generally applies in the case of a Code Sec. 301 distribution that exceeds the shareholder's basis (Code Sec. 301(c)(3)(A)). The collapsible corporation rules, however, required shareholders of a collapsible corporation to report as ordinary income gain from the sale or exchange of stock in the collapsible corporation or on a liquidating or other distribution from the corporation that would normally result in capital gain. Since the repeal of these rules, a shareholder's gain on a sale or exchange of stock or a liquidating distribution is generally taxed as capital gain at the applicable capital gain rates.

> **Comment:** The American Institute of Certified Public Accountants (AICPA) had long recommended repeal of the collapsible corporation rules in light of their ambiguity and because other laws already ensured corporate-level taxation upon the sale or liquidation of corporate assets. Code Sec. 341 had also been called "inordinately long and nearly incomprehensible." The provision was also criticized as at odds with the general preferential treatment of capital gain. The American Bar Association and the Senate Finance Committee Report on the Simplification of the Income Taxation of Corporations (September 22, 1993) also recommended repeal of the rules.

To reflect the repeal of the collapsible corporation rules, JGTRRA also made conforming amendments to other provisions. Thus, references to Code Sec. 341 were removed from Code Sec. 338 (regarding a corporation electing to treat a stock purchase as an asset purchase), Code Sec. 467 (related to deferred payments under rental agreements), Code Sec. 1255 (certain government cost-sharing program payments for conservation purposes), and Code Sec. 1257 (dispositions of converted wetland or highly erodible cropland).

Sunset provision. Under a sunset provision of JGTRRA, certain amendments made by the Act would not apply to tax years beginning after December 31, 2010 (Act Sec. 303 of P.L. 108-27, as amended by Act Sec. 102 of P.L. 109-222).

NEW LAW EXPLAINED

Repeal of collapsible corporation rules extended.—The repeal of the collapsible corporation rules of Code Sec. 341 is extended for two years, through December 31, 2012 (Act Sec. 102(a) of the Tax Relief, Unemployment Insurance Reauthorization, and Job Creation Act of 2010 (P.L. 111-312)). Thus, in tax years beginning in 2011 and 2012, shareholders of collapsible corporations will continue to report as capital gain, rather than ordinary income, any gain realized on sales or exchanges of their stock or on certain distributions that would normally result in capital gain treatment.

¶609

NEW LAW EXPLAINED

Under the sunset provision of the Jobs and Growth Tax Relief Reconciliation Act of 2003 (JGTRRA) (P.L. 108-27) (Act Sec. 303 of P.L. 108-27, as amended by Act Sec. 102(a) of the Tax Relief Act of 2010), the repeal of the collapsible corporation rules will expire for tax years beginning after December 31, 2012. Therefore, in such tax years the collapsible corporation rules (discussed below), as in effect prior to their repeal by JGTRRA, will apply.

Collapsible corporation definition in general. Generally, if a corporation meets the definition of a collapsible corporation, the shareholder's gain on a sale or exchange of the collapsible corporation's stock or a distribution to the shareholders in a complete or partial liquidation or under Code Sec. 301 that would otherwise result in capital gain may be treated as ordinary income (Code Sec. 341(a), prior to repeal by JGTRRA).

> **Comment:** The collapsible corporation rules apply only to gain, not loss, realized on a stock sale or distribution.

A corporation is collapsible if it is formed or availed of principally for (i) the manufacture, construction, or production of property, (ii) the purchase of inventory, property held for sale to customers, unrealized receivables and specified trade or business assets (Code Sec. 341 assets), or (iii) the holding of stock in another collapsible corporation, with a view to the sale or exchange of stock by its shareholders or a distribution to its shareholders before it has realized two-thirds of the taxable income to be derived from the property, and the realization of gain attributable to that property by the shareholders (Code Sec. 341(b)(1), prior to repeal by JGTRRA).

> **Comment:** Once a corporation reaches the requisite level of taxable income from the property, a subsequent sale or exchange of the stock by its shareholders or a subsequent distribution that would otherwise result in capital gain should be entitled to regular capital gain treatment. In addition, the collapsible corporation rules cannot be sidestepped by setting up a holding company that would hold the stock of a collapsible corporation since the definition specifically includes such holding companies.

> **Practical Note:** Although the law requires two-thirds of taxable income to be realized to avoid the collapsible corporation rules, courts have found that "substantiality" is the key focus. For example, in *J.B. Kelley* (CA-5, 61-2 USTC ¶9603, 293 F2d 904), "substantial part of the net income" referred to the portion of the net income that had been realized at the time stock was sold. One-third was a "substantial" portion of total net income, the corporation was determined not to be collapsible and the stockholders realized capital gain on the sale of their stock. Similarly, the IRS has ruled that a corporation, which has realized one-third of the taxable income to be derived from property manufactured, constructed, produced or purchased, is not on account of such manufacture, construction, production or purchase a collapsible corporation (Rev. Rul. 72-48, 1972-1 CB 102).

Production or purchase of property. For purposes of the collapsible corporation definition, a corporation is treated as having manufactured, constructed, produced or purchased property if it:

NEW LAW EXPLAINED

- engages in the manufacture, construction, or production of the property to any extent;
- holds property with a basis determined, in whole or in part, by reference to the cost of that property in the hands of a person who manufactured, constructed, produced or purchased the property; or
- holds property with a basis determined, in whole or in part, by reference to the cost of other property manufactured, constructed, produced or purchased by the corporation (Code Sec. 341(b)(2), prior to repeal by JGTRRA).

> **Comment:** Thus, it is not necessary for the corporation to start or complete the production of property. An engagement to any extent in the production process is enough to meet this test. The sweeping provision also coveres property acquired in a tax-free exchange, in which the basis of the acquired property is determined by reference to the basis of the transferred property. For example, property constructed by a person and transferred to a corporation in a Code Sec. 351 transfer will be deemed to have been constructed by the transferee corporation since the corporation's basis in that property is determined by reference to the basis of the property in the hands of the transferor under Code Sec. 362 (Reg. § 1.341-2(a)(5)).

Formed or availed with a view to stock sale or distribution. Under the collapsible corporation definition, a corporation must be formed or availed of for the manufacture, construction, production or purchase of certain property *with a view* to (i) the sale or exchange of the stock by its shareholders, or a distribution to them prior to the realization of two-thirds of the taxable income from the property, and (ii) the realization by the shareholders of gain attributable to that property (Code Sec. 341(b)(1), prior to repeal by JGTRRA). The Code Sec. 341 regulations provide that a corporation is formed or availed of with a view to these actions if the requisite view existed at any time during the property's manufacture, production, construction, or purchase. Thus, if the stock sale or distribution is attributable solely to circumstances arising after the manufacture, construction, production, or purchase of property (other than circumstances that reasonably could be anticipated at the time of the manufacture, construction, production, or purchase), the corporation will not be considered to have been formed or availed of with a view to collapse, absent compelling facts to the contrary (Reg. § 1.341-2(a)(3)).

> **Comment:** Referring to an identical provision in the regulations under the 1939 Code (Former Reg. § 39.117(m)-1(4)), the U.S. Court of Appeals for the Second Circuit found the narrow interpretation of the law in the regulations to be surprising (*A. Glickman*, CA-2, 58-2 USTC ¶ 9598). The court said that under the law, it was sufficient that the "view" existed when the corporation was "availed of," which could be at any time during its corporate life, rather than "during the manufacture, production, construction or purchase." However, it was not necessary for the court to pass upon the validity of the regulations since it held that the Tax Court had correctly found that the proscribed view had existed during "construction." The U.S. Supreme Court held in *B. Braunstein* (SCt, 63-2 USTC ¶ 9531), that gain from the sale of stock in a collapsible corporation is ordinary income even though the shareholders would have been entitled to capital gains

NEW LAW EXPLAINED

treatment if they had conducted the enterprise in their individual capacities without using a corporation. The Court found nothing to justify reading the additional requirement that the taxpayer must have been using the corporate form as a device to convert ordinary income into capital gain under the collapsible corporation provisions.

Practice Note: The courts have found various post-manufacture or post-purchase circumstances that qualify for the exception provided in the regulations, such as illness of an active shareholder, a shareholder's sudden need for funds to expand another business, dissent among the shareholders, and unanticipated changes in law or in the value of the property. If a shareholder is forced to sell his stock because of unforeseeable conditions beyond his control, there is no intent to collapse the corporation.

The requirement that a corporation be formed or availed of with a view to the stock sale or distribution is satisfied in the case where such an action was contemplated by the persons in a position to determine the policies of the corporation, such as the controlling or majority shareholders. The requirement is satisfied regardless of whether the action was contemplated unconditionally, conditionally, or as a recognized possibility. In addition, if the corporation was formed or availed of with a view to such actions, it is immaterial that a particular shareholder was not a shareholder at the time of the manufacture, construction, production, or purchase of the property, or if the shareholder did not share that view. The existence of a bona fide business reason for doing business in the corporate form does not, by itself, negate the fact that the corporation may also have been formed or availed of with a view to such actions (Reg. § 1.341-2(a)(2)).

Comment: The necessity for making a determination as to whether a corporation was formed or availed of with a view to the actions described above is obviated if a transaction comes within any of the Code Sec. 341(e) exceptions to the collapsible corporation rules, discussed below. If a transaction fails to qualify for these exceptions, the intent inquiries must be made.

Code Sec. 341 assets. For purposes of the collapsible corporation rules, Code Sec. 341 assets include:

- inventory property;

- property held primarily for sale to customers in the ordinary course of the corporation's business;

- unrealized receivables or fees (as defined below), except for receivables from sales of property that is not a Code Sec. 341 asset; and

- property described in Code Sec. 1231(b) to the extent it was not used in the manufacture, construction, production or sale of inventory or other property held for sale to customers (Code Sec. 341(b)(3), prior to repeal by JGTRRA).

The above property must be held for less than three years to be treated as a Code Sec. 341 asset. The Code Sec. 1223 rules generally apply in determining if the three-year holding period is satisfied. Thus, the time the assets were held by the transferor is taken into consideration. However, such a period will not be deemed to begin before

NEW LAW EXPLAINED

the completion of the manufacture, construction, production, or purchase of the property (Code Sec. 341(b)(3), prior to repeal by JGTRRA; Reg. § 1.341-2(b)).

For purposes of the Code Sec. 341 asset definition, unrealized receivables or fees include, to the extent not previously includible in income under the corporation's accounting method, any rights (contractual or otherwise) to payment for (i) goods delivered or to be delivered, to the extent the proceeds would be treated as received from the sale or exchange of a noncapital asset, or (ii) services rendered or to be rendered (Code Sec. 341(b)(4), prior to repeal by JGTRRA).

Presumption of collapsible corporation status. A corporation is presumed collapsible if, at the time of the stock sale or exchange or the distribution, the fair market value of its Code Sec. 341 assets is:

- 50 percent or more of the fair market value of its total assets, and
- 120 percent or more of the adjusted basis of the Code Sec. 341 assets (Code Sec. 341(c)(1), prior to repeal by JGTRRA).

In such a situation, it is up to the corporation to show that it is not collapsible. However, the fact that the value of the Code Sec. 341 assets is below these thresholds does not give rise to a presumption that the corporation is not a collapsible corporation. The total assets to be used for the percentage test in item (1), above, do not include cash, obligations that are capital assets of the corporation, short-term government obligations, or stock of another corporation (Code Sec. 341(c)(2), prior to repeal by JGTRRA).

> **Example 1:** On July 31, 2013, the XYZ corporation, which files its income tax returns on the accrual basis, owns assets with the following fair market values: cash ($175,000); note receivable held for investment ($130,000); stocks of other corporations ($545,000); rents receivable ($15,000); and a building constructed by the corporation in 2011 and held thereafter as rental property ($750,000). The adjusted basis of the building on that date is $600,000. The only debt outstanding is a $500,000 mortgage on the building. On July 31, 2013, the corporation liquidates and distributes all of its assets to its shareholders. In computing whether the fair market value of the Code Sec. 341 assets (which include only the building) is 50 percent or more of the fair market value of the total assets, the cash, note receivable, and stocks of other corporations are not taken into account in determining the value of the total assets. Thus, on the date of the distribution, the fair market value of the XYZ's total assets is $765,000 ($750,000 (building), plus $15,000 (rents receivable)). Therefore, the value of the building is 98 percent of the value of the total assets ($750,000 (value of building) / $765,000 (value of total assets)). The value of the building is also 125 percent of the adjusted basis of the building ($750,000 (value of building) / $600,000 (adjusted basis in building)). Accordingly, a presumption arises that XYZ is a collapsible corporation (Reg. § 1.341-3(b), Example).

Five-percent shareholder limitation. Capital gain treatment is disallowed under Code Sec. 341, prior to repeal by JGTRRA, only for gain realized by shareholders who owned

NEW LAW EXPLAINED

more than five percent of the value of the outstanding stock of the collapsible corporation at any time after the manufacture, construction or production of the property is begun, when the property is purchased, or at any time thereafter. Shareholders who owned stock that was considered as owned at such time by another shareholder who then owned more than five percent of the corporation's stock also fall under these rules (Code Sec. 341(d)(1), prior to repeal by JGTRRA). Thus, to avoid the collapsible treatment, a shareholder who sells stock or receives distribution must own directly or constructively five percent or less of the collapsible corporation's stock at such times.

> **Comment:** In determining stock ownership, treasury stock of the collapsible corporation is not treated as outstanding stock.

For purposes of applying the five-percent ownership test, a shareholder must take into account not only stock actually owned by the shareholder, but also stock that is constructively owned by the shareholder through the application of Code Sec. 544(a)(1), (2), (3), (5), and (6), which provide the rules for constructive stock ownership in the case of personal holding companies (Code Sec. 341(d), prior to repeal by JGTRRA). Thus, a shareholder of a collapsible corporation must apply the following constructive ownership rules to determine stock ownership:

- Stock owned, directly or indirectly, by or for a corporation, partnership, estate, or trust is considered as being owned proportionately by its shareholders, partners, or beneficiaries.

- An individual is considered as owning the stock owned, directly or indirectly, by or for his family, or by or for his partner. The family of an individual includes his brothers and sisters (whether by the whole or half blood), spouse, ancestors, lineal descendants, spouses of the individual's brothers and sisters (whether by the whole or half blood), and the spouses of the individual's lineal descendants.

- If any person has an option to acquire stock, the stock is considered as owned by that person. An option to acquire an option, and each one of a series of such options, is regarded as an option to acquire stock. Stock that an individual has an option to acquire from a partner or family member is considered as owned by the individual under the option rule and not under the partner or family attribution rule.

- Constructive ownership is treated as actual ownership but, if it results from the application of the family and partnership rule in item (2) above, it will not be considered as actual ownership in order to make another individual the constructive owner of such stock.

> **Comment:** The definition of "family" for purposes of the collapsible corporation rules is expanded to include spouses of the shareholder's brothers and sisters and the spouses of the shareholder's lineal descendants. The objective behind such broad rules of ownership is to forestall any attempt by the real owner of stock in a collapsible corporation to hide ownership by placing the stock in the names of close relatives.

70-percent gain limitation. Any gain recognized by a shareholder of a collapsible corporation on the sale or exchange of stock or a distribution escapes collapsible treatment unless more than 70 percent of the gain is attributable to collapsible

NEW LAW EXPLAINED

property described in Code Sec. 341(b)(1), prior to repeal by JGTRRA, (i.e., property for the manufacture, construction, production or purchase of which the corporation was formed or availed of with the view to a stock sale or a distribution before the corporation realizes two-third of the taxable income from such property) (Code Sec. 341(d)(2), prior to repeal by JGTRRA). For purposes of applying the 70-percent gain rule, inventory and property held primarily for sale to customers in the ordinary course of trade or business are treated as one item of property (Code Sec. 341(d), prior to repeal by JGTRRA).

> **Comment:** Even though a corporation is collapsible and a shareholder owns more than five percent of its stock, if the shareholder can prove that at least 30 percent of his gain in a tax year on a distribution from the corporation or on a sale or exchange of the shareholder's stock is not attributable to collapsible property, then no part of the gain is taxable as ordinary income and the entire gain qualifies for capital gain treatment. If more than 70 percent of the shareholder's gain is attributable to collapsible property, then all of the shareholder's gain is treated as ordinary income. Thus, if a collapsible corporation has two properties and has realized sufficient amount of income on one of the properties so that the property is not collapsible property, and 30 percent or more of the shareholder's gain is attributable to that noncollapsible property, then the entire gain escapes ordinary income treatment. However, a corporation cannot avoid collapsible status if it has property on which there is no adequate income realization even though it also holds other noncollapsible properties on which it has realized at least two-third of the taxable income from those properties.

> **Example 2:** On January 2, 2013, Smith forms the XYZ Corporation and contributes $1 million cash in exchange for all of the XYZ stock. XYZ invests $400,000 in one project for the purpose of building and selling residential houses. As of December 31, 2013, the residential houses in this project are all sold, resulting in a profit of $100,000 (after taxes). Simultaneously with the development of the first project and in connection with a second and separate project, XYZ invests $600,000 in land for the purpose of subdividing such land into lots suitable for sale as home sites and distributing such lots in liquidation before the realization by the corporation of a substantial part of the taxable income to be realized from this second project. As of December 31, 2013, XYZ has derived $60,000 in profits (after taxes) from the sale of some of the lots. On January 2, 2014, XYZ makes a distribution in complete liquidation to shareholder Smith who receives $560,000 in cash and notes and lots having a fair market value of $940,000.
>
> The gain recognized to Smith upon the liquidation is $500,000 ($1.5 million distribution, less $1 million basis in stock). The gain that would have been recognized to Smith if the second project had not been undertaken is $100,000 ($1.1 million distribution, less $1 million basis in stock). Therefore, the gain attributable to the second project, which is Code Sec. 341(b)(1) collapsible property, is $400,000 ($500,000 total gain, minus $100,000 gain attributable to the first project). Since this gain ($400,000) is more than 70 percent of the entire

NEW LAW EXPLAINED

> gain ($500,000) recognized to Smith on the liquidation ($350,000 = $500,000 x 70%), the entire gain recognized by Smith is subject to the collapsible treatment and converted into ordinary income (Reg. § 1.341-4(c)(4), Example).

Three-year limitation. Even if a corporation is collapsible, ordinary income treatment will not apply to any gain that would otherwise be capital gain if it is realized by a shareholder more than three years after the corporation has completed the manufacture, construction, production, or purchase of the collapsible property (Code Sec. 341(d)(3), prior to repeal by JGTRRA).

> **Planning Note:** On January 10, 2013, a taxpayer enters into an executory contract to sell his stock in a collapsible corporation. As of that date, the three-year limitation has not run. However, the sale of his stock will not be closed until July 2, 2013, at which time the three-year period will have run. Therefore, by waiting to close the sale the taxpayer would not be precluded from the application of the three-year limitation rule (Code Sec. 341(d)(3), prior to repeal by JGTRRA) (Rev. Rul. 67-100, 1967-1 CB 76).

> **Practical Note:** The 70-percent gain limitation, discussed above, operates independently of the three-year limitation. Thus, for example, any portion of the gain realized by a shareholders of a collapsible corporation that is attributable to a collapsible property the construction of which has been completed for more than three years is not subject to the collapsible treatment due to the three-year limitation, but it still remains gain attributable to a collapsible property for purposes of applying the 70-percent limitation (Rev. Rul. 65-184, 1965-2 CB 91).

Exception to collapsible treatment. An exception to the applicability of the collapsible corporation rules is provided by Code Sec. 341(e), prior to repeal by JGTRRA. A shareholder that comes within this exception will avoid application of the collapsible corporation provisions with respect to any sale or exchange of his or her stock even though the corporation is otherwise treated as collapsible.

> **Comment:** If this exception applies to any sale or exchange of stock by a shareholder, the corporation will not be treated as collapsible only with respect to that stock sale or exchange (i.e., the exception applies on a sale-by-sale and a shareholder-by-shareholder basis).

In general, the exception applies to avoid the collapsible corporation status and exempt a shareholder's gain on a sale or exchange of the shareholder's stock from ordinary income treatment if the net unrealized appreciation in certain ordinary income assets of the corporation, called "subsection (e) assets," does not exceed 15 percent of the net worth of the corporation (Code Sec. 341(e)(1), prior to repeal by JGTRRA).

The "net worth" of the corporation as of any day is the excess of (i) the fair market value of the corporation's assets at the close of such a day, plus the amount of any distribution in complete liquidation made on or before that day, over (ii) the corporation's liabilities at the close of such a day (Code Sec. 341(e)(7), prior to repeal by JGTRRA).

¶609

NEW LAW EXPLAINED

The subsection (e) assets of the corporation include:

- property not used in the trade or business if the corporation's gain on the sale of that property or, if such property is in the hands of a shareholder owning more than 20 percent of the corporation's stock, the shareholder's gain on the sale of the property would be taxed as ordinary income (generally, this includes property that is not a capital asset or a Code Sec. 1231(b) property);

- property used in the trade or business on which there is net unrealized depreciation;

- property used in the trade or business on which there is net unrealized appreciation if the gain on that property would be taxed as ordinary income if the property is in the hands of a more-than-20-percent shareholder; and

- a copyright, a literary, musical or artistic composition, a letter or memorandum, or similar property if it was created, in whole or in part, by the personal efforts of an individual owning more than five percent of the corporation's stock (Code Sec. 341(e)(5), prior to repeal by JGTRRA).

For purposes of the exception, net unrealized appreciation in the corporation's assets is generally the amount by which the unrealized appreciation in the assets in which there is such an appreciation exceeds the unrealized depreciation on the assets in which there is such a depreciation (Code Sec. 341(e)(6), prior to repeal by JGTRRA). For purposes of the "subsection (e) assets" definition, unrealized appreciation in any asset is the amount by which (i) the fair market value of the asset exceeds (ii) the adjusted basis in the asset used in determining gain from the sale or other disposition of the asset. Unrealized depreciation on any asset is the excess of the adjusted basis of the asset for determining gain from the asset's sale or other disposition, over the fair market value of the asset. If any portion of the gain on the sale of an asset would be taxed as ordinary income, the unrealized appreciation in the asset taken into account in applying these definitions will be equal to that portion.

If a shareholder owns five percent or less of the corporation's stock, the exception is applied by taking into account the net unrealized appreciation in the corporation's subsection (e) assets (Code Sec. 341(e)(1)(A), prior to repeal by JGTRRA). If a shareholder owns more than five percent of the corporation's stock, in applying the exception, the shareholder must take into account the net unrealized appreciation not only of the corporation's subsection (e) assets, but also the net unrealized appreciation in any other assets that would be subsection (e) assets under items (1) and (3), above, if the shareholder owned more than 20 percent of the corporation's stock (Code Sec. 341(e)(1)(B), prior to repeal by JGTRRA).

Different rules also apply for purposes of the exception if a shareholder owns more than 20 percent of the corporation's stock and owns (or owned at any time during the last three years) more than 20 percent of the stock of another corporation, more than 70 percent of the value of which assets are (or were during the time the shareholder held stock for the past three years) similar or related in service or use to assets of the corporation comprising more than 70 percent of the value of its total assets (Code Sec. 341(e)(1)(C), prior to repeal by JGTRRA). In this case, the exception is applied by taking into account, in addition to the net unrealized appreciation in the subsection

NEW LAW EXPLAINED

(e) assets, the net unrealized appreciation in assets that would be subsection (e) assets under items (1) and (3), above, if the determination whether the property in the hands of the shareholder would produce ordinary income gain if sold or exchanged is made by treating:

- any sale or exchange by the shareholder of stock in the other corporation within the preceding three years as a sale or exchange of his proportionate share of the assets of such other corporation, and

- any liquidating sale or exchange of property by such other corporation within such a three-year period as a sale or exchange by the shareholder of his proportionate share of the property sold or exchanged.

The exception does not apply in the case of a sale or exchange of the stock to the issuing corporation. Nor does it apply to a sale or exchange of stock by a shareholder who owns more than 20 percent of the corporation's stock to a person related to that shareholder (Code Sec. 341(e)(1), prior to repeal by JGTRRA). For this purpose, related person includes:

- in the case where the shareholder is an individual, the individual's spouse, ancestors, lineal descendants, and a corporation controlled by the individual; and

- in the case where the shareholder is a corporation, a corporation that controls, or is controlled by, the shareholder, and, if more than 50 percent of the shareholder's stock is owned by any person, a corporation more than 50 percent of which stock is owned by that same person (Code Sec. 341(e)(8), prior to repeal by JGTRRA).

In applying the related person definition, ownership of stock is determined under the rules of Code Sec. 267(c), except that the family of an individual includes only his spouse, ancestors, and lineal descendants. Control means ownership of at least 50 percent of a corporation's stock by vote or value.

In determining stock ownership for purposes of applying the exception, direct and constructive stock ownership is taken into account. Constructive ownership is determined under the same rules that apply for purposes of the Code Sec. 341(d) limitations on the collapsible corporation rules (discussed above) (Code Sec. 341(e)(10), prior to repeal by JGTRRA).

In determining what type of gain would be realized from the sale of an asset, Code Secs. 617(d)(1), 1245(a), 1250(a), 1252(a), 1254(a), and 1276(a) are inapplicable (Code Sec. 341(e)(12), prior to repeal by JGTRRA). These provisions treat gain from the disposition of certain depreciable property, to the extent of certain deductions previously taken for depreciation, as gain from the sale or exchange of property which is neither a capital asset nor property described in Code Sec. 1231. Code Secs. 1252(a), 1254(a), and 1276(a) deal with farmland expenditures, oil and gas interests, and disposition gain representing accrued market discount.

The fact that a corporation may not come within this exception does not mean that the corporation is a collapsible corporation. If the exception does not apply, a determination of a collapsible status has to be made as if the exception rules had not been enacted (Code Sec. 341(e)(11), prior to repeal by JGTRRA).

NEW LAW EXPLAINED

Collapsible treatment avoided by consent. The collapsible corporation provisions do not apply to the sale of stock in a corporation that consents to recognize gain on future disposition of certain assets (referred to as "subsection (f) assets") that the corporation owns, or has an option to acquire, on the date of the stock sale (Code Sec. 341(f), prior to repeal by JGTRRA). The consent applies to any sale of stock made within the six-month period beginning with the date on which the consent is filed (Code Sec. 341(f)(1), prior to repeal by JGTRRA). The consenting corporation must recognize any gain on the subsequent disposition of subsection (f) assets notwithstanding any other provision, but only to the extent that such gain is not recognized under any other provision (Code Sec. 341(f)(2), prior to repeal by JGTRRA).

> **Comment:** A consenting corporation does not become noncollapsible as a result of filing the consent. The consent simply provides relief for shareholders selling stock during the consent period (i.e., such shareholders enjoy capital gain treatment for such stock sales), but requires the corporation to recognize the collapsible gain after the shareholder sells his stock. The character of the gain recognized by the corporation on a subsequent sale of subsection (f) assets (capital or ordinary) will depend on the status of assets at the time of the disposition. Also, the consent relief does not apply to sales of stock by a shareholder to the issuing corporation.

A subsection (f) asset generally includes a noncapital asset that the corporation owns, or has an option to acquire, as of the date of the stock sale (Code Sec. 341(f)(4), prior to repeal by JGTRRA). Land or any interest in real property, other than a security interest, and unrealized receivables and fees, as defined in Code Sec. 341(b)(4), prior to repeal by JGTRRA, are also treated as noncapital assets for this purpose. In the case where such assets are being manufactured, constructed or produced at the time of the stock sale, any resulting property is also included the subsection (f) asset category. In the case of land or any real property interest, any improvements resulting from construction with respect to such property that commences within two years after the stock is sold are also included.

> **Compliance Note:** A corporation files consent on a statement signed by a duly authorized officer. The statement must state that the corporation consents to have the provisions of Code Sec. 341(f)(2), prior to repeal by, apply to any dispositions by it of its subsection (f) assets. The statement must also contain the names, addresses and employer identification numbers of any corporation, five percent or more in value of the stock of which is owned directly by the consenting corporation, and any other corporations related through a chain of stock ownership (Rev. Rul. 69-32, 1969-1 CB 100; Reg. § 1.341-7).

A shareholder selling stock of a consenting corporation within six months after the consent is filed should attach a copy of the consent to his income tax return for the tax year in which the sale is made. Each corporation that consents to the application of Code Sec. 341(f)(2), prior to repeal by JGTRRA, must maintain adequate records to permit specific identification of the consenting corporation's subsection (f) assets (Reg. § 1.341-7).

¶609

NEW LAW EXPLAINED

A consenting corporation does not have to take into account gain on the transfer of a subsection (f) asset to another corporation (other than a tax-exempt corporation) if the following conditions are met:

- the basis of such asset in the hands of the transferee corporation is determined by reference to its basis in the hands of the transferor by reason of the application of Code Sec. 332 (relating to tax-free liquidation of a controlled subsidiary), Code Sec. 351 (relating to transfers to a corporation controlled by the transferor), or Code Sec. 361 (relating to exchanges pursuant to certain reorganizations), and

- the transferee corporation agrees to have the provisions of Code Sec. 341(f)(2), prior to repeal by JGTRRA, apply to any disposition by it of such asset (Code Sec. 341(f)(3), prior to repeal by JGTRRA).

> **Compliance Note:** If a transferee in a reorganization or other tax-free transaction (a transaction where the transferee's basis of subsection (f) assets is determined by reference to the assets' basis in the hands of the transferor) consents to have Code Sec. 341(f)(2), prior to repeal by JGTRRA, apply, the amount of gain taxed to the transferor on the transaction is limited to the amount of gain recognized by it on the transfer. Rev. Rul. 69-33, 1969-1 CB 100, prescribes the following rules governing transferee agreements:
>
> - The transferee corporation's agreement should be filed before the subsection (f) assets are transferred.
>
> - The agreement should be filed and should be signed by any officer duly authorized to act for the transferee. If the transferee is in receivership or bankruptcy, the properly appointed fiduciary may sign the agreement.
>
> - The agreement should state that the transferee agrees to have the provisions of Code Sec. 341(f)(2), prior to repeal by JGTRRA, apply to any disposition by it of all subsection (f) assets received.
>
> - The agreement should identify the nature of the transaction in which the subsection (f) assets are acquired, including the names, addresses and taxpayer identification numbers of both transferor and transferee, and must include a schedule of the subsection (f) assets transferred.
>
> The transferor should, in addition, attach a copy of the transferee agreement to its tax return for the tax year in which the assets are transferred, and the transferee should maintain adequate records to permit specific identification of the transferred subsection (f) assets.

The relief does not apply to the sale of stock of a consenting corporation by a shareholder if, during the five-year period ending on the date of the sale, the shareholder (or any person related to the shareholder) sold stock of another consenting corporation within any six-month period beginning on a date on which a consent was filed by that other corporation (Code Sec. 341(f)(5), prior to repeal by JGTRRA). For this purpose, related person includes the shareholder's spouse, ancestors, lineal descendants and a corporation controlled by the shareholder (Code Sec. 341(e)(8)(A), prior to repeal by JGTRRA).

¶609

NEW LAW EXPLAINED

The consent provisions of Code Sec. 341(f) do not apply to foreign corporations, except as provided in regulations (Code Sec. 341(f)(8), prior to repeal by JGTRRA). Further, the exception from gain recognition in certain tax-free transactions under Code Sec. 341(f)(3), prior to repeal by JGTRRA, does not apply if the transferee is a foreign corporation.

A special rule applies in the case where the consenting corporation owns five percent or more of the outstanding stock of one or more other corporations. In such a case, the consent filed by the consenting corporation is not valid with respect to a sale of its stock during the applicable six-month period unless each of the other corporations, five percent or more of which stock is owned by the consenting corporation on the date of the sale, files a consent, within the six-month period ending on the date of such a sale, with respect to sales of its own stock. In the case of a chain of corporations connected by five-percent stock ownership, each corporation down the chain below the corporation whose stock is sold must also consent within the six-month period ending on the date the stock is sold (Code Sec. 341(f)(6), prior to repeal by JGTRRA).

> **Example 3:** The XYZ Corporation files a consent to the application of Code Sec. 341(f)(2), prior to repeal by JGTRRA, on January 1, 2013. Smith owns 100 percent of the outstanding stock of the consenting corporation on January 1, 2013, and sells five percent of the stock on January 2, 2013, ten percent on February 10, 2013, and one percent on May 1, 2013. No other sales of XYZ stock are made during the six-month period beginning on January 1, 2013. On that date, XYZ owns an apartment building and on March 1, 2013, XYZ purchases an office building. XYZ's subsection (f) assets include the apartment building owned on January 1 and the office building purchased on March 1.

> **Example 4:** Assume the same facts as in Example 3, above, except that on January 1, 2013, XYZ also owns a tract of raw land. On April 1, 2013, construction of a residential housing project is commenced on the tract of land. XYZ's subsection (f) assets will include the tract of land plus the resulting improvements to the land. This result would not be changed if construction of the residential housing project were not commenced until July 1, 2014, since the construction would have been commenced within two years after May 1, 2013.

> **Example 5:** ZYX Corporation files a consent to the application of Code Sec. 341(f)(2), prior to repeal by JGTRRA, on January 1, 2013. Smith owns 100 percent of the outstanding stock of the consenting corporation on January 1, 2013, and sells 10 percent of the stock on June 1, 2013. On April 1, 2013, ZYX acquires an option to purchase a motion picture when completed. On May 1, 2013, production is started on the motion picture. On February 1, 2015, production is completed, and ZYX exercises its option. ZYX holds the option and the

NEW LAW EXPLAINED

> motion picture for use in its trade or business. ZYX's subsection (f) assets initially include the option and ultimately include the motion picture. However, the exercise of the option is not a disposition of the option within the meaning of Code Sec. 341(f)(2), prior to repeal by JGTRRA.

Other provisions. Once the JGTRRA sunset takes effect in 2013, other provisions referencing the Code Sec. 341 collapsible corporation rules that were either amended or repealed by JGTRRA will also apply in tax years beginning after December 31, 2012. Thus, for purposes of Code Sec. 341(e)(12), prior to repeal by JGTRRA (see discussion of this rule, above), gain on the disposition of converted wetland or highly erodible cropland (Code Sec. 1257(d), prior to amendment by JGTRRA), certain government cost-sharing program payments for conservation purposes of Code Sec. 126 (Code Sec. 1255(b)(2), prior to amendment by JGTRRA), and deferred payments under Code Sec. 467 rental agreements (Code Sec. 467(c)(5)(C), prior to repeal by JGTRRA), will be treated as ordinary income in the same manner as amounts treated as ordinary income under Code Sec. 1245.

In addition, for purposes of determining whether Code Sec. 341, prior to repeal by JGTRRA, applies to a disposition within one year after the acquisition date of stock by a shareholder (other than the acquiring corporation) who held stock in the target corporation on the acquisition date, Code Sec. 341, prior to repeal by JGTRRA, will be applied without regard to Code Sec. 338 (Code Sec. 338(h)(14), prior to amendment by JGTRRA). Code Sec. 338 generally provides rules for a corporation electing to treat a stock purchase as an asset purchase.

Practical Analysis: Jasper L. Cummings, Jr., Alston & Bird LLP, Raleigh, N.C., observes that extension of the repeal of Code Sec. 341 by the 2010 Act will allow taxpayers to put off worrying about the pitfall of stumbling into this anachronistic rule. The pitfall is the conversion of capital gain into ordinary income. The rule is anachronistic because the transaction at which it was primarily aimed became economically undesirable as a result of the Tax Reform Act of 1986. That transaction depended for its success on (1) the existence of a large differential between the rates at which capital gains and ordinary income were taxed, and also (2) the ability of a corporation to liquidate and give its shareholders a stepped up basis in its assets without the corporation recognizing the appreciation in those assets (under what was called the *General Utilities* doctrine).

Example. Investors capitalized Newcorp with $2M, and Newcorp built 10 homes at a cost of $2M, which were worth $4M upon completion. Newcorp liquidated and did not recognize the $2M gain in its assets under pre-1986 law, and the shareholders reported $2M long-term capital gain, which was taxed at reduced rates, and took a $4M basis in the homes, sold them for $4M and paid no further tax. Thus, no taxpayer paid tax at ordinary income rates on the gain in the homes, which would have produced ordinary business income to Newcorp (or to Investors if they had built the homes in a partnership). Because

NEW LAW EXPLAINED

Newcorp was a collapsible corporation (*i.e.*, it was collapsed before it sold its inventory), Code Sec. 341 would require Investors to report the gain on their stock in the liquidation as $2M ordinary income. Obviously the repeal of the *General Utilities* doctrine in 1986 made this technique as described obsolete, because the corporation would pay tax at a rate near the Investors' ordinary income tax rate upon the gain the corporation was deemed to recognize. However, despite the repeal of the *General Utilities* doctrine, Investors' sale of the stock for close to $4M would still be advantageous if the gain were capital gain that was taxed at a lower rate. Such a sale is not usually possible because most buyers will not pay the value of the corporate assets for the stock of a corporation with built in gain. Nevertheless, Code Sec. 341 can apply to such stock sale gain, despite the reduced advantage to the Investors and Newcorp under current law (or even if there is no advantage).

Not only did the 1986 Act repeal the *General Utilities* doctrine (meaning that under Code Secs. 311 and 336 corporations now recognize gain in distributed property, just as if they had sold it to the shareholders for fair market value), but it eliminated the capital gains preference, which now has crept back into the Code. Thus, although the major precondition needed to plan into a collapsible corporation is gone (the *General Utilities* doctrine), a reduced penalty for falling into the collapsible corporation rule awaits a shareholder expecting to report a long-term capital gain, usually on selling the stock of the corporation that turns out to have been collapsible.

Therefore, the practice pointer for taxpayers is that after 2010 they need to refresh their ability to recognize the corporations to which Code Sec. 341 might be applied, despite the fact that no one actually intended to use a collapsible corporation the way it was originally used in planned tax reductions. In almost all cases the threat of Code Sec. 341 will come up on stock sales or redemptions that the taxpayer intends to report as producing long-term capital gains (because the Code section no longer can apply to liquidations of C corporations; in theory an S corporation can be collapsible, but that would be rare indeed). Such a selling shareholder should consider the possibility that the collapsible corporation rule might apply if (1) the corporation has built, constructed or manufactured property, whether real property, tangible personal property, including particularly films, or even intangible property such as goodwill, most of which it retains at the time of the stock sale; or (2) the corporation has bought inventory out of the ordinary course of business, most of which it retains at the time of the stock sale. Both of the foregoing situations may arise by virtue of shareholders building or buying such property and transferring it to a corporation under Code Sec. 351, and the construction or purchase occurred, or mostly occurred, within the last three years.

This description of problematic cases obviously could apply to a lot of new corporations and old corporations with substantial newly acquired and appreciated assets. Indeed it describes the type of investments venture capitalists like to make: in a business that will rapidly develop a valuable asset (patent, formula, etc.) and that they can sell quickly and recognize a capital gain. Therefore, recognizing the potential for Code Sec. 341 application will be important to a lot of investors.

Once recognized, however, there are several ways out, which is why the early detection of the collapsible corporation is the key. The most innocuous way out is a

NEW LAW EXPLAINED

Code Sec. 341(f) election that must be made by the corporation within six months before (not after) the stock sale. At very little cost to the corporation, it can restore the shareholder to capital gain status.

Practical Analysis: Paul C. Lau and Sandy Soltis, Blackman Kallick, Chicago, observe that under Code Sec. 341, a gain (otherwise taxable as capital gain) on a stock sale or liquidation of a collapsible corporation is treated as ordinary income. This provision was originally aimed to stop perceived abusive uses of the *General Utilities* doctrine that had been repealed in 1986. It was intended to prevent shareholders from collapsing (i.e., liquidating) a corporation holding ordinary income assets at capital gains rate. The shareholders would receive a basis step-up in the assets of the collapsible corporation at the cost of capital gains tax, while the corporation was not taxed at liquidation under the repealed *General Utilities* doctrine.

There has been no reported information that the IRS has taken enforcement action in this area in recent years. Presumably, this lack of enforcement action is attributable to the dubious and questionable role of Code Sec. 341.

The repeal of Code Sec. 341, which was scheduled to expire for tax years beginning after December 31, 2010 under the sunset provision of JGTRRA, was welcome news. During this holiday season, the extension of the repeal for two more years is wonderful news. Taxpayers will not need to worry and devote time and energy on the dubious application of Code Sec. 341 for at least two more years. It would be splendid news if the collapsible corporation rules are repealed permanently two years from now.

Practical Analysis: Mark R. Solomon, Walsh College, Troy, Michigan, notes that Code Sec. 341, providing for the ordinary income treatment of gain on the sale or liquidation of stock in a collapsible corporation, is a provision which has been inoperative since 2003, but which was scheduled under the sunset provisions of the Jobs and Growth Tax Relief Reconciliation Act of 2003 (JGTRRA) (P.L. 108-27) again to become effective for tax years beginning after December 31, 2010. Section 102 of the Tax Relief, Unemployment Insurance Reauthorization and Jobs Creation Act of 2010 (2010 Tax Relief Act) extends the period for which the collapsible corporation rules are suspended to December 31, 2012. Absent further legislation by Congress the collapsible corporation provisions will be reinstated as of January 1, 2013.

The scheduled reinstatement of the collapsible corporation provisions would be a significant departure from the idea of tax simplification and would be sure to generate significant work for tax practitioners (who will be required to ensure that their client's corporations will not fall under the ordinary income provisions of Code Sec. 341), all the while generating very little revenue for the federal government.

The collapsible corporations provisions are provisions designed to prevent taxpayers from achieving capital gains where a corporation with appreciated assets is sold or

NEW LAW EXPLAINED

liquidated (or distributed in a nonliquidating distribution) before the corporation realized at least two-thirds of the potential income from that property. Until the complete repeal of the General Utilities doctrine in the Tax Reform Act of 1986 (P.L. 99-514), taxpayers could sometimes construct property within a corporation, then liquidate the corporation without the corporation recognizing gain, or sell the stock of the corporation to a purchaser who could liquidate without the recognition of further gain. The original owner, absent application of the collapsible corporation rules, could then claim a capital gain on the disposition of the corporate stock. At one time this was particularly common in the real estate and movie production industries. However, with the repeal of the *General Utilities* doctrine, double taxation was virtually assured, and finally in 1993 Congress without comment in the legislative history repealed Code Sec. 341. Even with the scheduled reinstatement of Code Sec. 341 in 2013, there will be few opportunities to make affirmative use of collapsible corporations. Nevertheless, if section 341 is eventually reinstated, practitioners would be well-advised to stay attune to the collapsible corporation provisions, since they make it be possible for a tax disaster to occur. This would be the case if double taxation occurs, as is likely when using a C corporation, and the second tax, the tax at the shareholder level, is made ordinary income under Code Sec. 341, instead of capital gain. Most of the time this unfortunate outcome will be avoidable through the use of one of the numerous statutory exceptions to the application of Code Sec. 341, such as those provided in Code Secs. 341(e) or (f). However, because of the extreme complexity of those rules, more than ordinary care must be used in considering them.

It seems likely that the collapsible corporation provisions will eventually be permanently repealed (as they should be). However, given the political climate in Washington, which is unlikely to improve in 2012 (an election year), practitioners should remain alert for further developments in this unduly complex area.

▶ **Effective date.** The provision applies to tax years beginning after December 31, 2002 (Act Sec. 102(b) of the Tax Relief, Unemployment Insurance Reauthorization, and Job Creation Act of 2010 (P.L. 111-312); Act Sec. 302(f)(1) of the Jobs and Growth Tax Relief Reconciliation Act of 2003 (JGTRRA) (P.L. 108-27)). The provision shall not apply to tax years beginning after December 31, 2012 (Act Sec. 102(a) of the Tax Relief Act of 2010; Act Sec. 303 of JGTRRA). See ¶105 for a specific discussion of the sunset provision of JGTRRA and how it is applied.

Law source: Law at ¶5345, ¶5350, ¶5365, ¶5535, ¶5540, and ¶7015. Committee Report at ¶10,080.

— Act Sec. 102(a) of the Tax Relief, Unemployment Insurance Reauthorization, and Job Creation Act of 2010 (P.L. 111-312), amending Act. Sec. 303 of the Jobs and Growth Tax Relief Reconciliation Act of 2003 (JGTRRA) (P.L. 108-27);

— Act Sec. 102(b), providing the effective date.

Reporter references: For further information, consult the following CCH reporters.

— Standard Federal Tax Reporter, ¶16,312.01

— Tax Research Consultant, CCORP: 33,000, CCORP: 33,050 and CCORP: 33,100

— Practical Tax Explanation, §27,201

¶609

¶612 Alaska Native Settlement Trusts

SUMMARY OF NEW LAW

The provisions in Code Sec. 646 regarding the income tax treatment of an electing Alaska Settlement Trust and its beneficiaries will not apply to tax years beginning after December 31, 2012, pursuant to a two-year extension of the Economic Growth and Tax Relief Reconciliation Act of 2001 (EGTRRA) sunset. Also, for those years, reporting under Code Sec. 6039H is no longer required, nor is it available in lieu of the reporting requirements of Code Sec. 6034A.

BACKGROUND

The Economic Growth and Tax Relief Reconciliation Act of 2001 (EGTRRA) (P.L. 107-16) added Code Secs. 646 and 6039H, regarding the tax treatment of, and information with respect to, electing Alaska Native Settlement Trusts and sponsoring Native Corporations. Code Secs. 646 and 6039H apply to tax years ending after June 7, 2001 (the date of enactment of EGTRRA), and to contributions made to electing Settlement Trusts for such year or any subsequent year (Act Sec. 671(d) of P.L. 107-16).

The Alaska Native Claims Settlement Act (ANCSA) implemented the settlement of native Alaskans' aboriginal land claims by providing for the conveyance of certain lands and money (Alaska Native Fund, or "ANF") to Alaska Native Corporations ("ANCs") established by qualified Alaska natives as compensation (IRS Letter Ruling 200927022). The ANCSA allows the creation of Settlement Trusts by ANCs to "promote the health, education and welfare of its beneficiaries and preserve the heritage and culture of Natives" (43 U.S.C. § 1601 et seq.; 43 U.S.C. § 1629e). A Settlement Trust generally permits the separation of portfolio assets from the business assets of an ANC and allows these portfolio assets to be invested to provide income to Alaska Natives and their future generations free of business risks of the ANCs.

Pursuant to Code Secs. 646 and 6039H, as added by EGTRRA, a Settlement Trust may elect to have special rules apply to the trust and its beneficiaries with respect to the trust (Code Secs. 646 and 6039H). A "Settlement Trust" is defined as a trust that constitutes a settlement trust under section 3(t) of the Alaska Native Claims Settlement Act (43 U.S.C. § 1602(t)) (Code Sec. 646(h)(3)). In order to obtain tax treatment under the special rules, a Settlement Trust must make a one-time, irrevocable election under Code Sec. 646 on or before the due date (including extensions) for filing the trust's tax return for its first tax year ending after June 7, 2001. The election, made on Form 1041-N, applies to that tax year and all subsequent tax years (Code Sec. 646(c)).

If an election under Code Sec. 646 is in effect with respect to any Settlement Trust, the provisions of Code Sec. 646 apply in determining the income tax treatment of the Settlement Trust and its beneficiaries with respect to the Settlement Trust (Code Sec. 646(a)). An electing Settlement Trust pays tax on its income at the lowest rate

BACKGROUND

provided in Code Sec. 1(c) for ordinary income of an individual or corresponding capital gains rate (see ¶305 and ¶405) (Code Sec. 646(b)).

> **Comment:** The electing Settlement Trusts are taxed at the lowest tax rates because the majority of Alaska Natives are either taxed at the lowest rate or not taxed at all (Conference Committee Report to P.L. 107-16).

The Settlement Trust's taxable income is determined under Code Sec. 641(b) without regard to any deduction under Code Secs. 651 or 661 (Code Sec. 646(g)). Pursuant to Code Sec. 646(d), no amount is included in the gross income of a beneficiary by reason of contribution to the trust and the earnings and profits of the sponsoring ANC will not be reduced on account of any contribution to the Settlement Trust. However, the ANC earnings and profits would be reduced when distributions are made by the trust and taxed to beneficiaries. Amounts distributed by an electing Settlement Trust during a tax year have four characteristics in the hands of the recipient beneficiary:

(1) They are excludable from the gross income of the recipient beneficiary to the extent of the taxable income of the trust for the tax year for which an election is made, decreased by the income tax paid by the trust, plus any amounts excluded from gross income of the trust under Code Sec. 103;

(2) They are excludable from gross income to the extent of the amount described in (1) above for all tax years for which an election is in effect and not previously taken into account under (1) above.

(3) If distributions exceed the amounts described in (1) and (2) above, then excess distributions are reported and taxed to beneficiaries (as amounts described in Code Sec. 301(c)(1)), to the extent the ANC has current or accumulated earnings and profits. These distributed amounts are not treated as a corporate distribution subject to Code Sec. 311(b), and for purposes of determining the amount of a distribution and the basis to the recipients, Code Sec. 643(e) applies (and not Code Sec. 301(b) or (d));

(4) They are distributed by the trust in excess of the distributable net income of the trust for the tax year (Code Sec. 646(e)).

The special rules also contain a special loss disallowance rule (Code Sec. 646(i)) that reduces any loss that would otherwise be recognized by a shareholder upon the disposition of stock of a sponsoring ANC by a per share loss adjustment factor that reflects the aggregate of all contributions to an electing trust sponsored by an ANC made on or after the first day the trust is treated as an electing trust, expressed on a per share basis and determined as of the day of each contribution.

If in any tax year a beneficial interest in an electing Settlement Trust may be disposed of to a person in a manner which would not be permitted by section 7(h) of the ANCSA (43 U.S.C. §1606(h)) if the interest were Settlement Common Stock (defined in 43 U.S.C. §1602(p)), then the special provisions applicable to electing Settlement Trusts cease to apply as of the beginning of the tax year. The trust's distributable net income is increased up to the amount of current and accumulated earnings and profits of the sponsoring ANC as of the end of that year, but the increase will not exceed the fair market value of the trust assets as of the date the beneficial interests of

BACKGROUND

the trust became disposable. Thereafter, the trust and its beneficiaries are generally subject to the rules of subchapter J and to the generally applicable trust income tax rates. Likewise, if any stock of the ANC may be disposed of to a person in a manner that would not be permitted under ANCSA if the stock were Settlement Common Stock and the ANC makes a transfer to the trust. However, the surrender of an interest in an ANC or an electing Settlement Trust to accomplish the whole or partial redemption of the shareholder or beneficiary's interest in the ANC or trust, or to wholly or partially liquidate the ANC or trust, is deemed a permitted transfer under section 7(h) of the ANCSA (43 U.S.C. § 1606(h)) and will not result in the termination of Code Sec. 646 tax treatment.

A fiduciary of an electing Settlement Trust is required to provide the IRS with the trust tax return, the amount of distributions to each beneficiary, and the tax treatment to the beneficiary of distributions made either as exempt from tax or as a distribution deemed made by the ANC. Electing Settlement Trusts must complete Schedule K of Form 1041-N and file it with Form 1041-N. The electing trust is also required to furnish this information to the ANC and must provide a copy of Schedule K to the sponsoring ANC by the date Form 1041-N is required to be filed with the IRS. If the distribution is treated as made by the ANC, the ANC must report such amounts to the beneficiaries and indicate whether the distribution is a dividend or not, in accordance with the earnings and profits of the ANC. The Settlement Trust is not required to provide information to the beneficiaries on distributions made to them; the sponsoring ANC provides the beneficiaries with any required information (Code Sec. 6039H; Instructions for Form 1041-N (Rev. Dec. 2008)). This reporting requirement is in lieu of, and satisfies, the reporting requirements of Code Sec. 6034A (Code Sec. 6039H(b)).

Sunset provision. Under the sunset provision of EGTRRA, amendments made by the Act will not apply to tax years beginning after December 31, 2010 (Act Sec. 901 of P.L. 107-16).

NEW LAW EXPLAINED

Tax treatment and information requirements of Alaska Native Settlement Trusts extended.—The applicability of Code Secs. 646 and 6039H is extended for two years from December 31, 2010, to December 31, 2012 (Act Sec. 101(a)(1) of the Tax Relief, Unemployment Insurance Reauthorization, and Job Creation Act of 2010 (P.L. 111-312), amending Act Sec. 901 of the Economic Growth and Tax Relief Reconciliation Act of 2001 (EGTRRA) (P.L. 107-16). Thus, the special rules pursuant to Code Secs. 646 and 6039H will not apply to tax years beginning after December 31, 2012 (instead of December 31, 2010).

For tax years beginning after 2012, the provisions of Code Sec. 646 (regarding taxation of trust income, contributions to the trust, distributions to beneficiaries, transfer restrictions, and loss disallowance) will not apply in determining the income tax treatment of an electing Settlement Trust and its beneficiaries with respect to the trust. Also, reporting under Code Sec. 6039H will no longer require, nor will it be available in lieu

NEW LAW EXPLAINED

of, the reporting requirements of Code Sec. 6034A. Thus, beginning in 2013 Settlement Trust fiduciaries will have to comply with the applicable Code Sec. 6034A Form 1041, Schedule K-1, reporting requirements.

> **Comment:** The language in Code Sec. 646(c)(3)(A) that an election will apply to "all subsequent taxable years" is itself subject to the sunset, and therefore does not apply to tax years beginning after December 31, 2012.

Under the sunset provision, as amended, the Internal Revenue Code shall be applied and administered to tax years beginning after December 31, 2012, as if the provisions and amendments made by EGTRRA (including Code Secs. 646 and 6039H) had never been enacted (Act Sec. 101(a) of the Tax Relief Act of 2010; Act Sec. 901(b) of EGTRRA). According to the Conference Committee Report on EGTRRA, for the "post-sunset" tax years, the tax consequences of any Code Sec. 646 election previously made, and any right to make a future election, will be terminated, and any electing Settlement Trust then in existence, its beneficiaries, and the sponsoring ANC shall be taxed under the provisions of law in effect immediately prior to the enactment of Code Secs. 646 and 6039H (Conference Committee Report of EGTRRA).

> **Comment:** The loss disallowance rule in Code Sec. 646(i) also does not apply for tax years beginning after December 31, 2012.

Prior to the enactment of EGTRRA, the IRS indicated in several letter rulings that contributions to a Settlement Trust constituted distributions to the beneficiary-shareholders at the time of the contribution and were treated as dividends to the extent of earnings and profits as provided under Code Sec. 301 (IRS Letter Rulings 9824014; 9433021; 9329026 and 9326019). Also, a Settlement Trust and its beneficiaries were generally taxed subject to applicable trust rules (Code Sec. 641 et. seq.; Reg. § 301.7701-4).

> **Comment:** In these letter rulings, the IRS observed the congressional purpose expressed in the governing federal statute concerning Settlement Trusts, and ruled, under the facts and circumstances, that the Settlement Trust at issue was classified as a trust for federal tax purposes.

In addition, the IRS generally ruled that the corporations were not treated as owner of the trusts at issue under Code Secs. 671 through 678. Also, the IRS stated that, under ANCSA section 21(a), the shareholders' receipt of ANF proceeds is nontaxable. Accordingly, to the extent the corporation funded the trust with ANF proceeds, the deemed distribution reduced stock basis and, to the extent of the excess over basis, was treated as gain from the sale or exchange of property, in light of Code Sec. 301(c)(2) and (3). In IRS Letter Ruling 9326019, which involved an elder trust funded entirely from the corporation's earnings (with no trust funds coming from the original ANF payments made to the Native corporations under ANCSA), the IRS observed that neither the Internal Revenue Code, ANCSA, nor the amendments to ANCSA which authorized ANCs to create Settlement Trusts, specifically addressed the federal income tax treatment of a transfer of non-ANF funds or marketable securities to a Settlement Trust, and analyzed the transaction under generally applicable tax principles.

¶612

NEW LAW EXPLAINED

Several "pre-sunset" letter rulings issued after the enactment of EGTRRA provide an indication of how the IRS might address, for tax years beginning after December 31, 2012, a Settlement Trust which made a pre-sunset Code Sec. 646 election (see IRS Letter Rulings 200927022, 200835029, 200733013, 200329019, and 200329019). The IRS ruled, based on the current Code provisions at the time, that the sunset provision would not be treated as causing a taxable distribution from the corporation to the Settlement Trust or its beneficiaries, or to the corporation's shareholders, with respect to any contributions made by the corporation to the Settlement Trust during any years for which the Settlement Trust had a valid Code Sec. 646 election in effect. Further, the IRS generally ruled that the corporation would not be treated as the owner of any portion of the trust under current Code Secs. 673 through 678 for the tax years for which the election is not in effect, e.g., post sunset. Additionally, in several of the rulings, the IRS ruled that for tax years for which the trust does not have a Code Sec. 646(c) election in effect (e.g., after the sunset of Code Sec. 646), contributions by the corporation to the Settlement Trust will constitute constructive distributions to the shareholders (see IRS Letter Rulings 200927022 and 200835029).

> **Comment:** The legislative history explains that Code Sec. 646 was enacted out of a concern "that present law may inhibit many [Native Corporations] from establishing settlement trusts, due to the IRS present law treatment of a contribution by an [Alaska Native Corporation] to a trust as a dividend to the extent the [Native Corporation] has current or accumulated earnings and profits in the year of the contribution" (Senate Finance Committee, Technical Explanations of Provisions Approved by the Committee on May 15, 2001, at 148). Therefore, beneficiaries could be taxed on the Native Corporation's contributions to a settlement trust, even though they had received only an illiquid beneficial interest in a trust (Ruling Request As To Settlement Trusts Under ANCSA on behalf of Cook Inlet Region, Inc).

▶ **Effective date.** The provision applies to tax years ending after June 7, 2001, and to contributions made to electing Settlement Trusts for such year or any subsequent year (Act Sec. 101(a)(2) of the Tax Relief, Unemployment Insurance Reauthorization, and Job Creation Act of 2010 (P.L. 111-312); Act Sec. 671(d) of the Economic Growth and Tax Relief Reconciliation Act of 2001 (EGTRRA) (P.L. 107-16)). The provision shall not apply to tax years beginning after December 31, 2012 (Act Sec. 101(a)(1) of the Tax Relief Act of 2010; Act Sec. 901 of EGTRRA). See ¶105 for a specific discussion of the sunset provision of EGTRRA and how it is applied.

Law source: Law at ¶5410, ¶5775, and ¶7010. Committee Report at ¶10,070.

— Act Sec. 101(a)(1) of the Tax Relief, Unemployment Insurance Reauthorization, and Job Creation Act of 2010 (P.L. 111-312);

— Act Sec. 101(a)(2), providing the effective date.

Reporter references: For further information, consult the following CCH reporters.

— Standard Federal Tax Reporter, ¶24,359.01 and ¶24,359.06

— Tax Research Consultant, ESTTRST: 100

¶612

¶615 Tax Treatment of Payments to Controlling Exempt Organizations

SUMMARY OF NEW LAW

The application of special rules that permit the exclusion of certain qualifying payments by a controlled entity to a tax-exempt organization from that tax-exempt organization's unrelated business income is extended through December 31, 2011.

BACKGROUND

A tax-exempt organization is taxed on its unrelated business taxable income (UBTI), which is generally the organization's gross income from an unrelated trade or business, less the deductions related to that trade or business (Code Sec. 512). Among the items included in UBTI are specified payments that the organization receives or accrues from a controlled entity, to the extent they either reduce the controlled entity's net unrelated income or increase its net unrelated loss. Specified payments are interest, annuities, royalties or rents, but not dividends (Code Sec. 512(b)(13)(A) and (C)). For a controlled entity that is also tax-exempt, net unrelated income is the entity's UBTI. For a controlled entity that is taxable, net unrelated income is the portion of the entity's taxable income that would be UBTI if the entity were a tax-exempt organization with the same exempt purposes as the controlling organization. Net unrelated loss is determined under similar rules (Code Sec. 513(b)(13)(B)).

Two special rules apply to specified payments received or accrued after December 31, 2005, and before January 1, 2010 (Code Sec. 512(b)(13)(E)):

- Only the excess amount of qualifying specified payments are included in the controlling organization's UBTI.

  — A qualifying specified payment is one made in connection with a binding written contract that is in effect on August 17, 2006 (including a renewal of the contract under substantially similar terms).

  — A qualifying specified payment is excess to the extent it exceeds an amount that would meet the anti-abuse requirements of Code Sec. 482 (that is, to the extent it exceeds an amount that would be paid in an arm's-length transaction between unrelated parties).

- A valuation misstatement penalty applies to excess qualifying specified payments that are included in UBTI. Any federal income tax imposed on the controlling organization (including tax on UBTI) is increased by an amount equal to 20 percent of the excess payment, determined with (or, if larger, without) regard to return amendments or supplements.

NEW LAW EXPLAINED

Rules for payments to controlling exempt organizations extended.—The application of special rules that permit the exclusion of certain qualifying payments by a

NEW LAW EXPLAINED

controlled entity to a tax-exempt organization from that tax-exempt organization's unrelated business income is extended through December 31, 2011 (Code Sec. 512(b)(13)(E)(iv), as amended by the Tax Relief, Unemployment Insurance Reauthorization, and Job Creation Act of 2010 (P.L. 111-312)). Accordingly, payments of rent, royalties, annuities, or interest income by a controlled organization to a controlling organization pursuant to a binding written contract in effect on August 17, 2006 (or renewal of such a contract on substantially similar terms), may be includible in the unrelated business taxable income (UBTI) of the controlling organization only to the extent the payment exceeds the amount of the payment determined under the principles of Code Sec. 482 (i.e., at arm's length).

> **State Tax Consequences:** The extension of the special rules for interest, rents, royalties, and annuities received by an exempt entity from a controlled entity will not impact states like California that have specifically decoupled from the rules. Nor will it impact those states like New Jersey and Pennsylvania that do not tax the unrelated business income of exempt organizations. For those states that do incorporate the rules, whether the extension will be recognized depends on the state's Internal Revenue Code conformity date.

▶ **Effective date.** The extension of the special rules for excess qualifying specified payments is effective for payments received or accrued after December 31, 2009 (Act Sec. 747(b) of the Tax Relief, Unemployment Insurance Reauthorization, and Job Creation Act of 2010 (P.L. 111-312)).

Law source: Law at ¶5375. Committee Report at ¶10,520.

— Act Sec. 747(a) of the Tax Relief, Unemployment Insurance Reauthorization, and Job Creation Act of 2010 (P.L. 111-312), amending Code Sec. 512(b)(13)(E)(iv);

— Act Sec. 747(b), providing the effective date.

Reporter references: For further information, consult the following CCH reporters.

— Standard Federal Tax Reporter, ¶22,837.053

— Tax Research Consultant, EXEMPT: 15,304

— Practical Tax Explanation, §33,935.10

FOREIGN AND OTHER PROVISIONS

¶620 Look-Through Rule for FIRPTA Distributions

SUMMARY OF NEW LAW

The term "qualified investment entity" will continue to include regulated investment companies (RICs) that are U.S. real property holding companies (USRPHCs) through December 31, 2011.

BACKGROUND

Under the Foreign Investment in Real Property Tax Act (FIRPTA), as codified in Code Sec. 897, any gain realized by a nonresident alien or a foreign corporation from a disposition of a U.S. real property interest, including a disposition of an interest in a U.S. real property holding corporation (USRPHC), is treated as income effectively connected with the conduct of a U.S. trade or business. As a result, the foreign distributees are taxed on the net gain in the same manner as a U.S. citizen or domestic corporation and are required to report the gain on a U.S. tax return (Code Sec. 897(a)(1)).

A U.S. real property interest includes real property located in the U.S. or the Virgin Islands (Code Sec. 897(c)(1)(A)(i)) and any interest (e.g., stock) in a domestic corporation, unless the corporation was not a USRPHC during the five-year period ending on the date of disposition or, if shorter, during the period the taxpayer held the interest (Code Sec. 897(c)(1)(A)(ii)). A corporation is a USRPHC if the fair market value (FMV) of all of its U.S. real property interests equals or exceeds 50 percent of the total FMV of its real property interests within and outside the U.S. and any other assets used or held for use in a trade or business (Code Sec. 897(c)(2)). However, if any class of stock of a corporation is regularly traded on an established securities market, such class of stock is not treated as a U.S. real property interest in the case of a person who owns five percent or less of such class of stock during the five-year period ending on the date of disposition of the interest or during the period the taxpayer held the interest, if shorter (Code Sec. 897(c)(3)).

Look-through rule. Special rules apply to interests in qualified investment entities. A qualified investment entity includes any real estate investment trust (REIT), and any regulated investment company (RIC) (mutual fund) that is a USRPHC or would be a USRPHC if the exceptions for regularly traded stock (Code Sec. 897(c)(3)) and domestically controlled entities (Code Sec. 897(h)(2)) did not apply to the mutual fund's interest in any REIT or other mutual fund (Code Sec. 897(h)(4)(A)(i)).

Generally, under the look-through rule, any distribution by a qualified investment entity to a nonresident alien individual, a foreign corporation, or other qualified investment entity that is attributable to gain from a sale or exchange of a U.S. real property interest by the qualified investment entity is treated as gain recognized by the nonresident alien individual, foreign corporation, or other qualified investment entity from the sale or exchange of a U.S. real property interest (Code Sec. 897(h)(1) and (h)(4)(A)(i)(II)). The distributions are, therefore, subject to income taxation as effectively connected income under Code Secs. 897(a)(1) and 882(a)(1). The look-through rule does not apply to distributions involving regularly traded stock or entities that are domestically controlled.

Regularly traded stock exception. The look-through rule does not apply to distributions from a REIT or from a mutual fund that is a USRPHC to a nonresident alien individual or a foreign corporation based on any class of their stock that is regularly traded on an established securities market as long as the distributee did not own more than five percent of such class of stock during the one-year period ending on the date of distribution (Code Sec. 897(h)(1)). These distributions are recharacterized as dividends and are subject to the 30 percent withholding rate or a lower treaty rate, if applicable (Code Secs. 852(b)(3)(E) and 871(k)(2)(E)).

¶620

BACKGROUND

Domestically controlled entity exception. If less than 50 percent in value of the stock of a mutual fund or REIT is held directly or indirectly by foreign persons at all times during the shorter of:

- the period beginning on June 19, 1980, and ending on the date of the disposition or distribution,

- the five-year period ending on the date of the disposition or distribution, or

- the period during which the qualified investment entity was in existence (Code Sec. 897(h)(4)(D)),

then an interest in the mutual fund or REIT is not treated as a U.S. real property interest because the mutual fund or REIT is domestically controlled (Code Sec. 897(h)(4)(B) and (h)(2)).

Wash sale transactions. A nonresident alien, foreign corporation, or qualified investment entity that disposes of an interest in a domestically controlled qualified investment entity within 30 days prior to a distribution of FIRPTA income by that entity and acquires a substantially identical interest in the entity within a 61-day period, must pay FIRPTA tax on an amount equal to the amount of the distribution that was not taxed because of the disposition (Code Sec. 897(h)(5)(A)).

Withholding on qualified investment entity distributions. A REIT or mutual fund that is a USRPHC is required to withhold 35 percent from any distribution to a nonresident alien individual or a foreign corporation that is treated as gain realized from the sale or exchange of a U.S. real property interest (Code Sec. 1445(e)(6)). The withholding percentage may be reduced to 15 percent by regulations (20 percent in tax years beginning after 2010).

Modification of RIC termination date. A mutual fund that is a USRPHC is no longer treated as a qualified investment entity after December 31, 2009, except with respect to distributions it makes to a nonresident alien or foreign corporation that is attributable to a distribution the mutual fund that is a USRPHC received from a REIT, whether before or after December 31, 2009, for purposes of applying the look-through, wash sale and general withholding rules (Code Sec. 897(h)(4)(A)(ii)).

NEW LAW EXPLAINED

Qualified investment entity definition includes RICs through 2011.—The term "qualified investment entity," as used in Code Sec. 897, continues to include regulated investment companies (RICs) (mutual funds) that are U.S. real property holding companies (USRPHCs) through December 31, 2011, for all situations in which the inclusion would otherwise expire at the end of 2009 (Code Sec. 897(h)(4)(A)(ii), as amended by the Tax Relief, Unemployment Insurance Reauthorization, and Job Creation Act of 2010 (P.L. 111-312)).

> **Comment:** For purposes of applying the look-through, wash sale and general withholding rules, a mutual fund that is a USRPHC will continue to be treated as a qualified investment entity even after 2011 with respect to any distribution

¶620

NEW LAW EXPLAINED

it makes to a nonresident alien individual or a foreign corporation attributable to a distribution it received from a REIT.

The extension is effective on January 1, 2010, and any distributions made after December 17, 2010, the date of enactment, are subject to withholding. However, the withholding requirement under Code Sec. 1445 does not apply to any payments made during 2010 prior to December 17, 2010 (Act Sec. 749(b)(1) of the Tax Relief Act of 2010). Any investment company that makes a distribution during 2010 before December 17, 2010, that would have been subject to the withholding requirements if not for the exception applicable to 2010 distributions before December 17, 2010, is not liable to any distributee for any amounts it does actually withhold and pay to the Treasury (Act Sec. 749(b)(2) of the Tax Relief Act of 2010).

▶ **Effective date.** The provision is generally effective on January 1, 2010 (Act Sec. 749(b)(1) of the Tax Relief, Unemployment Insurance Reauthorization, and Job Creation Act of 2010 (P.L. 111-312)).

Law source: Law at ¶5470. Committee Report at ¶10,540.

— Act Sec. 749(a) of the Tax Relief, Unemployment Insurance Reauthorization, and Job Creation Act of 2010 (P.L. 111-312), amending Code Sec. 897(h)(4)(A)(ii);

— Act Sec. 749(b), providing the effective date.

Reporter references: For further information, consult the following CCH reporters.

— Standard Federal Tax Reporter, ¶27,711.033

— Tax Research Consultant, INTLIN: 6,068

— Practical Tax Explanation, § 19,205.30

¶623 Subpart F Exceptions for Active Financing Income

SUMMARY OF NEW LAW

The exceptions from subpart F income for so-called active financing income have been extended for two years, through 2011.

BACKGROUND

Under the subpart F rules, certain income earned by a controlled foreign corporation (CFC) may be currently taxed to U.S. shareholders, even though the earnings are not distributed to the shareholders (Code Secs. 951-965). For this purpose, a CFC is a foreign corporation with more than 50 percent of its stock owned (by vote or value) by 10-percent U.S. shareholders (Code Sec. 957). A U.S. shareholder is a shareholder that owns at least 10 percent of the voting stock of a foreign corporation (Code Sec. 951(b)).

¶623

BACKGROUND

A CFC's subpart F income that is currently taxed to its U.S. shareholders is made up of the following three categories of income: (1) insurance income (Code Sec. 953); (2) foreign base company income (Code Sec. 954); and (3) income related to international boycotts and other violations of public policy (Code Sec. 952(a)(3)-(5)).

Foreign base company income is made up of several categories of income, including foreign base company services income and foreign personal holding company income (FPHCI). Foreign base company services income is income from the performance of services outside of the CFC's home country, for, or on behalf of, a related person (Code Sec. 954(e)). FPHCI is generally passive type income, such as dividend, interest, rent and royalty income (Code Sec. 954(c)). FPHCI also includes the excess of gains over losses on the sale of non-inventory property (Code Sec. 954(c)(1)(B)). A regular dealer exception applies to gains from this type of property, if the gain is derived from a transaction entered into in the ordinary course of a dealer's trade or business, including a bona fide hedging transaction. However, dealers must treat interest, dividends, and equivalent amounts as FPHCI (Code Sec. 954(c)(2)(C)).

Temporary exceptions from subpart F income for active financing income. Income derived in the active conduct of a banking, finance or similar business, or in an insurance business (see ¶626) (so-called active financing income) is temporarily excepted from subpart F income. The temporary exceptions apply to tax years of a foreign corporation beginning after December 31, 1998, and before January 1, 2010, and to tax years of U.S. shareholders with or within which any such tax year of the foreign corporation ends (Code Sec. 954(h)(9)).

Under the exceptions, FPHCI does not include the active financing income of a CFC or its qualified business unit (QBU) (as defined under Code Sec. 989(a)). For the exception to apply, the CFC must be predominately engaged in the active conduct of a banking, financing or similar business and must conduct substantial activity with respect to that business. Further, the income must be earned by the CFC or its qualified business unit (QBU) in the active conduct of the business (Code Sec. 954(h)(2) and (3)). Only income earned in transactions with customers located outside of the United States where substantially all of the activities of the transaction are conducted in the corporation's or QBU's home country (i.e., where the CFC is created or organized or where the QBU has its principal office) is excepted. For cross-border transactions, the corporation or QBU must conduct substantial activities with respect to the business in the home country. The income must also be treated as earned by the corporation or QBU in its home country (Code Sec. 954(h)(3) and (5)(B)).

FPHCI also does not temporarily include income with respect to a securities dealer's interest, dividends and equivalent amounts from transactions, including hedging transactions, entered into in the ordinary course of the dealer's trade or business as a securities dealer. The income must be attributable to the dealer's activities in the country where the dealer is created or organized (or where the QBU of the dealer has its principal office and conducts substantial business activity) (Code Sec. 954(c)(2)(C)(ii)).

Finally, income that falls within the following temporary exceptions is not considered foreign base company services income (Code Sec. 954(e)(2)):

BACKGROUND

- the temporary exception from subpart F insurance income under Code Sec. 953(e);
- the temporary exception from FPHCI for insurance investment income under Code Sec. 954(i);
- the temporary exception from FPHCI for securities dealers under Code Sec. 954(c)(2)(C)(ii); and
- the temporary exception from FPHCI for income derived in the active conduct of a banking, financing or similar business.

NEW LAW EXPLAINED

Temporary exceptions from subpart F active financing income extended two years.—The exceptions from subpart F income for so-called active financing income, are extended for two years, through 2011 (Code Sec. 954(h)(9), as amended by the Tax Relief, Unemployment Insurance Reauthorization, and Job Creation Act of 2010 (P.L. 111-312)). The extension applies to the temporary exceptions from foreign personal holding company income for income derived in the active conduct of a banking, financing or similar business under Code Sec. 954(h), and income derived in the ordinary course of a security dealer's trade or business under Code Sec. 954(c)(2)(C)(ii). The extension also applies to the temporary exception from foreign base company services income for income that falls within the other temporary exceptions for active financing income (Code Sec. 954(e)(2)).

> **Comment:** Prior to the Tax Reform Act of 1986 (P.L. 99-514), exceptions from subpart F were provided for income earned in the active conduct of a banking, financing or similar business, or from certain investments made by insurance companies. The exceptions were eliminated and the income was subject to tax on a current basis under the general subpart F rules. Since 1997, Congress has enacted seven temporary exceptions from the subpart F rules.

The temporary exceptions apply to tax years of foreign corporations beginning after December 31, 1998, and before January 1, 2012, and to tax years of U.S. shareholders with or within which any such tax year of the foreign corporation ends.

> **Comment:** See ¶626 for a discussion of the extension of the temporary exceptions from subpart F insurance income under Code Sec. 953(e) and from foreign personal holding company income for insurance investment income under Code Sec. 954(i).

▶ **Effective date.** The amendments made by this provision apply to tax years of foreign corporations beginning after December 31, 2009, and to tax years of U.S. shareholders with or within which any such tax year of such foreign corporation ends (Act Sec. 750(c) of the Tax Relief, Unemployment Insurance Reauthorization, and Job Creation Act of 2010 (P.L. 111-312)).

Law source: Law at ¶5485. Committee Report at ¶10,550.

— Act Sec. 750(a) of the Tax Relief, Unemployment Insurance Reauthorization, and Job Creation Act of 2010 (P.L. 111-312), amending Code Sec. 954(h)(9);

— Act Sec. 750(c), providing the effective date.

¶623

NEW LAW EXPLAINED

Reporter references: For further information, consult the following CCH reporters.

— Standard Federal Tax Reporter, ¶28,543.0662

— Tax Research Consultant, INTLOUT: 9,106, INTLOUT: 9,106.30 and INTLOUT: 9,110

¶626 Subpart F Exceptions for Insurance Income

SUMMARY OF NEW LAW

The temporary exceptions from subpart F income for certain insurance and insurance investment income are extended for two years, through 2011.

BACKGROUND

Under the subpart F rules, certain income earned by a controlled foreign corporation (CFC) may be currently taxed to U.S. shareholders, even though the earnings are not distributed to the shareholders (Code Secs. 951-965). For this purpose, a CFC is a foreign corporation with more than 50 percent of its stock owned (by vote or value) by 10-percent U.S. shareholders (Code Sec. 957). A U.S. shareholder is a shareholder that owns at least 10 percent of the voting stock of a foreign corporation (Code Sec. 951(b)).

A CFC's subpart F income that is currently taxed to its U.S. shareholders is made up of the following three categories of income: (1) insurance income (Code Sec. 953); (2) foreign base company income (Code Sec. 954); and (3) income related to international boycotts and other violations of public policy (Code Sec. 952(a)(3)-(5)).

A CFC's subpart F insurance income is the corporation's income that is attributable to issuing or reinsuring an insurance or annuity contract. The income must be the type of income that would be taxed (with some modifications) under the rules of subchapter L, if the income were earned by a U.S. insurance company (Code Sec. 953(a)).

Foreign base company income is made up of several categories of income, one of which is foreign personal holding company income (FPHCI). FPHCI is generally passive type income, such as dividend, interest, rent and royalty income (Code Sec. 954(c)).

Temporary exception for insurance income. Under a temporary exception, the "exempt insurance income" of a qualifying insurance company or a qualifying insurance company branch is not considered subpart F income. In general, exempt insurance income is income from an insurance or annuity contract issued or reinsured by a qualifying insurance company or a qualifying insurance company branch in connection with risks located outside of the United States (Code Sec. 953(a) and (e)). However, the qualifying insurance company or branch must separately meet a minimum home country requirement—more than 30 percent of net premiums on exempt contracts must cover home country risks with respect to unrelated persons. Additionally, exempt income will not include income from covering home country

BACKGROUND

risks if, as a result of an arrangement, another company receives a substantially equal amount of consideration for covering non-home country risks.

If risks from both the home country and non-home country are covered under the contract, the income is not exempt unless the qualifying insurance company or branch conduct substantial activities in its home country with respect to the insurance business. Additionally, substantially all of the activities necessary to give rise to the contract must be performed in the home country (Code Sec. 953(e)(2)(C)).

The definition of a "qualifying insurance company" is intended to make sure that the exception applies to income from active insurance operations. Thus, a qualifying insurance company is a CFC that meets the following requirements (Code Sec. 953(e)(3) and (6)):

- it is regulated in its home country (i.e., country where the CFC is created or organized) as an insurance or reinsurance company and is allowed by the applicable insurance regulatory body to sell insurance, reinsurance or annuity contracts to unrelated persons;

- more than 50 percent of the aggregate net written premiums on the contracts of the CFC and each qualifying insurance company branch are from covering home country risks with respect to unrelated persons; and

- the CFC is engaged in the insurance business and would be taxed under subchapter L, if it were a U.S. company.

A "qualifying insurance company branch" is, in general, a separate and clearly identified qualified business unit of the CFC (under Code Sec. 989) that is a qualifying insurance company. The branch must maintain its own books and records, and must be allowed to sell insurance by the applicable insurance regulatory body in its home country (i.e., the country where the unit has its principal office) (Code Sec. 953(e)(4)).

Temporary exception for insurance investment income. Under a temporary exception, subpart F FPHCI does not include qualified insurance income of a qualifying insurance company (Code Sec. 954(i)).

Qualified insurance income is income received from an unrelated person derived from the investments made by the qualifying insurance company or qualifying insurance company branch of its reserves that are allocable to exempt contracts; or 80 percent of its unearned premiums from exempt contracts (Code Sec. 954(i)(2)(A)). Qualified insurance incomes may also include income received from an unrelated party and derived from investments made of the qualified insurance company's assets allocable to exempt contracts in an amount equal to: one-third of the premiums earned during the tax year on the property, casualty or health insurance contracts; and 10 percent of the loss reserves for life insurance or annuity contracts (Code Sec. 954(i)(2)(B)).

An exempt contract is defined the same way for both the subpart F insurance company exception, see above, and this exception. Thus, the amounts invested are allocable to the insuring or reinsuring of risks in the home country and other risks outside of the United States, if certain requirements are met (Code Sec. 954(i)(6)).

BACKGROUND

Application of temporary exceptions. The temporary exceptions from subpart F for insurance income apply to tax years of a foreign corporation beginning after December 31, 1998, and before January 1, 2010, and to tax years of U.S. shareholders with and within which such tax years of foreign corporations end (Code Sec. 953(e)(10)).

NEW LAW EXPLAINED

Temporary exceptions from subpart F income for insurance income extended two years.—The temporary exception from subpart F insurance income for "exempt insurance income" of a qualifying insurance company or a qualifying insurance company branch is extended for two years, through 2011 (Code Sec. 953(e)(10), as amended by the Tax Relief, Unemployment Insurance Reauthorization, and Job Creation Act of 2010 (P.L. 111-312)). The temporary exception from foreign personal holding company income for "qualified insurance income" of a qualifying insurance company or a qualifying insurance company branch is also extended for two years, through 2011 (Code Sec. 953(e)(10), as amended by the Tax Relief Act of 2010). The temporary exceptions apply to tax years of a foreign corporation beginning after December 31, 1998, and before January 1, 2012, and to tax years of U.S. shareholders with or within which any such tax years of the foreign corporation ends.

For tax years beyond the extension, Code Sec. 953(a), which defines subpart F insurance income, is applied as if the tax year of the foreign corporation began in 1998 (Code Sec. 953(e)(10), as amended by the Tax Relief Act of 2010). Consequently, only income attributable to insuring or reinsuring home country risks is excluded from subpart F insurance income. However, that income from issuing home country risks could be subpart F income if, as a result of an arrangement, another corporation receives a substantially equal amount for insuring non-home country risks (Code Sec. 953(a), prior to amendment by the Tax and Trade Relief Extension Act of 1998 (P.L. 105-277)).

> **Comment:** Prior to the Tax Reform Act of 1986 (P.L. 99-514), exceptions from subpart F were provided for income earned in the active conduct of a banking, financing or similar business, or from certain investments made by insurance companies. The exceptions were eliminated and the income was subject to tax on a current basis under the general subpart F rules. Since 1997, Congress has enacted seven temporary exceptions from the subpart F rules.

▶ **Effective date.** The amendments made by this provision apply to tax years of foreign corporations beginning after December 31, 2009, and to tax years of U.S. shareholders with or within which any such tax year of such foreign corporation ends (Act Sec. 750(c) of the Tax Relief, Unemployment Insurance Reauthorization, and Job Creation Act of 2010 (P.L. 111-312)).

Law source: Law at ¶5480. Committee Report at ¶10,550.

— Act Sec. 750(a) and (b) of the Tax Relief, Unemployment Insurance Reauthorization, and Job Creation Act of 2010 (P.L. 111-312), amending Code Sec. 953(e)(10);

— Act Sec. 750(c), providing the effective date.

NEW LAW EXPLAINED

Reporter references: For further information, consult the following CCH reporters.

— Standard Federal Tax Reporter, ¶28,518.066

— Tax Research Consultant, INTLOUT: 9,102, INTLOUT: 9,102.05 and INTLOUT: 9,106.30

¶629 Look-Through Rule for Related Controlled Foreign Corporation Payments

SUMMARY OF NEW LAW

Look-through treatment for related controlled foreign corporation payments is extended for two years, through 2011.

BACKGROUND

Under the subpart F rules, certain income earned by a controlled foreign corporation (CFC) may be currently taxed to U.S. shareholders, even though the earnings are not distributed to the shareholders (Code Secs. 951-965). For this purpose, a CFC is a foreign corporation with at least 50 percent of its stock owned (by vote or value) by 10-percent U.S. shareholders (Code Sec. 957). A U.S. shareholder is a shareholder that owns at least 10 percent of the voting stock of a foreign corporation (Code Sec. 951(b)).

One of the main categories of subpart F income is foreign base company income. Foreign base company income is made up of several subcategories of income, one of which is foreign personal holding company income (FPHCI). FPHCI generally includes dividends, interest, rents, royalties and annuities.

Amounts may be excluded from FPHCI and, therefore, escape current taxation under a look-through rule that applies to dividend, interest, rent and royalty payments received by a CFC from a related CFC (Code Sec. 954(c)(6)). To be eligible for the look-through rule, the payment must not be attributable to either subpart F income or income that is effectively connected to a U.S. trade or business. The look-though rule will not apply to the extent that an interest, rent or royalty payment either creates or increases a deficit under Code Sec. 952(c) that reduces subpart F income of either the payor or another CFC (Code Sec. 954(c)(6)(B)).

Prior to the addition of the look-through exception, an exception from FPHCI applied for payments received from a related corporation only where a same-country requirement was met. Under the same-country exception, in the case of dividends and interest, the related corporation must be created or organized under the law of the same country where the CFC was created or organized. In the case of rents and royalties, the exception applies only where property is used in the same country where the CFC is created or organized (Code Sec. 954(c)(3)).

BACKGROUND

The look-through exception applies to tax years of a foreign corporation beginning after December 31, 2005, and before January 1, 2010, and to tax years of U.S. shareholders with or within which such tax years of foreign corporations end (Code Sec. 954(c)(6)(C)).

NEW LAW EXPLAINED

Look-through treatment for related CFCs extended for two years.—The look-through rule that applies to dividend, interest, rent and royalty payments received by a controlled foreign corporation from a related corporation is extended for two years. The look-through rule applies to tax years of a foreign corporation beginning after December 31, 2005, and before January 1, 2012, and to tax years of U.S. shareholders with or within which any such tax year of such foreign corporation ends (Code Sec. 954(c)(6)(C), as amended by the Tax Relief, Unemployment Insurance Reauthorization, and Job Creation Act of 2010 (P.L. 111-312)).

> **Comment:** The application of the look-through rule was previously extended by the Emergency Economic Stabilization Act of 2008 (P.L. 110-343), to tax years beginning before January 1, 2010, and to tax years of U.S. shareholders with or within which such tax years of foreign corporations end.

▶ **Effective date.** The provision applies to tax years of foreign corporations beginning after December 31, 2009, and to tax years of U.S. shareholders with or within which any such tax year of such foreign corporation ends (Act Sec. 751(b) of the Tax Relief, Unemployment Insurance Reauthorization, and Job Creation Act of 2010 (P.L. 111-312)).

Law source: Law at ¶5485. Committee Report at ¶10,560.

— Act Sec. 751(a) of the Tax Relief, Unemployment Insurance Reauthorization, and Job Creation Act of 2010 (P.L. 111-312), amending Code Sec. 954(c)(6)(C);

— Act Sec. 751(b), providing the effective date.

Reporter references: For further information, consult the following CCH reporters.

— Standard Federal Tax Reporter, ¶28,543.0252

— Tax Research Consultant, INTLOUT: 9,106.105

¶632 Code Sec. 199 Deduction for Production Activities in Puerto Rico

SUMMARY OF NEW LAW

The special rule that allows Puerto Rico to be considered part of the United States in determining domestic production gross receipts (DPGR) under Code Sec. 199 is extended for two more years or for the first six tax years beginning after December 13, 2005, and before January 1, 2012.

BACKGROUND

A deduction may be claimed equal to an applicable percentage of the lesser of a taxpayer's qualified production activities income (QPAI) or taxable income (adjusted gross income in the case of an individual, estate or trust) (Code Sec. 199). The applicable percentage is nine percent for tax years beginning after 2009.

A taxpayer's QPAI is its DPGR attributable to the actual conduct of a trade or business by the taxpayer during the tax year, less the costs of goods sold, and other expenses, losses, or deductions properly allocable to those receipts. DPGR is the gross receipts of the taxpayer derived from:

- the lease, license, sale, exchange or other disposition of any:

  — qualifying production property (i.e., tangible personal property) manufactured, produced, grown or extracted (MPGE) by the taxpayer in whole or in significant part within the United States;

  — qualified film produced by the taxpayer within the United States; or

  — electricity, natural gas, or potable water produced by the taxpayer in the United States;

- the construction of real property that is performed by the taxpayer in the United States in the ordinary course of a taxpayer's construction trade or business; and

- architectural or engineering services that are performed by the taxpayer in the ordinary course of its architectural or engineering trade or business in the United States with respect to the construction of real property that is located in the United States.

The domestic production activities deduction cannot exceed more than 50 percent of the W-2 wages paid by the taxpayer to its employees for the calendar year ending during the tax year and properly allocable to the taxpayer's DPGR (those W-2 wages deducted in calculating QPAI). For this purpose, "wages" includes any amount paid by the taxpayer to its employees for services performed and that are subject to federal income tax withholding. Generally, no withholding is required on wages paid for services performed outside the United States, including wages paid to a bona fide resident of Puerto Rico for services performed in Puerto Rico.

Special rule for Puerto Rico. For purposes of the domestic production activities deduction (DPAD), the term "United States" only includes the 50 states and the District of Columbia, as well as U.S. territorial waters. It does not include U.S. possessions or territories. However, if a taxpayer has gross receipts from sources within the Commonwealth of Puerto Rico, then Puerto Rico will be considered part of the United States if all of those receipts are subject to the U.S. federal income tax (Code Sec. 199(d)(8)). Thus, if a taxpayer has gross receipts from qualified production activities within Puerto Rico and those receipts are subject to U.S. income tax, then such receipts will be considered DPGR. In such circumstances, wages paid by the taxpayer to a bona fide resident of Puerto Rico for services performed in Puerto Rico will be considered "wages" for purposes of calculating the 50-percent W-2 wage limitation. The treatment of Puerto Rico as part of the United States will only apply with respect to the first four tax years of a taxpayer beginning after December 31, 2005, and before January 1, 2010.

¶632

Code Sec. 199 deduction for production activities in Puerto Rico extended.— The special rule that permits Puerto Rico to be deemed part of the United States for purposes of the domestic production activities deduction (DPAD) under Code Sec. 199 is extended for two more years. Thus, a taxpayer with gross receipts from qualified production activities within Puerto Rico, which are subject to U.S. federal income taxes, may treat those receipts as domestic production gross receipts (DPGR) with respect to the first six tax years beginning after December 31, 2005, and before January 1, 2012 (Code Sec. 199(d)(8)(C), as amended by the Tax Relief, Unemployment Insurance Reauthorization, and Job Creation Act of 2010 (P.L. 111-312)).

> **Comment:** For calendar year taxpayers, this means that the rule will apply for tax years 2006 through 2011. For fiscal year taxpayers, the rule will apply for any tax year beginning in 2006 through 2011.

> **State Tax Consequences:** States such as Connecticut, Indiana, and New York that have decoupled from the domestic production activities deduction will not be impacted by the extension of the deduction for qualified activities in Puerto Rico. For those states that do incorporate the deduction, whether the extension will be recognized depends on the state's Internal Revenue Code conformity date. States that incorporate the Code as currently in effect will incorporate the amendment, whereas those states, such as New Hampshire, Kentucky, and Wisconsin, that have not updated their Code reference in years, will require an adjustment. Those states that update their Code conformity dates annually will most likely conform during their next legislative sessions.

▶ **Effective date.** The amendments made to this provision apply to tax years beginning after December 31, 2009 (Act Sec. 746(b) of the Tax Relief, Unemployment Insurance Reauthorization, and Job Creation Act of 2010 (P.L. 111-312)).

Law source: Law at ¶5295. Committee Report at ¶10,510.

— Act Sec. 746(a) of the Tax Relief, Unemployment Insurance Reauthorization, and Job Creation Act of 2010, amending Code Sec. 199(d)(8)(C);

— Act Sec. 746(b), providing the effective date.

Reporter references: For further information, consult the following CCH reporters.

— Standard Federal Tax Reporter, ¶12,476.0245

— Tax Research Consultant, BUSEXP: 6,054.05 and BUSEXP: 6,150

— Practical Tax Explanation, §6,010

¶635 Cover Over of Rum Excise Tax

SUMMARY OF NEW LAW

The $13.25 per proof gallon cover over amount paid to the treasuries of Puerto Rico and the U.S. Virgin Islands for rum imported into the United States from any source country is extended until January 1, 2012.

BACKGROUND

A $13.50 per proof gallon excise tax is imposed on all distilled spirits produced in or imported into the United States including the U.S. possessions of Puerto Rico and the U.S. Virgin Islands (Code Sec. 5001(a)(1)). The purpose of this excise tax is to minimize any advantage in the production of rum that Puerto Rico and the Virgin Islands would have over other mainland rum producers. To compensate Puerto Rico and the Virgin Islands for imposition of the excise tax on their rum, the amount of the excise tax imposed on the rum produced in these two U.S. possessions that is imported into the United States is paid back or "covered-over" to their respective possession treasuries. The amount of excise tax imposed on rum from any other source country is covered over in proportion to the U.S. market share of Puerto Rican and Virgin Island rum.

Puerto Rico and the Virgin Islands receive a payment ("cover over") limited to the amount of $10.50 per proof gallon of the excise tax imposed on rum brought into the United States (Code Sec. 7652(f)). This payment is made with respect to all rum imported into the United States from any source country. The cover over payment limit was temporarily increased to $13.25 per proof gallon for the period July 1, 1999, through December 31, 2009, by the Emergency Economic Stabilization Act of 2008 (P.L. 110-343).

NEW LAW EXPLAINED

Increased cover over limit extended.—The $13.25 per proof gallon cover over amount to Puerto Rico and the Virgin Islands for rum brought into the United States is extended for two additional years, until January 1, 2012 (Code Sec. 7652(f)(1), as amended by the Tax Relief, Unemployment Insurance Reauthorization, and Job Creation Act of 2010 (P.L. 111-312).

> **Comment:** Beginning on January 1, 2012, the cover over amount reverts to $10.50 per proof gallon.

▶ **Effective date.** The amendment made to this provision applies to distilled spirits brought into the United States after December 31, 2009 (Act Sec. 755(b) of the Tax Relief, Unemployment Insurance Reauthorization, and Job Creation Act of 2010 (P.L. 111-312).

Law source: Law at ¶5860. Committee Report at ¶10,610.

— Act Sec. 755(a) of the Tax Relief, Unemployment Insurance Reauthorization, and Job Creation Act of 2010, amending Code Sec. 7652(f)(1);

— Act Sec. 755(b), providing the effective date.

NEW LAW EXPLAINED

Reporter references: For further information, consult the following CCH reporters.

— Standard Federal Tax Reporter, ¶42,968F.01

¶638 Aviation Excise Taxes

SUMMARY OF NEW LAW

Excise taxes on aviation fuel, airline passenger tickets, and air cargo have been extended through March 31, 2011.

BACKGROUND

The Airport and Airway Trust Fund of the federal government provides funding for capital improvements to the U.S. airport and airway system, as well as supporting the Federal Aviation Administration (FAA) (Code Sec. 9502). The fund is financed through various excises taxes. For example, a 19.3 cents per gallon excise tax is imposed on aviation gasoline when it is removed from a terminal facility (Code Sec. 4081(a)(2)(A)(ii)).

For domestic air transportation, an excise tax of 7.5 percent is imposed on the amount a person pays for "taxable transportation" by air, as well as a flat rate for each domestic flight segment (Code Sec. 4261(a) and (b)). There is also an international air travel facilities tax that applies to the transportation of persons in international travel that begins or ends in the United States, and, at a different rate, to travel between the continental United States and Alaska or Hawaii (Code Sec. 4261(c)). Finally, an excise tax of 6.25 percent is imposed on the amount paid within or outside the United States for the "taxable transportation" of property by air (Code Sec. 4271). The tax is paid by the person making payment for the taxable transportation, but only if such payment is made to a person engaged in the business of transporting property by air for hire. All of these excise taxes are scheduled to expire after December 31, 2011.

NEW LAW EXPLAINED

Airport and Airway Trust Fund excise taxes extended.—The Airport and Airway Trust Fund excise taxes are extended through March 31, 2011 (Code Secs. 4081(d)(2), 4261(j)(1)(A), and 4271(d)(1)(A), as amended by the Airport and Airway Extension Act of 2010, Part IV (H.R. 6473)). The expenditure authority of the Airport and Airway Trust Fund has also been extended through March 31, 2011 (Code Sec. 9502(d)(1) and (e)(2), as amended by the Airport and Airway Extension Act, Part IV).

▶ **Effective date.** The amendments made by this section take effect on January 1, 2011 (Act Secs. 2(c) and 3(c) of the Airport and Airway Extension Act of 2010, Part IV (H.R. 6473)).

NEW LAW EXPLAINED

Law source: Law at ¶5747, ¶5748, ¶5749, and ¶5750.

— Act Sec. 2(a) of the Airport and Airway Extension Act of 2010, Part IV (H.R. 6473), amending Code Sec. 4081(d)(2)(B);

— Act Sec. 2(b), amending Code Secs. 4261(j)(1)(A)(ii) and 4271(d)(1)(A)(ii);

— Act Sec. 3(a) and (b), amending Code Sec. 9502(d)(1) and (e)(2);

— Act Secs. 2(c) and 3(c), providing the effective dates.

Reporter references: For further information, consult the following CCH reporters.

— Tax Research Consultant, EXCISE: 6,114.05, EXCISE: 9,102.05, and EXCISE: 9,106.05.

— Practical Tax Explanation, § 21,050, § 21,140, and § 21,145.

— Federal Excise Tax Reporter, ¶8919.01, ¶19,305.014, and ¶20,115.03.

Estate, Gift, and Generation-Skipping Taxes

7

TRANSFER TAXES

¶705   Sunset Extended; Transfer Taxes Reinstated

¶710   Transfer Tax Rates Lowered

¶715   Transfer Tax Exclusion and Exemption Amounts Increased

¶718   Deceased Spouse's Unused Applicable Exclusion Amount to be Portable

¶720   Qualified Family-Owned Business Interest Deduction

¶725   State Death Tax Credit

¶730   State Death Tax Deduction

¶735   Estate Tax Exclusion for Qualified Conservation Easements

BASIS RULES AND REPORTING REQUIREMENTS

¶740   Stepped-Up Basis for Property Acquired from a Decedent

¶745   Reporting and Penalty Provisions

¶750   Income Tax Exclusion for Sale of Principal Residence

¶755   Treatment of Appreciated Property Upon Distribution

¶760   Miscellaneous Amendments to Incorporate Carryover Basis Rules Repealed

GENERATION-SKIPPING TRUSTS

¶765   Deemed and Retroactive Allocations of GST Exemption

¶770   Severing of Trusts

¶775   Modification of Valuation Rules

¶780   Late Elections and Substantial Compliance

INSTALLMENT PAYMENTS

¶785   Allowable Number of Members for Closely Held Business

¶790   Election for Installment Payment of Estate Tax With Respect to Lending and Finance Businesses

¶795   Estate Tax Installment Payments and Stock of Holding Companies

TRANSFER TAXES

¶705 Sunset Extended; Transfer Taxes Reinstated

SUMMARY OF NEW LAW

The sunset of the transfer tax provisions of EGTRRA, which was scheduled to occur after December 31, 2010, pursuant to Act Sec. 901(a)(2) of EGTRRA, has been extended through December 31, 2012. In addition, federal estate and generation-skipping transfer (GST) taxes will apply to the estates of decedents dying and GSTs made after December 31, 2009, and before January 1, 2013, but with a higher estate tax applicable exclusion and GST exemption amount of $5 million (¶715) and lower tax rates (35 percent maximum) (¶710) than would have applied under the sunset provision. In addition, the modified adjusted carryover basis rules are repealed (¶740). However, for estates of decedents dying in 2010, executors may elect to have the EGTRRA rules (no estate tax, but modified carryover basis) apply. The gift tax will continue to apply, as it did in 2010, with a maximum tax rate of 35 percent, but with an applicable exclusion amount of $5 million for gifts made in 2011 and 2012 (¶715). Both the estate and gift tax applicable exclusion amounts will be subject to indexing for inflation beginning in 2012. Finally, the Tax Relief Act of 2010 provides an election to allow the unused portion of the applicable exclusion amount of a predeceased spouse to be available to the estate of his or her surviving spouse (¶718).

BACKGROUND

Under provisions of the Economic Growth and Tax Relief Reconciliation Act of 2001 (P.L. 107-16) (EGTRRA), federal transfer taxes, including the estate tax, the gift tax, and the generation-skipping transfer (GST) tax were drastically changed over the period from 2001 through 2010. These changes included a reduction in the maximum tax rates (¶710) and phased in increases in the applicable exclusion amount and (see ¶715). The changes made by EGTRRA culminated in the one-year repeal of the estate and GST taxes in 2010. Although the Bush Administration had proposed permanent repeal of the estate and GST taxes (see Code Secs. 2210(a) and 2664), the one-year suspension was necessary to overcome objections in the Senate to budgetary concerns about the legislation that would have required a 60-vote majority to cut off debate. During the years following 2001, several attempts to make the EGTRRA transfer tax changes permanent occurred, however, these attempts were unsuccessful in over-coming a filibuster in the Senate.

Example: The estate of William Alexander, who died on December 31, 2009, with a taxable estate of $5 million, would be liable for a federal estate tax of

NEW LAW EXPLAINED

Estate tax returns. Effective for decedents dying after December 31, 2009, and before December 17, 2010, the due date is extended to a date not earlier than September 19, 2011 (the date that is nine months after the date of enactment, December 17, 2010, but because September 17, 2011 is a Saturday, the date is extended to September 19, 2011), with respect to:

- filing any return due under Code Sec. 6018 (including any election required to be made on such a return), as that Code Section is in effect after December 17, 2010, the date of enactment of the Tax Relief Act of 2010, without regard to whether an election was made under Act Sec. 301(c) to apply the estate tax law or the carryover basis provisions;
- any payment of estate tax; and
- making any disclaimer under Code Sec. 2518(b) of an interest in property passing by reason of the death of such decedent (Act Sec. 301(d)(1) of the Tax Relief Act of 2010).

GST tax returns.—Effective for any GSTs made after December 31, 2009, and before December 17, 2010, the date of enactment, the due date for filing any returns due under Code Sec. 2662 (including any election required to be made on such a return) will be no earlier than September 19, 2011 (the date that is nine months after the date of enactment, December 17, 2010 (Act Sec. 301(d)(2) of the Tax Relief Act of 2010).

> **Comment:** In conjunction with reinstatement of the federal estate and GST taxes for estates of decedents and GSTs after December 31, 2009, the delayed application of the EGTRRA sunset provision until January 1, 2013 will mean that a number of provisions related to the estate tax that had either been eliminated or greatly changed by EGTRRA will not be reinstated. These provisions include the credit for state death taxes (Code Sec. 2011) and the qualified family owned business interest (QFOBI) deduction (Code Sec. 2057).

However, another provision that had been temporarily eliminated as a result of the one-year repeal of the estate tax will again have significance. Specifically, the concept of stepped-up basis at death (Code Sec. 1014) (see ¶740) will again apply to property acquired from a decedent. In addition, more liberal rules pertaining to the installment payment of estate taxes (Code Sec. 6166) (see ¶785, ¶790, and ¶795, respectively, for details) and conservation easements (Code Sec. 2031(c) (see ¶770) will remain in force. Similarly, several taxpayer-friendly changes to the rules governing the GST tax made by EGTRRA will also be continued (see ¶765, ¶770, ¶775, and ¶780).

Summary of Major Changes to Transfer Taxes Made by the Tax Relief Act of 2010

- Estate and GST taxes are reinstated for deaths and GSTs occurring after 2009 (however, for 2010 decedents, estates can elect to escape estate taxes) (Code Secs. 2001(a) and 2601).
- Maximum estate, gift, and GST tax rate: 35 percent, but for GSTs in 2010, the applicable GST rate is zero (Code Sec. 2001(c)(1)) (see ¶710).
- Applicable exclusion amount for both estate and gift taxes: $5 million, subject to inflation indexing beginning in 2012 (see ¶715).
- Exemption amount for GST tax: $5 million (Code Sec. 2631) (see ¶715).
- Stepped-up basis for assets acquired from a decedent restored (Code Sec. 1014) (see ¶740).

¶705

NEW LAW EXPLAINED

Timeline of Tax Relief Act of 2010 Rate and Applicable Exclusion Changes

2010 through 2012

- estate tax restored
- maximum estate tax rate: 35%
- estate tax applicable exclusion: $5 million
- special executor election to apply pre-Relief Act carryover basis law (estates of decedents dying in 2010)
- gift tax rate: 35% (35% in 2010 under EGTRRA)
- gift tax applicable exclusion: $1 million in 2010 ($5 million in 2011 and 2012)
- GST tax restored (but 0% applicable tax rate for 2010)
- GST tax rate: 0% in 2010 (35% in 2011 and 2012)
- GST exemption: $5 million

Unified credit against gift tax clarified.—A conforming amendment makes clear that on and after January 1, 2011, the gift tax applicable credit amount will not be limited to $1 million, but will be $5 million (Code Sec. 2505(a), as amended by the Tax Relief Act of 2010 (see ¶715).

Portability election.—Effective for deaths occurring in 2011 and 2012, the estate of a surviving spouse may qualify to utilize the unused portion of the estate tax applicable exclusion amount (as otherwise increased under the Tax Relief Act of 2010) of a predeceased spouse (Act Sec. 303 of the Tax Relief Act of 2010). To take advantage of this provision an election by the predeceased spouse's estate is required. The portability election is discussed in detail at ¶718.

EGTRRA sunset extended.—Under Act Sec. 101(a)(1) of the Tax Relief Act of 2010, the date that the tax provisions of EGTRRA were scheduled to sunset has been extended from December 31, 2010, to December 31, 2012. However, under Act Sec. 304 of the Tax Relief Act of 2010, the sunset provision of EGTRRA (Act Sec. 901), as amended by the Tax Relief Act of 2010, will apply to the transfer tax provisions of the 2010 Act. In other words, absent Congressional intervention in the interim, on January 1, 2013, federal estate, gift, and GST taxes will face the same possibility of a return to a lower applicable exclusion amount and higher rates as would have occurred on January 1, 2011, absent passage of the Tax Relief Act of 2010.

> **Practical Analysis:** Sidney Kess, New York, New York, CCH consulting editor, author and lecturer, observes that the exemption amount of $5 million is higher than it was in 2009 ($3.5 million) and the top estate tax rate of 35 percent is lower than the top rate in 2009 of 45 percent. The higher exemption amount was not a surprise, but setting the estate tax rate at the same level as the top individual income tax rate was unexpected by many tax professionals. However, the most surprising part of the new law is the fact that Congress did not enact any estate tax changes that could have

¶705

NEW LAW EXPLAINED

helped to pay for the extension, such as revisions to GRAT rules and caps on valuation discounts.

Practical Analysis: Michael Schlesinger, Schlesinger & Sussman, Beacon, New York and Clifton, New Jersey and Martin Miller, Miller & Miller, New York, New York, note that estate lawyers are going to be very busy revising wills and estate plans due to the changes brought by the Tax Relief Act of 2010. First, due to the fact that this new law will sunset in two years, lawyers will most likely be drafting disclaimer wills to cover the contingency that in 2013, the Tax Relief Act of 2010 may be repealed in whole or in part. Second, the marital rates of elderly citizens will probably increase dramatically, especially on deathbed situations where, because of Act Sec. 303(a) of the Tax Relief Act of 2010, elderly citizens will now have portability with their estate tax exclusion. Due to various factors, such as responsibility for a spouse for Medicare situations, this has served as a stumbling block to marriage among the elderly. But, now that there is this vast financial incentive of portability of the $5 million estate tax exclusion, both on death and during life for gift giving purposes, it is probable that the marital statistics for the elderly will rise for the next two years. Lastly, marital agreements will probably reflect this estate tax exclusion portability and given the size of it, namely $5 million, there will probably be extensive negotiations, especially if one senior citizen has assets greater than $5 million and the prospective spouse a minimal amount.

Practical Analysis: Sanford J. Schlesinger, Managing Partner, and Martin R. Goodman, Partner, Schlesinger Gannon & Lazetera LLP, New York, New York, comment that, pursuant to the Tax Relief Act of 2010, the estate of a person dying in 2010 or thereafter will have an applicable exclusion amount of $5 million (indexed for inflation from 2010, but starting in 2012) for estate tax purposes, the maximum estate tax rate will be 35 percent in 2010 and thereafter, and all such estates will have a full step-up in basis for income tax purposes with respect to the assets acquired from the decedent. However, the Tax Relief Act of 2010 also permits the estate of a person who dies in 2010 to instead elect not to be subject to any federal estate tax, but to be subject to the modified carryover basis regime that existed under prior law. Under this modified carryover basis regime, for income tax purposes the income tax cost basis of assets that are inherited will be the decedent's income tax cost basis of those assets, rather then the value of those assets at the date of the decedent's death, except that such estate can increase the basis of the decedent's assets to the extent of $1,300,000, and can also increase the basis of assets bequeathed to the decedent's surviving spouse outright, or bequeathed to a trust for the benefit of the decedent's spouse for which the estate receives an estate tax marital deduction (i.e., generally a QTIP trust), up to $3 million.

Election quandary. The estate of a person dying in 2010 who has a gross estate of less than the applicable exclusion amount of $5 million will generally not opt out of the estate tax regime, since such estate will not be required to pay any estate taxes,

NEW LAW EXPLAINED

due to the $5 million applicable exclusion amount, and will obtain a full income tax step-up in basis for the assets passing from the decedent. On the other hand, the estate of a person dying in 2010 that has a value in excess of the $5 million applicable exclusion amount may instead elect to not have the estate tax regime apply, and to have the modified carryover basis rules apply. However, in deciding whether or not to make such election, the executors of such estates will have to consider all the relevant factors, including the amount of income that the estate or its beneficiaries are likely to realize upon the eventual disposition of the inherited assets and when and at what rates they are likely to be required to pay income taxes on such income.

It appears that such election to opt out of the estate tax regime and to instead be subject to the modified carryover basis regime may have to be made on IRS Form 8939, Allocation of Increase in Basis for Property Acquired From a Decedent. The IRS has issued a draft of such Form, but it has not been finalized to date. However, the IRS has not yet definitively announced how such election must be made.

Due dates. The due date for the estate tax return and for the payment of any estate tax that may be due with respect to the estate of a person who dies prior to the enactment of the Act is extended to nine months after the date of the enactment of the Act. As the Act was enacted on December 17, 2010, the corresponding date which is nine months later is September 17, 2011. However, since September 17, 2011 is a Saturday, such due date will be the next following Monday, or September 19, 2011. Similarly, the due date for the filing of Form 8939 for estates of persons dying before the enactment of the Act is also extended to September 19, 2011.

Disclaimers. The Tax Relief Act of 2010 also provides that the time within which a beneficiary of an estate of a person who dies prior to the enactment of the Act must make a qualified disclaimer under Code Sec. 2518 is extended to nine months after the date of the enactment. Thus, such extended due date also is September 19, 2011. In this regard, issues may arise as to whether a beneficiary of inherited property can make a qualified disclaimer if the beneficiary already has accepted benefits from such property, or if applicable state law does not similarly extend the period in which a qualified disclaimer may be made.

Drafting issues. Wills and other documents that serve as testamentary substitutes may utilize a formula clause for dividing a decedent's estate between the portion of the estate that qualifies for the federal estate tax marital deduction and the balance of the estate, which may be bequeathed to or in trust for persons other than the decedent's surviving spouse. The application of such a formula with the advent of a $5 million applicable exclusion amount for estate tax purposes may result in a bequest of the first $5 million of the decedent's assets to or for the benefit of persons other than the decedent's surviving spouse, such as the decedent's children and more remote descendants, or to a trust of which the decedent's spouse is not the sole beneficiary. This dispositive result may be different from the disposition that the testator had intended by using such a formula clause in an instrument executed when the applicable exclusion amount for estate tax purposes was substantially less than $5 million. Therefore, it may be advisable to review estate planning documents to determine whether the dispositive plan in those documents, taking into account

NEW LAW EXPLAINED

the provisions of the Tax Relief Act of 2010 and applicable state laws, continue to reflect the testator's estate planning goals.

State law impact. In addition, it is important to note that, although the Tax Relief Act of 2010 increases the federal estate tax applicable exclusion amount to $5 million, the various states have their own laws regarding the imposition of state inheritance and estate taxes, and such state laws may not be ""coupled" with the federal estate tax applicable exclusion amount. In such cases, it is possible that an estate may not be required to pay any federal estate taxes, but may be required to pay a substantial amount of state estate taxes. Thus, consideration should be given to such state estate taxes when preparing estate plans.

Gift tax rules. Prior to the Tax Relief Act of 2010, the applicable exclusion amount (i.e., the exemption) for gift tax purposes was $1 million in 2010, and the maximum gift tax rate was 35 percent in 2010. The Tax Relief Act of 2010 did not change the applicable exclusion amount of $1 million for gift tax purposes with respect to gifts made in 2010. However, the Tax Relief Act of 2010 provides that after 2010, donors of gifts will have an applicable exclusion amount for gift tax purposes of $5 million (adjusted for inflation from 2010, but commencing in 2012), and the maximum gift tax rate is reduced to 35 percent for gifts made in 2010 and thereafter. Thus, a person who makes gifts in 2010 will have an applicable exclusion amount of $1 million with respect to such gifts, and such person's taxable gifts will be subject to a maximum gift tax rate of 35 percent. As a result, it generally would be preferable to make gifts in excess of $1 million in 2011, when the gift tax applicable exclusion amount will be increased to $5 million, rather than in 2010, when the gift tax applicable exclusion amount is limited to $1 million.

It should be noted that, as in the past, previously made gifts will "consume" part of this $5 million applicable exclusion amount, but at gift tax rates imposed at the time of the currently made gift. Thus, if a person previously made a gift of $1 million at a time when the maximum gift tax rate was 45 percent, rather than 35 percent, the person should still be able to make $4 million of additional gifts after 2010 and have such additional gifts "sheltered" from gift tax by the remaining $4 million of the person's applicable exclusion amount.

GST tax rules. Prior to the Tax Relief Act of 2010, there was no GST tax imposed on generation-skipping transfers that occurred in 2010. The Act creates an exemption of $5 million (indexed for inflation from 2010, but commencing in 2012) for GST tax purposes, beginning in 2010; provides that the GST tax rate for generation-skipping transfers occurring in 2010 is zero; and provides that the maximum tax rate for GST tax purposes is 35 percent for generation-skipping transfers that occur after 2010. The previously existing rules regarding the identification of the "transferor" of a transfer, and the automatic allocation rules regarding the allocation of the transferor's GST tax exemption, continue to apply, with respect to transfers made in 2010 and thereafter. The GST tax exemption of $5 million is available for the estate of a person who dies in 2010, whether or not such person's estate elects out of the estate tax regime for estate tax purposes. As a result of these rules, a person in 2010 can make a gift in an unlimited amount outright and free of trust to a grandchild or more remote descendant without incurring a GST tax, although the amount of the gift that exceeds

NEW LAW EXPLAINED

the unused portion of the donor's $1 million applicable exclusion amount for gift tax purposes will be subject to the payment of gift taxes at a 35-percent rate.

In addition, a person can make a gift in 2010 in trust for the benefit of the person's grandchild and more remote descendants, and no GST tax will be immediately imposed at the time of such transfer, as the transfer is a "direct skip" for GST tax purposes but the GST tax rate with respect to such transfer is zero. After the transfer, the donor, who is the "transferor" for GST tax purposes, will be treated as "moving down" one generation, so that the generation assignment of the donor's grandchild will only be one generation below that of the transferor. As a result, distributions by the trust to the grandchild after 2010 will not be generation-skipping transfers, and no GST tax will be payable on account of such transfers. However, if the trust also provides for the eventual distribution of the trust property to the donor's great grandchildren, then the death of the donor's grandchild after 2010 will be a taxable termination, and the GST tax will be due at that time, unless (1) the value of the trust remaining at the grandchild's death is includible in the grandchild's estate for estate tax purposes, or (2) if such value is not so includible, unless the trust is exempt from GST taxes as a result of the donor having allocated his or her GST tax exemption to the gift that he or she made to the trust.

Omitted provisions. It is also significant to note that the Tax Relief Act of 2010 does not contain any provisions requiring a minimum term for grantor retained annuity trusts (GRATs), as had been included in the President's Budget Proposal for the prior two years and in prior legislative proposals. Thus, short term GRATs continue to be a viable estate planning tool. In addition, the Tax Relief Act of 2010 does not contain any provisions restricting valuation discounts for transfer tax purposes, even though the President's prior Budget Proposal included such provisions. As a result, valuation discounts for family limited partnerships continue to apply for transfer tax purposes.

▶ **Effective date.** Except as otherwise provided, these amendments apply to the estates of decedents dying, and transfers made, after December 31, 2009 (Act Sec. 301(e) of the Tax Relief, Unemployment Insurance Reauthorization, and Job Creation Act of 2010 (P.L. 111-312)). The provision shall not apply to tax years beginning after December 31, 2012 (Act Sec. 101(a)(1) of the Tax Relief Act of 2010; Act Sec. 901 of EGTRRA). See ¶105 for a specific discussion of the sunset provision of EGTRRA and how it is applied.

Law source: Law at ¶5695, ¶5705, ¶5735, ¶5765, ¶7025, and ¶7035. Committee Report at ¶10,130.

— Act Sec. 301(a) of the Tax Relief, Unemployment Insurance Reauthorization, and Job Creation Act of 2010 (P.L. 111-312), amending subtitles A and E of title V of Economic Growth and Tax Relief Reconciliation Act of 2001 (EGTRRA) (P.L. 107-16);

— Act Sec. 301(b), amending Code Sec. 2505(a);

— Act Sec. 301(c), providing a special election for estates of decedents dying in 2010;

— Act Sec. 301(d)(1), affecting the due date of returns filed under Code Sec. 6018, tax payments under Chapter 11 of the Internal Revenue Code (estate tax), and disclaimers under Code Sec. 2518(b);

— Act Sec. 301(d)(2), affecting the due date of returns filed under Code Sec. 2662;

¶705

NEW LAW EXPLAINED

— Act Sec. 301(e), providing the effective date.

— Act Sec. 304, applying the EGTRRA sunset, as extended by Act Sec. 101(a)(1) the Tax Relief Act of 2010.

Reporter references: For further information, consult the following CCH reporters.

— Tax Research Consultant, ESTGIFT: 42,108.15, ESTGIFT: 51,000, ESTGIFT: 51,050, ESTGIFT: 57,000 and PLANIND: 15,402

— Practical Tax Explanation, § 34,001, § 34,701 and § 34,801

— Federal Estate and Gift Tax Reporter, ¶ 1250 and ¶ 12,085.01

¶710 Transfer Tax Rates Lowered

SUMMARY OF NEW LAW

In addition to the reinstatement of federal estate and generation-skipping transfer (GST) taxes for the estates of decedents dying and GSTs made after December 31, 2009, and before January 1, 2013 (¶705), and the addition of a special election for the estates of decedents dying in 2010 (¶740 and ¶745), a new rate structure will apply to the estates of decedents dying after December 31, 2009, and before January 1, 2013. Under that structure, the maximum estate tax rate will be 35 percent. Gifts will continue to be taxed at a maximum rate of 35 percent, as they were in 2010. The GST tax rate, which is tied to the maximum estate tax rate, will also be 35 percent for GSTs in 2011 and 2012, but is 0 percent for GSTs in 2010. In addition, the five-percent surtax, imposed on estates and gifts in excess of $10 million and up to $17,184,000, prior to 2002, will not be reinstated.

BACKGROUND

The Economic Growth and Tax Relief Reconciliation Act of 2001 (EGTRRA) (P.L. 107-16) increased the applicable estate tax exclusion amount (see ¶705 and ¶715) and decreased the top estate tax rate. Specifically, EGTRRA immediately eliminated the two highest tax brackets (53 and 55 percent, respectively) making the maximum rate 50 percent for decedents dying in 2002. Through the rest of the decade, the maximum tax rate continued to ratchet downward, ending at 45 percent in the years 2007 through 2009 (Code Sec. 2001(c)).

Gift tax rates.—The maximum gift tax rate ran parallel to the estate tax rate through 2009, but dropped to 35 percent for 2010—the year in which estate and GST taxes were temporarily suspended by EGTRRA (Code Sec. 2502).

Maximum Estate and Gift Tax Rates—2002 through 2010 under EGTRRA

- 2002: 50 percent
- 2003: 49 percent
- 2004: 48 percent

BACKGROUND

- 2005: 47 percent
- 2006: 46 percent
- 2007 through 2009: 45 percent
- 2010: No estate tax; Gift tax: 35 percent

Computation of the estate tax.—The estate tax is computed by applying the unified rate schedule to the decedent's taxable estate (Code Sec. 2001(b)). Under the unified transfer tax rate schedule, a tentative tax is computed on the sum of (1) the amount of the taxable estate and (2) the amount of taxable gifts made by the decedent after 1976, other than gifts that are includible in the gross estate, such as property transferred during life by means of a transfer where the decedent retained certain interests, rights or powers in the property and, in the case of decedents dying before 1982, property transferred within three years of death. The gift taxes payable on gifts made after 1976 (applying the rate schedule in effect in the year of the decedent's death) are then subtracted from this tentative tax.

GST tax rate.—The "applicable rate" for purposes of the generation-skipping transfer (GST) tax is computed pursuant to a formula based in part on the maximum estate tax rate (Code Secs. 2602 and 2641). Accordingly, the potential applicable rate for GST purposes dropped from a maximum of 55 percent in 2001 to 45 percent in 2007 through 2009.

Surtax on large estates.—EGTRRA also did away with the five-percent surtax that had previously been applied to estates and taxable gifts larger than $10 million and up to $17,184,000 (Code Sec. 2001(c)(2)). This surtax had been imposed to phase out the benefits of the graduated tax rates found in Code Sec. 2001. The surtax was repealed by EGTRRA for decedents dying after December 31, 2001.

NEW LAW EXPLAINED

Sunset delayed; maximum estate and gift tax rates to decrease.—The sunset of the transfer tax provisions of the Economic Growth and Tax Relief Reconciliation Act of 2001 (EGTRRA) (P.L. 107-16), which was scheduled to occur after December 31, 2010, has been extended for two years (Act Sec. 101(a)(1) of the Tax Relief, Unemployment Insurance Reauthorization, and Job Creation Act of 2010 (P.L. 111-312)). In addition, the Tax Relief Act of 2010 reinstates federal estate and generation-skipping transfer (GST) taxes for the estates of decedents dying and GSTs made after December 31, 2009, and before January 1, 2013 (¶ 705). And, a new rate structure will apply to the estates of decedents dying after December 31, 2009, and before January 1, 2013, under the Tax Relief Act of 2010. Under that structure, the maximum estate tax rate will be 35 percent (Code Sec. 2001(c)), as amended by the Tax Relief Act of 2010). Gifts will continue to be taxed at a maximum rate of 35 percent, as they were in 2010. However, the related gift tax section of the Code will no longer contain a separate rate structure, but will instead refer to the corresponding estate tax provision as it did prior to passage of EGTRRA (Code Sec. 2502(a), as amended by the Tax Relief Act of 2010). Thus, the estate and gift taxes are again "unified."

¶710

NEW LAW EXPLAINED

Unified Tax Rate Schedule 2010-2012 Under the Tax Relief Act of 2010

(A) Amount subject to tax equal to or more than—	(B) Amount subject to tax less than—	(C) Tax on amount in column (A)	(D) Rate of tax on excess over amount in column (A) Percent
. . . . .	$10,000	. . . . .	18
$10,000	20,000	$1,800	20
20,000	40,000	3,800	22
40,000	60,000	8,200	24
60,000	80,000	13,000	26
80,000	100,000	18,200	28
100,000	150,000	23,800	30
150,000	250,000	38,800	32
250,000	500,000	70,800	34
500,000		155,800	35

Surtax not reinstated.—The five-percent surtax that had been applied to estates and taxable gifts larger than $10 million and up to $17,184,000 prior to 2002 (Code Sec. 2001(c)(2)) will not be reinstated for the estates of decedents dying and taxable gifts made after December 31, 2009, and before January 1, 2013.

> **Example:** Miles Harrison, a single person, dies in 2011 with a taxable estate of $15 million. His estate will be subject to a federal estate tax of $3.5 million. If Harrison had instead died in 2010, no estate tax would have been due assuming his executor makes the election under Act Sec. 301(c) (see ¶740 and ¶745 for a discussion of this election available to the estates of decedents dying in 2010). However, if he had died in 2009, his estate would have owed an estate tax of $5,175,000. If the sunset of the EGTRRA transfer tax provisions had occurred, his estate would have owed $7,795,000 in federal estate taxes.

GST applicable rate decreased.—The "applicable rate" for GST purposes will be computed based on a maximum estate tax rate of 35 percent for GSTs occurring after December 31, 2010 and before January 1, 2013 (Code Sec. 2641). In addition, a separate provision of the 2010 Act confirms that, with respect to GSTs that occur after December 31, 2009, and before the January 1, 2011, the applicable rate for GST purposes is zero (Act Sec. 302(c) of Tax Relief Act of 2010).

> **Planning Note:** The 20-point differential between the 35-percent tax rate applicable to taxable gifts in 2010 through 2012, versus the 55-percent rate that would apply in 2013 and later pursuant to the extended EGTRRA sunset, coupled with an increase in the gift tax applicable exclusion amount to $5 million and with depressed asset values for many types of assets, creates an atmosphere that is conducive to making taxable gifts before January 1, 2013.

Modifications necessary to reflect impact of differences in tax rates.—The computation of both estate and gift taxes is clarified to reflect the changes in transfer tax rates made by the Tax Relief Act of 2010. According to the Joint Committee on Taxation (Technical Explanation of the Revenue Provisions Contained in the "Tax Relief, Unemployment Insurance Reauthorization, and Job Creation Act of 2010" (JCX-55-10), December 10, 2010), for purposes of determining the amount of gift tax

¶710

NEW LAW EXPLAINED

that would have been paid on one or more prior year gifts, the estate tax rates in effect under Code Sec. 2001(c) at the time of the decedent's death are used to compute both (1) the gift tax imposed by Chapter 12 of the Internal Revenue Code with respect to such gifts, and (2) the unified credit allowed against such gifts under Code Sec. 2505 (including the computation of the applicable credit amount under Code Sec. 2505(a)(1) and the sum of amounts allowed as a credit for all preceding periods under Code Sec. 2505(a)(2)).

EGTRRA sunset extended.—Under Act Sec. 101(a)(1) of the Tax Relief Act of 2010, the date that the tax provisions of EGTRRA were scheduled to sunset has been extended from December 31, 2010, to December 31, 2012. However, under Act Sec. 304 of the Tax Relief Act of 2010, the sunset provision of EGTRRA (Act Sec. 901), as amended by the Tax Relief Act of 2010, will apply to the transfer tax provisions of the 2010 Act. In other words, absent Congressional intervention in the interim, on January 1, 2013, federal estate, gift, and GST taxes will face the same possibility of a return to higher rates as would have occurred on January 1, 2011, absent passage of the Tax Relief Act of 2010.

▶ **Effective date.** Unless otherwise provided, these amendments apply to the estates of decedents dying, GSTs, and gifts made after December 31, 2009 (Act Sec. 301(e) of the Tax Relief, Unemployment Insurance Reauthorization, and Job Creation Act of 2010 (P.L. 111-312)). The provision shall not apply to tax years beginning after December 31, 2012 (Act Sec. 101(a)(1) of the Tax Relief Act of 2010; Act Sec. 901 of EGTRRA). See ¶105 for a specific discussion of the sunset provision of EGTRRA and how it is applied.

Law source: Law at ¶5600, ¶5610, ¶5700, ¶5705, ¶5710, ¶7030, and ¶7035. Committee Report at ¶10,130.

— Act Sec. 302(a)(2) of the Tax Relief, Unemployment Insurance Reauthorization, and Job Creation Act of 2010 (P.L. 111-312), amending Code Sec. 2001(c);

— Act Sec. 302(b)(2) amending Code Sec. 2502(a);

— Act Sec. 302(c) clarifying the applicable GST tax rate;

— Act Sec. 302(d)(1) amending Code Sec. 2001(b)(2) and adding Code Sec. 2001(g);

— Act Sec. 302(d)(2) amending Code Sec. 2505(a);

— Act Sec. 302(e) repealing Code Sec. 2511(c);

— Act Sec. 302(f), providing the effective date.

— Act Sec. 304, applying the EGTRRA sunset, as extended by Act Sec. 101(a)(1) of the Tax Relief Act of 2010.

Reporter references: For further information, consult the following CCH reporters.

— Tax Research Consultant, ESTGIFT: 51,050 and PLANIND: 15,402.20

— Practical Tax Explanation, § 34,010.30, § 34,715.10 and § 34,830

— Federal Estate and Gift Tax Reporter, ¶1250.015, ¶9494.05, and ¶12,730.01

¶710

¶715 Transfer Tax Exclusion and Exemption Amounts Increased

SUMMARY OF NEW LAW

In addition to the reinstatement of the federal estate and generation-skipping transfer (GST) taxes for the estates of decedents dying and GSTs made after December 31, 2009, and before January 1, 2013 (¶705), and the addition of a special election for the estates of decedents dying in 2010 (¶740 and ¶745), a larger applicable exclusion amount will be available to the estates of decedents dying after December 31, 2009, and before January 1, 2013, than would have been the case had the transfer tax provisions of the Economic Growth and Tax Relief Reconciliation Act of 2001 (EGT-RRA) (P.L. 107-16) been allowed to sunset. As a result, the estate tax applicable exclusion amount will increase to $5 million for the estates of decedents dying after December 31, 2009, and before January 1, 2013. The GST tax exemption amount, which is computed by reference to the estate tax applicable exclusion amount, will also be $5 million for GSTs occurring after 2009 and before 2013. Both the estate tax applicable exclusion amount and the GST tax exemption will be indexed for inflation beginning in 2012. The gift tax applicable exclusion amount, which had remained at $1 million since 2002, will also be $5 million, effective for gifts made after December 31, 2010, and before January 1, 2013, and will be indexed for inflation beginning in 2012. Finally, the estate of a surviving spouse may be entitled to the unused portion of his or her predeceased spouse's applicable exclusion amount, assuming the predeceased spouse's estate made an irrevocable election to take advantage of this provision. This election will be available beginning in 2011.

BACKGROUND

The Economic Growth and Tax Relief Reconciliation Act of 2001 (P.L. 107-16) (EGT-RRA) made significant changes to the federal estate, gift, and GST taxes, including changes made with respect to the estate tax applicable exclusion amount and the GST tax exemption amount. The estate tax applicable exclusion amount (Code Sec. 2010) reflects the amount of property protected from federal estate taxes by operation of the applicable credit allowable against such taxes. It also represents the filing threshold for the requirement to file an estate tax return (Code Sec. 6018(a)). The estate tax applicable exclusion amount, as well as the gift tax applicable exclusion amount (Code Sec. 2505) were scheduled to increase to $1 million for the estates of decedents dying and gifts made in 2006 under a provision of the Taxpayer Relief Act of 1997 (P.L. 105-34). However, EGTRRA accelerated the increase in the applicable exclusion amount for the estates of decedents dying beginning in 2002 through 2009.

BACKGROUND

Applicable Credit and Exclusion Amounts—2002 Through 2010 under EGTRRA

Year	Applicable Unified Credit	Applicable Exclusion Amount
2002 and 2003	$345,800	$1,000,000
2004 and 2005	555,800	1,500,000
2006 through 2008	780,800	2,000,000
2009	1,455,800	$3,500,000
2010	No estate tax	No estate tax

The GST exemption amount (Code Sec. 2631) was also altered by EGTRRA. For GSTs occurring in the years 2001 through 2003, the GST exemption amount was $1 million adjusted for inflation. Beginning in 2004, the GST exemption amount became tied to the estate tax applicable exclusion amount and was no longer adjusted for inflation.

GST Exemption Amount—2001 Through 2010 under EGTRRA

- 2001: $1,160,000 (adjusted)
- 2002: $1,100,000 (adjusted)
- 2003: $1,120,000 (adjusted)
- 2004 and 2005: $1,500,000
- 2006 through 2008: $2,000,000
- 2009: $3,500,000
- 2010: No GST tax

> **Comment:** Despite dramatic increases in the estate tax applicable exclusion amount and the GST tax exemption made by EGTRRA, the gift tax applicable exclusion amount (Code Sec. 2505) remained static at $1 million after 2003. This "de-unification" of estate and gift taxes tended to make lifetime gifts less attractive, unless those gifts effectively "leveraged" the applicable exclusion amount, such as those made via a grantor retained annuity trust (GRAT) or similar vehicle.

> **Example 1:** Rita Johnson, who died in 2009, could have passed on a taxable estate of up to $3.5 million without paying any federal estate tax. However, if Johnson had made a lifetime taxable gift in excess of $1 million, it would have generated a gift tax payable at a rate of 41 to 45 percent, depending on the amount of the gift.

> **Example 2:** Mike Leoni, who has not previously used any of his gift tax applicable exclusion, creates a GRAT and funds the GRAT with property worth $1 million. Using a "zeroed-out" or a "near-zero" GRAT, it is possible to effectively reduce the remainder (gift) interest transferred to a very small

¶715

BACKGROUND

> amount so as to leave most, if not all, of his gift tax applicable exclusion available for future gifts.

Comment: The increases in the estate tax applicable exclusion amount brought about under EGTRRA served to vastly reduce the number of estates required to file a federal estate tax return. IRS statistics reveal that the number of estates filing a federal estate tax return dropped from 108,071 in 2001 to 38,031 in 2007 (see "A Look at Estate Tax Returns Filed for Wealthy Decedents Since 2001," Brian G. Raub, IRS Statistics of Income Bulletin—Fall 2009, at http://www.irs.gov/pub/irs-soi/09fallbuletreturn.pdf). Separate statistics for returns filed in 2008 indicate little change from 2007, with 38,373 estate tax returns filed. Although the year the return was filed does not directly track the changes to the applicable exclusion amount, which relates to the year of death, the statistics do confirm a definite downward trend. Therefore, it would not be surprising if the estate tax filings for 2009 and 2010 were even lower as a result of the further increase in the applicable exclusion amount to $3.5 million for decedents dying in 2009.

NEW LAW EXPLAINED

Applicable exclusion amount increased.—In addition to extending the sunset date of the transfer tax provisions in the Economic Growth and Tax Relief Reconciliation Act of 2001 (EGTRRA) (P.L. 107-16) for two years, through December 31, 2012, and reinstating the federal estate and generation-skipping transfer (GST) taxes for the estates of decedents dying and GSTs made after December 31, 2009, and before January 1, 2013 (¶ 705), the estate tax applicable exclusion amount for decedents dying after 2009 and before 2013, will be $5 million (Code Sec. 2010(c)(2)(A), as amended by the Tax Relief, Unemployment Insurance Reauthorization and Job Creation Act of 2010 (P.L. 111-312)). The Tax Relief Act of 2010 also provides an election that would allow the estates of decedents dying in 2010 to be treated under an assumption of either (1) no estate tax and carryover basis on property acquired from a decedent or (2) an estate tax with stepped-up basis (see ¶ 740 and ¶ 745 for details).

> **Example:** Frank Gaines, a single person, dies in 2011 with a gross estate of $4.9 million. His estate would not be required to file an estate tax return. If Gaines had died in 2009, when the applicable exclusion amount and filing threshold was $3.5 million, an estate tax return would have been required. (See ¶740 and ¶745 for discussion of the election available to decedents dying in 2010, as mentioned above).

CCH Comment: As estimated by the Tax Policy Center and reported by the Congressional Research Service (*Estate Tax Legislation in the 111th Congress*, by Nonna A. Noto, July 16, 2010, Table A-1, p. 41, *www.crs.gov*, R40964), an applicable exclusion amount of $5 million that is indexed for inflation would result in

¶715

NEW LAW EXPLAINED

only 3,600 estates or 0.14 percent of deaths being subject to the federal estate tax in 2011. This is in contrast to 6,160 estates or 0.24 percent of deaths with an applicable exclusion of $3.5 million, indexed for inflation, and 6,410 estates or 0.25 percent with an applicable exclusion of $3.5 million, *not* indexed for inflation. However, if sunset of the EGTRRA provisions had occurred and the applicable exclusion amount was $1 million, not indexed for inflation, the result would be just under 46,000 estates and 1.76 percent of deaths.

Portability of unused exclusion amount available.—In a separate provision, the Tax Relief Act of 2010 would allow the unused portion of a deceased spouse's applicable exclusion amount to be utilized by the estate of his or her surviving spouse. As part of this change, the definition of the applicable exclusion amount has been modified to introduce the concept of the "basic exclusion amount." For further details of this portability option, see ¶718.

Inflation adjustment provided.—For the first time ever, the estate tax applicable exclusion amount will be subject to indexing for inflation beginning in 2012 (Code Sec. 2010(c)(2)(B), as amended by the Tax Relief Act of 2010).

Gift tax applicable exclusion amount re-unified.—For the first time since 2003, the gift tax applicable exclusion amount will again be equal to the estate tax applicable exclusion (at $5 million), beginning in 2011 (Code Secs. 2010(c)(2)(A), as added by the Tax Relief Act of 2010, and 2505(a), as amended by the Tax Relief Act of 2010). The gift tax applicable exclusion amount remains at $1 million for gifts made in 2010. Because the gift tax applicable exclusion will again be computed with reference to the estate tax applicable exclusion amount, it will also be subject to indexing for inflation beginning in 2012.

GST exemption amount raised.—Because the GST tax exemption amount is computed by reference to the estate tax applicable exclusion amount, the GST tax exemption amount for GSTs occurring after 2009 and before 2013 will also be $5 million and indexed for inflation beginning in 2012 (Code Sec. 2631(c), as amended by EGTRRA). However, for 2010, the applicable tax rate for GST purposes will be zero (Act Sec. 302(c) of the Tax Relief Act of 2010) (see ¶710 for further details on applicable rates).

EGTRRA sunset extended.—Under Act Sec. 101(a)(1) of the Tax Relief Act of 2010, the date that the tax provisions of EGTRRA were scheduled to sunset has been extended from December 31, 2010, to December 31, 2012. However, under Act Sec. 304 of the Tax Relief Act of 2010, the sunset provision of EGTRRA (Act Sec. 901), as amended by the Tax Relief Act of 2010, will apply to the transfer tax provisions of the 2010 Act. In other words, absent Congressional intervention in the interim, on January 1, 2013, federal estate, gift, and GST taxes will face the same possibility of a return to a lower applicable exclusion amount as would have occurred on January 1, 2011, absent passage of the Tax Relief Act of 2010.

▶ **Effective date.** Except as otherwise provided, these amendments apply to estates of decedents dying, GSTs, and gifts made after December 31, 2009 (Act Sec. 302(f) of the Tax Relief, Unemployment Insurance Reauthorization, and Job Creation Act of 2010 (P.L. 111-312)). The provision shall not apply to tax years beginning after December 31, 2012

¶715

NEW LAW EXPLAINED

(Act Sec. 101(a)(1) of the Tax Relief Act of 2010; Act Sec. 901 of EGTRRA). See ¶105 for a specific discussion of the sunset provision of EGTRRA and how it is applied.

Law source: Law at ¶5605, ¶5705, ¶5720, ¶5765, and ¶7030, and ¶7035. Committee Report at ¶10,130.

— Act Sec. 302(a)(1) of the Tax Relief, Unemployment Insurance Reauthorization, and Job Creation Act of 2010 (P.L. 111-312), amending Code Sec. 2010(c);

— Act Sec. 302(b)(1), amending Code Sec. 2505(a);

— Act Sec. 302(f), providing the effective date.

— Act Sec. 304, applying the EGTRRA sunset, as extended by Act Sec. 101(a) of the Tax Relief Act of 2010.

Reporter references: For further information, consult the following CCH reporters.

— Tax Research Consultant, ESTGIFT: 18,050, ESTGIFT: 51,052 and ESTGIFT: 57,106.05

— Practical Tax Explanation, §34,010.40, §34,725.05 and §34,820.20

— Federal Estate and Gift Tax Reporter, ¶1450.01, ¶10,448.03, and ¶12,605.01

¶718 Deceased Spouse's Unused Applicable Exclusion Amount to be Portable

SUMMARY OF NEW LAW

Effective for deaths occurring in 2011 and 2012, the estate of a surviving spouse may qualify to utilize the unused portion of the estate tax applicable exclusion amount (as otherwise increased under the Tax Relief, Unemployment Insurance Reauthorization, and Job Creation Act of 2010) of his or her last predeceased spouse. An election by the predeceased spouse's estate is required.

BACKGROUND

Prior to the temporary repeal of the federal estate tax by the Economic Growth and Tax Relief Reconciliation Act of 2001 (EGTRRA) (P.L. 107-16), the basic structure of the estate tax allowed for the effective exemption of a certain amount of property from taxation. Under that structure, the estate of every decedent is allowed a credit equal to the "applicable credit amount" (Code Sec. 2010) in determining the amount of estate tax due. The applicable credit amount is defined as the amount of the tentative tax that would be determined under the Code Sec. 2001(c) rate schedule if the amount with respect to which such tentative tax is to be computed were the applicable exclusion amount determined under the table set forth in Code Sec. 2001 (c). In application, Code Sec. 2010 works to exempt from the estate tax an amount equal to the "applicable exclusion amount" then in effect. The applicable exclusion amount for estates of decedents dying during 2009 (the last year the estate tax was in

BACKGROUND

effect) was $3,500,000. The corresponding applicable credit amount for the estates of decedents dying in 2009 was $1,455,800.

Separately, the Internal Revenue Code also provides an unlimited marital deduction for property that is includible in a decedent's gross estate and passes to a surviving spouse (Code Sec. 2056). To qualify for the deduction, the property must pass to the survivor outright, or in a form that does not violate the rule against terminable interests (Code Sec. 2056(b)). However, the marital deduction is effectively nothing more than a tax-deferral device because, assuming the property has not been consumed before then, it will be includible in the gross estate of the surviving spouse at his or her death.

Historically, the utilization of the applicable credit/exclusion from estate tax has been on a per-person basis. In other words, if the estate of a decedent did not fully take advantage of his or her applicable exclusion amount, whatever amount was left unused was lost. Accordingly, a married couple who were entitled to protect as much as $7 million in property from the estate tax in 2009, could, without proper planning, fail to take advantage of a portion of that amount.

> **Example:** David Engel died in 2006 when the applicable exclusion amount was $2 million. His entire estate of $3 million passed outright to his wife Sally. Pursuant to the unlimited marital deduction (Code Sec. 2056), no federal estate tax was paid at David's death. However, at Sally's death in 2009, her estate consisted of the $3 million she had received from her husband's estate, plus $2.5 million of her own property, or a total of $5.5 million. Of the total, $3.5 million would be protected from estate tax, but the remaining $2 million would not. If, instead, David's estate plan had placed $2 million of the property passing at his death into a credit shelter trust for the benefit of his wife and children, her estate could have saved $900,000 in federal estate taxes (0.45 ×$2 million).

NEW LAW EXPLAINED

Unused exclusion amount to be portable.—The unused portion of a decedent's applicable exclusion amount (as otherwise increased to $5 million under the Tax Relief, Unemployment Insurance Reauthorization, and Job Creation Act of 2010) may be utilized by the estate of the decedent's surviving spouse at his or her later death. To take advantage of this provision, a special election must have been made by the predeceased spouse's estate (Code Sec. 2010(c), as amended by the Tax Relief, Unemployment Insurance Reauthorization, and Job Creation Act of 2010 (P.L. 111-312)).

Computing exclusion amount of a surviving spouse. The applicable exclusion amount for a surviving spouse who dies in 2011 or 2012 is the sum of:

- the basic exclusion amount (see ¶ 715), and
- the aggregate deceased spousal unused exclusion amount (discussed below) (Code Sec. 2010(c)(2), as amended by the Tax Relief Act of 2010).

NEW LAW EXPLAINED

Any portion of the predeceased spouse's applicable exclusion amount that was used to reduce his or her estate tax liability may not be used to reduce the surviving spouse's estate tax liability under this new provision. The term "deceased spousal unused exclusion amount" is the lesser of:

- the basic exclusion amount, or
- the last deceased spouse's applicable exclusion amount, *minus*
- the amount with respect to which the tentative tax is determined under Code Sec. 2001(b)(1) on the estate of such deceased spouse (Code Sec. 2010(c)(4), as added by the Tax Relief Act of 2010).

Example 1: Gina Parsons died in 2011 with a taxable estate of $3 million. An election is made on Gina's estate tax return to permit her husband, Henry, to use any of her unused exclusion amount. Henry, who had not made any lifetime taxable gifts, dies in 2012 with a taxable estate of $10 million. The executor of Henry's estate computes Henry's deceased spousal unused exclusion amount as the lesser of: (1) Henry's basic exclusion amount of $5 million or (2) Gina's basic exclusion amount ($5 million) minus (3) the amount of Gina's taxable estate ($3 million), or: $2 million. Accordingly, the total applicable exclusion amount available to Henry's estate at his death is $7 million: his basic exclusion amount of $5 million, plus $2 million in deceased spousal unused exclusion from Gina's estate.

Caution: Note that the new provision refers to the applicable exclusion amount of the *last* deceased spouse. Accordingly, it is not possible for individuals who have been married multiple times to tack on multiple applicable exclusion amounts of their predeceased spouses.

Example 2: Assume the same facts as in Example 1, except that after Gina's death, Henry married a second spouse, Rita, who predeceased him leaving a taxable estate of $4 million. An election was made on Rita's estate tax return to permit Henry to use any of her unused exclusion amount. Although the combined unused applicable exclusion amounts of Gina and Rita is $3 million (Gina's $2 million and Rita's $1 million), only $1 million is available for use by Henry's estate because Henry's deceased spousal unused exclusion amount is the lesser of: (1) Henry's basic exclusion amount of $5 million or (2) Rita's basic exclusion amount ($5 million) minus (3) the amount of Rita's taxable estate ($4 million), or: $1 million. Accordingly, the total applicable exclusion amount available to Henry's estate at his death is $6 million, composed of his basic exclusion amount of $5 million, plus $1 million in deceased spousal unused exclusion from Rita's estate.

Caution: The JCT Report (Footnote 57, Joint Committee on Taxation, Technical Explanation of the Revenue Provisions Contained in the "Tax Relief, Unemploy-

¶718

NEW LAW EXPLAINED

ment Insurance Reauthorization, and Job Creation Act of 2010" (JCX-55-10), December 10, 2010) clarifies that the last deceased spouse limitation applies whether or not the last deceased spouse has any unused exclusion or the last deceased spouse's estate makes the election.

Caution: The JCT Report (Footnote 56, Joint Committee on Taxation, Technical Explanation of the Revenue Provisions Contained in the "Tax Relief, Unemployment Insurance Reauthorization, and Job Creation Act of 2010" (JCX-55-10), December 10, 2010) indicates that a surviving spouse is *not* allowed to use the unused GST tax exemption of a predeceased spouse.

Election required. In order for a decedent's estate to take advantage of the unused exclusion amount of the decedent's predeceased spouse, the executor of the predeceased spouse's estate must have:

- filed an estate tax return
- on which the amount of the deceased unused exclusion was computed, and
- made an election on the return that such amount may be taken into account by the surviving spouse's estate.

Once the above election is made, it is irrevocable. No such election will be allowed to be made if the deadline for filing the predeceased spouse's estate tax return (including extensions) had not been met (Code Sec. 2010(c)(5)(A), as added by the Tax Relief Act of 2010).

Examination of prior returns. To ensure compliance, the IRS is granted the authority to examine estate and gift tax returns of a predeceased spouse in order make determinations regarding the surviving spouse's claim to the unused portion of the predeceased spouse's exclusion amount (Code Sec. 2010(c)(5)(B), as added by the Tax Relief Act of 2010). This authority extends even after the statutory period of limitations has expired under Code Sec. 6501.

Regulations. The 2010 Act also directs the IRS to issue "such regulations as may be necessary or appropriate" to implement the new rules regarding the use of deceased spousal unused exclusion amounts (Code Sec. 2010(c)(6), as added by the Tax Relief Act of 2010).

Conforming amendments. In addition, conforming amendments are applied to the definitions of the (1) unified credit against gift taxes and the (2) generation shipping transfer (GST) tax exemption (Code Sec. 2505(a)(1), and Code Sec. 2631(c), respectively, as amended by the Tax Relief Act of 2010). A similar conforming amendment is made with respect to the estate tax return filing requirements (Code Sec. 6018(a)(1), as amended by the Tax Relief Act of 2010).

Comment: As noted at a hearing before the Senate Finance Committee on the future of the estate tax ("Outside the Box on Estate Tax Reform: Reviewing Ideas to Simplify Planning," Senate Finance Committee, April 3, 2008, testimony of Shirley L. Kovar, Esq.), the main impetus for the portability provision is undoubtedly simplicity. Although portability will not completely eliminate the need for trusts, for many couples, particularly those who have been married only once and who are in the lower echelons of exposure to the estate tax (e.g.,

NEW LAW EXPLAINED

estates of between $5 and $10 million under the new law), this change should prove to be beneficial. It was supported by, among others, the American College of Trust and Estate Counsel (ACTEC). However, additional suggestions made by ACTEC, including (1) allowing portability with respect to the GST exemption and (2) instead of requiring an election, allowing for the possibility of attaching a special schedule to the deceased spouse's income tax return as a means of alerting the IRS to the portability issue, were not incorporated into the changes made by the Tax Relief Act of 2010. Finally, the fact that the Tax Relief Act of 2010 is scheduled to sunset after 2012 (see discussion below), limits the utility of the portability election. Both spouses would have to die within the two-year term to take advantage of the provision.

EGTRRA sunset extended.—Under Act Sec. 101(a)(1) of the Tax Relief Act of 2010, the date that the tax provisions of EGTRRA were scheduled to sunset has been extended from December 31, 2010, to December 31, 2012. However, under Act Sec. 304 of the Tax Relief Act of 2010, the sunset provision of EGTRRA (Act Sec. 901), as amended by the Tax Relief Act of 2010, will apply to the transfer tax provisions of the 2010 Act. In other words, absent Congressional intervention in the interim, on January 1, 2013, the portability election will face the possibility of sunset.

Practical Analysis: Sanford J. Schlesinger, Managing Partner, and Martin R. Goodman, Partner, Schlesinger Gannon & Lazetera LLP, New York, New York, point out that the Tax Relief Act of 2010 provides that the unused applicable exclusion amount of the last deceased spouse of a person can be used by such a person for gift tax and/or estate tax purposes. However, these portability provisions do not apply to a person's GST tax exemption. It is important to note that these provisions apply only if the death of the first spouse to die occurs after 2010. Thus, both spouses must die after 2010 and before 2013 for these provisions to apply as to the estate of the second-to-die.

For example, if a husband dies in 2011 and he and his estate have used only $3 million of his $5 million estate tax applicable exclusion amount, then his surviving wife will have an aggregate applicable exclusion amount of $7 million (i.e., her own $5 million applicable exclusion amount, plus the unused $2 million of her deceased husband's applicable exclusion amount), assuming the widow does not remarry and she dies before 2013. Importantly, the Tax Relief Act of 2010 permits a person to use the unused portion of the applicable exclusion amount of only such person's *last* deceased spouse. Thus, a person cannot accumulate the unused portion of the applicable exclusion amount of more than one deceased spouse. In addition, the unused portion of the applicable exclusion amount of the deceased spouse that can be used by the surviving spouse is not itself indexed for inflation; only the applicable exclusion amount of the surviving spouse is indexed for inflation (see ¶715).

To apply the portability provisions, the estate of the first spouse to die must elect to do so on a timely filed federal estate tax return. Thus, the estate of the first spouse to die must file such return, even if that person's gross estate is less the applicable exclusion amount, if that person's estate wants to apply these portability provisions.

NEW LAW EXPLAINED

▶ **Effective date.** Unless otherwise provided, these amendments apply to the estates of decedents dying and gifts made after December 31, 2010 (Act Sec. 303(c) of the Tax Relief, Unemployment Insurance Reauthorization, and Job Creation Act of 2010 (P.L. 111-312)). The conforming amendment pertaining to the definition of the GST tax exemption is effective for GSTs after December 31, 2010. The provision shall not apply to tax years beginning after December 31, 2012 (Act Sec. 101(a)(1) of the Tax Relief Act of 2010; Act Sec. 901 of EGTRRA). See ¶105 for a specific discussion of the sunset provision of EGTRRA and how it is applied.

Law source: Law at ¶5605, ¶5705, ¶5720, and ¶5765, and ¶7035. Committee Report at ¶10,130.

— Act Sec. 303(a) of the Tax Relief, Unemployment Insurance Reauthorization, and Job Creation Act of 2010, amending Code Sec. 2010(c)(2) and adding Code Sec. 2010(c)(3)-(6);

— Act Sec. 303(b), amending Code Secs. 2505(a); 2631(c), and 6018(a)(1)

— Act Sec. 303(c), providing the effective date.

— Act Sec. 304, applying the EGTRRA sunset, as extended by Act Sec. 101(a)(1) of the Tax Relief Act of 2010.

Reporter references: For further information, consult the following CCH reporters.

— Tax Research Consultant, ESTGIFT: 18,050, ESTGIFT: 51,052 and ESTGIFT: 57,106.05

— Practical Tax Explanation, § 34,010.40, § 34,725.05 and § 34,820.20

— Federal Estate and Gift Tax Reporter, ¶1450.01, ¶10,448.03, and ¶12,605.01

¶720 Qualified Family-Owned Business Interest Deduction

SUMMARY OF NEW LAW

The qualified family-owned business interest (QFOBI) deduction (Code Sec. 2057) will be available for the estates of decedents dying after December 31, 2012, under the sunset provisions of EGTRRA (Act Sec. 901(a)(2)) of P.L. 107-16, as extended by the Tax Relief Act of 2010 (Act Sec. 101(a)(1)). Therefore, if the estate qualifies and elects to take the deduction, up to $675,000 of the adjusted value of QFOBIs may be deducted from the value of a decedent's gross estate.

BACKGROUND

The Economic Growth and Tax Relief Reconciliation Act of 2001 (EGTRRA) (P.L. 107-16) repealed the QFOBI deduction for the estates of decedents dying after December 31, 2003 (Act Sec. 521(d) of EGTRRA, repealing Code Sec. 2057). The deduction was considered unnecessary in light of the increased applicable exclusion amount allowed under EGTRRA and had long been criticized as overly complex and burdensome on qualified heirs.

BACKGROUND

Although EGTRRA did not specifically address the applicability of certain recapture tax provisions, the House Ways and Means Committee Report accompanying the Death Tax Elimination Bill of 2001 (H.R. Rep. No. 107-37) and the Senate Finance Committee Report accompanying the Restoring Earnings to Lift Individuals and Empower Families (RELIEF) Bill of 2001 (S. Rep. No. 107-30) state that certain estate tax recapture tax provisions will continue to apply after repeal of the estate tax becomes effective. The language regarding tax recapture provisions appeared to be implicitly included in the Conference Committee Report's explanation of EGTRRA, as the 2001 Act largely followed the Senate bill with respect to the transfer tax provisions. The recapture rules of Code Sec. 2057(f) were specifically identified in the House and Senate Committee Reports as being retained after repeal. Accordingly, if an estate elected to take the QFOBI deduction for the estate of a decedent dying prior to 2004, an additional estate tax would be imposed if specific recapture events occurred within 10 years of the decedent's death and before the death of the qualified heir, even if the event happened during the period that the deduction was repealed (between January 1, 2004, and December 31, 2010).

Sunset provision. Under the sunset provision of EGTRRA, amendments made by the Act will not apply to the estates of decedents dying after December 31, 2010 (Act Sec. 901 of P.L. 107-16).

NEW LAW EXPLAINED

QFOBI deduction reinstated beginning in 2013.—The qualified family-owned business interest (QFOBI) deduction is available to the estates of decedents dying after December 31, 2012, if the estate meets the requirements of Code Sec. 2057 and makes the election on the federal estate tax return, under the sunset provision of the Economic Growth and Tax Relief Reconciliation Act of 2001 (EGTRRA) (Act Sec. 901 of P.L. 107-16), as extended by the Tax Relief, Unemployment Insurance Reauthorization, and Job Creation Act of 2010 (the Tax Relief Act of 2010) (P.L. 111-312) (Act. Sec. 101(a)(1)).

> **Comment:** Prior to the repeal of the QFOBI election for the estates of decedents dying after 2003, the election was made by filing Schedule T (Qualified Family-Owned Business Interest Deduction), attaching all required statements, and deducting the value of the QFOBIs on Part 5, Recapitulation of Form 706, United States Estate (and Generation-Skipping Transfer) Tax Return. The post-EGTRRA sunset (as extended by the Tax Relief Act of 2010) QFOBI election will likely be made in a similar manner.

A qualified family owned-business interest is any interest in a trade or business with a principal place of business in the United States, the ownership of which is held (1) at least 50 percent by one family, (2) 70 percent by two families, or (3) 90 percent by three families. If the interest is held by more than one family, the decedent's family must own at least 30 percent of the trade or business.

The QFOBI provisions of Code Sec. 2057, as effective for the estates of decedents dying after December 31, 2012, work in conjunction with the applicable exclusion

NEW LAW EXPLAINED

amount available to all decedents (Code Sec. 2010) to protect up to $1.3 million in property from the estate tax. The maximum possible QFOBI deduction is $675,000. If an estate has $675,000 or more of QFOBIs, the deduction is $675,000 and the amount excluded by the applicable exclusion amount is $625,000, regardless of the date of death (Code Sec. 2057(a)(3)(A)). In order to coordinate the deduction with the applicable exclusion amount, if less than the maximum QFOBI deduction is elected, the $625,000 applicable exclusion amount is increased by the excess of $675,000 over the amount of the QFOBI deduction allowed. However, the applicable exclusion amount may not be increased above the amount that would apply to the estate under Code Sec. 2010 if no QFOBI deduction had been elected.

Example 1: Melissa Bell dies in 2013 when the Code Sec. 2010 applicable exclusion amount is $1,000,000. Her estate qualifies for and elects to deduct $1,000,000 worth of QFOBIs from the value of the gross estate. In this case, Bell's estate will be entitled to a $675,000 deduction under Code Sec. 2057 and an applicable exclusion amount of $625,000, for a total amount of $1.3 million.

Example 2: Assume the same facts as in Example 1, except that the value of the QFOBIs in Bell's estate is $550,000. The excess of the $675,000 QFOBI maximum deduction over the value of the QFOBIs in the estate ($125,000) may be used to increase the applicable exclusion beyond $625,000 on a dollar-for-dollar basis, up to a maximum of $1,000,000. In this case, the full $125,000 may be added to $625,000, making the applicable exclusion $750,000. Thus, the total amount of the QFOBI deduction and the applicable exclusion amount will be $1.3 million ($550,000 + $750,000).

Example 3: Assume the same facts as in Example 2, except that the value of the QFOBIs in Bell's estate is $275,000. The excess of the $675,000 QFOBI maximum deduction over the value of the QFOBIs in the estate ($400,000) may be used to increase the applicable exclusion beyond $625,000 on a dollar-for-dollar basis, up to a maximum of $1 million. Under these facts, the QFOBI deduction will be $275,000, and the applicable exclusion amount will be $1 million. Therefore, the total amount of the Code Sec. 2057 deduction and the applicable exclusion will be $1.275 million.

Planning Note: If a decedent's interest in a family-owned business exceeds the applicable exclusion amount, the QFOBI deduction should be considered in spite of the potential imposition of an additional estate tax and the restrictions placed on qualified heirs who receive the family-owned business interests. In Example 1, above, the total estate tax due if the maximum QFOBI deduction is claimed, assuming no credit is taken for state death taxes, is $500,000. On the other hand, if the QFOBI deduction is limited to $300,000 and the maximum applicable credit is taken, the total estate tax due is $533,000. The savings is

NEW LAW EXPLAINED

attributable to the tax being determined using a lower rate (45 percent vs. 49 percent) on a lower taxable estate ($1.825 million vs. $2.2 million).

Generally, to qualify for the QFOBI deduction, the aggregate value of a decedent's QFOBIs that are passed to qualified heirs must exceed 50 percent of the decedent's adjusted gross estate. In addition, the decedent must be a U.S. citizen or resident at the time of death; the executor must make a QFOBI election; a recapture agreement signed by each person having an interest in the property must be filed; and certain ownership and participation requirements must be met (Code Sec. 2057(b)(1)).

To meet the participation requirements, the decedent, or members of the decedent's family, must have owned and materially participated in the trade or business for at least five of the eight years preceding the decedent's death in order to qualify for the QFOBI deduction. In addition, a qualified heir is subject to a recapture tax if an heir, or a member of the qualified heir's family, does not materially participate in the trade or business for at least five of any eight-year period within 10 years following the decedent's death. The definition of "material participation" provided in Code Sec. 2032A and Reg. § 20.2032A-3, pertaining to special use valuation, apply. The principal factors to be considered include physical work and participation in management decisions. A qualified heir will not be treated as disposing of an interest in a trade or business by reason of ceasing to be engaged in a trade or business if any member of the qualified heir's family continues in the trade or business (Code Sec. 2057(f)(3)).

Although the QFOBI deduction affords some benefit to an estate, these benefits should be weighed against the risk of an additional recapture tax. An additional tax is imposed if any of the following recapture events occurs within 10 years of the decedent's death and before the qualified heir's death: (1) the qualified heir ceases to meet the material participation requirements; (2) the qualified heir disposes of any portion of his or her interest in the family-owned business, other than by a disposition to a member of the qualified heir's family or through a conservation contribution under Code Sec. 170(h); (3) the principal place of business of the trade or business ceases to be located in the United States; or (4) the qualified heir loses U.S. citizenship. The amount of the tax is based upon when the recapture event occurs in relation to the decedent's death.

If the recapture event occurs within the first six years of material participation, 100 percent of the reduction in estate tax attributable to the heir's interest, plus interest, is recaptured. Thereafter, the applicable percentage is 80 percent in the seventh year; 60 percent in the eighth year; 40 percent in the ninth year; and 20 percent in the tenth year. The total amount of tax potentially subject to recapture is the difference between the actual amount of estate tax liability for the estate and the amount of estate tax that would have been owed had the QFOBI deduction not been taken.

▶ **Effective date.** The repeal of the QFOBI deduction is effective for the estates of decedents dying after December 31, 2003 (Act Sec. 101(a)(2) of the Tax Relief, Unemployment Insurance Reauthorization, and Job Creation Act of 2010 (P.L. 111-312); Act Sec. 521(e)(3) of the Economic Growth and Tax Relief Reconciliation Act of 2001 (EGTRRA) (P.L. 107-16)). The repeal of the QFOBI deduction shall not apply to the estates of decedents dying after December 31, 2012 (Act Sec. 101(a)(1) of the Tax Relief Act of 2010; Act Sec.

¶720

NEW LAW EXPLAINED

901 of EGTRRA). See ¶105 for a specific discussion of the sunset provision of EGTRRA and how it is applied.

Law source: Law at ¶5655. Committee Report at ¶10,130.

— Act Sec. 101(a)(1) of the Tax Relief, Unemployment Insurance Reauthorization, and Job Creation Act of 2010 (P.L. 111-312), amending Act Sec. 901(a)(2) of the Economic Growth and Tax Relief Reconciliation Act of 2001 (EGTRRA) (P.L. 107-16);

— Act Sec. 101(a)(2) of the Tax Relief Act of 2010 providing the effective date.

Reporter references: For further information, consult the following CCH reporters.

— Tax Research Consultant, ESTGIFT: 15,700

— Practical Tax Explanation, § 34,325.05

— Federal Estate and Gift Tax Reporter, ¶7398.01

¶725 State Death Tax Credit

SUMMARY OF NEW LAW

The state death tax credit allowed for estate, inheritance, legacy, or succession taxes paid to any state or the District of Columbia (Code Sec. 2011) will be restored for the estates of decedents dying after December 31, 2012, under the sunset provisions of EGTRRA (Act Sec. 901(a)(2) of P.L. 107-16, as extended by the Tax Relief Act of 2010 (Act. Sec. 101(a)(1)). Correspondingly, the state death tax deduction (Code Sec. 2058) will no longer be applicable beginning in 2013 (see ¶730).

BACKGROUND

The Economic Growth and Tax Relief Reconciliation Act of 2001 (EGTRRA) (P.L. 107-16) amended Code Sec. 2011(b) to provide for the phase-out of the state death tax credit for the estates of decedents dying in 2002—2004 and the eventual repeal of the credit by Code Sec. 2011(f) for the estates of decedents dying after December 31, 2004. The state death tax credit was replaced by a deduction (Code Sec. 2058) for the estates of decedents dying after December 31, 2004 (see ¶730).

Beginning in 2002, the state death tax credit available under Code Sec. 2011 was reduced by 25 percent, with continuing reductions until its eventual repeal in 2005. The reduction in the credit was 50 percent for the estates of decedents dying in 2003 and 75 percent for the estates of decedents dying in 2004. The maximum state death tax credit allowable for decedents dying in 2002 through 2004 is summarized in the following chart.

BACKGROUND

2002

| If the adjusted taxable estate was: Over $10,040,000 | The maximum tax credit was: $812,100, plus 12% of the excess over $10,040,000 |

2003

| If the adjusted taxable estate was: Over $10,040,000 | The maximum tax credit was: $541,400, plus 8% of the excess over $10,040,000 |

2004

| If the adjusted taxable estate was: Over $10,040,000 | The maximum tax credit was: $270,700, plus 4% of the excess over $10,040,000 |

The amount of the credit was computed using the decedent's "adjusted taxable estate," which is the taxable estate less $60,000 (Code Sec. 2011(b)).

Example: Cody Littleton died in 2002, a resident of Virginia. His gross estate was valued at $3 million, less allowable deductions for funeral expenses and executor's and attorney's fees of $80,000. Accordingly, his taxable estate was equal to $2,920,000. For purposes of computing the state death tax credit, his adjusted taxable estate was $2,860,000 ($2.920 million − $60,000). The maximum state death tax credit allowable under Code Sec. 2011(b)(1) is $174,960. However, the state death tax credit is limited to $131,220 ($174,960 x (1 − .25). Because Littleton died in 2002, the amount computed under the state death tax credit is reduced by 25 percent. If Littleton had died in 2003, the state death tax credit is limited to $87,480, as the credit is reduced by 50 percent. If Littleton had died in 2004, the state death tax credit is limited to $43,740, as the credit is reduced by 75 percent. Had Littleton died in 2005, no credit would be allowed. His estate would be able to deduct state death taxes paid.

The credit for state death taxes was repealed completely for the estates of decedents dying after 2004 and was changed to a deduction, subject to the sunset of EGTRRA (see ¶ 730 for a discussion of the state death tax deduction).

Comment: When EGTRRA was signed into law on June 7, 2001, 37 states and the District of Columbia imposed only a "pick-up tax," which was designed to pick up no more state death tax from a decedent's estate than would be allowed by the federal credit under Code Sec. 2011. The loss of revenue experienced by many states attributable to the repeal of the federal state death tax credit was compounded by the reduction of the applicable credit beginning in 2002. The impact of the repeal of the credit and its replacement with a deduction meant that, instead of the near-uniform arrangement that existed prior to EGTRRA when every state took advantage of the state death tax credit and 37 states and the District of Columbia effectively based their state death tax on the amount allowable under the federal credit, estates faced a patchwork of different state laws with varying exemption amounts, effective dates, and other variations.

Sunset provision. Under the sunset provision of EGTRRA, amendments made by the Act will not apply to the estates of decedents dying after December 31, 2010 (Act Sec. 901 of P.L. 107-16).

NEW LAW EXPLAINED

State death tax credit restored beginning in 2013.—The state death tax credit allowed for estate, inheritance, legacy, or succession taxes actually paid to any state or the District of Columbia with respect to any property included in a decedent's gross estate (Code Sec. 2011) will be restored for the estates of decedents dying after December 31, 2012, under the sunset provision of the Economic Growth and Tax Relief Reconciliation Act of 2001 (EGTRRA) (Act Sec. 901 of P.L. 107-16), as extended by the Tax Relief, Unemployment Insurance Reauthorization, and Job Creation Act of 2010 (the Tax Relief Act of 2010) (Act Sec. 101(a)(1) of P.L. 111-312).

The credit does not include any taxes paid with respect to the estate of a person other than the decedent. The credit for state death taxes is available only to the extent that it does not exceed the estate's tax liability after reduction by the applicable credit amount. Although estates are not entitled to a credit under Code Sec. 2011 for death taxes paid to a possession of the United States, they may be entitled to a credit for foreign death taxes (Code Sec. 2014(g)).

The amount of the credit is based on the decedent's "adjusted taxable estate," which is defined as the taxable estate less $60,000 (Code Sec. 2011(b), prior to amendment by P.L. 107-16). The maximum allowable credit is computed under the following rate table. Pursuant to the table, the credit is allowed only for the portion of the adjusted taxable estate that exceeds $40,000.

If the adjusted taxable estate is:	The maximum tax credit shall be:
Not over $90,000	8/10ths of 1% of the amount by which the adjusted taxable estate exceeds $40,000
Over $90,000 but not over $140,000	$400 plus 1.6% of the excess over $90,000
Over $140,000 but not over $240,000	$1,200 plus 2.4% of the excess over $140,000
Over $240,000 but not over $440,000	$3,600 plus 3.2% of the excess over $240,000
Over $440,000 but not over $640,000	$10,000 plus 4% of the excess over $440,000
Over $640,000 but not over $840,000	$18,000 plus 4.8% of the excess over $640,000
Over $840,000 but not over $1,040,000	$27,600 plus 5.6% of the excess over $840,000
Over $1,040,000 but not over $1,540,000	$38,800 plus 6.4% of the excess over $1,040,000
Over $1,540,000 but not over $2,040,000	$70,800 plus 7.2% of the excess over $1,540,000
Over $2,040,000 but not over $2,540,000	$106,800 plus 8% of the excess over $2,040,000
Over $2,540,000 but not over $3,040,000	$146,800 plus 8.8% of the excess over $2,540,000
Over $3,040,000 but not over $3,540,000	$190,800 plus 9.6% of the excess over $3,040,000

¶725

NEW LAW EXPLAINED

If the adjusted taxable estate is:	The maximum tax credit shall be:
Over $3,540,000 but not over $4,040,000	$238,800 plus 10.4% of the excess over $3,540,000
Over $4,040,000 but not over $5,040,000	$290,800 plus 11.2% of the excess over $4,040,000
Over $5,040,000 but not over $6,040,000	$402,800 plus 12% of the excess over $5,040,000
Over $6,040,000 but not over $7,040,000	$522,800 plus 12.8% of the excess over $6,040,000
Over $7,040,000 but not over $8,040,000	$650,800 plus 13.6% of the excess over $7,040,000
Over $8,040,000 but not over $9,040,000	$786,800 plus 14.4% of the excess over $8,040,000
Over $9,040,000 but not over $10,040,000	$930,800 plus 15.2% of the excess over $9,040,000
Over $10,040,000	$1,082,800 plus 16% of the excess over $10,040,000

Example: Christine Ryan died on February 20, 2013, a resident of Virginia. As of the date of this publication, for the estates of decedents dying in 2013, Virginia imposes an estate tax equal to the federal state death tax credit available under Code Sec. 2011. Similar to federal law, Virginia also has an applicable exclusion amount equal to $1 million. On her date of death, Ryan's gross estate was valued at $3 million, less allowable deductions for funeral expenses and executor's and attorney's fees of $80,000. Accordingly, Ryan's taxable estate is $2.92 million.

Taxable estate	$2,920,000
Less: $60,000	60,000
Adjusted taxable estate (see below)	$2,860,000

In order to determine the "adjusted taxable estate," the taxable estate was reduced by $60,000. The state death tax credit was computed on the basis of the adjusted taxable estate, while the estate tax before credits is computed on the basis of the taxable estate, as can be seen below.

Estate tax on taxable estate	$1,248,400
Less: Unified credit (2013)	345,800
Less: State death tax credit	174,960
Tax payable (federal and assumed state tax paid)	$902,600

In response to the phaseout and eventual repeal of the federal tax credit, many states sought to protect the revenues generated by the credit in several ways, including decoupling their state tax from the federal credit, determining the state tax by reference to pre-EGTRRA law, or imposing stand-alone estate tax regimes.

NEW LAW EXPLAINED

State	Type of Tax
Connecticut	Stand-Alone Estate Tax
Delaware	Estate (de-coupled)
District of Columbia	Estate (de-coupled)
Hawaii	Estate (de-coupled)
Indiana	Inheritance
Iowa	Inheritance
Kentucky	Inheritance
Maine	Estate (de-coupled)
Maryland	Estate and Inheritance
Massachusetts	Estate (de-coupled)
Minnesota	Estate (de-coupled)
Nebraska	Inheritance
New Jersey	Estate and Inheritance
New York	Estate (de-coupled)
Ohio	Stand-Alone Estate Tax
Oregon	Estate (de-coupled)
Pennsylvania	Inheritance
Rhode Island	Estate (de-coupled)
Tennessee	Inheritance
Vermont	Estate (de-coupled)
Washington	Stand-Alone Estate Tax

Many states, including Virginia, which is referenced in the Example above, will see their state estate tax systems return in 2013 if the state death tax credit is restored. The estate tax will return in 2013 in the following states:

Alabama	Kentucky	North Dakota
Alaska	Louisiana	Pennsylvania
Arkansas	Michigan	South Carolina
California	Mississippi	South Dakota
Colorado	Missouri	Tennessee
Florida	Montana	Texas
Georgia	Nebraska	Utah
Idaho	Nevada	Virginia
Illinois	New Hampshire	West Virginia
Indiana	New Mexico	Wisconsin
Iowa	North Carolina	Wyoming

The following states have repealed their state estate tax systems: Arizona, Kansas, and Oklahoma.

Note: As a result of the extension of the EGTRRA sunset, it is possible that more states will modify their estate tax laws to de-couple from the federal system. For more information, see CCH's State Inheritance, Estate and Gift Tax Reporter for details.

¶725

NEW LAW EXPLAINED

Caution: Even if a state retained a state death tax, variations exist among the states and between the states and the federal law regarding the amount of the exclusion, effective dates, and other nuances. Each state's law should be analyzed. See CCH's STATE INHERITANCE, ESTATE AND GIFT TAX REPORTER for details.

Claiming the credit. Because the credit is allowed only as to the amount of state taxes actually paid, all required information must be supplied when the credit is claimed (Reg. § 20.2011-1(c)(2)). This information is particularly important where a deposit is made with the state as security for the payment of the state tax and where discounts or refunds may be allowed by the state. This information included data tending to show the actual amount of tax due the state that may be regarded as having been paid by a deposit, the amount of tax reasonably expected to be paid, and the identity of the property in respect to which the state tax has been paid or is to be paid.

The credit for state death taxes must generally be claimed within four years after the filing of the federal estate tax return (Reg. § 20.2011-1(c)(1)). However, exceptions are allowed if:

- A petition has been filed with the Tax Court. In such case, the claim for credit of state death taxes may be made within the four-year period or within 60 days after the decision of the Tax Court becomes final.

- An extension of time for payment of tax or deficiency has been granted. In such case, the claim for credit must be made within the four-year period or before the expiration of the extension period.

- The federal tax has been paid, a claim for credit or refund of federal estate taxes has been timely filed, and the claim is still pending on expiration of the four-year period. In such case, a claim for credit of state death taxes paid can be made within 60 days after the final disposition of the claim for credit or refund of federal estate taxes.

▶ **Effective date.** The phase-out of the state death tax credit is effective for the estates of decedents dying after December 31, 2001 (Act Sec. 101(a)(2) of the Tax Relief, Unemployment Insurance Reauthorization, and Job Creation Act of 2010 (P.L. 111-312); Act Sec. 531(b) of the Economic Growth and Tax Relief Reconciliation Act of 2001 (EGTRRA) (P.L. 107-16)). The phase-out of the state death tax credit shall not apply to the estates of decedents dying after December 31, 2012 (Act Sec. 101(a)(1) of the Tax Relief Act of 2010; Act Sec. 901 of EGTRRA). See ¶105 for a specific discussion of the sunset provision of EGTRRA and how it is applied.

Law source: Law at ¶5610. Committee Report at ¶10,130.

— Act Sec. 101(a)(1) of the Tax Relief, Unemployment Insurance Reauthorization, and Job Creation Act of 2010 (P.L. 111-312), amending Act Sec. 901(a)(2) of the Economic Growth and Tax Relief Reconciliation Act of 2001 (P.L. 107-16).

— Act Sec. 101(a)(2) of the Tax Relief Act of 2010, providing the effective date.

Reporter references: For further information, consult the following CCH reporters.

— Tax Research Consultant, ESTGIFT: 48,050

— Practical Tax Explanation, § 34,505.05

— Federal Estate and Gift Tax Reporter, ¶1651.01, ¶1651.03 and ¶7460.05

¶730 State Death Tax Deduction

SUMMARY OF NEW LAW

The state death tax deduction (Code Sec. 2058) is scheduled to expire for the estates of decedents dying after December 31, 2012, under the sunset provision of EGTRRA (Act Sec. 901(a)(2) of P.L. 107-16), as extended by the Tax Relief Act of 2010 (Act. Sec. 101(a)(1)). Accordingly, the estates of decedents dying after 2012 will not be able to deduct state death taxes paid to a state or the District of Columbia from a decedent's gross estate. However, although the state death tax deduction is no longer available, the state death tax credit will be restored beginning January 1, 2013 (see ¶725).

BACKGROUND

The Economic Growth and Tax Relief and Reconciliation Act of 2001 (EGTRRA) (P.L. 107-16) phased out the state death tax credit allowed under Code Sec. 2011 and added a deduction from the gross estate for state death taxes paid to any state or the District of Columbia (Code Sec. 2058(a)).

Beginning January 1, 2005, the state death tax credit was replaced with a deduction (Code Sec. 2058(a)). Therefore, for the estates of decedents dying after 2004, the value of a decedent's taxable estate was determined by deducting from the gross estate the amount of any estate, inheritance, legacy, or succession taxes actually paid to any state or the District of Columbia with respect to property included in the decedent's gross estate.

> **Compliance Note:** The state death tax deduction was taken on line 3b of Form 706, United States Estate (and Generation-Skipping Transfer) Tax Return (Rev. Sept. 2009). The deduction will likely be taken on line 3b or a similar line of the 2010 version of the Form 706. Although the estate tax has been reinstated for the estates of decedents dying in 2010 that do not elect to apply the Internal Revenue Code as if the estate tax and basis step-up rules of the Tax Relief, Unemployment Insurance Reauthorization, and Job Creation Act of 2010 (the Tax Relief Act) (P.L. 111-312) had not been enacted (see ¶740), the 2010 version of Form 706 has not been released and the filing deadlines for certain transfer tax returns have been extended (see ¶705).

A limitations period was imposed under which the deduction was allowed only for those state death taxes actually paid and for which a deduction was claimed before the later of:

- Four years after filing the estate tax return;

- In a case where a timely petition for redetermination has been filed with the Tax Court, 60 days after the Tax Court decision becomes final;

- When an extension of time has been granted for payment of estate tax or of a deficiency, the date the extension expires; or

BACKGROUND

- If a timely refund claim has been filed, then the latest of the expiration of (1) 60 days from the mailing of a notice to the taxpayer of a disallowance of the refund claim; (2) 60 days after a court decision on the merits of the claim becomes final; or (3) two years after a notice of waiver of disallowance is filed under Code Sec. 6523(a)(3) (Code Sec. 2058(b)).

   Comment: The state death tax deduction was not subject to dollar limits.

Conforming amendments were made to Code Secs. 2011(g) (redesignated as Code Sec. 2011(f) by P.L. 107-134), 2012(a), 2013(c)(1)(A), 2014(b)(2), 2015, 2016, 2053(d), 2056A(b)(10)(A), 2102(a), 2102(b)(5), 2102(c) (redesignated as Code Sec. 2102(b)), 2107(c)(3), 6511(i)(2), and 6612(c).

In addition, Code Sec. 2106(a)(4) was amended to provide a definition of "state death taxes" for purposes of determining the value of a nonresident noncitizen's taxable estate. The credit for state generation-skipping transfer (GST) taxes imposed on a GST (other than a direct skip) occurring as a result of death was also repealed (Code Sec. 2604(c)).

A related change was made to the definition of "additional estate tax" for purposes of the special exemption granted to the estates of members of the military who died in combat to include a reference to the state death tax credit, as in effect before repeal (Code Sec. 2201, as amended by P.L. 107-16). As with the other provisions related to the phase-out of the state death tax credit and eventual replacement with the state death tax deduction, this amendment was subject to the sunset provision of Act Sec. 901(a)(2). Following the September 11, 2001 terrorist attacks and the passage of the Victims of Terrorism Relief Act of 2001 (P.L. 107-134), this provision was retroactively repealed and never took effect (Act Sec. 103(b)(3) of P.L. 107-134).

   Note: Estate tax relief was extended to not only members of the Armed Forces but also to victims of certain terrorist attacks, including victims of the September 11, 2001 attacks and victims of the Oklahoma City terrorist attacks on April 19, 1995 (Code Sec. 2201, as amended by the Victims of Terrorism Relief Act of 2001 (P.L. 107-134)). The Military Tax Relief Act of 2003 (P.L. 108-121) further extended estate tax relief to astronauts who lose their lives on a space mission.

Sunset provision. Under the sunset provision of EGTRRA, amendments made by the Act will not apply to the estates of decedents dying after December 31, 2010 (Act Sec. 901 of P.L. 107-16).

NEW LAW EXPLAINED

State death tax deduction eliminated and credit restored beginning in 2013.— The state death tax deduction will no longer be available to the estates of decedents dying after December 31, 2012. Because Code Sec. 2058 expires under the sunset provision of the Economic Growth and Tax Relief Reconciliation Act of 2001 (EGTRRA) (P.L. 107-16), as extended by Act Sec. 101(a)(1) of the Tax Relief, Unemployment Insurance Reauthorization, and Job Creation Act of 2010 (the Tax Relief Act of 2010) (P.L. 111-312), the estates of decedents dying after 2012 will not be able to deduct

NEW LAW EXPLAINED

estate, inheritance, legacy, or succession taxes actually paid to any state or the District of Columbia from the value of the gross estate.

> **Comment:** By changing the state death tax credit to a deduction, the benefits to taxpayers were effectively reduced. A credit differs from a deduction in that the credit is subtracted from the tax itself, resulting in a dollar-for-dollar reduction in the tax liability. In the case of the state death tax credit, the credit is permitted only up to a statutorily allowed maximum. On the other hand, a deduction will be subtracted from the gross estate, resulting in a reduction of the property subject to estate tax. The return to the state death credit will presumably benefit estates of decedents dying after December 31, 2012.

With the expiration of the state death tax deduction comes the restoration of the state death tax credit, applicable to the estates of decedents dying after December 31, 2012. The credit will be available for estate, inheritance, legacy, or succession taxes paid to a state or the District of Columbia with respect to property included in the gross estate. The amount of the credit is based on the decedent's "adjusted taxable estate," which is defined as the taxable estate less $60,000 (Code Sec. 2011(b), prior to amendment by P.L. 107-16). The maximum allowable credit is computed under a progressive rate table (see ¶725). Pursuant to the table, the credit is allowed only for the portion of the adjusted taxable estate that exceeds $40,000. Under current law, the maximum state death credit allowable is $1,082,800, plus 16 percent of the adjusted taxable estate in excess of $10.04 million.

> **Comment:** The phase-out and ultimate repeal of the federal credit for state death taxes had a negative impact on the revenues of many states. Restoration of the state death tax credit by virtue of the EGTRRA sunset provision, as extended by the Tax Relief Act of 2010, will likely be welcomed by many states. Many states that had piggybacked on to the federal system prior to EGTRRA would benefit from this occurrence without making further changes. A few states, including Arizona, Kansas, and Oklahoma, which abandoned state death taxes or substantially altered their tax system subsequent to EGTRRA, may need to act to reinstate their state death tax systems.

A federal credit will be allowed for GST taxes paid to a state following a GST (other than a direct skip) that occurs as a result of the death of an individual after December 31, 2012. The credit for state GST taxes will be limited to five percent of the amount of federal GST taxes imposed on the transfer (Code Sec. 2604).

▶ **Effective date.** The provisions repealing the state death tax credit and replacing it with a deduction are effective for the estates of decedents dying after December 31, 2004 (Act Sec. 101(a)(2) of the Tax Relief, Unemployment Insurance Reauthorization, and Job Creation Act of 2010 (P.L. 111-312); Act Sec. 532(d) of the Economic Growth and Tax Relief Reconciliation Act of 2001 (EGTRRA) (P.L. 107-16). These provisions shall not apply to the estates of decedents dying after December 31, 2012 (Act Sec. 101(a)(1) of the Tax Relief Act of 2010; Act Sec. 901 of EGTRRA). See ¶105 for a specific discussion of the sunset provision of EGTRRA and how it is applied.

Law source: Law at ¶5610, ¶5615, ¶5620, ¶5625, ¶5630, ¶5635, ¶5645, ¶5650, ¶5660, ¶5670, ¶5680, ¶5685, ¶5715, ¶5835, and ¶5840. Committee Report at ¶10,130.

¶730

NEW LAW EXPLAINED

— Act Sec. 101(a)(1) of the Tax Relief, Unemployment Insurance Reauthorization, and Job Creation Act of 2010 (P.L. 111-312), amending Act Sec. 901(a)(2) of the Economic Growth and Tax Relief Reconciliation Act of 2001 (P.L. 107-16);

— Act Sec. 101(a)(2) of the Tax Relief Act of 2010, providing the effective date.

Reporter references: For further information, consult the following CCH reporters.

— Tax Research Consultant, ESTGIFT: 39,304

— Practical Tax Explanation, § 34,330

— Federal Estate and Gift Tax Reporter, ¶1651.01, ¶7460.05, ¶8075.05, ¶8375.10, and ¶12,205.10.

¶735 Estate Tax Exclusion for Qualified Conservation Easements

SUMMARY OF NEW LAW

The repeal of the distance requirements and clarification of the date used for determining the estate tax exclusion of a qualified conservation easement that were scheduled to expire for estates of decedent's dying after December 31, 2010, under the sunset provision of EGTRRA (Act Sec. 901(a)(2) of P.L. 107-16), have been extended. The repeal is scheduled to expire for estates of decedents dying after December 31, 2012. As a result, the exclusion for a qualified conservation easement is available to any otherwise qualifying real property without regard to the distance requirement for an additional two years (Code Sec. 2031(c)(8)(A)). In addition, Code Sec. 2031(c)(2) continues to clarify that the date to be used for determining the values to calculate the exclusion is the date of contribution (Code Sec. 2031(c)(2)).

BACKGROUND

The Economic Growth and Tax Relief Reconciliation Act of 2001 (EGTRRA) (P.L. 107-16) liberalized the rules governing the estate tax exclusion for qualified conservation easements by removing the prior law distance requirements (Code Sec. 2031(c)(8)(A)) and clarifying that the date such a contribution is made is the date to be used for determining the values necessary to calculate the exclusion amount (Code Sec. 2031(c)(2)).

For estates of decedent's dying after December 31, 2000, and before January 1, 2010, an executor may elect to exclude from the decedent's gross estate up to 40 percent of the value of the land subject to the qualified conservation easement (the "applicable percentage"). For purposes of computing the exclusion amount, the value of the land is reduced by the amount of any charitable deduction allowed under Code Sec. 2055(f) with respect to the land (Code Sec. 2031(c)). If the value of the easement is less than 30 percent of the overall value of the land (as determined without regard to the value of the easement), the applicable percentage is reduced by two percentage

BACKGROUND

points for each percentage point that the value of the easement falls below the 30 percent threshold. The amount of the exclusion is limited to the lesser of the applicable percentage of the value of the land or the exclusion limitation, which is $500,000 in 2002 and thereafter.

As amended by EGTRRA, the land subject to the conservation easement must:

- be located in the United States or any possession of the United States;
- have been owned by the decedent or a member of the decedent's family during the three-year period ending on the date of the decedent's death; and
- be subject to a qualified conservation easement granted by the decedent or a member of the decedent's family (Code Sec. 2031(c)(8)(A)).

The value of the land is determined without regard to the value of the easement and is reduced by the value of any retained development rights (i.e., rights retained for a commercial use that is not subordinate to and directly supportive of the land as a farm or for farming purposes within the meaning of Code Sec. 2032A(e)(5)). If the value of the easement is 10 percent or less of the value of the land before the easement, less the value of any retained development rights, the applicable percentage will be zero.

Pursuant to the changes made by EGTRRA, the values used in calculating the applicable percentage, including the value of the property subject to the easement and the value of the easement, are to be determined as of the date of contribution (Code Sec. 2031(c)(2)). If the property is encumbered with any acquisition indebtedness at the time of the decedent's death, the exclusion is limited to the decedent's net equity in the property (Code Sec. 2031(c)(4)(B)).

> **Caution:** In the event that a qualified conservation easement is created prior to the death of the decedent seeking the exclusion (such as an easement created by the decedent during life or a lineal ancestor of the decedent), the applicable percentage is to be determined as of the date of contribution of the easement, regardless of the then current values of the land and easement.

> **Example:** Pamela Harrison donated a conservation easement prior to her death at a time when the fair market value of the property was $600,000 without the conservation easement and $480,000 with the easement. The value of the conservation easement is $120,000 or 20 percent of the value of real property without the easement ($120,000/$600,000). The applicable percentage for the estate is 20% (40 percent reduced by twice the difference between 30 percent and 20 percent). Therefore, the exclusion amount is $96,000 (20 percent of $480,000 the date-of-death value with the easement).

The value of any development rights retained by the decedent is not taken into account for purposes of determining the exclusion amount (Code Sec. 2031(c)(5)). However, there may be estate tax ramifications depending on whether the heirs execute an agreement to extinguish some or all of the development rights. If the agreement to permanently extinguish the development rights is executed on or before the date the

BACKGROUND

estate tax return is due, the estate tax may be reduced accordingly (Code Sec. 2031(c)(5)(B)). But, if the agreement is not implemented by the earlier of the date that is two years after the decedent's death or the date of the sale of the land, an additional tax is imposed in the amount of the estate tax that would have been due on the retained development rights subject to the agreement (Code Sec. 2031(c)(5)(C)).

> **Caution:** According to the Conference Committee Report on the Economic Growth and Tax Relief Reconciliation Act of 2001 (P.L. 107-16) (H.R. Rep. No. 107-84), the provision relating to the additional tax is retained after repeal of the estate tax. The provision is retained so that those persons with an interest in the land who fail to execute the agreement will remain liable for any additional tax that may be due following repeal of the estate tax.

Sunset provision. Under the sunset provisions of EGTRRA, amendments made by the Act will not apply to decedents dying after December 31, 2010 (Act Sec. 901 of P.L. 107-16).

NEW LAW EXPLAINED

Removal of the distance requirements extended.—The repeal of the distance requirements for the exclusion of a qualified conservation easement (Code Sec. 2031(c)(8)(A), as amended by P.L. 107-16) will remain in force through December 31, 2012, as a result of the two-year extension of the EGTRRA sunset provision (Act Sec. 101(a)(1) of the Tax Relief, Unemployment Insurance Reauthorization, and Job Creation Act of 2010 (P.L. 111-312)). Accordingly, for estates of decedents dying after December 31, 2000, and before January 1, 2013, the exclusion for a qualified conservation easement will be available to any otherwise qualified real property that is located in the United States or any possession of the United States, that was owned by the decedent or a member of the decedent's family during the three-year period ending on the date of the decedent's death, and is subject to a qualified conservation easement granted by the decedent or a member of the decedent's family (Code Sec. 2031(c)(8)(A)).

For estates of decedents dying after December 31, 2012, the exclusion for a qualified conservation easement will be restricted to real property within 25 miles of a metropolitan area (as defined by the Office of Management and Budget), a national park, or a wilderness area (unless the land is not under significant development pressure as determined by the IRS) or 10 miles of an Urban National Forest (as designated by the Forest Service of the U.S. Department of Agriculture) (Code Sec. 2031(c)(8)(A)). The status of the property by the Office of Management and Budget, the IRS, or the Forest Service is determined as of the decedent's date of death.

Clarification of the date used to determine values extended. The clarification of the date used for determining the amount of the exclusion (Code Sec. 2031(c)(2), as amended by P.L. 107-16) is also extended for estates of decedent's dying before January 1, 2013, (Act Sec. 101(a)(2) of the Tax Relief Act of 2010). As a result, the values used in calculating the applicable percentage, including the value of the property subject to the

NEW LAW EXPLAINED

easement and the value of the easement, for estates of decedents dying after December 31, 2000 and before January 1, 2013, will be determined as of the date of contribution.

For estates of decedents dying after December 31, 2012, this clarification will be removed from Code Sec. 2031(c)(2), and will likely result in confusion regarding the values to be used in calculating the amount of the exclusion.

> **Caution:** The impact on estates of decedent's dying after December 31, 2012, of the expiration of both of these provisions is significant as both provisions have been in effect since January 1, 2001. Further guidance will be needed to assist executors in calculating the applicable percentage.

> **Compliance Note:** The qualified conservation exclusion election is made by filing Form 706 (United States Estate (and Generation-Skipping Transfer) Tax Return, Rev. September 2009), Schedule U (Qualified Conservation Easement Exclusion), and claiming the exclusion on Page 3, Part 5, line 11. Once made, the election is irrevocable.

▶ **Effective date.** This provision is effective for estates of decedents dying after December 31, 2000 (Act Sec. 101(a)(2) of the Tax Relief, Unemployment Insurance Reauthorization, and Job Creation Act of 2010 (P.L. 111-312); Act Sec. 551(c) of the Economic Growth and Tax Relief Reconciliation Act of 2001 (EGTRRA) (P.L. 107-16)). This provision shall not apply to estates of decedents dying after December 31, 2012 (Act Sec. 101(a)(1) of the Tax Relief Act of 2010 ; Act Sec. 901 of EGTRRA).

Law source: Law at ¶5640. Committee Report at ¶10,130.

— Act Sec. 101(a)(1) of the Tax Relief, Unemployment Insurance Reauthorization, and Job Creation Act of 2010 (P.L. 111-312), amending Act. Sec. 901 of the Economic Growth and Tax Relief Reconciliation Act of 2001 (EGTRRA) (P.L. 107-16);

— Act Sec. 101(a)(2) providing the effective date.

Reporter references: For further information, consult the following CCH reporters.

— Tax Research Consultant, ESTGIFT: 15,756

— Practical Tax Explanation, § 34,901

— Federal Estate and Gift Tax Reporter, ¶3185.10 and ¶3185.20.

BASIS RULES AND REPORTING REQUIREMENTS

¶740 Stepped-Up Basis for Property Acquired from a Decedent

SUMMARY OF NEW LAW

The modified carryover basis rules applicable to property acquired from a decedent (Code Sec. 1022) that were enacted by EGTRRA (P.L. 107-16) are replaced by the stepped-up basis rules of Code Sec. 1014 for decedents dying after December 31, 2009. Under the stepped-up basis rules, the income tax basis of property acquired

SUMMARY OF NEW LAW

from a decedent at death generally is stepped-up (or stepped down) to equal its value as of the date of the decedent's death (or on the date six months after the date of death, if alternate valuation (Code Sec. 2032) is elected on the decedent's estate tax return). However, executors for estates of decedents dying after December 31, 2009 and before January 1, 2011, may elect to have the EGTRRA rules apply to such estates, with the result that estate heirs will receive a carryover basis (rather than a stepped-up basis) in property received from a decedent.

BACKGROUND

Under the Economic Growth and Tax Relief Reconciliation Act of 2001 (EGTRRA) (P.L. 107-16), effective for property acquired from a decedent dying after December 31, 2009, the income tax basis of property acquired from a decedent is generally to be carried over from the decedent (Code Sec. 1022). More specifically, the recipient of property will receive a basis equal to the lesser of the adjusted basis of the property in the hands of the decedent, or the fair market value of the property on the date of the decedent's death. Although the Internal Revenue Code had long provided that the recipient of a lifetime gift received the donor's basis in the transferred property, this carryover basis rule previously did not apply to property received from a decedent.

Under the carryover basis at death rules, executors can elect to increase the basis of estate property by up to $1.3 million, and possibly an additional $3 million, in the case of property passing to a surviving spouse (Code Sec. 1022(b)).

Executor's power to allocate basis adjustments.—EGTRRA granted the executor of a decedent's estate the authority to increase—subject to stated maximums—the basis of assets passing from the decedent from their carryover value to a stepped-up, date-of-death, value. Once made, the allocation could only be changed pursuant to rules to be provided by the IRS (Code Sec. 1022(d)(3)).

Two separate basis increase provisions are generally available for property passing from decedents, although special rules apply to property passing from nonresident decedents who were not U.S. citizens. First, the executor generally can step up the basis of assets of the executor's choosing by a total of $1.3 million. (For purposes of this discussion, this basis increase will be referred to as the "general basis increase.") This step-up available under the general basis increase provision (Code Sec. 1022(b)(2)(B)) can be allocated to assets passing to any property recipient. Second, for properties that passed to the decedent's surviving spouse, an additional $3 million in basis step-up is available (Code Sec. 1022(c)). (This basis increase will be referred to as the "spousal property basis increase" for purposes of this discussion.) In order for the spousal property basis increase to be available, the property transferred must be "qualified spousal property" (discussed below).

Both the $1.3 million general basis increase and the $3 million spousal property basis increase can be applied to property passing to the surviving spouse. Thus, up to $4.3 million in date-of-death basis step up can be allocated to property received by a surviving spouse.

BACKGROUND

> **Example 1:** Frank Kenilworth died in 2010, leaving an estate that consisted entirely of 100,000 shares of Global Warming, Inc., having an aggregate date of death value of $7.5 million and an aggregate basis (determined under the carryover basis rules) of $2.2 million. Assuming that Kenilworth had a surviving spouse to whom he bequeathed all of this stock, his executor can increase the total basis of the stock to $6.5 million ($2.2 million carryover basis + $1.3 million general basis increase + $3 million spousal property basis increase). Had Kenilworth's spouse not survived him (or had he not bequeathed any stock to his surviving spouse), his executor could have only increased the basis of the stock to a maximum of $3.5 million ($2.2 million + $1.3 million).

Basis increase limited to fair market value. Basis increases made under any of the basis increase provisions of the carryover basis rules cannot be used to increase the basis of any property above its fair market value in the hands of the decedent on the date of his or her death (Code Sec. 1022(d)).

> **Example 2:** Assume the same facts as in Example 1, except that the aggregate date-of-death value of the stock going to Kenilworth's surviving spouse is $6 million. This $6 million amount limits the amount to which the stock can be stepped up; the potential additional $500,000 in basis step up would go unused.

Adjustments to $1.3 million amount. The $1.3 million general basis increase amount can be increased by:

- the sum of any capital loss carryover under Code Sec. 1212(b), and the amount of any net operating loss carryover under Code Sec. 172 that would have been carried over from the decedent's last tax year to a later tax year, but for the decedent's death, plus
- the sum of any losses that would have been allowable under Code Sec. 165, if the property acquired from the decedent had been sold at fair market value immediately before the decedent's death (Code Sec. 1022(b)(2)(C)).

Nonresidents who are not U.S. citizens. In place of the $1.3 million general basis increase amount that is available to the estates of U.S. citizens and residents, the estates of nonresidents who are not U.S. citizens are allowed an aggregate step up of $60,000 only (Code Sec. 1022(b)(3)(A)). Although the estates of nonresident, non-U.S. citizens are allowed the $3 million spousal property basis increase, they are not allowed adjustments for carryover basis under Code Sec. 1212(b), net operating loss carryovers under Code Sec. 172, or losses that would have been allowable under Code Sec. 165 (Code Sec. 1022(b)(3)(B)).

> **Comment:** EGTRRA's $1.3 million general basis increase provision of the carryover basis rule can be expected to generate additional challenges—and possibly lawsuits—against estate fiduciaries. EGTRRA gives executors the power to allocate the $1.3 million basis increase to property of their choosing. General principles of fiduciary law require that this allocation be made fairly. But, what is considered fair? If the amount of assets distributed to the beneficiaries is such

¶740

BACKGROUND

that the fully available $1.3 million basis increase cannot be utilized, each beneficiary will receive assets with basis increased to its date-of-death value Code Sec. 1022(a)(2)(B), and complaints about how the allocations were distributed should not arise. However, where the $1.3 million basis increase is fully utilized, and the basis of all assets cannot be raised to their date-of-death value, there may be disputes among beneficiaries. Even in the simplest situation, where all beneficiaries share equally in all property distributed, a pro-rata allocation of the basis increase among beneficiaries may not be perceived as fair by lower-income tax bracket beneficiaries, who will see a disproportionate share of actual benefits going to the higher-bracket beneficiaries. When different assets are distributed to different beneficiaries, the chances that some will feel unfairly treated with regard to the amount of their increased basis allocations would seemingly increase. With the return of the stepped-up basis rules, these increased basis allocation questions are no longer present, since all assets distributed from the estate will generally be received by beneficiaries with a basis computed on the assets' date-of-death value.

Spousal property basis increase.—In order for the $3 million spousal property basis increase to be available, the property transferred to the surviving spouse must be "qualified spousal property" (Code Sec. 1022(c)(3)). To be classified as qualified spousal property, the transferred property must be either "outright transfer property," or "qualified terminable interest property" (QTIP property).

Outright transfer property. As a general rule, outright transfer property means any interest in property acquired from a decedent by the decedent's surviving spouse (Code Sec. 1022(c)(4)). However, in order to so qualify, the property interest transferred to the surviving spouse must not terminate or fail on the lapse of time or on the occurrence, or the failure to occur, of some event or contingency. A property interest passing to the surviving spouse will fail this test if:

- an interest in the same property has passed (for less than adequate and full consideration) from the decedent to any person other than the surviving spouse or other than the estate of the surviving spouse; and

- by reason of its passing, such person, or his or her heirs or assigns, may possess or enjoy any part of the property after such termination or failure of the interest passing to the surviving spouse; or

- such interest is to be acquired for the surviving spouse pursuant to directions of the decedent, by the decedent's executor, or by a trustee of a trust (Code Sec. 1022(c)(4)(B)).

A provision of a decedent's will or trust that conditioned a marital bequest on the spouse surviving the decedent for up to six months, or on not dying in a common disaster with the decedent, will not disqualify property transferred to the surviving spouse from being an outright transfer for purposes of the spousal property basis increase, provided that the surviving spouse does in fact outlive these survivorship contingencies (Code Sec. 1022(b)(4)(C)).

Qualified terminable interest property. The definition of qualified terminable interest property (QTIP) for purposes of the spousal basis increase rules closely tracks the

BACKGROUND

statutory language of the QTIP provisions relating to the allowance of the estate tax marital deduction available under pre-2001 law (Code Sec. 2056(b)(7)(B)). In order to qualify as a QTIP for a spousal property basis increase under the modified carryover basis at death rules, the property must pass from the decedent to the surviving spouse, who must have a "qualified income interest for life" in the transferred property (Code Sec. 1022(b)(5)(A)).

Qualified income interest for life. A surviving spouse will be deemed to have a qualified income interest for life if:

- the surviving spouse is entitled to all income from the property, payable at least annually, or has a usufruct interest for life in the property under Louisiana law, and

- no person has a power to appoint any part of the property to anyone other than the surviving spouse during the surviving spouse's lifetime.

For purposes of determining the portion of the transferred property that may qualify as QTIP under the spousal property basis increase rules, a bequest of a specific portion of property will be treated as separate property. The term "specific portion" includes only a portion that is determined with reference to a fraction or percentage (Code Sec. 1022(c)(5)(D)).

Ownership by decedent.—In order for property to be eligible for either the $1.3 million general basis increase or the $3 million spousal property basis increase, the property must have been owned by the decedent at the time of his or her death (Code Sec. 1022(d)(1)(A)). Specific rules are provided to determine this ownership question for jointly held property, revocable trusts, property subject to a power of appointment, and community property.

Property acquired within three years of death.—The basis increase provisions of the modified carryover basis at death rules do not apply to property acquired by the decedent by gift or lifetime transfer for less than adequate and full consideration in money or money's worth during the three-year period ending on the date of the decedent's death (Code Sec. 1022(d)(1)(C)(i)). However, this prohibition does not apply to property received by the decedent from his or her spouse during the three-year period, provided that the spouse did not acquire the property in whole or in part by gift or by lifetime transfer for less than adequate and full consideration (Code Sec. 1022(d)(1)(C)(ii)).

Stock of certain entities.—The provisions of the modified carryover basis at death rules that allow basis increases generally do not apply to the stock of certain foreign entities, or to the stock of a DISC (Domestic International Sales Corporation) (Code Sec. 1022(d)(1)(D)).

Property acquired from a decedent.—In order for the carryover basis rules at death rules to apply, the property in question must be "acquired from the decedent." Accordingly, the following property will be deemed to be acquired from a decedent:

- property acquired by bequest, devise, or inheritance, or by the decedent's estate from the decedent,

¶740

BACKGROUND

- property transferred by the decedent during lifetime to (a) a "qualified revocable trust" under Code Sec. 645(b)(1) (a trust in which the deceased grantor retained revocation powers, thereby causing the trust's income to have been taxed to the grantor during life), or (b) any other trust with respect to which the decedent had reserved the right to change the enjoyment of the trust through the exercise of a power to alter, amend, or terminate the trust (powers that would also cause the trust income to be taxed to the grantor during life), or

- any other property passing from the decedent by reason of death to the extent that such property passed without consideration. Life insurance, death benefits and property passing by way of a survivorship provision of a jointly held property would qualify under this provision (Code Sec. 1022(e)).

> **Comment:** The above three categories were evidently designed to incorporate within the definition of "property acquired from the decedent," all property transfers not supported by consideration that cannot fairly be characterized as gifts.

Income in respect of a decedent. The carryover basis at death rules do not apply to property that constitutes an item of income in respect of a decedent under Code Sec. 691 (Code Sec. 1022(f)). (Income in respect of a decedent is income that the decedent had an enforceable right to during life, but was not received until after death, and thus, was not reportable on the decedent's final income tax return.)

Liabilities in excess of basis generally disregarded. For purposes of computing basis in property acquired from a decedent, and in determining whether gain is recognized on an acquisition of property, an asset's liabilities in excess of basis are generally disregarded (Code Sec. 1022(g)). This rule applies to property acquired from:

- a decedent by a decedent's estate or other beneficiary that is not tax exempt; and

- a decedent's estate by any beneficiary that is not tax exempt.

> **Comment:** The carryover basis at death rules enacted by EGTRRA did not contain a "fresh-start rule" that would step up the basis of property held by decedents to the effective date of the provision (that is, January 1, 2010). Because of this, no matter how long an investor owned property, if the investor dies after December 31, 2009, and still owns the property at death, his or her executor will be called upon to determine the tax basis of any noncash property that will pass to the investor's heirs or beneficiaries at death. Although this may less difficult with respect to readily marketable securities in some cases, it could be a particularly daunting task for other types of property, and could lead to uncertainty in establishing basis. This could invite the IRS to make its own determination of basis, which is rarely to the advantage of taxpayers.

Sunset provision. Under the sunset provision of EGTRRA, amendments made by the Act, including the carryover basis provisions of Code Sec. 1022, will not apply to decedents dying after December 31, 2010 (Act Sec. 901 of EGTRRA).

NEW LAW EXPLAINED

Carryover basis replaced with stepped-up basis rules.—Subject to a special election available to the executors of estates of decedents dying in 2010, the modified carryover basis rules for property acquired from a decedent (Code Sec. 1022, as added by P.L. 107-16) will not apply to decedents dying after December 31, 2009, under the Tax Relief, Unemployment Insurance Reauthorization, and Job Creation Act of 2010 (P.L. 111-312). Thus, for decedents dying after this date, the stepped-up basis rules of Code Sec. 1014 will apply. Under the stepped-up basis rules, the income tax basis of property acquired from a decedent at death generally is stepped up (or stepped down) to equal its value as of the date of the decedent's death (or on the date six months after the date of death, if alternate valuation (Code Sec. 2032), is elected on the decedent's estate tax return).

Executor election for estates of decedents dying in 2010. A special election provision (Act Sec. 301(c) of the Tax Relief Act of 2010) gives executors the power to elect application of the EGTRRA rules (that is, no estate or GST taxes, and carryover basis) for estates of decedents dying after December 31, 2009, and before January 1, 2011. This election must be made at the time and in the manner as provided by the IRS, and is revocable only with the consent of the IRS. See related discussion at ¶ 705.

For purposes of this election, an executor means the executor or administrator of the decedent's estate. If no executor or administrator is appointed, any person in actual or constructive possession of any property of the decedent is considered an executor (Code Sec. 2203).

Affect of sunset provision. In accordance with the amended sunset provision (Act Secs. 101(a) and 304 of the Tax Relief Act of 2010), the change related to the stepped-up basis provision will expire after December 31, 2012. After this expiration, the law relating to basis of property acquired from a decedent will revert to the law that was in effect before EGTRRA. Because pre-EGTRRA law included the stepped-up basis rules ofCode Sec. 1014, rather than the carryover basis rules of Code Sec. 1022, the stepped-up basis rules will also apply to estates of decedents dying on or after January 1, 2013. Seemingly, the only impact from the sunset provision would be that a change made by the American Jobs Creation Act of 2004 (P.L. 108-357) would no longer apply. This change to Code Sec. 1014(b)(5) terminated the rule providing that the basis of stock in a foreign personal holding company is the lower of its fair market value at the date of the decedent's death, or its basis in the hands of the decedent.

Where the property distributed was valued for estate tax purposes under the special valuation rules of Code Sec. 2032A, the basis of the property will equal its value determined under that Code Section.

Another special rule applies to appreciated property acquired by a decedent as a gift within one year of death if the property passes from the decedent to the original donor or to the donor's spouse (Code Sec. 1014(e)). The basis of such property in the hands of the original donor (or his or her spouse) is the decedent's adjusted basis in the property immediately prior to death, rather than its fair market value on the date of death.

¶740

NEW LAW EXPLAINED

Comment: This provision is intended to prevent individuals from transferring property in anticipation of a donee's death merely to obtain a tax-free step up in basis upon receipt of the property from the donee's estate.

Comment: In the typical situation where property acquired from a decedent had increased in value during the decedent's life, this basis rule allowed the recipient of the property to avoid income tax on any of the gain that occurred during the decedent's lifetime.

Example 1: At the death of his father, Simon, Jay Lynch received 2,500 shares of Family Corp. stock from his father's testamentary trust. At his death on January 1, 2011, Simon had a basis of $100 per share in his Family Corp. stock, and each Family Corp. share had a fair market value of $1,000. In each of the 2,500 shares received from his father, Jay will have a basis stepped up to its date of death value, that is, $1,000. If, upon receipt of his shares, Jay chooses to immediately sell them (assuming the value of each share is still $1,000), he will incur no taxable gain because his basis is equal to the stock's fair market value. Thus, the taxation of the $900 gain per share that had occurred during his father's lifetime is permanently excused: none of Jay's $2.25 million gain (2,500 shares × $900) will be taxed.

The stepped-up basis applicable for property acquired from a decedent is in sharp contrast to the basis of property computed under the carryover basis at death rules enacted by EGTRRA. Under the carryover basis rule, the basis of property transferred by a decedent to another person becomes the basis in the hands of the recipient; the decedent's basis is "carried over" to the recipient. If the property transferred at death had appreciated greatly in the decedent's lifetime, the recipient would face a significant capital gain on a later sale of the property.

Example 2: Assume the same facts as in Example 1, except that Simon died on December 31, 2010. The 2,500 shares transferred to his son, Jay, will have a basis equal to that of Simon ($100), assuming that the executor elects to have the EGTRRA rules apply. If Jay were to immediately sell his stock at $1,000 per share, he would incur a taxable gain of $900 per share. If the executor of Simon's estate allocates the full $1.3 million general basis increase to Jay's Family Corp. stock, upon sale, Jay will still have a taxable gain of $950,000 ($2.25 million – $1.3 million).

Under the stepped-basis rule, the recipient of property is also generally deemed to have met the one-year capital gains holding period, regardless of how long the decedent had owned the property before death (Code Sec. 1223(9)).

Although the recipient of property acquired from a decedent dying after December 31, 2010, generally receives a basis that is stepped up to its date of death value, there are exceptions to this rule:

¶740

NEW LAW EXPLAINED

- The income tax basis of property for which special use valuation has been elected will be equal to its special use value, as determined for estate tax purposes under Code Sec. 2032A (Code Sec. 1014(a)(2)).

- The basis of stock in a Domestic International Sales Corporation (DISC) acquired from a decedent must be reduced by the amount that would have been treated as ordinary income under Code Sec. 995 if the decedent had lived and sold the stock on the applicable estate valuation date (Code Sec. 1014(d)). (This rule is to prevent the recipient of stock from escaping taxation on the DISC income attributable to the stock when the recipient disposes it.)

- A decedent's executor may elect to exclude from the taxable estate up to 40 percent of the value of land subject to a qualified conservation exclusion under Code Sec. 2031(c). To the extent that the value of such land is excluded from the decedent's taxable estate, the basis of the property is not stepped up to its date of death value (Code Sec. 1014(a)(4)) (see ¶ 735).

    Planning Note: Under the stepped-up basis rules, an asset owner's poor record-keeping and/or general ignorance of an asset's basis is "cured" at his or her death, since the asset's basis will be stepped up to its date of death value. Because of this, assets with hard to determine basis are no longer a problem (at least from a tax basis perspective). If they are held until death, the owner's basis is generally stepped up to the asset's fair market value on date of death.

    Planning Note: A possible downside of the return of the stepped-up basis at death rules is that advisors may tend to pay inordinate attention to the tax advantage of the asset owner retaining the asset until death. Although the heirs and possibly the asset owner's estate will gain a tax advantages if an appreciated asset is retained until death, the overall economic affect of retaining an under-performing appreciated asset must be considered.

    Comment: Possibly the biggest advantage in the changeover from the carryover basis at death rules to the stepped-up basis at death rules relates to estate fiduciaries, and issues relating to uncertainty, fiduciary responsibilities of fairness, and tax compliance.

    Without a doubt, the carryover basis at death rules are much more complex than the stepped-up basis rules. Accordingly, estate fiduciaries may well charge higher estate settlement fees to compensate them for the additional time likely to be spent to establish asset bases and to deal with allocation of the $1.3 million and $3 million basis adjustments. Estate fiduciaries may also charge higher fees to deal with the additional time spent establishing basis for "problem assets," defending those basis calculations before the IRS, and for filing the additional tax returns required by the carryover basis rules (see the "Background" discussion at ¶ 745).

    State Tax Consequences: The replacement of the modified carryover basis rules with stepped-up basis rules for property acquired from a decedent dying after 2009 will affect states that adopted the modified carryover basis for decedents dying in 2010 and that have Code conformity dates that do not adopt this change. For these states, the basis of property received from a decedent dying

NEW LAW EXPLAINED

after 2009 will differ for federal and state purposes and an adjustment may be required on disposition of the property. However, under the federal law, an executor may elect to apply the carryover basis for decedents dying in 2010, which may mitigate the effects of this change on the states. There will be no affect on states that did not adopt the modified carryover basis.

Practical Analysis: Robert Keebler, Partner and Peter Melcher, Associate, with Keebler & Associates, Green Bay, Wisconsin, observe that a comparison of the tax impact of an environment with no estate tax, but a modified carryover basis (Code Sec. 1022, as opposed to a tax regime that includes an estate tax with stepped-up basis at death, may not be entirely clear cut. For decedents who are single or the second spouse to die and whose estate is less than $5 million (the applicable exclusion amount for decedents dying in 2010), no estate tax and a full step-up in basis would clearly be more valuable. However, in the case of decedents with estates over $5 million, quantitative analysis would be required to determine which is the more favorable tax regime. The independent variables that would need to be considered are the amount of basis that heirs would receive under the modified carryover basis rules and the size of the estate, the estate tax rate, and the capital gains tax rate.

With these points in mind, it is possible to calculate a "break-even" estate size given different amounts of carryover basis prior to addition of the allowable $1.3 million amount. Because the carryover basis alternative grows more favorable as estate size increases, any estate larger than the break-even point would be better off under Code Sec. 1022, and an estate smaller than the break-even point would be better off under the estate tax alternative (using the new 2010 estate tax parameters). This favorability comparison can be measured based on the sum of the estate tax that would be paid by the estate and the income tax that would be paid by the heirs, assuming they sold the assets immediately after receiving them.

Assuming the decedent has a carryover basis of $0 and the value of the estate is $5 million. Under these assumptions, the $1.3 million basis increase permitted under Code Sec. 1022 would increase the total basis to $1.3 million. Accordingly, the income tax payable (assuming a 15-percent capital gains rate) would be $555,000 [($5.0 million FMV – $1.3 million basis) x 0.15 = $555,000], and the amount of estate tax would be $0. Note that if the capital gains rate increased to the 20 percent, and the other assumptions were the same, the income tax payable would be $740,000, as noted in the following chart.

	Code Sec. 1022 (15% Capital Gains Rate)	Code Sec. 1022 (20% Capital Gains Rate)	2010 Estate Tax Rules
Estate Tax Payable	$0	$0	$0
Income Tax Payable	555,000	740,000	0
Total	555,000	740,000	0

The point at which the alternatives will break even is $5 million, plus the amount represented by the following formula.

NEW LAW EXPLAINED

(1) $555,000 + 0.15% (assuming 15-percent capital gains rate) = 0.35X

(2) Subtracting 0.15 from both sides of the equation, yields $555,000 = 0.20X

(3) Solving for X, yields $555,000/0.20 = $2,775,000

(4) Adding the amount in (3) to $5 million results in a break-even point of $7,775,000

This result can be checked. Looking at the Code Sec. 1022 alternative first, if the value of the assets is $7,775,000, the gain realized on the sale is $6,475,000 ($7,775,000 − $1.3 million). Assuming a 15-percent capital gains rate, the income tax payable would be $971,250 and there would be no estate tax. Instead, using the 2010 estate tax rules, $2,775,000 would be subject to estate tax ($7,775,000 − $5 million) and the tax payable on this amount would be 0.35 x $2,775,000 = $971,250.

	Code Sec. 1022 (15% Capital Gains Rate)	2010 Estate Tax Rules
Estate Tax Payable	$0	$971,250
Income Tax Payable	971,250	0
Total	971,250	971,250

Note that if the capital gains rate was instead 20 percent, applying the same formula would result in a break-even point of $9,933,333 and a tax payable amount of $1,726,667.

The break-even point is simply the estate tax value at which the estate tax payable equals the income tax payable. The following chart shows the break-even points for varying amounts of carryover basis, assuming either a 15- or 20-percent capital gains tax rate. When the carryover basis amount exceeds $3.7 million, the Code Sec. 1022 alternative is superior regardless of the size of the estate—there is no break-even point.

Carryover Basis	Break-Even Value (15% Capital Gains Rate)	Break-Even Value (20% Capital Gains Rate)
$0	$7,775,000	$9,933,333
500,000	7,400,000	9,266,667
1,000,000	7,025,000	8,600,000
1,500,000	6,650,000	7,933,333
2,000,000	6,275,000	7,266,667
3,700,000	5,000,000	5,000,000
>3,700,000*	None	None

* Assumes taxable estate exceeds $5 million, otherwise there would be no tax under either alternative.

Practical Analysis: Carol Cantrell, CPA, JD, CAP®, Briggs & Veselka Co., Bellaire, Texas, notes that the modified carryover basis rules introduced by EGTRRA have created a number of issues for practitioners to confront as described in the following points.

¶740

NEW LAW EXPLAINED

Code Sec. 1022 basis carryover and Code Sec. 754 elections. When a partner dies, the basis of his partnership interest is adjusted to its market value on the partner's death, or the alternate valuation date, reduced to the extent that the value is attributable to income in respect of a decedent (Code Sec. 1014(a) and Reg. § 1.742-1). In addition, the estate or successor partner receives a long-term holding period in his partnership interest (Code Sec. 1223(9)). But, this only affects the partnership interest and has no effect on the underlying partnership property. Thus, if the partnership sells an asset after a partner dies, the partner's estate or other successor will report his share of gain just like all the other partners as if no basis adjustment occurred.

However, if the partnership has a Code Sec. 754 election in effect, the basis of underlying partnership property is also adjusted as a result of the partner's death (Code Sec. 743(a)). A Code Sec. 754 election is effective regardless of whether the basis adjustment occurs as a result of Code Sec. 1014 or 1022. However, any basis adjustment under Code Sec. 1022 depends on the executor's affirmative election to allocate part of the decedent's $1.3 or $3 million spousal basis increase. If the partnership makes a Code Sec. 754 election, the successor partner acquires a basis in his share of the underlying partnership assets as if he had purchased an undivided interest in them at market value on the date of death. The Code Sec. 754 election has no effect on the holding period of the partnership assets. Nor does it affect the basis of any other partner (Reg. § 1.743-1(j)(1)).

This inside basis increase allows the successor partner to recognize a smaller share of gain or a larger share of loss than his partners when the partnership sells the assets on hand at the decedent's death. Once the partnership makes a Code Sec. 754 election, the IRS can bind the taxpayers to their original representations of value under the duty of consistency (FSA Letter Ruling 200234006).

Code Sec. 1022 basis carryover and smaller estates. The generous basis adjustments under Code Sec. 1022 will probably afford most estates worth less than $10 million a complete step up in basis, except for income in respect of a decedent (IRD), which cannot be stepped up under any circumstance. There are several reasons for this. First of all, the $1.3 and $3 million basis increases are added on to the decedent's existing basis and most people have a fair amount of basis in their property to begin with. Second, the estate, revocable trust, or any individual who acquires the decedent's personal residence may exclude up to $250,000 ($500,000 if married) of gain on a sale of the residence if they, together with the decedent, met the two out of five-year ownership and use requirements under Code Sec. 121(a). And third, the $1.3 and $3 million basis increases are further increased by any unused capital loss carryovers, net operating loss carryovers, and losses that would have been allowed under Code Sec. 165 if the property had been sold at fair market value immediately before the decedent's death. This last provision can be significant. Code Sec. 165 covers losses arising from the sale or disposition of business or investment property. In other words, if the decedent has any investment or business property that is worth less than its cost basis, the decline in value can provide additional basis step up, which can be used on any of the decedent's property.

NEW LAW EXPLAINED

Example: Joe Brown is married and died in 2010 with the following assets:

	Cost	FMV	Reallocate Built-in Losses	Allocate $4.3m Basis Increase	Adjusted Basis Under Code Sec. 1022
Residence	$500,000	$1,000,000		$250,000	$750,000
Vacation Home	250,000	700,000		450,000	700,000
Stocks	2,000,000	$1,500,000	(500,000)		1,500,000
Family Partnership	1,000,000	5,100,000	500,000	3,600,000	5,100,000
IRA (IRD)	-0-	800,000			-0-
Personal Use Property	500,000	150,000			150,000
Total	$4,250,000	$9,250,000	-0-	$4,300,000	$8,200,000

The modified carryover basis rules give Brown's estate a complete step up in basis to fair market value for all Brown's assets except the IRA, which is IRD, his residence, and his personal property. Not only does Brown's executor have $4.3 million of basis increase that he can allocate among assets as he chooses, but he has $500,000 of built-in losses that he can allocate as desired. In addition, any gain on sale of the residence can be offset by the $250,000/$500,000 gain exclusion under Code Sec. 121 if Brown and his successor together meet the use and ownership rules of Code Sec. 121(a). Note that Brown's personal property is not eligible for any additional basis increase because the loss would not be deductible under Code Sec. 165 if it were sold at fair market value. Therefore, most estates of this size with modest basis and appreciation in their assets will be afforded nearly a full step up to fair market value even under the carryover basis rules.

Code Sec. 1022 basis carryover and employee stock options. To the extent that the new carryover basis rules apply in 2010, the basis of incentive stock options (ISOs) will no longer be automatically stepped-up to the date-of-death values as they were under Code Sec. 1014. Instead, the decedent's cost basis of the ISOs (which is usually zero) carries over to the beneficiaries of the estate for both regular and the alternative minimum tax (AMT). If there is a large spread between the option's exercise price and the stock's fair market value at the time of death, the executor might consider applying some of the decedent's limited basis step-up to the options. The spread on an ISO is not an item of IRD like it would be for a nonqualified stock option (NQSO) taxed under Code Sec. 83. The executor cannot apply any step-up in basis to NQSOs because they are income in respect of a decedent under Code Sec. 691 (Code Sec. 691(a), Reg. § 1.83-1(d), and Code Sec. 1022(f)). Thus the basis of NQSOs received from a decedent is zero (as under the rules prior to 2010) and no part of the $1.3 million or $3 million special step-up or unused date of death losses may be applied to increase their basis. In effect, the treatment of NQs is the same under both Code Secs. 1014 and 1022.

Code Sec. 1022 basis carryover and revocable trusts. Not all property of the decedent or his estate qualifies for a basis increase under Code Sec. 1022. Only property that was owned by and acquired from the decedent is eligible (Code Sec. 1022(d)(1)(A)). Code Sec. 1022(d)(1)(B) provides that the decedent is treated as owning property transferred to a qualified revocable trust (as defined in Code Sec.

NEW LAW EXPLAINED

645(b)(1)). Code Sec. 645(b)(1) defines a qualified revocable trust as "any trust (or portion thereof) which was treated under section 676 as owned by the decedent of the estate referred to in subsection (a) by reason of a power of the grantor (determined without regard to section 672(e))." Code Sec. 1022(e)(2) provides that property is considered as having been acquired from the decedent if it was transferred by the decedent during his lifetime to a qualified revocable trust as defined in Code Sec. 645(b)(1) or to any other trust with respect to which the decedent reserved the right to make any change in the enjoyment thereof through the exercise of a power to alter, amend or terminate the trust.

This reference to qualified revocable trusts (QRTs) has led many to wonder whether a revocable trust must make the Code Sec. 645 election to be treated as part of the estate in order to qualify property owned by the trust for the special basis increases under Code Sec. 1022. However, the Conference Report to the Economic Growth and Tax Relief Reconciliation Act (EGTRRA) of 2001 (H.R. 107-84) and the Joint Committee on Taxation's General Explanation of Tax Legislation Enacted in the 107th Congress explain that property to which the modified carryover basis rules apply includes:

* * *

(3) property transferred by the decedent during his or her lifetime in trust to pay the income for life to or on the order of or on the direction of the decedent, with the right reserved to the decedent at all times before his death to revoke the trust, [fn 61. This is the same property the basis of which is stepped up to date of death fair market value under prior law section 1014(b)(2)]

(4) property transferred by the decedent during his lifetime in trust to pay the income for life to or on the order or direction of the decedent with the right reserved to the decedent at all times before his death to make any change to the enjoyment thereof through the exercise of a power to alter, amend, or terminate the trust. [fn 62. This is the same property the basis of which is stepped up to date of death fair market value under prior law section 1014(b)(3)" (Conference Report to the Economic Growth and Tax Relief Reconciliation Act (EGTRRA) of 2001 (H.R. 107-84), 2001-3 C.B. 306 (May 26, 2001); Joint Committee on Taxation's General Explanation of Tax Legislation Enacted in the 107th Congress, 2001-3 C.B. 596 (Jan. 24, 2003)).

Because the language above includes all revocable trusts, it seems clear that it is not necessary for a revocable trust to make a Code Sec. 645 election in order for the modified carryover basis rules to apply to property owned by the trust.

Practical Analysis: Michael J. Grace, Milbank, Tweed, Hadley & McCloy LLP, Washington, DC, observes that for decedents who died during 2010, an executor's option of electing to apply the estate tax under EGTRRA (i.e., no estate tax in 2010) instead of the newly amended and reinstated estate tax may influence a testamentary transferee's income tax planning for disposing of inherited property. That is because the executor's decision will affect a transferee's basis in inherited property

NEW LAW EXPLAINED

and, consequently, the amount of taxable gain or loss the transferee will realize upon disposing of the property. If the executor elects the estate tax under EGTRRA, then the transferee takes a modified carryover basis in the property. If, on the other hand, the estate is subject to the estate tax under the Tax Relief Act of 2010, then the transferee takes a basis equaling the property's fair market value on either the date of the decedent's death or an alternate valuation date. For example, if a transferred property's fair market value on the selected valuation date exceeds the decedent's basis in the property, then the transferee under the reinstated estate tax regime obtains a "stepped up" basis.

The Tax Relief Act of 2010 temporarily extends the maximum income tax rate of 15 percent on net capital gains for taxable years through December 31, 2012. Absent intervening legislation, that rate will increase to 20 percent beginning in 2013. See ¶405, Maximum Capital Gains Rates.

An executor's choice between the available estate tax regimes for 2010 may affect a transferee's income tax planning for disposing of inherited property, as follows. Assume that an executor elects to apply the federal estate tax under EGTRRA. The estate, thus, is not subject to federal estate tax, but a transferee of property from the estate takes a modified carryover basis in the property. Assume also that, had the estate instead become subject to the estate tax as amended and reinstated by the Tax Relief Act of 2010, the transferee would have taken a stepped-up basis in the transferred property exceeding the modified carryover basis. The transferee, thus, can anticipate recognizing a higher capital gain (or a smaller capital loss) upon the eventual sale of the transferred property compared to the property's basis having been stepped up. Assume also that the transferee does not anticipate having capital losses to shelter capital gain upon selling the inherited property. The transferee might consider selling the carryover basis property before 2013 when the tax rates on net capital gains are scheduled to increase.

▶ **Effective date.** The stepped-up basis at death rules of Code Sec. 1014 apply, and the carryover basis at death rules of Code Sec. 1022 do not apply, to estates of decedents dying after December 31, 2009, unless the executor of an estate of a decedent dying after December 31, 2009, and before January 1, 2011, elects application of EGTRRA estate tax and carryover basis rules (Act Sec. 301(c) of the Tax Relief, Unemployment Insurance Reauthorization, and Job Creation Act of 2010 (P.L. 111-312)).

Law source: Law at ¶5490, ¶5500, and ¶7025. Committee Report at ¶10,130.

— Act Sec. 301(a) of the Tax Relief, Unemployment Insurance Reauthorization, and Job Creation Act of 2010 (P.L. 111-312), amending subtitle E of title V of the Economic Growth and Tax Relief Reconciliation Act of 2001 (EGTRRA) (P.L. 107-16), and affecting Code Secs. 1014 and 1022.

— Act Sec. 301(c), providing a special election with respect to decedents dying in 2010;

— Act Sec. 301(e), providing the effective date.

¶740

NEW LAW EXPLAINED

Reporter references: For further information, consult the following CCH reporters.

— Standard Federal Tax Reporter, ¶29,380.01 and ¶29,498.01

— Tax Research Consultant, ESTGIFT: 54,000, ESTGIFT: 54,200, SALES: 6,150, and DEPR: 6,254

— Practical Tax Explanation, §16,301

— Federal Estate and Gift Tax Reporter, ¶18,115.01

¶745 Reporting and Penalty Provisions

SUMMARY OF NEW LAW

The stepped-up basis at death rules of Code Sec. 1014 have been reinstated for estates of decedents dying after December 31, 2009. Accordingly, the reporting requirements and penalty provisions relating to the carryover basis at death rules (Code Sec. 1022) no longer apply to estates of decedents dying after that date. However, the carryover basis reporting and penalty provisions will apply to estates of decedents dying in 2010 if executors elect to be bound by the EGTRRA estate tax and carryover basis provisions.

BACKGROUND

The Economic Growth and Tax Relief Reconciliation Act of 2001 (EGTRRA) (P.L. 107-16) provides that, effective for property acquired from a decedent dying after December 31, 2009, the income tax basis of property acquired from a decedent is generally to be carried over from the decedent (Code Sec. 1022). This rule replaces the stepped-up basis at death rule of Code Sec. 1014, which allowed the recipients of property acquired from a decedent to receive a basis in the property generally equal to its date-of-death value. The carryover basis rules are much more complex than the stepped-up basis rules they replaced, and are expected to raise more revenue through greater taxable gains to the property recipients, thereby partially offsetting the revenue loss caused by the one-year sunset of the estate and generation-skipping transfer (GST) taxes (see ¶740). Accordingly, the government has a vital interest in ensuring that individuals who receive property from a decedent after December 31, 2009 will have the information necessary to correctly calculate their tax liability on a later sale or exchange of the property. To do this, the recipient will have to know the property's basis, and the applicable holding period (to determine if capital gains or ordinary income tax rules apply). To this end, EGTRRA mandates rules for fiduciary reporting of basis and holding period information to property recipients, and backs up these rules with penalty provisions to encourage compliance.

Effective for estates of decedents dying after December 31, 2009, an executor of a decedent's estate must file an information return with the IRS, generally due with the decedent's last income tax return, for the following property transfers:

BACKGROUND

- property acquired from a decedent in a "large transfer;" that is, property with a fair market value that exceeds the Code Sec. 1022(b)(2)(B) dollar amount ($1.3 million), without regard to any increase for built-in losses or loss carryovers.

- appreciated property acquired from a decedent that was acquired by the decedent by gift or other lifetime transfer for less than adequate consideration during the three-year period ending on the date of the decedent's death, and for which the filing of a gift tax return was required (Code Sec. 6018(b)(1) and (2)).

Special rules apply in the case of nonresident alien decedents (Code Sec. 6018(b)(3)) and with respect to incomplete returns (Code Sec. 6018(b)(4)).

Information required to be furnished. Executors must provide the following information:

- the name and taxpayer identification number (TIN) of the recipient of the property,

- an accurate description of the property,

- the adjusted basis in the hands of the decedent, and its fair market value on the date of the decedent's death,

- the decedent's holding period for the property,

- sufficient information to determine if gain on any sale of the property would be ordinary income,

- the amount of basis increase allocated to the property: the portion of the $1.3 million general basis increase ($60,000 for nonresidents not citizens) under Code Sec. 1022(b) and the $3 million spousal property basis increase under Code Sec. 1022(c), and

- any additional information as may be prescribed by regulations issued by the IRS (Code Sec. 6075).

  Comment: As of the date of this publication, the IRS has not yet issued guidance regarding the information reporting requirements. Speaking at the AICPA Advanced Estate Planning Conference in Washington, D.C. on July 27, 2010, Catherine Hughes, Attorney–Advisor, Treasury Office of Tax Legislative Counsel, indicated that any guidance the IRS would issue would likely have a delayed effective date in order to grant taxpayers a reasonable amount of time to comply.

Statements to property recipients. In addition to the information return required to be filed with the IRS, the executor or other person required to file that return must provide a written statement to each person listed as a property recipient on the return. The statement must include:

- the name, address, and telephone number of the executor or other person required to make the return, and

- the decedent's adjusted basis in the property and its fair market value of the date of the decedent's death (Code Sec. 6018(e)).

The written statement must be furnished no later than 30 days after the date that the information return is filed.

¶745

BACKGROUND

Donor's written statement to lifetime gift recipients.—A donor who is required to file a gift tax return (Form 709) with respect to gifts made within a calendar year must also send the following written information to the donees listed on the return:

- the name, address, and telephone numbers of the person required to file the gift tax return, and

- the information specified in the gift tax return regarding the property the donee received.

    Comment: Generally, such information would include the donor's adjusted basis in the gifted property, the date of the gift, value of property at date of gift, whether the gift was a split gift between spouses, the description of the gift, and the CUSIP number, if the gifted property is stock (Schedule A, Form 709).

The above written statement must be furnished to the donee no later than 30 days after the gift tax return due date, which is generally April 15 following the calendar year in which the gifts were made (Code Sec. 6019(b)).

Penalties for noncompliance.—EGTRRA includes penalty provisions designed to encourage compliance with the reporting requirements related to the carryover basis at death rules. These penalties apply both to failures to provide information required for property received from a decedent, and property received from a living donor who was required to file a gift tax return relating to the transfer.

Information required to be filed with the IRS. Unless excused by a showing of reasonable cause, the executor or other person who fails to file a return required under Code Sec. 6018 by the applicable due date (including extensions) will be liable for a penalty of $10,000. Additionally, a failure to provide information to the IRS, as required by Code Sec. 6018(b)(2) (relating to appreciated property acquired by the decedent within three years of death), will subject the executor or other person required to file to a penalty of $500 for each such failure (Code Sec. 6716(b) and (c)).

Information required to be furnished to beneficiaries. If the person who is responsible for furnishing beneficiaries with a written statement under Code Sec. 6018(e) and Code Sec. 6019(b) does not do so, that person is subject to a $50 penalty for each such failure, unless the failure is excused by a showing of reasonable cause (Code Sec. 6716(b) and (c)).

Intentional disregard of reporting requirements. If the executor's failure to furnish a return or written information is due to intentional disregard of the carryover basis reporting requirements of Code Sec. 6018 or Code Sec. 6019(b), a five-percent penalty will be assessed. For property acquired from a decedent at death, this penalty will be applied against the fair market value of the property on the date of death. For property acquired by gift, the penalty will be applied against the fair market value of the property on the date of the gift (Code Sec. 6716(d)).

Sunset provision.—Under the sunset provision of EGTRRA, amendments made by the Act will not apply to decedents dying after December 31, 2010 (Act Sec. 901 of P.L. 107-16).

¶745

NEW LAW EXPLAINED

Simplified basis procedure.—Subject to a special election available to the executors of estates of decedents dying in 2010, the modified carryover basis at death rules for property acquired from a decedent (Code Sec. 1022, as added by P.L. 107-16) will not apply to decedents dying after December 31, 2009 (Act Sec. 301(a) of the Tax Relief, Unemployment Insurance Reauthorization, and Job Creation Act of 2010 (P.L. 111-312), amending Act Sec. 901 of the Economic Growth and Tax Relief Reconciliation Act of 2001 (EGTRRA) (P.L. 107-16)). Accordingly, the new reporting and penalty provisions associated with the carryover basis rules will also not apply after that date.

For estates of decedents dying after December 31, 2009, the stepped-up basis rules of Code Sec. 1014 will apply. Under the stepped-up basis rules, the income tax basis of property acquired from a decedent is generally stepped up (or stepped down) to equal its fair market value as of the date of the decedent's death (or on the date six months after date of death, if alternate valuation (Code Sec. 2032) is elected on the decedent's estate tax return). With the return of the stepped-up basis rules, the complicated compliance regime associated with implementing the carryover basis rules is no longer required. Under the stepped-up basis rules, ascertaining basis and holding period of property acquired from a decedent can be a straight-forward process, even without adequate records of the decedent, at least where marketable or readily appraisable assets are involved.

Executor election for estates of decedents dying in 2010. A special election provision (Act Sec. 301(c) of the Tax Relief Act of 2010) gives estate executors the power to elect application of the EGTRRA rules (that is, no estate or GST taxes, and carryover basis) for estates of decedents dying after December 31, 2009 and before January 1, 2011. This election must be made at the time and in the manner as provided by the IRS, and is revocable only with the consent of the IRS. If the election is made, all of the reporting and penalty provisions discussed in the "Background" section will apply. For further discussion of the 2010 election, see ¶ 705 and ¶ 740.

For purposes of this election, an executor means the executor or administrator of the decedent's estate. If no executor or administrator is appointed, any person in actual or constructive possession of any property of the decedent is considered as an executor (Code Sec. 2203).

Affect of sunset provision. In accordance with the amended sunset provision (Act Secs. 101(a) and 304 of the Tax Relief Act of 2010), the change related to the stepped-up basis provision will expire after December 31, 2012. After this expiration, the law relating to basis of property acquired from a decedent will revert to the law that was in effect before the enactment of EGTRRA. Because pre-EGTRRA law included the stepped-up basis rules of Code Sec. 1014, rather than the carryover basis rules of Code Sec. 1022, the stepped-up basis rules will also apply to estates of decedents dying on or after January 1, 2013. Seemingly, the only impact from the sunset provision would be that a change made by the American Jobs Creation Act of 2004 (P.L. 108-357) would no longer apply. This change to Code Sec. 1014(b)(5) terminated the rule providing that the basis of stock in a foreign personal holding company is the lower of its fair market value at the date of the decedent's death, or its basis in the hands of the decedent.

¶745

NEW LAW EXPLAINED

Practical Analysis: Carol Cantrell, CPA, JD, CAP®, Briggs & Veselka Co., Bellaire, Texas, notes that the special basis adjustments under Code Sec. 1022 are only available to the extent that the decedent's executor allocates them on a return required under Code Sec. 6018. Thus, the Code places the burden on the executor to make the basis allocation decisions (Code Sec. 6018(a)). If there is more than one executor, presumably the governing instrument or local law will address whether this decision can be made by only one executor, a majority, or requires a unanimous vote of all the executors. This is an onerous job for the executor. In addition, the Tax Relief Act of 2010 gives the executor discretion to choose whether to apply zero estate tax and the carryover basis rules or apply the reinstated estate tax with a $5 million exclusion amount and stepped-up basis. Thus, the job of many executors has become even more perilous.

Many decedents will not have executors because they transferred all their property during their lifetime to a revocable "will substitute" trust. In that case, the question arises as to who makes this decision to allocate carryover basis if there is no executor. Does the job fall to the trustee of the living trust? Code Sec. 2203 provides that the term executor means "the executor or administrator of the decedent, or if there is no executor or administrator appointed, qualified, and acting within the United States, then any person in actual or constructive possession of any property of the decedent."

Moreover, the Conference Report to the Economic Growth and Tax Relief Reconciliation Act (EGTRRA) of 2001 (H.R. 107-84) and the Joint Committee on Taxation's General Explanation of Tax Legislation Enacted in the 107th Congress explain that "For transfers at death of any non-cash assets in excess of $1.3 million and for appreciated property received by a decedent via reportable gift within three years of death, the executor of the estate (or the trustee of a revocable trust) would report to the IRS:" (Conference Report to the Economic Growth and Tax Relief Reconciliation Act (EGTRRA) of 2001 (H.R. 107-84), 2001-3 C.B. 308 (May 26, 2001); Joint Committee on Taxation's General Explanation of Tax Legislation Enacted in the 107th Congress, 2001-3 C.B. 598 (Jan. 24, 2003)).

Therefore, it is clear that the trustee of a revocable trust is charged with reporting under Code Sec. 6018. A decedent with property in both an estate and a revocable trust will conceivably have two fiduciaries charged with reporting obligations under Code Sec. 6018. How should they resolve disputes over allocating the decedent's $1.3 and $3 million basis increases? Do the executor's decisions trump the trustee's, given the express provision in Code Sec. 6018 charging the executor with the duty to report? How should they resolve disputes when each owes a fiduciary duty to their own beneficiaries?

▶ **Effective date.** The carryover basis reporting and penalty provisions do not apply to estates of decedents dying after December 31, 2009, unless the executor of an estate of a decedent dying after December 31, 2009, and before January 1, 2011, elects application of EGTRRA estate tax and carryover basis rules (see Act Sec. 301(e) of the Tax Relief, Unemployment Insurance Reauthorization, and Job Creation Act of 2010 (P.L. 111-312)).

Law source: Law at ¶5490, ¶5500, ¶5765, ¶5770, ¶5785, ¶5850, and ¶7025. Committee Report at ¶10,130.

NEW LAW EXPLAINED

— Act Sec. 301(a) of the Tax Relief, Unemployment Insurance Reauthorization, and Job Creation Act of 2010 (P.L. 111-312), amending subtitle E of title V, of the Economic Growth and Tax Relief Reconciliation Act of 2001 (EGTRRA) (P.L. 107-16), affecting Code Secs. 6018, 6019(b). 6075, and 6716.

— Act Sec. 301(e), providing the effective date.

Reporter references: For further information, consult the following CCH reporters.

— Tax Research Consultant, ESTGIFT: 54,050

— Practical Tax Explanation, § 16,301

— Federal Estate and Gift Tax Reporter, ¶20,085.09, ¶20,135.05 and ¶21,880.01

¶750 Income Tax Exclusion for Sale of Principal Residence

SUMMARY OF NEW LAW

The exclusion from gross income for gain realized on the sale of a decedent's principal residence sold by a decedent's estate, heir, or qualified revocable trust that was scheduled to expire for decedents dying after December 31, 2010, under the sunset provisions of EGTRRA (Act Sec. 901(a)(1) of P.L. 107-16), remains in effect, but only for estates electing to apply the modified carryover basis rules under Act Sec. 301(c) of the Tax Relief, Unemployment Insurance Reauthorization, and Job Creation Act of 2010. As a result, for estates of decedents dying in 2010, gain on the sale of the decedent's principal residence can be excluded from a decedent's gross income (Code Sec. 121(d)(11)), provided the estate elects to apply the modified carryover basis rules as enacted under EGTRRA. For estates of decedents dying in 2010 that do not make the modified carryover basis election and for estates of decedents dying after December 31, 2010, any gain on the sale of the decedent's principal residence will no longer be eligible for the exclusion.

BACKGROUND

The Economic Growth and Tax Relief Reconciliation Act of 2001 (EGTRRA) (P.L. 107-16) extended the income tax exclusion for gain realized on the sale of a principal residence to a decedent's personal residence sold by either:

- the decedent's estate;

- any individual who acquired the residence from the decedent (within the meaning of Code Sec. 1022) as a result of his or her death; or

- a trust established by the decedent that was a qualified revocable trust (within the meaning of Code Sec. 645(b)(1)) immediately prior to the decedent's death (Code Sec. 121(d)(11)).

BACKGROUND

Caution: This exclusion applies only to decedent's dying in the year 2010 during the repeal of the estate tax and reign of the modified carryover basis rules.

To exclude the gain, the decedent's ownership and use must be taken into account. Thus, the decedent must have owned and occupied the property as his or her principal residence for a total of two years during the five-year period prior to the sale by the estate.

Example 1: Ann Garret owned and occupied her property on Seashell Drive as her primary residence for three of the five years prior to her death. Garret purchased the property for $250,000 and the executor of her estate sold the property, which was part of her residuary estate, for $400,000. Garret died on August 1, 2010, her estate was allowed to exclude the $150,000 ($400,000 − $250,000) gain from income.

However, if a decedent's residence is sold by an heir who occupied the property as his or her principal residence after acquiring it from the decedent, the decedent's ownership and occupancy will be added to that of the heir's in determining whether the two-year ownership and use requirements are met (Senate Finance Committee Report (S. Rep. No. 107-30)). In addition, the decedent's period of occupancy can be combined with that of the heir's regardless of whether a qualified revocable trust owned the residence during such time (Conference Committee Report H.R. Rep. No. 107-84)).

Example 2: Assume the same facts as Example 1, except that Garret owned and occupied the property as her principal residence for one year during the five-year period preceding her death and the property passed to the decedent's daughter, Melissa, upon her death. Melissa occupied the property as her principal residence for one year prior to selling it. By adding Garret's and Melissa's periods of ownership and occupancy, the two-year limit is met and Melissa will be able to exclude the gain realized on the sale.

Planning Note: Under Code Sec. 121(d)(11), the exclusion applies only to sales by the decedent's estate, an individual heir, or a qualified revocable trust. Some commentators have suggested that if the decedent's property, for example, passes to a testamentary trust, the executor may be able to sell the property first and then fund the trust with the sale proceeds so the estate could exclude the gain from income.

Sunset provision. Under the sunset provision of EGTRRA, amendments made by the Act will not apply to decedents dying after December 31, 2010 (Act Sec. 901 of P.L. 107-16).

¶**750**

NEW LAW EXPLAINED

Exclusion of gain on sale of decedent's principal residence remains effective only for certain estates, heirs, and qualified revocable trusts.—For estates of decedent's dying in 2010 that elect to apply the modified carryover basis rules as originally enacted by P.L. 107-16 pursuant to Act Sec. 301(c) of the Tax Relief, Unemployment Insurance Reauthorization, and Job Creation Act of 2010 (P.L. 111-312), the income tax exclusion of gain from the sale of a principal residence will continue to be available with respect to a sale of the decedent's principal residence by the decedent's estate, a person who acquired the residence from the decedent upon his or her death, or a qualified revocable trust established by the decedent immediately prior to the decedent's death (Code Sec. 121(d)(11), as added by P.L. 107-16 and redesignated by P.L. 108-121 and P.L. 109-135). For further discussion of the special election to apply the modified carryover basis rules, see ¶ 740.

For estates of decedents dying in 2010 that do **not** make the election and estates of decedents dying after December 31, 2010, the income tax exclusion of gain from the sale of a decedent's principal residence will no longer be available (Act Sec. 301(e) of the Tax Relief Act of 2010).

> **Caution:** Beginning in 2011 (and in 2010, for estates that do not make the election to apply the carryover basis rules), successors to a decedent's personal residence will no longer be allowed to exclude gain from the sale under Code Sec. 121 unless the successor qualifies for the exclusion independent of the decedent.

> **Comment:** Because the Tax Relief Act of 2010 allows the executor of an estate of a decedent dying in 2010 to elect to apply the modified carryover basis rules, the income tax exclusion from gain on the sale of the decedent's principal residence is still needed to help soften the capital gains blow that estates and heirs could potentially have to pay upon the sale. If Code Sec. 121(d)(11) had not been enacted for 2010, estates and heirs would have had to pay capital gains tax on the sale of the decedent's residence based on the decedent's basis in the property (under the modified carryover basis rules of Code Sec. 1022). The gains could be significant in light of the length of time people generally own a home.

> **Caution:** The changes made to other subsections of Code Sec. 121 by Acts subsequent to EGTRRA are still valid, including the provisions regarding:

- suspension of the five-year period for ownership and use for absences due to:
  - service in the uniformed services or Foreign Service of the United States (Code Sec. 121(d)(9)(A), as added by P.L. 108-121 (Military Family Tax Relief Act of 2003)),
  - extended duty service as an employee of the intelligence community (Code Sec. 121(d)(9)(A), as revised by P.L. 109-432 (Tax Relief and Health Care Act of 2006)), and
  - service as a Peace Corps volunteer (Code Sec. 121(d)(12), as added by P.L. 110-245 (Heroes Earnings Assistance and Relief Tax Act of 2008));
- nonrecognition of gain in certain sales or exchanges in which the principal residence was acquired in a like-kind exchange (Code Sec. 121(d)(10), as

¶750

Limited recognition of gain on appreciated carryover basis property transferred to satisfy pecuniary bequest remains in effect for certain estates.—The limitation on the recognition of gain on appreciated carryover basis property in satisfaction of a pecuniary bequest or an equivalent distribution from a trust will continue to apply to the estates of decedents dying in 2010, provided the executor of the estate elects to apply the modified carryover basis rules (Code Sec. 1040, as amended by the Economic Growth and Tax Relief Reconciliation Act of 2001 (EGTRRA) (P.L. 107-16); Act Sec. 301(c) of the Tax Relief, Unemployment Insurance Reauthorization, and Job Creation Act of 2010 (P.L. 111-312)). For further discussion of the special election to apply the modified carryover basis rules, see ¶ 740

For the estates of decedents dying in 2010 that do not make the election and estates of decedents dying after December 31, 2010, the Code Sec. 1040 limitation on the recognition of gain by an estate or trust on the distribution of property will only apply to transfers of appreciated farm or closely held business real estate where the real estate had been valued for estate tax purposes under the special use valuation method of Code Sec. 2032A.

Therefore, with respect to estates of decedents dying in 2010 that do not elect to apply the modified carryover basis rules and estates of decedents dying after December 31, 2010, if an estate or trust transfers appreciated farm or closely held real property that has been valued for estate tax purposes under the special valuation rules of Code Sec. 2032A to a "qualified heir," the estate or trust must recognize gain only to the extent of the post-death appreciation on the property. Post-death appreciation is the difference between the property's fair market value on the date of transfer and its estate tax value as determined without regard to Code Sec. 2032A (Code Sec. 1040(a) and (b)).

> **Example 1:** Upon the death of Nancy Mathews, her trust directed that her niece, Anna Barlow, receive a parcel of real property used by Mathews for her closely held business. The property was valued for estate tax purposes at $500,000, without regard to its special use value. Although the special use valuation was elected for estate tax purposes, the special use value of $400,000 is disregarded. At the time the property was distributed to Anna, its fair market value grew to $525,000. Mathew's trust must recognize a gain on the property's post-death appreciation of $25,000 ($525,000 - $500,000).

A "qualified heir" is a member of the decedent's family, including a spouse, ancestors, lineal descendants (children, grandchildren and their spouses), parents, and aunts and uncles of the decedent and their descendants (Code Sec. 2032A(e)(1)).

Determination of basis. For estates of decedents dying in 2010 that have made the election to apply the modified carryover basis rules, the basis of the heir or beneficiary in property received in satisfaction of the pecuniary bequest is equal to the basis of the estate or trust immediately prior to the distribution plus the amount of the gain recognized by the estate or trust (Code Sec. 1040(c)). The gain of the estate or trust is

NEW LAW EXPLAINED

equal to the post-death appreciation in the property, that is, the fair market value of the property on the date of distribution less the date of death value.

For estates of decedents dying in 2010 that do not make the election and estates of decedents dying after December 31, 2010, the basis of the property in the hands of the heir or beneficiary is determined by adding the basis of the estate or trust in the property immediately before the transfer to the amount of gain recognized (the post-death appreciation) by the estate or trust on the transfer (Code Sec. 1040(c)). Generally, the basis of the estate or trust in the property immediately before the transfer is its estate tax value as determined under Code Sec. 2032A (Code Sec. 1014(a)(3)).

Example 2: Assuming the same facts as in Example 1, Anna's basis in the real property she received under the trust would be $425,000 (the estate tax value of the property under Code Sec. 2032A of $400,000 plus the $25,000 gain recognized by the trust).

Comment: When carryover basis was originally enacted by the Tax Reform Act of 1976 (P.L. 94-455), Code Sec. 1040 provided a gain limitation on transfers made by an estate or trust to any person of carryover basis property in satisfaction of a pecuniary bequest. After retroactive repeal of carryover basis by the Crude Oil Windfall Profit Tax Act of 1980 (P.L. 96-223), Code Sec. 1040 was amended to apply the gain limitation rule to transfers of farms and business property by estates and trusts to qualified heirs in satisfaction of pecuniary bequests. Under the Economic Recovery Tax Act of 1981 (P.L. 97-34), Code Sec. 1040 was amended once again to extend the gain limitation to all transfers of real estate to qualified heirs regardless of whether the transfer was in satisfaction of a pecuniary bequest. With the repeal of the estate tax in 2010 and the option to apply the carryover basis rules for estates of decedents dying in 2010, the gain limitation again applies to transfers of appreciated carryover basis property in satisfaction of a pecuniary bequest. However, for estates of decedents dying in 2010 that do not opt out of the estate tax and estates of decedents dying after December 31, 2010, Code Sec. 1040 once again applies the gain limitation rule to transfers of farms and business property by estates and trusts to qualified heirs regardless of whether the transfer was in satisfaction of a pecuniary bequest.

Practical Analysis: Carol Cantrell, CPA, JD, CAP®, Briggs & Veselka Co., Bellaire, Texas, notes that, in addition to the carryover basis rules in Code Sec. 1022, EGTRRA (P.L. 107-16) changed the tax consequences of funding pecuniary bequests with appreciated property in 2010 (Code Sec. 1040, as amended by P.L. 107-16). As amended, Code Sec. 1040 provides that an estate or trust recognizes a gain on the transfer of appreciated property to satisfy a pecuniary bequest only to the extent that the fair market value of the property at the time of the transfer exceeds the fair market value of the property on the date of the decedent's death. In other words, gain is recognized by the estate only to the extent of post-death appreciation, despite the carryover basis rules. The basis of the property in the hands of the

NEW LAW EXPLAINED

beneficiary is the decedent's basis immediately before the exchange increased by the gain recognized by the estate (Code Sec. 1022(a), as added by P.L. 107-16).

Without that provision, the estate or trust would recognize gain on funding a pecuniary bequest with appreciated property equal to the difference between the fair market value of the property and the carryover basis. This would have made funding pecuniary bequests with appreciated assets prohibitively expensive. It would also have run contrary to the intent of the carryover basis rules, which was to transfer the decedent's basis to the beneficiary.

The gain limitation under Code Sec. 1040 does not apply to income in respect of a decedent (IRD). Therefore, it is not advised to fund pecuniary bequests with IRD, such as nonqualified stock options, annuities, and IRAs because the funding is deemed to be a sale of the IRD property (Reg. § 1.691(a)-4(b)(2)) This is the same result as before EGTRRA.

▶ **Effective date.** This provision is effective for estates of decedents dying after December 31, 2009 (Act Sec. 301(e) of the Tax Relief, Unemployment Insurance Reauthorization, and Job Creation Act of 2010 (P.L. 111-312); Act Sec. 542(f)(1) of the Economic Growth and Tax Relief Reconciliation Act of 2001 (EGTRRA) (P.L. 107-16)). This provision shall not apply to estates of decedents dying after December 31, 2010 (Act Sec. 301 (c) of the Tax Relief Act of 2010; Act Sec. 901 of EGTRRA).

Law source: Law at ¶5490, ¶5505, and ¶7025. Committee Report at ¶10,130.

— Act Sec. 301(a) of the Tax Relief, Unemployment Insurance Reauthorization, and Job Creation Act of 2010 (P.L. 111-312) amending subtitle E of the Economic Growth and Tax Relief Reconciliation Act of 2001 (EGTRRA) (P.L. 107-16);

— Act Sec. 301(c), amending Act Sec. 901 of EGTRRA;

— Act Sec. 301(e), providing the effective date.

Reporter references: For further information, consult the following CCH reporters.

— Standard Federal Tax Reporter, ¶29,781.01

— Tax Research Consultant, ESTTRST: 21,152

— Practical Tax Explanation, § 34,210.30 and § 34,915

— Federal Estate and Gift Tax Reporter, ¶18,150.01 and ¶18,150.05

¶760 Miscellaneous Amendments to Incorporate Carryover Basis Rules Repealed

SUMMARY OF NEW LAW

The modified carryover basis rules (¶740) that were scheduled to expire for decedents dying after December 31, 2010, will remain in effect but only if the executor of an estate of a decedent dying in 2010 elects to apply the modified carryover basis rules as originally enacted. For estates of decedents dying in 2010 that do not make

SUMMARY OF NEW LAW

the election and for estates of decedents dying after December 31, 2010, these provisions have been repealed.

BACKGROUND

In conjunction with the imposition of the carryover basis regime (¶740), the Economic Growth and Tax Relief Reconciliation Act of 2001 (EGTRRA) (P.L. 107-16) also made various amendments to the Internal Revenue Code. These changes were made in order to maintain the effect of such provisions in light of the repeal of the estate tax and the enactment of modified carryover basis.

Recognition-of-gain rule for transfers to nonresident aliens and foreign trusts and estates. EGTRRA amended Code Sec. 684 to expand the recognition of gain rule to include transfers to nonresident aliens. Transfers of property after December 31, 2009, by a U.S. decedent to a nonresident alien or a foreign estate or trust are treated as a sale or exchange of such property for its fair market value on the date of the transfer (Code Sec. 684). Any gain on the transfer of property must be recognized by the U.S. person or the estate of the U.S. person in an amount equal to the excess of the fair market value of the property over the transferor's adjusted basis. Exceptions to the immediate recognition-of-gain rule under Code Sec. 684 are permitted when:

- a U.S. person is treated as the owner of a trust pursuant to the grantor trust rules of Code Sec. 671 or
- a U.S. person makes a lifetime transfer to a nonresident alien.

Prior to 2010, only transfers of property by U.S. persons to foreign estates or trusts were subject to the immediate recognition-of gain-rules.

Inherited self-created art not subject to capital gains treatment. EGTRRA amended Code Sec. 1221(a)(3)(C) to continue to treat self-created works of art, music, literature, or other similar property inherited from a decedent after 2009 as capital assets. Such creative works are excepted from the basis-by-reference rule under Code Sec. 1221(a)(3)(C). This rule would otherwise treat bequests of such items as ordinary income property. The determination of whether bequests of such property will be a capital asset is to be made without regard to the exception under Code Sec. 1221(a)(3)(C) for basis determined under the Code Sec. 1022 carryover basis rules (A similar rule applies in the case of charitable contributions (Code Sec. 170(e)(1)). Thus, when an heir or beneficiary exchanges such property, any gain thereon is subject to capital gains treatment.

> **Caution:** Subsequent amendments to Code Sec. 170(e)(1) were made by the American Jobs Creation Act of 2004 (P.L. 108-357), the Tax Increase Prevention and Reconciliation Act of 2005 (P.L. 109-222), the Pension Protection Act of 2006 (P.L. 109-280), and the Tax Technical Corrections Act of 2007 (P.L. 110-172).

Excise tax imposed on split-interest trusts. EGTRRA amended Code Sec. 4947(a)(2) to subject charitable split interest trusts to the private foundation rules that impose an excise tax on acts of self-dealing (Code Sec. 4941), excess business holdings (Code Sec. 4943), investments that jeopardize charitable purposes (Code Sec. 4944), and lobbying

¶760

BACKGROUND

expenditures (Code Sec. 4945) on income to be paid to trust beneficiaries under the terms of the trust instrument, effective for tax years beginning after 2009. These excise taxes apply only if a charitable deduction was allowed for the income interest, effective for deductions for tax years beginning in 2010 (Code Sec. 4947(2)(A)).

Executor defined. EGTRRA amended Code Sec. 7701(a) to include the definition of the term "executor." For decedent's dying after 2009, executor is defined by Code Sec. 7701(a)(47) as opposed to Code Sec. 2203. Although the definitions are essentially identical, the Code Sec. 2203 definition is used only in connection with the estate tax. Following the repeal of the estate tax in 2010, Code Sec. 2203 is not applicable and Code Sec. 7701(a)(47) applies. Under Code Sec. 7701(a)(47), an executor is an executor or administrator of the decedent, or if one is not appointed, qualified and living within the United States, then any person in actual or constructive possession of any of the decedent's property. Such person or persons has the power to make the basis allocations for purposes of the modified carryover basis regime (see ¶740).

Conforming amendments. The change in 2010 from stepped-up basis to carryover basis for property acquired from a decedent required certain conforming amendments to provisions in the Internal Revenue Code that operated with reference to the stepped-up basis rules (see ¶740) in the now inapplicable Code Sec. 1014. These changes, which apply only to the estates of decedents dying in 2010 include the following:

- rules pertaining to the interest on tax deferral with respect to a passive foreign investment company (Code Sec. 1291(e)) and

- rules concerning basis adjustments in connection with the mark-to-market election for stock in a passive foreign investment company acquired from a decedent (Code Sec. 1296(i)).

    Caution: Subsequent amendments to Code Sec. 1291(e) were made by both the American Jobs Creation Act of 2004 (P.L. 108-357) and the Hiring Incentives to Restore Employment Act (P.L. 111-147).

    Comment: Conforming amendments were also made to the rules relating to stock in a foreign investment company as acquired from a decedent (Code Sec. 1246(e)). However, the American Jobs Creation Act of 2004 (P.L. 108-357) repealed Code Sec. 1246(e), effective for tax years of foreign corporations beginning after December 31, 2004. Thus, these amendments do not apply to inherited assets in 2010.

Sunset provision. Under the sunset provision of EGTRRA, amendments made by the Act will not apply to decedents dying after December 31, 2010 (Act Sec. 901 of P.L. 107-16).

NEW LAW EXPLAINED

Miscellaneous amendments repealed, unless executors elect otherwise.—The miscellaneous amendments to incorporate the modified carryover basis rules are repealed for estates of decedents dying in 2010 unless the executor of the estate elects to apply the modified carryover basis rules (Act Sec. 301(a) of the Tax Relief, Unemploy-

NEW LAW EXPLAINED

ment Insurance Reauthorization, and Job Creation Act of 2010 (P.L. 111-312)). For a more detailed discussion of the election to apply the modified carryover basis rules, see ¶ 740. As a result, the following miscellaneous amendments made to the Internal Revenue Code apply to bequests from decedents dying in 2010, only if the executor elects for the estate to be subject to the modified carryover basis regime. Otherwise, the previous stepped up basis rules apply.

Recognition-of-gain rule for transfers to nonresident aliens. Transfers of property after December 31, 2009, by a U.S. decedent dying in 2010, whose executor elects to apply the modified carryover basis rules, to a nonresident alien are treated as a sale or exchange of such property for its fair market value on the date of the transfer.

Transfers of property made to nonresident aliens by U.S. decedents whose executors do not make the election and estates of decedents dying after December 31, 2010, are not subject to the immediate recognition-of-gain rules, but are instead subject to the estate tax pursuant to Code Sec. 2001 (Code Sec. 684).

Inherited self-created art subject to capital gains treatment. For estates of decedents dying in 2010 that have made the election to apply the modified carryover basis rules, self-created works of art, music, literature, or other similar property are treated as capital assets and are excepted from the basis-by-reference rule under Code Sec. 1221(a)(3)(C).

For estates of decedents not electing to apply the modified carryover basis rules and decedents dying after December 31, 2010, self-created art, literature, music, and other similar property are subject to stepped up basis regime. Under the stepped-up basis regime, an heir's basis in the property is determined by the fair market value of the asset and does not reference the decedent's basis in the property. As a result, such property will be treated as a capital asset and any gain on the sale or exchange of the property by the beneficiary will be subject to capital gains treatment.

Excise tax imposed on split-interest trusts. In cases where an executor of a decedent dying in 2010 elects the modified carryover basis regime, charitable split-interest trusts are subject to the private foundation excise taxes on acts of self-dealing pursuant to Code Sec. 4947(a)(2), as amended by P.L. 107-16. Such excise taxes only apply to acts of self dealing, excess business holdings, investments that would jeopardize charitable purposes, and lobbying expenditures, if a charitable deduction was allowed for the income interest.

For decedents dying after December 31, 2010, and decedents dying in 2010 for which the executor does not elect the modified carryover basis regime, the imposition of the private foundation excise taxes under Code Sec. 4947(a)(2)(A) does not apply to amounts payable from split-interest trusts to noncharitable income beneficiaries for which a deduction was allowed under Code Sec. 642(c). However, trust income to be paid to noncharitable beneficiaries where the trust received a charitable deduction for the income interest under Code Sec. 170(f)(2)(B), Code Sec. 2055(e)(2)(B), or Code Sec. 2522(c)(2)(B) is still subject to the excise taxes on self-dealing (Code Sec. 4941), excess business holdings (Code Sec. 4943), investments that jeopardize charitable

NEW LAW EXPLAINED

purposes (Code Sec. 4944), and certain taxable expenditures, such as lobbying expenditures (Code Sec. 4945) (Code Sec. 4947(a)(2)(A)).

Executor defined. With the reinstatement of the federal estate tax under Act Sec. 301(a) of the Tax Relief Act of 2010, (see ¶ 705) the term "executors" for decedents dying after 2009 will again be defined by Code Sec. 2203, unless the executor of a decedent dying in 2010 elects to subject the estate to the modified carryover basis regime. In such cases, the term "executors" will be defined under Code Sec. 7701(a)(47).

Conforming amendments. Following the repeal of the modified carryover basis provisions under Act Sec. 301(a) of the Tax Relief Act of 2010, inherited assets will be valued pursuant to Code Sec. 1014, unless an executor of a decedent dying in 2010 elects to subject the estate to the modified carryover basis regime. In such cases, the conforming amendments made to Code Sec. 1291(e) and Code Sec. 1296(i) will apply. For estates of decedents dying in 2010 that do not make the election and estates of decedents dying after December 31, 2010, the conforming amendments are no longer necessary.

▶ **Effective date.** This provision is effective for estates of decedents dying after December 31, 2009 (Act Sec. 301(e) of the Tax Relief, Unemployment Insurance Reauthorization Act of 2010 (P.L. 111-312); Act Sec. 542(e) of the Economic Growth and Tax Relief Reconciliation Act of 2001 (EGTRRA) (P.L. 107-16)). These provisions will not apply to estates of decedents dying after December 31, 2010 (Act Sec. 301(c) of the Tax Relief Act of 2010; Act Sec. 901 of EGTRRA).

Law source: Law at ¶5270, ¶5415, ¶5490, ¶5500, ¶5520, ¶5530, ¶5545, ¶5550, ¶5750, ¶5865, and ¶7025. Committee Report at ¶10,130.

— Act Sec. 301(a) of the Tax Relief, Unemployment Insurance Reauthorization, and Job Creation Act of 2010 (P.L. 111-312);

— Act Sec. 301(c);

— Act Sec. 301(e), providing the effective date.

Reporter references: For further information, consult the following CCH reporters.

— Standard Federal Tax Reporter, ¶24,892.01, ¶24,892.055, ¶24,892.06, ¶31,615.03, ¶34,143.01, ¶34,143.024 and ¶43,095.01

— Tax Research Consultant, INTL: 30,252, INTL: 30,252.10, SALES: 21,110, ESTGIFT: 45,252.454, ESTTRST: 15,354, FILEBUS: 9,350

— Practical Tax Explanation, § 16,301

— Federal Estate and Gift Tax Reporter, ¶18,115.35

GENERATION-SKIPPING TRUSTS

¶765 Deemed and Retroactive Allocations of GST Exemption

SUMMARY OF NEW LAW

The generation-skipping transfer (GST) deemed allocation and retroactive allocation provisions will remain in force through December 31, 2012, as a result of the two-year extension of the EGTRRA sunset date.

BACKGROUND

The Economic Growth and Tax Relief Reconciliation Act of 2001 (EGTRRA) (P.L. 107-16) made a number of what could be referred to as "taxpayer-friendly" changes to the GST tax rules. These included amendments to Code Sec. 2632 creating a new set of rules for the deemed allocation of GST exemption to certain lifetime transfers to trusts. Specifically, if an individual makes a lifetime "indirect skip," any unused portion of the individual's GST exemption is allocated to the property transferred to the extent necessary to make the inclusion ratio for such property equal to zero (Code Sec. 2632(c)(1)). If the amount of the indirect skip exceeds the unused portion of the GST exemption, then the entire unused portion is allocated to the property transferred. Under this deemed allocation rule, the unused portion of an individual's GST exemption is the portion of the exemption that has not previously been: (1) allocated by such individual; (2) treated as allocated under Code Sec. 2632(b) with respect to a direct skip occurring during or before the calendar year in which the indirect skip is made; or (3) treated as allocated under Code Sec. 2632(c)(1) with respect to a prior indirect skip.

Definitions. For purposes of the deemed allocation rule, the terms "indirect skip" and "GST trust" are defined as explained below.

Indirect skip. An "indirect skip" is defined as any transfer of property (other than a direct skip) subject to the gift tax made to a GST trust (Code Sec. 2632(c)(3)(A)).

GST trust. A "GST trust" is defined as a trust that could have a GST with respect to the transferor unless:

(1) the trust instrument provides that more than 25 percent of the trust corpus must be distributed to, or may be withdrawn by, one or more individuals who are non-skip persons (a) before the date that such individual attains age 46, (b) on or before one or more dates specified in the trust instrument that will occur before the date that such individual attains age 46, or (c) upon the occurrence of an event that is reasonably expected to occur before the date that such individual attains age 46;

(2) the trust instrument provides that more than 25 percent of the trust corpus must be distributed to, or may be withdrawn by, one or more individuals who are non-skip persons and who are living on the date of death of another person

BACKGROUND

identified in the instrument (either by name or by class) who is more than 10 years older than such individuals;

(3) the trust instrument provides that, if one or more individuals who are non-skip persons die on or before a date or event described in (1) or (2) above, more than 25 percent of the trust corpus (a) must be distributed to the estate or estates of one or more of such individuals or (b) is subject to a general power of appointment exercisable by one or more of such individuals;

(4) any portion of the trust would be included in the gross estate of a non-skip person (other than the transferor) if such person died immediately after the transfer;

(5) the trust is a charitable lead annuity trust (per Code Sec. 2642(e)(3)(A)), a charitable remainder annuity trust, or a charitable remainder unitrust (per Code Sec. 664(d)); or

(6) a gift tax charitable deduction was allowed under Code Sec. 2522 with respect to the trust for the amount of an interest in the form of the right to receive annual payments of a fixed percentage of the net fair market value of the trust property (determined yearly) and which trust is required to pay principal to a non-skip person if such person is alive when the yearly payments for which the deduction was allowed terminate (Code Sec. 2632(c)(3)(B)).

> **Example 1:** Gertrude Stack creates an irrevocable trust for the benefit of her lineal descendants. Stack funds the trust with stock worth $50,000 in 2008. Stack has one child, Andrew. The trust instrument provides that the trustee has discretion to distribute trust income or principal to Andrew during his lifetime. At Andrew's death, the remaining corpus is to be distributed to Andrew's issue, *per stirpes*. The trust is a "GST trust" because a GST may occur with respect to Stack and the trust does not fall within any of the exceptions specified in (1)—(6) above (Code Sec. 2632(c)(3)(B)(i)-(vi)).

For purposes of determining whether a trust is a "GST trust," the value of transferred property is not considered to be includible in the gross estate of a non-skip person or subject to a right of withdrawal by reason of such person holding a right to withdraw an amount that does not exceed the Code Sec. 2503(b) gift tax annual exclusion amount ($13,000 per donee in 2010 and 2011) with respect to any transferor. In addition, it is assumed that powers of appointment held by non-skip persons will not be exercised (Code Sec. 2632(c)(3)(B)).

In addition, an indirect skip to which Code Sec. 2642(f) applies is deemed to have been made only at the close of the estate tax inclusion period (ETIP). The value of such transfer is the fair market value of the trust property at the close of the ETIP (Code Sec. 2632(c)(4)).

> **Comment:** An ETIP is any period after a transfer during which the value of the transferred property would be includible in the gross estate of the transferor if he or she died (Code Sec. 2642(f)(3)).

BACKGROUND

Electing out of deemed allocation. An individual may opt out of the deemed allocation rule for lifetime indirect skips. An individual may elect to have Code Sec. 2632(c) not apply to (1) an indirect skip or (2) any or all transfers made by the individual to a particular trust. In addition, an individual may elect to treat any trust as a "GST trust" for purposes of Code Sec. 2632(c) with respect to any and all transfers made by the individual to the trust (Code Sec. 2632(c)(5)(A); see Reg. § 26.2632-1(b)(3)). An election to have Code Sec. 2632(c) not apply to an indirect skip is deemed to be timely if it is filed on a timely filed gift tax return for the calendar year in which the transfer was made or deemed to have been made under Code Sec. 2632(c)(4) (i.e., the close of the ETIP) (Code Sec. 2632(c)(5)(B)(i)). For other categories of elections permitted by Code Sec. 2632(c)(5)(A), the election may be made on a timely filed gift tax return for the calendar year for which the election is to become effective (Code Sec. 2632(c)(5)(B)(ii)).

> **Example 2:** Gertrude Stack decides that she does not want any of her GST exemption allocated to the transfer to the trust described in Example 1, above. Accordingly, on her 2008 Form 709, U.S. Gift (and Generation-Skipping Transfer) Tax Return, Stack elects to have Code Sec. 2632(c) not apply to the transfer of the stock.

Procedure for electing out. The transferor must attach an "election out" statement to a Form 709 filed on or before the due date for timely filing of the Form 709 for the calendar year in which the first transfer to be covered by the election out was made (Reg. § 26.2632-1(b)(2)(iii)(C)) (special rules apply in the case of a transfer subject to an ETIP). The election out statement must identify the trust and specifically must provide that the transferor is electing out of the automatic allocation of GST exemption with respect to the described transfer(s) (Reg. § 26.2632-1(b)(2)(iii)(B)). In addition, the current-year transfers and/or future transfers to which the election out is to apply must be specifically described or otherwise identified.

A transferor may terminate an election out made on a Form 709 for a prior year, to the extent that the election out applied to future transfers or to a transfer subject to an ETIP. The transferor must attach a "termination" statement to a Form 709 filed on or before the due date of the Form 709 for the calendar year in which is made the first transfer to which the election out is not to apply. The termination statement must identify the trust, describe the prior election out that is being terminated, specifically provide that the prior election out is being terminated, and either describe the extent to which the prior election out is being terminated or describe any current-year transfers to which the election out is not to apply (Reg. § 26.2632-1(b)(2)(iii)(E)).

Extension of time to make elections. A transferor may seek an extension of time to make an election described in Code Sec. 2632(b)(3) or (c)(5) under the provisions of Reg. § 301.9100-3 (Notice 2001-50, 2001-2 CB 189) (see, e.g., IRS Letter Rulings 200930033 and 200939012).

Retroactive allocations. In addition, EGTRRA amended Code Sec. 2632 to provide for the retroactive allocation of GST exemption if certain conditions are met. If the

BACKGROUND

requirements are satisfied, an individual will have the ability to make an allocation of unused GST exemption to any previous transfer(s) made to a trust, on a chronological basis (Code Sec. 2632(d)).

Availability. An individual may make a retroactive allocation of GST exemption if:

(1) a non-skip person has an interest or a future interest in a trust to which any transfer has been made;

(2) such person is a lineal descendant of a grandparent of the transferor or of a grandparent of the transferor's spouse or former spouse and such person is assigned to a generation below the generation assignment of the transferor; and

(3) such person predeceases the transferor (Code Sec. 2632(d)(1)).

If a transferor's retroactive allocation is made on a gift tax return that is filed on or before the due date for gifts made within the calendar year during which the non-skip person's death occurred, then:

(1) for purposes of Code Sec. 2642(a), the value of such transfer(s) is determined as if such allocation had been made on a timely filed gift tax return for each calendar year within which each transfer was made;

(2) such allocation is effective immediately before the non-skip person's death; and

(3) the amount of the transferor's unused GST exemption that is available for allocation is determined immediately before the non-skip person's death (Code Sec. 2632(d)(2)).

Example 3: In 1998, Gary Stack (no relation to Gertrude) creates an irrevocable trust for the primary benefit of his child, Anthony, who is age 31 and has two children. The trust instrument provides that (1) the trustee has discretion to distribute trust income to Anthony during his lifetime and (2) one-third of the trust corpus is to be distributed to Anthony at age 35, one-half of the remaining corpus at age 40, and the remainder of the corpus at age 45 (which will terminate the trust). If Anthony dies before reaching age 45, the corpus is to be distributed in equal shares to Anthony's children. Stack makes transfers to the trust in 1998, 1999 and 2000, but does not allocate any of his GST exemption to the transfers on the gift tax returns reporting the transfers. (Note that the deemed allocation rule of Code Sec. 2632(c) does not apply to the 1998, 1999, or 2000 transfers because the transfers predate the enactment of the rule.) On September 1, 2001, before reaching age 35, Anthony dies, which results in a taxable termination for GST tax purposes. Stack may retroactively allocate unused GST exemption to the transfers made in 1998, 1999, and 2000 and thereby exempt the trust property transferred to Anthony's children from the application of the GST tax.

Termination of GST tax. The GST tax is repealed with respect to generation-skipping transfers after December 31, 2009 (Code Sec. 2664). See further discussion at ¶ 705.

¶765

BACKGROUND

Sunset provision.—Under the sunset provision of EGTRRA, amendments made by the Act will not apply to generation-skipping transfers after December 31, 2010 (Act Sec. 901 of P.L. 107-16).

NEW LAW EXPLAINED

Deemed and retroactive GST allocation provisions remain in force through 2012.—The deemed and retroactive GST allocation provisions (Code Sec. 2632(c) and (d)) will remain in force through December 31, 2012, as a result of the two-year extension of the EGTRRA sunset provision (Act Sec. 101(a)(1) of the Tax Relief, Unemployment Insurance Reauthorization, and Job Creation Act of 2010 (P.L. 111-312)).

The application of the GST tax in 2010. As previously noted, EGTRRA provided that chapter 13 of subtitle B of the Code would not apply to generation-skipping transfers after December 31, 2009, effectively repealing the GST tax for 2010. This one-year termination of the tax was creating consternation among practitioners, who raised several questions concerning how the temporary lapse of the tax would impact the application and administration of the GST rules during 2010 and in subsequent years.

These concerns were highlighted by the ABA Section of Real Property, Trust & Estate Law in a December 1, 2010, letter to the heads of the House Ways & Means and Senate Finance Committees. The letter asked that Congress "resolve the systemic uncertainties" resulting from the one-year suspension of the estate and GST taxes in 2010. The letter noted that, while it is clear that the GST tax does not apply to generation-skipping transfers occurring in 2010, "there are many issues causing confusion, which could be resolved if Code Sec. 2664 were revised to clarify that the GST rules and definitions of Chapter 13 *otherwise* continue to apply during 2010."

As explained in greater detail at ¶ 705, the Tax Relief Act of 2010 repeals subtitle A of title V of EGTRRA, thereby reinstating the operation of chapter 13 for generation-skipping transfers occurring in 2010 (in essence, repealing the one-year repeal of the GST tax). The Tax Relief Act of 2010 further provides that the applicable rate under Code Sec. 2641(a) for generation-skipping transfers made in 2010 is zero. Because the GST tax is a product of the applicable rate and the taxable amount (Code Sec. 2602), no GST tax will be imposed on any generation-skipping transfers that occur during 2010, as any amount multiplied by zero is equal to zero. The Tax Relief Act of 2010 eliminates the GST tax in 2010 not by making chapter 13 inapplicable to generation-skipping transfers, as EGTRRA would have done, but by setting the effective GST tax rate at zero.

With the Tax Relief Act of 2010 cancelling the enactment of Code Sec. 2664, the "GST rules and definitions," to quote from the ABA letter, will continue to apply during 2010, including the deemed and retroactive GST allocation provisions. This should alleviate the concerns expressed by the ABA on behalf of the practitioner community with respect to 2010.

> **Comment:** The Joint Committee on Taxation (JCT) notes that the Tax Relief Act of 2010 reinstates the GST tax, effective for transfers made after December 31,

NEW LAW EXPLAINED

2009. After noting that the GST exemption amount is $5 million for 2010, the JCT explains that, "[t]herefore, up to $5 million in generation skipping transfer tax exemption may be allocated to a trust created or funded during 2010, depending on the amount of such exemption used by the taxpayer before 2010. Although the generation skipping transfer tax is applicable in 2010, the generation skipping transfer tax rate for transfers made during 2010 is zero percent" (Joint Committee on Taxation, *Technical Explanation of the Revenue Provisions Contained in the "Tax Relief, Unemployment Insurance Reauthorization, and Job Creation Act of 2010"* (JCX-55-10), December 10, 2010). The JCT report confirms that the GST rules and definitions that compose chapter 13 will apply during 2010.

Consequences of the EGTRRA sunset in 2013 and beyond. The amendments made by the Tax Relief Act of 2010—the elimination of Code Sec. 2664, along with the two-year extension of the sunset date—will keep the changes to the GST rules enacted by EGTRRA in force for 2010, 2011, and 2012. As a result, the deemed and retroactive GST allocation provisions will now become inoperative beginning in 2013.

Example 1: Gertrude Stack creates an irrevocable trust for the benefit of her lineal descendants. Stack funds the trust with stock worth $100,000 in 2013. Stack has one child, Andrew. The trust instrument provides that the trustee has discretion to distribute trust income or principal to Andrew during his lifetime. At Andrew's death, the remaining corpus is to be distributed to Andrew's issue, *per stirpes*.

Under Code Sec. 2632(c), prior to the EGTRRA sunset (as extended), the trust would have been a "GST trust" because a GST could occur with respect to Stack and the trust did not fall within any of the enumerated exceptions found in Code Sec. 2632(c)(3)(B)(i)-(vi). Accordingly, Stack's GST exemption would have been allocated to the transfer to the extent necessary to make the inclusion ratio equal to zero (unless she elected out of the allocation). However, because the deemed allocation provision is no longer operative in 2013, none of Stack's GST exemption would be allocated to the transfer unless she affirmatively makes an allocation on a gift tax return reporting the transfer.

Comment: The deemed allocation rule was designed to alleviate the problems that resulted when taxpayers failed to allocate GST exemption to an indirect skip and an allocation had been desired. The rule was intended to protect taxpayers from missed or defective allocations for transfers to a trust where there was a real possibility that a GST could occur. The sunsetting (i.e., elimination) of this provision will once again put the onus on taxpayers to make certain that they are properly allocating GST exemption to transfers made to a trust.

Compliance Note: Beginning with transfers made in 2013, taxpayers will no longer have the benefit of the deemed allocation rule to save them from the consequences of a missed allocation of GST exemption with respect to transfers to trusts that are not direct skips. As a result, tax advisers and return preparers will need to be especially vigilant to ensure that a taxpayer's GST exemption is being appropriately allocated in situations where a transfer is made to a trust.

NEW LAW EXPLAINED

> **Example 2:** In 2007, Gary Stack (no relation to Gertrude) creates an irrevocable trust for the primary benefit of his child, Anthony, who is age 28 and has two children. The trust instrument provides that (1) the trustee has discretion to distribute trust income to Anthony during his lifetime and (2) one-third of the trust corpus is to be distributed to Anthony at age 35, one-half of the remaining corpus at age 40, and the remainder of the corpus at age 45 (which will terminate the trust). If Anthony dies before reaching age 45, the corpus is to be distributed in equal shares to Anthony's children. Stack makes transfers to the trust in 2007, 2008 and 2009, but does not allocate any of his GST exemption to the transfers on the gift tax returns reporting the transfers. (Note that the deemed allocation rule of Code Sec. 2632(c) does not apply to the 2007, 2008, or 2009 transfers because the trust is not a "GST trust.") On September 1, 2013, before reaching age 35, Anthony dies, which results in a taxable termination for GST tax purposes.
>
> Under Code Sec. 2632(d), in the absence of the EGTRRA sunset, Stack would have had the ability to retroactively allocate unused GST exemption to the transfers made in 2007, 2008, and 2009 and thereby exempt the trust property transferred to Anthony's children from the application of the GST tax. But, because the retroactive allocation provision is no longer operative in 2013, Stack no longer has that opportunity.

> **Comment:** The retroactive allocation provision was designed to protect taxpayers in cases where there was an unexpected order of death, such as when the second generation predeceased the first generation transferor. In such cases, if the transferor knew that a child might predecease him or her, thereby causing a taxable termination, the transferor would probably have allocated GST exemption to the transfer at the time that it was made to the trust. The loss of this provision due to the EGTRRA sunset will close this avenue of relief to taxpayers.

Interpreting the sunset language. The EGTRRA sunset provision, as amended by the Tax Relief Act of 2010, states that "The Internal Revenue Code of 1986 . . . shall be applied and administered to years, estates, gifts, and transfers [after December 31, 2012] as if the provisions and amendments [made by EGTRRA] *had never been enacted*" (Act. Sec 901(b) of P.L. 107-16) (emphasis added). Various commentators have pointed out that the phrase, "had never been enacted," raises thorny interpretive issues with respect to the operation of the GST tax following the EGTRRA sunset.

> **Comment:** The Tax Relief Act of 2010 may have clarified the application of the GST rules in 2010, as previously discussed, but it did not address how the rules are to be construed following the sunset of EGTRRA. The two-year extension of the sunset date has simply postponed the day of reckoning as to those issues.

Representative of these concerns is a letter sent to the IRS by the ABA Section of Taxation on July 28, 2010 (ABA letter). The ABA letter, responding to the invitation to make recommendations for the 2010—11 IRS Priority Guidance Plan, states the following: "Guidance is needed as to whether this provision [the 'had never been enacted' phrase] will be interpreted to mean that after 2010 the Service will construe

NEW LAW EXPLAINED

the tax laws as if the provisions of EGTRRA were never in effect or, alternatively, that after 2010 the tax laws will be applied to transfers and events post-2010 without applying any of the provisions of EGTRRA to such transfers and events but without ignoring the fact that provisions of EGTRRA were in effect until 2011." The operative dates contained in the letter may have changed following enactment of the Tax Relief Act of 2010 (i.e., substitute "2012" for "2010"), but the need for guidance remains.

The ABA letter then lists several areas of the GST tax for which guidance is necessary to resolve the confusion over the appropriate interpretation of the EGTRRA sunset provision. With respect to the deemed allocation provision, the ABA letter asks the following: "If, during the years 2001 through 2009, a grantor created and funded a trust to which GST tax exemption was deemed allocated under section 2632(c), will the trust be exempt from GST tax after 2010 [now: 2012], when section 2632(c) will be treated as if it 'had never been enacted'?"

Example 3: Gertrude Stack creates an irrevocable trust for the benefit of her lineal descendants. Stack funds the trust with stock worth $250,000 in 2002. Stack has one child, Andrew. The trust instrument provides that the trustee has discretion to distribute trust income or principal to Andrew during his lifetime. At Andrew's death, the remaining corpus is to be distributed to Andrew's issue, *per stirpes*. The trust is a "GST trust," so $250,000 of Stack's GST exemption amount is deemed allocated to the transfer. As a result, the trust has an inclusion ratio of zero. Andrew dies in 2013, which results in a taxable termination for GST tax purposes.

If the EGTRRA sunset language is interpreted to mean that actions taken with respect to EGTRRA provisions will *not* be ignored for years after 2012, then the deemed allocation of Stack's GST exemption would remain valid and there would be no GST tax at Andrew's death. However, if the sunset language is construed in such a way so that any actions related to EGTRRA provisions are treated as if they never occurred, then there would be no deemed allocation of Stack's GST exemption. If no GST exemption was allocated to the transfer, the transfer of the trust corpus to Andrew's children would be subject to GST tax at the maximum estate tax rate in effect (55 percent in 2013).

Example 4: In 1998, Gary Stack creates an irrevocable trust for the primary benefit of his child, Anthony, who is age 31 and has two children. The trust instrument provides that (1) the trustee has discretion to distribute trust income to Anthony during his lifetime and (2) one-third of the trust corpus is to be distributed to Anthony at age 35, one-half of the remaining corpus at age 40, and the remainder of the corpus at age 45 (which will terminate the trust). If Anthony dies before reaching age 45, the corpus is to be distributed in equal shares to Anthony's children. Stack makes transfers to the trust in 1998, 1999 and 2000, but does not allocate any of his GST exemption to the transfers on the gift tax returns reporting the transfers. On September 1, 2001, before reaching

---

NEW LAW EXPLAINED

age 35, Anthony dies, which results in a taxable termination for GST tax purposes. Stack retroactively allocates his unused GST exemption to the transfers made in 1998, 1999, and 2000 and thereby exempts the trust property transferred to Anthony's children from the application of the GST tax.

If the EGTRRA sunset does not nullify any actions that were taken pursuant to EGTRRA provisions, then the retroactive allocation remains valid and there are no GST tax consequences resulting from the transfer to Anthony's children. But what if the retroactive allocation was considered to have never been made as a result of the sunset's application? Come January 1, 2013, would there be the possibility that GST tax could be imposed on the transfer retroactively?

The ABA letter also addressed the following scenario: "If a grantor created and funded a trust before 2001, neglected to timely allocate GST tax exemption to the trust, but obtained a ruling from the Service under Notice 2001-50, 2001-2 CB 189, permitting an extension of time to make that allocation, will the grantor's late allocation be effective after 2010 [now: 2012] even though section 2632(c), the statutory basis for the such [sic] an extension of time, will be treated as if it 'had never been enacted'?" As with the operation of the deemed and retroactive allocation provisions, the interpretation of the EGTRRA sunset language with respect to extensions of time to make GST allocations could have profound consequences.

> **Comment:** Prior to the enactment of the Tax Relief Act of 2010, the IRS never provided any guidance as to how it would interpret and apply the "had never been enacted" language in the EGTRRA sunset provision. The two-year extension of the EGTRRA sunset date, by alleviating the immediate need for clarification, probably means that such guidance will not forthcoming in the near future. However, until the ambiguities noted in the ABA letter are cleared up, whether by the IRS, Congress, or the courts, taxpayers will have to live with a considerable amount of uncertainty as to any actions predicated on the GST provisions added by EGTRRA, hampering long-term planning.

▶ **Effective date.** The deemed allocation provisions of Code Sec. 2632(c) apply to transfers subject to estate or gift tax made after December 31, 2000, and to estate tax inclusion periods ending after December 31, 2000 (Act Sec. 101(a)(2) of the Tax Relief, Unemployment Insurance Reauthorization, and Job Creation Act of 2010 (P.L. 111-312); Act Sec. 561(c)(1) of the Economic Growth and Tax Relief Reconciliation Act of 2001 (EGTRRA) (P.L. 107-16)). The retroactive allocation provisions of Code Sec. 2632(d) apply to deaths of non-skip persons occurring after December 31, 2000 (Act Sec. 101(a)(2) of the Tax Relief Act of 2010; Act Sec. 561(c)(2) of EGTRRA). The deemed allocation provisions of Code Sec. 2632(c) shall not apply to transfers subject to estate or gift tax made after December 31, 2012, and to estate tax inclusion periods ending after December 31, 2012 (Act Sec. 101(a)(1) of the Tax Relief Act of 2010; Act Sec. 901 of EGTRRA). The retroactive allocation provisions of Code Sec. 2632(d) shall not apply to deaths of non-skip persons occurring after December 31, 2012 (Act Sec. 101(a)(1) of the Tax Relief Act of 2010; Act Sec. 901 of EGTRRA). See ¶105 for a specific discussion of the sunset provision of EGTRRA and how it is applied.

¶765

NEW LAW EXPLAINED

Law source: Law at ¶5725 and ¶5735. Committee Report at ¶10,130.

— Act Sec. 101(a)(1) of the Tax Relief, Unemployment Insurance Reauthorization, and Job Creation Act of 2010 (P.L. 111-312), amending Act Sec. 901(a)(2) of the Economic Growth and Tax Relief Reconciliation Act of 2001 (P.L. 107-16).

— Act Sec. 101(a)(2), providing the effective date.

Reporter references: For further information, consult the following CCH reporters.

— Tax Research Consultant, ESTGIFT: 57,106.20

— Practical Tax Explanation, § 34,725.10

— Federal Estate and Gift Tax Reporter, ¶ 12,675.04 and ¶ 12,675.06

¶770 Severing of Trusts

SUMMARY OF NEW LAW

The provision allowing for a qualified severance of a trust for purposes of the generation-skipping transfer (GST) tax will remain in force through December 31, 2012, as a result of the two-year extension of the EGTRRA sunset date.

BACKGROUND

The Economic Growth and Tax Relief Reconciliation Act of 2001 (EGTRRA) (P.L. 107-16) amended Code Sec. 2642(a) to allow a taxpayer to make a "qualified severance." Specifically, if a trust is severed in a "qualified severance," the resulting trusts will be treated as separate trusts thereafter for purposes of the GST tax (Code Sec. 2642(a)(3)). This change provided a simplified means to achieve what is often the desired GST planning goal of having trusts that are either fully subject to GST tax (i.e., trusts with an inclusion ratio of one) or are completely exempt from GST tax (i.e., trusts with an inclusion ratio of zero), as opposed to having trusts that are partially exempt from GST tax (with an inclusion ratio between zero and one).

> **Comment:** The inclusion ratio is the key determinant with respect to the potential GST tax liability when transfers are made from a trust to skip persons (e.g., grandchildren). In computing the amount of GST tax, the maximum estate tax rate is multiplied by the inclusion ratio with respect to the transfer (Code Sec. 2641(a)). The inclusion ratio is a function of the amount of the transferor's GST exemption allocated to the transfer. Specifically, the inclusion ratio is equal to the excess of 1 over the applicable fraction. The numerator of the applicable fraction is the amount of GST exemption allocated to the trust and the denominator is the value of the property transferred to the trust (Code Sec. 2642(a)). Therefore, an applicable fraction equal to one, where the GST exemption allocated to the trust equals the value of the trust, yields an inclusion ratio of zero (making trust distributions fully exempt from GST tax), and an applicable

BACKGROUND

fraction equal to zero, where no GST exemption is allocated to the trust, yields an inclusion ratio of one (making trust distributions subject to GST tax at the highest possible rate).

A "qualified severance" is defined as the division of a single trust and the creation (by any means available under the governing instrument or local law) of two or more trusts if: (1) the single trust is divided on a fractional basis, and (2) the terms of the new trusts, in the aggregate, provide for the same succession of interests of beneficiaries as are provided for in the original trust (Code Sec. 2642(a)(3)(B)(i); see, e.g., IRS Letter Rulings 200644015 and 200508001).

The regulations provide that a qualified severance must satisfy each of the following requirements:

(1) The single trust is severed pursuant to the terms of the governing instrument or applicable local law.

(2) The severance is effective under local law.

(3) The date of severance is either the date selected by the trustee as of which the trust assets are to be valued in order to determine the funding of the resulting trusts, or the court-imposed date of funding in the case of an order of a local court. The funding must be commenced immediately upon, and funding must occur within a reasonable time (but in no event more than 90 days) after, the selected valuation date.

(4) The original trust is severed on a fractional basis, so that each resulting trust is funded with a fraction or percentage of the original trust, and the sum of those fractions or percentages is one or 100 percent, respectively. The fraction or percentage may be determined by use of a formula.

(5) The terms of the resulting trusts must provide, in the aggregate, for the same succession of interests of beneficiaries as are provided in the original trust (Reg. § 26.2642-6(d)).

In the case of a qualified severance of a trust with an inclusion ratio of either one or zero, each trust resulting from the severance will have an inclusion ratio equal to the inclusion ratio of the original trust.

A severance of a trust with an inclusion ratio of between zero and one is a "qualified severance" only if the single trust is divided into two trusts, one of which receives a fractional share of the total value of all trust assets equal to the applicable fraction of the single trust immediately before the severance. In such a case, the trust receiving the fractional share will have an inclusion ratio of zero and the other trust will have an inclusion ratio of one (Code Sec. 2642(a)(3)(B)(ii); Reg. § 26.2642-6(d)(7)).

Example: George Stack creates an irrevocable trust for the benefit of his grandson, Albert. The trust instrument provides that the trustee has discretion to distribute trust income and corpus to Albert during his lifetime. At Albert's death, the corpus is to be distributed in equal shares to Albert's children. The trust instrument also gives the trustee the discretion to sever the trust for GST

BACKGROUND

> tax purposes. Based on the amount of GST exemption allocated to the trust and the value of the trust property, the trust's applicable fraction is $2/5$, making the inclusion ratio equal to $3/5$ $(1 - 2/5 = 3/5)$. The trustee divides the trust into two trusts, each having terms identical to that of the original trust. One of the trusts receives a $2/5$-fractional share of the total value of the trust assets. The severance is a "qualified severance," with the trust receiving the $2/5$-fractional share having an inclusion ratio of zero, and the other trust having an inclusion ratio of one.

Effective date of severance. A qualified severance is applicable as of the date of the severance, as defined in Reg. § 26.2642-6(d)(3) (see requirement (3), above), and the resulting trusts are treated as separate trusts for GST tax purposes as of that date.

Time for making severance. A qualified severance under Code Sec. 2642(a)(3) may be made at any time prior to the termination of the trust (Code Sec. 2642(a)(3)(C); Reg. § 26.2642-6(f)(1)).

Reporting a qualified severance. A qualified severance is reported by filing Form 706-GS(T), "Generation-Skipping Transfer Tax Return for Terminations." The taxpayer should write "Qualified Severance" at the top of the form and attach a Notice of Qualified Severance (the Notice). The return and attached Notice is to be filed by April 15 of the year immediately following the year during which the severance occurred (not including any extensions of time to file) (Reg. § 26.2642-6(e)(1)).

With respect to the original trust being severed, the Notice should provide: (1) the transferor's name; (2) the original trust's name and date of creation; (3) the original trust's tax identification number (TIN); and (4) the inclusion ratio before the severance (Reg. § 26.2642-6(e)(2)). As to each of the resulting trusts created by the severance, the Notice should include: (1) the trust's name and TIN; (2) the date of severance; (3) the fraction of the total assets of the original trust received by the resulting trust; (4) other details explaining the basis for the funding of the resulting trust; and (5) the inclusion ratio (Reg. § 26.2642-6(e)(3)).

Nonqualified severances. Trusts resulting from a severance that does not meet the requirements of a qualified severance will be treated, after the date of the severance, as separate trusts for purposes of the GST tax, provided that such trusts are recognized as separate trusts under applicable state law (Reg. § 26.2642-6(h)). Separate trust treatment will generally permit the allocation of GST exemption, the making of various GST elections, and the occurrence of a taxable distribution or termination with regard to a particular resulting trust, with no GST tax impact on any other trust resulting from the severance. However, each trust resulting from a nonqualified severance will have the same inclusion ratio immediately after the severance as that of the original trust immediately before the severance.

Termination of GST tax. The GST tax is repealed with respect to generation-skipping transfers after December 31, 2009 (Code Sec. 2664). See further discussion at ¶ 705.

BACKGROUND

Sunset provision.—Under the sunset provision of EGTRRA, amendments made by the Act will not apply to generation-skipping transfers after December 31, 2010 (Act Sec. 901 of P.L. 107-16).

NEW LAW EXPLAINED

Qualified severance provision remains in force through 2012.—The qualified severance provision (Code Sec. 2642(a)(3)) will remain in force through December 31, 2012, as a result of the two-year extension of the EGTRRA sunset provision (Act Sec. 101(a)(1) of the Tax Relief, Unemployment Insurance Reauthorization, and Job Creation Act of 2010 (P.L. 111-312)).

The application of the GST tax in 2010. As previously noted, EGTRRA provided that chapter 13 of subtitle B of the Code would not apply to generation-skipping transfers after December 31, 2009, effectively repealing the GST tax for 2010. This one-year termination of the tax caused concern among estate planners, who wondered how the temporary lapse of the tax would affect the application and administration of the GST rules in 2010 and following years.

Seeking some answers, the ABA Section of Real Property, Trust & Estate Law sent a letter to the heads of the House Ways & Means and Senate Finance Committees. The letter, dated December 1, 2010, requested that Congress "resolve the systemic uncertainties" resulting from the one-year suspension of the estate and GST taxes in 2010. The letter observed that, while it was clear that the GST tax did not apply to generation-skipping transfers occurring in 2010, "there are many issues causing confusion, which would be resolved if IRC §2664 were revised to clarify that the GST rules and definitions of Chapter 13 *otherwise* continue to apply during 2010."

As discussed in greater detail at ¶ 705, the Tax Relief Act of 2010 repeals subtitle A of title V of EGTRRA, thereby reinstating the operation of chapter 13 for generation-skipping transfers occurring in 2010 (in essence, repealing the one-year repeal of the GST tax). The Tax Relief Act of 2010 further provides that the applicable rate under Code Sec. 2641(a) for generation-skipping transfers made in 2010 is zero. Because the GST tax is a product of the applicable rate and the taxable amount (Code Sec. 2602), no GST tax will be imposed on any generation-skipping transfers that occur during 2010, as any amount multiplied by zero is equal to zero. The Tax Relief Act of 2010 eliminates the GST tax in 2010 not by making chapter 13 inapplicable to generation-skipping transfers, as EGTRRA would have done, but by setting the effective GST tax rate at zero.

With the Tax Relief Act of 2010 cancelling the enactment of Code Sec. 2664, the "GST rules and definitions," as the ABA letter put it, will continue to apply during 2010, including the qualified severance provision. This should provide estate planning practitioners some of the clarity they were seeking in regard to the application of the GST tax in 2010.

Comment: The Joint Committee on Taxation (JCT) notes that the Tax Relief Act of 2010 reinstates the GST tax, effective for transfers made after December 31,

NEW LAW EXPLAINED

2009. After noting that the GST exemption amount is $5 million for 2010, the JCT explains that, "[t]herefore, up to $5 million in generation skipping transfer tax exemption may be allocated to a trust created or funded during 2010, depending on the amount of such exemption used by the taxpayer before 2010. Although the generation skipping transfer tax is applicable in 2010, the generation skipping transfer tax rate for transfers made during 2010 is zero percent" (Joint Committee on Taxation, *Technical Explanation of the Revenue Provisions Contained in the "Tax Relief, Unemployment Insurance Reauthorization, and Job Creation Act of 2010"* (JCX-55-10), December 10, 2010). The JCT report confirms that the GST rules and definitions that compose chapter 13 will apply during 2010.

Consequences of the EGTRRA sunset in 2013 and beyond.—The amendments made by the Tax Relief Act of 2010—the elimination of Code Sec. 2664, along with the two-year extension of the sunset date—will keep the changes to the GST rules enacted by EGTRRA in force for 2010, 2011, and 2012. As a result, the qualified severance provision will now become inoperative beginning in 2013.

Example 1: In 2000, George Stack creates an irrevocable trust for the benefit of his grandson, Albert. The trust instrument provides that the trustee has discretion to distribute trust income and corpus to Albert during his lifetime. At Albert's death, the corpus is to be distributed in equal shares to Albert's children. The trust instrument also gives the trustee the discretion to sever the trust for GST tax purposes. Based on the amount of GST exemption allocated to the trust and the value of the trust property, the trust's applicable fraction is $2/5$, making the inclusion ratio equal to $3/5$ ($1 - 2/5 = 3/5$). In 2011, the trustee makes a qualified severance of the trust. The trustee divides the trust into two trusts, each having terms identical to that of the original trust. One of the trusts receives a $2/5$-fractional share of the total value of the trust assets. The trust receiving the $2/5$-fractional share has an inclusion ratio of zero, and the other trust has an inclusion ratio of one. Prior to the severance, any distribution from the trust to Albert in 2009 (for example) would have been subject to a GST tax of 27 percent (45 percent × $3/5$). After the severance, a distribution can be made to Albert from the separate trust having the zero inclusion ratio with no GST tax consequences.

However, if the trustee waited until 2013, he would not have the ability to make a qualified severance due to the EGTRRA sunset (as extended). This would deprive the trustee of the ability to make distributions to Albert that were free from GST tax.

Comment: The qualified severance provision was prompted by the perceived need to reduce the complexity of GST tax administration. The provision was intended to make trust severance a less burdensome and complicated process, eliminating the need to draft the complex provisions that were necessary prior to EGTRRA. The sunsetting (i.e. elimination) of this provision will once again ramp up the difficulty of making trust severances for GST tax purposes.

NEW LAW EXPLAINED

> **Planning Point:** Beginning in 2013, with the loss of the qualified severance opportunity, careful and comprehensive document drafting will again be essential when it comes to planning for GST-motivated trust severances.

Interpreting the sunset language. The EGTRRA sunset provision, as amended by the Tax Relief act of 2010, states that "The Internal Revenue Code of 1986 . . . shall be applied and administered to years, estates, gifts, and transfers [after December 31, 2012] as if the provisions and amendments [made by EGTRRA] *had never been enacted*" (Act Sec. 901(b) of P.L. 107-16) (emphasis added). Various commentators have observed that the phrase, "had never been enacted," is a source of confusion in determining how the GST tax is to be applied after the EGTRRA sunset.

> **Comment:** The Tax Relief Act of 2010 may have clarified the application of the GST rules in 2010, as previously discussed, but it did not address how the rules are to be construed following the EGTRRA sunset. The two-year extension of the sunset date has only deferred the day of reckoning as to those matters.

An illustration of the concern in the practitioner community is a letter sent to the IRS by the ABA Section of Taxation, dated July 28, 2010 (ABA letter). The ABA letter, which is in response to the invitation to make suggestions for the 2010—11 IRS Priority Guidance List, reads: "Guidance is needed as to whether this provision [the 'had never been enacted' phrase] will be interpreted to mean that after 2010 the Service will construe the tax laws as if the provisions of EGTRRA were never in effect or, alternatively, that after 2010 the tax laws will be applied to transfers and events post-2010 without applying any of the provisions of EGTRRA to such transfers and events but without ignoring the fact that provisions of EGTRRA were in effect until 2011." The relevant dates cited in the letter may have changed with the enactment of the Tax Relief Act of 2010 (i.e., "2012" would now appear in place of "2010"), but the need for guidance remains.

The ABA letter lists several areas of the GST tax for which guidance would be helpful to clear up the confusion over the effect of the EGTRRA sunset provision. With respect to the qualified severance provision, the ABA letter asks: "If a trust was severed in the years 2001 to 2009 under the qualified severance rules of section 2642(a)(3), will the severance be respected after 2010 [now: 2012] when section 2642(a)(3) is treated as if it 'had never been enacted'?"

> **Example 2:** Assume the same facts as in Example 1, above, where the trustee made a qualified severance in 2011. If the EGTRRA sunset language is interpreted to mean that actions taken pursuant to provisions added by EGTRRA will not be ignored for years after 2012, then the qualified severance would remain valid. Therefore, for years after 2012, the trustee could continue the strategy of making GST tax-free distributions to Albert from the zero inclusion ratio separate trust.
>
> However, if the sunset language is applied in such a way that any actions related to EGTRRA provisions are treated as if they never occurred, there would be no qualified severance as of 2013. In the absence of the severance,

¶770

NEW LAW EXPLAINED

> there would be a single trust with an inclusion ratio of $\frac{3}{5}$ (assuming no further additions had been made to the trust). Any distribution to Albert would now be subject to the GST tax, at perhaps as high a rate as 33 percent (55 percent × $\frac{3}{5}$).

Comment: There are a host of questions that would arise if the EGTRRA sunset language is interpreted to mean that EGTRRA-specific actions are treated as if they never happened for years after 2012. For example, in the above Example, how would the inclusion ratio of a "reunified" trust be determined in 2013 where distributions had been made from the separate trusts following the qualified severance?

Comment: Prior to the enactment of the Tax Relief Act of 2010, the IRS never provided any guidance regarding how it would interpret and apply the "had never been enacted" language in the EGTRRA sunset provision. The two-year extension of the EGTRRA sunset date, by alleviating the immediate need for clarification, probably means that such guidance will not be arriving in the near future. However, until the issues highlighted by the ABA letter are dealt with by the IRS, Congress, or the courts, taxpayers and trustees will be facing a great deal of uncertainty with respect to the post-sunset environment.

▶ **Effective date.** The provision applies to severances after December 31, 2000 ((Act Sec. 101(a)(2) of the Tax Relief, Unemployment Insurance Reauthorization, and Job Creation Act of 2010 (P.L. 111-312); Act Sec. 562(b) of the Economic Growth and Tax Relief Reconciliation Act of 2001) (EGTRRA) (P.L. 107-16)). The provision shall not apply to severances after December 31, 2012 (Act Sec. 101(a)(1) of the Tax Relief Act of 2010; Act Sec. 901 of EGTRRA). See ¶105 for a specific discussion of the sunset provision of EGTRRA and how it is applied.

Law source: Law at ¶5730, ¶5735. Committee Report at ¶10,130.

— Act Sec. 101(a)(1) of the Tax Relief, Unemployment Insurance Reauthorization, and Job Creation Act of 2010 (P.L. 111-312), amending Act Sec. 901(a)(2) of the Economic Growth and Tax Relief Reconciliation Act of 2001 (P.L. 107-16);

— Act Sec. 101(a)(2), providing the effective date.

Reporter references: For further information, consult the following CCH reporters.

— Tax Research Consultant, ESTGIFT: 57,054.20

— Practical Tax Explanation, § 34,725.10

— Federal Estate and Gift Tax Reporter, ¶12,875.22

¶775 Modification of Valuation Rules

SUMMARY OF NEW LAW

The clarification of the valuation rules with respect to the determination of the inclusion ratio for generation-skipping transfer (GST) tax purposes will remain in

SUMMARY OF NEW LAW

force through December 31, 2012, as a result of the two-year extension of the EGTRRA sunset date.

BACKGROUND

The Economic Growth and Tax Relief Reconciliation Act of 2001 (EGTRRA) (P.L. 107-16) amended Code Sec. 2642(b) to clarify the valuation rules with respect to timely and automatic allocations of generation-skipping transfer (GST) tax exemption by including language similar to that of other provisions relating to valuation (e.g., Code Sec. 2001(f)). For transfers subject to estate or gift taxes after December 31, 2000, if an allocation of GST exemption to any transfer of property is made on a timely filed gift tax return or is deemed to be made under Code Sec. 2632(b)(1) (lifetime direct skips) or (c)(1) (lifetime indirect skips), then (1) the value of the property for purposes of calculating the inclusion ratio will be the value of the property as finally determined for gift tax purposes, and (2) the allocation will be effective on and after the date of the transfer. In the case of an allocation deemed to have been made at the close of an estate tax inclusion period (ETIP), the value of the property for inclusion ratio purposes will be the value at the time of the close of the ETIP, and the allocation will be effective on and after the close of the ETIP (Code Sec. 2642(b)(1)).

> **Comment:** An ETIP is any period after a transfer during which the value of the transferred property would be includible in the gross estate of the transferor if he or she died (Code Sec. 2642(f)(3)).

> **Comment:** The inclusion ratio is the key determinant with respect to the potential GST tax liability when transfers are made from a trust to skip persons (e.g., grandchildren). In computing the amount of GST tax, the maximum estate tax rate is multiplied by the inclusion ratio with respect to the transfer (Code Sec. 2641(a)). The inclusion ratio is a function of the amount of the transferor's GST exemption allocated to the transfer. Specifically, the inclusion ratio is equal to the excess of 1 over the applicable fraction. The numerator of the applicable fraction is the amount of GST exemption allocated to the trust and the denominator is the value of the property transferred to the trust (Code Sec. 2642(a)). Therefore, an applicable fraction equal to one, where the GST exemption allocated to the trust equals the value of the trust, yields an inclusion ratio of zero (making trust distributions fully exempt from GST tax), and an applicable fraction equal to zero, where no GST exemption is allocated to the trust, yields an inclusion ratio of one (making trust distributions subject to GST tax at the highest possible rate).

Similarly, for transfers made at death after December 31, 2000, the value of the transferred property for purposes of determining the inclusion ratio will be its value as finally determined for estate tax purposes. However, if the requirements respecting allocation of post-death changes in value are not met, the value of the property will be determined as of the time that the distribution occurred (Code Sec. 2642(b)(2)(A)).

BACKGROUND

Termination of estate and GST taxes. The estate tax is repealed with respect to the estates of decedents dying after December 31, 2009, and the GST tax is repealed with respect to generation-skipping transfers after December 31, 2009 (Code Secs. 2210 and 2664, respectively). See further discussion at ¶705.

Sunset provision. Under the sunset provision of EGTRRA, amendments made by the Act will not apply to decedents dying, gifts made, or generation-skipping transfers after December 31, 2010 (Act Sec. 901 of P.L. 107-16).

NEW LAW EXPLAINED

Clarification of valuation rules remains in force through 2012.—The valuation rules under Code Sec. 2642(b) with respect to the determination of the inclusion ratio for generation-skipping transfer (GST) tax purposes will remain in force through December 31, 2012, as a result of the two-year extension of the EGTRRA sunset provision (Act Sec. 101(a)(1) of the Tax Relief, Unemployment Insurance Reauthorization, and Job Creation Act of 2010 (P.L. 111-312)).

The application of the GST tax in 2010. As previously noted, EGTRRA provided that chapter 13 of subtitle B of the Code would not apply to generation-skipping transfers after December 31, 2009, effectively repealing the GST tax for 2010. This one-year termination of the tax created consternation among estate planners, who raised a number of questions about how the temporary lapse of the tax would impact the application and administration of the GST rules during 2010 and later years.

These concerns were voiced by the ABA Section of Real Property, Trust & Estate Law in a December 1, 2010, letter to the heads of the House Ways & Means and Senate Finance Committees. The letter asked that Congress "resolve the systemic uncertainties" resulting from the one-year suspension of the estate and GST taxes in 2010. The letter noted that, while it was clear that the GST tax did not apply to generation-skipping transfers occurring in 2010, "there are many issues causing confusion, which could be resolved if IRC § 2664 were revised to clarify that the GST rules and definitions of Chapter 13 *otherwise* continue to apply during 2010."

As explained in greater detail at ¶ 705, the Tax Relief Act of 2010 repeals subtitle A of title V of EGTRRA, thereby reinstating the operation of chapter 13 for generation-skipping transfers occurring in 2010 (in essence, repealing the one-year repeal of the GST tax). The Tax Relief Act of 2010 further provides that the applicable rate under Code Sec. 2641(a) for generation-skipping transfers made in 2010 is zero. Because the GST tax is a product of the applicable rate and the taxable amount (Code Sec. 2602), no GST tax will be imposed on any generation-skipping transfers that occur during 2010, as any amount multiplied by zero is equal to zero. The Tax Relief Act of 2010 eliminates the GST tax in 2010 not by making chapter 13 inapplicable to generation-skipping transfers, as EGTRRA would have done, but by setting the effective GST tax rate at zero.

With the Tax Relief Act of 2010 cancelling the enactment of Code Sec. 2664, the "GST rules and definitions," to use the language of the ABA letter, will continue to apply

¶775

NEW LAW EXPLAINED

during 2010, including the valuation rule clarification. This should address the concerns expressed by the ABA on behalf of estate planning practitioners with respect to 2010.

> **Comment:** The Joint Committee on Taxation (JCT) notes that the Tax Relief Act of 2010 reinstates the GST tax, effective for transfers made after December 31, 2009. After noting that the GST exemption amount is $5 million for 2010, the JCT explains that, "[t]herefore, up to $5 million in generation skipping transfer tax exemption may be allocated to a trust created or funded during 2010, depending on the amount of such exemption used by the taxpayer before 2010. Although the generation skipping transfer tax is applicable in 2010, the generation skipping transfer tax rate for transfers made during 2010 is zero percent" (Joint Committee on Taxation, *Technical Explanation of the Revenue Provisions Contained in the "Tax Relief, Unemployment Insurance Reauthorization, and Job Creation Act of 2010"* (JCX-55-10), December 10, 2010). The JCT report confirms that the GST rules and definitions that compose chapter 13 will apply during 2010.

Consequences of the EGTRRA sunset in 2013 and beyond.—The amendments made by the Tax Relief Act of 2010—the elimination of Code Sec. 2664, along with the two-year extension of the sunset date—will keep the changes to the GST rules enacted by EGTRRA in force for 2010, 2011, and 2012. The valuation rules under Code Sec. 2642(b) with respect to the determination of the inclusion ratio for generation-skipping transfer (GST) tax purposes will now revert to their "pre-clarified" incarnation for transfers made in 2013 and thereafter. The pre-EGTRRA version does not specifically address when the value of property is finally determined for estate or gift tax purposes.

> **Comment:** According to the House Ways and Means Committee report that accompanied the Death Tax Elimination Bill of 2001 (H.R. 8) (H. Rep. No. 107-37), the Ways and Means Committee believed that it was "appropriate to clarify" the valuation rules with respect to timely and automatic allocations of GST exemption. The phrase added to the rules by EGTRRA, "as finally determined," synchronizes with the language used elsewhere in the Code with respect to estate and gift tax valuation (see, in particular, Code Sec. 2001(f)(2)).

It is unclear what actual effect the sunsetting of the clarifying language will have. Because the modification of the valuation rules with respect to the determination of the inclusion ratio was characterized as a clarification, rather than a change, it would appear that Congress was not engaged in any policymaking when it amended Code Sec. 2642(b) as part of EGTRRA. If that is the case, the reversion to the pre-EGTRRA language in 2013 occasioned by the sunset provision would have no real practical effect.

▶ **Effective date.** The provision is effective for transfers subject to estate or gift tax made after December 31, 2000 (Act Sec. 101(a)(2) of the Tax Relief, Unemployment Insurance Reauthorization, and Job Creation Act of 2010) (P.L. 111-312); Act Sec. 563(c) of the Economic Growth and Tax Relief Reconciliation Act of 2001 (EGTRRA) (P.L. 107-16)). The provision shall not apply to transfers subject to estate or gift tax made after December 31, 2012 (Act Sec. 101(a)(1) of the Tax Relief Act of 2010; Act Sec. 901 of EGTRRA). See ¶105 for a specific discussion of the sunset provision of EGTRRA and how it is applied.

¶775

NEW LAW EXPLAINED

Law source: Law at ¶5695, ¶5730, and ¶5735. Committee Report at ¶10,130.

— Act Sec. 101(a)(1) of the Tax Relief, Unemployment Insurance Reauthorization, and Job Creation Act of 2010 (P.L. 111-312), amending Act Sec. 901(a)(2) of the Economic Growth and Tax Relief Reconciliation Act of 2001 (P.L. 107-16);

— Act Sec. 101(a)(2), providing the effective date.

Reporter references: For further information, consult the following CCH reporters.

— Tax Research Consultant, ESTGIFT: 57,108

— Practical Tax Explanation, § 34,715.15

— Federal Estate and Gift Tax Reporter, ¶12,875.25 and ¶12,875.30

¶780 Late Elections and Substantial Compliance

SUMMARY OF NEW LAW

The provisions providing relief from late generation-skipping transfer (GST) allocations and elections will remain in force through December 31, 2012, as a result of the two-year extension of the EGTRRA sunset date.

BACKGROUND

The Economic Growth and Tax Relief Reconciliation Act of 2001 (EGTRRA) (P.L. 107-16) added Code Sec. 2642(g), which directs the IRS to issue regulations that provide taxpayers the opportunity to request extensions of time with respect to certain generation-skipping transfer (GST) tax provisions. Specifically, the regulations are to include procedures under which extensions of time will be granted to make: (1) an allocation of GST exemption under Code Sec. 2642(b)(1) or (2), or (2) an election under Code Sec. 2632(b)(3) or (c)(5) (see ¶765 regarding deemed and retroactive allocations of GST exemption). In determining whether to grant relief, the IRS is directed to take into account "all relevant circumstances," such as evidence of intent contained in the trust instrument or instrument of transfer (Code Sec. 2642(g)(1)(B)). In addition, for purposes of whether to grant such relief, the time for making the allocation or election is to be treated as if not expressly prescribed by statute.

Interim guidance. In Notice 2001-50, 2001-2 CB 189, the IRS provided guidance regarding requests for the extensions of time covered by Code Sec. 2642(g). Under Notice 2001-50, effective with respect to requests for relief pending on, or filed after, December 31, 2000, taxpayers may seek an extension of time to allocate GST exemption to lifetime transfers and transfers at death, elect out of the automatic allocation rules, and elect to treat any trust as a GST trust, via the private letter ruling process under the provisions of Reg. § 301.9100-3. In general, relief will be granted if the taxpayer establishes that he or she acted reasonably and in good faith and that the grant of relief will not prejudice the interests of the government. If relief is granted

BACKGROUND

and the allocation is made, the amount of GST exemption necessary to reduce the inclusion ratio to zero is based on the value of the property on the date of the transfer and the allocation is effective as of the date of the transfer.

> **Example:** In 2002, Fred Miller transfers $1 million worth of stock to a generation-skipping trust for the benefit of Miller's grandchild, Marilyn Lee. If Miller's full GST exemption amount is allocated to this transfer on a timely filed gift tax return, then regardless of any future appreciation in the value of the stock, no GST tax will be owed on a later trust distribution or termination. If, however, Miller does not allocate the GST exemption on a timely filed gift tax return and the stock has grown to $1.5 million in value by the time that Miller makes the allocation, the allocation will fail to shelter the additional $500,000 (and any appreciation on that unsheltered amount) from future GST tax liability. If Miller was granted an extension of time to make an allocation pursuant to Code Sec. 2642(g)(1), then Miller could allocate his GST exemption based on the value of the stock as of the date of transfer ($1 million), as opposed to its later appreciated value.

> **Comment:** Since the enactment of EGTRRA, the IRS has granted many requests for an extension of time to allocate GST exemption. See ¶12,875.75 of CCH's FEDERAL ESTATE AND GIFT TAX REPORTER for a collection of some of these private letter rulings.

Alternate simplified method. In Rev. Proc. 2004-46, 2004-2 CB 142, the IRS detailed a simplified alternate method for certain taxpayers to obtain an extension of time under Reg. §301.9100-3 to make an allocation of GST exemption in accordance with Code Sec. 2642(b)(1). The alternate method may be used in lieu of the letter ruling process.

In order to use the alternate method, a taxpayer must satisfy the following requirements:

- On or before December 31, 2000, the taxpayer made a transfer by gift to a trust from which a GST could be made;
- At the time that the taxpayer files the request for relief, no taxable distributions had been made and no taxable terminations had occurred;
- The transfer qualified for the gift tax annual exclusion under Code Sec. 2503(b), and the amount of the transfer did not exceed the applicable annual exclusion amount for the year of the transfer;
- No GST exemption was allocated to the transfer (whether or not a gift tax return was filed);
- At the time that the taxpayer filed the request for relief, the taxpayer had unused GST exemption available to allocate to the transfer; and
- All of the procedural requirements contained in the revenue procedure are satisfied (see section 4 of Rev. Proc. 2004-46).

Proposed regulations. On April 17, 2008, the IRS issued proposed regulations pursuant to the mandate contained in Code Sec. 2642(g)(1). Under the proposed regula-

¶780

BACKGROUND

tions, requests for relief will be granted when the transferor (or the executor of the transferor's estate) establishes that he or she acted reasonably and in good faith, and the grant of relief would not prejudice the interests of the government (Proposed Reg. § 26.2642-7(d)(1)).

Under the proposed regulations, the relief will be provided through the IRS private letter ruling program. If an extension of time to allocate GST exemption is granted, the allocation will be considered effective as of the date of the transfer, and the value of the property transferred for estate or gift tax purposes will determine the amount of exemption to be allocated.

As to the determination of reasonableness and good faith, the IRS will consider the following factors (which are not meant to be exhaustive):

- the intent of the transferor to timely allocate GST exemption to a transfer or to timely make an election, as evidenced in the trust instrument or documents contemporaneous with the transfer, such as gift and estate tax returns and correspondence;

- intervening events beyond the control of the transferor or executor as the cause of the failure to allocate GST exemption to a transfer or the failure to make an election;

- lack of awareness by the transferor or the executor of the need to allocate GST exemption to the transfer, despite the exercise of reasonable diligence, taking into account the experience of the transferor or executor and the complexity of the GST issue;

- consistency by the transferor with regard to the allocation of his GST exemption in the past; and

- reasonable reliance by the transferor or executor on the advice of a qualified tax professional (Proposed Reg. § 26.2642-7(d)(2)).

With respect to the determination of whether the interests of the government have been prejudiced, the IRS will take into account the following considerations (again, which are not exhaustive):

- the extent to which the request for relief is an effort to benefit from hindsight, rather than to achieve the result that the transferor or the executor intended at the time when the transfer was made;

- the timing of the request for relief, where a delay in the filing of the request by the transferor or executor was intended to deprive the IRS of sufficient time to challenge any relevant aspect of the transfer; and

- the occurrence and effect of an intervening taxable termination or taxable distribution between the time for making a timely allocation or election and the time at which the request for relief was filed (Proposed Reg. § 26.2642-7(d)(3)).

The transferor or executor must submit a detailed affidavit describing the events that led to the failure to timely allocate GST exemption to a transfer or the failure to timely elect, and the events that led to the discovery of the failure (see Proposed Reg. § 26.2642-7(h)(2)). In addition, the transferor or executor must submit detailed affidavits from individuals who have knowledge or information about the events that led

BACKGROUND

to the failure to allocate GST exemption or to elect, and/or to the discovery of the failure (see Proposed Reg. § 26.2642-7(h)(3)).

Substantial compliance. In addition to the relief for late elections discussed above, EGTRRA added a substantial compliance provision to provide further assistance to transferors. Effective for transfers subject to estate or gift tax after December 31, 2000, an allocation of GST exemption under Code Sec. 2632 that demonstrated an intent to have the lowest possible inclusion ratio with respect to a transfer to a trust will be deemed to be an allocation of so much of the transferor's unused GST exemption as produces the lowest possible inclusion ratio (Code Sec. 2642(g)(2)). In determining whether there has been substantial compliance, "all relevant circumstances" are to be considered, including evidence of intent contained in the trust instrument or instrument of transfer (see, e.g., IRS Letter Rulings 201027034 and 200717002).

Termination of GST tax. The GST tax is repealed with respect to generation-skipping transfers after December 31, 2009 (Code Sec. 2664). See further discussion at ¶705.

Sunset provision. Under the sunset provision of EGTRRA, amendments made by the Act will not apply to generation-skipping transfers after December 31, 2010 (Act Sec. 901 of P.L. 107-16).

NEW LAW EXPLAINED

Provisions providing relief from late GST allocations and elections remain in force through 2012.—The provisions providing relief from late GST allocations and elections (Code Sec. 2642(g)(1)), as well as the provision pertaining to substantial compliance (Code Sec. 2642(g)(2)), will remain in force through December 31, 2012, as a result of the two-year extension of the EGTRRA sunset provision (Act Sec. 101(a)(1) of the Tax Relief, Unemployment Insurance Reauthorization, and Job Creation Act of 2010 (P.L. 111-312)).

The application of the GST tax in 2010. As previously noted, EGTRRA provided that chapter 13 of subtitle B of the Code would not apply to generation-skipping transfers after December 31, 2009, effectively repealing the GST tax for 2010. This one-year termination of the tax created difficulties for practitioners, who were confronted with the question of how the temporary lapse of the tax would impact the application and administration of the GST rules during 2010 and later years.

These concerns were expressed by the ABA Section of Real Property, Trust & Estate Law in a December 1, 2010, letter to the heads of the House Ways & Means and Senate Finance Committees. The letter asked that Congress "resolve the systemic uncertainties" resulting from the one-year suspension of the estate and GST taxes in 2010. The letter noted that, while it was clear that the GST tax did not apply to generation-skipping transfers occurring in 2010, "there are many issues causing confusion, which could be resolved if IRC § 2664 were revised to clarify that the GST rules and definitions of Chapter 13 *otherwise* continue to apply during 2010."

As explained in greater detail at ¶ 705, the Tax Relief Act of 2010 repeals subtitle A of title V of EGTRRA, thereby reinstating the operation of chapter 13 for generation-

NEW LAW EXPLAINED

skipping transfers occurring in 2010 (in essence, repealing the one-year repeal of the GST tax). The Tax Relief Act of 2010 further provides that the applicable rate under Code Sec. 2641(a) for generation-skipping transfers made in 2010 is zero. Because the GST tax is a product of the applicable rate and the taxable amount (Code Sec. 2602), no GST tax will be imposed on any generation-skipping transfers that occur during 2010, as any amount multiplied by zero is equal to zero. The Tax Relief Act of 2010 eliminates the GST tax in 2010 not by making chapter 13 inapplicable to generation-skipping transfers, as EGTRRA would have done, but by setting the effective GST tax rate at zero.

With the Tax Relief Act of 2010 cancelling the enactment of Code Sec. 2664, the "GST rules and definitions," to borrow the phrase from the ABA letter, will continue to apply during 2010, including the provision providing relief from late allocations and the substantial compliance provision. This should alleviate the concerns raised by the ABA on behalf of estate planners with respect to 2010.

> **Comment:** The Joint Committee on Taxation (JCT) notes that the Tax Relief Act of 2010 reinstates the GST tax, effective for transfers made after December 31, 2009. After noting that the GST exemption amount is $5 million for 2010, the JCT explains that, "[t]herefore, up to $5 million in generation skipping transfer tax exemption may be allocated to a trust created or funded during 2010, depending on the amount of such exemption used by the taxpayer before 2010. Although the generation skipping transfer tax is applicable in 2010, the generation skipping transfer tax rate for transfers made during 2010 is zero percent" (Joint Committee on Taxation, *Technical Explanation of the Revenue Provisions Contained in the "Tax Relief, Unemployment Insurance Reauthorization, and Job Creation Act of 2010"* (JCX-55-10), December 10, 2010). The JCT report confirms that the GST rules and definitions that compose chapter 13 will apply during 2010.

Consequences of the EGTRRA sunset in 2013 and beyond.—The amendments made by the Tax Relief Act of 2010—the elimination of Code Sec. 2664, along with the two-year extension of the sunset date—will keep the changes to the GST rules enacted by EGTRRA in force for 2010, 2011, and 2012. As a result, the provisions providing relief from late GST allocations and elections, as well as the provision pertaining to substantial compliance, will now become inoperative beginning in 2013.

> **Comment:** Code Sec. 2642(g) was added to provide taxpayers with the opportunity to obtain relief where they inadvertently failed to make a timely allocation of GST exemption to a transfer of property or where their allocation did not fully comply with the applicable statutory and regulatory requirements. The need for the relief provision was an acknowledgment that the requirements for allocating GST exemption are complex. The elimination of Code Sec. 2642(g) will deprive taxpayers of a statutory basis for obtaining relief in these situations.

Example 1: In 2013, Fred Miller transfers $1 million worth of stock to a generation-skipping trust for the benefit of Miller's grandchild, Marilyn Lee. Miller, who had $1 million of GST exemption available to be allocated at the

---

NEW LAW EXPLAINED

time of the transfer, inadvertently failed to allocate his GST exemption amount to the transfer on a timely filed gift tax return. In 2014, Miller became aware of the failure to allocate, by which time the value of the stock had increased to $1.5 million. Because the relief afforded by Code Sec. 2642(g) is no longer in force, Miller must use the value of the stock at the time of the late allocation to determine the inclusion ratio of the trust. This results in an inclusion ratio of $1/3$, rather than the zero inclusion ratio that would have resulted if Code Sec. 2642(g) had still been in effect (and assuming Miller's request for extension of time to allocate was granted).

Compliance Note: Beginning with transfers made in 2013, taxpayers will no longer have the benefit of the Code Sec. 2642(g) relief provisions to rectify their failures to make GST allocations. As a result, tax advisers and return preparers will need to exercise even greater care in making sure that the taxpayer's GST exemption is being properly allocated whenever the taxpayer makes a transfer with potential GST consequences.

Interpreting the sunset language. The EGTRRA sunset provision, as amended by the Tax Relief Act of 2010, states that "The Internal Revenue Code of 1986 . . . shall be applied and administered to years, estates, gifts, and transfers [after December 31, 2012] as if the provisions and amendments [made by EGTRRA] *had never been enacted*" (Act. Sec 901(b) of P.L. 107-16) (emphasis added). Various observers have noted that the phrase, "had never been enacted," creates some ambiguities in interpreting how the GST tax will operate in the years following the EGTRRA sunset.

Comment: The Tax Relief Act of 2010 may have clarified the application of the GST rules in 2010, as previously discussed, but it did not address how the rules will be construed following the sunset of EGTRRA. The two-year extension of the sunset date has simply postponed the day of reckoning as to those issues.

An example of these concerns is a letter sent to the IRS by the ABA Section of Taxation on July 28, 2010 (ABA letter). The ABA letter, responding to the invitation to make recommendations for the 2010—11 IRS Priority Guidance List, states the following: "Guidance is needed as to whether this provision [the 'had never been enacted' phrase] will be interpreted to mean that after 2010 the Service will construe the tax laws as if the provisions of EGTRRA were never in effect or, alternatively, that after 2010 the tax laws will be applied to transfers and events post-2010 without applying any of the provisions of EGTRRA to such transfers and events but without ignoring the fact that provisions of EGTRRA were in effect until 2011." The ABA letter then lists several areas of the GST tax for which guidance is necessary to resolve the confusion over the operation of the EGTRRA sunset provision.

Example 2: In 2002, Fred Miller transfers $1 million worth of stock to a generation-skipping trust for the benefit of his grandchild, Marilyn Lee. Miller inadvertently failed to allocate his GST exemption amount to the transfer on a timely filed gift tax return. In 2003, Miller became aware of the failure to

NEW LAW EXPLAINED

allocate. Miller requested and received an extension of time to allocate his GST exemption to the transfer pursuant to the relief made available under Code Sec. 2642(g). As a result, the allocation was effective as of the date of the transfer, and the inclusion ratio of the trust was zero.

If the EGTRRA sunset language is interpreted to mean that actions taken with respect to EGTRRA provisions will not be ignored for years after 2012, then the late allocation of Miller's GST exemption would remain valid and the trust would retain its zero inclusion ratio in 2013. However, if the sunset language is construed in such a way so that any actions related to EGTRRA provisions are treated as if they never occurred, then the allocation would be considered to have never been made. With no GST exemption having been allocated to the transfer, the trust's inclusion ratio would be one, not zero, in 2013. Rather than distributions being GST-tax free, they would be subject to GST tax at a 55-percent rate.

Comment: It appears that a case could be made that the IRS had already adopted the substantial compliance approach prior to the enactment of EGTRRA (see, e.g., IRS Letter Ruling 199937026, determining that a trust agreement attached to the estate tax return contained enough information to constitute substantial compliance with the requirements for making an allocation of GST exemption between two trusts). If that view was to prevail, then the EGTRRA sunset would have little practical effect with respect to the substantial compliance provision (Code Sec. 2642(g)(2)). See *Time Traveling and Generation-Skipping in 2010 and Beyond*, Carlyn S. McCaffrey and Pam H. Schneider, TAX NOTES, July 26, 2010.

Prior to the enactment of the Tax Relief Act of 2010, the IRS never provided any guidance as to how it would interpret and apply the "had never been enacted" language in the EGTRRA sunset provision. The two-year extension of the EGTRRA sunset date, by alleviating the immediate need for clarification, probably means that such guidance will not be forthcoming in the near future. However, until the uncertainty surrounding the administration of the GST tax post-sunset is resolved (whether by the IRS, Congress, or the courts), taxpayers looking ahead to 2013 and beyond will find themselves wondering about the continued viability of any actions that were made possible by EGTRRA provisions.

▶ **Effective date.** The provision relating to relief from late elections applies to requests pending on, or filed after, December 31, 2000 (Act Sec. 101(a)(2) of the Tax Relief, Unemployment Insurance Reauthorization, and Job Creation Act of 2010) (P.L. 111-312); Act Sec. 564(b)(1) of the Economic Growth and Tax Relief Reconciliation Act of 2001 (EGTRRA) (P.L. 107-16)). The provision relating to substantial compliance applies to transfers subject to estate or gift tax made after December 31, 2000 (Act Sec. 101(a)(2) of the Tax Relief Act of 2010; Act Sec. 564(b)(2) of EGTRRA). The provision relating to relief from late elections shall not apply to requests pending on, or filed after, December 31, 2012 (Act Sec. 101(a)(1) of the Tax Relief Act of 2010; Act Sec. 901 of EGTRRA). The provision relating to substantial compliance shall not apply to transfers subject to estate or gift tax made after December 31, 2012 (Act Sec. 101(a)(1) of the Tax Relief Act of 2010; Act Sec.

¶780

NEW LAW EXPLAINED

901 of EGTRRA). See ¶105 for a specific discussion of the sunset provision of EGTRRA and how it is applied.

Law source: Law at ¶5730 and ¶5735. Committee Report at ¶10,130.

— Act Sec. 101(a)(1) of the Tax Relief, Unemployment Insurance Reauthorization, and Job Creation Act of 2010 (P.L. 111-312), amending Act Sec. 901(a)(2) of the Economic Growth and Tax Relief Reconciliation Act of 2001 (P.L. 107-16);

— Act Sec. 101(a)(2), providing the effective date.

Reporter references: For further information, consult the following CCH reporters.

— Tax Research Consultant, ESTGIFT: 57,106.10

— Practical Tax Explanation, § 34,725.10

— Federal Estate and Gift Tax Reporter, ¶12,875.55 and ¶12,875.57

INSTALLMENT PAYMENTS

¶785 Allowable Number of Members for Closely Held Business

SUMMARY OF NEW LAW

The rule under Code Sec. 6166(b)(1)(B)(ii), Code Sec. 6166(b)(1)(C)(ii), and Code Sec. 6166(b)(9)(B)(iii)(I) providing that a decedent's estate cannot qualify for deferred payment of estate tax if the number of partners or shareholders in the decedent's closely held business exceeds 45 is extended to the estates of decedents dying before January 1, 2013.

BACKGROUND

The Economic Growth and Tax Relief Reconciliation Act of 2001 (EGTRRA) (P.L. 107-16) amended Code Sec. 6166 to expand the number of estates that qualify for deferral and payment of estate taxes in installments. Generally, any estate tax owed by a decedent's estate must be paid within nine months of the decedent's date of death. If more than 35 percent of the decedent's adjusted gross estate is an interest in a farm or other closely held business, under Code Sec. 6166 the executor may elect to extend the time for paying the estate tax that is attributable to the closely held business. The partnership or corporation must be an active entity that is carrying on a business at the time of the decedent's death (Code Sec. 6166(b)(9)).

If the election is made, the tax can be paid in installments. For the first five years, the estate can defer payment of principal and pay only interest. Following that, equal installments of principal and interest are paid on a yearly basis for up to 10 years. The installment payments will actually span the course of 14 years, instead of 15 years,

BACKGROUND

because the due date for the last interest-only payment coincides with the due date for the first installment of estate tax.

A special, reduced interest rate of two percent is applied to the first $1 million of taxable value of the closely held business (adjusted annually for inflation). The interest rate on the remaining amount of taxable value is paid at a rate of 45 percent of the rate applicable to underpayments of tax (Code Sec. 6601(j)(1)).

> **Comment:** For 2010, the dollar amount used to determine the "two-percent portion" for purposes of computing the interest due under Code Sec. 6601(j)(3) is $1,340,000 (Rev. Proc. 2009-50, IRB 2009-45, 617).

EGTRRA amended Code Sec. 6166 by liberalizing the rules governing the number of allowable partners or shareholders in a qualifying closely held entity. Accordingly, under Code Sec. 6166, an interest in a closely held business includes:

- a sole proprietorship;

- a partnership interest, if 20 percent or more of the assets are included in the decedent's gross estate or the partnership had no more than 45 partners (Code Sec. 6166(b)(1)(B)(ii)); or

- stock in a corporation, if 20 percent or more of the voting stock is included in determining the decedent's gross estate or the corporation had no more than 45 shareholders (Code Sec. 6166(b)(1)(C)(ii)).

> **Comment:** EGTRRA expanded the number of estates eligible for installment payment of estate taxes by increasing the maximum number of allowable partners or shareholders in a qualifying closely held business entity from 15 to 45. Prior to the EGTRRA amendment, the number of 15 allowable partners and shareholders had been unchanged since the addition of the Code Section by the Tax Reform Act of 1976 (P.L. 94-455). However, even with the maximum number of partners or shareholders being raised to 45, this was still considerably less than the number of shareholders allowed in an S corporation under Code Sec. 1361, which was 75 at the time EGTRRA was passed and is currently 100.

Sunset Provision.—Under the sunset provision of EGTRRA, amendments made by the Act will not apply to estates of decedent's dying after December 31, 2010 (Act Sec. 901 of P.L. 107-16).

NEW LAW EXPLAINED

Increase in number of members of closely held business extended.—For purposes of the rules governing qualification for installment payment of estate tax, the maximum allowable number of partners or shareholders in a closely held business owned by a decedent at the time of his or her death is extended to 45 for the estates of decedents dying before January 1, 2013 (Code Sec. 6166(b)(1)(B)(ii), Code Sec. 6166(b)(1)(C)(ii), and Code Sec. 6166(b)(9)(B)(iii)(I)) as amended by the Tax Relief, Unemployment Insurance Reauthorization, and Job Creation Act of 2010 (P.L. 111-312)). Under EGTRRA, this provision expired for a one-year period beginning on January 1,

NEW LAW EXPLAINED

2010. However, under the Tax Relief Act of 2010, this provision is extended to the estates of decedents dying before January 1, 2013.

> **Comment:** In addition to the rules governing the number of partners or shareholders allowed in a closely held entity for purposes of the estate tax installment payment provisions, other requirements are also imposed. For example, whether the decedent's business was a sole proprietorship, partnership or corporation, in order to qualify for installment payment of estate tax, it must be engaged in an active trade or business at the time of the decedent's death; the election is generally not available for passive assets (Code Sec. 6166(b)(9)). If the decedent had an interest in two or more closely held businesses, these businesses will be treated as a single, closely held business if 20 percent or more of the total value of each one is included in the decedent's gross estate (Code Sec. 6166(c)).

> **Comment:** In addition to extending the expanded number of allowable partners or shareholders for a closely held entity to qualify for paying the estate tax in installments, the Tax Relief Act of 2010 extends provisions that liberalized the rules for certain lending and finance businesses and holding companies to qualify for installment payment treatment (see ¶790 and ¶795, respectively, for details).

▶ **Effective date.** The provision is effective for estates of decedents dying after December 31, 2001 (Act Sec. 101(a)(2) of the Tax Relief, Unemployment Insurance Reauthorization, and Job Creation Act of 2010 (P.L. 111-312); Act Sec. 571(b) of the Economic Growth and Tax Relief Reconciliation Act of 2001 (EGTRRA) (P.L. 107-16)). The provision shall not apply to the estates of decedents dying after December 31, 2012 (Act Sec. 101(a)(1) of the Tax Relief Act of 2010; Act Sec. 901 of EGTRRA). See ¶105 for a specific discussion of the sunset provision of EGTRRA and how it is applied.

Law source: Law at ¶5790. Committee Report at ¶10,130.

— Act Sec. 101(a)(1) of the Tax Relief, Unemployment Insurance Reauthorization, and Job Creation Act of 2010 (P.L. 111-312), amending Code Sec. 6166(b)(1)(B)(ii); 6166(b)(1)(C)(ii) and 6166(b)(9)(B)(iii)(I)

— Act Sec. 101(a)(2), providing the effective date.

Reporter references: For further information, consult the following CCH reporters.

— Tax Research Consultant, ESTGIFT: 51,154

— Practical Tax Explanation, § 34,410.05 and § 34,935.20

— Federal Estate and Gift Tax Reporter, ¶20,665.02 and ¶20,665.023

¶785

¶790 Election for Installment Payment of Estate Tax With Respect to Lending and Finance Businesses

SUMMARY OF NEW LAW

The rule permitting stock in qualifying lending and financing entities to be treated as stock in an active trade or business for purposes of the election to pay estate tax in installments is extended to the estates of decedents dying before January 1, 2013.

BACKGROUND

The Economic Growth and Tax Relief Reconciliation Act of 2001 (EGTRRA) (P.L. 107-16) added Code Sec. 6166(b)(10), which expanded the definition of property that may be eligible for treatment as a closely held business asset under the rules governing the payment of estate tax in installments to include an interest in a lending and finance business. As a result, if a decedent's estate includes stock in a qualifying lending and finance business, the stock may be treated as stock in an active trade or business for purposes of the rules governing the installment payment of estate tax (Code Sec. 6166(b)(10)). However, unlike the case with other closely held interests (see ¶785), an estate holding interests in qualifying lending and finance entities is not entitled to defer principal for five years and is limited to making installment payments over five years instead of 10 years (Code Sec. 6166(b)(10)(A)).

In order to be considered a qualifying lending and finance business, the entity must have:

- conducted substantial activity relating to the lending and finance business immediately prior to the decedent's death; or

- employed at least one full-time manager and 10 full-time, non-owner employees during at least three of the five tax years prior to the decedent's death; and

- earned at least $5 million in gross receipts from lending and finance activities (Code Sec. 6166(b)(10)(B)(i)).

In addition, the term "lending and finance business" is defined as a business that is involved in:

(1) making loans;

(2) purchasing or discounting accounts receivable, notes or installment obligations;

(3) renting and leasing of real estate and tangible personal property; and

(4) rendering services or making facilities available in the ordinary course of a lending or financing business.

The term also includes providing services or making facilities available in connection with the activities that are listed in (1) through (4) above that are carried on by a corporation rendering such services or making facilities available, or another corporation that is a member of an affiliated group, as defined in Code Sec. 1504 (without

BACKGROUND

regard to Code Sec. 1504(b)(3)) (Code Sec. 6166(b)(10)(B)(ii)). However, the definition of a qualified lending and finance business does *not* include an interest in an entity if the stock or debt of that entity was readily tradable on an established securities market or secondary market at any time during the three years preceding the decedent's death (Code Sec. 6166(b)(10)(B)(iii)).

Sunset provision.—Under the sunset provision of EGTRRA, amendments made by the Act will not apply to the estates of decedent's dying after December 31, 2010 (Act Sec. 901 of P.L. 107-16).

NEW LAW EXPLAINED

Installment payment of estate tax for interest in lending and finance business extended.—The rule that permits a decedent's estate to pay estate tax in installments with respect to interests attributable to businesses that are engaged in lending and finance activities is extended to apply to the estates of decedents dying before January 1, 2013 (Code Sec. 6166(b)(10)), as amended by the Tax Relief, Unemployment Insurance Reauthorization, and Job Creation Act of 2010 (P.L. 111-312)). Under EGTRRA, this provision expired for a one-year period beginning on January 1, 2010. However, under the Tax Relief Act of 2010, this provision is extended to the estates of decedents dying before January 1, 2013. Therefore, stock held by the estate of a decedent who dies after December 31, 2012, will be treated as a passive asset that does not qualify for inclusion in the property used to compute the percentage threshold necessary to satisfy the requirements for the election to pay estate taxes in installments.

> **Comment:** In addition to extending the liberalized rules for certain lending and finance businesses to qualify for paying the estate tax in installments, the Tax Relief Act of 2010 extends the increased number of 45 allowable partners or shareholders for a closely held entity to qualify for installment payment treatment and limits the ability of certain holding companies to qualify (see ¶785 and ¶795, for details).

▶ **Effective date.** The provision is effective for estates of decedents dying after December 31, 2001 (Act Sec. 101(a)(2) of the Tax Relief, Unemployment Insurance Reauthorization, and Job Creation Act of 2010 (P.L. 111-312); Act Sec. 572(b) of the Economic Growth and Tax Relief Reconciliation Act of 2001 (EGTRRA) (P.L. 107-16)). The provision shall not apply to the estates of decedents dying after December 31, 2012 (Act Sec. 101(a)(1) of the Tax Relief Act of 2010; Act Sec. 901 of EGTRRA). See ¶105 for a specific discussion of the sunset provision of EGTRRA and how it is applied.

Law source: Law at ¶5790. Committee Report at ¶10,130.

— Act Sec. 101(a)(1) of the Tax Relief, Unemployment Insurance Reauthorization, and Job Creation Act of 2010 (P.L. 111-312), amending Code Sec. 6166(b)(10);

— Act Sec. 101(a)(2), providing the effective date.

Reporter references: For further information, consult the following CCH reporters.

— Tax Research Consultant, ESTGIFT: 51,154.05

— Practical Tax Explanation, § 34,410.05

— Federal Estate and Gift Tax Reporter, ¶20,665.025

¶790

¶795 Estate Tax Installment Payments and Stock of Holding Companies

SUMMARY OF NEW LAW

The rule under Code Sec. 6166(b)(8)(B) providing that only the stock of holding companies must be non-readily tradable in order for an executor to elect to pay estate tax in installments is extended to the estates of decedents dying before January 1, 2013.

BACKGROUND

The Economic Growth and Tax Relief Reconciliation Act of 2001 (EGTRRA) (P.L. 107-16) amended Code Sec. 6166 relating to the deferral and extension of estate tax payments. Code Sec. 6166 generally permits a decedent's closely held business to pay federal estate tax in installments. In addition to the rules regarding closely held businesses discussed at ¶785, the stock of a holding company that directly or indirectly owns stock in a closely held business will be considered stock in the business company, for purposes of the installment payment election under Code Sec. 6166.

A "holding company" refers to a corporation that holds stock in another corporation and a "business company" refers to a corporation with an active trade or business. In order to qualify for the deferral election under Code Sec. 6166, the holding company must satisfy the same requirements that apply to elections made for closely held business interests. Those requirements are:

- the corporation must have fewer than 45 shareholders; or

- at least 20 percent of the corporation's voting stock is included in the decedent's gross estate (Code Sec. 6166(b)(1)(C)).

In addition to the items listed above, the value of the business interest held by the holding company must exceed 35 percent of the value of the decedent's adjusted gross estate (Code Sec. 6166(a)(1)). The election to defer payments applies to stock that is "non-readily tradable," meaning there was no market for the stock at the time of the decedent's death (either on a stock exchange or over-the-counter). EGTRRA clarified that, in order to qualify for the election, only the stock of the holding company must be non-readily tradable, not the stock of the operating subsidiary (Code Sec. 6166(b)(8)(B)).

Sunset provision.—Under the sunset provision of EGTRRA, amendments made by the Act will not apply to the estates of decedent's dying after December 31, 2010 (Act Sec. 901 of P.L. 107-16).

NEW LAW EXPLAINED

Installment payment election application to stock of holding company extended.—The rule requiring that only stock in a holding company must be non-readily tradable in order to qualify for purposes of the installment payment rules is extended to include the estates of decedents dying before January 1, 2013 (Code Sec. 6166(b)(8)(B)), as amended by the Tax Relief, Unemployment Insurance Reauthorization, and Job Creation Act of 2010 (P.L. 111-312)). Under EGTRRA, this provision expired for a one-year period beginning on January 1, 2010. However, under the Tax Relief Act of 2010, this provision is extended to the estates of decedents dying before January 1, 2013.

> **Comment:** If the executor makes this election, the five-year period for deferring payment of principal does not apply. In addition, the two-percent interest rate that applies to installment payments will not be available (Code Sec. 6166(b)(8)(A)).

> **Comment:** In addition to extending provisions that liberalized the application of the installment payment rules for certain holding companies, the Tax Relief Act of 2010 extends the increased number of partners or shareholders that a closely held entity is allowed to have and still qualify for installment payment of estate taxes, as well as extending provisions that loosened the rules for certain lending and finance businesses to qualify for installment payments (see ¶785 and ¶790 for details).

▶ **Effective date.** The provision is effective for estates of decedents dying after December 31, 2001 (Act Sec. 101(a)(2) of the Tax Relief, Unemployment Insurance Reauthorization, and Job Creation Act of 2010 (P.L. 111-312); Act Sec. 572 [573](b) of the Economic Growth and Tax Relief Reconciliation Act of 2001 (EGTRRA) (P.L. 107-16)). The provision shall not apply to the estates of decedents dying after December 31, 2012 (Act Sec. 101(a)(1) of the Tax Relief Act of 2010; Act Sec. 901 of EGTRRA). See ¶105 for a specific discussion of the sunset provision of EGTRRA and how it is applied.

Law source: Law at ¶5790. Committee Report at ¶10,130.

— Act Sec. 101(a)(1) of the Tax Relief, Unemployment Insurance Reauthorization, and Job Creation Act of 2010 (P.L. 111-312), amending Code Sec. 6166(b)(8)(B);

— Act Sec. 101(a)(2), providing the effective date.

Reporter references: For further information, consult the following CCH reporters.

— Tax Research Consultant, ESTGIFT: 51,154.25

— Practical Tax Explanation, § 34,410.05

— Federal Estate and Gift Tax Reporter, ¶20,665.023

¶795

Regulated Investment Companies (RICs)

8

CAPITAL LOSS CARRYOVER

¶803   RIC Capital Loss Carryover

GROSS INCOME AND ASSET TESTS

¶806   RIC Asset and Gross Income Tests

DIVIDENDS AND OTHER DISTRIBUTIONS

¶809   RIC Dividend Distributions

¶812   Earnings and Profits of RICs

¶815   Pass-Through of Exempt-Interest Dividends and Foreign Tax Credits

¶818   Dividends Paid by RICs After Close of Tax Year

¶821   Return of Capital Distributions of RICs

¶824   Redemptions of Stock of RICs

¶827   Preferential Dividends of Publicly Offered RICs

¶830   Elective Deferral of Certain Late-Year Losses of RICs

¶833   Holding Period Requirement For Certain Regularly Declared Exempt-Interest Dividends

OTHER PROVISIONS

¶836   Excise Tax on RIC Distributions

¶839   Assessable Penalty with Respect to Tax Liability of RICs

¶842   Sale Load Basis Deferral Rule

CAPITAL LOSS CARRYOVER

¶803 RIC Capital Loss Carryover

SUMMARY OF NEW LAW

Regulated investment companies (RICs) can treat net capital loss carryovers in a manner that is similar to the present-law treatment of such carryovers by individuals.

BACKGROUND

In general, regulated investment companies (RICs) are electing domestic corporations that meet certain registration requirements under the Investment Company Act of 1940 (Code Sec. 851(a)). These companies, commonly known as mutual funds, act as investment agents for their shareholders, typically investing in government and corporate securities and distributing dividend and interest income earned from the investments to their shareholders. A RIC's income generally retains its character when distributed to shareholders, who may treat a dividend out of capital gain income as long-term capital gain and a dividend out of exempt-interest income as tax-exempt interest. If less than all of a RIC's earnings and profits are distributed but minimum distribution thresholds have been satisfied, the RIC is taxed only on undistributed ordinary and capital income (Code Sec. 852).

In general, a RIC must satisfy these requirements:

- at least 90 percent of a RIC's gross income must consist of income from investments in stock, securities or foreign currencies;

- at the close of each quarter of a RIC's tax year, at least 50 percent of the value of its assets must be made up of cash, government securities and securities of other issuers, and no more than 25 percent of the value of its assets may be invested in the securities of a single issuer;

- a RIC must distribute at least 90 percent of its ordinary income to its shareholders in the tax year earned; and

- a RIC must maintain records of all investments sufficient to demonstrate that all qualifications for RIC status have been met (Code Sec. 851(b)).

Generally, losses from the sale or exchange of capital assets are allowed only to the extent of the taxpayer's capital gain plus, for noncorporate taxpayers, $3,000 (Code Sec. 1211). However, a RIC can carry over a net capital loss to each of the eight tax years following the loss year as a short-term capital loss (Code Sec. 1212(a)(1)(C)(i)). The entire amount of a net capital loss is carried over to the first tax year succeeding the loss year and the portion of the loss that may be carried to each of the next seven years is the excess of the net capital loss over the net capital gain income (determined without regard to any net capital loss for the loss year or tax year thereafter) for each of the prior tax years to which the loss may be carried. Capital gain net income is the excess of gains from the sale or exchange of capital assets over losses from such sales or exchanges (Code Sec. 1222(9)).

¶803

BACKGROUND

In the case of a corporation other than a RIC, a net capital loss generally is carried back as a short-term capital loss to each of the three tax years preceding the loss year, and carried forward as short-term capital loss to each of the five tax years following the loss year (Code Sec. 1212(a)(1)(A)). The carryover amount is reduced in a manner similar to that applicable to RICs. A net capital loss may not be carried back to a tax year in which the corporation is a RIC (Code Sec. 1212(a)(3)(A)).

If a taxpayer other than a corporation has a net capital loss for any tax year, any excess of the net short-term capital loss over the net long-term capital gain is treated as a short-term capital loss in the succeeding tax year, and any excess of the net long-term capital loss over the net short-term capital gain is treated as a long-term capital loss in the succeeding tax year (Code Sec. 1212(b)). There is no limitation on the number of tax years that a net capital loss may be carried over.

NEW LAW EXPLAINED

Capital loss carryover treatment for regulated investment companies amended.—Net capital loss carryover rules similar to those applicable to individual taxpayers will also apply to regulated investment companies (RICs). If a RIC has a net capital loss for a tax year, any excess of the net short-term capital loss over the net long-term capital gain is treated as a short-term capital loss arising on the first day of the next tax year, and any excess of the net long-term capital loss over the net short-term capital gain is treated as a long-term capital loss arising on the first day of the next tax year (Code Sec. 1212(a)(3)(A), as added by the Regulated Investment Company Modernization Act of 2010 (H.R. 4337)). There is no limit to the number of tax years that a net capital loss of a RIC may be carried over.

Special rules coordinate the treatment of net capital loss carryovers under the pre-enactment law with the RIC's post-enactment tax years. These rules apply to capital loss carryovers from tax years beginning on or before the date of enactment of the carryover provision, and to capital loss carryovers from other tax years before the corporation became a RIC. Under these rules, amounts treated as a long-term or short-term capital loss arising on the first day of the next tax year under the new rules are determined without regard to amounts treated as a short-term capital loss under the pre-enactment carryover rule. In determining the reduction of a present-law carryover by capital gain net income for a prior tax year, any capital loss treated as arising on the first day of the prior tax year under the new rules is taken into account in determining capital gain net income for the prior year (Code Sec. 1212(a)(3)(B), as added by the 2010 RIC Act).

> **Example:** Mute Funds, a calendar year RIC, has no net capital loss for any tax year beginning before 2010; a net capital loss of $2 million for 2010 and a net capital loss of $1 million for 2011, all of which is a long-term capital loss; and $600,000 gain from the sale of a capital asset held less than one year on July 15, 2012.

NEW LAW EXPLAINED

For 2012, the RIC has (1) $600,000 short-term capital gain from the July 15 sale, (2) $2 million carryover from 2010, which is treated as a short-term capital loss (because the present-law treatment of net capital losses arising in tax years beginning before the date of enactment continues to apply) and (3) $1 million long-term capital loss from 2011 treated as arising on January 1, 2012. The capital loss allowed in 2012 is limited to $600,000, the amount of capital gain for the tax year.

For purposes of determining the amount of the $2 million net capital loss that may be carried over from 2010 to 2013, there is no capital gain net income for 2012 because the $600,000 gain does not exceed the $1 million long-term loss treated as arising on January 1, 2012; therefore, the entire 2010 net capital loss is carried over to 2013 as a short-term capital loss. $400,000 (the excess of the $1 million long-term capital loss treated as arising on January 1, 2012, over the $600,000 short-term capital gain for 2012) is treated as a long-term capital loss on January 1, 2013. The 2010 net capital loss may continue be carried over through 2018, subject to reduction by capital gain net income; no limitation applies on the number of tax years that the 2011 net capital loss may be carried over (Joint Committee on Taxation, *Technical Explanation of H.R. 4337, the "Regulated Investment Company Modernization Act of 2010,"* (JCX-49-10), September 28, 2010).

Practical Analysis: Dale S. Collinson, Director in the Financial Institutions and Products group of the Washington National Tax practice of KPMG LLP, observes that for those regulated investment companies ("RICs") that have pre-enactment capital loss carryovers a significant point to consider is that net capital losses arising in post-enactment years will be utilized prior to any of those carryover capital losses. That effect is illustrated by the example set forth in the explanation of the new law and results from a fundamental change in the statutory mechanics for handling net capital losses.

Under a regime that limits the number of years to which a net capital loss may be carried, it is necessary to identify the year in which a net capital loss arose and then to apply the carryover losses after the net capital gains and capital losses have been accounted for in the current tax year. With the change to an unlimited loss carryforward regime, it becomes unnecessary to treat prior year net capital losses any differently than current year losses.

So the new law takes net capital losses arising in a post-enactment year and treats them as arising on the first day of the following taxable year, while preserving their character as short-term or long-term. One might say that the new law "pours over" post-enactment losses rather than carrying them over.

In preparing its tax return for a year to which post-enactment losses have been poured over, a RIC will apply the capital gain and loss rules for that taxable year by combining the poured over post-enactment loss amounts with its current gains and

NEW LAW EXPLAINED

losses. As under current law, pre-enactment capital loss carryforwards will be taken into account only after the current year netting of gains and losses.

RICs that have pre-enactment capital losses may consider it useful to consider the effect that decisions regarding realization of current year gains and losses may have on their ultimate ability fully to utilize the carryover losses.

Practical Analysis: Paul Murphy, J.D., LL.M., Deloitte Tax LLP, observes that the effect of this rule is to require a RIC to use up all capital loss carryovers arising in post-enactment taxable years, which never expire, before taking into account capital loss carryovers of pre-enactment years, which expire after eight years. Previously, the oldest losses were applied first, so the transition to unlimited carryovers could result in the expiration of pre-enactment capital loss carryovers, which otherwise may have been utilized.

▶ **Effective date.** The regulated investment company carryover provision applies to net capital losses for tax years beginning after the date of enactment. The coordination rules apply to tax years beginning after the date of enactment (Act Sec. 101(c) of the Regulated Investment Company Modernization Act of 2010 (H.R. 4337)).

Law source: Law at ¶5515 and ¶5525. Committee Report at ¶15,010.

— Act Sec. 101(a) of the Regulated Investment Company Modernization Act of 2010 (H.R. 4337), redesignating Code Sec. 1212(a)(3) as (4) and adding new Code Sec. 1212(a)(3);

— Act Sec. 101(b), amending Code Sec. 1212(a)(1) and Code Sec. 1222(10);

— Act Sec. 101(c), providing the effective date.

Reporter references: For further information, consult the following CCH reporters.

— Standard Federal Tax Reporter, ¶30,402.04

— Tax Research Consultant, RIC: 3,252

— Practical Tax Explanation, § 16,535

GROSS INCOME AND ASSET TESTS

¶806 RIC Asset and Gross Income Tests

SUMMARY OF NEW LAW

Savings provisions are added under which certain companies that fail the regulated investment company (RIC) asset value or gross income tests can retain RIC status.

BACKGROUND

In general, at the close of each quarter of the tax year, at least 50 percent of the value of a regulated investment company's (RIC's) total assets must be represented by (i) cash and cash items (including receivables), government securities and securities of other RICs, and (ii) other securities, generally limited in respect of any one issuer to an amount not greater in value than five percent of the value of the total assets of the RIC and to not more than 10 percent of the outstanding voting securities of such issuer (Code Sec. 851(b)(3)(A)).

In addition, at the close of each quarter of the tax year, not more than 25 percent of the value of a RIC's total assets may be invested in (i) the securities (other than government securities or the securities of other RICs) of any one issuer, (ii) the securities (other than the securities of other RICs) of two or more issuers which the taxpayer controls and which are determined, under regulations prescribed by the Secretary, to be engaged in the same or similar trades or businesses or related trades or businesses, or (iii) the securities of one or more qualified publicly traded partnerships (as defined in Code Sec. 851(h)) (Sec. 851(b)(3)(B)).

Asset test savings provision. A RIC meeting both asset tests at the close of any quarter will not lose its status as a RIC because of a discrepancy during a subsequent quarter between the value of its various investments and the asset test requirements, unless such discrepancy exists immediately after the acquisition of any security or other property and is wholly or partly the result of such acquisition (Code Sec. 851(d)). This rule protects a RIC against inadvertent failures of the asset tests that may be caused by fluctuations in the relative values of its assets. A second rule (the 30-day rule) gives a RIC 30 days following the end of a quarter in which it fails an asset test to cure the failure, if the failure is by reason of a discrepancy, between the value of its various investments and the asset test requirements, that exists immediately after the acquisition of any security or other property which is wholly or partly the result of such acquisition during such quarter (Code Sec. 851(d)). Failure of any asset test (except where the failure is cured pursuant to the 30-day rule) will prevent a corporation from qualifying as a RIC.

Income test. A RIC must derive 90 percent of its gross income from qualifying income (Code Sec. 851(b)(2)). Under this rule, a RIC meets the gross income test as long as its gross income that is not qualifying income does not exceed one-ninth of the portion of its gross income that is qualifying income. For example, a RIC with $900 million of gross income from qualifying income can have up to $100 million of gross income from other sources without failing the test. Failure to meet the gross income test for a tax year prevents a corporation from qualifying as a RIC for that year.

NEW LAW EXPLAINED

Saving features are added for RICs that fail the gross income or asset tests.—The new law adds a rule for *de minimis* asset test failures, and a means by which a regulated investment company (RIC) can cure other asset test failures (Code Sec. 851(d), as amended by the Regulated Investment Company Modernization Act of 2010 (H.R.

¶806

NEW LAW EXPLAINED

4337)). In addition, a savings provision is added for failures of the gross income test if the failure to pass the test was due to reasonable cause (Code Sec. 851(i), as added by the 2010 RIC Act).

De minimis asset test failures. Under the *de minimis* asset test failure rule, the failure is forgiven if it is cured in a timely fashion. The rule is available if a RIC fails to meet one of the asset tests in Code Sec. 851(b)(3) due to the ownership of assets the total value of which does not exceed the lesser of:

- one percent of the total value of the RIC's assets at the end of the quarter for which the assets are valued, and

- $10 million (Code Sec. 851(d)(2)(B)(i), as added by the 2010 RIC Act).

Where the *de minimis* rule applies, the RIC is considered to have satisfied the asset tests if, within six months of the last day of the quarter in which the RIC identifies that it failed the asset test (or such other time period provided by the Secretary) the RIC:

- disposes of assets in order to meet the requirements of the asset tests, or

- the RIC otherwise meets the requirements of the asset tests (Code Sec. 851(d)(2)(B)(ii), as added by the 2010 RIC Act).

  Comment: No tax is imposed if the *de minimis* rules are satisfied. The *de minimis* rule is unavailable for any quarter in which a corporation's status as a RIC is preserved by the existing savings rule under Code Sec. 851(d)(1), as renumbered by the 2010 RIC Act (formerly Code Sec. 851(d)). (Code Sec. 851(d)(2), as added by the 2010 RIC Act).

Other (non-de minimis) asset test failures. A savings mechanism is available for other (non-*de minimis*) asset test failures, provided that:

- following the identification of the failure to satisfy the asset tests, the RIC sets forth in a schedule filed in the manner provided by the Secretary of the Treasury a description of each asset that causes the RIC to fail to satisfy the asset test (Code Sec. 851(d)(2)(A)(i), as added by the 2010 RIC Act);

- the failure to meet the asset tests is due to reasonable cause and not due to willful neglect (Code Sec. 851(d)(2)(A)(ii)), as added by the 2010 RIC Act); and

- within six months of the last day of the quarter in which the RIC identifies that it failed the asset test (or such other time period provided by the Secretary) the RIC (a) disposes of the assets which caused the asset test failure, or (b) otherwise meets the requirements of the asset tests (Code Sec. 851(d)(2)(A)(iii), as added by the 2010 RIC Act).

Tax imposed. In the case of an asset test failure other than a *de minimis* failure, a tax is imposed in an amount equal to the greater of:

- $50,000, or

- the amount determined (pursuant to regulations promulgated by the Secretary) by multiplying the highest rate of tax imposed on corporation specified in Code Sec. 11 (currently 35 percent) by the net income generated during the period of asset

NEW LAW EXPLAINED

test failure by the assets that caused the RIC to fail the asset test (Code Sec. 851(d)(2)(C)(i) and (C)(ii), as added by the 2010 RIC Act).

For purposes of subtitle F (relating to assessment and collection of tax), the tax imposed for an asset test failure is treated as an excise tax with respect to the application of the deficiency procedures (Code Sec. 851(d)(2)(C)(iii), as added by the 2010 RIC Act).

> **Comment:** This savings mechanism is also unavailable for any quarter in which a corporation's status as a RIC is preserved by the existing savings rule under Code Sec. 851(d)(1), as renumbered by the 2010 RIC Act) (formerly Code Sec. 851(d)) (Code Sec. 851(d)(2), as added by the 2010 RIC Act).

Gross income test failures. An RIC that fails to meet the gross income test shall nevertheless be considered to have satisfied the test if (following the identification of the failure to meet the test for the tax year):

- the RIC set forth in a schedule, filed in the manner provided by the Secretary of the Treasury, a description of each item of its gross income; and

- the failure to meet the gross income test is due to reasonable cause and is not due to willful neglect (Code Sec. 851(i)(1), as added by the 2010 RIC Act).

In addition, a tax is imposed on any RIC that fails to meet the gross income test equal to the amount by which the RIC's gross income from sources which are not qualifying income exceeds one-ninth of its gross income from sources which are qualifying income (Code Sec. 851(i)(2), as added by the 2010 RIC Act).

> **Example:** A RIC has $900 million of gross income from sources which are qualifying income, and $150 million of gross income from other sources. A tax of $50 million is imposed. The tax is the amount by which the $150 million gross income from sources which are not qualifying income exceeds $100 million, which is one ninth of $900 million (Joint Committee on Taxation, *Technical Explanation of H.R. 4337, the "Regulated Investment Company Modernization Act of 2010,"* (JCX-49-10)).

Calculation of investment company taxable income. Taxes imposed for failure of the asset or income tests are deductible for purposes of calculating investment company taxable income of a RIC (Code Sec. 851(b)(2)(G), as added by the 2010 RIC Act).

> **Practical Analysis:** Baruch J. Cohen, Deloitte Tax LLP, observes that while this change removes the severe consequences associated with gross income test failures, a tax of 100 percent of the excess of gross non-qualifying income over 1/9th of gross qualifying income, may still be significant.

▶ **Effective date.** The provision applies to tax years with respect to which the due date (determined with regard to extensions) of the return of tax is after the date of enactment (Act Sec. 201(d) of the Regulated Investment Company Modernization Act of 2010 (H.R. 4337)).

¶806

NEW LAW EXPLAINED

Law source: Law at ¶5425 and ¶5430. Committee Report at ¶15,030.

— Act Sec. 201(a) of the Regulated Investment Company Modernization Act of 2010 (H.R. 4337), renumbering Code Sec. 851(d) as 851(d)(1), and adding Code Sec. 851(d)(2);

— Act Sec. 201(b), adding Code Sec. 851(i);

— Act Sec. 201(c), adding Code Sec. 851(b)(2)(G);

— Act Sec. 201(d), providing the effective date.

Reporter references: For further information, consult the following CCH reporters.

— Standard Federal Tax Reporter, ¶26,408.021, ¶26,408.04

— Tax Research Consultant, RIC: 3,050, RIC: 3,064.20

— Practical Tax Explanation, § 19,201

DIVIDENDS AND OTHER DISTRIBUTIONS

¶809 RIC Dividend Distributions

SUMMARY OF NEW LAW

The rules relating to the various dividend distributions and other pass-through items of a regulated investment company (RIC) are amended, replacing written notice to shareholders with formal reporting, and revising the method of allocating excess distributions.

BACKGROUND

An attractive feature of investing in a regulated investment company (RIC) is that gains and income passed through the RIC to shareholders generally retain their character. Thus, a capital gain dividend is treated by shareholders as a gain from the sale of a capital asset held for more than one year (a long-term capital gain) (Code Sec. 852(b)(3)(B)). A capital gain dividend is any dividend paid by the RIC that it designates as a capital gain dividend in a written notice mailed to shareholders within 60 days after the close of the RIC's tax year (Code Sec. 852(b)(3)(C)). However, if the aggregate amount of capital gain dividends designated by the RIC after the end of the tax year exceeds the actual net capital gain of the RIC for the year, then a ratable portion of the capital gain dividends paid throughout the year loses its designation as a capital gain dividend and is treated as ordinary income (Code Sec. 852(b)(3)(C)).

> **Example:** A RIC makes quarterly distributions to its sole shareholder of $50 for an annual total of $200, designating the entirety as capital gain dividends. If, at the end of the year, the RIC only has $100 of net capital gain, only $25 of each

¶809

BACKGROUND

> quarterly distribution may be treated as long-term capital gain by the shareholder.

If there is a subsequent increase in the excess of the aggregate designated capital gain dividends over the RIC's net capital gain due to a determination (such as a ruling of the Tax Court, a closing agreement with the IRS, or a statement attached to the RIC's amended or supplemental tax return (Code Sec. 860(e)), then the RIC has 120 days after the determination to make a designation to the shareholder in a written notice (Code Sec. 852(b)(3)(C)).

In determining the amount of a RIC's net capital gain solely for purposes of designating capital gain dividends for a given year, net capital losses attributable to the transactions of a RIC after October 31 for the year are not treated as occurring in that year, but instead treated as occurring on the first day of the next tax year (Code Sec. 852(b)(3)(C)). A similar rule also applies to post-October 31st currency losses (Code Sec. 852(b)(8)).

> **Comment:** This provision was included to allow a RIC time to calculate its amount of designated capital gain dividends for a calendar year shareholder without having to worry about any transactions during the remainder of a calendar year that increase the excess of aggregate capital gain dividends over RIC net capital gain, and thereby increase the amount of tax on the receipt of the distributions, such as those that may occur in late December that require recalculation of the designations within the 60-day period for providing notice to shareholders.

Similar to capital gain dividends, a RIC may also designate a portion of dividends (other than capital gain dividends) as exempt-interest dividends, which then retain their tax-exempt character when received by the shareholder. In order to designate a dividend as an exempt-interest dividend, at least 50 percent of the assets of the RIC must consist of state or local bonds described in Code Sec. 103(a) (Code Sec. 852(b)(5)). Just as with capital gain dividends, the RIC must designate a dividend as an exempt-interest dividend in a written notice provided to shareholders within 60 days after the close of the RIC's tax year (Code Sec. 852(b)(5)(A)). If the amount designated as exempt-interest dividends exceeds the amount of exempt interest received by the RIC during the tax year, then a ratable portion of the designated exempt-interest dividends loses its tax-exempt status (Code Sec. 852(b)(5)(A)). Unlike capital gain dividends, there is no special rule pertaining to the post-October 31st activities of a RIC affecting its exempt income.

A RIC may also elect to pass through to its shareholders any foreign tax credits (Code Sec. 853), credits attributable to tax-credit bonds (Code Sec. 853A), and dividends received by the RIC that qualify for the dividends received deduction for corporate shareholders or the lower capital gain rates on dividends for individuals ("qualified dividends") (Code Sec. 854). In all of these cases, the RIC must provide to shareholders notice of the tax items being passed through within 60 days after the end of the RIC's tax year (Code Secs. 853(c) and (d), 853A(c) and (d), 854(b)(2)).

¶809

BACKGROUND

Comment: For a discussion of the lower capital gains rates that apply to qualified dividends received by individuals, estates, and trusts, see ¶ 420.

A RIC is excepted from the requirement to withhold 30 percent (Code Sec. 871) of dividends paid to certain foreign persons if the dividends are designated as interest-related dividends or short-term capital gain dividends (Code Sec. 871(k)(1)(C) and (2)(C)), and the dividends retain the character of the underlying earnings in the hands of the shareholders. Similar to the rules above, a RIC need only provide written notice to the shareholder of the designation within 60 days after the end of the RIC's tax year to qualify the dividends as either interest-related dividends or short-term capital gain dividends. Rules similar to the above rules relating to designated dividends in excess of actual amounts received by the RIC also apply (Code Sec. 871(k)(1)(C) and (2)(C)). For a discussion of these dividends, see ¶ 430.

Comment: In some cases, the method of providing written notice to shareholders is specifically provided in regulations, such as Reg. § 1.853-3 providing guidance on the notice to shareholders of the pass-through of the foreign tax credit. However, in other instances, such as the relatively new pass-through of credits related to tax-credit bonds, there is no guidance. Form 1099-DIV, can be used to report capital gain distributions and the amount of foreign tax paid, but it does not have specific boxes for all of the information required to be provided to shareholders. Finally, Notice 2004-39, 2004-2 CB 982, provides limited guidance on the reporting of the pass-through of qualified dividends under Code Sec. 854. The dearth of guidance relating to this notice can lead to often confusing statements received from RICs, which can lead to errors in reporting income.

NEW LAW EXPLAINED

Requirements and definitions of designated dividends enhanced.—For tax years beginning after the date of enactment, the requirements for a regulated investment company (RIC), more commonly known as a mutual fund, to designate certain tax items that are passed through to shareholders is replaced by a requirement to report the tax items.

Compliance Pointer: On its face, there is little noticeable difference between the use of the terms "designated," as effective prior to the Regulated Investment Company Modernization Act of 2010 (H.R. 4337), where notice must be provided to shareholders, and "reported." However, "reporting" indicates that the amount of the various tax items passed through or taken advantage of by shareholders will become known by the IRS, whereas before, written notice stayed between the RIC and the shareholder. Indeed, the Committee Reports for the 2010 RIC Act state that a Form 1099 may be used to satisfy the reporting requirement (Joint Committee on Taxation, *Technical Explanation of H.R. 4337, the "Regulated Investment Company Modernization Act of 2010,"* (JCX-49-10)).

Capital gains dividends. Under the new requirements, a capital gain dividend is any dividend, or part thereof, *reported* as such by a RIC in written statements furnished to shareholders (Code Sec. 852(b)(3)(C)(i), as added by the 2010 RIC Act). In the case of any excess reported amounts (meaning the excess of the aggregate reported amount

NEW LAW EXPLAINED

of capital gains dividend over the net capital gain of the RIC for the tax year (Code Sec. 852(b)(3)(C)(iv)(II), as added by the 2010 RIC Act)), a capital gain dividend is the excess of the reported capital gain dividend over the excess reported amount allocable to the reported capital gain dividend amount (Code Sec. 852(b)(3)(C)(ii), as added by the 2010 RIC Act). The amount of the excess reported amount allocable to the reported capital gain dividend amount is the portion of the excess reported amount that bears the same ratio to the excess reported amount as the reported capital gain dividend amount bears to the aggregate reported amount (Code Sec. 852(b)(3)(C)(iii)(I), as added by the 2010 RIC Act).

> **Comment:** Functionally, this general method of allocation is the same as the method used to account for excess capital gain dividend designations prior to the 2010 RIC Act.

A special allocation rule is provided for RICs that do not use a calendar tax year and have excess reported amounts of capital gain dividends. If the amount of post-December 31st reported amounts equal or exceed the aggregate excess reported amount for the entire tax year, the general allocation method is applied by substituting the post-December 31st reported amount for the aggregate reported amount, and none of the excess reported amount is allocated to any dividend paid on or before December 31 (Code Sec. 852(b)(3)(C)(iii)(II), as added by the 2010 RIC Act). Where the post-December 31 reported amounts are less than the aggregate excess reported amount for the entire tax year, the general allocation method is applied, and the excess aggregate reported amount is distributed among all reported dividends.

> **Example:** A RIC with a tax year ending June 30, 2012, makes quarterly distributions of $30,000 on September 30, 2011, December 31, 2011, March 31, 2012, and June 30, 2012, reporting the full amounts as capital gain dividends for a total of $120,000. However, the RIC only has $100,000 of net capital gain for the tax year, so the excess reported amount is $20,000. Because the amount of post-December 31 reported amount ($60,000) exceeds the excess reported amount ($20,000), the special allocation rule applies. Thus, the excess reported amount of $20,000 is allocated among only the post-December dividends in the same ratio that each dividend bears to the aggregate post-December amounts ($30,000/$60,000). Therefore, the $30,000 reported amounts for the March 31 and June 30 dividends are each reduced by $10,000 (1/2 of $20,000), or a final amount of $20,000 (Joint Committee on Taxation, *Technical Explanation of H.R. 4337, the "Regulated Investment Company Modernization Act of 2010," (JCX-49-10)*).

> **Comment:** This special allocation method helps to alleviate the need for RICs with non-calendar tax years with changes or miscalculations in net capital gains for the entire year to have to file amended Forms 1099 and the subsequent need for shareholders to amend returns based on the erroneous Forms 1099. Obviously, it does not completely eliminate the possibility of amended Forms 1099 and returns, as a RIC could have to lower prior-year dividends where the special allocation method does not apply.

¶809

NEW LAW EXPLAINED

The allowance for an increase in the amount of a capital gain dividend resulting from a "determination," as defined in Code Sec. 860(e), is retained, but subject to the limitations of the reporting requirements for capital gain dividends, eliminating the need to provide notice within 120 days, but adding the requirement to report the amount (Code Sec. 852(b)(3)(C)(v), as added by the 2010 RIC Act). Also, the special provision that allowed RICs to treat net capital losses from post-October 31st transactions as if they were incurred in the following year is eliminated.

Exempt interest dividends. The requirements for passing through to shareholders the benefits of tax-exempt interest from state and local bonds held as assets of a RIC in the form of exempt-interest dividends are also amended. Just as the case with capital gain dividends, mere designation in a written notice to shareholders within 60 days after the end of the RIC's tax year is no longer sufficient, but rather the amount of dividends treated as exempt-interest dividends must be reported (Code Sec. 852(b)(5)(A)(i), as added by the 2010 RIC Act). Also, the allocation of excess reported amounts of exempt-interest dividends, including the special allocation method used by non-calendar year RICs, is exactly the same as applied to capital gain dividends (Code Sec. 852(b)(5)(A)(ii) and (iii), as added by the 2010 RIC Act).

Foreign tax credits, credits for tax credit bonds and certain passed-through dividends. The elections to pass through to shareholders any applicable foreign tax credits, credits attributable to tax credit bonds, any dividends for which a dividends received deduction can be claimed or qualified dividends are also amended. Again, the requirement of providing written notice of the amounts within 60 days after the close of the RIC tax year is replaced with a requirement to report the amounts to the shareholder (Code Secs. 853(c), 853A(c), and 854(b)(1), as amended by the 2010 RIC Act).

> **Comment:** The amendments relating to the pass-through of dividends that are, if received by individuals, qualified dividends under Code Sec. 1(h) (Code Sec. 854(b)(1)(B)(i) and (C)(ii), are subject to the same sunset provision contained in Act Sec. 303 of the Jobs Growth and Tax Relief Reconciliation Act of 2003 (JGTRRA) (P.L. 108-27). That sunset date has been extended two years to December 31, 2012 by the Tax Relief, Unemployment Insurance Reauthorization, and Job Creation Act of 2010 (P.L. 111-312) (see ¶425). Thus, the provisions relating to reporting of the pass-through of these qualified dividends, like the dividends themselves, do not apply to tax years beginning after December 31, 2012. See ¶105 for a discussion of the JGTRRA sunset.

Interest-related dividends and short-term capital gain dividends paid to foreign persons. The provisions allowing for the pass-through of the character of both interest-related dividends and short-term capital gain dividends to nonresident aliens and other foreign persons are also subject to the new reporting requirement, again replacing written notice of a designation within 60 days after the end of the RIC tax year (Code Sec. 871(k)(1)(C)(i) and (2)(C)(i), as amended by the 2010 RIC Act). Also, the allocation of excess reported amounts of both types of dividends, including the special allocation method used by non-calendar year RICs, is exactly the same as applied to capital gain dividends (Code Sec. 871(k)(1)(C)(ii), (1)(C)(iii), (2)(C)(ii), and (2)(C)(iii) as added by the 2010 RIC Act).

NEW LAW EXPLAINED

Comment: The two provisions allowing for the pass-through of the character of both interest-related dividends and short-term capital gain dividends to nonresident aliens and other foreign persons under Code Sec. 871(k)(1)(C)(i) and (2)(C)(i) were both scheduled to terminate for tax years beginning after December 31, 2009. However, both were extended to apply to tax years beginning on or before December 31, 2011, by the 2010 Tax Relief Act. For a discussion of these two provisions, and their extension, see ¶430.

Practical Analysis: Baruch J. Cohen, Deloitte Tax LLP, observes that the elimination of this requirement will provide for less confusing shareholder information reporting.

▶ **Effective date.** The amendments apply to tax years beginning after the date of enactment (Act Sec. 301(h) of the Regulated Investment Company Modernization Act of 2010 (H.R. 4337)). The provisions relating to the requirements for reporting the pass-through of qualified dividends to individual shareholders shall not apply to tax years beginning after December 31, 2012 (Act Sec. 301(i) of the 2010 RIC Act; Act Sec. 102(a) of the Tax Relief Act of 2010 (P.L. 111-312), Act Sec. 303 of the Jobs Growth and Tax Relief Reconciliation Act of 2003 (P.L. 108-27)).

Law source: Law at ¶5430, ¶5435, ¶5440, ¶5445, ¶5450, ¶5460, and ¶5465. Committee Report at ¶15,040.

— Act Sec. 301(a)(1) of the Regulated Investment Company Modernization Act of 2010 (H.R. 4337), amending Code Sec. 852(b)(3);

— Act Sec. 301(a)(2), amending Code Sec. 860(f)(2);

— Act Sec. 301(b), amending Code Sec. 852(b)(5)(A);

— Act Sec. 301(c), amending Code Sec. 853(c) and (d);

— Act Sec. 301(d), amending Code Sec. 853A(c) and (d);

— Act Sec. 301(e), amending Code Sec. 854(b);

— Act Sec. 301(f)(1), amending Code Sec. 871(k)(1)(C);

— Act Sec. 301(f)(2), amending Code Sec. 871(k)(2)(C);

— Act Sec. 301(g), amending Code Sec. 855;

— Act Sec. 301(h), providing the effective date.

Reporter references: For further information, consult the following CCH reporters.

— Standard Federal Tax Reporter, ¶26,433.01, ¶26,433.075, ¶26,445.01, ¶26,452.01, ¶26,465.01, ¶27,343.0444

— Tax Research Consultant, RIC: 3,250, RIC: 3,300, RIC: 3,350

— Practical Tax Explanation, § 19,205.20, § 19,205.25

¶812 Earnings and Profits of RICs

SUMMARY OF NEW LAW

A net capital loss for a tax year is not taken into account in determining the earnings and profits of a regulated investment company (RIC), but any capital loss treated as arising on the first day of the following tax year is taken into account in determining earnings and profits for that year. Further, the deductions disallowed in computing regulated investment company taxable income with respect to tax-exempt interest are allowed in calculating a RIC's current (but not accumulated) earnings and profits.

BACKGROUND

Dividends from a regulated investment company (RIC), just like dividends from most other corporations, must be paid out of earnings and profits (Code Secs. 301, 312, 316, 561, 562(a) and 852(a)(1)). Thus, a RIC must be careful to maintain sufficient earnings and profits each year, or accumulated earnings and profits, to satisfy annual dividend distribution requirements. There should also be enough earnings and profits to avoid the excise tax on RICs (Code Sec. 4982). To help RICs keep a high level of earnings and profits, they may not reduce their earnings and profits for a tax year by any amount they are unable to claim as a deduction from taxable income in that year (Code Sec. 852(c)(1); Reg. §1.852-5(b)). Accumulated earnings may be reduced.

A RIC's earnings and profits are generally computed under the rules applicable to ordinary corporations. However, a RIC's earnings and profits for any tax year (but not its accumulated earnings and profits) are not reduced by any amount that is not allowable as a deduction in computing its taxable income for the tax year (Code Sec. 852(c)(1)). This rule for determining a RIC's earnings and profits applies even if the RIC does not satisfy the distribution requirements for pass-through treatment that year (Code Sec. 852(a) and (c)(1)).

Therefore, under the general rule, a RIC's current earnings and profits are not reduced by a net capital loss either in the tax year the loss arose or any tax year to which the loss is carried. The accumulated earnings and profits are reduced in the tax year the net capital loss arose.

In general, deductions are denied in computing current earnings and profits for amounts disallowed for expenses, interest and amortizable bond premium pertaining to tax-exempt interest (Code Secs. 171(a)(2) and 265). As a result, the current earnings and profits of a RIC with tax-exempt interest may exceed the amount that the RIC can distribute as interest-exempt dividends. Therefore, distributions by a RIC with only tax-exempt interest income may result in taxable dividends to its shareholders.

> **Example 1:** ABC investment company has $990,000 gross tax-exempt interest and $10,000 expenses disallowed as deductions under Code Sec. 265. ABC has no accumulated earnings and profits and no other item of current earnings and

BACKGROUND

profits. ABC distributes $990,000 to its shareholders during its tax year (which is $10,000 more than its economic income for the year). In this situation, $980,000 may be allocated as exempt-interest dividends, and the remaining $10,000 is taxable as ordinary dividends.

NEW LAW EXPLAINED

Rules for computing earnings and profits modified.—The rules applicable to the taxable income treatment of a net capital loss of a RIC apply for purposes of determining both current and accumulated earnings and profits (Code Sec. 852(c)(1)(A), as added by the Regulated Investment Company Modernization Act of 2010 (H.R. 4337)). As a result, a net capital loss for a tax year is not taken into account in determining earnings and profits; however, any capital loss treated as arising on the first day of the following tax year is taken into account in determining earnings and profits for that year (subject to the application of the net capital loss rule for that year).

> **Comment:** Note that the rules governing the carryover of losses by a RIC have been amended by the 2010 RIC Act. See ¶803 for a discussion of these changes.

The 2010 RIC Act also provides that the deductions disallowed in computing RIC taxable income with respect to tax-exempt interest are allowed in calculating a RIC's current earnings and profits (but not accumulated earnings and profits) (Code Sec. 852(c)(1)(B), as added by the 2010 RIC Act).

> **Example 2:** Assume the same facts as in Example 1 above, except that the tax year begins after the date of enactment of the 2010 RIC Act. In this case, ABC investment company's current earnings and profits are reduced from $990,000 to $980,000 and, if ABC distributes $990,000 to its shareholders during the tax year, $980,000 may be reported as exempt-interest dividends and the remaining $10,000 is treated as a return of capital (or gain to the shareholder).

The rules for determining a RIC's earnings and profits continue to apply even if the RIC does not satisfy the distribution requirements for pass-through treatment that year under Code Sec. 852(a) (Code Sec. 852(c)(4), as added by the 2010 RIC Act).

▶ **Effective date.** The provision applies to tax years beginning after the date of enactment (Act Sec. 302(c) of the Regulated Investment Company Modernization Act of 2010 (H.R. 4337)).

Law source: Law at ¶5430 and ¶5465. Committee Report at ¶15,050.

— Act Sec. 302(a) of the Regulated Investment Company Modernization Act of 2010 (H.R. 4337), amending Code Sec. 852(c)(1);

— Act Sec. 302(b)(1), adding Code Sec. 852(c)(4);

— Act Sec. 302(b)(2), amending Code Sec. 871(k);

— Act Sec. 302(c), providing the effective date.

¶812

NEW LAW EXPLAINED

Reporter references: For further information, consult the following CCH reporters.

— Standard Federal Tax Reporter, ¶26,433.034

— Tax Research Consultant, RIC: 3,204.15

— Practical Tax Explanation, §19,201

¶815 Pass-Through of Exempt-Interest Dividends and Foreign Tax Credits

SUMMARY OF NEW LAW

A qualified fund of funds may pass through exempt-interest dividends and foreign tax credits to its shareholders without meeting the 50-percent asset requirement.

BACKGROUND

A regulated investment company (RIC) may pass through tax-exemption interest earned on state and local bonds to its shareholders in the form of exempt interest dividends (Code Sec. 852(b)(5)). The RIC can pass on the tax exemption only if, at the close of each quarter of its tax year, at least 50 percent of the value of its total assets consist of bonds or other debt obligations issued by state or local governments that earn tax-exempt interest under Code Sec. 103(a).

A RIC may elect to have its foreign tax credits taken by its shareholders, instead of on its own return (Code Sec. 853(a)). In order to be eligible to pass through the foreign tax credits, more than 50 percent of the value of its total assets at the close of the tax year must consist of stock and securities in foreign corporations, and it must have distributed at least 90 percent of its investment company taxable income.

The value of securities (other than those of majority-owned subsidiaries) is the market value of the securities. The value of other securities and assets is the fair value of the securities and assets as determined in good faith by the board of directors. Fair value in the case of securities of a majority-owned subsidiary investment company cannot exceed market value or asset value, whichever is higher (Code Sec. 851(c)(4)).

Under a fund-of-funds structure, an upper-tier RIC holds stock in one or more lower-tier RICs, rather than directly investing in shares, bonds or other securities. Lower-tier RICs that meet the 50-percent asset requirement described above can pay exempt-interest dividends and pass through foreign tax credits to the upper-tier RIC. An upper-tier RIC, however, will not be able to pass through the exempt-interest dividends and foreign tax credits to its shareholders. Because the upper-tier RIC holds only stock in other RICs, it will not have assets invested in state and local bonds or foreign securities, which is necessary to meet the 50-percent asset requirement for passing through the exempt-interest dividends and foreign tax credits.

NEW LAW EXPLAINED

Pass through of exempt-interest dividends and foreign tax credits by qualified fund of funds allowed.—An upper-tier regulated investment company (RIC) that is a qualified fund of funds may pass through exempt-interest dividends and foreign tax credits to its shareholders, without having to meet the 50-percent asset requirement (Code Sec. 852(g), as added by the Regulated Investment Company Modernization Act of 2010 (H.R. 4337)). Specifically, the RIC may pass through exempt-interest dividends even though, at the close of each quarter of the tax year, it does not have at least 50 percent of the value of its total assets in bonds or other debt obligations issued by state or local governments that earn tax-exempt interest under Code Sec. 103(a) (Code Sec. 852(g)(1)(A), as added by the 2010 RIC Act). Similarly, the RIC may pass through foreign tax credits, even though, at the close of the tax year, not more than 50 percent of the value of its total assets consist of stock and securities in foreign corporations (Code Sec. 852(g)(1)(B), as added by the 2010 RIC Act).

A qualified fund of funds is a RIC if, at the close of each quarter of the tax year, at least 50 percent of the value of its total assets is represented by interests in other RICs (Code Sec. 852(g)(2), as added by the 2010 RIC Act).

> **Example:** At the close of each quarter of the tax year, RIC(U) has 30 percent of its total assets invested in RIC(L1) and 70 percent of its total assets invested in RIC(L2). At the close of its tax year, RIC(L1) owns stock in several foreign corporations. One foreign corporation, pays a dividend to RIC(L1) that is subject to withholding tax. Assume that RIC(L1) is eligible to, and does elect to pass through the foreign tax credits for the withholding tax paid to its shareholders, including RIC(U). Because at least 50 percent of the total value of RIC(U)'s total assets at the close of each quarter of the tax year consist of RIC interests, RIC(U) is a qualified fund-of-funds structure. RIC(U) may elect to pass the foreign tax credits for the withholding taxes paid by RIC(L1) on to its shareholders.

> **Practical Analysis:** Kristen M. Garry, Shearman & Sterling LLP, Washington, D.C., notes that new Code Sec. 852(g) improves the tax efficiency of qualifying fund of funds structures where the upper-tier RIC receives tax-exempt interest or foreign tax credits. That is, a qualifying fund of funds (which is a RIC if at the close of each quarter of the taxable year at least 50 percent of the value of its total assets is represented by interests in other RICs) is now able to pay exempt interest dividends and may elect to pass through foreign tax credits to its shareholders without regard to asset ownership requirements that do not make sense in the context of an upper-tier RIC.
>
> In recent years, the fund of funds structure has become more popular with investors and assets under management in fund of funds structures have multiplied in size. For example, according to the Investment Company Institute 2009 Factbook, assets of

NEW LAW EXPLAINED

funds of funds have grown from $35 billion of net assets at the end of 1998 to $489 billion of net assets at the end of 2008 (*See* ICI 2009 Factbook, available at *http:// www.icifactbook.org/fb_sec2.html*). A fund of funds is allowed to pass through to its shareholders capital gain dividends and qualifying dividends received from a lower-tier RIC without satisfying a test based on the upper-tier RIC's assets (See Code Secs. 852(b) and 854(b)(3)). Technical rules in Code Secs. 852(b)(5) and 853(a), however, require that a RIC hold more than 50 percent of the value of its total assets in tax-exempt state and local bonds to be eligible to passthrough tax-exempt interest or more than 50 percent of the value of its total assets in securities of foreign corporations to be eligible to elect to pass through foreign tax credits to the RIC's shareholders. These technical requirements did not provide any relief to take into account the fund of funds structure, in which the upper-tier RIC primarily holds and invests in shares of other RICs. The 2010 RIC Act provides much needed relief for fund of funds structures. New Code Sec. 852(g) allows investors in fund of funds structures the benefit of the flow-through provisions for tax-exempt interest and foreign tax credits and will improve the tax efficiency of an upper-tier RIC that receives tax-exempt interest or foreign tax credits from its investments in lower-tier RICs.

▶ **Effective date.** The provision applies to tax years beginning after the date of enactment (Act Sec. 303(b) of the Regulated Investment Company Modernization Act of 2010 (H.R. 4337)).

Law source: Law at ¶5430. Committee Report at ¶15,060.

— Act Sec. 303(a) of the Regulated Investment Company Modernization Act of 2010 (H.R. 4337), adding Code Sec. 852(g);

— Act Sec. 303(b), providing the effective date.

Reporter references: For further information, consult the following CCH reporters.

— Standard Federal Tax Reporter, ¶26,433.01, ¶26,433.024 and ¶26,445.01

— Tax Research Consultant, RIC: 3,300 and RIC: 3,500

— Practical Tax Explanation, § 19,201 and § 19,205.35

¶818 Dividends Paid by RICs After Close of Tax Year

SUMMARY OF NEW LAW

The requirements regarding when a regulated investment company (RICs) must declare and distribute spillover dividends have been modified.

BACKGROUND

A regulated investment company (RIC) is permitted to declare and pay dividends after the close of a tax year, yet still have those dividends considered as having been

BACKGROUND

paid during that preceding tax year for the limited purposes of the RIC distribution requirements and calculating the taxable income of the RIC (Code Sec. 855(a)). Such dividends payments are commonly referred to as "spillover dividends." To qualify for treatment as a spillover dividend, the company must:

- elect to have all (or any part) of the dividends paid after the end of the tax year related back to the tax year, and

- declare those dividends before the due date for filing the RIC's tax return for the prior tax year (including extensions) (Code Sec. 855(a)(1)).

In addition, the entire dividend must be distributed to the shareholders no later than:

- the date of the first regular dividend payment after the declaration, and

- within 12 months after the tax year is closed (Code Sec. 855(a)(2)).

The corporation may then treat the dividends as having been paid in that prior year. However, dividends distributed after the close of the RIC's tax year are included in the shareholder's income for the shareholder's tax year in which received despite being paid out of the RIC's earnings and profits for the prior year (Code Sec. 855(b)).

NEW LAW EXPLAINED

Spillover dividend rules modified.—The requirements a regulated investment company (RIC) must meet for spillover dividends have been modified as regards both when the declarations and the distributions must be made (Code Sec. 855(a), as amended by the Regulated Investment Company Modernization Act of 2010 (H.R. 4337)). A spillover dividend will have to be declared before the later of:

- the 15th day of the ninth month following the closing of the tax year, or

- the extended due date for filing the corporation's return for the tax year (when such a filing extension occurs) (Code Sec. 855(a)(1), as amended by the 2010 RIC Act).

Under the new rules, the entire dividend must be distributed to shareholders no later than the date of the first dividend payment *of the same type of dividend* (such as ordinary income dividend or capital gain dividend) after the declaration, and during the 12 months after the tax year is closed (Code Sec. 855(a)(2), as amended by the 2010 RIC Act).

For the purpose of classifying types of dividends, any dividend that is attributable to short-term capital gain and to which a notice is required under section 19 of the Investment Company Act of 1940 is to be treated as the same type of dividend as a capital gain dividend (Code Sec. 855(a), as amended by the 2010 RIC Act; Joint Committee on Taxation *Technical Explanation of H.R. 4337, the "Regulated Investment Company Modernization Act of 2010,"* (JCX-49-10)).

¶818

NEW LAW EXPLAINED

Practical Analysis: Baruch J. Cohen, Deloitte Tax LLP, observes that this change will assist in aligning RIC earnings and profits to the excise tax distribution requirements.

▶ **Effective date.** The provision applies to distributions in tax years beginning after the date of enactment (Act Sec. 304(d) of the Regulated Investment Company Modernization Act of 2010 (H.R. 4337)).

Law source: Law at ¶5450. Committee Report at ¶15,070.

— Act Sec. 304(a) of the Regulated Investment Company Modernization Act of 2010 (H.R. 4337), amending Code Sec. 855(a)(1);

— Act Sec. 304(b), amending Code Sec. 855(a)(2);

— Act Sec. 304(c), amending Code Sec. 855(a);

— Act Sec. 304(d), providing the effective date.

Reporter references: For further information, consult the following CCH reporters.

— Standard Federal Tax Reporter, ¶26,482.01

— Tax Research Consultant, RIC: 3,452.05 and RIC: 3,452.10

— Practical Tax Explanation, §19,201

¶821 Return of Capital Distributions of RICs

SUMMARY OF NEW LAW

When a regulated investment company (RIC) that is not a calendar-year taxpayer makes distributions with respect to a class of its stock during a year that exceed the current and accumulated earnings and profits (E&P) that may be used to make distributions with respect to that class of stock, current E&P is allocated first to those distributions that occurred in the portion of the RIC's tax year that precedes January 1.

BACKGROUND

A regulated investment company (RIC) is generally subject to tax on its undistributed income, but is allowed a deduction against its ordinary income for dividends paid to its shareholders, and shareholders are required to include the amount of such dividend in income, if otherwise taxable (Code Sec. 852).

The amount of a distribution from a RIC that is considered a dividend is generally determined the same as for other corporations. A distribution with respect to a share of stock is treated as a dividend to the extent of available earnings and profits (E&P) (Code Sec. 301(c)(1)). Any amount in excess of earnings and profits is first treated as a tax-free return of capital to the shareholder (Code Sec. 301(c)(2)), and once the

BACKGROUND

shareholder's basis is reduced to zero, any excess amount of the distribution is treated as gain from the sale or exchange of that share (Code Sec. 301(c)(3)). The primary question for any recipient of a distribution, then, is what portion of the distribution is a dividend—i.e., what portion is attributable to available earnings and profits.

> **Comment:** The type and amount of certain income recognized by a RIC, such as capital gains and exempt interest, may be essentially passed through to the RIC's shareholders. The IRS takes the position that a corporation does not use separate E&P accounts for ordinary income and capital gains dividends (GCM 39570). Instead, E&P is applied against distributions to determine the amount of the RIC's distributions to its shareholders that constitute dividends, and then the RIC determines how much of the dividend is ordinary and how much is capital gains.

A crucial aspect of Code Sec. 316 is that it treats as a dividend payments made not only out of a corporation's accumulated earnings and profits (which is a reasonably good measure of its accumulated economic income since the corporation's creation), but also out of any current earnings and profits that the corporation happened to earn during the tax year. Current earnings and profits is the earnings and profits for the current tax year, determined after the tax year has closed.

If current earnings and profits are greater than the total of all distributions made in the tax year, every dollar of every distribution is a dividend. Current earnings and profits are determined after the tax year has closed. A deficit in current earnings and profits at the time the distribution is made is of no consequence if current earnings and profits at year end is positive.

The computations become more complex if distributions exceed the amount of current earnings and profits during the year. First, in all cases, current earnings and profits are prorated among all the distributions made during the year (Reg. § 1.316-2(b)). Second, accumulated earnings and profits are not apportioned on a pro rata basis but instead are allocated on a "pay-as-you-go" basis, so that they are applied to the first distribution from the RIC during its tax year, and then to the second one and so forth, until used up. Finally, any remaining amount of a distribution is considered made out of sources other than E&P (Reg. § 1.316-2(a)). Generally, distribution amounts in excess of E&P are applied against the shareholder's basis in the stock on which the distribution is paid (Code Sec. 301(c)(2)). Any amount in excess of basis is considered a capital gain, unless it is out of an increase in value accrued before March 1, 1913 (Code Sec. 301(c)(3)).

NEW LAW EXPLAINED

Distributions by regulated investment companies in excess of earnings and profits.—Where a regulated investment company (RIC) that is not a calendar-year taxpayer makes distributions to its shareholders with respect to any class of stock of the company in excess of the sum of its current and accumulated E&P (i.e., where a portion of the distribution constitutes return of capital or capital gain), its current E&P is

NEW LAW EXPLAINED

allocated first to distributions during the RIC's tax year that are made before January 1 (Code Sec. 316(b)(4), as added by the Regulated Investment Company Modernization Act of 2010 (H.R. 4337)). Where a RIC has more than one class of stock, the provision will apply separately to each class of stock, so that distributions made during the corporation's tax year will be considered made to the shares with higher priority before they are made to shares with lower priority (Rev. Rul. 69-440, 1969-2 CB 46).

> **Example:** Fund, a RIC, has a tax year ending June 30. For the current year, Fund has $4 million of current E&P and no accumulated E&P. It makes distributions on its stock of $2 million a quarter on the last day of each quarter in its fiscal year. Fund's current E&P is allocated $2 million to the distribution that occurs with respect to its shares on September 30 and $2 million to the distribution that occurs with respect to its shares on December 31. Accordingly, those distributions are considered dividends. The distributions that occur on March 31 and June 30 are considered return of capital to the extent of basis or, if in excess of basis, capital gain.

> **Practical Analysis:** Deanna Flores, Principal in the Financial Institutions and Products group of the Washington National Tax practice of KPMG LLP in San Diego, notes that regulated Investment Companies (RICs) are required to distribute essentially all of their calendar-year income and capital gains to shareholders by December 31 to avoid an excise tax (Code Sec. 4982). To meet this distribution requirement, a RIC that is not a calendar-year taxpayer is required to estimate its earnings through December 31. The distributed amounts are reported to the RIC's shareholders and the IRS on Forms 1099 (or other required forms). Information reporting penalties will apply if previously-issued Forms 1099 are not amended to reflect a return of capital attributable to distributions made by the RIC during the pre-January 1 portion of its taxable year (Code Secs. 6721 and 6722). In addition, RICs generally will be required to report cost basis and holding period information on Forms 1099-B for redemptions of RIC shares acquired on or after January 1, 2012, including any adjustments required for return of capital distributions (Code Sec. 6045(g)). Under prior law, a problem could arise for a non-calendar-year RIC that incurred post-December losses reducing its E&P for its taxable year, because E&P is allocated proportionately among distributions during a taxable year. By allocating E&P first to distributions made during the pre-January 1 portion of a RIC's taxable year, the new law is expected to minimize the issuance of amended Forms 1099 to RIC shareholders due to returns of capital.

> **Practical Analysis:** Baruch J. Cohen, Deloitte Tax LLP, observes that this change will generally be more beneficial to RICs with significant distributions in the post-December period (*e.g.*, a RIC with a fiscal year end that falls later in the calendar

NEW LAW EXPLAINED

> year) than to RICs without significant distributions in the post-December period (*e.g.*, a RIC with a fiscal year end that falls earlier in the calendar year).

▶ **Effective date.** This provision applies to distributions made in tax years beginning after the date of enactment (Act Sec. 305(b) of the Regulated Investment Company Modernization Act of 2010 (H.R. 4337)).

Law source: Law at ¶5340. Committee Report at ¶15,080.

— Act Sec. 305(a) of the Regulated Investment Company Modernization Act of 2010 (H.R. 4337), adding Code Sec. 316(b)(4);

— Act Sec. 305(b), providing the effective date.

Reporter references: For further information, consult the following CCH reporters.

— Standard Federal Tax Reporter, ¶15,704.021, ¶15,704.022, ¶15,704.0255, ¶26,465.01

— Tax Research Consultant, CCORP: 6,052 , CCORP: 6,354.05, RIC: 3,000

— Practical Tax Explanation, § 19,205.05, § 26,215

¶824 Redemptions of Stock of RICs

SUMMARY OF NEW LAW

Certain redemptions of stock of publicly offered regulated investment companies (RICs) will be treated as exchanges. Losses on certain redemptions of stock by fund-of-funds RICs will not be disallowed.

BACKGROUND

A redemption of stock by a corporation is treated as an exchange of stock if the redemption falls within one of four categories of transactions (Code Sec. 302(a)): (i) a redemption that is not essentially equivalent to a dividend; (ii) a substantially disproportionate redemption; (iii) a redemption that terminates the shareholder's interest in the corporation; and (iv) a partial liquidation, in the case of a noncorporate shareholder (Code Sec. 302(b)). Because transactions that fall within one of the these four categories are treated as exchanges of stock, they result in capital gain treatment to the redeemed shareholder. If the redemption does not fall within any of these categories, it is treated as a Code Sec. 301 distribution of property that generally results in dividend treatment (Code Sec. 302(d)).

The courts have held that a redemption is not essentially equivalent to a dividend if it results in a meaningful reduction in the shareholder's proportionate ownership in the corporation. There is no specific rule in the Code regarding the application of the "not essentially equivalent to a dividend" test in the case of an open-end regulated investment company (RIC) whose shareholders "sell" their shares by having them

BACKGROUND

redeemed by the issuing RIC and where multiple redemptions by different shareholders may occur on a daily basis.

Losses from a sale or exchange of property between related persons are generally disallowed by Code Sec. 267(a)(1). For this purpose, persons are related if they bear the relationship described in Code Sec. 267(b). However, a loss on the sale or exchange of property between members of a controlled group of corporations is deferred until a transfer of the property outside the group occurs (Code Sec. 267(f)). The loss deferral rules do not apply in the case where:

- the transferor or the transferee is a domestic international sales corporation (DISC);

- the transferor or the transferee is a foreign corporation involved with the sale or exchange of inventory in the ordinary course of the transferor's trade or business (except when the income from the sale or resale of the inventory is taxable under Code Sec. 882, relating to effectively connected income); and

- the repayment of a loan is payable or denominated in a foreign currency and the loss is attributable to a reduction in the value of that foreign currency (Code Sec. 267(f)(3)).

In the case of a fund of funds, a lower-tier fund may be required to redeem shares in an upper-tier fund when the upper-tier fund shareholders demand redemption of their shares. Because the upper-tier fund and the lower-tier fund may be members of the same controlled group of corporations, any loss by the upper-tier fund on the disposition of the lower-tier fund shares may be deferred. A lower-tier fund and an upper-tier fund may be members of a controlled group and any intra-group transaction may be subject to the loss deferral rule.

In the case of a RIC having more than one fund, each fund of the RIC is treated as a separate corporation. For these purposes, a fund is a segregated portfolio of assets, the beneficial interest in which are owned by the holders of a class or series of stock of the RIC that is preferred over all other classes or series in respect of such portfolio of assets (Code Sec. 851(g)).

A publicly offered RIC is a RIC whose shares are (i) continuously offered pursuant to a public offering, (ii) regularly traded on an established securities market, or (iii) held by or for no fewer than 500 persons at all times during the tax year (Code Sec. 67(c)(2)(B)).

NEW LAW EXPLAINED

Certain redemptions by publicly offered RICs treated as exchanges; losses on redemptions by certain RICs not disallowed.—Except to the extent provided in regulations, a distribution in redemption of stock of a publicly offered regulated investment company (RIC) will be treated as an exchange for stock if (i) the redemption is upon the demand by the stockholder, and (ii) the RIC issues only stock that is redeemable upon the demand of the stockholder (Code Sec. 302(b)(5), as added by the Regulated Investment Company Modernization Act of 2010 (H.R. 4337)). For this purpose, the definition of a publicly offered RIC under Code Sec. 67(c)(2)(B) applies.

¶824

NEW LAW EXPLAINED

Except to the extent provided in regulations, the Code Sec. 267 loss disallowance and loss deferral rules will not apply to any redemption of stock of a fund-of-funds RIC if the RIC issues only stock that is redeemable upon the demand of the stockholder and the redemption is upon the demand of another RIC (Code Sec. 267(f)(3)(D), as added by the 2010 RIC Act).

Practical Analysis: Dale S. Collinson, Director in the Financial Institutions and Products group of the Washington National Tax practice of KPMG LLP, observes that regulated investment companies (RICs) are subchapter C corporations. As such, they are subject to all of the technical rules in subchapter C even though, in some cases, the tax policies implemented by those rules do not appear relevant to RICs. For example, Code Sec. 302 contains rules treating certain redemptions of corporate stock as dividends out of a concern that redemption transactions may be used inappropriately to distribute corporate earnings to shareholders while permitting shareholders to avoid tax at ordinary income tax rates. The distribution requirements that apply to RICs under Subchapter M of the code generally require RICs to distribute all of their earnings as declared dividends. As a result, it is not necessary to treat redemptions of RIC shares as dividends to prevent avoidance of tax at the shareholder level.

In principle, a strictly technical application of the rules for the application of Code Sec. 302 could result in a RIC's redemption of its shares being treated as a dividend. Rev. Rul. 76-385, 1976-2 CB 92, held that a relatively small reduction in the stock ownership of a minor shareholder, who owned several hundred shares out of a total of 28 million, caused the redemption not to be essentially equivalent to a dividend and, thus, the transaction would be respected as a redemption rather than being recast under Code Sec. 302 as a dividend. Most redemptions of shares in open-end RICs, which are obligated to redeem shares on demand of a shareholder, qualify as redemptions under that ruling. However, the constructive ownership rules of Code Sec. 318 apply to determine the number of shares owned by any particular RIC shareholder. In theory, a shareholder redeeming shares in an open-end RIC might not incur any reduction in ownership if other persons (whose ownership would be imputed to the redeeming shareholder) acquired additional shares at the same time. In that case, the redemption might be considered not to satisfy the requirement of *M.P. Davis*, SCt, 70-1 USTC ¶9289, 397 US 301 (1970) that there be a "meaningful reduction" in a shareholder's ownership percentage as a prerequisite to the conclusion that a redemption is not essentially equivalent to a dividend.

In practice, open-end RICs are unable to administer the "meaningful reduction" standard to the extent it involves the application of constructive ownership rules. The new law resolves this administrative problem and adjusts the literal language of Code Sec. 302 to the special circumstances of open-end RICs.

The new law resolves a similar unintended problem presented for open-end RICs by the potential application of the Code Sec. 267 loss deferral rule to a fund of funds structure in which an upper-tier RIC has a controlling ownership interest in a lower-tier RIC. As funds flow in or out of the upper-tier RIC, through share purchases and redemptions, that RIC will alter its investment in a lower-tier RIC. The new law makes

NEW LAW EXPLAINED

> the section 267 loss deferral rule inapplicable to the lower-tier RIC's redemption of shares held by the upper-tier RIC, except to the extent otherwise provided in regulations.

▶ **Effective date.** The provision applies to distributions after the date of enactment (Act Sec. 306(c) of the Regulated Investment Company Modernization Act of 2010 (H.R. 4337)).

Law source: Law at ¶5320 and ¶5330. Committee Report at ¶15,090.

— Act Sec. 306(a) of the Regulated Investment Company Modernization Act of 2010 (H.R. 4337), amending Code Sec. 302(a) and (b);

— Act Sec. 306(b), adding Code Sec. 267(f)(3)(D);

— Act Sec. 306(c), providing the effective date.

Reporter references: For further information, consult the following CCH reporters.

— Standard Federal Tax Reporter, ¶14,161.032 and ¶15,330.01

— Tax Research Consultant, CCORP: 21,100 and SALES: 39,112.05

— Practical Tax Explanation, § 17,605.30 and § 26,301

¶827 Preferential Dividends of Publicly Offered RICs

SUMMARY OF NEW LAW

The preferential dividend rule of Code Sec. 562(c) has been repealed for publicly offered regulated investment companies (RICs).

BACKGROUND

Regulate investment companies (RICs) are subject to tax on undistributed income (Code Sec. 852(b)(2)), but are generally allowed a deduction for dividends paid to their shareholders (Code Sec. 561). Special rules apply to determine if dividends are eligible for the dividends paid deduction (Code Sec. 562).

"Preferential dividends" are not treated as dividends that qualify for the dividends paid deduction (Code Sec. 562(c)). For this purpose, a dividend is preferential unless it is (i) distributed pro rata to shareholders, (ii) with no preference to any share of stock compared with other shares of the same class of stock, and (iii) with no preference to one class of stock as compared to another class of stock except to the extent the class is entitled to a preference. A distribution by a RIC to a shareholder who made an initial investment of at least $10 million in the RIC is not treated as not being pro rata or as being preferential solely if the distribution is increased to reflect reduced administrative expenses of the RIC with respect to the shareholder.

A publicly offered RIC is a RIC whose shares are (i) continuously offered pursuant to a public offering, (ii) regularly traded on an established securities market, or (iii) held

BACKGROUND

by or for no fewer than 500 persons at all times during the tax year (Code Sec. 67(c)(2)(B)).

Securities law regulations provide strict limits on the ability of RICs to issue shares with preferences.

NEW LAW EXPLAINED

Preferential dividend rule repealed for publicly offered RICs.—The preferential dividend rule, which applies in determining if dividends qualify for the dividends paid deduction, has been repealed for publicly offered regulated investment companies (RICs) (Code Sec. 562(c), as amended by the Regulated Investment Company Modernization Act of 2010 (H.R. 4337)). For this purpose, the definition of a publicly offered RIC under Code Sec. 67(c)(2)(B) applies.

Practical Analysis: Dale S. Collinson, Director in the Financial Institutions and Products group of the Washington National Tax practice of KPMG LLP, notes that regulated investment companies ("RICs") are not pure passthrough entities. RICs generally eliminate their taxable income through deductions for dividends paid. A key requirement for the deduction is that the dividends not be preferential, which generally means that the dividends must be pro rata among shares of the same class. RICs would be subject to tax at regular corporate rates on dividends treated as preferential and even could fail to qualify as RICs in certain situations due to the inability to take a dividends paid deduction for these amounts.

The prohibition on preferential dividends was originally enacted in 1936 to restrict certain tax minimization strategies of closely held corporations involving disproportionate distributions to low-bracket taxpayers in the context of the personal holding company tax and the accumulated earnings tax. (*See* Tax Section of the New York State Bar Association, Recommendation for the Repeal of Internal Revenue Code Section 562(c) for Regulated Investment Companies and Real Estate Investment Trusts (April 7, 2008), at 4.) It is not evident that its extension to RICs as a part of the dividends paid deduction mechanism ever served a particular tax policy goal. However, the application of this requirement to RICs has frequently presented interpretative and operational difficulties, particularly in the case of funds issuing multiple classes of common shares with different mechanisms for recovering distribution costs (such as front-end and back-end loads and annual fees). For example, errors in allocation of expenses and income among different share classes (that may affect dividends by only pennies a share) may trigger a highly technical exercise analyzing the effects of the errors as possibly constituting a violation of the preferential dividend rule.

The Ways and Means Committee explanation of the proposed change noted that "the 1940 Act and the Securities and Exchange Commission ensure that investors in mutual funds are treated equally and fairly" and that the preferential dividend rule has "largely served as an unintended trap for mutual funds that make inadvertent processing or computational errors." (Committee on Ways and Means, H.R. 4337: Regulated Investment Company Modernization Act of 2009 (Dec. 16, 2009); see

¶827

NEW LAW EXPLAINED

also, Letter from Dale S. Collinson and Louis W. Ricker to Donald C. Lubick, Acting Assistant Secretary of the Treasury (Feb. 3, 1998), 98 TNT 48-37.)

Practical Analysis: Baruch J. Cohen, Deloitte Tax LLP, observes that this change will allow RICs that inadvertently pay preferential dividends due to computational errors to satisfy the requirements necessary to claim a dividends paid deduction.

▶ **Effective date.** The provision applies to distributions in tax years beginning after the date of enactment (Act Sec. 307(c) of the Regulated Investment Company Modernization Act of 2010 (H.R. 4337)).

Law source: Law at ¶5395. Committee Report at ¶15,100.

— Act Sec. 307(a) and (b) of the Regulated Investment Company Modernization Act of 2010 (H.R. 4337), amending Code Sec. 562(c);

— Act Sec. 307(c), providing the effective date.

Reporter references: For further information, consult the following CCH reporters.

— Standard Federal Tax Reporter, ¶23,474.021

— Tax Research Consultant, RIC: 3,204.10

¶830 Elective Deferral of Certain Late-Year Losses of RICs

SUMMARY OF NEW LAW

A regulated investment company (RIC) may elect to defer to the first day of the next tax year, part or all of any qualified late-year losses. The election applies for purposes of determining taxable income, net capital gain, net short-term capital gain, and earnings and profits.

BACKGROUND

A regulated investment company (RIC) may pay a capital gain dividend to its shareholders to the extent of the RIC's net capital gain for the tax year. The shareholders treat capital gain dividends as long-term capital gain.

In determining the amount of a net capital gain dividend, the amount of net capital gain for a tax year is determined without regard to any net capital loss or net long-term capital loss attributable to transactions after October 31 of the tax year, and the post-October net capital loss or net long-term capital loss is treated as arising on the first day of the RIC's next tax year (Code Sec. 852(b)(3)(C)).

BACKGROUND

To the extent provided in regulations, the above rules relating to post-October net capital losses also apply for purposes of computing taxable income of a RIC. Regulations have been issued allowing RICs to elect to defer all or part of any net capital loss (or if there is no such net capital loss, any net long-term capital loss) attributable to the portion of the tax year after October 31 to the first day of the succeeding tax year (Reg. § 1.852-11).

There is no special rule that applies to short-term capital losses arising after October 31 of the tax year for purposes of defining a capital gain dividend. For purposes of determining capital gain dividends, the deferral of post-October capital losses is automatic, rather than elective. In contrast, the push forward of these losses is elective for RIC taxable income purposes.

In applying the excise tax under Code Sec. 4982(e)(5) and (6), net foreign currency losses and gains and ordinary loss or gain from the disposition of stock in a passive foreign investment company (PFIC) properly taken into account after October 31 are deferred to the following calendar year for purposes of the tax. To the extent provided in regulations, a RIC may elect to push the post-October net foreign currency losses and the net reduction in the value of stock in a PFIC with respect to which an election is in effect under Code Sec. 1296(k) forward to the next tax year. Regulations have been issued allowing RICs to elect to defer all or part of any post-October net foreign currency losses for the portion of the tax year after October 31 to the first day of the succeeding tax year (Code Sec. 852(b)(8) and (10); Reg. § 1.852-11).

Other ordinary losses of a RIC may not be moved forward. As a result, in the event that a RIC has net ordinary losses for the portion of the tax year after December 31 (other than a net foreign currency loss or loss on stock of a PFIC), the RIC may have insufficient earnings and profits to pay a dividend during the calendar year ending in the tax year in order to reduce or eliminate the excise tax.

NEW LAW EXPLAINED

Election for deferral of late-year losses provided.—Except to the extent provided in regulations, a regulated investment company (RIC) may elect to treat any portion of any qualified late-year loss as arising on the first day of the following tax year. *Qualified late-year loss* is any post-October capital loss and any late-year ordinary loss (Code Sec. 852(b)(8), as amended by the Regulated Investment Company Modernization Act of 2010 (H.R. 4337)).

A *post-October capital loss* is the greatest of: (1) the net capital loss attributable to the portion of the tax year after October 31; (2) the net long-term capital loss attributable to that portion of the tax year; or (3) the net short-term capital loss attributable to that portion of the tax year (Code Sec. 852(b)(8)(C), as added by the 2010 RIC Act).

A *late-year ordinary loss* is the excess of: (1) the sum of: (a) the specified losses attributable to the portion of the tax year after October 31, and (b) other ordinary losses not described in (a) that are attributable to the portion of the tax year after December 31, over (2) the sum of: (a) the specified gains attributable to the portion of the tax year after October 31, and (b) other ordinary income not described in (a) that is attributable

NEW LAW EXPLAINED

to the portion of the tax year after December 31 (Code Sec. 852(b)(8)(D), as added by the 2010 RIC Act). A specified loss is ordinary loss from the sale, exchange, or other disposition of property, (including the termination of a position with respect to such property (Code Sec. 4982(e)(5)(B)(ii)).

Special rule for companies determining capital gain distributions on tax year basis. RICs that have a tax year that ends with the month of November may elect to compute capital gain net income during their full tax year for purposes of the excise tax (Code Sec. 4982(e)(4)) must compute the amount of qualified late-year losses (if any) without regard to any income, gain or loss described in Code Sec. 852(b)(8)(C), (D)(i)(I), and (D)(ii)(I). The election to defer late-year losses under Code Sec. 852(b)(8)(A) does not apply to RICs that have a tax year ending with the month of December (Code Sec. 852(b)(8)(E), as added by the 2010 RIC Act). The special rule for certain losses on stock in a passive foreign investment company (PFIC) is removed (Code Sec. 852(b)(10), as stricken by the 2010 RIC Act).

For distributions made by a RIC with respect to any calendar year, the earnings and profits of the company are determined without regard to any net capital loss attributable to the portion of the tax year after October 31 and without regard to any late-year ordinary loss (Code Sec. 852(c)(2), as amended by the 2010 RIC Act).

For purposes of short-term capital gain dividends received by foreign persons, the net short-term gain of the RIC is computed by treating any short-term capital gain dividend includible in gross income with respect to stock of another RIC as short-term capital gain (Code Sec. 871(k)(2)(D), as amended by the 2010 RIC Act).

▶ **Effective date.** The provision applies to tax years beginning after the date of enactment (Act Sec. 308(c) of the Regulated Investment Company Modernization Act of 2010 (H.R. 4337)).

Law source: Law at ¶5430 and ¶5465. Committee Report at ¶15,110.

— Act Sec. 308(a) of the Regulated Investment Company Modernization Act of 2010 (H.R. 4337), amending Code Sec. 852(b)(8);

— Act Sec. 308(b)(1) of the 2010 RIC Act, striking Code Sec. 852(b)(10);

— Act Sec. 308(b)(2), amending Code Sec. 852(c)(2);

— Act Sec. 308(b)(3), amending Code Sec. 871(k)(2)(D);

— Act Sec. 308(c), providing the effective date.

Reporter references: For further information, consult the following CCH reporters.

— Standard Federal Tax Reporter, ¶26,433.01, ¶27,343.0444

— Tax Research Consultant, SALES: 15,202.55

— Practical Tax Explanation, § 19,205.05

¶833 Holding Period Requirement For Certain Regularly Declared Exempt-Interest Dividends

SUMMARY OF NEW LAW

The disallowance of a loss from the sale or exchange of any share of regulated investment company (RIC) stock with respect to which the shareholder received an exempt-interest dividend, does not apply to a regular dividend paid by a RIC which declares exempt-interest dividends on a daily basis in an amount equal to at least 90 percent of its tax-exempt interest and distributes such dividends on a monthly or more frequent basis.

BACKGROUND

If a shareholder of a regulated investment company (RIC) receives an exempt-interest dividend with respect to any share held for six months or less, then any loss on the sale or exchange of such share is disallowed to the extent of the amount of the exempt-interest dividend (Code Sec. 852(b)(4)(B)). To the extent provided in regulations, the loss disallowance rule does not apply to losses incurred on the sale or exchange of shares pursuant to a plan which provides for the periodic liquidation of the shares (Code Sec. 852(b)(4)(D)). In the case of a RIC which regularly distributes at least 90 percent of its net tax-exempt interest, the IRS may provide regulations which prescribe a holding period requirement shorter than six months, but not shorter than the greater of 31 days or the period between the regular distributions of exempt interest dividends (Code Sec. 852(b)(4)(E)).

NEW LAW EXPLAINED

Disallowance of loss not applicable to certain RICs.—The disallowance of a loss on the sale or exchange of regulated investment company (RIC) shares, on which exempt-interest dividends have been paid, does not apply, except as otherwise provided by regulations, to a regular dividend paid by a RIC which declares exempt-interest dividends on a daily basis in an amount not less than 90 percent of its net tax-exempt interest and distributes such dividends on a monthly or more frequent basis (Code Sec. 852(b)(4)(E)(i) as added by the Regulated Investment Company Modernization Act of 2010 (H.R. 4337)).

> **Comment:** New Code Sec. 852(b)(4)(E)(i) refers to RICs that declare exempt-interest dividends on a daily basis as "daily dividend companies."

In the case of a RIC, other than a daily dividend company, that regularly distributes at least 90 percent of its net tax-exempt interest, regulations may continue to provide that the loss disallowance rule under Code Sec. 852(b)(4)(B) be applied on the basis of a holding period requirement shorter than six months, but not shorter than the greater of 31 days or the period between the regular distributions of exempt-interest dividends (Code Sec. 852(b)(4)(E)(ii) as renumbered by the 2010 RIC Act).

NEW LAW EXPLAINED

▶ **Effective date.** This provision applies to losses incurred on shares of stock for which the taxpayer's holding period begins after the date of enactment (Act Sec. 309(c) of the Regulated Investment Company Modernization Act of 2010 (H.R. 4337)).

Law source: Law at ¶5430. Committee Report at ¶15,120.

— Act Sec. 309(a) of the Regulated Investment Company Modernization Act of 2010 (H.R. 4337)), amending Code Sec. 852(b)(4)(E);

— Act Sec. 309(c), providing the effective date.

Reporter references: For further information, consult the following CCH reporters.

— Standard Federal Tax Reporter, ¶26,433.042

— Tax Research Consultant, RIC: 3,258

— Practical Tax Explanation, § 19,230.15

OTHER PROVISIONS

¶836 Excise Tax on RIC Distributions

SUMMARY OF NEW LAW

Several modifications have been made regarding excise taxes that apply to regulated investment companies (RICs), including: (1) adding certain tax-exempt entities to the list of permitted shareholders allowing the RIC to remain exempt from the excise tax; (2) expanding the deferral or "push" rules for gains and losses to include ordinary gains and losses from the sale or exchange of certain property, including foreign currency gain and loss; (3) providing that a RIC may elect to increase the distributed amount for a calendar year by the amount of estimated tax payments made during the year; and (4) increasing the required distribution percentage of capital gain net income from 98 percent to 98.2 percent.

BACKGROUND

An excise tax is imposed on certain undistributed income of a regulated investment company (RIC) (Code Sec. 4982). The tax is equal to four percent of the excess of (1) the "required distribution" for the calendar year, over (2) the distributed amount for the calendar year.

> **Comment:** The RIC excise tax is payable on or before March 15 of the following calendar year. Form 8613, Return of Excise Tax on Undistributed Income of Regulated Investment Company, is used to report the RIC excise tax.

A "required distribution" is the sum of 98 percent of the RIC's ordinary income for the year (Code Sec. 4982(b)(1)(A)), plus 98 percent of the RIC's capital gain net income for the one-year period ending on October 31 of the calendar year. This is increased by any excess of "grossed up required distribution" over the distributed

BACKGROUND

amount for the preceding calendar year. For this purpose, the term "grossed up required distribution" for any year is the sum of the taxable income of the RIC for the year and all amounts from earlier years that are not treated as having been distributed under this provision.

The "distributed amount" under this provision is the sum of the dividends paid deduction during the calendar year and any amount taxed to the RIC as investment company taxable income or capital gains. This sum is increased by the distributed amount for the preceding calendar year to the extent that it exceeds the grossed up required distribution for that year. The dividends-paid deduction, for this purpose, is determined without regard to the rules regarding dividends paid after the close of the tax year and without taking into account any tax-exempt interest dividend (Code Sec. 4982(c)).

A RIC that is, for the entire calendar year, wholly owned by any combination of certain types of exempt organizations, or segregated asset accounts of a life insurance company, is exempt from the excise tax on its undistributed income. This exemption is in recognition of the fact that these types of organizations would not pay any tax on income distributed from a RIC, so there would be no incentive to accumulate earnings in the RIC for purposes of tax avoidance. In order to qualify for this exclusion, the exempt organization must be a qualified pension, profit-sharing, or stock bonus plan described in Code Sec. 401(a) and exempt from taxation under Code Sec. 501(a), and the segregated asset account of a life insurance company must be held in connection with variable contracts defined in Code Sec. 817(d). Shares attributable to an investment of less than $250,000 made in connection with the organization of a RIC will not prevent the RIC from qualifying for this exemption (Code Sec. 4982(f)).

The amount of net capital loss and income attributable to transactions after October 31 of a tax year is deferred or pushed to the following calendar year and is not included in determining the RIC distribution for a tax year (Code Sec. 4982(e)(2)). For this purpose, such loss and income is treated as arising on the first day of the next tax year.

A RIC cannot take into account, for purposes of ordinary income, foreign currency gains and losses (within the meaning of Code Sec. 988) that are properly taken into account for the portion of the calendar year after October 31. Any such gain or loss not taken into account in the current tax year due to this provision will be reflected in the following calendar year of the RIC. However, if the RIC has a tax year that ends with November or December and it elects to apply its tax year in the determination of the company's capital gain net income (in lieu of the one-year period ending on October 31), the preceding rule is applied by substituting the last day of the company's tax year for October 31 (Code Sec. 4982(e)(5)).

Caution: The IRS recently issued temporary guidance on stock distributions by RICs (Rev. Proc. 2010-12, 2010-3 I.R.B. 269, amplifying and superseding Rev. Proc. 2009-15, 2009-4 I.R.B. 356). As under the prior guidance, if a RIC makes a qualifying distribution, the IRS will treat the distribution of stock as a dividend. The amount of the stock distribution will be treated as equal to the amount of money that could have been received instead of stock. The new guidance further

¶836

BACKGROUND

provides that, if a RIC makes a qualifying distribution and some shareholders receive a combination of stock and money that differs from the combination received by other shareholders, and if the fair market value of the stock on the date of distribution differs from the amount of money that could have been received instead, those differences do not cause the distribution to be treated as a preferential dividend.

NEW LAW EXPLAINED

Excise tax provisions for RIC distributions modified.—Rules regarding the excise taxes that apply to regulated investment companies (RICs) under Code Sec. 4982 have been modified. The changes relate to a RIC's tax-exempt shareholders, the deferral of ordinary gains and losses (the "push" rule), an election to increase distributed amounts by estimated tax payments, and the required distribution percentage for capital gain.

The list of tax-exempt entities that may own stock in a RIC while still maintaining the RIC's exemption from the excise tax on undistributed income is expanded. That list now includes entities whose ownership of an interest in the RIC would not preclude the application of look-through rules under Code Sec. 817(h)(4) related to segregated accounts of certain annuity and life insurance contracts. Specifically, these entities include qualified annuity plans described in Code Sec. 403, IRAs, including Roth IRAs, certain government plans described in Code Secs. 414(d) or 457, and a pension plan described in Code Sec. 501(c)(18). In addition, another RIC not subject to Code Sec. 4982 may hold stock in a RIC without negating its exemption from the excise tax (Code Sec. 4982(f), as amended by the Regulated Investment Company Modernization Act of 2010 (H.R. 4337)).

The requirement for a RIC to defer or "push" certain gains and losses attributable to transactions after October 31 to the following tax year is expanded and applies to all "specified gains and losses." These include ordinary gains and losses from the sale, exchange, or other disposition of (or termination of a position with respect to) property, including foreign currency gain and loss, and amounts marked-to-market under Code Sec. 1296 (Code Sec. 4982(e), as amended by the 2010 RIC Act.) In addition, a RIC may elect to push net ordinary losses arising during the tax year to the following calendar year, without regard to ordinary gains and losses that must be pushed. This election allows an RIC to avoid making a distribution in the following calendar year, thereby avoiding the excise tax.

The distributed amount of RIC income for a tax year may be increased by the amount of estimated taxes paid during the calendar year in which the tax year begins. If this election is made, the distributed amount for the following calendar year is reduced by the amount of estimated taxes paid in the prior year (Code Sec. 4982(c), as amended by the 2010 RIC Act).

The required distribution percentage of capital gain net income is increased from 98 percent to 98.2 percent (Code Sec. 4982(b)(1)(B), as amended by the 2010 RIC Act).

NEW LAW EXPLAINED

> **Comment:** Practitioners should inform clients of the new investment opportunities that the expanded RIC provisions may provide for certain types of entities. In addition, clients should be encouraged to review their investment allocations for mutual funds; modifications under the 2010 RIC Act may stimulate mutual fund growth, which in turn may benefit both large and small investors.

Practical Analysis: Dale S. Collinson, Director in the Financial Institutions and Products group of the Washington National Tax practice of KPMG LLP, notes that prior to the enactment of the excise tax distribution requirements by the Tax Reform Act of 1986, shareholders of a RIC might be taxable on their share of the company's income in a later calendar year than the calendar year in which the income was earned. This could occur if the RIC's taxable year was a non-calendar taxable year or if the RIC distributed the income after the end of its taxable year as a "spillover dividend" under Code Sec. 855.

The excise tax distribution requirement was enacted to prevent such tax deferral by requiring RICs to distribute most of their income on a calendar-year basis. However, certain RICs were exempt from this requirement. These were RICs for which the deferral potential was not relevant because all of their shareholders were tax exempt entities or certain life insurance company segregated asset accounts.

The new law expands the list of permitted exempt entity shareholders. It also clarifies how the exemption applies to a fund of funds situation in which some of the shareholders of a RIC are themselves RICs that qualify for the exemption. Under the new law, such an "upper-tier" exempt RIC will be a qualified shareholder of the "lower-tier" RIC.

Other provisions of the new law also eliminate a technical issue in the application of the capital gains dividend designation rules for those RICs that are exempt from the excise tax. This primarily affects exempt RICs with calendar taxable years that do not want to push post-October capital losses into their next calendar year for income tax and excise tax purposes. However, Code Sec. 852(b)(3)(C) requires a RIC to push post-October capital losses for purposes of determining the maximum amount that may be designated as capital gains dividends unless the RIC has an election in effect under Code Sec. 4982(e)(4). Code Sec. 4982(e)(4) permits a RIC with a taxable year ending in November or December to elect to determine its capital gains excise tax distribution requirement on the basis of its taxable year rather than the 12-month period ending October 31. The issue was whether an exempt RIC could make that election given that the excise tax exemption in Code Sec. 4982(f) provides that Code Sec. 4982 shall not apply to an exempt RIC. Under the new law, the capital gains push provision is elective for all RICs (Code Sec. 852(b)(3)(C)(vi), as amended by Act Sec. 301(a)(1); Code Sec. 852(b)(8), as amended by Act Sec. 308(a)).

Practical Analysis: According to Stephen R. Baker, LECG, New York, New York, the RIC Modernization Act of 2010 (2010 RIC Act) will show that there is quite a bit more to consider relative to RIC tax compliance and planning. The impact of

¶836

NEW LAW EXPLAINED

elections from Subchapter M and Excise Tax perspectives has become more significant. For purposes of the excise tax, several issues present themselves:

Should a November or December fiscal year RIC elect to use its fiscal year instead of the standard October 31 computation date for required distributions?

Should an electing company try to revokes its election to use a November or December fiscal year instead of the standard October 31 computation date for required distributions?

Should an RIC elect to defer certain ordinary losses to the next calendar year?

Before the 2010 RIC Act, Code Sec. 4982(e)(5) and (6) required RICs to treat all post October 31 gains and losses, from foreign currency (as defined in Code Sec. 988) and all gains and losses from the mark-to-market of PFIC stock (under Code Sec. 1296) as being derived in the next calendar year. Section 402 of the Act expands the required deferral of post October 31 gains and losses to include all ordinary gains and losses from the sale, exchange, or other disposition of (or termination of a position with respect to) property, including foreign currency and amounts marked to market. The 2010 RIC Act labels these items "Specified Gains and Losses". In addition, the RIC Act now requires all mark to market transactions on Code Sec. 1256 Contracts, Marketable PFIC stock, and any other mark to market transaction governed by the Code to be taken to account as if the RIC has an October 31 year end.

Code Sec. 4982(e)(4) allows RICs operating on a November or December fiscal year end to elect to substitute the fiscal year end for October 31. The 2010 RIC Act still allows RICs to make this election. Given the significant increase in the quantity of items deferred into the next calendar year for purposes of computing ordinary income, RICs should re-evaluate November 30 or December 31 fiscal year ends under Code Sec. 4982(e)(4) or, consider the possibility of attempting to revoke an existing election.

The (e)(4) election is revocable only with consent of the Commissioner of the IRS. While a taxpayer cannot revoke the election to secure or preserve a tax benefit, a change in the tax law such as this, could arguably create enormous administrative burdens for RICs coping with the broad increase in deferred items and the resulting recalibration of their excise tax. For example, in LTRs 201019018 (Feb. 12, 2010), 200949027 (Aug. 6, 2009), 200915014 (Dec. 30, 2008) and 200652032 (Sep. 21, 2006) the respective RICs were permitted to revoke their elections. In each case the Commissioner acknowledged that the RICs had made the initial election in the belief that there would be significant efficiencies. However, after the promulgation of Treasury Regulations the result was the opposite. The dual calculations required for Subchapter M and the Excise Tax following promulgation of the Treasury Regulations was a significant and costly burden. In addition these companies found that greater accuracy in the computation of required ordinary income and capital gain income distributions could be achieved through the utilization of a one year period ending on October 31 for purposes of measuring foreign currency gains and losses and capital gain net income.

Section 402 of the 2010 RIC Act also provides another elective option as it added subsection 4982(e)(7). A RIC with a noncalendar fiscal year can now elect to

NEW LAW EXPLAINED

determine its ordinary income without regard to net ordinary loss (determined without regard to specified gains and losses discussed above) attributable to the portion of the fiscal year which is after the beginning of the taxable year which begins in such calendar year.

> *Example.* RIC uses a September 30 year end. RIC shows a $1,000,000 ordinary loss for the period October 1 to December 31, Y1 and $2,000,000 of ordinary income for the period beginning January 1 and ending September 30, Y2. Assuming no other items of income or loss, the RIC must distribute $1,960,000 during Y2 to avoid the excise tax. By making the election to treat the late year portion of the $1,000,000 loss as arising on January 1, Y2, the RIC will only be required to make a Y2 Distribution of $980,000 ($2,000,000 income less $1,000,000 late portion loss resulting in Y2 income of $1,000,000 for excise tax purposes).

The election permitting deferral of net ordinary loss will provide another tool for better excise tax management. If a fund has cash that it has not been able to invest, deferring losses may allow the fund to manage its excise taxes by increasing income in the current calendar year and permitted utilization of the deferred losses when income is expected to rise in the next calendar year. The section (e)(7) election is subject to any future Treasury Regulations.

Section 403 of the 2010 RIC Act modifies Code Sec. 4982(c) to allow a RIC to elect to include qualified estimated tax payments in the "amount distributed" during the calendar year and reduce the "amount distributed" in the succeeding calendar year by the same amount.

The election to include the qualified estimated tax payments in the distribution amount should provide a tool for some RICs to avoid tax on undistributed income, such as those RICs holding municipal bonds with market discount. If the RIC's shareholders demand tax-exempt distributions only, the RIC will pay the tax at the entity level and be required to make estimated tax payments. In addition, if a RIC fears that it will fail to qualify under Subchapter M for passthrough treatment and become subject to the corporate tax imposed by Code Sec. 11, it may choose to make estimated tax payments. The election could provide a benefit in this situation as well with respect to excise taxes. This election may actually cause the RIC to have distributions in excess of 100 percent of the ordinary income and capital gain net income. In such a circumstance, even though the included qualified estimated tax payments will need to be used to reduce the amount distributed in the succeeded calendar year, the over distribution will be available to increase the amount distributed in that succeeding calendar year under Code Sec. 4982(c)(2).

> *Example.* RIC has an investment portfolio focusing on tax-exempt income for its investors. RIC calculates 2011 Ordinary Income and Net Capital Gain totaling $1,000,000. Distributions other than qualified estimated tax payments total $950,000. RIC held several deep discount municipal bonds and made qualified estimated tax payments of $100,000 for the anticipated tax on the market discount so it could provide tax-exempt distributions to its shareholders. RIC can elect to include the $100,000 in its amount distributed in 2011, creating a calculated distribution of $1,050,000 and avoiding the excise tax. Distribution calculations for 2012 would normally be reduced by the $100,000

¶836

NEW LAW EXPLAINED

> taken in 2011. However, since over distributions exceeding 100 percent of ordinary income and net capital gain are allowed to be included in amounts calculated as distributed the $50,000 would be allowed and therefore the 2012 amounts distributed would only be reduced by $50,000.
>
> RICs for which the estimated tax payment election applies may see the reduction in the near term required distributions to be rather valuable.

> **Practical Analysis:** Paul Murphy, Deloitte Tax LLP, observes that in his experience, late, unforeseen ordinary income items, such as market discount, were responsible for many excise tax liabilities of RICs.

▶ **Effective date.** The amendments apply to calendar years beginning after the date of the enactment (Act Secs. 401(b), 402(b), 403(b), and 404(b) of the Regulated Investment Company Modernization Act of 2010 (H.R. 4337).

Law source: Law at ¶5760. Committee Reports at ¶15,130, ¶15,140, ¶15,150 and ¶15,160.

— Act Sec. 401(a) the Regulated Investment Company Modernization Act of 2010 (H.R. 4337), amending Code Sec. 4982(f);

— Act Sec. 402(a) amending Code Sec. 4982(e);

— Act Sec. 403(a), amending Code Sec. 4982(c);

— Act Sec. 404(a), amending Code Sec. 4982(b)(1)(B);

— Act Secs. 401(b), 402(b), 403(b), and 404(b), providing the effective date.

Reporter references: For further information, consult the following CCH reporters.

— Standard Federal Tax Reporter, ¶34,642.066

— Tax Research Consultant, RIC: 3,212

— Practical Tax Explanation, §45,430.10

¶839 Assessable Penalty with Respect to Tax Liability of RICs

SUMMARY OF NEW LAW

The assessable penalty imposed on a regulated investment company (RIC) claiming a deficiency dividend deduction has been repealed.

BACKGROUND

If there is a determination that a regulated investment company (RIC) has a tax deficiency with respect to a prior tax year, the RIC can distribute a deficiency

BACKGROUND

dividend (Code Sec. 860). A deficiency dividend is treated by the RIC as a dividend paid with respect to the prior tax year. As a result, the deficiency dividend increases the RIC's deduction for dividends paid for that year and eliminates the deficiency.

For this purpose, a determination includes:

- a final decision of the Tax Court or any other court of competent jurisdiction;
- a closing agreement under Code Sec. 7121;
- a tax liability agreement signed by the IRS and the taxpayer; and
- a statement by the taxpayer attached to its amendment or supplement to the tax return for the relevant tax year (Code Sec. 860(e)).

A deficiency dividend is a distribution to shareholders within 90 days after the determination that would otherwise qualify for the dividends paid deduction if it were paid during the tax year, and for which a deficiency dividend deduction is claimed within 120 days after the determination (Code Sec. 860(f) and (g)). A RIC making a deficiency dividend is subject to an interest charge as if the entire amount of the deficiency dividend were the amount of the tax deficiency (Code Sec. 860(c)).

An assessable penalty is also imposed on a RIC that uses the deficiency dividend procedure of Code Sec. 860 (Code Secs. 860(j) and 6697). The penalty is equal to the lesser of (i) the amount of the interest charge on the deficiency dividend, or (ii) one-half of the amount of the deficiency dividend deduction allowed under Code Sec. 860(a). The penalty may be assessed and collected without the normal deficiency procedures (Code Sec. 6697).

NEW LAW EXPLAINED

Penalty imposed on RICs claiming deficiency dividend deduction repealed.— The assessable penalty imposed on a regulated investment company (RIC) that claims a deficiency dividend deduction has been repealed for tax years beginning after the date of enactment (Act Sec. 501(a) and (b) of the Regulated Investment Company Modernization Act of 2010 (H.R. 4337), striking Code Secs. 860(j) and 6697).

> **Practical Analysis:** Baruch J. Cohen, Deloitte Tax LLP, observes that this change will align the deficiency dividend rules applicable to RICs with the deficiency dividend rules applicable to REITs.

▶ **Effective date.** The provision applies to tax years beginning after the date of enactment (Act Sec. 501(c) of the Regulated Investment Company Modernization Act of 2010 (H.R. 4337)).

Law source: Law at ¶5460 and ¶5845. Committee Report at ¶15,170.

— Act Sec. 501(a) of the Regulated Investment Company Modernization Act of 2010 (H.R. 4337), striking Code Sec. 6697;

— Act Sec. 501(b), striking Code Sec. 860(j);

— Act Sec. 501(c), providing the effective date.

¶839

NEW LAW EXPLAINED

Reporter references: For further information, consult the following CCH reporters.
— Standard Federal Tax Reporter, ¶26,586.068 and ¶39,990.01
— Tax Research Consultant, RIC: 3,506 and RIC: 3,508

¶842 Sale Load Basis Deferral Rule

SUMMARY OF NEW LAW

The sale load basis deferral rule for the acquisition of regulated investment company (RIC) stock is modified so that it will only apply to cases where the taxpayer acquires stock in the same or a different RIC by or before January 31 of the calendar year following the calendar year the original stock was disposed.

BACKGROUND

In certain circumstances, a sales or load charge will not be taken into account as part of the purchaser's basis for purposes of computing profit or loss on a sale of regulated investment company (RIC) stock (Code Sec. 852(f)(1)). A load charge is any sales or similar charge incurred in acquiring stock of a RIC (mutual fund). The term does not include a charge incurred by reason of the reinvestment of a dividend. A reinvestment right is the right to reinvest the proceeds from the sale or exchange of the shares at no load charge or a reduced charge in one or more mutual funds, including the original mutual fund (Code Sec. 852(f)(2)).

If:

- a taxpayer incurs a load charge in acquiring stock in a RIC and by reason of incurring the charge or making the acquisition, the taxpayer acquires a reinvestment right,

- the shares are disposed of within 90 days after the date on which such stock was acquired, and

- the taxpayer subsequently acquires stock of a RIC and the otherwise applicable load charge is reduced by reason of the reinvestment right,

then the load charge (to the extent it does not exceed the reduction) is not taken into account in determining gain or loss on the disposition of the original stock. To the extent that the load charge is not taken into account in determining such gain or loss, the charge is treated as incurred in the acquisition of the subsequently acquired stock (Code Sec. 852(f)(1)).

NEW LAW EXPLAINED

Sale load basis deferral rule modified.—The sale load basis deferral rule is changed so that after the original regulated investment company (RIC) stock is disposed of

NEW LAW EXPLAINED

within 90 days after the date it was originally acquired, the taxpayer must acquire stock in the same RIC or another RIC during the period beginning on the date of the disposition of the original stock, and ending on January 31 of the calendar year following the calendar year that includes the date of such disposition (Code Sec. 852(f)(1)(C), as amended by the Regulated Investment Company Modernization Act of 2010 (H.R. 4337)). If the later-acquired stock is acquired during this more limited period, and the otherwise applicable load charge on the later-acquired stock is reduced by a reinvestment right that the taxpayer received from making the original stock acquisition or incurring a load charge on that original acquisition, then the load charge incurred in the original acquisition (to the extent it does not exceed the load charge reduction due to the reinvestment right) is not taken into account for purposes of determining the amount of gain or loss on the disposition of the original stock.

> **Practical Analysis:** Deanna Flores, Principal in the Financial Institutions and Products group of the Washington National Tax practice of KPMG LLP in San Diego, notes that by providing a January 31 "cut-off" date for application of the sales load basis deferral rule, the new law will provide certainty to Regulated Investment Companies (RICs) and their shareholders with respect to the cost basis of previously-owned RIC shares, notwithstanding any reinvestment right related to those shares. The new law is particularly timely given that RICs generally will be required to report cost basis and holding period information on Forms 1099-B for redemptions of RIC shares acquired on or after January 1, 2012 (Code Sec. 6045(g)). Limiting the time period during which the sale load basis deferral rule applies is expected to minimize the issuance of amended Forms 1099-B to RIC shareholders. The new law also will reduce the complexity associated with tracking cost basis for RIC shares subject to reporting on Forms 1099-B.

▶ **Effective date.** This provision applies to charges incurred in tax years beginning after the date of enactment (Act Sec. 502(b) of the Regulated Investment Company Modernization Act of 2010 (H.R. 4337)).

Law source: Law at ¶5430. Committee Report at ¶15,180.

— Act Sec. 502(a) of the Regulated Investment Company Modernization Act of 2010 (H.R. 4337), amending Code Sec. 852(f)(1)(C);

— Act Sec. 502(b), providing the effective date.

Reporter references: For further information, consult the following CCH reporters.

— Standard Federal Tax Reporter, ¶26,433.046

— Tax Research Consultant, SALES: 6,068

— Practical Tax Explanation, § 19,215.05

¶842

Code Sections Added, Amended Or Repealed

[¶ 5001]

INTRODUCTION.

The Internal Revenue Code provisions amended by the Tax Relief, Unemployment Insurance Reauthorization, and Job Creation Act of 2010 (P.L. 111-312), the Regulated Investment Company Modernization Act of 2010 (H.R. 4337), the Claims Resolution Act of 2010 (P.L. 111-291), the Medicare and Medicaid Extenders Act of 2010 (P.L. 111-309), and the Airport and Airway Extension Act of 2010, Part IV (H.R. 6473) are shown in the following paragraphs. Deleted Code material or the text of the Code Section prior to amendment appears in the amendment notes following each amended Code provision. *Any changed or added material is set out in italics.* Also included are all Internal Revenue Code provisions to which the sunset provisions of the Economic Growth and Tax Relief Reconciliation Act of 2001 (P.L. 107-16), the Jobs and Growth Tax Relief Reconciliation Act of 2003 (P.L. 108-27), or the Patient Protection and Affordable Care Act (P.L. 111-148) are currently applicable.

[¶ 5005] CODE SEC. 1. TAX IMPOSED.

* * *

≫→ *Caution: The heading for Code Sec. 1(f), below, was amended by P.L. 107-16. For sunset provision, see P.L. 107-16, §901 [as amended by P.L. 111-312], in the amendment notes.*

(f) PHASEOUT OF MARRIAGE PENALTY IN 15-PERCENT BRACKET; ADJUSTMENTS IN TAX TABLES SO THAT INFLATION WILL NOT RESULT IN TAX INCREASES.—

(1) IN GENERAL.—Not later than December 15 of 1993, and each subsequent calendar year, the Secretary shall prescribe tables which shall apply in lieu of the tables contained in subsections (a), (b), (c), (d), and (e) with respect to taxable years beginning in the succeeding calendar year.

(2) METHOD OF PRESCRIBING TABLES.—The table which under paragraph (1) is to apply in lieu of the table contained in subsection (a), (b), (c), (d), or (e), as the case may be, with respect to taxable years beginning in any calendar year shall be prescribed—

≫→ *Caution: Code Sec. 1(f)(2)(A), below, was amended by P.L. 107-16. For sunset provision, see P.L. 107-16, §901 [as amended by P.L. 111-312], in the amendment notes.*

(A) except as provided in paragraph (8), by increasing the minimum and maximum dollar amounts for each rate bracket for which a tax is imposed under such table by the cost-of-living adjustment for such calendar year,

(B) by not changing the rate applicable to any rate bracket as adjusted under subparagraph (A), and

(C) by adjusting the amounts setting forth the tax to the extent necessary to reflect the adjustments in the rate brackets.

* * *

(6) ROUNDING.—

(A) IN GENERAL.—If any increase determined under paragraph (2)(A), section 63(c)(4), section 68(b)(2) or section 151(d)(4) is not a multiple of $50, such increase shall be rounded to the next lowest multiple of $50.

⇒→ *Caution: Code Sec. 1(f)(6)(B), below, was amended by P.L. 107-16. For sunset provision, see P.L. 107-16, §901 [as amended by P.L. 111-312], in the amendment notes.*

(B) TABLE FOR MARRIED INDIVIDUALS FILING SEPARATELY.—In the case of a married individual filing a separate return, subparagraph (A) (other than with respect to sections 63(c)(4) and 151(d)(4)(A)) shall be applied by substituting "$25" for "$50" each place it appears.

* * *

⇒→ *Caution: Code Sec. 1(f)(8), below, was added by P.L. 107-16 and amended by P.L. 108-27 and P.L. 108-311. For sunset provisions, see P.L. 107-16, §901 [as amended by P.L. 111-312], P.L. 108-27, §107, and P.L. 108-311, §105, in the amendment notes.*

(8) ELIMINATION OF MARRIAGE PENALTY IN 15-PERCENT BRACKET.—With respect to taxable years beginning after December 31, 2003, in prescribing the tables under paragraph (1)—

(A) the maximum taxable income in the 15-percent rate bracket in the table contained in subsection (a) (and the minimum taxable income in the next higher taxable income bracket in such table) shall be 200 percent of the maximum taxable income in the 15-percent rate bracket in the table contained in subsection (c) (after any other adjustment under this subsection), and

(B) the comparable taxable income amounts in the table contained in subsection (d) shall be ½ of the amounts determined under subparagraph (A).

* * *

[CCH Explanation at ¶310 and ¶315. Committee Reports at ¶10,040 and ¶10,160.]

Amendments

- **2004, Working Families Tax Relief Act of 2004 (P.L. 108-311)**

P.L. 108-311, §101(c):

Amended Code Sec. 1(f)(8). **Effective** for tax years beginning after 12-31-2003. Prior to amendment, Code Sec. 1(f)(8) read as follows:

(8) PHASEOUT OF MARRIAGE PENALTY IN 15-PERCENT BRACKET.—

(A) IN GENERAL.—With respect to taxable years beginning after December 31, 2002, in prescribing the tables under paragraph (1)—

(i) the maximum taxable income in the 15-percent rate bracket in the table contained in subsection (a) (and the minimum taxable income in the next higher taxable income bracket in such table) shall be the applicable percentage of the maximum taxable income in the 15-percent rate bracket in the table contained in subsection (c) (after any other adjustment under this subsection), and

(ii) the comparable taxable income amounts in the table contained in subsection (d) shall be ½ of the amounts determined under clause (i).

(B) APPLICABLE PERCENTAGE.—For purposes of subparagraph (A), the applicable percentage shall be determined in accordance with the following table:

For taxable years beginning in calendar year—	The applicable percentage is—
2003 and 2004	200
2005	180
2006	187
2007	193
2008 and thereafter	200.

(C) ROUNDING.—If any amount determined under subparagraph (A)(i) is not a multiple of $50, such amount shall be rounded to the next lowest multiple of $50.

P.L. 108-311, §105, provides:

SEC. 105. APPLICATION OF EGTRRA SUNSET TO THIS TITLE.

Each amendment made by this title shall be subject to title IX of the Economic Growth and Tax Relief Reconciliation Act of 2001 to the same extent and in the same manner as the provision of such Act to which such amendment relates.

- **2003, Jobs and Growth Tax Relief Reconciliation Act of 2003 (P.L. 108-27)**

P.L. 108-27, §102(a):

Amended the table contained in Code Sec. 1(f)(8)(B) by inserting a new item before the item relating to 2005. **Effective** for tax years beginning after 12-31-2002.

P.L. 108-27, §102(b)(1):

Amended Code Sec. 1(f)(8)(A) by striking "2004" and inserting "2002". **Effective** for tax years beginning after 12-31-2002.

P.L. 108-27, §107, provides:

SEC. 107. APPLICATION OF EGTRRA SUNSET TO THIS TITLE.

Each amendment made by this title shall be subject to title IX of the Economic Growth and Tax Relief Reconciliation Act of 2001 to the same extent and in the same manner as the provision of such Act to which such amendment relates.

- **2001, Economic Growth and Tax Relief Reconciliation Act of 2001 (P.L. 107-16)**

P.L. 107-16, §301(c)(1):

Amended Code Sec. 1(f)(6)(B) by striking "(other than with" and all that follows through "shall be applied" and inserting "(other than with respect to sections 63(c)(4) and 151(d)(4)(A)) shall be applied". **Effective** for tax years beginning after 12-31-2002 [**effective** date changed by P.L. 108-27, §103(b).—CCH]. Prior to amendment, Code Sec. 1(f)(6)(B) read as follows:

(B) Table for Married Individuals Filing Separately.—In the case of a married individual filing a separate return, subparagraph (A) (other than with respect to subsection (c)(4) of section 63 (as it applies to subsections (c)(5)(A) and (f) of such section) and section 151(d)(4)(A)) shall be applied by substituting "$25" for "$50" each place it appears.

P.L. 107-16, § 302(a):

Amended Code Sec. 1(f) by adding at the end a new paragraph (8). **Effective** for tax years beginning after 12-31-2002 [effective date changed by P.L. 108-27, § 102(c).—CCH].

P.L. 107-16, § 302(b)(1):

Amended Code Sec. 1(f)(2)(A) by inserting "except as provided in paragraph (8)," before "by increasing". **Effective** for tax years beginning after 12-31-2002 [effective date changed by P.L. 108-27, § 102(c).—CCH].

P.L. 107-16, § 302(b)(2):

Amended the heading for Code Sec. 1(f) by inserting "Phaseout of Marriage Penalty in 15-Percent Bracket;" before "Adjustments". **Effective** for tax years beginning af-

ter 12-31-2002 [effective date changed by P.L. 108-27, § 102(c).—CCH].

P.L. 107-16, § 901(a)-(b), as amended by P.L. 111-312, § 101(a)(1), provides:

SEC. 901. SUNSET OF PROVISIONS OF ACT.

(a) In General.—All provisions of, and amendments made by, this Act shall not apply—

(1) to taxable, plan, or limitation years beginning after December 31, 2012, or

(2) in the case of title V, to estates of decedents dying, gifts made, or generation skipping transfers, after December 31, 2012.

(b) Application of Certain Laws.—The Internal Revenue Code of 1986 and the Employee Retirement Income Security Act of 1974 shall be applied and administered to years, estates, gifts, and transfers described in subsection (a) as if the provisions and amendments described in subsection (a) had never been enacted.

(g) Certain Unearned Income of Children Taxed as if Parent's Income.—

* * *

(7) Election to Claim Certain Unearned Income of Child on Parent's Return.—

* * *

(B) Income Included on Parent's Return.—In the case of a parent making the election under this paragraph—

(i) the gross income of each child to whom such election applies (to the extent the gross income of such child exceeds twice the amount described in paragraph (4)(A)(ii)(I)) shall be included in such parent's gross income for the taxable year,

(ii) the tax imposed by this section for such year with respect to such parent shall be the amount equal to the sum of—

(I) the amount determined under this section after the application of clause (i), plus

≫→ *Caution: Code Sec. 1(g)(7)(B)(ii)(II), below, was amended by P.L. 107-16. For sunset provision, see P.L. 107-16, §901 [as amended by P.L. 111-312], in the amendment notes.*

(II) for each such child, 10 percent of the lesser of the amount described in paragraph (4)(A)(ii)(I) or the excess of the gross income of such child over the amount so described, and

(iii) any interest which is an item of tax preference under section 57(a)(5) of the child shall be treated as an item of tax preference of such parent (and not of such child).

[CCH Explanation at ¶ 305. Committee Reports at ¶ 10,010.]

Amendments

• **2004, Working Families Tax Relief Act of 2004 (P.L. 108-311)**

P.L. 108-311, § 408(a)(1):

Amended Code Sec. 1(g)(7)(B)(ii)(II) by striking "10 percent." and inserting "10 percent". **Effective** 10-4-2004.

• **2001, Economic Growth and Tax Relief Reconciliation Act of 2001 (P.L. 107-16)**

P.L. 107-16, § 101(c)(1):

Amended Code Sec. 1(g)(7)(B)(ii)(II) by striking "15 percent" and inserting "10 percent.". **Effective** for tax years beginning after 12-31-2000.

P.L. 107-16, § 901(a)-(b), as amended by P.L. 111-312, § 101(a)(1), provides:

SEC. 901. SUNSET OF PROVISIONS OF ACT.

(a) In General.—All provisions of, and amendments made by, this Act shall not apply—

(1) to taxable, plan, or limitation years beginning after December 31, 2012, or

(2) in the case of title V, to estates of decedents dying, gifts made, or generation skipping transfers, after December 31, 2012.

(b) Application of Certain Laws.—The Internal Revenue Code of 1986 and the Employee Retirement Income Security

Act of 1974 shall be applied and administered to years, estates, gifts, and transfers described in subsection (a) as if the provisions and amendments described in subsection (a) had never been enacted.

(h) MAXIMUM CAPITAL GAINS RATE.—

(1) IN GENERAL.—If a taxpayer has a net capital gain for any taxable year, the tax imposed by this section for such taxable year shall not exceed the sum of—

(A) a tax computed at the rates and in the same manner as if this subsection had not been enacted on the greater of—

(i) taxable income reduced by the net capital gain, or

(ii) the lesser of—

➤➤➤ *Caution: Code Sec. 1(h)(1)(A)(ii)(I), below, was amended by P.L. 107-16. For sunset provision, see P.L. 107-16, §901 [as amended by P.L. 111-312], in the amendment notes.*

(I) the amount of taxable income taxed at a rate below 25 percent; or

(II) taxable income reduced by the adjusted net capital gain;

➤➤➤ *Caution: Code Sec. 1(h)(1)(B), below, was amended by P.L. 108-27. For sunset provision, see P.L. 108-27, §303 [as amended by P.L. 111-312], in the amendment notes.*

(B) 5 percent (0 percent in the case of taxable years beginning after 2007) of so much of the adjusted net capital gain (or, if less, taxable income) as does not exceed the excess (if any) of—

➤➤➤ *Caution: Code Sec. 1(h)(1)(B)(i), below, was amended by P.L. 107-16. For sunset provision, see P.L. 107-16, §901 [as amended by P.L. 111-312], in the amendment notes.*

(i) the amount of taxable income which would (without regard to this paragraph) be taxed at a rate below 25 percent, over

(ii) the taxable income reduced by the adjusted net capital gain;

➤➤➤ *Caution: Code Sec. 1(h)(1)(C), below, was amended by P.L. 108-27. For sunset provision, see P.L. 108-27, §303 [as amended by P.L. 111-312], in the amendment notes.*

(C) 15 percent of the adjusted net capital gain (or, if less, taxable income) in excess of the amount on which a tax is determined under subparagraph (B);

(D) 25 percent of the excess (if any) of—

(i) the unrecaptured section 1250 gain (or, if less, the net capital gain (determined without regard to paragraph (11))), over

(ii) the excess (if any) of—

(I) the sum of the amount on which tax is determined under subparagraph (A) plus the net capital gain, over

(II) taxable income; and

(E) 28 percent of the amount of taxable income in excess of the sum of the amounts on which tax is determined under the preceding subparagraphs of this paragraph.

(2) NET CAPITAL GAIN TAKEN INTO ACCOUNT AS INVESTMENT INCOME.—For purposes of this subsection, the net capital gain for any taxable year shall be reduced (but not below zero) by the amount which the taxpayer takes into account as investment income under section 163(d)(4)(B)(iii).

➤➤➤ *Caution: Code Sec. 1(h)(3), below was amended by P.L. 108-27. For sunset provision, see P.L. 108-27, §303 [as amended by P.L. 111-312], in the amendment notes.*

(3) ADJUSTED NET CAPITAL GAIN.—For purposes of this subsection, the term "adjusted net capital gain" means the sum of—

(A) net capital gain (determined without regard to paragraph (11)) reduced (but not below zero) by the sum of—

(i) unrecaptured section 1250 gain, and

(ii) 28-percent rate gain, plus

(B) qualified dividend income (as defined in paragraph (11)).

(4) 28-PERCENT RATE GAIN.—For purposes of this subsection, the term "28-percent rate gain" means the excess (if any) of—

(A) the sum of—

(i) collectibles gain; and

(ii) section 1202 gain, over

(B) the sum of—

(i) collectibles loss;

(ii) the net short-term capital loss, and

(iii) the amount of long-term capital loss carried under section 1212(b)(1)(B) to the taxable year.

(5) COLLECTIBLES GAIN AND LOSS.—For purposes of this subsection—

(A) IN GENERAL.—The terms "collectibles gain" and "collectibles loss" mean gain or loss (respectively) from the sale or exchange of a collectible (as defined in section 408(m) without regard to paragraph (3) thereof) which is a capital asset held for more than 1 year but only to the extent such gain is taken into account in computing gross income and such loss is taken into account in computing taxable income.

(B) PARTNERSHIPS, ETC.—For purposes of subparagraph (A), any gain from the sale of an interest in a partnership, S corporation, or trust which is attributable to unrealized appreciation in the value of collectibles shall be treated as gain from the sale or exchange of a collectible. Rules similar to the rules of section 751 shall apply for purposes of the preceding sentence.

(6) UNRECAPTURED SECTION 1250 GAIN.—For purposes of this subsection—

(A) IN GENERAL.—The term "unrecaptured section 1250 gain" means the excess (if any) of—

(i) the amount of long-term capital gain (not otherwise treated as ordinary income) which would be treated as ordinary income if section 1250(b)(1) included all depreciation and the applicable percentage under section 1250(a) were 100 percent, over

(ii) the excess (if any) of—

(I) the amount described in paragraph (4)(B); over

(II) the amount described in paragraph (4)(A).

(B) LIMITATION WITH RESPECT TO SECTION 1231 PROPERTY.—The amount described in subparagraph (A)(i) from sales, exchanges, and conversions described in section 1231(a)(3)(A) for any taxable year shall not exceed the net section 1231 gain (as defined in section 1231(c)(3)) for such year.

(7) SECTION 1202 GAIN.—For purposes of this subsection, the term "section 1202 gain" means the excess of—

(A) the gain which would be excluded from gross income under section 1202 but for the percentage limitation in section 1202(a), over

(B) the gain excluded from gross income under section 1202.

(8) COORDINATION WITH RECAPTURE OF NET ORDINARY LOSSES UNDER SECTION 1231.—If any amount is treated as ordinary income under section 1231(c), such amount shall be allocated among the separate categories of net section 1231 gain (as defined in section 1231(c)(3)) in such manner as the Secretary may by forms or regulations prescribe.

(9) REGULATIONS.—The Secretary may prescribe such regulations as are appropriate (including regulations requiring reporting) to apply this subsection in the case of sales and exchanges by pass-thru entities and of interests in such entities.

(10) PASS-THRU ENTITY DEFINED.—For purposes of this subsection, the term "pass-thru entity" means—

(A) a regulated investment company;

(B) a real estate investment trust;

(C) an S corporation;

(D) a partnership;

(E) an estate or trust;

(F) a common trust fund; and

(G) a qualified electing fund (as defined in section 1295).

⟫→ *Caution: Code Sec. 1(h)(11), below, was added by P.L. 108-27 and amended by P.L. 108-311. For sunset provision, see P.L. 108-27, §303 [as amended by P.L. 111-312], in the amendment notes.*

(11) DIVIDENDS TAXED AS NET CAPITAL GAIN.—

(A) IN GENERAL.—For purposes of this subsection, the term "net capital gain" means net capital gain (determined without regard to this paragraph) increased by qualified dividend income.

(B) QUALIFIED DIVIDEND INCOME.—For purposes of this paragraph—

(i) IN GENERAL.—The term "qualified dividend income" means dividends received during the taxable year from—

(I) domestic corporations, and

(II) qualified foreign corporations.

(ii) CERTAIN DIVIDENDS EXCLUDED.—Such term shall not include—

(I) any dividend from a corporation which for the taxable year of the corporation in which the distribution is made, or the preceding taxable year, is a corporation exempt from tax under section 501 or 521,

(II) any amount allowed as a deduction under section 591 (relating to deduction for dividends paid by mutual savings banks, etc.), and

(III) any dividend described in section 404(k).

(iii) COORDINATION WITH SECTION 246(c).—Such term shall not include any dividend on any share of stock—

(I) with respect to which the holding period requirements of section 246(c) are not met (determined by substituting in section 246(c) "60 days" for "45 days" each place it appears and by substituting "121-day period" for "91-day period"), or

(II) to the extent that the taxpayer is under an obligation (whether pursuant to a short sale or otherwise) to make related payments with respect to positions in substantially similar or related property.

(C) QUALIFIED FOREIGN CORPORATIONS.—

(i) IN GENERAL.—Except as otherwise provided in this paragraph, the term "qualified foreign corporation" means any foreign corporation if—

(I) such corporation is incorporated in a possession of the United States, or

(II) such corporation is eligible for benefits of a comprehensive income tax treaty with the United States which the Secretary determines is satisfactory for purposes of this paragraph and which includes an exchange of information program.

(ii) DIVIDENDS ON STOCK READILY TRADABLE ON UNITED STATES SECURITIES MARKET.—A foreign corporation not otherwise treated as a qualified foreign corporation under clause (i) shall be so treated with respect to any dividend paid by such corporation if the stock with respect to which such dividend is paid is readily tradable on an established securities market in the United States.

(iii) EXCLUSION OF DIVIDENDS OF CERTAIN FOREIGN CORPORATIONS.—Such term shall not include any foreign corporation which for the taxable year of the corporation in which the dividend was paid, or the preceding taxable year, is a passive foreign investment company (as defined in section 1297).

(iv) COORDINATION WITH FOREIGN TAX CREDIT LIMITATION.—Rules similar to the rules of section 904(b)(2)(B) shall apply with respect to the dividend rate differential under this paragraph.

(D) SPECIAL RULES.—

(i) AMOUNTS TAKEN INTO ACCOUNT AS INVESTMENT INCOME.—Qualified dividend income shall not include any amount which the taxpayer takes into account as investment income under section 163(d)(4)(B).

(ii) EXTRAORDINARY DIVIDENDS.—If a taxpayer to whom this section applies receives, with respect to any share of stock, qualified dividend income from 1 or more dividends which are extraordinary dividends (within the meaning of section 1059(c)), any loss on the sale or exchange of such share shall, to the extent of such dividends, be treated as long-term capital loss.

(iii) TREATMENT OF DIVIDENDS FROM REGULATED INVESTMENT COMPANIES AND REAL ESTATE INVESTMENT TRUSTS.—A dividend received from a regulated investment company or a real estate investment trust shall be subject to the limitations prescribed in sections 854 and 857.

➤ *Caution: Code Sec. 1(h)(13) was stricken by P.L. 107-16. For sunset provision, see P.L. 107-16, §901 [as amended by P.L. 111-312], in the amendment notes.*

(13) [Stricken.]

[CCH Explanation at ¶305, ¶405, ¶410, ¶420 and ¶425. Committee Reports at ¶10,010 and ¶10,080.]

Amendments

• **2004, American Jobs Creation Act of 2004 (P.L. 108-357)**

P.L. 108-357, §413(c)(1)(A):

Amended Code Sec. 1(h)(10) by inserting "and" at the end of subparagraph (F), by striking subparagraph (G), and by redesignating subparagraph (H) as subparagraph (G). **Effective** for tax years of foreign corporations beginning after 12-31-2004, and for tax years of United States shareholders with or within which such tax years of foreign corporations end. Prior to being stricken, Code Sec. 1(h)(10)(G) read as follows:

(G) a foreign investment company which is described in section 1246(b)(1) and for which an election is in effect under section 1247; and

P.L. 108-357, §413(c)(1)(B):

Amended Code Sec. 1(h)(11)(C)(iii) by striking "a foreign personal holding company (as defined in section 552), a foreign investment company (as defined in section 1246(b)), or" immediately preceding "a passive foreign investment company". **Effective** for tax years of foreign corporations beginning after 12-31-2004, and for tax years of United States shareholders with or within which such tax years of foreign corporations end.

• **2004, Working Families Tax Relief Act of 2004 (P.L. 108-311)**

P.L. 108-311, §402(a)(1):

Amended Code Sec. 1(h)(1)(D)(i) by inserting "(determined without regard to paragraph (11))" after "net capital gain". **Effective** as if included in section 302 of the Jobs and

Growth Tax Relief Reconciliation Act of 2003 (P.L. 108-27) [effective generally for tax years beginning after 12-31-2002.—CCH].

P.L. 108-311, §402(a)(2)(A)-(C):

Amended Code Sec. 1(h)(11)(B)(iii)(I) by striking "section 246(c)(1)" and inserting "section 246(c)", by striking "120-day period" and inserting "121-day period", and by striking "90-day period" and inserting "91-day period". **Effective** as if included in section 302 of the Jobs and Growth Tax Relief Reconciliation Act of 2003 (P.L. 108-27) [effective generally for tax years beginning after 12-31-2002.—CCH].

P.L. 108-311, §402(a)(3):

Amended Code Sec. 1(h)(11)(D)(ii) by striking "an individual" and inserting "a taxpayer to whom this section applies". **Effective** as if included in section 302 of the Jobs and Growth Tax Relief Reconciliation Act of 2003 (P.L. 108-27) [effective generally for tax years beginning after 12-31-2002.—CCH].

P.L. 108-311, §408(a)(2)(A)-(B):

Amended Code Sec. 1(h)(6)(A)(ii) by striking "(5)(B)" in subclause (I) and inserting "(4)(B)", and by striking "(5)(A)" in subclause (II) and inserting "(4)(A)". **Effective** 10-4-2004.

• **2003, Jobs and Growth Tax Relief Reconciliation Act of 2003 (P.L. 108-27)**

P.L. 108-27, §301(a)(1):

Amended Code Sec. 1(h)(1)(B) by striking "10 percent" and inserting "5 percent (0 percent in the case of taxable years beginning after 2007)". **Effective** for tax years ending on or after 5-6-2003. For a transition rule, see Act Sec. 301(c), below.

P.L. 108-27, §301(a)(2)(A):

Amended Code Sec. 1(h)(1)(C) by striking "20 percent" and inserting "15 percent". **Effective** for tax years ending on or after 5-6-2003. For a transition rule, see Act Sec. 301(c), below.

P.L. 108-27, §301(b)(1)(A)-(C):

Amended Code Sec. 1(h) by striking paragraphs (2) and (9), by redesignating paragraphs (3) through (8) as paragraphs (2) through (7), respectively, and by redesignating paragraphs (10), (11), and (12) as paragraphs (8), (9), and (10), respectively. **Effective** for tax years ending on or after 5-6-2003. For a transition rule, see Act Sec. 301(c), below. Prior to being stricken, Code Sec. 1(h)(2) and (9) read as follows:

(2) REDUCED CAPITAL GAIN RATES FOR QUALIFIED 5-YEAR GAIN.—

(A) REDUCTION IN 10-PERCENT RATE.— In the case of any taxable year beginning after December 31, 2000, the rate under paragraph (1)(B) shall be 8 percent with respect to so much of the amount to which the 10-percent rate would otherwise apply as does not exceed qualified 5-year gain, and 10 percent with respect to the remainder of such amount.

(B) REDUCTION IN 20-PERCENT RATE.— The rate under paragraph (1)(C) shall be 18 percent with respect to so much of the amount to which the 20-percent rate would otherwise apply as does not exceed the lesser of—

(i) the excess of qualified 5-year gain over the amount of such gain taken into account under subparagraph (A) of this paragraph; or

(ii) the amount of qualified 5-year gain (determined by taking into account only property the holding period for which begins after December 31, 2000),

and 20 percent with respect to the remainder of such amount. For purposes of determining under the preceding sentence whether the holding period of property begins after December 31, 2000, the holding period of property acquired pursuant to the exercise of an option (or other right or obligation to acquire property) shall include the period such option (or other right or obligation) was held.

* * *

(9) QUALIFIED 5-YEAR GAIN.—For purposes of this subsection, the term "qualified 5-year gain" means the aggregate long-term capital gain from property held for more than 5 years. The determination under the preceding sentence shall be made without regard to collectibles gain, gain described in paragraph (7)(A)(i), and section 1202 gain.

P.L. 108-27, §301(c), provides:

(c) TRANSITIONAL RULES FOR TAXABLE YEARS WHICH INCLUDE MAY 6, 2003.—For purposes of applying section 1(h) of the Internal Revenue Code of 1986 in the case of a taxable year which includes May 6, 2003—

(1) The amount of tax determined under subparagraph (B) of section 1(h)(1) of such Code shall be the sum of—

(A) 5 percent of the lesser of—

(i) the net capital gain determined by taking into account only gain or loss properly taken into account for the portion of the taxable year on or after May 6, 2003 (determined without regard to collectibles gain or loss, gain described in section 1(h)(6)(A)(i) of such Code, and section 1202 gain), or

(ii) the amount on which a tax is determined under such subparagraph (without regard to this subsection),

(B) 8 percent of the lesser of—

(i) the qualified 5-year gain (as defined in section 1(h)(9) of the Internal Revenue Code of 1986, as in effect on the day before the date of the enactment of this Act) properly taken into account for the portion of the taxable year before May 6, 2003, or

(ii) the excess (if any) of—

(I) the amount on which a tax is determined under such subparagraph (without regard to this subsection), over

(II) the amount on which a tax is determined under subparagraph (A), plus

(C) 10 percent of the excess (if any) of—

(i) the amount on which a tax is determined under such subparagraph (without regard to this subsection), over

(ii) the sum of the amounts on which a tax is determined under subparagraphs (A) and (B).

(2) The amount of tax determined under subparagraph (C) of section (1)(h)(1) of such Code shall be the sum of—

(A) 15 percent of the lesser of—

(i) the excess (if any) of the amount of net capital gain determined under subparagraph (A)(i) of paragraph (1) of this subsection over the amount on which a tax is determined under subparagraph (A) of paragraph (1) of this subsection, or

(ii) the amount on which a tax is determined under such subparagraph (C) (without regard to this subsection), plus

(B) 20 percent of the excess (if any) of—

(i) the amount on which a tax is determined under such subparagraph (C) (without regard to this subsection), over

(ii) the amount on which a tax is determined under subparagraph (A) of this paragraph.

(3) For purposes of applying section 55(b)(3) of such Code, rules similar to the rules of paragraphs (1) and (2) of this subsection shall apply.

(4) In applying this subsection with respect to any pass-thru entity, the determination of when gains and losses are properly taken into account shall be made at the entity level.

(5) For purposes of applying section 1(h)(11) of such Code, as added by section 302 of this Act, to this subsection, dividends which are qualified dividend income shall be treated as gain properly taken into account for the portion of the taxable year on or after May 6, 2003.

(6) Terms used in this subsection which are also used in section 1(h) of such Code shall have the respective meanings that such terms have in such section.

P.L. 108-27, §302(a):

Amended Code Sec. 1(h), as amended by Act Sec. 301, by adding at the end a new paragraph (11). For the **effective** date, see Act Sec. 302(f), as amended by P.L. 108-311, §402(a)(6), below.

P.L. 108-27, §302(e)(1):

Amended Code Sec. 1(h)(3), as redesignated by Act Sec. 301. For the **effective** date, see Act Sec. 302(f), as amended by P.L. 108-311, §402(a)(6), below. Prior to amendment, but after redesignation, Code Sec. 1(h)(3) read as follows:

(3) ADJUSTED NET CAPITAL GAIN.—For purposes of this subsection, the term "adjusted net capital gain" means net capital gain reduced (but not below zero) by the sum of—

(A) unrecaptured section 1250 gain; and

(B) 28-percent rate gain.

P.L. 108-27, §302(f), as amended by P.L. 108-311, §402(a)(6), provides:

(f) EFFECTIVE DATE.—

(1) IN GENERAL.—Except as provided in paragraph (2), the amendments made by this section shall apply to taxable years beginning after December 31, 2002.

(2) PASS-THRU ENTITIES.—In the case of a pass-thru entity described in subparagraph (A), (B), (C), (D), (E), or (F) of section 1(h)(10) of the Internal Revenue Code of 1986, as amended by this Act, the amendments made by this section

shall apply to taxable years ending after December 31, 2002; except that dividends received by such an entity on or before such date shall not be treated as qualified dividend income (as defined in section 1(h)(11)(B) of such Code, as added by this Act).

P.L. 108-27, §303, as amended by P.L. 109-222, §102, and P.L. 111-312, §102(a), provides:

SEC. 303. SUNSET OF TITLE.

All provisions of, and amendments made by, this title shall not apply to taxable years beginning after December 31, 2012, and the Internal Revenue Code of 1986 shall be applied and administered to such years as if such provisions and amendments had never been enacted.

• **2001, Economic Growth and Tax Relief Reconciliation Act of 2001 (P.L. 107-16)**

P.L. 107-16, §101(c)(2)(A)-(B):

Amended Code Sec. 1(h) by striking "28 percent" both places it appears in paragraphs (1)(A)(ii)(I) and (1)(B)(i) and inserting "25 percent", and by striking paragraph (13). **Effective** for tax years beginning after 12-31-2000. Prior to being stricken, Code Sec. 1(h)(13) read as follows:

(13) SPECIAL RULES.—

(A) DETERMINATION OF 28-PERCENT RATE GAIN.—In applying paragraph (5)—

(i) the amount determined under subparagraph (A) of paragraph (5) shall include long-term capital gain (not otherwise described in such subparagraph)—

(I) which is properly taken into account for the portion of the taxable year before May 7, 1997; or

(II) from property held not more than 18 months which is properly taken into account for the portion of the taxable year after July 28, 1997, and before January 1, 1998;

(ii) the amount determined under subparagraph (B) of paragraph (5) shall include long-term capital loss (not otherwise described in such subparagraph)—

(I) which is properly taken into account for the portion of the taxable year before May 7, 1997; or

(II) from property held not more than 18 months which is properly taken into account for the portion of the taxable year after July 28, 1997, and before January 1, 1998; and

(iii) subparagraph (B) of paragraph (5) (as in effect immediately before the enactment of this clause) shall apply to amounts properly taken into account before January 1, 1998.

(B) DETERMINATION OF UNRECAPTURED SECTION 1250 GAIN.— The amount determined under paragraph (7)(A)(i) shall not include gain—

(i) which is properly taken into account for the portion of the taxable year before May 7, 1997; or

(ii) from property held not more than 18 months which is properly taken into account for the portion of the taxable year after July 28, 1997, and before January 1, 1998.

(C) SPECIAL RULES FOR PASS-THRU ENTITIES.—In applying this paragraph with respect to any pass-thru entity, the determination of when gains and loss are properly taken into account shall be made at the entity level.

(D) CHARITABLE REMAINDER TRUSTS.—Subparagraphs (A) and (B)(ii) shall not apply to any capital gain distribution made by a trust described in section 664.

P.L. 107-16, §901(a)-(b), as amended by P.L. 111-312, §101(a)(1), provides:

SEC. 901. SUNSET OF PROVISIONS OF ACT.

(a) IN GENERAL.—All provisions of, and amendments made by, this Act shall not apply—

(1) to taxable, plan, or limitation years beginning after December 31, 2012, or

(2) in the case of title V, to estates of decedents dying, gifts made, or generation skipping transfers, after December 31, 2012.

(b) APPLICATION OF CERTAIN LAWS.—The Internal Revenue Code of 1986 and the Employee Retirement Income Security Act of 1974 shall be applied and administered to years, estates, gifts, and transfers described in subsection (a) as if the provisions and amendments described in subsection (a) had never been enacted.

»»→ Caution: *Code Sec. 1(i), below, was added by P.L. 107-16 and amended by P.L. 108-27 and P.L. 108-311. For sunset provisions, see P.L. 107-16, §901 [as amended by P.L. 111-312], P.L. 108-27, §107, and P.L. 108-311, §105, in the amendment notes.*

(i) RATE REDUCTIONS AFTER 2000.—

(1) 10-PERCENT RATE BRACKET.—

(A) IN GENERAL.—In the case of taxable years beginning after December 31, 2000—

(i) the rate of tax under subsections (a), (b), (c), and (d) on taxable income not over the initial bracket amount shall be 10 percent, and

(ii) the 15 percent rate of tax shall apply only to taxable income over the initial bracket amount but not over the maximum dollar amount for the 15-percent rate bracket.

(B) INITIAL BRACKET AMOUNT.—For purposes of this paragraph, the initial bracket amount is—

(i) $14,000 in the case of subsection (a),

(ii) $10,000 in the case of subsection (b), and

(iii) ½ the amount applicable under clause (i) (after adjustment, if any, under subparagraph (C)) in the case of subsections (c) and (d).

(C) INFLATION ADJUSTMENT.—In prescribing the tables under subsection (f) which apply with respect to taxable years beginning in calendar years after 2003—

(i) the cost-of-living adjustment shall be determined under subsection (f)(3) by substituting "2002" for "1992" in subparagraph (B) thereof, and

(ii) the adjustments under clause (i) shall not apply to the amount referred to in subparagraph (B)(iii).

If any amount after adjustment under the preceding sentence is not a multiple of $50, such amount shall be rounded to the next lowest multiple of $50.

(2) REDUCTIONS IN RATES AFTER JUNE 30, 2001.—In the case of taxable years beginning in a calendar year after 2000, the corresponding percentage specified for such calendar year in the following table shall be substituted for the otherwise applicable tax rate in the tables under subsections (a), (b), (c), (d), and (e).

In the case of taxable years beginning during calendar year:	The corresponding percentages shall be substituted for the following percentages:			
	28%	31%	36%	39.6%
2001	27.5%	30.5%	35.5%	39.1%
2002	27.0%	30.0%	35.0%	38.6%
2003 and thereafter	25.0%	28.0%	33.0%	35.0%

(3) ADJUSTMENT OF TABLES.—The Secretary shall adjust the tables prescribed under subsection (f) to carry out this subsection.

[CCH Explanation at ¶305. Committee Reports at ¶10,010.]

Amendments

• 2008, Economic Stimulus Act of 2008 (P.L. 110-185)

P.L. 110-185, §101(f)(2):

Amended Code Sec. 1(i)(1) by striking subparagraph (D). **Effective** 2-13-2008. Prior to being stricken, Code Sec. 1(i)(1)(D) read as follows:

(D) COORDINATION WITH ACCELERATION OF 10 PERCENT RATE BRACKET BENEFIT FOR 2001.—This paragraph shall not apply to any taxable year to which section 6428 applies.

• 2004, Working Families Tax Relief Act of 2004 (P.L. 108-311)

P.L. 108-311, §101(d)(1):

Amended Code Sec. 1(i)(1)(B)(i) by striking "($12,000 in the case of taxable years beginning after December 31, 2004, and before January 1, 2008)" following "$14,000". **Effective** for tax years beginning after 12-31-2003.

P.L. 108-311, §101(d)(2):

Amended Code Sec. 1(i)(1)(C). **Effective** for tax years beginning after 12-31-2003. Prior to amendment, Code Sec. 1(i)(1)(C) read as follows:

(C) INFLATION ADJUSTMENT.—In prescribing the tables under subsection (f) which apply with respect to taxable years beginning in calendar years after 2000—

(i) except as provided in clause (ii) the Secretary shall make no adjustment to the initial bracket amounts for any taxable year beginning before January 1, 2009,

(ii) there shall be an adjustment under subsection (f) of such amounts which shall apply only to taxable years beginning in 2004, and such adjustment shall be determined under subsection (f)(3) by substituting "2002" for "1992" in subparagraph (B) thereof,

(iii) the cost-of-living adjustment used in making adjustments to the initial bracket amounts for any taxable year beginning after December 31, 2008, shall be determined under subsection (f)(3) by substituting "2007" for "1992" in subparagraph (B) thereof, and

(iv) the adjustments under clauses (ii) and (iii) shall not apply to the amount referred to in subparagraph (B)(iii).

If any amount after adjustment under the preceding sentence is not a multiple of $50, such amount shall be rounded to the next lowest multiple of $50.

P.L. 108-311, §105, provides:

SEC. 105. APPLICATION OF EGTRRA SUNSET TO THIS TITLE.

Each amendment made by this title shall be subject to title IX of the Economic Growth and Tax Relief Reconciliation Act of 2001 to the same extent and in the same manner as the provision of such Act to which such amendment relates.

• 2003, Jobs and Growth Tax Relief Reconciliation Act of 2003 (P.L. 108-27)

P.L. 108-27, §104(a):

Amended Code Sec. 1(i)(1)(B)(i) by striking "($12,000 in the case of taxable years beginning before January 1, 2008)" and inserting "($12,000 in the case of taxable years beginning after December 31, 2004, and before January 1, 2008))". **Effective** for tax years beginning after 12-31-2002. For a special rule, see Act Sec. 104(c)(2), below.

P.L. 108-27, §104(b):

Amended Code Sec. 1(i)(1)(C). **Effective** for tax years beginning after 12-31-2002. For a special rule, see Act Sec. 104(c)(2), below. Prior to amendment, Code Sec. 1(i)(1)(C) read as follows:

(C) INFLATION ADJUSTMENT.—In prescribing the tables under subsection (f) which apply with respect to taxable years beginning in calendar years after 2000—

(i) the Secretary shall make no adjustment to the initial bracket amount for any taxable year beginning before January 1, 2009,

(ii) the cost-of-living adjustment used in making adjustments to the initial bracket amount for any taxable year beginning after December 31, 2008, shall be determined under subsection (f)(3) by substituting "2007" for "1992" in subparagraph (B) thereof, and

(iii) such adjustment shall not apply to the amount referred to in subparagraph (B)(iii).

If any amount after adjustment under the preceding sentence is not a multiple of $50, such amount shall be rounded to the next lowest multiple of $50.

P.L. 108-27, §104(c)(2), provides:

(2) TABLES FOR 2003.—The Secretary of the Treasury shall modify each table which has been prescribed under section 1(f) of the Internal Revenue Code of 1986 for taxable years beginning in 2003 and which relates to the amendment made by subsection (a) to reflect such amendment.

P.L. 108-27, §105(a):

Amended the table contained in Code Sec. 1(i)(2). **Effective** for tax years beginning after 12-31-2002. Prior to amendment, the table contained in Code Sec. 1(i)(2) read as follows:

In the case of taxable years beginning during calendar year:	The corresponding percentages shall be substituted for the following percentages:			
	28%	31%	36%	39.6%
2001	27.5%	30.5%	35.5%	39.1%
2002 and 2003	27.0%	30.0%	35.0%	38.6%
2004 and 2005	26.0%	29.0%	34.0%	37.6%
2006 and thereafter	25.0%	28.0%	33.0%	35.0%

P.L. 108-27, §107, provides:

SEC. 107. APPLICATION OF EGTRRA SUNSET TO THIS TITLE.

Each amendment made by this title shall be subject to title IX of the Economic Growth and Tax Relief Reconciliation Act of 2001 to the same extent and in the same manner as the provision of such Act to which such amendment relates.

• **2001, Economic Growth and Tax Relief Reconciliation Act of 2001 (P.L. 107-16)**

P.L. 107-16, §101(a):

Amended Code Sec. 1 by adding at the end a new subsection (i). **Effective** for tax years beginning after 12-31-2000.

P.L. 107-16, §901(a)-(b), as amended by P.L. 111-312, §101(a)(1), provides:

SEC. 901. SUNSET OF PROVISIONS OF ACT.

(a) IN GENERAL.—All provisions of, and amendments made by, this Act shall not apply—

(1) to taxable, plan, or limitation years beginning after December 31, 2012, or

(2) in the case of title V, to estates of decedents dying, gifts made, or generation skipping transfers, after December 31, 2012.

(b) APPLICATION OF CERTAIN LAWS.—The Internal Revenue Code of 1986 and the Employee Retirement Income Security Act of 1974 shall be applied and administered to years, estates, gifts, and transfers described in subsection (a) as if the provisions and amendments described in subsection (a) had never been enacted.

[¶5010] CODE SEC. 15. EFFECT OF CHANGES.

* * *

》》→ Caution: *Code Sec. 15(f), below, was added by P.L. 107-16. For sunset provision, see P.L. 107-16, §901 [as amended by P.L. 111-312], in the amendment notes.*

(f) RATE REDUCTIONS ENACTED BY ECONOMIC GROWTH AND TAX RELIEF RECONCILIATION ACT OF 2001.— This section shall not apply to any change in rates under subsection (i) of section 1 (relating to rate reductions after 2000).

[CCH Explanation at ¶305. Committee Reports at ¶10,010.]

Amendments

• **2001, Economic Growth and Tax Relief Reconciliation Act of 2001 (P.L. 107-16)**

P.L. 107-16, §101(c)(3):

Amended Code Sec. 15 by adding at the end a new subsection (f). **Effective** for tax years beginning after 12-31-2000.

P.L. 107-16, §901(a)-(b), as amended by P.L. 111-312, §101(a)(1), provides:

SEC. 901. SUNSET OF PROVISIONS OF ACT.

(a) IN GENERAL.—All provisions of, and amendments made by, this Act shall not apply—

(1) to taxable, plan, or limitation years beginning after December 31, 2012, or

(2) in the case of title V, to estates of decedents dying, gifts made, or generation skipping transfers, after December 31, 2012.

(b) APPLICATION OF CERTAIN LAWS.—The Internal Revenue Code of 1986 and the Employee Retirement Income Security Act of 1974 shall be applied and administered to years, estates, gifts, and transfers described in subsection (a) as if the provisions and amendments described in subsection (a) had never been enacted.

[¶5015] CODE SEC. 21. EXPENSES FOR HOUSEHOLD AND DEPENDENT CARE SERVICES NECESSARY FOR GAINFUL EMPLOYMENT.

(a) ALLOWANCE OF CREDIT.—

* * *

⮕ *Caution: Code Sec. 21(a)(2), below, was amended by P.L. 107-16. For sunset provision, see P.L. 107-16, §901 [as amended by P.L. 111-312], in the amendment notes.*

(2) APPLICABLE PERCENTAGE DEFINED.—For purposes of paragraph (1), the term "applicable percentage" means 35 percent reduced (but not below 20 percent) by 1 percentage point for each $2,000 (or fraction thereof) by which the taxpayer's adjusted gross income for the taxable year exceeds $15,000.

* * *

[CCH Explanation at ¶365. Committee Reports at ¶10,060 and ¶10,120.]

Amendments

• **2001, Economic Growth and Tax Relief Reconciliation Act of 2001 (P.L. 107-16)**

P.L. 107-16, §204(b)(1)-(2):

Amended Code Sec. 21(a)(2) by striking "30 percent" and inserting "35 percent", and by striking "$10,000" and inserting "$15,000". **Effective** for tax years beginning after 12-31-2002.

P.L. 107-16, §901(a)-(b), as amended by P.L. 111-312, §101(a)(1), provides:

SEC. 901. SUNSET OF PROVISIONS OF ACT.

(a) IN GENERAL.—All provisions of, and amendments made by, this Act shall not apply—

(1) to taxable, plan, or limitation years beginning after December 31, 2012, or

(2) in the case of title V, to estates of decedents dying, gifts made, or generation skipping transfers, after December 31, 2012.

(b) APPLICATION OF CERTAIN LAWS.—The Internal Revenue Code of 1986 and the Employee Retirement Income Security Act of 1974 shall be applied and administered to years, estates, gifts, and transfers described in subsection (a) as if the provisions and amendments described in subsection (a) had never been enacted.

⮕ *Caution: Code Sec. 21(c)(1)-(2), below, was amended by P.L. 107-16. For sunset provision, see P.L. 107-16, §901 [as amended by P.L. 111-312], in the amendment notes.*

(c) DOLLAR LIMIT ON AMOUNT CREDITABLE.—The amount of the employment-related expenses incurred during any taxable year which may be taken into account under subsection (a) shall not exceed—

(1) $3,000 if there is 1 qualifying individual with respect to the taxpayer for such taxable year, or

(2) $6,000 if there are 2 or more qualifying individuals with respect to the taxpayer for such taxable year.

The amount determined under paragraph (1) or (2) (whichever is applicable) shall be reduced by the aggregate amount excludable from gross income under section 129 for the taxable year.

[CCH Explanation at ¶365. Committee Reports at ¶10,060 and ¶10,120.]

Amendments

• **2001, Economic Growth and Tax Relief Reconciliation Act of 2001 (P.L. 107-16)**

P.L. 107-16, §204(a)(1)-(2):

Amended Code Sec. 21(c) by striking "$2,400" in paragraph (1) and inserting "$3,000", and by striking "$4,800" in paragraph (2) and inserting "$6,000". **Effective** for tax years beginning after 12-31-2002.

P.L. 107-16, §901(a)-(b), as amended by P.L. 111-312, §101(a)(1), provides:

SEC. 901. SUNSET OF PROVISIONS OF ACT.

(a) IN GENERAL.—All provisions of, and amendments made by, this Act shall not apply—

(1) to taxable, plan, or limitation years beginning after December 31, 2012, or

(2) in the case of title V, to estates of decedents dying, gifts made, or generation skipping transfers, after December 31, 2012.

(b) APPLICATION OF CERTAIN LAWS.—The Internal Revenue Code of 1986 and the Employee Retirement Income Security Act of 1974 shall be applied and administered to years, estates, gifts, and transfers described in subsection (a) as if the provisions and amendments described in subsection (a) had never been enacted.

(d) EARNED INCOME LIMITATION.—

* * *

>>>→ *Caution: Code Sec. 21(d)(2), below, was amended by P.L. 107-147. For sunset provision, see P.L. 107-16, §901 [as amended by P.L. 111-312], in the amendment notes.*

(2) SPECIAL RULE FOR SPOUSE WHO IS A STUDENT OR INCAPABLE OF CARING FOR HIMSELF.—In the case of a spouse who is a student or a qualified individual described in subsection (b)(1)(C), for purposes of paragraph (1), such spouse shall be deemed for each month during which such spouse is a full-time student at an educational institution, or is such a qualifying individual, to be gainfully employed and to have earned income of not less than—

(A) $250 if subsection (c)(1) applies for the taxable year, or

(B) $500 if subsection (c)(2) applies for the taxable year.

In the case of any husband and wife, this paragraph shall apply with respect to only one spouse for any one month.

* * *

[CCH Explanation at ¶365. Committee Reports at ¶10,060 and ¶10,120.]

Amendments

- **2002, Job Creation and Worker Assistance Act of 2002 (P.L. 107-147)**

P.L. 107-147, §418(b)(1)-(2):

Amended Code Sec. 21(d)(2) by striking "$200" and inserting "$250" in subparagraph (A), and by striking "$400" and inserting "$500" in subparagraph (B). **Effective** as if included in the provision of P.L. 107-16 to which it relates [**effective** for tax years beginning after 12-31-2002.—CCH].

- **2001, Economic Growth and Tax Relief Reconciliation Act of 2001 (P.L. 107-16)**

P.L. 107-16, §901(a)-(b), as amended by P.L. 111-312, §101(a)(1), provides:

SEC. 901. SUNSET OF PROVISIONS OF ACT.

(a) IN GENERAL.—All provisions of, and amendments made by, this Act shall not apply—

(1) to taxable, plan, or limitation years beginning after December 31, 2012, or

(2) in the case of title V, to estates of decedents dying, gifts made, or generation skipping transfers, after December 31, 2012.

(b) APPLICATION OF CERTAIN LAWS.—The Internal Revenue Code of 1986 and the Employee Retirement Income Security Act of 1974 shall be applied and administered to years, estates, gifts, and transfers described in subsection (a) as if the provisions and amendments described in subsection (a) had never been enacted.

[¶5025] CODE SEC. 24. CHILD TAX CREDIT.

>>>→ *Caution: Code Sec. 24(a), below, was amended by P.L. 107-16, P.L. 108-27 and P.L. 108-311. For sunset provisions, see P.L. 107-16, §901 [as amended by P.L. 111-312], P.L. 108-27, §107, and P.L. 108-311, §105, in the amendment notes.*

(a) ALLOWANCE OF CREDIT.—There shall be allowed as a credit against the tax imposed by this chapter for the taxable year with respect to each qualifying child of the taxpayer for which the taxpayer is allowed a deduction under section 151 an amount equal to $1,000.

[CCH Explanation at ¶360. Committee Reports at ¶10,060 and ¶10,120.]

Amendments

- **2004, Working Families Tax Relief Act of 2004 (P.L. 108-311)**

P.L. 108-311, §101(a):

Amended Code Sec. 24(a). **Effective** for tax years beginning after 12-31-2003. Prior to amendment, Code Sec. 24(a) read as follows:

(a) ALLOWANCE OF CREDIT.—

(1) IN GENERAL.—There shall be allowed as a credit against the tax imposed by this chapter for the taxable year with respect to each qualifying child of the taxpayer an amount equal to the per child amount.

(2) PER CHILD AMOUNT.—For purposes of paragraph (1), the per child amount shall be determined as follows:

In the case of any taxable year beginning in—	The per child amount is—
2003 or 2004	$1,000
2005, 2006, 2007, or 2008	700
2009	800
2010 or thereafter	1,000.

P.L. 108-311, §105, provides:

SEC. 105. APPLICATION OF EGTRRA SUNSET TO THIS TITLE.

Each amendment made by this title shall be subject to title IX of the Economic Growth and Tax Relief Reconciliation Act of 2001 to the same extent and in the same manner as the provision of such Act to which such amendment relates.

• **2003, Jobs and Growth Tax Relief Reconciliation Act of 2003 (P.L. 108-27)**

P.L. 108-27, § 101(a):

Amended the item related to calendar years 2001 through 2004 in the table contained in Code Sec. 24(a)(2). **Effective** for tax years beginning after 12-31-2002. Prior to amendment, the item related to calendar years 2001 through 2004 in the table contained in Code Sec. 24(a)(2) read as follows:

2001, 2002, 2003, or 2004 . . . . $600

P.L. 108-27, § 107, provides:

SEC. 107. APPLICATION OF EGTRRA SUNSET TO THIS TITLE.

Each amendment made by this title shall be subject to title IX of the Economic Growth and Tax Relief Reconciliation Act of 2001 to the same extent and in the same manner as the provision of such Act to which such amendment relates.

• **2001, Economic Growth and Tax Relief Reconciliation Act of 2001 (P.L. 107-16)**

P.L. 107-16, § 201(a):

Amended Code Sec. 24(a). **Effective** for tax years beginning after 12-31-2000. Prior to amendment, Code Sec. 24(a) read as follows:

(a) ALLOWANCE OF CREDIT.—There shall be allowed as a credit against the tax imposed by this chapter for the taxable year with respect to each qualifying child of the taxpayer an amount equal to $500 ($400 in the case of taxable years beginning in 1998).

P.L. 107-16, § 901(a)-(b), as amended by P.L. 111-312, § 101(a)(1), provides:

SEC. 901. SUNSET OF PROVISIONS OF ACT.

(a) IN GENERAL.—All provisions of, and amendments made by, this Act shall not apply—

(1) to taxable, plan, or limitation years beginning after December 31, 2012, or

(2) in the case of title V, to estates of decedents dying, gifts made, or generation skipping transfers, after December 31, 2012.

(b) APPLICATION OF CERTAIN LAWS.—The Internal Revenue Code of 1986 and the Employee Retirement Income Security Act of 1974 shall be applied and administered to years, estates, gifts, and transfers described in subsection (a) as if the provisions and amendments described in subsection (a) had never been enacted.

⇛→ Caution: The headings for Code Sec. 24(b) and Code Sec. 24(b)(1), below, were amended by P.L. 107-16. For sunset provision, see P.L. 107-16, § 901 [as amended by P.L. 111-312], in the amendment notes.

(b) LIMITATIONS.—

(1) LIMITATION BASED ON ADJUSTED GROSS INCOME.—The amount of the credit allowable under subsection (a) shall be reduced (but not below zero) by $50 for each $1,000 (or fraction thereof) by which the taxpayer's modified adjusted gross income exceeds the threshold amount. For purposes of the preceding sentence, the term "modified adjusted gross income" means adjusted gross income increased by any amount excluded from gross income under section 911, 931, or 933.

* * *

(3) LIMITATION BASED ON AMOUNT OF TAX.—In the case of a taxable year to which section 26(a)(2) does not apply, the credit allowed under subsection (a) for any taxable year shall not exceed the excess of—

(A) the sum of the regular tax liability (as defined in section 26(b)) plus the tax imposed by section 55, over

⇛→ Caution: Code Sec. 24(b)(3)(B), below, as amended P.L. 111-312, applies to tax years on or after December 31, 2011. For sunset provision, see P.L. 111-148, § 10909(c) [as amended by P.L. 111-312], in the amendment notes.

(B) the sum of the credits allowable under this subpart (other than this section and sections 23, 25A(i), 25B, 25D, 30, 30B, and 30D) and section 27 for the taxable year.

* * *

[CCH Explanation at ¶ 360 and ¶ 370. Committee Reports at ¶ 10,030, ¶ 10,060 and ¶ 10,120.]

Amendments

- **2010, Tax Relief, Unemployment Insurance Reauthorization, and Job Creation Act of 2010 (P.L. 111-312)**

P.L. 111-312, § 101(b)(1):

Amended Code Sec. 24(b)(3)(B) to read as such provision would read if section 10909 of the Patient Protection and Affordable Care Act (P.L. 111-148) had never been enacted. **Effective** for tax years beginning after 12-31-2011.

- **2010, Patient Protection and Affordable Care Act (P.L. 111-148)**

P.L. 111-148, § 10909(b)(2)(A):

Amended Code Sec. 24(b)(3)(B) by striking "23," before "25A(i)". **Effective** for tax years beginning after 12-31-2009.

P.L. 111-148, § 10909(c), as amended by P.L. 111-312, § 101(b)(1), provides:

(c) SUNSET PROVISION.—Each provision of law amended by this section is amended to read as such provision would read if this section had never been enacted. The amendments made by the preceding sentence shall apply to taxable years beginning after December 31, 2011.

- **2001, Economic Growth and Tax Relief Reconciliation Act of 2001 (P.L. 107-16)**

P.L. 107-16, § 201(b)(1):

Amended Code Sec. 24(b) by adding at the end a new paragraph (3). **Effective** for tax years beginning after 12-31-2001. [But, see P.L. 107-147, § 601(b)(2), and P.L. 108-311, § 312(b)(2), above.—CCH.]

P.L. 107-16, § 201(b)(2)(A):

Amended the heading for Code Sec. 24(b). **Effective** for tax years beginning after 12-31-2001. [But, see P.L. 107-147, § 601(b)(2), and P.L. 108-311, § 312(b)(2), above.—CCH.] Prior to amendment, the heading for Code Sec. 24(b) read as follows:

LIMITATION BASED ON ADJUSTED GROSS INCOME.—

P.L. 107-16, § 201(b)(2)(B):

Amended the heading for Code Sec. 24(b)(1). **Effective** for tax years beginning after 12-31-2001. [But, see P.L. 107-147,

§ 601(b)(2), and P.L. 108-311, § 312(b)(2), above.—CCH.] Prior to amendment, the heading for Code Sec. 24(b)(1) read as follows:

IN GENERAL.—

P.L. 107-16, § 202(f)(2)(B):

Amended Code Sec. 24(b)(3)(B), as added by Act Sec. 201(b), by striking "this section" and inserting "this section and section 23". **Effective** for tax years beginning after 12-31-2001. [But, see P.L. 107-147, § 601(b)(2), and P.L. 108-311, § 312(b)(2), above.—CCH.]

P.L. 107-16, § 618(b)(2)(A) (as amended by P.L. 107-147, § 417(23)(A)):

Amended Code Sec. 24(b)(3)(B), as amended by Act Secs. 201(b) [added by Act Sec. 201(b)(1)] and 202(f), by striking "section 23" and inserting "sections 23 and 25B". **Effective** for tax years beginning after 12-31-2001. [But, see P.L. 107-147, § 601(b)(2), and P.L. 108-311, § 312(b)(2), above.—CCH.]

P.L. 107-16, § 901(a)-(b), as amended by P.L. 111-312, § 101(a)(1), provides [but see P.L. 109-280, § 811, and P.L. 111-148, § 10909(c), above]:

SEC. 901. SUNSET OF PROVISIONS OF ACT.

(a) IN GENERAL.—All provisions of, and amendments made by, this Act shall not apply—

(1) to taxable, plan, or limitation years beginning after December 31, 2012, or

(2) in the case of title V, to estates of decedents dying, gifts made, or generation skipping transfers, after December 31, 2012.

(b) APPLICATION OF CERTAIN LAWS.—The Internal Revenue Code of 1986 and the Employee Retirement Income Security Act of 1974 shall be applied and administered to years, estates, gifts, and transfers described in subsection (a) as if the provisions and amendments described in subsection (a) had never been enacted.

(d) PORTION OF CREDIT REFUNDABLE.—

⧉→ *Caution: Code Sec. 24(d)(1), below, was amended by P.L. 109-135. For sunset provision, see P.L. 109-135, § 402(i)(3)(H), in the amendment notes.*

(1) IN GENERAL.—The aggregate credits allowed to a taxpayer under subpart C shall be increased by the lesser of—

(A) the credit which would be allowed under this section without regard to this subsection and the limitation under section 26(a)(2) or subsection (b)(3), as the case may be, or

(B) the amount by which the aggregate amount of credits allowed by this subpart (determined without regard to this subsection) would increase if the limitation imposed by section 26(a)(2) or subsection (b)(3), as the case may be, were increased by the greater of—

(i) 15 percent of so much of the taxpayer's earned income (within the meaning of section 32) which is taken into account in computing taxable income for the taxable year as exceeds $10,000, or

(ii) in the case of a taxpayer with 3 or more qualifying children, the excess (if any) of—

(I) the taxpayer's social security taxes for the taxable year, over

(II) the credit allowed under section 32 for the taxable year.

The amount of the credit allowed under this subsection shall not be treated as a credit allowed under this subpart and shall reduce the amount of credit otherwise allowable under subsection (a) without regard to section 26(a)(2) or subsection (b)(3), as the case may be. For purposes of subparagraph (B), any amount excluded from gross income by reason of section 112 shall be treated as earned income which is taken into account in computing taxable income for the taxable year.

»»→ *Caution: Code Sec. 24(d)(2) was stricken by P.L. 107-16. For sunset provision, see P.L. 107-16, §901 [as amended by P.L. 111-312], in the amendment notes.*

(2) [Stricken.]

»»→ *Caution: Former Code Sec. 24(d)(3) was redesignated as Code Sec. 24(d)(2), below, by P.L. 107-16. For sunset provision, see P.L. 107-16, §901 [as amended by P.L. 111-312], in the amendment notes.*

(2) SOCIAL SECURITY TAXES.—For purposes of paragraph (1)—

(A) IN GENERAL.—The term "social security taxes" means, with respect to any taxpayer for any taxable year—

(i) the amount of the taxes imposed by sections 3101 and 3201(a) on amounts received by the taxpayer during the calendar year in which the taxable year begins,

(ii) 50 percent of the taxes imposed by section 1401 on the self-employment income of the taxpayer for the taxable year, and

(iii) 50 percent of the taxes imposed by section 3211(a) on amounts received by the taxpayer during the calendar year in which the taxable year begins.

(B) COORDINATION WITH SPECIAL REFUND OF SOCIAL SECURITY TAXES.—The term "social security taxes" shall not include any taxes to the extent the taxpayer is entitled to a special refund of such taxes under section 6413(c).

(C) SPECIAL RULE.—Any amounts paid pursuant to an agreement under section 3121(l) (relating to agreements entered into by American employers with respect to foreign affiliates) which are equivalent to the taxes referred to in subparagraph (A)(i) shall be treated as taxes referred to in such subparagraph.

* * *

(4) SPECIAL RULE FOR *2009, 2010, 2011 AND 2012.*—Notwithstanding paragraph (3), in the case of any taxable year beginning in 2009, *2010, 2011, or 2012,* the dollar amount in effect for such taxable year under paragraph (1)(B)(i) shall be $3,000.

* * *

[CCH Explanation at ¶360. Committee Reports at ¶10,030 and ¶10,120.]

Amendments

• **2010, Tax Relief, Unemployment Insurance Reauthorization, and Job Creation Act of 2010 (P.L. 111-312)**

P.L. 111-312, §103(b)(1)-(2):

Amended Code Sec. 24(d)(4) by striking "2009 AND 2010" in the heading and inserting "2009, 2010, 2011, AND 2012", and by striking "or 2010" and inserting ", 2010, 2011, or 2012". Effective for tax years beginning after 12-31-2010.

• **2005, Gulf Opportunity Zone Act of 2005 (P.L. 109-135)**

P.L. 109-135, §402(i)(3)(B)(ii):

Amended Code Sec. 24(d)(1). Effective for tax years beginning after 12-31-2005. Prior to amendment, Code Sec. 24(d)(1) read as follows:

(1) IN GENERAL.—The aggregate credits allowed to a taxpayer under subpart C shall be increased by the lesser of—

(A) the credit which would be allowed under this section without regard to this subsection and the limitation under subsection (b)(3), or

(B) the amount by which the aggregate amount of credits allowed by this subpart (determined without regard to this subsection) would increase if the limitation imposed by subsection (b)(3) were increased by the greater of—

(i) 15 percent of so much of the taxpayer's earned income (within the meaning of section 32) which is taken into account in computing taxable income for the taxable year as exceeds $10,000, or

(ii) in the case of a taxpayer with 3 or more qualifying children, the excess (if any) of—

(I) the taxpayer's social security taxes for the taxable year, over

(II) the credit allowed under section 32 for the taxable year.

The amount of the credit allowed under this subsection shall not be treated as a credit allowed under this subpart and shall reduce the amount of credit otherwise allowable under subsection (a) without regard to subsection (b)(3). For purposes of subparagraph (B), any amount excluded from gross income by reason of section 112 shall be treated as earned income which is taken into account in computing taxable income for the taxable year.

P.L. 109-135, §402(i)(3)(H), provides:

(H) APPLICATION OF EGTRRA SUNSET.—The amendments made by this paragraph (and each part thereof) shall be subject to title IX of the Economic Growth and Tax Relief Reconciliation Act of 2001 in the same manner as the provisions of such Act to which such amendment (or part thereof) relates.

• 2001, Economic Growth and Tax Relief Reconciliation Act of 2001 (P.L. 107-16)

P.L. 107-16, §201(b)(2)(C)(i)-(ii):

Amended Code Sec. 24(d), as amended by Act Sec. 201(c), by striking "section 26(a)" each place it appears and inserting "subsection (b)(3)", and in paragraph (1)(B) by striking "aggregate amount of credits allowed by this subpart" and inserting "amount of credit allowed by this section". [Note: The second part of this amendment was already made by Act Sec. 201(c)(1), applicable to tax years beginning after 12-31-2000.—CCH.] **Effective** for tax years beginning after 12-31-2001. [But, see P.L. 107-147, §601(b)(2), and P.L. 108-311, §312(b)(2), above.—CCH.]

P.L. 107-16, §201(c)(1):

Amended so much of Code Sec. 24(d) as precedes paragraph (2). **Effective** for tax years beginning after 12-31-2000. Prior to amendment, so much of Code Sec. 24(d) as preceded paragraph (2) read as follows:

(d) ADDITIONAL CREDIT FOR FAMILIES WITH 3 OR MORE CHILDREN.—

(1) IN GENERAL.—In the case of a taxpayer with three or more qualifying children for any taxable year, the aggregate credits allowed under subpart C shall be increased by the lesser of—

(A) the credit which would be allowed under this section without regard to this subsection and the limitation under section 26(a); or

(B) the amount by which the aggregate amount of credits allowed by this subpart (without regard to this subsection) would increase if the limitation imposed by section 26(a) were increased by the excess (if any) of—

(i) the taxpayer's social security taxes for the taxable year, over

(ii) the credit allowed under section 32 (determined without regard to subsection (n)) for the taxable year.

The amount of the credit allowed under this subsection shall not be treated as a credit allowed under this subpart and

shall reduce the amount of credit otherwise allowable under subsection (a) without regard to section 26(a).

P.L. 107-16, §201(c)(2):

Amended Code Sec. 24(d) by adding at the end a new paragraph (4). **Effective** for tax years beginning after 12-31-2000.

P.L. 107-16, §201(d)(1)-(2):

Amended Code Sec. 24(d) by striking paragraph (2) and by redesignating paragraphs (3) and (4) as paragraphs (2) and (3), respectively. **Effective** for tax years beginning after 12-31-2000. Prior to being stricken, Code Sec. 24(d)(2) read as follows:

(2) REDUCTION OF CREDIT TO TAXPAYER SUBJECT TO ALTERNATIVE MINIMUM TAX.—For taxable years beginning after December 31, 2001, the credit determined under this subsection for the taxable year shall be reduced by the excess (if any) of—

(A) the amount of tax imposed by section 55 (relating to alternative minimum tax) with respect to such taxpayer for such taxable year, over

(B) the amount of the reduction under section 32(h) with respect to such taxpayer for such taxable year.

P.L. 107-16, §203, provides:

SEC. 203. REFUNDS DISREGARDED IN THE ADMINISTRATION OF FEDERAL PROGRAMS AND FEDERALLY ASSISTED PROGRAMS.

Any payment considered to have been made to any individual by reason of section 24 of the Internal Revenue Code of 1986, as amended by section 201, shall not be taken into account as income and shall not be taken into account as resources for the month of receipt and the following month, for purposes of determining the eligibility of such individual or any other individual for benefits or assistance, or the amount or extent of benefits or assistance, under any Federal program or under any State or local program financed in whole or in part with Federal funds.

P.L. 107-16, §901(a)-(b) [as amended by P.L. 111-312, §101(a)(1)], provides:

SEC. 901. SUNSET OF PROVISIONS OF ACT.

(a) IN GENERAL.—All provisions of, and amendments made by, this Act shall not apply—

(1) to taxable, plan, or limitation years beginning after December 31, 2012, or

(2) in the case of title V, to estates of decedents dying, gifts made, or generation skipping transfers, after December 31, 2012.

(b) APPLICATION OF CERTAIN LAWS.—The Internal Revenue Code of 1986 and the Employee Retirement Income Security Act of 1974 shall be applied and administered to years, estates, gifts, and transfers described in subsection (a) as if the provisions and amendments described in subsection (a) had never been enacted.

[¶5030] CODE SEC. 25. INTEREST ON CERTAIN HOME MORTGAGES.

* * *

(e) SPECIAL RULES AND DEFINITIONS.—For purposes of this section—

(1) CARRYFORWARD OF UNUSED CREDIT.—

* * *

≫→ *Caution: Code Sec. 25(e)(1)(C), below, was amended by P.L. 107-16, P.L. 109-135, and P.L. 111-148. For sunset provisions, see P.L. 107-16, §901 [as amended by P.L. 111-312], P.L. 109-135, §402(i)(3)(H), and P.L. 111-148, §10909(c) [as amended by P.L. 111-312], in the amendment notes.*

(C) APPLICABLE TAX LIMIT.—For purposes of this paragraph, the term "applicable tax limit" means—

(i) in the case of a taxable year to which section 26(a)(2) applies, the limitation imposed by section 26(a)(2) for the taxable year reduced by the sum of the credits allowable under this subpart (other than this section and sections 23, 25D, and 1400C), and

(ii) in the case of a taxable year to which section 26(a)(2) does not apply, the limitation imposed by section 26(a)(1) for the taxable year reduced by the sum of the credits allowable under this subpart (other than this section and sections 23, 24, 25A(i), 25B, 25D, 30, 30B, 30D, and 1400C).

* * *

[CCH Explanation at ¶370. Committee Reports at ¶10,030 and ¶10,060.]

Amendments

• **2010, Tax Relief, Unemployment Insurance Reauthorization, and Job Creation Act of 2010 (P.L. 111-312)**

P.L. 111-312, §101(b)(1):

Amended Code Sec. 25(e)(1)(C) to read as such provision would read if section 10909 of the Patient Protection and Affordable Care Act (P.L. 111-148) had never been enacted. **Effective** for tax years beginning after 12-31-2011.

• **2010, Patient Protection and Affordable Care Act (P.L. 111-148)**

P.L. 111-148, §10909(b)(2)(B):

Amended Code Sec. 25(e)(1)(C) by striking "23," after "other than this section and sections" both places it appears. **Effective** for tax years beginning after 12-31-2009.

P.L. 111-148, §10909(c), as amended by P.L. 111-312, §101(b)(1), provides:

(c) SUNSET PROVISION.—Each provision of law amended by this section is amended to read as such provision would read if this section had never been enacted. The amendments made by the preceding sentence shall apply to taxable years beginning after December 31, 2011.

[¶5035] CODE SEC. 25A. HOPE AND LIFETIME LEARNING CREDITS.

* * *

≫→ *Caution: Code Sec. 25A(e), below, was amended by P.L. 107-16. For sunset provision, see P.L. 107-16, §901 [as amended by P.L. 111-312], in the amendment notes.*

(e) ELECTION NOT TO HAVE SECTION APPLY.—A taxpayer may elect not to have this section apply with respect to the qualified tuition and related expenses of an individual for any taxable year.

* * *

[CCH Explanation at ¶370. Committee Reports at ¶10,060 and ¶10,120.]

Amendments

• **2001, Economic Growth and Tax Relief Reconciliation Act of 2001 (P.L. 107-16)**

P.L. 107-16, §401(g)(2)(A):

Amended Code Sec. 25A(e). **Effective** for tax years beginning after 12-31-2001. Prior to amendment, Code Sec. 25A(e) read as follows:

(e) ELECTION TO HAVE SECTION APPLY.—

(1) IN GENERAL.—No credit shall be allowed under subsection (a) for a taxable year with respect to the qualified tuition and related expenses of an individual unless the taxpayer elects to have this section apply with respect to such individual for such year.

(2) COORDINATION WITH EXCLUSIONS.—An election under this subsection shall not take effect with respect to an individual for any taxable year if any portion of any distribution during such taxable year from an education individual retirement account is excluded from gross income under section 530(d)(2).

P.L. 107-16, §901(a)-(b), as amended by P.L. 111-312, §101(a)(1), provides:

SEC. 901. SUNSET OF PROVISIONS OF ACT.

(a) IN GENERAL.—All provisions of, and amendments made by, this Act shall not apply—

(1) to taxable, plan, or limitation years beginning after December 31, 2012, or

(2) in the case of title V, to estates of decedents dying, gifts made, or generation skipping transfers, after December 31, 2012.

(b) APPLICATION OF CERTAIN LAWS.—The Internal Revenue Code of 1986 and the Employee Retirement Income Security Act of 1974 shall be applied and administered to years, estates, gifts, and transfers described in subsection (a) as if the provisions and amendments described in subsection (a) had never been enacted.

(i) AMERICAN OPPORTUNITY TAX CREDIT.—In the case of any taxable year beginning in 2009, *2010, 2011, or 2012—*

(1) INCREASE IN CREDIT.—The Hope Scholarship Credit shall be an amount equal to the sum of—

(A) 100 percent of so much of the qualified tuition and related expenses paid by the taxpayer during the taxable year (for education furnished to the eligible student during any academic period beginning in such taxable year) as does not exceed $2,000, plus

(B) 25 percent of such expenses so paid as exceeds $2,000 but does not exceed $4,000.

(2) CREDIT ALLOWED FOR FIRST 4 YEARS OF POST-SECONDARY EDUCATION.—Subparagraphs (A) and (C) of subsection (b)(2) shall be applied by substituting "4" for "2".

(3) QUALIFIED TUITION AND RELATED EXPENSES TO INCLUDE REQUIRED COURSE MATERIALS.—Subsection (f)(1)(A) shall be applied by substituting "tuition, fees, and course materials" for "tuition and fees".

(4) INCREASE IN AGI LIMITS FOR HOPE SCHOLARSHIP CREDIT.—In lieu of applying subsection (d) with respect to the Hope Scholarship Credit, such credit (determined without regard to this paragraph) shall be reduced (but not below zero) by the amount which bears the same ratio to such credit (as so determined) as—

(A) the excess of—

(i) the taxpayer's modified adjusted gross income (as defined in subsection (d)(3)) for such taxable year, over

(ii) $80,000 ($160,000 in the case of a joint return), bears to

(B) $10,000 ($20,000 in the case of a joint return).

(5) CREDIT ALLOWED AGAINST ALTERNATIVE MINIMUM TAX.—In the case of a taxable year to which section 26(a)(2) does not apply, so much of the credit allowed under subsection (a) as is attributable to the Hope Scholarship Credit shall not exceed the excess of—

(A) the sum of the regular tax liability (as defined in section 26(b)) plus the tax imposed by section 55, over

>>>→ *Caution: Code Sec. 25A(i)(5)(B), below, as amended by P.L. 111-312, applies to tax years beginning after December 31, 2011. For sunset provision, see P.L. 111-148, §10909(c) [as amended by P.L. 111-312], in the amendment notes.*

(B) the sum of the credits allowable under this subpart (other than this subsection and sections 23, 25D, and 30D) and section 27 for the taxable year.

Any reference in this section or section 24, 25, 26, 25B, 904, or 1400C to a credit allowable under this subsection shall be treated as a reference to so much of the credit allowable under subsection (a) as is attributable to the Hope Scholarship Credit.

(6) PORTION OF CREDIT MADE REFUNDABLE.—40 percent of so much of the credit allowed under subsection (a) as is attributable to the Hope Scholarship Credit (determined after application of paragraph (4) and without regard to this paragraph and section 26(a)(2) or paragraph (5), as the case may be) shall be treated as a credit allowable under subpart C (and not allowed under subsection (a)). The preceding sentence shall not apply to any taxpayer for any taxable year if such taxpayer is a child to whom subsection (g) of section 1 applies for such taxable year.

(7) COORDINATION WITH MIDWESTERN DISASTER AREA BENEFITS.—In the case of a taxpayer with respect to whom section 702(a)(1)(B) of the Heartland Disaster Tax Relief Act of 2008 applies for any taxable year, such taxpayer may elect to waive the application of this subsection to such taxpayer for such taxable year.

* * *

[CCH Explanation at ¶370. Committee Reports at ¶10,060, ¶10,090 and ¶10,120.]

Amendments

- **2010, Tax Relief, Unemployment Insurance Reauthorization, and Job Creation Act of 2010 (P.L. 111-312)**

P.L. 111-312, §101(b)(1):

Amended Code Sec. 25A(i)(5)(B) to read as such provision would read if section 10909 of the Patient Protection and Affordable Care Act (P.L. 111-148) had never been enacted. **Effective** for tax years beginning after 12-31-2011.

P.L. 111-312, §103(a)(1):

Amended Code Sec. 25A(i) by striking "or 2010" and inserting ", 2010, 2011, or 2012". **Effective** for tax years beginning after 12-31-2010.

- **2010, Patient Protection and Affordable Care Act (P.L. 111-148)**

P.L. 111-148, §10909(b)(2)(C):

Amended Code Sec. 25A(i)(5)(B) by striking "23, 25D," and inserting "25D". **Effective** for tax years beginning after 12-31-2009.

P.L. 111-148, §10909(c), as amended by P.L. 111-312, §101(b)(1), provides:

(c) SUNSET PROVISION.—Each provision of law amended by this section is amended to read as such provision would read if this section had never been enacted. The amendments made by the preceding sentence shall apply to taxable years beginning after December 31, 2011.

[¶5037] CODE SEC. 25B. ELECTIVE DEFERRALS AND IRA CONTRIBUTIONS BY CERTAIN INDIVIDUALS.

* * *

(g) LIMITATION BASED ON AMOUNT OF TAX.—In the case of a taxable year to which section 26(a)(2) does not apply, the credit allowed under subsection (a) for the taxable year shall not exceed the excess of—

* * *

⟫→ Caution: *Code Sec. 25B(g)(2), below, as amended by P.L. 111-312, applies to tax year beginning after December 31, 2011. For sunset provision, see P.L. 111-148, §10909(c) [as amended by P.L. 111-312], in the amendment notes.*

(2) the sum of the credits allowable under this subpart (other than this section and sections 23, 25A(i), 25D, 30, 30B, and 30D) and section 27 for the taxable year.

[Committee Reports at ¶10,060.]

Amendments

- **2010, Tax Relief, Unemployment Insurance Reauthorization, and Job Creation Act of 2010 (P.L. 111-312)**

P.L. 111-312, §101(b)(1):

Amended Code Sec. 25B(g)(2) to read as such provision would read if section 10909 of the Patient Protection and Affordable Care Act (P.L. 111-148) had never been enacted. **Effective** for tax years beginning after 12-31-2011.

- **2010, Patient Protection and Affordable Care Act (P.L. 111-148)**

P.L. 111-148, §10909(b)(2)(D):

Amended Code Sec. 25B(g)(2) by striking "23," before "25A(i)". **Effective** for tax years beginning after 12-31-2009.

P.L. 111-148, §10909(c), as amended by P.L. 111-312, §101(b)(1), provides:

(c) SUNSET PROVISION..—Each provision of law amended by this section is amended to read as such provision would read if this section had never been enacted. The amendments made by the preceding sentence shall apply to taxable years beginning after December 31, 2011.

[¶5040] CODE SEC. 25C. NONBUSINESS ENERGY PROPERTY.

(a) ALLOWANCE OF CREDIT.—*In the case of an individual, there shall be allowed as a credit against the tax imposed by this chapter for the taxable year an amount equal to the sum of—*

(1) 10 percent of the amount paid or incurred by the taxpayer for qualified energy efficiency improvements installed during such taxable year, and

(2) the amount of the residential energy property expenditures paid or incurred by the taxpayer during such taxable year.

[CCH Explanation at ¶372. Committee Reports at ¶10,120 and ¶10,260.]

Amendments

- **2010, Tax Relief, Unemployment Insurance Reauthorization, and Job Creation Act of 2010 (P.L. 111-312)**

P.L. 111-312, §710(b)(1):

Amended Code Sec. 25C(a). **Effective** for property placed in service after 12-31-2010. Prior to amendment, Code Sec. 25C(a) read as follows:

(a) ALLOWANCE OF CREDIT.—In the case of an individual, there shall be allowed as a credit against the tax imposed by this chapter for the taxable year an amount equal to 30 percent of the sum of—

(1) the amount paid or incurred by the taxpayer during such taxable year for qualified energy efficiency improvements, and

(2) the amount of the residential energy property expenditures paid or incurred by the taxpayer during such taxable year.

(b) LIMITATIONS.—

(1) LIFETIME LIMITATION.—The credit allowed under this section with respect to any taxpayer for any taxable year shall not exceed the excess (if any) of $500 over the aggregate credits allowed under this section with respect to such taxpayer for all prior taxable years ending after December 31, 2005.

(2) WINDOWS.—In the case of amounts paid or incurred for components described in subsection (c)(2)(B) by any taxpayer for any taxable year, the credit allowed under this section with respect to such amounts for such year shall not exceed the excess (if any) of $200 over the aggregate credits allowed under this section with respect to such amounts for all prior taxable years ending after December 31, 2005.

(3) LIMITATION ON RESIDENTIAL ENERGY PROPERTY EXPENDITURES.—The amount of the credit allowed under this section by reason of subsection (a)(2) shall not exceed—

(A) $50 for any advanced main air circulating fan,

(B) $150 for any qualified natural gas, propane, or oil furnace or hot water boiler, and

(C) $300 for any item of energy-efficient building property.

[CCH Explanation at ¶372. Committee Reports at ¶10,120 and ¶10,260.]

Amendments

- **2010, Tax Relief, Unemployment Insurance Reauthorization, and Job Creation Act of 2010 (P.L. 111-312)**

P.L. 111-312, §710(b)(1):

Amended Code Sec. 25C(b). **Effective** for property placed in service after 12-31-2010. Prior to amendment, Code Sec. 25C(b) read as follows:

(b) LIMITATION.—The aggregate amount of the credits allowed under this section for taxable years beginning in 2009 and 2010 with respect to any taxpayer shall not exceed $1,500.

(c) QUALIFIED ENERGY EFFICIENCY IMPROVEMENTS.—For purposes of this section—

(1) IN GENERAL.—The term "qualified energy efficiency improvements" means any energy efficient building envelope component which meets the prescriptive criteria for such component established by the 2009 International Energy Conservation Code, as such Code (including supplements) is in effect on the date of the enactment of the American Recovery and Reinvestment Tax Act of 2009 (or, in the case of an exterior window, a skylight, an exterior door, a metal roof with appropriate pigmented coatings, or an asphalt roof with appropriate cooling granules, which meet the Energy Star program requirements), if—

(A) such component is installed in or on a dwelling unit located in the United States and owned and used by the taxpayer as the taxpayer's principal residence (within the meaning of section 121),

(B) the original use of such component commences with the taxpayer, and

(C) such component reasonably can be expected to remain in use for at least 5 years.

(2) BUILDING ENVELOPE COMPONENT.—The term "building envelope component" means—

(A) any insulation material or system which is specifically and primarily designed to reduce the heat loss or gain of a dwelling unit when installed in or on such dwelling unit,

(B) exterior windows (including skylights),

(C) exterior doors, and

(D) any metal roof or asphalt roof installed on a dwelling unit, but only if such roof has appropriate pigmented coatings or cooling granules which are specifically and primarily designed to reduce the heat gain of such dwelling unit.

* * *

(4) [*Stricken.*]

[CCH Explanation at ¶372. Committee Reports at ¶10,120 and ¶10,260.]

Amendments

- **2010, Tax Relief, Unemployment Insurance Reauthorization, and Job Creation Act of 2010 (P.L. 111-312)**

P.L. 111-312, §710(b)(2)(A):

Amended Code Sec. 25C(c)(1) by striking "2000" and all that follows through "this section" and inserting "2009 International Energy Conservation Code, as such Code (including supplements) is in effect on the date of the enactment of the American Recovery and Reinvestment Tax Act of 2009". **Effective** for property placed in service after 12-31-2010. Prior to being stricken, "2000" and all that followed through "this section" in Code Sec. 25C(c)(1) read as follows:

2000 International Energy Conservation Code, as such Code (including supplements) is in effect on the date of the enactment of this section

P.L. 111-312, §710(b)(2)(D)(i):

Amended Code Sec. 25C(c) by striking paragraph (4). **Effective** for property placed in service after 12-31-2010. Prior to being stricken, Code Sec. 25C(c)(4) read as follows:

(4) QUALIFICATIONS FOR EXTERIOR WINDOWS, DOORS, AND SKYLIGHTS.—Such term shall not include any component described in subparagraph (B) or (C) of paragraph (2) unless such component is equal to or below a U factor of 0.30 and SHGC of 0.30.

P.L. 111-312, §710(b)(2)(D)(ii):

Amended Code Sec. 25C(c)(1) by inserting "an exterior window, a skylight, an exterior door," after "in the case of" in the matter preceding subparagraph (A). **Effective** for property placed in service after 12-31-2010.

P.L. 111-312, §710(b)(2)(E):

Amended Code Sec. 25C(c)(2)(A) by striking "and meets the prescriptive criteria for such material or system established by the 2009 International Energy Conservation Code, as such Code (including supplements) is in effect on the date of the enactment of the American Recovery and Reinvestment Tax Act of 2009" before the comma at the end. **Effective** for property placed in service after 12-31-2010.

(d) RESIDENTIAL ENERGY PROPERTY EXPENDITURES.—For purposes of this section—

* * *

(2) QUALIFIED ENERGY PROPERTY.—

(A) IN GENERAL.—The term "qualified energy property" means—

* * *

(ii) a qualified natural gas, propane, or oil furnace or hot water boiler, or

* * *

(3) ENERGY-EFFICIENT BUILDING PROPERTY.—The term "energy-efficient building property" means—

* * *

(E) a stove which uses the burning of biomass fuel to heat a dwelling unit located in the United States and used as a residence by the taxpayer, or to heat water for use in such a dwelling unit, and which has a thermal efficiency rating of at least 75 percent.

(4) QUALIFIED NATURAL GAS, PROPANE, OR OIL FURNACE OR HOT WATER BOILER.—*The term "qualified natural gas, propane, or oil furnace or hot water boiler" means a natural gas, propane, or oil furnace or hot water boiler which achieves an annual fuel utilization efficiency rate of not less than 95.*

* * *

[CCH Explanation at ¶372. Committee Reports at ¶10,120 and ¶10,260.]

Amendments

- **2010, Tax Relief, Unemployment Insurance Reauthorization, and Job Creation Act of 2010 (P.L. 111-312)**

P.L. 111-312, §710(b)(2)(B):

Amended Code Sec. 25C(d)(3)(E) by striking ", as measured using a lower heating value" before the period at the

end. **Effective** for property placed in service after 12-31-2010.

P.L. 111-312, §710(b)(2)(C)(i):

Amended Code Sec. 25C(d)(4). **Effective** for property placed in service after 12-31-2010. Prior to amendment, Code Sec. 25C(d)(4) read as follows:

(4) QUALIFIED NATURAL GAS, PROPANE, AND OIL FURNACES AND HOT WATER BOILERS.—

(A) QUALIFIED NATURAL GAS FURNACE.—The term "qualified natural gas furnace" means any natural gas furnace which achieves an annual fuel utilization efficiency rate of not less than 95.

(B) QUALIFIED NATURAL GAS HOT WATER BOILER.—The term "qualified natural gas hot water boiler" means any natural gas hot water boiler which achieves an annual fuel utilization efficiency rate of not less than 90.

(C) QUALIFIED PROPANE FURNACE.—The term "qualified propane furnace" means any propane furnace which achieves an annual fuel utilization efficiency rate of not less than 95.

(D) QUALIFIED PROPANE HOT WATER BOILER.—The term "qualified propane hot water boiler" means any propane hot water boiler which achieves an annual fuel utilization efficiency rate of not less than 90.

(E) QUALIFIED OIL FURNACES.—The term "qualified oil furnace" means any oil furnace which achieves an annual fuel utilization efficiency rate of not less than 90.

(F) QUALIFIED OIL HOT WATER BOILER.—The term "qualified oil hot water boiler" means any oil hot water boiler which achieves an annual fuel utilization efficiency rate of not less than 90.

P.L. 111-312, §710(b)(2)(C)(ii):

Amended Code Sec. 25C(d)(2)(A)(ii). **Effective** for property placed in service after 12-31-2010. Prior to amendment, Code Sec. 25C(d)(2)(A)(ii) read as follows:

(ii) any qualified natural gas furnace, qualified propane furnace, qualified oil furnace, qualified natural gas hot water boiler, qualified propane hot water boiler, or qualified oil hot water boiler, or

(e) SPECIAL RULES.—For purposes of this section—

* * *

(3) *PROPERTY FINANCED BY SUBSIDIZED ENERGY FINANCING.—For purposes of determining the amount of expenditures made by any individual with respect to any property, there shall not be taken into account expenditures which are made from subsidized energy financing (as defined in section 48(a)(4)(C)).*

* * *

[CCH Explanation at ¶372. Committee Reports at ¶10,120 and ¶10,260.]
Amendments
- 2010, Tax Relief, Unemployment Insurance Reauthorization, and Job Creation Act of 2010 (P.L. 111-312)

P.L. 111-312, §710(b)(3):

Amended Code Sec. 25C(e) by adding at the end a new paragraph (3). **Effective** for property placed in service after 12-31-2010.

(g) TERMINATION.—This section shall not apply with respect to any property placed in service—

(1) after December 31, 2007, and before January 1, 2009, or

(2) after December 31, *2011.*

[CCH Explanation at ¶372. Committee Reports at ¶10,120 and ¶10,260.]
Amendments
- 2010, Tax Relief, Unemployment Insurance Reauthorization, and Job Creation Act of 2010 (P.L. 111-312)

P.L. 111-312, §710(a):

Amended Code Sec. 25C(g)(2) by striking "2010" and inserting "2011". **Effective** for property placed in service after 12-31-2010.

[¶5045] CODE SEC. 25D. RESIDENTIAL ENERGY EFFICIENT PROPERTY.

* * *

⟫→ *Caution: Code Sec. 25D(c), below, was amended by P.L. 109-135 and P.L. 110-343. For sunset provision, see P.L. 107-16, §901 [as amended by P.L. 111-312, §101(a)(1)], in the amendment notes.*

(c) LIMITATION BASED ON AMOUNT OF TAX; CARRYFORWARD OF UNUSED CREDIT.—

(1) LIMITATION BASED ON AMOUNT OF TAX.—In the case of a taxable year to which section 26(a)(2) does not apply, the credit allowed under subsection (a) for the taxable year shall not exceed the excess of—

(A) the sum of the regular tax liability (as defined in section 26(b)) plus the tax imposed by section 55, over

(B) the sum of the credits allowable under this subpart (other than this section) and section 27 for the taxable year.

(2) CARRYFORWARD OF UNUSED CREDIT.—

(A) RULE FOR YEARS IN WHICH ALL PERSONAL CREDITS ALLOWED AGAINST REGULAR AND ALTERNATIVE MINIMUM TAX.—In the case of a taxable year to which section 26(a)(2) applies, if the credit allowable under subsection (a) exceeds the limitation imposed by section 26(a)(2) for such taxable year reduced by the sum of the credits allowable under this subpart (other than this section), such excess shall be carried to the succeeding taxable year and added to the credit allowable under subsection (a) for such succeeding taxable year.

(B) RULE FOR OTHER YEARS.—In the case of a taxable year to which section 26(a)(2) does not apply, if the credit allowable under subsection (a) exceeds the limitation imposed by paragraph (1) for such taxable year, such excess shall be carried to the succeeding taxable year and added to the credit allowable under subsection (a) for such succeeding taxable year.

* * *

Amendments

● **2008, Energy Improvement and Extension Act of 2008 (P.L. 110-343)**

P.L. 110-343, Division B, §106(e)(1):

Amended Code Sec. 25D(c). **Effective** for tax years beginning after 12-31-2007. Prior to amendment, Code Sec. 25D(c) read as follows:

(c) CARRYFORWARD OF UNUSED CREDIT.—

(1) RULE FOR YEARS IN WHICH ALL PERSONAL CREDITS ALLOWED AGAINST REGULAR AND ALTERNATIVE MINIMUM TAX.—In the case of a taxable year to which section 26(a)(2) applies, if the credit allowable under subsection (a) exceeds the limitation imposed by section 26(a)(2) for such taxable year reduced by the sum of the credits allowable under this subpart (other than this section), such excess shall be carried to the succeeding taxable year and added to the credit allowable under subsection (a) for such succeeding taxable year.

(2) RULE FOR OTHER YEARS.—In the case of a taxable year to which section 26(a)(2) does not apply, if the credit allowable under subsection (a) exceeds the limitation imposed by section 26(a)(1) for such taxable year reduced by the sum of the credits allowable under this subpart (other than this section and sections 23, 24, and 25B), such excess shall be carried to the succeeding taxable year and added to the credit allowable under subsection (a) for such succeeding taxable year.

● **2005, Gulf Opportunity Zone Act of 2005 (P.L. 109-135)**

P.L. 109-135, §402(i)(3)(E):

Amended Code Sec. 25D(c). **Effective** for tax years beginning after 12-31-2005. Prior to amendment, Code Sec. 25D(c) read as follows:

(c) CARRYFORWARD OF UNUSED CREDIT.—If the credit allowable under subsection (a) exceeds the limitation imposed by section 26(a) for such taxable year reduced by the sum of the credits allowable under this subpart (other than this section), such excess shall be carried to the succeeding taxable year and added to the credit allowable under subsection (a) for such succeeding taxable year.

P.L. 109-135, §402(i)(3)(H), provides:

(H) APPLICATION OF EGTRRA SUNSET.—The amendments made by this paragraph (and each part thereof) shall be subject to title IX of the Economic Growth and Tax Relief Reconciliation Act of 2001 in the same manner as the provisions of such Act to which such amendment (or part thereof) relates.

● **2001, Economic Growth and Tax Relief Reconciliation Act of 2001 (P.L. 107-16)**

P.L. 107-16 §901(a)-(b), as amended by P.L. 111-312, §101(a)(1), provides:

SEC. 901. SUNSET OF PROVISIONS OF ACT.

(a) IN GENERAL.—All provisions of, and amendments made by, this Act shall not apply—

(1) to taxable, plan, or limitation years beginning after December 31, 2012, or

(2) in the case of title V, to estates of decedents dying, gifts made, or generation skipping transfers, after December 31, 2012.

(b) APPLICATION OF CERTAIN LAWS.—The Internal Revenue Code of 1986 and the Employee Retirement Income Security Act of 1974 shall be applied and administered to years, estates, gifts, and transfers described in subsection (a) as if the provisions and amendments described in subsection (a) had never been enacted.

[¶ 5050] CODE SEC. 26. LIMITATION BASED ON TAX LIABILITY; DEFINITION OF TAX LIABILITY.

(a) LIMITATION BASED ON AMOUNT OF TAX.—

⋙→ *Caution: Code Sec. 26(a)(1), below, as amended by P.L. 111-312, applies to tax years beginning after December 31, 2011. For sunset provision, see P.L. 111-148, §10909(c) [as amended by P.L. 111-312], in the amendment notes.*

(1) IN GENERAL.—The aggregate amount of credits allowed by this subpart (other than sections 23, 24, 25A(i), 25B, 25D, 30, 30B, and 30D) for the taxable year shall not exceed the excess (if any) of—

(A) the taxpayer's regular tax liability for the taxable year, over

(B) the tentative minimum tax for the taxable year (determined without regard to the alternative minimum tax foreign tax credit).

For purposes of subparagraph (B), the taxpayer's tentative minimum tax for any taxable year beginning during 1999 shall be treated as being zero.

(2) SPECIAL RULE FOR TAXABLE YEARS 2000 THROUGH 2011.—For purposes of any taxable year beginning during 2000, 2001, 2002, 2003, 2004, 2005, 2006, 2007, 2008, 2009, 2010, or 2011, the aggregate amount of credits allowed by this subpart for the taxable year shall not exceed the sum of—

(A) the taxpayer's regular tax liability for the taxable year reduced by the foreign tax credit allowable under section 27(a), and

(B) the tax imposed by section 55(a) for the taxable year.

* * *

[CCH Explanation at ¶ 360, ¶ 375 and ¶ 376. Committee Reports at ¶ 10,030, ¶ 10,060 and ¶ 10,120.]

Amendments

• **2010, Tax Relief, Unemployment Insurance Reauthorization, and Job Creation Act of 2010 (P.L. 111-312)**

P.L. 111-312, §101(b)(1):

Amended Code Sec. 26(a)(1) to read as such provision would read if section 10909 of the Patient Protection and Affordable Care Act (P.L. 111-148) had never been enacted. Effective for tax years beginning after 12-31-2011.

P.L. 111-312, §202(a)(1)–(2):

Amended Code Sec. 26(a)(2) by striking "or 2009" and inserting "2009, 2010, or 2011", and by striking "2009" in the heading thereof and inserting "2011". Effective for tax years beginning after 12-31-2009.

• **2010, Patient Protection and Affordable Care Act (P.L. 111-148)**

P.L. 111-148, §10909(b)(2)(E):

Amended Code Sec. 26(a)(1) by striking "23," before "24". Effective for tax years beginning after 12-31-2009.

P.L. 111-148, §10909(c), as amended by P.L. 111-312, §101(b)(1), provides:

(c) SUNSET PROVISION.—Each provision of law amended by this section is amended to read as such provision would read if this section had never been enacted. The amendments made by the preceding sentence shall apply to taxable years beginning after December 31, 2011.

[¶ 5055] CODE SEC. 30. CERTAIN PLUG-IN ELECTRIC VEHICLES.

* * *

(c) APPLICATION WITH OTHER CREDITS.—

* * *

(2) PERSONAL CREDIT.—

* * *

(B) LIMITATION BASED ON AMOUNT OF TAX.—In the case of a taxable year to which section 26(a)(2) does not apply, the credit allowed under subsection (a) for any taxable year (determined after application of paragraph (1)) shall not exceed the excess of—

(i) the sum of the regular tax liability (as defined in section 26(b)) plus the tax imposed by section 55, over

⫸→ *Caution: Code Sec. 30(c)(2)(B)(ii), below, as amended by P.L. 111-312, applies to tax years after December 31, 2011. For sunset provision, see P.L. 111-148, §10909(c) [as amended by P.L. 111-312], in the amendment notes.*

(ii) the sum of the credits allowable under subpart A (other than this section and sections 23, 25D, and 30D) and section 27 for the taxable year.

[CCH Explanation at ¶370. Committee Reports at ¶10,060.]

Amendments

• **2010, Tax Relief, Unemployment Insurance Reauthorization, and Job Creation Act of 2010 (P.L. 111-312)**

P.L. 111-312, §101(b)(1):

Amended Code Sec. 30(c)(2)(B)(ii) to read as such provision would read if section 10909 of the Patient Protection and Affordable Care Act (P.L. 111-148) had never been enacted. **Effective** for tax years beginning after 12-31-2011.

• **2010, Patient Protection and Affordable Care Act (P.L. 111-148)**

P.L. 111-148, §10909(b)(2)(F):

Amended Code Sec. 30(c)(2)(B)(ii) by striking "23, 25D," and inserting "25D". **Effective** for tax years beginning after 12-31-2009.

P.L. 111-148, §10909(c), as amended by P.L. 111-312, §101(b)(1), provides:

(c) SUNSET PROVISION.—Each provision of law amended by this section is amended to read as such provision would read if this section had never been enacted. The amendments made by the preceding sentence shall apply to taxable years beginning after December 31, 2011.

[¶5060] CODE SEC. 30B. ALTERNATIVE MOTOR VEHICLE CREDIT.

* * *

(g) APPLICATION WITH OTHER CREDITS.—

* * *

(2) PERSONAL CREDIT.—

* * *

(B) LIMITATION BASED ON AMOUNT OF TAX.—In the case of a taxable year to which section 26(a)(2) does not apply, the credit allowed under subsection (a) for any taxable year (determined after application of paragraph (1)) shall not exceed the excess of—

* * *

⫸→ *Caution: Code Sec. 30B(g)(2)(B)(ii), as amended by P.L. 111-312, applies to tax years after December 31, 2011. For sunset provision, see P.L. 111-148, §10909(c) [as amended by P.L. 111-312], in the amendment notes.*

(ii) the sum of the credits allowable under subpart A (other than this section and sections 23, 25D, 30, and 30D) and section 27 for the taxable year.

[CCH Explanation at ¶370. Committee Reports at ¶10,060.]

Amendments

• **2010, Tax Relief, Unemployment Insurance Reauthorization, and Job Creation Act of 2010 (P.L. 111-312)**

P.L. 111-312, §101(b)(1):

Amended Code Sec. 30B(g)(2)(B)(ii) to read as such provision would read if section 10909 of the Patient Protection and Affordable Care Act (P.L. 111-148) had never been enacted. **Effective** for tax years beginning after 12-31-2011.

• **2010, Patient Protection and Affordable Care Act (P.L. 111-148)**

P.L. 111-148, §10909(b)(2)(G):

Amended Code Sec. 30B(g)(2)(B)(ii) by striking "23," before "25D". **Effective** for tax years beginning after 12-31-2009.

P.L. 111-148, §10909(c), as amended by P.L. 111-312, §101(b)(1), provides:

(c) SUNSET PROVISION.—Each provision of law amended by this section is amended to read as such provision would read if this section had never been enacted. The amendments made by the preceding sentence shall apply to taxable years beginning after December 31, 2011.

[¶5065] CODE SEC. 30C. ALTERNATIVE FUEL VEHICLE REFUELING PROPERTY CREDIT.

* * *

(g) TERMINATION.—This section shall not apply to any property placed in service—

(1) in the case of property relating to hydrogen, after December 31, 2014, and

(2) in the case of any other property, after *December 31, 2011.*[sic].

[CCH Explanation at ¶548. Committee Reports at ¶10,270.]

Amendments

● **2010, Tax Relief, Unemployment Insurance Reauthorization, and Job Creation Act of 2010 (P.L. 111-312)**

P.L. 111-312, §711(a):

Amended Code Sec. 30C(g)(2) by striking "December 31, 2010" and inserting "December 31, 2011," [sic]. **Effective for** property placed in service after 12-31-2010.

[¶5070] CODE SEC. 30D. NEW QUALIFIED PLUG-IN ELECTRIC DRIVE MOTOR VEHICLES.

* * *

(c) APPLICATION WITH OTHER CREDITS.—

* * *

(2) PERSONAL CREDIT.—

* * *

(B) LIMITATION BASED ON AMOUNT OF TAX.—In the case of a taxable year to which section 26(a)(2) does not apply, the credit allowed under subsection (a) for any taxable year (determined after application of paragraph (1)) shall not exceed the excess of—

(i) the sum of the regular tax liability (as defined in section 26(b)) plus the tax imposed by section 55, over

⋙→ *Caution: Code Sec. 30D(c)(2)(B)(ii), below, as amended P.L. 111-312, applies to tax years after December 31, 2011. For sunset provision, see P.L. 111-148, §10909(c) [as amended by P.L. 111-312], in the amendment notes.*

(ii) the sum of the credits allowable under subpart A (other than this section and *sections 23 and* 25D) and section 27 for the taxable year.

[CCH Explanation at ¶370. Committee Reports at ¶10,060.]

Amendments

● **2010, Tax Relief, Unemployment Insurance Reauthorization, and Job Creation Act of 2010 (P.L. 111-312)**

P.L. 111-312, §101(b)(1):

Amended Code Sec. 30D(c)(2)(B)(ii) to read as such provision would read if section 10909 of the Patient Protection and Affordable Care Act (P.L. 111-148) had never been enacted. **Effective** for tax years beginning after 12-31-2011.

● **2010, Patient Protection and Affordable Care Act (P.L. 111-148)**

P.L. 111-148, §10909(b)(2)(H):

Amended Code Sec. 30D(c)(2)(B)(ii) by striking "sections 23 and" and inserting "section". **Effective** for tax years beginning after 12-31-2009.

P.L. 111-148, §10909(c), as amended by P.L. 111-312, §101(b)(1), provides:

(c) SUNSET PROVISION.—Each provision of law amended by this section is amended to read as such provision would read if this section had never been enacted. The amendments made by the preceding sentence shall apply to taxable years beginning after December 31, 2011.

[¶ 5075] CODE SEC. 32. EARNED INCOME.

(a) ALLOWANCE OF CREDIT.—

* * *

(2) LIMITATION.—The amount of the credit allowable to a taxpayer under paragraph (1) for any taxable year shall not exceed the excess (if any) of—

(A) the credit percentage of the earned income amount, over

»»→ *Caution: Code Sec. 32(a)(2)(B), below, was amended by P.L. 107-16. For sunset provision, see P.L. 107-16, §901 [as amended by P.L. 111-312], in the amendment notes.*

(B) the phaseout percentage of so much of the adjusted gross income (or, if greater, the earned income) of the taxpayer for the taxable year as exceeds the phaseout amount.

[CCH Explanation at ¶ 355. Committee Reports at ¶ 10,040 and ¶ 10,110.]

Amendments

• 2001, Economic Growth and Tax Relief Reconciliation Act of 2001 (P.L. 107-16)

P.L. 107-16, §303(d)(1):

Amended Code Sec. 32(a)(2)(B) by striking "modified" before "adjusted gross income". **Effective** for tax years beginning after 12-31-2001.

P.L. 107-16, §901(a)-(b), as amended by P.L. 111-312, §101(a)(1), provides:

SEC. 901. SUNSET OF PROVISIONS OF ACT.

(a) IN GENERAL.—All provisions of, and amendments made by, this Act shall not apply—

(1) to taxable, plan, or limitation years beginning after December 31, 2012, or

(2) in the case of title V, to estates of decedents dying, gifts made, or generation skipping transfers, after December 31, 2012.

(b) APPLICATION OF CERTAIN LAWS.—The Internal Revenue Code of 1986 and the Employee Retirement Income Security Act of 1974 shall be applied and administered to years, estates, gifts, and transfers described in subsection (a) as if the provisions and amendments described in subsection (a) had never been enacted.

(b) PERCENTAGES AND AMOUNTS.—For purposes of subsection (a)—

»»→ *Caution: Code Sec. 32(b)(2), below, was amended by P.L. 107-16. For sunset provision, see P.L. 107-16, §901 [as amended by P.L. 111-312], in the amendment notes.*

(2) AMOUNTS.—

(A) IN GENERAL.—Subject to subparagraph (B), the earned income amount and the phaseout amount shall be determined as follows:

In the case of an eligible individual with:	The earned income amount is:	The phaseout amount is:
1 qualifying child	$6,330	$11,610
2 or more qualifying children	$8,890	$11,610
No qualifying children	$4,220	$ 5,280

(B) JOINT RETURNS.—In the case of a joint return filed by an eligible individual and such individual's spouse, the phaseout amount determined under subparagraph (A) shall be increased by—

(i) $1,000 in the case of taxable years beginning in 2002, 2003, and 2004,

(ii) $2,000 in the case of taxable years beginning in 2005, 2006, and 2007, and

(iii) $3,000 in the case of taxable years beginning after 2007.

(3) SPECIAL RULES FOR *2009, 2010, 2011, AND 2012.*—In the case of any taxable year beginning in 2009 , *2010, 2011, or 2012*—

(A) INCREASED CREDIT PERCENTAGE FOR 3 OR MORE QUALIFYING CHILDREN.—In the case of a taxpayer with 3 or more qualifying children, the credit percentage is 45 percent.

(B) REDUCTION OF MARRIAGE PENALTY.—

(i) IN GENERAL.—The dollar amount in effect under paragraph (2)(B) shall be $5,000.

(ii) INFLATION ADJUSTMENT.—In the case of any taxable year beginning in 2010, the $5,000 amount in clause (i) shall be increased by an amount equal to—

(I) such dollar amount, multiplied by

(II) the cost of living adjustment determined under section 1(f)(3) for the calendar year in which the taxable year begins determined by substituting "calendar year 2008" for "calendar year 1992" in subparagraph (B) thereof.

(iii) ROUNDING.—Subparagraph (A) of subsection (j)(2) shall apply after taking into account any increase under clause (ii).

[CCH Explanation at ¶356. Committee Reports at ¶10,040 and ¶10,110.]

Amendments

- **2010, Tax Relief, Unemployment Insurance Reauthorization, and Job Creation Act of 2010 (P.L. 111-312)**

P.L. 111-312, §103(c)(1)-(2):

Amended Code Sec. 32(b)(3) by striking "2009 AND 2010" in the heading and inserting "2009, 2010, 2011, AND 2012", and by striking "or 2010" and inserting ", 2010, 2011, or 2012". **Effective** for tax years beginning after 12-31-2010.

- **2001, Economic Growth and Tax Relief Reconciliation Act of 2001 (P.L. 107-16)**

P.L. 107-16, §303(a)(1)(A)-(B):

Amended Code Sec. 32(b)(2). **Effective** for tax years beginning after 12-31-2001. Prior to amendment, Code Sec. 32(b)(2) read as follows:

(2) AMOUNTS.—The earned income amount and the phaseout amount shall be determined as follows:

In the case of an eligible individual with:	The earned income amount is:	The phaseout amount is:
1 qualifying child	$6,330	$11,610
2 or more qualifying children	$8,890	$11,610
No qualifying children	$4,220	$5,280

P.L. 107-16, §901(a)-(b) [as amended by P.L. 111-312, §101(a)(1)], provides:

SEC. 901. SUNSET OF PROVISIONS OF ACT.

(a) IN GENERAL.—All provisions of, and amendments made by, this Act shall not apply—

(1) to taxable, plan, or limitation years beginning after December 31, 2012, or

(2) in the case of title V, to estates of decedents dying, gifts made, or generation skipping transfers, after December 31, 2012.

(b) APPLICATION OF CERTAIN LAWS.—The Internal Revenue Code of 1986 and the Employee Retirement Income Security Act of 1974 shall be applied and administered to years, estates, gifts, and transfers described in subsection (a) as if the provisions and amendments described in subsection (a) had never been enacted.

(c) DEFINITIONS AND SPECIAL RULES.—For purposes of this section—

(1) ELIGIBLE INDIVIDUAL.—

* * *

(C) EXCEPTION FOR INDIVIDUAL CLAIMING BENEFITS UNDER SECTION 911.—The term "eligible individual" does not include any individual who claims the benefits of section 911 (relating to citizens or residents living abroad) for the taxable year.

* * *

(2) EARNED INCOME.—

(A) The term "earned income" means—

»»→ Caution: *Code Sec. 32(c)(2)(A)(i), below, was amended by P.L. 107-16. For sunset provision, see P.L. 107-16, §901 [as amended by P.L. 111-312], in the amendment notes.*

(i) wages, salaries, tips, and other employee compensation, but only if such amounts are includible in gross income for the taxable year, plus

(ii) the amount of the taxpayer's net earnings from self-employment for the taxable year (within the meaning of section 1402(a)), but such net earnings shall be determined with regard to the deduction allowed to the taxpayer by section 164(f).

(3) QUALIFYING CHILD.—

(A) IN GENERAL.—The term "qualifying child" means a qualifying child of the taxpayer (as defined in section 152(c), determined without regard to paragraph (1)(D) thereof and section 152(e)).

(B) MARRIED INDIVIDUAL.—The term "qualifying child" shall not include an individual who is married as of the close of the taxpayer's taxable year unless the taxpayer is entitled to a deduction under section 151 for such taxable year with respect to such individual (or would be so entitled but for section 152(e)).

(C) Place of Abode.—For purposes of subparagraph (A), the requirements of section 152(c)(1)(B) shall be met only if the principal place of abode is in the United States.

(D) Identification Requirements.—

(i) In General.—A qualifying child shall not be taken into account under subsection (b) unless the taxpayer includes the name, age, and TIN of the qualifying child on the return of tax for the taxable year.

(ii) Other Methods.—The Secretary may prescribe other methods for providing the information described in clause (i).

* * *

➽➔ *Caution: Code Sec. 32(c)(5), below, was stricken by P.L. 107-16. For sunset provision, see P.L. 107-16, §901 [as amended by P.L. 111-312], in the amendment notes.*

(5) [Stricken.]

* * *

[CCH Explanation at ¶355. Committee Reports at ¶10,040 and ¶10,110.]

Amendments

• 2004, Working Families Tax Relief Act of 2004 (P.L. 108-311)

P.L. 108-311, §205(a):

Amended Code Sec. 32(c)(3). **Effective** for tax years beginning after 12-31-2004. Prior to amendment, Code Sec. 32(c)(3) read as follows:

(3) Qualifying Child.—

(A) In General.—The term "qualifying child" means, with respect to any taxpayer for any taxable year, an individual—

(i) who bears a relationship to the taxpayer described in subparagraph (B),

(ii) who has the same principal place of abode as the taxpayer for more than one-half of such taxable year, and

(iii) who meets the age requirements of subparagraph (C).

(B) Relationship Test.—

(i) In General.—An individual bears a relationship to the taxpayer described in this subparagraph if such individual is—

(I) a son, daughter, stepson, or stepdaughter, or a descendant of any such individual,

(II) a brother, sister, stepbrother, or stepsister, or a descendant of any such individual, who the taxpayer cares for as the taxpayer's own child, or

(III) an eligible foster child of the taxpayer.

(ii) Married Children.—Clause (i) shall not apply to any individual who is married as of the close of the taxpayer's taxable year unless the taxpayer is entitled to a deduction under section 151 for such taxable year with respect to such individual (or would be so entitled but for paragraph (2) or (4) of section 152(e)).

(iii) Eligible Foster Child.—For purposes of clause (i), the term "eligible foster child" means an individual not described in subclause (I) or (II) of clause (i) who—

(I) is placed with the taxpayer by an authorized placement agency, and

(II) the taxpayer cares for as the taxpayer's own child.

(iv) Adoption.—For purposes of this subparagraph, a child who is legally adopted, or who is placed with the taxpayer by an authorized placement agency for adoption by the taxpayer, shall be treated as a child by blood.

(C) Age Requirements.—An individual meets the requirements of this subparagraph if such individual—

(i) has not attained the age of 19 as of the close of the calendar year in which the taxable year of the taxpayer begins,

(ii) is a student (as defined in section 151(c)(4)) who has not attained the age of 24 as of the close of such calendar year, or

(iii) is permanently and totally disabled (as defined in section 22(e)(3)) at any time during the taxable year.

(D) Identification Requirements.—

(i) In General.—A qualifying child shall not be taken into account under subsection (b) unless the taxpayer includes the name, age, and TIN of the qualifying child on the return of tax for the taxable year.

(ii) Other Methods.—The Secretary may prescribe other methods for providing the information described in clause (i).

(E) Abode Must Be In The United States.—The requirements of subparagraph (A)(ii) shall be met only if the principal place of abode is in the United States.

P.L. 108-311, §205(b)(1):

Amended Code Sec. 32(c)(1) by striking subparagraph (C) and by redesignating subparagraphs (D), (E), (F), and (G) as subparagraphs (C), (D), (E), and (F), respectively. **Effective** for tax years beginning after 12-31-2004. Prior to being stricken, Code Sec. 32(c)(1)(C) read as follows:

(C) 2 or More Claiming Qualifying Child.—

(i) In General.—Except as provided in clause (ii), if (but for this paragraph) an individual may be claimed, and is claimed, as a qualifying child by 2 or more taxpayers for a taxable year beginning in the same calendar year, such individual shall be treated as the qualifying child of the taxpayer who is—

(I) a parent of the individual, or

(II) if subclause (I) does not apply, the taxpayer with the highest adjusted gross income for such taxable year.

(ii) More Than 1 Claiming Credit.—If the parents claiming the credit with respect to any qualifying child do not file a joint return together, such child shall be treated as the qualifying child of—

(I) the parent with whom the child resided for the longest period of time during the taxable year, or

(II) if the child resides with both parents for the same amount of time during such taxable year, the parent with the highest adjusted gross income.

• 2001, Economic Growth and Tax Relief Reconciliation Act of 2001 (P.L. 107-16)

P.L. 107-16, § 303(b):

Amended Code Sec. 32(c)(2)(A)(i) by inserting ", but only if such amounts are includible in gross income for the taxable year" after "other employee compensation". **Effective** for tax years beginning after 12-31-2001.

P.L. 107-16, § 303(d)(2)(A):

Amended Code Sec. 32(c) by striking paragraph (5). **Effective** for tax years beginning after 12-31-2001. Prior to being stricken, Code Sec. 32(c)(5) read as follows:

(5) MODIFIED ADJUSTED GROSS INCOME.—

(A) IN GENERAL.—The term "modified adjusted gross income" means adjusted gross income determined without regard to the amounts described in subparagraph (B) and increased by the amounts described in subparagraph (C).

(B) CERTAIN AMOUNTS DISREGARDED.—An amount is described in this subparagraph if it is—

(i) the amount of losses from sales or exchanges of capital assets in excess of gains from such sales or exchanges to the extent such amount does not exceed the amount under section 1211(b)(1),

(ii) the net loss from estates and trusts,

(iii) the excess (if any) of amounts described in subsection (i)(2)(C)(ii) over the amounts described in subsection (i)(2)(C)(i) (relating to nonbusiness rents and royalties), or

(iv) 75 percent of the net loss from the carrying on of trades or businesses, computed separately with respect to—

(I) trades or businesses (other than farming) conducted as sole proprietorships,

(II) trades or businesses of farming conducted as sole proprietorships, and

(III) other trades or businesses.

For purposes of clause (iv), there shall not be taken into account items which are attributable to a trade or business which consists of the performance of services by the taxpayer as an employee.

(C) CERTAIN AMOUNTS INCLUDED.—An amount is described in this subparagraph if it is—

(i) interest received or accrued during the taxable year which is exempt from tax imposed by this chapter; or

(ii) amounts received as a pension or annuity, and any distributions or payments received from an individual retirement plan, by the taxpayer during the taxable year to the extent not included in gross income.

Clause (ii) shall not include any amount which is not includible in gross income by reason of a trustee-to-trustee transfer or a rollover distribution.

P.L. 107-16, § 303(e)(1):

Amended Code Sec. 32(c)(3)(B)(i). **Effective** for tax years beginning after 12-31-2001. Prior to amendment, Code Sec. 32(c)(3)(B)(i) read as follows:

(i) IN GENERAL.—An individual bears a relationship to the taxpayer described in this subparagraph if such individual is—

(I) a son or daughter of the taxpayer, or a descendant of either,

(II) a stepson or stepdaughter of the taxpayer, or

(III) an eligible foster child of the taxpayer.

P.L. 107-16, § 303(e)(2)(A):

Amended Code Sec. 32(c)(3)(B)(iii). **Effective** for tax years beginning after 12-31-2001. Prior to amendment, Code Sec. 32(c)(3)(B)(iii) read as follows:

(iii) ELIGIBLE FOSTER CHILD.—For purposes of clause (i)(III), the term "eligible foster child" means an individual not described in clause (i)(I) or (II) who—

(I) is a brother, sister, stepbrother, or stepsister of the taxpayer (or a descendant of any such relative) or is placed with the taxpayer by an authorized placement agency,

(II) the taxpayer cares for as the taxpayer's own child, and

(III) has the same principal place of abode as the taxpayer for the taxpayer's entire taxable year.

P.L. 107-16, § 303(e)(2)(B):

Amended Code Sec. 32(c)(3)(A)(ii) by striking "except as provided in subparagraph (B)(iii)," before "who has the". **Effective** for tax years beginning after 12-31-2001.

P.L. 107-16, § 303(f):

Amended Code Sec. 32(c)(1)(C). **Effective** for tax years beginning after 12-31-2001. Prior to amendment, Code Sec. 32(c)(1)(C) read as follows:

(C) 2 OR MORE ELIGIBLE INDIVIDUALS.—If 2 or more individuals would (but for this subparagraph and after application of subparagraph (B)) be treated as eligible individuals with respect to the same qualifying child for taxable years beginning in the same calendar year, only the individual with the highest modified adjusted gross income for such taxable years shall be treated as an eligible individual with respect to such qualifying child.

P.L. 107-16, § 303(h):

Amended Code Sec. 32(c)(3)(E) by striking "subparagraphs (A)(ii) and (B)(iii)(II)" and inserting "subparagraph (A)(ii)". **Effective** for tax years beginning after 12-31-2001.

P.L. 107-16, § 901(a)-(b), as amended by P.L. 111-312, § 101(a)(1), provides:

SEC. 901. SUNSET OF PROVISIONS OF ACT.

(a) IN GENERAL.—All provisions of, and amendments made by, this Act shall not apply—

(1) to taxable, plan, or limitation years beginning after December 31, 2012, or

(2) in the case of title V, to estates of decedents dying, gifts made, or generation skipping transfers, after December 31, 2012.

(b) APPLICATION OF CERTAIN LAWS.—The Internal Revenue Code of 1986 and the Employee Retirement Income Security Act of 1974 shall be applied and administered to years, estates, gifts, and transfers described in subsection (a) as if the provisions and amendments described in subsection (a) had never been enacted.

(f) Amount of Credit To Be Determined Under Tables.—

* * *

(2) Requirements for tables.—The tables prescribed under paragraph (1) shall reflect the provisions of subsections (a) and (b) and shall have income brackets of not greater than $50 each—

(A) for earned income between $0 and the amount of earned income at which the credit is phased out under subsection (b), and

»»→ *Caution: Code Sec. 32(f)(2)(B), below, was amended by P.L. 107-16. For sunset provision, see P.L. 107-16, §901 [as amended by P.L. 111-312], in the amendment notes.*

(B) for adjusted gross income between the dollar amount at which the phaseout begins under subsection (b) and the amount of adjusted gross income at which the credit is phased out under subsection (b).

* * *

[CCH Explanation at ¶355. Committee Reports at ¶10,040 and ¶10,110.]

Amendments

• **2001, Economic Growth and Tax Relief Reconciliation Act of 2001 (P.L. 107-16)**

P.L. 107-16, §303(d)(2)(B):

Amended Code Sec. 32(f)(2)(B) by striking "modified" each place it appears. **Effective** for tax years beginning after 12-31-2001. Prior to amendment, Code Sec. 32(f)(2)(B) read as follows:

(B) for modified adjusted gross income between the dollar amount at which the phaseout begins under subsection (b) and the amount of modified adjusted gross income at which the credit is phased out under subsection (b).

P.L. 107-16, §901(a)-(b), as amended by P.L. 111-312, §101(a)(1), provides:

SEC. 901. SUNSET OF PROVISIONS OF ACT.

(a) In General.—All provisions of, and amendments made by, this Act shall not apply—

(h) [Repealed.]

(1) to taxable, plan, or limitation years beginning after December 31, 2012, or

(2) in the case of title V, to estates of decedents dying, gifts made, or generation skipping transfers, after December 31, 2012.

(b) Application of Certain Laws.—The Internal Revenue Code of 1986 and the Employee Retirement Income Security Act of 1974 shall be applied and administered to years, estates, gifts, and transfers described in subsection (a) as if the provisions and amendments described in subsection (a) had never been enacted.

* * *

[CCH Explanation at ¶355. Committee Reports at ¶10,040 and ¶10,110.]

Amendments

• **2001, Economic Growth and Tax Relief Reconciliation Act of 2001 (P.L. 107-16)**

P.L. 107-16, §303(c):

Repealed Code Sec. 32(h). **Effective** for tax years beginning after 12-31-2001. Prior to repeal, Code Sec. 32(h) read as follows:

(h) Reduction of Credit to Taxpayers Subject to Alternative Minimum Tax.—The credit allowed under this section for the taxable year shall be reduced by the amount of tax imposed by section 55 (relating to alternative minimum tax) with respect to such taxpayer for such taxable year.

P.L. 107-16, §901(a)-(b), as amended by P.L. 111-312, §101(a)(1), provides:

SEC. 901. SUNSET OF PROVISIONS OF ACT.

(a) In General.—All provisions of, and amendments made by, this Act shall not apply—

(j) Inflation Adjustments.—

(1) In General.—In the case of any taxable year beginning after 1996, each of the dollar amounts in subsections (b)(2) and (i)(1) shall be increased by an amount equal to—

(1) to taxable, plan, or limitation years beginning after December 31, 2012, or

(2) in the case of title V, to estates of decedents dying, gifts made, or generation skipping transfers, after December 31, 2012.

(b) Application of Certain Laws.—The Internal Revenue Code of 1986 and the Employee Retirement Income Security Act of 1974 shall be applied and administered to years, estates, gifts, and transfers described in subsection (a) as if the provisions and amendments described in subsection (a) had never been enacted.

(A) such dollar amount, multiplied by

»»→ *Caution: Code Sec. 32(j)(1)(B), below, was amended by P.L. 107-16. For sunset provision, see P.L. 107-16, §901 [as amended by P.L. 111-312], in the amendment notes.*

(B) the cost-of-living adjustment determined under section 1(f)(3) for the calendar year in which the taxable year begins, determined—

(i) in the case of amounts in subsections (b)(2)(A) and (i)(1), by substituting "calendar year 1995" for "calendar year 1992" in subparagraph (B) thereof, and

(ii) in the case of the $3,000 amount in subsection (b)(2)(B)(iii), by substituting "calendar year 2007" for "calendar year 1992" in subparagraph (B) of such section 1.

(2) ROUNDING.—

»»→ *Caution: Code Sec. 32(j)(2)(A), below, was amended by P.L. 107-16. For sunset provision, see P.L. 107-16, §901 [as amended by P.L. 111-312], in the amendment notes.*

(A) IN GENERAL.—If any dollar amount in subsection (b)(2)(A) (after being increased under subparagraph (B) thereof), after being increased under paragraph (1), is not a multiple of $10, such dollar amount shall be rounded to the nearest multiple of $10.

* * *

[CCH Explanation at ¶355. Committee Reports at ¶10,040 and ¶10,110.]

Amendments

• **2001, Economic Growth and Tax Relief Reconciliation Act of 2001 (P.L. 107-16)**

P.L. 107-16, §303(a)(2):

Amended Code Sec. 32(j)(1)(B). **Effective** for tax years beginning after 12-31-2001. Prior to amendment, Code Sec. 32(j)(1)(B) read as follows:

(B) the cost-of-living adjustment determined under section 1(f)(3) for the calendar year in which the taxable year begins, determined by substituting "calendar year 1995" for "calendar year 1992" in subparagraph (B) thereof.

P.L. 107-16, §303(a)(3):

Amended Code Sec. 32(j)(2)(A) by striking "subsection (b)(2)" and inserting "subsection (b)(2)(A) (after being increased under subparagraph (B) thereof)". **Effective** for tax years beginning after 12-31-2001.

(n) [Stricken.]

P.L. 107-16, §901(a)-(b), as amended by P.L. 111-312, §101(a)(1), provides:

SEC. 901. SUNSET OF PROVISIONS OF ACT.

(a) IN GENERAL.—All provisions of, and amendments made by, this Act shall not apply—

(1) to taxable, plan, or limitation years beginning after December 31, 2012, or

(2) in the case of title V, to estates of decedents dying, gifts made, or generation skipping transfers, after December 31, 2012.

(b) APPLICATION OF CERTAIN LAWS.—The Internal Revenue Code of 1986 and the Employee Retirement Income Security Act of 1974 shall be applied and administered to years, estates, gifts, and transfers described in subsection (a) as if the provisions and amendments described in subsection (a) had never been enacted.

[CCH Explanation at ¶360. Committee Reports at ¶10,030.]

Amendments

• **2001, Economic Growth and Tax Relief Reconciliation Act of 2001 (P.L. 107-16)**

P.L. 107-16, §201(c)(3):

Amended Code Sec. 32 by striking subsection (n). **Effective** for tax years beginning after 12-31-2000. Prior to being stricken, Code Sec. 32(n) read as follows:

(n) SUPPLEMENTAL CHILD CREDIT.—

(1) IN GENERAL.—In the case of a taxpayer with respect to whom a credit is allowed under section 24(a) for the taxable year, the credit otherwise allowable under this section shall be increased by the lesser of—

(A) the excess of—

(i) the credits allowed under subpart A (determined after the application of section 26 and without regard to this subsection), over

(ii) the credits which would be allowed under subpart A after the application of section 26, determined without regard to section 24 and this subsection; or

(B) the excess of—

(i) the sum of the credits allowed under this part (determined without regard to sections 31, 33, and 34 and this subsection), over

(ii) the sum of the regular tax and the Social Security taxes (as defined in section 24(d)).

The credit determined under this subsection shall be allowed without regard to any other provision of this section, including subsection (d).

(2) COORDINATION WITH OTHER CREDITS.—The amount of the credit under this subsection shall reduce the amount of the credits otherwise allowable under subpart A for the taxable year (determined after the application of section 26), but the amount of the credit under this subsection (and such reduction) shall not be taken into account in determining the amount of any other credit allowable under this part.

P.L. 107-16, §901(a)-(b), as amended by P.L. 111-312, §101(a)(1), provides:

SEC. 901. SUNSET OF PROVISIONS OF ACT.

(a) IN GENERAL.—All provisions of, and amendments made by, this Act shall not apply—

(1) to taxable, plan, or limitation years beginning after December 31, 2012, or

(2) in the case of title V, to estates of decedents dying, gifts made, or generation skipping transfers, after December 31, 2012.

(b) APPLICATION OF CERTAIN LAWS.—The Internal Revenue Code of 1986 and the Employee Retirement Income Security Act of 1974 shall be applied and administered to years, estates, gifts, and transfers described in subsection (a) as if the provisions and amendments described in subsection (a) had never been enacted.

[¶ 5080] CODE SEC. 36B. REFUNDABLE CREDIT FOR COVERAGE UNDER A QUALIFIED HEALTH PLAN.

* * *

(f) RECONCILIATION OF CREDIT AND ADVANCE CREDIT.—

* * *

(2) EXCESS ADVANCE PAYMENTS.—

* * *

⋙→ *Caution: Code Sec. 36B(f)(2)(B), below, as amended by P.L. 111-309, applies to tax years beginning after December 31, 2013.*

(B) *LIMITATION ON INCREASE.—*

(i) *IN GENERAL.—In the case of a taxpayer whose household income is less than 500 percent of the poverty line for the size of the family involved for the taxable year, the amount of the increase under subparagraph (A) shall in no even exceed the applicable dollar amount determined in accordance with the following table (one-half of such amount in the case of a taxpayer whose tax is determined under section 1(c) for the taxable year):*

If the household income (expressed as a percentage of poverty line) is:	The applicable dollar amount is:
Less than 200%	$600
At least 200% but less than 250%	$1,000
At least 250% but less than 300%	$1,500
At least 300% but less than 350%	$2,000
At least 350% but less than 400%	$2,500
At least 400% but less than 450%	$3,000
At least 450% but less than 500%	$3,500

(ii) INDEXING OF AMOUNT.—In the case of any calendar year beginning after 2014, each of the dollar amounts *in the table contained* under clause (i) shall be increased by an amount equal to—

(I) such dollar amount, multiplied by

(II) the cost-of-living adjustment determined under section 1(f)(3) for the calendar year, determined by substituting "calendar year 2013" for "calendar year 1992" in subparagraph (B) thereof.

If the amount of any increase under clause (i) is not a multiple of $50, such increase shall be rounded to the next lowest multiple of $50.

[CCH Explanation at ¶ 373.]

Amendments

• **2010, Medicare and Medicaid Extenders Act of 2010 (P.L. 111-309)**

P.L. 111-309, § 208(a):

Amended Code Sec. 36B(f)(2)(B). **Effective** for tax years beginning after 12-31-2013. Prior to amendment, Code Sec. 36B(f)(2)(B) read as follows:

(B) LIMITATION ON INCREASE WHERE INCOME LESS THAN 400 PERCENT OF POVERTY LINE.—

(i) IN GENERAL.—In the case of an applicable taxpayer whose household income is less than 400 percent of the poverty line for the size of the family involved for the taxable year, the amount of the increase under subparagraph (A) shall in no event exceed $400 ($250 in the case of a taxpayer whose tax is determined under section 1(c) for the taxable year).

(ii) INDEXING OF AMOUNT.—In the case of any calendar year beginning after 2014, each of the dollar amounts under clause (i) shall be increased by an amount equal to—

(I) such dollar amount, multiplied by

(II) the cost-of-living adjustment determined under section 1(f)(3) for the calendar year, determined by substituting "calendar year 2013" for "calendar year 1992" in subparagraph (B) thereof.

If the amount of any increase under clause (i) is not a multiple of $50, such increase shall be rounded to the next lowest multiple of $50.

- **2010, Medicare and Medicaid Extenders Act of 2010 (P.L. 111-309)**

P.L. 111-309, §208(b):

Amended Code Sec. 36B(f)(2)(B)(ii) by inserting "in the table contained" after "each of the dollar amounts". **Effective** for tax years beginning after 12-31-2013.

>>>→ *Caution: Former Code Sec. 23 was redesignated as Code Sec. 36C, below, by P.L. 111-148, applicable to tax years beginning after December 31, 2009. Code Sec. 36C, below, was subsequently redesignated as Code Sec. 23 by P.L. 111-312, applicable to tax years beginning after December 31, 2011. For sunset provision, see P.L. 111-148, §10909(c) [as amended by P.L. 111-312], in the amendment notes.*

[¶5083] CODE SEC. 36C. ADOPTION EXPENSES.

(a) ALLOWANCE OF CREDIT.—

* * *

>>>→ *Caution: Code Sec. 36C(a)(3), below, was amended and redesignated as Code Sec. 23(a)(3) by P.L. 111-148, and further amended by P.L. 111-312, applicable to tax years beginning after December 31, 2011. For sunset provision, see P.L. 111-148, §10909(c) [as amended by P.L. 111-312], in the amendment notes.*

(3) *$10,000* CREDIT FOR ADOPTION OF CHILD WITH SPECIAL NEEDS REGARDLESS OF EXPENSES.—In the case of an adoption of a child with special needs which becomes final during a taxable year, the taxpayer shall be treated as having paid during such year qualified adoption expenses with respect to such adoption in an amount equal to the excess (if any) of *$10,000* over the aggregate qualified adoption expenses actually paid or incurred by the taxpayer with respect to such adoption during such taxable year and all prior taxable years.

[CCH Explanation at ¶373. Committee Reports at ¶10,060.]

Amendments

- **2010, Tax Relief, Unemployment Insurance Reauthorization, and Job Creation Act of 2010 (P.L. 111-312)**

P.L. 111-312, §101(b)(1):

Amended Code Sec. 23(a)(3) to read as such provision would read if section 10909 of the Patient Protection and Affordable Care Act (P.L. 111-148) had never been enacted. **Effective** for tax years beginning after 12-31-2011.

P.L. 111-312, §101(b)(1):

Amended Code Sec. 23 to read as such provision would read if section 10909 of the Patient Protection and Affordable Care Act (P.L. 111-148) had never been enacted. **Effective** for tax years beginning after 12-31-2011.

- **2010, Patient Protection and Affordable Care Act (P.L. 111-148)**

P.L. 111-148, §10909(a)(1)(B)(i)-(ii):

Amended Code Sec. 23(a)(3), in the text by striking "$10,000" and inserting "$13,170", and in the heading by striking "$10,000" and inserting "$13,170". **Effective for tax** years beginning after 12-31-2009.

P.L. 111-148, §10909(b)(1)(A)-(B):

Amended [subpart A of part IV of subchapter A of chapter 1] by redesignating Code Sec. 23, as amended by Act Sec. 10909(a), as Code Sec. 36C, and by moving it before Code Sec. 37 in subpart C of part IV of subchapter A of chapter 1. **Effective** for tax years beginning after 12-31-2009.

P.L. 111-148, §10909(c), as amended by P.L. 111-312, §101(b)(1), provides:

(c) SUNSET PROVISION.—Each provision of law amended by this section is amended to read as such provision would read if this section had never been enacted. The amendments made by the preceding sentence shall apply to taxable years beginning after December 31, 2011.

(b) LIMITATIONS.—

* * *

➤ *Caution: Code Sec. 36C(b)(1), below, was amended and redesignated as Code Sec. 23(b)(1) by P.L. 111-312, applicable to tax years beginning after December 31, 2011. For sunset provision, see P.L.111-148, §10909(c) [as amended by P.L. 111-312], in the amendment notes.*

(1) DOLLAR LIMITATION.—The aggregate amount of qualified adoption expenses which may be taken into account under subsection (a) for all taxable years with respect to the adoption of a child by the taxpayer shall not exceed *$10,000.*

(2) INCOME LIMITATION.—

(A) IN GENERAL.—The amount allowable as a credit under subsection (a) for any taxable year (determined without regard to subsection (c)) shall be reduced (but not below zero) by an amount which bears the same ratio to the amount so allowable (determined without regard to this paragraph but with regard to paragraph (1)) as—

➤ *Caution: Code Sec. 36C(b)(2)(A)(i), below, was amended by P.L. 107-16. For sunset provision, see P.L. 107-16, §901 [as amended by P.L. 111-312, §101(a)(1)], in the amendment notes.*

(i) the amount (if any) by which the taxpayer's adjusted gross income exceeds $150,000, bears to

(ii) $40,000.

* * *

➤ *Caution: Code Sec. 36C(b)(4), below, was redesignated as Code Sec. 23(b)(4), and amended by P.L. 111-312, applicable to tax years beginning after December 31, 2011. For sunset provision, see P.L. 111-148, §10909(c) [as amended by P.L. 111-312], in the amendment notes.*

(4) LIMITATION BASED ON AMOUNT OF TAX.—*In the case of a taxable year to which section 26(a)(2) does not apply, the credit allowed under subsection (a) for any taxable year shall not exceed the excess of—*

(A) *the sum of the regular tax liability (as defined in section 26(b)) plus the tax imposed by section 55, over*

(B) *the sum of the credits allowable under this subpart (other than this section and section 25D) and section 27 for the taxable year.*

[CCH Explanation at ¶373. Committee Reports at ¶10,060.]

Amendments

• 2010, Tax Relief, Unemployment Insurance Reauthorization, and Job Creation Act of 2010 (P.L. 111-312)

P.L. 111-312, §101(b)(1):

Amended Code Sec. 23(b)(1) to read as such provision would read if section 10909 of the Patient Protection and Affordable Care Act (P.L. 111-148) had never been enacted. **Effective** for tax years beginning after 12-31-2011.

P.L. 111-312, §101(b)(1):

Amended Code Sec. 36C(b)(4) to read as such provision would read if section 10909 of the Patient Protection and Affordable Care Act (P.L. 111-148) had never been enacted. **Effective** for tax years beginning after 12-31-2011.

• 2010, Patient Protection and Affordable Care Act (P.L. 111-148)

P.L. 111-148, 10909(a)(1)(A):

Amended Code Sec. 23(b)(1) by striking "$10,000" and inserting "$13,170". **Effective** for tax years beginning after 12-31-2009.

P.L. 111-148, 10909(b)(2)(I)(i):

Amended Code Sec. 36C, as redesignated, by striking paragraph (b)(4). **Effective** for tax years beginning after

12-31-2009. Prior to amendment, Code Sec. 36C(b)(4) read as follows:

(4) LIMITATION BASED ON AMOUNT OF TAX.—In the case of a taxable year to which section 26(a)(2) does not apply, the credit allowed under subsection (a) for any taxable year shall not exceed the excess of—

(A) the sum of the regular tax liability (as defined in section 26(b)) plus the tax imposed by section 55, over

(B) the sum of the credits allowable under this subpart (other than this section and section 25D) and section 27 for the taxable year.

P.L. 111-148, §10909(c), as amended by P.L. 111-312, §101(b)(1), provides:

(c) SUNSET PROVISION.—Each provision of law amended by this section is amended to read as such provision would read if this section had never been enacted. The amendments made by the preceding sentence shall apply to taxable years beginning after December 31, 2011.

• 2001, Economic Growth and Tax Relief Reconciliation Act of 2001 (P.L. 107-16)

P.L. 107-16, §202(b)(2)(A):

Act Sec. 202(b)(2)(A) amended Code Sec. 23(b)(2)(A)(i) by striking "$75,000" and inserting "$150,000". **Effective** for tax years beginning after 12-31-2001.

P.L. 107-16, §901(a)-(b), as amended by P.L. 111-312, §101(a)(1), provides:

SEC. 901. SUNSET OF PROVISIONS OF ACT.

(a) IN GENERAL.—All provisions of, and amendments made by, this Act shall not apply—

(1) to taxable, plan, or limitation years beginning after December 31, 2012, or

(2) in the case of title V, to estates of decedents dying, gifts made, or generation skipping transfers, after December 31, 2012.

(b) APPLICATION OF CERTAIN LAWS.—The Internal Revenue Code of 1986 and the Employee Retirement Income Security Act of 1974 shall be applied and administered to years, estates, gifts, and transfers described in subsection (a) as if the provisions and amendments described in subsection (a) had never been enacted.

⫸→ Caution: *Code Sec. 36C(c), below, was redesignated as Code Sec. 23(c), and amended by P.L. 111-312, applicable to tax years beginning after December 31, 2011. For sunset provision, see P.L. 111-148, §10909(c) [as amended by P.L. 111-312], in the amendment notes.*

(c) CARRYFORWARDS OF UNUSED CREDIT.—

(1) RULE FOR YEARS IN WHICH ALL PERSONAL CREDITS ALLOWED AGAINST REGULAR AND ALTERNATIVE MINIMUM TAX.—In the case of a taxable year to which section 26(a)(2) applies, if the credit allowable under subsection (a) for any taxable year exceeds the limitation imposed by section 26(a)(2) for such taxable year reduced by the sum of the credits allowable under this subpart (other than this section and sections 25D and 1400C), such excess shall be carried to the succeeding taxable year and added to the credit allowable under subsection (a) for such taxable year.

(2) RULE FOR OTHER YEARS.—In the case of a taxable year to which section 26(a)(2) does not apply, if the credit allowable under subsection (a) for any taxable year exceeds the limitation imposed by subsection (b)(4) for such taxable year, such excess shall be carried to the succeeding taxable year and added to the credit allowable under subsection (a) for such taxable year.

(3) LIMITATION.—No credit may be carried forward under this subsection to any taxable year following the fifth taxable year after the taxable year in which the credit arose. For purposes of the preceding sentence, credits shall be treated as used on a first-in first-out basis.

* * *

[CCH Explanation at ¶370. Committee Reports at ¶10,060.]

Amendments

- **2010, Tax Relief, Unemployment Insurance Reauthorization, and Job Creation Act of 2010 (P.L. 111-312)**

P.L. 111-312, §101(b)(1):

Amended Code Sec. 36C(c) to read as such provision would read if section 10909 of the Patient Protection and Affordable Care Act (P.L. 111-148) had never been enacted. **Effective** for tax years beginning after 12-31-2011.

- **2010, Patient Protection and Affordable Care Act (P.L. 111-148)**

P.L. 111-148, §10909(b)(2)(I)(ii):

Amended Code Sec. 36C, as redesignated, by striking subsection (c). **Effective** for tax years beginning after 12-31-2009. Prior to amendment, Code Sec. 36C(c) read as follows:

(c) CARRYFORWARDS OF UNUSED CREDIT.—

(1) RULE FOR YEARS IN WHICH ALL PERSONAL CREDITS ALLOWED AGAINST REGULAR AND ALTERNATIVE MINIMUM TAX.—In the case of a taxable year to which section 26(a)(2) applies, if the credit allowable under subsection (a) for any taxable year exceeds the limitation imposed by section 26(a)(2) for such

taxable year reduced by the sum of the credits allowable under this subpart (other than this section and sections 25D and 1400C), such excess shall be carried to the succeeding taxable year and added to the credit allowable under subsection (a) for such taxable year.

(2) RULE FOR OTHER YEARS.—In the case of a taxable year to which section 26(a)(2) does not apply, if the credit allowable under subsection (a) for any taxable year exceeds the limitation imposed by subsection (b)(4) for such taxable year, such excess shall be carried to the succeeding taxable year and added to the credit allowable under subsection (a) for such taxable year.

(3) LIMITATION.—No credit may be carried forward under this subsection to any taxable year following the fifth taxable year after the taxable year in which the credit arose. For purposes of the preceding sentence, credits shall be treated as used on a first-in first-out basis.

P.L. 111-148, §10909(c), as amended by P.L. 111-312, §101(b)(1), provides:

(c) SUNSET PROVISION.—Each provision of law amended by this section is amended to read as such provision would read if this section had never been enacted. The amendments made by the preceding sentence shall apply to taxable years beginning after December 31, 2011.

»»→ *Caution: Code Sec. 36C(h), below, was redesignated as Code Sec. 23(h), and amended by P.L. 111-312, applicable to tax years beginning after December 31, 2011. For sunset provision, P.L. 111-148, §10909(c) [as amended by P.L. 111-312], in the amendment notes.*

(h) ADJUSTMENTS FOR INFLATION.—In the case of a taxable year beginning after December 31, 2002, each of the dollar amounts in subsection (a)(3) and paragraphs (1) and (2)(A)(i) of subsection (b) shall be increased by an amount equal to—

(1) such dollar amount, multiplied by

(2) the cost-of-living adjustment determined under section 1(f)(3) for the calendar year in which the taxable year begins, determined by substituting "calendar year 2001" for "calendar year 1992" in subparagraph (B) thereof.

If any amount as increased under the preceding sentence is not a multiple of $10, such amount shall be rounded to the nearest multiple of $10.

[CCH Explanation at ¶370. Committee Reports at ¶10,060.]

Amendments

• **2010, Tax Relief, Unemployment Insurance Reauthorization, and Job Creation Act of 2010 (P.L. 111-312)**

P.L. 111-312, §101(b)(1):

Amended Code Sec. 23(h) to read as such provision would read if section 10909 of the Patient Protection and Affordable Care Act (P.L. 111-148) had never been enacted. **Effective** for tax years beginning after 12-31-2011. Prior to amendment, Code Sec. 23(h) read as follows:

(h) ADJUSTMENTS FOR INFLATION.—

(1) DOLLAR LIMITATIONS.—In the case of a taxable year beginning after December 31, 2010, each of the dollar amounts in subsections (a)(3) and (b)(1) shall be increased by an amount equal to—

(A) such dollar amount, multiplied by

(B) the cost-of-living adjustment determined under section 1(f)(3) for the calendar year in which the taxable year begins, determined by substituting "calendar year 2009" for "calendar year 1992" in subparagraph (B) thereof.

If any amount as increased under the preceding sentence is not a multiple of $10, such amount shall be rounded to the nearest multiple of $10.

(2) INCOME LIMITATION.—In the case of a taxable year beginning after December 31, 2002, the dollar amount in subsection (b)(2)(A)(i) shall be increased by an amount equal to—

(A) such dollar amount, multiplied by

(B) the cost-of-living adjustment determined under section 1(f)(3) for the calendar year in which the taxable year begins, determined by substituting "calendar year 2001" for "calendar year 1992" in subparagraph (B) thereof.

If any amount as increased under the preceding sentence is not a multiple of $10, such amount shall be rounded to the nearest multiple of $10.

• **2010, Patient Protection and Affordable Care Act (P.L. 111-148)**

P.L. 111-148, §10909(a)(1)(C):

Amended Code Sec. 23(h). **Effective** for tax years beginning after 12-31-2009. Prior to amendment, Code Sec. 23(h) read as follows:

(h) ADJUSTMENTS FOR INFLATION.—In the case of a taxable year beginning after December 31, 2002, each of the dollar amounts in subsection (a)(3) and paragraphs (1) and (2)(A)(i) of subsection (b) shall be increased by an amount equal to—

(1) such dollar amount, multiplied by

(2) the cost-of-living adjustment determined under section 1(f)(3) for the calendar year in which the taxable year begins, determined by substituting "calendar year 2001" for "calendar year 1992" in subparagraph (B) thereof.

If any amount as increased under the preceding sentence is not a multiple of $10, such amount shall be rounded to the nearest multiple of $10.

P.L. 111-148, §10909(c), as amended by P.L. 111-312, §101(b)(1), provides:

(c) SUNSET PROVISION.—Each provision of law amended by this section is amended to read as such provision would read if this section had never been enacted. The amendments made by the preceding sentence shall apply to taxable years beginning after December 31, 2011.

[¶5085] CODE SEC. 38. GENERAL BUSINESS CREDIT.

* * *

(b) CURRENT YEAR BUSINESS CREDIT.—For purposes of this subpart, the amount of the current year business credit is the sum of the following credits determined for the taxable year:

* * *

»»→ *Caution: Code Sec. 38(b)(13)-(15), below, was amended by P.L. 107-16. For sunset provision, see P.L. 107-16, §901 [as amended by P.L. 111-312], in the amendment notes.*

(13) the new markets tax credit determined under section 45D(a),

(14) in the case of an eligible employer (as defined in section 45E(c)), the small employer pension plan startup cost credit determined under section 45E(a),

(15) the employer-provided child care credit determined under section 45F(a),

* * *

[CCH Explanation at ¶ 522. Committee Reports at ¶ 10,060.]

Amendments

• **2004, American Jobs Creation Act of 2004 (P.L. 108-357)**

P.L. 108-357, § 245(c)(1):

Amended Code Sec. 38(b) by striking "plus" at the end of paragraph (14), by striking the period at the end of paragraph (15) and inserting ", plus", and by adding at the end a new paragraph (16). **Effective** for tax years beginning after 12-31-2004.

P.L. 108-357, § 302(b):

Amended Code Sec. 38(b), as amended by this Act, by striking "plus" at the end of paragraph (15), by striking the period at the end of paragraph (16) and inserting ", plus", and by inserting after paragraph (16) a new paragraph (17). **Effective** for fuel produced, and sold or used, after 12-31-2004, in tax years ending after such date.

• **2002, Job Creation and Worker Assistance Act of 2002 (P.L. 107-147)**

P.L. 107-147, § 411(d)(2):

Amended Code Sec. 38(b)(15) by striking "45F" and inserting "45F(a)". **Effective** as if included in the provision of P.L. 107-16 to which it relates [effective for tax years beginning after 12-31-2001.—CCH].

• **2001, Economic Growth and Tax Relief Reconciliation Act of 2001 (P.L. 107-16)**

P.L. 107-16, § 205(b)(1):

Amended Code Sec. 38(b), as amended by Act Sec. 619, by striking "plus" at the end of paragraph (13), by striking the period at the end of paragraph (14) and inserting ", plus", and by adding at the end a new paragraph (15). **Effective** for tax years beginning after 12-31-2001.

P.L. 107-16, § 901(a)-(b), as amended by P.L. 111-312, § 101(a)(1), provides:

SEC. 901. SUNSET OF PROVISIONS OF ACT.

(a) IN GENERAL.—All provisions of, and amendments made by, this Act shall not apply—

(1) to taxable, plan, or limitation years beginning after December 31, 2012, or

(2) in the case of title V, to estates of decedents dying, gifts made, or generation skipping transfers, after December 31, 2012.

(b) APPLICATION OF CERTAIN LAWS.—The Internal Revenue Code of 1986 and the Employee Retirement Income Security Act of 1974 shall be applied and administered to years, estates, gifts, and transfers described in subsection (a) as if the provisions and amendments described in subsection (a) had never been enacted.

[¶ 5090] CODE SEC. 40. ALCOHOL, etc., USED AS FUEL.

* * *

(e) TERMINATION.—

(1) IN GENERAL.—This section shall not apply to any sale or use—

(A) for any period after *December 31, 2011,* or

(B) for any period before *January 1, 2012,* during which the rates of tax under section 4081(a)(2)(A) are 4.3 cents per gallon.

* * *

[CCH Explanation at ¶ 546. Committee Reports at ¶ 10,240.]

Amendments

• **2010, Tax Relief, Unemployment Insurance Reauthorization, and Job Creation Act of 2010 (P.L. 111-312)**

P.L. 111-312, § 708(a)(1)(A)-(B):

Amended Code Sec. 40(e)(1) by striking "December 31, 2010" in subparagraph (A) and inserting "December 31, 2011", and by striking "January 1, 2011" in subparagraph (B) and inserting "January 1, 2012". **Effective** for periods after 12-31-2010.

(h) REDUCED CREDIT FOR ETHANOL BLENDERS.—

(1) IN GENERAL.—In the case of any alcohol mixture credit or alcohol credit with respect to any sale or use of alcohol which is ethanol during calendar years 2001 through *2011*—

(A) subsections (b)(1)(A) and (b)(2)(A) shall be applied by substituting "the blender amount" for "60 cents",

(B) subsection (b)(3) shall be applied by substituting "the low-proof blender amount" for "45 cents" and "the blender amount" for "60 cents", and

(C) subparagraphs (A) and (B) of subsection (d)(3) shall be applied by substituting "the blender amount" for "60 cents" and "the low-proof blender amount" for "45 cents".

(2) AMOUNTS.—For purposes of paragraph (1), the blender amount and the low-proof blender amount shall be determined in accordance with the following table:

In the case of any sale or use during calendar year:	The blender amount is:	The low-proof blender amount is:
2001 or 2002	53 cents	39.26 cents
2003 or 2004	52 cents	38.52 cents
2005, 2006, 2007, or 2008	51 cents	37.78 cents
2009 through 2011	45 cents	33.33 cents.

* * *

[CCH Explanation at ¶546. Committee Reports at ¶10,240.]
Amendments

• 2010, Tax Relief, Unemployment Insurance Reauthorization, and Job Creation Act of 2010 (P.L. 111-312)

P.L. 111-312, §708(a)(2):

Amended Code Sec. 40(h) by striking "2010" both places it appears and inserting "2011". **Effective** for periods after 12-31-2010.

[¶5095] CODE SEC. 40A. BIODIESEL AND RENEWABLE DIESEL USED AS FUEL.
* * *

(g) TERMINATION.—This section shall not apply to any sale or use after *December 31, 2011.*

[CCH Explanation at ¶544. Committee Reports at ¶10,170.]
Amendments

• 2010, Tax Relief, Unemployment Insurance Reauthorization, and Job Creation Act of 2010 (P.L. 111-312)

P.L. 111-312, §701(a):

Amended Code Sec. 40A(g) by striking "December 31, 2009" and inserting "December 31, 2011". **Effective** for fuel sold or used after 12-31-2009.

[¶5100] CODE SEC. 41. CREDIT FOR INCREASING RESEARCH ACTIVITIES.
* * *

(h) TERMINATION.—

    (1) IN GENERAL.—This section shall not apply to any amount paid or incurred—

        (A) after June 30, 1995, and before July 1, 1996, or

        (B) after *December 31, 2011.*

* * *

[CCH Explanation at ¶520. Committee Reports at ¶10,360.]
Amendments

• 2010, Tax Relief, Unemployment Insurance Reauthorization, and Job Creation Act of 2010 (P.L. 111-312)

P.L. 111-312, §731(a):

Amended Code Sec. 41(h)(1)(B) by striking "December 31, 2009" and inserting "December 31, 2011". **Effective** for amounts paid or incurred after 12-31-2009.

[¶5105] CODE SEC. 45. ELECTRICITY PRODUCED FROM CERTAIN RENEWABLE RESOURCES, etc. [sic]
* * *

(d) QUALIFIED FACILITIES.—For purposes of this section:
* * *

(8) REFINED COAL PRODUCTION FACILITY.—In the case of a facility that produces refined coal, the term "refined coal production facility" means—

(A) with respect to a facility producing steel industry fuel, any facility (or any modification to a facility) which is placed in service before January 1, 2010, and

(B) with respect to any other facility producing refined coal, any facility placed in service after the date of the enactment of the American Jobs Creation Act of 2004 and before *January 1, 2012.*

* * *

[CCH Explanation at ¶ 550. Committee Reports at ¶ 10,180.]
Amendments
• **2010, Tax Relief, Unemployment Insurance Reauthorization, and Job Creation Act of 2010 (P.L. 111-312)**

P.L. 111-312, § 702(a):

Amended Code Sec. 45(d)(8)(B) by striking "January 1, 2010" and inserting "January 1, 2012". **Effective** for facilities placed in service after 12-31-2009.

[¶ 5110] CODE SEC. 45A. INDIAN EMPLOYMENT CREDIT.

* * *

(f) TERMINATION.—This section shall not apply to taxable years beginning after *December 31, 2011.*

[CCH Explanation at ¶ 530. Committee Reports at ¶ 10,380.]
Amendments
• **2010, Tax Relief, Unemployment Insurance Reauthorization, and Job Creation Act of 2010 (P.L. 111-312)**

P.L. 111-312, § 732(a):

Amended Code Sec. 45A(f) by striking "December 31, 2009" and inserting "December 31, 2011". **Effective** for tax years beginning after 12-31-2009.

[¶ 5115] CODE SEC. 45C. CLINICAL TESTING EXPENSES FOR CERTAIN DRUGS FOR RARE DISEASES OR CONDITIONS.

* * *

(b) QUALIFIED CLINICAL TESTING EXPENSES.—For purposes of this section—

(1) QUALIFIED CLINICAL TESTING EXPENSES.—

* * *

(D) SPECIAL RULE.—For purposes of this paragraph, section 41 shall be deemed to remain in effect for periods after June 30, 1995, and before July 1, 1996, and periods after *December 31, 2011.*

* * *

[CCH Explanation at ¶ 520. Committee Reports at ¶ 10,370.]
Amendments
• **2010, Tax Relief, Unemployment Insurance Reauthorization, and Job Creation Act of 2010 (P.L. 111-312)**

P.L. 111-312, § 731(b):

Amended Code Sec. 45C(b)(1)(D) by striking "December 31, 2009" and inserting "December 31, 2011". **Effective** for amounts paid or incurred after 12-31-2009.

[¶5120] CODE SEC. 45D. NEW MARKETS TAX CREDIT.

* * *

(f) NATIONAL LIMITATION ON AMOUNT OF INVESTMENTS DESIGNATED.—

(1) IN GENERAL.—There is a new markets tax credit limitation for each calendar year. Such limitation is—

* * *

(E) $5,000,000,000 for 2008,

(F) $5,000,000,000 for 2009[, and]

(G) *$3,500,000,000 for 2010 and 2011.*

* * *

(3) CARRYOVER OF UNUSED LIMITATION.—If the new markets tax credit limitation for any calendar year exceeds the aggregate amount allocated under paragraph (2) for such year, such limitation for the succeeding calendar year shall be increased by the amount of such excess. No amount may be carried under the preceding sentence to any calendar year after *2016.*

* * *

[CCH Explanation at ¶528. Committee Reports at ¶10,380.]

Amendments

• **2010, Tax Relief, Unemployment Insurance Reauthorization, and Job Creation Act of 2010 (P.L. 111-312)**

P.L. 111-312, §733(a)(1)-(3):

Amended Code Sec. 45D(f)(1) by striking "and" at the end of subparagraph (E), by striking the period at the end of subparagraph (F), and by adding at the end a new subparagraph (G). **Effective** for calendar years beginning after 2009.

P.L. 111-312, §733(b):

Amended Code Sec. 45D(f)(3) by striking "2014" and inserting "2016". **Effective** for calendar years beginning after 2009.

⟫⟫→ *Caution: Code Sec. 45F, below, was added by P.L. 107-16. For sunset provision, see P.L. 107-16, §901 [as amended by P.L. 111-312], in the amendment notes.*

[¶5125] CODE SEC. 45F. EMPLOYER-PROVIDED CHILD CARE CREDIT.

(a) IN GENERAL.—For purposes of section 38, the employer-provided child care credit determined under this section for the taxable year is an amount equal to the sum of—

(1) 25 percent of the qualified child care expenditures, and

(2) 10 percent of the qualified child care resource and referral expenditures,

of the taxpayer for such taxable year.

(b) DOLLAR LIMITATION.—The credit allowable under subsection (a) for any taxable year shall not exceed $150,000.

(c) DEFINITIONS.—For purposes of this section—

(1) QUALIFIED CHILD CARE EXPENDITURE.—

(A) IN GENERAL.—The term "qualified child care expenditure" means any amount paid or incurred—

(i) to acquire, construct, rehabilitate, or expand property—

(I) which is to be used as part of a qualified child care facility of the taxpayer,

(II) with respect to which a deduction for depreciation (or amortization in lieu of depreciation) is allowable, and

(III) which does not constitute part of the principal residence (within the meaning of section 121) of the taxpayer or any employee of the taxpayer,

(ii) for the operating costs of a qualified child care facility of the taxpayer, including costs related to the training of employees, to scholarship programs, and to the providing of increased compensation to employees with higher levels of child care training, or

(iii) under a contract with a qualified child care facility to provide child care services to employees of the taxpayer.

(B) FAIR MARKET VALUE.—The term "qualified child care expenditures" shall not include expenses in excess of the fair market value of such care.

(2) QUALIFIED CHILD CARE FACILITY.—

(A) IN GENERAL.—The term "qualified child care facility" means a facility—

(i) the principal use of which is to provide child care assistance, and

(ii) which meets the requirements of all applicable laws and regulations of the State or local government in which it is located, including the licensing of the facility as a child care facility.

Clause (i) shall not apply to a facility which is the principal residence (within the meaning of section 121) of the operator of the facility.

(B) SPECIAL RULES WITH RESPECT TO A TAXPAYER.—A facility shall not be treated as a qualified child care facility with respect to a taxpayer unless—

(i) enrollment in the facility is open to employees of the taxpayer during the taxable year,

(ii) if the facility is the principal trade or business of the taxpayer, at least 30 percent of the enrollees of such facility are dependents of employees of the taxpayer, and

(iii) the use of such facility (or the eligibility to use such facility) does not discriminate in favor of employees of the taxpayer who are highly compensated employees (within the meaning of section 414(q)).

(3) QUALIFIED CHILD CARE RESOURCE AND REFERRAL EXPENDITURE.—

(A) IN GENERAL.—The term "qualified child care resource and referral expenditure" means any amount paid or incurred under a contract to provide child care resource and referral services to an employee of the taxpayer.

(B) NONDISCRIMINATION.—The services shall not be treated as qualified unless the provision of such services (or the eligibility to use such services) does not discriminate in favor of employees of the taxpayer who are highly compensated employees (within the meaning of section 414(q)).

(d) RECAPTURE OF ACQUISITION AND CONSTRUCTION CREDIT.—

(1) IN GENERAL.—If, as of the close of any taxable year, there is a recapture event with respect to any qualified child care facility of the taxpayer, then the tax of the taxpayer under this chapter for such taxable year shall be increased by an amount equal to the product of—

(A) the applicable recapture percentage, and

(B) the aggregate decrease in the credits allowed under section 38 for all prior taxable years which would have resulted if the qualified child care expenditures of the taxpayer described in subsection (c)(1)(A) with respect to such facility had been zero.

(2) APPLICABLE RECAPTURE PERCENTAGE.—

(A) IN GENERAL.—For purposes of this subsection, the applicable recapture percentage shall be determined from the following table:

If the recapture event occurs in:	The applicable recapture percentage is:
Years 1-3	100
Year 4	85
Year 5	70
Year 6	55
Year 7	40
Year 8	25
Years 9 and 10	10
Years 11 and thereafter	0.

(B) YEARS.—For purposes of subparagraph (A), year 1 shall begin on the first day of the taxable year in which the qualified child care facility is placed in service by the taxpayer.

(3) RECAPTURE EVENT DEFINED.—For purposes of this subsection, the term "recapture event" means—

(A) CESSATION OF OPERATION.—The cessation of the operation of the facility as a qualified child care facility.

(B) CHANGE IN OWNERSHIP.—

(i) IN GENERAL.—Except as provided in clause (ii), the disposition of a taxpayer's interest in a qualified child care facility with respect to which the credit described in subsection (a) was allowable.

(ii) AGREEMENT TO ASSUME RECAPTURE LIABILITY.—Clause (i) shall not apply if the person acquiring such interest in the facility agrees in writing to assume the recapture liability of the person disposing of such interest in effect immediately before such disposition. In the event of such an assumption, the person acquiring the interest in the facility shall be treated as the taxpayer for purposes of assessing any recapture liability (computed as if there had been no change in ownership).

(4) SPECIAL RULES.—

(A) TAX BENEFIT RULE.—The tax for the taxable year shall be increased under paragraph (1) only with respect to credits allowed by reason of this section which were used to reduce tax liability. In the case of credits not so used to reduce tax liability, the carryforwards and carrybacks under section 39 shall be appropriately adjusted.

(B) NO CREDITS AGAINST TAX.—Any increase in tax under this subsection shall not be treated as a tax imposed by this chapter for purposes of determining the amount of any credit under this chapter or for purposes of section 55.

(C) NO RECAPTURE BY REASON OF CASUALTY LOSS.—The increase in tax under this subsection shall not apply to a cessation of operation of the facility as a qualified child care facility by reason of a casualty loss to the extent such loss is restored by reconstruction or replacement within a reasonable period established by the Secretary.

[CCH Explanation at ¶ 522. Committee Reports at ¶ 10,060.]

Amendments

• 2002, Job Creation and Worker Assistance Act of 2002 (P.L. 107-147)

P.L. 107-147, §411(d)(1):

Amended Code Sec. 45F(d)(4)(B) by striking "subpart A, B, or D of this part" and inserting "this chapter or for purposes of section 55". Effective as if included in the provision of P.L. 107-16 to which it relates [effective for tax years beginning after 12-31-2001.—CCH].

(e) Special Rules.—For purposes of this section—

(1) Aggregation rules.—All persons which are treated as a single employer under subsections (a) and (b) of section 52 shall be treated as a single taxpayer.

(2) Pass-thru in the case of estates and trusts.—Under regulations prescribed by the Secretary, rules similar to the rules of subsection (d) of section 52 shall apply.

(3) Allocation in the case of partnerships.—In the case of partnerships, the credit shall be allocated among partners under regulations prescribed by the Secretary.

(f) No Double Benefit.—

(1) Reduction in basis.—For purposes of this subtitle—

(A) In General.—If a credit is determined under this section with respect to any property by reason of expenditures described in subsection (c)(1)(A), the basis of such property shall be reduced by the amount of the credit so determined.

(B) Certain dispositions.—If, during any taxable year, there is a recapture amount determined with respect to any property the basis of which was reduced under subparagraph (A), the basis of such property (immediately before the event resulting in such recapture) shall be increased by an amount equal to such recapture amount. For purposes of the preceding sentence, the term "recapture amount" means any increase in tax (or adjustment in carrybacks or carryovers) determined under subsection (d).

(2) Other deductions and credits.—No deduction or credit shall be allowed under any other provision of this chapter with respect to the amount of the credit determined under this section.

[CCH Explanation at ¶522. Committee Reports at ¶10,060.]
Amendments
• 2001, Economic Growth and Tax Relief Reconciliation Act of 2001 (P.L. 107-16)

P.L. 107-16, §205(a):

Amended subpart D of part IV of subchapter A of chapter 1, as amended by Act Sec. 619, by adding at the end a new Code Sec. 45F. Effective for tax years beginning after 12-31-2001.

P.L. 107-16, §901(a)-(b), as amended by P.L. 111-312, §101(a)(1), provides:

SEC. 901. SUNSET OF PROVISIONS OF ACT.

(a) In General.—All provisions of, and amendments made by, this Act shall not apply—

(1) to taxable, plan, or limitation years beginning after December 31, 2012, or

(2) in the case of title V, to estates of decedents dying, gifts made, or generation skipping transfers, after December 31, 2012.

(b) Application of Certain Laws.—The Internal Revenue Code of 1986 and the Employee Retirement Income Security Act of 1974 shall be applied and administered to years, estates, gifts, and transfers described in subsection (a) as if the provisions and amendments described in subsection (a) had never been enacted.

[¶5130] CODE SEC. 45G. RAILROAD TRACK MAINTENANCE CREDIT.

* * *

(f) Application of Section.—This section shall apply to qualified railroad track maintenance expenditures paid or incurred during taxable years beginning after December 31, 2004, and before January 1, 2012.

[CCH Explanation at ¶532. Committee Reports at ¶10,390.]
Amendments
• 2010, Tax Relief, Unemployment Insurance Reauthorization, and Job Creation Act of 2010 (P.L. 111-312)

P.L. 111-312, §734(a):

Amended Code Sec. 45G(f) by striking "January 1, 2010" and inserting "January 1, 2012". Effective for expenditures paid or incurred in tax years beginning after 12-31-2009.

[¶ 5135] CODE SEC. 45L. NEW ENERGY EFFICIENT HOME CREDIT.

* * *

(g) TERMINATION.—This section shall not apply to any qualified new energy efficient home acquired after *December 31, 2011.*

[CCH Explanation at ¶ 538. Committee Reports at ¶ 10,190.]

Amendments

• 2010, Tax Relief, Unemployment Insurance Reauthorization, and Job Creation Act of 2010 (P.L. 111-312)

P.L. 111-312, § 703(a):

Amended Code Sec. 45L(g) by striking "December 31, 2009" and inserting "December 31, 2011". **Effective** for homes acquired after 12-31-2009.

[¶ 5140] CODE SEC. 45M. ENERGY EFFICIENT APPLIANCE CREDIT.

* * *

(b) APPLICABLE AMOUNT.—For purposes of subsection (a)—

(1) DISHWASHERS.—The applicable amount is—

(A) $45 in the case of a dishwasher which is manufactured in calendar year 2008 or 2009 and which uses no more than 324 kilowatt hours per year and 5.8 gallons per cycle,

(B) $75 in the case of a dishwasher which is manufactured in calendar year 2008, 2009, or 2010 and which uses no more than 307 kilowatt hours per year and 5.0 gallons per cycle (5.5 gallons per cycle for dishwashers designed for greater than 12 place settings),

(C) $25 in the case of a dishwasher which is manufactured in calendar year 2011 and which uses no more than 307 kilowatt hours per year and 5.0 gallons per cycle (5.5 gallons per cycle for dishwashers designed for greater than 12 place settings),

(D) $50 in the case of a dishwasher which is manufactured in calendar year 2011 and which uses no more than 295 kilowatt hours per year and 4.25 gallons per cycle (4.75 gallons per cycle for dishwashers designed for greater than 12 place settings), and

(E) $75 in the case of a dishwasher which is manufactured in calendar year 2011 and which uses no more than 280 kilowatt hours per year and 4 gallons per cycle (4.5 gallons per cycle for dishwashers designed for greater than 12 place settings).

(2) CLOTHES WASHERS.—The applicable amount is—

* * *

(C) $150 in the case of a residential or commercial clothes washer manufactured in calendar year 2008, 2009, or 2010 which meets or exceeds 2.0 modified energy factor and does not exceed a 6.0 water consumption factor,

(D) $250 in the case of a residential or commercial clothes washer manufactured in calendar year 2008, 2009, or 2010 which meets or exceeds 2.2 modified energy factor and does not exceed a 4.5 water consumption factor,

(E) $175 in the case of a top-loading clothes washer manufactured in calendar year 2011 which meets or exceeds a 2.2 modified energy factor and does not exceed a 4.5 water consumption factor, and

(F) $225 in the case of a clothes washer manufactured in calendar year 2011—

(i) which is a top-loading clothes washer and which meets or exceeds a 2.4 modified energy factor and does not exceed a 4.2 water consumption factor, or

(ii) which is a front-loading clothes washer and which meets or exceeds a 2.8 modified energy factor and does not exceed a 3.5 water consumption factor.

(3) REFRIGERATORS.—The applicable amount is—

* * *

(C) $100 in the case of a refrigerator which is manufactured in calendar year 2008, 2009, or 2010, and consumes at least 25 percent but not more than 29.9 percent less kilowatt hours per year than the 2001 energy conservation standards,

(D) $200 in the case of a refrigerator manufactured in calendar year 2008, 2009, or 2010 and which consumes at least 30 percent less energy than the 2001 energy conservation standards,

(E) $150 in the case of a refrigerator manufactured in calendar year 2011 which consumes at least 30 percent less energy than the 2001 energy conservation standards, and

(F) $200 in the case of a refrigerator manufactured in calendar year 2011 which consumes at least 35 percent less energy than the 2001 energy conservation standards.

* * *

[CCH Explanation at ¶542. Committee Reports at ¶10,250.]

Amendments

- **2010, Tax Relief, Unemployment Insurance Reauthorization, and Job Creation Act of 2010 (P.L. 111-312)**

P.L. 111-312, §709(a):

Amended Code Sec. 45M(b)(1) by striking "and" at the end of subparagraph (A), by striking the period at the end of subparagraph (B) and inserting a comma, and by adding at the end new subparagraphs (C)-(E). **Effective** for appliances produced after 12-31-2010.

P.L. 111-312, §709(b):

Amended Code Sec. 45M(b)(2) by striking "and" at the end of subparagraph (C), by striking the period at the end of

subparagraph (D) and inserting a comma, and by adding at the end new subparagraphs (E)-(F). **Effective** for appliances produced after 12-31-2010.

P.L. 111-312, §709(c):

Amended Code Sec. 45M(b)(3) by striking "and" at the end of subparagraph (C), by striking the period at the end of subparagraph (D) and inserting a comma, and by adding at the end new subparagraphs (E)-(F). **Effective** for appliances produced after 12-31-2010.

(e) LIMITATIONS.—

(1) AGGREGATE CREDIT AMOUNT ALLOWED.—The aggregate amount of credit allowed under subsection (a) with respect to a taxpayer for any taxable year shall not exceed *$25,000,000* reduced by the amount of the credit allowed under subsection (a) to the taxpayer (or any predecessor) for all prior taxable years beginning after *December 31, 2010.*

(2) AMOUNT ALLOWED FOR CERTAIN REFRIGERATORS AND CLOTHES WASHERS.—Refrigerators described in *subsection (b)(3)(F)* and clothes washers described in *subsection (b)(2)(F)* shall not be taken into account under paragraph (1).

(3) LIMITATION BASED ON GROSS RECEIPTS.—The credit allowed under subsection (a) with respect to a taxpayer for the taxable year shall not exceed an amount equal to *4 percent* of the average annual gross receipts of the taxpayer for the 3 taxable years preceding the taxable year in which the credit is determined.

* * *

[CCH Explanation at ¶542. Committee Reports at ¶10,250.]

Amendments

- **2010, Tax Relief, Unemployment Insurance Reauthorization, and Job Creation Act of 2010 (P.L. 111-312)**

P.L. 111-312, §709(d)(1)(A)-(B):

Amended Code Sec. 45M(e)(1) by striking "$75,000,000" and inserting "$25,000,000", and by striking "December 31, 2007" and inserting "December 31, 2010". **Effective** for tax years beginning after 12-31-2010.

P.L. 111-312, §709(d)(2)(A)-(B):

Amended Code Sec. 45M(e)(2) by striking "subsection (b)(3)(D)" and inserting "subsection (b)(3)(F)", and by striking "subsection (b)(2)(D)" and inserting "subsection (b)(2)(F)". **Effective** for tax years beginning after 12-31-2010.

P.L. 111-312, §709(d)(3):

Amended Code Sec. 45M(e)(3) by striking "2 percent" and inserting "4 percent". **Effective** for tax years beginning after 12-31-2010.

[¶5145] CODE SEC. 45N. MINE RESCUE TEAM TRAINING CREDIT.

* * *

(e) TERMINATION.—This section shall not apply to taxable years beginning after *December 31, 2011.*

[CCH Explanation at ¶534. Committee Reports at ¶10,400.]

Amendments

• **2010, Tax Relief, Unemployment Insurance Reauthorization, and Job Creation Act of 2010 (P.L. 111-312)**

P.L. 111-312, §735(a):

Amended Code Sec. 45N(e) by striking "December 31, 2009" and inserting "December 31, 2011". **Effective** for tax years beginning after 12-31-2009.

[¶5150] CODE SEC. 45P. EMPLOYER WAGE CREDIT FOR EMPLOYEES WHO ARE ACTIVE DUTY MEMBERS OF THE UNIFORMED SERVICES.

* * *

(f) TERMINATION.—This section shall not apply to any payments made after *December 31, 2011.*

[CCH Explanation at ¶526. Committee Reports at ¶10,410.]

Amendments

• **2010, Tax Relief, Unemployment Insurance Reauthorization, and Job Creation Act of 2010 (P.L. 111-312)**

P.L. 111-312, §736(a):

Amended Code Sec. 45P(f) by striking "December 31, 2009" and inserting "December 31, 2011". **Effective** for payments made after 12-31-2009.

[¶5155] CODE SEC. 51. AMOUNT OF CREDIT.

* * *

(c) WAGES DEFINED.—For purposes of this subpart—

* * *

(4) TERMINATION.—The term "wages" shall not include any amount paid or incurred to an individual who begins work for the employer—

(A) after December 31, 1994, and before October 1, 1996, or

(B) after *December 31, 2011.*

* * *

[CCH Explanation at ¶524. Committee Reports at ¶10,630.]

Amendments

• **2010, Tax Relief, Unemployment Insurance Reauthorization, and Job Creation Act of 2010 (P.L. 111-312)**

P.L. 111-312, §757(a):

Amended Code Sec. 51(c)(4)(B) by striking "August 31, 2011" and inserting "December 31, 2011". **Effective** for individuals who begin work for the employer after 12-17-2010.

[¶5165] CODE SEC. 54E. QUALIFIED ZONE ACADEMY BONDS.

* * *

(c) LIMITATION ON AMOUNT OF BONDS DESIGNATED.—

(1) NATIONAL LIMITATION.—There is a national zone academy bond limitation for each calendar year. Such limitation is $400,000,000 for *2008,* $1,400,000,000 for 2009 and 2010, *and* $400,000,000 for 2011 and, except as provided in paragraph (4), zero thereafter.

* * *

[CCH Explanation at ¶ 465. Committee Reports at ¶ 10,640.]

Amendments

• **2010, Tax Relief, Unemployment Insurance Reauthorization, and Job Creation Act of 2010 (P.L. 111-312)**

P.L. 111-312, § 758(a)(1)-(2):

Amended Code Sec. 54E(c)(1) by striking "2008 and" and inserting "2008,", and by inserting "and $400,000,000 for 2011" after "2010,". **Effective** for obligations issued after 12-31-2010.

[¶ 5170] CODE SEC. 55. ALTERNATIVE MINIMUM TAX IMPOSED.

* * *

(b) TENTATIVE MINIMUM TAX.—For purposes of this part—

* * *

»»→ Caution: *Code Sec. 55(b)(3), below, was amended by P.L. 108-27. For sunset provision, see P.L. 108-27, § 303 [as amended by P.L. 111-312], in the amendment notes.*

(3) MAXIMUM RATE OF TAX ON NET CAPITAL GAIN OF NONCORPORATE TAXPAYERS.—The amount determined under the first sentence of paragraph (1)(A)(i) shall not exceed the sum of—

(A) the amount determined under such first sentence computed at the rates and in the same manner as if this paragraph had not been enacted on the taxable excess reduced by the lesser of—

(i) the net capital gain; or

(ii) the sum of—

(I) the adjusted net capital gain, plus

(II) the unrecaptured section 1250 gain, plus

(B) 5 percent (0 percent in the case of taxable years beginning after 2007) of so much of the adjusted net capital gain (or, if less, taxable excess) as does not exceed an amount equal to the excess described in section 1(h)(1)(B), plus

(C) 15 percent of the adjusted net capital gain (or, if less, taxable excess) in excess of the amount on which tax is determined under subparagraph (B), plus

(D) 25 percent of the amount of taxable excess in excess of the sum of the amounts on which tax is determined under the preceding subparagraphs of this paragraph.

Terms used in this paragraph which are also used in section 1(h) shall have the respective meanings given such terms by section 1(h) but computed with the adjustments under this part.

* * *

[CCH Explanation at ¶ 375, ¶ 405 and ¶ 410. Committee Reports at ¶ 10,080 and ¶ 10,120.]

Amendments

• **2003, Jobs and Growth Tax Relief Reconciliation Act of 2003 (P.L. 108-27)**

P.L. 108-27, § 301(a)(1):

Amended Code Sec. 55(b)(3)(B) by striking "10 percent" and inserting "5 percent (0 percent in the case of taxable years beginning after 2007)". **Effective** for tax years ending on or after 5-6-2003. For a transitional rule, see Act Sec. 301(c), below.

P.L. 108-27, § 301(a)(2)(B):

Amended Code Sec. 55(b)(3)(C) by striking "20 percent" and inserting "15 percent". **Effective** for tax years ending on or after 5-6-2003. For a transitional rule, see Act Sec. 301(c), below.

P.L. 108-27, § 301(b)(2):

Amended Code Sec. 55(b)(3) by striking "In the case of taxable years beginning after December 31, 2000, rules similar to the rules of section 1(h)(2) shall apply for purposes of subparagraphs (B) and (C)." before "Terms used in this paragraph which are also used in section 1(h) shall have the same respective meanings given such terms by section 1(h) but computed with the adjustments of this part.". **Effective** for tax years ending on or after 5-6-2003. For a transitional rule, see Act Sec. 301(c), below.

P.L. 108-27, § 301(c), provides:

(c) TRANSITIONAL RULES FOR TAXABLE YEARS WHICH INCLUDE MAY 6, 2003.—For purposes of applying section 1(h) of the Internal Revenue Code of 1986 in the case of a taxable year which includes May 6, 2003—

(1) The amount of tax determined under subparagraph (B) of section 1(h)(1) of such Code shall be the sum of—

(A) 5 percent of the lesser of—

(i) the net capital gain determined by taking into account only gain or loss properly taken into account for the portion of the taxable year on or after May 6, 2003 (determined without regard to collectibles gain or loss, gain described in section 1(h)(6)(A)(i) of such Code, and section 1202 gain), or

(ii) the amount on which a tax is determined under such subparagraph (without regard to this subsection),

(B) 8 percent of the lesser of—

(i) the qualified 5-year gain (as defined in section 1(h)(9) of the Internal Revenue Code of 1986, as in effect on the day before the date of the enactment of this Act) properly taken into account for the portion of the taxable year before May 6, 2003, or

(ii) the excess (if any) of—

(I) the amount on which a tax is determined under such subparagraph (without regard to this subsection), over

(II) the amount on which a tax is determined under subparagraph (A), plus

(C) 10 percent of the excess (if any) of—

(i) the amount on which a tax is determined under such subparagraph (without regard to this subsection), over

(ii) the sum of the amounts on which a tax is determined under subparagraphs (A) and (B).

(2) The amount of tax determined under subparagraph (C) of section (1)(h)(1) of such Code shall be the sum of—

(A) 15 percent of the lesser of—

(i) the excess (if any) of the amount of net capital gain determined under subparagraph (A)(i) of paragraph (1) of this subsection over the amount on which a tax is determined under subparagraph (A) of paragraph (1) of this subsection, or

(ii) the amount on which a tax is determined under such subparagraph (C) (without regard to this subsection), plus

(B) 20 percent of the excess (if any) of—

(i) the amount on which a tax is determined under such subparagraph (C) (without regard to this subsection), over

(ii) the amount on which a tax is determined under subparagraph (A) of this paragraph.

(3) For purposes of applying section 55(b)(3) of such Code, rules similar to the rules of paragraphs (1) and (2) of this subsection shall apply.

(4) In applying this subsection with respect to any pass-thru entity, the determination of when gains and losses are properly taken into account shall be made at the entity level.

(5) For purposes of applying section 1(h)(11) of such Code, as added by section 302 of this Act, to this subsection, dividends which are qualified dividend income shall be treated as gain properly taken into account for the portion of the taxable year on or after May 6, 2003.

(6) Terms used in this subsection which are also used in section 1(h) of such Code shall have the respective meanings that such terms have in such section.

P.L. 108-27, §303, as amended by P.L. 109-222, §102, and P.L. 111-312, §102(a), provides:

SEC. 303. SUNSET OF TITLE.

All provisions of, and amendments made by, this title shall not apply to taxable years beginning after December 31, 2012, and the Internal Revenue Code of 1986 shall be applied and administered to such years as if such provisions and amendments had never been enacted.

(d) EXEMPTION AMOUNT.—For purposes of this section—

(1) EXEMPTION AMOUNT FOR TAXPAYERS OTHER THAN CORPORATIONS.—In the case of a taxpayer other than a corporation, the term "exemption amount" means—

(A) $45,000 (*$72,450 in the case of taxable years beginning in 2010 and $74,450 in the case of taxable years beginning in 2011*) in the case of—

(i) a joint return, or

(ii) a surviving spouse,

(B) $33,750 (*$47,450 in the case of taxable years beginning in 2010 and $48,450 in the case of taxable years beginning in 2011*) in the case of an individual who—

(i) is not a married individual, and

(ii) is not a surviving spouse,

(C) 50 percent of the dollar amount applicable under paragraph (1)(A) in the case of a married individual who files a separate return, and

(D) $22,500 in the case of an estate or trust.

For purposes of this paragraph, the term "surviving spouse" has the meaning given to such term by section 2(a), and marital status shall be determined under section 7703.

* * *

[CCH Explanation at ¶375. Committee Reports at ¶10,120.]

Amendments

● **2010, Tax Relief, Unemployment Insurance Reauthorization, and Job Creation Act of 2010 (P.L. 111-312)**

P.L. 111-312, §201(a)(1)-(2):

Amended Code Sec. 55(d)(1) by striking "$70,950" and all that follows through "2009" in subparagraph (A) and inserting "$72,450 in the case of taxable years beginning in 2010 and $74,450 in the case of taxable years beginning in 2011", and by striking "$46,700" and all that follows

through "2009" in subparagraph (B) and inserting "$47,450 in the case of taxable years beginning in 2010 and $48,450 in the case of taxable years beginning in 2011". Effective for tax years beginning after 12-31-2009. Prior to amendment, Code Sec. 55(d)(1)(A)-(B) read as follows:

(A) $45,000 ($70,950 in the case of taxable years beginning in 2009) in the case of—

(i) a joint return, or

(ii) a surviving spouse,

(B) $33,750 ($46,700 in the case of taxable years beginning in 2009) in the case of an individual who—

(i) is not a married individual, and

(ii) is not a surviving spouse,

P.L. 111-312, §201(c), provides:

(c) REPEAL OF EGTRRA SUNSET.—Title IX of the Economic Growth and Tax Relief Reconciliation Act of 2001 (relating to

sunset of provisions of such Act) shall not apply to title VII of such Act (relating to alternative minimum tax).

[¶5175] CODE SEC. 57. ITEMS OF TAX PREFERENCE.

(a) GENERAL RULE.—For purposes of this part, the items of tax preference determined under this section are—

* * *

⋙→ Caution: *Code Sec. 57(a)(7), below, was amended by P.L. 108-27. For sunset provision, see P.L. 108-27, §303 [as amended by P.L. 111-222 and P.L. 111-312], in the amendment notes.*

(7) EXCLUSION FOR GAINS ON SALE OF CERTAIN SMALL BUSINESS STOCK.—An amount equal to 7 percent of the amount excluded from gross income for the taxable year under section 1202.

* * *

[CCH Explanation at ¶415. Committee Reports at ¶10,080.]

Amendments

● **2003, Jobs and Growth Tax Relief Reconciliation Act of 2003 (P.L. 108-27)**

P.L. 108-27, §301(b)(3)(A)-(B):

Amended Code Sec. 57(a)(7) by striking "42 percent" the first place it appears and inserting "7 percent", and by striking the last sentence. **Effective** for dispositions on or after 5-6-2003. Prior to amendment, the last sentence of Code Sec. 57(a)(7) read as follows:

In the case of stock the holding period of which begins after December 31, 2000 (determined with the application of

the last sentence of section 1(h)(2)(B)), the preceding sentence shall be applied by substituting "28 percent" for "42 percent".

P.L. 108-27, §303, as amended by P.L. 109-222, §102, and P.L. 111-312, §102(a), provides:

SEC. 303. SUNSET OF TITLE.

All provisions of, and amendments made by, this title shall not apply to taxable years beginning after December 31, 2012, and the Internal Revenue Code of 1986 shall be applied and administered to such years as if such provisions and amendments had never been enacted.

[¶5180] CODE SEC. 62. ADJUSTED GROSS INCOME DEFINED.

(a) GENERAL RULE.—For purposes of this subtitle, the term "adjusted gross income" means, in the case of an individual, gross income minus the following deductions:

* * *

(2) CERTAIN TRADE AND BUSINESS DEDUCTIONS OF EMPLOYEES.—

* * *

(D) CERTAIN EXPENSES OF ELEMENTARY AND SECONDARY SCHOOL TEACHERS.—In the case of taxable years beginning during 2002, 2003, 2004, 2005, 2006, 2007, 2008, *2009, 2010, or 2011*, the deductions allowed by section 162 which consist of expenses, not in excess of $250, paid or incurred by an eligible educator in connection with books, supplies (other than nonathletic supplies for courses of instruction in health or physical education), computer equipment (including related software and services) and other equipment, and supplementary materials used by the eligible educator in the classroom.

* * *

»»→ *Caution: Code Sec. 62(a)(18), below, was added by P.L. 107-16. For sunset provision, see P.L. 107-16, §901 [as amended by P.L. 111-312], in the amendment notes.*

(18) HIGHER EDUCATION EXPENSES.—The deduction allowed by section 222.

[CCH Explanation at ¶327 and ¶415. Committee Reports at ¶10,080 and ¶10,280.]

Amendments

• **2010, Tax Relief, Unemployment Insurance Reauthorization, and Job Creation Act of 2010 (P.L. 111-312)**

P.L. 111-312, §721(a):

Amended Code Sec. 62(a)(2)(D) by striking "or 2009" and inserting "2009, 2010, or 2011". **Effective** for tax years beginning after 12-31-2009.

• **2001, Economic Growth and Tax Relief Reconciliation Act of 2001 (P.L. 107-16)**

P.L. 107-16, §431(b):

Amended Code Sec. 62(a) by inserting after paragraph (17) a new paragraph (18). **Effective** for payments made in tax years beginning after 12-31-2001.

P.L. 107-16, §901(a)–(b) [as amended by P.L. 111-312, §101(a)(1)], provides:

SEC. 901. SUNSET OF PROVISIONS OF ACT.

(a) IN GENERAL.—All provisions of, and amendments made by, this Act shall not apply—

(1) to taxable, plan, or limitation years beginning after December 31, 2012, or

(2) in the case of title V, to estates of decedents dying, gifts made, or generation skipping transfers, after December 31, 2012.

(b) APPLICATION OF CERTAIN LAWS.—The Internal Revenue Code of 1986 and the Employee Retirement Income Security Act of 1974 shall be applied and administered to years, estates, gifts, and transfers described in subsection (a) as if the provisions and amendments described in subsection (a) had never been enacted.

[¶5185] CODE SEC. 63. TAXABLE INCOME DEFINED.

* * *

(c) STANDARD DEDUCTION.—For purposes of this subtitle—

* * *

»»→ *Caution: Code Sec. 63(c)(2), below, was amended by P.L. 107-16, P.L. 107-147, and P.L. 108-311. For sunset provisions, see P.L. 107-16, §901 [as amended by P.L. 111-312], and P.L. 108-311, §105, in the amendment notes.*

(2) BASIC STANDARD DEDUCTION.—For purposes of paragraph (1), the basic standard deduction is—

(A) 200 percent of the dollar amount in effect under subparagraph (C) for the taxable year in the case of—

(i) a joint return, or

(ii) a surviving spouse (as defined in section 2(a)),

(B) $4,400 in the case of a head of household (as defined in section 2(b)), or

(C) $3,000 in any other case.

* * *

»»→ *Caution: Code Sec. 63(c)(4), below, was amended by P.L. 107-16, P.L. 107-147, and P.L. 108-311. For sunset provisions, see P.L. 107-16, §901 [as amended by P.L. 111-312], and P.L. 108-311, §105, in the amendment notes.*

(4) ADJUSTMENTS FOR INFLATION.—In the case of any taxable year beginning in a calendar year after 1988, each dollar amount contained in paragraph (2)(B), (2)(C), or (5) or subsection (f) shall be increased by an amount equal to—

(A) such dollar amount, multiplied by

(B) the cost-of-living adjustment determined under section 1(f)(3) for the calendar year in which the taxable year begins, by substituting for "calendar year 1992" in subparagraph (B) thereof—

(i) "calendar year 1987" in the case of the dollar amounts contained in paragraph (2)(B), (2)(C), or (5)(A) or subsection (f), and

(ii) "calendar year 1997" in the case of the dollar amount contained in paragraph (5)(B).

* * *

P.L. 111-312, § 304, provides:

SEC. 304. APPLICATION OF EGTRRA SUNSET TO THIS TITLE.

Section 901 of the Economic Growth and Tax Relief Reconciliation Act of 2001 shall apply to the amendments made by this title.

- **2001, Economic Growth and Tax Relief Reconciliation Act of 2001 (P.L. 107-16)**

P.L. 107-16, § 542(c):

Amended Code Sec. 121(d) by adding at the end a new paragraph (9). **Effective** for estates of decedents dying after 12-31-2009.

P.L. 107-16, § 901(a)-(b), as amended by P.L. 111-312, § 101(a)(1), provides:

SEC. 901. SUNSET OF PROVISIONS OF ACT.

(a) IN GENERAL.—All provisions of, and amendments made by, this Act shall not apply—

(1) to taxable, plan, or limitation years beginning after December 31, 2012, or

(2) in the case of title V, to estates of decedents dying, gifts made, or generation skipping transfers, after December 31, 2012.

(b) APPLICATION OF CERTAIN LAWS.—The Internal Revenue Code of 1986 and the Employee Retirement Income Security Act of 1974 shall be applied and administered to years, estates, gifts, and transfers described in subsection (a) as if the provisions and amendments described in subsection (a) had never been enacted.

[¶ 5210] CODE SEC. 127. EDUCATIONAL ASSISTANCE PROGRAMS.

* * *

(c) DEFINITIONS; SPECIAL RULES.—For purposes of this section—

⧠→ *Caution: Code Sec. 127(c)(1), below, was amended by P.L. 107-16. For sunset provision, see P.L. 107-16, § 901 [as amended by P.L. 111-312], in the amendment notes.*

(1) EDUCATIONAL ASSISTANCE.—The term "educational assistance" means—

(A) the payment, by an employer, of expenses incurred by or on behalf of an employee for education of the employee (including, but not limited to, tuition, fees, and similar payments, books, supplies, and equipment), and

(B) the provision, by an employer, of courses of instruction for such employee (including books, supplies, and equipment),

but does not include payment for, or the provision of, tools or supplies which may be retained by the employee after completion of a course of instruction, or meals, lodging, or transportation. The term "educational assistance" also does not include any payment for, or the provision of any benefits with respect to, any course or other education involving sports, games, or hobbies.

* * *

[CCH Explanation at ¶ 335. Committee Reports at ¶ 10,050.]

Amendments

- **2001, Economic Growth and Tax Relief Reconciliation Act of 2001 (P.L. 107-16)**

P.L. 107-16, § 411(b):

Amended the last sentence of Code Sec. 127(c)(1) by striking before the period ", and such term also does not include any payment for, or the provision of any benefits with respect to, any graduate level course of a kind normally taken by an individual pursuing a program leading to a law, business, medical, or other advanced academic or professional degree". **Effective** with respect to expenses relating to courses beginning after 12-31-2001.

P.L. 107-16, § 901(a)-(b), as amended by P.L. 111-312, § 101(a)(1), provides:

SEC. 901. SUNSET OF PROVISIONS OF ACT.

(a) IN GENERAL.—All provisions of, and amendments made by, this Act shall not apply—

(1) to taxable, plan, or limitation years beginning after December 31, 2012, or

(2) in the case of title V, to estates of decedents dying, gifts made, or generation skipping transfers, after December 31, 2012.

(b) APPLICATION OF CERTAIN LAWS.—The Internal Revenue Code of 1986 and the Employee Retirement Income Security Act of 1974 shall be applied and administered to years, estates, gifts, and transfers described in subsection (a) as if the provisions and amendments described in subsection (a) had never been enacted.

»»→ *Caution: Code Sec. 127(d), below, was stricken by P.L. 107-16. For sunset provision, see P.L. 107-16, §901 [as amended by P.L. 111-312], in the amendment notes.*

(d) [Stricken.]

[CCH Explanation at ¶335. Committee Reports at ¶10,050.]

Amendments

• **2001, Economic Growth and Tax Relief Reconciliation Act of 2001 (P.L. 107-16)**

P.L. 107-16, §411(a):

Amended Code Sec. 127 by striking subsection (d) and by redesignating subsection (e) as subsection (d). Effective with respect to expenses relating to courses beginning after 12-31-2001. Prior to being stricken, Code Sec. 127(d) read as follows:

(d) TERMINATION.—This section shall not apply to expenses paid with respect to courses beginning after December 31, 2001.

P.L. 107-16, §901(a)-(b), as amended by P.L. 111-312, §101(a)(1), provides:

SEC. 901. SUNSET OF PROVISIONS OF ACT.

(a) IN GENERAL.—All provisions of, and amendments made by, this Act shall not apply—

(1) to taxable, plan, or limitation years beginning after December 31, 2012, or

(2) in the case of title V, to estates of decedents dying, gifts made, or generation skipping transfers, after December 31, 2012.

(b) APPLICATION OF CERTAIN LAWS.—The Internal Revenue Code of 1986 and the Employee Retirement Income Security Act of 1974 shall be applied and administered to years, estates, gifts, and transfers described in subsection (a) as if the provisions and amendments described in subsection (a) had never been enacted.

»»→ *Caution: Former Code Sec. 127(e), below, was redesignated as Code Sec. 127(d) by P.L. 107-16. For sunset provision, see P.L. 107-16, §901 [as amended by P.L. 111-312], in the amendment notes.*

(d) CROSS REFERENCE.—

For reporting and recordkeeping requirements, see section 6039D.

[CCH Explanation at ¶335. Committee Reports at ¶10,050.]

Amendments

• **2001, Economic Growth and Tax Relief Reconciliation Act of 2001 (P.L. 107-16)**

P.L. 107-16, §411(a):

Amended Code Sec. 127 by redesignating subsection (e) as subsection (d). Effective with respect to expenses relating to courses beginning after 12-31-2001.

P.L. 107-16, §901(a)-(b), as amended by P.L. 111-312, §101(a)(1), provides:

SEC. 901. SUNSET OF PROVISIONS OF ACT.

(a) IN GENERAL.—All provisions of, and amendments made by, this Act shall not apply—

(1) to taxable, plan, or limitation years beginning after December 31, 2012, or

(2) in the case of title V, to estates of decedents dying, gifts made, or generation skipping transfers, after December 31, 2012.

(b) APPLICATION OF CERTAIN LAWS.—The Internal Revenue Code of 1986 and the Employee Retirement Income Security Act of 1974 shall be applied and administered to years, estates, gifts, and transfers described in subsection (a) as if the provisions and amendments described in subsection (a) had never been enacted.

[¶5215] CODE SEC. 132. CERTAIN FRINGE BENEFITS.

* * *

(f) QUALIFIED TRANSPORTATION FRINGE.—

* * *

(2) LIMITATION ON EXCLUSION.—The amount of the fringe benefits which are provided by an employer to any employee and which may be excluded from gross income under subsection (a)(5) shall not exceed—

(A) $100 per month in the case of the aggregate of the benefits described in subparagraphs (A) and (B) of paragraph (1),

(B) $175 per month in the case of qualified parking, and

(C) the applicable annual limitation in the case of any qualified bicycle commuting reimbursement.

In the case of any month beginning on or after the date of the enactment of this sentence and before *January 1, 2012*, subparagraph (A) shall be applied as if the dollar amount therein were the same as the dollar amount in effect for such month under subparagraph (B).

* * *

[CCH Explanation at ¶380. Committee Reports at ¶10,340.]
Amendments
- **2010, Tax Relief, Unemployment Insurance Reauthorization, and Job Creation Act of 2010 (P.L. 111-312)**

P.L. 111-312, §727(a):

Amended Code Sec. 132(f)(2) by striking "January 1, 2011" and inserting "January 1, 2012". **Effective** for months after 12-31-2010.

[¶5220] CODE SEC. 135. INCOME FROM UNITED STATES SAVINGS BONDS USED TO PAY HIGHER EDUCATION TUITION AND FEES.

* * *

(c) Definitions.—For purposes of this section—

* * *

(4) Modified Adjusted Gross Income.—The term "modified adjusted gross income" means the adjusted gross income of the taxpayer for the taxable year determined—

⇨ *Caution: Code Sec. 135(c)(4)(A), below, was amended by P.L. 107-16. For sunset provision, see P.L. 107-16, §901 [as amended by P.L. 111-312], in the amendment notes.*

(A) without regard to this section and sections 137, 199, 221, 222, 911, 931, and 933, and

(B) after the application of sections 86, 469, and 219.

[CCH Explanation at ¶350. Committee Reports at ¶10,310.]
Amendments
- **2004, American Jobs Creation Act of 2004 (P.L. 108-357)**

P.L. 108-357, §102(d)(1):

Amended Code Sec. 135(c)(4)(A) by inserting "199," before "221". **Effective** for tax years beginning after 12-31-2004.

- **2001, Economic Growth and Tax Relief Reconciliation Act of 2001 (P.L. 107-16)**

P.L. 107-16, §431(c)(1):

Amended Code Sec. 135(c)(4) by inserting "222," after "221,". **Effective** for payments made in tax years beginning after 12-31-2001.

P.L. 107-16, §901(a)-(b), as amended by P.L. 111-312, §101(a)(1), provides:

SEC. 901. SUNSET OF PROVISIONS OF ACT.

(a) In General.—All provisions of, and amendments made by, this Act shall not apply—

(1) to taxable, plan, or limitation years beginning after December 31, 2012, or

(2) in the case of title V, to estates of decedents dying, gifts made, or generation skipping transfers, after December 31, 2012.

(b) Application of Certain Laws.—The Internal Revenue Code of 1986 and the Employee Retirement Income Security Act of 1974 shall be applied and administered to years, estates, gifts, and transfers described in subsection (a) as if the provisions and amendments described in subsection (a) had never been enacted.

(d) Special Rules.—

* * *

(2) Coordination with Other Higher Education Benefits.—The amount of the qualified higher education expenses otherwise taken into account under subsection (a) with respect to the education of an individual shall be reduced (before the application of subsection (b)) by—

⇨ *Caution: Code Sec. 135(d)(2)(A), below, was amended by P.L. 107-16. For sunset provision, see P.L. 107-16, §901 [as amended by P.L. 111-312], in the amendment notes.*

(A) the amount of such expenses which are taken into account in determining the credit allowed to the taxpayer or any other person under section 25A with respect to such expenses; and

(B) the amount of such expenses which are taken into account in determining the exclusions under sections 529(c)(3)(B) and 530(d)(2).

* * *

[CCH Explanation at ¶330. Committee Reports at ¶10,050.]

Amendments

• **2001, Economic Growth and Tax Relief Reconciliation Act of 2001 (P.L. 107-16)**

P.L. 107-16, §401(g)(2)(B):

Amended Code Sec. 135(d)(2)(A) by striking "allowable" and inserting "allowed". **Effective** for tax years beginning after 12-31-2001.

P.L. 107-16, §901(a)-(b), as amended by P.L. 111-312, §101(a)(1), provides:

SEC. 901. SUNSET OF PROVISIONS OF ACT.

(a) In General.—All provisions of, and amendments made by, this Act shall not apply—

(1) to taxable, plan, or limitation years beginning after December 31, 2012, or

(2) in the case of title V, to estates of decedents dying, gifts made, or generation skipping transfers, after December 31, 2012.

(b) Application of Certain Laws.—The Internal Revenue Code of 1986 and the Employee Retirement Income Security Act of 1974 shall be applied and administered to years, estates, gifts, and transfers described in subsection (a) as if the provisions and amendments described in subsection (a) had never been enacted.

[¶5225] CODE SEC. 137. ADOPTION ASSISTANCE PROGRAMS.

(a) Exclusion.—

≫≫→ *Caution: Code Sec. 137(a)(1), below, was amended by P.L. 107-16. For sunset provision, see P.L. 107-16, §901 [as amended by P.L. 111-312], in the amendment notes.*

(1) In General.—Gross income of an employee does not include amounts paid or expenses incurred by the employer for qualified adoption expenses in connection with the adoption of a child by an employee if such amounts are furnished pursuant to an adoption assistance program.

≫≫→ *Caution: Code Sec. 137(a)(2), below, as amended by P.L. 111-312, applies to tax years beginning after December 31, 2011. For sunset provisions, see P.L. 107-16, §901 [as amended by P.L. 111-312], and P.L. 111-148, §10909(c) [as amended by P.L. 111-312], in the amendment notes.*

(2) $10,000 Exclusion for Adoption of Child with Special Needs Regardless of Expenses.—In the case of an adoption of a child with special needs which becomes final during a taxable year, the qualified adoption expenses with respect to such adoption for such year shall be increased by an amount equal to the excess (if any) of $10,000 over the actual aggregate qualified adoption expenses with respect to such adoption during such taxable year and all prior taxable years.

[CCH Explanation at ¶370. Committee Reports at ¶10,060.]

Amendments

• **2010, Tax Relief, Unemployment Insurance Reauthorization, and Job Creation Act of 2010 (P.L. 111-312)**

P.L. 111-312, §101(b)(1):

Amended Code Sec. 137(a)(2) to read as such provision would read if section 10909 of the Patient Protection and Affordable Care Act (P.L. 111-148) had never been enacted. **Effective** for tax years beginning after 12-31-2011.

• **2010, Patient Protection and Affordable Care Act (P.L. 111-148)**

P.L. 111-148, §10909(a)(2)(B)(i)-(ii):

Amended Code Sec. 137(a)(2), in the text by striking "$10,000" and inserting "$13,170", and in the heading by striking "$10,000" and inserting "$13,170". **Effective** for tax years beginning after 12-31-2009.

P.L. 111-148, §10909(c), as amended by P.L. 111-312, §101(b)(1), provides:

(c) Sunset Provision.—Each provision of law amended by this section is amended to read as such provision would read if this section had never been enacted. The amend-

ments made by the preceding sentence shall apply to taxable years beginning after December 31, 2011.

• **2001, Economic Growth and Tax Relief Reconciliation Act of 2001 (P.L. 107-16)**

P.L. 107-16, §202(a)(2):

Amended Code Sec. 137(a). **Effective** for tax years beginning after 12-31-2002. Prior to amendment, Code Sec. 137(a) read as follows:

(a) In General.—Gross income of an employee does not include amounts paid or expenses incurred by the employer for qualified adoption expenses in connection with the adoption of a child by an employee if such amounts are furnished pursuant to an adoption assistance program.

P.L. 107-16, §901(a)-(b), as amended by P.L. 111-312, §101(a)(1), provides [but see P.L. 111-148, §10909(c), above]:

SEC. 901. SUNSET OF PROVISIONS OF ACT.

(a) In General.—All provisions of, and amendments made by, this Act shall not apply—

(1) to taxable, plan, or limitation years beginning after December 31, 2012, or

(2) in the case of title V, to estates of decedents dying, gifts made, or generation skipping transfers, after December 31, 2012.

(b) APPLICATION OF CERTAIN LAWS.—The Internal Revenue Code of 1986 and the Employee Retirement Income Security Act of 1974 shall be applied and administered to years, estates, gifts, and transfers described in subsection (a) as if the provisions and amendments described in subsection (a) had never been enacted.

(b) LIMITATIONS.—

>>>→ *Caution: Code Sec. 137(b)(1), below, as amended by P.L. 111-312, applies to tax years beginning after December 31, 2011. For sunset provisions, see P.L. 107-16, §901 [as amended by P.L. 111-312], and P.L. 111-148, §10909(c) [as amended by P.L. 111-312], in the amendment notes.*

(1) DOLLAR LIMITATION.—The aggregate of the amounts paid or expenses incurred which may be taken into account under subsection (a) for all taxable years with respect to the adoption of a child by the taxpayer shall not exceed $10,000.

>>>→ *Caution: Code Sec. 137(b)(2)-(3), below, was amended by P.L. 107-16. For sunset provision, see P.L. 107-16, §901 [as amended by P.L. 111-312], in the amendment notes.*

(2) INCOME LIMITATION.—The amount excludable from gross income under subsection (a) for any taxable year shall be reduced (but not below zero) by an amount which bears the same ratio to the amount so excludable (determined without regard to this paragraph but with regard to paragraph (1)) as—

>>>→ *Caution: Code Sec. 137(b)(2)(A), below, was amended by P.L. 107-16. For sunset provision, see P.L. 107-16, §901, in the amendment notes.*

(A) the amount (if any) by which the taxpayer's adjusted gross income exceeds $150,000, bears to

(B) $40,000.

(3) DETERMINATION OF ADJUSTED GROSS INCOME.—For purposes of paragraph (2), adjusted gross income shall be determined—

>>>→ *Caution: Code Sec. 137(b)(3)(A), below, was amended by P.L. 107-16. For sunset provision, see P.L. 107-16, §901, in the amendment notes.*

(A) without regard to this section and sections 199, 221, 222, 911, 931, and 933, and

(B) after the application of sections 86, 135, 219, and 469.

[CCH Explanation at ¶350 and ¶370. Committee Reports at ¶10,060 and ¶10,310.]

Amendments

• **2010, Tax Relief, Unemployment Insurance Reauthorization, and Job Creation Act of 2010 (P.L. 111-312)**

P.L. 111-312, §101(b)(1):

Amended Code Sec. 137(b)(1) to read as such provision would read if section 10909 of the Patient Protection and Affordable Care Act (P.L. 111-148) had never been enacted. **Effective** for tax years beginning after 12-31-2011.

• **2010, Patient Protection and Affordable Care Act (P.L. 111-148)**

P.L. 111-148, §10909(a)(2)(A):

Amended Code Sec. 137(b)(1) by striking "$10,000" and inserting "$13,170". **Effective** for tax years beginning after 12-31-2009.

P.L. 111-148, §10909(c), as amended by P.L. 111-312, §101(b)(1), provides:

(c) SUNSET PROVISION.—Each provision of law amended by this section is amended to read as such provision would read if this section had never been enacted. The amendments made by the preceding sentence shall apply to taxable years beginning after December 31, 2011.

• **2001, Economic Growth and Tax Relief Reconciliation Act of 2001 (P.L. 107-16)**

P.L. 107-16, §202(b)(1)(B)(i)-(iii):

Amended Code Sec. 137(b)(1) by striking "$5,000" and inserting "$10,000", by striking "($6,000, in the case of a child with special needs)" before the period, and by striking "subsection (a)" and inserting "subsection (a)(1)". **Effective** for tax years beginning after 12-31-2001.

P.L. 107-16, §202(b)(2)(B):

Amended Code Sec. 137(b)(2)(A) by striking "$75,000" and inserting "$150,000". **Effective** for tax years beginning after 12-31-2001.

P.L. 107-16, §431(c)(1):

Amended Code Sec. 137(b)(3) by inserting "222," after "221,". **Effective** for payments made in tax years beginning after 12-31-2001.

P.L. 107-16, §901(a)-(b), as amended by P.L. 111-312, §101(a)(1), provides [but see P.L. 111-148, §10909(c), above]:

SEC. 901. SUNSET OF PROVISIONS OF ACT.

(a) IN GENERAL.—All provisions of, and amendments made by, this Act shall not apply—

(1) to taxable, plan, or limitation years beginning after December 31, 2012, or

(2) in the case of title V, to estates of decedents dying, gifts made, or generation skipping transfers, after December 31, 2012.

(b) APPLICATION OF CERTAIN LAWS.—The Internal Revenue Code of 1986 and the Employee Retirement Income Security Act of 1974 shall be applied and administered to years, estates, gifts, and transfers described in subsection (a) as if the provisions and amendments described in subsection (a) had never been enacted.

>>>→ *Caution: Code Sec. 137(d), below, as amended by P.L. 111-312, applies to tax years beginning after December 31, 2011. For sunset provision, see P.L. 111-148, §10909(c) [as amended by P.L. 111-312], in the amendment notes.*

(d) QUALIFIED ADOPTION EXPENSES.—For purposes of this section, the term "qualified adoption expenses" has the meaning given such term by *section 23(d)* (determined without regard to reimbursements under this section).

[CCH Explanation at ¶370. Committee Reports at ¶10,060.]

Amendments

• **2010, Tax Relief, Unemployment Insurance Reauthorization, and Job Creation Act of 2010 (P.L. 111-312)**

P.L. 111-312, §101(b)(1):

Amended Code Sec. 137(d) to read as such provision would read if section 10909 of the Patient Protection and Affordable Care Act (P.L. 111-148) had never been enacted. **Effective** for tax years beginning after 12-31-2011.

• **2010, Patient Protection and Affordable Care Act (P.L. 111-148)**

P.L. 111-148, §10909(b)(2)(J)(i):

Amended Code Sec. 137(d) by striking "section 23(d)" and inserting "section 36C(d)". **Effective** for tax years beginning after 12-31-2009.

P.L. 111-148, §10909(c), as amended by P.L. 111-312, §101(b)(1), provides:

(c) SUNSET PROVISION.—Each provision of law amended by this section is amended to read as such provision would read if this section had never been enacted. The amendments made by the preceding sentence shall apply to taxable years beginning after December 31, 2011.

>>>→ *Caution: Code Sec. 137(e), below, as amended by P.L. 111-312, applies to tax years beginning after December 31, 2011. For sunset provision, see P.L. 111-148, §10909(c) [as amended by P.L. 111-312], in the amendment notes.*

(e) CERTAIN RULES TO APPLY.—Rules similar to the rules of subsections (e), (f), and (g) of *section 23* shall apply for purposes of this section.

[CCH Explanation at ¶370. Committee Reports at ¶10,060.]

Amendments

• **2010, Tax Relief, Unemployment Insurance Reauthorization, and Job Creation Act of 2010 (P.L. 111-312)**

P.L. 111-312, §101(b)(1):

Amended Code Sec. 137(e) to read as such provision would read if section 10909 of the Patient Protection and Affordable Care Act (P.L. 111-148) had never been enacted. **Effective** for tax years beginning after 12-31-2011.

• **2010, Patient Protection and Affordable Care Act (P.L. 111-148)**

P.L. 111-148, §10909(b)(2)(J)(ii):

Amended Code Sec. 137(e) by striking "section 23" and inserting "section 36C". **Effective** for tax years beginning after 12-31-2009.

P.L. 111-148, §10909(c), as amended by P.L. 111-312, §101(b)(1), provides:

(c) SUNSET PROVISION.—Each provision of law amended by this section is amended to read as such provision would read if this section had never been enacted. The amendments made by the preceding sentence shall apply to taxable years beginning after December 31, 2011.

>>>→ *Caution: Code Sec. 137(f), below, as amended by P.L. 111-312, applies to tax years beginning after December 31, 2011. For sunset provision, see P.L. 111-148, §10909(c) [as amended by P.L. 111-312], in the amendment notes.*

(f) ADJUSTMENTS FOR INFLATION.—In the case of a taxable year beginning after December 31, 2002, each of the dollar amounts in subsection (a)(2) and paragraphs (1) and (2)(A) of subsection (b) shall be increased by an amount equal to—

(1) such dollar amount, multiplied by

(2) the cost-of-living adjustment determined under section 1(f)(3) for the calendar year in which the taxable year begins, determined by substituting "calendar year 2001" for "calendar year 1992" in subparagraph (B) thereof.

If any amount as increased under the preceding sentence is not a multiple of $10, such amount shall be rounded to the nearest multiple of $10.

[CCH Explanation at ¶370.]
Amendments

• **2010, Tax Relief, Unemployment Insurance Reauthorization, and Job Creation Act of 2010 (P.L. 111-312)**

P.L. 111-312, §101(b)(1):

Amended Code Sec. 137(f) to read as such provision would read if section 10909 of the Patient Protection and Affordable Care Act (P.L. 111-148) had never been enacted. Effective for tax years beginning after 12-31-2011. Prior to amendment, Code Sec. 137(f) read as follows:

(f) ADJUSTMENTS FOR INFLATION.—

(1) DOLLAR LIMITATIONS.—In the case of a taxable year beginning after December 31, 2010, each of the dollar amounts in subsections (a)(2) and (b)(1) shall be increased by an amount equal to—

(A) such dollar amount, multiplied by

(B) the cost-of-living adjustment determined under section 1(f)(3) for the calendar year in which the taxable year begins, determined by substituting "calendar year 2009" for "calendar year 1992" in subparagraph (B) thereof.

If any amount as increased under the preceding sentence is not a multiple of $10, such amount shall be rounded to the nearest multiple of $10.

(2) INCOME LIMITATION.—In the case of a taxable year beginning after December 31, 2002, the dollar amount in subsection (b)(2)(A) shall be increased by an amount equal to—

(A) such dollar amount, multiplied by

(B) the cost-of-living adjustment determined under section 1(f)(3) for the calendar year in which the taxable year begins, determined by substituting "calendar year 2001" for "calendar year 1992" in subparagraph [(B)] thereof.

If any amount as increased under the preceding sentence is not a multiple of $10, such amount shall be rounded to the nearest multiple of $10.

• **2010, Patient Protection and Affordable Care Act (P.L. 111-148)**

P.L. 111-148, §10909(a)(2)(C):

Amended Code Sec. 137(f). Effective for tax years beginning after 12-31-2009. Prior to amendment, Code Sec. 137(f) read as follows:

(f) ADJUSTMENTS FOR INFLATION.—In the case of a taxable year beginning after December 31, 2002, each of the dollar amounts in subsection (a)(2) and paragraphs (1) and (2)(A) of subsection (b) shall be increased by an amount equal to—

(1) such dollar amount, multiplied by

(2) the cost-of-living adjustment determined under section 1(f)(3) for the calendar year in which the taxable year begins, determined by substituting "calendar year 2001" for "calendar year 1992" in subparagraph (B) thereof.

If any amount as increased under the preceding sentence is not a multiple of $10, such amount shall be rounded to the nearest multiple of $10.

P.L. 111-148, §10909(c), as amended by P.L. 111-312, §101(b)(1), provides:

(c) SUNSET PROVISION.—Each provision of law amended by this section is amended to read as such provision would read if this section had never been enacted. The amendments made by the preceding sentence shall apply to taxable years beginning after December 31, 2011.

[¶5230] CODE SEC. 142. EXEMPT FACILITY BOND.

(a) GENERAL RULE.—For purposes of this part, the term "exempt facility bond" means any bond issued as part of an issue 95 percent or more of the net proceeds of which are to be used to provide—

* * *

(11) high-speed intercity rail facilities,

(12) environmental enhancements of hydroelectric generating facilities,

⤞ *Caution: Code Sec. 142(a)(13), below, was added by P.L. 107-16. For sunset provision, see P.L. 107-16, §901 [as amended by P.L. 111-312], in the amendment notes.*

(13) qualified public educational facilities,

* * *

[CCH Explanation at ¶460. Committee Reports at ¶10,050.]
Amendments

• **2005, Safe, Accountable, Flexible, Efficient Transportation Equity Act: A Legacy for Users (P.L. 109-59)**

P.L. 109-59, §11143(a):

Amended Code Sec. 142(a) by striking "or" at the end of paragraph (13), by striking the period at the end of paragraph (14) and inserting ", or", and by adding at the end a new paragraph (15). Effective for bonds issued after 8-10-2005.

• 2004, American Jobs Creation Act of 2004 (P.L. 108-357)

P.L. 108-357, §701(a):

Amended Code Sec. 142(a) by striking "or" at the end of paragraph (12), by striking the period at the end of paragraph (13) and inserting ", or", and by inserting at the end a new paragraph (14). **Effective** for bonds issued after 12-31-2004.

• 2001, Economic Growth and Tax Relief Reconciliation Act of 2001 (P.L. 107-16)

P.L. 107-16, §422(a):

Amended Code Sec. 142(a) by striking "or" at the end of paragraph (11), by striking the period at the end of paragraph (12) and inserting ", or", and by adding at the end a new paragraph (13). **Effective** for bonds issued after 12-31-2001.

P.L. 107-16, §901(a)-(b), as amended by P.L. 111-312, §101(a)(1), provides:

SEC. 901. SUNSET OF PROVISIONS OF ACT.

(a) IN GENERAL.—All provisions of, and amendments made by, this Act shall not apply—

(1) to taxable, plan, or limitation years beginning after December 31, 2012, or

(2) in the case of title V, to estates of decedents dying, gifts made, or generation skipping transfers, after December 31, 2012.

(b) APPLICATION OF CERTAIN LAWS.—The Internal Revenue Code of 1986 and the Employee Retirement Income Security Act of 1974 shall be applied and administered to years, estates, gifts, and transfers described in subsection (a) as if the provisions and amendments described in subsection (a) had never been enacted.

»»→ *Caution: Code Sec. 142(k), below, was added by P.L. 107-16. For sunset provision, see P.L. 107-16, §901 [as amended by P.L. 111-312], in the amendment notes.*

(k) QUALIFIED PUBLIC EDUCATIONAL FACILITIES.—

(1) IN GENERAL.—For purposes of subsection (a)(13), the term "qualified public educational facility" means any school facility which is—

(A) part of a public elementary school or a public secondary school, and

(B) owned by a private, for-profit corporation pursuant to a public-private partnership agreement with a State or local educational agency described in paragraph (2).

(2) PUBLIC-PRIVATE PARTNERSHIP AGREEMENT DESCRIBED.—A public-private partnership agreement is described in this paragraph if it is an agreement—

(A) under which the corporation agrees—

(i) to do 1 or more of the following: construct, rehabilitate, refurbish, or equip a school facility, and

(ii) at the end of the term of the agreement, to transfer the school facility to such agency for no additional consideration, and

(B) the term of which does not exceed the term of the issue to be used to provide the school facility.

(3) SCHOOL FACILITY.—For purposes of this subsection, the term "school facility" means—

(A) any school building,

(B) any functionally related and subordinate facility and land with respect to such building, including any stadium or other facility primarily used for school events, and

(C) any property, to which section 168 applies (or would apply but for section 179), for use in a facility described in subparagraph (A) or (B).

(4) PUBLIC SCHOOLS.—For purposes of this subsection, the terms "elementary school" and "secondary school" have the meanings given such terms by section 14101 of the Elementary and Secondary Education Act of 1965 (20 U.S.C. 8801), as in effect on the date of the enactment of this subsection.

(5) ANNUAL AGGREGATE FACE AMOUNT OF TAX-EXEMPT FINANCING.—

(A) IN GENERAL.—An issue shall not be treated as an issue described in subsection (a)(13) if the aggregate face amount of bonds issued by the State pursuant thereto (when added to the aggregate face amount of bonds previously so issued during the calendar year) exceeds an amount equal to the greater of—

(i) $10 multiplied by the State population, or

(ii) $5,000,000.

(B) Allocation Rules.—

(i) In General.—Except as otherwise provided in this subparagraph, the State may allocate the amount described in subparagraph (A) for any calendar year in such manner as the State determines appropriate.

(ii) Rules for Carryforward of Unused Limitation.—A State may elect to carry forward an unused limitation for any calendar year for 3 calendar years following the calendar year in which the unused limitation arose under rules similar to the rules of section 146(f), except that the only purpose for which the carryforward may be elected is the issuance of exempt facility bonds described in subsection (a)(13).

* * *

[CCH Explanation at ¶ 460. Committee Reports at ¶ 10,050.]

Amendments

• **2001, Economic Growth and Tax Relief Reconciliation Act of 2001 (P.L. 107-16)**

P.L. 107-16, § 422(b):

Amended Code Sec. 142 by adding at the end a new subsection (k). **Effective** for bonds issued after 12-31-2001.

P.L. 107-16, § 901(a)-(b), as amended by P.L. 111-312, § 101(a)(1), provides:

SEC. 901. SUNSET OF PROVISIONS OF ACT.

(a) In General.—All provisions of, and amendments made by, this Act shall not apply—

(1) to taxable, plan, or limitation years beginning after December 31, 2012, or

(2) in the case of title V, to estates of decedents dying, gifts made, or generation skipping transfers, after December 31, 2012.

(b) Application of Certain Laws.—The Internal Revenue Code of 1986 and the Employee Retirement Income Security Act of 1974 shall be applied and administered to years, estates, gifts, and transfers described in subsection (a) as if the provisions and amendments described in subsection (a) had never been enacted.

[¶ 5235] CODE SEC. 146. VOLUME CAP.

* * *

(g) Exception for Certain Bonds.—Only for purposes of this section, the term "private activity bond" shall not include—

* * *

➤ *Caution: Code Sec. 146(g)(3), below, was amended by P.L. 107-16. For sunset provision, see P.L. 107-16, § 901 [as amended by P.L. 111-312], in the amendment notes.*

(3) any exempt facility bond issued as part of an issue described in paragraph (1), (2), (12), (13), (14), or (15) of section 142(a), and

* * *

[CCH Explanation at ¶ 460. Committee Reports at ¶ 10,050.]

Amendments

• **2005, Safe, Accountable, Flexible, Efficient Transportation Equity Act: A Legacy for Users (P.L. 109-59)**

P.L. 109-59, § 11143(c):

Amended Code Sec. 146(g)(3) by striking "or 14" and all that follows through the end of the paragraph and inserting "(14), or (15) or section 142(a), and". **Effective** for bonds issued after 8-10-2005. Prior to amendment, Code Sec. 146(g)(3) read as follows:

(3) any exempt facility bond issued as part of an issue described in paragraph (1), (2), (12), (13), or (14) of section 142(a) (relating to airports, docks and wharves, environmental enhancements of hydroelectric generating facilities, qualified public educational facilities, and qualified green building and sustainable design projects), and

• **2004, American Jobs Creation Act of 2004 (P.L. 108-357)**

P.L. 108-357, § 701(c)(1)-(2):

Amended Code Sec. 146(g)(3) by striking "or (13)" and inserting "(13), or (14)", and by striking "and qualified public educational facilities" and inserting "qualified public educational facilities, and qualified green building and sustainable design projects". **Effective** for bonds issued after 12-31-2004.

• **2001, Economic Growth and Tax Relief Reconciliation Act of 2001 (P.L. 107-16)**

P.L. 107-16, § 422(c)(1)-(2):

Amended Code Sec. 146(g)(3) by striking "or (12)" and inserting "(12), or (13)", and by striking "and environmental enhancements of hydroelectric generating facilities" and inserting "environmental enhancements of hydroelectric generating facilities, and qualified public educational facilities". **Effective** for bonds issued after 12-31-2001.

P.L. 107-16, §901(a)-(b), as amended by P.L. 111-312, §101(a)(1), provides:

SEC. 901. SUNSET OF PROVISIONS OF ACT.

(a) IN GENERAL.—All provisions of, and amendments made by, this Act shall not apply—

(1) to taxable, plan, or limitation years beginning after December 31, 2012, or

(2) in the case of title V, to estates of decedents dying, gifts made, or generation skipping transfers, after December 31, 2012.

(b) APPLICATION OF CERTAIN LAWS.—The Internal Revenue Code of 1986 and the Employee Retirement Income Security Act of 1974 shall be applied and administered to years, estates, gifts, and transfers described in subsection (a) as if the provisions and amendments described in subsection (a) had never been enacted.

[¶5240] CODE SEC. 147. OTHER REQUIREMENTS APPLICABLE TO CERTAIN PRIVATE ACTIVITY BONDS.

* * *

»»→ Caution: *The heading for Code Sec. 147(h), below, was amended by P.L. 107-16. For sunset provision, see P.L. 107-16, §901 [as amended by P.L. 111-312], in the amendment notes.*

(h) CERTAIN RULES NOT TO APPLY TO CERTAIN BONDS.—

* * *

»»→ Caution: *Code Sec. 147(h)(3), below, was added by P.L. 107-16. For sunset provision, see P.L. 107-16, §901 [as amended by P.L. 111-312], in the amendment notes.*

(3) EXEMPT FACILITY BONDS FOR QUALIFIED PUBLIC-PRIVATE SCHOOLS.—Subsection (c) shall not apply to any exempt facility bond issued as part of an issue described in section 142(a)(13) (relating to qualified public educational facilities).

[CCH Explanation at ¶460. Committee Reports at ¶10,050.]
Amendments

• **2001, Economic Growth and Tax Relief Reconciliation Act of 2001 (P.L. 107-16)**

P.L. 107-16, §422(d):

Amended Code Sec. 147(h) by adding at the end a new paragraph (3). **Effective** for bonds issued after 12-31-2001.

P.L. 107-16, §422(e):

Amended the heading for Code Sec. 147(h) by striking "MORTGAGE REVENUE BONDS, QUALIFIED STUDENT LOAN BONDS, AND QUALIFIED 501(c)(3) BONDS" and inserting "CERTAIN BONDS". **Effective** for bonds issued after 12-31-2001.

P.L. 107-16, §901(a)-(b), as amended by P.L. 111-312, §101(a)(1), provides:

SEC. 901. SUNSET OF PROVISIONS OF ACT.

(a) IN GENERAL.—All provisions of, and amendments made by, this Act shall not apply—

(1) to taxable, plan, or limitation years beginning after December 31, 2012, or

(2) in the case of title V, to estates of decedents dying, gifts made, or generation skipping transfers, after December 31, 2012.

(b) APPLICATION OF CERTAIN LAWS.—The Internal Revenue Code of 1986 and the Employee Retirement Income Security Act of 1974 shall be applied and administered to years, estates, gifts, and transfers described in subsection (a) as if the provisions and amendments described in subsection (a) had never been enacted.

[¶5245] CODE SEC. 148. ARBITRAGE.

* * *

(f) REQUIRED REBATE TO THE UNITED STATES.—

* * *

(4) SPECIAL RULES FOR APPLYING PARAGRAPH (2).—

* * *

(D) EXCEPTION FOR GOVERNMENTAL UNITS ISSUING $5,000,000 OR LESS OF BONDS.—

* * *

>>>→ *Caution: Code Sec. 148(f)(4)(D)(vii), below, was amended by P.L. 107-16. For sunset provision, see P.L. 107-16, §901 [as amended by P.L. 111-312], in the amendment notes.*

(vii) INCREASE IN EXCEPTION FOR BONDS FINANCING PUBLIC SCHOOL CAPITAL EXPENDITURES.—Each of the $5,000,000 amounts in the preceding provisions of this subparagraph shall be increased by the lesser of $10,000,000 or so much of the aggregate face amount of the bonds as are attributable to financing the construction (within the meaning of subparagraph (C)(iv)) of public school facilities.

* * *

[CCH Explanation at ¶455. Committee Reports at ¶10,050.]

Amendments

• **2001, Economic Growth and Tax Relief Reconciliation Act of 2001 (P.L. 107-16)**

P.L. 107-16, §421(a):

Amended Code Sec. 148(f)(4)(D)(vii) by striking "$5,000,000" the second place it appears and inserting "$10,000,000". Effective for obligations issued in calendar years beginning after 12-31-2001.

P.L. 107-16, §901(a)-(b), as amended by P.L. 111-312, §101(a)(1), provides:

SEC. 901. SUNSET OF PROVISIONS OF ACT.

(a) IN GENERAL.—All provisions of, and amendments made by, this Act shall not apply—

(1) to taxable, plan, or limitation years beginning after December 31, 2012, or

(2) in the case of title V, to estates of decedents dying, gifts made, or generation skipping transfers, after December 31, 2012.

(b) APPLICATION OF CERTAIN LAWS.—The Internal Revenue Code of 1986 and the Employee Retirement Income Security Act of 1974 shall be applied and administered to years, estates, gifts, and transfers described in subsection (a) as if the provisions and amendments described in subsection (a) had never been enacted.

[¶5250] CODE SEC. 151. ALLOWANCE OF DEDUCTIONS FOR PERSONAL EXEMPTIONS.

* * *

(d) EXEMPTION AMOUNT.—For purposes of this section—

* * *

>>>→ *Caution: Code Sec. 151(d)(3)(E)-(F), below, was added by P.L. 107-16. For sunset provision, see P.L. 107-16, §901 [as amended by P.L. 111-312], in the amendment notes.*

(3) PHASEOUT.—

* * *

(E) REDUCTION OF PHASEOUT.—

(i) IN GENERAL.—In the case of taxable years beginning after December 31, 2005, and before January 1, 2010, the reduction under subparagraph (A) shall be equal to the applicable fraction of the amount which would (but for this subparagraph) be the amount of such reduction.

(ii) APPLICABLE FRACTION.—For purposes of clause (i), the applicable fraction shall be determined in accordance with the following table:

For taxable years beginning in calendar year—	The applicable fraction is—
2006 and 2007	2/3
2008 and 2009	1/3.

(F) TERMINATION.—This paragraph shall not apply to any taxable year beginning after December 31, 2009.

* * *

[CCH Explanation at ¶325. Committee Reports at ¶10,020.]

Amendments

• **2001, Economic Growth and Tax Relief Reconciliation Act of 2001 (P.L. 107-16)**

P.L. 107-16, §102(a):

Amended Code Sec. 151(d)(3) by adding at the end new subparagraphs (E) and (F). **Effective** for tax years beginning after 12-31-2005.

P.L. 107-16, §901(a)-(b), as amended by P.L. 111-312, §101(a)(1), provides:

SEC. 901. SUNSET OF PROVISIONS OF ACT.

(a) IN GENERAL.—All provisions of, and amendments made by, this Act shall not apply—

(1) to taxable, plan, or limitation years beginning after December 31, 2012, or

(2) in the case of title V, to estates of decedents dying, gifts made, or generation skipping transfers, after December 31, 2012.

(b) APPLICATION OF CERTAIN LAWS.—The Internal Revenue Code of 1986 and the Employee Retirement Income Security Act of 1974 shall be applied and administered to years, estates, gifts, and transfers described in subsection (a) as if the provisions and amendments described in subsection (a) had never been enacted.

[¶5255] CODE SEC. 163. INTEREST.

* * *

(d) LIMITATION ON INVESTMENT INTEREST.—

* * *

(4) NET INVESTMENT INCOME.—For purposes of this subsection—

* * *

»»→ Caution: The flush sentence in Code Sec. 163(d)(4)(B), below, was added by P.L. 108-27. For sunset provision, see P.L. 108-27, §303 [as amended by P.L. 111-312], in the amendment notes.

(B) INVESTMENT INCOME.—The term "investment income" means the sum of—

(i) gross income from property held for investment (other than any gain taken into account under clause (ii)(I)),

(ii) the excess (if any) of—

(I) the net gain attributable to the disposition of property held for investment, over

(II) the net capital gain determined by only taking into account gains and losses from dispositions of property held for investment, plus

(iii) so much of the net capital gain referred to in clause (ii)(II) (or, if lesser, the net gain referred to in clause (ii)(I)) as the taxpayer elects to take into account under this clause.

Such term shall include qualified dividend income (as defined in section 1(h)(11)(B)) only to the extent the taxpayer elects to treat such income as investment income for purposes of this subsection.

* * *

[CCH Explanation at ¶420. Committee Reports at ¶10,080.]

Amendments

• **2003, Jobs and Growth Tax Relief Reconciliation Act of 2003 (P.L. 108-27)**

P.L. 108-27, §302(b):

Amended Code Sec. 163(d)(4)(B) by adding at the end a new flush sentence. For the effective date, see Act Sec. 302(f), as amended by P.L. 108-311, §402(a)(6), below.

P.L. 108-27, §302(f), as amended by P.L. 108-311, §402(a)(6), provides:

(f) EFFECTIVE DATE.—

(1) IN GENERAL.—Except as provided in paragraph (2), the amendments made by this section shall apply to taxable years beginning after December 31, 2002.

(2) PASS-THRU ENTITIES.—In the case of a pass-thru entity described in subparagraph (A), (B), (C), (D), (E), or (F) of section 1(h)(10) of the Internal Revenue Code of 1986, as amended by this Act, the amendments made by this section shall apply to taxable years ending after December 31, 2002; except that dividends received by such an entity on or before such date shall not be treated as qualified dividend income (as defined in section 1(h)(11)(B) of such Code, as added by this Act).

P.L. 108-27, §303, as amended by P.L. 109-222, §102, and P.L. 111-312, §102(a), provides:

SEC. 303. SUNSET OF TITLE.

All provisions of, and amendments made by, this title shall not apply to taxable years beginning after December

31, 2012, and the Internal Revenue Code of 1986 shall be applied and administered to such years as if such provisions and amendments had never been enacted.

(h) DISALLOWANCE OF DEDUCTION FOR PERSONAL INTEREST.—

* * *

(3) QUALIFIED RESIDENCE INTEREST.—For purposes of this subsection—

* * *

(E) MORTGAGE INSURANCE PREMIUMS TREATED AS INTEREST.—

* * *

(iv) TERMINATION.—Clause (i) shall not apply to amounts—

(I) paid or accrued after *December 31, 2011,* or

(II) properly allocable to any period after such date.

[CCH Explanation at ¶328. Committee Reports at ¶10,650.]

Amendments

● **2010, Tax Relief, Unemployment Insurance Reauthorization, and Job Creation Act of 2010 (P.L. 111-312)**

P.L. 111-312, §759(a):

Amended Code Sec. 163(h)(3)(E)(iv) by striking "December 31, 2010" and inserting "December 31, 2011". **Effective** for amounts paid or accrued after 12-31-2010.

[¶5260] CODE SEC. 164. TAXES.

* * *

(b) DEFINITIONS AND SPECIAL RULES.—For purposes of this section—

* * *

(5) GENERAL SALES TAXES.—For purposes of subsection (a)—

* * *

(I) APPLICATION OF PARAGRAPH.—This paragraph shall apply to taxable years beginning after December 31, 2003, and before *January 1, 2012.*

* * *

[CCH Explanation at ¶326. Committee Reports at ¶10,290.]

Amendments

● **2010, Tax Relief, Unemployment Insurance Reauthorization, and Job Creation Act of 2010 (P.L. 111-312)**

P.L. 111-312, §722(a):

Amended Code Sec. 164(b)(5)(I) by striking "January 1, 2010" and inserting "January 1, 2012". **Effective** for tax years beginning after 12-31-2009.

[¶5265] CODE SEC. 168. ACCELERATED COST RECOVERY SYSTEM.

* * *

(e) CLASSIFICATION OF PROPERTY.—For purposes of this section—

* * *

(3) CLASSIFICATION OF CERTAIN PROPERTY.—

* * *

(E) 15-YEAR PROPERTY.—The term "15-year property" includes—

* * *

(iv) any qualified leasehold improvement property placed in service before *January 1, 2012,*

(v) any qualified restaurant property placed in service before *January 1, 2012,*

* * *

(ix) any qualified retail improvement property placed in service after December 31, 2008, and before *January 1, 2012.*

* * *

(7) QUALIFIED RESTAURANT PROPERTY.—

(A) IN GENERAL.—The term "qualified restaurant property" means any section 1250 property which is—

(i) a building, or

(ii) an improvement to a building,

if more than 50 percent of the building's square footage is devoted to preparation of, and seating for on-premises consumption of, prepared meals.

(8) QUALIFIED RETAIL IMPROVEMENT PROPERTY.—

* * *

(E) [*Stricken.*]

* * *

[CCH Explanation at ¶ 508. Committee Reports at ¶ 10,420.]

Amendments

• 2010, Tax Relief, Unemployment Insurance Reauthorization, and Job Creation Act of 2010 (P.L. 111-312)

P.L. 111-312, § 737(a):

Amended Code Sec. 168(e)(3)(E)(iv), (v), and (ix) by striking "January 1, 2010" and inserting "January 1, 2012". **Effective** for property placed in service after 12-31-2009.

P.L. 111-312, § 737(b)(1):

Amended Code Sec. 168(e)(7)(A)(i) by striking "if such building is placed in service after December 31, 2008, and

before January 1, 2010," after "a building,". **Effective for** property placed in service after 12-31-2009.

P.L. 111-312, § 737(b)(2):

Amended Code Sec. 168(e)(8) by striking subparagraph (E). Effective for property placed in service after 12-31-2009. Prior to being stricken, Code Sec. 168(e)(8)(E) read as follows:

(E) TERMINATION.—Such term shall not include any improvement placed in service after December 31, 2009.

(i) DEFINITIONS AND SPECIAL RULES.—For purposes of this section—

* * *

(15) MOTORSPORTS ENTERTAINMENT COMPLEX.—

* * *

(D) TERMINATION.—Such term shall not include any property placed in service after *December 31, 2011.*

* * *

[CCH Explanation at ¶ 510. Committee Reports at ¶ 10,430.]

Amendments

• 2010, Tax Relief, Unemployment Insurance Reauthorization, and Job Creation Act of 2010 (P.L. 111-312)

P.L. 111-312, § 738(a):

Amended Code Sec. 168(i)(15)(D) by striking "December 31, 2009" and inserting "December 31, 2011". **Effective** for property placed in service after 12-31-2009.

(j) PROPERTY ON INDIAN RESERVATIONS.—

* * *

(8) TERMINATION.—This subsection shall not apply to property placed in service after *December 31, 2011.*

[CCH Explanation at ¶ 512. Committee Reports at ¶ 10,440.]
Amendments
• **2010, Tax Relief, Unemployment Insurance Reauthorization, and Job Creation Act of 2010 (P.L. 111-312)**

P.L. 111-312, § 739(a):

Amended Code Sec. 168(j)(8) by striking "December 31, 2009" and inserting "December 31, 2011". **Effective for** property placed in service after 12-31-2009.

(k) SPECIAL ALLOWANCE FOR CERTAIN PROPERTY ACQUIRED AFTER DECEMBER 31, 2007, AND BEFORE JANUARY 1, 2013.—

(1) ADDITIONAL ALLOWANCE.—In the case of any qualified property—

(A) the depreciation deduction provided by section 167(a) for the taxable year in which such property is placed in service shall include an allowance equal to 50 percent of the adjusted basis of the qualified property, and

(B) the adjusted basis of the qualified property shall be reduced by the amount of such deduction before computing the amount otherwise allowable as a depreciation deduction under this chapter for such taxable year and any subsequent taxable year.

(2) QUALIFIED PROPERTY.—For purposes of this subsection—

(A) IN GENERAL.—The term "qualified property" means property—

(i)(I) to which this section applies which has a recovery period of 20 years or less,

(II) which is computer software (as defined in section 167(f)(1)(B)) for which a deduction is allowable under section 167(a) without regard to this subsection,

(III) which is water utility property, or

(IV) which is qualified leasehold improvement property,

(ii) the original use of which commences with the taxpayer after December 31, 2007,

(iii) which is—

(I) acquired by the taxpayer after December 31, 2007, and before *January 1, 2013,* but only if no written binding contract for the acquisition was in effect before January 1, 2008, or

(II) acquired by the taxpayer pursuant to a written binding contract which was entered into after December 31, 2007, and before *January 1, 2013,* and

(iv) which is placed in service by the taxpayer before *January 1, 2013,* or, in the case of property described in subparagraph (B) or (C), before *January 1, 2014.*

(B) CERTAIN PROPERTY HAVING LONGER PRODUCTION PERIODS TREATED AS QUALIFIED PROPERTY.—

(i) IN GENERAL.—The term "qualified property" includes any property if such property—

(I) meets the requirements of clauses (i), (ii), (iii), and (iv) of subparagraph (A),

(II) has a recovery period of at least 10 years or is transportation property,

(III) is subject to section 263A, and

(IV) meets the requirements of clause (iii) of section 263A(f)(1)(B) (determined as if such clauses also apply to property which has a long useful life (within the meaning of section 263A(f))).

(ii) ONLY PRE-JANUARY 1, 2013, BASIS ELIGIBLE FOR ADDITIONAL ALLOWANCE.—In the case of property which is qualified property solely by reason of clause (i), paragraph (1) shall apply only to the extent of the adjusted basis thereof attributable to manufacture, construction, or production before *January 1, 2013.*

(iii) TRANSPORTATION PROPERTY.—For purposes of this subparagraph, the term "transportation property" means tangible personal property used in the trade or business of transporting persons or property.

(iv) APPLICATION OF SUBPARAGRAPH.—This subparagraph shall not apply to any property which is described in subparagraph (C).

(C) CERTAIN AIRCRAFT.—The term "qualified property" includes property—

(i) which meets the requirements of clauses (ii), (iii), and (iv) of subparagraph (A),

(ii) which is an aircraft which is not a transportation property (as defined in subparagraph (B)(iii)) other than for agricultural or firefighting purposes,

(iii) which is purchased and on which such purchaser, at the time of the contract for purchase, has made a nonrefundable deposit of the lesser of—

(I) 10 percent of the cost, or

(II) $100,000, and

(iv) which has—

(I) an estimated production period exceeding 4 months, and

(II) a cost exceeding $200,000.

(D) EXCEPTIONS.—

(i) ALTERNATIVE DEPRECIATION PROPERTY.—The term "qualified property" shall not include any property to which the alternative depreciation system under subsection (g) applies, determined—

(I) without regard to paragraph (7) of subsection (g) (relating to election to have system apply), and

(II) after application of section 280F(b) (relating to listed property with limited business use).

(ii) QUALIFIED NEW YORK LIBERTY ZONE LEASEHOLD IMPROVEMENT PROPERTY.—The term "qualified property" shall not include any qualified New York Liberty Zone leasehold improvement property (as defined in section 1400L(c)(2)).

(iii) ELECTION OUT.—If a taxpayer makes an election under this clause with respect to any class of property for any taxable year, this subsection shall not apply to all property in such class placed in service during such taxable year.

(E) SPECIAL RULES.—

(i) SELF-CONSTRUCTED PROPERTY.—In the case of a taxpayer manufacturing, constructing, or producing property for the taxpayer's own use, the requirements of clause (iii) of subparagraph (A) shall be treated as met if the taxpayer begins manufacturing, constructing, or producing the property after December 31, 2007, and before *January 1, 2013.*

(ii) SALE-LEASEBACKS.—For purposes of clause (iii) and subparagraph (A)(ii), if property is—

(I) originally placed in service after December 31, 2007, by a person, and

(II) sold and leased back by such person within 3 months after the date such property was originally placed in service,

such property shall be treated as originally placed in service not earlier than the date on which such property is used under the leaseback referred to in subclause (II).

(iii) SYNDICATION.—For purposes of subparagraph (A)(ii), if—

(I) property is originally placed in service after December 31, 2007, by the lessor of such property,

(II) such property is sold by such lessor or any subsequent purchaser within 3 months after the date such property was originally placed in service (or, in the case of multiple units of property subject to the same lease, within 3 months after the date the final unit is placed in service, so long as the period between the time the first unit is placed in service and the time the last unit is placed in service does not exceed 12 months), and

(III) the user of such property after the last sale during such 3-month period remains the same as when such property was originally placed in service,

such property shall be treated as originally placed in service not earlier than the date of such last sale.

(iv) LIMITATIONS RELATED TO USERS AND RELATED PARTIES.—The term "qualified property" shall not include any property if—

(I) the user of such property (as of the date on which such property is originally placed in service) or a person which is related (within the meaning of section 267(b) or 707(b)) to such user or to the taxpayer had a written binding contract in effect for the acquisition of such property at any time on or before December 31, 2007, or

(II) in the case of property manufactured, constructed, or produced for such user's or person's own use, the manufacture, construction, or production of such property began at any time on or before December 31, 2007.

(F) COORDINATION WITH SECTION 280F.—For purposes of section 280F—

(i) AUTOMOBILES.—In the case of a passenger automobile (as defined in section 280F(d)(5)) which is qualified property, the Secretary shall increase the limitation under section 280F(a)(1)(A)(i) by $8,000.

(ii) LISTED PROPERTY.—The deduction allowable under paragraph (1) shall be taken into account in computing any recapture amount under section 280F(b)(2).

(G) DEDUCTION ALLOWED IN COMPUTING MINIMUM TAX.—For purposes of determining alternative minimum taxable income under section 55, the deduction under subsection (a) for qualified property shall be determined under this section without regard to any adjustment under section 56.

(3) QUALIFIED LEASEHOLD IMPROVEMENT PROPERTY.—For purposes of this subsection—

(A) IN GENERAL.—The term "qualified leasehold improvement property" means any improvement to an interior portion of a building which is nonresidential real property if—

(i) such improvement is made under or pursuant to a lease (as defined in subsection (h)(7))—

(I) by the lessee (or any sublessee) of such portion, or

(II) by the lessor of such portion,

(ii) such portion is to be occupied exclusively by the lessee (or any sublessee) of such portion, and

(iii) such improvement is placed in service more than 3 years after the date the building was first placed in service.

(B) CERTAIN IMPROVEMENTS NOT INCLUDED.—Such term shall not include any improvement for which the expenditure is attributable to—

(i) the enlargement of the building,

(ii) any elevator or escalator,

(iii) any structural component benefiting a common area, and

(iv) the internal structural framework of the building.

(C) DEFINITIONS AND SPECIAL RULES.—For purposes of this paragraph—

(i) COMMITMENT TO LEASE TREATED AS LEASE.—A commitment to enter into a lease shall be treated as a lease, and the parties to such commitment shall be treated as lessor and lessee, respectively.

(ii) RELATED PERSONS.—A lease between related persons shall not be considered a lease. For purposes of the preceding sentence, the term "related persons" means—

(I) members of an affiliated group (as defined in section 1504), and

(II) persons having a relationship described in subsection (b) of section 267; except that, for purposes of this clause, the phrase "80 percent or more" shall be substituted for the phrase "more than 50 percent" each place it appears in such subsection.

(4) ELECTION TO ACCELERATE THE AMT AND RESEARCH CREDITS IN LIEU OF BONUS DEPRECIATION.—

(A) IN GENERAL.—If a corporation elects to have this paragraph apply for the first taxable year of the taxpayer ending after March 31, 2008, in the case of such taxable year and each subsequent taxable year—

(i) paragraph (1) shall not apply to any eligible qualified property placed in service by the taxpayer,

(ii) the applicable depreciation method used under this section with respect to such property shall be the straight line method, and

(iii) each of the limitations described in subparagraph (B) for any such taxable year shall be increased by the bonus depreciation amount which is—

(I) determined for such taxable year under subparagraph (C), and

(II) allocated to such limitation under subparagraph (E).

(B) LIMITATIONS TO BE INCREASED.—The limitations described in this subparagraph are—

(i) the limitation imposed by section 38(c), and

(ii) the limitation imposed by section 53(c).

(C) BONUS DEPRECIATION AMOUNT.—For purposes of this paragraph—

(i) IN GENERAL.—The bonus depreciation amount for any taxable year is an amount equal to 20 percent of the excess (if any) of—

(I) the aggregate amount of depreciation which would be allowed under this section for eligible qualified property placed in service by the taxpayer during such taxable year if paragraph (1) applied to all such property, over

(II) the aggregate amount of depreciation which would be allowed under this section for eligible qualified property placed in service by the taxpayer during such taxable year if paragraph (1) did not apply to any such property.

The aggregate amounts determined under subclauses (I) and (II) shall be determined without regard to any election made under subsection (b)(2)(C), (b)(3)(D), or (g)(7) and without regard to subparagraph (A)(ii).

(ii) MAXIMUM AMOUNT.—The bonus depreciation amount for any taxable year shall not exceed the maximum increase amount under clause (iii), reduced (but not below zero) by the sum of the bonus depreciation amounts for all preceding taxable years.

(iii) MAXIMUM INCREASE AMOUNT.—For purposes of clause (ii), the term "maximum increase amount" means, with respect to any corporation, the lesser of—

(I) $30,000,000, or

(II) 6 percent of the sum of the business credit increase amount, and the AMT credit increase amount, determined with respect to such corporation under subparagraph (E).

(iv) AGGREGATION RULE.—All corporations which are treated as a single employer under section 52(a) shall be treated—

(I) as 1 taxpayer for purposes of this paragraph, and

(II) as having elected the application of this paragraph if any such corporation so elects.

(D) ELIGIBLE QUALIFIED PROPERTY.—For purposes of this paragraph, the term "eligible qualified property" means qualified property under paragraph (2), except that in applying paragraph (2) for purposes of this paragraph—

(i) "March 31, 2008" shall be substituted for "December 31, 2007" each place it appears in subparagraph (A) and clauses (i) and (ii) of subparagraph (E) thereof,

(ii) "April 1, 2008" shall be substituted for "January 1, 2008" in subparagraph (A)(iii)(I) thereof, *and*

(iii) only adjusted basis attributable to manufacture, construction, *or production*—

(I) after March 31, 2008, and before January 1, 2010, and

(II) after December 31, 2010, and before January 1, 2013,

shall be taken into account under subparagraph (B)(ii) thereof.

(E) ALLOCATION OF BONUS DEPRECIATION AMOUNTS.—

(i) IN GENERAL.—Subject to clauses (ii) and (iii), the taxpayer shall, at such time and in such manner as the Secretary may prescribe, specify the portion (if any) of the bonus depreciation amount for the taxable year which is to be allocated to each of the limitations described in subparagraph (B) for such taxable year.

(ii) LIMITATION ON ALLOCATIONS.—The portion of the bonus depreciation amount which may be allocated under clause (i) to the limitations described in subparagraph (B) for any taxable year shall not exceed—

(I) in the case of the limitation described in subparagraph (B)(i), the excess of the business credit increase amount over the bonus depreciation amount allocated to such limitation for all preceding taxable years, and

(II) in the case of the limitation described in subparagraph (B)(ii), the excess of the AMT credit increase amount over the bonus depreciation amount allocated to such limitation for all preceding taxable years.

(iii) BUSINESS CREDIT INCREASE AMOUNT.—For purposes of this paragraph, the term "business credit increase amount" means the amount equal to the portion of the credit allowable under section 38 (determined without regard to subsection (c) thereof) for the first taxable year ending after March 31, 2008, which is allocable to business credit carryforwards to such taxable year which are—

(I) from taxable years beginning before January 1, 2006, and

(II) properly allocable (determined under the rules of section 38(d)) to the research credit determined under section 41(a).

(iv) AMT CREDIT INCREASE AMOUNT.—For purposes of this paragraph, the term "AMT credit increase amount" means the amount equal to the portion of the minimum tax credit under section 53(b) for the first taxable year ending after March 31, 2008, determined by taking into account only the adjusted minimum tax for taxable years beginning before January 1, 2006. For purposes of the preceding sentence, credits shall be treated as allowed on a first-in, first-out basis.

(F) CREDIT REFUNDABLE.—For purposes of section 6401(b), the aggregate increase in the credits allowable under part IV of subchapter A for any taxable year resulting from the application of this paragraph shall be treated as allowed under subpart C of such part (and not any other subpart).

(G) Other Rules.—

(i) Election.—Any election under this paragraph (including any allocation under subparagraph (E)) may be revoked only with the consent of the Secretary.

(ii) Partnerships with Electing Partners.—In the case of a corporation making an election under subparagraph (A) and which is a partner in a partnership, for purposes of determining such corporation's distributive share of partnership items under section 702—

(I) paragraph (1) shall not apply to any eligible qualified property, and

(II) the applicable depreciation method used under this section with respect to such property shall be the straight line method.

(iii) Special Rule for Passenger Aircraft.—In the case of any passenger aircraft, the written binding contract limitation under paragraph (2)(A)(iii)(I) shall not apply for purposes of subparagraphs (C)(i)(I) and (D).

(H) Special Rules for Extension Property.—

(i) Taxpayers Previously Electing Acceleration.—In the case of a taxpayer who made the election under subparagraph (A) for its first taxable year ending after March 31, 2008—

(I) the taxpayer may elect not to have this paragraph apply to extension property, but

(II) if the taxpayer does not make the election under subclause (I), in applying this paragraph to the taxpayer a separate bonus depreciation amount, maximum amount, and maximum increase amount shall be computed and applied to eligible qualified property which is extension property and to eligible qualified property which is not extension property.

(ii) Taxpayers Not Previously Electing Acceleration.—In the case of a taxpayer who did not make the election under subparagraph (A) for its first taxable year ending after March 31, 2008—

(I) the taxpayer may elect to have this paragraph apply to its first taxable year ending after December 31, 2008, and each subsequent taxable year, and

(II) if the taxpayer makes the election under subclause (I), this paragraph shall only apply to eligible qualified property which is extension property.

(iii) Extension Property.—For purposes of this subparagraph, the term "extension property" means property which is eligible qualified property solely by reason of the extension of the application of the special allowance under paragraph (1) pursuant to the amendments made by section 1201(a) of the American Recovery and Reinvestment Tax Act of 2009 (and the application of such extension to this paragraph pursuant to the amendment made by section 1201(b)(1) of such Act).

(I) Special Rules for Round 2 Extension Property.—

(i) In General.—In the case of round 2 extension property, this paragraph shall be applied without regard to—

(I) the limitation described in subparagraph (B)(i) thereof, and

(II) the business credit increase amount under subparagraph (E)(iii) thereof.

(ii) Taxpayers Previously Electing Acceleration.—In the case of a taxpayer who made the election under subparagraph (A) for its first taxable year ending after March 31, 2008, or a taxpayer who made the election under subparagraph (H)(ii) for its first taxable year ending after December 31, 2008—

(I) the taxpayer may elect not to have this paragraph apply to round 2 extension property, but

(II) *if the taxpayer does not make the election under subclause (I), in applying this paragraph to the taxpayer the bonus depreciation amount, maximum amount, and maximum increase amount shall be computed and applied to eligible qualified property which is round 2 extension property.*

The amounts described in subclause (II) shall be computed separately from any amounts computed with respect to eligible qualified property which is not round 2 extension property.

(iii) TAXPAYERS NOT PREVIOUSLY ELECTING ACCELERATION.—*In the case of a taxpayer who neither made the election under subparagraph (A) for its first taxable year ending after March 31, 2008, nor made the election under subparagraph (H)(ii) for its first taxable year ending after December 31, 2008—*

(I) *the taxpayer may elect to have this paragraph apply to its first taxable year ending after December 31, 2010, and each subsequent taxable year, and*

(II) *if the taxpayer makes the election under subclause (I), this paragraph shall only apply to eligible qualified property which is round 2 extension property.*

(iv) ROUND 2 EXTENSION PROPERTY.—*For purposes of this subparagraph, the term "round 2 extension property" means property which is eligible qualified property solely by reason of the extension of the application of the special allowance under paragraph (1) pursuant to the amendments made by section 401(a) of the Tax Relief, Unemployment Insurance Reauthorization, and Job Creation Act of 2010 (and the application of such extension to this paragraph pursuant to the amendment made by section 401(c)(1) of such Act).*

(5) SPECIAL RULE FOR PROPERTY ACQUIRED DURING CERTAIN PRE-2012 PERIODS.—*In the case of qualified property acquired by the taxpayer (under rules similar to the rules of clauses (ii) and (iii) of paragraph (2)(A)) after September 8, 2010, and before January 1, 2012, and which is placed in service by the taxpayer before January 1, 2012 (January 1, 2013, in the case of property described in subparagraph (2)(B) or (2)(C)), paragraph (1)(A) shall be applied by substituting "100 percent" for "50 percent".*

[CCH Explanation at ¶ 502 and 504. Committee Reports at ¶ 10,140.]

Amendments

- **2010, Tax Relief, Unemployment Insurance Reauthorization, and Job Creation Act of 2010 (P.L. 111-312)**

P.L. 111-312, § 401(a)(1)-(2):

Amended Code Sec. 168(k)(2) by striking "January 1, 2012" in subparagraph (A)(iv) and inserting "January 1, 2014", and by striking "January 1, 2011" each place it appears and inserting "January 1, 2013". **Effective** for property placed in service after 12-31-2010, in tax years ending after such date.

P.L. 111-312, § 401(b):

Amended Code Sec. 168(k) by adding at the end a new paragraph (5). **Effective** for property placed in service after 9-8-2010, in tax years ending after such date.

P.L. 111-312, § 401(c)(1):

Amended Code Sec. 168(k)(4)(D)(iii) by striking "or production" and all that follows and inserting "or production—", new subclauses (I) and (II), and new flush text. **Effective** for property placed in service after 12-31-2010, in tax years ending after such date. Prior to being stricken, all that followed "or production" in Code Sec. 168(k)(4)(D)(iii) read as follows:

or production after March 31, 2008, and before January 1, 2010, shall be taken into account under subparagraph (B)(ii) thereof,

P.L. 111-312, § 401(c)(2):

Amended Code Sec. 168(k)(4) by adding at the end a new subparagraph (I). **Effective** for property placed in service after 12-31-2010, in tax years ending after such date.

P.L. 111-312, § 401(d)(1):

Amended the heading for Code Sec. 168(k) by striking "JANUARY 1, 2011" and inserting "JANUARY 1, 2013". **Effective** for property placed in service after 12-31-2010, in tax years ending after such date.

P.L. 111-312, § 401(d)(2):

Amended the heading for Code Sec. 168(k)(2)(B)(ii) by striking "PRE-JANUARY 1, 2011" and inserting "PRE-JANUARY 1, 2013". **Effective** for property placed in service after 12-31-2010, in tax years ending after such date.

P.L. 111-312, § 401(d)(3)(A)-(C):

Amended Code Sec. 168(k)(4)(D) by striking clauses (iv) and (v), by inserting "and" at the end of clause (ii), and by striking the comma at the end of clause (iii) and inserting a period. **Effective** for property placed in service after 12-31-2010, in tax years ending after such date. Prior to being stricken, Code Sec. 168(k)(4)(D)(iv)-(v) read as follows:

(iv) "January 1, 2011" shall be substituted for "January 1, 2012" in subparagraph (A)(iv) thereof, and

(v) "January 1, 2010" shall be substituted for "January 1, 2011" each place it appears in subparagraph (A) thereof.

- **2003, Jobs and Growth Tax Relief Reconciliation Act of 2003 (P.L. 108-27)**

P.L. 108-27, § 201(a):

Amended Code Sec. 168(k) by adding at the end a new paragraph (4). **Effective** for tax years ending after 5-5-2003.

P.L. 108-27, §201(b)(1)(A):

Amended Code Sec. 168(k)(2)(B)(ii) and (D)(i) by striking "September 11, 2004" each place it appears in the text and inserting "January 1, 2005". **Effective** for tax years ending after 5-5-2003.

P.L. 108-27, §201(b)(1)(B):

Amended Code Sec. 168(k)(2)(B)(ii) by striking "PRE-SEPTEMBER 11, 2004" in the heading and inserting "PRE-JANUARY 1, 2005". **Effective** for tax years ending after 5-5-2003.

P.L. 108-27, §201(b)(2):

Amended Code Sec. 168(k)(2)(A)(iii) by striking "September 11, 2004" each place it appears and inserting "January 1, 2005". **Effective** for tax years ending after 5-5-2003.

P.L. 108-27, §201(b)(3):

Amended Code Sec. 168(k)(2)(C)(iii) by adding at the end a new sentence. **Effective** for tax years ending after 5-5-2003.

P.L. 108-27, §201(c)(1):

Amended the subsection heading for Code Sec. 168(k) by striking "SEPTEMBER 11, 2004" and inserting "JANUARY 1, 2005". **Effective** for tax years ending after 5-5-2003.

(l) SPECIAL ALLOWANCE FOR CELLULOSIC BIOFUEL PLANT PROPERTY.—

* * *

(5) SPECIAL RULES.—For purposes of this subsection, rules similar to the rules of subparagraph (E) of section 168(k)(2) shall apply, except that such subparagraph shall be applied—

(A) by substituting "the date of the enactment of subsection (l)" for "December 31, 2007" each place it appears therein, *and*

(B) by substituting "qualified cellulosic biofuel plant property" for "qualified property" in clause (iv) thereof.

* * *

[CCH Explanation at ¶502. Committee Reports at ¶10,140.]

Amendments

• **2010, Tax Relief, Unemployment Insurance Reauthorization, and Job Creation Act of 2010 (P.L. 111-312)**

P.L. 111-312, §401(d)(4)(A)-(C):

Amended Code Sec. 168(l)(5) by inserting "and" at the end of subparagraph (A), by striking subparagraph (B), and

by redesignating subparagraph (C) as subparagraph (B). **Effective** for property placed in service after 12-31-2010, in tax years ending after such date. Prior to being stricken, Code Sec. 168(l)(5)(B) read as follows:

(B) by substituting "January 1, 2013" for "January 1, 2011" in clause (i) thereof, and

(n) SPECIAL ALLOWANCE FOR QUALIFIED DISASTER ASSISTANCE PROPERTY.—

* * *

(2) QUALIFIED DISASTER ASSISTANCE PROPERTY.—For purposes of this subsection—

* * *

(C) SPECIAL RULES.—For purposes of this subsection, rules similar to the rules of subparagraph (E) of subsection (k)(2) shall apply, except that such subparagraph shall be applied—

* * *

(ii) without regard to "and before *January 1, 2013*" in clause (i) thereof, and

* * *

[CCH Explanation at ¶502. Committee Reports at ¶10,140.]

Amendments

• **2010, Tax Relief, Unemployment Insurance Reauthorization, and Job Creation Act of 2010 (P.L. 111-312)**

P.L. 111-312, §401(d)(5):

Amended Code Sec. 168(n)(2)(C) by striking "January 1, 2011" and inserting "January 1, 2013". **Effective** for property placed in service after 12-31-2010, in tax years ending after such date.

[¶5270] CODE SEC. 170. CHARITABLE, ETC., CONTRIBUTIONS AND GIFTS.

* * *

(b) PERCENTAGE LIMITATIONS.—

(1) INDIVIDUALS.—In the case of an individual, the deduction provided in subsection (a) shall be limited as provided in the succeeding subparagraphs.

* * *

(E) CONTRIBUTIONS OF QUALIFIED CONSERVATION CONTRIBUTIONS.—

* * *

(vi) TERMINATION.—This subparagraph shall not apply to any contribution made in taxable years beginning after *December 31, 2011.*

* * *

(2) CORPORATIONS.—In the case of a corporation—

* * *

(B) QUALIFIED CONSERVATION CONTRIBUTIONS BY CERTAIN CORPORATE FARMERS AND RANCHERS.—

* * *

(iii) TERMINATION.—This subparagraph shall not apply to any contribution made in taxable years beginning after *December 31, 2011.*

* * *

[CCH Explanation at ¶353. Committee Reports at ¶10,300.]

Amendments

• 2010, Tax Relief, Unemployment Insurance Reauthorization, and Job Creation Act of 2010 (P.L. 111-312)

P.L. 111-312, §723(a):

Amended Code Sec. 170(b)(1)(E)(vi) by striking "December 31, 2009" and inserting "December 31, 2011". Effective for contributions made in tax years beginning after 12-31-2009.

P.L. 111-312, §723(b):

Amended Code Sec. 170(b)(2)(B)(iii) by striking "December 31, 2009" and inserting "December 31, 2011". Effective for contributions made in tax years beginning after 12-31-2009.

(e) CERTAIN CONTRIBUTIONS OF ORDINARY INCOME AND CAPITAL GAIN PROPERTY.—

(1) GENERAL RULE.—The amount of any charitable contribution of property otherwise taken into account under this section shall be reduced by the sum of—

(A) the amount of gain which would not have been long-term capital gain (determined without regard to section 1221(b)(3)) if the property contributed had been sold by the taxpayer at its fair market value (determined at the time of such contribution), and

(B) in the case of a charitable contribution—

(i) of tangible personal property—

(I) if the use by the donee is unrelated to the purpose or function constituting the basis for its exemption under section 501 (or, in the case of a governmental unit, to any purpose or function described in subsection (c)), or

(II) which is applicable property (as defined in paragraph (7)(C), but without regard to clause (ii) thereof) which is sold, exchanged, or otherwise disposed of by the donee before the last day of the taxable year in which the contribution was made and with respect to which the donee has not made a certification in accordance with paragraph (7)(D),

(ii) to or for the use of a private foundation (as defined in section 509(a)), other than a private foundation described in subsection (b)(1)(F),

(iii) of any patent, copyright (other than a copyright described in section 1221(a)(3) or 1231(b)(1)(C)), trademark, trade name, trade secret, know-how, software (other than software described in section 197(e)(3)(A)(i)), or similar property, or applications or registrations of such property, or

(iv) of any taxidermy property which is contributed by the person who prepared, stuffed, or mounted the property or by any person who paid or incurred the cost of such preparation, stuffing, or mounting,

the amount of gain which would have been long-term capital gain if the property contributed had been sold by the taxpayer at its fair market value (determined at the time of such contribution).

≫→ *Caution: The flush text of Code Sec. 170(e)(1), below, as amended by P.L. 111-312, applies to estates of decedents dying, and transfers made, after December 31, 2009. For sunset provision, see P.L. 107-16, §901 [as amended by P.L. 111-312], in the amendment notes.*

For purposes of applying this paragraph (other than in the case of gain to which section 617(d)(1), 1245(a), 1250(a), 1252(a), or 1254(a) applies), property which is property used in the trade or business (as defined in section 1231(b)) shall be treated as a capital asset. For purposes of applying this paragraph in the case of a charitable contribution of stock in an S corporation, rules similar to the rules of section 751 shall apply in determining whether gain on such stock would have been long-term capital gain if such stock were sold by the taxpayer.

* * *

(3) SPECIAL RULE FOR CERTAIN CONTRIBUTIONS OF INVENTORY AND OTHER PROPERTY.—

* * *

(C) SPECIAL RULE FOR CONTRIBUTIONS OF FOOD INVENTORY.—

* * *

(iv) TERMINATION.—This subparagraph shall not apply to contributions made after *December 31, 2011.*

(D) SPECIAL RULE FOR CONTRIBUTIONS OF BOOK INVENTORY TO PUBLIC SCHOOLS.—

* * *

(iv) TERMINATION.—This subparagraph shall not apply to contributions made after *December 31, 2011.*

* * *

(6) SPECIAL RULE FOR CONTRIBUTIONS OF COMPUTER TECHNOLOGY AND EQUIPMENT FOR EDUCATIONAL PURPOSES.—

* * *

(G) TERMINATION.—This paragraph shall not apply to any contribution made during any taxable year beginning after *December 31, 2011.*

* * *

[CCH Explanation at ¶560, ¶563, ¶566, ¶705, and ¶760. Committee Reports at ¶10,130, ¶10,450, ¶10,460 and ¶10,470.]

Amendments

• 2010, Tax Relief, Unemployment Insurance Reauthorization, and Job Creation Act of 2010 (P.L. 111-312)

P.L. 111-312, §301(a):

Amended Code Sec. 170(e)(1) to read as such provision would read if subtitle E of title V of the Economic Growth and Tax Relief Reconciliation Act of 2001 (P.L. 107-16) had never been enacted. **Effective** for estates of decedents dying, and transfers made, after 12-31-2009. For a special rule, see Act Sec. 301(c), below. Prior to amendment by P.L. 111-312, the flush text following Code Sec. 170(e)(1) read as follows:

For purposes of applying this paragraph (other than in the case of gain to which section 617(d)(1), 1245(a), 1250(a), 1252(a), or 1254(a) applies), property which is property used

in the trade or business (as defined in section 1231(b)) shall be treated as a capital asset. For purposes of applying this paragraph in the case of a charitable contribution of stock in an S corporation, rules similar to the rules of section 751 shall apply in determining whether gain on such stock would have been long-term capital gain if such stock were sold by the taxpayer. For purposes of this paragraph, the determination of whether property is a capital asset shall be made without regard to the exception contained in section 1221(a)(3)(C) for basis determined under section 1022

P.L. 111-312, §301(c), provides:

(c) SPECIAL ELECTION WITH RESPECT TO ESTATES OF DECEDENTS DYING IN 2010.—Notwithstanding subsection (a), in the case of an estate of a decedent dying after December 31, 2009, and before January 1, 2011, the executor (within the meaning of section 2203 of the Internal Revenue Code of 1986) may elect to apply such Code as though the amendments made by subsection (a) do not apply with respect to chapter 11 of such Code and with respect to property acquired or passing from such decedent (within the meaning of section 1014(b) of such Code). Such election shall be made at such time and in such manner as the Secretary of the Treasury or the Secretary's delegate shall provide. Such an election once made shall be revocable only with the consent of the Secretary of the Treasury or the Secretary's delegate. For purposes of section 2652(a)(1) of such Code, the determination of whether any property is subject to the tax imposed by such chapter 11 shall be made without regard to any election made under this subsection.

P.L. 111-312, § 304, provides:

SEC. 304. APPLICATION OF EGTRRA SUNSET TO THIS TITLE.

Section 901 of the Economic Growth and Tax Relief Reconciliation Act of 2001 shall apply to the amendments made by this title.

P.L. 111-312, § 740(a):

Amended Code Sec. 170(e)(3)(C)(iv) by striking "December 31, 2009" and inserting "December 31, 2011". Effective for contributions made after 12-31-2009.

P.L. 111-312, § 741(a):

Amended Code Sec. 170(e)(3)(D)(iv) by striking "December 31, 2009" and inserting "December 31, 2011". Effective for contributions made after 12-31-2009.

P.L. 111-312, § 742(a):

Amended Code Sec. 170(e)(6)(G) by striking "December 31, 2009" and inserting "December 31, 2011". Effective for contributions made in tax years beginning after 12-31-2009.

● **2001, Economic Growth and Tax Relief Reconciliation Act of 2001 (P.L. 107-16)**

P.L. 107-16, § 542(e)(2)(B):

Amended Code Sec. 170(e)(1) by adding at the end a new sentence. Effective for estates of decedents dying after 12-31-2009.

P.L. 107-16, § 901(a)-(b), as amended by P.L. 111-312, § 101(a)(1), provides:

SEC. 901. SUNSET OF PROVISIONS OF ACT.

(a) IN GENERAL.—All provisions of, and amendments made by, this Act shall not apply—

(1) to taxable, plan, or limitation years beginning after December 31, 2012, or

(2) in the case of title V, to estates of decedents dying, gifts made, or generation skipping transfers, after December 31, 2012.

(b) APPLICATION OF CERTAIN LAWS.—The Internal Revenue Code of 1986 and the Employee Retirement Income Security Act of 1974 shall be applied and administered to years, estates, gifts, and transfers described in subsection (a) as if the provisions and amendments described in subsection (a) had never been enacted.

[¶ 5275] CODE SEC. 179. ELECTION TO EXPENSE CERTAIN DEPRECIABLE BUSINESS ASSETS.

* * *

(b) LIMITATIONS.—

(1) DOLLAR LIMITATION.—The aggregate cost which may be taken into account under subsection (a) for any taxable year shall not exceed—

(A) $250,000 in the case of taxable years beginning after 2007 and before 2010,

(B) $500,000 in the case of taxable years beginning in 2010 or 2011,

(C) *$125,000 in the case of taxable years beginning in 2012, and*

(D) *$25,000 in the case of taxable years beginning after 2012.*

(2) REDUCTION IN LIMITATION.—The limitation under paragraph (1) for any taxable year shall be reduced (but not below zero) by the amount by which the cost of section 179 property placed in service during such taxable year exceeds—

(A) $800,000 in the case of taxable years beginning after 2007 and before 2010,

(B) $2,000,000 in the case of taxable years beginning in 2010 or 2011,

(C) *$500,000 in the case of taxable years beginning in 2012, and*

(D) *$200,000 in the case of taxable years beginning after 2012.*

* * *

▶▶▶ *Caution: Code Sec. 179(b)(6), below, as added by P.L. 111-312, applies to tax years beginning after December 31, 2011.*

(6) INFLATION ADJUSTMENT.—

(A) IN GENERAL.—In the case of any taxable year beginning in calendar year 2012, the $125,000 and $500,000 amounts in paragraphs (1)(C) and (2)(C) shall each be increased by an amount equal to—

(i) *such dollar amount, multiplied by*

(ii) *the cost-of-living adjustment determined under section 1(f)(3) for the calendar year in which the taxable year begins, by substituting "calendar year 2006" for "calendar year 1992" in subparagraph (B) thereof.*

(B) ROUNDING.—

(i) DOLLAR LIMITATION.—*If the amount in paragraph (1) as increased under subparagraph (A) is not a multiple of $1,000, such amount shall be rounded to the nearest multiple of $1,000.*

(ii) PHASEOUT AMOUNT.—*If the amount in paragraph (2) as increased under subparagraph (A) is not a multiple of $10,000, such amount shall be rounded to the nearest multiple of $10,000.*

[CCH Explanation at ¶ 506. Committee Reports at ¶ 10,150.]

Amendments

● **2010, Tax Relief, Unemployment Insurance Reauthorization, and Job Creation Act of 2010 (P.L. 111-312)**

P.L. 111-312, § 402(a):

Amended Code Sec. 179(b)(1) by striking "and" at the end of subparagraph (B), by striking subparagraph (C), and inserting new subparagraphs (C) and (D). **Effective** for tax years beginning after 12-31-2011. Prior to being stricken, Code Sec. 179(b)(1)(C) read as follows:

(C) $25,000 in the case of taxable years beginning after 2011.

P.L. 111-312, § 402(b):

Amended Code Sec. 179(b)(2) by striking "and" at the end of subparagraph (B), by striking subparagraph (C), and inserting new subparagraphs (C) and (D). **Effective** for tax years beginning after 12-31-2011. Prior to being stricken, Code Sec. 179(b)(2)(C) read as follows:

(C) $200,000 in the case of taxable years beginning after 2011.

P.L. 111-312, § 402(c):

Amended Code Sec. 179(b) by adding at the end a new paragraph (6). **Effective** for tax years beginning after 12-31-2011.

● **2003, Jobs and Growth Tax Relief Reconciliation Act of 2003 (P.L. 108-27)**

P.L. 108-27, § 202(a):

Amended Code Sec. 179(b)(1). **Effective** for tax years beginning after 12-31-2002. Prior to amendment, Code Sec. 179(b)(1) read as follows:

(c) ELECTION.—

(1) DOLLAR LIMITATION.—The aggregate cost which may be taken into account under subsection (a) for any taxable year shall not exceed the following applicable amount:

If the taxable year begins in:	The applicable amount is:
1997	18,000
1998	18,500
1999	19,000
2000	20,000
2001 or 2002	24,000
2003 or thereafter	25,000

P.L. 108-27, § 202(b):

Amended Code Sec. 179(b)(2) by inserting "($400,000 in the case of taxable years beginning after 2002 and before 2006)" after "$200,000". **Effective** for tax years beginning after 12-31-2002.

P.L. 108-27, § 202(d):

Amended Code Sec. 179(b) by adding at the end a new paragraph (5). **Effective** for tax years beginning after 12-31-2002.

* * *

⯈ Caution: *Code Sec. 179(c)(2), below, as amended by P.L. 111-312, applies to tax years beginning after December 31, 2011.*

(2) ELECTION IRREVOCABLE.—Any election made under this section, and any specification contained in any such election, may not be revoked except with the consent of the Secretary. Any such election or specification with respect to any taxable year beginning after 2002 and before 2013 may be revoked by the taxpayer with respect to any property, and such revocation, once made, shall be irrevocable.

[CCH Explanation at ¶506. Committee Reports at ¶10,150.]

Amendments

- **2010, Tax Relief, Unemployment Insurance Reauthorization, and Job Creation Act of 2010 (P.L. 111-312)**

P.L. 111-312, §402(e):

Amended Code Sec. 179(c)(2) by striking "2012" and inserting "2013". **Effective** for tax years beginning after 12-31-2011.

- **2003, Jobs and Growth Tax Relief Reconciliation Act of 2003 (P.L. 108-27)**

P.L. 108-27, §202(e):

Amended Code Sec. 179(c)(2) by adding at the end a new sentence. **Effective** for tax years beginning after 12-31-2002.

(d) DEFINITIONS AND SPECIAL RULES.—

(1) SECTION 179 PROPERTY.—For purposes of this section, the term "section 179 property" means property—

(A) which is—

* * *

>>>→ *Caution: Code Sec. 179(d)(A)(ii), below, as amended by P.L. 111-312, applies to tax years beginning after December 31, 2011.*

(ii) computer software (as defined in section 197(e)(3)(B)) which is described in section 197(e)(3)(A)(i), to which section 167 applies, and which is placed in service in a taxable year beginning after 2002 and before 2013,

* * *

[CCH Explanation at ¶506. Committee Reports at ¶10,150.]

Amendments

- **2010, Tax Relief, Unemployment Insurance Reauthorization, and Job Creation Act of 2010 (P.L. 111-312)**

P.L. 111-312, §402(d):

Amended Code Sec. 179(d)(1)(A)(ii) by striking "2012" and inserting "2013". **Effective** for tax years beginning after 12-31-2011.

- **2003, Jobs and Growth Tax Relief Reconciliation Act of 2003 (P.L. 108-27)**

P.L. 108-27, §202(c):

Amended Code Sec. 179(d)(1). **Effective** for tax years beginning after 12-31-2002. Prior to amendment, Code Sec. 179(d)(1) read as follows:

(1) SECTION 179 PROPERTY.—For purposes of this section, the term "section 179 property" means any tangible property (to which section 168 applies) which is section 1245 property (as defined in section 1245(a)(3) and which is acquired by purchase for use in the active conduct of a trade or business. Such term shall not include any property described in section 50(b) and shall not include air conditioning or heating units.

(f) SPECIAL RULES FOR QUALIFIED REAL PROPERTY.—

* * *

(2) QUALIFIED REAL PROPERTY.—For purposes of this subsection, the term "qualified real property" means—

(A) qualified leasehold improvement property described in section 168(e)(6),

(B) qualified restaurant property described in section 168(e)(7), and

(C) qualified retail improvement property described in section 168(e)(8).

* * *

[CCH Explanation at ¶508. Committee Reports at ¶10,150.]

Amendments

• 2010, Tax Relief, Unemployment Insurance Reauthorization, and Job Creation Act of 2010 (P.L. 111-312)

P.L. 111-312, §737(b)(3)(A)-(B):

Amended Code Sec. 179(f)(2) by striking "(without regard to the dates specified in subparagraph (A)(i) thereof)" after "section 168(e)(7)" in subparagraph (B), and by striking "(without regard to subparagraph (E) thereof)" after "section 168(e)(8)" in subparagraph (C). **Effective** for property placed in service after 12-31-2009.

[¶5280] CODE SEC. 179E. ELECTION TO EXPENSE ADVANCED MINE SAFETY EQUIPMENT.

* * *

(g) TERMINATION.—This section shall not apply to property placed in service after *December 31, 2011.*

[CCH Explanation at ¶516. Committee Reports at ¶10,480.]

Amendments

• 2010, Tax Relief, Unemployment Insurance Reauthorization, and Job Creation Act of 2010 (P.L. 111-312)

P.L. 111-312, §743(a):

Amended Code Sec. 179E(g) by striking "December 31, 2009" and inserting "December 31, 2011". **Effective** for property placed in service after 12-31-2009.

[¶5285] CODE SEC. 181. TREATMENT OF CERTAIN QUALIFIED FILM AND TELEVISION PRODUCTIONS.

* * *

(f) TERMINATION.—This section shall not apply to qualified film and television productions commencing after *December 31, 2011.*

[CCH Explanation at ¶514. Committee Reports at ¶10,490.]

Amendments

• 2010, Tax Relief, Unemployment Insurance Reauthorization, and Job Creation Act of 2010 (P.L. 111-312)

P.L. 111-312, §744(a):

Amended Code Sec. 181(f) by striking "December 31, 2009" and inserting "December 31, 2011". **Effective** for productions commencing after 12-31-2009.

[¶5290] CODE SEC. 198. EXPENSING OF ENVIRONMENTAL REMEDIATION COSTS.

* * *

(h) TERMINATION.—This section shall not apply to expenditures paid or incurred after *December 31, 2011.*

[CCH Explanation at ¶518. Committee Reports at ¶10,500.]

Amendments

• 2010, Tax Relief, Unemployment Insurance Reauthorization, and Job Creation Act of 2010 (P.L. 111-312)

P.L. 111-312, §745(a):

Amended Code Sec. 198(h) by striking "December 31, 2009" and inserting "December 31, 2011". **Effective** for expenditures paid or incurred after 12-31-2009.

(2) ROUNDING.—If any amount as adjusted under paragraph (1) is not a multiple of $5,000, such amount shall be rounded to the next lowest multiple of $5,000.

[CCH Explanation at ¶345. Committee Reports at ¶10,050.]

Amendments

• **2001, Economic Growth and Tax Relief Reconciliation Act of 2001 (P.L. 107-16)**

P.L. 107-16, §412(a)(1):

Amended Code Sec. 221 by redesignating subsection (g) as subsection (f). Effective with respect to any loan interest paid after 12-31-2001, in tax years ending after such date.

P.L. 107-16, §412(b)(2), as amended by P.L. 108-311, §408(b)(5):

Amended Code Sec. 221(f)(1) by striking "$40,000 and $60,000 amounts" and inserting "$50,000 and $100,000 amounts". Effective for tax years ending after 12-31-2001.

P.L. 107-16, §901(a)-(b), as amended by P.L. 111-312, §101(a)(1), provides:

SEC. 901. SUNSET OF PROVISIONS OF ACT.

(a) IN GENERAL.—All provisions of, and amendments made by, this Act shall not apply—

(1) to taxable, plan, or limitation years beginning after December 31, 2012, or

(2) in the case of title V, to estates of decedents dying, gifts made, or generation skipping transfers, after December 31, 2012.

(b) APPLICATION OF CERTAIN LAWS.—The Internal Revenue Code of 1986 and the Employee Retirement Income Security Act of 1974 shall be applied and administered to years, estates, gifts, and transfers described in subsection (a) as if the provisions and amendments described in subsection (a) had never been enacted.

»»→ Caution: *Code Sec. 222, below, was added by P.L. 107-16. For sunset provision, see P.L. 107-16, §901 [as amended by P.L. 111-312], in the amendment notes.*

[¶5310] CODE SEC. 222. QUALIFIED TUITION AND RELATED EXPENSES.

(a) ALLOWANCE OF DEDUCTION.—In the case of an individual, there shall be allowed as a deduction an amount equal to the qualified tuition and related expenses paid by the taxpayer during the taxable year.

(b) DOLLAR LIMITATIONS.—

(1) IN GENERAL.—The amount allowed as a deduction under subsection (a) with respect to the taxpayer for any taxable year shall not exceed the applicable dollar limit.

(2) APPLICABLE DOLLAR LIMIT.—

(A) 2002 AND 2003.—In the case of a taxable year beginning in 2002 or 2003, the applicable dollar limit shall be equal to—

(i) in the case of a taxpayer whose adjusted gross income for the taxable year does not exceed $65,000 ($130,000 in the case of a joint return), $3,000, and—

(ii) in the case of any other taxpayer, zero.

(B) AFTER 2003.—In the case of any taxable year beginning after 2003, the applicable dollar amount shall be equal to—

(i) in the case of a taxpayer whose adjusted gross income for the taxable year does not exceed $65,000 ($130,000 in the case of a joint return), $4,000,

(ii) in the case of a taxpayer not described in clause (i) whose adjusted gross income for the taxable year does not exceed $80,000 ($160,000 in the case of a joint return), $2,000, and

(iii) in the case of any other taxpayer, zero.

(C) ADJUSTED GROSS INCOME.—For purposes of this paragraph, adjusted gross income shall be determined—

(i) without regard to this section and sections 199, 911, 931, and 933, and

(ii) after application of sections 86, 135, 137, 219, 221, and 469.

[CCH Explanation at ¶ 350. Committee Reports at ¶ 10,310.]

Amendments

• **2006, Tax Relief and Health Care Act of 2006 (P.L. 109-432)**

P.L. 109-432, Division A, § 101(b)(1)-(2):

Amended Code Sec. 222(b)(2)(B) by striking "a taxable year beginning in 2004 or 2005" and inserting "any taxable year beginning after 2003", and by striking "2004 AND 2005" in the heading and inserting "AFTER 2003". **Effective** for tax years beginning after 12-31-2005.

• **2004, American Jobs Creation Act of 2004 (P.L. 108-357)**

P.L. 108-357, § 102(d)(3):

Amended Code Sec. 222(b)(2)(C)(i) by inserting "199," before "911". **Effective** for tax years beginning after 12-31-2004.

(c) NO DOUBLE BENEFIT.—

(1) IN GENERAL.—No deduction shall be allowed under subsection (a) for any expense for which a deduction is allowed to the taxpayer under any other provision of this chapter.

(2) COORDINATION WITH OTHER EDUCATION INCENTIVES.—

(A) DENIAL OF DEDUCTION IF CREDIT ELECTED.—No deduction shall be allowed under subsection (a) for a taxable year with respect to the qualified tuition and related expenses with respect to an individual if the taxpayer or any other person elects to have section 25A apply with respect to such individual for such year.

(B) COORDINATION WITH EXCLUSIONS.—The total amount of qualified tuition and related expenses shall be reduced by the amount of such expenses taken into account in determining any amount excluded under section 135, 529(c)(1), or 530(d)(2). For purposes of the preceding sentence, the amount taken into account in determining the amount excluded under section 529(c)(1) shall not include that portion of the distribution which represents a return of any contributions to the plan.

(3) DEPENDENTS.—No deduction shall be allowed under subsection (a) to any individual with respect to whom a deduction under section 151 is allowable to another taxpayer for a taxable year beginning in the calendar year in which such individual's taxable year begins.

(d) DEFINITIONS AND SPECIAL RULES.—For purposes of this section—

(1) QUALIFIED TUITION AND RELATED EXPENSES.—The term "qualified tuition and related expenses" has the meaning given such term by section 25A(f). Such expenses shall be reduced in the same manner as under section 25A(g)(2).

(2) IDENTIFICATION REQUIREMENT.—No deduction shall be allowed under subsection (a) to a taxpayer with respect to the qualified tuition and related expenses of an individual unless the taxpayer includes the name and taxpayer identification number of the individual on the return of tax for the taxable year.

(3) LIMITATION ON TAXABLE YEAR OF DEDUCTION.—

(A) IN GENERAL.—A deduction shall be allowed under subsection (a) for qualified tuition and related expenses for any taxable year only to the extent such expenses are in connection with enrollment at an institution of higher education during the taxable year.

(B) CERTAIN PREPAYMENTS ALLOWED.—Subparagraph (A) shall not apply to qualified tuition and related expenses paid during a taxable year if such expenses are in connection with an academic term beginning during such taxable year or during the first 3 months of the next taxable year.

(4) NO DEDUCTION FOR MARRIED INDIVIDUALS FILING SEPARATE RETURNS.—If the taxpayer is a married individual (within the meaning of section 7703), this section shall apply only if the taxpayer and the taxpayer's spouse file a joint return for the taxable year.

(5) NONRESIDENT ALIENS.—If the taxpayer is a nonresident alien individual for any portion of the taxable year, this section shall apply only if such individual is treated as a resident alien of the United States for purposes of this chapter by reason of an election under subsection (g) or (h) of section 6013.

(6) REGULATIONS.—The Secretary may prescribe such regulations as may be necessary or appropriate to carry out this section, including regulations requiring recordkeeping and information reporting.

(e) TERMINATION.—This section shall not apply to taxable years beginning after *December 31, 2011.*

[CCH Explanation at ¶350. Committee Reports at ¶10,310.]

Amendments

• **2010, Tax Relief, Unemployment Insurance Reauthorization, and Job Creation Act of 2010 (P.L. 111-312)**

P.L. 111-312, §724(a):

Amended Code Sec. 222(e) by striking "December 31, 2009" and inserting "December 31, 2011". **Effective** for tax years beginning after 12-31-2009.

• **2001, Economic Growth and Tax Relief Reconciliation Act of 2001 (P.L. 107-16)**

P.L. 107-16, §431(a):

Amended part VII of subchapter B of chapter 1 by redesignating Code Sec. 222 as Code Sec. 223 and by inserting after Code Sec. 221 a new Code Sec. 222. **Effective** for payments made in tax years beginning after 12-31-2001.

P.L. 107-16, §901(a)-(b), as amended by P.L. 111-312, §101(a)(1), provides:

SEC. 901. SUNSET OF PROVISIONS OF ACT.

(a) IN GENERAL.—All provisions of, and amendments made by, this Act shall not apply—

(1) to taxable, plan, or limitation years beginning after December 31, 2012, or

(2) in the case of title V, to estates of decedents dying, gifts made, or generation skipping transfers, after December 31, 2012.

(b) APPLICATION OF CERTAIN LAWS.—The Internal Revenue Code of 1986 and the Employee Retirement Income Security Act of 1974 shall be applied and administered to years, estates, gifts, and transfers described in subsection (a) as if the provisions and amendments described in subsection (a) had never been enacted.

≫→ *Caution: Former Code Sec. 222, below, was redesignated as Code Sec. 223 by P.L. 107-16 and redesignated as Code Sec. 224 by P.L. 108-173. For sunset provision, see P.L. 107-16, §901 [as amended by P.L. 111-312], in the amendment notes.*

[¶5315] CODE SEC. 224. CROSS REFERENCE.

For deductions in respect of a decedent, see section 691.

[CCH Explanation at ¶350. Committee Reports at ¶10,310.]

Amendments

• **2003, Medicare Prescription Drug, Improvement, and Modernization Act of 2003 (P.L. 108-173)**

P.L. 108-173, §1201(a):

Amended part VII of subchapter B of chapter 1 by redesignating Code Sec. 223 as Code Sec. 224. **Effective** for tax years beginning after 12-31-2003.

• **2001, Economic Growth and Tax Relief Reconciliation Act of 2001 (P.L. 107-16)**

P.L. 107-16, §431(a):

Amended part VII of subchapter B of chapter 1 by redesignating Code Sec. 222 as Code Sec. 223. **Effective** for payments made in tax years beginning after 12-31-2001.

P.L. 107-16, §901(a)-(b), as amended by P.L. 111-312, §101(a)(1), provides:

SEC. 901. SUNSET OF PROVISIONS OF ACT.

(a) IN GENERAL.—All provisions of, and amendments made by, this Act shall not apply—

(1) to taxable, plan, or limitation years beginning after December 31, 2012, or

(2) in the case of title V, to estates of decedents dying, gifts made, or generation skipping transfers, after December 31, 2012.

(b) APPLICATION OF CERTAIN LAWS.—The Internal Revenue Code of 1986 and the Employee Retirement Income Security Act of 1974 shall be applied and administered to years, estates, gifts, and transfers described in subsection (a) as if the provisions and amendments described in subsection (a) had never been enacted.

[¶5320] CODE SEC. 267. LOSSES, EXPENSES, AND INTEREST WITH RESPECT TO TRANSACTIONS BETWEEN RELATED TAXPAYERS.

* * *

(f) CONTROLLED GROUP DEFINED; SPECIAL RULES APPLICABLE TO CONTROLLED GROUPS.—

* * *

(3) LOSS DEFERRAL RULES NOT TO APPLY IN CERTAIN CASES.—

* * *

(D) REDEMPTIONS BY FUND-OF-FUNDS REGULATED INVESTMENT COMPANIES.—Except to the extent provided in regulations prescribed by the Secretary, subsection (a)(1) shall not apply to any distribution in redemption of stock of a regulated investment company if—

(i) such company issues only stock which is redeemable upon the demand of the stockholder, and

(ii) such redemption is upon the demand of another regulated investment company.

* * *

[CCH Explanation at ¶ 824.]

Amendments

• 2010, Regulated Investment Company Modernization Act of 2010 (H.R. 4337)

H.R. 4337, § 306(b):

Amended Code Sec. 267(f)(3) by adding at the end a new subparagraph (D). Effective for distributions after the date of the enactment of this Act.

[¶ 5325] CODE SEC. 301. DISTRIBUTIONS OF PROPERTY.

* * *

(f) SPECIAL RULES.—

* * *

≫→ *Caution: Code Sec. 301(f)(4), below, was added by P.L. 108-27. For sunset provision, see P.L. 108-27, § 303 [as amended by P.L. 111-312], in the amendment notes.*

(4) For taxation of dividends received by individuals at capital gain rates, see section 1(h)(11).

[CCH Explanation at ¶ 420 and ¶ 425. Committee Reports at ¶ 10,080.]

Amendments

• 2003, Jobs and Growth Tax Relief Reconciliation Act of 2003 (P.L. 108-27)

P.L. 108-27, § 302(e)(2):

Amended Code Sec. 301(f) by adding at the end a new paragraph (4). For the effective date, see Act Sec. 302(f), as amended by P.L. 108-311, § 402(a)(6), below.

P.L. 108-27, § 302(f), as amended by P.L. 108-311, § 402(a)(6), provides:

(f) EFFECTIVE DATE.—

(1) IN GENERAL.—Except as provided in paragraph (2), the amendments made by this section shall apply to taxable years beginning after December 31, 2002.

(2) PASS-THRU ENTITIES.—In the case of a pass-thru entity described in subparagraph (A), (B), (C), (D), (E), or (F) of

section 1(h)(10) of the Internal Revenue Code of 1986, as amended by this Act, the amendments made by this section shall apply to taxable years ending after December 31, 2002; except that dividends received by such an entity on or before such date shall not be treated as qualified dividend income (as defined in section 1(h)(11)(B) of such Code, as added by this Act).

P.L. 108-27, § 303, as amended by P.L. 109-222, § 102, and P.L. 111-312, § 102(a), provides:

SEC. 303. SUNSET OF TITLE.

All provisions of, and amendments made by, this title shall not apply to taxable years beginning after December 31, 2012, and the Internal Revenue Code of 1986 shall be applied and administered to such years as if such provisions and amendments had never been enacted.

[¶ 5330] CODE SEC. 302. DISTRIBUTIONS IN REDEMPTION OF STOCK.

(a) GENERAL RULE.—If a corporation redeems its stock (within the meaning of section 317(b)), and if paragraph (1), (2), (3), (4), or (5) of subsection (b) applies, such redemption shall be treated as a distribution in part or full payment in exchange for the stock.

[CCH Explanation at ¶ 824.]

Amendments

• **2010, Regulated Investment Company Modernization Act of 2010 (H.R. 4337)**

H.R. 4337, § 306(a)(2):

Amended Code Sec. 302(a) by striking "or (4)" and inserting "(4), or (5)". **Effective** for distributions after the date of the enactment of this Act.

(b) REDEMPTIONS TREATED AS EXCHANGES.—

* * *

(5) REDEMPTIONS BY CERTAIN REGULATED INVESTMENT COMPANIES.—*Except to the extent provided in regulations prescribed by the Secretary, subsection (a) shall apply to any distribution in redemption of stock of a publicly offered regulated investment company (within the meaning of section 67(c)(2)(B)) if—*

(A) *such redemption is upon the demand of the stockholder, and*

(B) *such company issues only stock which is redeemable upon the demand of the stockholder.*

(6) APPLICATION OF PARAGRAPHS.—In determining whether a redemption meets the requirements of paragraph (1), the fact that such redemption fails to meet the requirements of paragraph (2), (3), or (4) shall not be taken into account. If a redemption meets the requirements of paragraph (3) and also the requirements of paragraph (1), (2), or (4), then so much of subsection (c) (2) as would (but for this sentence) apply in respect of the acquisition of an interest in the corporation within the 10-year period beginning on the date of the distribution shall not apply.

* * *

[CCH Explanation at ¶ 824.]

Amendments

• **2010, Regulated Investment Company Modernization Act of 2010 (H.R. 4337)**

H.R. 4337, § 306(a)(1):

Amended Code Sec. 302(b) by redesignating paragraph (5) as paragraph (6) and by inserting after paragraph (4) a new paragraph (5). **Effective** for distributions after the date of the enactment of this Act.

[¶ 5335] CODE SEC. 306. DISPOSITIONS OF CERTAIN STOCK.

(a) GENERAL RULE.—If a shareholder sells or otherwise disposes of section 306 stock (as defined in subsection (c))—

(1) DISPOSITIONS OTHER THAN REDEMPTIONS.—If such disposition is not a redemption (within the meaning of section 317(b))—

* * *

»»→ Caution: *Code Sec. 306(a)(1)(D), below, was added by P.L. 108-27. For sunset provision, see P.L. 108-27, § 303 [as amended by P.L. 111-312], in the amendment notes.*

(D) TREATMENT AS DIVIDEND.—For purposes of section 1(h)(11) and such other provisions as the Secretary may specify, any amount treated as ordinary income under this paragraph shall be treated as a dividend received from the corporation.

* * *

[CCH Explanation at ¶ 420 and ¶ 425. Committee Reports at ¶ 10,080.]

Amendments

• **2003, Jobs and Growth Tax Relief Reconciliation Act of 2003 (P.L. 108-27)**

P.L. 108-27, § 302(e)(3):

Amended Code Sec. 306(a)(1) by adding at the end a new subparagraph (D). For the effective date, see Act Sec. 302(f), as amended by P.L. 108-311, § 402(a)(6), below.

P.L. 108-27, § 302(f), as amended by P.L. 108-311, § 402(a)(6), provides:

(f) EFFECTIVE DATE.—

(1) IN GENERAL.—Except as provided in paragraph (2), the amendments made by this section shall apply to taxable years beginning after December 31, 2002.

(2) PASS-THRU ENTITIES.—In the case of a pass-thru entity described in subparagraph (A), (B), (C), (D), (E), or (F) of section 1(h)(10) of the Internal Revenue Code of 1986, as amended by this Act, the amendments made by this section shall apply to taxable years ending after December 31, 2002; except that dividends received by such an entity on or before such date shall not be treated as qualified dividend income (as defined in section 1(h)(11)(B) of such Code, as added by this Act).

P.L. 108-27, §303, as amended by P.L. 109-222, §102, and P.L. 111-312, §102(a), provides:

SEC. 303. SUNSET OF TITLE.

All provisions of, and amendments made by, this title shall not apply to taxable years beginning after December 31, 2012, and the Internal Revenue Code of 1986 shall be applied and administered to such years as if such provisions and amendments had never been enacted.

[¶5340] CODE SEC. 316. DIVIDEND DEFINED.

* * *

(b) SPECIAL RULES.—

* * *

(4) CERTAIN DISTRIBUTIONS BY REGULATED INVESTMENT COMPANIES IN EXCESS OF EARNINGS AND PROF- ITS.—In the case of a regulated investment company that has a taxable year other than a calendar year, if the distributions by the company with respect to any class of stock of such company for the taxable year exceed the company's current and accumulated earnings and profits which may be used for the payment of dividends on such class of stock, the company's current earnings and profits shall, for purposes of subsection (a), be allocated first to distributions with respect to such class of stock made during the portion of the taxable year which precedes January 1.

[CCH Explanation at ¶821.]
Amendments
• **2010, Regulated Investment Company Moderni- zation Act of 2010 (H.R. 4337)**

H.R. 4337, §305(a):

Amended Code Sec. 316(b) by adding at the end a new paragraph (4). **Effective** for distributions made in tax years beginning after the date of the enactment of this Act.

[¶5345] CODE SEC. 338. CERTAIN STOCK PURCHASES TREATED AS ASSET ACQUISITIONS.

* * *

(h) DEFINITIONS AND SPECIAL RULES.—For purposes of this section—

* * *

⨠→ *Caution: Code Sec. 338(h)(14), below, was stricken by P.L. 108-27. For sunset provision, see P.L. 108-27, §303 [as amended by P.L. 111-312], in the amendment notes.*

(14) [Stricken.]

* * *

[CCH Explanation at ¶425 and ¶609. Committee Reports at ¶10,080.]
Amendments
• **2003, Jobs and Growth Tax Relief Reconciliation Act of 2003 (P.L. 108-27)**

P.L. 108-27, §302(e)(4)(B)(i):

Amended Code Sec. 338(h) by striking paragraph (14). For the **effective** date, see Act Sec. 302(f), as amended by P.L. 108-311, §402(a)(6), below. Prior to being stricken, Code Sec. 338(h)(14) read as follows:

(14) COORDINATION WITH SECTION 341.—For purposes of determining whether section 341 applies to a disposition within 1 year after the acquisition date of stock by a share- holder (other than the acquiring corporation) who held stock in the target corporation on the acquisition date, sec- tion 341 shall be applied without regard to this section.

P.L. 108-27, §302(f), as amended by P.L. 108-311, §402(a)(6), provides:

(f) EFFECTIVE DATE.—

(1) IN GENERAL.—Except as provided in paragraph (2), the amendments made by this section shall apply to taxable years beginning after December 31, 2002.

(2) PASS-THRU ENTITIES.—In the case of a pass-thru entity described in subparagraph (A), (B), (C), (D), (E), or (F) of section 1(h)(10) of the Internal Revenue Code of 1986, as amended by this Act, the amendments made by this section shall apply to taxable years ending after December 31, 2002; except that dividends received by such an entity on or before such date shall not be treated as qualified dividend

income (as defined in section 1(h)(11)(B) of such Code, as added by this Act).

P.L. 108-27, §303, as amended by P.L. 109-222, §102, and P.L. 111-312, §102(a), provides:

SEC. 303. SUNSET OF TITLE.

➤➤➤ *Caution: Code Sec. 341, below, was repealed by P.L. 108-27. For sunset provision, see P.L. 108-27, §303 [as amended by P.L. 111-312], in the amendment notes.*

[¶5350] CODE SEC. 341. COLLAPSIBLE CORPORATIONS.

[Repealed.]

[CCH Explanation at ¶609. Committee Reports at ¶10,080.]

Amendments

● **2003, Jobs and Growth Tax Relief Reconciliation Act of 2003 (P.L. 108-27)**

P.L. 108-27, §302(e)(4)(A):

Repealed subpart C of part II of subchapter C of chapter 1 (Code Sec. 341). For the **effective** date, see Act Sec. 302(f), as amended by P.L. 108-311, §402(a)(6), below.

P.L. 108-27, §302(f), as amended by P.L. 108-311, §402(a)(6), provides:

(f) EFFECTIVE DATE.—

(1) IN GENERAL.—Except as provided in paragraph (2), the amendments made by this section shall apply to taxable years beginning after December 31, 2002.

(2) PASS-THRU ENTITIES.—In the case of a pass-thru entity described in subparagraph (A), (B), (C), (D), (E), or (F) of section 1(h)(10) of the Internal Revenue Code of 1986, as amended by this Act, the amendments made by this section shall apply to taxable years ending after December 31, 2002; except that dividends received by such an entity on or before such date shall not be treated as qualified dividend income (as defined in section 1(h)(11)(B) of such Code, as added by this Act).

P.L. 108-27, §303, as amended by P.L. 109-222, §102, and P.L. 111-312, §102(a), provides:

SEC. 303. SUNSET OF TITLE.

All provisions of, and amendments made by, this title shall not apply to taxable years beginning after December 31, 2012, and the Internal Revenue Code of 1986 shall be applied and administered to such years as if such provisions and amendments had never been enacted.

Prior to repeal, Code Sec. 341 read as follows:

SEC. 341. COLLAPSIBLE CORPORATIONS.

(a) TREATMENT OF GAIN TO SHAREHOLDERS.—Gain from—

(1) the sale or exchange of stock of a collapsible corporation,

(2) a distribution—

(A) in complete liquidation of a collapsible corporation if such distribution is treated under this part as in part or full payment in exchange for stock, or

(B) in partial liquidation (within the meaning of section 302(e)) of a collapsible corporation if such distribution is treated under section 302(b)(4) as in part or full payment in exchange for the stock, and

(3) a distribution made by a collapsible corporation which, under section 301(c)(3)(A), is treated, to the extent it exceeds the basis of the stock, in the same manner as a gain from the sale or exchange of property,

to the extent that it would be considered (but for the provisions of this section) as gain from the sale or exchange of a

capital asset shall, except as otherwise provided in this section, be considered as ordinary income.

(b) DEFINITIONS.—

(1) COLLAPSIBLE CORPORATION.—For purposes of this section, the term "collapsible corporation" means a corporation formed or availed of principally for the manufacture, construction, or production of property, for the purchase of property which (in the hands of the corporation) is property described in paragraph (3), or for the holding of stock in a corporation so formed or availed of, with a view to—

(A) the sale or exchange of stock by its shareholders (whether in liquidation or otherwise), or a distribution to its shareholders, before the realization by the corporation manufacturing, constructing, producing, or purchasing the property of ⅔ of the taxable income to be derived from such property, and

(B) the realization by such shareholders of gain attributable to such property.

(2) PRODUCTION OR PURCHASE OF PROPERTY.—For purposes of paragraph (1), a corporation shall be deemed to have manufactured, constructed, produced, or purchased property, if—

(A) it engaged in the manufacture, construction, or production of such property to any extent,

(B) it holds property having a basis determined, in whole or in part, by reference to the cost of such property in the hands of a person who manufactured, constructed, produced, or purchased the property, or

(C) it holds property having a basis determined, in whole or in part, by reference to the cost of property manufactured, constructed, produced, or purchased by the corporation.

(3) SECTION 341 ASSETS.—For purposes of this section, the term "section 341 assets" means property held for a period of less than 3 years which is—

(A) stock in trade of the corporation, or other property of a kind which would properly be included in the inventory of the corporation if on hand at the close of the taxable year;

(B) property held by the corporation primarily for sale to customers in the ordinary course of its trade or business;

(C) unrealized receivables or fees, except receivables from sales of property other than property described in this paragraph; or

(D) property described in section 1231(b) (without regard to any holding period therein provided), except such property which is or has been used in connection with the manufacture, construction, production, or sale of property described in subparagraph (A) or (B).

In determining whether the 3-year holding period specified in this paragraph has been satisfied, section 1223 shall apply, but no such period shall be deemed to begin before the completion of the manufacture, construction, production, or purchase.

(4) UNREALIZED RECEIVABLES.—For purposes of paragraph (3)(C), the term "unrealized receivables or fees" means, to the extent not previously includible in income under the method of accounting used by the corporation, any rights (contractual or otherwise) to payment for—

(A) goods delivered, or to be delivered, to the extent the proceeds therefrom would be treated as amounts received from the sale or exchange of property other than a capital asset, or

(B) services rendered or to be rendered.

(c) PRESUMPTION IN CERTAIN CASES.—

(1) IN GENERAL.—For purposes of this section, a corporation shall, unless shown to the contrary, be deemed to be a collapsible corporation if (at the time of the sale or exchange, or the distribution, described in subsection (a)) the fair market value of its section 341 assets (as defined in subsection (b)(3)) is—

(A) 50 percent or more of the fair market value of its total assets, and

(B) 120 percent or more of the adjusted basis of such section 341 assets.

Absence of the conditions described in subparagraphs (A) and (B) shall not give rise to a presumption that the corporation was not a collapsible corporation.

(2) DETERMINATION OF TOTAL ASSETS.—In determining the fair market value of the total assets of a corporation for purposes of paragraph (1)(A), there shall not be taken into account—

(A) cash,

(B) obligations which are capital assets in the hands of the corporation, and

(C) stock in any other corporation.

(d) LIMITATIONS ON APPLICATION OF SECTION.—In the case of gain realized by a shareholder with respect to his stock in a collapsible corporation, this section shall not apply—

(1) unless, at any time after the commencement of the manufacture, construction, or production of the property, or at the time of the purchase of the property described in subsection (b)(3) or at any time thereafter, such shareholder (A) owned (or was considered as owning) more than 5 percent in value of the outstanding stock of the corporation, or (B) owned stock which was considered as owned at such time by another shareholder who then owned (or was considered as owning) more than 5 percent in value of the outstanding stock of the corporation;

(2) to the gain recognized during a taxable year, unless more than 70 percent of such gain is attributable to property described in subsection (b)(1); and

(3) to gain realized after the expiration of 3 years following the completion of such manufacture, construction, production, or purchase.

For purposes of paragraph (1), the ownership of stock shall be determined in accordance with the rules prescribed in paragraphs (1), (2), (3), (5), and (6) of section 544(a) (relating to personal holding companies); except that, in addition to the persons prescribed by paragraph (2) of that section, the family of an individual shall include the spouses of that individual's brothers and sisters (whether by the whole or half blood) and the spouses of that individual's lineal descendants. In determining whether property is described in subsection (b)(1) for purposes of applying paragraph (2), all property described in section 1221(a)(1) shall, to the extent provided in regulations prescribed by the Secretary, be treated as one item of property.

(e) EXCEPTIONS TO APPLICATION OF SECTION.—

(1) SALES OR EXCHANGES OF STOCK.—For purposes of subsection (a)(1), a corporation shall not be considered to be a collapsible corporation with respect to any sale or exchange of stock of the corporation by a shareholder, if, at the time of such sale or exchange, the sum of—

(A) the net unrealized appreciation in subsection (e) assets of the corporation (as defined in paragraph (5)(A)), plus

(B) if the shareholder owns more than 5 percent in value of the outstanding stock of the corporation, the net unrealized appreciation in assets of the corporation (other than assets described in subparagraph (A)) which would be subsection (e) assets under clauses (i) and (iii) of paragraph (5)(A) if the shareholder owned more than 20 percent in value of such stock, plus

(C) if the shareholder owns more than 20 percent in value of the outstanding stock of the corporation and owns, or at any time during the preceding 3-year period owned, more than 20 percent in value of the outstanding stock of any other corporation more than 70 percent in value of the assets of which are, or were at any time during which such shareholder owned during such 3-year period more than 20 percent in value of the outstanding stock, assets similar or related in service or use to assets comprising more than 70 percent in value of the assets of the corporation, the net unrealized appreciation in assets of the corporation (other than assets described in subparagraph (A)) which would be subsection (e) assets under clauses (i) and (iii) of paragraph (5)(A) if the determination whether the property, in the hands of such shareholder, would be property gain from the sale or exchange of which would under any provision of this chapter be considered in whole or in part as ordinary income, were made—

(i) by treating any sale or exchange by such shareholder of stock in such other corporation within the preceding 3-year period (but only if at the time of such sale or exchange the shareholder owned more than 20 percent in value of the outstanding stock in such other corporation) as a sale or exchange by such shareholder of his proportionate share of the assets of such other corporation, and

(ii) by treating any liquidating sale or exchange of property by such other corporation within such 3-year period (but only if at the time of such sale or exchange the shareholder owned more than 20 percent in value of the outstanding stock in such other corporation), as a sale or exchange by such shareholder of his proportionate share of the property sold or exchanged,

does not exceed an amount equal to 15 percent of the net worth of the corporation. This paragraph shall not apply to any sale or exchange of stock to the issuing corporation or, in the case of a shareholder who owns more than 20 percent in value of the outstanding stock of the corporation, to any sale or exchange of stock by such shareholder to any person related to him (within the meaning of paragraph (8)).

(2) [Repealed.]

(3) [Repealed.]

(4) [Repealed.]

(5) SUBSECTION (e) ASSET DEFINED.—

(A) For purposes of paragraph (1), the term "subsection (e) asset" means, with respect to property held by any corporation—

(i) property (except property used in the trade or business, as defined in paragraph (9)) which in the hands of the corporation is, or, in the hands of a shareholder who owns more than 20 percent in value of the outstanding stock of the corporation, would be, property gain from the sale or exchange of which would under any provision of this chapter be considered in whole or in part as ordinary income;

(ii) property used in the trade or business (as defined in paragraph (9)), but only if the unrealized depreciation on all such property on which there is unrealized depreciation exceeds the unrealized appreciation on all such property on which there is unrealized appreciation;

(iii) if there is net unrealized appreciation on all property used in the trade or business (as defined in paragraph (9)), property used in the trade or business (as defined in paragraph (9)) which, in the hands of a shareholder who owns more than 20 percent in value of the outstanding stock of the corporation, would be property gain from the sale or exchange of which would under any provision of this chapter be considered in whole or in part as ordinary income; and

(iv) property (unless included under clause (i), (ii), or (iii)) which consists of a copyright, a literary, musical, or artistic composition, a letter or memorandum, or similar property, or any interest in any such property, if the property was created in whole or in part by the personal efforts of, or (in the case of a letter, memorandum, or similar property) was prepared, or produced in whole or in part for, any individual who owns more than 5 percent in value of the stock of the corporation.

The determination as to whether property of the corporation in the hands of the corporation is, or in the hands of a shareholder would be, property gain from the sale or exchange of which would under any provision in this chapter be considered in whole or in part as ordinary income shall be made as if all property of the corporation had been sold or exchanged to one person in one transaction.

(B) [Repealed.]

(6) NET UNREALIZED APPRECIATION DEFINED.—

(A) For purposes of this subsection, the term "net unrealized appreciation" means, with respect to the assets of a corporation, the amount by which—

(i) the unrealized appreciation in such assets on which there is unrealized appreciation, exceeds

(ii) the unrealized depreciation in such assets on which there is unrealized depreciation.

(B) For purposes of subparagraph (A) and paragraph (5)(A), the term "unrealized appreciation" means, with respect to any asset, the amount by which—

(i) the fair market value of such asset, exceeds

(ii) the adjusted basis for determining gain from the sale or other disposition of such asset.

(C) For purposes of subparagraph (A) and paragraph (5)(A), the term "unrealized depreciation" means, with respect to any asset, the amount by which—

(i) the adjusted basis for determining gain from the sale or other disposition of such asset, exceeds

(ii) the fair market value of such asset.

(D) For purposes of this paragraph (but not paragraph (5)(A)), in the case of any asset on the sale or exchange of which only a portion of the gain would under any provision of this chapter be considered as ordinary income, there shall be taken into account only an amount of the unrealized appreciation in such asset which is equal to such portion of the gain.

(7) NET WORTH DEFINED.—For purposes of this subsection, the net worth of a corporation, as of any day, is the amount by which—

(A)(i) the fair market value of all its assets at the close of such day, plus

(ii) the amount of any distribution in complete liquidation made by it on or before such day, exceeds

(B) all its liabilities at the close of such day.

For purposes of this paragraph, the net worth of a corporation as of any day shall not take into account any increase in net worth during the one-year period ending on such day to the extent attributable to any amount received by it for stock, or as a contribution to capital or as paid-in surplus, if

it appears that there was not a bona fide business purpose for the transaction in respect of which such amount was received.

(8) RELATED PERSON DEFINED.—For purposes of paragraphs (1) and (4), the following persons shall be considered to be related to a shareholder:

(A) If the shareholder is an individual—

(i) his spouse, ancestors, and lineal descendants, and

(ii) a corporation which is controlled by such shareholder.

(B) If the shareholder is a corporation—

(i) a corporation which controls, or is controlled by, the shareholder, and

(ii) if more than 50 percent in value of the outstanding stock of the shareholder is owned by any person, a corporation more than 50 percent in value of the outstanding stock of which is owned by the same person.

For purposes of determining the ownership of stock in applying subparagraphs (A) and (B), the rules of section 267(c) shall apply, except that the family of an individual shall include only his spouse, ancestors, and lineal descendants. For purposes of this paragraph, control means the ownership of stock possessing at least 50 percent of the total combined voting power of all classes of stock entitled to vote or at least 50 percent of the total value of shares of all classes of stock of the corporation.

(9) PROPERTY USED IN THE TRADE OR BUSINESS.—For purposes of this subsection, the term "property used in the trade or business" means property described in section 1231(b), without regard to any holding period therein provided.

(10) OWNERSHIP OF STOCK.—For purposes of this subsection (other than paragraph (8)), the ownership of stock shall be determined in the manner prescribed in subsection (d).

(11) CORPORATIONS AND SHAREHOLDERS NOT MEETING REQUIREMENTS.—In determining whether or not any corporation is a collapsible corporation within the meaning of subsection (b), the fact that such corporation, or such corporation with respect to any of its shareholders, does not meet the requirements of paragraph (1), (2), (3), or (4) of this subsection shall not be taken into account, and such determination, in the case of a corporation which does not meet such requirements, shall be made as if this subsection had not been enacted.

(12) NONAPPLICATION OF SECTION 1245(a), ETC.—For purposes of this subsection, the determination of whether gain from the sale or exchange of property would under any provision of this chapter be considered as ordinary income shall be made without regard to the application of sections 617(d)(1), 1245(a), 1250(a), 1252(a), 1254(a), and 1276(a).

(f) CERTAIN SALES OF STOCK OF CONSENTING CORPORATIONS.—

(1) IN GENERAL.—Subsection (a)(1) shall not apply to a sale of stock of a corporation (other than a sale to the issuing corporation) if such corporation (hereinafter in this subsection referred to as "consenting corporation") consents (at such time and in such manner as the Secretary may by regulations prescribe) to have the provisions of paragraph (2) apply. Such consent shall apply with respect to each sale of stock of such corporation made within the 6-month period beginning with the date on which such consent is filed.

(2) RECOGNITION OF GAIN.—Except as provided in paragraph (3), if a subsection (f) asset (as defined in paragraph (4)) is disposed of at any time by a consenting corporation (or, if paragraph (3) applies, by a transferee corporation), then the amount by which—

(A) in the case of a sale, exchange, or involuntary conversion, the amount realized, or

(B) in the case of any other disposition, the fair market value of such asset,

exceeds the adjusted basis of such asset shall be treated as gain from the sale or exchange of such asset. Such gain shall be recognized notwithstanding any other provision of this subtitle, but only to the extent such gain is not recognized under any other provision of this subtitle.

(3) EXCEPTION FOR CERTAIN TAX-FREE TRANSACTIONS.—If the basis of a subsection (f) asset in the hands of a transferee is determined by reference to its basis in the hands of the transferor by reason of the application of section 332, 351, or 361, then the amount of gain taken into account by the transferor under paragraph (2) shall not exceed the amount of gain recognized to the transferor on the transfer of such asset (determined without regard to this subsection). This paragraph shall apply only if the transferee—

(A) is not an organization which is exempt from tax imposed by this chapter, and

(B) agrees (at such time and in such manner as the Secretary may by regulations prescribe) to have the provisions of paragraph (2) apply to any disposition by it of such subsection (f) asset.

(4) SUBSECTION (f) ASSET DEFINED.—For purposes of this subsection—

(A) IN GENERAL.—The term "subsection (f) asset" means any property which, as of the date of any sale of stock referred to in paragraph (1), is not a capital asset and is property owned by, or subject to an option to acquire held by, the consenting corporation. For purposes of this subparagraph, land or any interest in real property (other than a security interest), and unrealized receivables or fees (as defined in subsection (b)(4)), shall be treated as property which is not a capital asset.

(B) PROPERTY UNDER CONSTRUCTION.—If manufacture, construction, or production with respect to any property described in subparagraph (A) has commenced before any date of sale described therein, the term "subsection (f) asset" includes the property resulting from such manufacture, construction, or production.

(C) SPECIAL RULE FOR LAND.—In the case of land or any interest in real property (other than a security interest) described in subparagraph (A), the term "subsection (f) asset" includes any improvements resulting from construction with respect to such property if such construction is commenced (by the consenting corporation or by a transferee corporation which has agreed to the application of paragraph (2)) within 2 years after the date of any sale described in subparagraph (A).

(5) 5-YEAR LIMITATION AS TO SHAREHOLDER.—Paragraph (1) shall not apply to the sale of stock of a corporation by a shareholder if, during the 5-year period ending on the date of such sale, such shareholder (or any related person within the meaning of subsection (e)(8)(A)) sold any stock of another consenting corporation within any 6-month period beginning on a date on which a consent was filed under paragraph (1) by such other corporation.

(6) SPECIAL RULE FOR STOCK OWNERSHIP IN OTHER CORPORATIONS.—If a corporation (hereinafter in this paragraph referred to as "owning corporation") owns 5 percent or more in value of the outstanding stock of another corporation on the date of any sale of stock of the owning corporation during a 6-month period with respect to which a consent under paragraph (1) was filed by the owning corporation, such consent shall not be valid with respect to such sale unless such other corporation has (within the 6-month period ending on the date of such sale) filed a valid consent under paragraph (1) with respect to sales of its stock. For purposes of applying paragraph (4) to such other corporation, a sale of stock of the owning corporation to which paragraph (1) applies shall be treated as a sale of stock of such other corporation. In the case of a chain of corporations connected by the 5-percent ownership requirements of this paragraph, rules similar to the rules of the two preceding sentences shall be applied.

(7) ADJUSTMENTS TO BASIS.—The Secretary shall prescribe such regulations as he may deem necessary to provide for adjustments to the basis of property to reflect gain recognized under paragraph (2).

(8) SPECIAL RULE FOR FOREIGN CORPORATIONS.—Except to the extent provided in regulations prescribed by the Secretary—

(A) any consent given by a foreign corporation under paragraph (1) shall not be effective, and

(B) paragraph (3) shall not apply if the transferee is a foreign corporation.

[¶5355] CODE SEC. 408. INDIVIDUAL RETIREMENT ACCOUNTS.

* * *

(d) TAX TREATMENT OF DISTRIBUTIONS.—

* * *

(8) DISTRIBUTIONS FOR CHARITABLE PURPOSES.—

* * *

(F) TERMINATION.—This paragraph shall not apply to distributions made in taxable years beginning after *December 31, 2011.*

* * *

[CCH Explanation at ¶352. Committee Reports at ¶10,320.]

Amendments

• **2010, Tax Relief, Unemployment Insurance Reauthorization, and Job Creation Act of 2010 (P.L. 111-312)**

P.L. 111-312, §725(a):

Amended Code Sec. 408(d)(8)(F) by striking "December 31, 2009" and inserting "December 31, 2011". **Effective for** distributions made in tax years beginning after 12-31-2009. For a special rule, see Act Sec. 725(b)(2), below.

P.L. 111-312, §725(b)(2), provides:

(2) SPECIAL RULE.—For purposes of subsections (a)(6), (b)(3), and (d)(8) of section 408 of the Internal Revenue Code of 1986, at the election of the taxpayer (at such time and in such manner as prescribed by the Secretary of the Treasury) any qualified charitable distribution made after December 31, 2010, and before February 1, 2011, shall be deemed to have been made on December 31, 2010.

[¶5360] CODE SEC. 451. GENERAL RULE FOR TAXABLE YEAR OF INCLUSION.

* * *

(i) SPECIAL RULE FOR SALES OR DISPOSITIONS TO IMPLEMENT FEDERAL ENERGY REGULATORY COMMISSION OR STATE ELECTRIC RESTRUCTURING POLICY.—

* * *

(3) QUALIFYING ELECTRIC TRANSMISSION TRANSACTION.—For purposes of this subsection, the term "qualifying electric transmission transaction" means any sale or other disposition before January 1, 2008 (before *January 1, 2012*, in the case of a qualified electric utility), of—

(A) property used in the trade or business of providing electric transmission services, or

(B) any stock or partnership interest in a corporation or partnership, as the case may be, whose principal trade or business consists of providing electric transmission services,

but only if such sale or disposition is to an independent transmission company.

* * *

[CCH Explanation at ¶554. Committee Reports at ¶10,210.]
Amendments

- **2010, Tax Relief, Unemployment Insurance Reauthorization, and Job Creation Act of 2010 (P.L. 111-312)**

P.L. 111-312, §705(a):

Amended Code Sec. 451(i)(3) by striking "January 1, 2010" and inserting "January 1, 2012". **Effective** for dispositions after 12-31-2009.

[¶5365] CODE SEC. 467. CERTAIN PAYMENTS FOR THE USE OF PROPERTY OR SERVICES.

* * *

(c) RECAPTURE OF PRIOR UNDERSTATED INCLUSIONS UNDER LEASEBACK OR LONG-TERM AGREEMENTS.—

* * *

(5) SPECIAL RULES.—Under regulations prescribed by the Secretary—

* * *

》》→ Caution: *Code Sec. 467(c)(5)(C), below, was amended by P.L. 108-27. For sunset provision, see P.L. 108-27, §303 [as amended by P.L. 111-312], in the amendment notes.*

(C) for purposes of sections 170(e) and 751(c), amounts treated as ordinary income under this section shall be treated in the same manner as amounts treated as ordinary income under section 1245 or 1250.

* * *

[CCH Explanation at ¶425 and ¶609. Committee Reports at ¶10,080.]
Amendments

- **2003, Jobs and Growth Tax Relief Reconciliation Act of 2003 (P.L. 108-27)**

P.L. 108-27, §302(e)(4)(B)(ii):

Amended Code Sec. 467(c)(5)(C) by striking ", 341(e)(12)", after "170(e)". For the effective date, see Act Sec. 302(f), as amended by P.L. 108-311, §402(a)(6), below.

P.L. 108-27, §302(f), as amended by P.L. 108-311, §402(a)(6), provides:

(f) EFFECTIVE DATE.—

(1) IN GENERAL.—Except as provided in paragraph (2), the amendments made by this section shall apply to taxable years beginning after December 31, 2002.

(2) PASS-THRU ENTITIES.—In the case of a pass-thru entity described in subparagraph (A), (B), (C), (D), (E), or (F) of section 1(h)(10) of the Internal Revenue Code of 1986, as amended by this Act, the amendments made by this section shall apply to taxable years ending after December 31, 2002; except that dividends received by such an entity on or before such date shall not be treated as qualified dividend income (as defined in section 1(h)(11)(B) of such Code, as added by this Act).

P.L. 108-27, §303, as amended by P.L. 109-222, §102, and P.L. 111-312, §102(a), provides:

SEC. 303. SUNSET OF TITLE.

All provisions of, and amendments made by, this title shall not apply to taxable years beginning after December 31, 2012, and the Internal Revenue Code of 1986 shall be applied and administered to such years as if such provisions and amendments had never been enacted.

[¶5370] CODE SEC. 469. PASSIVE ACTIVITY LOSSES AND CREDITS LIMITED.

* * *

(i) $25,000 OFFSET FOR RENTAL REAL ESTATE ACTIVITIES.—

* * *

(3) PHASE-OUT OF EXEMPTION.—

* * *

(F) ADJUSTED GROSS INCOME.—For purposes of this paragraph, adjusted gross income shall be determined without regard to—

(i) any amount includible in gross income under section 86,

(ii) the amounts excludable from gross income under sections 135 and 137,

»»→ Caution: Code Sec. 469(i)(3)(F)(iii), below, was amended by P.L. 107-16. For sunset provision, see P.L. 107-16, §901 [as amended by P.L. 111-312], in the amendment notes.

(iii) the amounts allowable as a deduction under sections 199, 219, 221, and 222 and

(iv) any passive activity loss or any loss allowable by reason of subsection (c)(7).

* * *

[CCH Explanation at ¶350. Committee Reports at ¶10,310.]

Amendments

• **2004, American Jobs Creation Act of 2004 (P.L. 108-357)**

P.L. 108-357, §102(d)(5):

Amended Code Sec. 469(i)(3)(F)(iii) by inserting "199," before "219,". Effective for tax years beginning after 12-31-2004.

• **2001, Economic Growth and Tax Relief Reconciliation Act of 2001 (P.L. 107-16)**

P.L. 107-16, §431(c)(3):

Amended Code Sec. 469(i)(3)(F)[(iii)] by striking "and 221" and inserting ", 221, and 222". Effective for payments made in tax years beginning after 12-31-2001.

P.L. 107-16, §901(a)-(b), as amended by P.L. 111-312, §101(a)(1), provides:

SEC. 901. SUNSET OF PROVISIONS OF ACT.

(a) IN GENERAL.—All provisions of, and amendments made by, this Act shall not apply—

(1) to taxable, plan, or limitation years beginning after December 31, 2012, or

(2) in the case of title V, to estates of decedents dying, gifts made, or generation skipping transfers, after December 31, 2012.

(b) APPLICATION OF CERTAIN LAWS.—The Internal Revenue Code of 1986 and the Employee Retirement Income Security Act of 1974 shall be applied and administered to years, estates, gifts, and transfers described in subsection (a) as if the provisions and amendments described in subsection (a) had never been enacted.

[¶5375] CODE SEC. 512. UNRELATED BUSINESS TAXABLE INCOME.

* * *

(b) MODIFICATIONS.—The modifications referred to in subsection (a) are the following:

* * *

(13) SPECIAL RULES FOR CERTAIN AMOUNTS RECEIVED FROM CONTROLLED ENTITIES.—

* * *

(E) PARAGRAPH TO APPLY ONLY TO CERTAIN EXCESS PAYMENTS.—

* * *

(iv) TERMINATION.—This subparagraph shall not apply to payments received or accrued after *December 31, 2011.*

* * *

[CCH Explanation at ¶615. Committee Reports at ¶10,520.]

Amendments

- **2010, Tax Relief, Unemployment Insurance Reauthorization, and Job Creation Act of 2010 (P.L. 111-312)**

P.L. 111-312, §747(a):

Amended Code Sec. 512(b)(13)(E)(iv) by striking "December 31, 2009" and inserting "December 31, 2011". **Effective** for payments received or accrued after 12-31-2009.

[¶5380] CODE SEC. 530. COVERDELL EDUCATION SAVINGS ACCOUNTS.

* * *

(b) DEFINITIONS AND SPECIAL RULES.—For purposes of this section—

⋙→ *Caution: Code Sec. 530(b)(1)-(2), below, was amended by P.L. 107-16. For sunset provision, see P.L. 107-16, §901 [as amended by P.L. 111-312], in the amendment notes.*

(1) COVERDELL EDUCATION SAVINGS ACCOUNT.—The term "Coverdell education savings account" means a trust created or organized in the United States exclusively for the purpose of paying the qualified education expenses of an individual who is the designated beneficiary of the trust (and designated as a Coverdell education savings account at the time created or organized), but only if the written governing instrument creating the trust meets the following requirements:

(A) No contribution will be accepted—

(i) unless it is in cash,

(ii) after the date on which such beneficiary attains age 18, or

(iii) except in the case of rollover contributions, if such contribution would result in aggregate contributions for the taxable year exceeding $2,000.

(B) The trustee is a bank (as defined in section 408(n)) or another person who demonstrates to the satisfaction of the Secretary that the manner in which that person will administer the trust will be consistent with the requirements of this section or who has so demonstrated with respect to any individual retirement plan.

(C) No part of the trust assets will be invested in life insurance contracts.

(D) The assets of the trust shall not be commingled with other property except in a common trust fund or common investment fund.

(E) Except as provided in subsection (d)(7), any balance to the credit of the designated beneficiary on the date on which the beneficiary attains age 30 shall be distributed within 30 days after such date to the beneficiary or, if the beneficiary dies before attaining age 30, shall be distributed within 30 days after the date of death of such beneficiary.

The age limitations in subparagraphs (A)(ii) and (E), and paragraphs (5) and (6) of subsection (d), shall not apply to any designated beneficiary with special needs (as determined under regulations prescribed by the Secretary).

(2) QUALIFIED EDUCATION EXPENSES.—

(A) IN GENERAL.—The term "qualified education expenses" means—

(i) qualified higher education expenses (as defined in section 529(e)(3)), and

(ii) qualified elementary and secondary education expenses (as defined in paragraph (3)).

➤➤➤ *Caution: Code Sec. 530(b)(3)-(4), below, was added by P.L. 107-16. For sunset provision, see P.L. 107-16, §901 [as amended by P.L. 111-312], in the amendment notes.*

(3) QUALIFIED ELEMENTARY AND SECONDARY EDUCATION EXPENSES.—

(A) IN GENERAL.—The term "qualified elementary and secondary education expenses" means—

(i) expenses for tuition, fees, academic tutoring, special needs services in the case of a special needs beneficiary, books, supplies, and other equipment which are incurred in connection with the enrollment or attendance of the designated beneficiary of the trust as an elementary or secondary school student at a public, private, or religious school,

(ii) expenses for room and board, uniforms, transportation, and supplementary items and services (including extended day programs) which are required or provided by a public, private, or religious school in connection with such enrollment or attendance, and

(iii) expenses for the purchase of any computer technology or equipment (as defined in section 170(e)(6)(F)(i)) or Internet access and related services, if such technology, equipment, or services are to be used by the beneficiary and the beneficiary's family during any of the years the beneficiary is in school.

Clause (iii) shall not include expenses for computer software designed for sports, games, or hobbies unless the software is predominantly educational in nature.

(B) SCHOOL.—The term "school" means any school which provides elementary education or secondary education (kindergarten through grade 12), as determined under State law.

(4) TIME WHEN CONTRIBUTIONS DEEMED MADE.—An individual shall be deemed to have made a contribution to a Coverdell education savings account on the last day of the preceding taxable year if the contribution is made on account of such taxable year and is made not later than the time prescribed by law for filing the return for such taxable year (not including extensions thereof).

[CCH Explanation at ¶330. Committee Reports at ¶10,050.]

Amendments

● **2005, Gulf Opportunity Zone Act of 2005 (P.L. 109-135)**

P.L. 109-135, §412(ff)(1):

Amended Code Sec. 530(b) by striking paragraph (3) and by redesignating paragraphs (4) and (5) as paragraphs (3) and (4), respectively. **Effective** 12-21-2005. Prior to being stricken, Code Sec. 530(b)(3) read as follows:

(3) ELIGIBLE EDUCATIONAL INSTITUTION.—The term "eligible educational institution" has the meaning given such term by section 529(e)(5).

P.L. 109-135, §412(ff)(2):

Amended Code Sec. 530(b)(2)(A)(ii) by striking "paragraph (4)" and inserting "paragraph (3)". **Effective** 12-21-2005.

● **2001 (P.L. 107-22)**

P.L. 107-22, §1(a)(1):

Amended Code Sec. 530 by striking "an education individual retirement account" each place it appears and inserting "a Coverdell education savings account". **Effective** 7-26-2001.

P.L. 107-22, §1(a)(3)(A)-(B):

Amended Code Sec. 530(b)(1) by striking "education individual retirement account" and inserting "Coverdell educa-

tion savings account", and by striking "EDUCATION INDIVIDUAL RETIREMENT ACCOUNT" in the heading and inserting "COVERDELL EDUCATION SAVINGS ACCOUNT". **Effective** 7-26-2001.

● **2001, Economic Growth and Tax Relief Reconciliation Act of 2001 (P.L. 107-16)**

P.L. 107-16, §401(a)(1):

Amended Code Sec. 530(b)(1)(A)(iii) by striking "$500" and inserting "$2,000". **Effective** for tax years beginning after 12-31-2001.

P.L. 107-16, §401(c)(1):

Amended Code Sec. 530(b)(2). **Effective** for tax years beginning after 12-31-2001. Prior to amendment, Code Sec. 530(b)(2) read as follows:

(2) QUALIFIED HIGHER EDUCATION EXPENSES.—

(A) IN GENERAL.—The term "qualified higher education expenses" has the meaning given such term by section 529(e)(3), reduced as provided in section 25A(g)(2).

(B) QUALIFIED STATE TUITION PROGRAMS.—Such term shall include amounts paid or incurred to purchase tuition credits or certificates, or to make contributions to an account, under a qualified State tuition program (as defined in section 529(b)) for the benefit of the beneficiary of the account.

P.L. 107-16, §401(c)(2):

Amended Code Sec. 530(b) by adding at the end a new paragraph (4). **Effective** for tax years beginning after 12-31-2001.

P.L. 107-16, §401(c)(3)(A):

Amended Code Sec. 530(b)(1) by striking "higher" after "qualified". **Effective** for tax years beginning after 12-31-2001.

P.L. 107-16, §401(d):

Amended Code Sec. 530(b)(1) by adding at the end a new flush sentence. **Effective** for tax years beginning after 12-31-2001.

P.L. 107-16, §401(f)(1):

Amended Code Sec. 530(b), as amended by Act Sec. 401(c)(2), by adding at the end a new paragraph (5). **Effective** for tax years beginning after 12-31-2001.

P.L. 107-16, §901(a)-(b), as amended by P.L. 111-312, §101(a)(1), provides:

SEC. 901. SUNSET OF PROVISIONS OF ACT.

(a) IN GENERAL.—All provisions of, and amendments made by, this Act shall not apply—

(1) to taxable, plan, or limitation years beginning after December 31, 2012, or

(2) in the case of title V, to estates of decedents dying, gifts made, or generation skipping transfers, after December 31, 2012.

(b) APPLICATION OF CERTAIN LAWS.—The Internal Revenue Code of 1986 and the Employee Retirement Income Security Act of 1974 shall be applied and administered to years, estates, gifts, and transfers described in subsection (a) as if the provisions and amendments described in subsection (a) had never been enacted.

(c) REDUCTION IN PERMITTED CONTRIBUTIONS BASED ON ADJUSTED GROSS INCOME.—

⟫→ Caution: *Code Sec. 530(c)(1), below, was amended by P.L. 107-16. For sunset provision, see P.L. 107-16, §901 [as amended by P.L. 111-312], in the amendment notes.*

(1) IN GENERAL.—In the case of a contributor who is an individual, the maximum amount the contributor could otherwise make to an account under this section shall be reduced by an amount which bears the same ratio to such maximum amount as—

    (A) the excess of—

        (i) the contributor's modified adjusted gross income for such taxable year, over

        (ii) $95,000 ($190,000 in the case of a joint return), bears to

    (B) $15,000 ($30,000 in the case of a joint return).

* * *

[CCH Explanation at ¶330. Committee Reports at ¶10,050.]

Amendments

• **2001, Economic Growth and Tax Relief Reconciliation Act of 2001 (P.L. 107-16)**

P.L. 107-16, §401(b)(1)-(2):

Amended Code Sec. 530(c)(1) by striking "$150,000" in subparagraph (A)(ii) and inserting "$190,000", and by striking "$10,000" in subparagraph (B) and inserting "$30,000". **Effective** for tax years beginning after 12-31-2001.

P.L. 107-16, §401(e):

Amended Code Sec. 530(c)(1) by striking "The maximum amount which a contributor" and inserting "In the case of a contributor who is an individual, the maximum amount the contributor". **Effective** for tax years beginning after 12-31-2001.

(d) TAX TREATMENT OF DISTRIBUTIONS.—

P.L. 107-16, §901(a)-(b), as amended by P.L. 111-312, §101(a)(1), provides:

SEC. 901. SUNSET OF PROVISIONS OF ACT.

(a) IN GENERAL.—All provisions of, and amendments made by, this Act shall not apply—

(1) to taxable, plan, or limitation years beginning after December 31, 2012, or

(2) in the case of title V, to estates of decedents dying, gifts made, or generation skipping transfers, after December 31, 2012.

(b) APPLICATION OF CERTAIN LAWS.—The Internal Revenue Code of 1986 and the Employee Retirement Income Security Act of 1974 shall be applied and administered to years, estates, gifts, and transfers described in subsection (a) as if the provisions and amendments described in subsection (a) had never been enacted.

* * *

⟫→ Caution: *Code Sec. 530(d)(2), below, was amended by P.L. 107-16 and P.L. 108-311, effective as if included in P.L. 107-16. For sunset provision, see P.L. 107-16, §901 [as amended by P.L. 111-312], in the amendment notes.*

(2) DISTRIBUTIONS FOR QUALIFIED EDUCATION EXPENSES.—

    (A) IN GENERAL.—No amount shall be includible in gross income under paragraph (1) if the qualified education expenses of the designated beneficiary during the taxable year are not less than the aggregate distributions during the taxable year.

(B) DISTRIBUTIONS IN EXCESS OF EXPENSES.—If such aggregate distributions exceed such expenses during the taxable year, the amount otherwise includible in gross income under paragraph (1) shall be reduced by the amount which bears the same ratio to the amount which would be includible in gross income under paragraph (1) (without regard to this subparagraph) as the qualified education expenses bear to such aggregate distributions.

(C) COORDINATION WITH HOPE AND LIFETIME LEARNING CREDITS AND QUALIFIED TUITION PROGRAMS.—For purposes of subparagraph (A)—

(i) CREDIT COORDINATION.—The total amount of qualified education expenses with respect to an individual for the taxable year shall be reduced—

(I) as provided in section 25A(g)(2), and

(II) by the amount of such expenses which were taken into account in determining the credit allowed to the taxpayer or any other person under section 25A.

(ii) COORDINATION WITH QUALIFIED TUITION PROGRAMS.—If, with respect to an individual for any taxable year—

(I) the aggregate distributions during such year to which subparagraph (A) and section 529(c)(3)(B) apply, exceed

(II) the total amount of qualified education expenses (after the application of clause (i)) for such year,

the taxpayer shall allocate such expenses among such distributions for purposes of determining the amount of the exclusion under subparagraph (A) and section 529(c)(3)(B).

(D) DISALLOWANCE OF EXCLUDED AMOUNTS AS DEDUCTION, CREDIT, OR EXCLUSION.—No deduction, credit, or exclusion shall be allowed to the taxpayer under any other section of this chapter for any qualified education expenses to the extent taken into account in determining the amount of the exclusion under this paragraph.

* * *

(4) ADDITIONAL TAX FOR DISTRIBUTIONS NOT USED FOR EDUCATIONAL EXPENSES.—

* * *

(B) EXCEPTIONS.—Subparagraph (A) shall not apply if the payment or distribution is—

* * *

⟫→ Caution: *Former Code Sec. 530(d)(4)(B)(iv), below, was redesignated as Code Sec. 530(d)(4)(B)(v) by P.L. 108-121, and amended by P.L. 107-147, effective as if included in P.L. 107-16. For sunset provision, see P.L. 107-16, §901 [as amended by P.L. 111-312], in the amendment notes.*

(iv) made on account of the attendance of the designated beneficiary at the United States Military Academy, the United States Naval Academy, the United States Air Force Academy, the United States Coast Guard Academy, or the United States Merchant Marine Academy, to the extent that the amount of the payment or distribution does not exceed the costs of advanced education (as defined by section 2005(e)(3) of title 10, United States Code, as in effect on the date of the enactment of this section) attributable to such attendance, or

* * *

⟫→ Caution: *Code Sec. 530(d)(4)(C), below, was amended by P.L. 107-16. For sunset provision, see P.L. 107-16, §901 [as amended by P.L. 111-312], in the amendment notes.*

(C) CONTRIBUTIONS RETURNED BEFORE CERTAIN DATE.—Subparagraph (A) shall not apply to the distribution of any contribution made during a taxable year on behalf of the designated beneficiary if—

(i) such distribution is made before the first day of the sixth month of the taxable year following the taxable year, and

(ii) such distribution is accompanied by the amount of net income attributable to such excess contribution.

Any net income described in clause (ii) shall be included in gross income for the taxable year in which such excess contribution was made.

* * *

[CCH Explanation at ¶330. Committee Reports at ¶10,050.]

Amendments

• **2004, Working Families Tax Relief Act of 2004 (P.L. 108-311)**

P.L. 108-311, §404(a):

Amended Code Sec. 530(d)(2)(C)(i) by striking "higher" after "qualified". **Effective** as if included in the provision of the Economic Growth and Tax Relief Reconciliation Act of 2001 (P.L. 107-16) to which it relates [**effective** for tax years beginning after 12-31-2001.—CCH].

• **2003, Military Family Tax Relief Act of 2003 (P.L. 108-121)**

P.L. 108-121, §107(a):

Amended Code Sec. 530(d)(4)(B) by striking "or" at the end of clause (iii), by redesignating clause (iv) as clause (v), and by inserting after clause (iii) a new clause (iv). **Effective** for tax years beginning after 12-31-2002.

• **2002, Job Creation and Worker Assistance Act of 2002 (P.L. 107-147)**

P.L. 107-147, §411(f):

Amended Code Sec. 530(d)(4)(B)(iv) by striking "because the taxpayer elected under paragraph (2)(C) to waive the application of paragraph (2)" and inserting "by application of paragraph (2)(C)(i)(II)". **Effective** as if included in the provision of P.L. 107-16 to which it relates [**effective** for tax years beginning after 12-31-2001.—CCH].

• **2001, Economic Growth and Tax Relief Reconciliation Act of 2001 (P.L. 107-16)**

P.L. 107-16, §401(c)(3)(A):

Amended Code Sec. 530(d)(2) by striking "higher" after "qualified" each place it appears. **Effective** for tax years beginning after 12-31-2001.

P.L. 107-16, §401(c)(3)(B):

Amended the heading for Code Sec. 530(d)(2) by striking "HIGHER" after "QUALIFIED". **Effective** for tax years beginning after 12-31-2001.

P.L. 107-16, §401(f)(2)(A)-(B):

Amended Code Sec. 530(d)(4)(C) by striking clause (i) and inserting a new clause (i), and by striking "DUE DATE OF RETURN" in the heading and inserting "CERTAIN DATE". **Effective** for tax years beginning after 12-31-2001. Prior to being stricken, Code Sec. 530(d)(4)(C)(i) read as follows:

(i) such distribution is made on or before the day prescribed by law (including extensions of time) for filing the beneficiary's return of tax for the taxable year or, if the beneficiary is not required to file such a return, the 15th day of the 4th month of the taxable year following the taxable year; and

P.L. 107-16, §401(g)(1):

Amended Code Sec. 530(d)(2)(C). **Effective** for tax years beginning after 12-31-2001. Prior to amendment, Code Sec. 530(d)(2)(C) read as follows:

(C) ELECTION TO WAIVE EXCLUSION.—A taxpayer may elect to waive the application of this paragraph for any taxable year.

P.L. 107-16, §401(g)(2)(C)(i)-(ii):

Amended Code Sec. 530(d)(2)(D) by striking "or credit" and inserting ", credit, or exclusion", and by striking "CREDIT OR DEDUCTION" in the heading and inserting "DEDUCTION, CREDIT, OR EXCLUSION". **Effective** for tax years beginning after 12-31-2001.

P.L. 107-16, §901(a)-(b), as amended by P.L. 111-312, §101(a)(1), provides:

SEC. 901. SUNSET OF PROVISIONS OF ACT.

(a) IN GENERAL.—All provisions of, and amendments made by, this Act shall not apply—

(1) to taxable, plan, or limitation years beginning after December 31, 2012, or

(2) in the case of title V, to estates of decedents dying, gifts made, or generation skipping transfers, after December 31, 2012.

(b) APPLICATION OF CERTAIN LAWS.—The Internal Revenue Code of 1986 and the Employee Retirement Income Security Act of 1974 shall be applied and administered to years, estates, gifts, and transfers described in subsection (a) as if the provisions and amendments described in subsection (a) had never been enacted.

➤ *Caution: Code Sec. 531, below, was amended by P.L. 107-16 and P.L. 108-27. For sunset provisions, see P.L. 107-16, §901 [as amended by P.L. 111-312], and P.L. 108-27, §303 [as amended by P.L. 111-312], in the amendment notes.*

[¶5385] CODE SEC. 531. IMPOSITION OF ACCUMULATED EARNINGS TAX.

In addition to other taxes imposed by this chapter, there is hereby imposed for each taxable year on the accumulated taxable income (as defined in section 535) of each corporation described in section 532, an accumulated earnings tax equal to 15 percent of the accumulated taxable income.

[CCH Explanation at ¶305, ¶425 and ¶603. Committee Reports at ¶10,010 and ¶10,080.]

Amendments

• **2003, Jobs and Growth Tax Relief Reconciliation Act of 2003 (P.L. 108-27)**

P.L. 108-27, §302(e)(5):

Amended Code Sec. 531 by striking "equal to" and all that follows and inserting "equal to 15 percent of the accumulated taxable income.". For the effective date, see Act Sec. 302(f), as amended by P.L. 108-311, §402(a)(6), below. Prior to amendment, Code Sec. 531 read as follows:

SEC. 531. IMPOSITION OF ACCUMULATED EARN-INGS TAX.

In addition to other taxes imposed by this chapter, there is hereby imposed for each taxable year on the accumulated taxable income (as defined in section 535) of each corporation described in section 532, an accumulated earnings tax equal to the product of the highest rate of tax under section 1(c) and the accumulated taxable income.

P.L. 108-27, §302(f), as amended by P.L. 108-311, §402(a)(6), provides:

(f) EFFECTIVE DATE.—

(1) IN GENERAL.—Except as provided in paragraph (2), the amendments made by this section shall apply to taxable years beginning after December 31, 2002.

(2) PASS-THRU ENTITIES.—In the case of a pass-thru entity described in subparagraph (A), (B), (C), (D), (E), or (F) of section 1(h)(10) of the Internal Revenue Code of 1986, as amended by this Act, the amendments made by this section shall apply to taxable years ending after December 31, 2002; except that dividends received by such an entity on or before such date shall not be treated as qualified dividend income (as defined in section 1(h)(11)(B) of such Code, as added by this Act).

P.L. 108-27, §303, as amended by P.L. 109-222, §102, and P.L. 111-312, §102(a), provides:

SEC. 303. SUNSET OF TITLE.

All provisions of, and amendments made by, this title shall not apply to taxable years beginning after December

31, 2012, and the Internal Revenue Code of 1986 shall be applied and administered to such years as if such provisions and amendments had never been enacted.

• **2001, Economic Growth and Tax Relief Reconciliation Act of 2001 (P.L. 107-16)**

P.L. 107-16, §101(c)(4):

Amended Code Sec. 531 by striking "equal to" and all that follows and inserting "equal to the product of the highest rate of tax under section 1(c) and the accumulated taxable income.". Effective for tax years beginning after 12-31-2000. Prior to amendment, Code Sec. 531 read as follows:

SEC. 531. IMPOSITION OF ACCUMULATED EARN-INGS TAX.

In addition to other taxes imposed by this chapter, there is hereby imposed for each taxable year on the accumulated taxable income (as defined in section 535) of each corporation described in section 532, an accumulated earnings tax equal to 39.6 percent of the accumulated taxable income.

P.L. 107-16, §901(a)-(b), as amended by P.L. 111-312, §101(a)(1), provides:

SEC. 901. SUNSET OF PROVISIONS OF ACT.

(a) IN GENERAL.—All provisions of, and amendments made by, this Act shall not apply—

(1) to taxable, plan, or limitation years beginning after December 31, 2012, or

(2) in the case of title V, to estates of decedents dying, gifts made, or generation skipping transfers, after December 31, 2012.

(b) APPLICATION OF CERTAIN LAWS.—The Internal Revenue Code of 1986 and the Employee Retirement Income Security Act of 1974 shall be applied and administered to years, estates, gifts, and transfers described in subsection (a) as if the provisions and amendments described in subsection (a) had never been enacted.

≫→ Caution: *Code Sec. 541, below, was amended by P.L. 107-16 and P.L. 108-27. For sunset provisions, see P.L. 107-16, §901 [as amended by P.L. 111-312], and P.L. 108-27, §303 [as amended by P.L. 111-312], in the amendment notes.*

[¶5390] CODE SEC. 541. IMPOSITION OF PERSONAL HOLDING COMPANY TAX.

In addition to other taxes imposed by this chapter, there is hereby imposed for each taxable year on the undistributed personal holding company income (as defined in section 545) of every personal holding company (as defined in section 542) a personal holding company tax equal to 15 percent of the undistributed personal holding company income.

[CCH Explanation at ¶305 and ¶425. Committee Reports at ¶10,010 and ¶10,080.]

Amendments

• **2003, Jobs and Growth Tax Relief Reconciliation Act of 2003 (P.L. 108-27)**

P.L. 108-27, §302(e)(6):

Amended Code Sec. 541 by striking "equal to" and all that follows and inserting "equal to 15 percent of the undistributed personal holding company income.". For the effective date, see Act Sec. 302(f), as amended by P.L. 108-311, §402(a)(6), below. Prior to amendment, Code Sec. 541 read as follows:

SEC. 541. IMPOSITION OF PERSONAL HOLDING COMPANY TAX.

In addition to other taxes imposed by this chapter, there is hereby imposed for each taxable year on the undistributed personal holding company income (as defined in section 545) of every personal holding company (as defined in section 542) a personal holding company tax equal to the product of the highest rate of tax under section 1(c) and the undistributed personal holding company income.

P.L. 108-27, §302(f), as amended by P.L. 108-311, §402(a)(6), provides:

(f) EFFECTIVE DATE.—

(1) IN GENERAL.—Except as provided in paragraph (2), the amendments made by this section shall apply to taxable years beginning after December 31, 2002.

(2) PASS-THRU ENTITIES.—In the case of a pass-thru entity described in subparagraph (A), (B), (C), (D), (E), or (F) of section 1(h)(10) of the Internal Revenue Code of 1986, as amended by this Act, the amendments made by this section shall apply to taxable years ending after December 31, 2002; except that dividends received by such an entity on or before such date shall not be treated as qualified dividend income (as defined in section 1(h)(11)(B) of such Code, as added by this Act).

P.L. 108-27, §303, as amended by P.L. 109-222, §102, and P.L. 111-312, §102(a), provides:

SEC. 303. SUNSET OF TITLE.

All provisions of, and amendments made by, this title shall not apply to taxable years beginning after December 31, 2012, and the Internal Revenue Code of 1986 shall be applied and administered to such years as if such provisions and amendments had never been enacted.

• **2001, Economic Growth and Tax Relief Reconciliation Act of 2001 (P.L. 107-16)**

P.L. 107-16, §101(c)(5):

Amended Code Sec. 541 by striking "equal to" and all that follows and inserting "equal to the product of the highest rate of tax under section 1(c) and the undistributed personal holding company income." **Effective** for tax years beginning after 12-31-2000. Prior to amendment, Code Sec. 541 read as follows:

SEC. 541. IMPOSITION OF PERSONAL HOLDING COMPANY TAX.

In addition to other taxes imposed by this chapter, there is hereby imposed for each taxable year on the undistributed personal holding company income (as defined in section 545) of every personal holding company (as defined in section 542) a personal holding company tax equal to 39.6 percent of the undistributed personal holding company income.

P.L. 107-16, §901(a)-(b), as amended by P.L. 111-312, §101(a)(1), provides:

SEC. 901. SUNSET OF PROVISIONS OF ACT.

(a) IN GENERAL.—All provisions of, and amendments made by, this Act shall not apply—

(1) to taxable, plan, or limitation years beginning after December 31, 2012, or

(2) in the case of title V, to estates of decedents dying, gifts made, or generation skipping transfers, after December 31, 2012.

(b) APPLICATION OF CERTAIN LAWS.—The Internal Revenue Code of 1986 and the Employee Retirement Income Security Act of 1974 shall be applied and administered to years, estates, gifts, and transfers described in subsection (a) as if the provisions and amendments described in subsection (a) had never been enacted.

[¶5395] CODE SEC. 562. RULES APPLICABLE IN DETERMINING DIVIDENDS ELIGIBLE FOR DIVIDENDS PAID DEDUCTION.

* * *

(c) PREFERENTIAL DIVIDENDS.—*Except in the case of a publicly offered regulated investment company (as defined in section 67(c)(2)(B)),* the amount of any distribution shall not be considered as a dividend for purposes of computing the dividends paid deduction, unless such distribution is pro rata, with no preference to any share of stock as compared with other shares of the same class, and with no preference to one class of stock as compared with another class except to the extent that the former is entitled (without reference to waivers of their rights by shareholders) to such preference. In the case of a distribution by a regulated investment company *(other than a publicly offered regulated investment company (as so defined))* to a shareholder who made an initial investment of at least $10,000,000 in such company, such distribution shall not be treated as not being pro rata or as being preferential solely by reason of an increase in the distribution by reason of reductions in administrative expenses of the company.

* * *

[CCH Explanation at ¶827.]

Amendments

• **2010, Regulated Investment Company Modernization Act of 2010 (H.R. 4337)**

H.R. 4337, §307(a):

Amended Code Sec. 562(c) by striking "The amount" and inserting "Except in the case of a publicly offered regulated investment company (as defined in section 67(c)(2)(B)), the amount". **Effective** for distributions in tax years beginning after the date of the enactment of this Act.

H.R. 4337, §307(b):

Amended Code Sec. 562(c) by inserting "(other than a publicly offered regulated investment company (as so defined))" after "regulated investment company" in the second sentence thereof. **Effective** for distributions in tax years beginning after the date of the enactment of this Act.

[¶5400] CODE SEC. 584. COMMON TRUST FUNDS.

* * *

»»→ *Caution: The flush sentence in Code Sec. 584(c), below, was added by P.L. 108-27. For sunset provision, see P.L. 108-27, §303 [as amended by P.L. 111-312], in the amendment notes.*

(c) INCOME OF PARTICIPANTS IN FUND.—Each participant in the common trust fund in computing its taxable income shall include, whether or not distributed and whether or not distributable—

(1) as part of its gains and losses from sales or exchanges of capital assets held for not more than 1 year, its proportionate share of the gains and losses of the common trust fund from sales or exchanges of capital assets held for not more than 1 year,

(2) as part of its gains and losses from sales or exchanges of capital assets held for more than 1 year, its proportionate share of the gains and losses of the common trust fund from sales or exchanges of capital assets held for more than 1 year, and

(3) its proportionate share of the ordinary taxable income or the ordinary net loss of the common trust fund, computed as provided in subsection (d).

The proportionate share of each participant in the amount of dividends received by the common trust fund and to which section 1(h)(11) applies shall be considered for purposes of such paragraph as having been received by such participant.

* * *

[CCH Explanation at ¶420 and ¶425. Committee Reports at ¶10,080.]

Amendments

• **2003, Jobs and Growth Tax Relief Reconciliation Act of 2003 (P.L. 108-27)**

P.L. 108-27, §302(e)(7):

Amended Code Sec. 584(c) by adding at the end a new flush sentence. For the effective date, see Act Sec. 302(f), as amended by P.L. 108-311, §402(a)(6), below.

P.L. 108-27, §302(f), as amended by P.L. 108-311, §402(a)(6), provides:

(f) EFFECTIVE DATE.—

(1) IN GENERAL.—Except as provided in paragraph (2), the amendments made by this section shall apply to taxable years beginning after December 31, 2002.

(2) PASS-THRU ENTITIES.—In the case of a pass-thru entity described in subparagraph (A), (B), (C), (D), (E), or (F) of

section 1(h)(10) of the Internal Revenue Code of 1986, as amended by this Act, the amendments made by this section shall apply to taxable years ending after December 31, 2002; except that dividends received by such an entity on or before such date shall not be treated as qualified dividend income (as defined in section 1(h)(11)(B) of such Code, as added by this Act).

P.L. 108-27, §303, as amended by P.L. 109-222, §102, and P.L. 111-312, §102(a), provides:

SEC. 303. SUNSET OF TITLE.

All provisions of, and amendments made by, this title shall not apply to taxable years beginning after December 31, 2012, and the Internal Revenue Code of 1986 shall be applied and administered to such years as if such provisions and amendments had never been enacted.

[¶5405] CODE SEC. 613A. LIMITATIONS ON PERCENTAGE DEPLETION IN CASE OF OIL AND GAS WELLS.

* * *

(c) EXEMPTION FOR INDEPENDENT PRODUCERS AND ROYALTY OWNERS.—

* * *

(6) OIL AND NATURAL GAS PRODUCED FROM MARGINAL PROPERTIES.—

* * *

(H) TEMPORARY SUSPENSION OF TAXABLE INCOME LIMIT WITH RESPECT TO MARGINAL PRODUCTION.—The second sentence of subsection (a) of section 613 shall not apply to so much of the allowance for depletion as is determined under subparagraph (A) for any taxable year—

(i) beginning after December 31, 1997, and before January 1, 2008, or

(ii) beginning after December 31, 2008, and before *January 1, 2012.*

* * *

[CCH Explanation at ¶ 552. Committee Reports at ¶ 10,220.]

Amendments

● **2010, Tax Relief, Unemployment Insurance Reauthorization, and Job Creation Act of 2010 (P.L. 111-312)**

P.L. 111-312, § 706(a):

Amended Code Sec. 613A(c)(6)(H)(ii) by striking "January 1, 2010" and inserting "January 1, 2012". **Effective** for tax years beginning after 12-31-2009.

》》→ *Caution: Code Sec. 646, below, was added by P.L. 107-16. For sunset provision, see P.L. 107-16, §901 [as amended by P.L. 111-312], in the amendment notes.*

[¶5410] CODE SEC. 646. TAX TREATMENT OF ELECTING ALASKA NATIVE SETTLEMENT TRUSTS.

(a) IN GENERAL.—If an election under this section is in effect with respect to any Settlement Trust, the provisions of this section shall apply in determining the income tax treatment of the Settlement Trust and its beneficiaries with respect to the Settlement Trust.

(b) TAXATION OF INCOME OF TRUST.—Except as provided in subsection (f)(1)(B)(ii)—

(1) IN GENERAL.—There is hereby imposed on the taxable income of an electing Settlement Trust, other than its net capital gain, a tax at the lowest rate specified in section 1(c).

(2) CAPITAL GAIN.—In the case of an electing Settlement Trust with a net capital gain for the taxable year, a tax is hereby imposed on such gain at the rate of tax which would apply to such gain if the taxpayer were subject to a tax on its other taxable income at only the lowest rate specified in section 1(c).

Any such tax shall be in lieu of the income tax otherwise imposed by this chapter on such income or gain.

(c) ONE-TIME ELECTION.—

(1) IN GENERAL.—A Settlement Trust may elect to have the provisions of this section apply to the trust and its beneficiaries.

(2) TIME AND METHOD OF ELECTION.—An election under paragraph (1) shall be made by the trustee of such trust—

(A) on or before the due date (including extensions) for filing the Settlement Trust's return of tax for the first taxable year of such trust ending after the date of the enactment of this section, and

(B) by attaching to such return of tax a statement specifically providing for such election.

(3) PERIOD ELECTION IN EFFECT.—Except as provided in subsection (f), an election under this subsection—

(A) shall apply to the first taxable year described in paragraph (2)(A) and all subsequent taxable years, and

(B) may not be revoked once it is made.

(d) CONTRIBUTIONS TO TRUST.—

(1) BENEFICIARIES OF ELECTING TRUST NOT TAXED ON CONTRIBUTIONS.—In the case of an electing Settlement Trust, no amount shall be includible in the gross income of a beneficiary of such trust by reason of a contribution to such trust.

(2) EARNINGS AND PROFITS.—The earnings and profits of the sponsoring Native Corporation shall not be reduced on account of any contribution to such Settlement Trust.

(e) Tax Treatment of Distributions to Beneficiaries.—Amounts distributed by an electing Settlement Trust during any taxable year shall be considered as having the following characteristics in the hands of the recipient beneficiary:

(1) First, as amounts excludable from gross income for the taxable year to the extent of the taxable income of such trust for such taxable year (decreased by any income tax paid by the trust with respect to the income) plus any amount excluded from gross income of the trust under section 103.

(2) Second, as amounts excludable from gross income to the extent of the amount described in paragraph (1) for all taxable years for which an election is in effect under subsection (c) with respect to the trust, and not previously taken into account under paragraph (1).

(3) Third, as amounts distributed by the sponsoring Native Corporation with respect to its stock (within the meaning of section 301(a)) during such taxable year and taxable to the recipient beneficiary as amounts described in section 301(c)(1), to the extent of current or accumulated earnings and profits of the sponsoring Native Corporation as of the close of such taxable year after proper adjustment is made for all distributions made by the sponsoring Native Corporation during such taxable year.

(4) Fourth, as amounts distributed by the trust in excess of the distributable net income of such trust for such taxable year.

Amounts distributed to which paragraph (3) applies shall not be treated as a corporate distribution subject to section 311(b), and for purposes of determining the amount of a distribution for purposes of paragraph (3) and the basis to the recipients, section 643(e) and not section 301(b) or (d) shall apply.

(f) Special Rules Where Transfer Restrictions Modified.—

(1) Transfer of beneficial interests.—If, at any time, a beneficial interest in an electing Settlement Trust may be disposed of to a person in a manner which would not be permitted by section 7(h) of the Alaska Native Claims Settlement Act (43 U.S.C. 1606(h)) if such interest were Settlement Common Stock—

(A) no election may be made under subsection (c) with respect to such trust, and

(B) if such an election is in effect as of such time—

(i) such election shall cease to apply as of the first day of the taxable year in which such disposition is first permitted,

(ii) the provisions of this section shall not apply to such trust for such taxable year and all taxable years thereafter, and

(iii) the distributable net income of such trust shall be increased by the current or accumulated earnings and profits of the sponsoring Native Corporation as of the close of such taxable year after proper adjustment is made for all distributions made by the sponsoring Native Corporation during such taxable year.

In no event shall the increase under clause (iii) exceed the fair market value of the trust's assets as of the date the beneficial interest of the trust first becomes so disposable. The earnings and profits of the sponsoring Native Corporation shall be adjusted as of the last day of such taxable year by the amount of earnings and profits so included in the distributable net income of the trust.

(2) Stock in corporation.—If—

(A) stock in the sponsoring Native Corporation may be disposed of to a person in a manner which would not be permitted by section 7(h) of the Alaska Native Claims Settlement Act (43 U.S.C. 1606(h)) if such stock were Settlement Common Stock, and

(B) at any time after such disposition of stock is first permitted, such corporation transfers assets to a Settlement Trust,

paragraph (1)(B) shall be applied to such trust on and after the date of the transfer in the same manner as if the trust permitted dispositions of beneficial interests in the trust in a manner not permitted by such section 7(h).

(3) CERTAIN DISTRIBUTIONS.—For purposes of this section, the surrender of an interest in a Native Corporation or an electing Settlement Trust in order to accomplish the whole or partial redemption of the interest of a shareholder or beneficiary in such corporation or trust, or to accomplish the whole or partial liquidation of such corporation or trust, shall be deemed to be a transfer permitted by section 7(h) of the Alaska Native Claims Settlement Act.

(g) TAXABLE INCOME.—For purposes of this title, the taxable income of an electing Settlement Trust shall be determined under section 641(b) without regard to any deduction under section 651 or 661.

(h) DEFINITIONS.—For purposes of this section—

(1) ELECTING SETTLEMENT TRUST.—The term "electing Settlement Trust" means a Settlement Trust which has made the election, effective for a taxable year, described in subsection (c).

(2) NATIVE CORPORATION.—The term "Native Corporation" has the meaning given such term by section 3(m) of the Alaska Native Claims Settlement Act (43 U.S.C. 1602(m)).

(3) SETTLEMENT COMMON STOCK.—The term "Settlement Common Stock" has the meaning given such term by section 3(p) of the Alaska Native Claims Settlement Act (43 U.S.C. 1602(p)).

(4) SETTLEMENT TRUST.—The term "Settlement Trust" means a trust that constitutes a settlement trust under section 3(t) of the Alaska Native Claims Settlement Act (43 U.S.C. 1602(t)).

(5) SPONSORING NATIVE CORPORATION.—The term "sponsoring Native Corporation" means the Native Corporation which transfers assets to an electing Settlement Trust.

(i) SPECIAL LOSS DISALLOWANCE RULE.—Any loss that would otherwise be recognized by a shareholder upon a disposition of a share of stock of a sponsoring Native Corporation shall be reduced (but not below zero) by the per share loss adjustment factor. The per share loss adjustment factor shall be the aggregate of all contributions to all electing Settlement Trusts sponsored by such Native Corporation made on or after the first day each trust is treated as an electing Settlement Trust expressed on a per share basis and determined as of the day of each such contribution.

(j) CROSS REFERENCE.—

For information required with respect to electing Settlement Trusts and sponsoring Native Corporations, see section 6039H.

[CCH Explanation at ¶ 612. Committee Reports at ¶ 10,070.]

Amendments

● 2001, Economic Growth and Tax Relief Reconciliation Act of 2001 (P.L. 107-16)

P.L. 107-16, § 671(a):

Amended subpart A of part I of subchapter J of chapter 1 by adding at the end a new Code Sec. 646. Effective for tax years ending after 6-7-2001, and to contributions made to electing Settlement Trusts for such year or any subsequent year.

P.L. 107-16, § 901(a)-(b), as amended by P.L. 111-312, § 101(a)(1), provides:

SEC. 901. SUNSET OF PROVISIONS OF ACT.

(a) IN GENERAL.—All provisions of, and amendments made by, this Act shall not apply—

(1) to taxable, plan, or limitation years beginning after December 31, 2012, or

(2) in the case of title V, to estates of decedents dying, gifts made, or generation skipping transfers, after December 31, 2012.

(b) APPLICATION OF CERTAIN LAWS.—The Internal Revenue Code of 1986 and the Employee Retirement Income Security Act of 1974 shall be applied and administered to years, estates, gifts, and transfers described in subsection (a) as if the provisions and amendments described in subsection (a) had never been enacted.

>»→ *Caution: The heading for Code Sec. 684, below, as amended by P.L. 111-312, applies to estates of decedents dying, and transfers made, after December 31, 2009. For sunset provision, see P.L. 107-16, §901 [as amended by P.L. 111-312], in the amendment notes.*

[¶5415] CODE SEC. 684. RECOGNITION OF GAIN ON CERTAIN TRANSFERS TO CERTAIN FOREIGN TRUSTS AND ESTATES.

>»→ *Caution: Code Sec. 684(a), below, as amended by P.L. 111-312, applies to estates of decedents dying, and transfers made, after December 31, 2009. For sunset provision, see P.L. 107-16, §901 [as amended by P.L. 111-312], in the amendment notes.*

(a) IN GENERAL.—Except as provided in regulations, in the case of any transfer of property by a United States person to a foreign estate or trust, for purposes of this subtitle, such transfer shall be treated as a sale or exchange for an amount equal to the fair market value of the property transferred, and the transferor shall recognize as gain the excess of—

    (1) the fair market value of the property so transferred, over

    (2) the adjusted basis (for purposes of determining gain) of such property in the hands of the transferor.

[CCH Explanation at ¶705 and ¶760. Committee Reports at ¶10,130.]

Amendments

- **2010, Tax Relief, Unemployment Insurance Reauthorization, and Job Creation Act of 2010 (P.L. 111-312)**

P.L. 111-312, §301(a):

Amended the heading of Code Sec. 684 and Code Sec. 684(a) to read as such provisions would read if subtitle E of title V of the Economic Growth and Tax Relief Reconciliation Act of 2001 (P.L. 107-16) had never been enacted. **Effective** for estates of decedents dying, and transfers made, after 12-31-2009. For a special rule, see Act Sec. 301(c), below. Prior to amendment by P.L. 111-312, the heading of Code Sec. 684 and Code Sec. 684(a) read as follows:

CODE SEC. 684. RECOGNITION OF GAIN ON CERTAIN TRANSFERS TO CERTAIN FOREIGN TRUSTS AND ESTATES AND NONRESIDENT ALIENS.

(a) IN GENERAL.—Except as provided in regulations, in the case of any transfer of property by a United States person to a foreign estate or trust, for purposes of this subtitle, such transfer shall be treated as a sale or exchange for an amount equal to the fair market value of the property transferred, and the transferor shall recognize as gain the excess of—

(1) the fair market value of the property so transferred, over

(2) the adjusted basis (for purposes of determining gain) of such property in the hands of the transferor.

P.L. 111-312, §301(c), provides:

(c) SPECIAL ELECTION WITH RESPECT TO ESTATES OF DECEDENTS DYING IN 2010.—Notwithstanding subsection (a), in the case of an estate of a decedent dying after December 31, 2009, and before January 1, 2011, the executor (within the meaning of section 2203 of the Internal Revenue Code of 1986) may elect to apply such Code as though the amendments made by subsection (a) do not apply with respect to chapter 11 of such Code and with respect to property acquired or passing from such decedent (within the meaning of section 1014(b) of such Code). Such election shall be made at such time and in such manner as the Secretary of the Treasury or the Secretary's delegate shall provide. Such an election once made shall be revocable only with the consent of the Secretary of the Treasury or the Secretary's delegate. For pur-

poses of section 2652(a)(1) of such Code, the determination of whether any property is subject to the tax imposed by such chapter 11 shall be made without regard to any election made under this subsection.

P.L. 111-312, §304, provides:

SEC. 304. APPLICATION OF EGTRRA SUNSET TO THIS TITLE.

Section 901 of the Economic Growth and Tax Relief Reconciliation Act of 2001 shall apply to the amendments made by this title.

- **2001, Economic Growth and Tax Relief Reconciliation Act of 2001 (P.L. 107-16)**

P.L. 107-16, §542(e)(1)(A):

Amended Code Sec. 684(a) by inserting "or to a nonresident alien" after "or trust". **Effective** for transfers after 12-31-2009.

P.L. 107-16, §542(e)(1)(C):

Amended the section heading for Code Sec. 684 by inserting "AND NONRESIDENT ALIENS" after "ESTATES". **Effective** for transfers after 12-31-2009.

P.L. 107-16, §901(a)-(b), as amended by P.L. 111-312, §101(a)(1), provides:

SEC. 901. SUNSET OF PROVISIONS OF ACT.

(a) IN GENERAL.—All provisions of, and amendments made by, this Act shall not apply—

(1) to taxable, plan, or limitation years beginning after December 31, 2012, or

(2) in the case of title V, to estates of decedents dying, gifts made, or generation skipping transfers, after December 31, 2012.

(b) APPLICATION OF CERTAIN LAWS.—The Internal Revenue Code of 1986 and the Employee Retirement Income Security Act of 1974 shall be applied and administered to years, estates, gifts, and transfers described in subsection (a) as if the provisions and amendments described in subsection (a) had never been enacted.

⟫→ *Caution: Code Sec. 684(b), below, as amended by P.L. 111-312, applies to estates of decedents dying, and transfers made, after December 31, 2009. For sunset provision, see P.L. 107-16, §901 [as amended by P.L. 111-312], in the amendment notes.*

(b) EXCEPTION.—Subsection (a) shall not apply to a transfer to a trust by a United States person to the extent that any person is treated as the owner of such trust under section 671.

* * *

[CCH Explanation at ¶705 and ¶760. Committee Reports at ¶10,130.]

Amendments

• **2010, Tax Relief, Unemployment Insurance Reauthorization, and Job Creation Act of 2010 (P.L. 111-312)**

P.L. 111-312, §301(a):

Amended Code Sec. 684(b) to read as such provision would read if subtitle E of title V of the Economic Growth and Tax Relief Reconciliation Act of 2001 (P.L. 107-16) had never been enacted. **Effective** for estates of decedents dying, and transfers made, after 12-31-2009. For a special rule, see Act Sec. 301(c), below. Prior to amendment by P.L. 111-312, Code Sec. 684(b) read as follows:

(b) EXCEPTIONS.—

(1) TRANSFERS TO CERTAIN TRUSTS.—Subsection (a) shall not apply to a transfer to a trust by a United States person to the extent that any United States person is treated as the owner of such trust under section 671.

(2) LIFETIME TRANSFERS TO NONRESIDENT ALIENS.—Subsection (a) shall not apply to a lifetime transfer to a nonresident alien.

P.L. 111-312, §301(c), provides:

(c) SPECIAL ELECTION WITH RESPECT TO ESTATES OF DECEDENTS DYING IN 2010.—Notwithstanding subsection (a), in the case of an estate of a decedent dying after December 31, 2009, and before January 1, 2011, the executor (within the meaning of section 2203 of the Internal Revenue Code of 1986) may elect to apply such Code as though the amendments made by subsection (a) do not apply with respect to chapter 11 of such Code and with respect to property acquired or passing from such decedent (within the meaning of section 1014(b) of such Code). Such election shall be made at such time and in such manner as the Secretary of the Treasury or the Secretary's delegate shall provide. Such an election once made shall be revocable only with the consent of the Secretary of the Treasury or the Secretary's delegate. For purposes of section 2652(a)(1) of such Code, the determination of whether any property is subject to the tax imposed by such chapter 11 shall be made without regard to any election made under this subsection.

P.L. 111-312, §304, provides:

SEC. 304. APPLICATION OF EGTRRA SUNSET TO THIS TITLE.

Section 901 of the Economic Growth and Tax Relief Reconciliation Act of 2001 shall apply to the amendments made by this title.

• **2001, Economic Growth and Tax Relief Reconciliation Act of 2001 (P.L. 107-16)**

P.L. 107-16, §542(e)(1)(B):

Amended Code Sec. 684(b). **Effective** for transfers after 12-31-2009. Prior to amendment, Code Sec. 684(b) read as follows:

(b) EXCEPTION.—Subsection (a) shall not apply to a transfer to a trust by a United States person to the extent that any person is treated as the owner of such trust under section 671.

P.L. 107-16, §901(a)-(b), as amended by P.L. 111-312, §101(a)(1), provides:

SEC. 901. SUNSET OF PROVISIONS OF ACT.

(a) IN GENERAL.—All provisions of, and amendments made by, this Act shall not apply—

(1) to taxable, plan, or limitation years beginning after December 31, 2012, or

(2) in the case of title V, to estates of decedents dying, gifts made, or generation skipping transfers, after December 31, 2012.

(b) APPLICATION OF CERTAIN LAWS.—The Internal Revenue Code of 1986 and the Employee Retirement Income Security Act of 1974 shall be applied and administered to years, estates, gifts, and transfers described in subsection (a) as if the provisions and amendments described in subsection (a) had never been enacted.

[¶5420] CODE SEC. 702. INCOME AND CREDITS OF PARTNER.

(a) GENERAL RULE.—In determining his income tax, each partner shall take into account separately his distributive share of the partnership's—

* * *

➤➤➤ Caution: *Code Sec. 702(a)(5), below, was amended by P.L. 108-27. For sunset provision, see P.L. 108-27, §303 [as amended by P.L. 111-312], in the amendment notes.*

(5) dividends with respect to which section 1(h)(11) or part VIII of subchapter B applies,

* * *

[CCH Explanation at ¶420 and ¶425. Committee Reports at ¶10,080.]

Amendments

• 2003, Jobs and Growth Tax Relief Reconciliation Act of 2003 (P.L. 108-27)

P.L. 108-27, §302(e)(8):

Amended Code Sec. 702(a)(5). For the **effective** date, see Act Sec. 302(f), as amended by P.L. 108-311, §402(a)(6), below. Prior to amendment, Code Sec. 702(a)(5) read as follows:

(5) dividends with respect to which there is a deduction under part VIII of subchapter B,

P.L. 108-27, §302(f), as amended by P.L. 108-311, §402(a)(6), provides:

(f) EFFECTIVE DATE.—

(1) IN GENERAL.—Except as provided in paragraph (2), the amendments made by this section shall apply to taxable years beginning after December 31, 2002.

(2) PASS-THRU ENTITIES.—In the case of a pass-thru entity described in subparagraph (A), (B), (C), (D), (E), or (F) of section 1(h)(10) of the Internal Revenue Code of 1986, as amended by this Act, the amendments made by this section shall apply to taxable years ending after December 31, 2002; except that dividends received by such an entity on or before such date shall not be treated as qualified dividend income (as defined in section 1(h)(11)(B) of such Code, as added by this Act).

P.L. 108-27, §303, as amended by P.L. 109-222, §102, and P.L. 111-312, §102(a), provides:

SEC. 303. SUNSET OF TITLE.

All provisions of, and amendments made by, this title shall not apply to taxable years beginning after December 31, 2012, and the Internal Revenue Code of 1986 shall be applied and administered to such years as if such provisions and amendments had never been enacted.

[¶5425] CODE SEC. 851. DEFINITION OF REGULATED INVESTMENT COMPANY.

* * *

(d) DETERMINATION OF STATUS.—

(1) IN GENERAL.—A corporation which meets the requirements of subsections (b)(3) and (c) at the close of any quarter shall not lose its status as a regulated investment company because of a discrepancy during a subsequent quarter between the value of its various investments and such requirements unless such discrepancy exists immediately after the acquisition of any security or other property and is wholly or partly the result of such acquisition. A corporation which does not meet such requirements at the close of any quarter by reason of a discrepancy existing immediately after the acquisition of any security or other property which is wholly or partly the result of such acquisition during such quarter shall not lose its status for such quarter as a regulated investment company if such discrepancy is eliminated within 30 days after the close of such quarter and in such cases it shall be considered to have met such requirements at the close of such quarter for purposes of applying the preceding sentence.

(2) SPECIAL RULES REGARDING FAILURE TO SATISFY REQUIREMENTS.—If paragraph (1) does not preserve a corporation's status as a regulated investment company for any particular quarter—

(A) IN GENERAL.—A corporation that fails to meet the requirements of subsection (b)(3) (other than a failure described in subparagraph (B)(i)) for such quarter shall nevertheless be considered to have satisfied the requirements of such subsection for such quarter if—

(i) following the corporation's identification of the failure to satisfy the requirements of such subsection for such quarter, a description of each asset that causes the corporation to fail to satisfy the requirements of such subsection at the close of such quarter is set forth in a schedule for such quarter filed in the manner provided by the Secretary,

(ii) the failure to meet the requirements of such subsection for such quarter is due to reasonable cause and not due to willful neglect, and

(iii)(I) the corporation disposes of the assets set forth on the schedule specified in clause (i) within 6 months after the last day of the quarter in which the corporation's identification of the failure to satisfy the requirements of such subsection occurred or such other time period prescribed by the Secretary and in the manner prescribed by the Secretary, or

(II) the requirements of such subsection are otherwise met within the time period specified in subclause (I).

(B) RULE FOR CERTAIN DE MINIMIS FAILURES.—A corporation that fails to meet the requirements of subsection (b)(3) for such quarter shall nevertheless be considered to have satisfied the requirements of such subsection for such quarter if—

(i) such failure is due to the ownership of assets the total value of which does not exceed the lesser of—

(I) 1 percent of the total value of the corporation's assets at the end of the quarter for which such measurement is done, or

(II) $10,000,000, and

(ii)(I) the corporation, following the identification of such failure, disposes of assets in order to meet the requirements of such subsection within 6 months after the last day of the quarter in which the corporation's identification of the failure to satisfy the requirements of such subsection occurred or such other time period prescribed by the Secretary and in the manner prescribed by the Secretary, or

(II) the requirements of such subsection are otherwise met within the time period specified in subclause (I).

(C) TAX.—

(i) TAX IMPOSED.—If subparagraph (A) applies to a corporation for any quarter, there is hereby imposed on such corporation a tax in an amount equal to the greater of—

(I) $50,000, or

(II) the amount determined (pursuant to regulations promulgated by the Secretary) by multiplying the net income generated by the assets described in the schedule specified in subparagraph (A)(i) for the period specified in clause (ii) by the highest rate of tax specified in section 11.

(ii) PERIOD.—For purposes of clause (i)(II), the period described in this clause is the period beginning on the first date that the failure to satisfy the requirements of subsection (b)(3) occurs as a result of the ownership of such assets and ending on the earlier of the date on which the corporation disposes of such assets or the end of the first quarter when there is no longer a failure to satisfy such subsection.

(iii) ADMINISTRATIVE PROVISIONS.—For purposes of subtitle F, a tax imposed by this subparagraph shall be treated as an excise tax with respect to which the deficiency procedures of such subtitle apply.

* * *

[CCH Explanation at ¶ 806.]

Amendments

● **2010, Regulated Investment Company Modernization Act of 2010 (H.R. 4337)**

H.R. 4337, § 201(a)(1)–(2):

Amended Code Sec. 851(d) by striking "A corporation which meets" and inserting the following: "(1) IN GENERAL.—

A corporation which meets", and by adding at the end a new paragraph (2). Effective for tax years with respect to which the due date (determined with regard to any extensions) of the return of tax for such tax year is after the date of the enactment of this Act.

(i) FAILURE TO SATISFY GROSS INCOME TEST.—

(1) DISCLOSURE REQUIREMENT.—A corporation that fails to meet the requirement of paragraph (2) of subsection (b) for any taxable year shall nevertheless be considered to have satisfied the requirement of such paragraph for such taxable year if—

(A) following the corporation's identification of the failure to meet such requirement for such taxable year, a description of each item of its gross income described in such paragraph is set forth in a schedule for such taxable year filed in the manner provided by the Secretary, and

(B) the failure to meet such requirement is due to reasonable cause and not due to willful neglect.

(2) IMPOSITION OF TAX ON FAILURES.—If paragraph (1) applies to a regulated investment company for any taxable year, there is hereby imposed on such company a tax in an amount equal to the excess of—

(A) the gross income of such company which is not derived from sources referred to in subsection (b)(2), over

(B) ⅓ of the gross income of such company which is derived from such sources.

[CCH Explanation at ¶ 806.]

Amendments

• **2010, Regulated Investment Company Modernization Act of 2010 (H.R. 4337)**

H.R. 4337, § 201(b):

Amended Code Sec. 851 by adding at the end a new subsection (i). **Effective** for tax years with respect to which

the due date (determined with regard to any extensions) of the return of tax for such tax year is after the date of the enactment of this Act.

[¶ 5430] CODE SEC. 852. TAXATION OF REGULATED INVESTMENT COMPANIES AND THEIR SHAREHOLDERS.

* * *

(b) METHOD OF TAXATION OF COMPANIES AND SHAREHOLDERS.—

* * *

(2) INVESTMENT COMPANY TAXABLE INCOME.—The investment company taxable income shall be the taxable income of the regulated investment company adjusted as follows:

* * *

(G) There shall be deducted an amount equal to the tax imposed by subsections (d)(2) and (i) of section 851 for the taxable year.

(3) CAPITAL GAINS.—

* * *

(C) DEFINITION OF CAPITAL GAIN DIVIDEND.—For purposes of this part—

(i) IN GENERAL.—Except as provided in clause (ii), a capital gain dividend is any dividend, or part thereof, which is reported by the company as a capital gain dividend in written statements furnished to its shareholders.

(ii) EXCESS REPORTED AMOUNTS.—If the aggregate reported amount with respect to the company for any taxable year exceeds the net capital gain of the company for such taxable year, a capital gain dividend is the excess of—

(I) the reported capital gain dividend amount, over

(II) the excess reported amount which is allocable to such reported capital gain dividend amount.

(iii) ALLOCATION OF EXCESS REPORTED AMOUNT.—

(I) IN GENERAL.—Except as provided in subclause (II), the excess reported amount (if any) which is allocable to the reported capital gain dividend amount is that portion of the excess reported amount which bears the same ratio to the excess reported amount as the reported capital gain dividend amount bears to the aggregate reported amount.

(II) SPECIAL RULE FOR NONCALENDAR YEAR TAXPAYERS.—In the case of any taxable year which does not begin and end in the same calendar year, if the post-December reported amount equals or exceeds the excess reported amount for such taxable year, subclause (I) shall be applied by substituting "post-December reported amount" for "aggregate reported amount" and no excess reported amount shall be allocated to any dividend paid on or before December 31 of such taxable year.

(iv) DEFINITIONS.—For purposes of this subparagraph—

(I) REPORTED CAPITAL GAIN DIVIDEND AMOUNT.—The term "reported capital gain dividend amount" means the amount reported to its shareholders under clause (i) as a capital gain dividend.

(II) Excess Reported Amount.—The term "excess reported amount" means the excess of the aggregate reported amount over the net capital gain of the company for the taxable year.

(III) Aggregate Reported Amount.—The term "aggregate reported amount" means the aggregate amount of dividends reported by the company under clause (i) as capital gain dividends for the taxable year (including capital gain dividends paid after the close of the taxable year described in section 855).

(IV) Post-December Reported Amount.—The term "post-December reported amount" means the aggregate reported amount determined by taking into account only dividends paid after December 31 of the taxable year.

(v) Adjustment for Determinations.—If there is an increase in the excess described in subparagraph (A) for the taxable year which results from a determination (as defined in section 860(e)), the company may, subject to the limitations of this subparagraph, increase the amount of capital gain dividends reported under clause (i).

(vi) Special Rule for Losses Late in the Calendar Year.—For [a] special rule for certain losses after October 31, see paragraph (8).

* * *

(4) Loss on Sale or Exchange of Stock Held 6 Months or Less.—

* * *

(E) Exception to Holding Period Requirement for Certain Regularly Declared Exempt-Interest Dividends.—

(i) Daily Dividend Companies.—Except as otherwise provided by regulations, subparagraph (B) shall not apply with respect to a regular dividend paid by a regulated investment company which declares exempt-interest dividends on a daily basis in an amount equal to at least 90 percent of its net tax-exempt interest and distributes such dividends on a monthly or more frequent basis.

(ii) Authority to Shorten Required Holding Period with Respect to Other Companies.—In the case of a regulated investment company (other than a company described in clause (i)) which regularly distributes at least 90 percent of its net tax-exempt interest, the Secretary may by regulations prescribe that subparagraph (B) (and subparagraph (C) to the extent it relates to subparagraph (B)) shall be applied on the basis of a holding period requirement shorter than 6 months; except that such shorter holding period requirement shall not be shorter than the greater of 31 days or the period between the regular distributions of exempt-interest dividends.

(5) Exempt-Interest Dividends.—If, at the close of each quarter of its taxable year, at least 50 percent of the value (as defined in section 851(c)(4)) of the total assets of the regulated investment company consists of obligations described in section 103(a), such company shall be qualified to pay exempt-interest dividends, as defined herein, to its shareholders.

(A) Definition of Exempt-Interest Dividend.—

(i) In General.—Except as provided in clause (ii), an exempt-interest dividend is any dividend or part thereof (other than a capital gain dividend) paid by a regulated investment company and reported by the company as an exempt-interest dividend in written statements furnished to its shareholders.

(ii) Excess Reported Amounts.—If the aggregate reported amount with respect to the company for any taxable year exceeds the exempt interest of the company for such taxable year, an exempt-interest dividend is the excess of—

(I) the reported exempt-interest dividend amount, over

(II) the excess reported amount which is allocable to such reported exempt-interest dividend amount.

(iii) ALLOCATION OF EXCESS REPORTED AMOUNT.—

(I) IN GENERAL.—Except as provided in subclause (II), the excess reported amount (if any) which is allocable to the reported exempt-interest dividend amount is that portion of the excess reported amount which bears the same ratio to the excess reported amount as the reported exempt-interest dividend amount bears to the aggregate reported amount.

(II) SPECIAL RULE FOR NONCALENDAR YEAR TAXPAYERS.—In the case of any taxable year which does not begin and end in the same calendar year, if the post-December reported amount equals or exceeds the excess reported amount for such taxable year, subclause (I) shall be applied by substituting "post-December reported amount" for "aggregate reported amount" and no excess reported amount shall be allocated to any dividend paid on or before December 31 of such taxable year.

(iv) DEFINITIONS.—For purposes of this subparagraph—

(I) REPORTED EXEMPT-INTEREST DIVIDEND AMOUNT.—The term "reported exempt-interest dividend amount" means the amount reported to its shareholders under clause (i) as an exempt-interest dividend.

(II) EXCESS REPORTED AMOUNT.—The term "excess reported amount" means the excess of the aggregate reported amount over the exempt interest of the company for the taxable year.

(III) AGGREGATE REPORTED AMOUNT.—The term "aggregate reported amount" means the aggregate amount of dividends reported by the company under clause (i) as exempt-interest dividends for the taxable year (including exempt-interest dividends paid after the close of the taxable year described in section 855).

(IV) POST-DECEMBER REPORTED AMOUNT.—The term "post-December reported amount" means the aggregate reported amount determined by taking into account only dividends paid after December 31 of the taxable year.

(V) EXEMPT INTEREST.—The term "exempt interest" means, with respect to any regulated investment company, the excess of the amount of interest excludable from gross income under section 103(a) over the amounts disallowed as deductions under sections 265 and 171(a)(2).

* * *

(8) ELECTIVE DEFERRAL OF CERTAIN LATE-YEAR LOSSES.—

(A) IN GENERAL.—Except as otherwise provided by the Secretary, a regulated investment company may elect for any taxable year to treat any portion of any qualified late-year loss for such taxable year as arising on the first day of the following taxable year for purposes of this title.

(B) QUALIFIED LATE-YEAR LOSS.—For purposes of this paragraph, the term "qualified late-year loss" means—

(i) any post-October capital loss, and

(ii) any late-year ordinary loss.

(C) POST-OCTOBER CAPITAL LOSS.—For purposes of this paragraph, the term "post-October capital loss" means the greatest of—

(i) the net capital loss attributable to the portion of the taxable year after October 31,

(ii) the net long-term capital loss attributable to such portion of the taxable year, or

(iii) the net short-term capital loss attributable to such portion of the taxable year.

(D) LATE-YEAR ORDINARY LOSS.—For purposes of this paragraph, the term "late-year ordinary loss" means the excess (if any) of—

(i) the sum of—

(I) the specified losses (as defined in section 4982(e)(5)(B)(ii)) attributable to the portion of the taxable year after October 31, plus

(II) the ordinary losses not described in subclause (I) attributable to the portion of the taxable year after December 31, over

(ii) the sum of—

(I) the specified gains (as defined in section 4982(e)(5)(B)(i)) attributable to the portion of the taxable year after October 31, plus

(II) the ordinary income not described in subclause (I) attributable to the portion of the taxable year after December 31.

(E) SPECIAL RULE FOR COMPANIES DETERMINING REQUIRED CAPITAL GAIN DISTRIBUTIONS ON TAXABLE YEAR BASIS.—In the case of a company to which an election under section 4982(e)(4) applies—

(i) if such company's taxable year ends with the month of November, the amount of qualified late-year losses (if any) shall be computed without regard to any income, gain, or loss described in subparagraphs (C), (D)(i)(I), and (D)(ii)(I), and

(ii) if such company's taxable year ends with the month of December, subparagraph (A) shall not apply.

* * *

(10) *[Stricken.]*

[CCH Explanation at ¶806, ¶830 and ¶833.]

Amendments

• **2010, Regulated Investment Company Modernization Act of 2010 (H.R. 4337)**

H.R. 4337, §201(c):

Amended Code Sec. 852(b)(2) by adding at the end a new subparagraph (G). **Effective** for tax years with respect to which the due date (determined with regard to any extensions) of the return of tax for such tax year is after the date of the enactment of this Act.

H.R. 4337, §301(a)(1):

Amended Code Sec. 852(b)(3)(C). **Effective** for tax years beginning after the date of the enactment of this Act. Prior to amendment, Code Sec. 852(b)(3)(C) read as follows:

(C) DEFINITION OF CAPITAL GAIN DIVIDEND.—For purposes of this part, a capital gain dividend is any dividend, or part thereof, which is designated by the company as a capital gain dividend in a written notice mailed to its shareholders not later than 60 days after the close of its taxable year. If the aggregate amount so designated with respect to a taxable year of the company (including capital gains dividends paid after the close of the taxable year described in section 855) is greater than the net capital gain of the taxable year, the portion of each distribution which shall be a capital gain dividend shall be only that proportion of the amounts so designated which such net capital gain bears to the aggregate amount so designated; except that, if there is an increase in the excess described in subparagraph (A) of this paragraph for such year which results from a determination (as defined in section 860(e)), such designation may be made with respect to such increase at any time before the expiration of 120 days after the date of such determination. For purposes of this subparagraph, the amount of the net capital gain for a taxable year (to which an election under section 4982(e)(4) does not apply) shall be determined without regard to any net capital loss or net long-term capital loss attributable to transactions after October 31 of such year, and any such net capital loss or net long-term capital loss shall be treated as arising on the 1st day of the next taxable year. To the extent provided in regulations, the preceding sentence shall apply also for purposes of computing the taxable income of the regulated investment company.

H.R. 4337, §301(b):

Amended Code Sec. 852(b)(5)(A). **Effective** for tax years beginning after the date of the enactment of this Act. Prior to amendment, Code Sec. 852(b)(5)(A) read as follows:

(A) DEFINITION.—An exempt-interest dividend means any dividend or part thereof (other than a capital gain dividend) paid by a regulated investment company and designated by it as an exempt-interest dividend in a written notice mailed to its shareholders not later than 60 days after the close of its taxable year. If the aggregate amount so designated with respect to a taxable year of the company (including exempt-interest dividends paid after the close of the taxable year as described in section 855) is greater than the excess of—

(i) the amount of interest excludable from gross income under section 103(a), over

(ii) the amounts disallowed as deductions under sections 265 and 171(a)(2), the portion of such distribution which shall constitute an exempt-interest dividend shall be only that proportion of the amount so designated as the amount of such excess for such taxable year bears to the amount so designated.

H.R. 4337, §308(a):

Amended Code Sec. 852(b)(8). **Effective** for tax years beginning after the date of the enactment of this Act. Prior to amendment, Code Sec. 852(b)(8) read as follows:

(8) SPECIAL RULE FOR TREATMENT OF CERTAIN FOREIGN CURRENCY LOSSES.—To the extent provided in regulations, the taxable income of a regulated investment company (other than a company to which an election under section 4982(e)(4) applies) shall be computed without regard to any net foreign currency loss attributable to transactions after October 31 of such year, and any such net foreign currency loss shall be treated as arising on the 1st day of the following taxable year.

H.R. 4337, §308(b)(1):

Amended Code Sec. 852(b) by striking paragraph (10). **Effective** for tax years beginning after the date of the enactment of this Act. Prior to being stricken, Code Sec. 852(b)(10) read as follows:

(10) SPECIAL RULE FOR CERTAIN LOSSES ON STOCK IN PASSIVE FOREIGN INVESTMENT COMPANY.—To the extent provided in regulations, the taxable income of a regulated investment company (other than a company to which an election under section 4982(e)(4) applies) shall be computed without regard to any net reduction in the value of any stock of a passive foreign investment company with respect to which an election under section 1296(k) is in effect occurring after October 31 of the taxable year, and any such reduction shall be treated as occurring on the first day of the following taxable year.

H.R. 4337, § 309(a):

Amended Code Sec. 852(b)(4)(E) by striking all that precedes "In the case of a regulated investment company" and

inserting a new subparagraph (E). **Effective** for losses incurred on shares of stock for which the taxpayer's holding period begins after the date of the enactment of this Act. Prior to being stricken, all that preceded "In the case of a regulated investment company" read as follows:

(E) AUTHORITY TO SHORTEN REQUIRED HOLDING PERIOD.—

H.R. 4337, § 309(b):

Amended Code Sec. 852(b)(4)(E)(ii), as amended by Act Sec. 309(a), by inserting "(other than a company described in clause (i))" after "regulated investment company". **Effective** for losses incurred on shares of stock for which the taxpayer's holding period begins after the date of the enactment of this Act.

(c) EARNINGS AND PROFITS.—

(1) TREATMENT OF NONDEDUCTIBLE ITEMS.—

(A) NET CAPITAL LOSS.—If a regulated investment company has a net capital loss for any taxable year—

(i) such net capital loss shall not be taken into account for purposes of determining the company's earnings and profits, and

(ii) any capital loss arising on the first day of the next taxable year by reason of clause (ii) or (iii) of section 1212(a)(3)(A) shall be treated as so arising for purposes of determining earnings and profits.

(B) OTHER NONDEDUCTIBLE ITEMS.—

(i) IN GENERAL.—The earnings and profits of a regulated investment company for any taxable year (but not its accumulated earnings and profits) shall not be reduced by any amount which is not allowable as a deduction (other than by reason of section 265 or 171(a)(2)) in computing its taxable income for such taxable year.

(ii) COORDINATION WITH TREATMENT OF NET CAPITAL LOSSES.—Clause (i) shall not apply to a net capital loss to which subparagraph (A) applies.

(2) COORDINATION WITH TAX ON UNDISTRIBUTED INCOME.—For purposes of applying this chapter to distributions made by a regulated investment company with respect to any calendar year, the earnings and profits of such company shall be determined without regard to any net capital loss attributable to the portion of the taxable year after October 31 and without regard to any late-year ordinary loss (as defined in subsection (b)(8)(D)). The preceding sentence shall apply—

(A) only to the extent that the amount distributed by the company with respect to the calendar year does not exceed the required distribution for such calendar year (as determined under section 4982 by substituting "100 percent" for each percentage set forth in section 4982(b)(1)), and

(B) except as provided in regulations, only if an election under section 4982(e)(4) is not in effect with respect to such company.

* * *

(4) REGULATED INVESTMENT COMPANY.—For purposes of this subsection, the term "regulated investment company" includes a domestic corporation which is a regulated investment company determined without regard to the requirements of subsection (a).

* * *

[CCH Explanation at ¶ 812 and ¶ 830.]

Amendments

• **2010, Regulated Investment Company Modernization Act of 2010 (H.R. 4337)**

H.R. 4337, § 302(a):

Amended Code Sec. 852(c)(1). **Effective** for tax years beginning after the date of the enactment of this Act. Prior to amendment, Code Sec. 852(c)(1) read as follows:

(1) IN GENERAL.—The earnings and profits of a regulated investment company for any taxable year (but not its accumulated earnings and profits) shall not reduced by any amount which is not allowable as a deduction in computing its taxable income for such taxable year. For purposes of this subsection, the term "regulated investment company" includes a domestic corporation which is a regulated investment company determined without regard to the requirements of subsection (a).

H.R. 4337, § 302(b)(1):

Amended Code Sec. 852(c) by adding at the end a new paragraph (4). **Effective** for tax years beginning after the date of the enactment of this Act.

H.R. 4337, § 308(b)(2):

Amended Code Sec. 852(c)(2) by striking the first sentence and inserting a new sentence. **Effective** for tax years beginning after the date of the enactment of this Act. Prior to being stricken, the first sentence of Code Sec. 852(c)(2) read as follows:

For purposes of applying this chapter to distributions made by a regulated investment company with respect to any calendar year, the earnings and profits of such company shall be determined without regard to any net capital loss (or net foreign currency loss) attributable to transactions after October 31 of such year, without regard to any net reduction in the value of any stock of a passive foreign investment company with respect to which an election under section 1296(k) is in effect occurring after October 31 of such year, and with such other adjustments as the Secretary may by regulations prescribe.

(f) TREATMENT OF CERTAIN LOAD CHARGES.—

(1) IN GENERAL.—If—

(A) the taxpayer incurs a load charge in acquiring stock in a regulated investment company and, by reason of incurring such charge or making such acquisition, the taxpayer acquires a reinvestment right,

(B) such stock is disposed of before the 91st day after the date on which such stock was acquired, and

(C) the taxpayer *acquires, during the period beginning on the date of the disposition referred to in subparagraph (B) and ending on January 31 of the calendar year following the calendar year that includes the date of such disposition,* stock in such regulated investment company or in another regulated investment company and the otherwise applicable load charge is reduced by reason of the reinvestment right.

the load charge referred to in subparagraph (A) (to the extent it does not exceed the reduction referred to in subparagraph (C)) shall not be taken into account for purposes of determining the amount of gain or loss on the disposition referred to in subparagraph (B). To the extent such charge is not taken into account in determining the amount of such gain or loss, such charge shall be treated as incurred in connection with the acquisition referred to in subparagraph (C) (including for purposes of reapplying this paragraph).

* * *

[CCH Explanation at ¶ 842.]

Amendments

• **2010, Regulated Investment Company Modernization Act of 2010 (H.R. 4337)**

H.R. 4337, § 502(a):

Amended Code Sec. 852(f)(1)(C) by striking "subsequently acquires" and inserting "acquires, during the period beginning on the date of the disposition referred to in subparagraph (B) and ending on January 31 of the calendar year following the calendar year that includes the date of such disposition,". **Effective** for charges incurred in tax years beginning after the date of the enactment of this Act.

(g) SPECIAL RULES FOR FUND OF FUNDS.—

(1) IN GENERAL.—*In the case of a qualified fund of funds—*

(A) *such fund shall be qualified to pay exempt-interest dividends to its shareholders without regard to whether such fund satisfies the requirements of the first sentence of subsection (b)(5), and*

(B) *such fund may elect the application of section 853 (relating to foreign tax credit allowed to shareholders) without regard to the requirement of subsection (a)(1) thereof.*

Code Sec. 852(g)(1)(B) ¶ 5430

(2) QUALIFIED FUND OF FUNDS.—*For purposes of this subsection, the term "qualified fund of funds" means a regulated investment company if (at the close of each quarter of the taxable year) at least 50 percent of the value of its total assets is represented by interests in other regulated investment companies.*

[CCH Explanation at ¶815.]

Amendments

• **2010, Regulated Investment Company Modernization Act of 2010 (H.R. 4337)**

H.R. 4337, §303(a):

Amended Code Sec. 852 by adding at the end a new subsection (g). **Effective** for tax years beginning after the date of the enactment of this Act.

[¶5435] CODE SEC. 853. FOREIGN TAX CREDIT ALLOWED TO SHAREHOLDERS.

* * *

(c) STATEMENTS TO SHAREHOLDERS.—The amounts to be treated by the shareholder, for purposes of subsection (b) (2), as his proportionate share of—

(1) taxes paid to any foreign country or possession of the United States, and

(2) gross income derived from sources within any foreign country or possession of the United States,

shall not exceed the amounts *so reported by the company in a written statement furnished to such shareholder.*

[CCH Explanation at ¶809.]

Amendments

• **2010, Regulated Investment Company Modernization Act of 2010 (H.R. 4337)**

H.R. 4337, §301(c)(1)(A)-(B):

Amended Code Sec. 853(c) by striking "so designated by the company in a written notice mailed to its shareholders not later than 60 days after the close of the taxable year" and inserting "so reported by the company in a written statement furnished to such shareholder", and by striking "NOTICE" in the heading and inserting "STATEMENTS". **Effective** for tax years beginning after the date of the enactment of this Act.

(d) MANNER OF MAKING ELECTION.—The election provided in subsection (a) shall be made in such manner as the Secretary may prescribe by regulations.

[CCH Explanation at ¶809.]

Amendments

• **2010, Regulated Investment Company Modernization Act of 2010 (H.R. 4337)**

H.R. 4337, §301(c)(2)(A)-(B):

Amended Code Sec. 853(d) by striking "and the notice to shareholders required by subsection (c)" after "subsection (a)" in the text thereof, and by striking "AND NOTIFYING SHAREHOLDERS" before the period at the end in the heading thereof. **Effective** for tax years beginning after the date of the enactment of this Act.

[¶5440] CODE SEC. 853A. CREDITS FROM TAX CREDIT BONDS ALLOWED TO SHAREHOLDERS.

* * *

(c) STATEMENTS TO SHAREHOLDERS.—For purposes of subsection (b)(3), the shareholder's proportionate share of—

(1) credits described in subsection (a), and

(2) gross income in respect of such credits, shall not exceed the amounts *so reported by the regulated investment company in a written statement furnished to such shareholder.*

[CCH Explanation at ¶809.]

Amendments

• **2010, Regulated Investment Company Modernization Act of 2010 (H.R. 4337)**

H.R. 4337, § 301(d)(1)(A)-(B):

Amended Code Sec. 853A(c) by striking "so designated by the regulated investment company in a written notice mailed to its shareholders not later than 60 days after the close of its taxable year" and inserting "so reported by the regulated investment company in a written statement furnished to such shareholder", and by striking "NOTICE" in the heading and inserting "STATEMENTS". **Effective** for tax years beginning after the date of the enactment of this Act.

(d) MANNER OF MAKING ELECTION.—The election provided in subsection (a) shall be made in such manner as the Secretary may prescribe.

[CCH Explanation at ¶809.]

Amendments

• **2010, Regulated Investment Company Modernization Act of 2010 (H.R. 4337)**

H.R. 4337, § 301(d)(2)(A)-(B):

Amended Code Sec. 853A(d) by striking "and the notice to shareholders required by subsection (c)" after "subsection (a)" in the text thereof, and by striking "AND NOTIFYING SHAREHOLDERS" before the period at the end in the heading thereof. **Effective** for tax years beginning after the date of the enactment of this Act.

>>→ *Caution: Code Sec. 854(a), below, was amended by P.L. 108-27. For sunset provision, see P.L. 108-27, § 303 [as amended by P.L. 111-312], in the amendment notes.*

[¶5445] CODE SEC. 854. LIMITATIONS APPLICABLE TO DIVIDENDS RECEIVED FROM REGULATED INVESTMENT COMPANY.

(a) CAPITAL GAIN DIVIDEND.—For purposes of section 1(h)(11) (relating to maximum rate of tax on dividends) and section 243 (relating to deductions for dividends received by corporations), a capital gain dividend (as defined in section 852(b)(3)) received from a regulated investment company shall not be considered as a dividend.

[CCH Explanation at ¶425. Committee Reports at ¶10,080.]

Amendments

• **2003, Jobs and Growth Tax Relief Reconciliation Act of 2003 (P.L. 108-27)**

P.L. 108-27, § 302(c)(1):

Amended Code Sec. 854(a) by inserting "section 1(h)(11) (relating to maximum rate of tax on dividends) and" after "For purposes of". For the **effective** date, see Act Sec. 302(f), as amended by P.L. 108-311, § 402(a)(6), below.

P.L. 108-27, § 302(f), as amended by P.L. 108-311, § 402(a)(6), provides:

(f) EFFECTIVE DATE.—

(1) IN GENERAL.—Except as provided in paragraph (2), the amendments made by this section shall apply to taxable years beginning after December 31, 2002.

(2) PASS-THRU ENTITIES.—In the case of a pass-thru entity described in subparagraph (A), (B), (C), (D), (E), or (F) of section 1(h)(10) of the Internal Revenue Code of 1986, as amended by this Act, the amendments made by this section shall apply to taxable years ending after December 31, 2002; except that dividends received by such an entity on or before such date shall not be treated as qualified dividend income (as defined in section 1(h)(11)(B) of such Code, as added by this Act).

P.L. 108-27, § 303, as amended by P.L. 109-222, § 102, and P.L. 111-312, § 102(a), provides:

SEC. 303. SUNSET OF TITLE.

All provisions of, and amendments made by, this title shall not apply to taxable years beginning after December 31, 2012, and the Internal Revenue Code of 1986 shall be applied and administered to such years as if such provisions and amendments had never been enacted.

(b) OTHER DIVIDENDS.—

(1) AMOUNT TREATED AS DIVIDEND.—

(A) DEDUCTION UNDER SECTION 243.—In any case in which—

(i) a dividend is received from a regulated investment company (other than a dividend to which subsection (a) applies), and

(ii) such investment company meets the requirements of section 852(a) for the taxable year during which it paid such dividend,

then, in computing any deduction under section 243, there shall be taken into account only that portion of such dividend *reported by the regulated investment company as eligible for such deduction in written statements furnished to its shareholders* and such dividend shall be treated as received from a corporation which is not a 20-percent owned corporation.

➤➤➤ *Caution: Code Sec. 854(b)(1)(B), below, was added by P.L. 108-27 and amended by H.R. 4337. For sunset provision, see P.L. 108-27, §303, in the amendment notes.*

(B) MAXIMUM RATE UNDER SECTION 1(h).—

(i) IN GENERAL.—In any case in which—

(I) a dividend is received from a regulated investment company (other than a dividend to which subsection (a) applies),

(II) such investment company meets the requirements of section 852(a) for the taxable year during which it paid such dividend, and

(III) the qualified dividend income of such investment company for such taxable year is less than 95 percent of its gross income,

then, in computing qualified dividend income, there shall be taken into account only that portion of such dividend *reported by the regulated investment company as qualified dividend income in written statements furnished to its shareholders.*

(ii) GROSS INCOME.—For purposes of clause (i), in the case of 1 or more sales or other dispositions of stock or securities, the term "gross income" includes only the excess of—

(I) the net short-term capital gain from such sales or dispositions, over

(II) the net long-term capital loss from such sales or dispositions.

➤➤➤ *Caution: Code Sec. 854(b)(1)(C), below, was added by P.L. 108-27 and amended by H.R. 4337. For sunset provision, see P.L. 108-27, §303, in the amendment notes.*

(C) LIMITATIONS.—

(i) SUBPARAGRAPH (A).—The aggregate amount which may be *reported* as dividends under subparagraph (A) shall not exceed the aggregate dividends received by the company for the taxable year.

(ii) SUBPARAGRAPH (B).—The aggregate amount which may be *reported* as qualified dividend income under subparagraph (B) shall not exceed the sum of—

(I) the qualified dividend income of the company for the taxable year, and

(II) the amount of any earnings and profits which were distributed by the company for such taxable year and accumulated in a taxable year with respect to which this part did not apply.

(2) AGGREGATE DIVIDENDS.—For purposes of this subsection—

(A) IN GENERAL.—In computing the amount of aggregate dividends received, there shall only be taken into account dividends received from domestic corporations.

(B) DIVIDENDS.—For purposes of subparagraph (A), the term "dividend" shall not include any distribution from—

(i) a corporation which, for the taxable year of the corporation in which the distribution is made, or for the next preceding taxable year of the corporation, is a corporation exempt from tax under section 501 (relating to certain charitable, etc., organizations) or section 521 (relating to farmers' cooperative associations), or

(ii) a real estate investment trust which, for the taxable year of the trust in which the dividend is paid, qualifies under part II of subchapter M (section 856 and following).

(C) LIMITATIONS ON DIVIDENDS FROM REGULATED INVESTMENT COMPANIES.—In determining the amount of any dividend for purposes of this paragraph, a dividend received from a regulated investment company shall be subject to the limitations prescribed in this section.

(3) SPECIAL RULE FOR COMPUTING DEDUCTION UNDER SECTION 243.—For purposes of subparagraph (A) of paragraph (1), an amount shall be treated as a dividend for the purpose of

paragraph (1) only if a deduction would have been allowable under section 243 to the regulated investment company determined—

  (A) as if section 243 applied to dividends received by a regulated investment company,

  (B) after the application of section 246 (but without regard to subsection (b) thereof), and

  (C) after the application of section 246A.

≫→ *Caution: Former Code Sec. 854(b)(5) was added by P.L. 108-27, amended by P.L. 108-311, and redesignated as Code Sec. 854(b)(4), below, by H.R. 4337. For sunset provision, see P.L. 108-27, §303, in the amendment notes.*

  (4) QUALIFIED DIVIDEND INCOME.—For purposes of this subsection, the term "qualified dividend income" has the meaning given such term by section 1(h)(11)(B).

[CCH Explanation at ¶425. Committee Reports at ¶10,080.]

Amendments

• **2010, Regulated Investment Company Modernization Act of 2010 (H.R. 4337)**

H.R. 4337, §301(e)(1)(A)-(D):

Amended Code Sec. 854(b)(1) by striking "designated under this subparagraph by the regulated investment company" in subparagraph (A) and inserting "reported by the regulated investment company as eligible for such deduction in written statements furnished to its shareholders", by striking "designated by the regulated investment company" in subparagraph (B)(i) and inserting "reported by the regulated investment company as qualified dividend income in written statements furnished to its shareholders", by striking "designated" in subparagraph (C)(i) and inserting "reported", and by striking "designated" in subparagraph (C)(ii) and inserting "reported". **Effective** for tax years beginning after the date of the enactment of this Act.

H.R. 4337, §301(e)(2):

Amended Code Sec. 854(b) by striking paragraph (2) and by redesignating paragraphs (3), (4), and (5), as paragraphs (2), (3), and (4), respectively. **Effective** for tax years beginning after the date of the enactment of this Act. Prior to being stricken, Code Sec. 854(b)(2) read as follows:

(2) NOTICE TO SHAREHOLDERS.—The amount of any distribution by a regulated investment company which may be taken into account as qualified dividend income for purposes of section 1(h)(11) and as dividends for purposes of the deduction under section 243 shall not exceed the amount so designated by the company in a written notice to its shareholders mailed not later than 60 days after the close of its taxable year.

H.R. 4337, §301(i):

(i) APPLICATION OF JGTRRA SUNSET.—Section 303 of the Jobs and Growth Tax Relief Reconciliation Act of 2003 shall apply to the amendments made by subparagraphs (B) and (D) of subsection (e)(1) to the same extent and in the same manner as section 303 of such Act applies to the amendments made by section 302 of such Act.

• **2004, Working Families Tax Relief Act of 2004 (P.L. 108-311)**

P.L. 108-311, §402(a)(5)(A)(i):

Amended Code Sec. 854(b)(1)(B) by striking clauses (iii) and (iv). **Effective** as if included in section 302 of the Jobs and Growth Tax Relief Reconciliation Act of 2003 (P.L. 108-27) [effective for tax years ending after 12-31-2002.—CCH]. Prior to being stricken, Code Sec. 854(b)(1)(B)(iii) and (iv) read as follows:

(iii) DIVIDENDS FROM REAL ESTATE INVESTMENT TRUSTS.—For purposes of clause (i)—

(I) paragraph (3)(B)(ii) shall not apply, and

(II) in the case of a distribution from a trust described in such paragraph, the amount of such distribution which is a dividend shall be subject to the limitations under section 857(c).

(iv) DIVIDENDS FROM QUALIFIED FOREIGN CORPORATIONS.—For purposes of clause (i), dividends received from qualified foreign corporations (as defined in section 1(h)(11)) shall also be taken into account in computing aggregate dividends received.

P.L. 108-311, §402(a)(5)(A)(ii):

Amended Code Sec. 854(b)(1)(B)(i). **Effective** as if included in section 302 of the Jobs and Growth Tax Relief Reconciliation Act of 2003 (P.L. 108-27) [effective for tax years ending after 12-31-2002.—CCH]. Prior to amendment, Code Sec. 854(b)(1)(B)(i) read as follows:

(i) IN GENERAL.—If the aggregate dividends received by a regulated investment company during any taxable year are less than 95 percent of its gross income, then, in computing the maximum rate under section 1(h)(11), rules similar to the rules of subparagraph (A) shall apply.

P.L. 108-311, §402(a)(5)(B):

Amended Code Sec. 854(b)(1)(C). **Effective** as if included in section 302 of the Jobs and Growth Tax Relief Reconciliation Act of 2003 (P.L. 108-27) [effective for tax years ending after 12-31-2002.—CCH]. Prior to amendment, Code Sec. 854(b)(1)(C) read as follows:

(C) LIMITATION.—The aggregate amount which may be designated as dividends under subparagraph (A) or (B) shall not exceed the aggregate dividends received by the company for the taxable year.

P.L. 108-311, §402(a)(5)(C):

Amended Code Sec. 854(b)(2) by striking "as a dividend for purposes of the maximum rate under section 1(h)(11) and" and inserting "as qualified dividend income for purposes of section 1(h)(11) and as dividends for purposes of". **Effective** as if included in section 302 of the Jobs and Growth Tax Relief Reconciliation Act of 2003 (P.L. 108-27) [effective for tax years ending after 12-31-2002.—CCH]. For a special rule, see Act. Sec. 402(a)(5)(F), below.

P.L. 108-311, §402(a)(5)(D):

Amended Code Sec. 854(b)(5). **Effective** as if included in section 302 of the Jobs and Growth Tax Relief Reconciliation Act of 2003 (P.L. 108-27) [effective for tax years ending after 12-31-2002.—CCH]. Prior to amendment, Code Sec. 854(b)(5) read as follows:

(5) COORDINATION WITH SECTION 1(h)(11).—For purposes of paragraph (1)(B), an amount shall be treated as a dividend

only if the amount is qualified dividend income (within the meaning of section 1(h)(11)(B)).

P.L. 108-311, §402(a)(5)(F), provides:

(F) With respect to any taxable year of a regulated investment company or real estate investment trust ending on or before November 30, 2003, the period for providing notice of the qualified dividend amount to shareholders under sections 854(b)(2) and 857(c)(2)(C) of the Internal Revenue Code of 1986, as amended by this section, shall not expire before the date on which the statement under section 6042(c) of such Code is required to be furnished with respect to the last calendar year beginning in such taxable year.

• **2003, Jobs and Growth Tax Relief Reconciliation Act of 2003 (P.L. 108-27)**

P.L. 108-27, §302(c)(2):

Amended Code Sec. 854(b)(1) by redesignating subparagraph (B) as subparagraph (C) and by inserting after subparagraph (A) a new subparagraph (B). For the **effective** date, see Act Sec. 302(f), as amended by P.L. 108-311, §402(a)(6), below.

P.L. 108-27, §302(c)(3):

Amended Code Sec. 854(b)(1)(C), as redesignating by Act Sec. 302(c)(2), by striking "subparagraph (A)" and inserting "subparagraph (A) or (B)". For the **effective** date, see Act Sec. 302(f), as amended by P.L. 108-311, §402(a)(6), below.

P.L. 108-27, §302(c)(4):

Amended Code Sec. 854(b)(2) by inserting "the maximum rate under section 1(h)(11) and" after "for purposes of". For the **effective** date, see Act Sec. 302(f), as amended by P.L. 108-311, §402(a)(6), below.

P.L. 108-27, §302(c)(5):

Amended Code Sec. 854(b) by adding at the end a new paragraph (5). For the **effective** date, see Act Sec. 302(f), as amended by P.L. 108-311, §402(a)(6), below.

P.L. 108-27, §302(f), as amended by P.L. 108-311, §402(a)(6), provides:

(f) EFFECTIVE DATE.—

(1) IN GENERAL.—Except as provided in paragraph (2), the amendments made by this section shall apply to taxable years beginning after December 31, 2002.

(2) PASS-THRU ENTITIES.—In the case of a pass-thru entity described in subparagraph (A), (B), (C), (D), (E), or (F) of section 1(h)(10) of the Internal Revenue Code of 1986, as amended by this Act, the amendments made by this section shall apply to taxable years ending after December 31, 2002; except that dividends received by such an entity on or before such date shall not be treated as qualified dividend income (as defined in section 1(h)(11)(B) of such Code, as added by this Act).

P.L. 108-27, §303, as amended by P.L. 109-222, §102, and P.L. 111-312, §102(a), provides:

SEC. 303. SUNSET OF TITLE.

All provisions of, and amendments made by, this title shall not apply to taxable years beginning after December 31, 2012, and the Internal Revenue Code of 1986 shall be applied and administered to such years as if such provisions and amendments had never been enacted.

[¶5450] CODE SEC. 855. DIVIDENDS PAID BY REGULATED INVESTMENT COMPANY AFTER CLOSE OF TAXABLE YEAR.

(a) GENERAL RULE.—For purposes of this chapter, if a regulated investment company—

(1) *declares a dividend before the later of—*

(A) *the 15th day of the 9th month following the close of the taxable year, or*

(B) *in the case of an extension of time for filing the company's return for the taxable year, the due date for filing such return taking into account such extension, and*

(2) distributes the amount of such dividend to shareholders in the 12-month period following the close of such taxable year and not later than the date of *the first dividend payment of the same type of dividend* made after such declaration,

the amount so declared and distributed shall, to the extent the company elects in such return in accordance with regulations prescribed by the Secretary, be considered as having been paid during such taxable year, except as provided in subsections (b) *and (c). For purposes of paragraph (2), a dividend attributable to any short-term capital gain with respect to which a notice is required under the Investment Company Act of 1940 shall be treated as the same type of dividend as a capital gain dividend.*

* * *

[CCH Explanation at ¶818.]
Amendments

• **2010, Regulated Investment Company Modernization Act of 2010 (H.R. 4337)**

H.R. 4337, §301(g)(2):

Amended Code Sec. 855(a) by striking ", (c) and (d)" and inserting "and (c)". **Effective** for tax years beginning after the date of the enactment of this Act.

H.R. 4337, §304(a):

Amended Code Sec. 855(a)(1). **Effective** for distributions in tax years beginning after the date of the enactment of this

Act. Prior to amendment, Code Sec. 855(a)(1) read as follows:

(1) declares a dividend prior to the time prescribed by law for the filing of its return for a taxable year (including the period of any extension of time granted for filing such return), and

H.R. 4337, §304(b):

Amended Code Sec. 855(a)(2) by striking "the first regular dividend payment" and inserting "the first dividend payment of the same type of dividend". **Effective** for distributions in tax years beginning after the date of the enactment of this Act.

H.R. 4337, §304(c):

Amended Code Sec. 855(a) by adding at the end a new sentence. **Effective** for distributions in tax years beginning after the date of the enactment of this Act.

(c) FOREIGN TAX ELECTION.—If an investment company to which section 853 is applicable for the taxable year makes a distribution as provided in subsection (a) of this section, the shareholders shall consider the amounts described in section 853(b)(2) allocable to such distribution as paid or received, as the case may be, in the taxable year in which the distribution is made.

[CCH Explanation at ¶818.]

Amendments

• **2010, Regulated Investment Company Modernization Act of 2010 (H.R. 4337)**

H.R. 4337, §301(g)(1):

Amended Code Sec. 855 by striking subsection (c) and redesignating subsection (d) as subsection (c). **Effective** for tax years beginning after the date of the enactment of this Act. Prior to being stricken, Code Sec. 855(c) read as follows:

(c) NOTICE TO SHAREHOLDERS.—In the case of amounts to which subsection (a) is applicable, any notice to shareholders required under this part with respect to such amounts shall be made not later than 60 days after the close of the taxable year in which the distribution is made.

[¶5455] CODE SEC. 857. TAXATION OF REAL ESTATE INVESTMENT TRUSTS AND THEIR BENEFICIARIES.

* * *

»»→ *Caution: Code Sec. 857(c), below, was amended by P.L. 108-27 and P.L. 108-311. For sunset provision, see P.L. 108-27, §303 [as amended by P.L. 111-312], in the amendment notes.*

(c) RESTRICTIONS APPLICABLE TO DIVIDENDS RECEIVED FROM REAL ESTATE INVESTMENT TRUSTS.—

(1) SECTION 243.—For purposes of section 243 (relating to deductions for dividends received by corporations), a dividend received from a real estate investment trust which meets the requirements of this part shall not be considered a dividend.

(2) SECTION (1)(h)(11).—

(A) IN GENERAL.—In any case in which—

(i) a dividend is received from a real estate investment trust (other than a capital gain dividend), and

(ii) such trust meets the requirements of section 856(a) for the taxable year during which it paid such dividend,

then, in computing qualified dividend income, there shall be taken into account only that portion of such dividend designated by the real estate investment trust.

(B) LIMITATION.—The aggregate amount which may be designated as qualified dividend income under subparagraph (A) shall not exceed the sum of—

(i) the qualified dividend income of the trust for the taxable year,

(ii) the excess of—

(I) the sum of the real estate investment trust taxable income computed under section 857(b)(2) for the preceding taxable year and the income subject to tax by reason of the application of the regulations under section 337(d) for such preceding taxable year, over

(II) the sum of the taxes imposed on the trust for such preceding taxable year under section 857(b)(1) and by reason of the application of such regulations, and

(iii) the amount of any earnings and profits which were distributed by the trust for such taxable year and accumulated in a taxable year with respect to which this part did not apply.

(C) NOTICE TO SHAREHOLDERS.—The amount of any distribution by a real estate investment trust which may be taken into account as qualified dividend income shall not exceed the amount so designated by the trust in a written notice to its shareholders mailed not later than 60 days after the close of its taxable year.

(D) QUALIFIED DIVIDEND INCOME.—For purposes of this paragraph, the term "qualified dividend income" has the meaning given such term by section 1(h)(11)(B).

* * *

[CCH Explanation at ¶ 425. Committee Reports at ¶ 10,080.]

Amendments

- **2004, Working Families Tax Relief Act of 2004 (P.L. 108-311)**

P.L. 108-311, § 402(a)(5)(E):

Amended Code Sec. 857(c)(2). **Effective** as if included in section 302 of the Jobs and Growth Tax Relief Reconciliation Act of 2003 (P.L. 108-27) [**effective** for tax years ending after 12-31-2002.—CCH]. For a special rule, see Act Sec. 402(a)(5)(F), below. Prior to amendment, Code Sec. 857(c)(2) read as follows:

(2) SECTION 1(h)(11).—For purposes of section 1(h)(11) (relating to maximum rate of tax on dividends)—

(A) rules similar to the rules of subparagraphs (B) and (C) of section 854(b)(1) shall apply to dividends received from a real estate investment trust which meets the requirements of this part, and

(B) for purposes of such rules, such a trust shall be treated as receiving qualified dividend income during any taxable year in an amount equal to the sum of—

(i) the excess of real estate investment trust taxable income computed under section 857(b)(2) for the preceding taxable year over the tax payable by the trust under section 857(b)(1) for such preceding taxable year, and

(ii) the excess of the income subject to tax by reason of the application of the regulations under section 337(d) for the preceding taxable year over the tax payable by the trust on such income for such preceding taxable year.

P.L. 108-311, § 402(a)(5)(F), provides:

(F) With respect to any taxable year of a regulated investment company or real estate investment trust ending on or before November 30, 2003, the period for providing notice of the qualified dividend amount to shareholders under sections 854(b)(2) and 857(c)(2)(C) of the Internal Revenue Code of 1986, as amended by this section, shall not expire before the date on which the statement under section 6042(c) of such Code is required to be furnished with respect to the last calendar year beginning in such taxable year.

- **2003, Jobs and Growth Tax Relief Reconciliation Act of 2003 (P.L. 108-27)**

P.L. 108-27, § 302(d):

Amended Code Sec. 857(c). For the **effective** date, see Act Sec. 302(f), as amended by P.L. 108-311, § 402(a)(6), below. Prior to amendment, Code Sec. 857(c) read as follows:

(c) RESTRICTIONS APPLICABLE TO DIVIDENDS RECEIVED FROM REAL ESTATE INVESTMENT TRUSTS.—For purposes of section 243 (relating to deductions for dividends received by corporations), a dividend received from a real estate investment trust which meets the requirements of this part shall not be considered as a dividend.

P.L. 108-27, § 302(f), as amended by P.L. 108-311, § 402(a)(6), provides:

(f) EFFECTIVE DATE.—

(1) IN GENERAL.—Except as provided in paragraph (2), the amendments made by this section shall apply to taxable years beginning after December 31, 2002.

(2) PASS-THRU ENTITIES.—In the case of a pass-thru entity described in subparagraph (A), (B), (C), (D), (E), or (F) of section 1(h)(10) of the Internal Revenue Code of 1986, as amended by this Act, the amendments made by this section shall apply to taxable years ending after December 31, 2002; except that dividends received by such an entity on or before such date shall not be treated as qualified dividend income (as defined in section 1(h)(11)(B) of such Code, as added by this Act).

P.L. 108-27, § 303, as amended by P.L. 109-222, § 102, and P.L. 111-312, § 102(a), provides:

SEC. 303. SUNSET OF TITLE.

All provisions of, and amendments made by, this title shall not apply to taxable years beginning after December 31, 2012, and the Internal Revenue Code of 1986 shall be applied and administered to such years as if such provisions and amendments had never been enacted.

[¶ 5460] CODE SEC. 860. DEDUCTION FOR DEFICIENCY DIVIDENDS.

* * *

(f) DEFICIENCY DIVIDENDS.—

* * *

(2) LIMITATIONS.—

* * *

(B) CAPITAL GAIN DIVIDENDS.—The amount of deficiency dividends qualifying as capital gain dividends paid by a qualified investment entity for the taxable year with respect to which the liability for tax resulting from the determination exists shall not exceed the amount by which (i) the increase referred to in subparagraph (B) of paragraph (1) or (2) of subsection (d) (whichever applies), exceeds (ii) the amount of any dividends paid during such taxable year which are designated *or reported (as the case may be)* as capital gain dividends after such determination.

* * *

[CCH Explanation at ¶ 809.]

Amendments

• **2010, Regulated Investment Company Modernization Act of 2010 (H.R. 4337)**

H.R. 4337, § 301(a)(2):

Amended Code Sec. 860(f)(2)(B) by inserting "or reported (as the case may be)" after "designated". **Effective** for tax years beginning after the date of the enactment of this Act.

(j) [*Stricken.*]

[CCH Explanation at ¶ 839.]

Amendments

• **2010, Regulated Investment Company Modernization Act of 2010 (H.R. 4337)**

H.R. 4337, § 501(b):

Amended Code Sec. 860 by striking subsection (j). **Effective** for tax years beginning after the date of the enactment

of this Act. Prior to amendment, Code Sec. 860(j) read as follows:

(j) PENALTY.—For assessable penalty with respect to liability for tax of a regulated investment company which is allowed a deduction under subsection (a), see section 6697.

[¶ 5465] CODE SEC. 871. TAX ON NONRESIDENT ALIEN INDIVIDUALS.

* * *

(k) EXEMPTION FOR CERTAIN DIVIDENDS OF REGULATED INVESTMENT COMPANIES.—

(1) INTEREST-RELATED DIVIDENDS.—

(A) IN GENERAL.—Except as provided in subparagraph (B), no tax shall be imposed under paragraph (1)(A) of subsection (a) on any interest-related dividend received from a regulated investment company *which meets the requirements of section 852(a) for the taxable year with respect to which the dividend is paid.*

* * *

(C) INTEREST-RELATED DIVIDEND.—*For purposes of this paragraph—*

(i) IN GENERAL.—*Except as provided in clause (ii), an interest related dividend is any dividend, or part thereof, which is reported by the company as an interest related dividend in written statements furnished to its shareholders.*

(ii) EXCESS REPORTED AMOUNTS.—*If the aggregate reported amount with respect to the company for any taxable year exceeds the qualified net interest income of the company for such taxable year, an interest related dividend is the excess of—*

(I) *the reported interest related dividend amount, over*

(II) *the excess reported amount which is allocable to such reported interest related dividend amount.*

(iii) ALLOCATION OF EXCESS REPORTED AMOUNT.—

(I) IN GENERAL.—*Except as provided in subclause (II), the excess reported amount (if any) which is allocable to the reported interest related dividend amount is that portion of the excess reported amount which bears the same ratio to the excess reported amount as the reported interest related dividend amount bears to the aggregate reported amount.*

(II) SPECIAL RULE FOR NONCALENDAR YEAR TAXPAYERS.—*In the case of any taxable year which does not begin and end in the same calendar year, if the post-December reported amount equals or exceeds the excess reported amount for such taxable year, subclause (I) shall be applied by substituting "post-December reported amount" for "aggregate reported amount" and no excess reported amount shall be allocated to any dividend paid on or before December 31 of such taxable year.*

(iv) DEFINITIONS.—*For purposes of this subparagraph—*

(I) REPORTED INTEREST RELATED DIVIDEND AMOUNT.—The term "reported interest related dividend amount" means the amount reported to its shareholders under clause (i) as an interest related dividend.

(II) EXCESS REPORTED AMOUNT.—The term "excess reported amount" means the excess of the aggregate reported amount over the qualified net interest income of the company for the taxable year.

(III) AGGREGATE REPORTED AMOUNT.—The term "aggregate reported amount" means the aggregate amount of dividends reported by the company under clause (i) as interest related dividends for the taxable year (including interest related dividends paid after the close of the taxable year described in section 855).

(IV) POST-DECEMBER REPORTED AMOUNT.—The term "post-December reported amount" means the aggregate reported amount determined by taking into account only dividends paid after December 31 of the taxable year.

(v) TERMINATION.—The term "interest related dividend" shall not include any dividend with respect to any taxable year of the company beginning after December 31, 2011.

* * *

(2) SHORT-TERM CAPITAL GAIN DIVIDENDS.—

(A) IN GENERAL.—Except as provided in subparagraph (B), no tax shall be imposed under paragraph (1)(A) of subsection (a) on any short-term capital gain dividend received from a regulated investment company which meets the requirements of section 852(a) for the taxable year with respect to which the dividend is paid.

* * *

(C) SHORT-TERM CAPITAL GAIN DIVIDEND.—For purposes of this paragraph—

(i) IN GENERAL.—Except as provided in clause (ii), the term "short-term capital gain dividend" means any dividend, or part thereof, which is reported by the company as a short-term capital gain dividend in written statements furnished to its shareholders.

(ii) EXCESS REPORTED AMOUNTS.—If the aggregate reported amount with respect to the company for any taxable year exceeds the qualified short-term gain of the company for such taxable year, the term "short-term capital gain dividend" means the excess of—

(I) the reported short-term capital gain dividend amount, over

(II) the excess reported amount which is allocable to such reported short-term capital gain dividend amount.

(iii) ALLOCATION OF EXCESS REPORTED AMOUNT.—

(I) IN GENERAL.—Except as provided in subclause (II), the excess reported amount (if any) which is allocable to the reported short-term capital gain dividend amount is that portion of the excess reported amount which bears the same ratio to the excess reported amount as the reported short-term capital gain dividend amount bears to the aggregate reported amount.

(II) SPECIAL RULE FOR NONCALENDAR YEAR TAXPAYERS.—In the case of any taxable year which does not begin and end in the same calendar year, if the post-December reported amount equals or exceeds the excess reported amount for such taxable year, subclause (I) shall be applied by substituting "post-December reported amount" for "aggregate reported amount" and no excess reported amount shall be allocated to any dividend paid on or before December 31 of such taxable year.

(iv) DEFINITIONS.—For purposes of this subparagraph—

(I) REPORTED SHORT-TERM CAPITAL GAIN DIVIDEND AMOUNT.—The term "reported short-term capital gain dividend amount" means the amount reported to its shareholders under clause (i) as a short-term capital gain dividend.

(II) Excess reported amount.—*The term "excess reported amount" means the excess of the aggregate reported amount over the qualified short-term gain of the company for the taxable year.*

(III) Aggregate reported amount.—*The term "aggregate reported amount" means the aggregate amount of dividends reported by the company under clause (i) as short-term capital gain dividends for the taxable year (including short-term capital gain dividends paid after the close of the taxable year described in section 855).*

(IV) Post-december reported amount.—*The term "post-December reported amount" means the aggregate reported amount determined by taking into account only dividends paid after December 31 of the taxable year.*

(v) Termination.—*The term "short-term capital gain dividend" shall not include any dividend with respect to any taxable year of the company beginning after December 31, 2011.*

(D) Qualified short-term gain.—For purposes of subparagraph (C), the term "qualified short-term gain" means the excess of the net short-term capital gain of the regulated investment company for the taxable year over the net long-term capital loss (if any) of such company for such taxable year. *For purposes of this subparagraph, the net short-term capital gain of the regulated investment company shall be computed by treating any short-term capital gain dividend includible in gross income with respect to stock of another regulated investment company as a short-term capital gain.*

* * *

[CCH Explanation at ¶430, ¶809, ¶812 and ¶830. Committee Reports at ¶10,530.]

Amendments

- **2010, Tax Relief, Unemployment Insurance Reauthorization, and Job Creation Act of 2010 (P.L. 111-312)**

P.L. 111-312, §748(a):

Amended Code Sec. 871(k)(1)(C)[(v)] and (2)(C)[(v)] by striking "December 31, 2009" and inserting "December 31, 2011". **Effective** for tax years beginning after 12-31-2009.

- **2010, Regulated Investment Company Modernization Act of 2010 (H.R. 4337)**

H.R. 4337, §301(f)(1):

Amended Code Sec. 871(k)(1)(C) by striking all that precedes "any taxable year of the company beginning" and inserting new text. **Effective** for tax years beginning after the date of the enactment of this Act. Prior to amendment, Code Sec. 871(k)(1)(C) read as follows:

(C) Interest-related dividend.—For purposes of this paragraph, the term "interest-related dividend" means any dividend (or part thereof) which is designated by the regulated investment company as an interest-related dividend in a written notice mailed to its shareholders not later than 60 days after the close of its taxable year. If the aggregate amount so designated with respect to a taxable year of the company (including amounts so designated with respect to dividends paid after the close of the taxable year described in section 855) is greater than the qualified net interest income of the company for such taxable year, the portion of each distribution which shall be an interest-related dividend shall be only that portion of the amounts so designated which such qualified net interest income bears to the aggregate amount so designated. Such term shall not include any dividend with respect to any taxable year of the company beginning after December 31, 2009.

H.R. 4337, §301(f)(2):

Amended Code Sec. 871(k)(2)(C) by striking all that precedes "any taxable year of the company beginning" and inserting new text. **Effective** for tax years beginning after

the date of the enactment of this Act. Prior to the amendment, Code Sec. 871(k)(2)(C) read as follows:

(C) Short-term capital gain dividend.—For purposes of this paragraph, the term "short-term capital gain dividend" means any dividend (or part thereof) which is designated by the regulated investment company as a short-term capital gain dividend in a written notice mailed to its shareholders not later than 60 days after the close of its taxable year. If the aggregate amount so designated with respect to a taxable year of the company (including amounts so designated with respect to dividends paid after the close of the taxable year described in section 855) is greater than the qualified short-term gain of the company for such taxable year, the portion of each distribution which shall be a short-term capital gain dividend shall be only that portion of the amounts so designated which such qualified short-term gain bears to the aggregate amount so designated. Such term shall not include any dividend with respect to any taxable year of the company beginning after December 31, 2009.

H.R. 4337, §302(b)(2):

Amended Code Sec. 871(k)(1)(A) and 871(k)(2)(A) by inserting "which meets the requirements of section 852(a) for the taxable year with respect to which the dividend is paid" before the period at the end. **Effective** for tax years beginning after the date of the enactment of this Act.

H.R. 4337, §308(b)(3):

Amended Code Sec. 871(k)(2)(D) by striking the last two sentences and inserting a new sentence. **Effective** for tax years beginning after the date of the enactment of this Act. Prior to amendment, Code Sec. 871(k)(2)(D) read as follows:

(D) Qualified short-term gain.—For purposes of subparagraph (C), the term "qualified short-term gain" means the excess of the net short-term capital gain of the regulated investment company for the taxable year over the net long-term capital loss (if any) of such company for such taxable year. For purposes of this subparagraph—

(i) the net short-term capital gain of the regulated investment company shall be computed by treating any short-term capital gain dividend includible in gross income with respect to stock of another regulated investment company as a short-term capital gain, and

(ii) the excess of the net short-term capital gain for a taxable year over the net long-term capital loss for a taxable year (to which an election under section 4982(e)(4) does not apply) shall be determined without regard to any net capital loss or net short-term capital loss attributable to transactions after October 31 of such year, and any such net capital loss or net short-term capital loss shall be treated as arising on the 1st day of the next taxable year.

To the extent provided in regulations, clause (ii) shall apply also for purposes of computing the taxable income of the regulated investment company.

[¶5470] CODE SEC. 897. DISPOSITION OF INVESTMENT IN UNITED STATES REAL PROPERTY.

* * *

(h) SPECIAL RULES FOR CERTAIN INVESTMENT ENTITIES.—For purposes of this section—

* * *

(4) DEFINITIONS.—

(A) QUALIFIED INVESTMENT ENTITY.—

* * *

(ii) TERMINATION.—Clause (i)(II) shall not apply after *December 31, 2011*. Notwithstanding the preceding sentence, an entity described in clause (i)(II) shall be treated as a qualified investment entity for purposes of applying paragraphs (1) and (5) and section 1445 with respect to any distribution by the entity to a nonresident alien individual or a foreign corporation which is attributable directly or indirectly to a distribution to the entity from a real estate investment trust.

* * *

[CCH Explanation at ¶620. Committee Reports at ¶10,540.]

Amendments

• **2010, Tax Relief, Unemployment Insurance Reauthorization, and Job Creation Act of 2010 (P.L. 111-312)**

P.L. 111-312, §749(a):

Amended Code Sec. 897(h)(4)(A)(ii) by striking "December 31, 2009" and inserting "December 31, 2011". For the effective date, see Act Sec. 749(b), below.

P.L. 111-312, §749(b), provides:

(b) EFFECTIVE DATE.—

(1) IN GENERAL.—The amendment made by subsection (a) shall take effect on January 1, 2010. Notwithstanding the preceding sentence, such amendment shall not apply with respect to the withholding requirement under section 1445 of the Internal Revenue Code of 1986 for any payment made before the date of the enactment of this Act.

(2) AMOUNTS WITHHELD ON OR BEFORE DATE OF ENACTMENT.— In the case of a regulated investment company—

(A) which makes a distribution after December 31, 2009, and before the date of the enactment of this Act; and

(B) which would (but for the second sentence of paragraph (1)) have been required to withhold with respect to such distribution under section 1445 of such Code,

such investment company shall not be liable to any person to whom such distribution was made for any amount so withheld and paid over to the Secretary of the Treasury.

[¶5475] CODE SEC. 904. LIMITATION ON CREDIT.

* * *

⟫→ *Caution: Code Sec. 904(i), below, as amended by P.L. 107-16, P.L. 107-147, P.L. 108-311, P.L. 108-357, P.L. 109-135, P.L. 111-5, P.L. 111-148, and P.L. 111-312, applies to tax years beginning after December 31, 2011. For sunset provisions, see P.L. 107-16, §901, P.L. 109-135, §402(i)(3)(H), and P.L. 111-148, §10909(c) [as amended by P.L. 111-312], in the amendment notes.*

(i) COORDINATION WITH NONREFUNDABLE PERSONAL CREDITS.—In the case of any taxable year of an individual to which section 26(a)(2) does not apply, for purposes of subsection (a), the tax against which the credit is taken is such tax reduced by the sum of the credits allowable under subpart A of part IV of subchapter A of this chapter (other than sections 23, 24, 25A(i), 25B, 30, 30B, and 30D).

[CCH Explanation at ¶ 360 and ¶ 370. Committee Reports at ¶ 10,030 and ¶ 10,060.]

Amendments

- **2010, Tax Relief, Unemployment Insurance Reauthorization, and Job Creation Act of 2010 (P.L. 111-312)**

P.L. 111-312, § 101(b)(1):

Amended Code Sec. 904(i) to read as such provision would read if section 10909 of the Patient Protection and Affordable Care Act (P.L. 111-148) had never been enacted. Effective for tax years beginning after 12-31-2011.

- **2010, Patient Protection and Affordable Care Act (P.L. 111-148)**

P.L. 111-148, § 10909(b)(2)(K):

Amended Code Sec. 904(i) by striking "23," before "24". Effective for tax years beginning after 12-31-2009.

P.L. 111-148, § 10909(c), as amended by P.L. 111-312, § 101(b)(1), provides:

(c) SUNSET PROVISION.—Each provision of law amended by this section is amended to read as such provision would read if this section had never been enacted. The amendments made by the preceding sentence shall apply to taxable years beginning after December 31, 2011.

[¶ 5480] CODE SEC. 953. INSURANCE INCOME.

* * *

(e) EXEMPT INSURANCE INCOME.—For purposes of this section—

* * *

(10) APPLICATION.—This subsection and section 954(i) shall apply only to taxable years of a foreign corporation beginning after December 31, 1998, and before *January 1, 2012,* and to taxable years of United States shareholders with or within which any such taxable year of such foreign corporation ends. If this subsection does not apply to a taxable year of a foreign corporation beginning after *December 31, 2011* (and taxable years of United States shareholders ending with or within such taxable year), then, notwithstanding the preceding sentence, subsection (a) shall be applied to such taxable years in the same manner as it would if the taxable year of the foreign corporation began in 1998.

* * *

[CCH Explanation at ¶ 623 and ¶ 626. Committee Reports at ¶ 10,550.]

Amendments

- **2010, Tax Relief, Unemployment Insurance Reauthorization, and Job Creation Act of 2010 (P.L. 111-312)**

P.L. 111-312, § 750(a):

Amended Code Sec. 953(e)(10) by striking "January 1, 2010" and inserting "January 1, 2012". Effective for tax years of foreign corporations beginning after 12-31-2009, and to tax years of United States shareholders with or within which any such tax year of such foreign corporation ends.

P.L. 111-312, § 750(b):

Amended Code Sec. 953(e)(10) by striking "December 31, 2009" and inserting "December 31, 2011". Effective for tax years of foreign corporations beginning after 12-31-2009, and to tax years of United States shareholders with or within which any such tax year of such foreign corporation ends.

[¶ 5485] CODE SEC. 954. FOREIGN BASE COMPANY INCOME.

* * *

(c) FOREIGN PERSONAL HOLDING COMPANY INCOME.—

* * *

(6) LOOK-THRU RULE FOR RELATED CONTROLLED FOREIGN CORPORATIONS.—

* * *

(C) APPLICATION.—Subparagraph (A) shall apply to taxable years of foreign corporations beginning after December 31, 2005, and before *January 1, 2012,* and to taxable years of United States shareholders with or within which such taxable years of foreign corporations end.

* * *

[CCH Explanation at ¶ 629. Committee Reports at ¶ 10,560.]

Amendments

• **2010, Tax Relief, Unemployment Insurance Reauthorization, and Job Creation Act of 2010 (P.L. 111-312)**

P.L. 111-312, § 751(a):

Amended Code Sec. 954(c)(6)(C) by striking "January 1, 2010" and inserting "January 1, 2012". **Effective** for tax years of foreign corporations beginning after 12-31-2009, and to tax years of United States shareholders with or within which any such tax year of such foreign corporation ends.

(h) SPECIAL RULE FOR INCOME DERIVED IN THE ACTIVE CONDUCT OF BANKING, FINANCING, OR SIMILAR BUSINESSES.—

* * *

(9) APPLICATION.—This subsection, subsection (c)(2)(C)(ii), and the last sentence of subsection (e)(2) shall apply only to taxable years of a foreign corporation beginning after December 31, 1998, and before *January 1, 2012,* and to taxable years of United States shareholders with or within which any such taxable year of such foreign corporation ends.

* * *

[CCH Explanation at ¶ 623. Committee Reports at ¶ 10,550.]

Amendments

• **2010, Tax Relief, Unemployment Insurance Reauthorization, and Job Creation Act of 2010 (P.L. 111-312)**

P.L. 111-312, § 750(a):

Amended Code Sec. 954(h)(9) by striking "January 1, 2010" and inserting "January 1, 2012". **Effective** for tax years of foreign corporations beginning after 12-31-2009, and to tax years of United States shareholders with or within which any such tax year of such foreign corporation ends.

[¶ 5490] CODE SEC. 1014. BASIS OF PROPERTY ACQUIRED FROM A DECEDENT.

* * *

⟫⟫→ *Caution: Code Sec. 1014(f) was added by P.L. 107-16, effective June 7, 2001. P.L. 111-312 removed Code Sec. 1014(f), applicable to estates of decedents dying, and transfers made, after December 31, 2009, but see P.L. 111-312, § 301(c), in the amendment notes. For sunset provision, see P.L. 107-16, § 901 [as amended by P.L. 111-312], in the amendment notes.*

(f) TERMINATION.—This section shall not apply with respect to decedents dying after December 31, 2009.

[CCH Explanation at ¶ 705, ¶ 740 and ¶ 760,. Committee Reports at ¶ 10,130.]

Amendments

• **2010, Tax Relief, Unemployment Insurance Reauthorization, and Job Creation Act of 2010 (P.L. 111-312)**

P.L. 111-312, § 301(a):

Amended Code Sec. 1014(f) to read as such provision would read if subtitle E of title V of the Economic Growth and Tax Relief Reconciliation Act of 2001 (P.L. 107-16) had never been enacted. **Effective** for estates of decedents dying, and transfers made, after 12-31-2009. For a special rule, see Act Sec. 301(c), below. Prior to amendment by P.L. 111-312, Code Sec. 1014(f) read as follows:

(f) TERMINATION.—This section shall not apply with respect to decedents dying after December 31, 2009.

P.L. 111-312, § 301(c), provides:

(c) SPECIAL ELECTION WITH RESPECT TO ESTATES OF DECEDENTS DYING IN 2010.—Notwithstanding subsection (a), in the case of an estate of a decedent dying after December 31, 2009, and before January 1, 2011, the executor (within the mean-ing of section 2203 of the Internal Revenue Code of 1986) may elect to apply such Code as though the amendments made by subsection (a) do not apply with respect to chapter 11 of such Code and with respect to property acquired or passing from such decedent (within the meaning of section 1014(b) of such Code). Such election shall be made at such time and in such manner as the Secretary of the Treasury or the Secretary's delegate shall provide. Such an election once made shall be revocable only with the consent of the Secretary of the Treasury or the Secretary's delegate. For pur-poses of section 2652(a)(1) of such Code, the determination of whether any property is subject to the tax imposed by such chapter 11 shall be made without regard to any elec-tion made under this subsection.

P.L. 111-312, § 304, provides:

SEC. 304. APPLICATION OF EGTRRA SUNSET TO THIS TITLE.

Section 901 of the Economic Growth and Tax Relief Rec-onciliation Act of 2001 shall apply to the amendments made by this title.

- **2001, Economic Growth and Tax Relief Reconciliation Act of 2001 (P.L. 107-16)**

P.L. 107-16, §541:

Amended Code Sec. 1014 by adding at the end a new subsection (f). Effective 6-7-2001.

P.L. 107-16, §901(a)-(b), as amended by P.L. 111-312, §101(a)(1), provides:

SEC. 901. SUNSET OF PROVISIONS OF ACT.

(a) In General.—All provisions of, and amendments made by, this Act shall not apply—

(1) to taxable, plan, or limitation years beginning after December 31, 2012, or

(2) in the case of title V, to estates of decedents dying, gifts made, or generation skipping transfers, after December 31, 2012.

(b) Application of Certain Laws.—The Internal Revenue Code of 1986 and the Employee Retirement Income Security Act of 1974 shall be applied and administered to years, estates, gifts, and transfers described in subsection (a) as if the provisions and amendments described in subsection (a) had never been enacted.

[¶5495] CODE SEC. 1016. ADJUSTMENTS TO BASIS.

(a) General Rule.—Proper adjustment in respect of the property shall in all cases be made—

* * *

⮕ *Caution: Code Sec. 1016(a)(26), below, as amended by P.L. 111-312, applies to tax years on or after December 31, 2011. For sunset provision, see P.L. 111-148, §10909(c) [as amended by P.L. 111-312], in the amendment notes.*

(26) to the extent provided in sections 23(g) and 137(e),

(27) in the case of a residence with respect to which a credit was allowed under section 1400C, to the extent provided in section 1400C(h),

⮕ *Caution: Code Sec. 1016(a)(28), below, was added by P.L. 107-16. For sunset provision, see P.L. 107-16, §901 [as amended by P.L. 111-312], in the amendment notes.*

(28) in the case of a facility with respect to which a credit was allowed under section 45F, to the extent provided in section 45F(f)(1),

* * *

[CCH Explanation at ¶370 and ¶522. Committee Reports at ¶10,060.]

Amendments

- **2010, Tax Relief, Unemployment Insurance Reauthorization, and Job Creation Act of 2010 (P.L. 111-312)**

P.L. 111-312, §101(b)(1):

Amended Code Sec. 1016(a)(26) to read as such provision would read if section 10909 of the Patient Protection and Affordable Care Act (P.L. 111-148) had never been enacted. Effective for tax years beginning after 12-31-2011.

- **2010, Patient Protection and Affordable Care Act (P.L. 111-148)**

P.L. 111-148, §10909(b)(2)(L):

Amended Code Sec. 1016(a)(26) by striking "23(g)" and inserting "36C(g)". Effective for tax years beginning after 12-31-2009.

P.L. 111-148, §10909(c), as amended by P.L. 111-312, §101(b)(1), provides:

(c) Sunset Provision.—Each provision of law amended by this section is amended to read as such provision would read if this section had never been enacted. The amendments made by the preceding sentence shall apply to taxable years beginning after December 31, 2011.

- **2001, Economic Growth and Tax Relief Reconciliation Act of 2001 (P.L. 107-16)**

P.L. 107-16, §205(b)(3):

Amended Code Sec. 1016(a) by striking "and" at the end of paragraph (26), by striking the period at the end of

paragraph (27) and inserting ", and", and by adding at the end a new subparagraph (28). Effective for tax years beginning after 12-31-2001.

P.L. 107-16, §901(a)-(b), as amended by P.L. 111-312, §101(a)(1), provides [but see P.L. 111-148, §10909(c), above]:

SEC. 901. SUNSET OF PROVISIONS OF ACT.

(a) In General.—All provisions of, and amendments made by, this Act shall not apply—

(1) to taxable, plan, or limitation years beginning after December 31, 2012, or

(2) in the case of title V, to estates of decedents dying, gifts made, or generation skipping transfers, after December 31, 2012.

(b) Application of Certain Laws.—The Internal Revenue Code of 1986 and the Employee Retirement Income Security Act of 1974 shall be applied and administered to years, estates, gifts, and transfers described in subsection (a) as if the provisions and amendments described in subsection (a) had never been enacted.

»»→ Caution: Code Sec. 1022 was added by P.L. 107-16, applicable to estates of decedents dying after December 31, 2009. P.L. 111-312 removed Code Sec. 1022, applicable to estates of decedents dying, and transfers made, after December 31, 2009, but see P.L. 111-312, §301(c), in the amendment notes. For sunset provision, see P.L. 107-16, §901 [as amended by P.L. 111-312], in the amendment notes.

[¶5500] CODE SEC. 1022. TREATMENT OF PROPERTY ACQUIRED FROM A DECEDENT DYING AFTER DECEMBER 31, 2009.

(a) IN GENERAL.—Except as otherwise provided in this section—

(1) property acquired from a decedent dying after December 31, 2009, shall be treated for purposes of this subtitle as transferred by gift, and

(2) the basis of the person acquiring property from such a decedent shall be the lesser of—

(A) the adjusted basis of the decedent, or

(B) the fair market value of the property at the date of the decedent's death.

(b) BASIS INCREASE FOR CERTAIN PROPERTY.—

(1) IN GENERAL.—In the case of property to which this subsection applies, the basis of such property under subsection (a) shall be increased by its basis increase under this subsection.

(2) BASIS INCREASE.—For purposes of this subsection—

(A) IN GENERAL.—The basis increase under this subsection for any property is the portion of the aggregate basis increase which is allocated to the property pursuant to this section.

(B) AGGREGATE BASIS INCREASE.—In the case of any estate, the aggregate basis increase under this subsection is $1,300,000.

(C) LIMIT INCREASED BY UNUSED BUILT-IN LOSSES AND LOSS CARRYOVERS.—The limitation under subparagraph (B) shall be increased by—

(i) the sum of the amount of any capital loss carryover under section 1212(b), and the amount of any net operating loss carryover under section 172, which would (but for the decedent's death) be carried from the decedent's last taxable year to a later taxable year of the decedent, plus

(ii) the sum of the amount of any losses that would have been allowable under section 165 if the property acquired from the decedent had been sold at fair market value immediately before the decedent's death.

(3) DECEDENT NONRESIDENTS WHO ARE NOT CITIZENS OF THE UNITED STATES.—In the case of a decedent nonresident not a citizen of the United States—

(A) paragraph (2)(B) shall be applied by substituting "$60,000" for "$1,300,000", and

(B) paragraph (2)(C) shall not apply.

(c) ADDITIONAL BASIS INCREASE FOR PROPERTY ACQUIRED BY SURVIVING SPOUSE.—

(1) IN GENERAL.—In the case of property to which this subsection applies and which is qualified spousal property, the basis of such property under subsection (a) (as increased under subsection (b)) shall be increased by its spousal property basis increase.

(2) SPOUSAL PROPERTY BASIS INCREASE.—For purposes of this subsection—

(A) IN GENERAL.—The spousal property basis increase for property referred to in paragraph (1) is the portion of the aggregate spousal property basis increase which is allocated to the property pursuant to this section.

(B) AGGREGATE SPOUSAL PROPERTY BASIS INCREASE.—In the case of any estate, the aggregate spousal property basis increase is $3,000,000.

(3) QUALIFIED SPOUSAL PROPERTY.—For purposes of this subsection, the term "qualified spousal property" means—

(A) outright transfer property, and

(B) qualified terminable interest property.

(4) OUTRIGHT TRANSFER PROPERTY.—For purposes of this subsection—

(A) IN GENERAL.—The term "outright transfer property" means any interest in property acquired from the decedent by the decedent's surviving spouse.

(B) EXCEPTION.—Subparagraph (A) shall not apply where, on the lapse of time, on the occurrence of an event or contingency, or on the failure of an event or contingency to occur, an interest passing to the surviving spouse will terminate or fail—

(i) (I) if an interest in such property passes or has passed (for less than an adequate and full consideration in money or money's worth) from the decedent to any person other than such surviving spouse (or the estate of such spouse), and

(II) if by reason of such passing such person (or his heirs or assigns) may possess or enjoy any part of such property after such termination or failure of the interest so passing to the surviving spouse, or

(ii) if such interest is to be acquired for the surviving spouse, pursuant to directions of the decedent, by his executor or by the trustee of a trust.

For purposes of this subparagraph, an interest shall not be considered as an interest which will terminate or fail merely because it is the ownership of a bond, note, or similar contractual obligation, the discharge of which would not have the effect of an annuity for life or for a term.

(C) INTEREST OF SPOUSE CONDITIONAL ON SURVIVAL FOR LIMITED PERIOD.—For purposes of this paragraph, an interest passing to the surviving spouse shall not be considered as an interest which will terminate or fail on the death of such spouse if—

(i) such death will cause a termination or failure of such interest only if it occurs within a period not exceeding 6 months after the decedent's death, or only if it occurs as a result of a common disaster resulting in the death of the decedent and the surviving spouse, or only if it occurs in the case of either such event, and

(ii) such termination or failure does not in fact occur.

(5) QUALIFIED TERMINABLE INTEREST PROPERTY.—For purposes of this subsection—

(A) IN GENERAL.—The term "qualified terminable interest property" means property—

(i) which passes from the decedent, and

(ii) in which the surviving spouse has a qualifying income interest for life.

(B) QUALIFYING INCOME INTEREST FOR LIFE.—The surviving spouse has a qualifying income interest for life if—

(i) the surviving spouse is entitled to all the income from the property, payable annually or at more frequent intervals, or has a usufruct interest for life in the property, and

(ii) no person has a power to appoint any part of the property to any person other than the surviving spouse.

Clause (ii) shall not apply to a power exercisable only at or after the death of the surviving spouse. To the extent provided in regulations, an annuity shall be treated in a manner similar to an income interest in property (regardless of whether the property from which the annuity is payable can be separately identified).

(C) PROPERTY INCLUDES INTEREST THEREIN.—The term "property" includes an interest in property.

(D) SPECIFIC PORTION TREATED AS SEPARATE PROPERTY.—A specific portion of property shall be treated as separate property. For purposes of the preceding sentence, the term "specific portion" only includes a portion determined on a fractional or percentage basis.

(d) DEFINITIONS AND SPECIAL RULES FOR APPLICATION OF SUBSECTIONS (b) AND (c).—

(1) PROPERTY TO WHICH SUBSECTIONS (b) AND (c) APPLY.—

(A) IN GENERAL.—The basis of property acquired from a decedent may be increased under subsection (b) or (c) only if the property was owned by the decedent at the time of death.

(B) RULES RELATING TO OWNERSHIP.—

(i) JOINTLY HELD PROPERTY.—In the case of property which was owned by the decedent and another person as joint tenants with right of survivorship or tenants by the entirety—

(I) if the only such other person is the surviving spouse, the decedent shall be treated as the owner of only 50 percent of the property,

(II) in any case (to which subclause (I) does not apply) in which the decedent furnished consideration for the acquisition of the property, the decedent shall be treated as the owner to the extent of the portion of the property which is proportionate to such consideration, and

(III) in any case (to which subclause (I) does not apply) in which the property has been acquired by gift, bequest, devise, or inheritance by the decedent and any other person as joint tenants with right of survivorship and their interests are not otherwise specified or fixed by law, the decedent shall be treated as the owner to the extent of the value of a fractional part to be determined by dividing the value of the property by the number of joint tenants with right of survivorship.

(ii) REVOCABLE TRUSTS.—The decedent shall be treated as owning property transferred by the decedent during life to a qualified revocable trust (as defined in section 645(b)(1)).

(iii) POWERS OF APPOINTMENT.—The decedent shall not be treated as owning any property by reason of holding a power of appointment with respect to such property.

(iv) COMMUNITY PROPERTY.—Property which represents the surviving spouse's one-half share of community property held by the decedent and the surviving spouse under the community property laws of any State or possession of the United States or any foreign country shall be treated for purposes of this section as owned by, and acquired from, the decedent if at least one-half of the whole of the community interest in such property is treated as owned by, and acquired from, the decedent without regard to this clause.

(C) PROPERTY ACQUIRED BY DECEDENT BY GIFT WITHIN 3 YEARS OF DEATH.—

(i) IN GENERAL.—Subsections (b) and (c) shall not apply to property acquired by the decedent by gift or by inter vivos transfer for less than adequate and full consideration in money or money's worth during the 3-year period ending on the date of the decedent's death.

(ii) EXCEPTION FOR CERTAIN GIFTS FROM SPOUSE.—Clause (i) shall not apply to property acquired by the decedent from the decedent's spouse unless, during such 3-year period, such spouse acquired the property in whole or in part by gift or by inter vivos transfer for less than adequate and full consideration in money or money's worth.

(D) STOCK OF CERTAIN ENTITIES.—Subsections (b) and (c) shall not apply to—

(i) stock or securities of a foreign personal holding company,

(ii) stock of a DISC or former DISC,

(iii) stock of a foreign investment company, or

(iv) stock of a passive foreign investment company unless such company is a qualified electing fund (as defined in section 1295) with respect to the decedent.

(2) FAIR MARKET VALUE LIMITATION.—The adjustments under subsections (b) and (c) shall not increase the basis of any interest in property acquired from the decedent above its fair market value in the hands of the decedent as of the date of the decedent's death.

(3) ALLOCATION RULES.—

(A) IN GENERAL.—The executor shall allocate the adjustments under subsections (b) and (c) on the return required by section 6018.

(B) CHANGES IN ALLOCATION.—Any allocation made pursuant to subparagraph (A) may be changed only as provided by the Secretary.

(4) INFLATION ADJUSTMENT OF BASIS ADJUSTMENT AMOUNTS.—

(A) IN GENERAL.—In the case of decedents dying in a calendar year after 2010, the $1,300,000, $60,000, and $3,000,000 dollar amounts in subsections (b) and (c)(2)(B) shall each be increased by an amount equal to the product of—

(i) such dollar amount, and

(ii) the cost-of-living adjustment determined under section 1(f)(3) for such calendar year, determined by substituting "2009" for "1992" in subparagraph (B) thereof.

(B) ROUNDING.—If any increase determined under subparagraph (A) is not a multiple of—

(i) $100,000 in the case of the $1,300,000 amount,

(ii) $5,000 in the case of the $60,000 amount, and

(iii) $250,000 in the case of the $3,000,000 amount,

such increase shall be rounded to the next lowest multiple thereof.

(e) PROPERTY ACQUIRED FROM THE DECEDENT.—For purposes of this section, the following property shall be considered to have been acquired from the decedent:

(1) Property acquired by bequest, devise, or inheritance, or by the decedent's estate from the decedent.

(2) Property transferred by the decedent during his lifetime—

(A) to a qualified revocable trust (as defined in section 645(b)(1)), or

(B) to any other trust with respect to which the decedent reserved the right to make any change in the enjoyment thereof through the exercise of a power to alter, amend, or terminate the trust.

(3) Any other property passing from the decedent by reason of death to the extent that such property passed without consideration.

(f) COORDINATION WITH SECTION 691.—This section shall not apply to property which constitutes a right to receive an item of income in respect of a decedent under section 691.

(g) CERTAIN LIABILITIES DISREGARDED.—

(1) IN GENERAL.—In determining whether gain is recognized on the acquisition of property—

(A) from a decedent by a decedent's estate or any beneficiary other than a tax-exempt beneficiary, and

(B) from the decedent's estate by any beneficiary other than a tax-exempt beneficiary,

and in determining the adjusted basis of such property, liabilities in excess of basis shall be disregarded.

(2) TAX-EXEMPT BENEFICIARY.—For purposes of paragraph (1), the term "tax-exempt beneficiary" means—

(A) the United States, any State or political subdivision thereof, any possession of the United States, any Indian tribal government (within the meaning of section 7871), or any agency or instrumentality of any of the foregoing,

(B) an organization (other than a cooperative described in section 521) which is exempt from tax imposed by chapter 1,

(C) any foreign person or entity (within the meaning of section 168(h)(2)), and

(D) to the extent provided in regulations, any person to whom property is transferred for the principal purpose of tax avoidance.

(h) REGULATIONS.—The Secretary shall prescribe such regulations as may be necessary to carry out the purposes of this section.

[CCH Explanation at ¶705, ¶740, ¶750, ¶760, ¶765, ¶770 and ¶775. Committee Reports at ¶10,130.]

Amendments

• **2010, Tax Relief, Unemployment Insurance Reauthorization, and Job Creation Act of 2010 (P.L. 111-312)**

P.L. 111-312, §301(a):

Amended Code Sec. 1022 to read as such provision would read if subtitle E of title V of the Economic Growth and Tax Relief Reconciliation Act of 2001 (P.L. 107-16) had never been enacted. **Effective** for estates of decedents dying, and transfers made, after 12-31-2009. For a special rule, see Act Sec. 301(c), below.

P.L. 111-312, §301(c), provides:

(c) SPECIAL ELECTION TO ESTATES OF DECEDENTS DYING IN 2010.—Notwithstanding subsection (a), in the case of an estate of a decedent dying after December 31, 2009, and before January 1, 2011, the executor (within the meaning of section 2203 of the Internal Revenue Code of 1986) may elect to apply such Code as though the amendments made by subsection (a) do not apply with respect to chapter 11 of such Code and with respect to property acquired or passing from such decedent (within the meaning of section 1014(b) of such Code). Such election shall be made at such time and in such manner as the Secretary of the Treasury or the Secretary's delegate shall provide. Such an election once made shall be revocable only with the consent of the Secretary of the Treasury or the Secretary's delegate. For purposes of section 2652(a)(1) of such Code, the determination of whether any property is subject to the tax imposed by such chapter 11 shall be made without regard to any election made under this subsection.

P.L. 111-312, §304, provides:

SEC. 304. APPLICATION OF EGTRRA SUNSET TO THIS TITLE.

Section 901 of the Economic Growth and Tax Relief Reconciliation Act of 2001 shall apply to the amendments made by this title.

• **2001, Economic Growth and Tax Relief Reconciliation Act of 2001 (P.L. 107-16)**

P.L. 107-16, §542(a):

Amended part II of subchapter O of chapter 1 by inserting after Code Sec. 1021 a new Code Sec. 1022. **Effective** for estates of decedents dying after 12-31-2009.

P.L. 107-16, §901(a)-(b), as amended by P.L. 111-312, §101(a)(1), provides:

SEC. 901. SUNSET OF PROVISIONS OF ACT.

(a) IN GENERAL.—All provisions of, and amendments made by, this Act shall not apply—

(1) to taxable, plan, or limitation years beginning after December 31, 2012, or

(2) in the case of title V, to estates of decedents dying, gifts made, or generation skipping transfers, after December 31, 2012.

(b) APPLICATION OF CERTAIN LAWS.—The Internal Revenue Code of 1986 and the Employee Retirement Income Security Act of 1974 shall be applied and administered to years, estates, gifts, and transfers described in subsection (a) as if the provisions and amendments described in subsection (a) had never been enacted.

⋙→ *Caution: Code Sec. 1040, below, as amended by P.L. 111-312, applies to estates of decedents dying, and transfers made, after December 31, 2009. For sunset provision, see P.L. 107-16, §901 [as amended by P.L. 111-312], in the amendment notes.*

[¶5505] CODE SEC. 1040. TRANSFER OF CERTAIN FARM, ETC., REAL PROPERTY.

(a) GENERAL RULE.—*If the executor of the estate of any decedent transfers to a qualified heir (within the meaning of section 2032A(e)(1) any property with respect to which an election was made under section 2032A, then gain on such transfer shall be recognized to the estate only to the extent that, on the date of such transfer, the fair market value of such property exceeds the value of such property for purposes of chapter 11 (determined without regard to section 2032A).*

(b) SIMILAR RULE FOR CERTAIN TRUSTS.—*To the extent provided in regulations prescribed by the Secretary, a rule similar to the rule provided in subsection (a) shall apply where the trustee of a trust (any portion of which is included in the gross estate of the decedent) transfers property with respect to which an election was made under section 2032A.*

(c) BASIS OF PROPERTY ACQUIRED IN TRANSFER DESCRIBED IN SUBSECTION (a) OR (b).—*The basis of property acquired in a transfer with respect to which gain realized is not recognized by reason of subsection (a) or (b) shall be the basis of such property immediately before the transfer increased by the amount of the gain recognized to the estate or trust on the transfer.*

[CCH Explanation at ¶705 and ¶755. Committee Reports at ¶10,130.]

Amendments

- **2010, Tax Relief, Unemployment Insurance Reauthorization, and Job Creation Act of 2010 (P.L. 111-312)**

P.L. 111-312, §301(a):

Amended Code Sec. 1040 to read as such provision would read if subtitle E of title V of the Economic Growth and Tax Relief Reconciliation Act of 2001 (P.L. 107-16) had never been enacted. **Effective** for estates of decedents dying, and transfers made, after 12-31-2009. For a special rule, see Act Sec. 301(c), below. Prior to amendment by P.L. 111-312, Code Sec. 1040 read as follows:

SEC. 1040. USE OF APPRECIATED CARRYOVER BASIS PROPERTY TO SATISFY PECUNIARY BEQUEST.

(a) In General.—If the executor of the estate of any decedent satisfies the right of any person to receive a pecuniary bequest with appreciated property, then gain on such exchange shall be recognized to the estate only to the extent that, on the date of such exchange, the fair market value of such property exceeds such value on the date of death.

(b) Similar Rule for Certain Trusts.—To the extent provided in regulations prescribed by the Secretary, a rule similar to the rule provided in subsection (a) shall apply where—

(1) by reason of the death of the decedent, a person has a right to receive from a trust a specific dollar amount which is the equivalent of a pecuniary bequest, and

(2) the trustee of a trust satisfies such right with property.

(c) Basis of Property Acquired in Exchange Described in Subsection (a) or (b).—The basis of property acquired in an exchange with respect to which gain realized is not recognized by reason of subsection (a) or (b) shall be the basis of such property immediately before the exchange increased by the amount of the gain recognized to the estate or trust on the exchange.

P.L. 111-312, §301(c), provides:

(c) Special Election With Respect to Estates of Decedents Dying in 2010.—Notwithstanding subsection (a), in the case of an estate of a decedent dying after December 31, 2009, and before January 1, 2011, the executor (within the meaning of section 2203 of the Internal Revenue Code of 1986) may elect to apply such Code as though the amendments made by subsection (a) do not apply with respect to chapter 11 of such Code and with respect to property acquired or passing from such decedent (within the meaning of section 1014(b) of such Code). Such election shall be made at such time and in such manner as the Secretary of the Treasury or the Secretary's delegate shall provide. Such an election once made shall be revocable only with the consent of the Secretary of the Treasury or the Secretary's delegate. For purposes of section 2652(a)(1) of such Code, the determination of whether any property is subject to the tax imposed by such chapter 11 shall be made without regard to any election made under this subsection.

P.L. 111-312, §304, provides:

SEC. 304. APPLICATION OF EGTRRA SUNSET TO THIS TITLE.

Section 901 of the Economic Growth and Tax Relief Reconciliation Act of 2001 shall apply to the amendments made by this title.

- **2001, Economic Growth and Tax Relief Reconciliation Act of 2001 (P.L. 107-16)**

P.L. 107-16, §542(d)(1):

Amended Code Sec. 1040. **Effective** for estates of decedents dying after 12-31-2009. Prior to amendment, Code Sec. 1040 read as follows:

SEC. 1040. TRANSFER OF CERTAIN FARM, ETC., REAL PROPERTY.

(a) General Rule.—If the executor of the estate of any decedent transfers to a qualified heir (within the meaning of section 2032A(e)(1) any property with respect to which an election was made under section 2032A, then gain on such transfer shall be recognized to the estate only to the extent that, on the date of such transfer, the fair market value of such property exceeds the value of such property for purposes of chapter 11 (determined without regard to section 2032A).

(b) Similar Rule for Certain Trusts.—To the extent provided in regulations prescribed by the Secretary, a rule similar to the rule provided in subsection (a) shall apply where the trustee of a trust (any portion of which is included in the gross estate of the decedent) transfers property with respect to which an election was made under section 2032A.

(c) Basis of Property Acquired in Transfer Described in Subsection (a) or (b).—The basis of property acquired in a transfer with respect to which gain realized is not recognized by reason of subsection (a) or (b) shall be the basis of such property immediately before the transfer increased by the amount of the gain recognized to the estate or trust on the transfer.

P.L. 107-16, §901(a)-(b), as amended by P.L. 111-312, §101(a)(1), provides:

SEC. 901. SUNSET OF PROVISIONS OF ACT.

(a) In General.—All provisions of, and amendments made by, this Act shall not apply—

(1) to taxable, plan, or limitation years beginning after December 31, 2012, or

(2) in the case of title V, to estates of decedents dying, gifts made, or generation skipping transfers, after December 31, 2012.

(b) Application of Certain Laws.—The Internal Revenue Code of 1986 and the Employee Retirement Income Security Act of 1974 shall be applied and administered to years, estates, gifts, and transfers described in subsection (a) as if the provisions and amendments described in subsection (a) had never been enacted.

[¶5510] CODE SEC. 1202. PARTIAL EXCLUSION FOR GAIN FROM CERTAIN SMALL BUSINESS STOCK.

(a) EXCLUSION.—

* * *

(2) EMPOWERMENT ZONE BUSINESSES.—

* * *

(C) GAIN AFTER *2016* NOT QUALIFIED.—Subparagraph (A) shall not apply to gain attributable to periods after *December 31, 2016.*

* * *

(4) 100 PERCENT EXCLUSION FOR STOCK ACQUIRED DURING CERTAIN PERIODS IN 2010 AND *2011.*—In the case of qualified small business stock acquired after the date of the enactment of the Creating Small Business Jobs Act of 2010 and before *January 1, 2012*—

(A) paragraph (1) shall be applied by substituting "100 percent" for "50 percent",

(B) paragraph (2) shall not apply, and

(C) paragraph (7) of section 57(a) shall not apply.

[CCH Explanation at ¶418 and ¶440. Committee Reports at ¶10,580 and ¶10,660.]

Amendments

● **2010, Tax Relief, Unemployment Insurance Reauthorization, and Job Creation Act of 2010 (P.L. 111-312)**

P.L. 111-312, §753(b)(1)-(2):

Amended Code Sec. 1202(a)(2)(C) by striking "December 31, 2014" and inserting "December 31, 2016"; and by strik-ing "2014" in the heading and inserting "2016". **Effective for** periods after 12-31-2009.

P.L. 111-312, §760(a)(1)-(2):

Amended Code Sec. 1202(a)(4) by striking "January 1, 2011" and inserting "January 1, 2012", and by inserting "AND 2011" after "2010" in the heading thereof. **Effective for** stock acquired after 12-31-2010.

[¶5515] CODE SEC. 1212. CAPITAL LOSS CARRYBACKS AND CARRYOVERS.

(a) CORPORATIONS.—

(1) IN GENERAL.—If a corporation has a net capital loss for any taxable year (hereinafter in this paragraph referred to as the "loss year"), the amount thereof shall be—

* * *

(C) *a capital loss carryover to each of the 10 taxable years succeeding the loss year, but only to the extent such loss is attributable to a foreign expropriation loss,*

* * *

(3) *REGULATED INVESTMENT COMPANIES.*—

(A) IN GENERAL.—*If a regulated investment company has a net capital loss for any taxable year*—

(i) *paragraph (1) shall not apply to such loss,*

(ii) *the excess of the net short-term capital loss over the net long-term capital gain for such year shall be a short-term capital loss arising on the first day of the next taxable year, and*

(iii) *the excess of the net long-term capital loss over the net short-term capital gain for such year shall be a long-term capital loss arising on the first day of the next taxable year.*

(B) COORDINATION WITH GENERAL RULE.—*If a net capital loss to which paragraph (1) applies is carried over to a taxable year of a regulated investment company*—

(i) *LOSSES TO WHICH THIS PARAGRAPH APPLIES.—Clauses (ii) and (iii) of subparagraph (A) shall be applied without regard to any amount treated as a short-term capital loss under paragraph (1).*

(ii) *LOSSES TO WHICH GENERAL RULE APPLIES.—Paragraph (1) shall be applied by substituting "net capital loss for the loss year or any taxable year thereafter (other than a net capital loss* to which paragraph (3)(A) applies)" for "net capital loss for the loss year or any taxable year thereafter".

(4) SPECIAL RULES ON CARRYBACKS.—A net capital loss of a corporation shall not be carried back under paragraph (1)(A) to a taxable year—

(A) for which it is a regulated investment company (as defined in section 851), or

(B) for which it is a real estate investment trust (as defined in section 856).

[CCH Explanation at ¶803.]

Amendments

• 2010, Regulated Investment Company Modernization Act of 2010 (H.R. 4337)

H.R. 4337, §101(a):

Amended Code Sec. 1212(a) by redesignating paragraph (3) as paragraph (4) and by inserting after paragraph (2) a new paragraph (3). **Effective** generally for net capital losses for tax years beginning after the date of the enactment of this Act. For a special rule, see Act Sec. 101(c)(2), below.

H.R. 4337, §101(b)(1):

Amended Code Sec. 1212(a)(1)(C). **Effective** for net capital losses for tax years beginning after the date of the enactment of this Act. Prior to amendment, Code Sec. 1212(a)(1)(C) read as follows:

(C) a capital loss carryover—

(i) in the case of a regulated investment company (as defined in section 851) to each of the 8 taxable years succeeding the loss year, and

(ii) to the extent such loss is attributable to a foreign expropriation capital loss, to each of the 10 taxable years succeeding the loss year,

H.R. 4337, §101(c)(2), provides:

(2) COORDINATION RULES.—Subparagraph (B) of section 1212(a)(3) of the Internal Revenue Code of 1986, as added by this section, shall apply to taxable years beginning after the date of the enactment of this Act.

[¶5520] CODE SEC. 1221. CAPITAL ASSET DEFINED.

(a) IN GENERAL.—For purposes of this subtitle, the term "capital asset" means property held by the taxpayer (whether or not connected with his trade or business), but does not include—

* * *

(3) a copyright, a literary, musical, or artistic composition, a letter or memorandum, or similar property, held by—

* * *

⟫→ Caution: *Code Sec. 1221(a)(3)(C), below, as amended by P.L. 111-312, applies to estates of decedents dying, and transfers made, after December 31, 2009. For sunset provision, see P.L. 107-16, §901 [as amended by P.L. 111-312], in the amendment notes.*

(C) a taxpayer in whose hands the basis of such property is determined, for purposes of determining gain from a sale or exchange, in whole or part by reference to the basis of such property in the hands of a taxpayer described in subparagraph (A) or (B);

* * *

[CCH Explanation at ¶705 and ¶760. Committee Reports at ¶10,130.]

Amendments

• 2010, Tax Relief, Unemployment Insurance Reauthorization, and Job Creation Act of 2010 (P.L. 111-312)

P.L. 111-312, §301(a):

Amended Code Sec. 1221(a)(3)(C) to read as such provision would read if subtitle E of title V of the Economic Growth and Tax Relief Reconciliation Act of 2001 (P.L. 107-16) had never been enacted. **Effective** for estates of decedents dying, and transfers made, after 12-31-2009. For a special rule, see Act Sec. 301(c), below. Prior to amendment by P.L. 111-312, Code Sec. 1221(c)(3)(C) read as follows:

(C) a taxpayer in whose hands the basis of such property is determined (other than by reason of section 1022), for purposes of determining gain from a sale or exchange, in whole or part by reference to the basis of such property in the hands of a taxpayer described in subparagraph (A) or (B);

P.L. 111-312, §301(c), provides:

(c) SPECIAL ELECTION WITH RESPECT TO ESTATES OF DECEDENTS DYING IN 2010.—Notwithstanding subsection (a), in the case of an estate of a decedent dying after December 31, 2009, and before January 1, 2011, the executor (within the meaning of section 2203 of the Internal Revenue Code of 1986) may elect to apply such Code as though the amendments made by subsection (a) do not apply with respect to chapter 11 of such Code and with respect to property acquired or passing from such decedent (within the meaning of section 1014(b) of such Code). Such election shall be made at such time and in such manner as the Secretary of the Treasury or the Secretary's delegate shall provide. Such an election once made shall be revocable only with the consent of the Secretary of the Treasury or the Secretary's delegate. For purposes of section 2652(a)(1) of such Code, the determination of whether any property is subject to the tax imposed by such chapter 11 shall be made without regard to any election made under this subsection.

P.L. 111-312, §304, provides:

SEC. 304. APPLICATION OF EGTRRA SUNSET TO THIS TITLE.

Section 901 of the Economic Growth and Tax Relief Reconciliation Act of 2001 shall apply to the amendments made by this title.

• **2001, Economic Growth and Tax Relief Reconciliation Act of 2001 (P.L. 107-16)**

P.L. 107-16, §542(e)(2)(A):

Amended Code Sec. 1221(a)(3)(C) by inserting "(other than by reason of section 1022)" after "is determined". **Effective** for estates of decedents dying after 12-31-2009.

P.L. 107-16, §901(a)-(b), as amended by P.L. 111-312, §101(a)(1), provides:

SEC. 901. SUNSET OF PROVISIONS OF ACT.

(a) In General.—All provisions of, and amendments made by, this Act shall not apply—

(1) to taxable, plan, or limitation years beginning after December 31, 2012, or

(2) in the case of title V, to estates of decedents dying, gifts made, or generation skipping transfers, after December 31, 2012.

(b) Application of Certain Laws.—The Internal Revenue Code of 1986 and the Employee Retirement Income Security Act of 1974 shall be applied and administered to years, estates, gifts, and transfers described in subsection (a) as if the provisions and amendments described in subsection (a) had never been enacted.

[¶5525] CODE SEC. 1222. OTHER TERMS RELATING TO CAPITAL GAINS AND LOSSES.

* * *

(10) Net Capital Loss.—The term "net capital loss" means the excess of the losses from sales or exchanges of capital assets over the sum allowed under section 1211. In the case of a corporation, for the purpose of determining losses under this paragraph, amounts which are short-term capital losses under *section 1212(a)(1)* shall be excluded.

* * *

[CCH Explanation at ¶803.]

Amendments

• **2010, Regulated Investment Company Modernization Act of 2010 (H.R. 4337)**

H.R. 4337, §101(b)(2):

Amended Code Sec. 1222(10) by striking "section 1212" and inserting "section 1212(a)(1)". **Effective** for net capital losses for tax years beginning after the date of the enactment of this Act.

[¶5530] CODE SEC. 1246. GAIN ON FOREIGN INVESTMENT COMPANY STOCK. [Repealed.]

[CCH Explanation at ¶705 and ¶760. Committee Reports at ¶10,130.]

Amendments

• **2010, Tax Relief, Unemployment Insurance Reauthorization, and Job Creation Act of 2010 (P.L. 111-312)**

P.L. 111-312, §301(a):

Amended Code Sec. 1246(e) to read as such provision would read if subtitle E of title V of the Economic Growth and Tax Relief Reconciliation Act of 2001 (P.L. 107-16) had never been enacted. **Effective** for estates of decedents dying, and transfers made, after 12-31-2009. For a special rule, see Act Sec. 301(c), below. [Note: P.L. 107-16 struck Code Sec. 301(c). Thus, the amendment by P.L. 111-312 effectively reinstates Code Sec. 1246(e) as it read prior to being stricken by P.L. 107-16. P.L. 108-357, §413(a)(2), however, repealed Code Sec. 1246 in its entirety, so this amendment made by P.L. 111-312 cannot be made.]

P.L. 111-312, §301(c), provides:

(c) Special Election With Respect to Estates of Decedents Dying in 2010.—Notwithstanding subsection (a), in the case of an estate of a decedent dying after December 31, 2009, and before January 1, 2011, the executor (within the meaning of section 2203 of the Internal Revenue Code of 1986) may elect to apply such Code as though the amendments made by subsection (a) do not apply with respect to chapter 11 of such Code and with respect to property acquired or passing from such decedent (within the meaning of section 1014(b) of such Code). Such election shall be made at such time and in such manner as the Secretary of the Treasury or the Secretary's delegate shall provide. Such an election once made shall be revocable only with the consent of the Secretary of the Treasury or the Secretary's delegate. For purposes of section 2652(a)(1) of such Code, the determination of whether any property is subject to the tax imposed by such chapter 11 shall be made without regard to any election made under this subsection.

P.L. 111-312, §304, provides:

SEC. 304. APPLICATION OF EGTRRA SUNSET TO THIS TITLE.

Section 901 of the Economic Growth and Tax Relief Reconciliation Act of 2001 shall apply to the amendments made by this title.

- **2004, American Jobs Creation Act of 2004 (P.L. 108-357)**

P.L. 108-357, § 413(a)(2):

Repealed Code Sec. 1246. **Effective** for tax years of foreign corporations beginning after 12-31-2004, and for tax years of United States shareholders with or within which such tax years of foreign corporations end. Prior to repeal, Code Sec. 1246(e) read as follows:

- **2001, Economic Growth and Tax Relief Reconciliation Act of 2001 (P.L. 107-16)**

P.L. 107-16, § 542(e)(5)(A):

Amended Code Sec. 1246 by striking subsection (e). **Effective** for estates of decedents dying after 12-31-2009. Prior to being stricken, Code Sec. 1246(e) read as follows:

(e) Rules Relating to Stock Acquired from a Decedent.—

(1) Basis.—In the case of stock of a foreign investment company acquired by bequest, devise, or inheritance (or by the decedent's estate) from a decedent dying after December 31, 1962, the basis determined under section 1014 shall be reduced (but not below the adjusted basis of such stock in the hands of the decedent immediately before his death) by the amount of the decedent's ratable share of the earnings and profits of such company accumulated after December 31, 1962. Any stock so acquired shall be treated as stock described in subsection (c).

(2) Deduction for estate tax.—If stock to which subsection (a) applies is acquired from a decedent, the taxpayer shall, under regulations prescribed by the Secretary or his delegate, be allowed (for the taxable year of the sale or exchange) a deduction from gross income equal to that portion of the decedent's estate tax deemed paid which is attributable to the excess of (A) the value at which such stock was taken into account for purposes of determining the value of the decedent's gross estate, over (B) the value at which it would have been so taken into account if such value had been reduced by the amount described in paragraph (1).

P.L. 107-16, § 901(a)-(b) [as amended by P.L. 111-312, § 101(a)(1)], provides:

SEC. 901. SUNSET OF PROVISIONS OF ACT.

(a) In General.—All provisions of, and amendments made by, this Act shall not apply—

(1) to taxable, plan, or limitation years beginning after December 31, 2012, or

(2) in the case of title V, to estates of decedents dying, gifts made, or generation skipping transfers, after December 31, 2012.

(b) Application of Certain Laws.—The Internal Revenue Code of 1986 and the Employee Retirement Income Security Act of 1974 shall be applied and administered to years, estates, gifts, and transfers described in subsection (a) as if the provisions and amendments described in subsection (a) had never been enacted.

[¶ 5535] CODE SEC. 1255. GAIN FROM DISPOSITION OF SECTION 126 PROPERTY.

* * *

(b) Special Rules.—Under regulations prescribed by the Secretary—

* * *

⟫⟶ Caution: *Code Sec. 1255(b)(2), below, was amended by P.L. 108-27. For sunset provision, see P.L. 108-27, §303 [as amended by P.L. 111-312], in the amendment notes.*

(2) for purposes of sections 170(e) and 751(c), amounts treated as ordinary income under this section shall be treated in the same manner as amounts treated as ordinary income under section 1245.

[CCH Explanation at ¶ 425 and ¶ 609. Committee Reports at ¶ 10,080.]

Amendments

- **2003, Jobs and Growth Tax Relief Reconciliation Act of 2003 (P.L. 108-27)**

P.L. 108-27, § 302(e)(4)(B)(ii):

Amended Code Sec. 1255(b)(2) by striking ", 341(e)(12)," after "170(e)". For the **effective** date, see Act Sec. 302(f), as amended by P.L. 108-311, § 402(a)(6), below.

P.L. 108-27, § 302(f), as amended by P.L. 108-311, § 402(a)(6), provides:

(f) Effective Date.—

(1) In General.—Except as provided in paragraph (2), the amendments made by this section shall apply to taxable years beginning after December 31, 2002.

(2) Pass-thru entities.—In the case of a pass-thru entity described in subparagraph (A), (B), (C), (D), (E), or (F) of section 1(h)(10) of the Internal Revenue Code of 1986, as amended by this Act, the amendments made by this section shall apply to taxable years ending after December 31, 2002; except that dividends received by such an entity on or before such date shall not be treated as qualified dividend income (as defined in section 1(h)(11)(B) of such Code, as added by this Act).

P.L. 108-27, § 303, as amended by P.L. 109-222, § 102, and P.L. 111-312, § 102(a), provides:

SEC. 303. SUNSET OF TITLE.

All provisions of, and amendments made by, this title shall not apply to taxable years beginning after December 31, 2012, and the Internal Revenue Code of 1986 shall be applied and administered to such years as if such provisions and amendments had never been enacted.

[¶ 5540] CODE SEC. 1257. DISPOSITION OF CONVERTED WETLANDS OR HIGHLY ERODIBLE CROPLANDS.

* * *

⟫→ *Caution: Code Sec. 1257(d), below, was amended by P.L. 108-27. For sunset provision, see P.L. 108-27, §303 [as amended by P.L. 111-312], in the amendment notes.*

(d) SPECIAL RULES.—Under regulations prescribed by the Secretary, rules similar to the rules applicable under section 1245 shall apply for purposes of subsection (a). For purposes of sections 170(e) and 751(c), amounts treated as ordinary income under subsection (a) shall be treated in the same manner as amounts treated as ordinary income under section 1245.

[CCH Explanation at ¶ 425 and ¶ 609. Committee Reports at ¶ 10,080.]

Amendments

• **2003, Jobs and Growth Tax Relief Reconciliation Act of 2003 (P.L. 108-27)**

P.L. 108-27, §302(e)(4)(B)(ii):

Amended Code Sec. 1257(d) by striking ", 341(e)(12)," after "170(e)". For the **effective** date, see Act Sec. 302(f), as amended by P.L. 108-311, §402(a)(6), below.

P.L. 108-27, §302(f), as amended by P.L. 108-311, §402(a)(6), provides:

(f) EFFECTIVE DATE.—

(1) IN GENERAL.—Except as provided in paragraph (2), the amendments made by this section shall apply to taxable years beginning after December 31, 2002.

(2) PASS-THRU ENTITIES.—In the case of a pass-thru entity described in subparagraph (A), (B), (C), (D), (E), or (F) of

section 1(h)(10) of the Internal Revenue Code of 1986, as amended by this Act, the amendments made by this section shall apply to taxable years ending after December 31, 2002; except that dividends received by such an entity on or before such date shall not be treated as qualified dividend income (as defined in section 1(h)(11)(B) of such Code, as added by this Act).

P.L. 108-27, §303, as amended by P.L. 109-222, §102, and P.L. 111-312, §102(a), provides:

SEC. 303. SUNSET OF TITLE.

All provisions of, and amendments made by, this title shall not apply to taxable years beginning after December 31, 2012, and the Internal Revenue Code of 1986 shall be applied and administered to such years as if such provisions and amendments had never been enacted.

[¶ 5545] CODE SEC. 1291. INTEREST ON TAX DEFERRAL.

* * *

⟫→ *Caution: Code Sec. 1291(e), below, as amended by P.L. 111-312, applies to estates of decedents dying, and transfers made, after December 31, 2009. For sunset provision, see P.L. 107-16, §901 [as amended by P.L. 111-312], in the amendment notes.*

(e) CERTAIN BASIS, ETC., RULES MADE APPLICABLE.—Except to the extent inconsistent with the regulations prescribed under subsection (f), rules similar to the rules of subsections (c), (d), (e), and (f) of section 1246 shall apply for purposes of this section; except that—

(1) the reduction under subsection (e) of such section shall be the excess of the basis determined under section 1014 over the adjusted basis of the stock immediately before the decedent's death, and

(2) such a reduction shall not apply in the case of a decedent who was a nonresident alien at all times during his holding period in the stock.

[CCH Explanation at ¶ 705 and ¶ 760. Committee Reports at ¶ 10,130.]

Amendments

• **2010, Tax Relief, Unemployment Insurance Reauthorization, and Job Creation Act of 2010 (P.L. 111-312)**

P.L. 111-312, §301(a):

Amended Code Sec. 1291(e) to read as such provision would read if subtitle E of title V of the Economic Growth and Tax Relief Reconciliation Act of 2001 (P.L. 107-16) had never been enacted. **Effective** for estates of decedents dying, and transfers made, after 12-31-2009. For a special rule, see Act Sec. 301(c), below. Prior to amendment by P.L. 111-312, Code Sec. 1291(e) read as follows:

(e) CERTAIN BASIS, ETC., RULES MADE APPLICABLE.—Except to the extent inconsistent with the regulations prescribed under subsection (f), rules similar to the rules of subsections (c) and (d) of section 1246 (as in effect on the day before the date of the enactment of the American Jobs Creation Act of 2004) shall apply for purposes of this section.

P.L. 111-312, §301(c), provides:

(c) SPECIAL ELECTION WITH RESPECT TO ESTATES OF DECEDENTS DYING IN 2010.—Notwithstanding subsection (a), in the case of an estate of a decedent dying after December 31, 2009, and before January 1, 2011, the executor (within the meaning of section 2203 of the Internal Revenue Code of 1986) may elect to apply such Code as though the amendments made by subsection (a) do not apply with respect to chapter 11 of such Code and with respect to property acquired or passing from such decedent (within the meaning of section 1014(b) of such Code). Such election shall be made at such time and in such manner as the Secretary of the Treasury or the Secretary's delegate shall provide. Such an election once made shall be revocable only with the consent of the Secretary of the Treasury or the Secretary's delegate. For purposes of section 2652(a)(1) of such Code, the determination of whether any property is subject to the tax imposed by such chapter 11 shall be made without regard to any election made under this subsection.

P.L. 111-312, §304, provides:

SEC. 304. APPLICATION OF EGTRRA SUNSET TO THIS TITLE.

Section 901 of the Economic Growth and Tax Relief Reconciliation Act of 2001 shall apply to the amendments made by this title.

• **2001, Economic Growth and Tax Relief Reconciliation Act of 2001 (P.L. 107-16)**

P.L. 107-16, §542(e)(5)(B)(i)-(ii):

Amended Code Sec. 1291(e) by striking "(e)," following "rules of subsections (c), (d),"; and by striking "; except that" and all that follows and inserting a period. **Effective** for estates of decedents dying after 12-31-2009. Prior to amendment Code Sec. 1291(e) read as follows:

(e) CERTAIN BASIS, ETC., RULES MADE APPLICABLE.—Except to the extent inconsistent with the regulations prescribed under subsection (f), rules similar to the rules of subsections (c), (d), (e), and (f) of section 1246 shall apply for purposes of this section; except that—

(1) the reduction under subsection (e) of such section shall be the excess of the basis determined under section 1014

over the adjusted basis of the stock immediately before the decedent's death, and

(2) such a reduction shall not apply in the case of a decedent who was a nonresident alien at all times during his holding period in the stock.

P.L. 107-16, §901(a)-(b), as amended by P.L. 111-312, §101(a)(1), provides:

SEC. 901. SUNSET OF PROVISIONS OF ACT.

(a) IN GENERAL.—All provisions of, and amendments made by, this Act shall not apply—

(1) to taxable, plan, or limitation years beginning after December 31, 2012, or

(2) in the case of title V, to estates of decedents dying, gifts made, or generation skipping transfers, after December 31, 2012.

(b) APPLICATION OF CERTAIN LAWS.—The Internal Revenue Code of 1986 and the Employee Retirement Income Security Act of 1974 shall be applied and administered to years, estates, gifts, and transfers described in subsection (a) as if the provisions and amendments described in subsection (a) had never been enacted.

[¶5550] CODE SEC. 1296. ELECTION OF MARK TO MARKET FOR MARKETABLE STOCK.

* * *

⫸→ Caution: *Code Sec. 1296(i), below, was stricken by P.L. 107-16, applicable to estates of decedents dying, after December 31, 2009, and then reinstated by P.L. 111-312, applicable to estates of decedents dying, and transfers made, after December 31, 2009. For sunset provision, see P.L. 107-16, §901 [as amended by P.L. 111-312], in the amendment notes.*

(i) STOCK ACQUIRED FROM A DECEDENT.—*In the case of stock of a passive foreign investment company which is acquired by bequest, devise, or inheritance (or by the decedent's estate) and with respect to which an election under this section was in effect as of the date of the decedent's death, notwithstanding section 1014, the basis of such stock in the hands of the person so acquiring it shall be the adjusted basis of such stock in the hands of the decedent immediately before his death (or, if lesser, the basis which would have been determined under section 1014 without regard to this subsection).*

* * *

[CCH Explanation at ¶705 and ¶760. Committee Reports at ¶10,130.]

Amendments

• **2010, Tax Relief, Unemployment Insurance Reauthorization, and Job Creation Act of 2010 (P.L. 111-312)**

P.L. 111-312, §301(a):

Amended Code Sec. 1296(i) to read as such provision would read if subtitle E of title V of the Economic Growth and Tax Relief Reconciliation Act of 2001 (P.L. 107-16) had never been enacted. **Effective** for estates of decedents dying, and transfers made, after 12-31-2009. For a special rule, see Act Sec. 301(c), below.

P.L. 111-312, §301(c), provides:

(c) SPECIAL ELECTION WITH RESPECT TO ESTATES OF DECEDENTS DYING IN 2010.—Notwithstanding subsection (a), in the case of an estate of a decedent dying after December 31, 2009, and before January 1, 2011, the executor (within the meaning of section 2203 of the Internal Revenue Code of 1986) may elect to apply such Code as though the amendments made by subsection (a) do not apply with respect to chapter 11 of such Code and with respect to property acquired or passing from such decedent (within the meaning of section 1014(a) of such Code). Such election shall be made at such time and in such manner as the Secretary of the Treasury or the Secretary's delegate shall provide. Such an election once

made shall be revocable only with the consent of the Secretary of the Treasury or the Secretary's delegate. For purposes of section 2652(a)(1) of such Code, the determination of whether any property is subject to the tax imposed by such chapter 11 shall be made without regard to any election made under this subsection.

P.L. 111-312, §304, provides:

SEC. 304. APPLICATION OF EGTRRA SUNSET TO THIS TITLE.

Section 901 of the Economic Growth and Tax Relief Reconciliation Act of 2001 shall apply to the amendments made by this title.

• **2001, Economic Growth and Tax Relief Reconciliation Act of 2001 (P.L. 107-16)**

P.L. 107-16, §542(e)(5)(C):

Amended Code Sec. 1296 by striking subsection (i). **Effective** for estates of decedents dying after 12-31-2009. Prior to being stricken, Code Sec. 1296(i) read as follows:

(i) STOCK ACQUIRED FROM A DECEDENT.—In the case of stock of a passive foreign investment company which is acquired by bequest, devise, or inheritance (or by the decedent's estate) and with respect to which an election under this section was in effect as of the date of the decedent's death, notwithstanding section 1014, the basis of such stock in the hands of the person so acquiring it shall be the adjusted basis of such stock in the hands of the decedent immediately before his death (or, if lesser, the basis which would have been determined under section 1014 without regard to this subsection).

P.L. 107-16, §901(a)-(b), as amended by P.L. 111-312, §101(a)(1), provides:

SEC. 901. SUNSET OF PROVISIONS OF ACT.

(a) IN GENERAL.—All provisions of, and amendments made by, this Act shall not apply—

(1) to taxable, plan, or limitation years beginning after December 31, 2012, or

(2) in the case of title V, to estates of decedents dying, gifts made, or generation skipping transfers, after December 31, 2012.

(b) APPLICATION OF CERTAIN LAWS.—The Internal Revenue Code of 1986 and the Employee Retirement Income Security Act of 1974 shall be applied and administered to years, estates, gifts, and transfers described in subsection (a) as if the provisions and amendments described in subsection (a) had never been enacted.

[¶5555] CODE SEC. 1367. ADJUSTMENTS TO BASIS OF STOCK OF SHAREHOLDERS, ETC.

(a) GENERAL RULE.—

* * *

(2) DECREASES IN BASIS.—The basis of each shareholder's stock in an S corporation shall be decreased for any period (but not below zero) by the sum of the following items determined with respect to the shareholder for such period:

(A) distributions by the corporation which were not includible in the income of the shareholder by reason of section 1368,

(B) the items of loss and deduction described in subparagraph (A) of section 1366(a)(1),

(C) any nonseparately computed loss determined under subparagraph (B) of section 1366(a)(1),

(D) any expense of the corporation not deductible in computing its taxable income and not properly chargeable to capital account, and

(E) the amount of the shareholder's deduction for depletion for any oil and gas property held by the S corporation to the extent such deduction does not exceed the proportionate share of the adjusted basis of such property allocated to such shareholder under section 613A(c)(11)(B).

The decrease under subparagraph (B) by reason of a charitable contribution (as defined in section 170(c)) of property shall be the amount equal to the shareholder's pro rata share of the adjusted basis of such property. The preceding sentence shall not apply to contributions made in taxable years beginning after *December 31, 2011.*

* * *

[CCH Explanation at ¶557. Committee Reports at ¶10,570.]
Amendments

• **2010, Tax Relief, Unemployment Insurance Reauthorization, and Job Creation Act of 2010 (P.L. 111-312)**

P.L. 111-312, §752(a):

Amended Code Sec. 1367(a)(2) by striking "December 31, 2009" and inserting "December 31, 2011". Effective for contributions made in tax years beginning after 12-31-2009.

[¶5560] CODE SEC. 1391. DESIGNATION PROCEDURE.

* * *

(d) PERIOD FOR WHICH DESIGNATION IS IN EFFECT.—

(1) IN GENERAL.—Any designation under this section shall remain in effect during the period beginning on the date of the designation and ending on the earliest of—

(A)(i) in the case of an empowerment zone, *December 31, 2011,* or

(ii) in the case of an enterprise community, the close of the 10th calendar year beginning on or after such date of designation,

(B) the termination date designated by the State and local governments as provided for in their nomination, or

(C) the date the appropriate Secretary revokes the designation.

[CCH Explanation at ¶440. Committee Reports at ¶10,580.]
Amendments

• 2010, Tax Relief, Unemployment Insurance Reauthorization, and Job Creation Act of 2010 (P.L. 111-312)

P.L. 111-312, §753(a)(1):

Amended Code Sec. 1391(d)(1)(A)(i) by striking "December 31, 2009" and inserting "December 31, 2011". **Effective** for periods after 12-31-2009.

(h) Additional Designations Permitted.—

* * *

(2) Period designations may be made and take effect.—A designation may be made under this subsection after the date of the enactment of this subsection and before January 1, 2002.

* * *

[CCH Explanation at ¶440. Committee Reports at ¶10,580.]
Amendments

• 2010, Tax Relief, Unemployment Insurance Reauthorization, and Job Creation Act of 2010 (P.L. 111-312)

P.L. 111-312, §753(a)(2):

Amended Code Sec. 1391(h)(2) by striking the last sentence. **Effective** for periods after 12-31-2009. Prior to being stricken, the last sentence of Code Sec. 1391(h)(2) read as follows:

Subject to subparagraphs (B) and (C) of subsection (d)(1), such designations shall remain in effect during the period beginning on January 1, 2002, and ending on December 31, 2009.

[¶5565] CODE SEC. 1400. ESTABLISHMENT OF DC ZONE.

* * *

(f) Time For Which Designation Applicable.—

(1) In general.—The designation made by subsection (a) shall apply for the period beginning on January 1, 1998, and ending on *December 31, 2011.*

(2) Coordination with DC enterprise community designated under subchapter U.—The designation under subchapter U of the census tracts referred to in subsection (b)(1) as an enterprise community shall terminate on *December 31, 2011.*

[CCH Explanation at ¶445. Committee Reports at ¶10,600.]
Amendments

• 2010, Tax Relief, Unemployment Insurance Reauthorization, and Job Creation Act of 2010 (P.L. 111-312)

P.L. 111-312, §754(a):

Amended Code Sec. 1400(f) by striking "December 31, 2009" each place it appears and inserting "December 31, 2011". **Effective** for periods after 12-31-2009.

[¶5570] CODE SEC. 1400A. TAX-EXEMPT ECONOMIC DEVELOPMENT BONDS.

* * *

(b) Period of Applicability.—This section shall apply to bonds issued during the period beginning on January 1, 1998, and ending on *December 31, 2011.*

[CCH Explanation at ¶445. Committee Reports at ¶10,600.]

Amendments

• 2010, Tax Relief, Unemployment Insurance Reauthorization, and Job Creation Act of 2010 (P.L. 111-312)

P.L. 111-312, §754(b):

Amended Code Sec. 1400A(b) by striking "December 31, 2009" and inserting "December 31, 2011". **Effective** for bonds issued after 12-31-2009.

[¶5575] CODE SEC. 1400B. ZERO PERCENT CAPITAL GAINS RATE.

* * *

(b) DC ZONE ASSET.—For purposes of this section—

* * *

(2) DC ZONE BUSINESS STOCK.—

(A) IN GENERAL.—The term "DC Zone business stock" means any stock in a domestic corporation which is originally issued after December 31, 1997, if—

(i) such stock is acquired by the taxpayer, before *January 1, 2012,* at its original issue (directly or through an underwriter) solely in exchange for cash,

* * *

(3) DC ZONE PARTNERSHIP INTEREST.—The term "DC Zone partnership interest" means any capital or profits interest in a domestic partnership which is originally issued after December 31, 1997, if—

(A) such interest is acquired by the taxpayer, before *January 1, 2012,* from the partnership solely in exchange for cash,

* * *

(4) DC ZONE BUSINESS PROPERTY.—

(A) IN GENERAL.—The term "DC Zone business property" means tangible property if—

(i) such property was acquired by the taxpayer by purchase (as defined in section 179(d)(2)) after December 31, 1997, and before *January 1, 2012,*

* * *

(B) SPECIAL RULE FOR BUILDINGS WHICH ARE SUBSTANTIALLY IMPROVED.—

(i) IN GENERAL.—The requirements of clauses (i) and (ii) of subparagraph (A) shall be treated as met with respect to—

(I) property which is substantially improved by the taxpayer before *January 1, 2012,* and

* * *

[CCH Explanation at ¶445. Committee Reports at ¶10,600.]

Amendments

• 2010, Tax Relief, Unemployment Insurance Reauthorization, and Job Creation Act of 2010 (P.L. 111-312)

P.L. 111-312, §754(c)(1):

Amended Code Sec. 1400B(b)(2)(A)(i), (3)(A), (4)(A)(i), and (4)(B)(i)(I) by striking "January 1, 2010" and inserting

"January 1, 2012". **Effective** for property acquired or substantially improved after 12-31-2009.

(e) OTHER DEFINITIONS AND SPECIAL RULES.—For purposes of this section—

* * *

(2) GAIN BEFORE 1998 OR AFTER *2016* NOT QUALIFIED.—The term "qualified capital gain" shall not include any gain attributable to periods before January 1, 1998, or after *December 31, 2016*.

* * *

[CCH Explanation at ¶445. Committee Reports at ¶10,600.]

Amendments

• **2010, Tax Relief, Unemployment Insurance Reauthorization, and Job Creation Act of 2010 (P.L. 111-312)**

P.L. 111-312, §754(c)(2)(A)(i)-(ii):

Amended Code Sec. 1400B(e)(2) by striking "December 31, 2014" and inserting "December 31, 2016"; and by strik-

ing "2014" in the heading and inserting "2016". **Effective for** property acquired or substantially improved after 12-31-2009.

(g) SALES AND EXCHANGES OF INTERESTS IN PARTNERSHIPS AND S CORPORATIONS WHICH ARE DC ZONE BUSINESSES.—In the case of the sale or exchange of an interest in a partnership, or of stock in an S corporation, which was a DC Zone business during substantially all of the period the taxpayer held such interest or stock, the amount of qualified capital gain shall be determined without regard to—

* * *

(2) any gain attributable to periods before January 1, 1998, or after *December 31, 2016*.

[CCH Explanation at ¶445. Committee Reports at ¶10,600.]

Amendments

• **2010, Tax Relief, Unemployment Insurance Reauthorization, and Job Creation Act of 2010 (P.L. 111-312)**

P.L. 111-312, §754(c)(2)(B):

Amended Code Sec. 1400B(g)(2) by striking "December 31, 2014" and inserting "December 31, 2016". **Effective for**

property acquired or substantially improved after 12-31-2009.

[¶5580] CODE SEC. 1400C. FIRST-TIME HOMEBUYER CREDIT FOR DISTRICT OF COLUMBIA.

* * *

⟫→ *Caution: Code Sec. 1400C(d) was amended by P.L. 107-16, P.L. 109-135, and P.L. 111-148. For sunset provisions, see P.L. 107-16, §901 [as amended by P.L. 111-312], P.L. 109-135, §402(i)(3)(H), and P.L. 111-148, §10909(c) [as amended by P.L. 111-312], in the amendment notes.*

(d) CARRYFORWARD OF UNUSED CREDIT.—

(1) RULE FOR YEARS IN WHICH ALL PERSONAL CREDITS ALLOWED AGAINST REGULAR AND ALTERNATIVE MINIMUM TAX.—In the case of a taxable year to which section 26(a)(2) applies, if the credit allowable under subsection (a) exceeds the limitation imposed by section 26(a)(2) for such taxable year reduced by the sum of the credits allowable under subpart A of part IV of subchapter A (other than this section and section 25D), such excess shall be carried to the succeeding taxable year and added to the credit allowable under subsection (a) for such taxable year.

⟫→ *Caution: Code Sec. 1400C(d)(2), below, as amended by P.L. 111-312, applies to tax years after December 31, 2011. For sunset provision, see P.L. 111-148, §10909(c) [as amended by P.L. 111-312], in the amendment notes.*

(2) RULE FOR OTHER YEARS.—In the case of a taxable year to which section 26(a)(2) does not apply, if the credit allowable under subsection (a) exceeds the limitation imposed by section 26(a)(1) for such taxable year reduced by the sum of the credits allowable under subpart A of part IV of subchapter A (other than this section and sections 23, 24, 25A(i), 25B, 25D, 30, and 30B, and 30D), such excess shall be carried to the succeeding taxable year and added to the credit allowable under subsection (a) for such taxable year.

* * *

[CCH Explanation at ¶360 and ¶370. Committee Reports at ¶10,030 and ¶10,060.]

Amendments

• **2010, Tax Relief, Unemployment Insurance Reauthorization, and Job Creation Act of 2010 (P.L. 111-312)**

P.L. 111-312, §101(b)(1):

Amended Code Sec. 1400C(d)[(2)] to read as such provision would read if section 10909 of the Patient Protection and Affordable Care Act (P.L. 111-148) had never been enacted. **Effective** for tax years beginning after 12-31-2011.

• **2010, Patient Protection and Affordable Care Act (P.L. 111-148)**

P.L. 111-148, §10909(b)(2)(M):

Amended Code Sec. 1400C(d)[(2)] by striking "23," before "24". **Effective** for tax years beginning after 12-31-2009.

P.L. 111-148, §10909(c), as amended by P.L. 111-312, §101(b)(1), provides:

(c) SUNSET PROVISION.—Each provision of law amended by this section is amended to read as such provision would read if this section had never been enacted. The amendments made by the preceding sentence shall apply to taxable years beginning after December 31, 2011.

• **2005, Gulf Opportunity Zone Act of 2005 (P.L. 109-135)**

P.L. 109-135, §402(i)(3)(F):

Amended Code Sec. 1400C(d). **Effective** for tax years beginning after 12-31-2005. Prior to amendment, Code Sec. 1400C(d) read as follows:

(d) CARRYOVER OF CREDIT.—If the credit allowable under subsection (a) exceeds the limitation imposed by section 26(a) for such taxable year reduced by the sum of the credits allowable under subpart A of part IV of subchapter A (other than this section and sections 23, 24, and 25B), such excess shall be carried to the succeeding taxable year and added to the credit allowable under subsection (a) for such taxable year.

P.L. 109-135, §402(i)(3)(H), provides:

(H) APPLICATION OF EGTRRA SUNSET.—The amendments made by this paragraph (and each part thereof) shall be subject to title IX of the Economic Growth and Tax Relief Reconciliation Act of 2001 [P.L. 107-16] in the same manner as the provisions of such Act to which such amendment (or part thereof) relates.

P.L. 109-135, §402(i)(4):

Amended Act Sec. 1335(b) of P.L. 109-58 by striking paragraphs (1), (2) and (3) and provided that the Internal Revenue Code of 1986 shall be applied and administered as if the amendments made by such paragraphs had never been enacted. **Effective** as if included in the provision of the Energy Policy Act of 2005 (P.L. 109-58) to which it relates. P.L. 109-58, §1335(b)(3), amended Code Sec. 1400C(d) by striking "this section" and inserting "this section and section 25D". This amendment reinstates the language "this section" to Code Sec. 1400C(d).

• **2001, Economic Growth and Tax Relief Reconciliation Act of 2001 (P.L. 107-16)**

P.L. 107-16, §201(b)(2)(H):

Amended Code Sec. 1400C(d) by inserting "and section 24" after "this section". **Effective** for tax years beginning after 12-31-2001. [But, see P.L. 107-147, §601(b)(2), and P.L. 108-311, §312(b)(2), above.—CCH].

P.L. 107-16, §202(f)(2)(C):

Amended Code Sec. 1400C(d), as amended by Act Sec. 201(b)(2)(H), by striking "section 24" and inserting "sections 23 and 24". **Effective** for tax years beginning after 12-31-2001. [But, see P.L. 107-147, §601(b)(2), and P.L. 108-311, §312(b)(2), above.—CCH].

P.L. 107-16, §618(b)(2)(E) (as amended by P.L. 107-147, §417(23)(B)):

Amended Code Sec. 1400C(d), as amended by Act Secs. 201(b)(2)(H) and 202(f), by striking "and 24" and inserting ", 24, and 25B". **Effective** for tax years beginning after 12-31-2001. [But, see P.L. 107-147, §601(b)(2), and P.L. 108-311, §312(b)(2), above.—CCH].

P.L. 107-16, §901(a)-(b), as amended by P.L. 111-312, §101(a), provides [but see P.L. 109-280, §811, and P.L. 111-148, §10909(c), above]:

SEC. 901. SUNSET OF PROVISIONS OF ACT.

(a) IN GENERAL.—All provisions of, and amendments made by, this Act shall not apply—

(1) to taxable, plan, or limitation years beginning after December 31, 2012, or

(2) in the case of title V, to estates of decedents dying, gifts made, or generation skipping transfers, after December 31, 2012.

(b) APPLICATION OF CERTAIN LAWS.—The Internal Revenue Code of 1986 and the Employee Retirement Income Security Act of 1974 shall be applied and administered to years, estates, gifts, and transfers described in subsection (a) as if the provisions and amendments described in subsection (a) had never been enacted.

(i) APPLICATION OF SECTION.—This section shall apply to property purchased after August 4, 1997, and before *January 1, 2012.*

[CCH Explanation at ¶445. Committee Reports at ¶10,600.]

Amendments

• **2010, Tax Relief, Unemployment Insurance Reauthorization, and Job Creation Act of 2010 (P.L. 111-312)**

P.L. 111-312, §754(d):

Amended Code Sec. 1400C(i) by striking "January 1, 2010" and inserting "January 1, 2012". **Effective** for homes purchased after 12-31-2009.

[¶5585] CODE SEC. 1400L. TAX BENEFITS FOR NEW YORK LIBERTY ZONE.

* * *

(b) SPECIAL ALLOWANCE FOR CERTAIN PROPERTY ACQUIRED AFTER SEPTEMBER 10, 2001.—

* * *

(2) QUALIFIED NEW YORK LIBERTY ZONE PROPERTY.—For purposes of this subsection—

* * *

(D) SPECIAL RULES.—For purposes of this subsection, rules similar to the rules of section 168(k)(2)(E) shall apply, except that clause (i) thereof shall be applied without regard to "and before *January 1, 2013*", and clause (iv) thereof shall be applied by substituting "qualified New York Liberty Zone property" for "qualified property".

* * *

[CCH Explanation at ¶502. Committee Reports at ¶10,140.]
Amendments
● **2010, Tax Relief, Unemployment Insurance Reauthorization, and Job Creation Act of 2010 (P.L. 111-312)**

P.L. 111-312, §401(d)(6):

Amended Code Sec. 1400L(b)(2)(D) by striking "January 1, 2011" and inserting "January 1, 2013". **Effective** for prop-erty placed in service after 12-31-2010, in tax years ending after such date.

(d) TAX-EXEMPT BOND FINANCING.—

* * *

(2) QUALIFIED NEW YORK LIBERTY BOND.—For purposes of this subsection, the term "qualified New York Liberty Bond" means any bond issued as part of an issue if—

* * *

(D) such bond is issued after the date of the enactment of this section and before *January 1, 2012.*

* * *

[CCH Explanation at ¶470. Committee Reports at ¶10,670.]
Amendments
● **2010, Tax Relief, Unemployment Insurance Reauthorization, and Job Creation Act of 2010 (P.L. 111-312)**

P.L. 111-312, §761(a):

Amended Code Sec. 1400L(d)(2)(D) by striking "January 1, 2010" and inserting "January 1, 2012". **Effective** for bonds issued after 12-31-2009.

[¶5590] CODE SEC. 1400N. TAX BENEFITS FOR GULF OPPORTUNITY ZONE.

(a) TAX-EXEMPT BOND FINANCING.—

* * *

(2) QUALIFIED GULF OPPORTUNITY ZONE BOND.—For purposes of this subsection, the term "qualified Gulf Opportunity Zone Bond" means any bond issued as part of an issue if—

* * *

(D) such bond is issued after the date of the enactment of this section and before *January 1, 2012,* and

* * *

(7) SPECIAL RULE FOR REPAIRS AND RECONSTRUCTIONS.—

* * *

(C) TERMINATION.—This paragraph shall apply only to owner-financing provided after the date of the enactment of this paragraph and before *January 1, 2012*.

* * *

[CCH Explanation at ¶450. Committee Reports at ¶10,700.]
Amendments
• **2010, Tax Relief, Unemployment Insurance Reauthorization, and Job Creation Act of 2010 (P.L. 111-312)**

P.L. 111-312, §764(a):

Amended Code Sec. 1400N(a)(2)(D) and (7)(C) by striking "January 1, 2011" and inserting "January 1, 2012". **Effective** 12-17-2010.

(c) LOW-INCOME HOUSING CREDIT.—

* * *

(5) TIME FOR MAKING LOW-INCOME HOUSING CREDIT ALLOCATIONS.—Section 42(h)(1)(B) shall not apply to an allocation of housing credit dollar amount to a building located in the Gulf Opportunity Zone, the Rita GO Zone, or the Wilma GO Zone, if such allocation is made in 2006, 2007, or 2008, and such building is placed in service before *January 1, 2012*.

* * *

[CCH Explanation at ¶450. Committee Reports at ¶10,690.]
Amendments
• **2010, Tax Relief, Unemployment Insurance Reauthorization, and Job Creation Act of 2010 (P.L. 111-312)**

P.L. 111-312, §763:

Amended Code Sec. 1400N(c)(5) by striking "January 1, 2011" and inserting "January 1, 2012". **Effective** 12-17-2010.

(d) SPECIAL ALLOWANCE FOR CERTAIN PROPERTY ACQUIRED ON OR AFTER AUGUST 28, 2005.—

* * *

(3) SPECIAL RULES.—For purposes of this subsection, rules similar to the rules of subparagraph (E) of section 168(k)(2) shall apply, except that such subparagraph shall be applied—

* * *

(B) without regard to "and before *January 1, 2013*" in clause (i) thereof, and

* * *

(6) EXTENSION FOR CERTAIN PROPERTY.—

* * *

(B) SPECIFIED GULF OPPORTUNITY ZONE EXTENSION PROPERTY.—For purposes of this paragraph, the term "specified Gulf Opportunity Zone extension property" means property—

* * *

(ii) which is—

(I) nonresidential real property or residential rental property which is placed in service by the taxpayer on or before *December 31, 2011*, or

(II) in the case of a taxpayer who places a building described in subclause (I) in service on or before *December 31, 2011*, property described in section 168(k)(2)(A)(i) if substantially all of the use of such property is in such building and such property is placed in service by the taxpayer not later than 90 days after such building is placed in service.

* * *

(D) ONLY PRE-*JANUARY 1, 2012,* BASIS OF REAL PROPERTY ELIGIBLE FOR ADDITIONAL ALLOWANCE.—In the case of property which is qualified Gulf Opportunity Zone property solely by reason of subparagraph (B)(ii)(I), paragraph (1) shall apply only to the extent of the adjusted basis thereof attributable to manufacture, construction, or production before *January 1, 2012.*

* * *

[CCH Explanation at ¶450 and ¶502. Committee Reports at ¶10,140 and 10,710.]

Amendments

• **2010, Tax Relief, Unemployment Insurance Reauthorization, and Job Creation Act of 2010 (P.L. 111-312)**

P.L. 111-312, §401(d)(7):

Amended Code Sec. 1400N(d)(3)(B) by striking "January 1, 2011" and inserting "January 1, 2013". **Effective** for property placed in service after 12-31-2010, in tax years ending after such date.

P.L. 111-312, §765(a)(1)-(2):

Amended Code Sec. 1400N(d)(6) by striking "December 31, 2010" both places it appears in subparagraph (B) and inserting "December 31, 2011", and by striking "January 1, 2010" in the heading and the text of subparagraph (D) and inserting "January 1, 2012". **Effective** for property placed in service after 12-31-2009.

(h) INCREASE IN REHABILITATION CREDIT.—In the case of qualified rehabilitation expenditures (as defined in section 47(c)) paid or incurred during the period beginning on August 28, 2005, and ending on *December 31, 2011,* with respect to any qualified rehabilitated building or certified historic structure (as defined in section 47(c)) located in the Gulf Opportunity Zone, subsection (a) of section 47 (relating to rehabilitation credit) shall be applied—

(1) by substituting "13 percent" for "10 percent" in paragraph (1) thereof, and

(2) by substituting "26 percent" for "20 percent" in paragraph (2) thereof.

* * *

[CCH Explanation at ¶450. Committee Reports at ¶10,680.]

Amendments

• **2010, Tax Relief, Unemployment Insurance Reauthorization, and Job Creation Act of 2010 (P.L. 111-312)**

P.L. 111-312, §762(a):

Amended Code Sec. 1400N(h) by striking "December 31, 2009" and inserting "December 31, 2011". **Effective** for amounts paid or incurred after 12-31-2009.

[¶5595] CODE SEC. 1445. WITHHOLDING OF TAX ON DISPOSITIONS OF UNITED STATES REAL PROPERTY INTERESTS.

* * *

⋙➤ *Caution: Code Sec. 1445(e)(1), below, was amended by P.L. 108-27. For sunset provision, see P.L. 108-27, §303 [as amended by P.L. 111-312], in the amendment notes.*

(e) SPECIAL RULES RELATING TO DISTRIBUTIONS, ETC., BY CORPORATIONS, PARTNERSHIPS, TRUSTS, OR ESTATES.—

(1) CERTAIN DOMESTIC PARTNERSHIPS, TRUSTS, AND ESTATES.—In the case of any disposition of a United States real property interest as defined in section 897(c) (other than a disposition described in paragraph (4) or (5)) by a domestic partnership, domestic trust, or domestic estate, such partnership, the trustee or such trust, or the executor of such estate (as the case may be) shall be required to deduct and withhold under subsection (a) a tax equal to 35 percent (or, to the extent provided in regulations, 15 percent) of the gain realized to the extent such gain—

(A) is allocable to a foreign person who is a partner or beneficiary of such partnership, trust, or estate, or

(B) is allocable to a portion of the trust treated as owned by a foreign person under subpart E of Part I of subchapter J.

* * *

[CCH Explanation at ¶405. Committee Reports at ¶10,080.]

Amendments

• **2003, Jobs and Growth Tax Relief Reconciliation Act of 2003 (P.L. 108-27)**

P.L. 108-27, §301(a)(2)(C):

Amended Code Sec. 1445(e)(1) by striking "20 percent" and inserting "15 percent". **Effective** for amounts paid after 5-28-2003.

P.L. 108-27, §303, as amended by P.L. 109-222, §102, and P.L. 111-312, §102(a), provides:

SEC. 303. SUNSET OF TITLE.

All provisions of, and amendments made by, this title shall not apply to taxable years beginning after December 31, 2012, and the Internal Revenue Code of 1986 shall be applied and administered to such years as if such provisions and amendments had never been enacted.

[¶5600] CODE SEC. 2001. IMPOSITION AND RATE OF TAX.

* * *

(b) COMPUTATION OF TAX.—The tax imposed by this section shall be the amount equal to the excess (if any) of—

* * *

⫸→ *Caution: Code Sec. 2001(b)(2), below, as amended by P.L. 111-312, applies to estates of decedents dying, generation-skipping transfers, and gifts made after December 31, 2009. For sunset provision, see P.L. 107-16, §901 [as amended by P.L. 111-312], in the amendment notes.*

(2) the aggregate amount of tax which would have been payable under chapter 12 with respect to gifts made by the decedent after December 31, 1976, *if the modifications described in subsection (g)* had been applicable at the time of such gifts.

* * *

[CCH Explanation at ¶705 and ¶710. Committee Reports at ¶10,130.]

Amendments

• **2010, Tax Relief, Unemployment Insurance Reauthorization, and Job Creation Act of 2010 (P.L. 111-312)**

P.L. 111-312, §302(d)(1)(A):

Amended Code Sec. 2001(b)(2) by striking "if the provisions of subsection (c) (as in effect at the decedent's death)" and inserting "if the modifications described in subsection (g)". **Effective** for estates of decedents dying, generation-skipping transfers, and gifts made, after 12-31-2009.

P.L. 111-312, §304, provides:

SEC. 304. APPLICATION OF EGTRRA SUNSET TO THIS TITLE.

Section 901 of the Economic Growth and Tax Relief Reconciliation Act of 2001 shall apply to the amendments made by this title.

• **2001, Economic Growth and Tax Relief Reconciliation Act of 2001 (P.L. 107-16)**

P.L. 107-16, §901(a)-(b), as amended by P.L. 111-312, §101(a)(1), provides:

SEC. 901. SUNSET OF PROVISIONS OF ACT.

(a) IN GENERAL.—All provisions of, and amendments made by, this Act shall not apply—

(1) to taxable, plan, or limitation years beginning after December 31, 2012, or

(2) in the case of title V, to estates of decedents dying, gifts made, or generation skipping transfers, after December 31, 2012.

(b) APPLICATION OF CERTAIN LAWS.—The Internal Revenue Code of 1986 and the Employee Retirement Income Security Act of 1974 shall be applied and administered to years, estates, gifts, and transfers described in subsection (a) as if the provisions and amendments described in subsection (a) had never been enacted.

»»→ *Caution: Code Sec. 2001(c), below, as amended by P.L. 111-312, applies to estates of decedents dying, generation-skipping transfers, and gifts made after December 31, 2009. For sunset provision, see P.L. 107-16, §901 [as amended by P.L. 111-312], in the amendment notes.*

(c) Rate Schedule.—

If the amount with respect to which the tentative tax to be computed is:	The tentative tax is:
Not over $10,000	18 percent of such amount.
Over $10,000 but not over $20,000	$1,800, plus 20 percent of the excess of such amount over $10,000.
Over $20,000 but not over $40,000	$3,800, plus 22 percent of the excess of such amount over $20,000.
Over $40,000 but not over $60,000	$8,200, plus 24 percent of the excess of such amount over $40,000.
Over $60,000 but not over $80,000	$13,000, plus 26 percent of the excess of such amount over $60,000.
Over $80,000 but not over $100,000	$18,200, plus 28 percent of the excess of such amount over $80,000.
Over $100,000 but not over $150,000	$23,800, plus 30 percent of the excess of such amount over $100,000.
Over $150,000 but not over $250,000	$38,800, plus 32 percent of the excess of such amount over $150,000.
Over $250,000 but not over $500,000	$70,800, plus 34 percent of the excess of such amount over $250,000.
Over $500,000	*$155,800, plus 35 percent of the excess of such amount over $500,000.*

(2) [*Stricken.*]

* * *

[CCH Explanation at ¶705 and ¶710. Committee Reports at ¶10,130.]

Amendments

• **2010, Tax Relief, Unemployment Insurance Reauthorization, and Job Creation Act of 2010 (P.L. 111-312)**

P.L. 111-312, §302(a)(2)(A)-(C):

Amended Code Sec. 2001(c) by striking "Over $500,000" and all that follows in the table contained in paragraph (1) and inserting a new table row, by striking "(1) In general.—" before the table, and by striking paragraph (2). **Effective** for estates of decedents dying, generation-skipping transfers, and gifts made, after 12-31-2009. Prior to being stricken, "Over $500,000" and all that followed in the table at Code Sec. 2001(c)(1) and (2) read as follows:

(1) In general.—

If the amount with respect to which the tentative tax to be computed is:	The tentative tax is:
Over $500,000 but not over $750,000	$155,800, plus 37 percent of the excess of such amount over $500,000.
Over $750,000 but not over $1,000,000	$248,300, plus 39 percent of the excess of such amount over $750,000.

If the amount with respect to which the tentative tax to be computed is:	The tentative tax is:
Over $1,000,000 but not over $1,250,000	$345,800, plus 41 percent of the excess of such amount over $1,000,000.
Over $1,250,000 but not over $1,500,000	$448,300, plus 43 percent of the excess of such amount over $1,250,000.
Over $1,500,000 but not over $2,000,000	$555,800, plus 45 percent of the excess of such amount over $1,500,000.
Over $2,000,000 but not over $2,500,000	$780,800, plus 49 percent of the excess of such amount over $2,000,000.
Over $2,500,000	$1,025,800, plus 50% of the excess over $2,500,000.

(2) PHASEDOWN OF MAXIMUM RATE OF TAX.—

(A) IN GENERAL.—In the case of estates of decedents dying, and gifts made, in calendar years after 2002 and before 2010, the tentative tax under this subsection shall be determined by using a table prescribed by the Secretary (in lieu of using the table contained in paragraph (1)) which is the same as such table; except that—

(i) the maximum rate of tax for any calendar year shall be determined in the table under subparagraph (B), and

(ii) the brackets and the amounts setting forth the tax shall be adjusted to the extent necessary to reflect the adjustments under subparagraph (A).

(B) MAXIMUM RATE.—

In calendar year:	The maximum rate is:
2003	49 percent
2004	48 percent
2005	47 percent
2006	46 percent
2007, 2008, and 2009	45 percent.

P.L. 111-312, § 304, provides:

SEC. 304. APPLICATION OF EGTRRA SUNSET TO THIS TITLE.

Section 901 of the Economic Growth and Tax Relief Reconciliation Act of 2001 shall apply to the amendments made by this title.

• 2001, Economic Growth and Tax Relief Reconciliation Act of 2001 (P.L. 107-16)

P.L. 107-16, § 511(a):

Amended the table contained in Code Sec. 2001(c)(1) by striking the two highest brackets and inserting a new

bracket. **Effective** for estates of decedents dying, and gifts made, after 12-31-2001. Prior to amendment, the two highest brackets in the table read as follows:

Over $2,500,000 but not over $3,000,000	$1,025,800, plus 53% of the excess over $2,500,000.
Over $3,000,000 . . .	$1,290,800, plus 55% of the excess over $3,000,000

P.L. 107-16, § 511(b):

Amended Code Sec. 2001(c) by striking paragraph (2). **Effective** for estates of decedents dying, and gifts made, after 12-31-2001. Prior to being stricken, Code Sec. 2001(c)(2) read as follows:

(2) PHASEOUT OF GRADUATED RATES AND UNIFIED CREDIT.—The tentative tax determined under paragraph (1) shall be increased by an amount equal to 5 percent of so much of the amount (with respect to which the tentative tax is to be computed) as exceeds $10,000,000 but does not exceed the amount at which the average tax rate under this section is 55 percent.

P.L. 107-16, § 511(c):

Amended Code Sec. 2001(c), as amended by Act Sec. 511(b), by adding at the end a new paragraph (2). **Effective** for estates of decedents dying, and gifts made, after 12-31-2002.

P.L. 107-16, § 901(a)-(b), as amended by P.L. 111-312, § 101(a)(1), provides:

SEC. 901. SUNSET OF PROVISIONS OF ACT.

(a) IN GENERAL.—All provisions of, and amendments made by, this Act shall not apply—

(1) to taxable, plan, or limitation years beginning after December 31, 2012, or

(2) in the case of title V, to estates of decedents dying, gifts made, or generation skipping transfers, after December 31, 2012.

(b) APPLICATION OF CERTAIN LAWS.—The Internal Revenue Code of 1986 and the Employee Retirement Income Security Act of 1974 shall be applied and administered to years, estates, gifts, and transfers described in subsection (a) as if the provisions and amendments described in subsection (a) had never been enacted.

»»→ *Caution: Code Sec. 2001(g), below, was added by P.L. 111-312, applicable to estates of decedents dying, generation-skipping transfers, and gifts made after December 31, 2009. For sunset provision, see P.L. 107-16, §901 [as amended by P.L. 111-312], in the amendment notes.*

(g) MODIFICATIONS TO GIFT TAX PAYABLE TO REFLECT DIFFERENT TAX RATES.—*For purposes of applying subsection (b)(2) with respect to 1 or more gifts, the rates of tax under subsection (c) in effect at the decedent's death shall, in lieu of the rates of tax in effect at the time of such gifts, be used both to compute—*

(1) *the tax imposed by chapter 12 with respect to such gifts, and*

(2) *the credit allowed against such tax under section 2505, including in computing—*

[CCH Explanation at ¶705 and ¶725. Committee Reports at ¶10,130.]

Amendments

- **2001, Economic Growth and Tax Relief Reconciliation Act of 2001 (P.L. 107-16)**

P.L. 107-16, §531(a)(1)-(3):

Amended Code Sec. 2011(b) by striking "CREDIT.—The credit allowed" and inserting "CREDIT.—(1) IN GENERAL.—Except as provided in paragraph (2), the credit allowed", by striking "For purposes" and inserting "(3) ADJUSTED TAXABLE ESTATE.—For purposes", and by inserting after paragraph (1) a new paragraph (2). **Effective** for estates of decedents dying after 12-31-2001.

P.L. 107-16, §901(a)-(b), as amended by P.L. 111-312, §101(a)(1), provides:

SEC. 901. SUNSET OF PROVISIONS OF ACT.

(a) IN GENERAL.—All provisions of, and amendments made by, this Act shall not apply—

(1) to taxable, plan, or limitation years beginning after December 31, 2012, or

(2) in the case of title V, to estates of decedents dying, gifts made, or generation skipping transfers, after December 31, 2012.

(b) APPLICATION OF CERTAIN LAWS.—The Internal Revenue Code of 1986 and the Employee Retirement Income Security Act of 1974 shall be applied and administered to years, estates, gifts, and transfers described in subsection (a) as if the provisions and amendments described in subsection (a) had never been enacted.

⋙➔ *Caution: Code Sec. 2011(f), below, as redesignated by P.L. 107-134, was added by P.L. 107-16. For sunset provision, see P.L. 107-16, §901 [as amended by P.L. 111-312], in the amendment notes.*

(f) TERMINATION.—This section shall not apply to the estates of decedents dying after December 31, 2004.

[CCH Explanation at ¶530.]

Amendments

- **2002, Victims of Terrorism Tax Relief Act of 2001 (P.L. 107-134)**

P.L. 107-134, §103(b)(1):

Amended Code Sec. 2011 by redesignating subsection (g) as subsection (f). **Effective** for estates of decedents dying on or after 9-11-2001; and in the case of individuals dying as a result of the 4-19-95 terrorist attack, dying on or after 4-19-95. For a waiver of limitations, see Act Sec. 103(d)(2) in the amendment notes for Code Sec. 2011(d).

- **2001, Economic Growth and Tax Relief Reconciliation Act of 2001 (P.L. 107-16)**

P.L. 107-16, §532(a):

Amended Code Sec. 2011 by adding at the end a new subsection (g). **Effective** for estates of decedents dying, and generation-skipping transfers, after 12-31-2004.

P.L. 107-16, §901(a)-(b), as amended by P.L. 111-312, §101(a)(1), provides:

SEC. 901. SUNSET OF PROVISIONS OF ACT.

(a) IN GENERAL.—All provisions of, and amendments made by, this Act shall not apply—

(1) to taxable, plan, or limitation years beginning after December 31, 2012, or

(2) in the case of title V, to estates of decedents dying, gifts made, or generation skipping transfers, after December 31, 2012.

(b) APPLICATION OF CERTAIN LAWS.—The Internal Revenue Code of 1986 and the Employee Retirement Income Security Act of 1974 shall be applied and administered to years, estates, gifts, and transfers described in subsection (a) as if the provisions and amendments described in subsection (a) had never been enacted.

[¶5615] CODE SEC. 2012. CREDIT FOR GIFT TAX.

⋙➔ *Caution: Code Sec. 2012(a), below, was amended by P.L. 107-16. For sunset provision, see P.L. 107-16, §901 [as amended by P.L. 111-312], in the amendment notes.*

(a) IN GENERAL.—If a tax on a gift has been paid under chapter 12 (sec. 2501 and following), or under corresponding provisions of prior laws, and thereafter on the death of the donor any amount in respect of such gift is required to be included in the value of the gross estate of the decedent for purposes of this chapter, then there shall be credited against the tax imposed by section 2001 the amount of the tax paid on a gift under chapter 12, or under corresponding provisions of prior laws, with respect to so much of the property which constituted the gift as is included in the gross estate, except that the amount of such credit shall not exceed an amount which bears the same ratio to the tax imposed by section 2001 (after deducting from such tax the unified credit provided by section 2010) as the value (at the time of the gift or at the time of the death, whichever is lower) of so much of the property which constituted the gift as is included in the gross estate bears to the value of the entire gross estate reduced by the aggregate amount of the charitable and marital deductions allowed under sections 2055, 2056, and 2106(a)(2).

* * *

[CCH Explanation at ¶705 and ¶730. Committee Reports at ¶10,130.]

Amendments

● **2001, Economic Growth and Tax Relief Reconciliation Act of 2001 (P.L. 107-16)**

P.L. 107-16, §532(c)(1):

Amended Code Sec. 2012(a) by striking "the credit for State death taxes provided by section 2011 and" following "(after deducting from such tax". **Effective** for estates of decedents dying, and generation-skipping transfers, after 12-31-2004.

P.L. 107-16, §901(a)-(b), as amended by P.L. 111-312, §101(a)(1), provides:

SEC. 901. SUNSET OF PROVISIONS OF ACT.

(a) IN GENERAL.—All provisions of, and amendments made by, this Act shall not apply—

(1) to taxable, plan, or limitation years beginning after December 31, 2012, or

(2) in the case of title V, to estates of decedents dying, gifts made, or generation skipping transfers, after December 31, 2012.

(b) APPLICATION OF CERTAIN LAWS.—The Internal Revenue Code of 1986 and the Employee Retirement Income Security Act of 1974 shall be applied and administered to years, estates, gifts, and transfers described in subsection (a) as if the provisions and amendments described in subsection (a) had never been enacted.

[¶5620] CODE SEC. 2013. CREDIT FOR TAX ON PRIOR TRANSFERS.

* * *

(c) LIMITATION ON CREDIT.—

(1) IN GENERAL.—The credit provided in this section shall not exceed the amount by which—

⋙→ Caution: *Code Sec. 2013(c)(1)(A), below, was amended by P.L. 107-16. For sunset provision, see P.L. 107-16, §901 [as amended by P.L. 111-312], in the amendment notes.*

(A) the estate tax imposed by section 2001 or section 2101 (after deducting the credits provided for in sections 2010, 2012, and 2014) computed without regard to this section, exceeds

(B) such tax computed by excluding from the decedent's gross estate the value of such property transferred and, if applicable, by making the adjustment hereinafter indicated.

[CCH Explanation at ¶705 and ¶730. Committee Reports at ¶10,130.]

Amendments

● **2001, Economic Growth and Tax Relief Reconciliation Act of 2001 (P.L. 107-16)**

P.L. 107-16, §532(c)(2):

Amended Code Sec. 2013(c)(1)(A) by striking "2011," following "in sections 2010,". **Effective** for estates of decedents dying, and generation-skipping transfers, after 12-31-2004.

P.L. 107-16, §901(a)-(b), as amended by P.L. 111-312, §101(a)(1), provides:

SEC. 901. SUNSET OF PROVISIONS OF ACT.

(a) IN GENERAL.—All provisions of, and amendments made by, this Act shall not apply—

(1) to taxable, plan, or limitation years beginning after December 31, 2012, or

(2) in the case of title V, to estates of decedents dying, gifts made, or generation skipping transfers, after December 31, 2012.

(b) APPLICATION OF CERTAIN LAWS.—The Internal Revenue Code of 1986 and the Employee Retirement Income Security Act of 1974 shall be applied and administered to years, estates, gifts, and transfers described in subsection (a) as if the provisions and amendments described in subsection (a) had never been enacted.

[¶5625] CODE SEC. 2014. CREDIT FOR FOREIGN DEATH TAXES.

* * *

(b) LIMITATIONS ON CREDIT.—The credit provided in this section with respect to such taxes paid to any foreign country—

* * *

⋙→ Caution: *Code Sec. 2014(b)(2), below, was amended by P.L. 107-16. For sunset provision, see P.L. 107-16, §901 [as amended by P.L. 111-312], in the amendment notes.*

(2) shall not, with respect to all such taxes, exceed an amount which bears the same ratio to the tax imposed by section 2001 (after deducting from such tax the credits provided by sections 2010 and 2012) as the value of property which is—

(A) situated within such foreign country,

(B) subjected to the taxes of such foreign country, and

(C) included in the gross estate

bears to the value of the entire gross estate reduced by the aggregate amount of the deductions allowed under sections 2055 and 2056.

* * *

[CCH Explanation at ¶705 and ¶730. Committee Reports at ¶10,130.]

Amendments

• 2001, Economic Growth and Tax Relief Reconciliation Act of 2001 (P.L. 107-16)

P.L. 107-16, §532(c)(3):

Amended Code Sec. 2014(b)(2) by striking ", 2011," following "provided by sections 2010". **Effective** for estates of decedents dying, and generation-skipping transfers, after 12-31-2004.

P.L. 107-16, §901(a)-(b), as amended by P.L. 111-312, §101(a)(1), provides:

SEC. 901. SUNSET OF PROVISIONS OF ACT.

(a) IN GENERAL.—All provisions of, and amendments made by, this Act shall not apply—

(1) to taxable, plan, or limitation years beginning after December 31, 2012, or

(2) in the case of title V, to estates of decedents dying, gifts made, or generation skipping transfers, after December 31, 2012.

(b) APPLICATION OF CERTAIN LAWS.—The Internal Revenue Code of 1986 and the Employee Retirement Income Security Act of 1974 shall be applied and administered to years, estates, gifts, and transfers described in subsection (a) as if the provisions and amendments described in subsection (a) had never been enacted.

Caution: Code Sec. 2015, below, was amended by P.L. 107-16. For sunset provision, see P.L. 107-16, §901, [as amended by P.L. 111-312], in the amendment notes.

[¶5630] CODE SEC. 2015. CREDIT FOR DEATH TAXES ON REMAINDERS.

Where an election is made under section 6163(a) to postpone payment of the tax imposed by section 2001 or 2101, such part of any estate, inheritance, legacy, or succession taxes allowable as a credit under section 2014, as is attributable to a reversionary or remainder interest may be allowed as a credit against the tax attributable to such interest, subject to the limitations on the amount of the credit contained in such sections, if such part is paid, and credit therefor claimed, at any time before the expiration of the time for payment of the tax imposed by section 2001 or 2101 as postponed and extended under section 6163.

[CCH Explanation at ¶705 and ¶730. Committee Reports at ¶10,130.]

Amendments

• 2001, Economic Growth and Tax Relief Reconciliation Act of 2001 (P.L. 107-16)

P.L. 107-16, §532(c)(4):

Amended Code Sec. 2015 by striking "2011 or" following "a credit under section". **Effective** for estates of decedents dying, and generation-skipping transfers, after 12-31-2004.

P.L. 107-16, §901(a)-(b), as amended by P.L. 111-312, §101(a)(1), provides:

SEC. 901. SUNSET OF PROVISIONS OF ACT.

(a) IN GENERAL.—All provisions of, and amendments made by, this Act shall not apply—

(1) to taxable, plan, or limitation years beginning after December 31, 2012, or

(2) in the case of title V, to estates of decedents dying, gifts made, or generation skipping transfers, after December 31, 2012.

(b) APPLICATION OF CERTAIN LAWS.—The Internal Revenue Code of 1986 and the Employee Retirement Income Security Act of 1974 shall be applied and administered to years, estates, gifts, and transfers described in subsection (a) as if the provisions and amendments described in subsection (a) had never been enacted.

Caution: Code Sec. 2016, below, was amended by P.L. 107-16 and P.L. 107-147. For sunset provision, see P.L. 107-16, §901 [as amended by P.L. 111-312], in the amendment notes.

[¶5635] CODE SEC. 2016. RECOVERY OF TAXES CLAIMED AS CREDIT.

If any tax claimed as a credit under section 2014 is recovered from any foreign country, the executor, or any other person or persons recovering such amount, shall give notice of such recovery to the Secretary at such time and in such manner as may be required by regulations prescribed by him, and the Secretary shall (despite the provisions of section 6501) redetermine the amount of the tax under this chapter and the amount, if any, of the tax due on such redetermination, shall be paid by the executor or such person or persons, as the case may be, on notice and demand. No interest shall be assessed or collected on any amount of tax due on any redetermination by the Secretary resulting from a refund to the executor of tax claimed as a credit under section 2014, for any period before the receipt of such refund, except to the extent interest was paid by the foreign country on such refund.

[CCH Explanation at ¶705 and ¶730. Committee Reports at ¶10,130.]

Amendments

• **2002, Job Creation and Worker Assistance Act of 2002 (P.L. 107-147)**

P.L. 107-147, §411(h):

Amended Code Sec. 2016 by striking "any State, any possession of the United States, or the District of Columbia," following "any foreign country,". Effective as if included in the provision of P.L. 107-16 to which it relates [applicable to estates of decedents dying, and generation-skipping transfers, after 12-31-2004.—CCH].

• **2001, Economic Growth and Tax Relief Reconciliation Act of 2001 (P.L. 107-16)**

P.L. 107-16, §532(c)(4):

Amended Code Sec. 2016 by striking "2011 or" following "If any tax claimed as a credit under section". Effective for estates of decedents dying, and generation-skipping transfers, after 12-31-2004.

P.L. 107-16, §901(a)-(b), as amended by P.L. 111-312, §101(a)(1), provides:

SEC. 901. SUNSET OF PROVISIONS OF ACT.

(a) In General.—All provisions of, and amendments made by, this Act shall not apply—

(1) to taxable, plan, or limitation years beginning after December 31, 2012, or

(2) in the case of title V, to estates of decedents dying, gifts made, or generation skipping transfers, after December 31, 2012.

(b) Application of Certain Laws.—The Internal Revenue Code of 1986 and the Employee Retirement Income Security Act of 1974 shall be applied and administered to years, estates, gifts, and transfers described in subsection (a) as if the provisions and amendments described in subsection (a) had never been enacted.

[¶5640] CODE SEC. 2031. DEFINITION OF GROSS ESTATE.

* * *

(c) Estate Tax With Respect to Land Subject to a Qualified Conservation Easement.—

* * *

⟫→ *Caution: Code Sec. 2031(c)(2), below, was amended by P.L. 107-16. For sunset provision, see P.L. 107-16, §901 [as amended by P.L. 111-312], in the amendment notes.*

(2) Applicable percentage.—For purposes of paragraph (1), the term "applicable percentage" means 40 percent reduced (but not below zero) by 2 percentage points for each percentage point (or fraction thereof) by which the value of the qualified conservation easement is less than 30 percent of the value of the land (determined without regard to the value of such easement and reduced by the value of any retained development right (as defined in paragraph (5)). The values taken into account under the preceding sentence shall be such values as of the date of the contribution referred to in paragraph (8)(B).

* * *

(8) Definitions.—For purposes of this subsection—

(A) Land subject to a qualified conservation easement.—The term "land subject to a qualified conservation easement" means land—

⟫→ *Caution: Code Sec. 2031(c)(8)(A)(i), below, was amended by P.L. 107-16. For sunset provision, see P.L. 107-16, §901 [as amended by P.L. 111-312], in the amendment notes.*

(i) which is located in the United States or any possession of the United States,

* * *

[CCH Explanation at ¶705 and ¶735. Committee Reports at ¶10,130.]

Amendments

• **2001, Economic Growth and Tax Relief Reconciliation Act of 2001 (P.L. 107-16)**

P.L. 107-16, §551(a):

Amended Code Sec. 2031(c)(8)(A)(i). Effective for estates of decedents dying after 12-31-2000. Prior to amendment, Code Sec. 2031(c)(8)(A)(i) read as follows:

(i) which is located—

(I) in or within 25 miles of an area which, on the date of the decedent's death, is a metropolitan area (as defined by the Office of Management and Budget),

(II) in or within 25 miles of an area which, on the date of the decedent's death, is a national park or wilderness area designated as part of the National Wilderness Preservation System (unless it is determined by the Secretary that land in or within 25 miles of such a park or wilderness area is not under significant development pressure), or

(III) in or within 10 miles of an area which, on the date of the decedent's death, is an Urban National Forest (as designated by the Forest Service),

P.L. 107-16, §551(b):

Amended Code Sec. 2031(c)(2) by adding at the end a new sentence. **Effective** for estates of decedents dying after 12-31-2000.

P.L. 107-16, §901(a)-(b), as amended by P.L. 111-312, §101(a)(1), provides:

SEC. 901. SUNSET OF PROVISIONS OF ACT.

(a) IN GENERAL.—All provisions of, and amendments made by, this Act shall not apply—

(1) to taxable, plan, or limitation years beginning after December 31, 2012, or

(2) in the case of title V, to estates of decedents dying, gifts made, or generation skipping transfers, after December 31, 2012.

(b) APPLICATION OF CERTAIN LAWS.—The Internal Revenue Code of 1986 and the Employee Retirement Income Security Act of 1974 shall be applied and administered to years, estates, gifts, and transfers described in subsection (a) as if the provisions and amendments described in subsection (a) had never been enacted.

[¶5645] CODE SEC. 2053. EXPENSES, INDEBTEDNESS, AND TAXES.

* * *

⟫→ Caution: *Code Sec. 2053(d), below, was amended by P.L. 107-16. For sunset provision, see P.L. 107-16, §901 [as amended by P.L. 111-312], in the amendment notes.*

(d) CERTAIN FOREIGN DEATH TAXES.—

(1) IN GENERAL.—Notwithstanding the provisions of subsection (c)(1)(B), for purposes of the tax imposed by section 2001, the value of the taxable estate may be determined, if the executor so elects before the expiration of the period of limitation for assessment provided in section 6501, by deducting from the value of the gross estate the amount (as determined in accordance with regulations prescribed by the Secretary) of any estate, succession, legacy, or inheritance tax imposed by and actually paid to any foreign country, in respect of any property situated within such foreign country and included in the gross estate of a citizen or resident of the United States, upon a transfer by the decedent for public, charitable, or religious uses described in section 2055. The determination under this paragraph of the country within which property is situated shall be made in accordance with the rules applicable under subchapter B (sec. 2101 and following) in determining whether property is situated within or without the United States. Any election under this paragraph shall be exercised in accordance with regulations prescribed by the Secretary.

(2) CONDITION FOR ALLOWANCE OF DEDUCTION.—No deduction shall be allowed under paragraph (1) for a foreign death tax specified therein unless the decrease in the tax imposed by section 2001 which results from the deduction provided in paragraph (1) will inure solely for the benefit of the public, charitable, or religious transferees described in section 2055 or section 2106(a)(2). In any case where the tax imposed by section 2001 is equitably apportioned among all the transferees of property included in the gross estate, including those described in sections 2055 and 2106(a)(2) (taking into account any exemptions, credits, or deductions allowed by this chapter), in determining such decrease, there shall be disregarded any decrease in the Federal estate tax which any transferees other than those described in sections 2055 and 2106(a)(2) are required to pay.

(3) EFFECT ON CREDIT FOR FOREIGN DEATH TAXES OF DEDUCTION UNDER THIS SUBSECTION.—

(A) ELECTION.—An election under this subsection shall be deemed a waiver of the right to claim a credit, against the Federal estate tax, under a death tax convention with any foreign country for any tax or portion thereof in respect of which a deduction is taken under this subsection.

(B) CROSS REFERENCE.—

See section 2014(f) for the effect of a deduction taken under this paragraph on the credit for foreign death taxes.

* * *

[CCH Explanation at ¶705 and ¶730. Committee Reports at ¶10,130.]

Amendments

• 2001, Economic Growth and Tax Relief Reconciliation Act of 2001 (P.L. 107-16)

P.L. 107-16, §532(c)(5):

Amended Code Sec. 2053(d). **Effective** for estates of decedents dying, and generation-skipping transfers, after 12-31-2004. Prior to amendment, Code Sec. 2053(d) read as follows:

(d) CERTAIN STATE AND FOREIGN DEATH TAXES.—

(1) GENERAL RULE.—Notwithstanding the provisions of subsection (c)(1)(B) of this section, for purposes of the tax imposed by section 2001 the value of the taxable estate may be determined, if the executor so elects before the expiration of the period of limitation for assessment provided in section 6501, by deducting from the value of the gross estate the amount (as determined in accordance with regulations prescribed by the Secretary) of—

(A) any estate, succession, legacy, or inheritance tax imposed by a State or the District of Columbia upon a transfer by the decedent for public, charitable, or religious uses described in section 2055 or 2106(a)(2), and

(B) any estate, succession, legacy, or inheritance tax imposed by and actually paid to any foreign country, in respect of any property situated within such foreign country and included in the gross estate of a citizen or resident of the United States, upon a transfer by the decedent for public, charitable, or religious uses described in section 2055.

The determination under subparagraph (B) of the country within which property is situated shall be made in accordance with the rules applicable under subchapter B (sec. 2101 and following) in determining whether property is situated within or without the United States. Any election under this paragraph shall be exercised in accordance with regulations prescribed by the Secretary.

(2) CONDITION FOR ALLOWANCE OF DEDUCTION.—No deduction shall be allowed under paragraph (1) for a State death tax or a foreign death tax specified therein unless the decrease in the tax imposed by section 2001 which results from the deduction provided in paragraph (1) will inure solely for the benefit of the public, charitable, or religious transferees described in section 2055 or section 2106(a)(2). In any case where the tax imposed by section 2001 is equitably apportioned among all the transferees of property included in the gross estate, including those described in sections 2055 and 2106(a)(2) (taking into account any exemptions, credits, or deductions allowed by this chapter), in determining such decrease, there shall be disregarded any decrease in the Federal estate tax which any transferees other than those described in sections 2055 and 2106(a)(2) are required to pay.

(3) EFFECT ON CREDITS FOR STATE AND FOREIGN DEATH TAXES OF DEDUCTION UNDER THIS SUBSECTION.—

(A) ELECTION.—An election under this subsection shall be deemed a waiver of the right to claim a credit, against the Federal estate tax, under a death tax convention with any foreign country for any tax or portion thereof in respect of which a deduction is taken under this subsection.

(B) CROSS REFERENCES.—

See section 2011(e) for the effect of a deduction taken under this subsection on the credit for State death taxes, and see section 2014(f) for the effect of a deduction taken under this subsection on the credit for foreign death taxes.

P.L. 107-16, §901(a)-(b), as amended by P.L. 111-312, §101(a)(1), provides:

SEC. 901. SUNSET OF PROVISIONS OF ACT.

(a) IN GENERAL.—All provisions of, and amendments made by, this Act shall not apply—

(1) to taxable, plan, or limitation years beginning after December 31, 2012, or

(2) in the case of title V, to estates of decedents dying, gifts made, or generation skipping transfers, after December 31, 2012.

(b) APPLICATION OF CERTAIN LAWS.—The Internal Revenue Code of 1986 and the Employee Retirement Income Security Act of 1974 shall be applied and administered to years, estates, gifts, and transfers described in subsection (a) as if the provisions and amendments described in subsection (a) had never been enacted.

[¶5650] CODE SEC. 2056A. QUALIFIED DOMESTIC TRUST.

* * *

(b) TAX TREATMENT OF TRUST.—

* * *

(10) CERTAIN BENEFITS ALLOWED.—

≫→ Caution: *Code Sec. 2056A(b)(10)(A), below, was amended by P.L. 107-16. For sunset provision, see P.L. 107-16, §901 [as amended by P.L. 111-312], in the amendment notes.*

(A) IN GENERAL.—If any property remaining in the qualified domestic trust on the date of the death of the surviving spouse is includible in the gross estate of such spouse for purposes of this chapter (or would be includible if such spouse were a citizen or resident of the United States), any benefit which is allowable (or would be allowable if such spouse were a citizen or resident of the United States) with respect to such property to the estate of such spouse under section 2014, 2032, 2032A, 2055, 2056, 2058, or 6166 shall be allowed for purposes of the tax imposed by paragraph (1)(B).

* * *

[CCH Explanation at ¶705 and ¶730. Committee Reports at ¶10,130.]

Amendments

• **2001, Economic Growth and Tax Relief Reconciliation Act of 2001 (P.L. 107-16)**

P.L. 107-16, §532(c)(6)(A)-(B):

Amended Code Sec. 2056A(b)(10)(A) by striking "2011," following "spouse under section", and by inserting "2058," after "2056,". Effective for estates of decedents dying, and generation-skipping transfers, after 12-31-2004.

P.L. 107-16, §901(a)-(b), as amended by P.L. 111-312, §101(a)(1), provides:

SEC. 901. SUNSET OF PROVISIONS OF ACT.

(a) In General.—All provisions of, and amendments made by, this Act shall not apply—

(1) to taxable, plan, or limitation years beginning after December 31, 2012, or

(2) in the case of title V, to estates of decedents dying, gifts made, or generation skipping transfers, after December 31, 2012.

(b) Application of Certain Laws.—The Internal Revenue Code of 1986 and the Employee Retirement Income Security Act of 1974 shall be applied and administered to years, estates, gifts, and transfers described in subsection (a) as if the provisions and amendments described in subsection (a) had never been enacted.

[¶5655] CODE SEC. 2057. FAMILY-OWNED BUSINESS INTERESTS.

* * *

➤➤➤ *Caution: Code Sec. 2057(j), below, was added by P.L. 107-16. For sunset provision, see P.L. 107-16, §901 [as amended by P.L. 111-312], in the amendment notes.*

(j) Termination.—This section shall not apply to the estates of decedents dying after December 31, 2003.

[CCH Explanation at ¶705 and ¶720. Committee Reports at ¶10,130.]

Amendments

• **2001, Economic Growth and Tax Relief Reconciliation Act of 2001 (P.L. 107-16)**

P.L. 107-16, §521(d):

Amended Code Sec. 2057 by adding at the end a new subsection (j). Effective for estates of decedents dying, and generation-skipping transfers, after 12-31-2003.

P.L. 107-16, §901(a)-(b), as amended by P.L. 111-312, §101(a)(1), provides:

SEC. 901. SUNSET OF PROVISIONS OF ACT.

(a) In General.—All provisions of, and amendments made by, this Act shall not apply—

(1) to taxable, plan, or limitation years beginning after December 31, 2012, or

(2) in the case of title V, to estates of decedents dying, gifts made, or generation skipping transfers, after December 31, 2012.

(b) Application of Certain Laws.—The Internal Revenue Code of 1986 and the Employee Retirement Income Security Act of 1974 shall be applied and administered to years, estates, gifts, and transfers described in subsection (a) as if the provisions and amendments described in subsection (a) had never been enacted.

➤➤➤ *Caution: Code Sec. 2058, below, was added by P.L. 107-16. For sunset provision, see P.L. 107-16, §901 [as amended by P.L. 111-312], in the amendment notes.*

[¶5660] CODE SEC. 2058. STATE DEATH TAXES.

(a) Allowance of Deduction.—For purposes of the tax imposed by section 2001, the value of the taxable estate shall be determined by deducting from the value of the gross estate the amount of any estate, inheritance, legacy, or succession taxes actually paid to any State or the District of Columbia, in respect of any property included in the gross estate (not including any such taxes paid with respect to the estate of a person other than the decedent).

(b) Period of Limitations.—The deduction allowed by this section shall include only such taxes as were actually paid and deduction therefor claimed before the later of—

(1) 4 years after the filing of the return required by section 6018, or

(2) if—

(A) a petition for redetermination of a deficiency has been filed with the Tax Court within the time prescribed in section 6213(a), the expiration of 60 days after the decision of the Tax Court becomes final,

(B) an extension of time has been granted under section 6161 or 6166 for payment of the tax shown on the return, or of a deficiency, the date of the expiration of the period of the extension, or

(C) a claim for refund or credit of an over-payment of tax imposed by this chapter has been filed within the time prescribed in section 6511, the latest of the expiration of—

(i) 60 days from the date of mailing by certified mail or registered mail by the Secretary to the taxpayer of a notice of the disallowance of any part of such claim,

(ii) 60 days after a decision by any court of competent jurisdiction becomes final with respect to a timely suit instituted upon such claim, or

(iii) 2 years after a notice of the waiver of disallowance is filed under section 6532(a)(3).

Notwithstanding sections 6511 and 6512, refund based on the deduction may be made if the claim for refund is filed within the period provided in the preceding sentence. Any such refund shall be made without interest.

[CCH Explanation at ¶705 and ¶730. Committee Reports at ¶10,130.]

Amendments

● **2001, Economic Growth and Tax Relief Reconciliation Act of 2001 (P.L. 107-16)**

P.L. 107-16, §532(b):

Amended part IV of subchapter A of chapter 11 by adding at the end a new Code Sec. 2058. Effective for estates of decedents dying, and generation-skipping transfers, after 12-31-2004.

P.L. 107-16, §901(a)-(b), as amended by P.L. 111-312, §101(a)(1), provides:

SEC. 901. SUNSET OF PROVISIONS OF ACT.

(a) IN GENERAL.—All provisions of, and amendments made by, this Act shall not apply—

(1) to taxable, plan, or limitation years beginning after December 31, 2012, or

(2) in the case of title V, to estates of decedents dying, gifts made, or generation skipping transfers, after December 31, 2012.

(b) APPLICATION OF CERTAIN LAWS.—The Internal Revenue Code of 1986 and the Employee Retirement Income Security Act of 1974 shall be applied and administered to years, estates, gifts, and transfers described in subsection (a) as if the provisions and amendments described in subsection (a) had never been enacted.

[¶5665] CODE SEC. 2101. TAX IMPOSED.

* * *

⟫→ Caution: *Code Sec. 2101(b), below, was amended by P.L. 107-147, effective as if included in P.L. 107-16. For sunset provision, see P.L. 107-16, §901 [as amended by P.L. 111-312], in the amendment notes.*

(b) COMPUTATION OF TAX.—The tax imposed by this section shall be the amount equal to the excess (if any) of—

(1) a tentative tax computed under section 2001(c) on the sum of—

(A) the amount of the taxable estate, and

(B) the amount of the adjusted taxable gifts, over

(2) a tentative tax computed under section 2001(c) on the amount of the adjusted taxable gifts.

* * *

[CCH Explanation at ¶705 and ¶710. Committee Reports at ¶10,130.]

Amendments

● **2002, Job Creation and Worker Assistance Act of 2002 (P.L. 107-147)**

P.L. 107-147, §411(g)(2):

Amended Code Sec. 2101(b) by striking the last sentence. Effective as if included in the provision of P.L. 107-16 to which it relates [effective for estates of decedents dying, and gifts made, after 12-31-2001.—CCH]. Prior to being stricken, the last sentence of Code Sec. 2101(b) read as follows:

For purposes of the preceding sentence, there shall be appropriate adjustments in the application of section 2001(c)(2) to reflect the difference between the amount of the credit provided under section 2102(c) and the amount of the credit provided under section 2010.

● **2001, Economic Growth and Tax Relief Reconciliation Act of 2001 (P.L. 107-16)**

P.L. 107-16, §901(a)-(b), as amended by P.L. 111-312, §101(a)(1), provides:

SEC. 901. SUNSET OF PROVISIONS OF ACT.

(a) IN GENERAL.—All provisions of, and amendments made by, this Act shall not apply—

(1) to taxable, plan, or limitation years beginning after December 31, 2012, or

(2) in the case of title V, to estates of decedents dying, gifts made, or generation skipping transfers, after December 31, 2012.

(b) APPLICATION OF CERTAIN LAWS.—The Internal Revenue Code of 1986 and the Employee Retirement Income Security Act of 1974 shall be applied and administered to years, estates, gifts, and transfers described in subsection (a) as if the provisions and amendments described in subsection (a) had never been enacted.

[¶5670] CODE SEC. 2102. CREDITS AGAINST TAX.

>>>→ *Caution: Code Sec. 2102(a), below, was amended by P.L. 107-16. For sunset provision, see P.L. 107-16, §901 [as amended by P.L. 111-312], in the amendment notes.*

(a) IN GENERAL.—The tax imposed by section 2101 shall be credited with the amounts determined in accordance with sections 2012 and 2013 (relating to gift tax and tax on prior transfers).

[CCH Explanation at ¶705 and ¶730. Committee Reports at ¶10,130.]

Amendments

• 2001, Economic Growth and Tax Relief Reconciliation Act of 2001 (P.L. 107-16)

P.L. 107-16, §532(c)(7)(A):

Amended Code Sec. 2102(a). **Effective** for estates of decedents dying, and generation-skipping transfers, after 12-31-2004. Prior to amendment, Code Sec. 2102(a) read as follows:

(a) IN GENERAL.—The tax imposed by section 2101 shall be credited with the amounts determined in accordance with sections 2011 to 2013, inclusive (relating to State death taxes, gift tax, and tax on prior transfers), subject to the special limitation provided in subsection (b).

P.L. 107-16, §901(a)-(b), as amended by P.L. 111-312, §101(a)(1), provides:

SEC. 901. SUNSET OF PROVISIONS OF ACT.

(a) IN GENERAL.—All provisions of, and amendments made by, this Act shall not apply—

(b) [Stricken.]

(1) to taxable, plan, or limitation years beginning after December 31, 2012, or

(2) in the case of title V, to estates of decedents dying, gifts made, or generation skipping transfers, after December 31, 2012.

(b) APPLICATION OF CERTAIN LAWS.—The Internal Revenue Code of 1986 and the Employee Retirement Income Security Act of 1974 shall be applied and administered to years, estates, gifts, and transfers described in subsection (a) as if the provisions and amendments described in subsection (a) had never been enacted.

[CCH Explanation at ¶705 and ¶730. Committee Reports at ¶10,130.]

Amendments

• 2001, Economic Growth and Tax Relief Reconciliation Act of 2001 (P.L. 107-16)

P.L. 107-16, §532(c)(7)(B):

Amended Code Sec. 2102 by striking subsection (b) and by redesignating subsection (c) as subsection (b). **Effective** for estates of decedents dying, and generation-skipping transfers, after 12-31-2004. Prior to being stricken, Code Sec. 2102(b) read as follows:

(b) SPECIAL LIMITATION.—The maximum credit allowed under section 2011 against the tax imposed by section 2101 for State death taxes paid shall be an amount which bears the same ratio to the credit computed as provided in section 2011(b) as the value of the property, as determined for purposes of this chapter, upon which State death taxes were paid and which is included in the gross estate under section 2103 bears to the value of the total gross estate under section 2103. For purposes of this subsection, the term "State death taxes" means the taxes described in section 2011(a).

P.L. 107-16, §901(a)-(b), as amended by P.L. 111-312, §101(a)(1), provides:

SEC. 901. SUNSET OF PROVISIONS OF ACT.

(a) IN GENERAL.—All provisions of, and amendments made by, this Act shall not apply—

(1) to taxable, plan, or limitation years beginning after December 31, 2012, or

(2) in the case of title V, to estates of decedents dying, gifts made, or generation skipping transfers, after December 31, 2012.

(b) APPLICATION OF CERTAIN LAWS.—The Internal Revenue Code of 1986 and the Employee Retirement Income Security Act of 1974 shall be applied and administered to years, estates, gifts, and transfers described in subsection (a) as if the provisions and amendments described in subsection (a) had never been enacted.

>>>→ *Caution: Former Code Sec. 2102(c), below, was redesignated as Code Sec. 2102(b) and amended by P.L. 107-16. For sunset provision, see P.L. 107-16, §901 [as amended by P.L. 111-312], in the amendment notes.*

(b) UNIFIED CREDIT.—

* * *

(5) APPLICATION OF OTHER CREDITS.—For purposes of subsection (a), sections 2012 and 2013 shall be applied as if the credit allowed under this subsection were allowed under section 2010.

[CCH Explanation at ¶705 and ¶730. Committee Reports at ¶10,130.]

Amendments

• 2001, Economic Growth and Tax Relief Reconciliation Act of 2001 (P.L. 107-16)

P.L. 107-16, §532(c)(7)(B):

Amended Code Sec. 2102 by striking subsection (b) and by redesignating subsection (c) as subsection (b). **Effective** for estates of decedents dying, and generation-skipping transfers, after 12-31-2004.

P.L. 107-16, §532(c)(7)(C):

Amended Code Sec. 2102(b)(5), as redesignated by Act Sec. 532(c)(7)(B), by striking "2011 to 2013, inclusive," and inserting "2012 and 2013". **Effective** for estates of decedents dying, and generation-skipping transfers, after 12-31-2004.

P.L. 107-16, §901(a)-(b), as amended by P.L. 111-312, §101(a)(1), provides:

SEC. 901. SUNSET OF PROVISIONS OF ACT.

(a) IN GENERAL.—All provisions of, and amendments made by, this Act shall not apply—

(1) to taxable, plan, or limitation years beginning after December 31, 2012, or

(2) in the case of title V, to estates of decedents dying, gifts made, or generation skipping transfers, after December 31, 2012.

(b) APPLICATION OF CERTAIN LAWS.—The Internal Revenue Code of 1986 and the Employee Retirement Income Security Act of 1974 shall be applied and administered to years, estates, gifts, and transfers described in subsection (a) as if the provisions and amendments described in subsection (a) had never been enacted.

[¶5675] CODE SEC. 2105. PROPERTY WITHOUT THE UNITED STATES.

* * *

(d) STOCK IN A RIC.—

* * *

(3) TERMINATION.—This subsection shall not apply to estates of decedents dying after *December 31, 2011.*

[CCH Explanation at ¶386. Committee Reports at ¶10,330.]

Amendments

• 2010, Tax Relief, Unemployment Insurance Reauthorization, and Job Creation Act of 2010 (P.L. 111-312)

P.L. 111-312, §726(a):

Amended Code Sec. 2105(d)(3) by striking "December 31, 2009" and inserting "December 31, 2011". **Effective** for estates of decedents dying after 12-31-2009.

[¶5680] CODE SEC. 2106. TAXABLE ESTATE.

(a) DEFINITION OF TAXABLE ESTATE.—For purposes of the tax imposed by section 2101, the value of the taxable estate of every decedent nonresident not a citizen of the United States shall be determined by deducting from the value of that part of his gross estate which at the time of his death is situated in the United States—

* * *

⯈ *Caution: Code Sec. 2106(a)(4), below, was added by P.L. 107-16. For sunset provision, see P.L. 107-16, §901 [as amended by P.L. 111-312], in the amendment notes.*

(4) STATE DEATH TAXES.—The amount which bears the same ratio to the State death taxes as the value of the property, as determined for purposes of this chapter, upon which State death taxes were paid and which is included in the gross estate under section 2103 bears to the value of the total gross estate under section 2103. For purposes of this paragraph, the term "State death taxes" means the taxes described in section 2011(a).

[CCH Explanation at ¶705 and ¶730. Committee Reports at ¶10,330.]

Amendments

• **2001, Economic Growth and Tax Relief Reconciliation Act of 2001 (P.L. 107-16)**

P.L. 107-16, §532(c)(8):

Amended Code Sec. 2106(a) by adding at the end a new paragraph (4). **Effective** for estates of decedents dying, and generation-skipping transfers, after 12-31-2004.

P.L. 107-16, §901(a)-(b), as amended by P.L. 111-312, §101(a)(1), provides:

SEC. 901. SUNSET OF PROVISIONS OF ACT.

(a) IN GENERAL.—All provisions of, and amendments made by, this Act shall not apply—

(1) to taxable, plan, or limitation years beginning after December 31, 2012, or

(2) in the case of title V, to estates of decedents dying, gifts made, or generation skipping transfers, after December 31, 2012.

(b) APPLICATION OF CERTAIN LAWS.—The Internal Revenue Code of 1986 and the Employee Retirement Income Security Act of 1974 shall be applied and administered to years, estates, gifts, and transfers described in subsection (a) as if the provisions and amendments described in subsection (a) had never been enacted.

[¶5685] CODE SEC. 2107. EXPATRIATION TO AVOID TAX.

* * *

(c) CREDITS.—

* * *

»»→ Caution: *Code Sec. 2107(c)(3), below, was amended by P.L. 107-16. For sunset provision, see P.L. 107-16, §901 [as amended by P.L. 111-312], in the amendment notes.*

(3) OTHER CREDITS.—The tax imposed by subsection (a) shall be credited with the amounts determined in accordance with subsections (a) and (b) of section 2102. For purposes of subsection (a) of section 2102, sections 2012 and 2013 shall be applied as if the credit allowed under paragraph (1) were allowed under section 2010.

* * *

[CCH Explanation at ¶705 and ¶730. Committee Reports at ¶10,330.]

Amendments

• **2001, Economic Growth and Tax Relief Reconciliation Act of 2001 (P.L. 107-16)**

P.L. 107-16, §532(c)(7)(C):

Amended Code Sec. 2107(c)(3) by striking "2011 to 2013, inclusive," and inserting "2012 and 2013". **Effective** for estates of decedents dying, and generation-skipping transfers, after 12-31-2004.

P.L. 107-16, §901(a)-(b), as amended by P.L. 111-312, §101(a)(1), provides:

SEC. 901. SUNSET OF PROVISIONS OF ACT.

(a) IN GENERAL.—All provisions of, and amendments made by, this Act shall not apply—

(1) to taxable, plan, or limitation years beginning after December 31, 2012, or

(2) in the case of title V, to estates of decedents dying, gifts made, or generation skipping transfers, after December 31, 2012.

(b) APPLICATION OF CERTAIN LAWS.—The Internal Revenue Code of 1986 and the Employee Retirement Income Security Act of 1974 shall be applied and administered to years, estates, gifts, and transfers described in subsection (a) as if the provisions and amendments described in subsection (a) had never been enacted.

»»→ Caution: *Code Sec. 2210 was added by P.L. 107-16, applicable to estates of decedents dying, and generation-skipping transfers, after December 31, 2009. P.L. 111-312 removed Code Sec. 2210, applicable to estates of decedents dying, and transfers made, after December 31, 2009, but see P.L. 111-312, §301(c), in the amendment notes. For sunset provision, see P.L. 107-16, §901 [as amended by P.L. 111-312], in the amendment notes.*

[¶5695] CODE SEC. 2210. TERMINATION.

(a) IN GENERAL.—Except as provided in subsection (b), this chapter shall not apply to the estates of decedents dying after December 31, 2009.

(b) CERTAIN DISTRIBUTIONS FROM QUALIFIED DOMESTIC TRUSTS.—In applying section 2056A with respect to the surviving spouse of a decedent dying before January 1, 2010—

(1) section 2056A(b)(1)(A) shall not apply to distributions made after December 31, 2020, and

(2) section 2056A(b)(1)(B) shall not apply after December 31, 2009.

[CCH Explanation at ¶705 and ¶775. Committee Reports at ¶10,130.]

Amendments

- **2010, Tax Relief, Unemployment Insurance Reauthorization, and Job Creation Act of 2010 (P.L. 111-312)**

P.L. 111-312, §301(a):

Amended Code Sec. 2210 to read as such provision would read if subtitle A of title V of the Economic Growth and Tax Relief Reconciliation Act of 2001 (P.L. 107-16) had never been enacted. **Effective** for estates of decedents dying, and transfers made, after 12-31-2009. For a special rule, see Act Sec. 301(c), below.

P.L. 111-312, §301(c), provides:

(c) SPECIAL ELECTION WITH RESPECT TO ESTATES OF DECEDENTS DYING IN 2010.—Notwithstanding subsection (a), in the case of an estate of a decedent dying after December 31, 2009, and before January 1, 2011, the executor (within the meaning of section 2203 of the Internal Revenue Code of 1986) may elect to apply such Code as though the amendments made by subsection (a) do not apply with respect to chapter 11 of such Code and with respect to property acquired or passing from such decedent (within the meaning of section 1014(b) of such Code). Such election shall be made at such time and in such manner as the Secretary of the Treasury or the Secretary's delegate shall provide. Such an election once made shall be revocable only with the consent of the Secretary of the Treasury or the Secretary's delegate. For purposes of section 2652(a)(1) of such Code, the determination of whether any property is subject to the tax imposed by such chapter 11 shall be made without regard to any election made under this subsection.

P.L. 111-312, §304, provides:

SEC. 304. APPLICATION OF EGTRRA SUNSET TO THIS TITLE.

Section 901 of the Economic Growth and Tax Relief Reconciliation Act of 2001 shall apply to the amendments made by this title.

- **2001, Economic Growth and Tax Relief Reconciliation Act of 2001 (P.L. 107-16)**

P.L. 107-16, §501(a):

Amended subchapter C of chapter 11 of subtitle B by adding at the end a new Code Sec. 2210. **Effective** for the estates of decedents dying, and generation-skipping transfers, after 12-31-2009.

P.L. 107-16, §901(a)-(b), as amended by P.L. 111-312, §101(a)(1), provides:

SEC. 901. SUNSET OF PROVISIONS OF ACT.

(a) IN GENERAL.—All provisions of, and amendments made by, this Act shall not apply—

(1) to taxable, plan, or limitation years beginning after December 31, 2012, or

(2) in the case of title V, to estates of decedents dying, gifts made, or generation skipping transfers, after December 31, 2012.

(b) APPLICATION OF CERTAIN LAWS.—The Internal Revenue Code of 1986 and the Employee Retirement Income Security Act of 1974 shall be applied and administered to years, estates, gifts, and transfers described in subsection (a) as if the provisions and amendments described in subsection (a) had never been enacted.

[¶5700] CODE SEC. 2502. RATE OF TAX.

⇒ Caution: *Code Sec. 2502(a), below, as amended by P.L. 111-312, is effective on and after January 1, 2011. For sunset provision, see P.L. 107-16, §901 [as amended by P.L. 111-312], in the amendment notes.*

(a) COMPUTATION OF TAX.—*The tax imposed by section section 2501 for each calendar year shall be an amount equal to the excess of*—

(1) *a tentative tax, computed under section 2001(c), on the aggregate sum of the taxable gifts for such calendar year and for each of the preceding calendar periods, over*

(2) *a tentative tax, computed under such section, on the aggregate sum of the taxable gifts for each of the preceding calendar periods.*

* * *

[CCH Explanation at ¶705 and ¶710. Committee Reports at ¶10,130.]

Amendments

- **2010, Tax Relief, Unemployment Insurance Reauthorization, and Job Creation Act of 2010 (P.L. 111-312)**

P.L. 111-312, §302(b)(2):

Amended Code Sec. 2502(a) to read as such subsection would read if section 511(d) of the Economic Growth and Tax Relief Reconciliation Act of 2001 (P.L. 107-16) had never been enacted. **Effective** on and after 1-1-2011. Prior to amendment by P.L. 111-312, Code Sec. 2502(a) read as follows:

(a) COMPUTATION OF TAX.—

(1) IN GENERAL.—The tax imposed by section 2501 for each calendar year shall be an amount equal to the excess of—

(A) a tentative tax, computed under paragraph (2), on the aggregate sum of the taxable gifts for such calendar year and for each of the preceding calendar periods, over

(B) a tentative tax, computed under paragraph (2), on the aggregate sum of the taxable gifts for each of the preceding calendar periods.

(2) RATE SCHEDULE.—

If the amount with respect to which the tentative tax to be computed is:	The tentative tax is:
Not over $10,000 . . .	18% of such amount.
Over $10,000 but not over $20,000	$1,800, plus 20% of the excess over $10,000.
Over $20,000 but not over $40,000	$3,800, plus 22% of the excess over $20,000.
Over $40,000 but not over $60,000	$8,200, plus 24% of the excess over $40,000.
Over $60,000 but not over $80,000	$13,000, plus 26% of the excess over $60,000.
Over $80,000 but not over $100,000	$18,200, plus 28% of the excess over $80,000.
Over $100,000 but not over $150,000.	$23,800, plus 30% of the excess over $100,000.
Over $150,000 but not over $250,000.	$38,800, plus 32% of the excess over $150,000.
Over $250,000 but not over $500,000.	$70,800, plus 34% of the excess over $250,000.
Over $500,000	$155,800, plus 35% of the excess over $500,000.

P.L. 111-312, §304, provides:

SEC. 304. APPLICATION OF EGTRRA SUNSET TO THIS TITLE.

Section 901 of the Economic Growth and Tax Relief Reconciliation Act of 2001 shall apply to the amendments made by this title.

● **2001, Economic Growth and Tax Relief Reconciliation Act of 2001 (P.L. 107-16)**

P.L. 107-16, §511(d):

Amended Code Sec. 2502(a). **Effective** for gifts made after 12-31-2009. Prior to amendment, Code Sec. 2502(a) read as follows:

(a) COMPUTATION OF TAX.—The tax imposed by section 2501 for each calendar year shall be an amount equal to the excess of—

(1) a tentative tax, computed under section 2001(c), on the aggregate sum of the taxable gifts for such calendar year and for each of the preceding calendar periods, over

(2) a tentative tax, computed under such section, on the aggregate sum of the taxable gifts for each of the preceding calendar periods.

P.L. 107-16, §901(a)-(b), as amended by P.L. 111-312, §101(a)(1), provides:

SEC. 901. SUNSET OF PROVISIONS OF ACT.

(a) IN GENERAL.—All provisions of, and amendments made by, this Act shall not apply—

(1) to taxable, plan, or limitation years beginning after December 31, 2012, or

(2) in the case of title V, to estates of decedents dying, gifts made, or generation skipping transfers, after December 31, 2012.

(b) APPLICATION OF CERTAIN LAWS.—The Internal Revenue Code of 1986 and the Employee Retirement Income Security Act of 1974 shall be applied and administered to years, estates, gifts, and transfers described in subsection (a) as if the provisions and amendments described in subsection (a) had never been enacted.

[¶5705] CODE SEC. 2505. UNIFIED CREDIT AGAINST GIFT TAX.

》》》→ Caution: *Code Sec. 2505(a), below, was amended by P.L. 111-312. For sunset provision, see P.L. 107-16, §901 [as amended by P.L. 111-312], in the amendment notes.*

(a) GENERAL RULE.—In the case of a citizen or resident of the United States, there shall be allowed as a credit against the tax imposed by section 2501 for each calendar year an amount equal to—

》》》→ Caution: *Code Sec. 2505(a)(1), below, as amended by P.L. 111-312, §301(b), but prior to amendment by §302(b)(1)(A) and §303(b)(1), is effective on and after January 1, 2011. For sunset provision, see P.L. 107-16, §901 [as amended by P.L. 111-312], in the amendment notes.*

(1) the applicable credit amount in effect under section 2010(c) for such calendar year (determined as if the applicable exclusion amount were $1,000,000), reduced by

》》》→ Caution: *Code Sec. 2505(a)(1), below, as amended by P.L. 111-312, §301(b) and §302(b)(1)(A), but prior to amendment by §303(b)(1), applies to gifts made after December 31, 2010. For sunset provision, see P.L. 107-16, §901 [as amended by P.L. 111-312], in the amendment notes.*

(1) the applicable credit amount in effect under section 2010(c) for such calendar year, reduced by

》》》→ Caution: *Code Sec. 2505(a)(1), below, as amended by P.L. 111-312, §301(b), §302(b)(1)(A) and §303(b)(1), applies to estates of decedents dying and gifts made after December 31, 2010. For sunset provision, see P.L. 107-16, §901 [as amended by P.L. 111-312], in the amendment notes.*

(1) The applicable credit amount in effect under section 2010(c) which would apply if the donor died as of the end of the calendar year, reduced by

(2) the sum of the amounts allowable as a credit to the individual under this section for all preceding calendar periods.

For purposes of applying paragraph (2) for any calendar year, the rates of tax in effect under section 2502(a)(2) for such calendar year shall, in lieu of the rates of tax in effect for preceding calendar periods, be used in determining the amounts allowable as a credit under this section for all preceding calendar periods.

* * *

[CCH Explanation at ¶705, ¶710, ¶715 and ¶718. Committee Reports at ¶10,130.]

Amendments

• **2010, Tax Relief, Unemployment Insurance Reauthorization, and Job Creation Act of 2010 (P.L. 111-312)**

P.L. 111-312, §301(b):

Amended Code Sec. 2505(a)(1) to read as such paragraph would read if section 521(b)(2) of the Economic Growth and Tax Relief Reconciliation Act of 2001 (P.L. 107-16) had never been enacted. **Effective** on and after 1-1-2011. Prior to amendment by P.L. 111-312, Code Sec. 2505(a)(1) read as follows:

(1) the amount of the tentative tax which would be determined under the rate schedule set forth in section 2502(a)(2) if the amount with respect to which such tentative tax is to be computed were $1,000,000, reduced by

P.L. 111-312, §302(b)(1)(A):

Amended Code Sec. 2505(a)(1), after the application of Act Sec. 301(b), by striking "(determined as if the applicable exclusion amount were $1,000,000)" after "such calendar year". **Effective** for gifts made after 12-31-2010.

P.L. 111-312, §302(d)(2):

Amended Code Sec. 2505(a) by adding at the end a new flush sentence. **Effective** for estates of decedents dying, generation-skipping transfers, and gifts made, after 12-31-2009.

P.L. 111-312, §303(b)(1):

Amended Code Sec. 2505(a)(1), as amended by Act Sec. 302(b)(1). **Effective** for estates of decedents dying and gifts made after 12-31-2010. Prior to amendment, Code Sec. 2505(a)(1) read as follows:

(1) the applicable credit amount in effect under section 2010(c) for such calendar year, reduced by

P.L. 111-312, §304, provides:

SEC. 304. APPLICATION OF EGTRRA SUNSET TO THIS TITLE.

Section 901 of the Economic Growth and Tax Relief Reconciliation Act of 2001 shall apply to the amendments made by this title.

• **2001, Economic Growth and Tax Relief Reconciliation Act of 2001 (P.L. 107-16)**

P.L. 107-16, §521(b)(1):

Amended Code Sec. 2505(a)(1) by inserting "(determined as if the applicable exclusion amount were $1,000,000)" after "calendar year". **Effective** for estates of decedents dying, and gifts made, after 12-31-2001.

P.L. 107-16, §521(b)(2):

Amended Code Sec. 2505(a)(1), as amended by Act Sec. 521(b)(1). **Effective** for gifts made after 12-31-2009. Prior to amendment, Code Sec. 2505(a)(1) read as follows:

(1) the applicable credit amount in effect under section 2010(c) for such calendar year (determined as if the applicable exclusion amount were $1,000,000), reduced by

P.L. 107-16, §901(a)-(b), as amended by P.L. 111-312, §101(a)(1), provides:

SEC. 901. SUNSET OF PROVISIONS OF ACT.

(a) IN GENERAL.—All provisions of, and amendments made by, this Act shall not apply—

(1) to taxable, plan, or limitation years beginning after December 31, 2012, or

(2) in the case of title V, to estates of decedents dying, gifts made, or generation skipping transfers, after December 31, 2012.

(b) APPLICATION OF CERTAIN LAWS.—The Internal Revenue Code of 1986 and the Employee Retirement Income Security Act of 1974 shall be applied and administered to years, estates, gifts, and transfers described in subsection (a) as if the provisions and amendments described in subsection (a) had never been enacted.

[¶5710] CODE SEC. 2511. TRANSFERS IN GENERAL.

* * *

⋙➔ *Caution: Code Sec. 2511(c), below, was stricken by P.L. 111-312, applicable to estates of decedents dying, generation-skipping transfers, and gifts made after December 31, 2009. For sunset provision, see P.L. 107-16, §901 [as amended by P.L. 111-312], in the amendment notes.*

(c) TREATMENT OF CERTAIN TRANSFERS IN TRUST.—Notwithstanding any other provision of this section and except as provided in regulations, a transfer in trust shall be treated as a transfer of property by gift, unless the trust is treated as wholly owned by the donor or the donor's spouse under subpart E of part I of subchapter J of chapter 1.

[CCH Explanation at ¶705 and ¶710. Committee Reports at ¶10,130.]

Amendments

● **2010, Tax Relief, Unemployment Insurance Reauthorization, and Job Creation Act of 2010 (P.L. 111-312)**

P.L. 111-312, §302(e):

Amended Code Sec. 2511 by striking subsection (c). **Effective** for estates of decedents dying, generation-skipping transfers, and gifts made, after 12-31-2009. Prior to being stricken, Code Sec. 2511(c) read as follows:

(c) TREATMENT OF CERTAIN TRANSFERS IN TRUST.—Notwithstanding any other provision of this section and except as provided in regulations, a transfer in trust shall be treated as a transfer of property by gift, unless the trust is treated as wholly owned by the donor or the donor's spouse under subpart E of part I of subchapter J of chapter 1.

P.L. 111-312, §304, provides:

SEC. 304. APPLICATION OF EGTRRA SUNSET TO THIS TITLE.

Section 901 of the Economic Growth and Tax Relief Reconciliation Act of 2001 shall apply to the amendments made by this title.

● **2002, Job Creation and Worker Assistance Act of 2002 (P.L. 107-147)**

P.L. 107-147, §411(g)(1):

Amended Code Sec. 2511(c) by striking "taxable gift under section 2503," and inserting "transfer of property by

gift,". **Effective** as if included in the provision of P.L. 107-16 to which it relates [effective for gifts made after 12-31-2009.—CCH].

● **2001, Economic Growth and Tax Relief Reconciliation Act of 2001 (P.L. 107-16)**

P.L. 107-16, §511(e):

Amended Code Sec. 2511 by adding at the end a new subsection (c). **Effective** for gifts made after 12-31-2009.

P.L. 107-16, §901(a)-(b), as amended by P.L. 111-312, §101(a)(1), provides:

SEC. 901. SUNSET OF PROVISIONS OF ACT.

(a) IN GENERAL.—All provisions of, and amendments made by, this Act shall not apply—

(1) to taxable, plan, or limitation years beginning after December 31, 2012, or

(2) in the case of title V, to estates of decedents dying, gifts made, or generation skipping transfers, after December 31, 2012.

(b) APPLICATION OF CERTAIN LAWS.—The Internal Revenue Code of 1986 and the Employee Retirement Income Security Act of 1974 shall be applied and administered to years, estates, gifts, and transfers described in subsection (a) as if the provisions and amendments described in subsection (a) had never been enacted.

[¶5715] CODE SEC. 2604. CREDIT FOR CERTAIN STATE TAXES.

* * *

➤ *Caution: Code Sec. 2604(c), below, was added by P.L. 107-16. For sunset provision, see P.L. 107-16, §901 [as amended by P.L. 111-312], in the amendment notes.*

(c) TERMINATION.—This section shall not apply to the generation-skipping transfers after December 31, 2004.

[CCH Explanation at ¶705, ¶715 and ¶730. Committee Reports at ¶10,130.]

Amendments

● **2001, Economic Growth and Tax Relief Reconciliation Act of 2001 (P.L. 107-16)**

P.L. 107-16, §532(c)(10):

Amended Code Sec. 2604 by adding at the end a new subsection (c). **Effective** for estates of decedents dying, and generation-skipping transfers, after 12-31-2004.

P.L. 107-16, §901(a)-(b), as amended by P.L. 111-312, §101(a)(1), provides:

SEC. 901. SUNSET OF PROVISIONS OF ACT.

(a) IN GENERAL.—All provisions of, and amendments made by, this Act shall not apply—

(1) to taxable, plan, or limitation years beginning after December 31, 2012, or

(2) in the case of title V, to estates of decedents dying, gifts made, or generation skipping transfers, after December 31, 2012.

(b) APPLICATION OF CERTAIN LAWS.—The Internal Revenue Code of 1986 and the Employee Retirement Income Security Act of 1974 shall be applied and administered to years, estates, gifts, and transfers described in subsection (a) as if the provisions and amendments described in subsection (a) had never been enacted.

[¶5720] CODE SEC. 2631. GST EXEMPTION.

➤ *Caution: Code Sec. 2631(a), below, was amended by P.L. 107-16. For sunset provision, see P.L. 107-16, §901 [as amended by P.L. 111-312], in the amendment notes.*

(a) GENERAL RULE.—For purposes of determining the inclusion ratio, every individual shall be allowed a GST exemption amount which may be allocated by such individual (or his executor) to any property with respect to which such individual is the transferor.

* * *

[CCH Explanation at ¶705 and ¶715. Committee Reports at ¶10,130.]

Amendments

● **2001, Economic Growth and Tax Relief Reconciliation Act of 2001 (P.L. 107-16)**

P.L. 107-16, §521(c)(1):

Amended Code Sec. 2631(a) by striking "of $1,000,000" and inserting "amount". Effective for estates of decedents dying, and generation-skipping transfers, after 12-31-2003.

P.L. 107-16, §901(a)-(b), as amended by P.L. 111-312, §101(a)(1), provides:

SEC. 901. SUNSET OF PROVISIONS OF ACT.

(a) IN GENERAL.—All provisions of, and amendments made by, this Act shall not apply—

(1) to taxable, plan, or limitation years beginning after December 31, 2012, or

(2) in the case of title V, to estates of decedents dying, gifts made, or generation skipping transfers, after December 31, 2012.

(b) APPLICATION OF CERTAIN LAWS.—The Internal Revenue Code of 1986 and the Employee Retirement Income Security Act of 1974 shall be applied and administered to years, estates, gifts, and transfers described in subsection (a) as if the provisions and amendments described in subsection (a) had never been enacted.

⟫➔ Caution: Code Sec. 2631(c), below, was amended by P.L. 107-16 and P.L. 111-312. For sunset provision, see P.L. 107-16, §901 [as amended by P.L. 111-312], in the amendment notes.

(c) GST EXEMPTION AMOUNT.—For purposes of subsection (a), the GST exemption amount for any calendar year shall be equal to *the basic exclusion amount* under section 2010(c) for such calendar year.

[CCH Explanation at ¶705, ¶715 and ¶718. Committee Reports at ¶10,130.]

Amendments

● **2010, Tax Relief, Unemployment Insurance Reauthorization, and Job Creation Act of 2010 (P.L. 111-312)**

P.L. 111-312, §303(b)(2):

Amended Code Sec. 2631(c) by striking "the applicable exclusion amount" and inserting "the basic exclusion amount". Effective for generation-skipping transfers after 12-31-2010.

P.L. 111-312, §304, provides:

SEC. 304. APPLICATION OF EGTRRA SUNSET TO THIS TITLE.

Section 901 of the Economic Growth and Tax Relief Reconciliation Act of 2001 shall apply to the amendments made by this title.

● **2001, Economic Growth and Tax Relief Reconciliation Act of 2001 (P.L. 107-16)**

P.L. 107-16, §521(c)(2):

Amended Code Sec. 2631(c). Effective for estates of decedents dying, and generation-skipping transfers, after 12-31-2003. Prior to amendment, Code Sec. 2631(c) read as follows:

(c) INFLATION ADJUSTMENT.—

(1) IN GENERAL.—In the case of any calendar year after 1998, the $1,000,000 amount contained in subsection (a) shall be increased by an amount equal to—

(A) $1,000,000, multiplied by

(B) the cost-of-living adjustment determined under section 1(f)(3) for such calendar year by substituting "calendar year 1997" for "calendar year 1992" in subparagraph (B) thereof.

If any amount as adjusted under the preceding sentence is not a multiple of $10,000, such amount shall be rounded to the next lowest multiple of $10,000.

(2) ALLOCATION OF INCREASE.—Any increase under paragraph (1) for any calendar year shall apply only to generation-skipping transfers made during or after such calendar year; except that no such increase for calendar years after the calendar year in which the transferor dies shall apply to transfers by such transferor.

P.L. 107-16, §901(a)-(b), as amended by P.L. 111-312, §101(a)(1), provides:

SEC. 901. SUNSET OF PROVISIONS OF ACT.

(a) IN GENERAL.—All provisions of, and amendments made by, this Act shall not apply—

(1) to taxable, plan, or limitation years beginning after December 31, 2012, or

(2) in the case of title V, to estates of decedents dying, gifts made, or generation skipping transfers, after December 31, 2012.

(b) APPLICATION OF CERTAIN LAWS.—The Internal Revenue Code of 1986 and the Employee Retirement Income Security Act of 1974 shall be applied and administered to years, estates, gifts, and transfers described in subsection (a) as if the provisions and amendments described in subsection (a) had never been enacted.

[¶5725] CODE SEC. 2632. SPECIAL RULES FOR ALLOCATION OF GST EXEMPTION.

* * *

(b) DEEMED ALLOCATION TO CERTAIN LIFETIME DIRECT SKIPS.—

* * *

>>>→ *Caution: Code Sec. 2632(b)(2), below, was amended by P.L. 107-16. For sunset provision, see P.L. 107-16; § 901 [as amended by P.L. 111-312], in the amendment notes.*

(2) UNUSED PORTION.—For purposes of paragraph (1), the unused portion of an individual's GST exemption is that portion of such exemption which has not previously been allocated by such individual (or treated as allocated under paragraph (1) or subsection (c)(1)).

* * *

[CCH Explanation at ¶705 and ¶765. Committee Reports at ¶10,130.]

Amendments

• **2001, Economic Growth and Tax Relief Reconciliation Act of 2001 (P.L. 107-16)**

P.L. 107-16, §561(b):

Amended Code Sec. 2632(b)(2) by striking "with respect to a prior direct skip" and inserting "or subsection (c)(1)". Effective for transfers subject to chapter 11 or 12 made after 12-31-2000, and to estate tax inclusion periods ending after 12-31-2000.

P.L. 107-16, §901(a)-(b), as amended by P.L. 111-312, §101(a)(1), provides:

SEC. 901. SUNSET OF PROVISIONS OF ACT.

(a) IN GENERAL.—All provisions of, and amendments made by, this Act shall not apply—

(1) to taxable, plan, or limitation years beginning after December 31, 2012, or

(2) in the case of title V, to estates of decedents dying, gifts made, or generation skipping transfers, after December 31, 2012.

(b) APPLICATION OF CERTAIN LAWS.—The Internal Revenue Code of 1986 and the Employee Retirement Income Security Act of 1974 shall be applied and administered to years, estates, gifts, and transfers described in subsection (a) as if the provisions and amendments described in subsection (a) had never been enacted.

>>>→ *Caution: Code Sec. 2632(c), below, was added by P.L. 107-16. For sunset provision, see P.L. 107-16, §901 [as amended by P.L. 111-312], in the amendment notes.*

(c) DEEMED ALLOCATION TO CERTAIN LIFETIME TRANSFERS TO GST TRUSTS.—

(1) IN GENERAL.—If any individual makes an indirect skip during such individual's lifetime, any unused portion of such individual's GST exemption shall be allocated to the property transferred to the extent necessary to make the inclusion ratio for such property zero. If the amount of the indirect skip exceeds such unused portion, the entire unused portion shall be allocated to the property transferred.

(2) UNUSED PORTION.—For purposes of paragraph (1), the unused portion of an individual's GST exemption is that portion of such exemption which has not previously been—

(A) allocated by such individual,

(B) treated as allocated under subsection (b) with respect to a direct skip occurring during or before the calendar year in which the indirect skip is made, or

(C) treated as allocated under paragraph (1) with respect to a prior indirect skip.

(3) DEFINITIONS.—

(A) INDIRECT SKIP.—For purposes of this subsection, the term "indirect skip" means any transfer of property (other than a direct skip) subject to the tax imposed by chapter 12 made to a GST trust.

(B) GST TRUST.—The term "GST trust" means a trust that could have a generation-skipping transfer with respect to the transferor unless—

(i) the trust instrument provides that more than 25 percent of the trust corpus must be distributed to or may be withdrawn by one or more individuals who are non-skip persons—

(I) before the date that the individual attains age 46,

(II) on or before one or more dates specified in the trust instrument that will occur before the date that such individual attains age 46, or

(III) upon the occurrence of an event that, in accordance with regulations prescribed by the Secretary, may reasonably be expected to occur before the date that such individual attains age 46,

(ii) the trust instrument provides that more than 25 percent of the trust corpus must be distributed to or may be withdrawn by one or more individuals who are non-skip persons and who are living on the date of death of another person identified in the instrument (by name or by class) who is more than 10 years older than such individuals,

(iii) the trust instrument provides that, if one or more individuals who are non-skip persons die on or before a date or event described in clause (i) or (ii), more than 25 percent of the trust corpus either must be distributed to the estate or estates of one or more of such individuals or is subject to a general power of appointment exercisable by one or more of such individuals,

(iv) the trust is a trust any portion of which would be included in the gross estate of a non-skip person (other than the transferor) if such person died immediately after the transfer,

(v) the trust is a charitable lead annuity trust (within the meaning of section 2642(e)(3)(A)) or a charitable remainder annuity trust or a charitable remainder unitrust (within the meaning of section 664(d)), or

(vi) the trust is a trust with respect to which a deduction was allowed under section 2522 for the amount of an interest in the form of the right to receive annual payments of a fixed percentage of the net fair market value of the trust property (determined yearly) and which is required to pay principal to a non-skip person if such person is alive when the yearly payments for which the deduction was allowed terminate.

For purposes of this subparagraph, the value of transferred property shall not be considered to be includible in the gross estate of a non-skip person or subject to a right of withdrawal by reason of such person holding a right to withdraw so much of such property as does not exceed the amount referred to in section 2503(b) with respect to any transferor, and it shall be assumed that powers of appointment held by non-skip persons will not be exercised.

(4) AUTOMATIC ALLOCATIONS TO CERTAIN GST TRUSTS.—For purposes of this subsection, an indirect skip to which section 2642(f) applies shall be deemed to have been made only at the close of the estate tax inclusion period. The fair market value of such transfer shall be the fair market value of the trust property at the close of the estate tax inclusion period.

(5) APPLICABILITY AND EFFECT.—

(A) IN GENERAL.—An individual—

(i) may elect to have this subsection not apply to—

(I) an indirect skip, or

(II) any or all transfers made by such individual to a particular trust, and

(ii) may elect to treat any trust as a GST trust for purposes of this subsection with respect to any or all transfers made by such individual to such trust.

(B) ELECTIONS.—

(i) ELECTIONS WITH RESPECT TO INDIRECT SKIPS.—An election under subparagraph (A)(i)(I) shall be deemed to be timely if filed on a timely filed gift tax return for the calendar year in which the transfer was made or deemed to have been made pursuant to paragraph (4) or on such later date or dates as may be prescribed by the Secretary.

(ii) OTHER ELECTIONS.—An election under clause (i)(II) or (ii) of subparagraph (A) may be made on a timely filed gift tax return for the calendar year for which the election is to become effective.

[CCH Explanation at ¶705 and ¶765. Committee Reports at ¶10,130.]

Amendments

• **2001, Economic Growth and Tax Relief Reconciliation Act of 2001 (P.L. 107-16)**

P.L. 107-16, §561(a):

Amended Code Sec. 2632 by redesignating subsection (c) as subsection (e) and by inserting after subsection (b) a new subsection (c). **Effective** for transfers subject to chapter 11 or 12 made after 12-31-2000, and to estate tax inclusion periods ending after 12-31-2000.

P.L. 107-16, §901(a)-(b), as amended by P.L. 111-312, §101(a)(1), provides:

SEC. 901. SUNSET OF PROVISIONS OF ACT.

(a) IN GENERAL.—All provisions of, and amendments made by, this Act shall not apply—

(1) to taxable, plan, or limitation years beginning after December 31, 2012, or

(2) in the case of title V, to estates of decedents dying, gifts made, or generation skipping transfers, after December 31, 2012.

(b) APPLICATION OF CERTAIN LAWS.—The Internal Revenue Code of 1986 and the Employee Retirement Income Security Act of 1974 shall be applied and administered to years, estates, gifts, and transfers described in subsection (a) as if the provisions and amendments described in subsection (a) had never been enacted.

⟫⟫→ *Caution: Code Sec. 2632(d), below, was added by P.L. 107-16. For sunset provision, see P.L. 107-16, §901 [as amended by P.L. 111-312], in the amendment notes.*

(d) RETROACTIVE ALLOCATIONS.—

(1) IN GENERAL.—If—

(A) a non-skip person has an interest or a future interest in a trust to which any transfer has been made,

(B) such person—

(i) is a lineal descendant of a grandparent of the transferor or of a grandparent of the transferor's spouse or former spouse, and

(ii) is assigned to a generation below the generation assignment of the transferor, and

(C) such person predeceases the transferor,

then the transferor may make an allocation of any of such transferor's unused GST exemption to any previous transfer or transfers to the trust on a chronological basis.

(2) SPECIAL RULES.—If the allocation under paragraph (1) by the transferor is made on a gift tax return filed on or before the date prescribed by section 6075(b) for gifts made within the calendar year within which the non-skip person's death occurred—

(A) the value of such transfer or transfers for purposes of section 2642(a) shall be determined as if such allocation had been made on a timely filed gift tax return for each calendar year within which each transfer was made,

(B) such allocation shall be effective immediately before such death, and

(C) the amount of the transferor's unused GST exemption available to be allocated shall be determined immediately before such death.

(3) FUTURE INTEREST.—For purposes of this subsection, a person has a future interest in a trust if the trust may permit income or corpus to be paid to such person on a date or dates in the future.

[CCH Explanation at ¶705 and ¶765. Committee Reports at ¶10,130.]

Amendments

• **2001, Economic Growth and Tax Relief Reconciliation Act of 2001 (P.L. 107-16)**

P.L. 107-16, §561(a):

Amended Code Sec. 2632 by redesignating subsection (c) as subsection (e) and by inserting after new subsection (c), as added by Act Sec. 561(a), a new subsection (d). **Effective** for deaths of non-skip persons occurring after 12-31-2000.

P.L. 107-16, §901(a)-(b), as amended by P.L. 111-312, §101(a)(1), provides:

SEC. 901. SUNSET OF PROVISIONS OF ACT.

(a) IN GENERAL.—All provisions of, and amendments made by, this Act shall not apply—

(1) to taxable, plan, or limitation years beginning after December 31, 2012, or

(2) in the case of title V, to estates of decedents dying, gifts made, or generation skipping transfers, after December 31, 2012.

(b) APPLICATION OF CERTAIN LAWS.—The Internal Revenue Code of 1986 and the Employee Retirement Income Security Act of 1974 shall be applied and administered to years, estates, gifts, and transfers described in subsection (a) as if the provisions and amendments described in subsection (a) had never been enacted.

»»→ Caution: *Former Code Sec. 2632(c) was redesignated as Code Sec. 2632(e), below, by P.L. 107-16. For sunset provision, see P.L. 107-16, §901 [as amended by P.L. 111-312], in the amendment notes.*

(e) ALLOCATION OF UNUSED GST EXEMPTION.—

(1) IN GENERAL.—Any portion of an individual's GST exemption which has not been allocated within the time prescribed by subsection (a) shall be deemed to be allocated as follows—

(A) first, to property which is the subject of a direct skip occurring at such individual's death, and

(B) second, to trusts with respect to which such individual is the transferor and from which a taxable distribution or a taxable termination might occur at or after such individual's death.

(2) ALLOCATION WITHIN CATEGORIES.—

(A) IN GENERAL.—The allocation under paragraph (1) shall be made among the properties described in subparagraph (A) thereof and the trust described in subparagraph (B) thereof, as the case may be, in proportion to the respective amounts (at the time of allocation) of the nonexempt portions of such properties or trusts.

(B) NONEXEMPT PORTION.—For purposes of subparagraph (A), the term "nonexempt portion" means the value (at the time of allocation) of the property or trust, multiplied by the inclusion ratio with respect to such property or trust.

Amendments

• **2001, Economic Growth and Tax Relief Reconciliation Act of 2001 (P.L. 107-16)**

P.L. 107-16, §561(a):

Amended Code Sec. 2632 by redesignating subsection (c) as subsection (e). **Effective 6-7-2001.**

P.L. 107-16, §901(a)-(b), as amended by P.L. 111-312, §101(a)(1), provides:

SEC. 901. SUNSET OF PROVISIONS OF ACT.

(a) IN GENERAL.—All provisions of, and amendments made by, this Act shall not apply—

(1) to taxable, plan, or limitation years beginning after December 31, 2012, or

(2) in the case of title V, to estates of decedents dying, gifts made, or generation skipping transfers, after December 31, 2012.

(b) APPLICATION OF CERTAIN LAWS.—The Internal Revenue Code of 1986 and the Employee Retirement Income Security Act of 1974 shall be applied and administered to years, estates, gifts, and transfers described in subsection (a) as if the provisions and amendments described in subsection (a) had never been enacted.

[¶5730] CODE SEC. 2642. INCLUSION RATIO.

(a) INCLUSION RATIO DEFINED.—For purposes of this chapter—

* * *

»»→ Caution: *Code Sec. 2642(a)(3), below, was added by P.L. 107-16. For sunset provision, see P.L. 107-16, §901 [as amended by P.L. 111-312], in the amendment notes.*

(3) SEVERING OF TRUSTS.—

(A) IN GENERAL.—If a trust is severed in a qualified severance, the trusts resulting from such severance shall be treated as separate trusts thereafter for purposes of this chapter.

(B) QUALIFIED SEVERANCE.—For purposes of subparagraph (A)—

(i) IN GENERAL.—The term "qualified severance" means the division of a single trust and the creation (by any means available under the governing instrument or under local law) of two or more trusts if—

(I) the single trust was divided on a fractional basis, and

(II) the terms of the new trusts, in the aggregate, provide for the same succession of interests of beneficiaries as are provided in the original trust.

(ii) Trusts with Inclusion Ratio Greater than Zero.—If a trust has an inclusion ratio of greater than zero and less than 1, a severance is a qualified severance only if the single trust is divided into two trusts, one of which receives a fractional share of the total value of all trust assets equal to the applicable fraction of the single trust immediately before the severance. In such case, the trust receiving such fractional share shall have an inclusion ratio of zero and the other trust shall have an inclusion ratio of 1.

(iii) Regulations.—The term "qualified severance" includes any other severance permitted under regulations prescribed by the Secretary.

(C) Timing and Manner of Severances.—A severance pursuant to this paragraph may be made at any time. The Secretary shall prescribe by forms or regulations the manner in which the qualified severance shall be reported to the Secretary.

[CCH Explanation at ¶705 and ¶770. Committee Reports at ¶10,130.]

Amendments

• **2001, Economic Growth and Tax Relief Reconciliation Act of 2001 (P.L. 107-16)**

P.L. 107-16, §562(a):

Amended Code Sec. 2642(a) by adding at the end a new paragraph (3). Effective for severances after 12-31-2000.

P.L. 107-16, §901(a)-(b), as amended by P.L. 111-312, §101(a)(1), provides:

SEC. 901. SUNSET OF PROVISIONS OF ACT.

(a) In General.—All provisions of, and amendments made by, this Act shall not apply—

(1) to taxable, plan, or limitation years beginning after December 31, 2012, or

(2) in the case of title V, to estates of decedents dying, gifts made, or generation skipping transfers, after December 31, 2012.

(b) Application of Certain Laws.—The Internal Revenue Code of 1986 and the Employee Retirement Income Security Act of 1974 shall be applied and administered to years, estates, gifts, and transfers described in subsection (a) as if the provisions and amendments described in subsection (a) had never been enacted.

(b) Valuation Rules, Etc.—Except as provided in subsection (f)—

⇛➤ Caution: *Code Sec. 2642(b)(1), below, was amended by P.L. 107-16. For sunset provision, see P.L. 107-16, §901 [as amended by P.L. 111-312], in the amendment notes.*

(1) Gifts for Which Gift Tax Return Filed or Deemed Allocation Made.—If the allocation of the GST exemption to any transfers of property is made on a gift tax return filed on or before the date prescribed by section 6075(b) for such transfer or is deemed to be made under section 2632(b)(1) or (c)(1)—

(A) the value of such property for purposes of subsection (a) shall be its value as finally determined for purposes of chapter 12 (within the meaning of section 2001(f)(2)), or, in the case of an allocation deemed to have been made at the close of an estate tax inclusion period, its value at the time of the close of the estate tax inclusion period, and

(B) such allocation shall be effective on and after the date of such transfer, or, in the case of an allocation deemed to have been made at the close of an estate tax inclusion period, on and after the close of such estate tax inclusion period.

(2) Transfers and Allocations at or After Death.—

⇛➤ Caution: *Code Sec. 2642(b)(2)(A), below, was amended by P.L. 107-16. For sunset provision, see P.L. 107-16, §901 [as amended by P.L. 111-312], in the amendment notes.*

(A) Transfers at Death.—If property is transferred as a result of the death of the transferor, the value of such property for purposes of subsection (a) shall be its value as finally determined for purposes of chapter 11; except that, if the requirements prescribed by the Secretary respecting allocation of post-death changes in value are not met, the value of such property shall be determined as of the time of the distribution concerned.

* * *

[CCH Explanation at ¶705 and ¶775. Committee Reports at ¶10,130.]

Amendments

• **2001, Economic Growth and Tax Relief Reconciliation Act of 2001 (P.L. 107-16)**

P.L. 107-16, §563(a):

Amended Code Sec. 2642(b)(1). **Effective** for transfers subject to chapter 11 or 12 of the Internal Revenue Code of 1986 made after 12-31-2000. Prior to amendment, Code Sec. 2642(b)(1) read as follows:

(1) GIFTS FOR WHICH GIFT TAX RETURN FILED OR DEEMED ALLOCATION MADE.—If the allocation of the GST exemption to any property is made on a gift tax return filed on or before the date prescribed by section 6075(b) or is deemed to be made under section 2632(b)(1)—

(A) the value of such property for purposes of subsection (a) shall be its value for purposes of chapter 12, and

(B) such allocation shall be effective on and after the date of such transfer.

P.L. 107-16, §563(b):

Amended Code Sec. 2642(b)(2)(A). **Effective** for transfers subject to chapter 11 or 12 of the Internal Revenue Code of 1986 made after 12-31-2000. Prior to amendment, Code Sec. 2642(b)(2)(A) read as follows:

(A) TRANSFERS AT DEATH.—If property is transferred as a result of the death of the transferor, the value of such property for purposes of subsection (a) shall be its value for purposes of chapter 11; except that, if the requirements prescribed by the Secretary respecting allocation of post-death changes in value are not met, the value of such property shall be determined as of the time of the distribution concerned.

P.L. 107-16, §901(a)-(b), as amended by P.L. 111-312, §101(a)(1), provides:

SEC. 901. SUNSET OF PROVISIONS OF ACT.

(a) IN GENERAL.—All provisions of, and amendments made by, this Act shall not apply—

(1) to taxable, plan, or limitation years beginning after December 31, 2012, or

(2) in the case of title V, to estates of decedents dying, gifts made, or generation skipping transfers, after December 31, 2012.

(b) APPLICATION OF CERTAIN LAWS.—The Internal Revenue Code of 1986 and the Employee Retirement Income Security Act of 1974 shall be applied and administered to years, estates, gifts, and transfers described in subsection (a) as if the provisions and amendments described in subsection (a) had never been enacted.

⟫→ *Caution: Code Sec. 2642(g), below, was added by P.L. 107-16. For sunset provision, see P.L. 107-16, §901 [as amended by P.L. 111-312], in the amendment notes.*

(g) RELIEF PROVISIONS.—

(1) RELIEF FROM LATE ELECTIONS.—

(A) IN GENERAL.—The Secretary shall by regulation prescribe such circumstances and procedures under which extensions of time will be granted to make—

(i) an allocation of GST exemption described in paragraph (1) or (2) of subsection (b), and

(ii) an election under subsection (b)(3) or (c)(5) of section 2632.

Such regulations shall include procedures for requesting comparable relief with respect to transfers made before the date of the enactment of this paragraph.

(B) BASIS FOR DETERMINATIONS.—In determining whether to grant relief under this paragraph, the Secretary shall take into account all relevant circumstances, including evidence of intent contained in the trust instrument or instrument of transfer and such other factors as the Secretary deems relevant. For purposes of determining whether to grant relief under this paragraph, the time for making the allocation (or election) shall be treated as if not expressly prescribed by statute.

(2) SUBSTANTIAL COMPLIANCE.—An allocation of GST exemption under section 2632 that demonstrates an intent to have the lowest possible inclusion ratio with respect to a transfer or a trust shall be deemed to be an allocation of so much of the transferor's unused GST exemption as produces the lowest possible inclusion ratio. In determining whether there has been substantial compliance, all relevant circumstances shall be taken into account, including evidence of intent contained in the trust instrument or instrument of transfer and such other factors as the Secretary deems relevant.

[CCH Explanation at ¶705, ¶765, ¶770, ¶775 and ¶780. Committee Reports at ¶10,130.]

Amendments

• **2001, Economic Growth and Tax Relief Reconciliation Act of 2001 (P.L. 107-16)**

P.L. 107-16, §564(a):

Amended Code Sec. 2642 by adding at the end a new subsection (g). For the **effective** date, see Act Sec. 564(b)(1)-(2), below.

P.L. 107-16, §564(b)(1)-(2), provides:

(b) EFFECTIVE DATES.—

(1) RELIEF FROM LATE ELECTIONS.—Section 2642(g)(1) of the Internal Revenue Code of 1986 (as added by subsection (a)) shall apply to requests pending on, or filed after, December 31, 2000.

(2) SUBSTANTIAL COMPLIANCE.—Section 2642(g)(2) of such Code (as so added) shall apply to transfers subject to chapter 11 or 12 of the Internal Revenue Code of 1986 made after December 31, 2000. No implication is intended with respect to the availability of relief from late elections or the applica-tion of a rule of substantial compliance on or before such date.

P.L. 107-16, §901(a)-(b), as amended by P.L. 111-312, §101(a)(1), provides:

SEC. 901. SUNSET OF PROVISIONS OF ACT.

(a) IN GENERAL.—All provisions of, and amendments made by, this Act shall not apply—

(1) to taxable, plan, or limitation years beginning after December 31, 2012, or

(2) in the case of title V, to estates of decedents dying, gifts made, or generation skipping transfers, after December 31, 2012.

(b) APPLICATION OF CERTAIN LAWS.—The Internal Revenue Code of 1986 and the Employee Retirement Income Security Act of 1974 shall be applied and administered to years, estates, gifts, and transfers described in subsection (a) as if the provisions and amendments described in subsection (a) had never been enacted.

⨠⨠→ *Caution: Code Sec. 2664, below, was added by P.L. 107-16, applicable to estates of decedents dying, and generation-skipping transfers, after December 31, 2009. P.L. 111-312 removed Code Sec. 2664, applicable to estates of decedents dying, and transfers made, after December 31, 2009, but see P.L. 111-312, §301(c), in the amendment notes. For sunset provision, see P.L. 107-16, §901 [as amended by P.L. 111-312], in the amendment notes.*

[¶5735] CODE SEC. 2664. TERMINATION.

This chapter shall not apply to generation-skipping transfers after December 31, 2009.

[CCH Explanation at ¶705, ¶765, ¶770, ¶775 and ¶780. Committee Reports at ¶10,130.]

Amendments

• **2010, Tax Relief, Unemployment Insurance Reauthorization, and Job Creation Act of 2010 (P.L. 111-312)**

P.L. 111-312, §301(a):

Amended Code Sec. 2664 to read as such provision would read if subtitle A of title V of the Economic Growth and Tax Relief Reconciliation Act of 2001 (P.L. 107-16) had never been enacted. **Effective** for estates of decedents dying, and transfers made, after 12-31-2009. For a special rule, see Act Sec. 301(c), below. Prior to amendment by P.L. 111-312, Code Sec. 2664 read as follows:

SEC. 2664. TERMINATION.

This chapter shall not apply to generation-skipping trans-fers after December 31, 2009.

P.L. 111-312, §301(c), provides:

(c) SPECIAL ELECTION WITH RESPECT TO ESTATES OF DECEDENTS DYING IN 2010.—Notwithstanding subsection (a), in the case of an estate of a decedent dying after December 31, 2009, and before January 1, 2011, the executor (within the meaning of section 2203 of the Internal Revenue Code of 1986) may elect to apply such Code as though the amendments made by subsection (a) do not apply with respect to chapter 11 of such Code and with respect to property acquired or passing from such decedent (within the meaning of section 1014(b) of such Code). Such election shall be made at such time and in such manner as the Secretary of the Treasury or the Secretary's delegate shall provide. Such an election once made shall be revocable only with respect to the Secretary of the Treasury or the Secretary's delegate. For pur-poses of section 2652(a)(1) of such Code, the determination of whether any property is subject to the tax imposed by such chapter 11 shall be made without regard to any elec-tion made under this subsection.

P.L. 111-312, §304, provides:

SEC. 304. APPLICATION OF EGTRRA SUNSET TO THIS TITLE.

Section 901 of the Economic Growth and Tax Relief Rec-onciliation Act of 2001 shall apply to the amendments made by this title.

• **2001, Economic Growth and Tax Relief Reconciliation Act of 2001 (P.L. 107-16)**

P.L. 107-16, §501(b):

Amended subchapter G of chapter 13 of subtitle B by adding at the end a new Code Sec. 2664. **Effective** for the estates of decedents dying, and generation-skipping trans-fers, after 12-31-2009.

P.L. 107-16, §901(a)-(b), as amended by P.L. 111-312, §101(a)(1), provides:

SEC. 901. SUNSET OF PROVISIONS OF ACT.

(a) IN GENERAL.—All provisions of, and amendments made by, this Act shall not apply—

(1) to taxable, plan, or limitation years beginning after December 31, 2012, or

(2) in the case of title V, to estates of decedents dying, gifts made, or generation skipping transfers, after December 31, 2012.

(b) APPLICATION OF CERTAIN LAWS.—The Internal Revenue Code of 1986 and the Employee Retirement Income Security Act of 1974 shall be applied and administered to years, estates, gifts, and transfers described in subsection (a) as if the provisions and amendments described in subsection (a) had never been enacted.

[¶5740] CODE SEC. 3402. INCOME TAX COLLECTED AT SOURCE.

* * *

(p) Voluntary Withholding Agreements.—

(1) Certain federal payments.—

* * *

»»→ Caution: *Code Sec. 3402(p)(1)(B), below, was amended by P.L. 107-16. For sunset provision, see P.L. 107-16, §901 [as amended by P.L. 111-312], in the amendment notes.*

(B) Amount withheld.—The amount to be deducted and withheld under this chapter from any payment to which any request under subparagraph (A) applies shall be an amount equal to the percentage of such payment specified in such request. Such a request shall apply to any payment only if the percentage specified is 7 percent, any percentage applicable to any of the 3 lowest income brackets in the table under section 1(c), or such other percentage as is permitted under regulations prescribed by the Secretary.

* * *

»»→ Caution: *Code Sec. 3402(p)(2), below, was amended by P.L. 107-16. For sunset provision, see P.L. 107-16, §901 [as amended by P.L. 111-312], in the amendment notes.*

(2) Voluntary withholding on unemployment benefits.—If, at the time a payment of unemployment compensation (as defined in section 85(b)) is made to any person, a request by such person is in effect that such payment be subject to withholding under this chapter, then for purposes of this chapter and so much of subtitle F as relates to this chapter, such payment shall be treated as if it were a payment of wages by an employer to an employee. The amount to be deducted and withheld under this chapter from any payment to which any request under this paragraph applies shall be an amount equal to 10 percent of such payment.

* * *

[CCH Explanation at ¶305. Committee Reports at ¶10,010.]

Amendments

● **2001, Economic Growth and Tax Relief Reconciliation Act of 2001 (P.L. 107-16)**

P.L. 107-16, §101(c)(6):

Amended Code Sec. 3402(p)(1)(B) by striking "7, 15, 28, or 31 percent" and inserting "7 percent, any percentage applicable to any of the 3 lowest income brackets in the table under section 1(c),". For the **effective** date of the above amendment, see Act Sec. 101(d)(2), below.

P.L. 107-16, §101(c)(7):

Amended Code Sec. 3402(p)(2) by striking "15 percent" and inserting "10 percent". For the **effective** date of the above amendment, see Act Sec. 101(d)(2), below.

P.L. 107-16, §101(d)(2), provides:

(2) Amendments to withholding provisions.—The amendments made by paragraphs (6), (7), (8), (9), (10), and (11) of subsection (c) shall apply to amounts paid after the 60th day after the date of the enactment of this Act. References to income brackets and rates of tax in such paragraphs shall be

applied without regard to section 1(i)(1)(D) of the Internal Revenue Code of 1986.

P.L. 107-16, §901(a)-(b), as amended by P.L. 111-312, §101(a)(1), provides:

SEC. 901. SUNSET OF PROVISIONS OF ACT.

(a) In General.—All provisions of, and amendments made by, this Act shall not apply—

(1) to taxable, plan, or limitation years beginning after December 31, 2012, or

(2) in the case of title V, to estates of decedents dying, gifts made, or generation skipping transfers, after December 31, 2012.

(b) Application of Certain Laws.—The Internal Revenue Code of 1986 and the Employee Retirement Income Security Act of 1974 shall be applied and administered to years, estates, gifts, and transfers described in subsection (a) as if the provisions and amendments described in subsection (a) had never been enacted.

(q) Extension of Withholding to Certain Gambling Winnings.—

»»→ Caution: *Code Sec. 3402(q)(1), below, was amended by P.L. 107-16. For sunset provision, see P.L. 107-16, §901 [as amended by P.L. 111-312], in the amendment notes.*

(1) General rule.—Every person, including the Government of the United States, a State, or a political subdivision thereof, or any instrumentalities of the foregoing, making any payment of winnings which are subject to withholding shall deduct and withhold from such payment a tax in an amount equal to the product of the third lowest rate of tax applicable under section 1(c) and such payment.

* * *

[CCH Explanation at ¶305. Committee Reports at ¶10,010.]

Amendments

• **2001, Economic Growth and Tax Relief Reconciliation Act of 2001 (P.L. 107-16)**

P.L. 107-16, §101(c)(8):

Amended Code Sec. 3402(q)(1) by striking "equal to 28 percent of such payment" and inserting "equal to the product of the third lowest rate of tax applicable under section 1(c) and such payment". For the **effective** date of the above amendment, see Act Sec. 101(d)(2) in the amendment notes to Code Sec. 3402(p).

P.L. 107-16, §901(a)-(b), as amended by P.L. 111-312, §101(a)(1), provides:

SEC. 901. SUNSET OF PROVISIONS OF ACT.

(a) IN GENERAL.—All provisions of, and amendments made by, this Act shall not apply—

(1) to taxable, plan, or limitation years beginning after December 31, 2012, or

(2) in the case of title V, to estates of decedents dying, gifts made, or generation skipping transfers, after December 31, 2012.

(b) APPLICATION OF CERTAIN LAWS.—The Internal Revenue Code of 1986 and the Employee Retirement Income Security Act of 1974 shall be applied and administered to years, estates, gifts, and transfers described in subsection (a) as if the provisions and amendments described in subsection (a) had never been enacted.

(r) EXTENSION OF WITHHOLDING TO CERTAIN TAXABLE PAYMENTS OF INDIAN CASINO PROFITS.—

* * *

➤ *Caution: Code Sec. 3402(r)(3), below, was amended by P.L. 107-16. For sunset provision, see P.L. 107-16, §901 [as amended by P.L. 111-312], in the amendment notes.*

(3) ANNUALIZED TAX.—For purposes of paragraph (1), the term "annualized tax" means, with respect to any payment, the amount of tax which would be imposed by section 1(c) (determined without regard to any rate of tax in excess of the fourth lowest rate of tax applicable under section 1(c)) on an amount of taxable income equal to the excess of—

(A) the annualized amount of such payment, over

(B) the amount determined under paragraph (2).

* * *

[CCH Explanation at ¶305. Committee Reports at ¶10,010.]

Amendments

• **2001, Economic Growth and Tax Relief Reconciliation Act of 2001 (P.L. 107-16)**

P.L. 107-16, §101(c)(9):

Amended Code Sec. 3402(r)(3) by striking "31 percent" and inserting "the fourth lowest rate of tax applicable under section 1(c)". For the **effective** date of the above amendment, see Act Sec. 101(d)(2) in the amendment notes to Code Sec. 3402(p).

P.L. 107-16, §901(a)-(b), as amended by P.L. 111-312, §101(a)(1), provides:

SEC. 901. SUNSET OF PROVISIONS OF ACT.

(a) IN GENERAL.—All provisions of, and amendments made by, this Act shall not apply—

(1) to taxable, plan, or limitation years beginning after December 31, 2012, or

(2) in the case of title V, to estates of decedents dying, gifts made, or generation skipping transfers, after December 31, 2012.

(b) APPLICATION OF CERTAIN LAWS.—The Internal Revenue Code of 1986 and the Employee Retirement Income Security Act of 1974 shall be applied and administered to years, estates, gifts, and transfers described in subsection (a) as if the provisions and amendments described in subsection (a) had never been enacted.

[¶5745] CODE SEC. 3406. BACKUP WITHHOLDING.

(a) REQUIREMENT TO DEDUCT AND WITHHOLD.—

➤ *Caution: Code Sec. 3406(a)(1), below, was amended by P.L. 107-16. For sunset provision, see P.L. 107-16, §901 [as amended by P.L. 111-312], in the amendment notes.*

(1) IN GENERAL.—In the case of any reportable payment, if—

(A) the payee fails to furnish his TIN to the payor in the manner required,

(B) the Secretary notifies the payor that the TIN furnished by the payee is incorrect,

(C) there has been a notified payee underreporting described in subsection (c), or

(D) there has been a payee certification failure described in subsection (d),

then the payor shall deduct and withhold from such payment a tax equal to the product of the fourth lowest rate of tax applicable under section 1(c) and such payment.

* * *

[CCH Explanation at ¶305. Committee Reports at ¶10,010.]

Amendments

• 2001, Economic Growth and Tax Relief Reconciliation Act of 2001 (P.L. 107-16)

P.L. 107-16, §101(c)(10):

Amended Code Sec. 3406(a)(1) by striking "equal to 31 percent of such payment" and inserting "equal to the product of the fourth lowest rate of tax applicable under section 1(c) and such payment". **Effective,** generally, for amounts paid after 6-7-2001. For special rules, see Act Sec. 101(d)(2), below.

P.L. 107-16, §101(d)(2), provides:

(2) AMENDMENTS TO WITHHOLDING PROVISIONS.—The amendments made by paragraphs (6), (7), (8), (9), (10), and (11) of subsection (c) shall apply to amounts paid after the 60th day after the date of the enactment of this Act. References to income brackets and rates of tax in such paragraphs shall be applied without regard to section 1(i)(1)(D) of the Internal Revenue Code of 1986.

P.L. 107-16, §901(a)-(b), as amended by P.L. 111-312, §101(a)(1), provides:

SEC. 901. SUNSET OF PROVISIONS OF ACT.

(a) IN GENERAL.—All provisions of, and amendments made by, this Act shall not apply—

(1) to taxable, plan, or limitation years beginning after December 31, 2012, or

(2) in the case of title V, to estates of decedents dying, gifts made, or generation skipping transfers, after December 31, 2012.

(b) APPLICATION OF CERTAIN LAWS.—The Internal Revenue Code of 1986 and the Employee Retirement Income Security Act of 1974 shall be applied and administered to years, estates, gifts, and transfers described in subsection (a) as if the provisions and amendments described in subsection (a) had never been enacted.

[¶5747] CODE SEC. 4081. IMPOSITION OF TAX.

* * *

(d) TERMINATION.—

* * *

(2) AVIATION FUELS.—The rates of tax specified in subsections (a)(2)(A)(ii) and (a)(2)(C)(ii) shall be 4.3 cents per gallon—

(A) after December 31, 1996, and before the date which is 7 days after the date of the enactment of the Airport and Airway Trust Fund Tax Reinstatement Act of 1997, and

(B) after *March 31, 2011.*

* * *

[CCH Explanation at ¶638.]

Amendments

• 2010, Airport and Airway Extension Act of 2010, Part IV (H.R. 6473)

H.R. 6473, §2(a):

Amended Code Sec. 4081(d)(2)(B) by striking "December 31, 2010" and inserting "March 31, 2011". **Effective** 01-01-2011.

[¶5748] CODE SEC. 4261. IMPOSITION OF TAX.

* * *

(j) APPLICATION OF TAXES.—

(1) IN GENERAL.—The taxes imposed by this section shall apply to—

(A) transportation beginning during the period—

(i) beginning on the 7th day after the date of the enactment of the Airport and Airway Trust Fund Tax Reinstatement Act of 1997, and

(ii) ending on *March 31, 2011,* and

(B) amounts paid during such period for transportation beginning after such period.

* * *

[CCH Explanation at ¶ 638.]

Amendments
● 2010, Airport and Airway Extension Act of 2010,
Part IV (H.R. 6473)

H.R. 6473, § 2(b)(1):

Amended Code Sec. 4261(j)(1)(A)(ii) by striking "December 31, 2010" and inserting "March 31, 2011". Effective 01-01-2011.

[¶ 5749] CODE SEC. 4271. IMPOSITION OF TAX.

* * *

(d) APPLICATION OF TAX.—

(1) IN GENERAL.—The tax imposed by subsection (a) shall apply to—

(A) transportation beginning during the period—

(i) beginning on the 7th day after the date of the enactment of the Airport and Airway Trust Fund Tax Reinstatement Act of 1997, and

(ii) ending on *March 31, 2011,* and

(B) amounts paid during such period for transportation beginning after such period.

* * *

[CCH Explanation at ¶ 638.]

Amendments
● 2010, Airport and Airway Extension Act of 2010,
Part IV (H.R. 6473)

H.R. 6473, § 2(b)(2):

Amended Code Sec. 4271(d)(1)(A)(ii) by striking "December 31, 2010" and inserting "March 31, 2011". Effective 01-01-2011.

[¶ 5750] CODE SEC. 4947. APPLICATION OF TAXES TO CERTAIN NONEXEMPT TRUSTS.

(a) APPLICATION OF TAX.—

* * *

(2) SPLIT-INTEREST TRUSTS.—In the case of a trust which is not exempt from tax under section 501(a), not all of the unexpired interests in which are devoted to one or more of the purposes described in section 170(c)(2)(B), and which has amounts in trust for which a deduction was allowed under section 170, 545(b)(2), 642(c), 2055, 2106(a)(2), or 2522, section 507 (relating to termination of private foundation status), section 508(e) (relating to governing instruments) to the extent applicable to a trust described in this paragraph, section 4941 (relating to taxes on self-dealing), section 4943 (relating to taxes on excess business holdings) except as provided in subsection (b)(3), section 4944 (relating to investments which jeopardize charitable purpose) except as provided in subsection (b)(3), and section 4945 (relating to taxes on taxable expenditures) shall apply as if such trust were a private foundation. This paragraph shall not apply with respect to—

➤➤➤ *Caution: Code Sec. 4947(a)(2)(A), below, as amended by P.L. 111-312, applies to estates of decedents dying, and transfers made, after December 31, 2009. For sunset provision, see P.L. 107-16, § 901 [as amended by P.L. 111-312], in the amendment notes.*

(A) any amounts payable under the terms of such trust to income beneficiaries, unless a deduction was allowed under section 170(f)(2)(B), 2055(e)(2)(B), or 2522(c)(2)(B),

(B) any amounts in trust other than amounts for which a deduction was allowed under section 170, 545(b)(2), 642(c), 2055, 2106(a)(2), or 2522, if such other amounts are segregated from amounts for which no deduction was allowable, or

(C) any amounts transferred in trust before May 27, 1969.

[CCH Explanation at ¶705 and ¶760. Committee Reports at ¶10,130.]

Amendments

• **2010, Tax Relief, Unemployment Insurance Reauthorization, and Job Creation Act of 2010 (P.L. 111-312)**

P.L. 111-312, §301(a):

Amended Code Sec. 4947(a)(2)(A) to read as such provision would read if subtitle E of title V of the Economic Growth and Tax Relief Reconciliation Act of 2001 (P.L. 107-16) had never been enacted. **Effective** for estates of decedents dying, and transfers made, after 12-31-2009. For a special rule, see Act Sec. 301(c), below. Prior to amendment by P.L. 111-312, Code Sec. 4947(a)(2)(A) read as follows:

(A) any amounts payable under the terms of such trust to income beneficiaries, unless a deduction was allowed under section 170(f)(2)(B), 642(c), 2055(e)(2)(B), or 2522(c)(2)(B),

P.L. 111-312, §301(c), provides:

(c) SPECIAL ELECTION WITH RESPECT TO ESTATES OF DECEDENTS DYING IN 2010.—Notwithstanding subsection (a), in the case of an estate of a decedent dying after December 31, 2009, and before January 1, 2011, the executor (within the meaning of section 2203 of the Internal Revenue Code of 1986) may elect to apply such Code as though the amendments made by subsection (a) do not apply with respect to chapter 11 of such Code and with respect to property acquired or passing from such decedent (within the meaning of section 1014(b) of such Code). Such election shall be made at such time and in such manner as the Secretary of the Treasury or the Secretary's delegate shall provide. Such an election once made shall be revocable only with the consent of the Secretary of the Treasury or the Secretary's delegate. For purposes of section 2652(a)(1) of such Code, the determination of whether any property is subject to the tax imposed by such chapter 11 shall be made without regard to any election made under this subsection.

P.L. 111-312, §304, provides:

SEC. 304. APPLICATION OF EGTRRA SUNSET TO THIS TITLE.

Section 901 of the Economic Growth and Tax Relief Reconciliation Act of 2001 shall apply to the amendments made by this title.

• **2001, Economic Growth and Tax Relief Reconciliation Act of 2001 (P.L. 107-16)**

P.L. 107-16, §542(e)(4):

Amended Code Sec. 4947(a)(2)(A) by inserting "642(c)," after "170(f)(2)(B),". **Effective** for deductions for tax years beginning after 12-31-2009.

P.L. 107-16, §901(a)-(b), as amended by P.L. 111-312, §101(a)(1), provides:

SEC. 901. SUNSET OF PROVISIONS OF ACT.

(a) IN GENERAL.—All provisions of, and amendments made by, this Act shall not apply—

(1) to taxable, plan, or limitation years beginning after December 31, 2012, or

(2) in the case of title V, to estates of decedents dying, gifts made, or generation skipping transfers, after December 31, 2012.

(b) APPLICATION OF CERTAIN LAWS.—The Internal Revenue Code of 1986 and the Employee Retirement Income Security Act of 1974 shall be applied and administered to years, estates, gifts, and transfers described in subsection (a) as if the provisions and amendments described in subsection (a) had never been enacted.

[¶5755] CODE SEC. 4973. TAX ON EXCESS CONTRIBUTIONS TO CERTAIN TAX-FAVORED ACCOUNTS AND ANNUITIES.

* * *

(e) EXCESS CONTRIBUTIONS TO COVERDELL EDUCATION SAVINGS ACCOUNTS.—For purposes of this section—

»»→ *Caution: Code Sec. 4973(e)(1), below, was amended by P.L. 107-16 and P.L. 107-22. For sunset provision, see P.L. 107-16, §901 [as amended by P.L. 111-312] in the amendment notes.*

(1) IN GENERAL.—In the case of Coverdell education savings accounts maintained for the benefit of any one beneficiary, the term "excess contributions" means the sum of—

(A) the amount by which the amount contributed for the taxable year to such accounts exceeds $2,000 (or, if less, the sum of the maximum amounts permitted to be contributed under section 530(c) by the contributors to such accounts for such year); and

(B) the amount determined under this subsection for the preceding taxable year, reduced by the sum of—

(i) the distributions out of the accounts for the taxable year (other than rollover distributions), and

(ii) the excess (if any) of the maximum amount which may be contributed to the accounts for the taxable year over the amount contributed to the accounts for the taxable year.

(2) SPECIAL RULES.—For purposes of paragraph (1), the following contributions shall not be taken into account:

(A) Any contribution which is distributed out of the Coverdell education savings account in a distribution to which section 530(d)(4)(C) applies.

(B) Any rollover contribution.

* * *

[CCH Explanation at ¶ 330. Committee Reports at ¶ 10,050.]

Amendments

• **2001 (P.L. 107-22)**

P.L. 107-22, § 1(b)(2)(B):

Amended Code Sec. 4973(e) by striking "education individual retirement" each place it appears in the text and inserting "Coverdell education savings". **Effective** 7-26-2001.

P.L. 107-22, § 1(b)(4):

Amended the heading for Code Sec. 4973(e) by striking "EDUCATION INDIVIDUAL RETIREMENT" and inserting "COVERDELL EDUCATION SAVINGS". **Effective** 7-26-2001.

• **2001, Economic Growth and Tax Relief Reconciliation Act of 2001 (P.L. 107-16)**

P.L. 107-16, § 401(a)(2):

Amended Code Sec. 4973(e)(1)(A) by striking "$500" and inserting "$2,000". **Effective** for tax years beginning after 12-31-2001.

P.L. 107-16, § 401(g)(2)(D):

Amended Code Sec. 4973(e)(1) by adding "and" at the end of subparagraph (A), by striking subparagraph (B), and by redesignating subparagraph (C) as subparagraph (B). **Effective** for tax years beginning after 12-31-2001. Prior to being stricken, Code Sec. 4973(e)(1)(B) read as follows:

(B) if any amount is contributed (other than a contribution described in section 530(b)(2)(B)) during such year to a qualified State tuition program for the benefit of such beneficiary, any amount contributed to such accounts for such taxable year; and

P.L. 107-16, § 901(a)-(b), as amended by P.L. 111-312, § 101(a)(1), provides [but see P.L. 109-280, § 1304(a), above]:

SEC. 901. SUNSET OF PROVISIONS OF ACT.

(a) IN GENERAL.—All provisions of, and amendments made by, this Act shall not apply—

(1) to taxable, plan, or limitation years beginning after December 31, 2012, or

(2) in the case of title V, to estates of decedents dying, gifts made, or generation skipping transfers, after December 31, 2012.

(b) APPLICATION OF CERTAIN LAWS.—The Internal Revenue Code of 1986 and the Employee Retirement Income Security Act of 1974 shall be applied and administered to years, estates, gifts, and transfers described in subsection (a) as if the provisions and amendments described in subsection (a) had never been enacted.

[¶ 5760] CODE SEC. 4982. EXCISE TAX ON UNDISTRIBUTED INCOME OF REGULATED INVESTMENT COMPANIES.

* * *

(b) REQUIRED DISTRIBUTION.—For purposes of this section—

(1) IN GENERAL.—The term "required distribution" means, with respect to any calendar year, the sum of—

* * *

(B) *98.2 percent* of the regulated investment company's capital gain net income for the 1-year period ending on October 31 of such calendar year.

* * *

[CCH Explanation at ¶ 836.]

Amendments

• **2010, Regulated Investment Company Modernization Act of 2010 (H.R. 4337)**

H.R. 4337, § 404(a):

Amended Code Sec. 4982(b)(1)(B) by striking "98 percent" and inserting "98.2 percent". **Effective** for calendar years beginning after the date of the enactment of this Act.

(c) DISTRIBUTED AMOUNT.—For purposes of this section—

* * *

(4) SPECIAL RULE FOR ESTIMATED TAX PAYMENTS.—

(A) IN GENERAL.—In the case of a regulated investment company which elects the application of this paragraph for any calendar year—

(i) the distributed amount with respect to such company for such calendar year shall be increased by the amount on which qualified estimated tax payments are made by such company during such calendar year, and

(ii) the distributed amount with respect to such company for the following calendar year shall be reduced by the amount of such increase.

(B) QUALIFIED ESTIMATED TAX PAYMENTS.—For purposes of this paragraph, the term "qualified estimated tax payments" means, with respect to any calendar year, payments of estimated tax of a tax described in paragraph (1)(B) for any taxable year which begins (but does not end) in such calendar year.

* * *

[CCH Explanation at ¶ 836.]
Amendments
• 2010, Regulated Investment Company Modernization Act of 2010 (H.R. 4337)

H.R. 4337, § 403(a):

Amended Code Sec. 4982(c) by adding at the end a new paragraph (4). **Effective** for calendar years beginning after the date of the enactment of this Act.

(e) DEFINITIONS AND SPECIAL RULES.—For purposes of this section—

* * *

(5) TREATMENT OF SPECIFIED GAINS AND LOSSES AFTER OCTOBER 31 OF CALENDAR YEAR.—

(A) IN GENERAL.—Any specified gain or specified loss which (but for this paragraph) would be properly taken into account for the portion of the calendar year after October 31 shall be treated as arising on January 1 of the following calendar year.

(B) SPECIFIED GAINS AND LOSSES.—For purposes of this paragraph—

(i) SPECIFIED GAIN.—The term "specified gain" means ordinary gain from the sale, exchange, or other disposition of property (including the termination of a position with respect to such property). Such term shall include any foreign currency gain attributable to a section 988 transaction (within the meaning of section 988) and any amount includible in gross income under section 1296(a)(1).

(ii) SPECIFIED LOSS.—The term "specified loss" means ordinary loss from the sale, exchange, or other disposition of property (including the termination of a position with respect to such property). Such term shall include any foreign currency loss attributable to a section 988 transaction (within the meaning of section 988) and any amount allowable as a deduction under section 1296(a)(2).

(C) SPECIAL RULE FOR COMPANIES ELECTING TO USE THE TAXABLE YEAR.—In the case of any company making an election under paragraph (4), subparagraph (A) shall be applied by substituting the last day of the company's taxable year for October 31.

(6) TREATMENT OF MARK TO MARKET GAIN.—

(A) IN GENERAL.—For purposes of determining a regulated investment company's ordinary income, notwithstanding paragraph (1)(C), each specified mark to market provision shall be applied as if such company's taxable year ended on October 31. In the case of a company making an election under paragraph (4), the preceding sentence shall be applied by substituting the last day of the company's taxable year for October 31.

(B) SPECIFIED MARK TO MARKET PROVISION.—*For purposes of this paragraph, the term "specified mark to market provision" means sections 1256 and 1296 and any other provision of this title (or regulations thereunder) which treats property as disposed of on the last day of the taxable year.*

(7) ELECTIVE DEFERRAL OF CERTAIN ORDINARY LOSSES.—*Except as provided in regulations prescribed by the Secretary, in the case of a regulated investment company which has a taxable year other than the calendar year—*

(A) *such company may elect to determine its ordinary income for the calendar year without regard to any net ordinary loss (determined without regard to specified gains and losses taken into account under paragraph (5)) which is attributable to the portion of such calendar year which is after the beginning of the taxable year which begins in such calendar year, and*

(B) *any amount of net ordinary loss not taken into account for a calendar year by reason of subparagraph (A) shall be treated as arising on the 1st day of the following calendar year.*

[CCH Explanation at ¶836.]

Amendments

- **2010, Regulated Investment Company Modernization Act of 2010 (H.R. 4337)**

H.R. 4337, §402(a):

Amended Code Sec. 4982(e) by striking paragraphs (5) and (6) and inserting new paragraphs (5), (6), and (7). **Effective** for calendar years beginning after the date of the enactment of this Act. Prior to being stricken, Code Sec. 4982(e)(5)-(6) read as follows:

(5) TREATMENT OF FOREIGN CURRENCY GAINS AND LOSSES AFTER OCTOBER 31 OF CALENDAR YEAR.—Any foreign currency gain or loss which is attributable to a section 988 transaction and which is properly taken into account for the portion of the calendar year after October 31 shall not be taken into account in determining the amount of the ordinary income of the regulated investment company for such calendar year but shall be taken into account in determining the ordinary income of the investment company for the following calendar year. In the case of any company making an election

under paragraph (4), the preceding sentence shall be applied by substituting the last day of the company's taxable year for October 31.

(6) TREATMENT OF GAIN RECOGNIZED UNDER SECTION 1296.— For purposes of determining a regulated investment company's ordinary income—

(A) notwithstanding paragraph (1)(C), section 1296 shall be applied as if such company's taxable year ended on October 31, and

(B) any ordinary gain or loss from an actual disposition of stock in a passive foreign investment company during the portion of the calendar year after October 31 shall be taken into account in determining such regulated investment company's ordinary income for the following calendar year.

In the case of a company making an election under paragraph (4), the preceding sentence shall be applied by substituting the last day of the company's taxable year for October 31.

(f) EXCEPTION FOR CERTAIN REGULATED INVESTMENT COMPANIES.—This section shall not apply to any regulated investment company for any calendar year if at all times during such calendar year each shareholder in such company was—

(1) a trust described in section 401(a) and exempt from tax under section 501(a),

(2) a segregated asset account of a life insurance company held in connection with variable contracts (as defined in section 817(d))[,]

(3) *any other tax-exempt entity whose ownership of beneficial interests in the company would not preclude the application of section 817(h)(4), or*

(4) *another regulated investment company described in this subsection.*

For purposes of the preceding sentence, any shares attributable to an investment in the regulated investment company (not exceeding $250,000) made in connection with the organization of such company shall not be taken into account.

[CCH Explanation at ¶836.]

Amendments

- **2010, Regulated Investment Company Modernization Act of 2010 (H.R. 4337)**

H.R. 4337, §401(a)(1)-(4):

Amended Code Sec. 4982(f) by striking "either" following "company was" in the matter preceding paragraph (1), by

striking "or" at the end of paragraph (1), by striking the period [sic] at the end of paragraph (2), and by inserting after paragraph (2) the new paragraphs (3) and (4). **Effective** for calendar years beginning after the date of the enactment of this Act.

»»→ *Caution: Code Sec. 6018, below, as amended by P.L. 111-312, applies to estates of decedents dying, and transfers made, after December 31, 2009. For sunset provision, see P.L. 107-16, §901 [as amended by P.L. 111-312], in the amendment notes.*

[¶ 5765] CODE SEC. 6018. ESTATE TAX RETURNS.

(a) RETURNS BY EXECUTOR.—

(1) CITIZENS OR RESIDENTS.—*In all cases where the gross estate at the death of a citizen or resident exceeds the basic exclusion amount in effect under section 2010(c) for the calendar year which includes the date of death, the executor shall make a return with respect to the estate tax imposed by subtitle B.*

(2) NONRESIDENTS NOT CITIZENS OF THE UNITED STATES.—*In the case of the estate of every nonresident not a citizen of the United States if that part of the gross estate which is situated in the United States exceeds $60,000, the executor shall make a return with respect to the estate tax imposed by subtitle B.*

(3) ADJUSTMENT FOR CERTAIN GIFTS.—*The amount applicable under paragraph (1) and the amount set forth in paragraph (2) shall each be reduced (but not below zero) by the sum of—*

(A) *the amount of the adjusted taxable gifts (within the meaning of section 2001(b)) made by the decedent after December 31, 1976, plus*

(B) *the aggregate amount allowed as a specific exemption under section 2521 (as in effect before its repeal by the Tax Reform Act of 1976) with respect to gifts made by the decedent after September 8, 1976.*

(b) RETURNS BY BENEFICIARIES.—*If the executor is unable to make a complete return as to any part of the gross estate of the decedent, he shall include in his return a description of such part and the name of every person holding a legal or beneficial interest therein. Upon notice from the Secretary such person shall in like manner make a return as to such part of the gross estate.*

[CCH Explanation at ¶ 705, ¶ 715, ¶ 718 and ¶ 745. Committee Reports at ¶ 10,130.]

Amendments

● **2010, Tax Relief, Unemployment Insurance Reauthorization, and Job Creation Act of 2010 (P.L. 111-312)**

P.L. 111-312, § 301(a):

Amended Code Sec. 6018 to read as such provision would read if subtitle E of title V of the Economic Growth and Tax Relief Reconciliation Act of 2001 (P.L. 107-16) had never been enacted. **Effective** for estates of decedents dying, and transfers made, after 12-31-2009. For special rules, see Act Sec. 301(c) and (d)(1), below. Prior to amendment by P.L. 111-312, Code Sec. 6018 read as follows:

SEC. 6018. RETURNS RELATING TO LARGE TRANSFERS AT DEATH.

(a) IN GENERAL.—If this section applies to property acquired from a decedent, the executor of the estate of such decedent shall make a return containing the information specified in subsection (c) with respect to such property.

(b) PROPERTY TO WHICH SECTION APPLIES.—

(1) LARGE TRANSFERS.—This section shall apply to all property (other than cash) acquired from a decedent if the fair market value of such property acquired from the decedent exceeds the dollar amount applicable under section 1022(b)(2)(B) (without regard to section 1022(b)(2)(C)).

(2) TRANSFERS OF CERTAIN GIFTS RECEIVED BY DECEDENT WITHIN 3 YEARS OF DEATH.—This section shall apply to any appreciated property acquired from the decedent if—

(A) subsections (b) and (c) of section 1022 do not apply to such property by reason of section 1022(d)(1)(C), and

(B) such property was required to be included on a return required to be filed under section 6019.

(3) NONRESIDENTS NOT CITIZENS OF THE UNITED STATES.—In the case of a decedent who is a nonresident not a citizen of the United States, paragraphs (1) and (2) shall be applied—

(A) by taking into account only—

(i) tangible property situated in the United States, and

(ii) other property acquired from the decedent by a United States person, and

(B) by substituting the dollar amount applicable under section 1022(b)(3) for the dollar amount referred to in paragraph (1).

(4) RETURNS BY TRUSTEES OR BENEFICIARIES.—If the executor is unable to make a complete return as to any property acquired from or passing from the decedent, the executor shall include in the return a description of such property and the name of every person holding a legal or beneficial interest therein. Upon notice from the Secretary, such person shall in like manner make a return as to such property.

(c) INFORMATION REQUIRED TO BE FURNISHED.—The information specified in this subsection with respect to any property acquired from the decedent is—

(1) the name and TIN of the recipient of such property,

(2) an accurate description of such property,

(3) the adjusted basis of such property in the hands of the decedent and its fair market value at the time of death,

(4) the decedent's holding period for such property,

(5) sufficient information to determine whether any gain on the sale of the property would be treated as ordinary income,

(6) the amount of basis increase allocated to the property under subsection (b) or (c) of section 1022, and

(7) such other information as the Secretary may by regulations prescribe.

(d) PROPERTY ACQUIRED FROM DECEDENT.—For purposes of this section, section 1022 shall apply for purposes of determining the property acquired from a decedent.

(e) STATEMENTS TO BE FURNISHED TO CERTAIN PERSONS.— Every person required to make a return under subsection (a) shall furnish to each person whose name is required to be set forth in such return (other than the person required to make such return) a written statement showing—

(1) the name, address, and phone number of the person required to make such return, and

(2) the information specified in subsection (c) with respect to property acquired from, or passing from, the decedent to the person required to receive such statement.

The written statement required under the preceding sentence shall be furnished not later than 30 days after the date that the return required by subsection (a) is filed.

P.L. 111-312, § 301(c) and (d)(1), provide:

(c) SPECIAL ELECTION WITH RESPECT TO ESTATES OF DECEDENTS DYING IN 2010.—Notwithstanding subsection (a), in the case of an estate of a decedent dying after December 31, 2009, and before January 1, 2011, the executor (within the meaning of section 2203 of the Internal Revenue Code of 1986) may elect to apply such Code as though the amendments made by subsection (a) do not apply with respect to chapter 11 of such Code and with respect to property acquired or passing from such decedent (within the meaning of section 1014(b) of such Code). Such election shall be made at such time and in such manner as the Secretary of the Treasury or the Secretary's delegate shall provide. Such an election once made shall be revocable only with the consent of the Secretary of the Treasury or the Secretary's delegate. For purposes of section 2652(a)(1) of such Code, the determination of whether any property is subject to the tax imposed by such chapter 11 shall be made without regard to any election made under this subsection.

(d) EXTENSION OF TIME FOR PERFORMING CERTAIN ACTS.—

(1) ESTATE TAX.—In the case of the estate of a decedent dying after December 31, 2009, and before the date of the enactment of this Act, the due date for—

(A) filing any return under section 6018 of the Internal Revenue Code of 1986 (including any election required to be made on such a return) as such section is in effect after the date of the enactment of this Act without regard to any election under subsection (c),

(B) making any payment of tax under chapter 11 of such Code, and

(C) making any disclaimer described in section 2518(b) of such Code of an interest in property passing by reason of the death of such decedent,

shall not be earlier than the date which is 9 months after the date of the enactment of this Act.

P.L. 111-312, § 303(b)(3):

Amended Code Sec. 6018(a)(1) by striking "the applicable exclusion amount" and inserting "the basic exclusion amount". **Effective** for estates of decedents dying and gifts made after 12-31-2010.

P.L. 111-312, § 304, provides:

SEC. 304. APPLICATION OF EGTRRA SUNSET TO THIS TITLE.

Section 901 of the Economic Growth and Tax Relief Reconciliation Act of 2001 shall apply to the amendments made by this title.

• 2001, Economic Growth and Tax Relief Reconciliation Act of 2001 (P.L. 107-16)

P.L. 107-16, § 542(b)(1):

Amended so much of subpart C of part II of subchapter A of chapter 61 as precedes Code Sec. 6019 (Code Sec. 6018). **Effective** for estates of decedents dying after 12-31-2009. Prior to amendment, so much of subpart C of part II of subchapter A of chapter 61 as preceded section 6019 (Code Sec. 6018) read as follows:

SEC. 6018. ESTATE TAX RETURNS.

(a) RETURNS BY EXECUTOR.—

(1) CITIZENS OR RESIDENTS.—In all cases where the gross estate at the death of a citizen or resident exceeds the applicable exclusion amount in effect under section 2010(c) for the calendar year which includes the date of death, the executor shall make a return with respect to the estate tax imposed by subtitle B.

(2) NONRESIDENTS NOT CITIZENS OF THE UNITED STATES.—In the case of the estate of every nonresident not a citizen of the United States if that part of the gross estate which is situated in the United States exceeds $60,000, the executor shall make a return with respect to the estate tax imposed by subtitle B.

(3) ADJUSTMENT FOR CERTAIN GIFTS.—The amount applicable under paragraph (1) and the amount set forth in paragraph (2) shall each be reduced (but not below zero) by the sum of—

(A) the amount of the adjusted taxable gifts (within the meaning of section 2001(b)) made by the decedent after December 31, 1976, plus

(B) the aggregate amount allowed as a specific exemption under section 2521 (as in effect before its repeal by the Tax Reform Act of 1976) with respect to gifts made by the decedent after September 8, 1976.

(b) RETURNS BY BENEFICIARIES.—If the executor is unable to make a complete return as to any part of the gross estate of the decedent, he shall include in his return a description of such part and the name of every person holding a legal or beneficial interest therein. Upon notice from the Secretary such person shall in like manner make a return as to such part of the gross estate.

P.L. 107-16, § 901(a)-(b), as amended by P.L. 111-312, § 101(a)(1), provides:

SEC. 901. SUNSET OF PROVISIONS OF ACT.

(a) IN GENERAL.—All provisions of, and amendments made by, this Act shall not apply—

(1) to taxable, plan, or limitation years beginning after December 31, 2012, or

(2) in the case of title V, to estates of decedents dying, gifts made, or generation skipping transfers, after December 31, 2012.

(b) APPLICATION OF CERTAIN LAWS.—The Internal Revenue Code of 1986 and the Employee Retirement Income Security Act of 1974 shall be applied and administered to years, estates, gifts, and transfers described in subsection (a) as if the provisions and amendments described in subsection (a) had never been enacted.

≫→ *Caution: Code Sec. 6019, below, as amended by P.L. 111-312, applies to estates of decedents dying, and transfers made, after December 31, 2009. For sunset provision, see P.L. 107-16, §901 [as amended by P.L. 111-312], in the amendment notes.*

[¶5770] CODE SEC. 6019. GIFT TAX RETURNS.

Any individual who in any calendar year makes any transfer by gift other than—

(1) a transfer which under subsection (b) or (e) of section 2503 is not to be included in the total amount of gifts for such year,

(2) a transfer of an interest with respect to which a deduction is allowed under section 2523, or

(3) a transfer with respect to which a deduction is allowed under section 2522 but only if—

(A)(i) such transfer is of the donor's entire interest in the property transferred, and

(ii) no other interest in such property is or has been transferred (for less than adequate and full consideration in money or money's worth) from the donor to a person, or for a use, not described in subsection (a) or (b) of section 2522, or

(B) such transfer is described in section 2522(d),

shall make a return for such year with respect to the gift tax imposed by subtitle B.

[CCH Explanation at ¶705 and ¶745. Committee Reports at ¶10,130.]

Amendments

• **2010, Tax Relief, Unemployment Insurance Reauthorization, and Job Creation Act of 2010 (P.L. 111-312)**

P.L. 111-312, §301(a):

Amended Code Sec. 6019 to read as such provision would read if subtitle E of title V of the Economic Growth and Tax Relief Reconciliation Act of 2001 (P.L. 107-16) had never been enacted. **Effective** for estates of decedents dying, and transfers made, after 12-31-2009. For a special rule, see Act Sec. 301(c), below. Prior to amendment by P.L. 111-312, Code Sec. 6019(a) read as follows:

(a) IN GENERAL.—Any individual who in any calendar year makes any transfer by gift other than—

(1) a transfer which under subsection (b) or (e) of section 2503 is not to be included in the total amount of gifts for such year,

(2) a transfer of an interest with respect to which a deduction is allowed under section 2523, or

(3) a transfer with respect to which a deduction is allowed under section 2522 but only if—

(A)(i) such transfer is of the donor's entire interest in the property transferred, and

(ii) no other interest in such property is or has been transferred (for less than adequate and full consideration in money or money's worth) from the donor to a person, or for a use, not described in subsection (a) or (b) of section 2522, or

(B) such transfer is described in section 2522(d),

shall make a return for such year with respect to the gift tax imposed by subtitle B.

(b) STATEMENTS TO BE FURNISHED TO CERTAIN PERSONS.—Every person required to make a return under subsection (a) shall furnish to each person whose name is required to be set forth in such return (other than the person required to make such return) a written statement showing—

(1) the name, address, and phone number of the person required to make such return, and

(2) the information specified in such return with respect to property received by the person required to receive such statement.

The written statement required under the preceding sentence shall be furnished not later than 30 days after the date that the return required by subsection (a) is filed.

P.L. 111-312, §301(c), provides:

(c) SPECIAL ELECTION WITH RESPECT TO ESTATES OF DECEDENTS DYING IN 2010.—Notwithstanding subsection (a), in the case of an estate of a decedent dying after December 31, 2009, and before January 1, 2011, the executor (within the meaning of section 2203 of the Internal Revenue Code of 1986) may elect to apply such Code as though the amendments made by subsection (a) do not apply with respect to chapter 11 of such Code and with respect to property acquired or passing from such decedent (within the meaning of section 1014(b) of such Code). Such election shall be made at such time and in such manner as the Secretary of the Treasury or the Secretary's delegate shall provide. Such an election once made shall be revocable only with the consent of the Secretary of the Treasury or the Secretary's delegate. For purposes of section 2652(a)(1) of such Code, the determination of whether any property is subject to the tax imposed by such chapter 11 shall be made without regard to any election made under this subsection.

P.L. 111-312, §304, provides:

SEC. 304. APPLICATION OF EGTRRA SUNSET TO THIS TITLE.

Section 901 of the Economic Growth and Tax Relief Reconciliation Act of 2001 shall apply to the amendments made by this title.

• **2001, Economic Growth and Tax Relief Reconciliation Act of 2001 (P.L. 107-16)**

P.L. 107-16, §542(b)(2)(A):

Amended Code Sec. 6019 by striking "Any individual" and inserting "(a) IN GENERAL.—Any individual". **Effective** for estates of decedents dying after 12-31-2009.

P.L. 107-16, §542(b)(2)(B):

Amended Code Sec. 6019 by adding at the end a new subsection (b). **Effective** for estates of decedents dying after 12-31-2009.

P.L. 107-16, §901(a)-(b), as amended by P.L. 111-312, §101(a)(1), provides:

SEC. 901. SUNSET OF PROVISIONS OF ACT..—(a) IN GENERAL.—All provisions of, and amendments made by, this Act shall not apply—

(1) to taxable, plan, or limitation years beginning after December 31, 2012, or

(2) in the case of title V, to estates of decedents dying, gifts made, or generation skipping transfers, after December 31, 2012.

(b) APPLICATION OF CERTAIN LAWS.—The Internal Revenue Code of 1986 and the Employee Retirement Income Security Act of 1974 shall be applied and administered to years, estates, gifts, and transfers described in subsection (a) as if the provisions and amendments described in subsection (a) had never been enacted.

>>> *Caution: Code Sec. 6039H, below, was added by P.L. 107-16. For sunset provision, see P.L. 107-16, §901 [as amended by P.L. 111-312], in the amendment notes.*

[¶5775] CODE SEC. 6039H. INFORMATION WITH RESPECT TO ALASKA NATIVE SETTLEMENT TRUSTS AND SPONSORING NATIVE CORPORATIONS.

(a) REQUIREMENT.—The fiduciary of an electing Settlement Trust (as defined in section 646(h)(1)) shall include with the return of income of the trust a statement containing the information required under subsection (c).

(b) APPLICATION WITH OTHER REQUIREMENTS.—The filing of any statement under this section shall be in lieu of the reporting requirements under section 6034A to furnish any statement to a beneficiary regarding amounts distributed to such beneficiary (and such other reporting rules as the Secretary deems appropriate).

(c) REQUIRED INFORMATION.—The information required under this subsection shall include—

(1) the amount of distributions made during the taxable year to each beneficiary,

(2) the treatment of such distribution under the applicable provision of section 646, including the amount that is excludable from the recipient beneficiary's gross income under section 646, and

(3) the amount (if any) of any distribution during such year that is deemed to have been made by the sponsoring Native Corporation (as defined in section 646(h)(5)).

(d) SPONSORING NATIVE CORPORATION.—

(1) IN GENERAL.—The electing Settlement Trust shall, on or before the date on which the statement under subsection (a) is required to be filed, furnish such statement to the sponsoring Native Corporation (as so defined).

(2) DISTRIBUTEES.—The sponsoring Native Corporation shall furnish each recipient of a distribution described in section 646(e)(3) a statement containing the amount deemed to have been distributed to such recipient by such corporation for the taxable year.

[CCH Explanation at ¶612. Committee Reports at ¶10,070.]

Amendments

• 2001, Economic Growth and Tax Relief Reconciliation Act of 2001 (P.L. 107-16)

P.L. 107-16, §671(b):

Amended subpart A of part III of subchapter A of chapter 61 of subtitle F by inserting after Code Sec. 6039G a new Code Sec. 6039H. **Effective** for tax years ending after 6-7-2001, and to contributions made to electing Settlement Trusts for such year or any subsequent year.

P.L. 107-16, §901(a)-(b), as amended by P.L. 111-312, §101(a)(1), provides:

SEC. 901. SUNSET OF PROVISIONS OF ACT.

(a) IN GENERAL.—All provisions of, and amendments made by, this Act shall not apply—

(1) to taxable, plan, or limitation years beginning after December 31, 2012, or

(2) in the case of title V, to estates of decedents dying, gifts made, or generation skipping transfers, after December 31, 2012.

(b) APPLICATION OF CERTAIN LAWS.—The Internal Revenue Code of 1986 and the Employee Retirement Income Security Act of 1974 shall be applied and administered to years, estates, gifts, and transfers described in subsection (a) as if the provisions and amendments described in subsection (a) had never been enacted.

[¶5780] CODE SEC. 6050S. RETURNS RELATING TO HIGHER EDUCATION TUITION AND RELATED EXPENSES.

* * *

》》→ Caution: *Code Sec. 6050S(e), below, was amended by P.L. 107-16. For sunset provision, see P.L. 107-16, §901 [as amended by P.L. 111-312], in the amendment notes.*

(e) DEFINITIONS.—For purposes of this section, the terms "eligible educational institution" and "qualified tuition and related expenses" have the meanings given such terms by section 25A (without regard to subsection (g)(2) thereof), and except as provided in regulations, the term "qualified education loan" has the meaning given such term by section 221(d)(1).

* * *

[CCH Explanation at ¶345. Committee Reports at ¶10,050.]

Amendments

● **2001, Economic Growth and Tax Relief Reconciliation Act of 2001 (P.L. 107-16)**

P.L. 107-16, §412(a)(2):

Amended Code Sec. 6050S(e) by striking "section 221(e)(1)" and inserting "section 221(d)(1)". Effective with respect to any loan interest paid after 12-31-2001, in tax years ending after such date.

P.L. 107-16, §901(a)-(b), as amended by P.L. 111-312, §101(a)(1), provides:

SEC. 901. SUNSET OF PROVISIONS OF ACT.

(a) IN GENERAL.—All provisions of, and amendments made by, this Act shall not apply—

(1) to taxable, plan, or limitation years beginning after December 31, 2012, or

(2) in the case of title V, to estates of decedents dying, gifts made, or generation skipping transfers, after December 31, 2012.

(b) APPLICATION OF CERTAIN LAWS.—The Internal Revenue Code of 1986 and the Employee Retirement Income Security Act of 1974 shall be applied and administered to years, estates, gifts, and transfers described in subsection (a) as if the provisions and amendments described in subsection (a) had never been enacted.

[¶5785] CODE SEC. 6075. TIME FOR FILING ESTATE AND GIFT TAX RETURNS.

》》→ Caution: *Code Sec. 6075(a), below, as amended by P.L. 111-312, applies to estates of decedents dying, and transfers made, after December 31, 2009. For sunset provision, see P.L. 107-16, §901 [as amended by P.L. 111-312], in the amendment notes.*

(a) ESTATE TAX RETURNS.—*Returns made under section 6018(a) (relating to estate taxes) shall be filed within 9 months after the date of the decedent's death.*

[CCH Explanation at ¶705 and ¶745. Committee Reports at ¶10,130.]

Amendments

● **2010, Tax Relief, Unemployment Insurance Reauthorization, and Job Creation Act of 2010 (P.L. 111-312)**

P.L. 111-312, §301(a):

Amended Code Sec. 6075(a) to read as such provision would read if subtitle E of title V of the Economic Growth and Tax Relief Reconciliation Act of 2001 (P.L. 107-16) had never been enacted. Effective for estates of decedents dying, and transfers made, after 12-31-2009. For a special rule, see Act Sec. 301(c), below. Prior to amendment by P.L. 111-312, Code Sec. 6075(a) read as follows:

(a) RETURNS RELATING TO LARGE TRANSFERS AT DEATH.—The return required by section 6018 with respect to a decedent shall be filed with the return of the tax imposed by chapter 1 for the decedent's last taxable year or such later date specified in regulations prescribed by the Secretary.

P.L. 111-312, §301(c), provides:

(c) SPECIAL ELECTION WITH RESPECT TO ESTATES OF DECEDENTS DYING IN 2010.—Notwithstanding subsection (a), in the case of an estate of a decedent dying after December 31, 2009, and before January 1, 2011, the executor (within the meaning of section 2203 of the Internal Revenue Code of 1986) may elect to apply such Code as though the amendments made by subsection (a) do not apply with respect to chapter 11 of such Code and with respect to property acquired or

passing from such decedent (within the meaning of section 1014(b) of such Code). Such election shall be made at such time and in such manner as the Secretary of the Treasury or the Secretary's delegate shall provide. Such an election once made shall be revocable only with the consent of the Secretary of the Treasury or the Secretary's delegate. For purposes of section 2652(a)(1) of such Code, the determination of whether any property is subject to the tax imposed by such chapter 11 shall be made without regard to any election made under this subsection.

P.L. 111-312, §304, provides:

SEC. 304. APPLICATION OF EGTRRA SUNSET TO THIS TITLE.

Section 901 of the Economic Growth and Tax Relief Reconciliation Act of 2001 shall apply to the amendments made by this title.

● **2001, Economic Growth and Tax Relief Reconciliation Act of 2001 (P.L. 107-16)**

P.L. 107-16, §542(b)(3)(A):

Amended Code Sec. 6075(a). Effective for estates of decedents dying after 12-31-2009. Prior to amendment, Code Sec. 6075(a) read as follows:

(a) ESTATE TAX RETURNS.—Returns made under section 6018 (a) (relating to estate taxes) shall be filed within 9 months after the date of the decedent's death.

P.L. 107-16, §901(a)-(b), as amended by P.L. 111-312, §101(a)(1), provides:

SEC. 901. SUNSET OF PROVISIONS OF ACT.

(a) In General.—All provisions of, and amendments made by, this Act shall not apply—

(1) to taxable, plan, or limitation years beginning after December 31, 2012, or

(2) in the case of title V, to estates of decedents dying, gifts made, or generation skipping transfers, after December 31, 2012.

(b) Gift Tax Returns.—

(b) Application of Certain Laws.—The Internal Revenue Code of 1986 and the Employee Retirement Income Security Act of 1974 shall be applied and administered to years, estates, gifts, and transfers described in subsection (a) as if the provisions and amendments described in subsection (a) had never been enacted.

* * *

⟫→ *Caution: Code Sec. 6075(b)(3), below, as amended by P.L. 111-312, applies to estates of decedents dying, and transfers made, after December 31, 2009. For sunset provision, see P.L. 107-16, §901 [as amended by P.L. 111-312], in the amendment notes.*

(3) Coordination with Due Date for Estate Tax Return.—Notwithstanding paragraphs (1) and (2), the time for filing the return made under section 6019 for the calendar year which includes the date of death of the donor shall not be later than the time (including extensions) for filing the return made under section 6018 (relating to estate tax returns) with respect to such donor.

[CCH Explanation at ¶705 and ¶745. Committee Reports at ¶10,130.]

Amendments

• 2010, Tax Relief, Unemployment Insurance Reauthorization, and Job Creation Act of 2010 (P.L. 111-312)

P.L. 111-312, §301(a):

Amended Code Sec. 6075(b)(3) to read as such provision would read if subtitle E of title V of the Economic Growth and Tax Relief Reconciliation Act of 2001 (P.L. 107-16) had never been enacted. **Effective** for estates of decedents dying, and transfers made, after 12-31-2009. For a special rule, see Act Sec. 301(c), below. Prior to amendment by P.L. 111-312, Code Sec. 6075(b)(3) read as follows:

(3) Coordination with Due Date for Section 6018 Return.—Notwithstanding paragraphs (1) and (2), the time for filing the return made under section 6019 for the calendar year which includes the date of death of the donor shall not be later than the time (including extensions) for filing the return made under section 6018 (relating to returns relating to large transfers at death) with respect to such donor.

P.L. 111-312, §301(c), provides:

(c) Special Election With Respect to Estates of Decedents Dying in 2010.—Notwithstanding subsection (a), in the case of an estate of a decedent dying after December 31, 2009, and before January 1, 2011, the executor (within the meaning of section 2203 of the Internal Revenue Code of 1986) may elect to apply such Code as though the amendments made by subsection (a) do not apply with respect to chapter 11 of such Code and with respect to property acquired or passing from such decedent (within the meaning of section 1014(b) of such Code). Such election shall be made at such time and in such manner as the Secretary of the Treasury or the Secretary's delegate shall provide. Such an election once made shall be revocable only with the consent of the Secretary of the Treasury or the Secretary's delegate. For purposes of section 2652(a)(1) of such Code, the determination of whether any property is subject to the tax imposed by such chapter 11 shall be made without regard to any election made under this subsection.

P.L. 111-312, §304, provides:

SEC. 304. APPLICATION OF EGTRRA SUNSET TO THIS TITLE.

Section 901 of the Economic Growth and Tax Relief Reconciliation Act of 2001 shall apply to the amendments made by this title.

• 2001, Economic Growth and Tax Relief Reconciliation Act of 2001 (P.L. 107-16)

P.L. 107-16, §542(b)(3)(B)(i)-(ii):

Amended Code Sec. 6075(b)(3) by striking "estate tax return" in the heading and inserting "section 6018 return", and by striking "(relating to estate tax returns)" and inserting "(relating to returns relating to large transfers at death)". **Effective** for estates of decedents dying after 12-31-2009.

P.L. 107-16, §901(a)-(b), as amended by P.L. 111-312, §101(a)(1), provides:

SEC. 901. SUNSET OF PROVISIONS OF ACT.

(a) In General.—All provisions of, and amendments made by, this Act shall not apply—

(1) to taxable, plan, or limitation years beginning after December 31, 2012, or

(2) in the case of title V, to estates of decedents dying, gifts made, or generation skipping transfers, after December 31, 2012.

(b) Application of Certain Laws.—The Internal Revenue Code of 1986 and the Employee Retirement Income Security Act of 1974 shall be applied and administered to years, estates, gifts, and transfers described in subsection (a) as if the provisions and amendments described in subsection (a) had never been enacted.

[¶5790] CODE SEC. 6166. EXTENSION OF TIME FOR PAYMENT OF ESTATE TAX WHERE ESTATE CONSISTS LARGELY OF INTEREST IN CLOSELY HELD BUSINESS.

* * *

(b) DEFINITIONS AND SPECIAL RULES.—

(1) INTEREST IN CLOSELY HELD BUSINESS.—For purposes of this section, the term "interest in a closely held business" means—

* * *

(B) an interest as a partner in a partnership carrying on a trade or business, if—

(i) 20 percent or more of the total capital interest in such partnership is included in determining the gross estate of the decedent, or

⇨ Caution: *Code Sec. 6166(b)(1)(B)(ii), below, was amended by P.L. 107-16. For sunset provision, see P.L. 107-16, §901 [as amended by P.L. 111-312], in the amendment notes.*

(ii) such partnership had 45 or fewer partners; or

(C) stock in a corporation carrying on a trade or business if—

(i) 20 percent or more in value of the voting stock of such corporation is included in determining the gross estate of the decedent, or

⇨ Caution: *Code Sec. 6166(b)(1)(C)(ii), below, was amended by P.L. 107-16. For sunset provision, see P.L. 107-16, §901 [as amended by P.L. 111-312], in the amendment notes.*

(ii) such corporation had 45 or fewer shareholders.

* * *

(8) STOCK IN HOLDING COMPANY TREATED AS BUSINESS COMPANY STOCK IN CERTAIN CASES.—

* * *

⇨ Caution: *Code Sec. 6166(b)(8)(B), below, was amended by P.L. 107-16. For sunset provision, see P.L. 107-16, §901 [as amended by P.L. 111-312], in the amendment notes.*

(B) ALL STOCK MUST BE NON-READILY-TRADABLE STOCK.—

(i) IN GENERAL.—No stock shall be taken into account for purposes of applying this paragraph unless it is non-readily-tradable stock (within the meaning of paragraph (7)(B)).

(ii) SPECIAL APPLICATION WHERE ONLY HOLDING COMPANY STOCK IS NON-READILY-TRADABLE STOCK.—If the requirements of clause (i) are not met, but all of the stock of each holding company taken into account is non-readily-tradable, then this paragraph shall apply, but subsection (a)(1) shall be applied by substituting "5" for "10".

* * *

(9) DEFERRAL NOT AVAILABLE FOR PASSIVE ASSETS.—

* * *

(B) PASSIVE ASSET DEFINED.—For purposes of this paragraph—

* * *

(iii) EXCEPTION FOR ACTIVE CORPORATIONS.—If—

⇨ Caution: *Code Sec. 6166(b)(9)(B)(iii)(I), below, was amended by P.L. 107-16. For sunset provision, see P.L. 107-16, §901 [as amended by P.L. 111-312], in the amendment notes.*

(I) a corporation owns 20 percent or more in value of the voting stock of another corporation, or such other corporation has 45 or fewer shareholders, and

(II) 80 percent or more of the value of the assets of each such corporation is attributable to assets used in carrying on a trade or business,

then such corporations shall be treated as 1 corporation for purposes of clause (ii). For purposes of applying subclause (II) to the corporation holding the stock of the other corporation, such stock shall not be taken into account.

➤➤➤ *Caution: Code Sec. 6166(b)(10), below, was added by P.L. 107-16. For sunset provision, see P.L. 107-16, §901 [as amended by P.L. 111-312], in the amendment notes.*

(10) Stock in Qualifying Lending and Finance Business Treated as Stock in an Active Trade or Business Company.—

(A) In General.—If the executor elects the benefits of this paragraph, then—

(i) Stock in Qualifying Lending and Finance Business Treated as Stock in an Active Trade or Business Company.—For purposes of this section, any asset used in a qualifying lending and finance business shall be treated as an asset which is used in carrying on a trade or business.

(ii) 5-year Deferral for Principal Not to Apply.—The executor shall be treated as having selected under subsection (a)(3) the date prescribed by section 6151(a).

(iii) 5 Equal Installments Allowed.—For purposes of applying subsection (a)(1), "5" shall be substituted for "10".

(B) Definitions.—For purposes of this paragraph—

(i) Qualifying Lending and Finance Business.—The term "qualifying lending and finance business" means a lending and finance business, if—

(I) based on all the facts and circumstances immediately before the date of the decedent's death, there was substantial activity with respect to the lending and finance business, or

(II) during at least 3 of the 5 taxable years ending before the date of the decedent's death, such business had at least 1 full-time employee substantially all of whose services were the active management of such business, 10 full-time, nonowner employees substantially all of whose services were directly related to such business, and $5,000,000 in gross receipts from activities described in clause (ii).

(ii) Lending and Finance Business.—The term "lending and finance business" means a trade or business of—

(I) making loans,

(II) purchasing or discounting accounts receivable, notes, or installment obligations,

(III) engaging in rental and leasing of real and tangible personal property, including entering into leases and purchasing, servicing, and disposing of leases and leased assets,

(IV) rendering services or making facilities available in the ordinary course of a lending or finance business, and

(V) rendering services or making facilities available in connection with activities described in subclauses (I) through (IV) carried on by the corporation rendering services or making facilities available, or another corporation which is a member of the same affiliated group (as defined in section 1504 without regard to section 1504(b)(3)).

(iii) Limitation.—The term "qualifying lending and finance business" shall not include any interest in an entity, if the stock or debt of such entity or a controlled group (as defined in section 267(f)(1)) of which such entity was a member was readily tradable on an established securities market or secondary market (as defined by the Secretary) at any time within 3 years before the date of the decedent's death.

[CCH Explanation at ¶705, 785, 790 and ¶795. Committee Reports at ¶10,130.]

Amendments

• **2001, Economic Growth and Tax Relief Reconciliation Act of 2001 (P.L. 107-16)**

P.L. 107-16, §571(a):

Amended Code Sec. 6166(b)(1)(B)(ii), (b)(1)(C)(ii), and (b)(9)(B)(iii)(I) by striking "15" and inserting "45". **Effective** for estates of decedents dying after 12-31-2001.

P.L. 107-16, §572(a):

Amended Code Sec. 6166(b) by adding at the end a new paragraph (10). **Effective** for estates of decedents dying after 12-31-2001.

P.L. 107-16, §573(a):

Amended Code Sec. 6166(b)(8)(B). **Effective** for estates of decedents dying after 12-31-2001. Prior to amendment, Code Sec. 6166(b)(8)(B) read as follows:

(B) ALL STOCK MUST BE NON-READILY-TRADABLE STOCK.—No stock shall be taken into account for purposes of applying this paragraph unless it is non-readily-tradable stock (within the meaning of paragraph (7)(B)).

P.L. 107-16, §901(a)-(b), as amended by P.L. 111-312, §101(a)(1), provides:

SEC. 901. SUNSET OF PROVISIONS OF ACT.

(a) IN GENERAL.—All provisions of, and amendments made by, this Act shall not apply—

(1) to taxable, plan, or limitation years beginning after December 31, 2012, or

(2) in the case of title V, to estates of decedents dying, gifts made, or generation skipping transfers, after December 31, 2012.

(b) APPLICATION OF CERTAIN LAWS.—The Internal Revenue Code of 1986 and the Employee Retirement Income Security Act of 1974 shall be applied and administered to years, estates, gifts, and transfers described in subsection (a) as if the provisions and amendments described in subsection (a) had never been enacted.

[¶5793] CODE SEC. 6211. DEFINITION OF A DEFICIENCY.

* * *

(b) RULES FOR APPLICATION OF SUBSECTION (a).—For purposes of this section—

* * *

(4) For purposes of subsection (a)—

* * *

⧉→ *Caution: Code Sec. 6211(b)(4)(A), below, as amended by P.L. 111-312, applies to tax years beginning after December 31, 2011. For sunset provision, see P.L. 111-148, §10909(c) [as amended by P.L. 111-312], in the amendment notes.*

(A) any excess of the sum of the credits allowable under sections 24(d), 25A by reason of subsection (i)(6) thereof, 32, 34, 35, 36, 36A, 36B, 53(e), 168(k)(4), 6428, and 6431 over the tax imposed by subtitle A (determined without regard to such credits), and

* * *

[CCH Explanation at ¶370. Committee Reports at ¶10,060.]

Amendments

• **2010, Tax Relief, Unemployment Insurance Reauthorization, and Job Creation Act of 2010 (P.L. 111-312)**

P.L. 111-312, §101(b)(1):

Amended Code Sec. 6211(b)(4)(A) to read as such provision would read if section 10909 of the Patient Protection and Affordable Care Act (P.L. 111-148) had never been enacted. **Effective** for tax years beginning after 12-31-2011.

• **2010, Patient Protection and Affordable Care Act (P.L. 111-148)**

P.L. 111-148, §10105(d):

Amended Act Sec. 1401(d) by adding at the end a new Act Sec. 1401(d)(3), which amends Code Sec. 6211(b)(4)(A) by inserting "36B," after "36A,". **Effective** 3-23-2010.

P.L. 111-148, §10909(b)(2)(N):

Amended Code Sec. 6211(b)(4)(A) by inserting "36C," before "53(e)". **Effective** for tax years beginning after 12-31-2009.

P.L. 111-148, §10909(c), as amended by P.L. 111-312, §101(b)(1), provides:

(c) SUNSET PROVISION..—Each provision of law amended by this section is amended to read as such provision would read if this section had never been enacted. The amendments made by the preceding sentence shall apply to taxable years beginning after December 31, 2011.

[¶5795] CODE SEC. 6213. RESTRICTIONS APPLICABLE TO DEFICIENCIES; PETITION TO TAX COURT.

* * *

(g) DEFINITIONS.—For purposes of this section—

* * *

(2) MATHEMATICAL OR CLERICAL ERROR.—The term "mathematical or clerical error" means—

* * *

(K) an omission of information required by section 32(k)(2) (relating to taxpayers making improper prior claims of earned income credit),

(L) the inclusion on a return of a TIN required to be included on the return under section 21, 24, 32, or 6428 if—

(i) such TIN is of an individual whose age affects the amount of the credit under such section, and

(ii) the computation of the credit on the return reflects the treatment of such individual as being of an age different from the individual's age based on such TIN,

>>> *Caution: Code Sec. 6213(g)(2)(M), below, was added by P.L. 107-16. For sunset provision, see P.L. 107-16, §901 [as amended by P.L. 111-312], in the amendment notes.*

(M) the entry on the return claiming the credit under section 32 with respect to a child if, according to the Federal Case Registry of Child Support Orders established under section 453(h) of the Social Security Act, the taxpayer is a non-custodial parent of such child,

* * *

[CCH Explanation at ¶355. Committee Reports at ¶10,040.]

Amendments

● 2001, Economic Growth and Tax Relief Reconciliation Act of 2001 (P.L. 107-16)

P.L. 107-16, §303(g):

Amended Code Sec. 6213(g)(2) by striking "and" at the end of subparagraph (K), by striking the period at the end of subparagraph (L) and inserting ", and", and by inserting after subparagraph (L) a new subparagraph (M). **Effective** 1-1-2004.

P.L. 107-16, §901(a)-(b), as amended by P.L. 111-312, §101(a)(1), provides:

SEC. 901. SUNSET OF PROVISIONS OF ACT.

(a) IN GENERAL.—All provisions of, and amendments made by, this Act shall not apply—

(1) to taxable, plan, or limitation years beginning after December 31, 2012, or

(2) in the case of title V, to estates of decedents dying, gifts made, or generation skipping transfers, after December 31, 2012.

(b) APPLICATION OF CERTAIN LAWS.—The Internal Revenue Code of 1986 and the Employee Retirement Income Security Act of 1974 shall be applied and administered to years, estates, gifts, and transfers described in subsection (a) as if the provisions and amendments described in subsection (a) had never been enacted.

[¶5800] CODE SEC. 6402. AUTHORITY TO MAKE CREDITS OR REFUNDS.

* * *

(f) COLLECTION OF UNEMPLOYMENT COMPENSATION DEBTS.—

* * *

(3) NOTICE; CONSIDERATION OF EVIDENCE.—No State may take action under this subsection until such State—

(A) notifies the person owing the covered unemployment compensation debt that the State proposes to take action pursuant to this section;

(B) provides such person at least 60 days to present evidence that all or part of such liability is not legally enforceable or *is not a covered unemployment compensation debt*;

(C) considers any evidence presented by such person and determines that an amount of such debt is legally enforceable and *is a covered unemployment compensation debt*; and

* * *

(4) COVERED UNEMPLOYMENT COMPENSATION DEBT.—For purposes of this subsection, the term "covered unemployment compensation debt" means—

(A) a past-due debt for erroneous payment of unemployment compensation due to fraud *or the person's failure to report earnings* which has become final under the law of a State certified by the Secretary of Labor pursuant to section 3304 and which remains uncollected;

(B) contributions due to the unemployment fund of a State for which the State has determined the person to be liable and which remain uncollected; and

(5) REGULATIONS.—

* * *

(6) ERRONEOUS PAYMENT TO STATE.—Any State receiving notice from the Secretary that an erroneous payment has been made to such State under paragraph (1) shall pay promptly to the Secretary, in accordance with such regulations as the Secretary may prescribe, an amount equal to the amount of such erroneous payment (without regard to whether any other amounts payable to such State under such paragraph have been paid to such State).

* * *

[CCH Explanation at ¶ 382.]
Amendments

• **2010, Tax Relief, Unemployment Insurance Reauthorization, and Job Creation Act of 2010 (P.L. 111-312)**

P.L. 111-312, § 503(a):

Amended Code Sec. 6402(f)(3)(C), as amended by section 801 of the Claims Resolution Act of 2010 (P.L. 111-291), by striking "is not a covered unemployment compensation debt" and inserting "is a covered unemployment compensation debt". **Effective** as if included in section 801 of the Claims Resolution Act of 2010 (P.L. 111-291) [effective for refunds payable under Code Sec. 6402 on or after 12-8-2010.—CCH].

• **2010, Claims Resolution Act of 2010 (P.L. 111-291)**

P.L. 111-291, § 801(a)(1)-(4):

Amended Code Sec. 6402(f) by striking "RESULTING FROM FRAUD" following "COMPENSATION DEBTS" in the heading; by striking paragraphs (3) and (8) and redesignating paragraphs (4) through (7) as paragraphs (3) through (6), respectively; in paragraph (3), as so redesignated, by striking "by certified mail with return receipt" following "noti-

fies" in subparagraph (A); by striking "due to fraud" and inserting "is not a covered unemployment compensation debt" in subparagraph (B); by striking " due to fraud" and inserting "is not [sic] a covered unemployment compensation debt" in subparagraph (C); and in paragraph (4), as so redesignated, in subparagraph (A), by inserting "or the person's failure to report earnings" after "due to fraud"; and by striking "for not more than 10 years" following "which remains uncollected"; and in subparagraph (B), by striking "due to fraud" following "the person to be liable"; and by striking "for not more than 10 years" following "which remain uncollected". **Effective** for refunds payable under Code Sec. 6402 on or after 12-8-2010. Prior to being stricken, Code Sec. 6402(f)(3) and (8) read as follows:

(3) OFFSET PERMITTED ONLY AGAINST RESIDENTS OF STATE SEEKING OFFSET.—Paragraph (1) shall apply to an overpayment by any person for a taxable year only if the address shown on the Federal return for such taxable year of the overpayment is an address within the State seeking the offset.

* * *

(8) TERMINATION.—This section shall not apply to refunds payable after the date which is 10 years after the date of the enactment of this subsection.

[¶ 5805] *CODE SEC. 6409. REFUNDS DISREGARDED IN THE ADMINISTRATION OF FEDERAL PROGRAMS AND FEDERALLY ASSISTED PROGRAMS.*

(a) IN GENERAL.—Notwithstanding any other provision of law, any refund (or advance payment with respect to a refundable credit) made to any individual under this title shall not be taken into account as income, and shall not be taken into account as resources for a period of 12 months from receipt, for purposes of determining the eligibility of such individual (or any other individual) for benefits or assistance (or the amount or extent of benefits or assistance) under any Federal program or under any State or local program financed in whole or in part with Federal funds.

(b) TERMINATION.—Subsection (a) shall not apply to any amount received after December 31, 2012.

[CCH Explanation at ¶ 384. Committee Reports at ¶ 10,350.]
Amendments

• **2010, Tax Relief, Unemployment Insurance Reauthorization, and Job Creation Act of 2010 (P.L. 111-312)**

P.L. 111-312, § 728(a):

Amended subchapter A of chapter 65 by adding at the end a new Code Sec. 6409. **Effective** for amounts received after 12-31-2009.

[¶5810] CODE SEC. 6426. CREDIT FOR ALCOHOL FUEL, BIODIESEL, AND ALTERNATIVE FUEL MIXTURES.

* * *

(b) ALCOHOL FUEL MIXTURE CREDIT.—

* * *

(6) TERMINATION.—This subsection shall not apply to any sale, use, or removal for any period after *December 31, 2011.*

[CCH Explanation at ¶546. Committee Reports at ¶10,240.]
Amendments

• **2010, Tax Relief, Unemployment Insurance Reauthorization, and Job Creation Act of 2010 (P.L. 111-312)**

P.L. 111-312, §708(b)(1):

Amended Code Sec. 6426(b)(6) by striking "December 31, 2010" and inserting "December 31, 2011". **Effective** for periods after 12-31-2010.

(c) BIODIESEL MIXTURE CREDIT.—

* * *

(6) TERMINATION.—This subsection shall not apply to any sale, use, or removal for any period after *December 31, 2011.*

[CCH Explanation at ¶544. Committee Reports at ¶10,170.]
Amendments

• **2010, Tax Relief, Unemployment Insurance Reauthorization, and Job Creation Act of 2010 (P.L. 111-312)**

P.L. 111-312, §701(b)(1):

Amended Code Sec. 6426(c)(6) by striking "December 31, 2009" and inserting "December 31, 2011". **Effective** for fuel sold or used after 12-31-2009.

(d) ALTERNATIVE FUEL CREDIT.—

* * *

(2) ALTERNATIVE FUEL.—For purposes of this section, the term "alternative fuel" means—

* * *

(G) liquid fuel derived from biomass (as defined in section 45K(c)(3)). Such term does not include ethanol, methanol, *biodiesel, or any fuel (including lignin, wood residues, or spent pulping liquors) derived from the production of paper or pulp.*

* * *

(5) TERMINATION.—This subsection shall not apply to any sale or use for any period after *December 31, 2011* (September 30, 2014, in the case of any sale or use involving liquefied hydrogen).

[CCH Explanation at ¶544. Committee Reports at ¶10,200.]
Amendments

• **2010, Tax Relief, Unemployment Insurance Reauthorization, and Job Creation Act of 2010 (P.L. 111-312)**

P.L. 111-312, §704(a):

Amended Code Sec. 6426(d)(5) by striking "December 31, 2009" and inserting "December 31, 2011". **Effective** for fuel sold or used after 12-31-2009. For a special rule, see Act Sec. 704(c), below.

P.L. 111-312, §704(b):

Amended the last sentence of Code Sec. 6426(d)(2) by striking "or biodiesel" and inserting "biodiesel (including lignin, wood residues, or spent pulping liquors) derived from the production of paper or pulp". **Effective** for fuel sold or used after 12-31-2009. For a special rule, see Act Sec. 704(c), below:

P.L. 111-312, § 704(c), provides:

(c) SPECIAL RULE FOR 2010.—Notwithstanding any other provision of law, in the case of any alternative fuel credit or any alternative fuel mixture credit properly determined under subsection (d) or (e) of section 6426 of the Internal Revenue Code of 1986 for periods during 2010, such credit shall be allowed, and any refund or payment attributable to such credit (including any payment under section 6427(e) of such Code) shall be made, only in such manner as the Secretary of the Treasury (or the Secretary's delegate) shall

provide. Such Secretary shall issue guidance within 30 days after the date of the enactment of this Act providing for a one-time submission of claims covering periods during 2010. Such guidance shall provide for a 180-day period for the submission of such claims (in such manner as prescribed by such Secretary) to begin not later than 30 days after such guidance is issued. Such claims shall be paid by such Secretary not later than 60 days after receipt. If such Secretary has not paid pursuant to a claim filed under this subsection within 60 days after the date of the filing of such claim, the claim shall be paid with interest from such date determined by using the overpayment rate and method under section 6621 of such Code.

(e) ALTERNATIVE FUEL MIXTURE CREDIT.—

* * *

(3) TERMINATION.—This subsection shall not apply to any sale or use for any period after December 31, 2011 (September 30, 2014, in the case of any sale or use involving liquefied hydrogen).

* * *

[CCH Explanation at ¶ 544. Committee Reports at ¶ 10,200.]

Amendments

• **2010, Tax Relief, Unemployment Insurance Reauthorization, and Job Creation Act of 2010 (P.L. 111-312)**

P.L. 111-312, § 704(a):

Amended Code Sec. 6426(e)(3) by striking "December 31, 2009" and inserting "December 31, 2011". Effective for fuel sold or used after 12-31-2009. For a special rule, see Act Sec. 704(c), below:

P.L. 111-312, § 704(c), provides:

(c) SPECIAL RULE FOR 2010.—Notwithstanding any other provision of law, in the case of any alternative fuel credit or any alternative fuel mixture credit properly determined under subsection (d) or (e) of section 6426 of the Internal Revenue Code of 1986 for periods during 2010, such credit

shall be allowed, and any refund or payment attributable to such credit (including any payment under section 6427(e) of such Code) shall be made, only in such manner as the Secretary of the Treasury (or the Secretary's delegate) shall provide. Such Secretary shall issue guidance within 30 days after the date of the enactment of this Act providing for a one-time submission of claims covering periods during 2010. Such guidance shall provide for a 180-day period for the submission of such claims (in such manner as prescribed by such Secretary) to begin not later than 30 days after such guidance is issued. Such claims shall be paid by such Secretary not later than 60 days after receipt. If such Secretary has not paid pursuant to a claim filed under this subsection within 60 days after the date of the filing of such claim, the claim shall be paid with interest from such date determined by using the overpayment rate and method under section 6621 of such Code.

[¶ 5815] CODE SEC. 6427. FUELS NOT USED FOR TAXABLE PURPOSES.

* * *

(e) ALCOHOL, BIODIESEL, OR ALTERNATIVE FUEL.—Except as provided in subsection (k)—

* * *

(6) TERMINATION.—This subsection shall not apply with respect to—

(A) any alcohol fuel mixture (as defined in section 6426(b)(3)) sold or used after December 31, 2011,

(B) any biodiesel mixture (as defined in section 6426(c)(3)) sold or used after December 31, 2011,

(C) except as provided in subparagraph (D), any alternative fuel or alternative fuel mixture (as defined in subsection (d)(2) or (e)(3) of section 6426) sold or used after December 31, 2011, and

* * *

[CCH Explanation at ¶544 and ¶546. Committee Reports a t¶10,170, ¶10,200 and ¶10,240.]

Amendments

• **2010, Tax Relief, Unemployment Insurance Reauthorization, and Job Creation Act of 2010 (P.L. 111-312)**

P.L. 111-312, §701(b)(2):

Amended Code Sec. 6427(e)(6)(B) by striking "December 31, 2009" and inserting "December 31, 2011". Effective for fuel sold or used after 12-31-2009.

P.L. 111-312, §704(a):

Amended Code Sec. 6427(e)(6)(C) by striking "December 31, 2009" and inserting "December 31, 2011". Effective for fuel sold or used after 12-31-2009. For a special rule, see Act Sec. 704(c), below.

P.L. 111-312, §704(c), provides:

(c) SPECIAL RULE FOR 2010.—Notwithstanding any other provision of law, in the case of any alternative fuel credit or any alternative fuel mixture credit properly determined under subsection (d) or (e) of section 6426 of the Internal Revenue Code of 1986 for periods during 2010, such credit shall be allowed, and any refund or payment attributable to such credit (including any payment under section 6427(e) of such Code) shall be made, only in such manner as the Secretary of the Treasury (or the Secretary's delegate) shall provide. Such Secretary shall issue guidance within 30 days after the date of the enactment of this Act providing for a one-time submission of claims covering periods during 2010. Such guidance shall provide for a 180-day period for the submission of such claims (in such manner as prescribed by such Secretary) to begin not later than 30 days after such guidance is issued. Such claims shall be paid by such Secretary not later than 60 days after receipt. If such Secretary has not paid pursuant to a claim filed under this subsection within 60 days after the date of the filing of such claim, the claim shall be paid with interest from such date determined by using the overpayment rate and method under section 6621 of such Code.

P.L. 111-312, §708(c)(1):

Amended Code Sec. 6427(e)(6)(A) by striking "December 31, 2010" and inserting "December 31, 2011". Effective for sales and uses after 12-31-2010.

≫→ *Caution: Code Sec. 6428, below, was added by P.L. 107-16, and amended by P.L. 107-147, P.L. 110-185 and P.L. 110-245. For sunset provision, see P.L. 107-16, §901 [as amended by P.L. 111-312], in the amendment notes.*

[¶5820] CODE SEC. 6428. 2008 RECOVERY REBATES FOR INDIVIDUALS.

(a) IN GENERAL.—In the case of an eligible individual, there shall be allowed as a credit against the tax imposed by subtitle A for the first taxable year beginning in 2008 an amount equal to the lesser of—

(1) net income tax liability, or

(2) $600 ($1,200 in the case of a joint return).

(b) SPECIAL RULES.—

(1) IN GENERAL.—In the case of a taxpayer described in paragraph (2)—

(A) the amount determined under subsection (a) shall not be less than $300 ($600 in the case of a joint return), and

(B) the amount determined under subsection (a) (after the application of subparagraph (A)) shall be increased by the product of $300 multiplied by the number of qualifying children (within the meaning of section 24(c)) of the taxpayer.

(2) TAXPAYER DESCRIBED.—A taxpayer is described in this paragraph if the taxpayer—

(A) has qualifying income of at least $3,000, or

(B) has—

(i) net income tax liability which is greater than zero, and

(ii) gross income which is greater than the sum of the basic standard deduction plus the exemption amount (twice the exemption amount in the case of a joint return).

(c) TREATMENT OF CREDIT.—The credit allowed by subsection (a) shall be treated as allowed by subpart C of part IV of subchapter A of chapter 1.

(d) LIMITATION BASED ON ADJUSTED GROSS INCOME.—The amount of the credit allowed by subsection (a) (determined without regard to this subsection and subsection (f)) shall be reduced (but not below zero) by 5 percent of so much of the taxpayer's adjusted gross income as exceeds $75,000 ($150,000 in the case of a joint return).

(e) DEFINITIONS.—For purposes of this section—

(1) QUALIFYING INCOME.—The term "qualifying income" means—

(A) earned income,

(B) social security benefits (within the meaning of section 86(d)), and

(C) any compensation or pension received under chapter 11, chapter 13, or chapter 15 of title 38, United States Code.

(2) NET INCOME TAX LIABILITY.—The term "net income tax liability" means the excess of—

(A) the sum of the taxpayer's regular tax liability (within the meaning of section 26(b)) and the tax imposed by section 55 for the taxable year, over

(B) the credits allowed by part IV (other than section 24 and subpart C thereof) of subchapter A of chapter 1.

(3) ELIGIBLE INDIVIDUAL.—The term "eligible individual" means any individual other than—

(A) any nonresident alien individual,

(B) any individual with respect to whom a deduction under section 151 is allowable to another taxpayer for a taxable year beginning in the calendar year in which the individual's taxable year begins, and

(C) an estate or trust.

(4) EARNED INCOME.—The term "earned income" has the meaning set forth in section 32(c)(2) except that such term shall not include net earnings from self-employment which are not taken into account in computing taxable income.

(5) BASIC STANDARD DEDUCTION; EXEMPTION AMOUNT.—The terms "basic standard deduction" and "exemption amount" shall have the same respective meanings as when used in section 6012(a).

[CCH Explanation at ¶305. Committee Reports at ¶10,010.]

Amendments

• 2008, Heroes Earnings Assistance and Relief Tax Act of 2008 (P.L. 110-245)

P.L. 110-245, §102(b):

Amended Code Sec. 6428(e)(4) by striking "except that—" "and all that follows through "(B) such term shall" and inserting "except that such term shall". **Effective** for tax years ending after 12-31-2007. Prior to amendment, Code Sec. 6428(e)(4) read as follows:

(4) EARNED INCOME.—The term "earned income" has the meaning set forth in section 32(c)(2) except that—

(A) subclause (II) of subparagraph (B)(vi) thereof shall be applied by substituting "January 1, 2009" for "January 1, 2008", and

(B) such term shall not include net earnings from self-employment which are not taken into account in computing taxable income.

(f) COORDINATION WITH ADVANCE REFUNDS OF CREDIT.—

(1) IN GENERAL.—The amount of credit which would (but for this paragraph) be allowable under this section shall be reduced (but not below zero) by the aggregate refunds and credits made or allowed to the taxpayer under subsection (g). Any failure to so reduce the credit shall be treated as arising out of a mathematical or clerical error and assessed according to section 6213(b)(1).

(2) JOINT RETURNS.—In the case of a refund or credit made or allowed under subsection (g) with respect to a joint return, half of such refund or credit shall be treated as having been made or allowed to each individual filing such return.

(g) ADVANCE REFUNDS AND CREDITS.—

(1) IN GENERAL.—Each individual who was an eligible individual for such individual's first taxable year beginning in 2007 shall be treated as having made a payment against the tax imposed by chapter 1 for such first taxable year in an amount equal to the advance refund amount for such taxable year.

(2) ADVANCE REFUND AMOUNT.—For purposes of paragraph (1), the advance refund amount is the amount that would have been allowed as a credit under this section for such first taxable year if this section (other than subsection (f) and this subsection) had applied to such taxable year.

(3) TIMING OF PAYMENTS.—The Secretary shall, subject to the provisions of this title, refund or credit any overpayment attributable to this section as rapidly as possible. No refund or credit shall be made or allowed under this subsection after December 31, 2008.

(4) NO INTEREST.—No interest shall be allowed on any overpayment attributable to this section.

(h) IDENTIFICATION NUMBER REQUIREMENT.—

(1) IN GENERAL.—No credit shall be allowed under subsection (a) to an eligible individual who does not include on the return of tax for the taxable year—

(A) such individual's valid identification number,

(B) in the case of a joint return, the valid identification number of such individual's spouse, and

(C) in the case of any qualifying child taken into account under subsection (b)(1)(B), the valid identification number of such qualifying child.

(2) VALID IDENTIFICATION NUMBER.—For purposes of paragraph (1), the term "valid identification number" means a social security number issued to an individual by the Social Security Administration. Such term shall not include a TIN issued by the Internal Revenue Service.

(3) SPECIAL RULE FOR MEMBERS OF THE ARMED FORCES.—Paragraph (1) shall not apply to a joint return where at least 1 spouse was a member of the Armed Forces of the United States at any time during the taxable year.

[CCH Explanation at ¶305. Committee Reports at ¶10,010.]

Amendments

• **2008, Heroes Earnings Assistance and Relief Tax Act of 2008 (P.L. 110-245)**

P.L. 110-245, §101(a):

Amended Code Sec. 6428(h) by adding at the end a new paragraph (3). **Effective** as if included in the amendments made by section 101 of the Economic Stimulus Act of 2008 (P.L. 110-185) [**effective 2-13-2008.**—CCH].

• **2008, Economic Stimulus Act of 2008 (P.L. 110-185)**

P.L. 110-185, §101(a):

Amended Code Sec. 6428. **Effective** 2-13-2008. Prior to amendment, Code Sec. 6428 read as follows:

SEC. 6428. ACCELERATION OF 10 PERCENT INCOME TAX RATE BRACKET BENEFIT FOR 2001.

[Sec. 6428(a)]

(a) IN GENERAL.—In the case of an eligible individual, there shall be allowed as a credit against the tax imposed by chapter 1 for the taxpayer's first taxable year beginning in 2001 an amount equal to 5 percent of so much of the taxpayer's taxable income as does not exceed the initial bracket amount (as defined in section 1(i)(1)(B)).

[Sec. 6428(b)]

(b) CREDIT TREATED AS NONREFUNDABLE PERSONAL CREDIT.—For purposes of this title, the credit allowed under this section shall be treated as a credit allowable under subpart A of part IV of subchapter A of chapter 1.

Amendments

• **2002, Job Creation and Worker Assistance Act of 2002 (P.L. 107-147)**

P.L. 107-147, §411(a)(1):

Amended Code Sec. 6428(b). **Effective** as if included in the provision of P.L. 107-16 to which it relates [**effective for**

tax years beginning after 12-31-2000.—CCH]. Prior to amendment, Code Sec. 6428(b) read as follows:

(b) LIMITATION BASED ON AMOUNT OF TAX.—The credit allowed by subsection (a) shall not exceed the excess (if any) of—

(1) the sum of the regular tax liability (as defined in section 26(b)) plus the tax imposed by section 55, over

(2) the sum of the credits allowable under part IV of subchapter A of chapter 1 (other than the credits allowable under subpart C thereof, relating to refundable credits).

• **2001, Economic Growth and Tax Relief Reconciliation Act of 2001 (P.L. 107-16)**

P.L. 107-16, §901(a)-(b), as amended by P.L. 111-312, §101(a)(1), provides:

SEC. 901. SUNSET OF PROVISIONS OF ACT.

(a) IN GENERAL.—All provisions of, and amendments made by, this Act shall not apply—

(1) to taxable, plan, or limitation years beginning after December 31, 2012, or

(2) in the case of title V, to estates of decedents dying, gifts made, or generation skipping transfers, after December 31, 2012.

(b) APPLICATION OF CERTAIN LAWS.—The Internal Revenue Code of 1986 and the Employee Retirement Income Security Act of 1974 shall be applied and administered to years, estates, gifts, and transfers described in subsection (a) as if the provisions and amendments described in subsection (a) had never been enacted.

[Sec. 6428(c)]

(c) ELIGIBLE INDIVIDUAL.—For purposes of this section, the term "eligible individual" means any individual other than—

(1) any estate or trust,

(2) any nonresident alien individual, and

(3) any individual with respect to whom a deduction under section 151 is allowable to another taxpayer for a taxable year beginning in the calendar year in which the individual's taxable year begins.

[Sec. 6428(d)]

(d) COORDINATION WITH ADVANCE REFUNDS OF CREDIT.—

(1) IN GENERAL.—The amount of credit which would (but for this paragraph) be allowable under this section shall be reduced (but not below zero) by the aggregate refunds and credits made or allowed to the taxpayer under subsection (e). Any failure to so reduce the credit shall be treated as arising out of a mathematical or clerical error and assessed according to section 6213(b)(1).

(2) JOINT RETURNS.—In the case of a refund or credit made or allowed under subsection (e) with respect to a joint return, half of such refund or credit shall be treated as having been made or allowed to each individual filing such return.

Amendments

● **2002, Job Creation and Worker Assistance Act of 2002 (P.L. 107-147)**

P.L. 107-147, §411(a)(2)(A):

Amended Code Sec. 6428(d). **Effective** as if included in the provision of P.L. 107-16 to which it relates [effective for tax years beginning after 12-31-2000.—CCH]. Prior to amendment, Code Sec. 6428(d) read as follows:

(d) SPECIAL RULES.—

(1) COORDINATION WITH ADVANCE REFUNDS OF CREDIT.—

(A) IN GENERAL.—The amount of credit which would (but for this paragraph) be allowable under this section shall be reduced (but not below zero) by the aggregate refunds and credits made or allowed to the taxpayer under subsection (e). Any failure to so reduce the credit shall be treated as arising out of a mathematical or clerical error and assessed according to section 6213(b)(1).

(B) JOINT RETURNS.—In the case of a refund or credit made or allowed under subsection (e) with respect to a joint return, half of such refund or credit shall be treated as having been made or allowed to each individual filing such return.

(2) COORDINATION WITH ESTIMATED TAX.—The credit under this section shall be treated for purposes of section 6654(f) in the same manner as a credit under subpart A of part IV of subchapter A of chapter 1.

● **2001, Economic Growth and Tax Relief Reconciliation Act of 2001 (P.L. 107-16)**

P.L. 107-16, §901(a)-(b), as amended by P.L. 111-312, §101(a)(1), provides:

SEC. 901. SUNSET OF PROVISIONS OF ACT.

(a) IN GENERAL.—All provisions of, and amendments made by, this Act shall not apply—

(1) to taxable, plan, or limitation years beginning after December 31, 2012, or

(2) in the case of title V, to estates of decedents dying, gifts made, or generation skipping transfers, after December 31, 2012.

(b) APPLICATION OF CERTAIN LAWS.—The Internal Revenue Code of 1986 and the Employee Retirement Income Security Act of 1974 shall be applied and administered to years, estates, gifts, and transfers described in subsection (a) as if the provisions and amendments described in subsection (a) had never been enacted.

[Sec. 6428(e)]

(e) ADVANCE REFUNDS OF CREDIT BASED ON PRIOR YEAR DATA.—

(1) IN GENERAL.—Each individual who was an eligible individual for such individual's first taxable year beginning in 2000 shall be treated as having made a payment against the tax imposed by chapter 1 for such first taxable year in an amount equal to the advance refund amount for such taxable year.

(2) ADVANCE REFUND AMOUNT.—For purposes of paragraph (1), the advance refund amount is the amount that would have been allowed as a credit under this section for such first taxable year if—

(A) this section (other than subsections (b) and (d) and this subsection) had applied to such taxable year, and

(B) the credit for such taxable year were not allowed to exceed the excess (if any) of—

(i) the sum of the regular tax liability (as defined in section 26(b)) plus the tax imposed by section 55, over

(ii) the sum of the credits allowable under part IV of subchapter A of chapter 1 (other than the credits allowable under subpart C thereof, relating to refundable credits).

(3) TIMING OF PAYMENTS.—In the case of any overpayment attributable to this subsection, the Secretary shall, subject to the provisions of this title, refund or credit such overpayment as rapidly as possible and, to the extent practicable, before October 1, 2001. No refund or credit shall be made or allowed under this subsection after December 31, 2001.

(4) NO INTEREST.—No interest shall be allowed on any overpayment attributable to this subsection.

Amendments

● **2002, Job Creation and Worker Assistance Act of 2002 (P.L. 107-147)**

P.L. 107-147, §411(a)(2)(B):

Amended Code Sec. 6428(e)(2). **Effective** as if included in the provision of P.L. 107-16 to which it relates [effective for tax years beginning after 12-31-2000.—CCH]. Prior to amendment, Code Sec. 6428(e)(2) read as follows:

(2) ADVANCE REFUND AMOUNT.—For purposes of paragraph (1), the advance refund amount is the amount that would have been allowed as a credit under this section for such first taxable year if this section (other than subsection (d) and this subsection) had applied to such taxable year.

● **2001, Economic Growth and Tax Relief Reconciliation Act of 2001 (P.L. 107-16)**

P.L. 107-16, §101(b)(1):

Amended subchapter B of chapter 65 by adding at the end a new Code Sec. 6428. **Effective** for tax years beginning after 12-31-2000.

P.L. 107-16, §901(a)-(b), as amended by P.L. 111-312, §101(a)(1), provides:

SEC. 901. SUNSET OF PROVISIONS OF ACT.

(a) IN GENERAL.—All provisions of, and amendments made by, this Act shall not apply—

(1) to taxable, plan, or limitation years beginning after December 31, 2012, or

(2) in the case of title V, to estates of decedents dying, gifts made, or generation skipping transfers, after December 31, 2012.

(b) APPLICATION OF CERTAIN LAWS.—The Internal Revenue Code of 1986 and the Employee Retirement Income Security

Act of 1974 shall be applied and administered to years, estates, gifts, and transfers described in subsection (a) as if the provisions and amendments described in subsection (a) had never been enacted.

P.L. 110-185, §101(c)-(d), provides:

(c) TREATMENT OF POSSESSIONS.—

(1) PAYMENTS TO POSSESSIONS.—

(A) MIRROR CODE POSSESSION.—The Secretary of the Treasury shall make a payment to each possession of the United States with a mirror code tax system in an amount equal to the loss to that possession by reason of the amendments made by this section. Such amount shall be determined by the Secretary of the Treasury based on information provided by the government of the respective possession.

(B) OTHER POSSESSIONS.—The Secretary of the Treasury shall make a payment to each possession of the United States which does not have a mirror code tax system in an amount estimated by the Secretary of the Treasury as being equal to the aggregate benefits that would have been provided to residents of such possession by reason of the amendments made by this section if a mirror code tax system had been in effect in such possession. The preceding sentence shall not apply with respect to any possession of the United States unless such possession has a plan, which has been approved by the Secretary of the Treasury, under which such possession will promptly distribute such payment to the residents of such possession.

(2) COORDINATION WITH CREDIT ALLOWED AGAINST UNITED STATES INCOME TAXES.—No credit shall be allowed against United States income taxes under section 6428 of the Internal Revenue Code of 1986 (as amended by this section) to any person—

(A) to whom a credit is allowed against taxes imposed by the possession by reason of the amendments made by this section, or

(B) who is eligible for a payment under a plan described in paragraph (1)(B).

(3) DEFINITIONS AND SPECIAL RULES.—

(A) POSSESSION OF THE UNITED STATES.—For purposes of this subsection, the term "possession of the United States" includes the Commonwealth of Puerto Rico and the Commonwealth of the Northern Mariana Islands.

(B) MIRROR CODE TAX SYSTEM.—For purposes of this subsection, the term "mirror code tax system" means, with respect to any possession of the United States, the income tax system of such possession if the income tax liability of the residents of such possession under such system is determined by reference to the income tax laws of the United States as if such possession were the United States.

(C) TREATMENT OF PAYMENTS.—For purposes of section 1324(b)(2) of title 31, United States Code, the payments under this subsection shall be treated in the same manner as a refund due from the credit allowed under section 6428 of the Internal Revenue Code of 1986 (as amended by this section).

(d) REFUNDS DISREGARDED IN THE ADMINISTRATION OF FEDERAL PROGRAMS AND FEDERALLY ASSISTED PROGRAMS.—Any credit or refund allowed or made to any individual by reason of section 6428 of the Internal Revenue Code of 1986 (as amended by this section) or by reason of subsection (c) of this section shall not be taken into account as income and shall not be taken into account as resources for the month of receipt and the following 2 months, for purposes of determining the eligibility of such individual or any other individual for benefits or assistance, or the amount or extent of benefits or assistance, under any Federal program or under any State or local program financed in whole or in part with Federal funds.

≫→ Caution: *Code Sec. 6429, below, was added by P.L. 108-27. For sunset provision, see P.L. 108-27, §107 [as amended by P.L. 111-312], in the amendment notes.*

[¶5825] CODE SEC. 6429. ADVANCE PAYMENT OF PORTION OF INCREASED CHILD CREDIT FOR 2003.

(a) IN GENERAL.—Each taxpayer who was allowed a credit under section 24 on the return for the taxpayer's first taxable year beginning in 2002 shall be treated as having made a payment against the tax imposed by chapter 1 for such taxable year in an amount equal to the child tax credit refund amount (if any) for such taxable year.

(b) CHILD TAX CREDIT REFUND AMOUNT.—For purposes of this section, the child tax credit refund amount is the amount by which the aggregate credits allowed under part IV of subchapter A of chapter 1 for such first taxable year would have been increased if—

(1) the per child amount under section 24(a)(2) for such year were $1,000,

(2) only qualifying children (as defined in section 24(c)) of the taxpayer for such year who had not attained age 17 as of December 31, 2003, were taken into account, and

(3) section 24(d)(1)(B)(ii) did not apply.

(c) TIMING OF PAYMENTS.—In the case of any overpayment attributable to this section, the Secretary shall, subject to the provisions of this title, refund or credit such overpayment as rapidly as possible and, to the extent practicable, before October 1, 2003. No refund or credit shall be made or allowed under this section after December 31, 2003.

(d) COORDINATION WITH CHILD TAX CREDIT.—

(1) IN GENERAL.—The amount of credit which would (but for this subsection and section 26) be allowed under section 24 for the taxpayer's first taxable year beginning in 2003 shall be reduced (but not below zero) by the payments made to the taxpayer under this section. Any

failure to so reduce the credit shall be treated as arising out of a mathematical or clerical error and assessed according to section 6213(b)(1).

(2) JOINT RETURNS.—In the case of a payment under this section with respect to a joint return, half of such payment shall be treated as having been made to each individual filing such return.

(e) NO INTEREST.—No interest shall be allowed on any overpayment attributable to this section.

[CCH Explanation at ¶360. Committee Reports at ¶10,030.]

Amendments

• **2003, Jobs and Growth Tax Relief Reconciliation Act of 2003 (P.L. 108-27)**

P.L. 108-27, §101(b)(1):

Amended subchapter B of chapter 65 by inserting after Code Sec. 6428 a new Code Sec. 6429. **Effective on** 5-28-2003.

P.L. 108-27, §107, provides:

SEC. 107. APPLICATION OF EGTRRA SUNSET TO THIS TITLE.

Each amendment made by this title shall be subject to title IX of the Economic Growth and Tax Relief Reconciliation Act of 2001 to the same extent and in the same manner as the provision of such Act to which such amendment relates.

• **2001, Economic Growth and Tax Relief Reconciliation Act of 2001 (P.L. 107-16)**

P.L. 107-16, §901(a)-(b), as amended by P.L. 111-312, §101(a)(1), provides:

SEC. 901. SUNSET OF PROVISIONS OF ACT.

(a) IN GENERAL.—All provisions of, and amendments made by, this Act shall not apply—

(1) to taxable, plan, or limitation years beginning after December 31, 2012, or

(2) in the case of title V, to estates of decedents dying, gifts made, or generation skipping transfers, after December 31, 2012.

(b) APPLICATION OF CERTAIN LAWS.—The Internal Revenue Code of 1986 and the Employee Retirement Income Security Act of 1974 shall be applied and administered to years, estates, gifts, and transfers described in subsection (a) as if the provisions and amendments described in subsection (a) had never been enacted.

[¶5830] CODE SEC. 6431. CREDIT FOR QUALIFIED BONDS ALLOWED TO ISSUER.

* * *

(f) APPLICATION OF SECTION TO CERTAIN QUALIFIED TAX CREDIT BONDS.—

* * *

(3) SPECIFIED TAX CREDIT BOND.—For purposes of this subsection, the term "specified tax credit bond" means any qualified tax credit bond (as defined in section 54A(d)) if—

(A) such bond is—

* * *

(iii) a qualified zone academy bond (as defined in section 54E) *determined without regard to any allocation relating to the national zone academy bond limitation for 2011 or any carryforward of such allocation,* or

* * *

[CCH Explanation at ¶465. Committee Reports at ¶10,640.]

Amendments

• **2010, Tax Relief, Unemployment Insurance Reauthorization, and Job Creation Act of 2010 (P.L. 111-312)**

P.L. 111-312, §758(b):

Amended Code Sec. 6431(f)(3)(A)(iii) by inserting "determined without regard to any allocation relating to the na-

tional zone academy bond limitation for 2011 or any carryforward of such allocation" after "54E)". **Effective for** obligations issued after 12-31-2010.

[¶5835] CODE SEC. 6511. LIMITATIONS ON CREDIT OR REFUND.

* * *

(i) CROSS REFERENCES.—

* * *

»»→ *Caution: Code Sec. 6511(i)(2), below, was amended by P.L. 107-16. For sunset provision, see P.L. 107-16, §901 [as amended by P.L. 111-312], in the amendment notes.*

(2) For limitations with respect to certain credits against estate tax, see sections 2014(b) and 2015.

* * *

[CCH Explanation at ¶705 and ¶730. Committee Reports at ¶10,130.]

Amendments

• **2001, Economic Growth and Tax Relief Reconciliation Act of 2001 (P.L. 107-16)**

P.L. 107-16, §532(c)(11):

Amended Code Sec. 6511(i)(2) by striking "2011(c), 2014(b)," and inserting "2014(b)". **Effective** for estates of decedents dying, and generation-skipping transfers, after 12-31-2004.

P.L. 107-16, §901(a)-(b), as amended by P.L. 111-312, §101(a)(1), provides:

SEC. 901. SUNSET OF PROVISIONS OF ACT.

(a) IN GENERAL.—All provisions of, and amendments made by, this Act shall not apply—

(1) to taxable, plan, or limitation years beginning after December 31, 2012, or

(2) in the case of title V, to estates of decedents dying, gifts made, or generation skipping transfers, after December 31, 2012.

(b) APPLICATION OF CERTAIN LAWS.—The Internal Revenue Code of 1986 and the Employee Retirement Income Security Act of 1974 shall be applied and administered to years, estates, gifts, and transfers described in subsection (a) as if the provisions and amendments described in subsection (a) had never been enacted.

[¶5840] CODE SEC. 6612. CROSS REFERENCES.

* * *

»»→ *Caution: Code Sec. 6612(c), below, was amended by P.L. 107-16. For sunset provision, see P.L. 107-16, §901 [as amended by P.L. 111-312], in the amendment notes.*

(c) OTHER RESTRICTIONS ON INTEREST.—For other restrictions on interest, see [sections] 2014(e) (relating to refunds attributable to foreign tax credits), 6412 (relating to floor stock refunds), 6413(d) (relating to taxes under the Federal Unemployment Tax Act), 6416 (relating to certain taxes on sales and services), 6419 (relating to the excise tax on wagering), 6420 (relating to payments in the case of gasoline used on the farm for farming purposes) and 6421 (relating to payments in the case of gasoline used for certain nonhighway purposes or by local transit systems).

[CCH Explanation at ¶705 and ¶730. Committee Reports at ¶10,130.]

Amendments

• **2001, Economic Growth and Tax Relief Reconciliation Act of 2001 (P.L. 107-16)**

P.L. 107-16, §532(c)(12):

Amended Code Sec. 6612(c) by striking "section 2011(c) (relating to refunds due to credit for State taxes)," following "For other restrictions on interest, see". **Effective** for estates of decedents dying, and generation-skipping transfers, after 12-31-2004.

P.L. 107-16, §901(a)-(b), as amended by P.L. 111-312, §101(a)(1), provides:

SEC. 901. SUNSET OF PROVISIONS OF ACT.

(a) IN GENERAL.—All provisions of, and amendments made by, this Act shall not apply—

(1) to taxable, plan, or limitation years beginning after December 31, 2012, or

(2) in the case of title V, to estates of decedents dying, gifts made, or generation skipping transfers, after December 31, 2012.

(b) APPLICATION OF CERTAIN LAWS.—The Internal Revenue Code of 1986 and the Employee Retirement Income Security Act of 1974 shall be applied and administered to years, estates, gifts, and transfers described in subsection (a) as if the provisions and amendments described in subsection (a) had never been enacted.

[¶ 5845] CODE SEC. 6697. ASSESSABLE PENALTIES WITH RESPECT TO LIABLITY FOR TAX OF REGULATED INVESTMENT COMPANIES. [Stricken.]

[CCH Explanation at ¶ 839.]

Amendments

• 2010, Regulated Investment Company Modernization Act of 2010 (H.R. 4337)

H.R. 4337, § 501(a):

Amended part I of subchapter B of chapter 68 by striking section 6697 (and by striking the item relating to such section in the table of sections of such part). Effective for tax years beginning after the date of the enactment of this Act. Prior to being stricken, Code Sec. 6697 read as follows:

SEC. 6697. ASSESSABLE PENALTIES WITH RESPECT TO LIABILITY FOR TAX OF REGULATED INVESTMENT COMPANIES.

(a) CIVIL PENALTY.—In addition to any other penalty provided by law, any regulated investment company whose tax liability for any taxable year is deemed to be increased pursuant to section 860(c)(1)(A) shall pay a penalty in an amount equal to the amount of the interest (for which such company is liable) which is attributable solely to such increase.

(b) 50-PERCENT LIMITATION.—The penalty payable under this section with respect to any determination shall not exceed one-half of the amount of the deduction allowed by section 860(a) for such taxable year.

(c) DEFICIENCY PROCEDURES NOT TO APPLY.—Subchapter B of chapter 63 (relating to deficiency procedure for income, estate, gift, and certain excise taxes) shall not apply in respect of the assessment or collection of any penalty imposed by subsection (a).

⧉→ Caution: *Code Sec. 6716 was added by P.L. 107-16, applicable to estates of decedents dying after December 31, 2009. P.L. 111-312 removed Code Sec. 6716, applicable to estates of decedents dying, and transfers made, after December 31, 2009, but see P.L. 111-312, §301(c), in the amendment notes. For sunset provision, see P.L. 107-16, §901 [as amended by P.L. 111-312], in the amendment notes.*

[¶ 5850] CODE SEC. 6716. FAILURE TO FILE INFORMATION WITH RESPECT TO CERTAIN TRANSFERS AT DEATH AND GIFTS.

(a) INFORMATION REQUIRED TO BE FURNISHED TO THE SECRETARY.—Any person required to furnish any information under section 6018 who fails to furnish such information on the date prescribed therefor (determined with regard to any extension of time for filing) shall pay a penalty of $10,000 ($500 in the case of information required to be furnished under section 6018(b)(2)) for each such failure.

(b) INFORMATION REQUIRED TO BE FURNISHED TO BENEFICIARIES.—Any person required to furnish in writing to each person described in section 6018(e) or 6019(b) the information required under such section who fails to furnish such information shall pay a penalty of $50 for each such failure.

(c) REASONABLE CAUSE EXCEPTION.—No penalty shall be imposed under subsection (a) or (b) with respect to any failure if it is shown that such failure is due to reasonable cause.

(d) INTENTIONAL DISREGARD.—If any failure under subsection (a) or (b) is due to intentional disregard of the requirements under sections 6018 and 6019(b), the penalty under such subsection shall be 5 percent of the fair market value (as of the date of death or, in the case of section 6019(b), the date of the gift) of the property with respect to which the information is required.

(e) DEFICIENCY PROCEDURES NOT TO APPLY.—Subchapter B of chapter 63 (relating to deficiency procedures for income, estate, gift, and certain excise taxes) shall not apply in respect of the assessment or collection of any penalty imposed by this section.

[CCH Explanation at ¶ 705 and ¶ 745. Committee Reports at ¶ 10,130.]

Amendments

• 2010, Tax Relief, Unemployment Insurance Reauthorization, and Job Creation Act of 2010 (P.L. 111-312)

P.L. 111-312, § 301(a):

Amended Code Sec. 6716 to read as such provision would read if subtitle E of title V of the Economic Growth and Tax Relief Reconciliation Act of 2001 (P.L. 107-16) had never been enacted. Effective for estates of decedents dying, and transfers made, after 12-31-2009. For a special rule, see Act Sec. 301(c), below. Prior to amendment by P.L. 111-312, Code Sec. 6716 read as follows:

SEC. 6716. FAILURE TO FILE INFORMATION WITH RESPECT TO CERTAIN TRANSFERS AT DEATH AND GIFTS.

(a) INFORMATION REQUIRED TO BE FURNISHED TO THE SECRETARY.—Any person required to furnish any information under section 6018 who fails to furnish such information on the date prescribed therefor (determined with regard to any extension of time for filing) shall pay a penalty of $10,000 ($500 in the case of information required to be furnished under section 6018(b)(2)) for each such failure.

(b) INFORMATION REQUIRED TO BE FURNISHED TO BENEFICIARIES.—Any person required to furnish in writing to each person described in section 6018(e) or 6019(b) the information required under such section who fails to furnish such information shall pay a penalty of $50 for each such failure.

(c) REASONABLE CAUSE EXCEPTION.—No penalty shall be imposed under subsection (a) or (b) with respect to any failure if it is shown that such failure is due to reasonable cause.

(d) INTENTIONAL DISREGARD.—If any failure under subsection (a) or (b) is due to intentional disregard of the requirements under sections 6018 and 6019(b), the penalty under such subsection shall be 5 percent of the fair market value (as of the date of death or, in the case of section 6019(b), the date of the gift) of the property with respect to which the information is required.

(e) DEFICIENCY PROCEDURES NOT TO APPLY.—Subchapter B of chapter 63 (relating to deficiency procedures for income, estate, gift, and certain excise taxes) shall not apply in respect of the assessment or collection of any penalty imposed by this section.

P.L. 111-312, §301(c), provides:

(c) SPECIAL ELECTION WITH RESPECT TO ESTATES OF DECEDENTS DYING IN 2010.—Notwithstanding subsection (a), in the case of an estate of a decedent dying after December 31, 2009, and before January 1, 2011, the executor (within the meaning of section 2203 of the Internal Revenue Code of 1986) may elect to apply such Code as though the amendments made by subsection (a) do not apply with respect to chapter 11 of such Code and with respect to property acquired or passing from such decedent (within the meaning of section 1014(b) of such Code). Such election shall be made at such time and in such manner as the Secretary of the Treasury or the Secretary's delegate shall provide. Such an election once made shall be revocable only with the consent of the Secretary of the Treasury or the Secretary's delegate. For purposes of section 2652(a)(1) of such Code, the determination of whether any property is subject to the tax imposed by such chapter 11 shall be made without regard to any election made under this subsection.

P.L. 111-312, §304, provides:

SEC. 304. APPLICATION OF EGTRRA SUNSET TO THIS TITLE.

Section 901 of the Economic Growth and Tax Relief Reconciliation Act of 2001 shall apply to the amendments made by this title.

• 2001, Economic Growth and Tax Relief Reconciliation Act of 2001 (P.L. 107-16)

P.L. 107-16, §542(b)(4):

Amended part I of subchapter B of chapter 68 by adding at the end a new Code Sec. 6716. **Effective for estates of** decedents dying after 12-31-2009.

P.L. 107-16, §901(a)-(b), as amended by P.L. 111-312, §101(a)(1), provides:

SEC. 901. SUNSET OF PROVISIONS OF ACT.

(a) IN GENERAL.—All provisions of, and amendments made by, this Act shall not apply—

(1) to taxable, plan, or limitation years beginning after December 31, 2012, or

(2) in the case of title V, to estates of decedents dying, gifts made, or generation skipping transfers, after December 31, 2012.

(b) APPLICATION OF CERTAIN LAWS.—The Internal Revenue Code of 1986 and the Employee Retirement Income Security Act of 1974 shall be applied and administered to years, estates, gifts, and transfers described in subsection (a) as if the provisions and amendments described in subsection (a) had never been enacted.

⨠➔ *Caution: Code Sec. 7518, below, was amended by P.L. 108-27. For sunset provision, see P.L. 108-27, §303, in the amendment notes.*

[¶5855] CODE SEC. 7518. TAX INCENTIVES RELATING TO MERCHANT MARINE CAPITAL CONSTRUCTION FUNDS.

* * *

(g) TAX TREATMENT OF NONQUALIFIED WITHDRAWALS.—

* * *

(6) NONQUALIFIED WITHDRAWALS TAXED AT HIGHEST MARGINAL RATE.—

⨠➔ *Caution: Code Sec. 7518(g)(6)(A), below, was amended by P.L. 108-27. For sunset provision, see P.L. 108-27, §303 [as amended by P.L. 111-312], in the amendment notes.*

(A) IN GENERAL.—In the case of any taxable year for which there is a nonqualified withdrawal (including any amount so treated under paragraph (5)), the tax imposed by chapter 1 shall be determined—

(i) by excluding such withdrawal from gross income, and

(ii) by increasing the tax imposed by chapter 1 by the product of the amount of such withdrawal and the highest rate of tax specified in section 1 (section 11 in the case of a corporation).

With respect to the portion of any nonqualified withdrawal made out of the capital gain account during a taxable year to which section 1(h) or 1201(a) applies, the rate of tax taken into account under the preceding sentence shall not exceed 15 percent (34 percent in the case of a corporation).

* * *

[CCH Explanation at ¶405. Committee Reports at ¶10,080.]

Amendments

- **2003, Jobs and Growth Tax Relief Reconciliation Act of 2003 (P.L. 108-27)**

P.L. 108-27, §301(a)(2)(D):

Amended the second sentence of Code Sec. 7518(g)(6)(A) by striking "20 percent" and inserting "15 percent". **Effective** for tax years ending on or after 5-6-2003.

P.L. 108-27, §303, as amended by P.L. 109-222, §102, and P.L. 111-312, §102(a), provides:

SEC. 303. SUNSET OF TITLE.

All provisions of, and amendments made by, this title shall not apply to taxable years beginning after December 31, 2012, and the Internal Revenue Code of 1986 shall be applied and administered to such years as if such provisions and amendments had never been enacted.

[¶5860] CODE SEC. 7652. SHIPMENTS TO THE UNITED STATES.

* * *

(f) LIMITATION ON COVER OVER OF TAX ON DISTILLED SPIRITS.—For purposes of this section, with respect to taxes imposed under section 5001 or this section on distilled spirits, the amount covered into the treasuries of Puerto Rico and the Virgin Islands shall not exceed the lesser of the rate of—

(1) $10.50 ($13.25 in the case of distilled spirits brought into the United States after June 30, 1999, and before *January 1, 2012*), or

(2) the tax imposed under section 5001(a)(1), on each proof gallon.

* * *

[CCH Explanation at ¶635. Committee Reports at ¶10,610.]

Amendments

- **2010, Tax Relief, Unemployment Insurance Reauthorization, and Job Creation Act of 2010 (P.L. 111-312)**

P.L. 111-312, §755(a):

Amended Code Sec. 7652(f)(1) by striking "January 1, 2010" and inserting "January 1, 2012". **Effective** for distilled spirits brought into the United States after 12-31-2009.

[¶5865] CODE SEC. 7701. DEFINITIONS.

(a) When used in this title, where not otherwise distinctly expressed or manifestly incompatible with the intent thereof—

* * *

⧉→ Caution: *Code Sec. 7701(a)(47) was added by P.L. 107-16, applicable to estates of decedents dying after December 31, 2009. P.L. 111-312 removed Code Sec. 7701(a)(47), applicable to estates of decedents dying, and transfers made, after December 31, 2009, but see P.L. 111-312, §301(c), in the amendment notes. For sunset provision, see P.L. 107-16, §901 [as amended by P.L. 111-312], in the amendment notes.*

(47) EXECUTOR.—The term "executor" means the executor or administrator of the decedent, or, if there is no executor or administrator appointed, qualified, and acting within the United States, then any person in actual or constructive possession of any property of the decedent.

* * *

[CCH Explanation at ¶705 and ¶760. Committee Reports at ¶10,130.]

Amendments

- **2010, Tax Relief, Unemployment Insurance Reauthorization, and Job Creation Act of 2010 (P.L. 111-312)**

P.L. 111-312, §301(a):

Amended Code Sec. 7701(a)(47) to read as such provision would read if subtitle E of title V of the Economic Growth and Tax Relief Reconciliation Act of 2001 (P.L. 107-16) had

never been enacted. **Effective** for estates of decedents dying, and transfers made, after 12-31-2009. For a special rule, see Act Sec. 301(c), below. Prior to amendment by P.L. 111-312, Code Sec. 7701(a)(47) read as follows:

(47) EXECUTOR.—The term "executor" means the executor or administrator of the decedent, or, if there is no executor or administrator appointed, qualified, and acting within the United States, then any person in actual or constructive possession of any property of the decedent.

P.L. 111-312, § 301(c), provides:

(c) SPECIAL ELECTION WITH RESPECT TO ESTATES OF DECEDENTS DYING IN 2010.—Notwithstanding subsection (a), in the case of an estate of a decedent dying after December 31, 2009, and before January 1, 2011, the executor (within the meaning of section 2203 of the Internal Revenue Code of 1986) may elect to apply such Code as though the amendments made by subsection (a) do not apply with respect to chapter 11 of such Code and with respect to property acquired or passing from such decedent (within the meaning of section 1014(b) of such Code). Such election shall be made at such time and in such manner as the Secretary of the Treasury or the Secretary's delegate shall provide. Such an election once made shall be revocable only with the consent of the Secretary of the Treasury or the Secretary's delegate. For purposes of section 2652(a)(1) of such Code, the determination of whether any property is subject to the tax imposed by such chapter 11 shall be made without regard to any election made under this subsection.

P.L. 111-312, § 304, provides:

SEC. 304. APPLICATION OF EGTRRA SUNSET TO THIS TITLE.

Section 901 of the Economic Growth and Tax Relief Reconciliation Act of 2001 shall apply to the amendments made by this title.

● **2001, Economic Growth and Tax Relief Reconciliation Act of 2001 (P.L. 107-16)**

P.L. 107-16, § 542(e)(3):

Amended Code Sec. 7701(a) by adding at the end a new paragraph (47). **Effective** for estates of decedents dying after 12-31-2009.

P.L. 107-16, § 901(a)-(b), as amended by P.L. 111-312, § 101(a)(1), provides:

SEC. 901. SUNSET OF PROVISIONS OF ACT.

(a) IN GENERAL.—All provisions of, and amendments made by, this Act shall not apply—

(1) to taxable, plan, or limitation years beginning after December 31, 2012, or

(2) in the case of title V, to estates of decedents dying, gifts made, or generation skipping transfers, after December 31, 2012.

(b) APPLICATION OF CERTAIN LAWS.—The Internal Revenue Code of 1986 and the Employee Retirement Income Security Act of 1974 shall be applied and administered to years, estates, gifts, and transfers described in subsection (a) as if the provisions and amendments described in subsection (a) had never been enacted.

[¶ 5870] CODE SEC. 9502. AIRPORT AND AIRWAY TRUST FUND.

* * *

(d) EXPENDITURES FROM AIRPORT AND AIRWAY TRUST FUND.—

(1) AIRPORT AND AIRWAY PROGRAM.—Amounts in the Airport and Airway Trust Fund shall be available, as provided by appropriation Acts, for making expenditures before *April 1, 2011,* to meet those obligations of the United States—

(A) incurred under title I of the Airport and Airway Development Act of 1970 or of the Airport and Airway Development Act Amendments of 1976 or of the Aviation Safety and Noise Abatement Act of 1979 (as such Acts were in effect on the date of enactment of the Fiscal Year 1981 Airport Development Authorization Act) or under the Fiscal Year 1981 Airport Development Authorization Act or the provisions of the Airport and Airway Improvement Act of 1982 or the Airport and Airway Safety and Capacity Expansion Act of 1987 or the Federal Aviation Administration Research, Engineering, and Development Authorization Act of 1990 or the Aviation Safety and Capacity Expansion Act of 1990 or the Airport and Airway Safety, Capacity, Noise Improvement, and Intermodal Transportation Act of 1992 or the Airport Improvement Program Temporary Extension Act of 1994 or the Federal Aviation Administration Authorization Act of 1994 or the Federal Aviation Reauthorization Act of 1996 or the provisions of the Omnibus Consolidated and Emergency Supplemental Appropriations Act, 1999 providing for payments from the Airport and Airway Trust Fund or the Interim Federal Aviation Administration Authorization Act or section 6002 of the 1999 Emergency Supplemental Appropriations Act, Public Law 106-59, or the Wendell H. Ford Aviation Investment and Reform Act for the 21st Century or the Aviation and Transportation Security Act or the Vision 100—Century of Aviation Reauthorization Act or any joint resolution making continuing appropriations for the fiscal year 2008 or the Department of Transportation Appropriations Act, 2008 or the Airport and Airway Extension Act of 2008 or the Federal Aviation Administration Extension Act of 2008 or the Federal Aviation Administration Extension Act of 2008, Part II or the Federal Aviation Administration Extension Act of 2009 or any joint resolution making continuing appropriations for the fiscal year 2010 or the Fiscal Year 2010 Federal Aviation Administration Extension Act or the Fiscal Year 2010 Federal Aviation Administration Extension Act, Part II or the Federal Aviation Administration Extension Act of 2010 or the Airport and Airway Extension Act of 2010 or the Airport and Airway Extension Act of 2010, Part II or the Airline Safety and Federal Aviation Administration Extension Act of 2010 or the Airport and Airway Extension Act of 2010, Part III *or the Airport and Airway Extension Act of 2010, Part IV;*

* * *

Any reference in subparagraph (A) to an Act shall be treated as a reference to such Act and the corresponding provisions (if any) of title 49, United States Code, as such Act and provisions were in effect on the date of the enactment of the last Act referred to in subparagraph (A).

* * *

[CCH Explanation at ¶ 000. Committee Reports at ¶ 0,000.]

Amendments

• **2010, Airport and Airway Extension Act of 2010, Part IV (H.R. 6473)**

H.R. 6473, § 3(a)(1)-(2):

Amended Code Sec. 9502(d)(1) by striking "January 1, 2011" and inserting "April 1, 2011", and by inserting "or the Airport and Airway Extension Act of 2010, Part IV" before the semicolon at the end of subparagraph (A). **Effective** 01-01-2011.

(e) LIMITATION ON TRANSFERS TO TRUST FUND.—

* * *

(2) EXCEPTION FOR PRIOR OBLIGATIONS.—Paragraph (1) shall not apply to any expenditure to liquidate any contract entered into (or for any amount otherwise obligated) before *April 1, 2011*, in accordance with the provisions of this section.

[CCH Explanation at ¶ 638.]

Amendments

• **2010, Airport and Airway Extension Act of 2010, Part IV (H.R. 6473)**

H.R. 6473, § 3(b):

Amended Code Sec. 9502(e)(2) by striking "January 1, 2011" and inserting "April 1, 2011". **Effective** 01-01-2011.

Act Sections Not Amending Code Sections

TAX RELIEF, UNEMPLOYMENT INSURANCE REAUTHORIZATION, AND JOB CREATION ACT OF 2010

[¶7005] ACT SEC. 1. SHORT TITLE; ETC.

(a) SHORT TITLE.—This Act may be cited as the "Tax Relief, Unemployment Insurance Reauthorization, and Job Creation Act of 2010".

* * *

TITLE I—TEMPORARY EXTENSION OF TAX RELIEF

[¶7010] ACT SEC. 101. TEMPORARY EXTENSION OF 2001 TAX RELIEF.

(a) TEMPORARY EXTENSION.—

(1) IN GENERAL.—Section 901 of the Economic Growth and Tax Relief Reconciliation Act of 2001 is amended by striking "December 31, 2010" both places it appears and inserting "December 31, 2012".

• • *ECONOMIC GROWTH AND TAX RELIEF RECONCILIATION ACT OF 2001 ACT SEC. 901(a) AS AMENDED*————————————————————————

ACT SEC. 901. SUNSET OF PROVISIONS OF ACT.

(a) IN GENERAL.—All provisions of, and amendments made by, this Act shall not apply—

(1) to taxable, plan, or limitation years beginning after *December 31, 2012*, or

(2) in the case of title V, to estates of decedents dying, gifts made, or generation skipping transfers, after *December 31, 2012*.

* * *

(2) EFFECTIVE DATE.—The amendment made by this subsection shall take effect as if included in the enactment of the Economic Growth and Tax Relief Reconciliation Act of 2001.

(b) SEPARATE SUNSET FOR EXPANSION OF ADOPTION BENEFITS UNDER THE PATIENT PROTECTION AND AFFORDABLE CARE ACT.—

(1) IN GENERAL.—Subsection (c) of section 10909 of the Patient Protection and Affordable Care Act is amended to read as follows:

"(c) SUNSET PROVISION.—Each provision of law amended by this section is amended to read as such provision would read if this section had never been enacted. The amendments made by the preceding sentence shall apply to taxable years beginning after December 31, 2011.".

• • *PATIENT PROTECTION AND AFFORDABLE CARE ACT OF 2010 ACT SEC. 10909(c) PRIOR TO AMENDMENT*————————————————————————

ACT SEC. 10909. EXPANSION OF ADOPTION CREDIT AND ADOPTION ASSISTANCE PROGRAMS.

* * *

(c) APPLICATION AND EXTENSION OF EGTRRA SUNSET.—Notwithstanding section 901 of the Economic Growth and Tax Relief Reconciliation Act of 2001, such section shall apply to the amendments made by this section and the amendments made by section 202 of such Act by substituting "December 31, 2011" for "December 31, 2010" in subsection (a)(1) thereof.

(2) CONFORMING AMENDMENT.—Subsection (d) of section 10909 of such Act is amended by striking "The amendments" and inserting "Except as provided in subsection (c), the amendments".

• • *PATIENT PROTECTION AND AFFORDABLE CARE ACT OF 2010 ACT SEC. 10909(d) AS AMENDED*————————————————————————

ACT SEC. 10909. EXPANSION OF ADOPTION CREDIT AND ADOPTION ASSISTANCE PROGRAMS.

* * *

(d) EFFECTIVE DATE.—*Except as provided in subsection (c), the amendments* made by this section shall apply to taxable years beginning after December 31, 2009.

[CCH Explanation at ¶305, ¶310, ¶315,¶320, ¶325,¶330, ¶335,¶340, ¶345,¶350, ¶355,¶360, ¶365,¶370, ¶375,¶455, ¶460,¶522, ¶603,¶606, ¶612,¶720, ¶725,¶730, ¶735,¶765, ¶770,¶775, ¶780,¶785, ¶790, and ¶795. **Committee Reports at ¶10,010,** ¶10,020,¶10,030,¶10,040,¶10,050,¶10,060, and ¶10,070.]

[¶7015] ACT SEC. 102. TEMPORARY EXTENSION OF 2003 TAX RELIEF.

(a) IN GENERAL.—Section 303 of the Jobs and Growth Tax Relief Reconciliation Act of 2003 is amended by striking "December 31, 2010" and inserting "December 31, 2012".

• • *JOBS AND GROWTH TAX RELIEF RECONCILIATION ACT OF 2003 ACT SEC. 303 [as amended by P.L. 109-222, §102] AS AMENDED*————————————————————————

ACT SEC. 303. SUNSET OF TITLE.

All provisions of, and amendments made by, this title shall not apply to taxable years beginning after *December 31, 2012*, and the Internal Revenue Code of 1986 shall be applied and administered to such years as if such provisions and amendments had never been enacted.

(b) EFFECTIVE DATE.—The amendment made by this section shall take effect as if included in the enactment of the Jobs and Growth Tax Relief Reconciliation Act of 2003.

* * *

[CCH Explanation at ¶305, ¶310, ¶315, ¶360, ¶375, ¶405, ¶410, ¶415, ¶420, ¶425, ¶603, ¶606, and ¶609. Committee Reports at ¶10,080.]

[¶7017] ACT SEC. 103. TEMPORARY EXTENSION OF 2009 TAX RELIEF.

(a) AMERICAN OPPORTUNITY TAX CREDIT.—

* * *

(2) TREATMENT OF POSSESSIONS.—Section 1004(c)(1) of the American Recovery and Reinvestment Tax Act of 2009 is amended by striking "and 2010" each place it appears and inserting ", 2010, 2011, and 2012".

* * *

• • *AMERICAN RECOVERY AND REINVESTMENT ACT OF 2009 ACT SEC. 1004(c)(1) AS AMENDED*—————————————————————————————

ACT SEC. 1004. AMERICAN OPPORTUNITY TAX CREDIT.

* * *

(c) TREATMENT OF POSSESSIONS.—

(1) PAYMENTS TO POSSESSIONS.—

(A) MIRROR CODE POSSESSION.—The Secretary of the Treasury shall pay to each possession of the United States with a mirror code tax system amounts equal to the loss to that possession by reason of the application of section 25A(i)(6) of the Internal Revenue Code of 1986 (as added by this section) with respect to taxable years beginning in 2009, *2010, 2011, and 2012*. Such amounts shall be determined by the Secretary of the Treasury based on information provided by the government of the respective possession.

(B) OTHER POSSESSIONS.—The Secretary of the Treasury shall pay to each possession of the United States which does not have a mirror code tax system amounts estimated by the Secretary of the Treasury as being equal to the aggregate benefits that would have been provided to residents of such possession by reason of the application of section 25A(i)(6) of such Code (as so added) for taxable years beginning in 2009, *2010, 2011, and 2012* if a mirror code tax system had been in effect in such possession. The preceding sentence shall not apply with respect to any possession of the United States unless such possession has a plan, which has been approved by the Secretary of the Treasury, under which such possession will promptly distribute such payments to the residents of such possession.

* * *

(d) EFFECTIVE DATE.—The amendments made by this section shall apply to taxable years beginning after December 31, 2008.

* * *

---

* * *

[CCH Explanation at ¶371. Committee Reports at ¶10,090.]

TITLE II—TEMPORARY EXTENSION OF INDIVIDUAL AMT RELIEF

[¶7020] ACT SEC. 201. TEMPORARY EXTENSION OF INCREASED ALTERNATIVE MINIMUM TAX EXEMPTION AMOUNT.

* * *

(c) Repeal of EGTRRA Sunset.—Title IX of the Economic Growth and Tax Relief Reconciliation Act of 2001 (relating to sunset of provisions of such Act) shall not apply to title VII of such Act (relating to alternative minimum tax).

* * *

[CCH Explanation at ¶375. Committee Reports at ¶10,120.]

* * *

TITLE III—TEMPORARY ESTATE TAX RELIEF

[¶7025] ACT SEC. 301. REINSTATEMENT OF ESTATE TAX; REPEAL OF CARRYOVER BASIS.

(a) In General.—Each provision of law amended by subtitle A or E of title V of the Economic Growth and Tax Relief Reconciliation Act of 2001 is amended to read as such provision would read if such subtitle had never been enacted.

(b) Conforming Amendment.—On and after January 1, 2011, paragraph (1) of section 2505(a) of the Internal Revenue Code of 1986 is amended to read as such paragraph would read if section 521(b)(2) of the Economic Growth and Tax Relief Reconciliation Act of 2001 had never been enacted.

(c) Special Election With Respect to Estates of Decedents Dying in 2010.—Notwithstanding subsection (a), in the case of an estate of a decedent dying after December 31, 2009, and before January 1, 2011, the executor (within the meaning of section 2203 of the Internal Revenue Code of 1986) may elect to apply such Code as though the amendments made by subsection (a) do not apply with respect to chapter 11 of such Code and with respect to property acquired or passing from such decedent (within the meaning of section 1014(b) of such Code). Such election shall be made at such time and in such manner as the Secretary of the Treasury or the Secretary's delegate shall provide. Such an election once made shall be revocable only with the consent of the Secretary of the Treasury or the Secretary's delegate. For purposes of section 2652(a)(1) of such Code, the determination of whether any property is subject to the tax imposed by such chapter 11 shall be made without regard to any election made under this subsection.

(d) Extension of Time for Performing Certain Acts.—

(1) Estate Tax.—In the case of the estate of a decedent dying after December 31, 2009, and before the date of the enactment of this Act, the due date for—

(A) filing any return under section 6018 of the Internal Revenue Code of 1986 (including any election required to be made on such a return) as such section is in effect after the date of the enactment of this Act without regard to any election under subsection (c),

(B) making any payment of tax under chapter 11 of such Code, and

(C) making any disclaimer described in section 2518(b) of such Code of an interest in property passing by reason of the death of such decedent,

shall not be earlier than the date which is 9 months after the date of the enactment of this Act.

(2) Generation-skipping Tax.—In the case of any generation-skipping transfer made after December 31, 2009, and before the date of the enactment of this Act, the due date for filing any return under section 2662 of the Internal Revenue Code of 1986 (including any election required to be made on such a return) shall not be earlier than the date which is 9 months after the date of the enactment of this Act.

(e) Effective Date.—Except as otherwise provided in this section, the amendments made by this section shall apply to estates of decedents dying, and transfers made, after December 31, 2009.

[CCH Explanation at ¶705, ¶740, ¶745, ¶750, ¶755, and ¶760. Committee Reports at ¶10,130.]

[¶7030] ACT SEC. 302. MODIFICATIONS TO ESTATE, GIFT, AND GENERATION-SKIPPING TRANSFER TAXES.

* * *

(b) MODIFICATIONS TO GIFT TAX.—

* * *

(2) MODIFICATION OF GIFT TAX RATE.—On and after January 1, 2011, subsection (a) of section 2502 is amended to read as such subsection would read if section 511(d) of the Economic Growth and Tax Relief Reconciliation Act of 2001 had never been enacted.

(c) MODIFICATION OF GENERATION-SKIPPING TRANSFER TAX.—In the case of any generation-skipping transfer made after December 31, 2009, and before January 1, 2011, the applicable rate determined under section 2641(a) of the Internal Revenue Code of 1986 shall be zero.

* * *

(f) EFFECTIVE DATE.—Except as otherwise provided in this subsection, the amendments made by this section shall apply to estates of decedents dying, generation-skipping transfers, and gifts made, after December 31, 2009.

* * *

[CCH Explanation at ¶710. Committee Reports at ¶10,130.]

[¶7035] ACT SEC. 304. APPLICATION OF EGTRRA SUNSET TO THIS TITLE.

Section 901 of the Economic Growth and Tax Relief Reconciliation Act of 2001 shall apply to the amendments made by this title.

* * *

[Committee Reports at ¶10,130.]

TITLE VI—TEMPORARY EMPLOYEE PAYROLL TAX CUT

[¶7040] ACT SEC. 601. TEMPORARY EMPLOYEE PAYROLL TAX CUT.

(a) IN GENERAL.—Notwithstanding any other provision of law—

(1) with respect to any taxable year which begins in the payroll tax holiday period, the rate of tax under section 1401(a) of the Internal Revenue Code of 1986 shall be 10.40 percent, and

(2) with respect to remuneration received during the payroll tax holiday period, the rate of tax under 3101(a) of such Code shall be 4.2 percent (including for purposes of determining the applicable percentage under section 3201(a) and 3211(a)(1) of such Code).

(b) COORDINATION WITH DEDUCTIONS FOR EMPLOYMENT TAXES.—

(1) DEDUCTION IN COMPUTING NET EARNINGS FROM SELF-EMPLOYMENT.—For purposes of applying section 1402(a)(12) of the Internal Revenue Code of 1986, the rate of tax imposed by subsection 1401(a) of such Code shall be determined without regard to the reduction in such rate under this section.

(2) INDIVIDUAL DEDUCTION.—In the case of the taxes imposed by section 1401 of such Code for any taxable year which begins in the payroll tax holiday period, the deduction under section 164(f) with respect to such taxes shall be equal to the sum of—

(A) 59.6 percent of the portion of such taxes attributable to the tax imposed by section 1401(a) (determined after the application of this section), plus

(B) one-half of the portion of such taxes attributable to the tax imposed by section 1401(b).

(c) PAYROLL TAX HOLIDAY PERIOD.—The term "payroll tax holiday period" means calendar year 2011.

(d) EMPLOYER NOTIFICATION.—The Secretary of the Treasury shall notify employers of the payroll tax holiday period in any manner the Secretary deems appropriate.

(e) TRANSFERS OF FUNDS.—

(1) TRANSFERS TO FEDERAL OLD-AGE AND SURVIVORS INSURANCE TRUST FUND.—There are hereby appropriated to the Federal Old-Age and Survivors Trust Fund and the Federal Disability Insurance Trust Fund established under section 201 of the Social Security Act (42 U.S.C. 401) amounts equal to the reduction in revenues to the Treasury by reason of the application of subsection (a). Amounts appropriated by the preceding sentence shall be transferred from the general fund at such times and in such manner as to replicate to the extent possible the transfers which would have occurred to such Trust Fund had such amendments not been enacted.

(2) TRANSFERS TO SOCIAL SECURITY EQUIVALENT BENEFIT ACCOUNT.—There are hereby appropriated to the Social Security Equivalent Benefit Account established under section 15A(a) of the Railroad Retirement At of 1974 (45 U.S.C. 231n-1(a)) amounts equal to the reduction in revenues to the Treasury by reason of the application of subsection (a)(2). Amounts appropriated by the preceding sentence shall be transferred from the general fund at such times and in such manner as to replicate to the extent possible the transfers which would have occurred to such Account had such amendments not been enacted.

(3) COORDINATION WITH OTHER FEDERAL LAWS.—For purposes of applying any provision of Federal law other than the provisions of the Internal Revenue Code of 1986, the rate of tax in effect under section 3101(a) of such Code shall be determined without regard to the reduction in such rate under this section.

[CCH Explanation at ¶312. Committee Reports at ¶10,160.]

TITLE VII—TEMPORARY EXTENSION OF CERTAIN EXPIRING PROVISIONS

Subtitle A—Energy

[¶7045] ACT SEC. 701. INCENTIVES FOR BIODIESEL AND RENEWABLE DIESEL.

* * *

(c) SPECIAL RULE FOR 2010.—Notwithstanding any other provision of law, in the case of any biodiesel mixture credit properly determined under section 6426(c) of the Internal Revenue Code of 1986 for periods during 2010, such credit shall be allowed, and any refund or payment attributable to such credit (including any payment under section 6427(e) of such Code) shall be made, only in such manner as the Secretary of the Treasury (or the Secretary's delegate) shall provide. Such Secretary shall issue guidance within 30 days after the date of the enactment of this Act providing for a one-time submission of claims covering periods during 2010. Such guidance shall provide for a 180-day period for the submission of such claims (in such manner as prescribed by such Secretary) to begin not later than 30 days after such guidance is issued. Such claims shall be paid by such Secretary no later than 60 days after receipt. If such Secretary has not paid pursuant to a claim filed under this subsection within 60 days after the date of the filing of such claim, the claim shall be paid with interest from such date determined by using the overpayment rate and method under section 6621 of such Code.

* * *

[CCH Explanation at ¶544. Committee Reports at ¶10,170.]

* * *

[¶7050] ACT SEC. 704. EXCISE TAX CREDITS AND OUTLAY PAYMENTS FOR ALTERNATIVE FUEL AND ALTERNATIVE FUEL MIXTURES.

* * *

(c) SPECIAL RULE FOR 2010.—Notwithstanding any other provision of law, in the case of any alternative fuel credit or any alternative fuel mixture credit properly determined under subsection (d) or (e) of section 6426 of the Internal Revenue Code of 1986 for periods during 2010, such credit shall be allowed, and any refund or payment attributable to such credit (including any payment under section 6427(e) of such Code) shall be made, only in such manner as the Secretary of the Treasury (or the Secretary's delegate) shall provide. Such Secretary shall issue guidance within 30 days after the date of the enactment of this Act providing for a one-time submission of claims covering periods during 2010. Such guidance shall provide for a 180-day period for the submission of such claims (in such manner as prescribed by such Secretary) to begin not later than 30 days after such guidance is issued. Such claims shall be paid by such Secretary no later than 60 days after receipt. If such Secretary has not paid pursuant to a claim filed under this subsection within 60 days after the date of the filing of such claim, the claim shall be paid with interest from such date determined by using the overpayment rate and method under section 6621 of such Code.

* * *

[CCH Explanation at ¶544. Committee Reports at ¶10,200.]

* * *

[¶7055] ACT SEC. 707. EXTENSION OF GRANTS FOR SPECIFIED ENERGY PROPERTY IN LIEU OF TAX CREDITS.

(a) IN GENERAL.—Subsection (a) of section 1603 of division B of the American Recovery and Reinvestment Act of 2009 is amended—

(1) in paragraph (1), by striking "2009 or 2010" and inserting "2009, 2010, or 2011", and

(2) in paragraph (2)—

(A) by striking "after 2010" and inserting "after 2011", and

(B) by striking "2009 or 2010" and inserting "2009, 2010, or 2011".

(b) CONFORMING AMENDMENT.—Subsection (j) of section 1603 of division B of such Act is amended by striking "2011" and inserting "2012".

• • *AMERICAN RECOVERY AND REINVESTMENT ACT OF 2009, DIVISION B, ACT SEC. 1603(a)(1)-(2) AND (j) AS AMENDED*———————————————

ACT SEC. 1603. GRANTS FOR SPECIFIED ENERGY PROPERTY IN LIEU OF TAX CREDITS.

(a) IN GENERAL.—Upon application, the Secretary of the Treasury shall, subject to the requirements of this section, provide a grant to each person who places in service specified energy property to reimburse such person for a portion of the expense of such property as provided in subsection (b). No grant shall be made under this section with respect to any property unless such property—

(1) is placed in service during *2009, 2010, or 2011*, or

(2) is placed in service *after 2011* and before the credit termination date with respect to such property, but only if the construction of such property began during *2009, 2010, or 2011*.

* * *

(j) TERMINATION.—The Secretary of the Treasury shall not make any grant to any person under this section unless the application of such person for such grant is received before October 1, 2012.

* * *

[CCH Explanation at ¶540. Committee Reports at ¶10,230.]

Subtitle B—Individual Tax Relief
* * *

[¶7060] ACT SEC. 725. TAX-FREE DISTRIBUTIONS FROM INDIVIDUAL RETIREMENT PLANS FOR CHARITABLE PURPOSES.
* * *

(b) EFFECTIVE DATE; SPECIAL RULE.—
* * *

(2) SPECIAL RULE.—For purposes of subsections (a)(6), (b)(3), and (d)(8) of section 408 of the Internal Revenue Code of 1986, at the election of the taxpayer (at such time and in such manner as prescribed by the Secretary of the Treasury) any qualified charitable distribution made after December 31, 2010, and before February 1, 2011, shall be deemed to have been made on December 31, 2010.

[CCH Explanation at ¶352. Committee Reports at ¶10,320.]
* * *

Subtitle C—Business Tax Relief
* * *

[¶7065] ACT SEC. 753. EMPOWERMENT ZONE TAX INCENTIVES.
* * *

(c) TREATMENT OF CERTAIN TERMINATION DATES SPECIFIED IN NOMINATIONS.—In the case of a designation of an empowerment zone the nomination for which included a termination date which is contemporaneous with the date specified in subparagraph (A)(i) of section 1391(d)(1) of the Internal Revenue Code of 1986 (as in effect before the enactment of this Act), subparagraph (B) of such section shall not apply with respect to such designation if, after the date of the enactment of this section, the entity which made such nomination amends the nomination to provide for a new termination date in such manner as the Secretary of the Treasury (or the Secretary's designee) may provide.
* * *

[CCH Explanation at ¶440. Committee Reports at ¶10,580.]

[¶7070] ACT SEC. 756. AMERICAN SAMOA ECONOMIC DEVELOPMENT CREDIT.

(a) IN GENERAL.—Subsection (d) of section 119 of division A of the Tax Relief and Health Care Act of 2006 is amended—

(1) by striking "first 4 taxable years" and inserting "first 6 taxable years", and

(2) by striking "January 1, 2010" and inserting "January 1, 2012".

• • *TAX RELIEF AND HEALTH CARE ACT OF 2006 DIVISION A, ACT SEC. 119(d) [as amended by P.L. 110-343, Division C, §309(a)(1)-(2)] AS AMENDED*————————

ACT SEC. 119. AMERICAN SAMOA ECONOMIC DEVELOPMENT CREDIT.
* * *

(d) APPLICATION OF SECTION.—Notwithstanding section 30A(h) or section 936(j) of such Code, this section (and so much of section 30A and section 936 of such Code as relates to this section) shall apply to the *first 6 taxable years* of a corporation to which subsection (a) applies which begin after December 31, 2005, and before *January 1, 2012*.

(b) Effective Date.—The amendments made by this section shall apply to taxable years beginning after December 31, 2009.

* * *

[CCH Explanation at ¶ 536. Committee Reports at ¶ 10,620.]

[¶ 7075] ACT SEC. 764. TAX-EXEMPT BOND FINANCING.

* * *

(b) Conforming Amendments.—Sections 702(d)(1) and 704(a) of the Heartland Disaster Tax Relief Act of 2008 are each amended by striking "January 1, 2011" each place it appears and inserting "January 1, 2012".

● ● *HEARTLAND DISASTER TAX RELIEF ACT OF 2008 ACT SECS. 702(d)(1) and 704(a) AS AMENDED*———————————————————————————————————

ACT SEC. 702. TEMPORARY TAX RELIEF FOR AREAS DAMAGED BY 2008 MIDWESTERN SEVERE STORMS, TORNADOS, AND FLOODING.

* * *

(d) Modifications to 1986 Code.—The following provisions of the Internal Revenue Code of 1986 shall be applied with the following modifications:

(1) Tax-exempt bond financing.—Section 1400N(a)—

* * *

(D) by substituting "January 1, 2013" for "*January 1, 2012*" in paragraph (2)(D),

* * *

(G) by substituting "after the date of the enactment of the Heartland Disaster Tax Relief Act of 2008 and before January 1, 2013" for "after the date of the enactment of this paragraph and before *January 1, 2012*" in paragraph (7)(C), and

* * *

ACT SEC. 704. TEMPORARY TAX-EXEMPT BOND FINANCING AND LOW-INCOME HOUSING TAX RELIEF FOR AREAS DAMAGED BY HURRICANE IKE.

(a) Tax-exempt bond financing.—Section 1400N(a) of the Internal Revenue Code of 1986 shall apply to any Hurricane Ike disaster areas in addition to any other area referenced in such section, but with the following modifications:

* * *

(4) by substituting "January 1, 2013" for "*January 1, 2012*" in paragraph (2)(D),

* * *

(7) by substituting "after the date of the enactment of the Heartland Disaster Tax Relief Act of 2008 and before January 1, 2013" for "after the date of the enactment of this paragraph and before *January 1, 2012*" in paragraph (7)(C), and

* * *

---

* * *

[CCH Explanation at ¶ 450. Committee Reports at ¶ 10,700.]

Committee Reports

The Tax Relief, Unemployment Insurance Reauthorization, and Job Creation Act of 2010

¶10,001 Introduction

The Tax Relief, Unemployment Insurance Reauthorization, and Job Creation Act of 2010 (P.L. 111-312) was passed by Congress on December 16, 2010, and signed by the President on December 17, 2010. The Joint Committee on Taxation produced a Technical Explanation of certain revenue provisions of the bill on December 10, 2010 (JCX-55-10). This report explains the intent of Congress regarding the provisions of the Act. There was no conference report issued for this Act. The Technical Explanation from the Joint Committee on Taxation is included in this section to aid the reader's understanding, but may not be cited as the official Conference Committee Report accompanying the Act. At the end of each section, references are provided to the corresponding CCH explanation and the Internal Revenue Code provisions. Subscribers to the electronic version can link from these references to the corresponding material. *The pertinent sections of the Technical Explanation relating to the Tax Relief, Unemployment Insurance Reauthorization, and Job Creation Act of 2010 appear in Act Section order beginning at ¶10,010.*

¶10,005 Background

The Middle Class Tax Relief Act of 2010 was introduced in the House of Representatives on December 1, 2010. The bill passed the House on December 2, 2010. The Senate passed the bill, as amended, on December 15, 2010, as the Tax Relief, Unemployment Insurance Reauthorization, and Job Creation Act of 2010. The House passed the bill, as amended by the Senate, on December 16, 2010. The bill was signed by the President on December 17, 2010.

References are to the following report:

• The Joint Committee on Taxation, Technical Explanation of the Revenue Provisions Contained in the "Tax Relief, Unemployment Insurance Reauthorization, and Job Creation Act of 2010" Scheduled for Consideration by the Senate, December 10, 2010, is referred to as Joint Committee on Taxation (J.C.T. Rep. No. JCX-55-10).

[¶10,010] Act Sec. 101. Marginal individual income tax rate reductions

Joint Committee on Taxation (J.C.T. REP. NO. JCX-55-10)

[Code Sec. 1]

Present Law

In general

The Economic Growth and Tax Relief Reconciliation Act of 2001[2] ("EGTRRA") created a new 10-percent regular income tax bracket for a portion of taxable income that was previously taxed at 15 percent. EGTRRA also reduced the other regular income tax rates. The otherwise applicable regular income tax rates of 28 percent, 31 percent, 36 percent and 39.6 percent were reduced to 25 percent, 28 percent, 33 percent, and 35 percent, respectively. These provisions of

EGTRRA shall cease to apply for taxable years beginning after December 31, 2010.

Tax rate schedules

To determine regular tax liability, a taxpayer generally must apply the tax rate schedules (or the tax tables) to his or her regular taxable income. The rate schedules are broken into several ranges of income, known as income brackets, and the marginal tax rate increases as a taxpayer's income increases. Separate rate schedules apply based on an individual's filing status. For 2010, the regular individual income tax rate schedules are as follows:

Table 1.-Federal Individual Income Tax Rates for 2010

If taxable income is:	Then income tax equals:
Single Individuals	
Not over $8,375	10% of the taxable income
Over $8,375 but not over $34,000	$837.50 plus 15% of the excess over $8,375
Over $34,000 but not over $82,400	$4,681.25 plus 25% of the excess over $34,000
Over $82,400 but not over $171,850	$16,781.25 plus 28% of the excess over $82,400
Over $171,850 but not over $373,650	$41,827.25 plus 33% of the excess over $171,850
Over $373,650	$108,421.25 plus 35% of the excess over $373,650
Heads of Households	
Not over $11,950	10% of the taxable income
Over $11,950 but not over $45,550	$1,195 plus 15% of the excess over $11,950
Over $45,550 but not over $117,650	$6,235 plus 25% of the excess over $45,550
Over $117,650 but not over $190,550	$24,260 plus 28% of the excess over $117,650
Over $190,550 but not over $373,650	$44,672 plus 33% of the excess over $190,550
Over $373,650	$105,095 plus 35% of the excess over $373,650
Married Individuals Filing Joint Returns and Surviving Spouses	
Not over $16,750	10% of the taxable income
Over $16,750 but not over $68,000	$1,675 plus 15% of the excess over $16,750
Over $68,000 but not over $137,300	$9,362.50 plus 25% of the excess over $68,000
Over $137,300 but not over $209,250	$26,687.50 plus 28% of the excess over $137,300

[2] Pub. L. No. 107-16.

If taxable income is:	Then income tax equals:
Over $209,250 but not over $373,650	$46,833.50 plus 33% of the excess over $209,250
Over $373,650	$101,085.50 plus 35% of the excess over $373,650
Married Individuals Filing Separate Returns	
Not over $8,375	10% of the taxable income
Over $8,375 but not over $34,000	$837.50 plus 15% of the excess over $8,375
Over $34,000 but not over $68,650	$4,681.25 plus 25% of the excess over $34,000
Over $68,650 but not over $104,625	$13,343.75 plus 28% of the excess over $68,650
Over $104,625 but not over $186,825	$23,416.75 plus 33% of the excess over $104,625
Over $186,825	$50,542.75 plus 35% of the excess over $186,825

Explanation of Provision

The provision extends the 10-percent, 15-percent, 25-percent, 28-percent, 33-percent and 35-percent individual income tax rates for two years (through 2012).

The rate structure is indexed for inflation.

A comparison of Table 2, below, with Table 1, above, illustrates the tax rate changes. Note that Table 2 also incorporates the provision to retain the marriage penalty relief with respect to the size of the 15 percent rate bracket, as discussed below.

Table 2.-Federal Individual Income Tax Rates for 2011

If taxable income is:	Then income tax equals:
Single Individuals	
Not over $8,500	10% of the taxable income
Over $8,500 but not over $34,500	$850 plus 15% of the excess over $8,500
Over $34,500 but not over $83,600	$4,750 plus 25% of the excess over $34,500
Over $83,600 but not over $174,400	$17,025 plus 28% of the excess over $83,600
Over $174,400 but not over $379,150	$42,449 plus 33% of the excess over $174,400
Over $379,150	$110,016.50 plus 35% of the excess over $379,150
Heads of Households	
Not over $12,150	10% of the taxable income
Over $12,150 but not over $46,250	$1,215 plus 15% of the excess over $12,150
Over $46,250 but not over $119,400	$6,330 plus 25% of the excess over $46,250
Over $119,400 but not over $193,350	$24,617.50 plus 28% of the excess over $119,350
Over $193,350 but not over $379,150	$45,323.50 plus 33% of the excess over $193,350
Over $379,150	$106,637.50 plus 35% of the excess over $379,150
Married Individuals Filing Joint Returns and Surviving Spouses	
Not over $17,000	10% of the taxable income
Over $17,000 but not over $69,000	$1,700 plus 15% of the excess over $17,000
Over $69,000 but not over $139,350	$9,500 plus 25% of the excess over $69,000

If taxable income is:	Then income tax equals:
Over $139,350 but not over $212,300	$27,087.50 plus 28% of the excess over $139,350
Over $212,300 but not over $379,150	$47,513.50 plus 33% of the excess over $379,150
Over $379,150	$102,574 plus 35% of the excess over $379,150
Married Individuals Filing Separate Returns	
Not over $8,500	10% of the taxable income
Over $8,500 but not over $34,500	$850 plus 15% of the excess over $8,500
Over $34,500 but not over $69,675	$4,750 plus 25% of the excess over $34,500
Over $69,675 but not over $106,150	$13,543.75 plus 28% of the excess over $69,675
Over $106,150 but not over $189,575	$23,756.75 plus 33% of the excess over $106,150
Over $189,575	$51,287 plus 35% of the excess over $189,575

Effective Date

The provision applies to taxable years beginning after December 31, 2010.

[Law at ¶5005 and ¶7010. CCH Explanation at ¶305.]

[¶10,020] Act Sec. 101. The overall limitation on itemized deductions and the personal exemption phase-out

Joint Committee on Taxation (J.C.T. REP. NO. JCX-55-10)

[Code Secs. 68 and 151]

Present Law

Overall limitation on itemized deductions ("Pease" limitation)

Unless an individual elects to claim the standard deduction for a taxable year, the taxpayer is allowed to deduct his or her itemized deductions. Itemized deductions generally are those deductions which are not allowed in computing adjusted gross income ("AGI"). Itemized deductions include unreimbursed medical expenses, investment interest, casualty and theft losses, wagering losses, charitable contributions, qualified residence interest, State and local income and property taxes, unreimbursed employee business expenses, and certain other miscellaneous expenses.

Prior to 2010, the total amount of otherwise allowable itemized deductions (other than medical expenses, investment interest, and casualty, theft, or wagering losses) was limited for upper-income taxpayers. In computing this reduction of total itemized deductions, all limitations applicable to such deductions (such as the separate floors) were first applied and, then, the otherwise allowable total amount of itemized deductions was reduced by three percent of the amount by which the taxpayer's AGI exceeded a threshold amount which was indexed annually for inflation. The otherwise allowable itemized deductions could not be reduced by more than 80 percent.

EGTRRA repealed this overall limitation on itemized deductions with the repeal phased-in over five years. EGTRRA provided: (1) a one-third reduction of the otherwise applicable limitation in 2006 and 2007; (2) a two-thirds reduction in 2008, and 2009; and (3) no overall limitation on itemized deductions in 2010. Thus in 2009, for example, the total amount of otherwise allowable itemized deductions (other than medical expenses, investment interest, and casualty, theft, or wagering losses) was reduced by three percent of the amount of the taxpayer's AGI in excess of $166,800 ($83,400 for married couples filing separate returns). Then the overall reduction in itemized deductions was phased-down to 1/3 of the full reduction amount (that is, the limitation was reduced by two-thirds).

Pursuant to the general EGTRRA sunset, the phased-in repeal of the Pease limitation sunsets and the limitation becomes fully effective again in 2011. Adjusting for inflation, the AGI threshold is $169,550 for 2011.

Personal exemption phase-out for certain taxpayers ("PEP")

Personal exemptions generally are allowed for the taxpayer, his or her spouse, and any dependents. For 2010, the amount deductible for each personal exemption is $3,650. This amount is indexed annually for inflation.

Prior to 2010, the deduction for personal exemptions was reduced or eliminated for taxpayers with incomes over certain thresholds, which were indexed annually for inflation. Specifically, the total amount of exemptions that could be claimed by a taxpayer was reduced by two percent for each $2,500 (or portion thereof) by which the taxpayer's AGI exceeded the applicable threshold. (The phase-out rate was two percent for each $1,250 for married taxpayers filing separate returns.) Thus, the deduction for personal exemptions was phased out over a $122,500 range (which was not indexed for inflation), beginning at the applicable threshold.

In 2009, for example, the applicable thresholds were $166,800 for single individuals, $250,200 for married individuals filing a joint return and surviving spouses, $208,500 for heads of households, and $125,100 for married individuals filing separate returns.

EGTRRA repealed PEP with the repeal phased-in over five years. EGTRRA provided: (1) a one-third reduction of the otherwise applicable limitation in 2006 and 2007: (2) a two-thirds reduction in 2008, and 2009; and (3) no PEP in 2010. However, under the EGTRRA sunset, the PEP becomes fully effective again in 2011. Adjusted for inflation, the PEP thresholds for 2011 are: (1) $169,550 for unmarried individuals; (2) $254,350 for married couples filing joint returns; and (3) $211,950 for heads of households.

Explanation of Provision

Overall limitation on itemized deductions ("Pease" limitation)

Under the provision the overall limitation on itemized deductions does not apply for two additional years (through 2012).

Personal exemption phase-out for certain taxpayers ("PEP")

Under the provision the personal exemption phase-out does not apply for two additional years (through 2012).

Effective Date

The provision applies to taxable years beginning after December 31, 2010.

[Law at ¶ 5190, ¶ 5250 and ¶ 7010. CCH Explanation at ¶ 320 and ¶ 325.]

[¶ 10,030] Act Secs. 101 and 103. Child tax credit

Joint Committee on Taxation (J.C.T. Rep. No. JCX-55-10)

[Code Sec. 24]

Present Law

An individual may claim a tax credit for each qualifying child under the age of 17. The maximum amount of the credit per child is $1,000 through 2010 and $500 thereafter. A child who is not a citizen, national, or resident of the United States cannot be a qualifying child.

The aggregate amount of child credits that may be claimed is phased out for individuals with income over certain threshold amounts. Specifically, the otherwise allowable aggregate child tax credit amount is reduced by $50 for each $1,000 (or fraction thereof) of modified adjusted gross income ("modified AGI") over $75,000 for single individuals or heads of households, $110,000 for married individuals filing joint returns, and $55,000 for married individuals

filing separate returns. For purposes of this limitation, modified AGI includes certain otherwise excludable income earned by U.S. citizens or residents living abroad or in certain U.S. territories.

The credit is allowable against the regular tax and, for taxable years beginning before January 1, 2011, is allowed against the alternative minimum tax ("AMT"). To the extent the child tax credit exceeds the taxpayer's tax liability, the taxpayer is eligible for a refundable credit (the additional child tax credit) equal to 15 percent of earned income in excess of a threshold dollar amount (the "earned income" formula). EGTRRA provided, in general, that this threshold dollar amount is $10,000 indexed for inflation from 2001. The American Recovery and Reinvestment Act of 2009 ("ARRA")[3] set the threshold at $3,000 for both 2009 and 2010. After 2010,

---

[3] Pub. L. No.111-5.

the ability to determine the refundable child credit based on earned income in excess of the threshold dollar amount expires.

Families with three or more qualifying children may determine the additional child tax credit using the "alternative formula" if this results in a larger credit than determined under the earned income formula. Under the alternative formula, the additional child tax credit equals the amount by which the taxpayer's social security taxes exceed the taxpayer's earned income tax credit ("EITC"). After 2010, due to the expiration of the earned income formula, this is the only manner of obtaining a refundable child credit.

Earned income is defined as the sum of wages, salaries, tips, and other taxable employee compensation plus net self-employment earnings. Unlike the EITC, which also includes the preceding items in its definition of earned income, the additional child tax credit is based only on earned income to the extent it is included in computing taxable income. For example, some ministers' parsonage allowances are considered self-employment income, and thus are considered earned income for purposes of computing the EITC, but are excluded from gross income for individual income tax purposes. Therefore, these allowances are not considered earned income for purposes of the additional child tax credit.

Explanation of Provision

The provision extends the $1,000 child tax credit and allows the child tax credit against the individual's regular income tax and AMT for two years (through 2012). The provision also extends the EGTRRA repeal of a prior-law provision that reduced the refundable child credit by the amount of the AMT for two years (through 2012). The provision extends the earned income formula for determining the refundable child credit, with the earned income threshold of $3,000 (also, the provision stops indexation for inflation of the $3,000 earnings threshold) for two years (through 2012).[4] Finally, the provision extends the rule that the refundable portion of the child tax credit does not constitute income and shall not be treated as resources for purposes of determining eligibility or the amount or nature of benefits or assistance under any Federal program or any State or local program financed with Federal funds for two years (through 2012).

Effective Date

The provision applies to taxable years beginning after December 31, 2010.

[Law at ¶5025 and ¶7010. CCH Explanation at ¶360.]

[¶10,040] Act Sec. 101. Marriage penalty relief and earned income tax credit simplification

Joint Committee on Taxation (J.C.T. Rep. No. JCX-55-10)

[Code Secs. 1, 32 and 63]

Present Law

Marriage penalty

A married couple generally is treated as one tax unit that must pay tax on the couple's total taxable income. Although married couples may elect to file separate returns, the rate schedules and other provisions are structured so that filing separate returns usually results in a higher tax than filing a joint return. Other rate schedules apply to single persons and to single heads of households.

A "marriage penalty" exists when the combined tax liability of a married couple filing a joint return is greater than the sum of the tax liabilities of each individual computed as if they were not married. A "marriage bonus" exists when the combined tax liability of a married couple filing a joint return is less than the sum of the tax liabilities of each individual computed as if they were not married.

Basic standard deduction

EGTRRA increased the basic standard deduction for a married couple filing a joint return to twice the basic standard deduction for an unmarried individual filing a single return. The basic standard deduction for a married taxpayer filing separately continued to equal one-half of the basic standard deduction for a married

---

[4] Section 101 of the bill extends the EGTRRA modifications to the provision. Section 103 of the bill extends the modifications to the provision (including reduction in the earnings threshold for the refundable portion of the child tax credit to $3,000). See Title I, section J for additional discussion of the child tax credit.

couple filing jointly; thus, the basic standard deduction for unmarried individuals filing a single return and for married couples filing separately are the same.

Fifteen percent rate bracket

EGTRRA increased the size of the 15-percent regular income tax rate bracket for a married couple filing a joint return to twice the size of the corresponding rate bracket for an unmarried individual filing a single return.

Earned income tax credit

The earned income tax credit ("EITC") is a refundable credit available to certain low-income taxpayers. Generally, the amount of an individual's allowable earned income credit is dependent on the individual's earned income, adjusted gross income, the number of qualifying children and (through 2010) filing status.

Explanation of Provision

Basic standard deduction

The provision increases the basic standard deduction for a married couple filing a joint return to twice the basic standard deduction for an unmarried individual filing a single return for two years (through 2012).

Fifteen percent rate bracket

The provision increases the size of the 15-percent regular income tax rate bracket for a married couple filing a joint return to twice the 15-percent regular income tax rate bracket for an unmarried individual filing a single return for two years (through 2012).

Earned income tax credit

The provision extends certain EITC provisions adopted by EGTRRA for two years (through 2012). These include: (1) a simplified definition of earned income; (2) a simplified relationship test; (3) use of AGI instead of modified AGI; (4) a simplified tie-breaking rule; (5) additional math error authority for the Internal Revenue Service; (6) a repeal of the prior-law provision that reduced an individual's EITC by the amount of his alternative minimum tax liability; and (7) increases in the beginning and ending points of the credit phase-out for married taxpayers by $5,000.[5]

Effective Date

The provision applies to taxable years beginning after December 31, 2010.

[Law at ¶5005, ¶5075, ¶5185 and ¶7010. CCH Explanation at ¶310, ¶315 and ¶355.]

[¶10,050] Act Sec. 101. Education incentives

Joint Committee on Taxation (J.C.T. REP. NO. JCX-55-10)

[Code Secs. 117, 127, 142, 146, 147, 148, 221 and 530]

Present Law

Income and wage exclusion for awards under the National Health Service Corps Scholarship Program and the F. Edward Hebert Armed Forces Health Professions Scholarship and Financial Assistance Program

Section 117 excludes from gross income amounts received as a qualified scholarship by an individual who is a candidate for a degree and used for tuition and fees required for the enrollment or attendance (or for fees, books, supplies, and equipment required for courses of instruction) at a primary, secondary, or postsecondary educational institution. The tax-free treatment provided by section 117 does not extend to scholarship amounts covering regular living expenses, such as room and board. In addition to the exclusion for qualified scholarships, section 117 provides an exclusion from gross income for qualified tuition reductions for certain education provided to employees (and their spouses and dependents) of certain educational organizations. Amounts excludable from gross income under section 117 are also excludable from wages for payroll tax purposes.[6]

The exclusion for qualified scholarships and qualified tuition reductions does not apply to any amount received by a student that represents payment for teaching, research, or other services by the student required as a condition for receiving the scholarship or tuition reduction. An exception to this rule applies in the case of the National Health Service Corps Scholarship Program (the "NHSC Scholarship Program") and the F. Edward Hebert Armed Forces Health Professions Scholarship and Financial Assistance

---

[5] The amount is indexed for inflation annually. See Title I, section K for a more complete description of the EITC.

[6] Sec. 3121(a)(20).

Program (the "Armed Forces Scholarship Program").

The NHSC Scholarship Program and the Armed Forces Scholarship Program provide education awards to participants on the condition that the participants provide certain services. In the case of the NHSC Scholarship Program, the recipient of the scholarship is obligated to provide medical services in a geographic area (or to an underserved population group or designated facility) identified by the Public Health Service as having a shortage of health care professionals. In the case of the Armed Forces Scholarship Program, the recipient of the scholarship is obligated to serve a certain number of years in the military at an armed forces medical facility.

Under the sunset provisions of EGTRRA, the exclusion from gross income and wages for the NHSC Scholarship Program and the Armed Forces Scholarship Program will no longer apply for taxable years beginning after December 31, 2010.

Income and wage exclusion for employer-provided educational assistance

If certain requirements are satisfied, up to $5,250 annually of educational assistance provided by an employer to an employee is excludable from gross income for income tax purposes and from wages for employment tax purposes.[7] This exclusion applies to both graduate and undergraduate courses.[8] For the exclusion to apply, certain requirements must be satisfied. The educational assistance must be provided pursuant to a separate written plan of the employer. The employer's educational assistance program must not discriminate in favor of highly compensated employees. In addition, no more than five percent of the amounts paid or incurred by the employer during the year for educational assistance under a qualified educational assistance program can be provided for the class of individuals consisting of more than five-percent owners of the employer and the spouses or dependents of such more than five-percent owners.

For purposes of the exclusion, educational assistance means the payment by an employer of expenses incurred by or on behalf of the employee for education of the employee including, but not limited to, tuition, fees, and similar payments, books, supplies, and equipment. Educational assistance also includes the provision by the employer of courses of instruction for the employee (including books, supplies, and equipment). Educational assistance does not include (1) tools or supplies that may be retained by the employee after completion of a course, (2) meals, lodging, or transportation, or (3) any education involving sports, games, or hobbies. The exclusion for employer-provided educational assistance applies only with respect to education provided to the employee (e.g., it does not apply to education provided to the spouse or a child of the employee).

In the absence of the specific exclusion for employer-provided educational assistance under section 127, employer-provided educational assistance is excludable from gross income and wages only if the education expenses qualify as a working condition fringe benefit.[9] In general, education qualifies as a working condition fringe benefit if the employee could have deducted the education expenses under section 162 if the employee paid for the education. In general, education expenses are deductible by an individual under section 162 if the education (1) maintains or improves a skill required in a trade or business currently engaged in by the taxpayer, or (2) meets the express requirements of the taxpayer's employer, applicable law, or regulations imposed as a condition of continued employment. However, education expenses are generally not deductible if they relate to certain minimum educational requirements or to education or training that enables a taxpayer to begin working in a new trade or business. In determining the amount deductible for this purpose, the two-percent floor on miscellaneous itemized deductions is disregarded.

The specific exclusion for employer-provided educational assistance was originally enacted on a temporary basis and was subsequently extended 10 times.[10] EGTRRA deleted the exclusion's explicit expiration date and extended the exclusion to graduate courses. However, those changes are subject to EGT-

---

[7] Secs. 127, 3121(a)(18).

[8] The exclusion has not always applied to graduate courses. The exclusion was first made inapplicable to graduate-level courses by the Technical and Miscellaneous Revenue Act of 1988. The exclusion was reinstated with respect to graduate-level courses by the Omnibus Budget Reconciliation Act of 1990, effective for taxable years beginning after December 31, 1990. The exclusion was again made inapplicable to graduate-level courses by the Small Business Job

Protection Act of 1996, effective for courses beginning after June 30, 1996. The exclusion for graduate-level courses was reinstated by EGTRRA, although that change does not apply to taxable years beginning after December 31, 2010 (under EGTRRA's sunset provision).

[9] Sec. 132(d).

[10] The exclusion was first enacted as part of the Revenue Act of 1978 (with a 1983 expiration date).

RRA's sunset provision so that the exclusion will not be available for taxable years beginning after December 31, 2010. Thus, at that time, educational assistance will be excludable from gross income only if it qualifies as a working condition fringe benefit (i.e., the expenses would have been deductible as business expenses if paid by the employee). As previously discussed, to meet such requirement, the expenses must be related to the employee's current job.[11]

Deduction for student loan interest

Certain individuals who have paid interest on qualified education loans may claim an above-the-line deduction for such interest expenses, subject to a maximum annual deduction limit.[12] Required payments of interest generally do not include voluntary payments, such as interest payments made during a period of loan forbearance. No deduction is allowed to an individual if that individual is claimed as a dependent on another taxpayer's return for the taxable year.

A qualified education loan generally is defined as any indebtedness incurred solely to pay for the costs of attendance (including room and board) of the taxpayer, the taxpayer's spouse, or any dependent of the taxpayer as of the time the indebtedness was incurred in attending an eligible educational institution on at least a half-time basis. Eligible educational institutions are (1) post-secondary educational institutions and certain vocational schools defined by reference to section 481 of the Higher Education Act of 1965, or (2) institutions conducting internship or residency programs leading to a degree or certificate from an institution of higher education, a hospital, or a health care facility conducting postgraduate training. Additionally, to qualify as an eligible educational institution, an institution must be eligible to participate in Department of Education student aid programs.

The maximum allowable deduction per year is $2,500. For 2010, the deduction is phased out ratably for single taxpayers with AGI between $60,000 and $75,000 and between $120,000 and $150,000 for married taxpayers filing a joint return. The income phaseout ranges are indexed for inflation and rounded to the next lowest multiple of $5,000.

Effective for taxable years beginning after December 31, 2010, the changes made by EGT-RRA to the student loan provisions no longer apply. The EGTRRA changes scheduled to expire are: (1) increases that were made in the AGI phaseout ranges for the deduction and (2) rules that extended deductibility of interest beyond the first 60 months that interest payments are required. With the expiration of EGTRRA, the phaseout ranges will revert to a base level of $40,000 to $55,000 ($60,000 to $75,000 in the case of a married couple filing jointly), but with an adjustment for inflation occurring since 2002.

Coverdell education savings accounts

A Coverdell education savings account is a trust or custodial account created exclusively for the purpose of paying qualified education expenses of a named beneficiary.[13] Annual contributions to Coverdell education savings accounts may not exceed $2,000 per designated beneficiary and may not be made after the designated beneficiary reaches age 18 (except in the case of a special needs beneficiary). The contribution limit is phased out for taxpayers with modified AGI between $95,000 and $110,000 ($190,000 and $220,000 for married taxpayers filing a joint return); the AGI of the contributor, and not that of the beneficiary, controls whether a contribution is permitted by the taxpayer.

Earnings on contributions to a Coverdell education savings account generally are subject to tax when withdrawn.[14] However, distributions from a Coverdell education savings account are excludable from the gross income of the distributee (i.e., the student) to the extent that the distribution does not exceed the qualified education expenses incurred by the beneficiary during the year the distribution is made. The earnings portion of a Coverdell education savings account distribution not used to pay qualified education expenses is includible in the gross income of the distributee and generally is subject to an additional 10-percent tax.[15]

Tax-free (including free of additional 10-percent tax) transfers or rollovers of account balances from one Coverdell education savings account benefiting one beneficiary to another Coverdell education savings account benefiting another beneficiary (as well as redesignations of

---

[11] Treas. Reg. sec. 1.162-5.

[12] Sec. 221.

[13] Sec. 530.

[14] In addition, Coverdell education savings accounts are subject to the unrelated business income tax imposed by section 511.

[15] This 10-percent additional tax does not apply if a distribution from an education savings account is made on account of the death or disability of the designated beneficiary, or if made on account of a scholarship received by the designated beneficiary.

the named beneficiary) are permitted, provided that the new beneficiary is a member of the family of the prior beneficiary and is under age 30 (except in the case of a special needs beneficiary). In general, any balance remaining in a Coverdell education savings account is deemed to be distributed within 30 days after the date that the beneficiary reaches age 30 (or, if the beneficiary dies before attaining age 30, within 30 days of the date that the beneficiary dies).

Qualified education expenses include "qualified higher education expenses" and "qualified elementary and secondary education expenses."

The term "qualified higher education expenses" includes tuition, fees, books, supplies, and equipment required for the enrollment or attendance of the designated beneficiary at an eligible education institution, regardless of whether the beneficiary is enrolled at an eligible educational institution on a full-time, half-time, or less than half-time basis.[16] Moreover, qualified higher education expenses include certain room and board expenses for any period during which the beneficiary is at least a half-time student. Qualified higher education expenses include expenses with respect to undergraduate or graduate-level courses. In addition, qualified higher education expenses include amounts paid or incurred to purchase tuition credits (or to make contributions to an account) under a qualified tuition program for the benefit of the beneficiary of the Coverdell education savings account.[17]

The term "qualified elementary and secondary education expenses," means expenses for: (1) tuition, fees, academic tutoring, special needs services, books, supplies, and other equipment incurred in connection with the enrollment or attendance of the beneficiary at a public, private, or religious school providing elementary or secondary education (kindergarten through grade 12) as determined under State law; (2) room and board, uniforms, transportation, and supplementary items or services (including extended day programs) required or provided by such a school in connection with such enrollment or attendance of the beneficiary; and (3) the purchase of any computer technology or equipment (as defined in section 170(e)(6)(F)(i)) or Internet access and related services, if such technology, equipment, or services are to be used by the beneficiary and the beneficiary's family during any of the years the beneficiary is in elementary or sec-

ondary school. Computer software primarily involving sports, games, or hobbies is not considered a qualified elementary and secondary education expense unless the software is predominantly educational in nature.

Qualified education expenses generally include only out-of-pocket expenses. Such qualified education expenses do not include expenses covered by employer-provided educational assistance or scholarships for the benefit of the beneficiary that are excludable from gross income. Thus, total qualified education expenses are reduced by scholarship or fellowship grants excludable from gross income under section 117, as well as any other tax-free educational benefits, such as employer-provided educational assistance, that are excludable from the employee's gross income under section 127.

Effective for taxable years beginning after December 31, 2010, the changes made by EGTRRA to Coverdell education savings accounts no longer apply. The EGTRRA changes scheduled to expire are: (1) the increase in the contribution limit to $2,000 from $500; (2) the increase in the phaseout range for married taxpayers filing jointly to $190,000-$220,000 from $150,000-$160,000; (3) the expansion of qualified expenses to include elementary and secondary education expenses; (4) special age rules for special needs beneficiaries; (5) clarification that corporations and other entities are permitted to make contributions, regardless of the income of the corporation or entity during the year of the contribution; (6) certain rules regarding when contributions are deemed made and extending the time during which excess contributions may be returned without additional tax; (7) certain rules regarding coordination with the Hope and Lifetime Learning credits; and (8) certain rules regarding coordination with qualified tuition programs.

Amount of governmental bonds that may be issued by governments qualifying for the "small governmental unit" arbitrage rebate exception

To prevent State and local governments from issuing more Federally subsidized tax-exempt bonds than is necessary for the activity being financed or from issuing such bonds earlier than needed for the purpose of the borrowing, the Code includes arbitrage restrictions limiting the ability to profit from investment of

---

[16] Qualified higher education expenses are defined in the same manner as for qualified tuition programs.

[17] Sec. 530(b)(2)(B).

tax-exempt bond proceeds.[18] The Code also provides certain exceptions to the arbitrage restrictions. Under one such exception, small issuers of governmental bonds issued for local governmental activities are not subject to the rebate requirement.[19] To qualify for this exception the governmental bonds must be issued by a governmental unit with general taxing powers that reasonably expects to issue no more than $5 million of tax-exempt governmental bonds in a calendar year.[20] Prior to EGTRRA, the $5 million limit was increased to $10 million if at least $5 million of the bonds are used to finance public schools. EGTRRA provided the additional amount of governmental bonds for public schools that small governmental units may issue without being subject to the arbitrage rebate requirements is increased from $5 million to $10 million.[21] Thus, these governmental units may issue up to $15 million of governmental bonds in a calendar year provided that at least $10 million of the bonds are used to finance public school construction expenditures. This increase is subject to the EGTRRA sunset.

Issuance of tax-exempt private activity bonds for public school facilities

Interest on bonds that nominally are issued by State or local governments, but the proceeds of which are used (directly or indirectly) by a private person and payment of which is derived from funds of such a private person is taxable unless the purpose of the borrowing is approved specifically in the Code or in a non-Code provision of a revenue act. These bonds are called "private activity bonds."[22] The term "private person" includes the Federal government and all other individuals and entities other than State or local governments.

Only specified private activity bonds are tax-exempt. EGTRRA added a new type of private activity bond that is subject to the EGTRRA sunset. This category is bonds for elementary and secondary public school facilities that are owned by private, for-profit corporations pursuant to public-private partnership agreements with a State or local educational agency.[23] The term school facility includes school buildings

and functionally related and subordinate land (including stadiums or other athletic facilities primarily used for school events) and depreciable personal property used in the school facility. The school facilities for which these bonds are issued must be operated by a public educational agency as part of a system of public schools.

A public-private partnership agreement is defined as an arrangement pursuant to which the for-profit corporate party constructs, rehabilitates, refurbishes, or equips a school facility for a public school agency (typically pursuant to a lease arrangement). The agreement must provide that, at the end of the contract term, ownership of the bond-financed property is transferred to the public school agency party to the agreement for no additional consideration.

Issuance of these bonds is subject to a separate annual per-State private activity bond volume limit equal to $10 per resident ($5 million, if greater) in lieu of the present-law State private activity bond volume limits. As with the present-law State private activity bond volume limits, States can decide how to allocate the bond authority to State and local government agencies. Bond authority that is unused in the year in which it arises may be carried forward for up to three years for public school projects under rules similar to the carryforward rules of the present-law private activity bond volume limits.

Explanation of Provision

The provision delays the EGTRRA sunset as it applies to the NHSC Scholarship Program and the Armed Forces Scholarship Program, the section 127 exclusion from income and wages for employer-provided educational assistance, the student loan interest deduction, and Coverdell education savings accounts for two years. The provision also delays the EGTRRA sunset as it applies to the expansion of the small government unit exception to arbitrage rebate and allowing issuance of tax-exempt private activity bonds for public school facilities. Thus, all of these tax benefits for education continue to be available through 2012.

---

[18] The exclusion from gross income for interest on State and local bonds does not apply to any arbitrage bond (sec. 103(a), (b)(2)). A bond is an arbitrage bond if it is part of an issue that violates the restrictions against investing in higher-yielding investments under section 148(a) or that fails to satisfy the requirement to rebate arbitrage earnings under section 148(f).

[19] Ninety-five percent or more of the net proceeds of governmental bond issue are to be used for local governmental activities of the issuer. Sec. 148(f)(4)(D).

[20] Under the Treasury regulations, an issuer may apply a fact-based rather than an expectations-based test. Treas. Reg. 1.148-8(c)(1).

[21] Sec. 148(f)(4)(D)(vii).

[22] The Code provides that the exclusion from gross income does not apply to interest on private activity bonds that are not qualified bonds within the meaning of section 141. See secs. 103(b)(1), 141.

[23] Sec. 142(a)(13), (k).

Effective Date

The provision is effective on the date of enactment.

[Law at ¶5200, ¶5210, ¶5230, ¶5245, ¶5305, ¶5380 and ¶7010. CCH Explanation at ¶330, ¶335, ¶340, ¶345, ¶455 and ¶460]

[¶10,060] Act Sec. 101. Other incentives for families and children (includes extension of the adoption tax credit, employer-provided child care tax credit, and dependent care tax credit)

Joint Committee on Taxation (J.C.T. REP. No. JCX-55-10)

[Code Secs. 21, 23 [redesignated 36C], 36C, 45D [sic; should be 45F] and 137]

Present Law

Adoption credit and exclusion from income for employer-provided adoption assistance

Present law for 2010 provides: (1) a maximum adoption credit of $13,170 per eligible child (both special needs and non-special needs adoptions); and (2) a maximum exclusion of $13,170 per eligible child (both special needs and non-special needs adoptions).[24] These dollar amounts are adjusted annually for inflation. These benefits are phased-out over a $40,000 range for taxpayers with modified adjusted gross income ("modified AGI") in excess of certain dollar levels. For 2010, the phase-out range is between $182,520 and $222,520. The phase-out threshold is adjusted for inflation annually, but the phase-out range remains a $40,000 range.

For taxable years beginning after December 31, 2011, the adoption credit and employer-provided adoption assistance exclusion are available only to special needs adoptions and the maximum credit and exclusion are reduced to $6,000, respectively. The phase-out range is reduced to lower income levels (i.e., between $75,000 and $115,000). The maximum credit, exclusion, and phase-out range are not indexed for inflation.

Employer-provided child care tax credit

Taxpayers receive a tax credit equal to 25 percent of qualified expenses for employee child care and 10 percent of qualified expenses for child care resource and referral services. The maximum total credit that may be claimed by a taxpayer cannot exceed $150,000 per taxable year.

Qualified child care expenses include costs paid or incurred: (1) to acquire, construct, rehabilitate or expand property that is to be used as part of the taxpayer's qualified child care facility; (2) for the operation of the taxpayer's qualified child care facility, including the costs of training and certain compensation for employees of the child care facility, and scholarship programs; or (3) under a contract with a qualified child care facility to provide child care services to employees of the taxpayer. To be a qualified child care facility, the principal use of the facility must be for child care (unless it is the principal residence of the taxpayer), and the facility must meet all applicable State and local laws and regulations, including any licensing laws. A facility is not treated as a qualified child care facility with respect to a taxpayer unless: (1) it has open enrollment to the employees of the taxpayer; (2) use of the facility (or eligibility to use such facility) does not discriminate in favor of highly compensated employees of the taxpayer (within the meaning of section 414(q) of the Code); and (3) at least 30 percent of the children enrolled in the center are dependents of the taxpayer's employees, if the facility is the principal trade or business of the taxpayer. Qualified child care resource and referral expenses are amounts paid or incurred under a contract to provide child care resource and referral services to the employees of the taxpayer. Qualified child care services and qualified child care resource and referral expenditures must be provided (or be eligible for use) in a way that does not discriminate in favor

---

[24] EGTRRA increased the maximum credit and exclusion to $10,000 (indexed for inflation after 2002) for both non-special needs and special needs adoptions, increased the phase-out starting point to $150,000 (indexed for inflation after 2002), and allowed the credit against the AMT. Section 10909 of the Patient Protection and Affordable Care Act (Pub. L. No. 111-148): (1) extended the EGTRRA expansion

of the adoption credit and exclusion from income for employer-provided adoption assistance for one year (for 2011); (2) increased by $1,000 (to $13,170, indexed for inflation) the maximum adoption credit and exclusion from income for employer-provided adoption assistance for two years (2010 and 2011); and (3) made the credit refundable for two years (2010 and 2011).

of highly compensated employees of the taxpayer (within the meaning of section 414(q) of the Code).

Any amounts for which the taxpayer may otherwise claim a tax deduction are reduced by the amount of these credits. Similarly, if the credits are taken for expenses of acquiring, constructing, rehabilitating, or expanding a facility, the taxpayer's basis in the facility is reduced by the amount of the credits.

Credits taken for the expenses of acquiring, constructing, rehabilitating, or expanding a qualified facility are subject to recapture for the first ten years after the qualified child care facility is placed in service. The amount of recapture is reduced as a percentage of the applicable credit over the 10-year recapture period. Recapture takes effect if the taxpayer either ceases operation of the qualified child care facility or transfers its interest in the qualified child care facility without securing an agreement to assume recapture liability for the transferee. The recapture tax is not treated as a tax for purposes of determining the amount of other credits or determining the amount of the alternative minimum tax. Other rules apply.

This tax credit expires for taxable years beginning after December 31, 2010.

Dependent care tax credit

The maximum dependent care tax credit is $1,050 (35 percent of up to $3,000 of eligible expenses) if there is one qualifying individual, and $2,100 (35 percent of up to $6,000 of eligible expenses) if there are two or more qualifying individuals. The 35-percent credit rate is reduced, but not below 20 percent, by one percent-

age point for each $2,000 (or fraction thereof) of adjusted gross income ("AGI") above $15,000. Therefore, the credit percentage is reduced to 20 percent for taxpayers with AGI over $43,000.

The level of this credit is reduced for taxable years beginning after December 31, 2010, under the EGTRRA sunset.

Explanation of Provision

Adoption credit and exclusion from income for employer-provided adoption assistance

The provision extends the EGTRRA expansion of these two benefits for one year (2012). Therefore, for 2012, the maximum benefit is $12,170 (indexed for inflation after 2010). The adoption credit and exclusion are phased out ratably for taxpayers with modified adjusted gross income between $182,520 and $222,520 (indexed for inflation after 2010).[25]

Employer-provided child care tax credit

The provision extends this tax benefit for two years (through 2012).

Expansion of dependent care tax credit

The provision extends the dependent care tax credit EGTRRA expansion for two years (through 2012).

Effective Date

The provisions apply to taxable years beginning after December 31, 2010.

[Law at ¶5015, ¶5083, ¶5125 and ¶7010. CCH Explanation at ¶365, ¶370 and ¶522.]

[¶10,070] Act Sec. 101. Alaska native settlement trusts

Joint Committee on Taxation (J.C.T. REP. No. JCX-55-10)

[Code Sec. 646]

Present Law

The Alaska Native Claims Settlement Act ("ANCSA")[26] established Alaska Native Corporations to hold property for Alaska Natives. Alaska Natives are generally the only permitted common shareholders of those corporations under section 7(h) of ANCSA, unless an Alaska

Native Corporation specifically allows other shareholders under specified procedures.

ANCSA permits an Alaska Native Corporation to transfer money or other property to an Alaska Native Settlement Trust ("Settlement Trust") for the benefit of beneficiaries who constitute all or a class of the shareholders of the Alaska Native Corporation, to promote the

---

[25] The changes to the adoption credit and exclusion from employer-provided adoption assistance for 2010 and 2011 (relating to the $1,000 increase in the maximum credit and exclusion and the refundability of the credit) enacted as part

of the Patient Protection and Affordable Care Act (Pub. L. No. 111-148) are not extended by the provision.

[26] 43 U.S.C. 1601 *et. seq.*

health, education and welfare of beneficiaries and to preserve the heritage and culture of Alaska Natives.[27]

Alaska Native Corporations and Settlement Trusts, as well as their shareholders and beneficiaries, are generally subject to tax under the same rules and in the same manner as other taxpayers that are corporations, trusts, shareholders, or beneficiaries.

Special tax rules enacted in 2001 allow an election to use a more favorable tax regime for transfers of property by an Alaska Native Corporation to a Settlement Trust and for income taxation of the Settlement Trust. There is also simplified reporting to beneficiaries.

Under the special tax rules, a Settlement Trust may make an irrevocable election to pay tax on taxable income at the lowest rate specified for individuals, (rather than the highest rate that is generally applicable to trusts) and to pay tax on capital gains at a rate consistent with being subject to such lowest rate of tax. As described further below, beneficiaries may generally thereafter exclude from gross income distributions from a trust that has made this election. Also, contributions from an Alaska Native Corporation to an electing Settlement Trust generally will not result in the recognition of gross income by beneficiaries on account of the contribution. An electing Settlement Trust remains subject to generally applicable requirements for classification and taxation as a trust.

A Settlement Trust distribution is excludable from the gross income of beneficiaries to the extent of the taxable income of the Settlement Trust for the taxable year and all prior taxable years for which an election was in effect, decreased by income tax paid by the Trust, plus tax-exempt interest from State and local bonds for the same period. Amounts distributed in excess of the amount excludable is taxed to the beneficiaries as if distributed by the sponsoring Alaska Native Corporation in the year of distribution by the Trust, which means that the beneficiaries must include in gross income as dividends the amount of the distribution, up to the current and accumulated earnings and profits of the Alaska Native Corporation. Amounts distributed in excess of the current and accumulated earnings and profits are not included in gross income by the beneficiaries.

A special loss disallowance rule reduces (but not below zero) any loss that would otherwise be recognized upon disposition of stock of a sponsoring Alaska Native Corporation by a proportion, determined on a per share basis, of all contributions to all electing Settlement Trusts by the sponsoring Alaska Native Corporation. This rule prevents a stockholder from being able to take advantage of a decrease in value of an Alaska Native Corporation that is caused by a transfer of assets from the Alaska Native Corporation to a Settlement Trust.

The fiduciary of an electing Settlement Trust is obligated to provide certain information relating to distributions from the trust in lieu of reporting requirements under Section 6034A.

The earnings and profits of an Alaska Native Corporation are not reduced by the amount of its contributions to an electing Trust at the time of the contributions. However, the Alaska Native Corporation earnings and profits are reduced as and when distributions are thereafter made by the electing Trust that are taxed to the beneficiaries as dividends from the Alaska Native Corporation to the beneficiaries.

The election to pay tax at the lowest rate is not available in certain disqualifying cases: (a) where transfer restrictions have been modified either to allow a transfer of a beneficial interest that would not be permitted by section 7(h) of the Alaska Native Claims Settlement Act if the interest were Settlement Common stock, or (b) where transfer restrictions have been modified to allow a transfer of any Stock in an Alaska Native Corporation that would not be permitted by section 7(h) if it were Settlement Common Stock and the Alaska Native Corporation thereafter makes a transfer to the Trust. Where an election is already in effect at the time of such disqualifying situations, the special rules applicable to an electing trust cease to apply and rules generally applicable to trusts apply. In addition, the distributable net income of the trust is increased by undistributed current and accumulated earnings and profits of the trust, limited by the fair market value of trust assets at the date the trust becomes so disposable. The effect is to cause the trust to be taxed at regular trust rates on the amount of recomputed distributable net income not distributed to beneficiaries, and to cause the beneficiaries to be taxed on the amount of any

---

[27] With certain exceptions, once an Alaska Native Corporation has made a conveyance to a Settlement Trust, the assets conveyed shall not be subject to attachment, distraint, or sale or execution of judgment, except with respect to the lawful debts and obligations of the Settlement Trust.

distributions received consistent with the applicable tax rate bracket.[28]

Explanation of Provision

The provision delays for two years the EGTRRA sunset as it applies to electing Settlement Trusts.

Effective Date

The provision is effective for taxable years of electing Settlement Trusts, their beneficiaries, and sponsoring Alaska Native Corporations beginning after December 31, 2010.

[Law at ¶5410 and ¶7010. CCH Explanation at ¶612.]

[¶10,080] Act Sec. 102. Reduced rate on dividends and capital gains

Joint Committee on Taxation (J.C.T. REP. NO. JCX-55-10)

[Code Sec. 1(h)]

Present Law

Dividends

In general

A dividend is the distribution of property made by a corporation to its shareholders out of its after-tax earnings and profits.

Tax rates before 2011

An individual's qualified dividend income is taxed at the same rates that apply to net capital gain. This treatment applies for purposes of both the regular tax and the alternative minimum tax. Thus, for taxable years beginning before 2011, an individual's qualified dividend income is taxed at rates of zero and 15 percent. The zero-percent rate applies to qualified dividend income which otherwise would be taxed at a 10- or 15-percent rate if the special rates did not apply.

Qualified dividend income generally includes dividends received from domestic corporations and qualified foreign corporations. The term "qualified foreign corporation" includes a foreign corporation that is eligible for the benefits of a comprehensive income tax treaty with the United States which the Treasury Department determines to be satisfactory and which includes an exchange of information program. In addition, a foreign corporation is treated as a qualified foreign corporation for any dividend paid by the corporation with respect to stock that is readily tradable on an established securities market in the United States.

If a shareholder does not hold a share of stock for more than 60 days during the 121-day period beginning 60 days before the ex-dividend date (as measured under section 246(c)), dividends received on the stock are not eligible for the reduced rates. Also, the reduced rates are not available for dividends to the extent that the taxpayer is obligated to make related payments with respect to positions in substantially similar or related property.

Dividends received from a corporation that is a passive foreign investment company (as defined in section 1297) in either the taxable year of the distribution, or the preceding taxable year, are not qualified dividends.

Special rules apply in determining a taxpayer's foreign tax credit limitation under section 904 in the case of qualified dividend income. For these purposes, rules similar to the rules of section 904(b)(2)(B) concerning adjustments to the foreign tax credit limitation to reflect any capital gain rate differential will apply to any qualified dividend income.

If a taxpayer receives an extraordinary dividend (within the meaning of section 1059(c)) eligible for the reduced rates with respect to any share of stock, any loss on the sale of the stock is treated as a long-term capital loss to the extent of the dividend.

A dividend is treated as investment income for purposes of determining the amount of deductible investment interest only if the taxpayer elects to treat the dividend as not eligible for the reduced rates.

---

[28] These provisions were enacted by the Economic Growth and Tax Relief Reconciliation Act of 2001, Pub. L. No. 107-16, sec. 671 (June 7, 2001), scheduled to sunset in taxable years beginning after December 31, 2010. See H.R. Rep. No. 107-84 (2001).

The amount of dividends qualifying for reduced rates that may be paid by a regulated investment company ("RIC") for any taxable year in which the qualified dividend income received by the RIC is less than 95 percent of its gross income (as specially computed) may not exceed the sum of (1) the qualified dividend income of the RIC for the taxable year and (2) the amount of earnings and profits accumulated in a non-RIC taxable year that were distributed by the RIC during the taxable year.

The amount of dividends qualifying for reduced rates that may be paid by a real estate investment trust ("REIT") for any taxable year may not exceed the sum of (1) the qualified dividend income of the REIT for the taxable year, (2) an amount equal to the excess of the income subject to the taxes imposed by section 857(b)(1) and the regulations prescribed under section 337(d) for the preceding taxable year over the amount of these taxes for the preceding taxable year, and (3) the amount of earnings and profits accumulated in a non-REIT taxable year that were distributed by the REIT during the taxable year.

The reduced rates do not apply to dividends received from an organization that was exempt from tax under section 501 or was a tax-exempt farmers' cooperative in either the taxable year of the distribution or the preceding taxable year; dividends received from a mutual savings bank that received a deduction under section 591; or deductible dividends paid on employer securities.[29]

Tax rates after 2010

For taxable years beginning after 2010, dividends received by an individual are taxed at ordinary income tax rates.

Capital gains

In general

In general, gain or loss reflected in the value of an asset is not recognized for income tax purposes until a taxpayer disposes of the asset. On the sale or exchange of a capital asset, any gain generally is included in income. Any net capital gain of an individual generally is taxed at rates lower than rates applicable to ordinary income. Net capital gain is the excess of the net long-term capital gain for the taxable year over the net short-term capital loss for the year. Gain or loss is treated as long-term if the asset is held for more than one year.

Capital losses generally are deductible in full against capital gains. In addition, individual taxpayers may deduct capital losses against up to $3,000 of ordinary income in each year. Any remaining unused capital losses may be carried forward indefinitely to another taxable year.

A capital asset generally means any property except (1) inventory, stock in trade, or property held primarily for sale to customers in the ordinary course of the taxpayer's trade or business, (2) depreciable or real property used in the taxpayer's trade or business, (3) specified literary or artistic property, (4) business accounts or notes receivable, (5) certain U.S. publications, (6) certain commodity derivative financial instruments, (7) hedging transactions, and (8) business supplies. In addition, the net gain from the disposition of certain property used in the taxpayer's trade or business is treated as long-term capital gain. Gain from the disposition of depreciable personal property is not treated as capital gain to the extent of all previous depreciation allowances. Gain from the disposition of depreciable real property is generally not treated as capital gain to the extent of the depreciation allowances in excess of the allowances available under the straight-line method of depreciation.

Tax rates before 2011

Under present law, for taxable years beginning before January 1, 2011, the maximum rate of tax on the adjusted net capital gain of an individual is 15 percent. Any adjusted net capital gain which otherwise would be taxed at a 10- or 15-percent rate is taxed at a zero rate. These rates apply for purposes of both the regular tax and the AMT.

Under present law, the "adjusted net capital gain" of an individual is the net capital gain reduced (but not below zero) by the sum of the 28-percent rate gain and the unrecaptured section 1250 gain. The net capital gain is reduced by the amount of gain that the individual treats as investment income for purposes of determining the investment interest limitation under section 163(d).

The term "28-percent rate gain" means the excess of the sum of the amount of net gain attributable to long-term capital gains and losses

---

[29] In addition, for taxable years beginning before 2011, amounts treated as ordinary income on the disposition of certain preferred stock (sec. 306) are treated as dividends for purposes of applying the reduced rates; the tax rate for the accumulated earnings tax (sec. 531) and the personal holding company tax (sec. 541) is reduced to 15 percent; and the collapsible corporation rules (sec. 341) are repealed.

from the sale or exchange of collectibles (as defined in section 408(m) without regard to paragraph (3) thereof) and the amount of gain equal to the additional amount of gain that would be excluded from gross income under section 1202 (relating to certain small business stock) if the percentage limitations of section 1202(a) did not apply, over the sum of the net short-term capital loss for the taxable year and any long-term capital loss carryover to the taxable year.

"Unrecaptured section 1250 gain" means any long-term capital gain from the sale or exchange of section 1250 property (i.e., depreciable real estate) held more than one year to the extent of the gain that would have been treated as ordinary income if section 1250 applied to all depreciation, reduced by the net loss (if any) attributable to the items taken into account in computing 28-percent rate gain. The amount of unrecaptured section 1250 gain (before the reduction for the net loss) attributable to the disposition of property to which section 1231 (relating to certain property used in a trade or business) applies may not exceed the net section 1231 gain for the year.

An individual's unrecaptured section 1250 gain is taxed at a maximum rate of 25 percent, and the 28-percent rate gain is taxed at a maximum rate of 28 percent. Any amount of unrecaptured section 1250 gain or 28-percent rate gain otherwise taxed at a 10- or 15-percent rate is taxed at the otherwise applicable rate.

Tax rates after 2010

For taxable years beginning after December 31, 2010, the maximum rate of tax on the adjusted net capital gain of an individual is 20 percent. Any adjusted net capital gain which otherwise would be taxed at the 15-percent rate is taxed at a 10-percent rate.

In addition, any gain from the sale or exchange of property held more than five years that would otherwise have been taxed at the 10-percent capital gain rate is taxed at an 8-percent rate. Any gain from the sale or exchange of property held more than five years and the holding period for which began after December 31, 2000, that would otherwise have been taxed at a 20-percent rate is taxed at an 18-percent rate.

The tax rates on 28-percent gain and unrecaptured section 1250 gain are the same as for taxable years beginning before 2011.

Explanation of Provision

Under the provision, the regular and minimum tax rates for qualified dividend income and capital gain in effect before 2011 are extended for two additional years (through 2012).

Effective Date

The provision applies to taxable years beginning after December 31, 2010.

[Law at ¶5005 and ¶7015. CCH Explanation at ¶405, ¶410, ¶420 and ¶425.]

[¶10,090] Act Sec. 103. Extend American Opportunity Tax Credit

Joint Committee on Taxation (J.C.T. Rep. No. JCX-55-10)

[Code Sec. 25A]

Present Law

Hope credit

For taxable years beginning before 2009 and after 2010, individual taxpayers are allowed to claim a nonrefundable credit, the Hope credit, against Federal income taxes of up to $1,800 (for 2008) per eligible student per year for qualified tuition and related expenses paid for the first two years of the student's post-secondary education in a degree or certificate program. The Hope credit rate is 100 percent on the first $1,200 of qualified tuition and related expenses, and 50 percent on the next $1,200 of qualified tuition and related expenses; these dollar amounts are indexed for inflation, with the amount rounded down to the next lowest multiple of $100. Thus,

for example, a taxpayer who incurs $1,200 of qualified tuition and related expenses for an eligible student is eligible (subject to the adjusted gross income phaseout described below) for a $1,200 Hope credit. If a taxpayer incurs $2,400 of qualified tuition and related expenses for an eligible student, then he or she is eligible for a $1,800 Hope credit.

The Hope credit that a taxpayer may otherwise claim is phased out ratably for taxpayers with modified AGI between $48,000 and $58,000 ($96,000 and $116,000 for married taxpayers filing a joint return) for 2008. The beginning points of the AGI phaseout ranges are indexed for inflation, with the amount rounded down to the next lowest multiple of $1,000. The size of the phaseout ranges are always $10,000 and $20,000 respectively.

The qualified tuition and related expenses must be incurred on behalf of the taxpayer, the taxpayer's spouse, or a dependent of the taxpayer. The Hope credit is available with respect to an individual student for two taxable years, provided that the student has not completed the first two years of post-secondary education before the beginning of the second taxable year.

The Hope credit is available in the taxable year the expenses are paid, subject to the requirement that the education is furnished to the student during that year or during an academic period beginning during the first three months of the next taxable year. Qualified tuition and related expenses paid with the proceeds of a loan generally are eligible for the Hope credit. The repayment of a loan itself is not a qualified tuition or related expense.

A taxpayer may claim the Hope credit with respect to an eligible student who is not the taxpayer or the taxpayer's spouse (e.g., in cases in which the student is the taxpayer's child) only if the taxpayer claims the student as a dependent for the taxable year for which the credit is claimed. If a student is claimed as a dependent, the student is not entitled to claim a Hope credit for that taxable year on the student's own tax return. If a parent (or other taxpayer) claims a student as a dependent, any qualified tuition and related expenses paid by the student are treated as paid by the parent (or other taxpayer) for purposes of determining the amount of qualified tuition and related expenses paid by such parent (or other taxpayer) under the provision. In addition, for each taxable year, a taxpayer may elect either the Hope credit, the Lifetime Learning credit, or an above-the-line deduction for qualified tuition and related expenses with respect to an eligible student.

The Hope credit is available for "qualified tuition and related expenses," which include tuition and fees (excluding nonacademic fees) required to be paid to an eligible educational institution as a condition of enrollment or attendance of an eligible student at the institution. Charges and fees associated with meals, lodging, insurance, transportation, and similar personal, living, or family expenses are not eligible for the credit. The expenses of education involving sports, games, or hobbies are not qualified tuition and related expenses unless this education is part of the student's degree program.

Qualified tuition and related expenses generally include only out-of-pocket expenses. Qualified tuition and related expenses do not include expenses covered by employer-provided educational assistance and scholarships that are not required to be included in the gross income of either the student or the taxpayer claiming the credit. Thus, total qualified tuition and related expenses are reduced by any scholarship or fellowship grants excludable from gross income under section 117 and any other tax-free educational benefits received by the student (or the taxpayer claiming the credit) during the taxable year. The Hope credit is not allowed with respect to any education expense for which a deduction is claimed under section 162 or any other section of the Code.

An eligible student for purposes of the Hope credit is an individual who is enrolled in a degree, certificate, or other program (including a program of study abroad approved for credit by the institution at which such student is enrolled) leading to a recognized educational credential at an eligible educational institution. The student must pursue a course of study on at least a halftime basis. A student is considered to pursue a course of study on at least a half-time basis if the student carries at least one half the normal full-time work load for the course of study the student is pursuing for at least one academic period that begins during the taxable year. To be eligible for the Hope credit, a student must not have been convicted of a Federal or State felony consisting of the possession or distribution of a controlled substance.

Eligible educational institutions generally are accredited post-secondary educational institutions offering credit toward a bachelor's degree, an associate's degree, or another recognized post-secondary credential. Certain proprietary institutions and post-secondary vocational institutions also are eligible educational institutions. To qualify as an eligible educational institution, an institution must be eligible to participate in Department of Education student aid programs.

Effective for taxable years beginning after December 31, 2010, the changes to the Hope credit made by EGTRRA no longer apply. The principal EGTRRA change scheduled to expire is the change that permits a taxpayer to claim a Hope credit in the same year that he or she claims an exclusion from a Coverdell education savings account. Thus, after 2010, a taxpayer cannot claim a Hope credit in the same year he or she claims an exclusion from a Coverdell education savings account.

American opportunity tax credit

The American Opportunity Tax Credit refers to modifications to the Hope credit that apply for taxable years beginning in 2009 or 2010. The maximum allowable modified credit is $2,500 per eligible student per year for qualified tuition and related expenses paid for each of the first four years of the student's post-secondary education in a degree or certificate program. The modified credit rate is 100 percent on the first $2,000 of qualified tuition and related expenses, and 25 percent on the next $2,000 of qualified tuition and related expenses. For purposes of the modified credit, the definition of qualified tuition and related expenses is expanded to include course materials.

Under the provision, the modified credit is available with respect to an individual student for four years, provided that the student has not completed the first four years of post-secondary education before the beginning of the fourth taxable year. Thus, the modified credit, in addition to other modifications, extends the application of the Hope credit to two more years of post-secondary education.

The modified credit that a taxpayer may otherwise claim is phased out ratably for taxpayers with modified AGI between $80,000 and $90,000 ($160,000 and $180,000 for married taxpayers filing a joint return). The modified credit may be claimed against a taxpayer's AMT liability.

Forty percent of a taxpayer's otherwise allowable modified credit is refundable. However, no portion of the modified credit is refundable if the taxpayer claiming the credit is a child to whom section 1(g) applies for such taxable year (generally, any child who has at least one living parent, does not file a joint return, and is either under age 18 or under age 24 and a student providing less than one-half of his or her own support).

Bona fide residents of the U.S. possessions are not permitted to claim the refundable portion of the modified credit in the United States. Rather, a bona fide resident of a mirror code possession (Commonwealth of the Northern Mariana Islands, Guam, and the Virgin Islands) may claim the refundable portion of the credit in the possession in which the individual is a resident. Similarly, a bona fide resident of a non-mirror code possession (Commonwealth of Puerto Rico and American Samoa) may claim the refundable portion of the credit in the possession in which the individual is resident, but only if the possession establishes a plan for permitting the claim under its internal law. The U.S. Treasury will make payments to the possession in respect of credits allowable to their residents under their internal laws.

Explanation of Provision

The provision extends for two years (through 2012) the temporary modifications to the Hope credit for taxable years beginning in 2009 and 2010 that are known as the American Opportunity Tax Credit, including the rules governing the treatment of the U.S. possessions.

Effective Date

The provision is effective for taxable years beginning after December 31, 2010.

[Law at ¶5035 and ¶7017. CCH Explanation at ¶371.]

[¶10,100] Act Sec. 103. Child tax credit

Joint Committee on Taxation (J.C.T. REP. NO. JCX-55-10)

[Code Sec. 24]

Present Law

An individual may claim a tax credit for each qualifying child under the age of 17. The maximum amount of the credit per child is $1,000 through 2010 and $500 thereafter. A child who is not a citizen, national, or resident of the United States cannot be a qualifying child.

The aggregate amount of child credits that may be claimed is phased out for individuals with income over certain threshold amounts. Specifically, the otherwise allowable aggregate child tax credit amount is reduced by $50 for each $1,000 (or fraction thereof) of modified adjusted gross income ("modified AGI") over $75,000 for single individuals or heads of households, $110,000 for married individuals filing joint returns, and $55,000 for married individuals filing separate returns. For purposes of this limitation, modified AGI includes certain otherwise excludable income earned by U.S. citizens or residents living abroad or in certain U.S. territories.

The credit is allowable against the regular tax and, for taxable years beginning before January 1, 2011, is allowed against the alternative minimum tax ("AMT"). To the extent the child tax credit exceeds the taxpayer's tax liability, the taxpayer is eligible for a refundable credit (the additional child tax credit) equal to 15 percent of earned income in excess of a threshold dollar amount (the "earned income" formula). EGTRRA provided, in general, that this threshold dollar amount is $10,000 indexed for inflation from 2001. The American Recovery and Reinvestment Act of 2009 set the threshold at $3,000 for both 2009 and 2010. After 2010, the ability to determine the refundable child credit based on earned income in excess of the threshold dollar amount expires.

Families with three or more qualifying children may determine the additional child tax credit using the "alternative formula" if this results in a larger credit than determined under the earned income formula. Under the alternative formula, the additional child tax credit equals the amount by which the taxpayer's social security taxes exceed the taxpayer's earned income tax credit ("EITC"). After 2010, due to the expiration of the earned income formula, this is the only manner of obtaining a refundable child credit.

Earned income is defined as the sum of wages, salaries, tips, and other taxable employee compensation plus net self-employment earnings. Unlike the EITC, which also includes the preceding items in its definition of earned income, the additional child tax credit is based only on earned income to the extent it is included in computing taxable income. For example, some ministers' parsonage allowances are considered self-employment income, and thus are considered earned income for purposes of computing the EITC, but the allowances are excluded from gross income for individual income tax purposes, and thus are not considered earned income for purposes of the additional child tax credit since the income is not included in taxable income.

Explanation of Provision

The provision extends for two years the earned income threshold of $3,000. Also, the provision stops indexation for inflation of the $3,000 earnings threshold for that period.

Effective Date

The provision applies to taxable years beginning after December 31, 2010.

[Law at ¶5025. CCH Explanation at ¶360.]

[¶10,110] Act Sec. 103. Increase in the earned income tax credit

Joint Committee on Taxation (J.C.T. Rep. No. JCX-55-10)

[Code Sec. 32]

Present Law

Overview

Low-and moderate-income workers may be eligible for the refundable earned income tax credit ("EITC"). Eligibility for the EITC is based on earned income, adjusted gross income, investment income, filing status, number of children, and immigration and work status in the United States. The amount of the EITC is based on the presence and number of qualifying children in the worker's family, as well as on adjusted gross income and earned income.

The EITC generally equals a specified percentage of earned income up to a maximum dollar amount. The maximum amount applies over a certain income range and then diminishes to zero over a specified phaseout range. For taxpayers with earned income (or adjusted gross income ("AGI"), if greater) in excess of the beginning of the phaseout range, the maximum EITC amount is reduced by the phaseout rate multiplied by the amount of earned income (or AGI, if greater) in excess of the beginning of the phaseout range. For taxpayers with earned income (or AGI, if greater) in excess of the end of the phaseout range, no credit is allowed.

An individual is not eligible for the EITC if the aggregate amount of disqualified income of the taxpayer for the taxable year exceeds $3,100 (for 2010). This threshold is indexed for inflation. Disqualified income is the sum of: (1) interest (both taxable and tax exempt); (2) dividends; (3) net rent and royalty income (if greater than zero); (4) capital gains net income; and (5) net passive income that is not self-employment income (if greater than zero).

The EITC is a refundable credit, meaning that if the amount of the credit exceeds the taxpayer's Federal income tax liability, the excess is payable to the taxpayer as a direct transfer payment.

Filing status

An unmarried individual may claim the EITC if he or she files as a single filer or as a head of household. Married individuals generally may not claim the EITC unless they file jointly. An exception to the joint return filing requirement applies to certain spouses who are separated. Under this exception, a married taxpayer who is separated from his or her spouse for the last six months of the taxable year is not considered to be married (and, accordingly, may file a return as head of household and claim the EITC), provided that the taxpayer maintains a household that constitutes the principal place of abode for a dependent child (including a son, stepson, daughter, stepdaughter, adopted child, or a foster child) for over half the taxable year, and pays over half the cost of maintaining the household in which he or she resides with the child during the year.

Presence of qualifying children and amount of the earned income credit

Four separate credit schedules apply: one schedule for taxpayers with no qualifying children, one schedule for taxpayers with one qualifying child, one schedule for taxpayers with two qualifying children, and one schedule for taxpayers with three or more qualifying children.

Taxpayers with no qualifying children may claim a credit if they are over age 24 and below age 65. The credit is 7.65 percent of earnings up to $5,980, resulting in a maximum credit of $457 for 2010. The maximum is available for those with incomes between $5,980 and $7,480 ($12,490 if married filing jointly). The credit begins to phase out at a rate of 7.65 percent of earnings above $7,480 ($12,480 if married filing jointly) resulting in a $0 credit at $13,460 of earnings ($18,470 if married filing jointly).

Taxpayers with one qualifying child may claim a credit in 2010 of 34 percent of their earnings up to $8,970, resulting in a maximum credit of $3,050. The maximum credit is available for those with earnings between $8,970 and $16,450 ($21,460 if married filing jointly). The credit begins to phase out at a rate of 15.98 percent of earnings above $16,450 ($21,460 if married filing jointly). The credit is completely phased out at $35,535 of earnings ($40,545 if married filing jointly).

Taxpayers with two qualifying children may claim a credit in 2010 of 40 percent of earnings up to $12,590, resulting in a maximum credit of $5,036. The maximum credit is available for those with earnings between $12,590 and $16,450 ($21,460 if married filing jointly). The credit begins to phase out at a rate of 21.06 percent of earnings above $16,450 ($21,460 if married filing jointly). The credit is completely phased out at $40,363 of earnings ($45,373 if married filing jointly).

A temporary provision enacted by ARRA allows taxpayers with three or more qualifying children to claim a credit of 45 percent for 2009 and 2010. For example, in 2010 taxpayers with three or more qualifying children may claim a credit of 45 percent of earnings up to $12,590, resulting in a maximum credit of $5,666. The maximum credit is available for those with earnings between $12,590 and $16,450 ($21,460 if married filing jointly). The credit begins to phase out at a rate of 21.06 percent of earnings above $16,450 ($21,460 if married filing jointly). The credit is completely phased out at $43,352 of earnings ($48,362 if married filing jointly).

Under another provision of ARRA, the phase-out thresholds for married couples were raised to an amount $5,000 above that for other filers for 2009 (and indexed for inflation). The increase is $5,010 for 2010. Formerly, the phase-out thresholds for married couples were $3,000 (indexed for inflation from 2008) greater than those for other filers as provided for in EGTRRA.

If more than one taxpayer lives with a qualifying child, only one of these taxpayers may claim the child for purposes of the EITC. If multiple eligible taxpayers actually claim the same qualifying child, then a tiebreaker rule determines which taxpayer is entitled to the EITC with respect to the qualifying child. Any eligible taxpayer with at least one qualifying child who does not claim the EITC with respect to qualifying children due to failure to meet certain identification requirements with respect to such children (i.e., providing the name, age and taxpayer identification number of each of such children) may not claim the EITC for taxpayers without qualifying children.

Explanation of Provision

The provision extends the EITC at a rate of 45 percent for three or more qualifying children for two years (through 2012).

The provision extends the higher phase-out thresholds for married couples filing joint returns enacted as part of ARRA for two years (through 2012).

Effective Date

The provision applies to taxable years beginning after December 31, 2010.

[Law at ¶ 5075. CCH Explanation at ¶ 356.]

[¶10,120] Act Secs. 201 and 202. Extension of alternative minimum tax relief for nonrefundable personal credits and increased alternative minimum tax exemption amount

Joint Committee on Taxation (J.C.T. Rep. No. JCX-55-10)

[Code Secs. 26 and 55]

Present Law

Present law imposes an alternative minimum tax ("AMT") on individuals. The AMT is the amount by which the tentative minimum tax exceeds the regular income tax. An individual's tentative minimum tax is the sum of (1) 26 percent of so much of the taxable excess as does not exceed $175,000 ($87,500 in the case of a married individual filing a separate return) and (2) 28 percent of the remaining taxable excess. The taxable excess is so much of the alternative minimum taxable income ("AMTI") as exceeds the exemption amount. The maximum tax rates on net capital gain and dividends used in computing the regular tax are used in computing the tentative minimum tax. AMTI is the individual's taxable income adjusted to take account of specified preferences and adjustments.

The exemption amounts are: (1) $70,950 for taxable years beginning in 2009 and $45,000 in taxable years beginning after 2009 in the case of married individuals filing a joint return and surviving spouses; (2) $46,700 for taxable years beginning in 2009 and $33,750 in taxable years beginning after 2009 in the case of other unmarried individuals; (3) $35,475 for taxable years beginning in 2009 and $22,500 in taxable years beginning after 2009 in the case of married individuals filing separate returns; and (4) $22,500 in the case of an estate or trust. The exemption amount is phased out by an amount equal to 25 percent of the amount by which the individual's AMTI exceeds (1) $150,000 in the case of married individuals filing a joint return and surviving spouses, (2) $112,500 in the case of other unmarried individuals, and (3) $75,000 in the case of married individuals filing separate returns or an estate or a trust. These amounts are not indexed for inflation.

Present law provides for certain nonrefundable personal tax credits (i.e., the dependent care credit, the credit for the elderly and disabled, the child credit, the credit for interest on certain home mortgages, the Hope Scholarship and Life-time Learning credits, the credit for savers, the credit for certain nonbusiness energy property, the credit for residential energy efficient property, the credit for certain plug-in electric vehicles, the credit for alternative motor vehicles, the credit for new qualified plug-in electric drive motor vehicles, and the D.C. first-time homebuyer credit).

For taxable years beginning before 2010, the nonrefundable personal credits are allowed to the extent of the full amount of the individual's regular tax and alternative minimum tax.

For taxable years beginning after 2009, the nonrefundable personal credits (other than the child credit, the credit for savers, the credit for residential energy efficient property, the credit for certain plug-in electric drive motor vehicles, the credit for alternative motor vehicles, and credit for new qualified plug-in electric drive motor vehicles) are allowed only to the extent that the individual's regular income tax liability exceeds the individual's tentative minimum tax, determined without regard to the minimum tax foreign tax credit. The remaining nonrefundable personal credits are allowed to the full extent of the individual's regular tax and alternative minimum tax.[30]

Explanation of Provisions

The provision allows an individual to offset the entire regular tax liability and alternative minimum tax liability by the nonrefundable personal credits for 2010 and 2011.

The provision provides that the individual AMT exemption amount for taxable years beginning in 2010 is (1) $72,450, in the case of married individuals filing a joint return and surviving spouses; (2) $47,450 in the case of other unmarried individuals; and (3) $36,225 in the case of married individuals filing separate returns.

The provision provides that the individual AMT exemption amount for taxable years beginning in 2011 is (1) $74,450, in the case of married individuals filing a joint return and surviving spouses; (2) $48,450 in the case of other unmar-

---

[30] The rule applicable to the child credit after 2010 is subject to the EGTRRA sunset. The adoption credit is refundable in 2010 and 2011 and beginning in 2012 is nonrefundable and treated for purposes of the AMT in the same manner as the child credit.

ried individuals; and (3) $37,225 in the case of married individuals filing separate returns.

[Law at ¶5050, ¶5170 and ¶7020. CCH Explanation at ¶375 and ¶376.]

Effective Date

The provision is effective for taxable years beginning after 2009.

[¶10,130] Act Secs. 301-304. Modify and extend the estate, gift, and generation skipping transfer taxes after 2009

Joint Committee on Taxation (J.C.T. Rep. No. JCX-55-10)

[Code Secs. 2001, 2010, 2502, 2505, 2511, 2631 and 6018]

Present and Prior Law

In general

In general, a gift tax is imposed on certain lifetime transfers and an estate tax is imposed on certain transfers at death. A generation skipping transfer tax generally is imposed on certain transfers, either directly or in trust or similar arrangement, to a "skip person" (i.e., a beneficiary in a generation more than one generation younger than that of the transferor). Transfers subject to the generation skipping transfer tax include direct skips, taxable terminations, and taxable distributions.

The estate and generation skipping transfers taxes are repealed for decedents dying and gifts made during 2010, but are reinstated for decedents dying and gifts made after 2010.

Exemption equivalent amounts and applicable tax rates

In general

Under present law in effect through 2009 and after 2010, a unified credit is available with respect to taxable transfers by gift and at death.[31] The unified credit offsets tax computed at the lowest estate and gift tax rates.

Before 2004, the estate and gift taxes were fully unified, such that a single graduated rate schedule and a single effective exemption amount of the unified credit applied for purposes of determining the tax on cumulative taxable transfers made by a taxpayer during his or her lifetime and at death. For years 2004 through 2009, the gift tax and the estate tax continued to be determined using a single graduated rate schedule, but the effective exemption amount allowed for estate tax purposes was higher than the effective exemption amount allowed for gift

tax purposes. In 2009, the highest estate and gift tax rate was 45 percent. The unified credit effective exemption amount was $3.5 million for estate tax purposes and $1 million for gift tax purposes.

For 2009 and after 2010, the generation skipping transfer tax is imposed using a flat rate equal to the highest estate tax rate on cumulative generation skipping transfers in excess of the exemption amount in effect at the time of the transfer. The generation skipping transfer tax exemption for a given year (prior to and after repeal, discussed below) is equal to the unified credit effective exemption amount for estate tax purposes.

Repeal of estate and generation skipping transfer taxes in 2010; modifications to gift tax

Under EGTRRA, the estate and generation skipping transfer taxes are repealed for decedents dying and generation skipping transfers made during 2010. The gift tax remains in effect during 2010, with a $1 million exemption amount and a gift tax rate of 35 percent. Also in 2010, except as provided in regulations, certain transfers in trust are treated as transfers of property by gift, unless the trust is treated as wholly owned by the donor or the donor's spouse under the grantor trust provisions of the Code.

Reinstatement of the estate and generation skipping transfer taxes for decedents dying and generation skipping transfers made after December 31, 2010

The estate, gift, and generation skipping transfer tax provisions of EGTRRA sunset at the end of 2010, such that those provisions (including repeal of the estate and generation skipping transfer taxes) do not apply to estates of decedents dying, gifts made, or generation skipping transfers made after December 31, 2010. As a result, in general, the estate, gift, and generation

---

[31] Sec. 2010.

skipping transfer tax rates and exemption amounts that would have been in effect had EGTRRA not been enacted apply for estates of decedents dying, gifts made, or generation skipping transfers made in 2011 or later years. A single graduated rate schedule with a top rate of 55 percent and a single effective exemption amount of $1 million applies for purposes of determining the tax on cumulative taxable transfers by lifetime gift or bequest.

Basis in property received

In general

Gain or loss, if any, on the disposition of property is measured by the taxpayer's amount realized (i.e., gross proceeds received) on the disposition, less the taxpayer's basis in such property.[32] Basis generally represents a taxpayer's investment in property, with certain adjustments required after acquisition. For example, basis is increased by the cost of capital improvements made to the property and decreased by depreciation deductions taken with respect to the property.

Basis in property received by lifetime gift

Property received from a donor of a lifetime gift generally takes a carryover basis.[33] "Carryover basis" means that the basis in the hands of the donee is the same as it was in the hands of the donor. The basis of property transferred by lifetime gift also is increased, but not above fair market value, by any gift tax paid by the donor. The basis of a lifetime gift, however, generally cannot exceed the property's fair market value on the date of the gift. If the basis of property is greater than the fair market value of the property on the date of the gift, then, for purposes of determining loss, the basis is the property's fair market value on the date of the gift.

Basis in property received from a decedent who died in 2009

Property passing from a decedent who died during 2009 generally takes a "stepped-up" basis.[34] In other words, the basis of property passing from such a decedent's estate generally is the fair market value on the date of the decedent's death (or, if the alternate valuation date is elected, the earlier of six months after the decedent's death or the date the property is sold or distributed by the estate).[35] This step up in basis generally eliminates the recognition of income on any appreciation of the property that occurred prior to the decedent's death. If the value of property on the date of the decedent's death was less than its adjusted basis, the property takes a stepped-down basis when it passes from a decedent's estate. This stepped-down basis eliminates the tax benefit from any unrealized loss.

Basis in property received from a decedent who dies during 2010

The rules providing for stepped-up basis in property acquired from a decedent are repealed for assets acquired from decedents dying in 2010, and a modified carryover basis regime applies.[36] Under this regime, recipients of property acquired from a decedent at the decedent's death receive a basis equal to the lesser of the decedent's adjusted basis or the fair market value of the property on the date of the decedent's death. The modified carryover basis rules apply to property acquired by bequest, devise, or inheritance, or property acquired by the decedent's estate from the decedent, property passing from the decedent to the extent such property passed without consideration, and certain other property to which the prior law rules apply, other than property that is income in respect of a decedent. Property acquired from a decedent is treated as if the property had been acquired by gift. Thus, the character of gain on the sale of property received from a decedent's estate is carried over to the heir. For example, real estate that has been depreciated and would be subject to recapture if sold by the decedent will be subject to recapture if sold by the heir.

An executor generally may increase the basis in assets owned by the decedent and acquired by the beneficiaries at death, subject to certain

---

[32] Sec. 1001.

[33] Sec. 1015.

[34] Sec. 1014.

[35] There is an exception to the rule that assets subject to the Federal estate tax receive stepped-up basis in the case of "income in respect of a decedent." Sec. 1014(c). The basis of assets that are "income in respect of a decedent" is a carryover basis (i.e., the basis of such assets to the estate or heir is the same as it was in the hands of the decedent) increased by estate tax paid on that asset. Income in respect of a decedent includes rights to income that has been earned, but not recognized, by the date of death (e.g., wages that were

earned, but not paid, before death), individual retirement accounts (IRAs), and assets held in accounts governed by section 401(k).

In community property states, a surviving spouse's one-half share of community property held by the decedent and the surviving spouse generally is treated as having passed from the decedent and, thus, is eligible for stepped-up basis. Under 2009 law, this rule applies if at least one-half of the whole of the community interest is includible in the decedent's gross estate.

[36] Sec. 1022.

---

special rules and exceptions. Under these rules, each decedent's estate generally is permitted to increase the basis of assets transferred by up to a total of $1.3 million. The $1.3 million is increased by the amount of unused capital losses, net operating losses, and certain "built-in" losses of the decedent. Nonresidents who are not U.S. citizens may be allowed to increase the basis of property by up to $60,000. In addition, the basis of property transferred to a surviving spouse may be increased by an additional $3 million. Thus, the basis of property transferred to surviving spouses generally may be increased by up to $4.3 million.

Repeal of modified carryover basis regime for determining basis in property received from a decedent who dies after December 31, 2010

As a result of the EGTRRA sunset at the end of 2010, the modified carryover basis regime in effect for determining basis in property passing from a decedent who dies during 2010 does not apply for purposes of determining basis in property received from a decedent who dies after December 31, 2010. Instead, the law in effect prior to 2010, which generally provides for stepped-up basis in property passing from a decedent, applies.

State death tax credit; deduction for State death taxes paid

State death tax credit under prior law

Before 2005, a credit was allowed against the Federal estate tax for any estate, inheritance, legacy, or succession taxes ("death taxes") actually paid to any State or the District of Columbia with respect to any property included in the decedent's gross estate.[37] The maximum amount of credit allowable for State death taxes was determined under a graduated rate table, the top rate of which was 16 percent, based on the size of the decedent's adjusted taxable estate. Most States imposed a "pick-up" or "soak-up" estate tax, which served to impose a State tax equal to the maximum Federal credit allowed.

Phase-out of State death tax credit; deduction for State death taxes paid

Under EGTRRA, the amount of allowable State death tax credit was reduced from 2002 through 2004. For decedents dying after 2004, the State death tax credit was repealed and replaced with a deduction for death taxes actually paid to any State or the District of Columbia, in respect of property included in the gross estate of the decedent.[38] Such State taxes must have been paid and claimed before the later of: (1) four years after the filing of the estate tax return; or (2) (a) 60 days after a decision of the U.S. Tax Court determining the estate tax liability becomes final, (b) the expiration of the period of extension to pay estate taxes over time under section 6166, or (c) the expiration of the period of limitations in which to file a claim for refund or generally 60 days after a decision of a court in which such refund suit has become final.

Reinstatement of State death tax credit for decedents dying after December 31, 2010

As described above, the estate, gift, and generation skipping transfer tax provisions of EGTRRA sunset at the end of 2010, such that those provisions will not apply to estates of decedents dying, gifts made, or generation skipping transfers made after December 31, 2010. As a result, neither the EGTRRA modifications to the State death tax credit nor the replacement of the credit with a deduction applies for decedents dying after December 31, 2010. Instead, the State death tax credit as in effect for decedents who died prior to 2002 applies.

Exclusions and deductions

Gift tax annual exclusion

Donors of lifetime gifts are provided an annual exclusion of $13,000 (for 2010 and 2011) on transfers of present interests in property to each donee during the taxable year.[39] If the non-donor spouse consents to split the gift with the donor spouse, then the annual exclusion is $26,000 for 2010 and 2011. The dollar amounts are indexed for inflation.

Transfers to a surviving spouse

In general.–A 100-percent marital deduction generally is permitted for estate and gift tax purposes for the value of property transferred between spouses.[40] Transfers of "qualified terminable interest property" are eligible for the marital deduction. "Qualified terminable interest property" is property: (1) that passes from the decedent; (2) in which the surviving spouse has a "qualifying income interest for life"; and (3) to which an election applies. A "qualifying income interest for life" exists if: (1) the surviving spouse is entitled to all the income from the property (payable annually or at more frequent intervals) or has the right to use the property during the

---

[37] Sec. 2011.
[38] Sec. 2058.

[39] Sec. 2503(b).
[40] Secs. 2056 & 2523.

spouse's life; and (2) no person has the power to appoint any part of the property to any person other than the surviving spouse.

Transfers to surviving spouses who are not U.S. citizens.–A marital deduction generally is denied for property passing to a surviving spouse who is not a citizen of the United States.[41] A marital deduction is permitted, however, for property passing to a qualified domestic trust of which the noncitizen surviving spouse is a beneficiary. A qualified domestic trust is a trust that has as its trustee at least one U.S. citizen or U.S. corporation. No corpus may be distributed from a qualified domestic trust unless the U.S. trustee has the right to withhold any estate tax imposed on the distribution.

For years when the estate tax is in effect, the estate tax is imposed on (1) any distribution from a qualified domestic trust before the date of the death of the noncitizen surviving spouse and (2) the value of the property remaining in a qualified domestic trust on the date of death of the noncitizen surviving spouse. The tax is computed as an additional estate tax on the estate of the first spouse to die.

Conservation easements

For years when an estate tax is in effect, an executor generally may elect to exclude from the taxable estate 40 percent of the value of any land subject to a qualified conservation easement, up to a maximum exclusion of $500,000.[42] The exclusion percentage is reduced by two percentage points for each percentage point (or fraction thereof) by which the value of the qualified conservation easement is less than 30 percent of the value of the land (determined without regard to the value of such easement and reduced by the value of any retained development right).

Before 2001, a qualified conservation easement generally was one that met the following requirements: (1) the land was located within 25 miles of a metropolitan area (as defined by the Office of Management and Budget) or a national park or wilderness area, or within 10 miles of an Urban National Forest (as designated by the Forest Service of the U.S. Department of Agriculture); (2) the land had been owned by the decedent or a member of the decedent's family at all times during the three-year period ending on the date of the decedent's death; and (3) a qualified conservation contribution (within the meaning of sec. 170(h)) of a qualified real property interest (as generally defined in sec.

170(h)(2)(C)) was granted by the decedent or a member of his or her family. Preservation of a historically important land area or a certified historic structure does not qualify as a conservation purpose.

Effective for estates of decedents dying after December 31, 2000, EGTRRA expanded the availability of qualified conservation easements by eliminating the requirement that the land be located within a certain distance of a metropolitan area, national park, wilderness area, or Urban National Forest. A qualified conservation easement may be claimed with respect to any land that is located in the United States or its possessions. EGTRRA also clarifies that the date for determining easement compliance is the date on which the donation is made.

As a result of the EGTRRA sunset at the end of 2010, the EGTRRA modifications to expand the availability of qualified conservation contributions do not apply for decedents dying after December 31, 2010.

Provisions affecting small and family-owned businesses and farms

Special-use valuation

For years when an estate tax is in effect, an executor may elect to value for estate tax purposes certain "qualified real property" used in farming or another qualifying closely-held trade or business at its current-use value, rather than its fair market value.[43] The maximum reduction in value for such real property was $1 million for 2009. Real property generally can qualify for special-use valuation if at least 50 percent of the adjusted value of the decedent's gross estate consists of a farm or closely-held business assets in the decedent's estate (including both real and personal property) and at least 25 percent of the adjusted value of the gross estate consists of farm or closely-held business real property. In addition, the property must be used in a qualified use (e.g., farming) by the decedent or a member of the decedent's family for five of the eight years immediately preceding the decedent's death.

If, after a special-use valuation election is made, the heir who acquired the real property ceases to use it in its qualified use within 10 years of the decedent's death, an additional estate tax is imposed in order to recapture the entire estate-tax benefit of the special-use valuation.

---

[41] Secs. 2056(d)(1) & 2523(i)(1).

[42] Sec. 2031(c).

[43] Sec. 2032A.

Family-owned business deduction

Prior to 2004, an estate was permitted to deduct the adjusted value of a qualified family-owned business interest of the decedent, up to $675,000.[44] A qualified family-owned business interest generally is defined as any interest in a trade or business (regardless of the form in which it is held) with a principal place of business in the United States if the decedent's family owns at least 50 percent of the trade or business, two families own 70 percent, or three families own 90 percent, as long as the decedent's family owns, in the case of the 70-percent and 90-percent rules, at least 30 percent of the trade or business.

To qualify for the deduction, the decedent (or a member of the decedent's family) must have owned and materially participated in the trade or business for at least five of the eight years preceding the decedent's date of death. In addition, at least one qualified heir (or member of the qualified heir's family) is required to materially participate in the trade or business for at least 10 years following the decedent's death. The qualified family-owned business rules provide a graduated recapture based on the number of years after the decedent's death within which a disqualifying event occurred.

In general, there is no requirement that the qualified heir (or members of his or her family) continue to hold or participate in the trade or business more than 10 years after the decedent's death. However, the 10-year recapture period can be extended for a period of up to two years if the qualified heir does not begin to use the property for a period of up to two years after the decedent's death.

EGTRRA repealed the qualified family-owned business deduction for estates of decedents dying after December 31, 2003. As a result of the EGTRRA sunset at the end of 2010, the qualified family-owned business deduction applies to estates of decedents dying after December 31, 2010.

Installment payment of estate tax for closely held businesses

Estate tax generally is due within nine months of a decedent's death. However, an executor generally may elect to pay estate tax attributable to an interest in a closely held business in two or more installments (but no more than 10).[45] An estate is eligible for payment of estate tax in installments if the value of the decedent's interest in a closely held business exceeds 35 percent of the decedent's adjusted gross estate (i.e., the gross estate less certain deductions). If the election is made, the estate may defer payment of principal and pay only interest for the first five years, followed by up to 10 annual installments of principal and interest. This provision effectively extends the time for paying estate tax by 14 years from the original due date of the estate tax. A special two-percent interest rate applies to the amount of deferred estate tax attributable to the first $1.34 million[46] (as adjusted annually for inflation occurring after 1998; the original amount for 1998 was $1 million) in taxable value of a closely held business. The interest rate applicable to the amount of estate tax attributable to the taxable value of the closely held business in excess of $1.34 million is equal to 45 percent of the rate applicable to underpayments of tax under section 6621 of the Code (i.e., 45 percent of the Federal short-term rate plus two percentage points). Interest paid on deferred estate taxes is not deductible for estate or income tax purposes.

Under pre-EGTRRA law, for purposes of these rules an interest in a closely held business was: (1) an interest as a proprietor in a sole proprietorship; (2) an interest as a partner in a partnership carrying on a trade or business if 20 percent or more of the total capital interest of such partnership was included in the decedent's gross estate or the partnership had 15 or fewer partners; and (3) stock in a corporation carrying on a trade or business if 20 percent or more of the value of the voting stock of the corporation was included in the decedent's gross estate or such corporation had 15 or fewer shareholders.

Under present and pre-EGTRRA law, the decedent may own the interest directly or, in certain cases, indirectly through a holding company. If ownership is through a holding company, the stock must be non-readily tradable. If stock in a holding company is treated as business company stock for purposes of the installment payment provisions, the five-year deferral for principal and the two-percent interest rate do not apply. The value of any interest in a closely

---

[44] Sec. 2057. The qualified family-owned business deduction and the unified credit effective exemption amount are coordinated. If the maximum deduction amount of $675,000 is elected, then the unified credit effective exemption amount is $625,000, for a total of $1.3 million. Because of the coordination between the qualified family-owned business deduction and the unified credit effective exemption

amount, the qualified family-owned business deduction would not provide a benefit in any year in which the applicable exclusion amount exceeds $1.3 million.

[45] Sec. 6166.

[46] Rev. Proc. 2009-50, I.R.B. 2009-45 (Nov. 9, 2009).

held business does not include the value of that portion of such interest attributable to passive assets held by such business.

Effective for estates of decedents dying after December 31, 2001, EGTRRA expands the definition of a closely held business for purposes of installment payment of estate tax. EGTRRA increases from 15 to 45 the maximum number of partners in a partnership and shareholders in a corporation that may be treated as a closely held business in which a decedent held an interest, and thus will qualify the estate for installment payment of estate tax.

EGTRRA also expands availability of the installment payment provisions by providing that an estate of a decedent with an interest in a qualifying lending and financing business is eligible for installment payment of the estate tax. EGTRRA provides that an estate with an interest in a qualifying lending and financing business that claims installment payment of estate tax must make installment payments of estate tax (which will include both principal and interest) relating to the interest in a qualifying lending and financing business over five years.

EGTRRA clarifies that the installment payment provisions require that only the stock of holding companies, not the stock of operating subsidiaries, must be non-readily tradable to qualify for installment payment of the estate tax. EGTRRA provides that an estate with a qualifying property interest held through holding companies that claims installment payment of estate tax must make all installment payments of estate tax (which will include both principal and interest) relating to a qualifying property interest held through holding companies over five years.

As a result of the EGTRRA sunset at the end of 2010, the EGTRRA modifications to the estate tax installment payment rules described above do not apply for estates of decedents dying after December 31, 2010.

Generation-skipping transfer tax rules

In general

For years before and after 2010, a generation skipping transfer tax generally is imposed on transfers, either directly or in trust or similar arrangement, to a "skip person" (as defined above).[47] Transfers subject to the generation skipping transfer tax include direct skips, taxable terminations, and taxable distributions.[48] An ex-

emption generally equal to the estate tax effective exemption amount is provided for each person making generation skipping transfers. The exemption may be allocated by a transferor (or his or her executor) to transferred property.

A direct skip is any transfer subject to estate or gift tax of an interest in property to a skip person.[49] Natural persons or certain trusts may be skip persons. All persons assigned to the second or more remote generation below the transferor are skip persons (e.g., grandchildren and great-grandchildren). Trusts are skip persons if (1) all interests in the trust are held by skip persons, or (2) no person holds an interest in the trust and at no time after the transfer may a distribution (including distributions and terminations) be made to a non-skip person. A taxable termination is a termination (by death, lapse of time, release of power, or otherwise) of an interest in property held in trust unless, immediately after such termination, a non-skip person has an interest in the property, or unless at no time after the termination may a distribution (including a distribution upon termination) be made from the trust to a skip person.[50] A taxable distribution is a distribution from a trust to a skip person (other than a taxable termination or direct skip).[51] If a transferor allocates generation skipping transfer tax exemption to a trust prior to the taxable distribution, generation skipping transfer tax may be avoided.

The tax rate on generation skipping transfers is a flat rate of tax equal to the maximum estate and gift tax rate in effect at the time of the transfer multiplied by the "inclusion ratio." The inclusion ratio with respect to any property transferred in a generation skipping transfer indicates the amount of "generation skipping transfer tax exemption" allocated to a trust. The allocation of generation skipping transfer tax exemption effectively reduces the tax rate on a generation skipping transfer.

If an individual makes a direct skip during his or her lifetime, any unused generation-skipping transfer tax exemption is automatically allocated to a direct skip to the extent necessary to make the inclusion ratio for such property equal to zero. An individual can elect out of the automatic allocation for lifetime direct skips.

Under pre-EGTRRA law, for lifetime transfers made to a trust that were not direct skips, the transferor had to make an affirmative alloca-

---

[47] Sec. 2601.
[48] Sec. 2611.
[49] Sec. 2612(c).

[50] Sec. 2612(a).
[51] Sec. 2612(b).

tion of generation skipping transfer tax exemption; the allocation was not automatic. If generation skipping transfer tax exemption was allocated on a timely filed gift tax return, then the portion of the trust that was exempt from generation skipping transfer tax was based on the value of the property at the time of the transfer. If, however, the allocation was not made on a timely filed gift tax return, then the portion of the trust that was exempt from generation skipping transfer tax was based on the value of the property at the time the allocation of generation skipping transfer tax exemption was made.

An election to allocate generation skipping transfer tax to a specific transfer generally may be made at any time up to the time for filing the transferor's estate tax return.

Modifications to the generation skipping transfer tax rules under EGTRRA

Generally effective after 2000, EGTRRA modifies and adds certain mechanical rules related to the generation skipping transfer tax. First, EGTRRA generally provides that generation skipping transfer tax exemption will be allocated automatically to transfers made during life that are "indirect skips." An indirect skip is any transfer of property (that is not a direct skip) subject to the gift tax that is made to a generation skipping transfer trust, as defined in the Code. If any individual makes an indirect skip during the individual's lifetime, then any unused portion of such individual's generation skipping transfer tax exemption is allocated to the property transferred to the extent necessary to produce the lowest possible inclusion ratio for such property. An individual can elect out of the automatic allocation or may elect to treat a trust as a generation skipping transfer trust attracting the automatic allocation.

Second, EGTRRA provides that, under certain circumstances, generation skipping transfer tax exemption can be allocated retroactively when there is an unnatural order of death. In general, if a lineal descendant of the transferor predeceases the transferor, then the transferor can allocate any unused generation skipping transfer exemption to any previous transfer or transfers to the trust on a chronological basis.

Third, EGTRRA provides that a trust that is only partially subject to generation skipping transfer tax because its inclusion ratio is less than one can be severed in a "qualified severance." A qualified severance generally is defined as the division of a single trust and the creation of two or more trusts, one of which would be exempt from generation skipping transfer tax and an-

other of which would be fully subject to generation skipping transfer tax, if (1) the single trust was divided on a fractional basis, and (2) the terms of the new trusts, in the aggregate, provide for the same succession of interests of beneficiaries as are provided in the original trust.

Fourth, EGTRRA provides that in connection with timely and automatic allocations of generation skipping transfer tax exemption, the value of the property for purposes of determining the inclusion ratio shall be its finally determined gift tax value or estate tax value depending on the circumstances of the transfer. In the case of a generation skipping transfer tax exemption allocation deemed to be made at the conclusion of an estate tax inclusion period, the value for purposes of determining the inclusion ratio shall be its value at that time.

Fifth, under EGTRRA, the Secretary of the Treasury generally is authorized and directed to grant extensions of time to make the election to allocate generation skipping transfer tax exemption and to grant exceptions to the time requirement, without regard to whether any period of limitations has expired. If such relief is granted, then the gift tax or estate tax value of the transfer to trust would be used for determining generation skipping transfer tax exemption allocation.

Sixth, EGTRRA provides that substantial compliance with the statutory and regulatory requirements for allocating generation skipping transfer tax exemption will suffice to establish that generation skipping transfer tax exemption was allocated to a particular transfer or a particular trust. If a taxpayer demonstrates substantial compliance, then so much of the transferor's unused generation skipping transfer tax exemption will be allocated as produces the lowest possible inclusion ratio.

Sunset of EGTRRA modifications to the generation skipping transfer tax rules

The estate and generation skipping transfer taxes are repealed for decedents dying and gifts made in 2010. As a result of the EGTRRA sunset at the end of 2010, the generation skipping transfer tax again will apply after December 31, 2010. However, the EGTRRA modifications to the generation skipping transfer tax rules described above do not apply to generation skipping transfers made after December 31, 2010. Instead, in general, the rules as in effect prior to 2001 apply.

Explanation of Provision

In general

The provision reinstates the estate and generation skipping transfer taxes effective for decedents dying and transfers made after December 31, 2009. The estate tax applicable exclusion amount is $5 million under the provision and is indexed for inflation for decedents dying in calendar years after 2011, and the maximum estate tax rate is 35 percent. For gifts made in 2010, the applicable exclusion amount for gift tax purposes is $1 million, and the gift tax rate is 35 percent. For gifts made after December 31, 2010, the gift tax is reunified with the estate tax, with an applicable exclusion amount of $5 million and a top estate and gift tax rate of 35 percent.[52]

The generation skipping transfer tax exemption for decedents dying or gifts made after December 31, 2009, is equal to the applicable exclusion amount for estate tax purposes (e.g., $5 million for 2010).[53] Therefore, up to $5 million in generation skipping transfer tax exemption may be allocated to a trust created or funded during 2010, depending upon the amount of such exemption used by the taxpayer before 2010. Although the generation skipping transfer tax is applicable in 2010, the generation skipping transfer tax rate for transfers made during 2010 is zero percent. The generation skipping transfer tax rate for transfers made after 2010 is equal to the highest estate and gift tax rate in effect for such year (35 percent for 2011 and 2012).

The provision allows a deduction for certain death taxes paid to any State or the District of Columbia for decedents dying after December 31, 2009.

The provision generally repeals the modified carryover basis rules that, under EGTRRA, would apply for purposes of determining basis in property acquired from a decedent who dies in 2010. Under the provision, a recipient of property acquired from a decedent who dies after December 31, 2009, generally will receive fair market value basis (i.e., "stepped up" basis) under the basis rules applicable to assets acquired from decedents who died in 2009.[54]

The provision extends the EGTRRA modifications to the rules regarding (1) qualified conservation easements, (2) installment payment of estate taxes, and (3) various technical aspects of the generation skipping transfer tax, described in the present-law section, above.

Election for decedents who die during 2010

In the case of a decedent who dies during 2010, the provision generally allows the executor of such decedent's estate to elect to apply the Internal Revenue Code as if the new estate tax and basis step-up rules described in the preceding section had not been enacted. In other words, instead of applying the above-described new estate tax and basis step-up rules of the provision, the executor may elect to have present law (as enacted under EGTRRA) apply. In general, if such an election is made, the estate would not be subject to estate tax, and the basis of assets acquired from the decedent would be determined under the modified carryover basis rules of section 1022.[55] This election will have no effect on the continued applicability of the generation skipping transfer tax. In addition, in applying the definition of transferor in section 2652(a)(1), the determination of whether any property is subject to the tax imposed by chapter 11 of the Code is made without regard to an election made under this provision.

The Secretary of the Treasury or his delegate shall determine the time and manner for making the election. The election, once made, is revocable only with the consent of the Secretary or his delegate.

Extension of certain filing deadlines

The provision also provides for the extension of filing deadlines for certain transfer tax returns. Specifically, in the case of a decedent dying after December 31, 2009, and before the

---

[52] The provision clarifies current law regarding the computation of estate and gift taxes. Under present law, the gift tax on taxable transfers for a year is determined by computing a tentative tax on the cumulative value of current year transfers and all gifts made by a decedent after December 31, 1976, and subtracting from the tentative tax the amount of gift tax that would have been paid by the decedent on taxable gifts after December 31, 1976, if the tax rate schedule in effect in the current year had been in effect on the date of the prior-year gifts. Under the provision, for purposes of determining the amount of gift tax that would have been paid on one or more prior year gifts, the estate tax rates in effect under section 2001(c) at the time of the decedent's death are used to compute both (1) the gift tax imposed by chapter 12 with respect to such gifts, and (2) the unified credit allowed against such gifts under section 2505 (including in computing the applicable credit amount under sec-

tion 2505(a)(1) and the sum of amounts allowed as a credit for all preceding periods under section 2505(a)(2)).

[53] The $5 million generation skipping transfer tax exemption is available in 2010 regardless of whether the executor of an estate of a decedent who dies in 2010 makes the election described below to apply the EGTRRA 2010 estate tax rules and section 1022 basis rules.

[54] See generally Sec. 1014.

[55] Therefore, an heir who acquires an asset from the estate of a decedent who died in 2010 and whose executor elected application of the 2010 EGTRRA rules has a basis in the asset determined under the modified carryover basis rules of section 1022. Such basis is applicable for the determination of any gain or loss on the sale or disposition of the asset in any future year regardless of the status of the sunset provision described below.

¶10,130   Act Sec.301

date of enactment, the due date shall not be earlier than the date which is nine months after the date of enactment for: (1) filing an estate tax return required under section 6018; (2) making the payment of estate tax under Chapter 11; and (3) making any disclaimer described in section 2518(b) of an interest in property passing by reason of the death of such a decedent. In the case of a generation skipping transfer made after December 31, 2009, and before the date of enactment, the due date for filing any return required under section 2662 (including the making of any election required to be made on the return) shall not be earlier than the date which is nine months after the date of enactment.

Portability of unused exemption between spouses

Under the provision, any applicable exclusion amount that remains unused as of the death of a spouse who dies after December 31, 2010 (the "deceased spousal unused exclusion amount"), generally is available for use by the surviving spouse, as an addition to such surviving spouse's applicable exclusion amount.[56]

If a surviving spouse is predeceased by more than one spouse, the amount of unused exclusion that is available for use by such surviving spouse is limited to the lesser of $5 million or the unused exclusion of the last such deceased spouse.[57] A surviving spouse may use the predeceased spousal carryover amount in addition to such surviving spouse's own $5 million exclusion for taxable transfers made during life or at death.

A deceased spousal unused exclusion amount is available to a surviving spouse only if an election is made on a timely filed estate tax return (including extensions) of the predeceased spouse on which such amount is computed, regardless of whether the estate of the predeceased spouse otherwise is required to file an estate tax return. In addition, notwithstanding the statute of limitations for assessing estate or gift tax with respect to a predeceased spouse, the Secretary of the Treasury may examine the return of a predeceased spouse for purposes of determining the deceased spousal unused exclusion amount available for use by the surviving spouse. The Secretary of the Treasury shall prescribe regulations as may be appropriate and necessary to carry out the rules described in this paragraph.

Example 1.—Assume that Husband 1 dies in 2011, having made taxable transfers of $3 million and having no taxable estate. An election is made on Husband 1's estate tax return to permit Wife to use Husband 1's deceased spousal unused exclusion amount. As of Husband 1's death, Wife has made no taxable gifts. Thereafter, Wife's applicable exclusion amount is $7 million (her $5 million basic exclusion amount plus $2 million deceased spousal unused exclusion amount from Husband 1), which she may use for lifetime gifts or for transfers at death.

Example 2.—Assume the same facts as in Example 1, except that Wife subsequently marries Husband 2. Husband 2 also predeceases Wife, having made $4 million in taxable transfers and having no taxable estate. An election is made on Husband 2's estate tax return to permit Wife to use Husband 2's deceased spousal unused exclusion amount. Although the combined amount of unused exclusion of Husband 1 and Husband 2 is $3 million ($2 million for Husband 1 and $1 million for Husband 2), only Husband 2's $1 million unused exclusion is available for use by Wife, because the deceased spousal unused exclusion amount is limited to the lesser of the basic exclusion amount ($5 million) or the unused exclusion of the last deceased spouse of the surviving spouse (here, Husband 2's $1 million unused exclusion). Thereafter, Wife's applicable exclusion amount is $6 million (her $5 million basic exclusion amount plus $1 million deceased spousal unused exclusion amount from Husband 2), which she may use for lifetime gifts or for transfers at death.

Example 3.—Assume the same facts as in Examples 1 and 2, except that Wife predeceases Husband 2. Following Husband 1's death, Wife's applicable exclusion amount is $7 million (her $5 million basic exclusion amount plus $2 million deceased spousal unused exclusion amount from Husband 1). Wife made no taxable transfers and has a taxable estate of $3 million. An election is made on Wife's estate tax return to permit Husband 2 to use Wife's deceased spousal unused exclusion amount, which is $4 million (Wife's $7 million applicable exclusion amount less her $3 million taxable estate). Under the provision, Husband 2's applicable exclusion amount is increased by $4 million, i.e., the amount of deceased spousal unused exclusion amount of Wife.

---

[56] The provision does not allow a surviving spouse to use the unused generation skipping transfer tax exemption of a predeceased spouse.

[57] The last deceased spouse limitation applies whether or not the last deceased spouse has any unused exclusion or the last deceased spouse's estate makes a timely election.

Sunset provision

Under the bill, the sunset of the EGTRRA estate, gift, and generation skipping transfer tax provisions, scheduled to apply to estates of decedents dying, gifts made, or generation skipping transfers after December 31, 2010, is extended to apply to estates of decedents dying, gifts made, or generation skipping transfers after December 31, 2012. The EGTRRA sunset, as extended by the bill, applies to the amendments made by the provision. Therefore, neither the EGTRRA rules nor the new rules of the provision will apply to estates of decedents dying, gifts made, or generation skipping transfers made after December 31, 2012.

Effective Date

The estate and generation skipping transfer tax provisions generally are effective for dece-

dents dying, gifts made, and generation skipping transfers made after December 31, 2009. The modifications to the gift tax exemption and rate generally are effective for gifts made after December 31, 2010. The new rules providing for portability of unused exemption between spouses generally are effective for decedents dying and gifts made after December 31, 2010.

[**Law at** ¶5205, ¶5490, ¶5500, ¶5600, ¶5605, ¶5695, ¶5700, ¶5705, ¶5710, ¶5720, ¶5765, ¶5770, ¶5785, ¶5850, ¶7025, ¶7030 **and** ¶7035. **CCH Explanation at** ¶705, ¶710, ¶715, ¶718, ¶740, ¶745, ¶750, ¶755 **and** ¶760.]

[¶10,140] Act Sec. 401. Extension of bonus depreciation; temporary 100 percent expensing for certain business assets

Joint Committee on Taxation (J.C.T. Rep. No. JCX-55-10)

[Code Sec. 168(k)]

Present Law

In general

An additional first-year depreciation deduction is allowed equal to 50 percent of the adjusted basis of qualified property placed in service during 2008, 2009, and 2010 (2009, 2010, and 2011 for certain longer-lived and transportation property).[58] The additional first-year depreciation deduction is allowed for both regular tax and alternative minimum tax purposes, but is not allowed for purposes of computing earnings and profits. The basis of the property and the depreciation allowances in the year of purchase and later years are appropriately adjusted to reflect the additional first-year depreciation deduction. In addition, there are no adjustments to the allowable amount of depreciation for purposes of computing a taxpayer's alternative minimum taxable income with respect to property to which the provision applies. The amount of the additional first-year depreciation deduction is not affected by a short taxable year. The taxpayer may elect out of additional first-year depreciation for any class of property for any taxable year.

The interaction of the additional first-year depreciation allowance with the otherwise applicable depreciation allowance may be illustrated as follows. Assume that in 2009, a taxpayer purchased new depreciable property and placed it in service.[59] The property's cost is $1,000, and it is five-year property subject to the half-year convention. The amount of additional first-year depreciation allowed is $500. The remaining $500 of the cost of the property is depreciable under the rules applicable to five-year property. Thus, 20 percent, or $100, is also allowed as a depreciation deduction in 2009. The total depreciation deduction with respect to the property for 2009 is $600. The remaining $400 adjusted basis of the property generally is recovered through otherwise applicable depreciation rules.

Property qualifying for the additional first-year depreciation deduction must meet all of the following requirements. First, the property must be (1) property to which MACRS applies with an applicable recovery period of 20 years or less; (2) water utility property (as defined in section 168(e)(5)); (3) computer software other than computer software covered by section 197; or (4) qualified leasehold improvement property (as

---

[58] Sec. 168(k). The additional first-year depreciation deduction is subject to the general rules regarding whether an item must be capitalized under section 263 or section 263A.

[59] Assume that the cost of the property is not eligible for expensing under section 179.

¶10,140   Act Sec. 401

defined in section 168(k)(3)).[60] Second, the original use[61] of the property must commence with the taxpayer after December 31, 2007.[62] Third, the taxpayer must purchase the property within the applicable time period. Finally, the property must be placed in service after December 31, 2007, and before January 1, 2011. An extension of the placed in service date of one year (i.e., to January 1, 2012) is provided for certain property with a recovery period of 10 years or longer and certain transportation property.[63] Transportation property is defined as tangible personal property used in the trade or business of transporting persons or property.

To qualify, property must be acquired (1) after December 31, 2007, and before January 1, 2011, but only if no binding written contract for the acquisition is in effect before January 1, 2008, or (2) pursuant to a binding written contract which was entered into after December 31, 2007, and before January 1, 2011.[64] With respect to property that is manufactured, constructed, or produced by the taxpayer for use by the taxpayer, the taxpayer must begin the manufacture, construction, or production of the property after December 31, 2007, and before January 1, 2011. Property that is manufactured, constructed, or produced for the taxpayer by another person under a contract that is entered into prior to the manufacture, construction, or production of the property is considered to be manufactured, constructed, or produced by the taxpayer. For property eligible for the extended placed in service date, a special rule limits the amount of costs eligible for the additional first-year depreciation. With respect to such property, only the portion of the basis that is properly attributable to the costs incurred before January 1, 2011 ("progress expenditures") is eligible for the additional first-year depreciation.[65]

Property does not qualify for the additional first-year depreciation deduction when the user of such property (or a related party) would not have been eligible for the additional first-year depreciation deduction if the user (or a related party) were treated as the owner. For example, if a taxpayer sells to a related party property that was under construction prior to January 1, 2008, the property does not qualify for the additional first-year depreciation deduction. Similarly, if a taxpayer sells to a related party property that was subject to a binding written contract prior to January 1, 2008, the property does not qualify for the additional first-year depreciation deduction. As a further example, if a taxpayer (the lessee) sells property in a sale-leaseback arrangement, and the property otherwise would not have qualified for the additional first-year depreciation deduction if it were owned by the taxpayer-lessee, then the lessor is not entitled to the additional first-year depreciation deduction.

The limitation under section 280F on the amount of depreciation deductions allowed with respect to certain passenger automobiles is increased in the first year by $8,000 for automobiles that qualify (and for which the taxpayer does not elect out of the additional first-year deduction). The $8,000 increase is not indexed for inflation.

Election to accelerate certain credits in lieu of claiming bonus depreciation

A corporation otherwise eligible for additional first year depreciation under section 168(k) may elect to claim additional research or mini-

---

[60] The additional first-year depreciation deduction is not available for any property that is required to be depreciated under the alternative depreciation system of MACRS. The additional first-year depreciation deduction is also not available for qualified New York Liberty Zone leasehold improvement property as defined in section 1400L(c)(2).

[61] The term "original use" means the first use to which the property is put, whether or not such use corresponds to the use of such property by the taxpayer.

If in the normal course of its business a taxpayer sells fractional interests in property to unrelated third parties, then the original use of such property begins with the first user of each fractional interest (i.e., each fractional owner is considered the original user of its proportionate share of the property).

[62] A special rule applies in the case of certain lease d property. In the case of any property that is originally placed in service by a person and that is sold to the taxpayer and leased back to such person by the taxpayer within three months after the date that the property was placed in service, the property would be treated as originally placed in

service by the taxpayer not earlier than the date that the property is used under the leaseback.

If property is originally placed in service by a lessor (including by operation of section 168(k)(2)(E)(i)), such property is sold within three months after the date that the property was placed in service, and the user of such property does not change, then the property is treated as originally placed in service by the taxpayer not earlier than the date of such sale.

[63] Property qualifying for the extended placed in service date must have an estimated production period exceeding one year and a cost exceeding $1 million.

[64] Property does not fail to qualify for the additional first-year depreciation merely because a binding written contract to acquire a component of the property is in effect prior to January 1, 2008.

[65] For purposes of determining the amount of eligible progress expenditures, it is intended that rules similar to section 46(d)(3) as in effect prior to the Tax Reform Act of 1986 apply.

mum tax credits in lieu of claiming depreciation under section 168(k) for "eligible qualified property" placed in service after March 31, 2008 and before December 31, 2008.[66] A corporation making the election forgoes the depreciation deductions allowable under section 168(k) and instead increases the limitation under section 38(c) on the use of research credits or section 53(c) on the use of minimum tax credits.[67] The increases in the allowable credits are treated as refundable. The depreciation for qualified property is calculated for both regular tax and AMT purposes using the straight-line method in place of the method that would otherwise be used absent the election under this provision.

The research credit or minimum tax credit limitation is increased by the bonus depreciation amount, which is equal to 20 percent of bonus depreciation[68] for certain eligible qualified property that could be claimed absent an election under this provision. Generally, eligible qualified property included in the calculation is bonus depreciation property that meets the following requirements: (1) the original use of the property must commence with the taxpayer after March 31, 2008; (2) the taxpayer must purchase the property either (a) after March 31, 2008, and before January 1, 2010, but only if no binding written contract for the acquisition is in effect before April 1, 2008,[69] or (b) pursuant to a binding written contract which was entered into after March 31, 2008, and before January 1, 2010;[70] and (3) the property must be placed in service after March 31, 2008, and before January 1, 2010 (January 1, 2011 for certain longer-lived and transportation property).

The bonus depreciation amount is limited to the lesser of: (1) $30 million, or (2) six percent of the sum of research credit carryforwards from taxable years beginning before January 1, 2006 and minimum tax credits allocable to the adjusted minimum tax imposed for taxable years beginning before January 1, 2006. All corporations treated as a single employer under section 52(a) are treated as one taxpayer for purposes of

the limitation, as well as for electing the application of this provision.

A corporation may make a separate election to increase the research credit or minimum tax credit limitation by the bonus depreciation amount with respect to certain property placed in service in 2009 (2010 in the case of certain longer-lived and transportation property). The election applies with respect to extension property, which is defined as property that is eligible qualified property solely because it meets the requirements under the extension of the special allowance for certain property acquired during 2009.

A corporation that has made an election to increase the research credit or minimum tax credit limitation for eligible qualified property for its first taxable year ending after March 31, 2008, may choose not to make this election for extension property. Further, a corporation that has not made an election for eligible qualified property for its first taxable year ending after March 31, 2008, is permitted to make the election for extension property for its first taxable year ending after December 31, 2008, and for each subsequent year. In the case of a taxpayer electing to increase the research or minimum tax credit for both eligible qualified property and extension property, a separate bonus depreciation amount, maximum amount, and maximum increase amount is computed and applied to each group of property.[71]

Explanation of Provision

The provision extends and expands the additional first-year depreciation to equal 100 percent of the cost of qualified property placed in service after September 8, 2010 and before January 1, 2012 (before January 1, 2013 for certain longer-lived and transportation property), and provides for a 50 percent first-year additional depreciation deduction for qualified property placed in service after December 31, 2011 and before January 1, 2013 (after December 31, 2012

---

[66] Sec. 168(k)(4). In the case of an electing corporation that is a partner in a partnership, the corporate partner's distributive share of partnership items is determined as if section 168(k) does not apply to any eligible qualified property and the straight line method is used to calculate depreciation of such property.

[67] Special rules apply to an applicable partnership.

[68] For this purpose, bonus depreciation is the difference between (i) the aggregate amount of depreciation for all eligible qualified property determined if section 168(k)(1) applied using the most accelerated depreciation method (determined without regard to this provision), and shortest life allowable for each property, and (ii) the amount of

depreciation that would be determined if section 168(k)(1) did not apply using the same method and life for each property.

[69] In the case of passenger aircraft, the written binding contract limitation does not apply.

[70] Special rules apply to property manufactured, constructed, or produced by the taxpayer for use by the taxpayer.

[71] In computing the maximum amount, the maximum increase amount for extension property is reduced by bonus depreciation amounts for preceding taxable years only with respect to extension property.

and before January 1, 2014 for certain longer-lived and transportation property). Rules similar to those in section 168(k)(2)(A)(ii) and (iii), which provide that qualified property does not include property acquired pursuant to a written binding contract that was in effect prior to January 1, 2008, apply for purposes of determining whether property is eligible for the temporary 100 percent additional first-year depreciation deduction. Thus under the provision, property acquired pursuant to a written binding contract entered into after December 31, 2007 is qualified property for purposes of the 100 percent additional first-year depreciation deduction assuming all other requirements of section 168(k)(2) are met.

The provision generally permits a corporation to increase the minimum tax credit limitation by the bonus depreciation amount with respect to certain property placed in service after December 31, 2010 and before January 1, 2013 (January 1, 2014 in the case of certain longer-lived and transportation property).[72] The provision applies with respect to round 2 extension property, which is defined as property that is eligible qualified property solely because it meets the requirements under the extension of the additional first-year depreciation deduction for certain property placed in service after December 31, 2010.[73]

Under the provision, a taxpayer that has made an election to increase the research credit

or minimum tax credit limitation for eligible qualified property for its first taxable year ending after March 31, 2008 or for extension property may choose not to make this election for round 2 extension property. Further, the provision allows a taxpayer that has not made an election for eligible qualified property for its first taxable year ending after March 31, 2008 or for extension property, to make the election for round 2 extension property for its first taxable year ending after December 31, 2010, and for each subsequent year. In the case of a taxpayer electing to increase the research or minimum tax credit for eligible qualified property and extension property and the minimum tax credit for round 2 extension property a separate bonus depreciation amount, maximum amount, and maximum increase amount is computed and applied to each group of property.[74]

Effective Date

The provision generally applies to property placed in service by the taxpayer after December 31, 2010, in taxable years ending after such date. The provision expanding the additional first-year depreciation deduction to 100 percent of the basis of qualified property applies to property placed in service by the taxpayer after September 8, 2010, in taxable years ending after such date.

[Law at ¶5265. CCH Explanation at ¶502 and ¶504.]

[¶10,150] Act Sec. 402. Temporary extension of increased small business expensing

Joint Committee on Taxation (J.C.T. Rep. No. JCX-55-10)

[Code Sec. 179]

Present Law

Subject to certain limitations, a taxpayer that invests in certain qualifying property may elect

under section 179 to deduct (or "expense") the cost of qualifying property, rather than to recover such costs through depreciation deductions.[75] For taxable years beginning in 2010 and 2011, the maximum amount that a taxpayer may

---

[72] A taxpayer does not compute a bonus depreciation amount under section 168(k)(4)(C) for any bonus depreciation allowable with respect to property placed in service during 2010. For example, assume in its taxable year beginning October 1, 2010 and ending September 30, 2011, a corporation places into service qualified property with a total cost of $1,000,000, of which $250,000 was placed in service before December 31, 2010. The corporation computes its bonus depreciation amount under section 168(k)(4)(C) taking into account only the bonus depreciation computed with respect to the $750,000 of property placed in service after December 31, 2010.

[73] An election under new section 168(k)(4)(I) with respect to round 2 extension property is binding for any property that is eligible qualified property solely by reason of the amendments made by section 401(a) of the Tax Relief, Un-

employment Insurance Reauthorization, and Job Creation Act of 2010 (and the application of such extension to this paragraph pursuant to the amendment made by section 401(c)(1) of such Act), even if such property is placed in service in 2012.

[74] In computing the maximum amount, the maximum increase amount for extension property or for round 2 extension property is reduced by bonus depreciation amounts for preceding taxable years only with respect to extension property or round 2 extension property, respectively.

[75] Additional section 179 incentives are provided with respect to qualified property meeting applicable requirements that is used by a business in an empowerment zone (sec. 1397A), a renewal community (sec. 1400J), or the Gulf Opportunity Zone (sec. 1400N(e)). In addition, section

expense is $500,000 of the cost of qualifying property placed in service for the taxable year.[76] The $500,000 amount is reduced (but not below zero) by the amount by which the cost of qualifying property placed in service during the taxable year exceeds $2,000,000.[77] Off-the-shelf computer software placed in service in taxable years beginning before 2012 is treated as qualifying property.

The amount eligible to be expensed for a taxable year may not exceed the taxable income for a taxable year that is derived from the active conduct of a trade or business (determined without regard to this provision). Any amount that is not allowed as a deduction because of the taxable income limitation generally may be carried forward to succeeding taxable years (subject to similar limitations).[78] No general business credit under section 38 is allowed with respect to any amount for which a deduction is allowed under section 179. An expensing election is made under rules prescribed by the Secretary.[79]

For taxable years beginning in 2012 and thereafter, a taxpayer with a sufficiently small amount of annual investment may elect to deduct up to $25,000 of the cost of qualifying property placed in service for the taxable year. The $25,000 amount is reduced (but not below zero) by the amount by which the cost of qualifying property placed in service during the taxable year exceeds $200,000. The $25,000 and $200,000 amounts are not indexed. In general, qualifying property is defined as depreciable tangible personal property that is purchased for use in the active conduct of a trade or business (not including off-the-shelf computer software).

Explanation of Provision

Under the provision, for taxable years beginning in 2012, the maximum amount a taxpayer may expense is $125,000 of the cost of qualifying property placed in service for the taxable year. The $125,000 amount is reduced (but not below zero) by the amount by which the cost of qualifying property placed in service during the taxable year exceeds $500,000. The $125,000 and $500,000 amounts are indexed for inflation.

In addition, the provision extends the treatment of off-the-shelf computer software as qualifying property,[80] as well as the provision permitting a taxpayer to amend or irrevocably revoke an election for a taxable year under section 179 without the consent of the Commissioner for one year (through 2012).

For taxable years beginning in 2013, and thereafter, the maximum amount a taxpayer may expense is $25,000 of the cost of qualifying property placed in service for the taxable year. The $25,000 amount is reduced (but not below zero) by the amount by which the cost of qualifying property placed in service during the taxable year exceeds $200,000.

Effective Date

The provision is effective for taxable years beginning after December 31, 2011.

[Law at ¶ 5275. CCH Explanation at ¶ 506.]

(Footnote Continued)

179(e) provides for an enhanced section 179 deduction for qualified disaster assistance property.

[76] The definition of qualifying property was temporarily (for 2010 and 2011) expanded to include up to $250,000 of qualified leasehold improvement property, qualified restaurant property, and qualified retail improvement property. See section 179(f)(2).

[77] The temporary $500,000 and $2,000,000 amounts were enacted in the Small Business Jobs Act of 2010, Pub. L. No. 111-240.

[78] Special rules apply to limit the carryover of unused section 179 deductions attributable to qualified leasehold improvement property, qualified restaurant property, and qualified retail improvement property. See section 179(f)(4).

[79] Sec. 179(c)(1). Under Treas. Reg. sec. 1.179-5, applicable to property placed in service in taxable years beginning after 2002 and before 2008, a taxpayer is permitted to make or revoke an election under section 179 without the consent of the Commissioner on an amended Federal tax return for that taxable year. This amended return must be filed within the time prescribed by law for filing an amended return for the taxable year. T.D. 9209, July 12, 2005.

[80] The temporary extension of the definition of qualifying property to include qualified leasehold improvement property, qualified restaurant property, and qualified retail improvement property is not extended.

[¶10,160] Act Sec. 601. Payroll tax cut

Joint Committee on Taxation (J.C.T. REP. NO. JCX-55-10)

[Act Sec. 601]

Present Law

Federal Insurance Contributions Act ("FICA") tax

The FICA tax applies to employers based on the amount of covered wages paid to an employee during the year.[81] Generally, covered wages means all remuneration for employment, including the cash value of all remuneration paid in any medium other than cash.[82] Certain exceptions from covered wages are also provided. The tax imposed is composed of two parts: (1) the old age, survivors, and disability insurance ("OASDI") tax equal to 6.2 percent of covered wages up to the taxable wage base ($106,800 in 2010); and (2) the Medicare hospital insurance ("HI") tax amount equal to 1.45 percent of covered wages.

In addition to the tax on employers, each employee is subject to FICA taxes equal to the amount of tax imposed on the employer (the "employee portion").[83] The employee portion generally must be withheld and remitted to the Federal government by the employer.

Self-Employment Contributions Act ("SECA") tax

As a parallel to FICA taxes, the SECA tax applies to the self-employment income of self-employed individuals.[84] The rate of the OASDI portion of SECA taxes is 12.4 percent, which is equal to the combined employee and employer OASDI FICA tax rates, and applies to self-employment income up to the FICA taxable wage base. Similarly, the rate of the HI portion is 2.9 percent, the same as the combined employer and employee HI rates under the FICA tax, and there is no cap on the amount of self-employment income to which the rate applies.[85]

An individual may deduct, in determining net earnings from self-employment under the SECA tax, the amount of the net earnings from self-employment (determined without regard to this deduction) for the taxable year multiplied by one half of the combined OASDI and HI rates.[86]

Additionally, a deduction, for purposes of computing the income tax of an individual, is allowed for one half of the amount of the SECA tax imposed on the individual's self-employment income for the taxable year.[87]

Railroad retirement tax

The Railroad Retirement System has two main components. Tier I of the system is financed by taxes on employers and employees equal to the Social Security payroll tax and provides qualified railroad retirees (and their qualified spouses, dependents, widows, or widowers) with benefits that are roughly equal to Social Security. Covered railroad workers and their employers pay the Tier I tax instead of the Social Security payroll tax, and most railroad retirees collect Tier I benefits instead of Social Security. Tier II of the system replicates a private pension plan, with employers and employees contributing a certain percentage of pay toward the system to finance defined benefits to eligible railroad retirees (and qualified spouses, dependents, widows, or widowers) upon retirement; however, the Federal Government collects the Tier II payroll contribution and pays out the benefits.

Explanation of Provision

The provision reduces the employee OASDI tax rate under the FICA tax by two percentage points to 4.2 percent for one year (2011). Similarly, the provision reduces the OASDI tax rate under the SECA tax by two percentage points to 10.4 percent for taxable years of individuals that begin in 2011. A similar reduction applies to railroad retirement tax.

The provision provides rules for coordination with deductions for employment taxes. The rate reduction is not taken into account in determining the SECA tax deduction allowed for determining the amount of the net earnings from self-employment for the taxable year. Thus, the deduction for 2011 remains at 7.65 percent of self-employment income (determined without regard to the deduction).

---

[81] Sec. 3111.

[82] Sec. 3121.

[83] Sec. 3101. For taxable years beginning after 2012, an additional HI tax applies.

[84] Sec. 1401.

[85] For taxable years beginning after 2012, an additional HI tax applies.

[86] Sec. 1402(a)(12).

[87] Sec. 164(f).

The income tax deduction allowed under section 164(f) for taxable years beginning in 2011 is computed at the rate of 59.6 percent of the OASDI tax paid, plus one half of the HI tax paid.[88]

The provision provides that the Treasury Secretary is to notify employers of the payroll tax cut.

The Federal Old-Age and Survivors Trust Fund, the Federal Disability Insurance Trust Fund, and the Social Security Equivalent Benefit Account established under the Railroad Retirement Act of 1974[89] will receive transfers from the General Fund of the United States Treasury equal to any reduction in payroll taxes attributable to this provision. The amounts will be transferred from the General Fund at such times and in such a manner as to replicate to the extent possible the transfers which would have occurred to the Trust Funds or Benefit Account had the provision not been enacted.

For purposes of applying any provision of Federal law other than the provisions of the Internal Revenue Code of 1986, the rate of tax in effect under section 3101(a) is determined without regard to the reduction in that rate under this provision.

Effective Date

The provision is effective for remuneration received during 2011 and for self-employment income for taxable years beginning in 2011.

[Law at ¶ 7040. CCH Explanation at ¶ 312.]

[¶ 10,170] Act Sec. 701. Incentives for biodiesel and renewable diesel

Joint Committee on Taxation (J.C.T. Rep. No. JCX-55-10)

[Code Secs. 40A, 6426 and 6427]

Present Law

Biodiesel

The Code provides an income tax credit for biodiesel fuels (the "biodiesel fuels credit").[90] The biodiesel fuels credit is the sum of three credits: (1) the biodiesel mixture credit, (2) the biodiesel credit, and (3) the small agri-biodiesel producer credit. The biodiesel fuels credit is treated as a general business credit. The amount of the biodiesel fuels credit is includable in gross income. The biodiesel fuels credit is coordinated to take into account benefits from the biodiesel excise tax credit and payment provisions discussed below. The credit does not apply to fuel sold or used after December 31, 2009.

Biodiesel is monoalkyl esters of long chain fatty acids derived from plant or animal matter that meet (1) the registration requirements established by the EPA under section 211 of the Clean Air Act (42 U.S.C. sec. 7545) and (2) the requirements of the American Society of Testing and Materials ("ASTM") D6751. Agri-biodiesel is biodiesel derived solely from virgin oils including oils from corn, soybeans, sunflower seeds, cottonseeds, canola, crambe, rapeseeds, safflowers, flaxseeds, rice bran, mustard seeds, camelina, or animal fats.

Biodiesel may be taken into account for purposes of the credit only if the taxpayer obtains a certification (in such form and manner as prescribed by the Secretary) from the producer or importer of the biodiesel that identifies the product produced and the percentage of biodiesel and agri-biodiesel in the product.

Biodiesel mixture credit

The biodiesel mixture credit is $1.00 for each gallon of biodiesel (including agri-biodiesel) used by the taxpayer in the production of a qualified biodiesel mixture. A qualified biodiesel mixture is a mixture of biodiesel and diesel fuel that is (1) sold by the taxpayer producing such mixture to any person for use as a fuel, or (2) used as a fuel by the taxpayer producing such mixture. The sale or use must be in the trade or business of the taxpayer and is to be taken into account for the taxable year in which such sale or use occurs. No credit is allowed with respect to any casual off-farm production of a qualified biodiesel mixture.

---

[88] This percentage replaces the rate of one half (50 percent) allowed under present law for this portion of the deduction. The new percentage is necessary to continue to allow the self-employed taxpayer to deduct the full amount of the employer portion of SECA taxes. The employer OASDI tax rate remains at 6.2 percent, while the employee portion falls to 4.2 percent. Thus, the employer share of total OASDI taxes is 6.2 divided by 10.4, or 59.6 percent of the OASDI portion of SECA taxes.

[89] 45 U.S.C. 231n-1(a).

[90] Sec. 40A.

Per IRS guidance a mixture need only contain 1/10th of one percent of diesel fuel to be a qualified mixture.[91] Thus, a qualified biodiesel mixture can contain 99.9 percent biodiesel and 0.1 percent diesel fuel.

Biodiesel credit (B-100)

The biodiesel credit is $1.00 for each gallon of biodiesel that is not in a mixture with diesel fuel (100 percent biodiesel or B-100) and which during the taxable year is (1) used by the taxpayer as a fuel in a trade or business or (2) sold by the taxpayer at retail to a person and placed in the fuel tank of such person's vehicle.

Small agri-biodiesel producer credit

The Code provides a small agri-biodiesel producer income tax credit, in addition to the biodiesel and biodiesel fuel mixture credits. The credit is 10-cents-per-gallon for up to 15 million gallons of agri-biodiesel produced by small producers, defined generally as persons whose agri-biodiesel production capacity does not exceed 60 million gallons per year. The agri-biodiesel must (1) be sold by such producer to another person (a) for use by such other person in the production of a qualified biodiesel mixture in such person's trade or business (other than casual off-farm production), (b) for use by such other person as a fuel in a trade or business, or, (c) who sells such agri-biodiesel at retail to another person and places such agri-biodiesel in the fuel tank of such other person; or (2) used by the producer for any purpose described in (a), (b), or (c).

Biodiesel mixture excise tax credit

The Code also provides an excise tax credit for biodiesel mixtures.[92] The credit is $1.00 for each gallon of biodiesel used by the taxpayer in producing a biodiesel mixture for sale or use in a trade or business of the taxpayer. A biodiesel mixture is a mixture of biodiesel and diesel fuel that (1) is sold by the taxpayer producing such mixture to any person for use as a fuel or (2) is used as a fuel by the taxpayer producing such mixture. No credit is allowed unless the taxpayer obtains a certification (in such form and manner as prescribed by the Secretary) from the producer of the biodiesel that identifies the product produced and the percentage of biodiesel and agri-biodiesel in the product.[93]

The credit is not available for any sale or use for any period after December 31, 2009. This excise tax credit is coordinated with the income tax credit for biodiesel such that credit for the same biodiesel cannot be claimed for both income and excise tax purposes.

Payments with respect to biodiesel fuel mixtures

If any person produces a biodiesel fuel mixture in such person's trade or business, the Secretary is to pay such person an amount equal to the biodiesel mixture credit.[94] The biodiesel fuel mixture credit must first be taken against tax liability for taxable fuels. To the extent the biodiesel fuel mixture credit exceeds such tax liability, the excess may be received as a payment. Thus, if the person has no section 4081 liability, the credit is refundable. The Secretary is not required to make payments with respect to biodiesel fuel mixtures sold or used after December 31, 2009.

Renewable diesel

"Renewable diesel" is liquid fuel that (1) is derived from biomass (as defined in section 45K(c)(3)), (2) meets the registration requirements for fuels and fuel additives established by the EPA under section 211 of the Clean Air Act, and (3) meets the requirements of the ASTM D975 or D396, or equivalent standard established by the Secretary. ASTM D975 provides standards for diesel fuel suitable for use in diesel engines. ASTM D396 provides standards for fuel oil intended for use in fuel-oil burning equipment, such as furnaces. Renewable diesel also includes fuel derived from biomass that meets the requirements of a Department of Defense specification for military jet fuel or an ASTM for aviation turbine fuel.

For purposes of the Code, renewable diesel is generally treated the same as biodiesel. In the case of renewable diesel that is aviation fuel, kerosene is treated as though it were diesel fuel for purposes of a qualified renewable diesel mixture. Like biodiesel, the incentive may be taken as an income tax credit, an excise tax credit, or as a payment from the Secretary.[95] The incentive for renewable diesel is $1.00 per gallon. There is no small producer credit for renewable diesel.

---

[91] Notice 2005-62, I.R.B. 2005-35, 443 (2005). "A biodiesel mixture is a mixture of biodiesel and diesel fuel containing at least 0.1 percent (by volume) of diesel fuel. Thus, for example, a mixture of 999 gallons of biodiesel and 1 gallon of diesel fuel is a biodiesel mixture." Ibid.

[92] Sec. 6426(c).

[93] Sec. 6426(c)(4).

[94] Sec. 6427(e).

[95] Secs. 40A(f), 6426(c), and 6427(e).

The incentives for renewable diesel expire after December 31, 2009.

Explanation of Provision

The provision extends the income tax credit, excise tax credit and payment provisions for biodiesel and renewable diesel for two additional years (through December 31, 2011).

In light of the retroactive nature of the provision, the provision creates a special rule to address claims regarding excise credits and claims for payment associated with periods occurring during 2010. In particular the provision directs the Secretary to issue guidance within 30 days of the date of enactment. Such guidance is to provide for a one-time submission of claims covering periods occurring during 2010. The guidance is to provide for a 180-day period for the submission of such claims (in such manner as prescribed by the Secretary) to begin no later than 30 days after such guidance is issued. Such claims shall be paid by the Secretary of the Treasury not later than 60 days after receipt. If the claim is not paid within 60 days of the date of the filing, the claim shall be paid with interest from such date determined by using the overpayment rate and method under section 6621 of such Code.

Effective Date

The provision is effective for sales and uses after December 31, 2009.

[Law at ¶5095, ¶5810, ¶5815, and ¶7045. CCH Explanation at ¶544.]

[¶10,180] Act Sec. 702. Credit for refined coal facilities

Joint Committee on Taxation (J.C.T. REP. NO. JCX-55-10)

[Code Sec. 45]

Present Law

In general

A credit is available for refined coal. In general, refined coal is a fuel produced from coal that is (1) used to produce steam or (2) used to produce steel industry fuel.

Refined coal used to produce steam

An income tax credit is allowed for the production at qualified facilities of certain refined coal sold to an unrelated person for use to produce steam. The amount of the refined coal credit is $4.375 per ton (adjusted for inflation using 1992 as the base year; $6.27 for 2010). A taxpayer may generally claim the credit during the 10-year period commencing with the date the qualified facility is placed in service.

A qualifying refined coal facility is a facility producing refined coal that is placed in service after October 22, 2004, and before January 1, 2010. Refined coal is a qualifying liquid, gaseous, or solid synthetic fuel produced from coal (including lignite) or high-carbon fly ash, including such fuel used as a feedstock. A qualifying fuel is a fuel that, when burned, emits 20 percent less nitrogen oxides and either sulfur dioxide or mercury than the burning of feedstock coal or comparable coal predominantly available in the marketplace as of January 1, 2003, but only if the fuel sells at prices at least 50 percent greater than the prices of the feedstock coal or comparable coal. In addition, to be qualified refined coal, the taxpayer must sell the fuel with the reasonable expectation that it will be used for the primary purpose of producing steam.

The refined coal credit is reduced over an $8.75 phase-out range as the reference price of the fuel used as feedstock for the refined coal exceeds an amount equal to 1.7 times the reference price for such fuel in 2002 (adjusted for inflation). The amount of the credit a taxpayer may claim is reduced by reason of grants, tax-exempt bonds, subsidized energy financing, and other credits, but the reduction cannot exceed 50 percent of the otherwise allowable credit.

The credit is a component of the general business credit,[96] allowing excess credits to be carried back one year and forward up to 20 years. The credit is also subject to the alternative minimum tax.

Facilities placed in service after 2008 that make refined coal used to produce steam

For refined coal facilities placed in service after 2008, the requirement that the qualified refined coal fuel sell at a price at least 50 percent greater than the price of the feedstock coal does not apply. However, to be credit-eligible, refined coal produced by such facilities must reduce by 40 percent (not 20 percent) the amount by which refined coal must reduce, when burned, emissions of either sulfur dioxide or mercury com-

---

[96] Sec. 38(b)(8).

pared to the emissions released by the feedstock coal or comparable coal predominantly available in the marketplace as of January 1, 2003.

Refined coal that is steel industry fuel

Each barrel-of-oil equivalent (defined as 5.8 million British thermal units) of steel industry fuel produced at a qualified facility during the credit period receives a $2 credit (adjusted for inflation using 1992 as the base year; $2.87 for 2010). A qualified facility is any facility capable of producing steel industry fuel (or any modification to a facility making it so capable) that is placed in service before January 1, 2010. For facilities capable of producing steel industry fuel on or before October 1, 2008, the credit is available for fuel produced and sold on or after such date and before January 1, 2010. For facilities placed in service or modified to produce steel industry fuel after October 1, 2008, the credit period begins on the placed-in-service or modification date and ends one year after such date or December 31, 2009, whichever is later.

Steel industry fuel is defined as a fuel produced through a process of liquefying coal waste sludge, distributing the liquefied product on coal, and using the resulting mixture as a feedstock for the manufacture of coke. Coal waste sludge includes tar decanter sludge and related byproducts of the coking process.

Explanation of Provision

The provision extends for two years (through December 31, 2011) the placed-in-service period for new refined coal facilities other than refined coal facilities that produce steel industry fuel.

Effective Date

The modifications to the placed-in-service period are effective on the date of enactment.

[Law at ¶5105. CCH Explanation at ¶550.]

[¶10,190] Act Sec. 703. New energy efficient home credit

Joint Committee on Taxation (J.C.T. Rep. No. JCX-55-10)

[Code Sec. 45L]

Present Law

The Code provides a credit to an eligible contractor for each qualified new energy-efficient home that is constructed by the eligible contractor and acquired by a person from such eligible contractor for use as a residence during the taxable year. To qualify as a new energy-efficient home, the home must be: (1) a dwelling located in the United States, (2) substantially completed after August 8, 2005, and (3) certified in accordance with guidance prescribed by the Secretary to have a projected level of annual heating and cooling energy consumption that meets the standards for either a 30-percent or 50-percent reduction in energy usage, compared to a comparable dwelling constructed in accordance with the standards of chapter 4 of the 2003 International Energy Conservation Code as in effect (including supplements) on August 8, 2005, and any applicable Federal minimum efficiency standards for equipment. With respect to homes that meet the 30-percent standard, one-third of such 30-percent savings must come from the building envelope, and with respect to homes that meet the 50-percent standard, one-fifth of such 50-percent savings must come from the building envelope.

Manufactured homes that conform to Federal manufactured home construction and safety standards are eligible for the credit provided all the criteria for the credit are met. The eligible contractor is the person who constructed the home, or in the case of a manufactured home, the producer of such home.

The credit equals $1,000 in the case of a new home that meets the 30-percent standard and $2,000 in the case of a new home that meets the 50-percent standard. Only manufactured homes are eligible for the $1,000 credit.

In lieu of meeting the standards of chapter 4 of the 2003 International Energy Conservation Code, manufactured homes certified by a method prescribed by the Administrator of the Environmental Protection Agency under the Energy Star Labeled Homes program are eligible for the $1,000 credit provided criteria (1) and (2), above, are met.

The credit applies to homes that are purchased prior to January 1, 2010. The credit is part of the general business credit.

Explanation of Provision

The provision extends the credit to homes that are purchased prior to January 1, 2012.

Effective Date

The provision applies to homes acquired after December 31, 2009.

[Law at ¶5135. CCH Explanation at ¶538.]

[¶ 10,200] Act Sec. 704. Excise tax credits and outlay payments for alternative fuel and alternative fuel mixtures

Joint Committee on Taxation (J.C.T. REP. NO. JCX-55-10)

[Code Secs. 6426 and 6427(e)]

Present Law

The Code provides two per-gallon excise tax credits with respect to alternative fuel: the alternative fuel credit, and the alternative fuel mixture credit. For this purpose, the term "alternative fuel" means liquefied petroleum gas, P Series fuels (as defined by the Secretary of Energy under 42 U.S.C. sec. 13211(2)), compressed or liquefied natural gas, liquefied hydrogen, liquid fuel derived from coal through the Fischer-Tropsch process ("coal-to-liquids"), compressed or liquified gas derived from biomass, or liquid fuel derived from biomass. Such term does not include ethanol, methanol, or biodiesel.

For coal-to-liquids produced after September 30, 2009 through December 30, 2009, the fuel must be certified as having been derived from coal produced at a gasification facility that separates and sequesters 50 percent of such facility's total carbon dioxide emissions. The sequestration percentage increases to 75 percent for fuel produced after December 30, 2009.

The alternative fuel credit is allowed against section 4041 liability, and the alternative fuel mixture credit is allowed against section 4081 liability. Neither credit is allowed unless the taxpayer is registered with the Secretary. The alternative fuel credit is 50 cents per gallon of alternative fuel or gasoline gallon equivalents[97] of nonliquid alternative fuel sold by the taxpayer for use as a motor fuel in a motor vehicle or motorboat, sold for use in aviation or so used by the taxpayer.

The alternative fuel mixture credit is 50 cents per gallon of alternative fuel used in producing an alternative fuel mixture for sale or use in a trade or business of the taxpayer. An "alternative fuel mixture" is a mixture of alternative fuel and taxable fuel that contains at least 1/10 of one percent taxable fuel. The mixture must be sold by the taxpayer producing such mixture to any person for use as a fuel, or used by the taxpayer producing the mixture as a fuel. The credits generally expired after December 31, 2009 (September 30, 2014 for liquefied hydrogen).

A person may file a claim for payment equal to the amount of the alternative fuel credit and alternative fuel mixture credits. These payment provisions generally also expired after December 31, 2009. With respect to liquefied hydrogen, the payment provisions expire after September 30, 2014. The alternative fuel credit and alternative fuel mixture credit must first be applied to excise tax liability for special and alternative fuels, and any excess credit may be taken as a payment.

Explanation of Provision

The provision extends the alternative fuel credit, alternative fuel mixture credit, and related payment provisions, for two additional years (through December 31, 2011). For purposes of the alternative fuel credit, alternative fuel mixture credit and related payment provisions, the provision excludes fuel (including lignin, wood residues, or spent pulping liquors) derived from the production of paper or pulp.

In light of the retroactive nature of the provision, the provision creates a special rule to address claims regarding excise credits and claims for payment associated with periods occurring during 2010. In particular the provision directs the Secretary to issue guidance within 30 days of the date of enactment. Such guidance is to provide for a one-time submission of claims covering periods occurring during 2010. The guidance is to provide for a 180-day period for the submission of such claims (in such manner as prescribed by the Secretary) to begin no later than 30 days after such guidance is issued. Such claims shall be paid by the Secretary of the Treasury not later than 60 days after receipt. If the claim is not paid within 60 days of the date of the filing, the claim shall be paid with interest from such date determined by using the overpayment rate and method under section 6621 of such Code.

Effective Date

The provision is effective for fuel sold or used after December 31, 2009.

[Law at ¶ 5810, ¶ 5815 and ¶ 7050. CCH Explanation at ¶ 544.]

---

[97] "Gasoline gallon equivalent" means, with respect to any nonliquid alternative fuel (for example, compressed natural gas), the amount of such fuel having a Btu (British thermal unit) content of 124,800 (higher heating value).

[¶10,210] Act Sec. 705. Special rule for sales or dispositions to implement FERC or state electric restructuring policy for qualified electric utilities

Joint Committee on Taxation (J.C.T. REP. NO. JCX-55-10)

[Code Sec. 451(i)]

Present Law

A taxpayer selling property generally recognizes gain to the extent the sales price (and any other consideration received) exceeds the seller's basis in the property. The recognized gain is subject to current income tax unless the gain is deferred or not recognized under a special tax provision.

One such special tax provision permits taxpayers to elect to recognize gain from qualifying electric transmission transactions ratably over an eight-year period beginning in the year of sale if the amount realized from such sale is used to purchase exempt utility property within the applicable period[98] (the "reinvestment property").[99] If the amount realized exceeds the amount used to purchase reinvestment property, any realized gain is recognized to the extent of such excess in the year of the qualifying electric transmission transaction.

A qualifying electric transmission transaction is the sale or other disposition of property used by a qualified electric utility to an independent transmission company prior to January 1, 2010. A qualified electric utility is defined as an electric utility, which as of the date of the qualifying electric transmission transaction, is vertically integrated in that it is both (1) a transmitting utility (as defined in the Federal Power Act)[100] with respect to the transmission facilities to which the election applies, and (2) an electric utility (as defined in the Federal Power Act).[101]

In general, an independent transmission company is defined as: (1) an independent transmission provider[102] approved by the Federal Energy Regulatory Commission ("FERC"); (2) a person (i) who the FERC determines under section 203 of the Federal Power Act (or by declaratory order) is not a "market participant" and (ii) whose transmission facilities are placed under the operational control of a FERC-approved independent transmission provider no later than four years after the close of the taxable year in which the transaction occurs; or (3) in the case of facilities subject to the jurisdiction of the Public Utility Commission of Texas, (i) a person which is approved by that Commission as consistent with Texas State law regarding an independent transmission organization, or (ii) a political subdivision, or affiliate thereof, whose transmission facilities are under the operational control of an organization described in (i).

Exempt utility property is defined as: (1) property used in the trade or business of generating, transmitting, distributing, or selling electricity or producing, transmitting, distributing, or selling natural gas, or (2) stock in a controlled corporation whose principal trade or business consists of the activities described in (1). Exempt utility property does not include any property that is located outside of the United States.

If a taxpayer is a member of an affiliated group of corporations filing a consolidated return, the reinvestment property may be purchased by any member of the affiliated group (in lieu of the taxpayer).

---

[98] The applicable period for a taxpayer to reinvest the proceeds is four years after the close of the taxable year in which the qualifying electric transmission transaction occurs.

[99] Sec. 451(i).

[100] Sec. 3(23), 16 U.S.C. 796, defines "transmitting utility" as any electric utility, qualifying cogeneration facility, qualifying small power production facility, or Federal power marketing agency which owns or operates electric power transmission facilities which are used for the sale of electric energy at wholesale.

[101] Sec. 3(22), 16 U.S.C. 796, defines "electric utility" as any person or State agency (including any municipality) which sells electric energy; such term includes the Tennessee Valley Authority, but does not include any Federal power marketing agency.

[102] For example, a regional transmission organization, an independent system operator, or an independent transmission company.

Explanation of Provision

The provision extends the treatment under the present-law deferral provision to sales or dispositions by a qualified electric utility that occur prior to January 1, 2012.

Effective Date

The extension provision applies to dispositions after December 31, 2009.

[Law at ¶ 5360. CCH Explanation at ¶ 554.]

[¶ 10,220] Act Sec. 706. Suspension of limitation on percentage depletion for oil and gas from marginal wells

Joint Committee on Taxation (J.C.T. REP. NO. JCX-55-10)

[Code Sec. 613A]

Present Law

The Code permits taxpayers to recover their investments in oil and gas wells through depletion deductions. Two methods of depletion are currently allowable under the Code: (1) the cost depletion method, and (2) the percentage depletion method.[103] Under the cost depletion method, the taxpayer deducts that portion of the adjusted basis of the depletable property which is equal to the ratio of units sold from that property during the taxable year to the number of units remaining as of the end of taxable year plus the number of units sold during the taxable year. Thus, the amount recovered under cost depletion may never exceed the taxpayer's basis in the property.

The Code generally limits the percentage depletion method for oil and gas properties to independent producers and royalty owners.[104] Generally, under the percentage depletion method, 15 percent of the taxpayer's gross income from an oil- or gas-producing property is allowed as a deduction in each taxable year.[105] The amount deducted generally may not exceed 100 percent of the net income from that property in any year (the "net-income limitation").[106] The 100-percent net-income limitation for marginal production has been suspended for taxable years beginning before January 1, 2010.

Marginal production is defined as domestic crude oil and natural gas production from stripper well property or from property substantially all of the production from which during the calendar year is heavy oil. Stripper well property is property from which the average daily production is 15 barrel equivalents or less, determined by dividing the average daily production of domestic crude oil and domestic natural gas from producing wells on the property for the calendar year by the number of wells. Heavy oil is domestic crude oil with a weighted average gravity of 20 degrees API or less (corrected to 60 degrees Fahrenheit).[107]

Explanation of Provision

The provision extends the suspension of the 100-percent net-income limitation for marginal production for two years (to apply to tax years beginning before January 1, 2012).

Effective Date

The provision is effective for taxable years beginning after December 31, 2009.

[Law at ¶ 5405. CCH Explanation at ¶ 552.]

---

[103] Secs. 611-613.
[104] Sec. 613A.
[105] Sec. 613A(c).
[106] Sec. 613(a).

[107] The American Petroleum Institute gravity, or API gravity, is a measure of how heavy or light a petroleum liquid is compared to water.

[¶10,230] Act Sec. 707. Extension of grants for specified energy property in lieu of tax credits

Joint Committee on Taxation (J.C.T. Rep. No. JCX-55-10)

[Act Sec. 707]

Present Law

Renewable electricity production credit

An income tax credit is allowed for the production of electricity from qualified energy resources at qualified facilities (the "renewable electricity production credit").[108] Qualified energy resources comprise wind, closed-loop biomass, open-loop biomass, geothermal energy, solar energy, small irrigation power, municipal solid waste, qualified hydropower production, and marine and hydrokinetic renewable energy. Qualified facilities are, generally, facilities that generate electricity using qualified energy resources. To be eligible for the credit, electricity produced from qualified energy resources at qualified facilities must be sold by the taxpayer to an unrelated person.

Summary of Credit for Electricity Produced from Certain Renewable Resources		
Eligible electricity production activity (sec. 45)	Credit amount for 2010[1] (cents per kilowatt-hour)	Expiration[2]
Wind	2.2	December 31, 2012
Closed-loop biomass	2.2	December 31, 2013
Open-loop biomass (including agricultural livestock waste nutrient facilities)	1.1	December 31, 2013
Geothermal	2.2	December 31, 2013
Solar (pre-2006 facilities only)	2.2	December 31, 2005
Small irrigation power	1.1	December 31, 2013
Municipal solid waste (including landfill gas facilities and trash combustion facilities)	1.1	December 31, 2013
Qualified hydropower	1.1	December 31, 2013
Marine and hydrokinetic	1.1	December 31, 2013

[1] In general, the credit is available for electricity produced during the first 10 years after a facility has been placed in service.
[2] Expires for property placed in service after this date.

Energy credit

An income tax credit is also allowed for certain energy property placed in service. Qualifying property includes certain fuel cell property, solar property, geothermal power production property, small wind energy property, combined heat and power system property, and geothermal heat pump property.[109]

---

[108] Sec. 45. In addition to the renewable electricity production credit, section 45 also provides income tax credits for the production of Indian coal and refined coal at qualified facilities.

[109] Sec. 48.

Summary of Energy Investment Tax Credit			
	Credit rate	Maximum credit	Expiration
Energy credit (sec. 48) Equipment to produce a geothermal deposit	10%	None	None
Equipment to use ground or ground water for heating or cooling	10%	None	December 31, 2016
Microturbine property (< 2 Mw electrical generation power plants of >26% efficiency)	10%	$200 per Kw of capacity	December 31, 2016
Combined heat and power property (simultaneous production of electrical/ mechanical power and useful heat > 60% efficiency)	10%	None	December 31, 2016
Solar electric or solar hot water property	30% (10% after December 31, 2016)	None	None
Fuel cell property (generates electricity through electrochemical process)	30%	$1,500 for each 1/2 Kw of capacity	December 31, 2016
Small (<100 Kw capacity) wind electrical generation property	30%	None	December 31, 2016

Election to claim energy credit in lieu of renewable electricity production credit

A taxpayer may make an irrevocable election to have certain property which is part of a qualified renewable electricity production facility be treated as energy property eligible for a 30 percent investment credit under section 48. For this purpose, qualified facilities are facilities otherwise eligible for the renewable electricity production credit with respect to which no credit under section 45 has been allowed. A taxpayer electing to treat a facility as energy property may not claim the renewable electricity production credit. The eligible basis for the investment credit for taxpayers making this election is the basis of the depreciable (or amortizable) property that would comprise a facility capable of generating electricity eligible for the renewable electricity production credit.

Grants in lieu of credits

The Secretary of the Treasury is authorized to provide a grant to each person who places in service depreciable property that is either (1) part of a qualified renewable electricity production facility or (2) qualifying property otherwise eligible for the energy credit. In general, the grant amount is 30 percent of the basis of the qualified property. For qualified microturbine, combined heat and power system, and geothermal heat pump property, the amount is 10 percent of the basis of the property. Otherwise eligible property must be placed in service in calendar years 2009 or 2010, or its construction must begin during that period and must be completed prior to 2013 (in the case of wind facility property), 2014 (in the case of other renewable power facility property eligible for credit under section 45), or 2017 (in the case of any specified energy property described in section 48).

The grant provision mimics the operation of the energy credit. For example, the amount of the grant is not includable in gross income. However, the basis of the property is reduced by 50 percent of the amount of the grant. In addition, some or all of each grant is subject to recapture if the grant-eligible property is disposed of by the grant recipient within five years of being placed in service.

Under the provision, if a grant is paid, no renewable electricity credit or energy credit may be claimed with respect to the grant-eligible property. In general, tax-exempt entities are not eligible to receive a grant. No grant may be made unless the application for the grant has been received before October 1, 2011.

Description of Proposal

The proposal extends the Secretary's authority to provide grants in lieu of credits for one year (through 2011). Otherwise eligible property must thus be placed in service in calendar years 2009, 2010, or 2011, or its construction must begin during that period and must be completed prior to 2013 (in the case of wind facility property), 2014 (in the case of other renewable power facility property eligible for credit under section 45), or 2017 (in the case of any specified energy property described in section 48).

Effective Date

The proposal is effective on the date of enactment.

[Law at ¶ 7055. CCH Explanation at ¶ 540.]

[¶ 10,240] Act Sec. 708. Extension of provisions related to alcohol used as fuel

Joint Committee on Taxation (J.C.T. Rep. No. JCX-55-10)

[Code Secs. 40, 6426 and 6427(e)]

Present Law

Sections 40, 6426 and 6427(e) provide per-gallon tax incentives for the sale, use and production of alcohol fuel and alcohol fuel mixtures. The incentives for alcohol generally do not apply after December 31, 2010. For cellulosic biofuel (discussed infra), the incentive is unavailable after December 31, 2012.

"Alcohol" includes methanol and ethanol, and the alcohol gallon equivalent of ethyl tertiary butyl ether, or other ethers produced from such alcohol. It does not include alcohol produced from petroleum, natural gas, or coal, or any alcohol with a proof of less than 150 (190 proof for purposes of the credit taken under 6426 or payment under section 6427). Denaturants (additives that make the alcohol unfit for human consumption) are disregarded for purposes of determining proof. However, denaturants are taken into account in determining the volume of alcohol eligible for the per-gallon incentive. In calculating alcohol volume, denaturants cannot exceed two percent of volume.

The section 40 alcohol fuels credit is an income tax credit comprised of four components: (1) the alcohol mixture credit, (2) the alcohol credit, (3) the small ethanol producer credit, and (4) the cellulosic biofuel producer credit. Sections 6426 and 6427(e) pertain to alcohol fuel mixtures only.

Alcohol mixture credits and payments

The alcohol fuel mixture credit may be taken as part of the section 40 income tax credit, the section 6426 excise tax credit, or as a payment under section 6427. For section 40, an alcohol fuel mixture is a mixture of alcohol and gasoline or alcohol and a special fuel. Since the excise tax credit is taken against the liability for taxable fuels (gasoline, kerosene, or diesel), for purposes of the excise tax payments and credits, an alcohol fuel mixture is a mixture of alcohol and a taxable fuel.

The fuel must be either sold for use as a fuel to another person or used as fuel in the mixture producer's trade or business. The addition of denaturants does not constitute production of a mixture. The credit is allowed only for the gallons of alcohol used to produce the mixture. For alcohol that is ethanol, the amount of the incentive is 45 cents per gallon. For other alcohol, the incentive is generally 60 cents per gallon.

The alcohol mixture credit is most often taken as an excise tax credit or payment. Persons who blend alcohol with gasoline, diesel fuel, or kerosene to produce an alcohol fuel mixture must pay tax on the volume of alcohol in the mixture when the mixture is sold or removed. The alcohol fuel mixture credit must first be taken to reduce excise tax liability for gasoline, diesel fuel or kerosene. Any excess credit may be taken as a payment or income tax credit.

Alcohol credit (straight or "neat" alcohol)

The second component of the section 40 income tax credit is the alcohol credit. The credit is available for alcohol (not in a mixture) that is either (1) used as a fuel in the taxpayer's trade or business, or (2) sold at retail and placed in the fuel tank of the retail buyer. The credit cannot be claimed for alcohol bought at retail, even if the buyer uses it as a fuel in a trade or business. This credit is not available as an excise tax credit or payment.

Small ethanol producer credit

The third component of the section 40 income tax credit is the small ethanol producer credit. It is in addition to the credits described above and is an extra 10 cents per gallon available for up to 15 million gallons of qualified ethanol fuel production for any tax year. The 15 million gallon limitation is waived for ethanol that is cellulosic ethanol. The credit is available to eligible small ethanol producers, defined as producers who have an annual productive capacity of not more than 60 million gallons of any type of alcohol. Qualified ethanol fuel production is ethanol produced and sold by such producer to another person (a) for use by such other person in the production of a qualified alcohol fuel mixture in such person's trade or business (other than casual off-farm production), (b) for use by such other person as a fuel in a trade or business, or (c) who sells such ethanol at retail to another person and places such ethanol in the fuel tank of such other person. Qualified ethanol fuel production also includes use or sale by the producer for any purpose described in (a), (b), or (c). A cooperative may pass through the small ethanol producer credit to its patrons. The small ethanol producer credit is not available as an excise tax credit or payment.

Cellulosic biofuel producer credit

The cellulosic biofuel producer credit is a nonrefundable income tax credit for each gallon of qualified cellulosic fuel production of the producer for the taxable year. The amount of the credit per gallon is $1.01, except in the case of cellulosic biofuel that is alcohol. In the case of cellulosic biofuel that is alcohol, the $1.01 credit amount is reduced by (1) the credit amount applicable for such alcohol under the alcohol mixture credit as in effect at the time cellulosic biofuel is produced and (2) in the case of cellulosic biofuel that is also ethanol, the credit amount for small ethanol producers as in effect at the time the cellulosic biofuel fuel is produced. The reduction applies regardless of whether the producer claims the alcohol mixture credit or small ethanol producer credit with respect to the cellulosic alcohol. When the alcohol mixture credit and small ethanol producer credit expire after December 31, 2010, cellulosic biofuel that is alcohol is entitled to the $1.01 without reduction.

Duties on ethanol

Heading 9901.00.50 of the Harmonized Tariff Schedule of the United States imposes a cumulative general duty of 14.27 cents per liter (approximately 54 cents per gallon) on imports of ethyl alcohol, and any mixture containing ethyl alcohol, if used as a fuel or in producing a mixture to be used as a fuel, that are entered into the United States prior to January 1, 2011. Heading 9901.00.52 of the Harmonized Tariff Schedule of the United States imposes a general duty of 5.99 cents per liter on imports of ethyl tertiary-butyl ether, and any mixture containing ethyl tertiary-butyl ether, that are entered into the United States prior to January 1, 2011.

Explanation of Provision

Extension of income tax credit

The provision extends the present-law income tax credit for alcohol fuels (other than the cellulosic biofuel producer credit) an additional year, through December 31, 2011.

Extension of excise tax credit and outlay payment provisions for alcohol used as a fuel

The provision extends the present-law excise tax credit and outlay payments for alcohol fuel mixtures for an additional year, through December 31, 2011.

Extension of additional duties on ethanol

The provision extends the present-law duties on ethanol and ethyl tertiary butyl ether for an additional year, through December 31, 2011.

Effective Date

The extension of the income tax credit is effective for periods after December 31, 2010. The extension of excise tax credit for alcohol fuel mixtures applies to periods after December 31, 2010. The extension of the payment provisions for alcohol fuel mixtures apply to sales and uses after December 31, 2010. The extension of additional duties on ethanol takes effect on January 1, 2011.

[Law at ¶5090, ¶5810 and ¶5815. CCH Explanation at ¶546.]

[¶10,250] Act Sec. 709. Energy efficient appliance credit

Joint Committee on Taxation (J.C.T. Rep. No. JCX-55-10)

[Code Sec. 45M]

Present Law

In general

A credit is allowed for the eligible production of certain energy-efficient dishwashers, clothes washers, and refrigerators. The credit is part of the general business credit.

The credits are as follows:

Dishwashers

$45 in the case of a dishwasher that is manufactured in calendar year 2008 or 2009 that uses no more than 324 kilowatt hours per year and 5.8 gallons per cycle, and

$75 in the case of a dishwasher that is manufactured in calendar year 2008, 2009, or 2010 and that uses no more than 307 kilowatt hours per year and 5.0 gallons per cycle (5.5 gallons per cycle for dishwashers designed for greater than 12 place settings).

Clothes washers

$75 in the case of a residential top-loading clothes washer manufactured in calendar year 2008 that meets or exceeds a 1.72 modified energy factor and does not exceed a 8.0 water consumption factor, and

$125 in the case of a residential top-loading clothes washer manufactured in calendar year 2008 or 2009 that meets or exceeds a 1.8 modified energy factor and does not exceed a 7.5 water consumption factor,

$150 in the case of a residential or commercial clothes washer manufactured in calendar year 2008, 2009, or 2010 that meets or exceeds a 2.0 modified energy factor and does not exceed a 6.0 water consumption factor, and

$250 in the case of a residential or commercial clothes washer manufactured in calendar year 2008, 2009, or 2010 that meets or exceeds a 2.2 modified energy factor and does not exceed a 4.5 water consumption factor.

Refrigerators

$50 in the case of a refrigerator manufactured in calendar year 2008 that consumes at least 20 percent but not more than 22.9 percent less kilowatt hours per year than the 2001 energy conservation standards,

$75 in the case of a refrigerator that is manufactured in calendar year 2008 or 2009 that consumes at least 23 percent but not more than 24.9 percent less kilowatt hours per year than the 2001 energy conservation standards,

$100 in the case of a refrigerator that is manufactured in calendar year 2008, 2009, or 2010 that consumes at least 25 percent but not more than 29.9 percent less kilowatt hours per year than the 2001 energy conservation standards, and

$200 in the case of a refrigerator manufactured in calendar year 2008, 2009, or 2010 that consumes at least 30 percent less energy than the 2001 energy conservation standards.

Definitions

A dishwasher is any residential dishwasher subject to the energy conservation standards established by the Department of Energy. A refrigerator must be an automatic defrost refrigerator-freezer with an internal volume of at least 16.5 cubic feet to qualify for the credit. A clothes washer is any residential clothes washer, including a residential style coin operated washer, that satisfies the relevant efficiency standard.

The term "modified energy factor" means the modified energy factor established by the Department of Energy for compliance with the Federal energy conservation standard.

The term "gallons per cycle" means, with respect to a dishwasher, the amount of water, expressed in gallons, required to complete a normal cycle of a dishwasher.

The term "water consumption factor" means, with respect to a clothes washer, the quotient of the total weighted per-cycle water consumption divided by the cubic foot (or liter) capacity of the clothes washer.

Other rules

Appliances eligible for the credit include only those produced in the United States and that exceed the average amount of U.S. production from the two prior calendar years for each category of appliance. The aggregate credit amount allowed with respect to a taxpayer for all taxable years beginning after December 31, 2007 may not exceed $75 million, with the exception that the $200 refrigerator credit and the $250 clothes washer credit are not limited. Additionally, the credit allowed in a taxable year for all appliances may not exceed two percent of the average annual gross receipts of the taxpayer for the three taxable years preceding the taxable year in which the credit is determined.

Explanation of Provision

The provision extends the credit for one year, for appliances manufactured in 2011, and changes the aggregate credit limitation to permit up to $25 million in credits to be claimed per manufacturer for appliances manufactured in 2011. Additionally, the provision changes the two percent gross receipts limitation on the credit to four percent. The credit modifies the standards and credit amounts as follows:

Dishwashers

$25 in the case of a dishwasher which is manufactured in calendar year 2011 and which uses no more than 307 kilowatt hours per year and 5.0 gallons per cycle (5.5 gallons per cycle for dishwashers designed for greater than 12 place settings),

$50 in the case of a dishwasher which is manufactured in calendar year 2011 and which uses no more than 295 kilowatt hours per year and 4.25 gallons per cycle (4.75 gallons per cycle for dishwashers designed for greater than 12 place settings), and

$75 in the case of a dishwasher which is manufactured in calendar year 2011 and which uses no more than 280 kilowatt hours per year and 4 gallons per cycle (4.5 gallons per cycle for dishwashers designed for greater than 12 place settings).

Clothes washers

$175 in the case of a top-loading clothes washer manufactured in calendar year 2011 which meets or exceeds a 2.2 modified energy factor and does not exceed a 4.5 water consumption factor, and

$225 in the case of a clothes washer manufactured in calendar year 2011 which (1) is a top-loading clothes washer and which meets or exceeds a 2.4 modified energy factor and does not exceed a 4.2 water consumption factor, or (2) is a front-loading clothes washer and which meets or exceeds a 2.8 modified energy factor and does not exceed a 3.5 water consumption factor.

Refrigerators

$150 in the case of a refrigerator manufactured in calendar year 2011 which consumes at least 30 percent less energy than the 2001 energy conservation standards, and

$200 in the case of a refrigerator manufactured in calendar year 2011 which consumes at least 35 percent less energy than the 2001 energy conservation standards.

Effective Date

The provision applies to appliances produced after December 31, 2010. The provision related to the gross receipts limitation applies to taxable years beginning after December 31, 2010.

[Law at ¶5140. CCH Explanation at ¶542.]

[¶10,260] Act Sec. 710. Credit for nonbusiness energy property

Joint Committee on Taxation (J.C.T. Rep. No. JCX-55-10)

[Code Sec. 25C]

Present Law

In general

Section 25C provides a 30-percent credit for the purchase of qualified energy efficiency improvements to the envelope of existing homes. Additionally, section 25C provides a 30 percent credit for the purchase of (1) qualified natural gas, propane, or oil furnace or hot water boilers, (2) qualified energy efficient property, and (3) advanced main air circulating fans.

The credit applies to expenditures made after December 31, 2008, for property placed in service after December 31, 2008, and prior to January 1, 2011.[110] The aggregate amount of the credit allowed for a taxpayer for taxable years beginning in 2009 and 2010 is $1,500.

---

[110] With the exception of biomass fuel property, property placed in service after December 31, 2008 and prior to February 17, 2009 qualifies for the new 30 percent credit rate (and $1,500 aggregate cap) if it met the efficiency standards of prior law for property placed in service during 2009. Biomass fuel property placed in service at any point in 2009 is governed by the new efficiency standard.

Building envelope improvements

A qualified energy efficiency improvement is any energy efficiency building envelope component (1) that meets or exceeds the prescriptive criteria for such a component established by the 2000 International Energy Conservation Code[111] as supplemented and as in effect on August 8, 2005 (or, in the case of metal roofs with appropriate pigmented coatings, meets the Energy Star program requirements); (2) that is installed in or on a dwelling located in the United States and owned and used by the taxpayer as the taxpayer's principal residence; (3) the original use of which commences with the taxpayer; and (4) that reasonably can be expected to remain in use for at least five years. The credit is nonrefundable.

Building envelope components are: (1) insulation materials or systems which are specifically and primarily designed to reduce the heat loss or gain for a dwelling and which meet the prescriptive criteria for such material or system established by the 2009 International Energy Conservation Code, as such Code (including supplements) is in effect on the date of the enactment of the American Recovery and Reinvestment Tax Act of 2009 (February 17, 2009); (2) exterior windows (including skylights) and doors provided such component has a U-factor and a seasonal heat gain coefficient ("SHGC") of 0.3 or less; and (3) metal or asphalt roofs with appropriate pigmented coatings or cooling granules that are specifically and primarily designed to reduce the heat gain for a dwelling.

Other eligible property

Qualified natural gas, propane, or oil furnace or hot water boilers

A qualified natural gas, propane, or oil hot water boiler is a natural gas, propane, or oil hot water boiler with an annual fuel utilization efficiency rate of at least 90. A qualified natural gas or propane furnace is a natural gas or propane furnace with an annual fuel utilization efficiency rate of at least 95. A qualified oil furnace is an oil furnace with an annual fuel utilization efficiency rate of at least 90.

Qualified energy-efficient property

Qualified energy-efficient property is: (1) an electric heat pump water heater which yields an energy factor of at least 2.0 in the standard Department of Energy test procedure, (2) an electric heat pump which achieves the highest efficiency tier established by the Consortium for Energy Efficiency, as in effect on January 1, 2009,[112] (3) a central air conditioner which achieves the highest efficiency tier established by the Consortium for Energy Efficiency as in effect on Jan. 1, 2009,[113] (4) a natural gas, propane, or oil water heater which has an energy factor of at least 0.82 or thermal efficiency of at least 90 percent, and (5) biomass fuel property.

Biomass fuel property is a stove that burns biomass fuel to heat a dwelling unit located in the United States and used as a principal residence by the taxpayer, or to heat water for such dwelling unit, and that has a thermal efficiency rating of at least 75 percent as measured using a lower heating value. Biomass fuel is any plant-derived fuel available on a renewable or recurring basis, including agricultural crops and trees, wood and wood waste and residues (including wood pellets), plants (including aquatic plants), grasses, residues, and fibers.

Advanced main air circulating fan

An advanced main air circulating fan is a fan used in a natural gas, propane, or oil furnace and which has an annual electricity use of no more than two percent of the total annual energy use of the furnace (as determined in the standard Department of Energy test procedures).

Additional rules

The taxpayer's basis in the property is reduced by the amount of the credit. Special proration rules apply in the case of jointly owned property, condominiums, and tenant-stockholders in cooperative housing corporations. If less than 80 percent of the property is used for nonbusiness purposes, only that portion of expenditures that is used for nonbusiness purposes is taken into account.

---

[111] This reference to the 2000 International Energy Conservation Code is superseded by the additional requirements described in the paragraph below regarding building envelope components.

[112] These standards are a seasonal energy efficiency ratio ("SEER") greater than or equal to 15, an energy efficiency ratio ("EER") greater than or equal to 12.5, and heating seasonal performance factor ("HSPF") greater than or equal

to 8.5 for split heat pumps, and SEER greater than or equal to 14, EER greater than or equal to 12, and HSPF greater than or equal to 8.0 for packaged heat pumps.

[113] These standards are a SEER greater than or equal to 16 and EER greater than or equal to 13 for split systems, and SEER greater than or equal to 14 and EER greater than or equal to 12 for packaged systems.

Explanation of Provision

The provision extends the credits for one year but utilizes the credit structure and credit rates that existed prior to the enactment of the American Recovery and Reinvestment Act of 2009. The provision reinstates the rule that expenditures made from subsidized energy financing are not qualifying expenditures. Additionally, certain efficiency standards that were weakened in the American Recovery and Reinvestment Act are restored to their prior levels. Lastly, the provision provides that windows, skylights and doors that meet the Energy Star standards are qualified improvements.

The following describes the operation of the credit under the provision:

Section 25C provides a 10-percent credit for the purchase of qualified energy efficiency improvements to existing homes. A qualified energy efficiency improvement is any energy efficiency building envelope component (1) that meets or exceeds the prescriptive criteria for such a component established by the 2009 International Energy Conservation Code as such Code (including supplements) is in effect on the date of the enactment of the American Recovery and Reinvestment Tax Act of 2009 (February 17, 2009) (or, in the case of windows, skylights and doors, and metal roofs with appropriate pigmented coatings or asphalt roofs with appropriate cooling granules, meets the Energy Star program requirements); (2) that is installed in or on a dwelling located in the United States and owned and used by the taxpayer as the taxpayer's principal residence; (3) the original use of which commences with the taxpayer; and (4) that reasonably can be expected to remain in use for at least five years. The credit is nonrefundable.

Building envelope components are: (1) insulation materials or systems which are specifically and primarily designed to reduce the heat loss or gain for a dwelling and which meet the prescriptive criteria for such material or system established by the 2009 International Energy Conservation Code, as such Code (including supplements) is in effect on the date of the enactment of the American Recovery and Reinvestment Tax Act of 2009 (February 17, 2009); (2) exterior windows (including skylights) and

doors; and (3) metal or asphalt roofs with appropriate pigmented coatings or cooling granules that are specifically and primarily designed to reduce the heat gain for a dwelling.

Additionally, section 25C provides specified credits for the purchase of specific energy efficient property originally placed in service by the taxpayer during the taxable year. The allowable credit for the purchase of certain property is (1) $50 for each advanced main air circulating fan, (2) $150 for each qualified natural gas, propane, or oil furnace or hot water boiler, and (3) $300 for each item of qualified energy efficient property.

An advanced main air circulating fan is a fan used in a natural gas, propane, or oil furnace and which has an annual electricity use of no more than two percent of the total annual energy use of the furnace (as determined in the standard Department of Energy test procedures).

A qualified natural gas, propane, or oil furnace or hot water boiler is a natural gas, propane, or oil furnace or hot water boiler with an annual fuel utilization efficiency rate of at least 95.

Qualified energy-efficient property is: (1) an electric heat pump water heater which yields an energy factor of at least 2.0 in the standard Department of Energy test procedure, (2) an electric heat pump which achieves the highest efficiency tier established by the Consortium for Energy Efficiency, as in effect on January 1, 2009,[114] (3) a central air conditioner which achieves the highest efficiency tier established by the Consortium for Energy Efficiency as in effect on Jan. 1, 2009,[115] (4) a natural gas, propane, or oil water heater which has an energy factor of at least 0.82 or thermal efficiency of at least 90 percent, and (5) biomass fuel property.

Biomass fuel property is a stove that burns biomass fuel to heat a dwelling unit located in the United States and used as a principal residence by the taxpayer, or to heat water for such dwelling unit, and that has a thermal efficiency rating of at least 75 percent. Biomass fuel is any plant-derived fuel available on a renewable or recurring basis, including agricultural crops and trees, wood and wood waste and residues (in-

---

[114] These standards are a seasonal energy efficiency ratio ("SEER") greater than or equal to 15, an energy efficiency ratio ("EER") greater than or equal to 12.5, and heating seasonal performance factor ("HSPF") greater than or equal to 8.5 for split heat pumps, and SEER greater than or equal to 14, EER greater than or equal to 12, and HSPF greater than or equal to 8.0 for packaged heat pumps.

[115] These standards are a SEER greater than or equal to 16 and EER greater than or equal to 13 for split systems, and SEER greater than or equal to 14 and EER greater than or equal to 12 for packaged systems.

cluding wood pellets), plants (including aquatic plants), grasses, residues, and fibers.

Under section 25C, the maximum credit for a taxpayer for all taxable years is $500, and no more than $200 of such credit may be attributable to expenditures on windows.

The taxpayer's basis in the property is reduced by the amount of the credit. Special proration rules apply in the case of jointly owned property, condominiums, and tenant-stockholders in cooperative housing corporations. If less than 80 percent of the property is used for nonbusiness purposes, only that portion of expenditures that is used for nonbusiness purposes is taken into account.

For purposes of determining the amount of expenditures made by any individual with respect to any dwelling unit, expenditures which are made from subsidized energy financing are not taken into account. The term "subsidized energy financing" means financing provided under a Federal, State, or local program a principal purpose of which is to provide subsidized financing for projects designed to conserve or produce energy.

Effective Date

The provision applies to property placed in service after December 31. 2010.

[Law at ¶ 5040. CCH Explanation at ¶ 372.]

[¶ 10,270] Act Sec. 711. Alternative fuel vehicle refueling property

Joint Committee on Taxation (J.C.T. REP. No. JCX-55-10)

[Code Sec. 30C]

Present Law

Taxpayers may claim a 30-percent credit for the cost of installing qualified clean-fuel vehicle refueling property to be used in a trade or business of the taxpayer or installed at the principal residence of the taxpayer.[116] The credit may not exceed $30,000 per taxable year per location, in the case of qualified refueling property used in a trade or business and $1,000 per taxable year per location, in the case of qualified refueling property installed on property which is used as a principal residence.

For property placed in service in 2009 or 2010, the maximum credit available for business property is increased to $200,000 for qualified hydrogen refueling property and to $50,000 for other qualified refueling property. For nonbusiness property, the maximum credit is increased to $2,000 for refueling property other than hydrogen refueling property. In addition, during these years, the credit rate is increased from 30 percent to 50 percent for refueling property other than hydrogen refueling property.

Qualified refueling property is property (not including a building or its structural components) for the storage or dispensing of a clean-burning fuel or electricity into the fuel tank or battery of a motor vehicle propelled by such fuel or electricity, but only if the storage or dispensing of the fuel or electricity is at the point of delivery into the fuel tank or battery of the mo-

tor vehicle. The original use of such property must begin with the taxpayer.

Clean-burning fuels are any fuel at least 85 percent of the volume of which consists of ethanol, natural gas, compressed natural gas, liquefied natural gas, liquefied petroleum gas, or hydrogen. In addition, any mixture of biodiesel and diesel fuel, determined without regard to any use of kerosene and containing at least 20 percent biodiesel, qualifies as a clean fuel.

Credits for qualified refueling property used in a trade or business are part of the general business credit and may be carried back for one year and forward for 20 years. Credits for residential qualified refueling property cannot exceed for any taxable year the difference between the taxpayer's regular tax (reduced by certain other credits) and the taxpayer's tentative minimum tax. Generally, in the case of qualified refueling property sold to a tax-exempt entity, the taxpayer selling the property may claim the credit.

A taxpayer's basis in qualified refueling property is reduced by the amount of the credit. In addition, no credit is available for property used outside the United States or for which an election to expense has been made under section 179.

The credit is available for property placed in service after December 31, 2005, and (except in the case of hydrogen refueling property) before January 1, 2011. In the case of hydrogen refuel-

---

[116] Sec. 30C.

ing property, the property must be placed in service before January 1, 2015.

Explanation of Provision

The provision extends through 2011 the 30-percent credit for alternative fuel refueling property (other than hydrogen refueling property, the credit for which continues under pre-sent law through 2014), subject to the pre-2009 maximum credit amounts.

Effective Date

The provision is effective for property placed in service after December 31, 2010.

[Law at ¶5065. CCH Explanation at ¶548.]

[¶10,280] Act Sec. 721. Deduction for certain expenses of elementary and secondary school teachers

Joint Committee on Taxation (J.C.T. REP. No. JCX-55-10)

[Code Sec. 62]

Present Law

In general, ordinary and necessary business expenses are deductible. However, un-reimbursed employee business expenses generally are deductible only as an itemized deduction and only to the extent that the individual's total miscellaneous deductions (including employee business expenses) exceed two percent of adjusted gross income. With the exception of taxable years beginning in 2010, an individual's otherwise allowable itemized deductions may be further limited by the overall limitation on itemized deductions, which reduces itemized deductions for taxpayers with adjusted gross income in excess of a threshold amount. In addition, miscellaneous itemized deductions are not allowable under the alternative minimum tax.

Certain expenses of eligible educators are allowed as an above-the-line deduction. Specifically, for taxable years beginning prior to January 1, 2010, an above-the-line deduction is allowed for up to $250 annually of expenses paid or incurred by an eligible educator for books, supplies (other than nonathletic supplies for courses of instruction in health or physical education), computer equipment (including related software and services) and other equipment, and supplementary materials used by the eligible educator in the classroom.[117] To be eligible for this deduction, the expenses must be otherwise deductible under section 162 as a trade or business expense. A deduction is allowed only to the extent the amount of expenses exceeds the amount excludable from income under section 135 (relating to education savings bonds), 529(c)(1) (relating to qualified tuition programs), and section 530(d)(2) (relating to Coverdell education savings accounts).

An eligible educator is a kindergarten through grade twelve teacher, instructor, counselor, principal, or aide in a school for at least 900 hours during a school year. A school means any school that provides elementary education or secondary education, as determined under State law.

The above-the-line deduction for eligible educators is not allowed for taxable years beginning after December 31, 2009.

Explanation of Provision

The provision extends the deduction for eligible educator expenses for two years so that it is available for taxable years beginning before January 1, 2012.

Effective Date

The provision is effective for expenses incurred in taxable years beginning after December 31, 2009.

[Law at ¶5180. CCH Explanation at ¶327.]

---

[117] Sec. 62(a)(2)(D).

[¶10,290] Act Sec. 722. Deduction of state and local sales taxes

Joint Committee on Taxation (J.C.T. Rep. No. JCX-55-10)

[Code Sec. 164]

Present Law

For purposes of determining regular tax liability, an itemized deduction is permitted for certain State and local taxes paid, including individual income taxes, real property taxes, and personal property taxes. The itemized deduction is not permitted for purposes of determining a taxpayer's alternative minimum taxable income. For taxable years beginning in 2004-2009, at the election of the taxpayer, an itemized deduction may be taken for State and local general sales taxes in lieu of the itemized deduction provided under present law for State and local income taxes. As is the case for State and local income taxes, the itemized deduction for State and local general sales taxes is not permitted for purposes of determining a taxpayer's alternative minimum taxable income. Taxpayers have two options with respect to the determination of the sales tax deduction amount. Taxpayers may deduct the total amount of general State and local sales taxes paid by accumulating receipts showing general sales taxes paid. Alternatively, taxpayers may use tables created by the Secretary that show the allowable deduction. The tables are based on average consumption by taxpayers on a State-by-State basis taking into account number of dependents, modified adjusted gross income and rates of State and local general sales taxation. Taxpayers who live in more than one jurisdiction during the tax year are required to pro-rate the table amounts based on the time they live in each jurisdiction. Taxpayers who use the tables created by the Secretary may, in addition to the table amounts, deduct eligible general sales taxes paid with respect to the purchase of motor vehicles, boats and other items specified by the Secretary. Sales taxes for items that may be added to the tables are not reflected in the tables themselves.

The term "general sales tax" means a tax imposed at one rate with respect to the sale at retail of a broad range of classes of items. However, in the case of items of food, clothing, medical supplies, and motor vehicles, the fact that the tax does not apply with respect to some or all of such items is not taken into account in determining whether the tax applies with respect to a broad range of classes of items, and the fact that the rate of tax applicable with respect to some or all of such items is lower than the general rate of tax is not taken into account in determining whether the tax is imposed at one rate. Except in the case of a lower rate of tax applicable with respect to food, clothing, medical supplies, or motor vehicles, no deduction is allowed for any general sales tax imposed with respect to an item at a rate other than the general rate of tax. However, in the case of motor vehicles, if the rate of tax exceeds the general rate, such excess shall be disregarded and the general rate is treated as the rate of tax.

A compensating use tax with respect to an item is treated as a general sales tax, provided such tax is complementary to a general sales tax and a deduction for sales taxes is allowable with respect to items sold at retail in the taxing jurisdiction that are similar to such item.

Explanation of Provision

The provision allowing taxpayers to elect to deduct State and local sales taxes in lieu of State and local income taxes is extended for two years (through December 31, 2011).

Effective Date

The provision applies to taxable years beginning after December 31, 2009.

[Law at ¶5260. CCH Explanation at ¶326.]

[¶10,300] Act Sec. 723. Contributions of capital gain real property made for conservation purposes

Joint Committee on Taxation (J.C.T. REP. NO. JCX-55-10)

[Code Sec. 170]

Present Law

Charitable contributions generally

In general, a deduction is permitted for charitable contributions, subject to certain limitations that depend on the type of taxpayer, the property contributed, and the donee organization. The amount of deduction generally equals the fair market value of the contributed property on the date of the contribution. Charitable deductions are provided for income, estate, and gift tax purposes.[118]

In general, in any taxable year, charitable contributions by a corporation are not deductible to the extent the aggregate contributions exceed 10 percent of the corporation's taxable income computed without regard to net operating or capital loss carrybacks. For individuals, the amount deductible is a percentage of the taxpayer's contribution base, (i.e., taxpayer's adjusted gross income computed without regard to any net operating loss carryback). The applicable percentage of the contribution base varies depending on the type of donee organization and property contributed. Cash contributions by an individual taxpayer to public charities, private operating foundations, and certain types of private nonoperating foundations may not exceed 50 percent of the taxpayer's contribution base. Cash contributions to private foundations and certain other organizations generally may be deducted up to 30 percent of the taxpayer's contribution base.

In general, a charitable deduction is not allowed for income, estate, or gift tax purposes if the donor transfers an interest in property to a charity while also either retaining an interest in that property or transferring an interest in that property to a noncharity for less than full and adequate consideration. Exceptions to this general rule are provided for, among other interests, remainder interests in charitable remainder annuity trusts, charitable remainder unitrusts, and pooled income funds, present interests in the form of a guaranteed annuity or a fixed percentage of the annual value of the property, and qualified conservation contributions.

Capital gain property

Capital gain property means any capital asset or property used in the taxpayer's trade or business the sale of which at its fair market value, at the time of contribution, would have resulted in gain that would have been long-term capital gain. Contributions of capital gain property to a qualified charity are deductible at fair market value within certain limitations. Contributions of capital gain property to charitable organizations described in section 170(b)(1)(A) (e.g., public charities, private foundations other than private non-operating foundations, and certain governmental units) generally are deductible up to 30 percent of the taxpayer's contribution base. An individual may elect, however, to bring all these contributions of capital gain property for a taxable year within the 50-percent limitation category by reducing the amount of the contribution deduction by the amount of the appreciation in the capital gain property. Contributions of capital gain property to charitable organizations described in section 170(b)(1)(B) (e.g., private non-operating foundations) are deductible up to 20 percent of the taxpayer's contribution base.

For purposes of determining whether a taxpayer's aggregate charitable contributions in a taxable year exceed the applicable percentage limitation, contributions of capital gain property are taken into account after other charitable contributions. Contributions of capital gain property that exceed the percentage limitation may be carried forward for five years.

Qualified conservation contributions

Qualified conservation contributions are not subject to the "partial interest" rule, which generally bars deductions for charitable contributions of partial interests in property.[119] A qualified conservation contribution is a contribution of a qualified real property interest to a qualified organization exclusively for conservation purposes. A qualified real property interest is defined as: (1) the entire interest of the donor other than a qualified mineral interest; (2) a remainder interest; or (3) a restriction (granted in perpetuity) on the use that may be made of the

---

[118] Secs. 170, 2055, and 2522, respectively.

[119] Secs. 170(f)(3)(B)(iii) and 170(h).

real property. Qualified organizations include certain governmental units, public charities that meet certain public support tests, and certain supporting organizations. Conservation purposes include: (1) the preservation of land areas for outdoor recreation by, or for the education of, the general public; (2) the protection of a relatively natural habitat of fish, wildlife, or plants, or similar ecosystem; (3) the preservation of open space (including farmland and forest land) where such preservation will yield a significant public benefit and is either for the scenic enjoyment of the general public or pursuant to a clearly delineated Federal, State, or local governmental conservation policy; and (4) the preservation of an historically important land area or a certified historic structure.

Qualified conservation contributions of capital gain property are subject to the same limitations and carryover rules as other charitable contributions of capital gain property.

Special rule regarding contributions of capital gain real property for conservation purposes

In general

Under a temporary provision that is effective for contributions made in taxable years beginning after December 31, 2005,[120] the 30-percent contribution base limitation on contributions of capital gain property by individuals does not apply to qualified conservation contributions (as defined under present law). Instead, individuals may deduct the fair market value of any qualified conservation contribution to an organization described in section 170(b)(1)(A) to the extent of the excess of 50 percent of the contribution base over the amount of all other allowable charitable contributions. These contributions are not taken into account in determining the amount of other allowable charitable contributions.

Individuals are allowed to carry over any qualified conservation contributions that exceed the 50-percent limitation for up to 15 years.

For example, assume an individual with a contribution base of $100 makes a qualified conservation contribution of property with a fair market value of $80 and makes other charitable contributions subject to the 50-percent limitation of $60. The individual is allowed a deduction of $50 in the current taxable year for the non-conservation contributions (50 percent of the $100

contribution base) and is allowed to carry over the excess $10 for up to 5 years. No current deduction is allowed for the qualified conservation contribution, but the entire $80 qualified conservation contribution may be carried forward for up to 15 years.

Farmers and ranchers

In the case of an individual who is a qualified farmer or rancher for the taxable year in which the contribution is made, a qualified conservation contribution is allowable up to 100 percent of the excess of the taxpayer's contribution base over the amount of all other allowable charitable contributions.

In the above example, if the individual is a qualified farmer or rancher, in addition to the $50 deduction for non-conservation contributions, an additional $50 for the qualified conservation contribution is allowed and $30 may be carried forward for up to 15 years as a contribution subject to the 100-percent limitation.

In the case of a corporation (other than a publicly traded corporation) that is a qualified farmer or rancher for the taxable year in which the contribution is made, any qualified conservation contribution is allowable up to 100 percent of the excess of the corporation's taxable income (as computed under section 170(b)(2)) over the amount of all other allowable charitable contributions. Any excess may be carried forward for up to 15 years as a contribution subject to the 100-percent limitation.[121]

As an additional condition of eligibility for the 100 percent limitation, with respect to any contribution of property in agriculture or livestock production, or that is available for such production, by a qualified farmer or rancher, the qualified real property interest must include a restriction that the property remain generally available for such production. (There is no requirement as to any specific use in agriculture or farming, or necessarily that the property be used for such purposes, merely that the property remain available for such purposes.) Such additional condition does not apply to contributions made on or before August 17, 2006.

A qualified farmer or rancher means a taxpayer whose gross income from the trade or business of farming (within the meaning of section 2032A(e)(5)) is greater than 50 percent of the taxpayer's gross income for the taxable year.

---

[120] Sec. 170(b)(1)(E).

[121] Sec. 170(b)(2)(B).

Termination

The special rule regarding contributions of capital gain real property for conservation purposes does not apply to contributions made in taxable years beginning after December 31, 2009.[122]

Explanation of Provision

The Act extends the special rule regarding contributions of capital gain real property for conservation purposes for two years for contributions made in taxable years beginning before January 1, 2012.

Effective Date

The provision is effective for contributions made in taxable years beginning after December 31, 2009.

[Law at ¶5270. CCH Explanation at ¶353.]

[¶10,310] Act Sec. 724. Above-the-line deduction for qualified tuition and related expenses

Joint Committee on Taxation (J.C.T. REP. NO. JCX-55-10)

[Code Sec. 222]

Present Law

An individual is allowed an above-the-line deduction for qualified tuition and related expenses for higher education paid by the individual during the taxable year.[123] The term qualified tuition and related expenses is defined in the same manner as for the Hope and Lifetime Learning credits, and includes tuition and fees required for the enrollment or attendance of the taxpayer, the taxpayer's spouse, or any dependent of the taxpayer with respect to whom the taxpayer may claim a personal exemption, at an eligible institution of higher education for courses of instruction of such individual at such institution.[124] The expenses must be in connection with enrollment at an institution of higher education during the taxable year, or with an academic period beginning during the taxable year or during the first three months of the next taxable year. The deduction is not available for tuition and related expenses paid for elementary or secondary education.

The maximum deduction is $4,000 for an individual whose adjusted gross income for the taxable year does not exceed $65,000 ($130,000 in the case of a joint return), or $2,000 for other individuals whose adjusted gross income does not exceed $80,000 ($160,000 in the case of a joint return). No deduction is allowed for an individual whose adjusted gross income exceeds the relevant adjusted gross income limitations, for a married individual who does not file a joint return, or for an individual with respect to whom a personal exemption deduction may be claimed by another taxpayer for the taxable year. The deduction is not available for taxable years beginning after December 31, 2009.

The amount of qualified tuition and related expenses must be reduced by certain scholarships, educational assistance allowances, and other amounts paid for the benefit of such individual,[125] and by the amount of such expenses taken into account for purposes of determining any exclusion from gross income of: (1) income from certain U.S. savings bonds used to pay higher education tuition and fees; and (2) income from a Coverdell education savings account.[126] Additionally, such expenses must be reduced by the earnings portion (but not the return of principal) of distributions from a qualified tuition program if an exclusion under section 529 is claimed with respect to expenses eligible for the qualified tuition deduction. No deduction is allowed for any expense for which a deduction is otherwise allowed or with respect to an individual for whom a Hope or Lifetime Learning credit is elected for such taxable year.

Explanation of Provision

The provision extends the qualified tuition deduction for two years so that it is generally available for taxable years beginning before January 1, 2012.

Effective Date

The provision is effective for taxable years beginning after December 31, 2009.

[Law at ¶5310. CCH Explanation at ¶350.]

---

[122] Secs. 170(b)(1)(E)(vi) and 170(b)(2)(B)(iii).

[123] Sec. 222.

[124] The deduction generally is not available for expenses with respect to a course or education involving sports, games, or hobbies, and is not available for student activity fees, athletic fees, insurance expenses, or other expenses unrelated to an individual's academic course of instruction.

[125] Secs. 222(d)(1) and 25A(g)(2).

[126] Sec. 222(c). These reductions are the same as those that apply to the Hope and Lifetime Learning credits.

[¶10,320] Act Sec. 725. Tax-free distributions from individual retirement plans for charitable purposes

Joint Committee on Taxation (J.C.T. Rep. No. JCX-55-10)

[Code Sec. 408]

Present Law

In general

If an amount withdrawn from a traditional individual retirement arrangement ("IRA") or a Roth IRA is donated to a charitable organization, the rules relating to the tax treatment of withdrawals from IRAs apply to the amount withdrawn and the charitable contribution is subject to the normally applicable limitations on deductibility of such contributions. An exception applies in the case of a qualified charitable distribution.

Charitable contributions

In computing taxable income, an individual taxpayer who itemizes deductions generally is allowed to deduct the amount of cash and up to the fair market value of property contributed to the following entities: (1) a charity described in section 501(c)(3); (2) certain veterans' organizations, fraternal societies, and cemetery companies;[127] and (3) a Federal, State, or local governmental entity, but only if the contribution is made for exclusively public purposes.[128] The deduction also is allowed for purposes of calculating alternative minimum taxable income.

The amount of the deduction allowable for a taxable year with respect to a charitable contribution of property may be reduced depending on the type of property contributed, the type of charitable organization to which the property is contributed, and the income of the taxpayer.[129]

A taxpayer who takes the standard deduction (i.e., who does not itemize deductions) may not take a separate deduction for charitable contributions.[130]

A payment to a charity (regardless of whether it is termed a "contribution") in exchange for which the donor receives an economic benefit is not deductible, except to the extent that the donor can demonstrate, among other things, that the payment exceeds the fair market value of the benefit received from the charity. To facilitate distinguishing charitable contributions from purchases of goods or services from charities, present law provides that no charitable contribution deduction is allowed for a separate contribution of $250 or more unless the donor obtains a contemporaneous written acknowledgement of the contribution from the charity indicating whether the charity provided any good or service (and an estimate of the value of any such good or service provided) to the taxpayer in consideration for the contribution.[131] In addition, present law requires that any charity that receives a contribution exceeding $75 made partly as a gift and partly as consideration for goods or services furnished by the charity (a "quid pro quo" contribution) is required to inform the contributor in writing of an estimate of the value of the goods or services furnished by the charity and that only the portion exceeding the value of the goods or services may be deductible as a charitable contribution.[132]

Under present law, total deductible contributions of an individual taxpayer to public charities, private operating foundations, and certain types of private nonoperating foundations generally may not exceed 50 percent of the taxpayer's contribution base, which is the taxpayer's adjusted gross income for a taxable year (disregarding any net operating loss carryback). To the extent a taxpayer has not exceeded the 50-percent limitation, (1) contributions of capital gain property to public charities generally may be deducted up to 30 percent of the taxpayer's contribution base, (2) contributions of cash to private foundations and certain other charitable organizations generally may be deducted up to 30 percent of the taxpayer's contribution base, and (3) contributions of capital gain property to private foundations and certain other charitable organizations generally may be deducted up to 20 percent of the taxpayer's contribution base.

---

[127] Secs. 170(c)(3)-(5).
[128] Sec. 170(c)(1).
[129] Secs. 170(b) and (e).
[130] Sec. 170(a).
[131] Sec. 170(f)(8). For any contribution of a cash, check, or other monetary gift, no deduction is allowed unless the

donor maintains as a record of such contribution a bank record or written communication from the donee charity showing the name of the donee organization, the date of the contribution, and the amount of the contribution. Sec. 170(f)(17).
[132] Sec. 6115.

Contributions by individuals in excess of the 50-percent, 30-percent, and 20-percent limits generally may be carried over and deducted over the next five taxable years, subject to the relevant percentage limitations on the deduction in each of those years.

In general, a charitable deduction is not allowed for income, estate, or gift tax purposes if the donor transfers an interest in property to a charity (e.g., a remainder) while also either retaining an interest in that property (e.g., an income interest) or transferring an interest in that property to a noncharity for less than full and adequate consideration.[133] Exceptions to this general rule are provided for, among other interests, remainder interests in charitable remainder annuity trusts, charitable remainder unitrusts, and pooled income funds, and present interests in the form of a guaranteed annuity or a fixed percentage of the annual value of the property.[134] For such interests, a charitable deduction is allowed to the extent of the present value of the interest designated for a charitable organization.

IRA rules

Within limits, individuals may make deductible and nondeductible contributions to a traditional IRA. Amounts in a traditional IRA are includible in income when withdrawn (except to the extent the withdrawal represents a return of nondeductible contributions). Certain individuals also may make nondeductible contributions to a Roth IRA (deductible contributions cannot be made to Roth IRAs). Qualified withdrawals from a Roth IRA are excludable from gross income. Withdrawals from a Roth IRA that are not qualified withdrawals are includible in gross income to the extent attributable to earnings. Includible amounts withdrawn from a traditional IRA or a Roth IRA before attainment of age 59-1/2 are subject to an additional 10-percent early withdrawal tax, unless an exception applies. Under present law, minimum distributions are required to be made from tax-favored retirement arrangements, including IRAs. Minimum required distributions from a traditional IRA must generally begin by April 1 of the calendar year following the year in which the IRA owner attains age 70-1/2.[135]

If an individual has made nondeductible contributions to a traditional IRA, a portion of each distribution from an IRA is nontaxable until the total amount of nondeductible contributions has been received. In general, the amount of a distribution that is nontaxable is determined by multiplying the amount of the distribution by the ratio of the remaining nondeductible contributions to the account balance. In making the calculation, all traditional IRAs of an individual are treated as a single IRA, all distributions during any taxable year are treated as a single distribution, and the value of the contract, income on the contract, and investment in the contract are computed as of the close of the calendar year.

In the case of a distribution from a Roth IRA that is not a qualified distribution, in determining the portion of the distribution attributable to earnings, contributions and distributions are deemed to be distributed in the following order: (1) regular Roth IRA contributions; (2) taxable conversion contributions;[136] (3) nontaxable conversion contributions; and (4) earnings. In determining the amount of taxable distributions from a Roth IRA, all Roth IRA distributions in the same taxable year are treated as a single distribution, all regular Roth IRA contributions for a year are treated as a single contribution, and all conversion contributions during the year are treated as a single contribution.

Distributions from an IRA (other than a Roth IRA) are generally subject to withholding unless the individual elects not to have withholding apply.[137] Elections not to have withholding apply are to be made in the time and manner prescribed by the Secretary.

Qualified charitable distributions

Present law provides an exclusion from gross income for otherwise taxable IRA distributions from a traditional or a Roth IRA in the case of qualified charitable distributions.[138] The exclusion may not exceed $100,000 per taxpayer per taxable year. Special rules apply in determining the amount of an IRA distribution that is otherwise taxable. The otherwise applicable rules regarding taxation of IRA distributions and the deduction of charitable contributions continue to apply to distributions from an IRA that

---

[133] Secs. 170(f), 2055(e)(2), and 2522(c)(2).

[134] Sec. 170(f)(2).

[135] Minimum distribution rules also apply in the case of distributions after the death of a traditional or Roth IRA owner.

[136] Conversion contributions refer to conversions of amounts in a traditional IRA to a Roth IRA.

[137] Sec. 3405.

[138] Sec. 408(d)(8). The exclusion does not apply to distributions from employer-sponsored retirement plans, including SIMPLE IRAs and simplified employee pensions ("SEPs").

are not qualified charitable distributions. A qualified charitable distributions is taken into account for purposes of the minimum distribution rules applicable to traditional IRAs to the same extent the distribution would have been taken into account under such rules had the distribution not been directly distributed under the qualified charitable distribution provision. An IRA does not fail to qualify as an IRA as a result of qualified charitable distributions being made from the IRA.

A qualified charitable distribution is any distribution from an IRA directly by the IRA trustee to an organization described in section 170(b)(1)(A) (other than an organization described in section 509(a)(3) or a donor advised fund (as defined in section 4966(d)(2)). Distributions are eligible for the exclusion only if made on or after the date the IRA owner attains age 70-1/2 and only to the extent the distribution would be includible in gross income (without regard to this provision).

The exclusion applies only if a charitable contribution deduction for the entire distribution otherwise would be allowable (under present law), determined without regard to the generally applicable percentage limitations. Thus, for example, if the deductible amount is reduced because of a benefit received in exchange, or if a deduction is not allowable because the donor did not obtain sufficient substantiation, the exclusion is not available with respect to any part of the IRA distribution.

If the IRA owner has any IRA that includes nondeductible contributions, a special rule applies in determining the portion of a distribution that is includible in gross income (but for the qualified charitable distribution provision) and thus is eligible for qualified charitable distribution treatment. Under the special rule, the distribution is treated as consisting of income first, up to the aggregate amount that would be includible in gross income (but for the qualified charitable distribution provision) if the aggregate balance of all IRAs having the same owner were distributed during the same year. In determining the amount of subsequent IRA distributions includible in income, proper adjustments are to be made to reflect the amount treated as a qualified charitable distribution under the special rule.

Distributions that are excluded from gross income by reason of the qualified charitable distribution provision are not taken into account in determining the deduction for charitable contributions under section 170.

The exclusion for qualified charitable distributions applies to distributions made in taxable years beginning after December 31, 2005. Under present law, the exclusion does not apply to distributions made in taxable years beginning after December 31, 2009.

Explanation of Provision

The provision extends the exclusion for qualified charitable distributions to distributions made in taxable years beginning after December 31, 2009 and before January 1, 2012. The provision contains a special rule permitting taxpayers to elect (in such form and manner as the Secretary may prescribe) to have qualified charitable distributions made in January 2011 treated as having been made on December 31, 2010 for purposes of sections 408(a)(6), 408(b)(3), and 408(d)(8). Thus, a qualified charitable distribution made in January 2011 is permitted to be (1) treated as made in the taxpayer's 2010 taxable year and thus permitted to count against the 2010 $100,000 limitation on the exclusion, and (2) treated as made in the 2010 calendar year and thus permitted to be used to satisfy the taxpayer's minimum distribution requirement for 2010.

Effective Date

The provision is effective for distributions made in taxable years beginning after December 31, 2009.

[Law at ¶ 5355 and ¶ 7060. CCH Explanation at ¶ 352.]

[¶10,330] Act Sec. 726. Look-thru of certain regulated investment company stock in determining gross estate of nonresidents

Joint Committee on Taxation (J.C.T. REP. NO. JCX-55-10)

[Code Sec. 2105]

Present Law

The gross estate of a decedent who was a U.S. citizen or resident generally includes all property – real, personal, tangible, and intangible – wherever situated.[139] The gross estate of a nonresident non-citizen decedent, by contrast, generally includes only property that at the time of the decedent's death is situated within the United States.[140] Property within the United States generally includes debt obligations of U.S. persons, including the Federal government and State and local governments, but does not include either bank deposits or portfolio obligations the interest on which would be exempt from U.S. income tax under section 871.[141] Stock owned and held by a nonresident non-citizen generally is treated as property within the United States if the stock was issued by a domestic corporation.[142]

Treaties may reduce U.S. taxation of transfers of the estates of nonresident non-citizens. Under recent treaties, for example, U.S. tax generally may be eliminated except insofar as the property transferred includes U.S. real property or business property of a U.S. permanent establishment.

Although stock issued by a domestic corporation generally is treated as property within the United States, stock of a regulated investment company ("RIC") that was owned by a nonresident non-citizen is not deemed property within the United States in the proportion that, at the end of the quarter of the RIC's taxable year immediately before a decedent's date of death, the assets held by the RIC are debt obligations, deposits, or other property that would be treated as situated outside the United States if held directly by the estate (the "estate tax look-through rule for RIC stock").[143] This estate tax look-through rule for RIC stock does not apply to estates of decedents dying after December 31, 2009.

Explanation of Provision

The provision permits the estate tax look-through rule for RIC stock to apply to estates of decedents dying before January 1, 2012.

Effective Date

The provision is effective for decedents dying after December 31, 2009.

[Law at ¶5675. CCH Explanation at ¶386.]

[¶10,340] Act Sec. 727. Parity for exclusion from income for employer-provided mass transit and parking benefits

Joint Committee on Taxation (J.C.T. REP. NO. JCX-55-10)

[Code Sec. 132]

Present Law

In general

Qualified transportation fringe benefits provided by an employer are excluded from an employee's gross income for income tax pur-

poses and from an employee's wages for payroll tax purposes.[144] Qualified transportation fringe benefits include parking, transit passes, vanpool benefits, and qualified bicycle commuting reimbursements. No amount is includible in the income of an employee merely because the employer offers the employee a choice between

---

[139] Sec. 2031. The Economic Growth and Tax Relief Reconciliation Act of 2001 ("EGTRRA") repealed the estate tax for estates of decedents dying after December 31, 2009. EGTRRA, however, included a termination provision under which EGTRRA's rules, including estate tax repeal, do not apply to estates of decedents dying after December 31, 2010.

[140] Sec. 2103.

[141] Secs. 2104(c), 2105(b).

[142] Sec. 2104(a); Treas. Reg. sec. 20.2104-1(a)(5)).

[143] Sec. 2105(d).

[144] Secs. 132(f), 3121(b)(2), and 3306(b)(16) and 3401(a)(19).

cash and qualified transportation fringe benefits (other than a qualified bicycle commuting reimbursement). Qualified transportation fringe benefits also include a cash reimbursement by an employer to an employee. In the case of transit passes, however, a cash reimbursement is considered a qualified transportation fringe benefit only if a voucher or similar item which may be exchanged only for a transit pass is not readily available for direct distribution by the employer to the employee.

Prior to February 17, 2009, the amount that could be excluded as qualified transportation fringe benefits was limited to $100 per month in combined vanpooling and transit pass benefits and $175 per month in qualified parking benefits. All limits were adjusted annually for inflation, using 1998 as the base year (in 2009 the limits were $120 and $230, respectively). The

American Recovery and Reinvestment Act of 2009, however, temporarily increased the monthly exclusion for employer-provided vanpool and transit pass benefits to the same level as the exclusion for employer-provided parking ($230 for 2010). The American Recovery and Reinvestment Act of 2009 limits are set to expire on December 31, 2010.

Explanation of Provision

The provision extends the parity in qualified transportation fringe benefits for one year (through December 31, 2011).

Effective Date

The provision is effective for months after December, 2010.

[Law at ¶ 5215. CCH Explanation at ¶ 380.]

[¶ 10,350] Act Sec. 728. Refunds disregarded in the administration of federal programs and federally assisted programs

Joint Committee on Taxation (J.C.T. REP. NO. JCX-55-10)

[Code Sec. 6409]

Present Law

Qualifying individuals may receive refundable credits under various provisions in the Code. Some of these credits are not taken into account for purposes of determining eligibility for benefits or assistance under Federal programs, but the treatment of such credits is not uniform. For example, for purposes of determining an individual's eligibility under any Federal program or federally funded State or local program, the child tax credit[145] is not considered a resource for the month of receipt and the following month,[146] but the making work pay credit[147] is not so considered for the month of receipt and the following two months.[148] The earned income credit has a similar rule to the child tax credit but only with respect to certain specifically listed benefit programs.[149]

Explanation of Provision

Under this provision, any tax refund (or advance payment with respect to a refundable

credit) received by an individual after December 31, 2009 begins a period of 12 months during which such refund may not be taken into account as a resource for purposes of determining the eligibility of such individual (or any other individual) for benefits or assistance (or the amount or extent of benefits or assistance) under any Federal program or under any State or local program financed in whole or in part with Federal funds. The provision terminates on December 31, 2012.

Effective Date

The provision is effective for amounts received after December 31, 2009 and on or before December 31, 2012.

[Law at ¶ 5805. CCH Explanation at ¶ 384.]

---

[145] Sec. 24.

[146] Economic Growth and Tax Relief Reconciliation Act of 2001, Pub. L. No. 107-16, sec. 203.

[147] Sec. 36A.

[148] American Recovery and Reinvestment Act of 2009, Pub. L. No. 111-5, sec. 1001(c).

[149] Sec. 32(l).

[¶10,360] Act Sec. 731. Research credit

Joint Committee on Taxation (J.C.T. REP. No. JCX-55-10)

[Code Sec. 41]

Present Law

General rule

A taxpayer may claim a research credit equal to 20 percent of the amount by which the taxpayer's qualified research expenses for a taxable year exceed its base amount for that year.[150] Thus, the research credit is generally available with respect to incremental increases in qualified research.

A 20-percent research tax credit is also available with respect to the excess of (1) 100 percent of corporate cash expenses (including grants or contributions) paid for basic research conducted by universities (and certain nonprofit scientific research organizations) over (2) the sum of (a) the greater of two minimum basic research floors plus (b) an amount reflecting any decrease in nonresearch giving to universities by the corporation as compared to such giving during a fixed-base period, as adjusted for inflation. This separate credit computation is commonly referred to as the university basic research credit.[151]

Finally, a research credit is available for a taxpayer's expenditures on research undertaken by an energy research consortium. This separate credit computation is commonly referred to as the energy research credit. Unlike the other research credits, the energy research credit applies to all qualified expenditures, not just those in excess of a base amount.

The research credit, including the university basic research credit and the energy research credit, expires for amounts paid or incurred after December 31, 2009.[152]

Computation of allowable credit

Except for energy research payments and certain university basic research payments made by corporations, the research tax credit applies only to the extent that the taxpayer's qualified research expenses for the current taxable year exceed its base amount. The base amount for the current year generally is computed by multiplying the taxpayer's fixed-base percentage by the average amount of the taxpayer's gross receipts for the four preceding years. If a taxpayer both incurred qualified research expenses and had gross receipts during each of at least three years from 1984 through 1988, then its fixed-base percentage is the ratio that its total qualified research expenses for the 1984-1988 period bears to its total gross receipts for that period (subject to a maximum fixed-base percentage of 16 percent). All other taxpayers (so-called start-up firms) are assigned a fixed-base percentage of three percent.[153]

In computing the credit, a taxpayer's base amount cannot be less than 50 percent of its current-year qualified research expenses.

To prevent artificial increases in research expenditures by shifting expenditures among commonly controlled or otherwise related entities, a special aggregation rule provides that all members of the same controlled group of corporations are treated as a single taxpayer.[154] Under regulations prescribed by the Secretary, special rules apply for computing the credit when a major portion of a trade or business (or unit thereof) changes hands, under which qualified research expenses and gross receipts for periods prior to the change of ownership of a trade or business are treated as transferred with the trade or business that gave rise to those expenses and

---

[150] Sec. 41.

[151] Sec. 41(e).

[152] Sec. 41(h).

[153] The Small Business Job Protection Act of 1996 expanded the definition of start-up firms under section 41(c)(3)(B)(i) to include any firm if the first taxable year in which such firm had both gross receipts and qualified research expenses began after 1983. A special rule (enacted in 1993) is designed to gradually recompute a start-up firm's fixed-base percentage based on its actual research experience. Under this special rule, a start-up firm is assigned a

fixed-base percentage of three percent for each of its first five taxable years after 1993 in which it incurs qualified research expenses. A start-up firm's fixed-base percentage for its sixth through tenth taxable years after 1993 in which it incurs qualified research expenses is a phased-in ratio based on the firm's actual research experience. For all subsequent taxable years, the taxpayer's fixed-base percentage is its actual ratio of qualified research expenses to gross receipts for any five years selected by the taxpayer from its fifth through tenth taxable years after 1993. Sec. 41(c)(3)(B).

[154] Sec. 41(f)(1).

receipts for purposes of recomputing a taxpayer's fixed-base percentage.[155]

Alternative simplified credit

Taxpayers may elect to claim an alternative simplified credit for qualified research expenses. The alternative simplified research credit is equal to 14 percent of qualified research expenses that exceed 50 percent of the average qualified research expenses for the three preceding taxable years. The rate is reduced to six percent if a taxpayer has no qualified research expenses in any one of the three preceding taxable years. An election to use the alternative simplified credit applies to all succeeding taxable years unless revoked with the consent of the Secretary.

Eligible expenses

Qualified research expenses eligible for the research tax credit consist of: (1) in-house expenses of the taxpayer for wages and supplies attributable to qualified research; (2) certain time-sharing costs for computer use in qualified research; and (3) 65 percent of amounts paid or incurred by the taxpayer to certain other persons for qualified research conducted on the taxpayer's behalf (so-called contract research expenses).[156] Notwithstanding the limitation for contract research expenses, qualified research expenses include 100 percent of amounts paid or incurred by the taxpayer to an eligible small business, university, or Federal laboratory for qualified energy research.

To be eligible for the credit, the research not only has to satisfy the requirements of present-law section 174 (described below) but also must be undertaken for the purpose of discovering information that is technological in nature, the application of which is intended to be useful in the development of a new or improved business component of the taxpayer, and substantially all of the activities of which constitute elements of a process of experimentation for functional aspects, performance, reliability, or quality of a business component. Research does not qualify for the credit if substantially all of the activities relate to style, taste, cosmetic, or seasonal design factors.[157] In addition, research does not qualify for the credit: (1) if conducted after the beginning of commercial production of the business component; (2) if related to the adaptation of an existing business component to a particular customer's requirements; (3) if related to the duplication of an existing business component from a physical examination of the component itself or certain other information; or (4) if related to certain efficiency surveys, management function or technique, market research, market testing, or market development, routine data collection or routine quality control.[158] Research does not qualify for the credit if it is conducted outside the United States, Puerto Rico, or any U.S. possession.

Relation to deduction

Under section 174, taxpayers may elect to deduct currently the amount of certain research or experimental expenditures paid or incurred in connection with a trade or business, notwithstanding the general rule that business expenses to develop or create an asset that has a useful life extending beyond the current year must be capitalized.[159] However, deductions allowed to a taxpayer under section 174 (or any other section) are reduced by an amount equal to 100 percent of the taxpayer's research tax credit determined for the taxable year.[160] Taxpayers may alternatively elect to claim a reduced research tax credit amount under section 41 in lieu of reducing deductions otherwise allowed.[161]

Explanation of Provision

The provision extends the research credit for two years, through December 31, 2011.

Effective Date

The provision is effective for amounts paid or incurred after December 31, 2009.

[Law at ¶ 5100. CCH Explanation at ¶ 520.]

---

[155] Sec. 41(f)(3).

[156] Under a special rule, 75 percent of amounts paid to a research consortium for qualified research are treated as qualified research expenses eligible for the research credit (rather than 65 percent under the general rule under section 41(b)(3) governing contract research expenses) if (1) such research consortium is a tax-exempt organization that is described in section 501(c)(3) (other than a private foundation) or section 501(c)(6) and is organized and operated primarily to conduct scientific research, and (2) such qualified research is conducted by the consortium on behalf of

the taxpayer and one or more persons not related to the taxpayer. Sec. 41(b)(3)(C).

[157] Sec. 41(d)(3).

[158] Sec. 41(d)(4).

[159] Taxpayers may elect 10-year amortization of certain research expenditures allowable as a deduction under section 174(a). Secs. 174(f)(2) and 59(e).

[160] Sec. 280C(c).

[161] Sec. 280C(c)(3).

[¶10,370] Act Sec. 732. Indian employment tax credit

Joint Committee on Taxation (J.C.T. REP. NO. JCX-55-10)

[Code Sec. 45A]

Present Law

In general, a credit against income tax liability is allowed to employers for the first $20,000 of qualified wages and qualified employee health insurance costs paid or incurred by the employer with respect to certain employees.[162] The credit is equal to 20 percent of the excess of eligible employee qualified wages and health insurance costs during the current year over the amount of such wages and costs incurred by the employer during 1993. The credit is an incremental credit, such that an employer's current-year qualified wages and qualified employee health insurance costs (up to $20,000 per employee) are eligible for the credit only to the extent that the sum of such costs exceeds the sum of comparable costs paid during 1993. No deduction is allowed for the portion of the wages equal to the amount of the credit.

Qualified wages means wages paid or incurred by an employer for services performed by a qualified employee. A qualified employee means any employee who is an enrolled member of an Indian tribe or the spouse of an enrolled member of an Indian tribe, who performs substantially all of the services within an Indian reservation, and whose principal place of abode while performing such services is on or near the reservation in which the services are performed. An "Indian reservation" is a reservation as defined in section 3(d) of the Indian Financing Act of 1974[163] or section 4(10) of the Indian Child Welfare Act of 1978.[164] For purposes of the preceding sentence, section 3(d) is applied by treating "former Indian reservations in Oklahoma" as including only lands that are (1) within the jurisdictional area of an Oklahoma Indian tribe as determined by the Secretary of the Interior, and

(2) recognized by such Secretary as an area eligible for trust land status under 25 C.F.R. Part 151 (as in effect on August 5, 1997).

An employee is not treated as a qualified employee for any taxable year of the employer if the total amount of wages paid or incurred by the employer with respect to such employee during the taxable year exceeds an amount determined at an annual rate of $30,000 (which after adjusted for inflation is currently $45,000 for 2009). In addition, an employee will not be treated as a qualified employee under certain specific circumstances, such as where the employee is related to the employer (in the case of an individual employer) or to one of the employer's shareholders, partners, or grantors. Similarly, an employee will not be treated as a qualified employee where the employee has more than a five percent ownership interest in the employer. Finally, an employee will not be considered a qualified employee to the extent the employee's services relate to gaming activities or are performed in a building housing such activities.

The wage credit is available for wages paid or incurred in taxable years that begin before January 1, 2010.

Explanation of Provision

The provision extends for two years the present-law employment credit provision (through taxable years beginning on or before December 31, 2011).

Effective Date

The provision is effective for taxable years beginning after December 31, 2009.

[Law at ¶5110. CCH Explanation at ¶530.]

[¶10,380] Act Sec. 733. New markets tax credit

Joint Committee on Taxation (J.C.T. REP. NO. JCX-55-10)

[Code Sec. 45D]

Present Law

Section 45D provides a new markets tax credit for qualified equity investments made to acquire stock in a corporation, or a capital inter-

est in a partnership, that is a qualified community development entity ("CDE").[165] The amount of the credit allowable to the investor (either the original purchaser or a subsequent holder) is (1) a five-percent credit for the year in which the equity interest is purchased from the CDE and

---

[162] Sec. 45A.

[163] Pub. L. No. 93-262.

[164] Pub. L. No. 95-608.

[165] Section 45D was added by section 121(a) of the Community Renewal Tax Relief Act of 2000, Pub. L. No. 106-554 (December 21, 2000).

for each of the following two years, and (2) a six-percent credit for each of the following four years.[166] The credit is determined by applying the applicable percentage (five or six percent) to the amount paid to the CDE for the investment at its original issue, and is available to the taxpayer who holds the qualified equity investment on the date of the initial investment or on the respective anniversary date that occurs during the taxable year.[167] The credit is recaptured if at any time during the seven-year period that begins on the date of the original issue of the investment the entity (1) ceases to be a qualified CDE, (2) the proceeds of the investment cease to be used as required, or (3) the equity investment is redeemed.[168]

A qualified CDE is any domestic corporation or partnership: (1) whose primary mission is serving or providing investment capital for low-income communities or low-income persons; (2) that maintains accountability to residents of low-income communities by their representation on any governing board of or any advisory board to the CDE; and (3) that is certified by the Secretary as being a qualified CDE.[169] A qualified equity investment means stock (other than nonqualified preferred stock) in a corporation or a capital interest in a partnership that is acquired directly from a CDE for cash, and includes an investment of a subsequent purchaser if such investment was a qualified equity investment in the hands of the prior holder.[170] Substantially all of the investment proceeds must be used by the CDE to make qualified low-income community investments. For this purpose, qualified low-income community investments include: (1) capital or equity investments in, or loans to, qualified active low-income community businesses; (2) certain financial counseling and other services to businesses and residents in low-income communities; (3) the purchase from another CDE of any loan made by such entity that is a qualified low-income community investment; or (4) an equity investment in, or loan to, another CDE.[171]

A "low-income community" is a population census tract with either (1) a poverty rate of at least 20 percent or (2) median family income which does not exceed 80 percent of the greater of metropolitan area median family income or statewide median family income (for a non-metropolitan census tract, does not exceed 80 percent of statewide median family income). In the case of a population census tract located within a high migration rural county, low-income is defined by reference to 85 percent (as opposed to 80 percent) of statewide median family income.[172] For this purpose, a high migration rural county is any county that, during the 20-year period ending with the year in which the most recent census was conducted, has a net out-migration of inhabitants from the county of at least 10 percent of the population of the county at the beginning of such period.

The Secretary is authorized to designate "targeted populations" as low-income communities for purposes of the new markets tax credit.[173] For this purpose, a "targeted population" is defined by reference to section 103(20) of the Riegle Community Development and Regulatory Improvement Act of 1994[174] (the "Act") to mean individuals, or an identifiable group of individuals, including an Indian tribe, who are low-income persons or otherwise lack adequate access to loans or equity investments. Section 103(17) of the Act provides that "low-income" means (1) for a targeted population within a metropolitan area, less than 80 percent of the area median family income; and (2) for a targeted population within a non-metropolitan area, less than the greater of—80 percent of the area median family income, or 80 percent of statewide non-metropolitan area median family income.[175] A targeted population is not required to be within any census tract. In addition, a population census tract with a population of less than 2,000 is treated as a low-income community for purposes of the credit if such tract is within an empowerment zone, the designation of which is in effect under section 1391 of the Code, and is contiguous to one or more low-income communities.

A qualified active low-income community business is defined as a business that satisfies, with respect to a taxable year, the following requirements: (1) at least 50 percent of the total gross income of the business is derived from the active conduct of trade or business activities in any low-income community; (2) a substantial portion of the tangible property of the business is used in a low-income community; (3) a substantial portion of the services performed for the business by its employees is performed in a low-income community; and (4) less than five percent of the average of the aggregate unadjusted

[166] Sec. 45D(a)(2).
[167] Sec. 45D(a)(3).
[168] Sec. 45D(g).
[169] Sec. 45D(c).
[170] Sec. 45D(b).

[171] Sec. 45D(d).
[172] Sec. 45D(e).
[173] Sec. 45D(e)(2).
[174] Pub. L. No. 103-325.
[175] Pub. L. No. 103-325.

bases of the property of the business is attributable to certain financial property or to certain collectibles.[176]

The maximum annual amount of qualified equity investments was $5.0 billion for calendar years 2008 and 2009. The new markets tax credit expired on December 31, 2009.

Explanation of Provision

The provision extends the new markets tax credit for two years, through 2011, permitting up to $3.5 billion in qualified equity investments for each of the 2010 and 2011 calendar years. The provision also extends for two years, through 2016, the carryover period for unused new markets tax credits.

Effective Date

The provision applies to calendar years beginning after December 31, 2009.

[Law at ¶ 5120. CCH Explanation at ¶ 528.]

[¶ 10,390] Act Sec. 734. Railroad track maintenance credit

Joint Committee on Taxation (J.C.T. REP. NO. JCX-55-10)

[Code Sec. 45G]

Present Law

Present law provides a 50-percent business tax credit for qualified railroad track maintenance expenditures paid or incurred by an eligible taxpayer during taxable years beginning before January 1, 2010.[177] The credit is limited to the product of $3,500 times the number of miles of railroad track (1) owned or leased by an eligible taxpayer as of the close of its taxable year, and (2) assigned to the eligible taxpayer by a Class II or Class III railroad that owns or leases such track at the close of the taxable year.[178] Each mile of railroad track may be taken into account only once, either by the owner of such mile or by the owner's assignee, in computing the per-mile limitation. The credit may also reduce a taxpayer's tax liability below its tentative minimum tax.[179]

Qualified railroad track maintenance expenditures are defined as gross expenditures (whether or not otherwise chargeable to capital account) for maintaining railroad track (including roadbed, bridges, and related track structures) owned or leased as of January 1, 2005, by a Class II or Class III railroad (determined without regard to any consideration for such expenditure given by the Class II or Class III railroad which made the assignment of such track).[180]

An eligible taxpayer means any Class II or Class III railroad, and any person who transports property using the rail facilities of a Class II or Class III railroad or who furnishes railroad-related property or services to a Class II or Class III railroad, but only with respect to miles of railroad track assigned to such person by such railroad under the provision.[181]

The terms Class II or Class III railroad have the meanings given by the Surface Transportation Board.[182]

Explanation of Provision

The provision extends the present law credit for two years, for qualified railroad track maintenance expenses paid or incurred during taxable years beginning after December 31, 2009 and before January 1, 2012.

Effective Date

The provision is effective for expenses paid or incurred in taxable years beginning after December 31, 2009.

[Law at ¶ 5130. CCH Explanation at ¶ 532.]

---

[176] Sec. 45D(d)(2).
[177] Sec. 45G(a).
[178] Sec. 45G(b)(1).
[179] Sec. 38(c)(4).

[180] Sec. 45G(d).
[181] Sec. 45G(c).
[182] Sec. 45G(e)(1).

[¶10,400] Act Sec. 735. Mine rescue team training credit

Joint Committee on Taxation (J.C.T. REP. No. JCX-55-10)

[Code Sec. 45N]

Present Law

An eligible employer may claim a general business credit against income tax with respect to each qualified mine rescue team employee equal to the lesser of: (1) 20 percent of the amount paid or incurred by the taxpayer during the taxable year with respect to the training program costs of the qualified mine rescue team employee (including the wages of the employee while attending the program); or (2) $10,000. A qualified mine rescue team employee is any full-time employee of the taxpayer who is a miner eligible for more than six months of a taxable year to serve as a mine rescue team member by virtue of either having completed the initial 20 hour course of instruction prescribed by the Mine Safety and Health Administration's Office of Educational Policy and Development, or receiving at least 40 hours of refresher training in such instruction. The credit is not allowable for purposes of computing the alternative minimum tax.[183]

An eligible employer is any taxpayer which employs individuals as miners in underground mines in the United States. The term "wages" has the meaning given to such term by section 3306(b)[184] (determined without regard to any dollar limitation contained in that section).

No deduction is allowed for the portion of the expenses otherwise deductible that is equal to the amount of the credit.[185] The credit does not apply to taxable years beginning after December 31, 2009. Additionally, the credit may not offset the alternative minimum tax.

Explanation of Provision

The provision extends the credit for two years through taxable years beginning on or before December 31, 2011.

Effective Date

The provision generally is effective for taxable years beginning after December 31, 2009.

[Law at ¶5145. CCH Explanation at ¶534.]

[¶10,410] Act Sec. 736. Employer wage credit for employees who are active duty members of the uniformed services

Joint Committee on Taxation (J.C.T. REP. No. JCX-55-10)

[Code Sec. 45P]

Present Law

Differential pay

In general, compensation paid by an employer to an employee is deductible by the employer under section 162(a)(1), unless the expense must be capitalized. In the case of an employee who is called to active duty with respect to the armed forces of the United States, some employers voluntarily pay the employee the difference between the compensation that the employer would have paid to the employee during the period of military service less the amount of pay received by the employee from the military. This payment by the employer is often referred to as "differential pay."

Wage credit for differential pay

If an employer qualifies as an eligible small business employer, the employer is allowed to take a credit against its income tax liability for a taxable year in an amount equal to 20 percent of the sum of the eligible differential wage payments for each of the employer's qualified employees for the taxable year.[186]

An eligible small business employer means, with respect to a taxable year, any taxpayer which: (1) employed on average less than 50 employees on business days during the taxable year; and (2) under a written plan of the taxpayer, provides eligible differential wage payments to every qualified employee of the taxpayer. Taxpayers under common control are

---

[183] Sec. 38(c).
[184] Section 3306(b) defines wages for purposes of Federal Unemployment Tax.

[185] Sec. 280C(e).
[186] Sec. 45P.

aggregated for purposes of determining whether a taxpayer is an eligible small business employer. The credit is not available with respect to a taxpayer who has failed to comply with the employment and reemployment rights of members of the uniformed services (as provided under Chapter 43 of Title 38 of the United States Code).

Differential wage payment means any payment which: (1) is made by an employer to an individual with respect to any period during which the individual is performing service in the uniformed services of the United States while on active duty for a period of more than 30 days; and (2) represents all or a portion of the wages that the individual would have received from the employer if the individual were performing services for the employer. The term eligible differential wage payments means so much of the differential wage payments paid to a qualified employee as does not exceed $20,000. A qualified employee is an individual who has been an employee for the 91-day period immediately preceding the period for which any differential wage payment is made.

No deduction may be taken for that portion of compensation which is equal to the credit. In addition, the amount of any other credit otherwise allowable under Chapter 1 (Normal Taxes and Surtaxes) of Subtitle A (Income Taxes) of the Code with respect to compensation paid to an employee must be reduced by the differential wage payment credit allowed with respect to such employee.

The differential wage payment credit is part of the general business credit, and thus this credit is subject to the rules applicable to business credits. For example, an unused credit generally may be carried back to the taxable year that precedes an unused credit year or carried forward to each of the 20 taxable years following the unused credit year. Any credit that is included in the general business credit, however, cannot be carried back to a tax year before the first tax year for which that credit is allowable

under the effective date of that credit. Thus, the differential wage payment credit, if disallowed under section 38(c), cannot be carried back to tax years ending before June 18, 2008. In addition, unlike many of the other credits that are included in the general business credit, the differential wage payment credit is not a "qualified business credit" under section 196(c). Thus, a taxpayer cannot deduct under section 196(c) any differential wage payment credits that remain unused at the end of the 20-year carryforward period.

Rules similar to the rules in section 52(c), which bars the work opportunity tax credit for tax-exempt organizations other than certain farmer's cooperatives, apply to the differential wage payment credit. Additionally, rules similar to the rules in section 52(e), which limits the work opportunity tax credit allowable to regulated investment companies, real estate investment trusts, and certain cooperatives, apply to the differential wage payment credit.

The credit is not allowable against a taxpayer's alternative minimum tax liability. The amount of credit otherwise allowable under the income tax rules for compensation paid to any employee must be reduced by the differential wage payment credit with respect to that employee.

There are special rules for trusts and estates and their beneficiaries.

The credit is available with respect to amounts paid after June 17, 2008[187] and before January 1, 2010.

Explanation of Provision

The provision extends the availability of the credit to amounts paid before January 1, 2012.

Effective Date

The provision applies to payments made after December 31, 2009.

[Law at ¶5150. CCH Explanation at ¶526.]

---

[187] This date is the date of enactment of the Heroes Earnings Assistance and Relief Tax Act of 2008, Pub. L. No. 110-245.

[¶10,420] Act Sec. 737. 15-year straight-line cost recovery for qualified leasehold improvements, qualified restaurant buildings and improvements, and qualified retail improvements

Joint Committee on Taxation (J.C.T. REP. NO. JCX-55-10)

[Code Sec. 168]

Present Law

In general

A taxpayer generally must capitalize the cost of property used in a trade or business and recover such cost over time through annual deductions for depreciation or amortization. Tangible property generally is depreciated under the modified accelerated cost recovery system ("MACRS"), which determines depreciation by applying specific recovery periods, placed-in-service conventions, and depreciation methods to the cost of various types of depreciable property.[188] The cost of nonresidential real property is recovered using the straight-line method of depreciation and a recovery period of 39 years. Nonresidential real property is subject to the mid-month placed-in-service convention. Under the mid-month convention, the depreciation allowance for the first year property is placed in service is based on the number of months the property was in service, and property placed in service at any time during a month is treated as having been placed in service in the middle of the month.

Depreciation of leasehold improvements

Generally, depreciation allowances for improvements made on leased property are determined under MACRS, even if the MACRS recovery period assigned to the property is longer than the term of the lease. This rule applies regardless of whether the lessor or the lessee places the leasehold improvements in service. If a leasehold improvement constitutes an addition or improvement to nonresidential real property already placed in service, the improvement generally is depreciated using the straight-line method over a 39-year recovery period, beginning in the month the addition or improvement was placed in service. However, exceptions exist for certain qualified leasehold improvements, qualified restaurant property, and qualified retail improvement property.

Qualified leasehold improvement property

Section 168(e)(3)(E)(iv) provides a statutory 15-year recovery period for qualified leasehold improvement property placed in service before January 1, 2010. Qualified leasehold improvement property is recovered using the straight-line method and a half-year convention. Leasehold improvements placed in service after December 31, 2009 will be subject to the general rules described above.

Qualified leasehold improvement property is any improvement to an interior portion of a building that is nonresidential real property, provided certain requirements are met. The improvement must be made under or pursuant to a lease either by the lessee (or sublessee), or by the lessor, of that portion of the building to be occupied exclusively by the lessee (or sublessee). The improvement must be placed in service more than three years after the date the building was first placed in service. Qualified leasehold improvement property does not include any improvement for which the expenditure is attributable to the enlargement of the building, any elevator or escalator, any structural component benefiting a common area, or the internal structural framework of the building.

If a lessor makes an improvement that qualifies as qualified leasehold improvement property, such improvement does not qualify as qualified leasehold improvement property to any subsequent owner of such improvement. An exception to the rule applies in the case of death and certain transfers of property that qualify for non-recognition treatment.

Qualified restaurant property

Section 168(e)(3)(E)(v) provides a statutory 15-year recovery period for qualified restaurant property placed in service before January 1, 2010. Qualified restaurant property is any section 1250 property that is a building (if the building is placed in service after December 31, 2008 and

---

[188] Sec. 168.

before January 1, 2010) or an improvement to a building, if more than 50 percent of the building's square footage is devoted to the preparation of, and seating for on-premises consumption of, prepared meals.[189] Qualified restaurant property is recovered using the straight-line method and a half-year convention. Additionally, qualified restaurant property is not eligible for bonus depreciation.[190] Restaurant property placed in service after December 31, 2009 is subject to the general rules described above.

Qualified retail improvement property

Section 168(e)(3)(E)(ix) provides a statutory 15-year recovery period and for qualified retail improvement property placed in service after December 31, 2008 and before January 1, 2010. Qualified retail improvement property is any improvement to an interior portion of a building which is nonresidential real property if such portion is open to the general public[191] and is used in the retail trade or business of selling tangible personal property to the general public, and such improvement is placed in service more than three years after the date the building was first placed in service. Qualified retail improvement property does not include any improvement for which the expenditure is attributable to the enlargement of the building, any elevator or escalator, or the internal structural framework of the building. In the case of an improvement made by the owner of such improvement, the improvement is a qualified retail improvement only so long as the improvement is held by such owner.

Retail establishments that qualify for the 15-year recovery period include those primarily engaged in the sale of goods. Examples of these retail establishments include, but are not limited to, grocery stores, clothing stores, hardware stores and convenience stores. Establishments primarily engaged in providing services, such as professional services, financial services, personal services, health services, and entertainment, do not qualify. It is generally intended that businesses defined as a store retailer under the current North American Industry Classification System (industry sub-sectors 441 through 453) qualify while those in other industry classes do not qualify.

Qualified retail improvement property is recovered using the straight-line method and a half-year convention. Additionally, qualified retail improvement property is not eligible for bonus depreciation.[192] Qualified retail improvement property placed in service on or after January 1, 2010 is subject to the general rules described above.

Explanation of Provision

The present law provisions for qualified leasehold improvement property, qualified restaurant property, and qualified retail improvement property are extended for two years to apply to property placed in service on or before December 31, 2011.

Effective Date

The provision is effective for property placed in service after December 31, 2009.

[Law at ¶5265. CCH Explanation at ¶508.]

[¶10,430] Act Sec. 738. 7-year recovery period for motorsports entertainment complexes

Joint Committee on Taxation (J.C.T. REP. NO. JCX-55-10)

[Code Sec. 168]

Present Law

A taxpayer generally must capitalize the cost of property used in a trade or business and recover such cost over time through annual deductions for depreciation or amortization. Tangible property generally is depreciated under the modified accelerated cost recovery system ("MACRS"), which determines depreciation by applying specific recovery periods, placed-in-service conventions, and depreciation methods to the cost of various types of depreciable property.[193] The cost of nonresidential real property

---

[189] Sec. 168(e)(7)((A).

[190] Property that satisfies the definition of both qualified leasehold improvement property and qualified restaurant property is eligible for bonus depreciation.

[191] Improvements to portions of a building not open to the general public (e.g., stock room in back of retail space) do not qualify under the provision.

[192] Property that satisfies the definition of both qualified leasehold improvement property and qualified retail property is eligible for bonus depreciation.

[193] Sec. 168.

¶10,430   Act Sec. 738

is recovered using the straight-line method of depreciation and a recovery period of 39 years. Nonresidential real property is subject to the mid-month placed-in-service convention. Under the mid-month convention, the depreciation allowance for the first year property is placed in service is based on the number of months the property was in service, and property placed in service at any time during a month is treated as having been placed in service in the middle of the month. Land improvements (such as roads and fences) are recovered over 15 years. An exception exists for the theme and amusement park industry, whose assets are assigned a recovery period of seven years. Additionally, a motorsports entertainment complex placed in service before December 31, 2009 is assigned a recovery period of seven years.[194] For these purposes, a motorsports entertainment complex means a racing track facility which is permanently situated on land and which during the 36-month period

following its placed-in-service date hosts a racing event.[195] The term motorsports entertainment complex also includes ancillary facilities, land improvements (e.g., parking lots, sidewalks, fences), support facilities (e.g., food and beverage retailing, souvenir vending), and appurtenances associated with such facilities (e.g., ticket booths, grandstands).

Explanation of Provision

The provision extends the present law seven-year recovery period for motorsports entertainment complexes two years to apply to property placed in service before January 1, 2012.

Effective Date

The provision is effective for property placed in service after December 31, 2009.

[Law at ¶5265. CCH Explanation at ¶510.]

[¶10,440] Act Sec. 739. Accelerated depreciation for business property on an Indian reservation

Joint Committee on Taxation (J.C.T. REP. NO. JCX-55-10)

[Code Sec. 168(j)]

Present Law

With respect to certain property used in connection with the conduct of a trade or business within an Indian reservation, depreciation deductions under section 168(j) are determined using the following recovery periods:

3-year property	2 years
5-year property	3 years
7-year property	4 years
10-year property	6 years
15-year property	9 years
20-year property	12 years
Nonresidential real property	22 years

"Qualified Indian reservation property" eligible for accelerated depreciation includes property described in the table above which is: (1) used by the taxpayer predominantly in the active conduct of a trade or business within an Indian reservation; (2) not used or located outside the reservation on a regular basis; (3) not acquired (directly or indirectly) by the taxpayer from a person who is related to the taxpayer;[196] and (4) is not property placed in service for purposes of conducting gaming activities.[197] Certain "qualified infrastructure property" may be eligible for

the accelerated depreciation even if located outside an Indian reservation, provided that the purpose of such property is to connect with qualified infrastructure property located within the reservation (e.g., roads, power lines, water systems, railroad spurs, and communications facilities).[198]

An "Indian reservation" means a reservation as defined in section 3(d) of the Indian Financing Act of 1974[199] or section 4(10) of the Indian Child Welfare Act of 1978 (25 U.S.C.

---

[194] Sec. 168(e)(3)(C)(ii).
[195] Sec. 168(i)(15).
[196] For these purposes, related persons is defined in Sec. 465(b)(3)(C).

[197] Sec. 168(j)(4)(A).
[198] Sec. 168(j)(4)(C).
[199] Pub. L. No. 93-262.

1903(10)).[200] For purposes of the preceding sentence, section 3(d) is applied by treating "former Indian reservations in Oklahoma" as including only lands that are (1) within the jurisdictional area of an Oklahoma Indian tribe as determined by the Secretary of the Interior, and (2) recognized by such Secretary as an area eligible for trust land status under 25 C.F.R. Part 151 (as in effect on August 5, 1997).

The depreciation deduction allowed for regular tax purposes is also allowed for purposes of the alternative minimum tax. The accelerated depreciation for qualified Indian reservation property is available with respect to property placed in service on or after January 1, 1994, and before January 1, 2010.

Explanation of Provision

The provision extends for two years the present-law accelerated MACRS recovery periods for qualified Indian reservation property to apply to property placed in service before January 1, 2012.

Effective Date

The provision is effective for property placed in service after December 31, 2009.

[Law at ¶ 5265. CCH Explanation at ¶ 512.]

[¶ 10,450]   Act Sec. 740. Enhanced charitable deduction for contributions of food inventory

Joint Committee on Taxation (J.C.T. REP. NO. JCX-55-10)

[Code Sec. 170]

Present Law

Charitable contributions in general

In general, an income tax deduction is permitted for charitable contributions, subject to certain limitations that depend on the type of taxpayer, the property contributed, and the donee organization.[201]

Charitable contributions of cash are deductible in the amount contributed. In general, contributions of capital gain property to a qualified charity are deductible at fair market value with certain exceptions. Capital gain property means any capital asset or property used in the taxpayer's trade or business the sale of which at its fair market value, at the time of contribution, would have resulted in gain that would have been long-term capital gain. Contributions of other appreciated property generally are deductible at the donor's basis in the property. Contributions of depreciated property generally are deductible at the fair market value of the property.

General rules regarding contributions of food inventory

Under present law, a taxpayer's deduction for charitable contributions of inventory gener-

ally is limited to the taxpayer's basis (typically, cost) in the inventory, or if less the fair market value of the inventory.

For certain contributions of inventory, C corporations may claim an enhanced deduction equal to the lesser of (1) basis plus one-half of the item's appreciation (i.e., basis plus one-half of fair market value in excess of basis) or (2) two times basis.[202] In general, a C corporation's charitable contribution deductions for a year may not exceed 10 percent of the corporation's taxable income.[203] To be eligible for the enhanced deduction, the contributed property generally must be inventory of the taxpayer, contributed to a charitable organization described in section 501(c)(3) (except for private nonoperating foundations), and the donee must (1) use the property consistent with the donee's exempt purpose solely for the care of the ill, the needy, or infants, (2) not transfer the property in exchange for money, other property, or services, and (3) provide the taxpayer a written statement that the donee's use of the property will be consistent with such requirements.[204] In the case of contributed property subject to the Federal Food, Drug, and Cosmetic Act, as amended, the property must satisfy the applicable requirements of such Act on the date of transfer and for 180 days prior to the transfer.[205]

---

[200] Pub. L. No. 95-608.
[201] Sec. 170.
[202] Sec. 170(e)(3).

[203] Sec. 170(b)(2).
[204] Sec. 170(e)(3)(A)(i)-(iii).
[205] Sec. 170(e)(3)(A)(iv).

A donor making a charitable contribution of inventory must make a corresponding adjustment to the cost of goods sold by decreasing the cost of goods sold by the lesser of the fair market value of the property or the donor's basis with respect to the inventory.[206] Accordingly, if the allowable charitable deduction for inventory is the fair market value of the inventory, the donor reduces its cost of goods sold by such value, with the result that the difference between the fair market value and the donor's basis may still be recovered by the donor other than as a charitable contribution.

To use the enhanced deduction, the taxpayer must establish that the fair market value of the donated item exceeds basis. The valuation of food inventory has been the subject of disputes between taxpayers and the IRS.[207]

Temporary rule expanding and modifying the enhanced deduction for contributions of food inventory

Under a special temporary provision, any taxpayer, whether or not a C corporation, engaged in a trade or business is eligible to claim the enhanced deduction for donations of food inventory.[208] For taxpayers other than C corporations, the total deduction for donations of food inventory in a taxable year generally may not exceed 10 percent of the taxpayer's net income for such taxable year from all sole proprietorships, S corporations, or partnerships (or other non C corporation) from which contributions of apparently wholesome food are made. For example, if a taxpayer is a sole proprietor, a shareholder in an S corporation, and a partner in a partnership, and each business makes charitable contributions of food inventory, the taxpayer's deduction for donations of food inventory is limited to 10 percent of the taxpayer's net income from the sole proprietorship and the taxpayer's interests in the S corporation and partnership. However, if only the sole proprietorship and the S corporation made charitable contributions of food inventory, the taxpayer's deduction would be limited to 10 percent of the net income from the trade or business of the sole proprietorship and the taxpayer's interest in the S corporation, but not the taxpayer's interest in the partnership.[209]

Under the temporary provision, the enhanced deduction for food is available only for food that qualifies as "apparently wholesome food." Apparently wholesome food is defined as food intended for human consumption that meets all quality and labeling standards imposed by Federal, State, and local laws and regulations even though the food may not be readily marketable due to appearance, age, freshness, grade, size, surplus, or other conditions.

The temporary provision does not apply to contributions made after December 31, 2009.

Explanation of Provision

The provision extends the expansion of, and modifications to, the enhanced deduction for charitable contributions of food inventory to contributions made before January 1, 2012.

Effective Date

The provision is effective for contributions made after December 31, 2009.

[Law at ¶5270. CCH Explanation at ¶560.]

---

[206] Treas. Reg. sec. 1.170A-4A(c)(3).

[207] *Lucky Stores Inc. v. Commissioner*, 105 T.C. 420 (1995) (holding that the value of surplus bread inventory donated to charity was the full retail price of the bread rather than half the retail price, as the IRS asserted).

[208] Sec. 170(e)(3)(C).

[209] The 10 percent limitation does not affect the application of the generally applicable percentage limitations. For example, if 10 percent of a sole proprietor's net income from the proprietor's trade or business was greater than 50 per-

cent of the proprietor's contribution base, the available deduction for the taxable year (with respect to contributions to public charities) would be 50 percent of the proprietor's contribution base. Consistent with present law, such contributions may be carried forward because they exceed the 50 percent limitation. Contributions of food inventory by a taxpayer that is not a C corporation that exceed the 10 percent limitation but not the 50 percent limitation could not be carried forward.

[¶ 10,460] Act Sec. 741. Enhanced charitable deduction for contributions of book inventories to public schools

Joint Committee on Taxation (J.C.T. REP. NO. JCX-55-10)

[Code Sec. 170]

Present Law

Charitable contributions in general

In general, an income tax deduction is permitted for charitable contributions, subject to certain limitations that depend on the type of taxpayer, the property contributed, and the donee organization.[210]

Charitable contributions of cash are deductible in the amount contributed. In general, contributions of capital gain property to a qualified charity are deductible at fair market value with certain exceptions. Capital gain property means any capital asset or property used in the taxpayer's trade or business the sale of which at its fair market value, at the time of contribution, would have resulted in gain that would have been long-term capital gain. Contributions of other appreciated property generally are deductible at the donor's basis in the property. Contributions of depreciated property generally are deductible at the fair market value of the property.

General rules regarding contributions of book inventory

Under present law, a taxpayer's deduction for charitable contributions of inventory generally is limited to the taxpayer's basis (typically, cost) in the inventory, or, if less, the fair market value of the inventory.

In general, for certain contributions of inventory, C corporations may claim an enhanced deduction equal to the lesser of (1) basis plus one-half of the item's appreciation (i.e., basis plus one-half of fair market value in excess of basis) or (2) two times basis.[211] In general, a C corporation's charitable contribution deductions for a year may not exceed 10 percent of the corporation's taxable income.[212] To be eligible for the enhanced deduction, the contributed property generally must be inventory of the taxpayer contributed to a charitable organization described in section 501(c)(3) (except for private

nonoperating foundations), and the donee must (1) use the property consistent with the donee's exempt purpose solely for the care of the ill, the needy, or infants, (2) not transfer the property in exchange for money, other property, or services, and (3) provide the taxpayer a written statement that the donee's use of the property will be consistent with such requirements.[213] In the case of contributed property subject to the Federal Food, Drug, and Cosmetic Act, as amended, the property must satisfy the applicable requirements of such Act on the date of transfer and for 180 days prior to the transfer.[214]

A donor making a charitable contribution of inventory must make a corresponding adjustment to the cost of goods sold by decreasing the cost of goods sold by the lesser of the fair market value of the property or the donor's basis with respect to the inventory.[215] Accordingly, if the allowable charitable deduction for inventory is the fair market value of the inventory, the donor reduces its cost of goods sold by such value, with the result that the difference between the fair market value and the donor's basis may still be recovered by the donor other than as a charitable contribution.

To use the enhanced deduction, the taxpayer must establish that the fair market value of the donated item exceeds basis.

Special rule expanding and modifying the enhanced deduction for contributions of book inventory

The generally applicable enhanced deduction for C corporations is expanded and modified to include certain qualified book contributions made after August 28, 2005, and before January 1, 2010.[216] A qualified book contribution means a charitable contribution of books to a public school that provides elementary education or secondary education (kindergarten through grade 12) and that is an educational organization that normally maintains a regular faculty and curriculum and normally has a regularly enrolled body of pupils or

---

[210] Sec. 170.
[211] Sec. 170(e)(3).
[212] Sec. 170(b)(2).
[213] Sec. 170(e)(3)(A)(i)-(iii).

[214] Sec. 170(e)(3)(A)(iv).
[215] Treas. Reg. sec. 1.170A-4A(c)(3).
[216] Sec. 170(e)(3)(D).

students in attendance at the place where its educational activities are regularly carried on. The enhanced deduction for qualified book contributions is not allowed unless the donee organization certifies in writing that the contributed books are suitable, in terms of currency, content, and quantity, for use in the donee's educational programs and that the donee will use the books in such educational programs. The donee also must make the certifications required for the generally applicable enhanced deduction, i.e., the donee will (1) use the property consistent with the donee's exempt purpose solely for the care of the ill, the needy, or infants, (2) not transfer the property in exchange for money, other property, or services, and (3) provide the taxpayer a written statement that the donee's use of the property will be consistent with such requirements.

Explanation of Provision

The provision extends the expansion of, and modifications to, the enhanced deduction for contributions of book inventory to contributions made before January 1, 2012.

Effective Date

The provision is effective for contributions made after December 31, 2009.

[Law at ¶ 5270. CCH Explanation at ¶ 563.]

[¶ 10,470] Act Sec. 742. Enhanced charitable deduction for corporate contributions of computer inventory for educational purposes

Joint Committee on Taxation (J.C.T. REP. No. JCX-55-10)

[Code Sec. 170]

Present Law

In the case of a charitable contribution of inventory or other ordinary-income or short-term capital gain property, the amount of the charitable deduction generally is limited to the taxpayer's basis in the property. In the case of a charitable contribution of tangible personal property, the deduction is limited to the taxpayer's basis in such property if the use by the recipient charitable organization is unrelated to the organization's tax-exempt purpose. In cases involving contributions to a private foundation (other than certain private operating foundations), the amount of the deduction is limited to the taxpayer's basis in the property.[217]

Explanation of Provision

A taxpayer's deduction for charitable contributions of computer technology and equipment generally is limited to the taxpayer's basis (typically, cost) in the property. Under a special, temporary provision, certain corporations may claim a deduction in excess of basis for a "qualified computer contribution."[218] This enhanced deduction is equal to the lesser of (1) basis plus one-half of the item's appreciation (i.e., basis plus one half of fair market value in excess of basis) or (2) two times basis. The enhanced deduction for qualified computer contributions expires for any contribution made during any taxable year beginning after December 31, 2009.[219]

A qualified computer contribution means a charitable contribution of any computer technology or equipment, which meets several requirements. The contribution must meet standards of functionality and suitability as established by the Secretary of the Treasury. The contribution must be to certain educational organizations or public libraries and made not later than three years after the taxpayer acquired the property (or, if the taxpayer constructed or assembled the property, the date construction or assembly of the property is substantially completed).[220] The original use of the property must be by the donor or the donee,[221] and substantially all of the donee's use of the property must be within the United States for educational purposes related to the function or purpose of the donee. The property must fit productively into the donee's education plan. The donee may not transfer the property in exchange for money, other property, or services, except for shipping, installation, and transfer

---

[217] Sec. 170(e)(1).

[218] Sec. 170(e)(6).

[219] Sec. 170(e)(6)(G).

[220] If the taxpayer constructed the property and reacquired such property, the contribution must be within three years of the date the original construction was substantially completed. Sec. 170(e)(6)(D)(i).

[221] This requirement does not apply if the property was reacquired by the manufacturer and contributed. Sec. 170(e)(6)(D)(ii).

costs. To determine whether property is constructed or assembled by the taxpayer, the rules applicable to qualified research contributions apply. Contributions may be made to private foundations under certain conditions.[222]

Explanation of Provision

The provision extends the enhanced deduction for computer technology and equipment to contributions made before January 1, 2012.

Effective Date

The provision is effective for contributions made in taxable years beginning after December 31, 2009.

[Law at ¶5270. CCH Explanation at ¶566.]

[¶10,480] Act Sec. 743. Election to expense mine safety equipment

Joint Committee on Taxation (J.C.T. Rep. No. JCX-55-10)

[Code Sec. 179E]

Present Law

A taxpayer is allowed to recover, through annual depreciation deductions, the cost of certain property used in a trade or business or for the production of income. The amount of the depreciation deduction allowed with respect to tangible property for a taxable year is determined under the modified accelerated cost recovery system ("MACRS").[223] Under MACRS, different types of property generally are assigned applicable recovery periods and depreciation methods. The recovery periods applicable to most tangible personal property (generally tangible property other than residential rental property and nonresidential real property) range from three to 20 years. The depreciation methods generally applicable to tangible personal property are the 200-percent and 150-percent declining balance methods, switching to the straight-line method for the taxable year in which the depreciation deduction would be maximized.

In lieu of depreciation, a taxpayer with a sufficiently small amount of annual investment may elect to deduct (or "expense") such costs under section 179. Present law provides that the maximum amount a taxpayer may expense for taxable years beginning in 2010 is $500,000 of the cost of the qualifying property for the taxable year. In general, qualifying property is defined as depreciable tangible personal property that is purchased for use in the active conduct of a trade or business.[224] The $500,000 amount is reduced (but not below zero) by the amount by which the cost of qualifying property placed in service during the taxable year exceeds $2,000,000.

A taxpayer may elect to treat 50 percent of the cost of any qualified advanced mine safety equipment property as an expense in the taxable year in which the equipment is placed in service.[225] The deduction under section 179E is allowed for both regular and alternative minimum tax purposes, including adjusted current earnings. In computing earnings and profits, the amount deductible under section 179E is allowed as a deduction ratably over five taxable years beginning with the year the amount is deductible under section 179E.[226]

"Qualified advanced mine safety equipment property" means any advanced mine safety equipment property for use in any underground mine located in the United States the original use of which commences with the taxpayer and which is placed in service before January 1, 2010.[227]

Advanced mine safety equipment property means any of the following: (1) emergency communication technology or devices used to allow a miner to maintain constant communication with an individual who is not in the mine; (2) electronic identification and location devices that allow individuals not in the mine to track at all times the movements and location of miners

---

[222] Sec. 170(e)(6)(C).

[223] Sec. 168.

[224] The definition of qualifying property was temporarily (for 2010 and 2011) expanded to include up to $250,000 of qualified leasehold improvement property, qualified restaurant property, and qualified retail improvement property. See section 179(c).

[225] Sec. 179E(a).

[226] Sec. 312(k)(3). Section 56(g)(4)(C)(i) does not apply to a deduction under section 179E (or under sections 179, 179A, 179B, and 179D), as such deduction is permitted for purposes of computing earnings and profits.

[227] Secs. 179E(c) and (g).

working in or at the mine; (3) emergency oxygen-generating, self-rescue devices that provide oxygen for at least 90 minutes; (4) pre-positioned supplies of oxygen providing each miner on a shift the ability to survive for at least 48 hours; and (5) comprehensive atmospheric monitoring systems that monitor the levels of carbon monoxide, methane and oxygen that are present in all areas of the mine and that can detect smoke in the case of a fire in a mine.[228]

The portion of the cost of any property with respect to which an expensing election under section 179 is made may not be taken into account for purposes of the 50-percent deduction under section 179E.[229] In addition, a taxpayer making an election under section 179E must file

with the Secretary a report containing information with respect to the operation of the mines of the taxpayer as required by the Secretary.[230]

Explanation of Provision

The provision extends for two years, to December 31, 2011, the present-law placed in service date relating to expensing of mine safety equipment.

Effective Date

The provision applies to property placed in service after December 31, 2009.

[Law at ¶5280. CCH Explanation at ¶516.]

[¶10,490] Act Sec. 744. Special expensing rules for certain film and television productions

Joint Committee on Taxation (J.C.T. Rep. No. JCX-55-10)

[Code Sec. 181]

Present Law

The modified accelerated cost recovery system ("MACRS") does not apply to certain property, including any motion picture film, video tape, or sound recording, or to any other property if the taxpayer elects to exclude such property from MACRS and the taxpayer properly applies a unit-of-production method or other method of depreciation not expressed in a term of years. Section 197 does not apply to certain intangible property, including property produced by the taxpayer or any interest in a film, sound recording, video tape, book or similar property not acquired in a transaction (or a series of related transactions) involving the acquisition of assets constituting a trade or business or substantial portion thereof. Thus, the recovery of the cost of a film, video tape, or similar property that is produced by the taxpayer or is acquired on a "stand-alone" basis by the taxpayer may not be determined under either the MACRS depreciation provisions or under the section 197 amortization provisions. The cost recovery of such property may be determined under section 167, which allows a depreciation deduction for the reasonable allowance for the exhaustion, wear and tear, or obsolescence of the property. A tax-

payer is allowed to recover, through annual depreciation deductions, the cost of certain property used in a trade or business or for the production of income. Section 167(g) provides that the cost of motion picture films, sound recordings, copyrights, books, and patents are eligible to be recovered using the income forecast method of depreciation.

Under section 181, taxpayers may elect[231] to deduct the cost of any qualifying film and television production, commencing prior to January 1, 2010, in the year the expenditure is incurred in lieu of capitalizing the cost and recovering it through depreciation allowances.[232] Taxpayers may elect to deduct up to $15 million of the aggregate cost of the film or television production under this section.[233] The threshold is increased to $20 million if a significant amount of the production expenditures are incurred in areas eligible for designation as a low-income community or eligible for designation by the Delta Regional Authority as a distressed county or isolated area of distress.[234]

A qualified film or television production means any production of a motion picture (whether released theatrically or directly to video cassette or any other format) or television program if at least 75 percent of the total com-

---

[228] Sec. 179E(d).
[229] Sec. 179E(e).
[230] Sec. 179E(f).
[231] See Treas. Reg. section 1.181-2T for rules on making an election under this section.

[232] For this purpose, a production is treated as commencing on the first date of principal photography.
[233] Sec. 181(a)(2)(A).
[234] Sec. 181(a)(2)(B).

pensation expended on the production is for services performed in the United States by actors, directors, producers, and other relevant production personnel.[235] The term "compensation" does not include participations and residuals (as defined in section 167(g)(7)(B)).[236] With respect to property which is one or more episodes in a television series, each episode is treated as a separate production and only the first 44 episodes qualify under the provision.[237] Qualified property does not include sexually explicit productions as defined by section 2257 of title 18 of the U.S. Code.[238]

For purposes of recapture under section 1245, any deduction allowed under section 181 is treated as if it were a deduction allowable for amortization.[239]

Explanation of Provision

The provision extends the present law expensing provision for two years, to qualified film and television productions commencing prior to January 1, 2012.

Effective Date

The provision applies to qualified film and television productions commencing after December 31, 2009.

[Law at ¶ 5285. CCH Explanation at ¶ 514.]

[¶ 10,500] Act Sec. 745. Expensing of environmental remediation costs

Joint Committee on Taxation (J.C.T. REP. NO. JCX-55-10)

[Code Sec. 198]

Present Law

Present law allows a deduction for ordinary and necessary expenses paid or incurred in carrying on any trade or business.[240] Treasury regulations provide that the cost of incidental repairs that neither materially add to the value of property nor appreciably prolong its life, but keep it in an ordinarily efficient operating condition, may be deducted currently as a business expense.[241] Section 263(a)(1) limits the scope of section 162 by prohibiting a current deduction for certain capital expenditures. Treasury regulations define "capital expenditures" as amounts paid or incurred to materially add to the value, or substantially prolong the useful life, of property owned by the taxpayer, or to adapt property to a new or different use.[242] Amounts paid for repairs and maintenance do not constitute capital expenditures. The determination of whether an expense is deductible or capitalizable is based on all relevant facts and circumstances.

Taxpayers may elect to treat certain environmental remediation expenditures paid or incurred before January 1, 2010, that would otherwise be chargeable to capital account as deductible in the year paid or incurred.[243] The deduction applies for both regular and alternative minimum tax purposes. The expenditure must be incurred in connection with the abatement or control of hazardous substances at a qualified contaminated site. In general, any expenditure for the acquisition of depreciable property used in connection with the abatement or control of hazardous substances at a qualified contaminated site does not constitute a qualified environmental remediation expenditure. However, depreciation deductions allowable for such property that would otherwise be allocated to the site under the principles set forth in *Commissioner v. Idaho Power Co.*[244] and section 263A are treated as qualified environmental remediation expenditures.

A "qualified contaminated site" (a so-called "brownfield") generally is any property that is held for use in a trade or business, for the production of income, or as inventory and is certified by the appropriate State environmental agency to be an area at or on which there has been a release (or threat of release) or disposal of a hazardous substance. Both urban and rural property may qualify. However, sites that are identified on the national priorities list under the Comprehensive Environmental Response, Compensation, and Liability Act of 1980 ("CER-

---

[235] Sec. 181(d)(3)(A).
[236] Sec. 181(d)(3)(B).
[237] Sec. 181(d)(2)(B).
[238] Sec. 181(d)(2)(C).
[239] Sec. 1245(a)(2)(C).

[240] Sec. 162.
[241] Treas. Reg. sec. 1.162-4.
[242] Treas. Reg. sec. 1.263(a)-1(b).
[243] Sec. 198.
[244] 418 U.S. 1 (1974).

CLA")[245] cannot qualify as targeted areas. Hazardous substances generally are defined by reference to sections 101(14) and 102 of CERCLA, subject to additional limitations applicable to asbestos and similar substances within buildings, certain naturally occurring substances such as radon, and certain other substances released into drinking water supplies due to deterioration through ordinary use, as well as petroleum products defined in section 4612(a)(3) of the Code.

In the case of property to which a qualified environmental remediation expenditure otherwise would have been capitalized, any deduction allowed under section 198 is treated as a depreciation deduction and the property is treated as section 1245 property. Thus, deductions for qualified environmental remediation expenditures are subject to recapture as ordinary

income upon a sale or other disposition of the property. In addition, sections 280B (demolition of structures) and 468 (special rules for mining and solid waste reclamation and closing costs) do not apply to amounts that are treated as expenses under section 198.

Explanation of Provision

The provision extends the present law expensing for two years to include expenditures paid or incurred before January 1, 2012.

Effective Date

The provision is effective for expenditures paid or incurred after December 31, 2009.

[Law at ¶ 5290. CCH Explanation at ¶ 518.]

[¶ 10,510] Act Sec. 746. Deduction allowable with respect to income attributable to domestic production activities in Puerto Rico

Joint Committee on Taxation (J.C.T. Rep. No. JCX-55-10)

[Code Sec. 199]

Present Law

General

Present law provides a deduction from taxable income (or, in the case of an individual, adjusted gross income) that is equal to nine percent of the lesser of the taxpayer's qualified production activities income or taxable income for the taxable year. For taxpayers subject to the 35-percent corporate income tax rate, the nine-percent deduction effectively reduces the corporate income tax rate to just under 32 percent on qualified production activities income.

In general, qualified production activities income is equal to domestic production gross receipts reduced by the sum of: (1) the costs of goods sold that are allocable to those receipts; and (2) other expenses, losses, or deductions which are properly allocable to those receipts.

Domestic production gross receipts generally are gross receipts of a taxpayer that are

derived from: (1) any sale, exchange, or other disposition, or any lease, rental, or license, of qualifying production property[246] that was manufactured, produced, grown or extracted by the taxpayer in whole or in significant part within the United States; (2) any sale, exchange, or other disposition, or any lease, rental, or license, of qualified film[247] produced by the taxpayer; (3) any lease, rental, license, sale, exchange, or other disposition of electricity, natural gas, or potable water produced by the taxpayer in the United States; (4) construction of real property performed in the United States by a taxpayer in the ordinary course of a construction trade or business; or (5) engineering or architectural services performed in the United States for the construction of real property located in the United States.

The amount of the deduction for a taxable year is limited to 50 percent of the wages paid by the taxpayer, and properly allocable to domestic production gross receipts, during the calendar year that ends in such taxable year.[248] Wages paid to bona fide residents of Puerto Rico gener-

---

[245] Pub. L. No. 96-510 (1980).

[246] Qualifying production property generally includes any tangible personal property, computer software, and sound recordings.

[247] Qualified film includes any motion picture film or videotape (including live or delayed television programming, but not including certain sexually explicit productions) if 50 percent or more of the total compensation

relating to the production of the film (including compensation in the form of residuals and participations) constitutes compensation for services performed in the United States by actors, production personnel, directors, and producers.

[248] For purposes of the provision, "wages" include the sum of the amounts of wages as defined in section 3401(a) and elective deferrals that the taxpayer properly reports to the Social Security Administration with respect to the em-

ally are not included in the definition of wages for purposes of computing the wage limitation amount.[249]

Rules for Puerto Rico

When used in the Code in a geographical sense, the term "United States" generally includes only the States and the District of Columbia.[250] A special rule for determining domestic production gross receipts, however, provides that in the case of any taxpayer with gross receipts from sources within the Commonwealth of Puerto Rico, the term "United States" includes the Commonwealth of Puerto Rico, but only if all of the taxpayer's Puerto Rico-sourced gross receipts are taxable under the Federal income tax for individuals or corporations.[251] In computing the 50-percent wage limitation, the taxpayer is permitted to take into account wages paid to bona fide residents of Puerto Rico for services performed in Puerto Rico.[252]

The special rules for Puerto Rico apply only with respect to the first four taxable years of a taxpayer beginning after December 31, 2005 and before January 1, 2010.

Explanation of Provision

The provision allows the special domestic production activities rules for Puerto Rico to apply for the first six taxable years of a taxpayer beginning after December 31, 2005 and before January 1, 2012.

Effective Date

The provision is effective for taxable years beginning after December 31, 2009.

[Law at ¶ 5295. CCH Explanation at ¶ 632.]

[¶ 10,520] Act Sec. 747. Modification of tax treatment of certain payments to controlling exempt organizations

Joint Committee on Taxation (J.C.T. REP. NO. JCX-55-10)

[Code Sec. 512]

Present Law

In general, organizations exempt from Federal income tax are subject to the unrelated business income tax on income derived from a trade or business regularly carried on by the organization that is not substantially related to the performance of the organization's tax-exempt functions.[253] In general, interest, rents, royalties, and annuities are excluded from the unrelated business income of tax-exempt organizations.[254]

Section 512(b)(13) provides special rules regarding income derived by an exempt organization from a controlled subsidiary. In general, section 512(b)(13) treats otherwise excluded rent, royalty, annuity, and interest income as unrelated business income if such income is received from a taxable or tax-exempt subsidiary that is 50-percent controlled by the parent tax-exempt organization to the extent the payment reduces the net unrelated income (or increases any net unrelated loss) of the controlled entity (deter-

mined as if the entity were tax exempt). However, a special rule provides that, for payments made pursuant to a binding written contract in effect on August 17, 2006 (or renewal of such a contract on substantially similar terms), the general rule of section 512(b)(13) applies only to the portion of payments received or accrued in a taxable year that exceeds the amount of the payment that would have been paid or accrued if the amount of such payment had been determined under the principles of section 482 (i.e., at arm's length).[255] In addition, the special rule imposes a 20-percent penalty on the larger of such excess determined without regard to any amendment or supplement to a return of tax, or such excess determined with regard to all such amendments and supplements.

In the case of a stock subsidiary, "control" means ownership by vote or value of more than 50 percent of the stock. In the case of a partnership or other entity, "control" means ownership of more than 50 percent of the profits, capital, or beneficial interests. In addition, present law ap-

---

(Footnote Continued)

ployment of employees of the taxpayer during the calendar year ending during the taxpayer's taxable year.

[249] Section 3401(a)(8)(C) excludes wages paid to United States citizens who are bona fide residents of Puerto Rico from the term wages for purposes of income tax withholding.

[250] Sec. 7701(a)(9).

[251] Sec. 199(d)(8)(A).

[252] Sec. 199(d)(8)(B).

[253] Sec. 511.

[254] Sec. 512(b).

[255] Sec. 512(b)(13)(E).

plies the constructive ownership rules of section 318 for purposes of section 512(b)(13). Thus, a parent exempt organization is deemed to control any subsidiary in which it holds more than 50 percent of the voting power or value, directly (as in the case of a first-tier subsidiary) or indirectly (as in the case of a second-tier subsidiary).

The special rule does not apply to payments received or accrued after December 31, 2009.

Explanation of Provision

The provision extends the special rule to payments received or accrued before January 1, 2012. Accordingly, under the provision, payments of rent, royalties, annuities, or interest income by a controlled organization to a controlling organization pursuant to a binding written contract in effect on August 17, 2006 (or renewal of such a contract on substantially similar terms), may be includible in the unrelated business taxable income of the controlling organization only to the extent the payment exceeds the amount of the payment determined under the principles of section 482 (i.e., at arm's length). Any such excess is subject to a 20-percent penalty on the larger of such excess determined without regard to any amendment or supplement to a return of tax, or such excess determined with regard to all such amendments and supplements.

Effective Date

The provision is effective for payments received or accrued after December 31, 2009.

[Law at ¶5375. CCH Explanation at ¶615.]

[¶10,530] Act Sec. 748. Treatment of certain dividends of regulated investment companies

Joint Committee on Taxation (J.C.T. Rep. No. JCX-55-10)

[Code Sec. 871(k)]

Present Law[256]

In general

A regulated investment company ("RIC") is an entity that meets certain requirements, including a requirement that its income generally be derived from passive investments such as dividends and interest, that it distribute 90 percent of its income, and that it elects to be taxed under a special tax regime. Unlike an entity taxed as a corporation, an entity that is taxed as a RIC can deduct amounts paid to its shareholders as dividends. In this manner, tax on RIC income is generally not paid by the RIC but rather by its shareholders. However, income of a RIC is treated as a dividend by those shareholders, unless other special rules apply. Dividends received by foreign persons from a RIC are generally subject to gross-basis tax under sections 871(a) or 881, and the RIC payor of such dividends is obligated to withhold such tax under sections 1441 and 1442.

Under present law, a RIC that earns certain interest income that would not be subject to U.S. tax if earned by a foreign person directly may, to the extent of such net income, designate a dividend it pays as derived from such interest income. A foreign person who is a shareholder in the RIC generally can treat such a dividend as exempt from gross-basis U.S. tax, as if the foreign person had earned the interest directly. Also, subject to certain requirements, the RIC is exempt from withholding the gross basis tax on such dividends. Similar rules apply with respect to the designation of certain short term capital gain dividends. However, these provisions relating to certain dividends with respect to interest income and short term capital gain of the RIC do not apply to dividends with respect to any taxable year of a RIC beginning after December 31, 2009.

Explanation of Provision

The provision extends the rules exempting from gross basis tax and from withholding tax the interest-related dividends and short term capital gain dividends received from a RIC, to dividends with respect to taxable years of a RIC beginning before January 1, 2012.

Effective Date

The provision applies to dividends paid with respect to any taxable year of the RIC beginning after December 31, 2009.

[Law at ¶5465. CCH Explanation at ¶430.]

---

[256] Secs. 871(k), 881, 1441 and 1442.

[¶10,540] Act Sec. 749. RIC qualified investment entity treatment under FIRPTA

Joint Committee on Taxation (J.C.T. Rep. No. JCX-55-10)

[Code Secs. 897 and 1445]

Present law

Special U.S. tax rules apply to capital gains of foreign persons that are attributable to dispositions of interests in U.S. real property. In general, although a foreign person (a foreign corporation or a nonresident alien individual) is not generally taxed on U.S. source capital gains unless certain personal presence or active business requirements are met, a foreign person who sells a U.S. real property interest ("USRPI") is subject to tax at the same rates as a U.S. person, under the Foreign Investment in Real Property Tax Act ("FIRPTA") provisions codified in section 897 of the Code. Withholding tax is also imposed under section 1445.

A USRPI includes stock or a beneficial interest in any domestic corporation unless such corporation has not been a U.S. real property holding corporation (as defined) during the testing period. A USRPI does not include an interest in a domestically controlled "qualified investment entity." A distribution from a "qualified investment entity" that is attributable to the sale of a USRPI is also subject to tax under FIRPTA unless the distribution is with respect to an interest that is regularly traded on an established securities market located in the United States and the recipient foreign corporation or nonresident alien individual did not hold more than 5 percent of that class of stock or beneficial interest within the 1-year period ending on the date of distribution.[257] Special rules apply to situations involving tiers of qualified investment entities.

The term "qualified investment entity" includes a real estate investment trust ("REIT") and also includes a regulated investment company ("RIC") that meets certain requirements, although the inclusion of a RIC in that definition does not apply for certain purposes after December 31, 2009.[258]

Explanation of Provision

The provision extends the inclusion of a RIC within the definition of a "qualified investment entity" under section 897 of the Code through December 31, 2011, for those situations in which that inclusion would otherwise have expired at the end of 2009.

Effective Date

The provision is generally effective on January 1, 2010.

The provision does not apply with respect to the withholding requirement under section 1445 for any payment made before the date of enactment, but a RIC that withheld and remitted tax under section 1445 on distributions made after December 31, 2009 and before the date of enactment is not liable to the distributee with respect to such withheld and remitted amounts.

[Law at ¶5470. CCH Explanation at ¶620.]

[¶10,550] Act Sec. 750. Exceptions for active financing income

Joint Committee on Taxation (J.C.T. Rep. No. JCX-55-10)

[Code Secs. 953 and 954]

Present Law

Under the subpart F rules,[259] 10-percent-or-greater U.S. shareholders of a controlled foreign corporation ("CFC") are subject to U.S. tax currently on certain income earned by the CFC, whether or not such income is distributed to the shareholders. The income subject to current inclusion under the subpart F rules includes, among other things, insurance income and foreign base company income. Foreign base company income includes, among other things, foreign personal holding company income and foreign base company services income (i.e., income derived from services performed for or on behalf of a related person outside the country in which the CFC is organized).

---

[257] Sections 857(b)(3)(F), 852(b)(3)(E), and 871(k)(2)(E) require dividend treatment, rather than capital gain treatment, for certain distributions to which FIRPTA does not apply by reason of this exception. See also section 881(e)(2).

[258] Section 897(h).

[259] Secs. 951-964.

Foreign personal holding company income generally consists of the following: (1) dividends, interest, royalties, rents, and annuities; (2) net gains from the sale or exchange of (a) property that gives rise to the preceding types of income, (b) property that does not give rise to income, and (c) interests in trusts, partnerships, and real estate mortgage investment conduits ("REMICs"); (3) net gains from commodities transactions; (4) net gains from certain foreign currency transactions; (5) income that is equivalent to interest; (6) income from notional principal contracts; (7) payments in lieu of dividends; and (8) amounts received under personal service contracts.

Insurance income subject to current inclusion under the subpart F rules includes any income of a CFC attributable to the issuing or reinsuring of any insurance or annuity contract in connection with risks located in a country other than the CFC's country of organization. Subpart F insurance income also includes income attributable to an insurance contract in connection with risks located within the CFC's country of organization, as the result of an arrangement under which another corporation receives a substantially equal amount of consideration for insurance of other country risks. Investment income of a CFC that is allocable to any insurance or annuity contract related to risks located outside the CFC's country of organization is taxable as subpart F insurance income.[260]

Temporary exceptions from foreign personal holding company income, foreign base company services income, and insurance income apply for subpart F purposes for certain income that is derived in the active conduct of a banking, financing, or similar business, as a securities dealer, or in the conduct of an insurance business (so-called "active financing income"). These provisions were enacted in the Taxpayer Relief Act of 1997 as one-year temporary exceptions, and in 1998, 1999, 2002, 2006, and 2008, the provisions were extended, and in some cases, modified.[261]

With respect to income derived in the active conduct of a banking, financing, or similar business, a CFC is required to be predominantly engaged in such business and to conduct substantial activity with respect to such business in order to qualify for the active financing exceptions. In addition, certain nexus requirements apply, which provide that income derived by a CFC or a qualified business unit ("QBU") of a CFC from transactions with customers is eligible for the exceptions if, among other things, substantially all of the activities in connection with such transactions are conducted directly by the CFC or QBU in its home country, and such income is treated as earned by the CFC or QBU in its home country for purposes of such country's tax laws. Moreover, the exceptions apply to income derived from certain cross border transactions, provided that certain requirements are met. Additional exceptions from foreign personal holding company income apply for certain income derived by a securities dealer within the meaning of section 475 and for gain from the sale of active financing assets.

In the case of a securities dealer, the temporary exception from foreign personal holding company income applies to certain income. The income covered by the exception is any interest or dividend (or certain equivalent amounts) from any transaction, including a hedging transaction or a transaction consisting of a deposit of collateral or margin, entered into in the ordinary course of the dealer's trade or business as a dealer in securities within the meaning of section 475. In the case of a QBU of the dealer, the income is required to be attributable to activities of the QBU in the country of incorporation, or to a QBU in the country in which the QBU both maintains its principal office and conducts substantial business activity. A coordination rule provides that this exception generally takes precedence over the exception for income of a banking, financing or similar business, in the case of a securities dealer.

In the case of insurance, a temporary exception from foreign personal holding company in-

---

[260] Prop. Treas. Reg. sec. 1.953-1(a).

[261] Temporary exceptions from the subpart F provisions for certain active financing income applied only for taxable years beginning in 1998 (Taxpayer Relief Act of 1997, Pub. L. No. 105-34). Those exceptions were modified and extended for one year, applicable only for taxable years beginning in 1999 (the Tax and Trade Relief Extension Act of 1998, Pub. L. No. 105-277). The Tax Relief Extension Act of 1999 (Pub. L. No. 106-170) clarified and extended the temporary exceptions for two years, applicable only for taxable years beginning after 1999 and before 2002. The Job Creation and

Worker Assistance Act of 2002 (Pub. L. No. 107-147) modified and extended the temporary exceptions for five years, for taxable years beginning after 2001 and before 2007. The Tax Increase Prevention and Reconciliation Act of 2005 (Pub. L. No. 109-222) extended the temporary provisions for two years, for taxable years beginning after 2006 and before 2009. The Energy Improvement and Extension Act of 2008 (Pub. L. No. 110-343) extended the temporary provisions for one year, for taxable years beginning after 2008 and before 2010.

come applies for certain income of a qualifying insurance company with respect to risks located within the CFC's country of creation or organization. In the case of insurance, temporary exceptions from insurance income and from foreign personal holding company income also apply for certain income of a qualifying branch of a qualifying insurance company with respect to risks located within the home country of the branch, provided certain requirements are met under each of the exceptions. Further, additional temporary exceptions from insurance income and from foreign personal holding company income apply for certain income of certain CFCs or branches with respect to risks located in a country other than the United States, provided that the requirements for these exceptions are met. In the case of a life insurance or annuity contract, reserves for such contracts are determined under rules specific to the temporary exceptions. Present law also permits a taxpayer in certain circumstances, subject to approval by the IRS through the ruling process or in published guidance, to establish that the reserve of a life insurance company for life insurance and annuity contracts is the amount taken into account in determining the foreign statement reserve for the contract (reduced by catastrophe, equalization, or deficiency reserve or any similar reserve). IRS approval is to be based on whether the method, the interest rate, the mortality and morbidity assumptions, and any other factors taken into account in determining foreign statement reserves (taken together or separately) provide an appropriate means of measuring income for Federal income tax purposes.

Explanation of Provision

The provision extends for two years (for taxable years beginning before 2012) the present-law temporary exceptions from subpart F foreign personal holding company income, foreign base company services income, and insurance income for certain income that is derived in the active conduct of a banking, financing, or similar business, or in the conduct of an insurance business.

Effective Date

The provision is effective for taxable years of foreign corporations beginning after December 31, 2009, and for taxable years of U.S. shareholders with or within which such taxable years of such foreign corporations end.

[Law at ¶5480 and ¶5485. CCH Explanation at ¶623 and ¶626.]

[¶10,560] Act Sec. 751. Look-thru treatment of payments between related controlled foreign corporations under foreign personal holding company rules

Joint Committee on Taxation (J.C.T. REP. NO. JCX-55-10)

[Code Sec. 954(c)(6)]

Present Law

In general

The rules of subpart F[262] require U.S. shareholders with a 10-percent or greater interest in a controlled foreign corporation ("CFC") to include certain income of the CFC (referred to as "subpart F income") on a current basis for U.S. tax purposes, regardless of whether the income is distributed to the shareholders.

Subpart F income includes foreign base company income. One category of foreign base company income is foreign personal holding company income. For subpart F purposes, foreign personal holding company income generally includes dividends, interest, rents, and royalties, among other types of income. There are several exceptions to these rules. For example, foreign personal holding company income does not include dividends and interest received by a CFC from a related corporation organized and operating in the same foreign country in which the CFC is organized, or rents and royalties received by a CFC from a related corporation for the use of property within the country in which the CFC is organized. Interest, rent, and royalty payments do not qualify for this exclusion to the extent that such payments reduce the subpart F income of the payor. In addition, subpart F income of a CFC does not include any item of income from sources within the United States that is effectively connected with the conduct by such CFC of a trade or business within the United States ("ECI") unless such item is exempt from taxation (or is subject to a reduced rate of tax) pursuant to a tax treaty.

---

[262] Secs. 951-964.

The "look-thru rule"

Under the "look-thru rule" (sec. 954(c)(6)), dividends, interest (including factoring income that is treated as equivalent to interest under section 954(c)(1)(E)), rents, and royalties received by one CFC from a related CFC are not treated as foreign personal holding company income to the extent attributable or properly allocable to income of the payor that is neither subpart F income nor treated as ECI. For this purpose, a related CFC is a CFC that controls or is controlled by the other CFC, or a CFC that is controlled by the same person or persons that control the other CFC. Ownership of more than 50 percent of the CFC's stock (by vote or value) constitutes control for these purposes.

The Secretary is authorized to prescribe regulations that are necessary or appropriate to carry out the look-thru rule, including such regulations as are appropriate to prevent the abuse of the purposes of such rule.

The look-thru rule is effective for taxable years of foreign corporations beginning before January 1, 2010, and for taxable years of U.S. shareholders with or within which such taxable years of such foreign corporations end.

Explanation of Provision

The provision extends for two years the application of the look-thru rule, to taxable years of foreign corporations beginning before January 1, 2012, and for taxable years of U.S. shareholders with or within which such taxable years of such foreign corporations end.

Effective Date

The provision is effective for taxable years of foreign corporations beginning after December 31, 2009, and for taxable years of U.S. shareholders with or within which such taxable years of such foreign corporations end.

[Law at ¶5485. CCH Explanation at ¶629.]

[¶10,570] Act Sec. 752. Basis adjustment to stock of S corps making charitable contributions of property

Joint Committee on Taxation (J.C.T. REP. NO. JCX-55-10)

[Code Sec. 1367]

Present Law

Under present law, if an S corporation contributes money or other property to a charity, each shareholder takes into account the shareholder's pro rata share of the contribution in determining its own income tax liability.[263] A shareholder of an S corporation reduces the basis in the stock of the S corporation by the amount of the charitable contribution that flows through to the shareholder.[264]

In the case of contributions made in taxable years beginning before January 1, 2010, the amount of a shareholder's basis reduction in the stock of an S corporation by reason of a charitable contribution made by the corporation is equal to the shareholder's pro rata share of the

adjusted basis of the contributed property. For contributions made in taxable years beginning after December 31, 2009, the amount of the reduction is the shareholder's pro rata share of the fair market value of the contributed property.

Explanation of Provision

The provision extends the rule relating to the basis reduction on account of charitable contributions of property for two years to contributions made in taxable years beginning before January 1, 2012.

Effective Date

The provision applies to contributions made in taxable years beginning after December 31, 2009.

[Law at ¶5555. CCH Explanation at ¶557.]

---

[263] Sec. 1366(a)(1)(A).

[264] Sec. 1367(a)(2)(B).

[¶10,580] Act Sec. 753. Empowerment zone tax incentives

Joint Committee on Taxation (J.C.T. Rep. No. JCX-55-10)

[Code Secs. 1202 and 1391]

Present Law

The Omnibus Budget Reconciliation Act of 1993 ("OBRA 93")[265] authorized the designation of nine empowerment zones ("Round I empowerment zones") to provide tax incentives for businesses to locate within certain targeted areas[266] designated by the Secretaries of the Department of Housing and Urban Development ("HUD") and the U.S Department of Agriculture ("USDA"). The Taxpayer Relief Act of 1997[267] authorized the designation of two additional Round I urban empowerment zones, and 20 additional empowerment zones ("Round II empowerment zones"). The Community Renewal Tax Relief Act of 2000 ("2000 Community Renewal Act")[268] authorized a total of ten new empowerment zones ("Round III empowerment zones"), bringing the total number of authorized empowerment zones to 40.[269] In addition, the 2000 Community Renewal Act conformed the tax incentives that are available to businesses in the Round I, Round II, and Round III empowerment zones, and extended the empowerment zone incentives through December 31, 2009.[270]

The tax incentives available within the designated empowerment zones include a Federal income tax credit for employers who hire qualifying employees, accelerated depreciation deductions on qualifying equipment, tax-exempt bond financing, deferral of capital gains tax on sale of qualified assets sold and replaced, and partial exclusion of capital gains tax on certain sales of qualified small business stock.

The following is a description of the tax incentives.

Employment credit

A 20-percent wage credit is available to employers for the first $15,000 of qualified wages paid to each employee (i.e., a maximum credit of $3,000 with respect to each qualified employee) who (1) is a resident of the empowerment zone, and (2) performs substantially all employment services within the empowerment zone in a trade or business of the employer.[271]

The wage credit rate applies to qualifying wages paid before January 1, 2010. Wages paid to a qualified employee who earns more than $15,000 are eligible for the wage credit (although only the first $15,000 of wages is eligible for the credit). The wage credit is available with respect to a qualified full-time or part-time employee (employed for at least 90 days), regardless of the number of other employees who work for the employer. In general, any taxable business carrying out activities in the empowerment zone may claim the wage credit, regardless of whether the employer meets the definition of an "enterprise zone business."[272]

---

[265] Pub. L. No. 103-66.

[266] The targeted areas are those that have pervasive poverty, high unemployment, and general economic distress, and that satisfy certain eligibility criteria, including specified poverty rates and population and geographic size limitations.

[267] Pub. L. No. 105-34.

[268] Pub. L. No. 106-554.

[269] The urban part of the program is administered by HUD and the rural part of the program is administered by the USDA. The eight Round I urban empowerment zones are Atlanta, GA; Baltimore, MD; Chicago, IL; Cleveland, OH; Detroit, MI; Los Angeles, CA; New York, NY; and Philadelphia, PA/Camden, NJ. Atlanta relinquished its empowerment zone designation in Round III. The three Round I rural empowerment zones are Kentucky Highlands, KY; Mid-Delta, MI; and Rio Grande Valley, TX. The 15 Round II urban empowerment zones are Boston, MA; Cincinnati, OH; Columbia, SC; Columbus, OH; Cumberland County, NJ; El Paso, TX; Gary/Hammond/East Chicago, IN; Ironton, OH/Huntington, WV; Knoxville, TN; Miami/Dade County, FL; Minneapolis, MN; New Haven, CT; Norfolk/Portsmouth, VA; Santa Ana, CA; and St. Louis, Missouri/East St. Louis, IL. The five Round II rural empowerment zones are Desert Communities, CA; Griggs-Steele, ND; Oglala Sioux Tribe, SD; Southernmost Illinois Delta, IL; and Southwest Georgia United, GA. The eight Round III urban empowerment zones are Fresno, CA; Jacksonville, FL; Oklahoma City, OK; Pulaski County, AR; San Antonio, TX; Syracuse, NY; Tucson, AZ; and Yonkers, NY. The two Round III rural empowerment zones are Aroostook County, ME; and Futuro, TX.

[270] If an empowerment zone designation were terminated prior to December 31, 2009, the tax incentives would cease to be available as of the termination date.

[271] Sec. 1396. The $15,000 limit is annual, not cumulative such that the limit is the first $15,000 of wages paid in a calendar year which ends with or within the taxable year.

[272] Secs. 1397C(b) and 1397C(c). However, the wage credit is not available for wages paid in connection with certain business activities described in section 144(c)(6)(B), including a golf course, country club, massage parlor, hot tub facility, suntan facility, racetrack, or liquor store, or certain farming activities. In addition, wages are not eligible for the wage credit if paid to: (1) a person who owns more than five percent of the stock (or capital or profits interests) of the employer, (2) certain relatives of the employer, or (3) if the employer is a corporation or partnership, certain

An employer's deduction otherwise allowed for wages paid is reduced by the amount of wage credit claimed for that taxable year.[273] Wages are not to be taken into account for purposes of the wage credit if taken into account in determining the employer's work opportunity tax credit under section 51 or the welfare-to-work credit under section 51A.[274] In addition, the $15,000 cap is reduced by any wages taken into account in computing the work opportunity tax credit or the welfare-to-work credit.[275] The wage credit may be used to offset up to 25 percent of alternative minimum tax liability.[276]

Increased section 179 expensing limitation

An enterprise zone business is allowed an additional $35,000 of section 179 expensing (for a total of up to $285,000 in 2009)[277] for qualified zone property placed in service before January 1, 2010.[278] The section 179 expensing allowed to a taxpayer is phased out by the amount by which 50 percent of the cost of qualified zone property placed in service during the year by the taxpayer exceeds $500,000.[279] The term "qualified zone property" is defined as depreciable tangible property (including buildings) provided that (i) the property is acquired by the taxpayer (from an unrelated party) after the designation took effect, (ii) the original use of the property in an empowerment zone commences with the taxpayer, and (iii) substantially all of the use of the property is in an empowerment zone in the active conduct of a trade or business by the taxpayer. Special rules are provided in the case of property that is substantially renovated by the taxpayer.

An enterprise zone business means any qualified business entity and any qualified proprietorship. A qualified business entity means, any corporation or partnership if for such year: (1) every trade or business of such entity is the active conduct of a qualified business within an empowerment zone; (2) at least 50 percent of the total gross income of such entity is derived from the active conduct of such business; (3) a substantial portion of the use of the tangible property of such entity (whether owned or leased) is within an empowerment zone; (4) a substantial

portion of the intangible property of such entity is used in the active conduct of any such business; (5) a substantial portion of the services performed for such entity by its employees are performed in an empowerment zone; (6) at least 35 percent of its employees are residents of an empowerment zone; (7) less than five percent of the average of the aggregate unadjusted bases of the property of such entity is attributable to collectibles other than collectibles that are held primarily for sale to customers in the ordinary course of such business; and (8) less than 5 percent of the average of the aggregate unadjusted bases of the property of such entity is attributable to nonqualified financial property.[280]

A qualified proprietorship is any qualified business carried on by an individual as a proprietorship if for such year: (1) at least 50 percent of the total gross income of such individual from such business is derived from the active conduct of such business in an empowerment zone; (2) a substantial portion of the use of the tangible property of such individual in such business (whether owned or leased) is within an empowerment zone; (3) a substantial portion of the intangible property of such business is used in the active conduct of such business; (4) a substantial portion of the services performed for such individual in such business by employees of such business are performed in an empowerment zone; (5) at least 35 percent of such employees are residents of an empowerment zone; (6) less than 5 percent of the average of the aggregate unadjusted bases of the property of such individual which is used in such business is attributable to collectibles other than collectibles that are held primarily for sale to customers in the ordinary course of such business; and (7) less than 5 percent of the average of the aggregate unadjusted bases of the property of such individual which is used in such business is attributable to nonqualified financial property.[281]

A qualified business is defined as any trade or business other than a trade or business that consists predominantly of the development or holding of intangibles for sale or license or any business prohibited in connection with the em-

---

(Footnote Continued)

relatives of a person who owns more than 50 percent of the business.

[273] Sec. 280C(a).

[274] Secs. 1396(c)(3)(A) and 51A(d)(2).

[275] Secs. 1396(c)(3)(B) and 51A(d)(2).

[276] Sec. 38(c)(2).

[277] For each of 2010 and 2011, the 179 expensing limitation will be a total of up to $535,000. The Small Business

Jobs Act of 2010, Pub. L. No. 111-240. See discussion above at IV.B.

[278] Secs. 1397A, 1397D.

[279] Sec. 1397A(a)(2), 179(b)(2), (7). For 2008 and 2009, the limit is $800,000.

[280] Sec. 1397C(b).

[281] Sec. 1397C(c).

ployment credit.[282] In addition, the leasing of real property that is located within the empowerment zone is treated as a qualified business only if (1) the leased property is not residential property, and (2) at least 50 percent of the gross rental income from the real property is from enterprise zone businesses. The rental of tangible personal property is not a qualified business unless at least 50 percent of the rental of such property is by enterprise zone businesses or by residents of an empowerment zone.

Expanded tax-exempt financing for certain zone facilities

States or local governments can issue enterprise zone facility bonds to raise funds to provide an enterprise zone business with qualified zone property.[283] These bonds can be used in areas designated enterprise communities as well as areas designated empowerment zones. To qualify, 95 percent (or more) of the net proceeds from the bond issue must be used to finance: (1) qualified zone property whose principal user is an enterprise zone business, and (2) certain land functionally related and subordinate to such property.

The term enterprise zone business is the same as that used for purposes of the increased section 179 deduction limitation (discussed above) with certain modifications for start-up businesses. First, a business will be treated as an enterprise zone business during a start-up period if (1) at the beginning of the period, it is reasonable to expect the business to be an enterprise zone business by the end of the start-up period, and (2) the business makes bona fide efforts to be an enterprise zone business. The start-up period is the period that ends with the start of the first tax year beginning more than two years after the later of (1) the issue date of the bond issue financing the qualified zone property, and (2) the date this property is first placed in service (or, if earlier, the date that is three years after the issue date).[284]

Second, a business that qualifies as at the end of the start-up period must continue to qualify during a testing period that ends three tax years after the start-up period ends. After the three-year testing period, a business will continue to be treated as an enterprise zone business as long as 35 percent of its employees are residents of an empowerment zone or enterprise community.

The face amount of the bonds may not exceed $60 million for an empowerment zone in a rural area, $130 million for an empowerment zone in an urban area with zone population of less than 100,000, and $230 million for an empowerment zone in an urban area with zone population of at least 100,000.

Elective roll over of capital gain from the sale or exchange of any qualified empowerment zone asset purchased after December 21, 2000

Taxpayers can elect to defer recognition of gain on the sale of a qualified empowerment zone asset[285] held for more than one year and replaced within 60 days by another qualified empowerment zone asset in the same zone.[286] The deferral is accomplished by reducing the basis of the replacement asset by the amount of the gain recognized on the sale of the asset.

Partial exclusion of capital gains on certain small business stock

Individuals generally may exclude 50 percent (60 percent for certain empowerment zone businesses) of the gain from the sale of certain small business stock acquired at original issue and held for at least five years.[287] The amount of gain eligible for the exclusion by an individual with respect to any corporation is the greater of

---

[282] Sec. 1397C(d). Excluded businesses include any private or commercial golf course, country club, massage parlor, hot tub facility, sun tan facility, racetrack, or other facility used for gambling or any store the principal business of which is the sale of alcoholic beverages for off-premises consumption. Sec. 144(c)(6).

[283] Sec. 1394.

[284] Sec. 1394(b)(3).

[285] The term "qualified empowerment zone asset" means any property which would be a qualified community asset (as defined in section 1400F, relating to certain tax benefits for renewal communities) if in section 1400F: (i) references to empowerment zones were substituted for references to renewal communities, (ii) references to enterprise zone businesses (as defined in section 1397C) were substituted for references to renewal community businesses, and (iii) the date of the enactment of this paragraph were substituted for

"December 31, 2001" each place it appears. Sec. 1397B(b)(1)(A).

A "qualified community asset" includes: (1) qualified community stock (meaning original-issue stock purchased for cash in an enterprise zone business), (2) a qualified community partnership interest (meaning a partnership interest acquired for cash in an enterprise zone business), and (3) qualified community business property (meaning tangible property originally used in a enterprise zone business by the taxpayer) that is purchased or substantially improved after the date of the enactment of this paragraph.

For the definition of "enterprise zone business," see text accompanying *supra* note 280. For the definition of "qualified business," see text accompanying *supra* note 280.

[286] Sec. 1397B.

[287] Sec. 1202.

(1) ten times the taxpayer's basis in the stock or (2) $10 million. To qualify as a small business, when the stock is issued, the gross assets of the corporation may not exceed $50 million. The corporation also must meet certain active trade or business requirements.

The portion of the gain includible in taxable income is taxed at a maximum rate of 28 percent under the regular tax.[288] A percentage of the excluded gain is an alternative minimum tax preference;[289] the portion of the gain includible in alternative minimum taxable income is taxed at a maximum rate of 28 percent under the alternative minimum tax.

Gain from the sale of qualified small business stock generally is taxed at effective rates of 14 percent under the regular tax[290] and (i) 14.98 percent under the alternative minimum tax for dispositions before January 1, 2011; (ii) 19.88 percent under the alternative minimum tax for dispositions after December 31, 2010, in the case of stock acquired before January 1, 2001; and (iii) 17.92 percent under the alternative minimum tax for dispositions after December 31, 2010, in the case of stock acquired after December 31, 2000.[291]

Temporary increases in exclusion

The percentage exclusion for qualified small business stock acquired after February 17, 2009, and on or before September 27, 2010, is increased to 75 percent.

The percentage exclusion for qualified small business stock acquired after September 27, 2010, and before January 1, 2011, is increased to 100 percent.[292]

The temporary increases in the exclusion percentage apply for all qualified small business stock, including stock of empowerment zone businesses.[293]

Other tax incentives

Other incentives not specific to empowerment zones but beneficial to these areas include the work opportunity tax credit for employers based on the first year of employment of certain targeted groups, including empowerment zone residents (up to $2,400 per employee), and qualified zone academy bonds for certain public schools located in an empowerment zone, or expected (as of the date of bond issuance) to have at least 35 percent of its students receiving free or reduced lunches.

Explanation of Provision

The provision extends for two years, through December 31, 2011, the period for which the designation of an empowerment zone is in effect, thus extending for two years the empowerment zone tax incentives, including the wage credit, accelerated depreciation deductions on qualifying equipment, tax-exempt bond financing, and deferral of capital gains tax on sale of qualified assets sold and replaced. In the case of a designation of an empowerment zone the nomination for which included a termination date which is December 31, 2009, termination shall not apply with respect to such designation if the entity which made such nomination amends the nomination to provide for a new termination date in such manner as the Secretary may provide.

The provision extends for two years, through December 31, 2016, the period for which the percentage exclusion for qualified small business stock (of a corporation which is a qualified business entity) acquired on or before February 17, 2009 is 60 percent. Gain attributable to periods after December 31, 2016 for qualified small business stock acquired on or before February 17, 2009 or after December 31, 2011 is subject to the general rule which provides for a percentage exclusion of 50 percent.

Effective Date

The provision relating to the designation of an empowerment zone and the provision relating to the exclusion of gain from the sale or exchange of qualified small business stock held for more than five years applies to periods after December 31, 2009.

[Law at ¶5510 and ¶5560, ¶7065. CCH Explanation at ¶440.]

---

[288] Sec. 1(h).

[289] Sec. 57(a)(7). In the case of qualified small business stock, the percentage of gain excluded from gross income which is an alternative minimum tax preference is (i) seven percent in the case of stock disposed of in a taxable year beginning before 2011; (ii) 42 percent in the case of stock acquired before January 1, 2001, and disposed of in a taxable year beginning after 2010; and (iii) 28 percent in the case of stock acquired after December 31, 2000, and disposed of in a taxable year beginning after 2010.

[290] The 50 percent of gain included in taxable income is taxed at a maximum rate of 28 percent.

[291] The amount of gain included in alternative minimum tax is taxed at a maximum rate of 28 percent. The amount so included is the sum of (i) 50 percent (the percentage included in taxable income) of the total gain and (ii) the applicable preference percentage of the one-half gain that is excluded from taxable income.

[292] Sec. 760 of the bill extends the January 1, 2011, date to January 1, 2012.

[293] Secs. 1202(a)(3)(B) and 1202(a)(4)(B).

[¶10,600] Act Sec. 754. Tax incentives for investment in the District of Columbia

Joint Committee on Taxation (J.C.T. Rep. No. JCX-55-10)

[Code Secs. 1400, 1400A, 1400B and 1400C]

Present Law

In general

The Taxpayer Relief Act of 1997 designated certain economically depressed census tracts within the District of Columbia as the "District of Columbia Enterprise Zone," or "DC Zone," within which businesses and individual residents are eligible for special tax incentives. The census tracts that comprise the District of Columbia Enterprise Zone are (1) all census tracts that presently are part of the D.C. enterprise community designated under section 1391 (i.e., portions of Anacostia, Mt. Pleasant, Chinatown, and the easternmost part of the District of Columbia), and (2) all additional census tracts within the District of Columbia where the poverty rate is not less than 20 percent. The District of Columbia Enterprise Zone designation remains in effect for the period from January 1, 1998, through December 31, 2009.

The following tax incentives are available for businesses located in an empowerment zone and the District of Columbia Enterprise Zone is treated as an empowerment zone for this purpose: (1) 20-percent wage credit, (2) an additional $35,000 of section 179 expensing for qualified zone property, and (3) expanded tax-exempt financing for certain zone facilities. In addition, a zero-percent capital gains rate applies to capital gains from the sale of certain qualified DC Zone assets held for more than five years.

Present law also provides for a nonrefundable tax credit for first-time homebuyers of a principal residence in the District of Columbia.

Employment credit

A 20-percent wage credit is available to employers for the first $15,000 of qualified wages paid to each employee (i.e., a maximum credit of $3,000 with respect to each qualified employee) who (1) is a resident of the District of Columbia, and (2) performs substantially all employment services within an empowerment zone in a trade or business of the employer.

The wage credit rate applies to qualifying wages paid after December 31, 2001, and before January 1, 2010. Wages paid to a qualified employee who earns more than $15,000 are eligible for the wage credit (although only the first $15,000 of wages is eligible for the credit). The wage credit is available with respect to a qualified full-time or part-time employee (employed for at least 90 days), regardless of the number of other employees who work for the employer. In general, any taxable business carrying out activities in the empowerment zone may claim the wage credit, regardless of whether the employer meets the definition of an "enterprise zone business," as defined below.

An employer's deduction otherwise allowed for wages paid is reduced by the amount of wage credit claimed for that taxable year. Wages are not to be taken into account for purposes of the wage credit if taken into account in determining the employer's work opportunity tax credit under section 51 or the welfare-to-work credit under section 51A. In addition, the $15,000 cap is reduced by any wages taken into account in computing the work opportunity tax credit or the welfare-to-work credit. The wage credit may be used to offset up to 25 percent of alternative minimum tax liability.

Increased section 179 expensing limitation

An enterprise zone business is allowed an additional $35,000 of section 179 expensing (for a total of up to $285,000 in 2009)[294] for qualified zone property placed in service after December 31, 2001, and before January 1, 2010. The section 179 expensing allowed to a taxpayer is phased out by the amount by which 50 percent of the cost of qualified zone property placed in service during the year by the taxpayer exceeds $500,000. The term "qualified zone property" is defined as depreciable tangible property (including buildings) provided that (i) the property is

---

[294] For each of 2010 and 2011, the 179 expensing limitation will be a total of up to $535,000. The Small Business Jobs Act of 2010, Pub. L. No. 111-240. See discussion above at IV.B.

acquired by the taxpayer (from an unrelated party) after the designation took effect, (ii) the original use of the property in an empowerment zone commences with the taxpayer, and (iii) substantially all of the use of the property is in an empowerment zone in the active conduct of a trade or business by the taxpayer. For this purpose, special rules are provided in the case of property that is substantially renovated by the taxpayer.

An enterprise zone business means any qualified business entity and any qualified proprietorship. A qualified business entity means, any corporation or partnership if for such year: (1) every trade or business of such entity is the active conduct of a qualified business within an empowerment zone; (2) at least 50 percent of the total gross income of such entity is derived from the active conduct of such business; (3) a substantial portion of the use of the tangible property of such entity (whether owned or leased) is within an empowerment zone; (4) a substantial portion of the intangible property of such entity is used in the active conduct of any such business; (5) a substantial portion of the services performed for such entity by its employees are performed in an empowerment zone; (6) at least 35 percent of its employees are residents of an empowerment zone; (7) less than five percent of the average of the aggregate unadjusted bases of the property of such entity is attributable to collectibles other than collectibles that are held primarily for sale to customers in the ordinary course of such business; and (8) less than 5 percent of the average of the aggregate unadjusted bases of the property of such entity is attributable to nonqualified financial property.

A qualified proprietorship is any qualified business carried on by an individual as a proprietorship if for such year: (1) at least 50 percent of the total gross income of such individual from such business is derived from the active conduct of such business in an empowerment zone; (2) a substantial portion of the use of the tangible property of such individual in such business (whether owned or leased) is within an empowerment zone; (3) a substantial portion of the intangible property of such business is used in the active conduct of such business; (4) a substantial portion of the services performed for such individual in such business by employees of such business are performed in an empowerment zone; (5) at least 35 percent of such employees are residents of an empowerment zone; (6) less than 5 percent of the average of the aggregate unadjusted bases of the property of such individual which is used in such business is attributable to collectibles other than collectibles that

are held primarily for sale to customers in the ordinary course of such business; and (7) less than 5 percent of the average of the aggregate unadjusted bases of the property of such individual which is used in such business is attributable to nonqualified financial property.

A qualified business is defined as any trade or business other than a trade or business that consists predominantly of the development or holding of intangibles for sale or license or any business prohibited in connection with the employment credit. In addition, the leasing of real property that is located within the empowerment zone is treated as a qualified business only if (1) the leased property is not residential property, and (2) at least 50 percent of the gross rental income from the real property is from enterprise zone businesses. The rental of tangible personal property is not a qualified business unless at least 50 percent of the rental of such property is by enterprise zone businesses or by residents of an empowerment zone.

Expanded tax-exempt financing for certain zone facilities

An enterprise zone business is permitted to borrow proceeds from the issuance of tax-exempt enterprise zone facility bonds (as defined in section 1394, without regard to the employee residency requirement) issued by the District of Columbia. To qualify, 95 percent (or more) of the net proceeds must be used to finance: (1) qualified zone property whose principal user is an enterprise zone business, and (2) certain land functionally related and subordinate to such property. Accordingly, most of the proceeds have to be used to finance certain facilities within the DC Zone. The aggregate face amount of all outstanding qualified enterprise zone facility bonds per enterprise zone business may not exceed $15 million and may be issued only while the DC Zone designation is in effect, from January 1, 1998 through December 31, 2009.

The term enterprise zone business is the same as that used for purposes of the increased section 179 deduction limitation with certain modifications for start-up businesses. First, a business will be treated as an enterprise zone business during a start-up period if (1) at the beginning of the period, it is reasonable to expect the business to be an enterprise zone business by the end of the start-up period, and (2) the business makes bona fide efforts to be an enterprise zone business. The start-up period is the period that ends with the start of the first tax year beginning more than two years after the later of (1) the issue date of the bond issue financing the qualified zone property, and (2) the date this property is first placed in service (or, if earlier, the date that is three years after the issue date).

Second, a business that qualifies as at the end of the start-up period must continue to qualify during a testing period that ends three tax years after the start-up period ends. After the three-year testing period, a business will continue to be treated as an enterprise zone business as long as 35 percent of its employees are residents of an empowerment zone or enterprise community.

Zero-percent capital gains

A zero-percent capital gains rate applies to capital gains from the sale of certain qualified DC Zone assets held for more than five years. In general, a "qualified DC Zone asset" means stock or partnership interests held in, or tangible property held by, a DC Zone business. For purposes of the zero-percent capital gains rate, the DC Zone is defined to include all census tracts within the District of Columbia where the poverty rate is not less than ten percent.

In general, gain eligible for the zero-percent tax rate is that from the sale or exchange of a qualified DC Zone asset that is (1) a capital asset or (2) property used in a trade or business, as defined in section 1231(b). Gain that is attributable to real property, or to intangible assets, qualifies for the zero-percent rate, provided that such real property or intangible asset is an integral part of a qualified DC Zone business. However, no gain attributable to periods before January 1, 1998, and after December 31, 2014, is qualified capital gain.

District of Columbia homebuyer tax credit

First-time homebuyers of a principal residence in the District of Columbia qualify for a tax credit of up to $5,000. The $5,000 maximum credit amount applies both to individuals and married couples. The credit phases out for individual taxpayers with adjusted gross income between $70,000 and $90,000 ($110,000 and $130,000 for joint filers). The credit is available with respect to purchases of existing property as well as new construction.

A "first-time homebuyer" means any individual if such individual (and, if married, such individual's spouse) did not have a present ownership interest in a principal residence in the District of Columbia during the one-year period ending on the date of the purchase of the principal residence to which the credit applies. A taxpayer will be treated as a first-time homebuyer with respect to only one residence—i.e., a taxpayer may claim the credit only once. A tax-

payer's basis in a property is reduced by the amount of any homebuyer tax credit claimed with respect to such property.

The first-time homebuyer credit is a nonrefundable personal credit and may offset the regular tax and the alternative minimum tax. Any credit in excess of tax liability may be carried forward indefinitely. The homebuyer credit is generally available for property purchased after August 4, 1997, and before January 1, 2010. However, the credit does not apply to the purchase of a residence after December 31, 2008 to which the national first-time homebuyer credit under Section 36 of the Code applies.

Explanation of Provision

The provision extends for two years, through December 31, 2011, the designation of the District of Columbia Enterprise Zone. The provision also extends for two years through December 31, 2011, the special $15 million per-user bond limitation and the relief from resident and employee requirements for certain tax-exempt bonds issued in the District of Columbia Enterprise Zone.

The provision extends for two years the zero-percent capital gains rate applicable to capital gains from the sale or exchange of any DC Zone asset held for more than five years (and, as amended, acquired or substantially improved before January 1, 2012). The provision also extends for two years the period to which the term "qualified capital gain" refers. As amended, the term "qualified capital gain" shall not include any gain attributable to periods before January 1, 1998, or after December 31, 2016.

The provision extends the first-time D.C. homebuyer credit for two years (as amended, to apply to property purchased before January 1, 2012).

Effective Date

The provision extending the period of designation of the District of Columbia Enterprise Zone and the provision extending the period for which the term "qualified capital gain" refers applies to periods after December 31, 2009. The provision extending tax-exempt financing for certain zone facilities applies to bonds issued after December 31, 2009. The provision amending the definitions of DC Zone business stock, DC Zone partnership interest, and DC Zone business property applies to property acquired or substantially improved after December 31, 2009. The provision extending the first-time homebuyer credit applies to homes purchased after December 31, 2009.

[Law at ¶5565, ¶5570, ¶5575 and ¶5580. CCH Explanation at ¶445.]

[¶10,610] Act Sec. 755. Temporary increase in limit on cover over of rum excise taxes to Puerto Rico and the Virgin Islands

Joint Committee on Taxation (J.C.T. REP. No. JCX-55-10)

[Code Sec. 7652(f)]

Present Law

A $13.50 per proof gallon[295] excise tax is imposed on distilled spirits produced in or imported into the United States.[296] The excise tax does not apply to distilled spirits that are exported from the United States, including exports to U.S. possessions (e.g., Puerto Rico and the Virgin Islands).[297]

The Code provides for cover over (payment) to Puerto Rico and the Virgin Islands of the excise tax imposed on rum imported (or brought) into the United States, without regard to the country of origin.[298] The amount of the cover over is limited under Code section 7652(f) to $10.50 per proof gallon ($13.25 per proof gallon before January 1, 2010).

Tax amounts attributable to shipments to the United States of rum produced in Puerto Rico are covered over to Puerto Rico. Tax amounts attributable to shipments to the United States of rum produced in the Virgin Islands are covered over to the Virgin Islands. Tax amounts attributable to shipments to the United States of rum produced in neither Puerto Rico nor the Virgin Islands are divided and covered over to the two possessions under a formula.[299] Amounts covered over to Puerto Rico and the Virgin Islands are deposited into the treasuries of the two possessions for use as those possessions determine.[300] All of the amounts covered over are subject to the limitation.

Explanation of Provision

The provision suspends for two years the $10.50 per proof gallon limitation on the amount of excise taxes on rum covered over to Puerto Rico and the Virgin Islands. Under the provision, the cover over limitation of $13.25 per proof gallon is extended for rum brought into the United States after December 31, 2009 and before January 1, 2012. After December 31, 2011, the cover over amount reverts to $10.50 per proof gallon.

Effective Date

The provision is effective for distilled spirits brought into the United States after December 31, 2009.

[Law at ¶5860. CCH Explanation at ¶635.]

[¶10,620] Act Sec. 756. American Samoa economic development credit

Joint Committee on Taxation (J.C.T. REP. No. JCX-55-10)

[Act Sec. 756]

Present Law

A domestic corporation that was an existing credit claimant with respect to American Samoa and that elected the application of section 936 for its last taxable year beginning before January 1, 2006 is allowed a credit based on the corporation's economic activity-based limitation with respect to American Samoa. The credit is not part of the Code but is computed based on the rules of sections 30A and 936. The credit is allowed for the first four taxable years of a corporation that begin after December 31, 2005, and before January 1, 2010.

---

[295] A proof gallon is a liquid gallon consisting of 50 percent alcohol. See sec. 5002(a)(10) and (11).

[296] Sec. 5001(a)(1).

[297] Secs. 5214(a)(1)(A), 5002(a)(15), 7653(b) and (c).

[298] Secs. 7652(a)(3), (b)(3), and (e)(1). One percent of the amount of excise tax collected from imports into the United

States of articles produced in the Virgin Islands is retained by the United States under section 7652(b)(3).

[299] Sec. 7652(e)(2).

[300] Secs. 7652(a)(3), (b)(3), and (e)(1).

A corporation was an existing credit claimant with respect to a American Samoa if (1) the corporation was engaged in the active conduct of a trade or business within American Samoa on October 13, 1995, and (2) the corporation elected the benefits of the possession tax credit[301] in an election in effect for its taxable year that included October 13, 1995.[302] A corporation that added a substantial new line of business (other than in a qualifying acquisition of all the assets of a trade or business of an existing credit claimant) ceased to be an existing credit claimant as of the close of the taxable year ending before the date on which that new line of business was added.

The amount of the credit allowed to a qualifying domestic corporation under the provision is equal to the sum of the amounts used in computing the corporation's economic activity-based limitation with respect to American Samoa, except that no credit is allowed for the amount of any American Samoa income taxes. Thus, for any qualifying corporation the amount of the credit equals the sum of (1) 60 percent of the corporation's qualified American Samoa wages and allocable employee fringe benefit expenses and (2) 15 percent of the corporation's depreciation allowances with respect to short-life qualified American Samoa tangible property,

plus 40 percent of the corporation's depreciation allowances with respect to medium-life qualified American Samoa tangible property, plus 65 percent of the corporation's depreciation allowances with respect to long-life qualified American Samoa tangible property.

The section 936(c) rule denying a credit or deduction for any possessions or foreign tax paid with respect to taxable income taken into account in computing the credit under section 936 does not apply with respect to the credit allowed by the provision.

The credit applies to the first four taxable years of a taxpayer which begin after December 31, 2005, and before January 1, 2010.

Explanation of Provision

The provision allows the credit to apply to the first six taxable years of a taxpayer beginning after December 31, 2005, and before January 1, 2012.

Effective Date

The provision is effective for taxable years beginning after December 31, 2009.

[Law at ¶7070. CCH Explanation at ¶536.]

---

[301] For taxable years beginning before January 1, 2006, certain domestic corporations with business operations in the U.S. possessions were eligible for the possession tax credit. Secs. 27(b), 936. This credit offset the U.S. tax imposed on certain income related to operations in the U.S. possessions. Subject to certain limitations, discussed below, the amount of the possession tax credit allowed to any domestic corporation equaled the portion of that corporation's U.S. tax that was attributable to the corporation's non-U.S. source taxable income from (1) the active conduct of a trade or business within a U.S. possession, (2) the sale or exchange of substantially all of the assets that were used in such a trade or business, or (3) certain possessions investment. No deduction or foreign tax credit was allowed for any possessions or foreign tax paid or accrued with respect to taxable income that was taken into account in computing the credit under section 936.

Under the economic activity-based limit, the amount of the credit could not exceed an amount equal to the sum of (1) 60 percent of the taxpayer's qualified possession wages and allocable employee fringe benefit expenses, (2) 15 percent of depreciation allowances with respect to short-life qualified tangible property, plus 40 percent of depreciation allowances with respect to medium-life qualified tangible property, plus 65 percent of depreciation allowances with

respect to long-life qualified tangible property, and (3) in certain cases, a portion of the taxpayer's possession income taxes. A taxpayer could elect, instead of the economic activity-based limit, a limit equal to the applicable percentage of the credit that otherwise would have been allowable with respect to possession business income, beginning in 1998, the applicable percentage was 40 percent.

To qualify for the possession tax credit for a taxable year, a domestic corporation was required to satisfy two conditions. First, the corporation was required to derive at least 80 percent of its gross income for the three-year period immediately preceding the close of the taxable year from sources within a possession. Second, the corporation was required to derive at least 75 percent of its gross income for that same period from the active conduct of a possession business. Sec. 936(a)(2). The section 936 credit generally expired for taxable years beginning after December 31, 2005.

[302] A corporation will qualify as an existing credit claimant if it acquired all the assets of a trade or business of a corporation that (1) actively conducted that trade or business in a possession on October 13, 1995, and (2) had elected the benefits of the possession tax credit in an election in effect for the taxable year that included October 13, 1995.

[¶10,630] Act Sec. 757. Work opportunity credit

Joint Committee on Taxation (J.C.T. Rep. No. JCX-55-10)

[Code Sec. 51]

Present Law

In general

The work opportunity tax credit is available on an elective basis for employers hiring individuals from one or more of nine targeted groups. The amount of the credit available to an employer is determined by the amount of qualified wages paid by the employer. Generally, qualified wages consist of wages attributable to service rendered by a member of a targeted group during the one-year period beginning with the day the individual begins work for the employer (two years in the case of an individual in the long-term family assistance recipient category).

Targeted groups eligible for the credit

Generally, an employer is eligible for the credit only for qualified wages paid to members of a targeted group.

(1) Families receiving TANF

An eligible recipient is an individual certified by a designated local employment agency (e.g., a State employment agency) as being a member of a family eligible to receive benefits under the Temporary Assistance for Needy Families Program ("TANF") for a period of at least nine months part of which is during the 18-month period ending on the hiring date. For these purposes, members of the family are defined to include only those individuals taken into account for purposes of determining eligibility for the TANF.

(2) Qualified veteran

There are two subcategories of qualified veterans related to eligibility for food stamps and compensation for a service-connected disability.

Food stamps

A qualified veteran is a veteran who is certified by the designated local agency as a member of a family receiving assistance under a food stamp program under the Food Stamp Act of 1977 for a period of at least three months part of which is during the 12-month period ending on the hiring date. For these purposes, members of a family are defined to include only those individuals taken into account for purposes of determining eligibility for a food stamp program under the Food Stamp Act of 1977.

Entitled to compensation for a service-connected disability

A qualified veteran also includes an individual who is certified as entitled to compensation for a service-connected disability and: (1) having a hiring date which is not more than one year after having been discharged or released from active duty in the Armed Forces of the United States; or (2) having been unemployed for six months or more (whether or not consecutive) during the one-year period ending on the date of hiring.

Definitions

For these purposes, being entitled to compensation for a service-connected disability is defined with reference to section 101 of Title 38, U.S. Code, which means having a disability rating of 10 percent or higher for service connected injuries.

For these purposes, a veteran is an individual who has served on active duty (other than for training) in the Armed Forces for more than 180 days or who has been discharged or released from active duty in the Armed Forces for a service-connected disability. However, any individual who has served for a period of more than 90 days during which the individual was on active duty (other than for training) is not a qualified veteran if any of this active duty occurred during the 60-day period ending on the date the individual was hired by the employer. This latter rule is intended to prevent employers who hire current members of the armed services (or those departed from service within the last 60 days) from receiving the credit.

(3) Qualified ex-felon

A qualified ex-felon is an individual certified as: (1) having been convicted of a felony under any State or Federal law; and (2) having a hiring date within one year of release from prison or the date of conviction.

(4) Designated community residents

A designated community resident is an individual certified as being at least age 18 but not yet age 40 on the hiring date and as having a principal place of abode within an empowerment zone, enterprise community, renewal community or a rural renewal community. For these purposes, a rural renewal county is a county outside a metropolitan statistical area (as defined by the Office of Management and Budget) which had a net population loss during the five-year periods 1990-1994 and 1995-1999. Qualified wages do not include wages paid or incurred for services performed after the individual moves outside an empowerment zone, enterprise community, renewal community or a rural renewal community.

(5) Vocational rehabilitation referral

A vocational rehabilitation referral is an individual who is certified by a designated local agency as an individual who has a physical or mental disability that constitutes a substantial handicap to employment and who has been referred to the employer while receiving, or after completing: (a) vocational rehabilitation services under an individualized, written plan for employment under a State plan approved under the Rehabilitation Act of 1973; (b) under a rehabilitation plan for veterans carried out under Chapter 31 of Title 38, U.S. Code; or (c) an individual work plan developed and implemented by an employment network pursuant to subsection (g) of section 1148 of the Social Security Act. Certification will be provided by the designated local employment agency upon assurances from the vocational rehabilitation agency that the employee has met the above conditions.

(6) Qualified summer youth employee

A qualified summer youth employee is an individual: (1) who performs services during any 90-day period between May 1 and September 15; (2) who is certified by the designated local agency as being 16 or 17 years of age on the hiring date; (3) who has not been an employee of that employer before; and (4) who is certified by the designated local agency as having a principal place of abode within an empowerment zone, enterprise community, or renewal community. As with designated community residents, no credit is available on wages paid or incurred for service performed after the qualified summer youth moves outside of an empowerment zone, enterprise community, or renewal community. If, after the end of the 90-day period, the employer continues to employ a youth who was certified during the 90-day period as a member of another targeted group, the limit on qualified first-year wages will take into account wages paid to the youth while a qualified summer youth employee.

(7) Qualified food stamp recipient

A qualified food stamp recipient is an individual at least age 18 but not yet age 40 certified by a designated local employment agency as being a member of a family receiving assistance under a food stamp program under the Food Stamp Act of 1977 for a period of at least six months ending on the hiring date. In the case of families that cease to be eligible for food stamps under section 6(o) of the Food Stamp Act of 1977, the six-month requirement is replaced with a requirement that the family has been receiving food stamps for at least three of the five months ending on the date of hire. For these purposes, members of the family are defined to include only those individuals taken into account for purposes of determining eligibility for a food stamp program under the Food Stamp Act of 1977.

(8) Qualified SSI recipient

A qualified SSI recipient is an individual designated by a local agency as receiving supplemental security income ("SSI") benefits under Title XVI of the Social Security Act for any month ending within the 60-day period ending on the hiring date.

(9) Long-term family assistance recipients

A qualified long-term family assistance recipient is an individual certified by a designated local agency as being: (1) a member of a family that has received family assistance for at least 18 consecutive months ending on the hiring date; (2) a member of a family that has received such family assistance for a total of at least 18 months (whether or not consecutive) after August 5, 1997 (the date of enactment of the welfare-to-work tax credit)[303] if the individual is hired within two years after the date that the 18-month total is reached; or (3) a member of a family who is no longer eligible for family assistance because of either Federal or State time limits, if the individual is hired within two years after the Federal or State time limits made the family ineligible for family assistance.

(10) Unemployed veterans and disconnected youth hired in 2009 and 2010

Unemployed veterans and disconnected youth who begin work for the employer in 2009 or 2010 are treated as a targeted category under

---

[303] The welfare-to-work tax credit was consolidated into the work opportunity tax credit in the Tax Relief and Health Care Act of 2006, for qualified individuals who begin to work for an employer after December 31, 2006.

section 1221(a) of the American Recovery and Reinvestment Act of 2009.[304]

An unemployed veteran is defined as an individual certified by the designated local agency as someone who: (1) has served on active duty (other than for training) in the Armed Forces for more than 180 days or who has been discharged or released from active duty in the Armed Forces for a service-connected disability; (2) has been discharged or released from active duty in the Armed Forces during the five-year period ending on the hiring date; and (3) has received unemployment compensation under State or Federal law for not less than four weeks during the one-year period ending on the hiring date.

A disconnected youth is defined as an individual certified by the designated local agency as someone: (1) at least age 16 but not yet age 25 on the hiring date; (2) not regularly attending any secondary, technical, or post-secondary school during the six-month period preceding the hiring date; (3) not regularly employed during the six-month period preceding the hiring date; and (4) not readily employable by reason of lacking a sufficient number of skills.

Qualified wages

Generally, qualified wages are defined as cash wages paid by the employer to a member of a targeted group. The employer's deduction for wages is reduced by the amount of the credit.

For purposes of the credit, generally, wages are defined by reference to the FUTA definition of wages contained in sec. 3306(b) (without regard to the dollar limitation therein contained). Special rules apply in the case of certain agricultural labor and certain railroad labor.

Calculation of the credit

The credit available to an employer for qualified wages paid to members of all targeted groups except for long-term family assistance recipients equals 40 percent (25 percent for employment of 400 hours or less) of qualified first-year wages. Generally, qualified first-year wages are qualified wages (not in excess of $6,000) attributable to service rendered by a member of a targeted group during the one-year period beginning with the day the individual began work for the employer. Therefore, the maximum credit per employee is $2,400 (40 percent of the first $6,000 of qualified first-year wages). With respect to qualified summer youth employees, the maximum credit is $1,200 (40 percent of the first

$3,000 of qualified first-year wages). Except for long-term family assistance recipients, no credit is allowed for second-year wages.

In the case of long-term family assistance recipients, the credit equals 40 percent (25 percent for employment of 400 hours or less) of $10,000 for qualified first-year wages and 50 percent of the first $10,000 of qualified second-year wages. Generally, qualified second-year wages are qualified wages (not in excess of $10,000) attributable to service rendered by a member of the long-term family assistance category during the one-year period beginning on the day after the one-year period beginning with the day the individual began work for the employer. Therefore, the maximum credit per employee is $9,000 (40 percent of the first $10,000 of qualified first-year wages plus 50 percent of the first $10,000 of qualified second-year wages).

In the case of a qualified veteran who is entitled to compensation for a service connected disability, the credit equals 40 percent of $12,000 of qualified first-year wages. This expanded definition of qualified first-year wages does not apply to the veterans qualified with reference to a food stamp program, as defined under present law.

Certification rules

An individual is not treated as a member of a targeted group unless: (1) on or before the day on which an individual begins work for an employer, the employer has received a certification from a designated local agency that such individual is a member of a targeted group; or (2) on or before the day an individual is offered employment with the employer, a pre-screening notice is completed by the employer with respect to such individual, and not later than the 28th day after the individual begins work for the employer, the employer submits such notice, signed by the employer and the individual under penalties of perjury, to the designated local agency as part of a written request for certification. For these purposes, a pre-screening notice is a document (in such form as the Secretary may prescribe) which contains information provided by the individual on the basis of which the employer believes that the individual is a member of a targeted group.

Minimum employment period

No credit is allowed for qualified wages paid to employees who work less than 120 hours in the first year of employment.

---

[304] (Pub. L. No. 111-5)

Other rules

The work opportunity tax credit is not allowed for wages paid to a relative or dependent of the taxpayer. No credit is allowed for wages paid to an individual who is a more than fifty-percent owner of the entity. Similarly, wages paid to replacement workers during a strike or lockout are not eligible for the work opportunity tax credit. Wages paid to any employee during any period for which the employer received on-the-job training program payments with respect to that employee are not eligible for the work opportunity tax credit. The work opportunity tax credit generally is not allowed for wages paid to individuals who had previously been employed by the employer. In addition, many other technical rules apply.

Expiration

The work opportunity tax credit is not available for individuals who begin work for an employer after August 31, 2011.

Explanation of Provision

The provision extends the work opportunity tax credit for four months (for individuals who begin work for an employer after August 31, 2011 before January 1, 2012).[305]

Effective Date

The provisions are effective for individuals who begin work for an employer after August 31, 2011.

[Law at ¶ 5155. CCH Explanation at ¶ 524.]

[¶10,640] Act Sec. 758. Qualified zone academy bonds

Joint Committee on Taxation (J.C.T. Rep. No. JCX-55-10)

[Code Sec. 54E]

Present Law

Tax-exempt bonds

Interest on State and local governmental bonds generally is excluded from gross income for Federal income tax purposes if the proceeds of the bonds are used to finance direct activities of these governmental units or if the bonds are repaid with revenues of the governmental units. These can include tax-exempt bonds which finance public schools.[306] An issuer must file with the Internal Revenue Service certain information about the bonds issued in order for that bond issue to be tax-exempt.[307] Generally, this information return is required to be filed no later than the 15th day of the second month after the close of the calendar quarter in which the bonds were issued.

The tax exemption for State and local bonds does not apply to any arbitrage bond.[308] An arbitrage bond is defined as any bond that is part of an issue if any proceeds of the issue are reasonably expected to be used (or intentionally are used) to acquire higher yielding investments or to replace funds that are used to acquire higher yielding investments.[309] In general, arbitrage profits may be earned only during specified periods (e.g., defined "temporary periods")

before funds are needed for the purpose of the borrowing or on specified types of investments (e.g., "reasonably required reserve or replacement funds"). Subject to limited exceptions, investment profits that are earned during these periods or on such investments must be rebated to the Federal Government.

Qualified zone academy bonds

As an alternative to traditional tax-exempt bonds, States and local governments were given the authority to issue "qualified zone academy bonds."[310] A total of $400 million of qualified zone academy bonds is authorized to be issued annually in calendar years 1998 through 2008. That is increased to $1,400 million in 2009 and 2010. Each calendar year's bond limitation is allocated to the States according to their respective populations of individuals below the poverty line. Each State, in turn, allocates the credit authority to qualified zone academies within such State.

A taxpayer holding a qualified zone academy bond on the credit allowance date is entitled to a credit. The credit is includible in gross income (as if it were a taxable interest payment on the bond), and may be claimed against regular income tax and alternative minimum tax liability.

---

[305] The rule to allow unemployed veterans and disconnected youth who begin work for the employer in 2009 or 2010 to be treated as members of a targeted group is not extended.

[306] Sec. 103.

[307] Sec. 149(e).

[308] Sec. 103(a) and (b)(2).

[309] Sec. 148.

[310] See secs. 54E and 1397E.

The Treasury Department sets the credit rate at a rate estimated to allow issuance of qualified zone academy bonds without discount and without interest cost to the issuer.[311] The Secretary determines credit rates for tax credit bonds based on general assumptions about credit quality of the class of potential eligible issuers and such other factors as the Secretary deems appropriate. The Secretary may determine credit rates based on general credit market yield indexes and credit ratings. The maximum term of the bond is determined by the Treasury Department, so that the present value of the obligation to repay the principal on the bond is 50 percent of the face value of the bond.

"Qualified zone academy bonds" are defined as any bond issued by a State or local government, provided that (1) at least 95 percent of the proceeds are used for the purpose of renovating, providing equipment to, developing course materials for use at, or training teachers and other school personnel in a "qualified zone academy" and (2) private entities have promised to contribute to the qualified zone academy certain equipment, technical assistance or training, employee services, or other property or services with a value equal to at least 10 percent of the bond proceeds.

A school is a "qualified zone academy" if (1) the school is a public school that provides education and training below the college level, (2) the school operates a special academic program in cooperation with businesses to enhance the academic curriculum and increase graduation and employment rates, and (3) either (a) the school is located in an empowerment zone or enterprise community designated under the Code, or (b) it is reasonably expected that at least 35 percent of the students at the school will be eligible for free or reduced-cost lunches under the school lunch program established under the National School Lunch Act.

The arbitrage requirements which generally apply to interest-bearing tax-exempt bonds also generally apply to qualified zone academy bonds. In addition, an issuer of qualified zone academy bonds must reasonably expect to and actually spend 100 percent or more of the proceeds of such bonds on qualified zone academy property within the three-year period that begins on the date of issuance. To the extent less than 100 percent of the proceeds are used to finance qualified zone academy property during the

three-year spending period, bonds will continue to qualify as qualified zone academy bonds if unspent proceeds are used within 90 days from the end of such three-year period to redeem any nonqualified bonds. The three-year spending period may be extended by the Secretary if the issuer establishes that the failure to meet the spending requirement is due to reasonable cause and the related purposes for issuing the bonds will continue to proceed with due diligence.

Two special arbitrage rules apply to qualified zone academy bonds. First, available project proceeds invested during the three-year period beginning on the date of issue are not subject to the arbitrage restrictions (i.e., yield restriction and rebate requirements). Available project proceeds are proceeds from the sale of an issue of qualified zone academy bonds, less issuance costs (not to exceed two percent) and any investment earnings on such proceeds. Thus, available project proceeds invested during the three-year spending period may be invested at unrestricted yields, but the earnings on such investments must be spent on qualified zone academy property. Second, amounts invested in a reserve fund are not subject to the arbitrage restrictions to the extent: (1) such fund is funded at a rate not more rapid than equal annual installments; (2) such fund is funded in a manner reasonably expected to result in an amount not greater than an amount necessary to repay the issue; and (3) the yield on such fund is not greater than the average annual interest rate of tax-exempt obligations having a term of 10 years or more that are issued during the month the qualified zone academy bonds are issued.

Issuers of qualified zone academy bonds are required to report issuance to the Internal Revenue Service in a manner similar to the information returns required for tax-exempt bonds.

For bonds originally issued after March 18, 2010, an issuer of qualified zone academy bonds may make an irrevocable election on or before the issue date of such bonds to receive a payment under section 6431 in lieu of providing a tax credit to the holder of the bonds. The payment to the issuer on each payment date is equal to the lesser of (1) the amount of interest payable on such bond by such issuer with respect to such date or (2) the amount of the interest which would have been payable under such bond on such date if such interest were determined at the applicable tax credit bond rate.

---

[311] Given the differences in credit quality and other characteristics of individual issuers, the Secretary cannot set credit rates in a manner that will allow each issuer to issue tax credit bonds at par.

Explanation of Provision

In general

The provision extends the qualified zone academy bond program for one year. The provision authorizes issuance of up to $400 million of qualified zone academy bonds for 2011.

The issuer election to receive a payment in lieu of providing a tax credit to the holder of the qualified zone academy bond is not available for bonds issued with the 2011 national limitation. The provision has no effect on bonds issued with limitation carried forward from 2009 or 2010.

Effective Date

The provision applies to obligations issued after December 31, 2010.

[Law at ¶5165 and ¶5830. CCH Explanation at ¶465.]

[¶10,650] Act Sec. 759. Mortgage insurance premiums

Joint Committee on Taxation (J.C.T. Rep. No. JCX-55-10)

[Code Sec. 163]

Present Law

In general

Present law provides that qualified residence interest is deductible notwithstanding the general rule that personal interest is nondeductible (sec. 163(h)).

Acquisition indebtedness and home equity indebtedness

Qualified residence interest is interest on acquisition indebtedness and home equity indebtedness with respect to a principal and a second residence of the taxpayer. The maximum amount of home equity indebtedness is $100,000. The maximum amount of acquisition indebtedness is $1 million. Acquisition indebtedness means debt that is incurred in acquiring constructing, or substantially improving a qualified residence of the taxpayer, and that is secured by the residence. Home equity indebtedness is debt (other than acquisition indebtedness) that is secured by the taxpayer's principal or second residence, to the extent the aggregate amount of such debt does not exceed the difference between the total acquisition indebtedness with respect to the residence, and the fair market value of the residence.

Private mortgage insurance

Certain premiums paid or accrued for qualified mortgage insurance by a taxpayer during the taxable year in connection with acquisition indebtedness on a qualified residence of the taxpayer are treated as interest that is qualified residence interest and thus deductible. The amount allowable as a deduction is phased out ratably by 10 percent for each $1,000 by which the taxpayer's adjusted gross income exceeds $100,000 ($500 and $50,000, respectively, in the case of a married individual filing a separate return). Thus, the deduction is not allowed if the taxpayer's adjusted gross income exceeds $110,000 ($55,000 in the case of married individual filing a separate return).

For this purpose, qualified mortgage insurance means mortgage insurance provided by the Veterans Administration, the Federal Housing Administration,[312] or the Rural Housing Administration, and private mortgage insurance (defined in section 2 of the Homeowners Protection Act of 1998 as in effect on the date of enactment of the provision).

Amounts paid for qualified mortgage insurance that are properly allocable to periods after the close of the taxable year are treated as paid in the period to which they are allocated. No deduction is allowed for the unamortized balance if the mortgage is paid before its term (except in the case of qualified mortgage insurance provided by the Department of Veterans Affairs or Rural Housing Service).

The provision does not apply with respect to any mortgage insurance contract issued before January 1, 2007. The provision terminates for any amount paid or accrued after December 31, 2010, or properly allocable to any period after that date.

Reporting rules apply under the provision.

Explanation of Provision

The provision extends the deduction for private mortgage insurance premiums for one year (only with respect to contracts entered into after

---

[312] The Veterans Administration and the Rural Housing Administration have been succeeded by the Department of Veterans Affairs and the Rural Housing Service, respectively.

December 31, 2006). Thus, the provision applies to amounts paid or accrued in 2011 (and not properly allocable to any period after 2011).

[Law at ¶ 5255. CCH Explanation at ¶ 328.]

Effective Date

The provision is effective for amounts paid or accrued after December 31, 2010.

[¶10,660] Act Sec. 760. Temporary exclusion of 100 percent of gain on certain small business stock

Joint Committee on Taxation (J.C.T. Rep. No. JCX-55-10)

[Code Sec. 1202]

Present Law

In general

Individuals generally may exclude 50 percent (60 percent for certain empowerment zone businesses) of the gain from the sale of certain small business stock acquired at original issue and held for at least five years.[313] The amount of gain eligible for the exclusion by an individual with respect to any corporation is the greater of (1) ten times the taxpayer's basis in the stock or (2) $10 million. To qualify as a small business, when the stock is issued, the gross assets of the corporation may not exceed $50 million. The corporation also must meet certain active trade or business requirements.

The portion of the gain includible in taxable income is taxed at a maximum rate of 28 percent under the regular tax.[314] A percentage of the excluded gain is an alternative minimum tax preference;[315] the portion of the gain includible in alternative minimum taxable income is taxed at a maximum rate of 28 percent under the alternative minimum tax.

Gain from the sale of qualified small business stock generally is taxed at effective rates of 14 percent under the regular tax[316] and (i) 14.98 percent under the alternative minimum tax for dispositions before January 1, 2011; (ii) 19.88 percent under the alternative minimum tax for dispositions after December 31, 2010, in the case of stock acquired before January 1, 2001; and (iii) 17.92 percent under the alternative minimum tax for dispositions after December 31, 2010, in the case of stock acquired after December 31, 2000.[317]

Temporary increases in exclusion

The percentage exclusion for qualified small business stock acquired after February 17, 2009, and on or before September 27, 2010, is increased to 75 percent. As a result of the increased exclusion, gain from the sale of this qualified small business stock held at least five years is taxed at effective rates of seven percent under the regular tax[318] and 12.88 percent under the alternative minimum tax.[319]

The percentage exclusion for qualified small business stock acquired after September 27, 2010, and before January 1, 2011, is increased to 100 percent and the minimum tax preference does not apply.[320] The minimum tax preference does not apply.

---

[313] Sec. 1202.

[314] Sec. 1(h).

[315] Sec. 57(a)(7). In the case of qualified small business stock, the percentage of gain excluded from gross income which is an alternative minimum tax preference is (i) seven percent in the case of stock disposed of in a taxable year beginning before 2011; (ii) 42 percent in the case of stock acquired before January 1, 2001, and disposed of in a taxable year beginning after 2010; and (iii) 28 percent in the case of stock acquired after December 31, 2000, and disposed of in a taxable year beginning after 2010. Section 102 of the bill extends the 2010 and 2011 dates by two years.

[316] The 50 percent of gain included in taxable income is taxed at a maximum rate of 28 percent.

[317] The amount of gain included in alternative minimum tax is taxed at a maximum rate of 28 percent. The amount so included is the sum of (i) 50 percent (the percentage included in taxable income) of the total gain and (ii) the applicable preference percentage of the one-half gain that is excluded from taxable income.

[318] The 25 percent of gain included in taxable income is taxed at a maximum rate of 28 percent.

[319] The 46 percent of gain included in alternative minimum tax is taxed at a maximum rate of 28 percent. Forty-six percent is the sum of 25 percent (the percentage of total gain included in taxable income) plus 21 percent (the percentage of total gain which is an alternative minimum tax preference).

[320] Sec. 1202(a)(4)(A) and (C).

Explanation of Provision

The provision extends the 100-percent exclusion and the exception from minimum tax preference treatment for one year (for stock acquired before January 1, 2012).

Effective Date

The provision is effective for stock acquired after December 31, 2010.

[Law at ¶ 5510. CCH Explanation at ¶ 418.]

[¶10,670] Act Sec. 761. New York Liberty Zone tax-exempt bond financing

Joint Committee on Taxation (J.C.T. REP. NO. JCX-55-10)

[Code Sec. 1400L]

Present Law

An aggregate of $8 billion in tax-exempt private activity bonds is authorized for the purpose of financing the construction and repair of infrastructure in New York City ("Liberty Zone bonds"). The bonds must be issued before January 1, 2010.

Explanation of Provision

The provision extends authority to issue Liberty Zone bonds for two years (through December 31, 2011).

Effective Date

The provision is effective for bonds issued after December 31, 2009.

[Law at ¶ 5585. CCH Explanation at ¶ 470.]

[¶10,680] Act Sec. 762. Increase in rehabilitation credit in the Gulf Opportunity Zone

Joint Committee on Taxation (J.C.T. REP. NO. JCX-55-10)

[Code Sec. 1400N(h)]

Present Law

Present law provides a two-tier tax credit for rehabilitation expenditures.

A 20-percent credit is provided for qualified rehabilitation expenditures with respect to a certified historic structure. For this purpose, a certified historic structure means any building that is listed in the National Register, or that is located in a registered historic district and is certified by the Secretary of the Interior to the Secretary of the Treasury as being of historic significance to the district.

A 10-percent credit is provided for qualified rehabilitation expenditures with respect to a qualified rehabilitated building, which generally means a building that was first placed in service before 1936. The pre-1936 building must meet requirements with respect to retention of existing external walls and internal structural framework of the building in order for expenditures with respect to it to qualify for the 10-percent credit. A building is treated as having met the substantial rehabilitation requirement under the 10-percent credit only if the rehabilitation expenditures during the 24-month period selected by the taxpayer and ending within the taxable year exceed the

greater of (1) the adjusted basis of the building (and its structural components), or (2) $5,000.

The provision requires the use of straight-line depreciation or the alternative depreciation system in order for rehabilitation expenditures to be treated as qualified under the provision.

Present law increases from 20 to 26 percent, and from 10 to 13 percent, respectively, the credit under section 47 with respect to any certified historic structure or qualified rehabilitated building located in the Gulf Opportunity Zone, provided the qualified rehabilitation expenditures with respect to such buildings or structures are incurred on or after August 28, 2005, and before January 1, 2010. The provision is effective for expenditures incurred on or after August 28, 2005, for taxable years ending on or after August 28, 2005.

Explanation of Provision

The provision extends for two additional years the increase in the rehabilitation credit from 20 to 26 percent, and from 10 to 13 percent, respectively, with respect to any certified historic structure or qualified rehabilitated building located in the Gulf Opportunity Zone. Thus, the increase applies for qualified rehabilitation expenditures with respect to such buildings or structures incurred before January 1, 2012.

[Law at ¶5590. CCH Explanation at ¶450.]

Effective Date

The provision is effective for amounts paid or incurred after December 31, 2009.

[¶10,690] Act Sec. 763. Low-income housing credit rules for buildings in Gulf Opportunity Zones

Joint Committee on Taxation (J.C.T. REP. No. JCX-55-10)

[Code Sec. 1400N(c)(5)]

Present Law

In general

The low-income housing credit may be claimed over a 10-year period for the cost of rental housing occupied by tenants having incomes below specified levels. The amount of the credit for any taxable year in the credit period is the applicable percentage of the qualified basis of each qualified low-income building. The qualified basis of any qualified low-income building for any taxable year equals the applicable fraction of the eligible basis of the building.

The credit percentage for newly constructed or substantially rehabilitated housing that is not Federally subsidized is adjusted monthly by the Internal Revenue Service so that the 10 annual installments have a present value of 70 percent of the total qualified basis. The credit percentage for newly constructed or substantially rehabilitated housing that is Federally subsidized and for existing housing that is substantially rehabilitated is calculated to have a present value of 30 percent of qualified basis. These are referred to as the 70-percent credit and 30-percent credit, respectively.

Volume limit

Generally, a low-income housing credit is allowable only if the owner of a qualified building receives a housing credit allocation from the State or local housing credit agency. Each State has a limited amount of low-income housing credit available to allocate. This amount is called the aggregate housing credit dollar amount (or the "State housing credit ceiling"). For each State, the State housing credit ceiling is the sum of four components: (1) the unused housing credit ceiling, if any, of such State from the prior calendar year; (2) the credit ceiling for the year (either a per capital amount or the small State minimum annual cap); (3) any returns of credit ceiling to the State during the calendar year from previous allocations; and (4) the State's share, if any, of the national pool of unused credits from other States that failed to use them (only States which allocated their entire credit ceiling for the preceding calendar year are eligible for a share of the national pool. For calendar year 2010, each State's credit ceiling is $2.10 per resident, with a minimum annual cap of $2,430,000 for certain small population States.[321] These amounts are indexed for inflation. These limits do not apply in the case of projects that also receive financing with proceeds of tax-exempt bonds issued subject to the private activity bond volume limit.

Under section 1400N(c) of the Code, the otherwise applicable State housing credit ceiling is increased for each of the States within the Gulf Opportunity Zone. This increase applies to calendar years 2006, 2007, and 2008. The additional volume for each of the affected States equals $18.00 times the number of such State's residents within the Gulf Opportunity Zone. This amount is not adjusted for inflation. This additional volume limit expires unless the applicable low-income buildings are placed in service before January 1, 2011.

Explanation of Provision

The provision extends the placed-in-service deadline (for one year) to December 31, 2011.

Effective Date

The provision is effective on the date of enactment.

[Law at ¶5590. CCH Explanation at ¶450.]

[321] Rev. Proc. 2009-50.

[¶10,700] Act Sec. 764. Tax-exempt bond financing for the Gulf Opportunity Zones

Joint Committee on Taxation (J.C.T. Rep. No. JCX-55-10)

[Code Sec. 1400N(a)]

Present Law

In general

Under present law, gross income does not include interest on State or local bonds. State and local bonds are classified generally as either governmental bonds or private activity bonds. Governmental bonds are bonds which are primarily used to finance governmental functions or which are repaid with governmental funds. Private activity bonds are bonds with respect to which the State or local government serves as a conduit providing financing to nongovernmental persons (e.g., private businesses or individuals). The exclusion from income for State and local bonds does not apply to private activity bonds, unless the bonds are issued for certain permitted purposes ("qualified private activity bonds"). The definition of a qualified private activity bond includes an exempt facility bond and a qualified mortgage bond.

Exempt facility bonds

The definition of exempt facility bond includes bonds issued to finance certain transportation facilities (airports, ports, mass commuting, and high-speed intercity rail facilities); qualified residential rental projects; privately owned and/or operated utility facilities (sewage, water, solid waste disposal, and local district heating and cooling facilities, certain private electric and gas facilities, and hydroelectric dam enhancements); public/private educational facilities; qualified green building and sustainable design projects; and qualified highway or surface freight transfer facilities (sec. 142(a)).

Residential rental property may be financed with exempt facility bonds if the financed project is a "qualified residential rental project." A project is a qualified residential rental project if 20 percent or more of the residential units in such project are occupied by individuals whose income is 50 percent or less of area median gross income (the "20-50 test"). Alternatively, a project is a qualified residential rental project if 40 percent or more of the residential units in such project are occupied by individuals whose income is 60 percent or less of area median gross income (the "40-60 test").

Qualified mortgage bonds

Qualified mortgage bonds are tax-exempt bonds issued to make mortgage loans to eligible mortgagors for the purchase, improvement, or rehabilitation of owner-occupied residences. The Code imposes several limitations on qualified mortgage bonds, including income limitations for eligible mortgagors, purchase price limitations on the home financed with bond proceeds, and a "first-time homebuyer" requirement. In addition, bond proceeds generally only can be used for new mortgages, i.e., proceeds cannot be used to acquire or replace existing mortgages.

Exceptions to the new mortgage requirement are provided for the replacement of construction period loans, bridge loans, and other similar temporary initial financing. In addition, qualified rehabilitation loans may be used, in part, to replace existing mortgages. A qualified rehabilitation loan means certain loans for the rehabilitation of a building if there is a period of at least 20 years between the date on which the building was first used (the "20 year rule") and the date on which the physical work on such rehabilitation begins and the existing walls and basis requirements are met. The existing walls requirement for a rehabilitated building is met if 50 percent or more of the existing external walls are retained in place as external walls, 75 percent or more of the existing external walls are retained in place as internal or external walls, and 75 percent or more of the existing internal structural framework is retained in place. The basis requirement is met if expenditures for rehabilitation are 25 percent or more of the mortgagor's adjusted basis in the residence, determined as of the later of the completion of the rehabilitation or the date on which the mortgagor acquires the residence.

Qualified mortgage bonds also may be used to finance qualified home-improvement loans. Qualified home-improvement loans are defined as loans to finance alterations, repairs, and improvements on an existing residence, but only if such alterations, repairs, and improvements substantially protect or improve the basic livability or energy efficiency of the property. Qualified home-improvement loans may not exceed $15,000, and may not be used to refinance existing mortgages.

As with most qualified private activity bonds, issuance of qualified mortgage bonds is subject to annual State volume limitations (the "State volume cap")..

Gulf Opportunity Zone Bonds

The Gulf Opportunity Zone Act of 2005 authorizes Alabama, Louisiana, and Mississippi (or any political subdivision of those States) to issue qualified private activity bonds to finance the construction and rehabilitation of residential and nonresidential property located in the Gulf Opportunity Zone ("Gulf Opportunity Zone Bonds"). Gulf Opportunity Zone Bonds are not subject to the State volume cap. Rather, the maximum aggregate amount of Gulf Opportunity Zone Bonds that may be issued in any eligible State is limited to $2,500 multiplied by the population of the respective State within the Gulf Opportunity Zone.

Depending on the purpose for which such bonds are issued, Gulf Opportunity Zone Bonds are treated as either exempt facility bonds or qualified mortgage bonds. Gulf Opportunity Zone Bonds are treated as exempt facility bonds if 95 percent or more of the net proceeds of such bonds are to be used for qualified project costs located in the Gulf Opportunity Zone. Qualified project costs include the cost of acquisition, construction, reconstruction, and renovation of non-residential real property (including buildings and their structural components and fixed improvements associated with such property), qualified residential rental projects (as defined in section 142(d) with certain modifications), and public utility property. Bond proceeds may not be used to finance movable fixtures and equipment.

Rather than applying the 20-50 and 40-60 test from section142, a project is a qualified residential rental project under the provision if 20 percent or more of the residential units in such project are occupied by individuals whose income is 60 percent or less of area median gross income or if 40 percent or more of the residential units in such project are occupied by individuals whose income is 70 percent or less of area median gross income.

Gulf Opportunity Zone Bonds issued to finance residences located in the Gulf Opportunity Zone are treated as qualified mortgage bonds if the general requirements for qualified mortgage bonds are met. The Code also provides special rules for Gulf Opportunity Zone Bonds issued to finance residences located in the Gulf Opportunity Zone. For example, the first-time homebuyer rule is waived and the income and purchase price rules are relaxed for residences financed in the GO Zone, the Rita GO Zone, or the Wilma GO Zone. In addition, the Code increases from $15,000 to $150,000 the amount of a qualified home-improvement loan with respect to residences located in the specified disaster areas.

Also, a qualified GO Zone repair or reconstruction loan is treated as a qualified rehabilitation loan for purposes of the qualified mortgage bond rules. Thus, such loans financed with the proceeds of qualified mortgage bonds and Gulf Opportunity Zone Bonds may be used to acquire or replace existing mortgages, without regard to the existing walls or 20 year rule under present law. A qualified GO Zone repair or reconstruction loan is any loan used to repair damage caused by Hurricane Katrina, Hurricane Rita, or Hurricane Wilma to a building located in the GO Zones (or reconstruction of such building in the case of damage constituting destruction) if the expenditures for such repair or reconstruction are 25 percent or more of the mortgagor's adjusted basis in the residence. For these purposes, the mortgagor's adjusted basis is determined as of the later of (1) the completion of the repair or reconstruction or (2) the date on which the mortgagor acquires the residence.

Gulf Opportunity Zone Bonds must be issued before January 1, 2011.

Explanation of Provision

The provision extends authority to issue Gulf Opportunity Zone Bonds for one year (through December 31, 2011).

Effective Date

The provision is effective on the date of enactment.

[Law at ¶ 5590. CCH Explanation at ¶ 450.]

Act Sec. 764   ¶ 10,700

[¶10,710] Act Sec. 765. Bonus depreciation deduction applicable to specified Gulf Opportunity Zone extension property

Joint Committee on Taxation (J.C.T. REP. NO. JCX-55-10)

[Code Sec. 1400N(d)(6)]

Present Law

In general

An additional first-year depreciation deduction is allowed equal to 50 percent of the adjusted basis of qualified property placed in service during 2008, 2009, and 2010 (2009, 2010, and 2011 for certain longer-lived and transportation property).[322] The additional first-year depreciation deduction is allowed for both regular tax and alternative minimum tax purposes, but is not allowed for purposes of computing earnings and profits. The basis of the property and the depreciation allowances in the year of purchase and later years are appropriately adjusted to reflect the additional first-year depreciation deduction. In addition, there are no adjustments to the allowable amount of depreciation for purposes of computing a taxpayer's alternative minimum taxable income with respect to property to which the provision applies. The amount of the additional first-year depreciation deduction is not affected by a short taxable year. The taxpayer may elect out of additional first-year depreciation for any class of property for any taxable year.

Property qualifying for the additional first-year depreciation deduction must meet all of the following requirements. First, the property must be (1) property to which MACRS applies with an applicable recovery period of 20 years or less; (2) water utility property (as defined in section 168(e)(5)); (3) computer software other than computer software covered by section 197; or (4) qualified leasehold improvement property (as defined in section 168(k)(3)).[323] Second, the original use[324] of the property must commence with the taxpayer after December 31, 2007.[325] Third, the taxpayer must purchase the property within the applicable time period. Finally, the property must be placed in service after December 31, 2007, and before January 1, 2011. An extension of the placed in service date of one year (i.e., to January 1, 2012) is provided for certain property with a recovery period of 10 years or longer and certain transportation property.[326] Transportation property is defined as tangible personal property used in the trade or business of transporting persons or property.

The applicable time period for acquired property is (1) after December 31, 2007, and before January 1, 2011, but only if no binding written contract for the acquisition is in effect before January 1, 2008, or (2) pursuant to a binding written contract which was entered into after December 31, 2007, and before January 1, 2011.[327] With respect to property that is manufactured, constructed, or produced by the taxpayer for use by the taxpayer, the taxpayer must begin the manufacture, construction, or production of the property after December 31, 2007, and

---

[322] Sec. 168(k). The additional first-year depreciation deduction is subject to the general rules regarding whether an item must be capitalized under section 263 or section 263A.

[323] The additional first-year depreciation deduction is not available for any property that is required to be depreciated under the alternative depreciation system of MACRS. The additional first-year depreciation deduction is also not available for qualified New York Liberty Zone leasehold improvement property as defined in section 1400L(c)(2).

[324] The term "original use" means the first use to which the property is put, whether or not such use corresponds to the use of such property by the taxpayer.

If in the normal course of its business a taxpayer sells fractional interests in property to unrelated third parties, then the original use of such property begins with the first user of each fractional interest (i.e., each fractional owner is considered the original user of its proportionate share of the property).

[325] A special rule applies in the case of certain leased property. In the case of any property that is originally placed in service by a person and that is sold to the taxpayer and leased back to such person by the taxpayer within three months after the date that the property was placed in service, the property would be treated as originally placed in service by the taxpayer not earlier than the date that the property is used under the leaseback.

If property is originally placed in service by a lessor (including by operation of section 168(k)(2)(D)(i)), such property is sold within three months after the date that the property was placed in service, and the user of such property does not change, then the property is treated as originally placed in service by the taxpayer not earlier than the date of such sale.

[326] Property qualifying for the extended placed in service date must have an estimated production period exceeding one year and a cost exceeding $1 million.

[327] Property does not fail to qualify for the additional first-year depreciation merely because a binding written contract to acquire a component of the property is in effect prior to January 1, 2008.

before January 1, 2011. Property that is manufactured, constructed, or produced for the taxpayer by another person under a contract that is entered into prior to the manufacture, construction, or production of the property is considered to be manufactured, constructed, or produced by the taxpayer. For property eligible for the extended placed in service date, a special rule limits the amount of costs eligible for the additional first-year depreciation. With respect to such property, only the portion of the basis that is properly attributable to the costs incurred before January 1, 2011 ("progress expenditures") is eligible for the additional first-year depreciation.[328]

Gulf Opportunity Zone Additional Depreciation

Present law provides an additional first-year depreciation deduction equal to 50 percent of the adjusted basis of specified qualified Gulf Opportunity Zone extension property. To qualify, property generally must be placed in service on or before December 31, 2010. Specified Gulf Opportunity Zone extension property is defined as property substantially all the use of which is in one or more specified portions of the Gulf Opportunity Zone and which is either: (1) nonresidential real property or residential rental property which is placed in service by the taxpayer on or before December 31, 2010, or (2) in the case of a taxpayer who places in service a building described in (1), property described in section 168(k)(2)(A)(i),[329] if substantially all the use of such property is in such building and such property is placed in service within 90 days of the date the building is placed in service. However, in the case of nonresidential real property or residential rental property, only the adjusted basis of such property attributable to manufacture, construction, or production before January 1, 2010 is eligible for the additional first-year depreciation.

The specified portions of the Gulf Opportunity Zone are defined as those portions of the Gulf Opportunity Zone which are in a county or parish which is identified by the Secretary of the Treasury (or his delegate) as being a county or parish in which hurricanes occurring in 2005 damaged (in the aggregate) more than 60 percent of the housing units in such county or parish which were occupied (determined according to the 2000 Census).

Explanation of Provision

The provision extends for one year through December 31, 2011, the date by which specified Gulf Opportunity Zone extension property must be placed in service to be eligible for the additional first-year depreciation deduction. In the case of nonresidential real property or residential rental property, the adjusted basis of such property attributable to manufacture, construction, or production before January 1, 2012 is eligible for the additional first-year depreciation.

Effective Date

The provision applies to property placed in service after December 31, 2009.

[Law at ¶ 5590. CCH Explanation at ¶ 450.]

---

[328] For purposes of determining the amount of eligible progress expenditures, it is intended that rules similar to section 46(d)(3) as in effect prior to the Tax Reform Act of 1986 apply.

[329] Generally, property described in section 168(k)(2)(A)(i) is (1) property to which the general rules of the Modified Accelerated Cost Recovery System ("MACRS") apply with an applicable recovery period of 20 years or less, (2) computer software other than computer software covered by section 197, (3) water utility property (as defined in section 168(e)(5)), or (4) certain leasehold improvement property.

Committee Reports

Regulated Investment Company Modernization Act of 2010

¶15,001 Introduction

The Regulated Investment Company Modernization Act of 2010 was passed by Congress on December 15, 2010, and sent that day to the President for his signature. The Joint Committee on Taxation produced a Technical Explanation of the bill on September 28, 2010 (JCX-49-10). This report explains the intent of Congress regarding the provisions of the Act. There was no conference report issued for this Act. The Technical Explanation from the Joint Committee on Taxation is included in this section to aid the reader's understanding, but may not be cited as the official Conference Committee Report accompanying the Act. At the end of each section, references are provided to the corresponding CCH explanation and the Internal Revenue Code provisions. Subscribers to the electronic version can link from these references to the corresponding material. *The pertinent sections of the Technical Explanation relating to the Regulated Investment Company Modernization Act of 2010 appear in Act Section order beginning at ¶15,010.*

¶15,005 Background

The Regulated Investment Company Modernization Act of 2010, H.R. 4337, was introduced in the House of Representatives on December 16, 2009. The bill passed the House by voice vote on September 28, 2010. The Senate amended the bill and passed its version by voice vote on December 15, 2010. The House passed the bill, as amended by the Senate, on December 15, 2010. The bill was sent to the President for his signature on December 17, 2010.

References are to the following report:

• The Joint Committee on Taxation, Technical Explanation of H.R. 4337, the "Regulated Investment Company Modernization Act of 2010" for Consideration on the Floor of the House of Representatives, September 28, 2010, is referred to as Joint Committee on Taxation (J.C.T. REP. NO. JCX-49-10).

¶15,007 Overview of regulated investment companies

In general, a regulated investment company ("RIC") is an electing domestic corporation that either meets (or is excepted from) certain registration requirements under the Investment Company Act of 1940,[2] that derives at least 90 percent of its ordinary income from specified sources considered passive investment income,[3] that has a portfolio of investments that meet certain diversification requirements,[4] and meets certain other requirements.[5]

---

[2] Secs. 851(a) and (b)(1).
[3] Sec. 851(b)(2).

[4] Sec. 851(b)(3).
[5] Secs. 851 and 852.

Many RICs are "open-end" companies (mutual funds) which have a continuously changing number of shares that are bought from, and redeemed by, the company and that are not otherwise available for purchase or sale in the secondary market. Shareholders of open-end RICs generally have the right to have the company redeem shares at "net asset value." Other RICs are "closed-end" companies, which have a fixed number of shares that are normally traded on national securities exchanges or in the over-the-counter market and are not redeemable upon the demand of the shareholder.

In the case of a RIC that distributes at least 90 percent of its net ordinary income and net tax-exempt interest to its shareholders, a deduction for dividends paid is allowed to the RIC in computing its tax.[6] Thus, no corporate income tax is imposed on income distributed to its shareholders. Dividends of a RIC generally are includible in the income of the shareholders; a RIC can pass through the character of (1) its long-term capital gain income, by paying "capital gain dividends" and (2) in certain cases, tax-exempt interest, by paying "exempt-interest dividends." A RIC may also pass through certain foreign tax credits and credits on tax-credit bonds, as well as the character of certain other income received by the RIC.

---

[6] Sec. 852(a) and (b).

[¶ 15,010] Act Sec. 101. Capital loss carryovers of RICs

Joint Committee on Taxation (J.C.T. REP. NO. JCX-49-10)

[Code Sec. 1212(a)]

Present Law

Limitation on capital losses

Losses from the sale or exchange of capital assets are allowed only to the extent of the taxpayer's gains from the sale or exchange of capital assets plus, in the case of a taxpayer other than a corporation, $3,000.[7]

Carryover of net capital losses

RICs

If a RIC has a net capital loss (i.e., losses from the sale or exchanges of capital assets in excess of gains from sales or exchanges of capital assets) for any taxable year, the amount of the net capital loss is a capital loss carryover to each of the eight taxable years following the loss year, and is treated as a short-term capital loss in each of those years.[8] The entire amount of a net capital loss is carried over to the first taxable year succeeding the loss year and the portion of the loss which may be carried to each of the next seven years is the excess of the net capital loss over the net capital gain income[9] (determined without regard to any net capital loss for the loss year or taxable year thereafter) for each of the prior taxable year to which the loss may be carried.

Corporations other than RICs

In the case of a corporation other than a RIC, a net capital loss generally is treated as a capital loss carryback to each of the three taxable years preceding the loss year and a capital loss carryover the each of the five taxable years following the loss year and is treated as a short-term capital loss in each of those years.[10] The carryover amount is reduced in a manner similar to that described above applicable to RICs. A net capital loss may not be carried back to a taxable year for which a corporation is a RIC.[11]

Individual taxpayers

If a taxpayer other than a corporation has a net capital loss for any taxable year, the excess (if any) of the net short-term capital loss over the net long-term capital gain is treated as a short-term capital loss in the succeeding taxable year, and the excess (if any) of the net long-term capital loss over the net short-term capital gain is treated as a long-term capital loss in the succeeding taxable year.[12] There is no limitation on the number of taxable years that a net capital loss may be carried over.

Explanation of Provision

In general

The bill provides capital loss carryover treatment for RICs similar to the present-law treatment of net capital loss carryovers applicable to individuals. Under the bill, if a RIC has a net capital loss for a taxable year, the excess (if any) of the net short-term capital loss over the net long-term capital gain is treated as a short-term capital loss arising on the first day of the next taxable year, and the excess (if any) of the net long-term capital loss over the net short-term capital gain is treated as a long-term capital loss arising on the first day of the next taxable year.[13] The number of taxable years that a net capital loss of a RIC may be carried over under the provision is not limited.

Coordination with present-law carryovers

The bill provides for the treatment of net capital loss carryovers under the present law rules to taxable years of a RIC beginning after the date of enactment. These rules apply to (1) capital loss carryovers from taxable years beginning on or before the date of enactment of the provision and (2) capital loss carryovers from other taxable years prior to the taxable year the corporation becoming a RIC.

---

[7] Sec. 1211.

[8] Sec. 1212(a)(1)(C)(i).

[9] Capital gain net income is the excess of gains from the sale or exchange of capital assets over losses from such sales or exchanges. Sec. 1222(9).

[10] Sec. 1212(a)(1)(A).

[11] Sec. 1212(a)(3)(A).

[12] Sec. 1212(b). Adjustments are made to take account of the $3,000 amount allowed against ordinary income

[13] For earnings and profits treatment of a RIC's net capital loss, see sec. 302 of the bill.

Amounts treated as a long-term or short-term capital loss arising on the first day of the next taxable year under the provision are determined without regard to amounts treated as a short-term capital loss under the present-law carryover rule. In determining the amount by which a present-law carryover is reduced by capital gain net income for a prior taxable year, any capital loss treated as arising on the first day of the prior taxable year under the provision is taken into account in determining capital gain net income for the prior year.

The following example illustrates these rules:

Assume a calendar year RIC has no net capital loss for any taxable year beginning before 2010, a net capital loss of $2 million for 2010; a net capital loss of $1 million for 2011, all of which is a long-term capital loss; and $600,000 gain from the sale of a capital asset held less than one year on July 15, 2012.[14]

For 2012, the RIC has (1) $600,000 short-term capital gain from the July 15 sale, (2) $2 million carryover from 2010 which is treated as a short-term capital loss,[15] and (3) $1 million long-term capital loss from 2011 treated as arising on January 1, 2012. The capital loss allowed in 2012 is limited to $600,000, the amount of capital gain for the taxable year.

For purposes of determining the amount of the $2 million net capital loss that may be carried over from 2010 to 2013, there is no capital gain net income for 2012 because the $600,000 gain does not exceed the $1 million long-term loss treated as arising on January 1, 2012; therefore the entire 2010 net capital loss is carried over to 2013 and treated as a short-term capital loss in 2013. $400,000 (the excess of the $1 million long-term capital loss treated as arising on January 1, 2012, over the $600,000 short-term capital gain for 2012) is treated as a long-term capital loss on January 1, 2013. The 2010 net capital loss may continue be carried over through 2018, subject to reduction by capital gain net income; no limitation applies on the number of taxable years that the 2011 net capital loss may be carried over.

Effective Date

The provision generally applies to net capital losses for taxable years beginning after the date of enactment. The provision relating to the treatment of present-law carryovers applies to taxable years beginning after the date of enactment.

[Law at ¶5515 and ¶5525. CCH Explanation at ¶803.]

[¶15,020] Act Sec. 201. Income from commodities counted toward gross income test of RICs

Joint Committee on Taxation (J.C.T. Rep. No. JCX-49-10)

[Code Sec. 851(b) (sic - 851(d))]

Present Law

A RIC must derive 90 percent of its gross income for a taxable year from certain types of income.[16] These types of income ("qualifying income") are (1) dividends, interest, payments with respect to securities loans (as defined in section 512(a)(5)), and gains from the sale or other disposition of stock or securities (as defined in section 2(a)(36) of the Investment Company Act of 1940, as amended)[17] or foreign currencies, or other income (including but not limited to gains from options, futures or forward contracts) derived with respect to the business of investing in such stock, securities, or currencies,

---

[14] Assume, for purposes of this example, that the provision is enacted in 2010.

[15] The present-law treatment of net capital losses arising in taxable years beginning before the date of enactment continues to apply.

[16] Sec. 851(b)(2).

[17] Section 2(a)(36) of the Investment Company Act of 1940 defines a "security" as "any note, stock, treasury stock, security future, bond, debenture, evidence of indebtedness, certificate of interest or participation in any profit-sharing agreement, collateral-trust certificate, preorganization certificate or subscription, transferable share, investment contract, voting-trust certificate, certificate of deposit for a security, fractional undivided interest in oil, gas, or other mineral rights, any put, call, straddle, option, or privilege on any security (including a certificate of deposit) or on any group or index of securities (including any interest therein or based on the value thereof), or any put, call, straddle, option, or privilege entered into on a national securities exchange relating to foreign currency, or, in general, any interest or instrument commonly known as a 'security,' or any certificate of interest or participation in, temporary or interim certificate for, receipt for, guarantee of, or warrant or right to subscribe to or purchase, any of the foregoing."

and (2) net income derived from an interest in a qualified publicly traded partnership.[18]

In general, because direct investments in commodities are not "securities" under section 2(a)(36) of the Investment Company Act of 1940, they do not generate "qualifying income" for purposes of the 90 percent gross income test. Similarly, the IRS has ruled that derivative contracts with respect to commodity indexes are not securities for the purposes of the gross income tests.[19] On the other hand, in a series of private rulings, the IRS has held that certain notes, with payout formulas determined with reference to a commodities index, produce qualifying income for purposes of the gross income test.[20] The IRS also has held that income of a RIC derived from investments in commodities by a wholly owned foreign subsidiary of the RIC is qualifying income for purposes of the gross income test.[21]

The Secretary has the regulatory authority to exclude from qualifying income foreign currency gains which are not directly related to the RIC's principal business of investing in stock or securities (or options and futures with respect to stock or securities).[22]

Explanation of Provision

The provision modifies the qualifying income test to provide that (i) a RIC's gains from the sale or other disposition of commodities and (ii) other income of a RIC (including but not limited to gains from options, futures or forward contracts) derived with respect to its business of investing in commodities, are qualifying income for purposes of the gross income test. As a result, income earned by a RIC from derivative contracts with respect to commodity indices will be qualifying income for purposes of the gross income test.[23] In general, these changes are not intended to change the present law treatment of RICs' income from foreign currencies. However, because the provision allows RICs to derive qualifying income from investments in commodities (including foreign currencies), the provision repeals the regulatory authority given to the Secretary to exclude certain foreign currency gains from qualifying income.[24]

Effective Date

The provision is effective for taxable years beginning after the date of enactment.

[Law at ¶5425 and ¶5430. CCH Explanation at ¶806.]

[¶15,030] Act Sec. 202. Savings provisions for failures of RICs to satisfy gross income and asset tests

Joint Committee on Taxation (J.C.T. REP. NO. JCX-49-10)

[Code Sec. 851(d) and (i)]

Present Law

Asset tests

In general, at the close of each quarter of the taxable year, at least 50 percent of the value of a RIC's total assets must be represented by (i) cash and cash items (including receivables), Government securities and securities of other RICs, and (ii) other securities, generally limited in respect of any one issuer to an amount not greater in value than five percent of the value of the total assets of the RIC and to not more than 10 percent of the outstanding voting securities of such issuer.[25]

---

[18] A "qualified publicly traded partnership" means a publicly traded partnership (within the meaning of section 7704(b)), other than a publicly traded partnership whose gross income is qualifying income (other than income of another publicly traded partnership). Sec. 851(h).

[19] See Rev. Rul. 2006-31, 2006-1 C.B. 1133.

[20] See, e.g., PLRs 201031007, 200822012, 200705026, 200701020, 200647017, 200637018, 200628001.

[21] See, e.g., PLRs 200936002, 200932007.

[22] Sec. 851(b)(3).

[23] Cf. Rev. Rul. 2006-31, 2006-1 C.B. 1133 (holding that a RIC's income from a derivative contract with respect to a commodity index is not qualifying income for purposes of section 851(b)(2), because the income from the contract is not derived with respect to the RIC's business of investing in stocks, securities, or currencies.)

[24] The bill contains several conforming amendments to retain the present law definition of qualifying income for purposes of provisions relating to publicly traded partnerships.

[25] Sec. 851(b)(3)(A).

In addition, at the close of each quarter of the taxable year, not more than 25 percent of the value of a RIC's total assets may be invested in (i) the securities (other than Government securities or the securities of other RICs) of any one issuer, (ii) the securities (other than the securities of other RICs) of two or more issuers which the taxpayer controls and which are determined, under regulations prescribed by the Secretary, to be engaged in the same or similar trades or businesses or related trades or businesses, or (iii) the securities of one or more qualified publicly traded partnerships (as defined in section 851(h)).[26]

A RIC meeting both asset tests at the close of any quarter will not lose its status as a RIC because of a discrepancy during a subsequent quarter between the value of its various investments and the asset test requirements, unless such discrepancy exists immediately after the acquisition of any security or other property and is wholly or partly the result of such acquisition.[27] This rule protects a RIC against inadvertent failures of the asset tests that may be caused by fluctuations in the relative values of its assets. A second rule (the "30-day rule") gives a RIC 30 days following the end of a quarter in which it fails an asset test to cure the failure, if the failure is by reason of a discrepancy, between the value of its various investments and the asset test requirements, that exists immediately after the acquisition of any security or other property which is wholly or partly the result of such acquisition during such quarter.[28] Failure of any asset test (except where the failure is cured pursuant to the 30-day rule) will prevent a corporation from qualifying as a RIC.

Gross income test

A RIC must derive 90 percent of its gross income from qualifying income.[29] Thus, a RIC meets the gross income test provided its gross income that is not qualifying income does not exceed one-ninth of the portion of its gross income that is qualifying income. For example, a RIC with $90x of gross income from qualifying income can have up to $10x of gross income from other sources without failing the test. Failure to meet the gross income test for a taxable year prevents a corporation from qualifying as a RIC for that year.

Explanation of Provision

Saving provision for asset test failures

The bill provides a special rule for *de minimis* asset test failures and a mechanism by which a RIC can cure other asset test failures and pay a penalty tax. The rule for *de minimis* asset test failures applies if a RIC fails to meet one of the asset tests in section 851(b)(3) due to the ownership of assets the total value of which does not exceed the lesser of (i) one percent of the total value of the RIC's assets at the end of the quarter for which the assets are valued, and (ii) $10 million. Where the *de minimis* rule applies, the RIC shall nevertheless be considered to have satisfied the asset tests if, within six months of the last day of the quarter in which the RIC identifies that it failed the asset test (or such other time period provided by the Secretary) the RIC: (i) disposes of assets in order to meet the requirements of the asset tests, or (ii) the RIC otherwise meets the requirements of the asset tests.

In the case of other asset test failures, a RIC shall nevertheless be considered to have met the asset tests if: (i) the RIC sets forth in a schedule filed in the manner provided by the Secretary a description of each asset that causes the RIC to fail to satisfy the asset test; (ii) the failure to meet the asset tests is due to reasonable cause and not due to willful neglect; and (iii) within six months of the last day of the quarter in which the RIC identifies that it failed the asset test (or such other time period provided by the Secretary) the RIC (I) disposes of the assets which caused the asset test failure, or (II) otherwise meets the requirements of the asset tests. In cases of asset test failures other than *de minimis* failures, the provision imposes a tax in an amount equal to the greater of (i) $50,000 or (ii) the amount determined (pursuant to regulations promulgated by the Secretary) by multiplying the highest rate of tax specified in section 11 (currently 35 percent) by the net income generated during the period of asset test failure by the assets that caused the RIC to fail the asset test. For purposes of subtitle F, the tax imposed for an asset test failure is treated as excise tax with respect to which the deficiency procedures apply.

---

[26] Sec. 851(b)(3)(B).

[27] Sec. 851(d).

[28] *Ibid.*

[29] See present-law explanation of section 201 of the bill for a description of qualifying income.

These provisions added by the bill do not apply to any quarter in which a corporation's status of a RIC is preserved under the provision of present law.

Saving provision for gross income test failures

The bill provides that a corporation that fails to meet the gross income test shall nevertheless be considered to have satisfied the test if, following the corporation's failure to meet the test for the taxable year, the corporation (i) sets forth in a schedule, filed in the manner provided by the Secretary, a description of each item of its gross income and (ii) the failure to meet the gross income test is due to reasonable cause and is not due to willful neglect.

In addition, under the bill, a tax is imposed on any RIC that fails to meet the gross income test equal to the amount by which the RIC's gross income from sources which are not qualifying income exceeds one-ninth of its gross income

from sources which are qualifying income. For example, if a RIC has $90x of gross income of sources which are qualifying income and $15x of gross income from other sources, a tax of $5x is imposed. The tax is the amount by which the $15x gross income from sources which are not qualifying income exceeds the $10x permitted under present law.

Calculation of investment company taxable income

Taxes imposed for failure of the asset or income tests are deductible for purposes of calculating investment company taxable income.

Effective Date

The provision applies to taxable years with respect to which the due date (determined with regard to extensions) of the return of tax is after the date of enactment.

[**Law at ¶ 5425 and ¶ 5430. CCH Explanation at ¶ 806.**]

[¶ 15,040] Act Sec. 301. Modification of dividend designation requirements and allocation rules for RICs

Joint Committee on Taxation (J.C.T. REP. NO. JCX-49-10)

[Code Sec. 852(b)]

Present Law

Capital gain dividends

In general

In general, a capital gain dividend paid by a RIC is treated by the RIC's shareholders as long-term capital gain.[30] In addition, a RIC is allowed a dividend paid deduction for its capital gain dividends in computing the tax imposed on its net capital gain.[31]

A capital gain dividend is any dividend, or part thereof, which is designated by the RIC as a capital gain dividend in a written notice mailed to the RIC's shareholders not later than 60 days after the close of the RIC's taxable year,[32] except that in the event a RIC designates an aggregate

amount of capital gain dividends for a taxable year that exceeds the RIC's net capital gain, the portion of each distribution that is a capital gain dividend is only that proportion of the designated amount that the RIC's net capital gain bears to the total amount so designated by the RIC. For example, assume a RIC makes quarterly distributions of $30, designated entirely as capital gain dividends. If the RIC has only $100 of net capital gain for its taxable year, only $25 of each quarterly distribution is a capital gain dividend (i.e., $30 × ($100/$120) = $25).

Other designated items

Exempt-interest dividends

A RIC may designate any portion of a dividend (other than a capital gain dividend) as an "exempt-interest dividend," if at least half of the

---

[30] Sec. 852(b)(3)(B). This provision applies only with respect to RICs which meet the requirements of section 852(a) for the taxable year.

[31] Sec. 852(b)(3)(A).

[32] Sec. 852(b)(3)(C). If there is an increase in the amount by which a RIC's net capital gain exceeds the deduction for dividends paid (determined with reference to capital gain dividends only) as a result of a "determination," the RIC has 120 days after the date of the determination to make a designation with respect to such increase. A determination

is defined in section 860(e) as: (1) a decision by the Tax Court, or a judgment, decree, or other order by any court of competent jurisdiction, which has become final; (2) a closing agreement made under section 7121; (3) under regulations prescribed by the Secretary, an agreement signed by the Secretary and by, or on behalf of, the qualified investment entity relating to the liability of such entity for tax; or (4) a statement by the taxpayer attached to its amendment or supplement to a return of tax for the relevant tax year. See Rev. Proc. 2009-28, 2009-20 I.R.B. 1011.

RICs assets consist of tax-exempt State and local bonds. The shareholder treats an exempt-interest dividend as an item of tax-exempt interest.[33]

Exempt-interest dividends are defined as any dividend, or part thereof, which is designated by the RIC as an exempt interest dividend in a written notice mailed to the RIC's shareholders not later than 60 days after the close of the RIC's taxable year,[34] except that in the event a RIC designates an aggregate amount of exempt-interest dividends for a taxable year that exceeds the RIC's tax exempt interest (net of related deductions disallowed under sections 265 and 171(a)(2) by reason of the interest being tax exempt), the portion of each distribution that will be an exempt interest dividend is only that proportion of the designated amount that net exempt interest bears to the amount so designated.

Foreign tax credits; credits for tax-credit bonds; dividends received by RIC

RICs may pass through to shareholders certain foreign tax credits, credits for tax-credit bonds, and dividends received by the RIC that qualify, in the case of corporate shareholders, for the dividends received deduction, or, in the case of individual shareholders, the capital gain rates in effect for dividends received in taxable years beginning before January 1, 2011. In each case the qualifying amount must be designated in a written notice mailed to its shareholders not later than 60 days after the close of the RIC's taxable year.

Dividends paid to certain foreign persons.

Certain dividends paid to nonresident alien individuals and foreign corporations in taxable years of the RIC beginning before January 1, 2010, retain their character as interest or short term-capital gain.[35] These dividends must be designated in a written notice mailed to its shareholders not later than 60 days after the close of the RIC's taxable year. Rules similar to the rules described above relating to capital gain dividends and exempt-interest dividends apply to designated amounts in excess of actual amounts.

Explanation of Provision

Capital gain dividends

Reporting requirements

The provision replaces the present-law designation requirement for a capital gain dividend with a requirement that a capital gain dividend be *reported* by the RIC in written statements furnished to its shareholders. A written statement furnishing this information to a shareholder may be a Form 1099.

Allocation by fiscal year RICs

The provision provides a special rule allocating the excess reported amount[36] for taxable year RICs in order to reduce the need for RICs to amend Form 1099s and shareholders to file amended income tax returns. This special allocation rule applies to a taxable year of a RIC which includes more than one calendar year if the RIC's post-December reported amount[37] exceeds the excess reported amount for the taxable year.

For example, assume a RIC for its taxable year ending June 30, 2012, makes quarterly distributions of $30,000 on September 30, 2011, December 31, 2011, March 31, 2012, and June 30, 2012, and reports the amounts as capital gain dividends. If the RIC has only $100,000 net capital gain for its taxable year, the excess reported amount is $20,000. Because the post-December reported amount ($60,000) exceeds the excess reported amount ($20,000), the excess reported amount is allocated among the post-December reported capital gain dividends in proportion to the amount of each such distribution reported as a capital gain dividend. Thus, one-half of the excess reported amount (i.e., 1/2 of $20,000 = $10,000) is allocated to each post-December distribution, reducing the amount of each post-December distribution treated as a capital gain dividend from $30,000 to $20,000. Because no excess reported amount is allocated to either of the quarterly distributions made on or before December 31, 2011, the entire $30,000 of each of the distributions retains its character as a capital gain dividend.

---

[33] Sec. 852(b)(5)(B).

[34] Sec. 852(b)(5)(A).

[35] Secs. 871(k) and 881(e).

[36] The "excess reported amount" is the excess of the aggregate amount reported as capital gain dividends for the taxable year over the RIC's net capital gain for the taxable year.

[37] The "post-December reported amount" is the aggregate amount reported with respect to items arising after December 31 of the RIC's taxable year.

If, in the above example, the RIC has only $40,000 net capital gain for its taxable year, the excess reported amount is $80,000. Because the post-December reported amount ($60,000) does not exceed the excess reported amount ($80,000), the excess reported amount is allocated among all the reported capital gain dividends for the taxable year in proportion to the amount of each distribution reported as a capital gain dividend. Thus, one-fourth of the excess reported amount (i.e., 1/4 of $80,000 = $20,000) is allocated to each distribution, reducing the amount of each distribution treated as a capital gain dividend from $30,000 to $10,000.

Other designated items

The provision replaces the other designation requirements described under present law with a requirement that amounts be *reported* by the RIC in written statements furnished to its shareholders.[38]

The provision also provides allocation rules for excess reported amounts of exempt-interest dividends and certain dividends paid to nonresident alien individuals and foreign corporations by fiscal year RICs similar to the rule described above applicable capital gain dividends.

Effective Date

The provision applies to taxable years beginning after the date of enactment.[39]

[Law at ¶5430, ¶5435, ¶5440, ¶5445, ¶5450, ¶5460 and ¶5465. CCH Explanation at ¶809.]

[¶15,050] Act Sec. 302. Earnings and profits of RICs

Joint Committee on Taxation (J.C.T. REP. No. JCX-49-10)

[Code Sec. 852(c)(1)]

Present Law

The current earnings and profits of a RIC are not reduced by any amount that is not allowable as a deduction in computing taxable income for the taxable year.[40]

Application to net capital loss

Thus, under the general rule, the current earnings and profits of a RIC are not reduced by a net capital loss either in the taxable year the loss arose or any taxable year to which the loss is carried.[41] The accumulated earnings and profits are reduced in the taxable year the net capital loss arose.

Application to exempt-interest expenses

Because the general rule denies deductions in computing current earnings and profits for amounts disallowed for expenses, interest, and amortizable bond premium relating to tax-exempt interest,[42] the current earnings and profits

of a RIC with tax-exempt interest may exceed the amount which the RIC can distribute as exempt-interest dividends.[43] Thus, distributions by a RIC with only tax-exempt interest income may result in taxable dividends to its shareholders. For example, assume a RIC has $1 million gross tax-exempt interest and $10,000 expenses disallowed under section 265 (and no accumulated earnings and profits and no other item of current earnings and profits). If the RIC were to distribute $1 million to its shareholders during its taxable year (which is $10,000 more than its economic income for the year), $990,000 may be designated as exempt-interest dividends, and the remaining $10,000 is taxable as ordinary dividends.

Explanation of Provision

Net capital loss

The rules applicable to the taxable income treatment of a net capital loss of a RIC apply for purposes of determining earnings and profits (both current earnings and profits and accumu-

---

[38] The bill does not change the method of designation of undistributed capital gain taken into account by shareholders under section 852(b)(3)(D)(i).

[39] Each amendment to a provision relating to qualified dividends of individual shareholders will sunset when the provision to which the amendment was made sunsets pursuant to section 303 of the Jobs and Growth Tax Relief Reconciliation Act. Under present law, these provisions sunset in taxable years beginning after December 31, 2010.

[40] Sec. 852(c)(1). The provision applies to a RIC without regard to whether it meets the requirements of section 852(a) for the taxable year.

[41] See sec. 101 of the bill for the treatment of carryovers of a net capital loss under present law and as amended by the bill.

[42] Secs. 171(a)(2) and 265.

[43] For a description of exempt-interest dividends, see explanation of section 301 of the bill.

lated earnings and profits). Thus, a net capital loss for a taxable year is not taken into account in determining earnings and profits, but any capital loss treated as arising on the first day of the next taxable year is taken into account in determining earnings and profits for the next taxable year (subject to the application of the net capital loss rule for that year).

Exempt-interest expenses

The deductions disallowed in computing investment company taxable income relating to tax-exempt interest are allowed in computing current earnings and profits of a RIC.

In the example under present law, the provision reduces the RIC's current earnings and profits from $1 million to $990,000 and if the RIC were to distribute $1 million to its shareholders during the taxable year, $990,000 may be reported as exempt-interest dividends and the remaining $10,000 is treated as a return of capital (or gain to the shareholder).

Effective Date

The provision applies to taxable years beginning after the date of enactment.

[Law at ¶ 5430 and ¶ 5465. CCH Explanation at ¶ 812.]

[¶ 15,060] Act Sec. 303. Pass-thru of exempt-interest dividends and foreign tax credits in fund of funds structures

Joint Committee on Taxation (J.C.T. REP. NO. JCX-49-10)

[Code Sec. 852(g)]

Present Law

In a so-called "fund of funds" structure, one RIC ("upper-tier fund") holds stock in one or more other RICs ("lower-tier funds"). Generally, the character of certain types of income and gain, such as capital gain and qualified dividends, of a lower-tier fund pass through from the lower-tier RIC to the upper-tier RIC and then pass through to the shareholders of the upper-tier RIC.

Exempt-interest dividends and foreign tax credits may be passed through by a RIC only if at least 50 percent of the value of the total assets of a RIC consist of tax-exempt obligations (in the case of exempt-interest dividends) or more than 50 percent of the value of the total assets consist of stock or securities in foreign corporations (in the case of the foreign tax credit). Because an upper-tier RIC holds stock in other RICs, it does not meet the 50-percent asset requirements. As a result, it may not pass through these items to its shareholders, even though the items were passed through to it by a lower tier RIC meeting these requirements.

Explanation of Provision

Under the provision, in the case of a qualified fund of funds, the RIC may (1) pay exempt-interest dividends without regard to the requirement that at least 50 percent of the value of its total assets consist of tax-exempt State and local bonds and (2) elect to allow its shareholders foreign tax credit without regard to the requirement that more than 50 percent of the value of its total assets consist of stock or securities in foreign corporations.

For this purpose, a qualified fund of funds means a RIC at least 50 percent of the value of the total assets of which (at the close of each quarter of the taxable year) is represented by interests in other RICs.

Effective Date

The provision applies to taxable years beginning after the date of enactment.

[Law at ¶ 5430. CCH Explanation at ¶ 815.]

[¶ 15,070] Act Sec. 304. Modification of rules for spillover dividends of RICs

Joint Committee on Taxation (J.C.T. REP. NO. JCX-49-10)

[Code Sec. 855]

Present Law

A RIC may elect to have certain dividends paid after the close of a taxable year considered

as having been paid during that year for purposes of the RIC distribution requirements and determining the taxable income of the RIC.[44] These dividends are referred to as "spillover dividends." In order to qualify as a spillover dividend, the dividend must be declared prior to the time prescribed for filing the tax return for the taxable year (determined with regard to extensions) and the distribution must be made in the 12-month period following the close of the taxable year and not later than the date of the first dividend payment made after the declaration.

Explanation of Provision

The time for declaring a spillover dividend is the later of the 15th day of the 9th month following the close of the taxable year or the extended due date for filing the return. Also, the requirement that the distribution be made not later than the date of the first dividend payment after the declaration is changed. The provision provides that the distribution must be made not later than the date of the first dividend payment of the same type of dividend (for example, an ordinary income dividend or a capital gain dividend) made after the declaration. For this purpose, a dividend attributable to short-term capital gain with respect to which a notice is required under the Investment Company Act of 1940 shall be treated as the same type of dividend as a capital gain dividend.[45]

Effective Date

The provision applies to distributions in taxable years beginning after the date of enactment.

[Law at ¶5450. CCH Explanation at ¶818.]

[¶15,080] Act Sec. 305. Return of capital distributions of RICs

Joint Committee on Taxation (J.C.T. Rep. No. JCX-49-10)

[Code Sec. 316]

Present Law

A dividend is a distribution of property by a corporation (1) out of its earnings and profits accumulated after February 28, 1913 ("accumulated earnings and profits"), and (2) out of its earnings and profits of the taxable year ("current earnings and profits").[46] The current earnings and profits are prorated among current year distributions.[47] Distributions of property which are not a dividend reduce the adjusted basis of a shareholder's stock and are treated as gain to the extent in excess of the stock's adjusted basis.[48]

For example, assume a RIC, with a taxable year ending June 30 and with no accumulated earnings and profits, has current earnings and profits of $4 million and distributes $3 million to its shareholders on September 15 and $3 million on March 15. Under present law, $2 million of each distribution is out of current earnings and profits and is treated as dividend income to its shareholders. The remaining amounts are applied against the adjusted basis of the each shareholder's stock or taken into account as gain by the shareholders.

Explanation of Provision

In the case of a non-calendar year RIC which makes distributions of property with respect to the taxable year in an amount in excess of the current and accumulated and earnings and profits, the current earnings and profits are allocated first to distributions made on or before December 31 of the taxable year.

Thus, under the provision, in the above example, all $3 million of the distribution made on September 15 is out of current earnings and profits and thus treated as dividend income. Only $1 million of the distribution made on March 15 is out of current earnings and profits and treated as dividend income. The remaining $2 million of the March 15 distribution is applied against the adjusted basis of each shareholder's stock or taken into account as gain by the shareholders.

In the case of a RIC with more than one class of stock, the provision applies separately to each class of stock.[49]

Effective Date

The provision applies to distributions made in taxable years beginning after the date of enactment.

[Law at ¶5340. CCH Explanation at ¶821.]

---

[44] Sec. 855.
[45] See section 19 of the Investment Company Act of 1940, as amended, for rules requiring notice to shareholders identifying source of distribution.
[46] Sec. 316.

[47] Treas. Reg. sec. 1.316-2(b).
[48] Sec. 301(c).
[49] See Rev. Rul. 69-440.

[¶15,090] Act Sec. 306. Distributions in redemption of stock of RICs

Joint Committee on Taxation (J.C.T. Rep. No. JCX-49-10)

[Code Secs. 267 and 302]

Present Law

Exchange treatment

The redemption of stock by a corporation is treated as an exchange of stock if the redemption fits into one of four categories of transactions.[50] If the redemption does not fit into one of these categories, the redemption is treated as a distribution of property. One of the four categories of transactions is that the redemption "is not essentially equivalent to a dividend."[51] A redemption "is not essentially equivalent to a dividend" if the redemption results in a "meaningful reduction in the shareholder's proportionate ownership in the corporation."[52] Other categories include a substantially disproportionate redemption, a redemption that terminates the shareholder's interest in the corporation, and a partial liquidation (if the redeemed shareholder is not a corporation).[53]

The Code provides no specific rule regarding the application of the "not essentially equivalent to a dividend" test in the case of an open-end RIC whose shareholders "sell" their shares by having them redeemed by the issuing RIC and where multiple redemptions by different shareholders may occur daily.

Loss deferral

Any deduction in respect of a loss from the sale or exchange of property between members of a controlled group of corporation is deferred until the transfer of the property outside the group.[54] In the case of a fund of funds, a lower-tier fund may be required to redeem shares in an upper-tier fund when the upper-tier fund shareholders demand redemption of their shares. Because the upper-tier fund and lower-tier fund may be members of the same controlled group of corporations, any loss by the upper-tier fund on the disposition of the lower-tier fund shares may be deferred.

Explanation of Provision

Exchange treatment

The bill provides that, except to the extent provided in regulations, the redemption of stock of a publicly offered RIC is treated as an exchange if the redemption is upon the demand of the shareholder and the company issues only stock which is redeemable upon the demand of the shareholder. A publicly offered RIC is a RIC the shares of which are (1) continuously offered pursuant to a public offering, (2) regularly traded on an established securities market, or (3) held by no fewer than 500 persons at all times during the taxable year.

Loss disallowance

The bill provides that, except to the extent provided in regulations, the loss deferral rule does not apply to any redemption of stock of a RIC if the RIC issues only stock which is redeemable upon the demand of the shareholder and the redemption is upon the demand of a shareholder which is another RIC.

Effective Date

The provision applies to distributions after the date of enactment.

[Law at ¶5320 and ¶5330. CCH Explanation at ¶824.]

---

[50] Sec. 302.
[51] Sec. 302(b)(1).
[52] *United States v. Davis*, 397 U.S. 301 (1970).

[53] Sec. 302(b)(2)-(4).
[54] Sec. 267(f).

[¶15,100] Act Sec. 307. Repeal of preferential dividend rule for publicly offered RICs

Joint Committee on Taxation (J.C.T. Rep. No. JCX-49-10)

[Code Sec. 562]

Present Law

RICs are allowed a deduction for dividends paid to their shareholders. In order to qualify for the deduction, a dividend must not be a "preferential dividend."[55] For this purpose, a dividend is preferential unless it is distributed pro rata to shareholders, with no preference to any share of stock compared with other shares of the same class, and with no preference to one class as compared with another except to the extent the class is entitled to a preference. A distribution by a RIC to a shareholder whose initial investment was $10 million or more is not treated as preferential if the distribution is increased to reflect reduced administrative cost of the RIC with respect to the shareholder.

Securities law, administered by the Securities Exchange Commission, provides strict limits on the ability of RICs to issue shares with preferences.[56]

Explanation of Provision

The provision repeals the preferential dividend rule for publicly offered RICs. For this purpose, a RIC is publicly offered if its shares are (1) continuously offered pursuant to a public offering, (2) regularly traded on an established securities market, or (3) held by no fewer than 500 persons at all times during the taxable year.

Effective Date

The provision applies to distributions in taxable years beginning after the date of enactment.

[Law at ¶5395. CCH Explanation at ¶827.]

[¶15,110] Act Sec. 308. Elective deferral of certain late-year losses of RICs

Joint Committee on Taxation (J.C.T. Rep. No. JCX-49-10)

[Code Sec. 852(b)(8)]

Present Law

Capital gains and losses

In general

In general, a RIC may pay a capital gain dividend to its shareholders to the extent of the RIC's net capital gain for the taxable year. The shareholders treat capital gain dividends as long-term capital gain.[57]

Under present law, an excise tax is imposed on a RIC for a calendar year equal to four percent of the excess (if any) of the required distribution over the distributed amount. The required distribution is the sum of 98 percent of the RIC's ordinary income for the calendar year and 98 percent of the capital gain net income for the one-year period ending October 31 of such calendar year. The distributed amount is the sum of the deduction for dividends paid during the calendar year and the amount on which a corporate income tax is imposed on the RIC for taxable years ending during the calendar year.[58]

Deferral of net capital losses and long-term capital losses

Under present law, for purposes of determining the amount of a net capital gain dividend, the amount of net capital gain for a taxable year is determined without regard to any net capital loss or net long-term capital loss attributable to transactions after October 31 of the taxable year, and the post-October net capital loss or net long term capital loss is treated as arising on the first day of the RIC's next taxable year.[59]

Present law provides that to the extent provided in regulations, the above rules relating to

---

[55] Sec. 562(c).

[56] See, for example, section 18 of the Investment Company Act of 1940.

[57] See explanation of section 301 of the bill.

[58] Sec. 4982.

[59] Section 852(b)(3)(C). Certain RICs with taxable years ending with the month of November or December are not subject to this rule.

post-October net capital losses also apply for purposes of computing taxable income of a RIC.[60] Regulations have been issued allowing RICs to elect to defer all or part of any net capital loss (or if there is no such net capital loss, any net long-term capital loss) attributable to the portion of the taxable year after October 31 to the first day of the succeeding taxable year.[61]

The following example illustrates the application of the post-October capital loss rules.

Assume a RIC with a taxable year ending June 30, 2011, recognizes a long-term capital gain of $1,000,000 on September 15, 2010. In order to avoid the excise tax, the RIC distributes $980,000 on December 15, 2010, which it designates as a capital gain dividend. On January 15, 2011, the RIC recognizes a $600,000 long-term capital loss. The RIC has no other income or loss during 2010 and 2011, and has no accumulated earnings and profits.

Absent the post-October loss rule, the RIC would have a net capital gain (and current earnings and profits) of only $400,000 for the taxable year ending June 30, 2011. Only $400,000 of the December 15, 2010, distribution would be a capital gain dividend; the remaining $580,000 of the $980,000 distributed on December 15 would be a return of capital. Because the "distributed amount" for excise tax purposes takes into account only those distributions for which a dividend paid deduction is allowed, the RIC's distributed amount for calendar year 2010 would be $400,000, which is less than the distributed amount required to avoid the excise tax. In addition, the shareholders may have improperly reported the distribution as a capital gain dividend on the 2010 income tax returns.

By "pushing" the post-October long-term capital loss to July 1, 2011, in the above example the entire $980,000 paid on December 15, 2010, is a capital gain dividend. The distribution is fully deductible in computing the excise tax. No excise tax is imposed for 2010 because the RIC has no undistributed income.

Short-term capital losses not deferred

No special rule applies to short-term capital losses arising after October 31 of the taxable year for purposes of defining a capital gain dividend.

The following example illustrates the present-law treatment of a RIC with a post-October 31 short-term capital loss:

Assume a RIC with a taxable year ending June 30, 2011, recognizes a short-term capital gain of $1 million on September 15, 2010. In order to avoid the excise tax, the RIC distributes $980,000 on December 15, 2010. On May 15, 2011, the RIC recognizes a $1 million long-term capital gain and $1 million short term-capital loss. The RIC has no other income or loss during 2010, 2011, or 2012 (and has no accumulated earnings and profits).

Under present law, the shareholders receive Forms 1099 for 2010 reporting the dividends as other than capital gain dividends and they report the dividends accordingly on their 2010 income tax returns. Because the RIC has only $1 million of current earnings and profits for its taxable year, the RIC may not pay an additional distribution designated as a capital gain dividend for its taxable year in order to be allowed a dividend paid deduction in computing the RIC's tax on net capital gain. Instead, the RIC could designate the December 15 distribution as a capital gain dividend, but that would require shareholders to file amended income tax returns for 2010.

Deferral partly elective

Under present law, for purposes of determining capital gain dividends, the "push" forward of post-October capital losses is automatic, rather than elective; in contrast the push forward of these losses is elective for RIC taxable income purposes. Assume for example that a RIC has no net capital gain for the portion of its taxable year on or before October 31, and makes no distributions before January 1 of the taxable year. For the remainder of its taxable year, the RIC has a $1 million short-term capital gain and a $1 million long-term capital loss. Under present law, for purposes of determining the amount of capital gain dividends, the $1 million long-term capital loss is automatically pushed forward to the next taxable year. But for purposes of determining its taxable income, the capital loss is pushed forward only if the RIC elects. If no election is made and the RIC has a $1 million long-term capital gain in the next taxable year and pays a $1 million dividend, the dividend may not be designated a capital gain dividend, although the RIC had $1 million long-term capital gain that year. If an election is made, the RIC must distribute the $1 million of short-term capital gain as an ordinary dividend in the current taxable year although the gains were economically offset by the long-term capital loss.

---

[60] The last sentence of Sec. 852(b)(3)(C).

[61] Treas. Reg. 1.852-11.

Ordinary gains and losses

Net foreign currency losses and losses on stock in a passive foreign investment company

In applying the excise tax described above, net foreign currency losses and gains and ordinary loss or gain from the disposition of stock in a passive foreign investment company ("PFIC") properly taken into account after October 31 are "pushed" to the following calendar year for purposes of the tax.[62]

Under present law, to the extent provided in regulations, a RIC may elect to push the post-October net foreign currency losses and the net reduction in the value of stock in a PFIC with respect to which an election is in effect under section 1296(k) forward to the next taxable year.[63] Regulations have been issued allowing RICs to elect to defer all or part of any post-October net foreign currency losses for the portion of the taxable year after October 31 to the first day of the succeeding taxable year.[64]

Other ordinary losses

Other ordinary losses of a RIC may not be "pushed" forward. As a result, in the event that a RIC has net ordinary losses for the portion of the taxable year after December 31 (other than a net foreign currency loss or loss on stock of a PFIC), the RIC may have insufficient earnings and profits to pay a dividend during the calendar year ending in the taxable year in order to reduce or eliminate the excise tax.

For example, assume a RIC for its taxable year ending June 30, 2012, has ordinary income of $1 million for the portion of its taxable year ending on December 31, 2011. In order to avoid the excise tax, the RIC distributes $980,000 on December 15, 2011. The RIC has no accumulated earnings and profits. For the period beginning January 1, 2012, and ending on June 30, 2012, the RIC has a net ordinary loss of $1 million. Because the RIC has no earnings and profits, the distribution in 2011 is not a dividend; the distributed amount for calendar year 2011 is zero; and an excise tax is imposed.

Explanation of Provision

Post-October capital losses

Under the provision, except to the extent provided in regulations, a RIC may elect to "push" to the first day of the next taxable year part or all of any post-October capital loss. The post-October capital loss means the greatest of the RIC's net capital loss, net long-term capital loss, or the net short-term capital loss (attributable to the portion of the taxable year after October 31).[65]

The election[66] applies for all purposes of the Code, including determining taxable income, net capital gain, net short-term capital gain, and earnings and profits.

The application of the provision to short-term capital losses may be illustrated by the following example:

Assume a RIC for its taxable year ending June 30, 2012, recognizes a short-term capital gain of $1 million on September 15, 2011. In order to avoid the excise tax, the RIC distributes $980,000 on December 15, 2011. On May 15, 2012, the RIC recognizes a $1 million long-term capital gain and $1 million short term-capital loss. The RIC has no other income or loss during 2011, 2012, or 2013 (and has no accumulated earnings and profits).

The RIC may elect to treat the short-term capital loss as arising on July 1, 2012. If the RIC so elects and makes an additional $1 million distribution before July 1, 2012, it may report the distribution as a capital gain dividend and be allowed a dividends paid deduction in computing the tax on its net capital gain for the 2011-2012 taxable year. No amended Forms 1099 and no amended tax returns by the shareholders are required.

Late-year ordinary losses

Under the provision, except to the extent provided in regulations, a RIC may elect to "push" to the first day of the next taxable year part or all of any qualified late-year ordinary loss. The qualified late year ordinary loss is the excess of (1) the sum of the specified losses attributable to the portion of the taxable year after October 31 and other ordinary losses attributable to the portion of the taxable year after December 31, over (2) the sum of the specified gains attributable to the portion of the taxable year after October 31 and other ordinary income attributable to the portion of the taxable year after December 31. Specified losses and gains have the

---

[62] Sec. 4982(e)(5) and (6).

[63] Sec. 852(b)(8) and (10).

[64] Treas. Reg. 1.852-11.

[65] Special rules apply to certain RICs with taxable years ending with the month of November or December.

[66] The principles of Treasury Regulation 1.852-11 are to apply to a qualified late-year loss for which an election is made under this provision, subject to any subsequent change in the regulations.

same meaning as used for purposes of the excise tax under section 4982.[67]

The election applies for all purposes of the Code.

Effective Date

The provision applies to taxable years beginning after the date of enactment.

[Law at ¶5430 and ¶5465. CCH Explanation at ¶830.]

[¶15,120] Act Sec. 309. Exception to holding period requirement for exempt-interest dividends declared on daily basis

Joint Committee on Taxation (J.C.T. Rep. No. JCX-49-10)

[Code Sec. 852(b)(4)]

Present Law

If a shareholder receives an exempt-interest dividend with respect to a share of RIC stock held for 6 months or less, any loss on the sale or exchange of the stock, to the extent of the amount of the exempt-interest dividend, is disallowed. To the extent provided by regulations, the loss disallowance rule does not apply to losses on shares which are sold or exchanged pursuant to a plan which involves the periodic liquidation of the shares. In the case of a RIC which regularly distributes at least 90 percent of its net tax-exempt interest, the Secretary may by regulations prescribe a shorter holding period not shorter than the greater of 31 days or the period between the regular distributions.

Explanation of Provision

The provision makes the loss disallowance rule inapplicable, except as otherwise provided by regulations, with respect to a regular dividend paid by a RIC that declares exempt-interest dividends on a daily basis in amount equal to at least 90 percent of its net tax-exempt interest and distributes the dividends on a monthly or more frequent basis.

Effective Date

The provision applies to stock for which the taxpayer's holding period begins after the date of enactment of this provision.

[Law at ¶5430. CCH Explanation at ¶833.]

[¶15,130] Act Sec. 401. Excise tax exemption for certain RICs owned by tax exempt entities

Joint Committee on Taxation (J.C.T. Rep. No. JCX-49-10)

[Code Sec. 4982(f)]

Present Law

An excise tax is imposed on a RIC for a calendar year equal to four percent of the excess (if any) of the required distribution over the distributed amount. The required distribution is the sum of 98 percent of the RIC's ordinary income for the calendar year and 98 percent of the capital gain net income for the one-year period ending October 31 of such calendar year. The distributed amount is the sum of the deduction for dividends paid during the calendar year and the amount on which a corporate income tax

is imposed on the RIC for taxable years ending during the calendar year.[68]

The excise tax does not apply to a RIC for any calendar year if at all times during the calendar year each shareholder in the RIC is either a qualified pension plan exempt from tax or a segregated asset account of a life insurance company held in connection with variable contracts.

Explanation of Provision

The provision adds tax-exempt entities whose ownership of beneficial interests in the RIC would not preclude the application of sec-

---

[67] See explanation of section 402 of the bill.

[68] Sec. 4982.

tion 817(h)(4) (regarding segregated asset accounts of a variable annuity or life insurance contract) to the list of persons who may hold stock in a RIC that is exempt from the excise tax. These persons include qualified annuity plans described in section 403, IRAs, including Roth IRAs, certain government plans described in section 414(d) or 457, and a pension plan described in section 501(c)(18).[69] Also, another RIC to which section 4982 does not apply may hold stock in a RIC exempt from the excise tax.

Effective Date

The provision applies to calendar years beginning after the date of enactment.

[Law at ¶5760. CCH Explanation at ¶836.]

[¶15,140] Act Sec. 402. Deferral of certain gains and losses of RICs for excise tax purposes

Joint Committee on Taxation (J.C.T. Rep. No. JCX-49-10)

[Code Sec. 4982(e)]

Present Law

Special rules apply to certain items of income and loss in computing the excise tax under section 4982.[70] Any foreign currency gains and losses attributable to a section 988 transaction properly taken into account after October 31 of any calendar year generally are "pushed" to the following calendar year.[71] Any post-October positive or negative adjustments, and income or loss, on contingent payment debt instruments is treated in the same manner as foreign currency gain or loss from a section 988 transaction.[72] Any gain recognized under section 1296 (relating to mark-to-market for marketable stock in a passive foreign investment company ("PFIC")) generally is determined as if the RIC's taxable year ends October 31, and any gain or loss from an actual disposition of stock in an electing PFIC after October 31 generally is "pushed" to the following calendar year.[73]

To the extent provided in regulations, any net foreign currency loss of a RIC and any net reduction in the value of the stock of a PFIC held by a RIC attributable to transactions after October 31 of the taxable year may be "pushed" to the first day of the following taxable year for purposes of computing taxable income.[74] Similar rules apply for purposes of computing earnings and profits in order to allow a RIC a distribution deduction for purposes of the excise tax.[75]

Explanation of Provision

Under the provision, the present-law excise tax "push" rules applicable to foreign currency gains and losses are expanded to include all "specified gains and losses," i.e., ordinary gains and losses from the sale, exchange, or other disposition of (or termination of a position with respect to) property, including foreign currency gain and loss, and amounts marked-to-market under section 1296. Thus, these post-October 31 gains and losses are "pushed" to the next calendar year.[76]

The provision also provides that, for purposes of determining a RIC's ordinary income, the present-law rule treating PFIC stock as disposed of on October 31 is made applicable to all property held by a RIC which under any provision of the Code (including regulations thereunder) is treated as disposed of on the last day of the taxable year.

Finally, for purposes of the excise tax, the provision allows a taxable year RIC, except as provided in regulations, to elect to "push" any net ordinary loss (determined without regard to ordinary gains and losses which are automatically "pushed" to the next calendar year) attributable to the portion of the calendar year after the beginning of the taxable year which begins in the calendar year to the first day of the next calendar year.

---

[69] See Rev. Rul. 94-62, 1994-2 C.B. 164, as supplemented by Rev. Rul. 2007-58, I.R.B. 2007-37 (Sept. 10, 2007).

[70] See section 401 for a description of the tax.

[71] Sec. 4982(e)(5).

[72] See Treas. Reg. 1.1275-4(b)(9)(v).

[73] Sec. 4982(e)(6).

[74] Sec 852(b)(8) and (10). See Treas. Reg. 1.852-11 for rules relating to the treatment of losses attributable to periods after October 31 of a taxable year.

[75] Sec. 852(c)(2).

[76] For treatment of these losses for income tax purposes, see section 852(b)(8) of the Code, as amended by section 308 of the bill.

For example, assume a RIC for its taxable year ending June 30, 2012, has ordinary loss of $1 million for the portion of its taxable year ending on December 31, 2011, and $1 million ordinary income for the remainder of the taxable year. The RIC has no other items of income or loss in 2011, 2012, or 2013. The RIC must distribute $980,000 in 2012 to avoid the excise tax, notwithstanding that it has no taxable income (or earnings and profits) for a taxable year which includes any portion of 2012. Under the provision, if the RIC makes an election, the $1 million ordinary loss will be treated as arising on January 1, 2012, for purposes of the excise tax and the RIC will not be required to make a distribution in 2012 to avoid the excise tax.

Effective Date

The provision applies to calendar years beginning after the date of enactment.

[Law at ¶ 5760. CCH Explanation at ¶ 836.]

[¶15,150] Act Sec. 403. Distributed amount for excise tax purposes determined on basis of taxes paid by RIC

Joint Committee on Taxation (J.C.T. Rep. No. JCX-49-10)

[Code Sec. 4982(c)(4)]

Present Law

In computing the excise tax under section 4982,[77] a RIC is treated as having distributed amounts on which a tax is imposed on the RIC during the calendar year in which the taxable year of the RIC ends, regardless of the calendar year in which estimated tax payments are made.[78]

Explanation of Provision

Under the provision, a RIC making estimated tax payments of the taxes imposed on investment company taxable income and undistributed net capital gain for a taxable year beginning (but not ending) during any calendar year may elect to increase the distributed amount for that calendar year by the amount on which the estimated tax payments of these taxes are made during that calendar year. The distributed amount for the following calendar year is reduced by the amount of the prior year's increase.

Effective Date

The provision applies to calendar years beginning after the date of enactment.

[Law at ¶ 5760. CCH Explanation at ¶ 836.]

[¶15,160] Act Sec. 404. Increase in Required distribution of capital gain net income

Joint Committee on Taxation (J.C.T. Rep. No. JCX-49-10)

[Code Sec. 4982]

Present Law

An excise tax is imposed on a RIC for a calendar year equal to four percent of the excess (if any) of the required distribution over the distributed amount. The required distribution is the sum of 98 percent of the RIC's ordinary income for the calendar year and 98 percent of the capital gain net income for the one-year period ending October 31 of such calendar year. The distributed amount is the sum of the deduction for dividends paid during the calendar year and the amount on which a corporate income tax is imposed on the RIC for taxable years ending during the calendar year.[79]

Explanation of Provision

The provision increases the required distribution percentage of the capital gain net income from 98 percent to 98.2 percent

Effective Date

The provision applies to calendar years beginning after the date of enactment.

[Law at ¶ 5760. CCH Explanation at ¶ 836.]

---

[77] See section 401 for a description of the tax.
[78] Sec. 4982(c)(1)(B).

[79] Sec. 4982.

[¶15,170] Act Sec. 501. Repeal of assessable penalty with respect to liability for tax of RICs

Joint Committee on Taxation (J.C.T. REP. No. JCX-49-10)

[Code Sec. 6697]

Present Law

If there is a determination that a RIC has a tax deficiency with respect to a prior taxable year, the RIC can distribute a "deficiency dividend."[80] A deficiency dividend is treated by the RIC as a dividend paid with respect to the prior taxable year. As a result, the deficiency dividend increases the RIC's deduction for dividends paid for that year and eliminates the deficiency. A RIC making a deficiency dividend is subject to an interest charge as if the entire amount of the deficiency dividend were the amount of the tax deficiency. An additional penalty is also imposed equal to the lesser of (1) the amount of the interest charge, or (2) one-half of the amount of the deficiency dividend.[81]

Explanation of Provision

The provision repeals the additional penalty with respect to deficiency dividends.

Effective Date

The provision applies to taxable years beginning after the date of enactment.

[Law at ¶5845. CCH Explanation at ¶839.]

[¶15,180] Act Sec. 502. Modification of sale load basis deferral rule for RICs

Joint Committee on Taxation (J.C.T. REP. No. JCX-49-10)

[Code Sec. 852(f)(1)]

Present Law

If (1) a taxpayer incurs a load charge in acquiring stock in a RIC and by reason of incurring the charge or making the acquisition, acquires a reinvestment right, (2) the stock is disposed of within 90 days of the acquisition, and (3) the taxpayer subsequently acquires stock in a RIC and the otherwise applicable load charge is reduced by reason of the reinvestment right, the load charge (to the extent it does not exceed the reduction) is not taken into account in determining gain or loss of the original stock but is treated as incurred in acquiring the subsequently acquired stock.[82]

Explanation of Provision

The provision limits the applicability of the provision described under present law to cases where the taxpayer subsequently acquires stock before January 31 of the calendar year following the calendar year the original stock is disposed of.

Effective Date

The provision applies to charges incurred in taxable years beginning after the date of enactment.

[Law at ¶5430. CCH Explanation at ¶842.]

---

[80] Sec. 860.
[81] Sec. 6697.

[82] Sec. 852(f).

Act Sec. 502   ¶15,180

¶20,001 Effective Dates

Tax Relief, Unemployment Insurance Reauthorization, and Job Creation Act of 2010

This CCH-prepared table presents the general effective dates for major law provisions added, amended or repealed by the Tax Relief, Unemployment Insurance Reauthorization, and Job Creation Act of 2010 (P.L. 111-312), enacted December 17, 2010. Entries are listed in Code Section order.

Code Sec.	Act Sec.	Act Provision Subject	Effective Date
1(f)	101(a)(1)	Temporary Extension of 2001 Tax Relief—Temporary Extension	Tax years beginning after December 31, 2004
1(f)(2)(A)	101(a)(1)	Temporary Extension of 2001 Tax Relief—Temporary Extension	Tax years beginning after December 31, 2004
1(f)(6)(B)	101(a)(1)	Temporary Extension of 2001 Tax Relief—Temporary Extension	Tax years beginning after December 31, 2004
1(f)(8)	101(a)(1)	Temporary Extension of 2001 Tax Relief—Temporary Extension	Tax years beginning after December 31, 2004
1(f)(8)(A)	102(a)	Temporary Extension of 2003 Tax Relief	Tax years beginning after December 31, 2002
1(f)(8)(B)	102(a)	Temporary Extension of 2003 Tax Relief	Tax years beginning after December 31, 2002
1(g)(7)(B)	101(a)(1)	Temporary Extension of 2001 Tax Relief—Temporary Extension	Tax years beginning after December 31, 2000
1(h)(1)(A)(ii)(I)	101(a)(1)	Temporary Extension of 2001 Tax Relief—Temporary Extension	Tax years beginning after December 31, 2000
1(h)(1)(B)	102(a)	Temporary Extension of 2003 Tax Relief	Tax years ending on or after May 6, 2003
1(h)(1)(B)(i)	101(a)(1)	Temporary Extension of 2001 Tax Relief—Temporary Extension	Tax years beginning after December 31, 2000
1(h)(1)(C)	102(a)	Temporary Extension of 2003 Tax Relief	Tax years ending on or after May 6, 2003
1(h)(2)	102(a)	Temporary Extension of 2003 Tax Relief	Tax years ending on or after May 6, 2003
1(h)(3)	102(a)	Temporary Extension of 2003 Tax Relief	Tax years ending on or after May 6, 2003
1(h)(4)	102(a)	Temporary Extension of 2003 Tax Relief	Tax years ending on or after May 6, 2003
1(h)(5)	102(a)	Temporary Extension of 2003 Tax Relief	Tax years ending on or after May 6, 2003
1(h)(6)	102(a)	Temporary Extension of 2003 Tax Relief	Tax years ending on or after May 6, 2003
1(h)(7)	102(a)	Temporary Extension of 2003 Tax Relief	Tax years ending on or after May 6, 2003
1(h)(8)	102(a)	Temporary Extension of 2003 Tax Relief	Tax years ending on or after May 6, 2003
1(h)(9)	102(a)	Temporary Extension of 2003 Tax Relief	Tax years ending on or after May 6, 2003
1(h)(10)	102(a)	Temporary Extension of 2003 Tax Relief	Tax years ending on or after May 6, 2003

Code Sec.	Act Sec.	Act Provision Subject	Effective Date
1(h)(11)	102(a)	Temporary Extension of 2003 Tax Relief	Tax years beginning after December 31, 2002
1(h)(11)	102(a)	Temporary Extension of 2003 Tax Relief	Tax years ending on or after May 6, 2003
1(h)(12)	102(a)	Temporary Extension of 2003 Tax Relief	Tax years ending on or after May 6, 2003
1(h)(13)	101(a)(1)	Temporary Extension of 2001 Tax Relief—Temporary Extension	Tax years beginning after December 31, 2000
1(i)	101(a)(1)	Temporary Extension of 2001 Tax Relief—Temporary Extension	Tax years beginning after December 31, 2000
1(i)(1)(B)	102(a)	Temporary Extension of 2003 Tax Relief	Tax years beginning after December 31, 2002
1(i)(1)(C)	102(a)	Temporary Extension of 2003 Tax Relief	Tax years beginning after December 31, 2002
1(i)(2)	102(a)	Temporary Extension of 2003 Tax Relief	Tax years beginning after December 31, 2002
15(f)	101(a)(1)	Temporary Extension of 2001 Tax Relief—Temporary Extension	Tax years beginning after December 31, 2000
21(a)(2)	101(a)(1)	Temporary Extension of 2001 Tax Relief—Temporary Extension	Tax years beginning after December 31, 2002
21(c)(1)	101(a)(1)	Temporary Extension of 2001 Tax Relief—Temporary Extension	Tax years beginning after December 31, 2002
21(c)(2)	101(a)(1)	Temporary Extension of 2001 Tax Relief—Temporary Extension	Tax years beginning after December 31, 2004
23	101(a)(1)	Temporary Extension of 2001 Tax Relief—Temporary Extension	Tax years beginning after December 31, 2001
23	101(b)(1)	Temporary Extension of 2001 Tax Relief—Separate Sunset for Expansion of Adoption Benefits Under the Patient Protection and Affordable Care Act	Amended to read as if Sec. 10909(c) of the Patient Protection and Affordable Care Act had never been enacted; tax years beginning after December 31, 2011
23(a)(1)	101(a)(1)	Temporary Extension of 2001 Tax Relief—Temporary Extension	Tax years beginning after December 31, 2001
23(a)(2)	101(a)(1)	Temporary Extension of 2001 Tax Relief—Temporary Extension	Tax years beginning after December 31, 2001
23(a)(3)	101(b)(1)	Temporary Extension of 2001 Tax Relief—Separate Sunset for Expansion of Adoption Benefits Under the Patient Protection and Affordable Care Act	Amended to read as if Sec. 10909(c) of the Patient Protection and Affordable Care Act had never been enacted; tax years beginning after December 31, 2011
23(b)(1)	101(a)(1)	Temporary Extension of 2001 Tax Relief—Temporary Extension	Tax years beginning after December 31, 2001

Code Sec.	Act Sec.	Act Provision Subject	Effective Date
23(b)(1)	101(b)(1)	Temporary Extension of 2001 Tax Relief—Separate Sunset for Expansion of Adoption Benefits Under the Patient Protection and Affordable Care Act	Amended to read as if Sec. 10909(c) of the Patient Protection and Affordable Care Act had never been enacted; tax years beginning after December 31, 2011
23(b)(2)(A)	101(a)(1)	Temporary Extension of 2001 Tax Relief—Temporary Extension	Tax years beginning after December 31, 2001
23(b)(4)	101(a)(1)	Temporary Extension of 2001 Tax Relief—Temporary Extension	Tax years beginning after December 31, 2001
23(c)	101(a)(1)	Temporary Extension of 2001 Tax Relief—Temporary Extension	Tax years beginning after December 31, 2001
23(d)(2)	101(a)(1)	Temporary Extension of 2001 Tax Relief—Temporary Extension	Tax years beginning after December 31, 2001
23(h)	101(a)(1)	Temporary Extension of 2001 Tax Relief—Temporary Extension	Tax years beginning after December 31, 2001
23(h)	101(b)(1)	Temporary Extension of 2001 Tax Relief—Separate Sunset for Expansion of Adoption Benefits Under the Patient Protection and Affordable Care Act	Amended to read as if Sec. 10909(c) of the Patient Protection and Affordable Care Act had never been enacted; tax years beginning after December 31, 2011
24(a)	101(a)(1)	Temporary Extension of 2001 Tax Relief—Temporary Extension	Tax years beginning after December 31, 2000
24(a)(2)	102(a)	Temporary Extension of 2003 Tax Relief	Tax years beginning after December 31, 2002
24(b)	101(a)(1)	Temporary Extension of 2001 Tax Relief—Temporary Extension	Tax years beginning after December 31, 2004
24(b)(1)	101(a)(1)	Temporary Extension of 2001 Tax Relief—Temporary Extension	Tax years beginning after December 31, 2001
24(b)(3)	101(a)(1)	Temporary Extension of 2001 Tax Relief—Temporary Extension	Tax years beginning after December 31, 2001
24(b)(3)(B)	101(a)(1)	Temporary Extension of 2001 Tax Relief—Temporary Extension	Tax years beginning after December 31, 2001
24(b)(3)B	101(b)(1)	Temporary Extension of 2001 Tax Relief—Separate Sunset for Expansion of Adoption Benefits Under the Patient Protection and Affordable Care Act	Amended to read as if Sec. 10909(c) of the Patient Protection and Affordable Care Act had never been enacted; tax years beginning after December 31, 2011
24(d)	101(a)(1)	Temporary Extension of 2001 Tax Relief—Temporary Extension	Tax years beginning after December 31, 2001
24(d)(2)	101(a)(1)	Temporary Extension of 2001 Tax Relief—Temporary Extension	Tax years beginning after December 31, 2000
24(d)(3)	101(a)(1)	Temporary Extension of 2001 Tax Relief—Temporary Extension	Tax years beginning after December 31, 2004
24(d)(4)	101(a)(1)	Temporary Extension of 2001 Tax Relief—Temporary Extension	Tax years beginning after December 31, 2004

Code Sec.	Act Sec.	Act Provision Subject	Effective Date
24(d)(4)	103(b)(1)-(2)	Temporary Extension of 2009 Tax Relief—Child Tax Credit	Tax years beginning after December 31, 2010
25(e)(1)(C)	101(a)(1)	Temporary Extension of 2001 Tax Relief—Temporary Extension	Tax years beginning after December 31, 2001
25(e)(1)(C)	101(b)(1)	Temporary Extension of 2001 Tax Relief—Separate Sunset for Expansion of Adoption Benefits Under the Patient Protection and Affordable Care Act	Amended to read as if Sec. 10909(c) of the Patient Protection and Affordable Care Act had never been enacted; tax years beginning after December 31, 2011
25A(e)	101(a)(1)	Temporary Extension of 2001 Tax Relief—Temporary Extension	Tax years beginning after December 31, 2001
25A(i)	103(a)(1)	Temporary Extension of 2009 Tax Relief—American Opportunity Credit	Tax years beginning after December 31, 2010
25A(i)(5)(B)	101(b)(1)	Temporary Extension of 2001 Tax Relief—Separate Sunset for Expansion of Adoption Benefits Under the Patient Protection and Affordable Care Act	Amended to read as if Sec. 10909(c) of the Patient Protection and Affordable Care Act had never been enacted; tax years beginning after December 31, 2011
25B	101(a)(1)	Temporary Extension of 2001 Tax Relief—Temporary Extension	Tax years beginning after December 31, 2001
25B(g)	101(a)(1)	Temporary Extension of 2001 Tax Relief—Temporary Extension	Tax years beginning after December 31, 2001
25B(g)(2)	101(b)(1)	Temporary Extension of 2001 Tax Relief—Separate Sunset for Expansion of Adoption Benefits Under the Patient Protection and Affordable Care Act	Amended to read as if Sec. 10909(c) of the Patient Protection and Affordable Care Act had never been enacted; tax years beginning after December 31, 2011
25C(a)-(b)	710(b)(1)	Credit for Nonbusiness Energy Property—Return to Pre-ARRA Limitations and Standards	Property placed in service after December 31, 2010
25C(c)(1)	710(b)(2)(A)	Credit for Nonbusiness Energy Property—Return to Pre-ARRA Limitations and Standards—Modification of Standards	Property placed in service after December 31, 2010
25C(c)(1)	710(b)(2)(D)(ii)	Credit for Nonbusiness Energy Property—Return to Pre-ARRA Limitations and Standards—Exterior Windows, Doors, and Skylights—Application of energy star standards	Property placed in service after December 31, 2010
25C(c)(2)(A)	710(b)(2)(E)	Credit for Nonbusiness Energy Property—Return to Pre-ARRA Limitations and Standards—Insulation	Property placed in service after December 31, 2010
25C(c)(4)	710(b)(2)(D)(i)	Credit for Nonbusiness Energy Property—Return to Pre-ARRA Limitations and Standards—Exterior Windows, Doors, and Skylights	Property placed in service after December 31, 2010

¶20,001

Code Sec.	Act Sec.	Act Provision Subject	Effective Date
25C(d)(2)(A)(ii)	710(b)(2)(C)(ii)	Credit for Nonbusiness Energy Property—Return to Pre-ARRA Limitations and Standards—Oil Furnaces and Hot Water Boilers—Conforming amendment	Property placed in service after December 31, 2010
25C(d)(3)(E)	710(b)(2)(B)	Credit for Nonbusiness Energy Property—Return to Pre-ARRA Limitations and Standards—Wood Stoves	Property placed in service after December 31, 2010
25C(d)(4)	710(b)(2)(C)(i)	Credit for Nonbusiness Energy Property—Return to Pre-ARRA Limitations and Standards—Oil Furnaces and Hot Water Boilers	Property placed in service after December 31, 2010
25C(e)(3)	710(b)(3)	Credit for Nonbusiness Energy Property—Subsidized Energy Financing	Property placed in service after December 31, 2010
25C(g)(2)	710(a)	Credit for Nonbusiness Energy Property—Extension	Property placed in service after December 31, 2010
26(a)(1)	101(a)(1)	Temporary Extension of 2001 Tax Relief—Temporary Extension	Tax years beginning after December 31, 2001
26(a)(1)	101(b)(1)	Temporary Extension of 2001 Tax Relief—Separate Sunset for Expansion of Adoption Benefits Under the Patient Protection and Affordable Care Act	Amended to read as if Sec. 10909(c) of the Patient Protection and Affordable Care Act had never been enacted; tax years beginning after December 31, 2011
26(a)(2)	202(a)(1)–(2)	Temporary Extension of Alternative Minimum Tax Relief for Nonrefundable Personal Credits	Tax years beginning after December 31, 2009
30(c)(2)(B)(ii)	101(b)(1)	Temporary Extension of 2001 Tax Relief—Separate Sunset for Expansion of Adoption Benefits Under the Patient Protection and Affordable Care Act	Amended to read as if Sec. 10909(c) of the Patient Protection and Affordable Care Act had never been enacted; tax years beginning after December 31, 2011
30B(g)(2)(B)(ii)	101(b)(1)	Temporary Extension of 2001 Tax Relief—Separate Sunset for Expansion of Adoption Benefits Under the Patient Protection and Affordable Care Act	Amended to read as if Sec. 10909(c) of the Patient Protection and Affordable Care Act had never been enacted; tax years beginning after December 31, 2011
30C(g)(2)	711(a)	Alternative Fuel Vehicle Refueling Property	Property placed in service after December 31, 2010

Code Sec.	Act Sec.	Act Provision Subject	Effective Date
30D(c)(2)(B)(ii)	101(b)(1)	Temporary Extension of 2001 Tax Relief—Separate Sunset for Expansion of Adoption Benefits Under the Patient Protection and Affordable Care Act	Amended to read as if Sec. 10909(c) of the Patient Protection and Affordable Care Act had never been enacted; tax years beginning after December 31, 2011
32(a)(2)(B)	101(a)(1)	Temporary Extension of 2001 Tax Relief—Temporary Extension	Tax years beginning after December 31, 2001
32(b)(2)	101(a)(1)	Temporary Extension of 2001 Tax Relief—Temporary Extension	Tax years beginning after December 31, 2001
32(b)(2)B)	101(a)(1)	Temporary Extension of 2001 Tax Relief—Temporary Extension	Tax years beginning after December 31, 2001
32(b)(3)	103(c)(1)-(2)	Temporary Extension of 2009 Tax Relief—Earned Income Credit	Tax years beginning after December 31, 2010
32(c)(1)(C)	101(a)(1)	Temporary Extension of 2001 Tax Relief—Temporary Extension	Tax years beginning after December 31, 2001
32(c)(2)(A)	101(a)(1)	Temporary Extension of 2001 Tax Relief—Temporary Extension	Tax years beginning after December 31, 2001
32(c)(3)(A)	101(a)(1)	Temporary Extension of 2001 Tax Relief—Temporary Extension	Tax years beginning after December 31, 2001
32(c)(3)(B)	101(a)(1)	Temporary Extension of 2001 Tax Relief—Temporary Extension	Tax years beginning after December 31, 2001
32(c)(3)(E)	101(a)(1)	Temporary Extension of 2001 Tax Relief—Temporary Extension	Tax years beginning after December 31, 2001
32(c)(5)	101(a)(1)	Temporary Extension of 2001 Tax Relief—Temporary Extension	Tax years beginning after December 31, 2001
32(f)(2)(B)	101(a)(1)	Temporary Extension of 2001 Tax Relief—Temporary Extension	Tax years beginning after December 31, 2001
32(h)	101(a)(1)	Temporary Extension of 2001 Tax Relief—Temporary Extension	Tax years beginning after December 31, 2001
32(j)(1)(B)	101(a)(1)	Temporary Extension of 2001 Tax Relief—Temporary Extension	Tax years beginning after December 31, 2001
32(j)(2)(A)	101(a)(1)	Temporary Extension of 2001 Tax Relief—Temporary Extension	Tax years beginning after December 31, 2001
32(n)	101(a)(1)	Temporary Extension of 2001 Tax Relief—Temporary Extension	Tax years beginning after December 31, 2001
36C	101(a)(1)	Temporary Extension of 2001 Tax Relief—Temporary Extension	Tax years beginning after December 31, 2001
36C	101(b)(1)	Temporary Extension of 2001 Tax Relief—Separate Sunset for Expansion of Adoption Benefits Under the Patient Protection and Affordable Care Act	Amended to read as if Sec. 10909(c) of the Patient Protection and Affordable Care Act had never been enacted; tax years beginning after December 31, 2011
36C(a)(1)	101(a)(1)	Temporary Extension of 2001 Tax Relief—Temporary Extension	Tax years beginning after December 31, 2001
36C(a)(2)	101(a)(1)	Temporary Extension of 2001 Tax Relief—Temporary Extension	Tax years beginning after December 31, 2001
36C(b)(1)	101(a)(1)	Temporary Extension of 2001 Tax Relief—Temporary Extension	Tax years beginning after December 31, 2001

¶20,001

Code Sec.	Act Sec.	Act Provision Subject	Effective Date
36C(b)(2)(A)	101(a)(1)	Temporary Extension of 2001 Tax Relief—Temporary Extension	Tax years beginning after December 31, 2001
36C(b)(4)	101(a)(1)	Temporary Extension of 2001 Tax Relief—Temporary Extension	Tax years beginning after December 31, 2001
36C(b)(4)	101(b)(1)	Temporary Extension of 2001 Tax Relief—Separate Sunset for Expansion of Adoption Benefits Under the Patient Protection and Affordable Care Act	Amended to read as if Sec. 10909(c) of the Patient Protection and Affordable Care Act had never been enacted; tax years beginning after December 31, 2011
36C(c)	101(a)(1)	Temporary Extension of 2001 Tax Relief—Temporary Extension	Tax years beginning after December 31, 2001
36C(c)	101(b)(1)	Temporary Extension of 2001 Tax Relief—Separate Sunset for Expansion of Adoption Benefits Under the Patient Protection and Affordable Care Act	Amended to read as if Sec. 10909(c) of the Patient Protection and Affordable Care Act had never been enacted; tax years beginning after December 31, 2011
36C(d)(2)	101(a)(1)	Temporary Extension of 2001 Tax Relief—Temporary Extension	Tax years beginning after December 31, 2001
36C(h)	101(a)(1)	Temporary Extension of 2001 Tax Relief—Temporary Extension	Tax years beginning after December 31, 2001
38(b)(14)	101(a)(1)	Temporary Extension of 2001 Tax Relief—Temporary Extension	Costs paid or incurred in tax years beginning after December 31, 2001, with respect to qualified plans
38(b)(15)	101(a)(1)	Temporary Extension of 2001 Tax Relief—Temporary Extension	Costs paid or incurred in tax years beginning after December 31, 2001, with respect to qualified plans
39(d)(10)	101(a)(1)	Temporary Extension of 2001 Tax Relief—Temporary Extension	Costs paid or incurred in tax years beginning after December 31, 2001, with respect to qualified plans
40(e)(1)(A)-(B)	708(a)(1)(A)-(B)	Extension of Provisions Related to Alcohol Used as Fuel—Extension of Income Tax Credit for Alcohol Used as Fuel	Periods after December 31, 2010
40(h)	708(a)(2)	Extension of Provisions Related to Alcohol Used as Fuel—Extension of Income Tax Credit for Alcohol Used as Fuel--Reduced Amount for Ethanol Blenders	Periods after December 31, 2010
40A(g)	701(a)	Incentives for Biodiesel and Renewable Diesel—Credits for Biodiesel and Renewable Diesel Used as Fuel	Fuel sold or used after December 31, 2009

Code Sec.	Act Sec.	Act Provision Subject	Effective Date
41(h)(1)(B)	731(a)	Research Credit	Amounts paid or incurred after December 31, 2009
45(d)(8)(B)	702(a)	Credit for Refined Coal Facilities	Facilities placed in service after December 31, 2009
45A(f)	732(a)	Indian Employment Tax Credit	Tax years beginning after December 31, 2009
45C(b)(1)(D)	731(b)	Research Credit—Conforming Amendment	Amounts paid or incurred after December 31, 2009
45D(f)(1)(E)-(G)	733(a)(1)-(3)	New Markets Credit	Calendar years beginning after 2009
45D(f)(3)	733(b)	New Markets Credit—Conforming Amendment	Calendar years beginning after 2009
45E	101(a)(1)	Temporary Extension of 2001 Tax Relief—Temporary Extension	Costs paid or incurred in tax years beginning after December 31, 2001, with respect to qualified plans
45F	101(a)(1)	Temporary Extension of 2001 Tax Relief—Temporary Extension	Tax years beginning after December 31, 2001
45G(f)	734(a)	Railroad Track Maintenance Credit	Expenditures paid or incurred in tax years beginning after December 31, 2009
45L(g)	703(a)	New Energy Efficient Home Credit	Homes acquired after December 31, 2009
45M(b)(1)(A)-(E)	709(a)	Energy Efficient Appliance Credit—Dishwashers	Appliances produced after December 31, 2010
45M(b)(2)(C)-(F)	709(b)	Energy Efficient Appliance Credit—Clothes Washers	Appliances produced after December 31, 2010
45M(b)(3)(C)-(F)	709(c)	Energy Efficient Appliance Credit—Refrigerators	Appliances produced after December 31, 2010
45M(e)(1)	709(d)(1)(A)-(B)	Energy Efficient Appliance Credit—Rebasing of Limitations	Tax years beginning after December 31, 2010
45M(e)(2)	709(d)(2)(A)-(B)	Energy Efficient Appliance Credit—Rebasing of Limitations—Exception For Certain Refrigerators and Clothes Washers	Tax years beginning after December 31, 2010
45M(e)(3)	709(d)(3)	Energy Efficient Appliance Credit—Rebasing of Limitations	Tax years beginning after December 31, 2010
45N(e)	735(a)	Mine Rescue Team Training Credit	Tax years beginning after December 31, 2009
45P(f)	736(a)	Employer Wage Credit for Employees Who are Active Duty Members of the Uniformed Services	Payments made after December 31, 2009
51(c)(4)(B)	757(a)	Work Opportunity Credit	Individuals who begin work for the employer after December 17, 2010

¶20,001

Code Sec.	Act Sec.	Act Provision Subject	Effective Date
51A(b)(5)(B)(iii)	101(a)(1)	Temporary Extension of 2001 Tax Relief— Temporary Extension	Expenses relating to courses beginning after December 31, 2001
54E(c)(1)	758(a)(1)–(2)	Qualified Zone Academy Bonds	Obligations issued after December 31, 2010
55(b)(3)	102(a)	Temporary Extension of 2003 Tax Relief	Tax years ending on or after May 6, 2003
55(b)(3)	102(a)	Temporary Extension of 2003 Tax Relief	Tax years ending on or after May 6, 2003
55(b)(3)(B)	102(a)	Temporary Extension of 2003 Tax Relief	Tax years ending on or after May 6, 2003
55(b)(3)(C)	102(a)	Temporary Extension of 2003 Tax Relief	Tax years ending on or after May 6, 2003
55(d)(1)(A)	101(a)(1)	Temporary Extension of 2001 Tax Relief— Temporary Extension	Tax years beginning after December 31, 2001
55(d)(1)(A)	102(a)	Temporary Extension of 2003 Tax Relief	Tax years beginning after December 31, 2002
55(d)(1)(A)–(B)	201(a)(1)–(2)	Temporary Extension of Increased Alternative Minimum Tax Exemption Amount	Tax years beginning after December 31, 2009
55(d)(1)(B)	101(a)(1)	Temporary Extension of 2001 Tax Relief— Temporary Extension	Tax years beginning after December 31, 2001
55(d)(1)(B)	102(a)	Temporary Extension of 2003 Tax Relief	Tax years beginning after December 31, 2002
55(d)(1)(C)	101(a)(1)	Temporary Extension of 2001 Tax Relief— Temporary Extension	Tax years beginning after December 31, 2001
55(d)(1)(D)	101(a)(1)	Temporary Extension of 2001 Tax Relief— Temporary Extension	Tax years beginning after December 31, 2000
55(d)(3)	101(a)(1)	Temporary Extension of 2001 Tax Relief— Temporary Extension	Tax years beginning after December 31, 2000
55(d)(3)(C)	101(a)(1)	Temporary Extension of 2001 Tax Relief— Temporary Extension	Tax years beginning after December 31, 2001
57(a)(7)	102(a)	Temporary Extension of 2003 Tax Relief	Dispositions on or after May 6, 2003
62(a)(2)(D)	721(a)	Deduction for Certain Expenses of Elementary and Secondary School Teachers	Tax years beginning after December 31, 2009
62(a)(18)	101(a)(1)	Temporary Extension of 2001 Tax Relief— Temporary Extension	Payments made in tax years beginning after December 31, 2001
63(c)(2)	101(a)(1)	Temporary Extension of 2001 Tax Relief— Temporary Extension	Tax years beginning after December 31, 2004
63(c)(4)	101(a)(1)	Temporary Extension of 2001 Tax Relief— Temporary Extension	Tax years beginning after December 31, 2004
63(c)(7)	101(a)(1)	Temporary Extension of 2001 Tax Relief— Temporary Extension	Tax years beginning after December 31, 2004
63(c)(17)	102(a)	Temporary Extension of 2003 Tax Relief	Tax years beginning after December 31, 2002
68(f)	101(a)(1)	Temporary Extension of 2001 Tax Relief— Temporary Extension	Tax years beginning after December 31, 2005
68(g)	101(a)(1)	Temporary Extension of 2001 Tax Relief— Temporary Extension	Tax years beginning after December 31, 2005
72(e)(9)	101(a)(1)	Temporary Extension of 2001 Tax Relief— Temporary Extension	Tax years beginning after December 31, 2001

Code Sec.	Act Sec.	Act Provision Subject	Effective Date
72(f)	101(a)(1)	Temporary Extension of 2001 Tax Relief—Temporary Extension	Years beginning after December 31, 2001
72(o)(4)	101(a)(1)	Temporary Extension of 2001 Tax Relief—Temporary Extension	Distributions after December 31, 2001
72(t)(9)	101(a)(1)	Temporary Extension of 2001 Tax Relief—Temporary Extension	Distributions after December 31, 2001, generally
86(b)(2)	101(a)(1)	Temporary Extension of 2001 Tax Relief—Temporary Extension	Payments made in tax years beginning after December 31, 2001
117(c)	101(a)(1)	Temporary Extension of 2001 Tax Relief—Temporary Extension	Amounts received in tax years beginning after December 31, 2001
121(d)(9)	101(a)(1)	Temporary Extension of 2001 Tax Relief—Temporary Extension	Estates of decedents dying after December 31, 2009
121(d)(9)	301(a)	Reinstatement of Estate Tax; Repeal of Carryover Basis	Estates of decedents dying after December 31, 2009
127(c)(1)	101(a)(1)	Temporary Extension of 2001 Tax Relief—Temporary Extension	Expenses relating to courses beginning after December 31, 2001
127(d)	101(a)(1)	Temporary Extension of 2001 Tax Relief—Temporary Extension	Expenses relating to courses beginning after December 31, 2001
127(e)	101(a)(1)	Temporary Extension of 2001 Tax Relief—Temporary Extension	Expenses relating to courses beginning after December 31, 2001
132(a)(7)	101(a)(1)	Temporary Extension of 2001 Tax Relief—Temporary Extension	Years beginning after December 31, 2001
132(f)(2)	727(a)	Parity for Exclusion From Income For Employer-Provided Mass Transit and Parking Benefits	Months after December 31, 2010
132(m)	101(a)(1)	Temporary Extension of 2001 Tax Relief—Temporary Extension	Years beginning after December 31, 2001
132(m)	101(a)(1)	Temporary Extension of 2001 Tax Relief—Temporary Extension	Years beginning after December 31, 2001
135(c)(2)(C)	101(a)(1)	Temporary Extension of 2001 Tax Relief—Temporary Extension	Tax years beginning after December 31, 2001
135(c)(4)(A)	101(a)(1)	Temporary Extension of 2001 Tax Relief—Temporary Extension	Payments made in tax years beginning after December 31, 2001
135(d)(1)(D)	101(a)(1)	Temporary Extension of 2001 Tax Relief—Temporary Extension	Tax years beginning after December 31, 2001
135(d)(2)(A)	101(a)(1)	Temporary Extension of 2001 Tax Relief—Temporary Extension	Tax years beginning after December 31, 2001
135(d)(2)(B)	101(a)(1)	Temporary Extension of 2001 Tax Relief—Temporary Extension	Tax years beginning after December 31, 2001

¶20,001

Code Sec.	Act Sec.	Act Provision Subject	Effective Date
137	101(b)(1)	Temporary Extension of 2001 Tax Relief— Separate Sunset for Expansion of Adoption Benefits Under the Patient Protection and Affordable Care Act	Amended to read as if Sec. 10909(c) 0f the Patient Protection and Affordable Care Act had never been enacted; tax years beginning after December 31, 2011
137(a)	101(a)(1)	Temporary Extension of 2001 Tax Relief— Temporary Extension	Tax years beginning after December 31, 2001
137(a)(2)	101(b)(1)	Temporary Extension of 2001 Tax Relief— Separate Sunset for Expansion of Adoption Benefits Under the Patient Protection and Affordable Care Act	Amended to read as if Sec. 10909(c) 0f the Patient Protection and Affordable Care Act had never been enacted; tax years beginning after December 31, 2011
137(b)(1)	101(a)(1)	Temporary Extension of 2001 Tax Relief— Temporary Extension	Tax years beginning after December 31, 2001
137(b)(1)	101(b)(1)	Temporary Extension of 2001 Tax Relief— Separate Sunset for Expansion of Adoption Benefits Under the Patient Protection and Affordable Care Act	Amended to read as if Sec. 10909(c) 0f the Patient Protection and Affordable Care Act had never been enacted; tax years beginning after December 31, 2011
137(b)(2)(A)	101(a)(1)	Temporary Extension of 2001 Tax Relief— Temporary Extension	Tax years beginning after December 31, 2001
137(b)(3)	101(a)(1)	Temporary Extension of 2001 Tax Relief— Temporary Extension	Payments made in tax years beginning after December 31, 2001
137(d)	101(b)(1)	Temporary Extension of 2001 Tax Relief— Separate Sunset for Expansion of Adoption Benefits Under the Patient Protection and Affordable Care Act	Amended to read as if Sec. 10909(c) 0f the Patient Protection and Affordable Care Act had never been enacted; tax years beginning after December 31, 2011
137(e)	101(b)(1)	Temporary Extension of 2001 Tax Relief— Separate Sunset for Expansion of Adoption Benefits Under the Patient Protection and Affordable Care Act	Amended to read as if Sec. 10909(c) 0f the Patient Protection and Affordable Care Act had never been enacted; tax years beginning after December 31, 2011
137(f)	101(a)(1)	Temporary Extension of 2001 Tax Relief— Temporary Extension	Tax years beginning after December 31, 2001

Code Sec.	Act Sec.	Act Provision Subject	Effective Date
137(f)	101(b)(1)	Temporary Extension of 2001 Tax Relief—Separate Sunset for Expansion of Adoption Benefits Under the Patient Protection and Affordable Care Act	Amended to read as if Sec. 10909(c) 0f the Patient Protection and Affordable Care Act had never been enacted; tax years beginning after December 31, 2011
142(a)(11)	101(a)(1)	Temporary Extension of 2001 Tax Relief—Temporary Extension	Bonds issued after December 31, 2001
142(a)(12)	101(a)(1)	Temporary Extension of 2001 Tax Relief—Temporary Extension	Bonds issued after December 31, 2001
142(a)(13)	101(a)(1)	Temporary Extension of 2001 Tax Relief—Temporary Extension	Bonds issued after December 31, 2001
142(k)	101(a)(1)	Temporary Extension of 2001 Tax Relief—Temporary Extension	Bonds issued after December 31, 2001
146(g)(3)	101(a)(1)	Temporary Extension of 2001 Tax Relief—Temporary Extension	Bonds issued after December 31, 2001
147(h)	101(a)(1)	Temporary Extension of 2001 Tax Relief—Temporary Extension	Bonds issued after December 31, 2001
147(h)(3)	101(a)(1)	Temporary Extension of 2001 Tax Relief—Temporary Extension	Bonds issued after December 31, 2001
148(f)(4)(D)	101(a)(1)	Temporary Extension of 2001 Tax Relief—Temporary Extension	Obligations issued in calendar years beginning after December 31, 2001
151(d)(3)	101(a)(1)	Temporary Extension of 2001 Tax Relief—Temporary Extension	Tax years beginning after December 31, 2005
163(d)(4)(B)	102(a)	Temporary Extension of 2003 Tax Relief	Tax years beginning after December 31, 2002
163(h)(3)(E)(iv)	759(a)	Mortgage Insurance Premiums	Amounts paid or accrued after December 31, 2010
164(b)(5)(I)	722(a)	Deduction of State and Local Sales Taxes	Tax years beginning after December 31, 2009
168(e)(3)(E)(iv)-(v)	737(a)	15-Year Straight-Line Cost Recovery for Qualified Leasehold Improvements, Qualified Restaurant Buildings and Improvements, and Qualified Retail Improvements	Property placed in service after December 31, 2009
168(e)(3)(E)(ix)	737(a)	15-Year Straight-Line Cost Recovery for Qualified Leasehold Improvements, Qualified Restaurant Buildings and Improvements, and Qualified Retail Improvements	Property placed in service after December 31, 2009
168(e)(7)(A)(i)	737(b)(1)	15-Year Straight-Line Cost Recovery for Qualified Leasehold Improvements, Qualified Restaurant Buildings and Improvements, and Qualified Retail Improvements—Conforming Amendments	Property placed in service after December 31, 2009

¶20,001

Code Sec.	Act Sec.	Act Provision Subject	Effective Date
168(e)(8)(E)	737(b)(2)	15-Year Straight-Line Cost Recovery for Qualified Leasehold Improvements, Qualified Restaurant Buildings and Improvements, and Qualified Retail Improvements—Conforming Amendments	Property placed in service after December 31, 2009
168(i)(15)(D)	738(a)	7-Year Recovery Period For Motorsports Entertainment Complexes	Property placed in service after December 31, 2009
168(j)(8)	739(a)	Accelerated Depreciation For Business Property on an Indian Reservation	Property placed in service after December 31, 2009
168(k)	102(a)	Temporary Extension of 2003 Tax Relief	Tax years ending after May 5, 2003
168(k)	401(d)(1)	Extension of Bonus Depreciation; Temporary 100 Percent Expensing for Certain Business Assets—Conforming Amendments	Property placed in service after December 31, 2010, in tax years ending after such date
168(k)(2)	401(a)(1)-(2)	Extension of Bonus Depreciation; Temporary 100 Percent Expensing for Certain Business Assets	Property placed in service after December 31, 2010, in tax years ending after such date
168(k)(2)(A)	102(a)	Temporary Extension of 2003 Tax Relief	Tax years ending after May 5, 2003
168(k)(2)(B)	102(a)	Temporary Extension of 2003 Tax Relief	Tax years ending after May 5, 2003
168(k)(2)(B)(ii)	401(d)(2)	Extension of Bonus Depreciation; Temporary 100 Percent Expensing for Certain Business Assets—Conforming Amendments	Property placed in service after December 31, 2010, in tax years ending after such date
168(k)(2)(C)	102(a)	Temporary Extension of 2003 Tax Relief	Tax years ending after May 5, 2003
168(k)(2)(D)	102(a)	Temporary Extension of 2003 Tax Relief	Tax years ending after May 5, 2003
168(k)(4)	102(a)	Temporary Extension of 2003 Tax Relief	Tax years ending after May 5, 2003
168(k)(4)(D)(ii)-(v)	401(d)(3)(A)-(C)	Extension of Bonus Depreciation; Temporary 100 Percent Expensing for Certain Business Assets—Conforming Amendments	Property placed in service after December 31, 2010, in tax years ending after such date
168(k)(4)(D)(iii)	401(c)(1)	Extension of Bonus Depreciation; Temporary 100 Percent Expensing for Certain Business Assets—Extension of Election to Accelerate the AMT Credit in Lieu of Bonus Depreciation—Extension	Property placed in service after December 31, 2010, in tax years ending after such date

Code Sec.	Act Sec.	Act Provision Subject	Effective Date
168(k)(4)(I)	401(c)(2)	Extension of Bonus Depreciation; Temporary 100 Percent Expensing for Certain Business Assets—Extension of Election to Accelerate the AMT Credit in Lieu of Bonus Depreciation—Rules for Round 2 Extension Property	Property placed in service after December 31, 2010, in tax years ending after such date
168(k)(5)	401(b)	Extension of Bonus Depreciation; Temporary 100 Percent Expensing for Certain Business Assets—Temporary 100 Percent Expensing	Property placed in service after September 8, 2010, in tax years ending after such date
168(l)(5)(A)-(C)	401(d)(4)(A)-(C)	Extension of Bonus Depreciation; Temporary 100 Percent Expensing for Certain Business Assets—Conforming Amendments	Property placed in service after December 31, 2010, in tax years ending after such date
168(n)(2)(C)	401(d)(5)	Extension of Bonus Depreciation; Temporary 100 Percent Expensing for Certain Business Assets—Conforming Amendments	Property placed in service after December 31, 2010, in tax years ending after such date
170(b)(1)(E)(vi)	723(a)	Contributions of Capital Gain Real Property Made for Conservation Purposes	Contributions made in tax years beginning after December 31, 2009
170(b)(2)(B)(iii)	723(b)	Contributions of Capital Gain Real Property Made for Conservation Purposes—Contributions by Certain Corporate Farmers and Ranchers	Contributions made in tax years beginning after December 31, 2009
170(e)(1)	101(a)(1)	Temporary Extension of 2001 Tax Relief—Temporary Extension	Estates of decedents dying after December 31, 2009
170(e)(1)	301(a)	Reinstatement of Estate Tax; Repeal of Carryover Basis	Estates of decedents dying after December 31, 2009
170(e)(3)(C)(iv)	740(a)	Enhanced Charitable Deduction for Contributions of Food Inventory	Contributions made in tax years after December 31, 2009
170(e)(3)(D)(iv)	741(a)	Enhanced Charitable Deduction for Contributions of Book Inventories to Public Schools	Contributions made in tax years after December 31, 2009
170(e)(6)(G)	742(a)	Enhanced Charitable Deduction for Corporate Contributions of Computer Technology and Equipment for Educational Purposes	Contributions made in tax years beginning after December 31, 2009
179(b)(1)	102(a)	Temporary Extension of 2003 Tax Relief	Tax years beginning after December 31, 2002
179(b)(1)(B)-(D)	402(a)	Temporary Extension of Increased Small Business Expensing—Dollar Limitation	Tax years beginning after December 31, 2011
179(b)(2)	102(a)	Temporary Extension of 2003 Tax Relief	Tax years beginning after December 31, 2002

¶20,001

Code Sec.	Act Sec.	Act Provision Subject	Effective Date
179(b)(2)(B)-(D)	402(b)	Temporary Extension of Increased Small Business Expensing—Reduction in Limitation	Tax years beginning after December 31, 2011
179(b)(5)	102(a)	Temporary Extension of 2003 Tax Relief	Tax years beginning after December 31, 2002
179(b)(6)	402(c)	Temporary Extension of Increased Small Business Expensing—Inflation Adjustment	Tax years beginning after December 31, 2011
179(c)(2)	102(a)	Temporary Extension of 2003 Tax Relief	Tax years beginning after December 31, 2002
179(c)(2)	402(e)	Temporary Extension of Increased Small Business Expensing—Conforming Amendment	Tax years beginning after December 31, 2011
179(d)(1)	102(a)	Temporary Extension of 2003 Tax Relief	Tax years beginning after December 31, 2002
179(d)(1)(A)(ii)	402(d)	Temporary Extension of Increased Small Business Expensing—Computer Software	Tax years beginning after December 31, 2011
179(f)(2)(B)-(C)	737(b)(3)(A)-(B)	15-Year Straight-Line Cost Recovery for Qualified Leasehold Improvements, Qualified Restaurant Buildings and Improvements, and Qualified Retail Improvements—Conforming Amendments	Property placed in service after December 31, 2009
179E(g)	743(a)	Election to Expense Advanced Mine Safety Equipment	Property placed in service after December 31, 2009
181(f)	744(a)	Special Expensing Rules for Certain Film and Television Productions	Productions commencing after December 31, 2009
196(c)(10)	101(a)(1)	Temporary Extension of 2001 Tax Relief—Temporary Extension	Costs paid or incurred in tax years beginning after December 31, 2001, with respect to qualified plans
198(h)	745(a)	Expensing of Environmental Remediation Costs	Expenditures paid or incurred after December 31, 2009
199(d)(8)(C)	746(a)(1)-(2)	Deduction Allowable with Respect to Income Attributable to Domestic Production Activities in Puerto Rico	Tax years beginning after December 31, 2009
219(b)(1)(A)	101(a)(1)	Temporary Extension of 2001 Tax Relief—Temporary Extension	Tax years beginning after December 31, 2001
219(b)(5)	101(a)(1)	Temporary Extension of 2001 Tax Relief—Temporary Extension	Tax years beginning after December 31, 2001
219(d)(2)	101(a)(1)	Temporary Extension of 2001 Tax Relief—Temporary Extension	Distributions after December 31, 2001
219(g)(3)	101(a)(1)	Temporary Extension of 2001 Tax Relief—Temporary Extension	Payments made in tax years beginning after December 31, 2001
221(b)(2)(B)	101(a)(1)	Temporary Extension of 2001 Tax Relief—Temporary Extension	Tax years beginning after December 31, 2001
221(b)(2)(C)	101(a)(1)	Temporary Extension of 2001 Tax Relief—Temporary Extension	Payments made in tax years beginning after December 31, 2001

¶20,001

Code Sec.	Act Sec.	Act Provision Subject	Effective Date
221(d)	101(a)(1)	Temporary Extension of 2001 Tax Relief— Temporary Extension	Loan interest paid after December 31, 2001, in tax years ending after such date
221(e)	101(a)(1)	Temporary Extension of 2001 Tax Relief— Temporary Extension	Loan interest paid after December 31, 2001, in tax years ending after such date
221(e)(2)(A)	101(a)(1)	Temporary Extension of 2001 Tax Relief— Temporary Extension	Tax years beginning after December 31, 2001
221(f)	101(a)(1)	Temporary Extension of 2001 Tax Relief— Temporary Extension	Loan interest paid after December 31, 2001, in tax years ending after such date
221(g)	101(a)(1)	Temporary Extension of 2001 Tax Relief— Temporary Extension	Loan interest paid after December 31, 2001, in tax years ending after such date
221(g)(1)	101(a)(1)	Temporary Extension of 2001 Tax Relief— Temporary Extension	Tax years ending after December 31, 2001
222	101(a)(1)	Temporary Extension of 2001 Tax Relief— Temporary Extension	Payments made in tax years beginning after December 31, 2001
222(e)	724(a)	Above-the-Line Deduction for Qualified Tuition and Related Expenses	Tax years beginning after December 31, 2009
301(f)(4)	102(a)	Temporary Extension of 2003 Tax Relief	Tax years beginning after December 31, 2002
306(a)(1)(D)	102(a)	Temporary Extension of 2003 Tax Relief	Tax years beginning after December 31, 2002
338(h)(14)	102(a)	Temporary Extension of 2003 Tax Relief	Tax years beginning after December 31, 2002
341	102(a)	Temporary Extension of 2003 Tax Relief	Tax years beginning after December 31, 2002
401(a)(17)	101(a)(1)	Temporary Extension of 2001 Tax Relief— Temporary Extension	Years beginning after December 31, 2001
401(a)(17)(B)	101(a)(1)	Temporary Extension of 2001 Tax Relief— Temporary Extension	Years beginning after December 31, 2001
401(a)(31)	101(a)(1)	Temporary Extension of 2001 Tax Relief— Temporary Extension	Distributions made after final regulations implementing subsection (c)(2)(A) of this section 657 are prescribed
401(a)(31)(B)	101(a)(1)	Temporary Extension of 2001 Tax Relief— Temporary Extension	Distributions made after final regulations implementing subsection (c)(2)(A) of this section 657 are prescribed
401(a)(31)(C)	101(a)(1)	Temporary Extension of 2001 Tax Relief— Temporary Extension	Distributions made after final regulations implementing subsection (c)(2)(A) of this section 657 are prescribed

¶20,001

Code Sec.	Act Sec.	Act Provision Subject	Effective Date
401(a)(31)(D)	101(a)(1)	Temporary Extension of 2001 Tax Relief— Temporary Extension	Distributions made after final regulations implementing subsection (c)(2)(A) of this section 657 are prescribed
401(a)(31)(E)	101(a)(1)	Temporary Extension of 2001 Tax Relief— Temporary Extension	Distributions made after final regulations implementing subsection (c)(2)(A) of this section 657 are prescribed
401(c)(2)(A)	101(a)(1)	Temporary Extension of 2001 Tax Relief— Temporary Extension	Years beginning after December 31, 2001
401(k)(2)(B)	101(a)(1)	Temporary Extension of 2001 Tax Relief— Temporary Extension	Distributions after December 31, 2001
401(k)(10)	101(a)(1)	Temporary Extension of 2001 Tax Relief— Temporary Extension	Distributions after December 31, 2001
401(k)(10)(A)	101(a)(1)	Temporary Extension of 2001 Tax Relief— Temporary Extension	Distributions after December 31, 2001
401(k)(10)(B)	101(a)(1)	Temporary Extension of 2001 Tax Relief— Temporary Extension	Distributions after December 31, 2001
401(k)(10)(C)	101(a)(1)	Temporary Extension of 2001 Tax Relief— Temporary Extension	Distributions after December 31, 2001
401(k)(11)(B)	101(a)(1)	Temporary Extension of 2001 Tax Relief— Temporary Extension	Years beginning after December 31, 2001
401(k)(11)(E)	101(a)(1)	Temporary Extension of 2001 Tax Relief— Temporary Extension	Years beginning after December 31, 2001
401(m)(9)	101(a)(1)	Temporary Extension of 2001 Tax Relief— Temporary Extension	Years beginning after December 31, 2001
402(c)(2)	101(a)(1)	Temporary Extension of 2001 Tax Relief— Temporary Extension	Distributions made after December 31, 2001
402(c)(3)	101(a)(1)	Temporary Extension of 2001 Tax Relief— Temporary Extension	Distributions made after December 31, 2001
402(c)(4)(C)	101(a)(1)	Temporary Extension of 2001 Tax Relief— Temporary Extension	Distributions made after December 31, 2001
402(c)(8)(B)	101(a)(1)	Temporary Extension of 2001 Tax Relief— Temporary Extension	Distributions after December 31, 2001, generally
402(c)(8)(B)	101(a)(1)	Temporary Extension of 2001 Tax Relief— Temporary Extension	Tax years beginning after December 31, 2005
402(c)(9)	101(a)(1)	Temporary Extension of 2001 Tax Relief— Temporary Extension	Distributions after December 31, 2001, generally
402(c)(10)	101(a)(1)	Temporary Extension of 2001 Tax Relief— Temporary Extension	Distributions after December 31, 2001, generally
402(f)(1)	101(a)(1)	Temporary Extension of 2001 Tax Relief— Temporary Extension	Distributions after December 31, 2001, generally

Code Sec.	Act Sec.	Act Provision Subject	Effective Date
402(f)(1)(A)	101(a)(1)	Temporary Extension of 2001 Tax Relief—Temporary Extension	Distributions made after final regulations implementing subsection (c)(2)(A) of this section 657 are prescribed
402(f)(1)(B)	101(a)(1)	Temporary Extension of 2001 Tax Relief—Temporary Extension	Distributions after December 31, 2001, generally
402(f)(1)(E)	101(a)(1)	Temporary Extension of 2001 Tax Relief—Temporary Extension	Distributions after December 31, 2001, generally
402(f)(2)(A)	101(a)(1)	Temporary Extension of 2001 Tax Relief—Temporary Extension	Distributions after December 31, 2001
402(g)(1)	101(a)(1)	Temporary Extension of 2001 Tax Relief—Temporary Extension	Years beginning after December 31, 2001
402(g)(1)(A)	101(a)(1)	Temporary Extension of 2001 Tax Relief—Temporary Extension	Tax years beginning after December 31, 2005
402(g)(2)(A)	101(a)(1)	Temporary Extension of 2001 Tax Relief—Temporary Extension	Tax years beginning after December 31, 2005
402(g)(4)	101(a)(1)	Contribution Limits—Stricken	Years beginning after December 31, 2001
402(g)(5)	101(a)(1)	Temporary Extension of 2001 Tax Relief—Temporary Extension	Years beginning after December 31, 2001
402(g)(6)	101(a)(1)	Temporary Extension of 2001 Tax Relief—Temporary Extension	Years beginning after December 31, 2001
402(g)(7)	101(a)(1)	Temporary Extension of 2001 Tax Relief—Temporary Extension	Years beginning after December 31, 2001
402(g)(7)(B)	101(a)(1)	Temporary Extension of 2001 Tax Relief—Temporary Extension	Years beginning after December 31, 2001
402(g)(8)	101(a)(1)	Temporary Extension of 2001 Tax Relief—Temporary Extension	Years beginning after December 31, 2001
402(g)(9)	101(a)(1)	Temporary Extension of 2001 Tax Relief—Temporary Extension	Years beginning after December 31, 2001
402A	101(a)(1)	Temporary Extension of 2001 Tax Relief—Temporary Extension	Tax years beginning after December 31, 2005
403(b)(1)	101(a)(1)	Temporary Extension of 2001 Tax Relief—Temporary Extension	Distributions after December 31, 2001, generally
403(b)(1)	101(a)(1)	Temporary Extension of 2001 Tax Relief—Temporary Extension	Years beginning after December 31, 2001
403(b)(2)	101(a)(1)	Temporary Extension of 2001 Tax Relief—Temporary Extension	Years beginning after December 31, 2001
403(b)(3)	101(a)(1)	Temporary Extension of 2001 Tax Relief—Temporary Extension	Years beginning after December 31, 2001
403(b)(7)(A)	101(a)(1)	Temporary Extension of 2001 Tax Relief—Temporary Extension	Distributions after December 31, 2001
403(b)(8)(A)	101(a)(1)	Temporary Extension of 2001 Tax Relief—Temporary Extension	Distributions after December 31, 2001
403(b)(8)(B)	101(a)(1)	Temporary Extension of 2001 Tax Relief—Temporary Extension	Distributions after December 31, 2001
403(b)(11)	101(a)(1)	Temporary Extension of 2001 Tax Relief—Temporary Extension	Distributions after December 31, 2001
403(b)(11)(A)	101(a)(1)	Temporary Extension of 2001 Tax Relief—Temporary Extension	Distributions after December 31, 2001

Code Sec.	Act Sec.	Act Provision Subject	Effective Date
403(b)(13)	101(a)(1)	Temporary Extension of 2001 Tax Relief—Temporary Extension	Trustee-to-trustee transfers after December 31, 2001
404(a)(1)(A)	101(a)(1)	Temporary Extension of 2001 Tax Relief—Temporary Extension	Tax years beginning after December 31, 2001
404(a)(1)(D)	10(a)(1)	Temporary Extension of 2001 Tax Relief—Temporary Extension	Plan years beginning after December 31, 2001
404(a)(3)(A)	101(a)(1)	Temporary Extension of 2001 Tax Relief—Temporary Extension	Years beginning after December 31, 2001
404(a)(3)(B)	101(a)(1)	Temporary Extension of 2001 Tax Relief—Temporary Extension	Years beginning after December 31, 2001
404(a)(10)(B)	101(a)(1)	Temporary Extension of 2001 Tax Relief—Temporary Extension	Years beginning after December 31, 2001
404(a)(12)	101(a)(1)	Temporary Extension of 2001 Tax Relief—Temporary Extension	Years beginning after December 31, 2001
404(h)(1)(C)	101(a)(1)	Temporary Extension of 2001 Tax Relief—Temporary Extension	Years beginning after December 31, 2001
404(h)(2)	101(a)(1)	Temporary Extension of 2001 Tax Relief—Temporary Extension	Years beginning after December 31, 2001
404(k)(2)(A)	101(a)(1)	Temporary Extension of 2001 Tax Relief—Temporary Extension	Tax years beginning after December 31, 2001
404(k)(5)(A)	101(a)(1)	Temporary Extension of 2001 Tax Relief—Temporary Extension	Tax years beginning after December 31, 2001
404(l)	101(a)(1)	Temporary Extension of 2001 Tax Relief—Temporary Extension	Years beginning after December 31, 2001
404(n)	101(a)(1)	Temporary Extension of 2001 Tax Relief—Temporary Extension	Years beginning after December 31, 2001
408(a)(1)	101(a)(1)	Temporary Extension of 2001 Tax Relief—Temporary Extension	Distributions after December 31, 2001, generally
408(a)(1)	101(a)(1)	Temporary Extension of 2001 Tax Relief—Temporary Extension	Tax years beginning after December 31, 2001
408(b)	101(a)(1)	Temporary Extension of 2001 Tax Relief—Temporary Extension	Tax years beginning after December 31, 2001
408(b)(2)(B)	101(a)(1)	Temporary Extension of 2001 Tax Relief—Temporary Extension	Tax years beginning after December 31, 2001
408(d)(3)(A)	101(a)(1)	Temporary Extension of 2001 Tax Relief—Temporary Extension	Distributions after December 31, 2001, generally
408(d)(3)(D)	101(a)(1)	Temporary Extension of 2001 Tax Relief—Temporary Extension	Distributions after December 31, 2001, generally
408(d)(3)(G)	101(a)(1)	Temporary Extension of 2001 Tax Relief—Temporary Extension	Distributions after December 31, 2001, generally
408(d)(3)(H)	101(a)(1)	Temporary Extension of 2001 Tax Relief—Temporary Extension	Distributions after December 31, 2001
408(d)(3)(I)	101(a)(1)	Temporary Extension of 2001 Tax Relief—Temporary Extension	Distributions after December 31, 2001
408(d)(8)(F)	725(a)	Tax-Free Distributions From Individual Retirement Plans For Charitable Purposes	Distributions made in tax years beginning after December 31, 2009
408(j)	101(a)(1)	Temporary Extension of 2001 Tax Relief—Temporary Extension	Tax years beginning after December 31, 2001

Code Sec.	Act Sec.	Act Provision Subject	Effective Date
408(k)	101(a)(1)	Temporary Extension of 2001 Tax Relief—Temporary Extension	Years beginning after December 31, 2001
408(p)(2)(A)	101(a)(1)	Temporary Extension of 2001 Tax Relief—Temporary Extension	Years beginning after December 31, 2001
408(p)(2)(E)	101(a)(1)	Temporary Extension of 2001 Tax Relief—Temporary Extension	Years beginning after December 31, 2001
408(p)(6)(A)	101(a)(1)	Temporary Extension of 2001 Tax Relief—Temporary Extension	Years beginning after December 31, 2001
408(p)(8)	101(a)(1)	Temporary Extension of 2001 Tax Relief—Temporary Extension	Tax years beginning after December 31, 2001
408(q)	101(a)(1)	Temporary Extension of 2001 Tax Relief—Temporary Extension	Plan years beginning after December 31, 2002
408(r)	101(a)(1)	Temporary Extension of 2001 Tax Relief—Temporary Extension	Plan years beginning after December 31, 2002
408A(e)	101(a)(1)	Temporary Extension of 2001 Tax Relief—Temporary Extension	Tax years beginning after December 31, 2005
409(p)	101(a)(1)	Temporary Extension of 2001 Tax Relief—Temporary Extension	Plan years beginning after December 31, 2004, generally
411(a)(2)	101(a)(1)	Temporary Extension of 2001 Tax Relief—Temporary Extension	Contributions for plan years beginning after December 31, 2001, generally
411(a)(11)(D)	101(a)(1)	Temporary Extension of 2001 Tax Relief—Temporary Extension	Distributions after December 31, 2001
411(a)(12)	101(a)(1)	Temporary Extension of 2001 Tax Relief—Temporary Extension	Contributions for plan years beginning after December 31, 2001, generally
411(d)(6)(B)	101(a)(1)	Temporary Extension of 2001 Tax Relief—Temporary Extension	June 7, 2001; regulations issued pursuant to directive to apply to plan years beginning after December 31, 2003, or earlier as specified by the Treasury
411(d)(6)(D)	101(a)(1)	Temporary Extension of 2001 Tax Relief—Temporary Extension	Years beginning after December 31, 2001
411(d)(6)(E)	101(a)(1)	Temporary Extension of 2001 Tax Relief—Temporary Extension	Years beginning after December 31, 2001
412(c)(7)(A)	101(a)(1)	Temporary Extension of 2001 Tax Relief—Temporary Extension	Plan years beginning after December 31, 2001
412(c)(7)(F)	101(a)(1)	Temporary Extension of 2001 Tax Relief—Temporary Extension	Plan years beginning after December 31, 2001
412(c)(9)	101(a)(1)	Temporary Extension of 2001 Tax Relief—Temporary Extension	Plan years beginning after December 31, 2001

¶20,001

Code Sec.	Act Sec.	Act Provision Subject	Effective Date
414(p)(10)	101(a)(1)	Temporary Extension of 2001 Tax Relief—Temporary Extension	Transfers, distributions, and payments made after December 31, 2001
414(p)(11)	101(a)(1)	Temporary Extension of 2001 Tax Relief—Temporary Extension	Transfers, distributions, and payments made after December 31, 2001
414(p)(12)	101(a)(1)	Temporary Extension of 2001 Tax Relief—Temporary Extension	Transfers, distributions, and payments made after December 31, 2001
414(p)(13)	101(a)(1)	Temporary Extension of 2001 Tax Relief—Temporary Extension	Transfers, distributions, and payments made after December 31, 2001
414(v)	101(a)(1)	Temporary Extension of 2001 Tax Relief—Temporary Extension	Contributions in tax years beginning after December 31, 2001
415(a)(2)	101(a)(1)	Temporary Extension of 2001 Tax Relief—Temporary Extension	Years beginning after December 31, 2001
415(b)(1)(A)	101(a)(1)	Temporary Extension of 2001 Tax Relief—Temporary Extension	Years ending after December 31, 2001
415(b)(2)(A)	101(a)(1)	Temporary Extension of 2001 Tax Relief—Temporary Extension	Distributions after December 31, 2001, generally
415(b)(2)(B)	101(a)(1)	Temporary Extension of 2001 Tax Relief—Temporary Extension	Distributions after December 31, 2001, generally
415(b)(2)(C)	101(a)(1)	Temporary Extension of 2001 Tax Relief—Temporary Extension	Years ending after December 31, 2001
415(b)(2)(D)	101(a)(1)	Temporary Extension of 2001 Tax Relief—Temporary Extension	Years ending after December 31, 2001
415(b)(2)(F)	101(a)(1)	Temporary Extension of 2001 Tax Relief—Temporary Extension	Years ending after December 31, 2001
415(b)(7)	101(a)(1)	Temporary Extension of 2001 Tax Relief—Temporary Extension	Years ending after December 31, 2001
415(b)(9)	101(a)(1)	Temporary Extension of 2001 Tax Relief—Temporary Extension	Years ending after December 31, 2001
415(b)(10)(C)	101(a)(1)	Temporary Extension of 2001 Tax Relief—Temporary Extension	Years ending after December 31, 2001
415(b)(11)	101(a)(1)	Temporary Extension of 2001 Tax Relief—Temporary Extension	Years beginning after December 31, 2001
415(c)(1)(A)	101(a)(1)	Temporary Extension of 2001 Tax Relief—Temporary Extension	Years beginning after December 31, 2001
415(c)(1)(B)	101(a)(1)	Temporary Extension of 2001 Tax Relief—Temporary Extension	Years beginning after December 31, 2001
415(c)(2)	101(a)(1)	Temporary Extension of 2001 Tax Relief—Temporary Extension	Distributions after December 31, 2001, generally
415(c)(3)(E)	101(a)(1)	Temporary Extension of 2001 Tax Relief—Temporary Extension	Years beginning after December 31, 2001
415(c)(4)	101(a)(1)	Temporary Extension of 2001 Tax Relief—Temporary Extension	Years beginning after December 31, 2001

Code Sec.	Act Sec.	Act Provision Subject	Effective Date
415(c)(7)	101(a)(1)	Temporary Extension of 2001 Tax Relief—Temporary Extension	Years beginning after December 31, 2001
415(d)(1)(A)	101(a)(1)	Temporary Extension of 2001 Tax Relief—Temporary Extension	Years beginning after December 31, 2001
415(d)(1)(C)	101(a)(1)	Temporary Extension of 2001 Tax Relief—Temporary Extension	Years beginning after December 31, 2001
415(d)(3)(A)	101(a)(1)	Temporary Extension of 2001 Tax Relief—Temporary Extension	Years beginning after December 31, 2001
415(d)(3)(D)	101(a)(1)	Temporary Extension of 2001 Tax Relief—Temporary Extension	Years beginning after December 31, 2001
415(d)(4)	101(a)(1)	Temporary Extension of 2001 Tax Relief—Temporary Extension	Years beginning after December 31, 2001
415(f)(3)	101(a)(1)	Temporary Extension of 2001 Tax Relief—Temporary Extension	Years beginning after December 31, 2001
415(g)	101(a)(1)	Temporary Extension of 2001 Tax Relief—Temporary Extension	Years beginning after December 31, 2001
415(k)(4)	101(a)(1)	Temporary Extension of 2001 Tax Relief—Temporary Extension	Limitation years beginning after December 31, 1999, generally
416(c)(1)(C)	101(a)(1)	Temporary Extension of 2001 Tax Relief—Temporary Extension	Years beginning after December 31, 2001
416(c)(2)(A)	101(a)(1)	Temporary Extension of 2001 Tax Relief—Temporary Extension	Years beginning after December 31, 2001
416(g)(3)	101(a)(1)	Temporary Extension of 2001 Tax Relief—Temporary Extension	Years beginning after December 31, 2001
416(g)(4)(E)	101(a)(1)	Temporary Extension of 2001 Tax Relief—Temporary Extension	Years beginning after December 31, 2001
416(g)(4)(H)	101(a)(1)	Temporary Extension of 2001 Tax Relief—Temporary Extension	Years beginning after December 31, 2001
416(i)(1)(A)	101(a)(1)	Temporary Extension of 2001 Tax Relief—Temporary Extension	Years beginning after December 31, 2001
416(i)(1)(B)	101(a)(1)	Temporary Extension of 2001 Tax Relief—Temporary Extension	Years beginning after December 31, 2001
451(i)(3)	705(a)	Special Rule for Sales or Dispositions to Implement FERC or State Electric Restructuring Policy for Qualified Electric Utilities	Dispositions after December 31, 2009
457(a)	101(a)(1)	Temporary Extension of 2001 Tax Relief—Temporary Extension	Distributions after December 31, 2001
457(b)(2)	101(a)(1)	Temporary Extension of 2001 Tax Relief—Temporary Extension	Distributions after December 31, 2001, generally
457(b)(2)(A)	101(a)(1)	Temporary Extension of 2001 Tax Relief—Temporary Extension	Years beginning after December 31, 2001
457(b)(2)(B)	101(a)(1)	Temporary Extension of 2001 Tax Relief—Temporary Extension	Years beginning after December 31, 2001
457(b)(3)(A)	101(a)(1)	Temporary Extension of 2001 Tax Relief—Temporary Extension	Years beginning after December 31, 2001
457(c)(1)	101(a)(1)	Temporary Extension of 2001 Tax Relief—Temporary Extension	Years beginning after December 31, 2001
457(c)(2)	101(a)(1)	Temporary Extension of 2001 Tax Relief—Temporary Extension	Years beginning after December 31, 2001
457(d)(1)	101(a)(1)	Temporary Extension of 2001 Tax Relief—Temporary Extension	Distributions after December 31, 2001, generally

Code Sec.	Act Sec.	Act Provision Subject	Effective Date
457(d)(1)(A)	101(a)(1)	Temporary Extension of 2001 Tax Relief— Temporary Extension	Distributions after December 31, 2001, generally
457(d)(2)	101(a)(1)	Temporary Extension of 2001 Tax Relief— Temporary Extension	Distributions after December 31, 2001
457(d)(3)	101(a)(1)	Temporary Extension of 2001 Tax Relief— Temporary Extension	Distributions after December 31, 2001
457(e)(9)	101(a)(1)	Temporary Extension of 2001 Tax Relief— Temporary Extension	Distributions after December 31, 2001
457(e)(9)(A)	101(a)(1)	Temporary Extension of 2001 Tax Relief— Temporary Extension	Distributions after December 31, 2001
457(e)(15)	101(a)(1)	Temporary Extension of 2001 Tax Relief— Temporary Extension	Years beginning after December 31, 2001
457(e)(16)	101(a)(1)	Temporary Extension of 2001 Tax Relief— Temporary Extension	Distributions after December 31, 2001
457(e)(17)	101(a)(1)	Temporary Extension of 2001 Tax Relief— Temporary Extension	Trustee-to-trustee transfers after December 31, 2001
467(c)(5)(C)	102(a)	Temporary Extension of 2003 Tax Relief	Tax years beginning after December 31, 2002
469(i)(3)(F)	101(a)(1)	Temporary Extension of 2001 Tax Relief— Temporary Extension	Payments made in tax years beginning after December 31, 2001
501(c)(18)(D)	101(a)(1)	Temporary Extension of 2001 Tax Relief— Temporary Extension	Years beginning after December 31, 2001
505(b)(7)	101(a)(1)	Temporary Extension of 2001 Tax Relief— Temporary Extension	Years beginning after December 31, 2001
512(b)(13)(E)(iv)	747(a)	Modification of Tax Treatment of Certain Payments to Controlling Exempt Organizations	Payments received or accrued after December 31, 2009
529	101(a)(1)	Temporary Extension of 2001 Tax Relief— Temporary Extension	Tax years beginning after December 31, 2001
529(b)	101(a)(1)	Temporary Extension of 2001 Tax Relief— Temporary Extension	Tax years beginning after December 31, 2001
529(b)(1)	101(a)(1)	Temporary Extension of 2001 Tax Relief— Temporary Extension	Tax years beginning after December 31, 2001
529(b)(1)(A)	101(a)(1)	Temporary Extension of 2001 Tax Relief— Temporary Extension	Tax years beginning after December 31, 2001
529(c)(3)(B)	101(a)(1)	Temporary Extension of 2001 Tax Relief— Temporary Extension	Tax years beginning after December 31, 2001
529(c)(3)(C)	101(a)(1)	Temporary Extension of 2001 Tax Relief— Temporary Extension	Tax years beginning after December 31, 2001
529(c)(3)(D)	101(a)(1)	Temporary Extension of 2001 Tax Relief— Temporary Extension	Tax years beginning after December 31, 2001
529(c)(6)	101(a)(1)	Temporary Extension of 2001 Tax Relief— Temporary Extension	Tax years beginning after December 31, 2001
529(d)	101(a)(1)	Temporary Extension of 2001 Tax Relief— Temporary Extension	Tax years beginning after December 31, 2001
529(e)(2)	101(a)(1)	Temporary Extension of 2001 Tax Relief— Temporary Extension	Tax years beginning after December 31, 2001
529(e)(3)(A)	101(a)(1)	Temporary Extension of 2001 Tax Relief— Temporary Extension	Tax years beginning after December 31, 2001
529(e)(3)(B)(ii)	101(a)(1)	Temporary Extension of 2001 Tax Relief— Temporary Extension	Tax years beginning after December 31, 2001

Code Sec.	Act Sec.	Act Provision Subject	Effective Date
530(b)(1)	101(a)(1)	Temporary Extension of 2001 Tax Relief—Temporary Extension	Tax years beginning after December 31, 2001
530(b)(1)(A)	101(a)(1)	Temporary Extension of 2001 Tax Relief—Temporary Extension	Tax years beginning after December 31, 2001
530(b)(2)	101(a)(1)	Temporary Extension of 2001 Tax Relief—Temporary Extension	Tax years beginning after December 31, 2001
530(b)(2)(B)	101(a)(1)	Temporary Extension of 2001 Tax Relief—Temporary Extension	Tax years beginning after December 31, 2001
530(b)(4)	101(a)(1)	Temporary Extension of 2001 Tax Relief—Temporary Extension	Tax years beginning after December 31, 2001
530(b)(5)	101(a)(1)	Temporary Extension of 2001 Tax Relief—Temporary Extension	Tax years beginning after December 31, 2001
530(c)(1)	101(a)(1)	Temporary Extension of 2001 Tax Relief—Temporary Extension	Tax years beginning after December 31, 2001
530(d)(2)	101(a)(1)	Temporary Extension of 2001 Tax Relief—Temporary Extension	Tax years beginning after December 31, 2001
530(d)(2)(C)	101(a)(1)	Temporary Extension of 2001 Tax Relief—Temporary Extension	Tax years beginning after December 31, 2001
530(d)(2)(D)	101(a)(1)	Temporary Extension of 2001 Tax Relief—Temporary Extension	Tax years beginning after December 31, 2001
530(d)(4)(C)	101(a)(1)	Temporary Extension of 2001 Tax Relief—Temporary Extension	Tax years beginning after December 31, 2001
531	101(a)(1)	Temporary Extension of 2001 Tax Relief—Temporary Extension	Tax years beginning after December 31, 2000
531	102(a)	Temporary Extension of 2003 Tax Relief	Tax years beginning after December 31, 2002
541	101(a)(1)	Temporary Extension of 2001 Tax Relief—Temporary Extension	Tax years beginning after December 31, 2000
541	102(a)	Temporary Extension of 2003 Tax Relief	Tax years beginning after December 31, 2002
584(c)	102(a)	Temporary Extension of 2003 Tax Relief	Tax years beginning after December 31, 2002
613A(c)(6)(H)(ii)	706(a)	Suspension of Limitation on Percentage Depletion for Oil and Gas From Marginal Wells	Tax years beginning after December 31, 2009
646	101(a)(1)	Temporary Extension of 2001 Tax Relief—Temporary Extension	Tax years ending after June 7, 2001 and contributions made to electing settlement trusts for such year or any subsequent year
664(g)(3)(E)	101(a)(1)	Temporary Extension of 2001 Tax Relief—Temporary Extension	Years beginning after December 31, 2001
664(g)(7)	101(a)(1)	Temporary Extension of 2001 Tax Relief—Temporary Extension	Years beginning after December 31, 2001
684	101(a)(1)	Temporary Extension of 2001 Tax Relief—Temporary Extension	Transfers after December 31, 2009
684(a)	101(a)(1)	Temporary Extension of 2001 Tax Relief—Temporary Extension	Transfers after December 31, 2009
684(a)	301(a)	Reinstatement of Estate Tax; Repeal of Carryover Basis	Transfers after December 31, 2009
684(b)	101(a)(1)	Temporary Extension of 2001 Tax Relief—Temporary Extension	Transfers after December 31, 2009

Code Sec.	Act Sec.	Act Provision Subject	Effective Date
684(b)	301(a)	Reinstatement of Estate Tax; Repeal of Carryover Basis	Transfers after December 31, 2009
702(a)(5)	102(a)	Temporary Extension of 2003 Tax Relief	Tax years beginning after December 31, 2002
854(a)	102(a)	Temporary Extension of 2003 Tax Relief	Tax years ending after December 31, 2002, generally
854(b)(1)(B)	102(a)	Temporary Extension of 2003 Tax Relief	Tax years ending after December 31, 2002, generally
854(b)(1)(B)	102(a)	Temporary Extension of 2003 Tax Relief	Tax years ending after December 31, 2002, generally
854(b)(1)(C)	102(a)	Temporary Extension of 2003 Tax Relief	Tax years ending after December 31, 2002, generally
854(b)(2)	102(a)	Temporary Extension of 2003 Tax Relief	Tax years ending after December 31, 2002, generally
854(b)(5)	102(a)	Temporary Extension of 2003 Tax Relief	Tax years ending after December 31, 2002, generally
857(c)	102(a)	Temporary Extension of 2003 Tax Relief	Tax years ending after December 31, 2002, generally
861(a)(3)	101(a)(1)	Temporary Extension of 2001 Tax Relief— Temporary Extension	Remuneration for services performed for plan years beginning after December 31, 2001
871(k)(1)(C)	748(a)	Treatment of Certain Dividends and Assets of Regulated Investment Companies	Tax years beginning after December 31, 2009
871(k)(2)(C)	748(a)	Treatment of Certain Dividends and Assets of Regulated Investment Companies	Tax years beginning after December 31, 2009
897(h)(4)(A)(ii)	749(a)	RIC Qualified Investment Entity Treatment Under FIRPTA	January 1, 2010, generally
904(h)	101(a)(1)	Temporary Extension of 2001 Tax Relief— Temporary Extension	Tax years beginning after December 31, 2001
904(i)	101(b)(1)	Temporary Extension of 2001 Tax Relief— Separate Sunset for Expansion of Adoption Benefits Under the Patient Protection and Affordable Care Act	Amended to read as if Sec. 10909(c) 0f the Patient Protection and Affordable Care Act had never been enacted; tax years beginning after December 31, 2011

¶20,001

Code Sec.	Act Sec.	Act Provision Subject	Effective Date
953(e)(10)	750(a)	Exceptions for Active Financing Income	Tax years of foreign corporations beginning after December 31, 2009, and to tax years of United States shareholders with or within which any such tax year of such foreign corporation ends
953(e)(10)	750(b)	Exceptions for Active Financing Income—Conforming Amendment	Tax years of foreign corporations beginning after December 31, 2009, and to tax years of United States shareholders with or within which any such tax year of such foreign corporation ends
954(c)(6)(C)	751(a)	Look-Thru Treatment of Payments Between Related Controlled Foreign Corporations Under Foreign Personal Holding Company Rules	Tax years of foreign corporations beginning after December 31, 2009, and to tax years of United States shareholders with or within which any such tax year of such foreign corporation ends
954(h)(9)	750(a)	Exceptions for Active Financing Income	Tax years of foreign corporations beginning after December 31, 2009, and to tax years of United States shareholders with or within which any such tax year of such foreign corporation ends
1014(f)	101(a)(1)	Temporary Extension of 2001 Tax Relief—Temporary Extension	June 7, 2001
1014(f)	301(a)	Reinstatement of Estate Tax; Repeal of Carryover Basis	June 7, 2001
1016(a)(26)	101(b)(1)	Temporary Extension of 2001 Tax Relief—Separate Sunset for Expansion of Adoption Benefits Under the Patient Protection and Affordable Care Act	Amended to read as if Sec. 10909(c) 0f the Patient Protection and Affordable Care Act had never been enacted; tax years beginning after December 31, 2011
1016(a)(28)	101(a)(1)	Temporary Extension of 2001 Tax Relief—Temporary Extension	Tax years beginning after December 31, 2001

Code Sec.	Act Sec.	Act Provision Subject	Effective Date
1022	101(a)(1)	Temporary Extension of 2001 Tax Relief—Temporary Extension	Estates of decedents dying after December 31, 2009
1022	301(a)	Reinstatement of Estate Tax; Repeal of Carryover Basis	Estates of decedents dying after December 31, 2009
1040	101(a)(1)	Temporary Extension of 2001 Tax Relief—Temporary Extension	Estates of decedents dying after December 31, 2009
1040	301(a)	Reinstatement of Estate Tax; Repeal of Carryover Basis	Estates of decedents dying after December 31, 2009
1202(a)(2)(C)	753(b)(1)-(2)	Empowerment Zone Tax Incentives—Increased Exclusion of Gain on Stock of Empowerment Zone Businesses	Periods after December 31, 2009
1202(a)(4)	760(a)(1)-(2)	Temporary Exclusion of 100 Percent of Gain on Certain Small Business Stock	Stock acquired after December 31, 2010
1221(a)(3)(C)	101(a)(1)	Temporary Extension of 2001 Tax Relief—Temporary Extension	Estates of decedents dying after December 31, 2009
1221(a)(3)(C)	301(a)	Reinstatement of Estate Tax; Repeal of Carryover Basis	Estates of decedents dying after December 31, 2009
1246(e)	101(a)(1)	Temporary Extension of 2001 Tax Relief—Temporary Extension	Estates of decedents dying after December 31, 2009
1246(e)	301(a)	Reinstatement of Estate Tax; Repeal of Carryover Basis	Estates of decedents dying after December 31, 2009
1255(b)(2)	102(a)	Temporary Extension of 2003 Tax Relief	Tax years beginning after December 31, 2002
1257(d)	102(a)	Temporary Extension of 2003 Tax Relief	Tax years beginning after December 31, 2002
1291(e)	101(a)(1)	Temporary Extension of 2001 Tax Relief—Temporary Extension	Estates of decedents dying after December 31, 2009
1291(e)	301(a)	Reinstatement of Estate Tax; Repeal of Carryover Basis	Estates of decedents dying after December 31, 2009
1296(i)	101(a)(1)	Temporary Extension of 2001 Tax Relief—Temporary Extension	Estates of decedents dying after December 31, 2009
1296(i)	301(a)	Reinstatement of Estate Tax; Repeal of Carryover Basis	Estates of decedents dying after December 31, 2009
1367(a)(2)	752(a)	Basis Adjustment to Stock of S Corporations Making Charitable Contributions of Property	Contributions made in tax years beginning after December 31, 2009
1391(d)(1)(A)(i)	753(a)(1)	Empowerment Zone Tax Incentives	Periods after December 31, 2009
1391(h)(2)	753(a)(2)	Empowerment Zone Tax Incentives	Periods after December 31, 2009

Code Sec.	Act Sec.	Act Provision Subject	Effective Date
1400(f)	754(a)	Tax Incentives for Investment in the District of Columbia	Periods after December 31, 2009
1400A(b)	754(b)	Tax Incentives for Investment in the District of Columbia—Tax-Exempt Empowerment Zone Bonds	Bonds issued after December 31, 2009
1400B(b)(2)(A)(i)	754(c)(1)	Tax Incentives for Investment in the District of Columbia—Zero-Percent Capital Gains Rate—Acquisition Date	Property acquired or substantially improved after December 31, 2009
1400B(b)(3)(A)	754(c)(1)	Tax Incentives for Investment in the District of Columbia—Zero-Percent Capital Gains Rate—Acquisition Date	Property acquired or substantially improved after December 31, 2009
1400B(b)(4)(A)(i)	754(c)(1)	Tax Incentives for Investment in the District of Columbia—Zero-Percent Capital Gains Rate—Acquisition Date	Property acquired or substantially improved after December 31, 2009
1400B(b)(4)(B)(i)(I)	754(c)(1)	Tax Incentives for Investment in the District of Columbia—Zero-Percent Capital Gains Rate—Acquisition Date	Property acquired or substantially improved after December 31, 2009
1400B(e)(2)	754(c)(2)(A)(i)-(ii)	Tax Incentives for Investment in the District of Columbia—Zero-Percent Capital Gains Rate—Limitation on Period of Gains	Property acquired or substantially improved after December 31, 2009
1400B(g)(2)	754(c)(2)(B)	Tax Incentives for Investment in the District of Columbia—Zero-Percent Capital Gains Rate—Limitation on Period of Zero-Percent Capital Gains—Partnership and S Corps	Property acquired or substantially improved after December 31, 2009
1400C(d)	101(a)(1)	Temporary Extension of 2001 Tax Relief—Temporary Extension	Tax years beginning after December 31, 2001
1400C(d)	101(b)(1)	Temporary Extension of 2001 Tax Relief—Separate Sunset for Expansion of Adoption Benefits Under the Patient Protection and Affordable Care Act	Amended to read as if Sec. 10909(c) 0f the Patient Protection and Affordable Care Act had never been enacted; tax years beginning after December 31, 2011
1400C(i)	754(d)	Tax Incentives for Investment in the District of Columbia—First-Time Homebuyer Credit	Homes purchased after December 31, 2009
1400L(b)(2)(C)(i)	102(a)	Temporary Extension of 2003 Tax Relief	Tax years ending on or after May 5, 2003
1400L(b)(2)(D)	401(d)(6)	Extension of Bonus Depreciation; Temporary 100 Percent Expensing for Certain Business Assets—Conforming Amendments	Property placed in service after December 31, 2010, in tax years ending after such date
1400L(d)(2)(D)	761(a)	Tax-Exempt Bond Financing	Bonds issued after December 31, 2009
1400N(a)(2)(D)	764(a)	Tax-Exempt Bond Financing	Date of enactment
1400N(a)(7)(C)	764(a)	Tax-Exempt Bond Financing	Date of enactment

¶20,001

Code Sec.	Act Sec.	Act Provision Subject	Effective Date
1400N(c)(5)	763	Low-Income Housing Credit Rules For Buildings in GO Zones	Date of enactment
1400N(d)(3)(B)	401(d)(7)	Extension of Bonus Depreciation; Temporary 100 Percent Expensing for Certain Business Assets—Conforming Amendments	Property placed in service after December 31, 2010, in tax years ending after such date
1400N(d)(6)	765(a)(1)-(2)	Bonus Depreciation Deduction Applicable to the GO Zone	Property placed in service after December 31, 2009
1400N(h)	762(a)	Increase in Rehabilitation Credit	Amounts paid or incurred after December 31, 2009
1445(e)(1)	102(a)	Temporary Extension of 2003 Tax Relief	Amounts paid after May 28, 2003
1603(a)(1)	707(a)(1)	Extension of Grants For Specified Energy Property in Lieu of Tax Credits	Date of enactment
1603(a)(2)	707(a)(2)(A)-(B)	Extension of Grants For Specified Energy Property in Lieu of Tax Credits	Date of enactment
1603(j)	707(b)	Extension of Grants For Specified Energy Property in Lieu of Tax Credits—Conforming Amendment	Date of enactment
2001(b)(2)	302(d)(1)(A)	Modifications to Estate, Gift, and Generation-Skipping Transfer Taxes—Modifications of Estate and Gift Taxes to Reflect Differences in Credit Resulting From Different Tax Rates—Estate Tax	Estates of decedents dying, generation-skipping transfers, and gifts made, after December 31, 2009
2001(c)	302(a)(2)(A)-(C)	Modifications to Estate, Gift, and Generation-Skipping Transfer Taxes—Modifications to Estate Tax—Maximum Estate Tax Rate Equal to 35 Percent	Estates of decedents dying, generation-skipping transfers, and gifts made, after December 31, 2009
2001(c)(1)	101(a)(1)	Temporary Extension of 2001 Tax Relief—Temporary Extension	Estates of decedents dying after December 31, 2001
2001(c)(2)	101(a)(1)	Temporary Extension of 2001 Tax Relief—Temporary Extension	Estates of decedents dying after December 31, 2002
2001(g)	302(d)(1)(B)	Modifications to Estate, Gift, and Generation-Skipping Transfer Taxes—Modifications of Estate and Gift Taxes to Reflect Differences in Credit Resulting From Different Tax Rates—Estate Tax	Estates of decedents dying, generation-skipping transfers, and gifts made, after December 31, 2009
2010(c)	101(a)(1)	Temporary Extension of 2001 Tax Relief—Temporary Extension	Estates of decedents dying after December 31, 2009
2010(c)	302(a)(1)	Modifications to Estate, Gift, and Generation-Skipping Transfer Taxes—Modifications to Estate Tax	Estates of decedents dying, generation-skipping transfers, and gifts made, after December 31, 2009

Code Sec.	Act Sec.	Act Provision Subject	Effective Date
2010(c)(2)-(6)	303(a)	Applicable Exclusion Amount Increased by Unused Exclusion Amount of Deceased Spouse	Estates of decedents dying and gifts made after December 31, 2010
2011(b)	101(a)(1)	Temporary Extension of 2001 Tax Relief—Temporary Extension	Estates of decedents dying after December 31, 2001
2011(b)(2)	101(a)(1)	Temporary Extension of 2001 Tax Relief—Temporary Extension	Estates of decedents dying after December 31, 2001
2011(g)	101(a)(1)	Temporary Extension of 2001 Tax Relief—Temporary Extension	Estates of decedents dying and generation-skipping transfers after December 31, 2004
2012(a)	101(a)(1)	Temporary Extension of 2001 Tax Relief—Temporary Extension	Estates of decedents dying and generation-skipping transfers after December 31, 2004
2013(c)(1)(A)	101(a)(1)	Temporary Extension of 2001 Tax Relief—Temporary Extension	Estates of decedents dying and generation-skipping transfers after December 31, 2004
2014(b)(2)	101(a)(1)	Temporary Extension of 2001 Tax Relief—Temporary Extension	Estates of decedents dying and generation-skipping transfers after December 31, 2004
2015	101(a)(1)	Temporary Extension of 2001 Tax Relief—Temporary Extension	Estates of decedents dying and generation-skipping transfers after December 31, 2004
2016	101(a)(1)	Temporary Extension of 2001 Tax Relief—Temporary Extension	Estates of decedents dying and generation-skipping transfers after December 31, 2004
2031(c)(2)	101(a)(1)	Temporary Extension of 2001 Tax Relief—Temporary Extension	Estates of decedents dying after December 31, 2000
2031(c)(8)(A)	101(a)(1)	Temporary Extension of 2001 Tax Relief—Temporary Extension	Estates of decedents dying after December 31, 2000
2053(d)	101(a)(1)	Temporary Extension of 2001 Tax Relief—Temporary Extension	Estates of decedents dying and generation-skipping transfers after December 31, 2004

¶20,001

Code Sec.	Act Sec.	Act Provision Subject	Effective Date
2056A(b)(10)(A)	101(a)(1)	Temporary Extension of 2001 Tax Relief—Temporary Extension	Estates of decedents dying and generation-skipping transfers after December 31, 2004
2057(j)	101(a)(1)	Temporary Extension of 2001 Tax Relief—Temporary Extension	Estates of decedents dying and generation-skipping transfers after December 31, 2003
2058	101(a)(1)	Temporary Extension of 2001 Tax Relief—Temporary Extension	Estates of decedents dying and generation-skipping transfers after December 31, 2004
2102(a)	101(a)(1)	Temporary Extension of 2001 Tax Relief—Temporary Extension	Estates of decedents dying and generation-skipping transfers after December 31, 2004
2102(b)	101(a)(1)	Temporary Extension of 2001 Tax Relief—Temporary Extension	Estates of decedents dying and generation-skipping transfers after December 31, 2004
2102(c)	101(a)(1)	Temporary Extension of 2001 Tax Relief—Temporary Extension	Estates of decedents dying and generation-skipping transfers after December 31, 2004
2105(d)(3)	726(a)	Look-Thru of Certain Regulated Investment Company Stock in Determining Gross Estate of Nonresidents	Estates of decedents dying after December 31, 2009
2106(a)(4)	101(a)(1)	Temporary Extension of 2001 Tax Relief—Temporary Extension	Estates of decedents dying and generation-skipping transfers after December 31, 2004
2107(c)(3)	101(a)(1)	Temporary Extension of 2001 Tax Relief—Temporary Extension	Estates of decedents dying and generation-skipping transfers after December 31, 2004
2201	101(a)(1)	Temporary Extension of 2001 Tax Relief—Temporary Extension	Estates of decedents dying and generation-skipping transfers after December 31, 2004
2210	101(a)(1)	Temporary Extension of 2001 Tax Relief—Temporary Extension	Estates of decedents dying and generation-skipping transfers after December 31, 2009

Code Sec.	Act Sec.	Act Provision Subject	Effective Date
2210	301(a)	Reinstatement of Estate Tax; Repeal of Carryover Basis	Estates of decedents dying and generation-skipping transfers after December 31, 2009
2502(a)	101(a)(1)	Temporary Extension of 2001 Tax Relief—Temporary Extension	Gifts made after December 31, 2009
2502(a)	302(b)(2)	Modifications to Estate, Gift, and Generation-Skipping Transfer Taxes—Modifications to Gift Tax—Modification of Gift Tax Rate	On or after January 1, 2011
2505(a)	302(d)(2)	Modifications to Estate, Gift, and Generation-Skipping Transfer Taxes—Modifications of Estate and Gift Taxes to Reflect Differences in Credit Resulting From Different Tax Rates—Gift Tax	Estates of decedents dying, generation-skipping transfers and gifts made, after December 31, 2009
2505(a)(1)	101(a)(1)	Temporary Extension of 2001 Tax Relief—Temporary Extension	Estates of decedents dying and gifts made after December 31, 2001
2505(a)(1)	101(a)(1)	Temporary Extension of 2001 Tax Relief—Temporary Extension	Gifts made after December 31, 2009
2505(a)(1)	302(b)(1)(A)	Modifications to Estate, Gift, and Generation-Skipping Transfer Taxes—Modifications to Gift Tax—Restoration of Unified Credit Against Gift Tax	Gifts made after December 31, 2010
2505(a)(1)	303(b)(1)	Applicable Exclusion Amount Increased by Unused Exclusion Amount of Deceased Spouse—Conforming Amendments	Estates of decedents dying and gifts made after December 31, 2010
2505(a)(1)	301(b)	Reinstatement of Estate Tax; Repeal of Carryover Basis—Conforming Amendment	On or after January 1, 2011
2511(c)	101(a)(1)	Temporary Extension of 2001 Tax Relief—Temporary Extension	Gifts made after December 31, 2009
2511(c)	302(e)	Modifications to Estate, Gift, and Generation-Skipping Transfer Taxes—Conforming Amendment	Estates of decedents dying, generation-skipping transfers and gifts made, after December 31, 2009
2604(c)	101(a)(1)	Temporary Extension of 2001 Tax Relief—Temporary Extension	Estates of decedents dying and generation-skipping transfers after December 31, 2004
2631(a)	101(a)(1)	Temporary Extension of 2001 Tax Relief—Temporary Extension	Estates of decedents dying and generation-skipping transfers after December 31, 2003

¶20,001

Code Sec.	Act Sec.	Act Provision Subject	Effective Date
2631(c)	101(a)(1)	Temporary Extension of 2001 Tax Relief—Temporary Extension	Estates of decedents dying and generation-skipping transfers after December 31, 2003
2631(c)	303(b)(2)	Applicable Exclusion Amount Increased by Unused Exclusion Amount of Deceased Spouse—Conforming Amendments	Generation-skipping transfers after December 31, 2010
2632(b)(2)	101(a)(1)	Temporary Extension of 2001 Tax Relief—Temporary Extension	Transfers subject to Chapter 11 or 12 made after December 31, 2000, and to estate tax inclusion periods ending after December 31, 2000
2632(c)	101(a)(1)	Temporary Extension of 2001 Tax Relief—Temporary Extension	Transfers subject to Chapter 11 or 12 made after December 31, 2000, and to estate tax inclusion periods ending after December 31, 2000
2632(d)	101(a)(1)	Temporary Extension of 2001 Tax Relief—Temporary Extension	Deaths of non-skip persons occurring after December 31, 2000
2632(e)	101(a)(1)	Temporary Extension of 2001 Tax Relief—Temporary Extension	June 7, 2001
2642(a)(3)	101(a)(1)	Temporary Extension of 2001 Tax Relief—Temporary Extension	Severances after December 31, 2000
2642(b)(1)	101(a)(1)	Temporary Extension of 2001 Tax Relief—Temporary Extension	Transfers subject to Chapter 11 or 12 made after December 31, 2000
2642(b)(2)(A)	101(a)(1)	Temporary Extension of 2001 Tax Relief—Temporary Extension	Transfers subject to Chapter 11 or 12 made after December 31, 2000
2642(g)(1)	101(a)(1)	Temporary Extension of 2001 Tax Relief—Temporary Extension	Requests pending on or filed after December 31, 2000
2642(g)(2)	101(a)(1)	Temporary Extension of 2001 Tax Relief—Temporary Extension	Transfers subject to Chapter 11 or 12 made after December 31, 2000
2664	101(a)(1)	Temporary Extension of 2001 Tax Relief—Temporary Extension	Estates of decedents dying and generation-skipping transfers after December 31, 2009
2664	301(a)	Reinstatement of Estate Tax; Repeal of Carryover Basis	Estates of decedents dying and generation-skipping transfers after December 31, 2009

Code Sec.	Act Sec.	Act Provision Subject	Effective Date
3401(a)(12)(E)	101(a)(1)	Temporary Extension of 2001 Tax Relief— Temporary Extension	Distributions after December 31, 2001, generally
3402(p)(1)(B)	101(a)(1)	Temporary Extension of 2001 Tax Relief— Temporary Extension	Amounts paid after August 6, 2001
3402(p)(2)	101(a)(1)	Temporary Extension of 2001 Tax Relief— Temporary Extension	Amounts paid after August 6, 2001
3402(q)(1)	101(a)(1)	Temporary Extension of 2001 Tax Relief— Temporary Extension	Amounts paid after August 6, 2001
3402(r)(3)	101(a)(1)	Temporary Extension of 2001 Tax Relief— Temporary Extension	Amounts paid after August 6, 2001
3405(c)(3)	101(a)(1)	Temporary Extension of 2001 Tax Relief— Temporary Extension	Distributions after December 31, 2001, generally
3405(d)(2)(B)	101(a)(1)	Temporary Extension of 2001 Tax Relief— Temporary Extension	Distributions after December 31, 2001, generally
3406(a)(1)	101(a)(1)	Temporary Extension of 2001 Tax Relief— Temporary Extension	Amounts paid after August 6, 2001
4947(a)(2)(A)	101(a)(1)	Temporary Extension of 2001 Tax Relief— Temporary Extension	Deductions for tax years beginning after December 31, 2009
4947(a)(2)(A)	301(a)	Reinstatement of Estate Tax; Repeal of Carryover Basis	Deductions for tax years beginning after December 31, 2009
4972(c)(6)	101(a)(1)	Temporary Extension of 2001 Tax Relief— Temporary Extension	Plan years beginning after December 31, 2001
4972(c)(6)	101(a)(1)	Temporary Extension of 2001 Tax Relief— Temporary Extension	Tax years beginning after December 31, 2001
4972(c)(6)(B)	101(a)(1)	Temporary Extension of 2001 Tax Relief— Temporary Extension	Years beginning after December 31, 2001
4972(c)(6)(C)	101(a)(1)	Temporary Extension of 2001 Tax Relief— Temporary Extension	Tax years beginning after December 31, 2001
4972(c)(7)	101(a)(1)	Temporary Extension of 2001 Tax Relief— Temporary Extension	Years beginning after December 31, 2001
4973(b)(1)(A)	101(a)(1)	Temporary Extension of 2001 Tax Relief— Temporary Extension	Distributions after December 31, 2001, generally
4973(e)	101(a)(1)	Temporary Extension of 2001 Tax Relief— Temporary Extension	Tax years beginning after December 31, 2001
4973(e)(1)	101(a)(1)	Temporary Extension of 2001 Tax Relief— Temporary Extension	Tax years beginning after December 31, 2001
4975(e)(7)	101(a)(1)	Temporary Extension of 2001 Tax Relief— Temporary Extension	Plan years beginning after December 31, 2004
4975(f)(6)(B)	101(a)(1)	Temporary Extension of 2001 Tax Relief— Temporary Extension	Years beginning after December 31, 2001
4979A(a)	101(a)(1)	Temporary Extension of 2001 Tax Relief— Temporary Extension	Plan years beginning after December 31, 2001
4979A(c)	101(a)(1)	Temporary Extension of 2001 Tax Relief— Temporary Extension	Plan years beginning after December 31, 2001

¶20,001

Code Sec.	Act Sec.	Act Provision Subject	Effective Date
4979A(e)	101(a)(1)	Temporary Extension of 2001 Tax Relief—Temporary Extension	Plan years beginning after December 31, 2001
4980F	101(a)(1)	Temporary Extension of 2001 Tax Relief—Temporary Extension	Plan amendments taking effect on or after June 7, 2001
6018	101(a)(1)	Temporary Extension of 2001 Tax Relief—Temporary Extension	Estates of decedents dying after December 31, 2009
6018	301(a)	Reinstatement of Estate Tax; Repeal of Carryover Basis	Estates of decedents dying after December 31, 2009
6018(a)(1)	303(b)(3)	Applicable Exclusion Amount Increased by Unused Exclusion Amount of Deceased Spouse—Conforming Amendments	Estates of decedents dying and gifts made after December 31, 2010
6019	101(a)(1)	Temporary Extension of 2001 Tax Relief—Temporary Extension	Estates of decedents dying after December 31, 2009
6019	301(a)	Reinstatement of Estate Tax; Repeal of Carryover Basis	Estates of decedents dying after December 31, 2009
6039H	101(a)(1)	Temporary Extension of 2001 Tax Relief—Temporary Extension	Tax years ending after June 7, 2001 and contributions made to electing settlement trusts for such year or any subsequent year
6047(f)	101(a)(1)	Temporary Extension of 2001 Tax Relief—Temporary Extension	Tax years beginning after December 31, 2005
6047(g)	101(a)(1)	Temporary Extension of 2001 Tax Relief—Temporary Extension	Tax years beginning after December 31, 2005
6050S(e)	101(a)(1)	Temporary Extension of 2001 Tax Relief—Temporary Extension	Loan interest paid after December 31, 2001, in tax years ending after such date
6051(a)(8)	101(a)(1)	Temporary Extension of 2001 Tax Relief—Temporary Extension	Tax years beginning after December 31, 2001
6075(a)	101(a)(1)	Temporary Extension of 2001 Tax Relief—Temporary Extension	Estates of decedents dying after December 31, 2009
6075(a)	301(a)	Reinstatement of Estate Tax; Repeal of Carryover Basis	Estates of decedents dying after December 31, 2009
6075(b)(3)	101(a)(1)	Temporary Extension of 2001 Tax Relief—Temporary Extension	Estates of decedents dying after December 31, 2009
6075(b)(3)	301(a)	Reinstatement of Estate Tax; Repeal of Carryover Basis	Estates of decedents dying after December 31, 2009
6166(b)(1)(B)	101(a)(1)	Temporary Extension of 2001 Tax Relief—Temporary Extension	Estates of decedents dying after December 31, 2001

Code Sec.	Act Sec.	Act Provision Subject	Effective Date
6166(b)(1)(C)	101(a)(1)	Temporary Extension of 2001 Tax Relief—Temporary Extension	Estates of decedents dying after December 31, 2001
6166(b)(8)(B)	101(a)(1)	Temporary Extension of 2001 Tax Relief—Temporary Extension	Estates of decedents dying after December 31, 2001
6166(b)(9)(B)	101(a)(1)	Temporary Extension of 2001 Tax Relief—Temporary Extension	Estates of decedents dying after December 31, 2001
6166(b)(10)	101(a)(1)	Temporary Extension of 2001 Tax Relief—Temporary Extension	Estates of decedents dying after December 31, 2001
6211(b)(4)(A)	101(b)(1)	Temporary Extension of 2001 Tax Relief—Separate Sunset for Expansion of Adoption Benefits Under the Patient Protection and Affordable Care Act	Amended to read as if Sec. 10909(c) 0f the Patient Protection and Affordable Care Act had never been enacted; tax years beginning after December 31, 2011
6213(g)(2)(K)	101(a)(1)	Temporary Extension of 2001 Tax Relief—Temporary Extension	January 1, 2004
6213(g)(2)(L)	101(a)(1)	Temporary Extension of 2001 Tax Relief—Temporary Extension	January 1, 2004
6213(g)(2)(M)	101(a)(1)	Temporary Extension of 2001 Tax Relief—Temporary Extension	January 1, 2004
6402(f)(3)(C)	503(a)	Technical Amendment Relating to Collection of Unemployment Compensation Debts	Refunds payable under section Code Sec. 6402 on or after December 8, 2010
6409	728(a)	Refunds Disregarded in the Administration of Federal Programs and Federally Assisted Programs	Amounts received after December 31, 2009
6426(b)(6)	708(b)(1)	Extension of Provisions Related to Alcohol Used as Fuel—Extension of Excise Tax Credit for Alcohol Used as Fuel	Periods after December 31, 2010
6426(c)(6)	701(b)(1)	Incentives for Biodiesel and Renewable Diesel—Excise Tax Credits and Outlay Payments for Biodiesel and Renewable Diesel Fuel Mixtures	Fuel sold or used after December 31, 2009
6426(d)(2)	704(b)	Excise Tax Credits and Outlay Payments for Alternative Fuel and Alternative Fuel Mixtures—Exclusion of Black Liquor From Credit Eligibility	Fuel sold or used after December 31, 2009
6426(d)(5)	704(a)	Excise Tax Credits and Outlay Payments for Alternative Fuel and Alternative Fuel Mixtures	Fuel sold or used after December 31, 2009
6426(e)(3)	704(a)	Excise Tax Credits and Outlay Payments for Alternative Fuel and Alternative Fuel Mixtures	Fuel sold or used after December 31, 2009
6427(e)(6)(A)	708(c)(1)	Extension of Provisions Related to Alcohol Used as Fuel—Extension of Payment for Alcohol Fuel Mixture	Sales and uses after December 31, 2010

¶20,001

Code Sec.	Act Sec.	Act Provision Subject	Effective Date
6427(e)(6)(B)	701(b)(2)	Incentives for Biodiesel and Renewable Diesel—Excise Tax Credits and Outlay Payments for Biodiesel and Renewable Diesel Fuel Mixtures	Fuel sold or used after December 31, 2009
6427(e)(6)(C)	704(a)	Excise Tax Credits and Outlay Payments for Alternative Fuel and Alternative Fuel Mixtures	Fuel sold or used after December 31, 2009
6428	101(a)(1)	Temporary Extension of 2001 Tax Relief—Temporary Extension	Tax years beginning after December 31, 2000
6429	102(a)	Temporary Extension of 2003 Tax Relief	May 28, 2003
6431(f)(3)(A)	758(b)	Qualified Zone Academy Bonds	Obligations issued after December 31, 2010
6462(d)(5)	704(a)	Excise Tax Credits and Outlay Payments for Alternative Fuel and Alternative Fuel Mixtures	Fuel sold or used after December 31, 2009
6511(i)(2)	101(a)(1)	Temporary Extension of 2001 Tax Relief—Temporary Extension	Estates of decedents dying and generation-skip transfers after December 31, 2004
6612(c)	101(a)(1)	Temporary Extension of 2001 Tax Relief—Temporary Extension	Estates of decedents dying and generation-skip transfers after December 31, 2004
6693(a)(2)(C)	101(a)(1)	Temporary Extension of 2001 Tax Relief—Temporary Extension	Tax years beginning after December 31, 2001
6716	101(a)(1)	Temporary Extension of 2001 Tax Relief—Temporary Extension	Estates of decedents dying after December 31, 2009
6716	301(a)	Reinstatement of Estate Tax; Repeal of Carryover Basis	Estates of decedents dying after December 31, 2009
7508A(a)	101(a)(1)	Temporary Extension of 2001 Tax Relief—Temporary Extension	June 7, 2001
7518(g)(6)(A)	102(a)	Temporary Extension of 2003 Tax Relief	Tax years ending on or after May 6, 2003
7652(f)(1)	755(a)	Temporary Increase in Limit on Cover Over of Rum Excise Taxes to Puerto Rico and the Virgin Islands	Distilled spirits brought into the United States after December 31, 2009
7701(a)(47)	101(a)(1)	Temporary Extension of 2001 Tax Relief—Temporary Extension	Estates of decedents dying after December 31, 2009
7701(a)(47)	301(a)	Reinstatement of Estate Tax, Repeal of Carryover Basis	Estates of decedents dying after December 31, 2009
I(h)(3)	102(a)	Temporary Extension of 2003 Tax Relief	Tax years beginning after December 31, 2002
. . .	103(a)(2)	Temporary Extension of 2009 Tax Relief—American Opportunity Credit	Tax years beginning after December 31, 2010
. . .	301(c)	Reinstatement of Estate Tax; Repeal of Carryover Basis—Special Election With Respect to Estates of Decedents Dying in 2010	Estates of decedents dying, and transfers made, after December 31, 2009

¶20,001

Code Sec.	Act Sec.	Act Provision Subject	Effective Date
...	301(d)(1)(A)-(C)	Reinstatement of Estate Tax; Repeal of Carryover Basis—Extension of time for Performing Certain Acts—Estate Tax	Estates of decedents dying, and transfers made, after December 31, 2009
...	301(d)(2)	Reinstatement of Estate Tax; Repeal of Carryover Basis—Extension of time for Performing Certain Acts—Generation-Skipping Tax	Estates of decedents dying, and transfers made, after December 31, 2009
...	302(c)	Modifications to Estate, Gift, and Generation-Skipping Transfer Taxes—Modifications to Generation-Skipping Transfer Tax	Date of enactment
...	756(a)(1)-(2)	American Samoa Economic Development Credit	Tax years beginning after December 31, 2009

¶20,005 Effective Dates

Regulated Investment Company Modernization Act of 2010

This CCH-prepared table presents the general effective dates for major law provisions added, amended or repealed by the Regulated Investment Company Modernization Act of 2010 (H.R. 4337). Entries are listed in Code Section order.

Code Sec.	Act Sec.	Act Provision Subject	Effective Date
267(f)(3)(D)	306(b)	Distributions in Redemption of Stock of a Regulated Investment Company—Losses on Redemptions Not Disallowed For Fund-of-Funds Regulated Investment Companies	Distributions after date of enactment
302(a)	306(a)(2)	Distributions in Redemption of Stock of a Regulated Investment Company—Redemptions Treated as Exchanges—Conforming Amendment	Distributions after date of enactment
302(b)(5)-(6)	306(a)(1)	Distributions in Redemption of Stock of a Regulated Investment Company—Redemptions Treated as Exchanges	Distributions after date of enactment
316(b)(4)	305(a)	Return of Capital Distributions of Regulated Investment Companies	Distributions made in tax years beginning after date of enactment
562(c)	307(a)	Repeal of Preferential Dividend Rule For Publicly Offered Regulated Investment Companies	Distributions in tax years beginning after date of enactment
562(c)	307(b)	Repeal of Preferential Dividend Rule For Publicly Offered Regulated Investment Companies—Conforming Amendment	Distributions in tax years beginning after date of enactment
851(d)(1)-(2)	201(a)(1)-(2)	Savings Provisions For Failures of Regulated Investment Companies to Satisfy Gross Income and Asset Tests—Asset Test	Tax years with respect to which the due date (determined with regard to any extensions) of the return of tax for such tax year is after the date of enactment
851(i)	201(b)	Savings Provisions For Failures of Regulated Investment Companies to Satisfy Gross Income and Asset Tests—Gross Income Test	Tax years with respect to which the due date (determined with regard to any extensions) of the return of tax for such tax year is after the date of enactment

Code Sec.	Act Sec.	Act Provision Subject	Effective Date
852(b)(2)(G)	201(c)	Savings Provisions For Failures of Regulated Investment Companies to Satisfy Gross Income and Asset Tests—Deduction of Taxes Paid From Investment Company Taxable Income	Tax years with respect to which the due date (determined with regard to any extensions) of the return of tax for such tax year is after the date of enactment
852(b)(3)(C)	301(a)(1)	Modification of Dividend Designation Requirements and Allocation Rules For Regulated Investment Companies—Capital Gain Dividends	Tax years beginning after date of enactment
852(b)(4)(E)	309(a)	Exception to Holding Period Requirement For Certain Regularly Declared Exempt-Interest Dividends	Losses incurred on shares of stock for which the taxpayer's holding period begins after date of enactment
852(b)(4)(E)(ii)	309(b)	Exception to Holding Period Requirement For Certain Regularly Declared Exempt-Interest Dividends—Conforming Amendment	Losses incurred on shares of stock for which the taxpayer's holding period begins after date of enactment
852(b)(5)(A)	301(b)	Modification of Dividend Designation Requirements and Allocation Rules For Regulated Investment Companies—Exempt-Interest Dividends	Tax years beginning after date of enactment
852(b)(8)	308(a)	Elective Deferral of Certain Late-Year Losses of Regulated Investment Companies	Tax years beginning after date of enactment
852(b)(10)	308(b)(1)	Elective Deferral of Certain Late-Year Losses of Regulated Investment Companies—Conforming Amendments	Tax years beginning after date of enactment
852(c)(1)	302(a)	Earnings and Profits of Regulated Investment Companies	Tax years beginning after date of enactment
852(c)(2)	308(b)(2)	Elective Deferral of Certain Late-Year Losses of Regulated Investment Companies—Conforming Amendments	Tax years beginning after date of enactment
852(c)(4)	302(b)(1)	Earnings and Profits of Regulated Investment Companies—Conforming Amendments	Tax years beginning after date of enactment
852(f)(1)(C)	502(a)	Modification of Sales Load Basis Deferral Rules for Regulated Investment Companies	Charges incurred in tax years beginning after date of enactment
852(g)	303(a)	Pass-Thru of Exempt-Interest Dividends and Foreign Tax Credits in Fund of Funds Structure	Tax years beginning after date of enactment
853(c)	301(c)(1)(A)-(B)	Modification of Dividend Designation Requirements and Allocation Rules For Regulated Investment Companies—Foreign Tax Credits	Tax years beginning after date of enactment

¶20,005

Code Sec.	Act Sec.	Act Provision Subject	Effective Date
853(d)	301(c)(2)(A)-(B)	Modification of Dividend Designation Requirements and Allocation Rules For Regulated Investment Companies—Foreign Tax Credits—Conforming Amendments	Tax years beginning after date of enactment
853A(c)	301(d)(1)(A)-(B)	Modification of Dividend Designation Requirements and Allocation Rules For Regulated Investment Companies—Credits For Tax Credit Bonds	Tax years beginning after date of enactment
853A(d)	301(d)(2)(A)-(B)	Modification of Dividend Designation Requirements and Allocation Rules For Regulated Investment Companies—Credits For Tax Credit Bonds—Conforming Amendments	Tax years beginning after date of enactment
854(b)(1)(A)	301(e)(1)(A)	Modification of Dividend Designation Requirements and Allocation Rules For Regulated Investment Companies—Dividend Received Deduction, Etc.	Tax years beginning after date of enactment
854(b)(1)(B)(i)	301(e)(1)(B)	Modification of Dividend Designation Requirements and Allocation Rules For Regulated Investment Companies—Dividend Received Deduction, Etc.	Tax years beginning after date of enactment
854(b)(1)(C)(i)-(ii)	301(e)(1)(C)-(D)	Modification of Dividend Designation Requirements and Allocation Rules For Regulated Investment Companies—Dividend Received Deduction, Etc.	Tax years beginning after date of enactment
854(b)(2)-(5)	301(e)(2)	Modification of Dividend Designation Requirements and Allocation Rules For Regulated Investment Companies—Dividend Received Deduction, Etc.—Conforming Amendments	Tax years beginning after date of enactment
855(a)	301(g)(2)	Modification of Dividend Designation Requirements and Allocation Rules For Regulated Investment Companies—Conforming Amendments	Tax years beginning after date of enactment
855(a)	304(c)	Modification of Rules For Spillover Dividends of Regulated Investment Companies—Short-Term Capital Gain	Distributions in tax years beginning after date of enactment
855(a)(1)	304(a)	Modification of Rules For Spillover Dividends of Regulated Investment Companies—Deadline For Declaration of Dividend	Distributions in tax years beginning after date of enactment
855(a)(2)	304(b)	Modification of Rules For Spillover Dividends of Regulated Investment Companies—Deadline For Distribution of Dividend	Distributions in tax years beginning after date of enactment
855(c)-(d)	301(g)(1)	Modification of Dividend Designation Requirements and Allocation Rules For Regulated Investment Companies—Conforming Amendments	Tax years beginning after date of enactment

¶20,005

Code Sec.	Act Sec.	Act Provision Subject	Effective Date
860(f)(2)(B)	301(a)(2)	Modification of Dividend Designation Requirements and Allocation Rules For Regulated Investment Companies—Conforming Amendment	Tax years beginning after date of enactment
860(j)	501(b)	Repeal of Assessable Penalty With Respect to Liability For Tax on Regulated Investment Companies—Conforming Amendment	Tax years beginning after date of enactment
871(k)(1)(A)	302(b)(2)	Earnings and Profits of Regulated Investment Companies—Conforming Amendments	Tax years beginning after date of enactment
871(k)(1)(C)	301(f)(1)	Modification of Dividend Designation Requirements and Allocation Rules For Regulated Investment Companies—Dividends Paid to Certain Foreign Persons—Interest-Related Deductions	Tax years beginning after date of enactment
871(k)(2)(A)	302(b)(2)	Earnings and Profits of Regulated Investment Companies—Conforming Amendments	Tax years beginning after date of enactment
871(k)(2)(C)	301(f)(2)	Modification of Dividend Designation Requirements and Allocation Rules For Regulated Investment Companies—Dividends Paid to Certain Foreign Persons—Short-Term Capital Gain Dividends	Tax years beginning after date of enactment
871(k)(2)(D)	308(b)(3)	Elective Deferral of Certain Late-Year Losses of Regulated Investment Companies—Conforming Amendments	Tax years beginning after date of enactment
1212(a)(1)(C)	101(b)(1)	Capital Loss Carryovers of Regulated Investment Companies—Conforming Amendments	Net Capital Losses for tax years beginning after date of enactment
1212(a)(3)	101(a)	Capital Loss Carryovers of Regulated Investment Companies	Tax years beginning after date of enactment
1212(a)(4)	101(a)	Capital Loss Carryovers of Regulated Investment Companies	Net Capital Losses for tax years beginning after date of enactment
1222(10)	101(b)(2)	Capital Loss Carryovers of Regulated Investment Companies—Conforming Amendments	Net Capital Losses for tax years beginning after date of enactment
4982(b)(1)(B)	404(a)	Increase in Required Distribution of Capital Gain Net Income	Calendar years beginning after date of enactment
4982(c)(4)	403(a)	Distributed Amount For Excise Tax Purposes Determined on Basis of Taxes Paid By Regulated Investment Company	Calendar years beginning after date of enactment
4982(e)(5)–(7)	402(a)	Deferral of Certain Gains and Losses of Regulated Investment Companies For Excise Tax Purposes	Calendar years beginning after date of enactment
4982(f)(1)–(4)	401(a)(1)–(4)	Excise Tax Exemption For Certain Regulated Investment Companies Owned By Tax-Exempt Entities	Calendar years beginning after date of enactment
6697	501(a)	Repeal of Assessable Penalty With Respect to Liability For Tax on Regulated Investment Companies	Tax years beginning after date of enactment

¶20,005

¶25,001 Code Section to Explanation Table

Code Sec.	Explanation
24(d)(4)	¶360
25A(i)	¶371
25C(a)	¶372
25C(b)	¶372
25C(c)(1)	¶372
25C(c)(2)(A)	¶372
25C(d)(2)(A)(ii)	¶372
25C(d)(3)(E)	¶372
25C(d)(4)	¶372
25C(e)(3)	¶372
25C(g)(2)	¶372
26(a)(2)	¶376
30C(g)(2)	¶548
32(b)(3)	¶356
36B(f)(2)(B)	¶373
36B(f)(2)(B)(ii)	¶373
40(e)(1)	¶546
40(h)	¶546
40A(g)	¶544
41(h)(1)(B)	¶520
45(d)(8)(B)	¶550
45A(f)	¶530
45C(b)(1)(D)	¶520
45D(f)(1)	¶528
45D(f)(3)	¶528
45G(f)	¶532
45L(g)	¶538
45M(b)(1)	¶542
45M(b)(2)	¶542
45M(b)(3)	¶542
45M(e)(1)	¶542
45M(e)(2)	¶542
45M(e)(3)	¶542
45N(e)	¶534
45P(f)	¶526
51(c)(4)(B)	¶524
54E(c)(1)	¶465
55(d)	¶375
62(a)(2)(D)	¶327
132(f)(2)	¶380
163(h)(3)(E)(iv)	¶328
164(b)(5)(I)	¶326
168(e)(3)(E)	¶508
168(e)(7)(A)(i)	¶508
168(e)(8)(E)	¶508
168(i)(15)(D)	¶510
168(j)(8)	¶512

Code Sec.	Explanation
168(k)	¶502
168(k)(2)	¶502
168(k)(2)(B)(ii)	¶502
168(k)(4)(D)	¶504
168(k)(4)(D)(iii)	¶504
168(k)(4)(I)	¶504
168(k)(5)	¶502
168(l)(5)	¶502
168(n)(2)(C)	¶502
170(b)(1)(E)(vi)	¶353
170(b)(2)(B)(iii)	¶353
170(e)(3)(C)(iv)	¶560
170(e)(3)(D)(iv)	¶563
170(e)(6)(G)	¶566
179(b)(1)	¶506
179(b)(2)	¶506
179(b)(6)	¶506
179(c)(2)	¶506
179(d)(1)(A)(ii)	¶506
179(f)(2)	¶508
179E(g)	¶516
181(f)	¶514
198(h)	¶518
199(d)(8)(C)	¶632
222(e)	¶350
267(f)(3)(D)	¶824
302(a)	¶824
302(b)	¶824
316(b)(4)	¶822
408(d)(8)(F)	¶352
451(i)(3)	¶554
512(b)(13)(E)(iv)	¶615
562(c)	¶827
613A(c)(6)(H)(ii)	¶552
851(b)(2)(G)	¶806
851(d)(1)	¶806
851(d)(2)	¶806
851(i)	¶806
852(b)(3)	¶809
852(b)(4)(E)	¶833
852(b)(5)(A)	¶809
852(b)(8)	¶830
852(b)(10)	¶830
852(c)(1)	¶812
852(c)(2)	¶830
852(c)(4)	¶812
852(f)(1)(C)	¶842

Code Sec.	Explanation
852(g)	¶815
853(c)	¶809
853(d)	¶809
853A(c)	¶809
853A(d)	¶809
854(b)	¶809
855	¶809
855(a)	¶818
855(a)(1)	¶818
855(a)(2)	¶818
860(f)(2)	¶809
860(j)	¶839
871(k)	¶812
871(k)(1)(C)	¶430; ¶809
871(k)(2)(C)	¶430; ¶809
871(k)(2)(D)	¶830
897(h)(4)(A)(ii)	¶620
953(e)(10)	¶626
954(c)(6)(C)	¶629
954(h)(9)	¶623
1014	¶740
1022	¶740
1202(a)(2)(C)	¶440
1202(a)(4)	¶418
1212(a)(1)	¶803
1212(a)(3)	¶803
1212(a)(4)	¶803
1222(10)	¶803
1367(a)(2)	¶557
1391(d)(1)(A)(i)	¶440
1391(h)(2)	¶440
1400(f)	¶445
1400A(b)	¶445
1400B(b)(2)(A)(i)	¶445
1400B(b)(3)(A)	¶445
1400B(b)(4)(A)(i)	¶445
1400B(b)(4)(B)(i)(I)	¶445
1400B(e)(2)	¶445
1400B(g)(2)	¶445
1400C(i)	¶445
1400L(b)(2)(D)	¶502
1400L(d)(2)(D)	¶470; ¶502
1400N(a)	¶450
1400N(c)(5)	¶450
1400N(d)	¶450
1400N(d)(3)(B)	¶502
1400N(h)	¶450
2001(b)(2)	¶710
2001(c)	¶710
2001(g)	¶710
2010(c)	¶715
2010(c)(2)	¶718
2010(c)(3)	¶718
2010(c)(4)	¶718
2010(c)(5)	¶718
2010(c)(6)	¶718
2105(d)(3)	¶386
2502(a)	¶710
2505(a)	¶705; ¶710; ¶715; ¶718
2511(c)	¶710
2518(b)	¶705
2631(c)	¶718
2662	¶705
4081(d)(2)(B)	¶638
4261(j)(1)(A)(ii)	¶638
4271(d)(1)(A)(ii)	¶638
4982(b)(1)(B)	¶836
4982(c)	¶836
4982(e)	¶836
4982(f)	¶836
6018	¶705; ¶745
6018(a)(1)	¶718
6019(b)	¶745
6075	¶745
6166(b)(1)(B)(ii)	¶785
6166(b)(1)(C)(ii)	¶785
6166(b)(8)(B)	¶795
6166(b)(9)(B)(iii)(I)	¶785
6166(b)(10)	¶790
6402(f)(3)	¶382
6402(f)(3)(C)	¶382
6402(f)(4)	¶382
6402(f)(5)	¶382
6402(f)(6)	¶382
6409	¶384
6426(b)(6)	¶546
6426(c)(6)	¶544
6426(d)(2)	¶544
6426(d)(5)	¶544
6426(e)(3)	¶544
6427(e)(6)(A)	¶546
6427(e)(6)(B)	¶544
6427(e)(6)(C)	¶544
6431(f)(3)(A)(iii)	¶465
6697	¶839
6716	¶745
7652(f)(1)	¶635
9502(d)(1)	¶638
9502(e)(2)	¶638

¶25,001

¶25,005 Code Sections Added, Amended or Repealed

The list below notes all the Code Sections or subsections of the Internal Revenue Code that were added, amended or repealed by the Tax Relief, Unemployment Insurance Reauthorization, and Job Creation Act of 2010 (P.L. 111-312), enacted December 17, 2010, the Regulated Investment Company Modernization Act of 2010 (H.R. 4337), the Airport and Airway Extension Act of 2010, Part IV (H.R. 6473), the Claims Resolution Act of 2010 (P.L. 111-291), enacted December 8, 2010, and the Medicare and Medicaid Extenders Act of 2010 (P.L. 111-309), enacted December 15, 2010. The first column indicates the Code Section added, amended or repealed, and the second column indicates the Act Section.

Tax Relief, Unemployment Insurance Reauthorization, and Job Creation Act of 2010

Code Sec.	Act Sec.	Code Sec.	Act Sec.
24(b)(3)(B)	101(b)	45C(b)(1)(D)	731(b)
24(d)(4)	103(b)(1)-(2)	45D(f)(1)(E)-(G)	733(a)(1)-(3)
25(e)(1)(E)	101(b)	45D(f)(3)	733(b)
25A(i)	103(a)(1)	45G(f)	734(a)
25A(i)(5)(B)	101(b)	45L(g)	703(a)
25B(g)(2)	101(b)	45M(b)(1)(A)-(E)	709(a)
25C(a)-(b)	710(b)(1)	45M(b)(2)(C)-(F)	709(b)
25C(c)(1)	710(b)(2)(A)	45M(b)(3)(C)-(F)	709(c)
25C(c)(1)	710(b)(2)(D)(ii)	45M(e)(1)	709(d)(1)(A)-(B)
25C(c)(2)(A)	710(b)(2)(E)	45M(e)(2)	709(d)(2)(A)-(B)
25C(c)(4)	710(b)(2)(D)(i)	45M(e)(3)	709(d)(3)
25C(d)(2)(A)(ii)	710(b)(2)(C)(ii)	45N(e)	735(a)
25C(d)(3)(E)	710(b)(2)(B)	45P(f)	736(a)
25C(d)(4)	710(b)(2)(C)(i)	51(c)(4)(B)	757(a)
25C(e)(3)	710(b)(3)	54E(c)(1)	758(a)(1)-(2)
25C(g)(2)	710(a)	55(d)(1)(A)-(B)	201(a)(1)-(2)
26(a)(1)	101(b)	62(a)(2)(D)	721(a)
26(a)(2)	202(a)(1)-(2)	121(d)(9)	301(a)
30(i)(2)(B)(ii)	101(b)	132(f)(2)	727(a)
30B(g)(2)(B)(ii)	101(b)	137(a)(2)	101(b)
30C(g)(2)	711(a)	137(b)(4)	101(b)
30D(c)(2)(B)(ii)	101(b)	137(d)-(e)	101(b)
32(b)(3)	103(c)(1)-(2)	137(f)	101(b)
36C	101(b)	163(h)(3)(E)(iv)	759(a)
36C(a)(3)	101(b)	164(b)(5)(I)	722(a)
36C(b)(4)	101(b)	168(e)(3)(E)	737(a)
36C(h)	101(b)	168(e)(7)(A)(i)	737(b)(1)
40(e)(1)(A)-(B)	708(a)(1)(A)-(B)	168(e)(8)(E)	737(b)(2)
40(h)	708(a)(2)	168(i)(15)(D)	738(a)
40A(g)	701(a)	168(j)(8)	739(a)
41(h)(1)(B)	731(a)	168(k)	401(d)(1)
45(d)(8)(B)	702(a)	168(k)(2)	401(a)(1)-(2)
45A(f)	732(a)	168(k)(2)(B)(ii)	401(d)(2)

Code Sec.	Act Sec.	Code Sec.	Act Sec.
168(k)(4)(D)(ii)-(v)	401(d)(3)(A)-(C)	1400(f)	754(a)
168(k)(4)(D)(iii)	401(c)(1)	1400A(b)	754(b)
168(k)(4)(I)	401(c)(2)	1400B(b)(2)-(4)	754(c)(1)
168(k)(5)	401(b)	1400B(e)(2)	754(c)(2)(A)(i)-(ii)
168(l)(5)(A)-(C)	401(d)(4)(A)-(C)	1400B(g)(2)	754(c)(2)(B)
168(n)(2)(C)	401(d)(5)	1400C(i)	754(d)
170(b)(1)(E)(vi)	723(a)	1400C(d)[(2)]	101(b)
170(b)(2)(B)(iii)	723(b)	1400L(b)(2)(D)	401(d)(6)
170(e)(1)	301(a)	1400L(d)(2)(D)	761(a)
170(e)(3)(C)(iv)	740(a)	1400N(a)	764(a)
170(e)(3)(D)(iv)	741(a)	1400N(c)(5)	763
170(e)(6)(G)	742(a)	1400N(d)(3)(B)	401(d)(7)
179(b)(1)(B)-(D)	402(a)	1400N(d)(6)	765(a)(1)-(2)
179(b)(2)(B)-(D)	402(b)	1400N(h)	762(a)
179(b)(6)	402(c)	2001(b)(2)	302(d)(1)(A)
179(c)(2)	402(e)	2001(c)(1)-(2)	302(a)(2)(A)-(C)
179(d)(1)(A)(ii)	402(d)	2001(g)	302(d)(1)(B)
179(f)(2)(B)-(C)	737(b)(3)(A)-(B)	2010(c)	302(a)(1)
179E(g)	743(a)	2010(c)(2)-(6)	303(a)
181(f)	744(a)	2105(d)(3)	726(a)
198(h)	745(a)	2210	303(a)
199(d)(8)(C)	746(a)(1)-(2)	2502(a)	302(b)(2)
222(e)	724(a)	2505(a)	302(d)(2)
408(d)(8)(F)	725(a)	2505(a)(1)	301(b)
451(i)(3)	705(a)	2505(a)(1)	302(b)(1)(A)
512(b)(13)(E)(iv)	747(a)	2505(a)(1)	303(b)(1)
613A(c)(6)(H)(ii)	706(a)	2511(c)	302(e)
684	301(a)	2631(c)	303(b)(2)
684(a)	301(a)	2664	301(a)
684(b)	301(a)	4947(a)(2)(A)	301(a)
871(k)(1)-(2)	748(a)	6018	301(a)
897(h)(4)(A)(ii)	749(a)	6018(a)(1)	303(b)(3)
904(i)	101(b)	6019	301(a)
953(e)(10)	750(a)	6075(a)	301(a)
953(e)(10)	750(b)	6075(b)(3)	301(a)
954(c)(6)(C)	751(a)	6211(b)(4)(A)	101(b)
954(h)(9)	750(a)	6402(f)(3)(C)	503(a)
1014(f)	301(a)	6409	728(a)
1016(a)(26)	101(b)	6426(b)(6)	708(b)(1)
1022	301(a)	6426(c)(6)	701(b)(1)
1040	301(a)	6426(d)(2)	704(b)
1202(a)(2)(C)	753(b)(1)-(2)	6426(d)(5)	704(a)
1202(a)(4)	760(a)(1)-(2)	6426(e)(3)	704(a)
1221(a)(3)(C)	301(a)	6427(e)(6)(A)	708(c)(1)
1246(e)	301(a)	6427(e)(6)(B)	701(b)(2)
1291(e)	301(a)	6427(e)(6)(C)	704(a)
1296(i)	301(a)	6431(f)(3)(A)(iii)	758(b)
1367(a)(2)	752(a)	6716	301(a)
1391(d)(1)(A)(i)	753(a)(1)	7652(f)(1)	755(a)
1391(h)(2)	753(a)(2)	7701(a)(47)	301(a)

¶25,005

Regulated Investment Company Modernization Act of 2010

Code Sec.	Act Sec.	Code Sec.	Act Sec.
267(f)(3)(D)	306(b)	853A(c)	301(d)(1)(A)-(B)
302(a)	306(a)(2)	853A(d)	301(d)(2)(A)-(B)
302(b)(5)-(6)	306(a)(1)	854(b)(1)	301(e)(1)(A)-(D)
316(b)(4)	305(a)	854(b)(2)-(5)	301(e)(2)
562(c)	307(a)	855	301(g)(1)-(2)
562(c)	307(b)	855(a)	304(c)
851(d)	201(a)(1)-(2)	855(a)(1)	304(a)
851(i)	201(b)	855(a)(2)	304(b)
852(b)(2)(G)	201(c)	860(f)(2)(B)	301(a)(2)
852(b)(3)(C)	301(a)(1)	860(j)	501(b)
852(b)(4)(E)	309(a)	871(k)(1)(C)	301(f)(1)
852(b)(4)(E)(ii)	309(b)	871(k)(1)-(2)	302(b)(2)
852(b)(5)(A)	301(b)	871(k)(2)(C)	301(f)(2)
852(b)(8)	308(a)	871(k)(2)(D)	308(b)(3)
852(b)(10)	308(b)(1)	1212(a)(1)(C)	101(b)(1)
852(c)(1)	302(a)	1212(a)(3)-(4)	101(a)
852(c)(2)	308(b)(2)	1222(10)	101(b)(2)
852(c)(4)	302(b)(1)	4982(b)(1)(B)	404(a)
852(f)(1)(C)	502(a)	4982(c)(4)	403(a)
852(g)	303(a)	4982(e)(5)-(7)	402(a)
853(c)	301(c)(1)(A)-(B)	4982(f)(1)-(4)	401(a)(1)-(4)
853(d)	301(c)(2)(A)-(B)	6697	501(a)

Airport and Airway Extension Act of 2010, Part IV

Code Sec.	Act Sec.	Code Sec.	Act Sec.
4081(d)(2)(B)	2(a)	9502(d)(1)	3(a)(1)-(2)
4261(j)(1)(A)(ii)	2(b)(1)	9502(e)(2)	3(b)
4271(d)(1)(A)(ii)	2(b)(2)		

Claims Resolution Act of 2010

Code Sec.	Act Sec.
6402(f)	801(a)(1)-(4)

Medicare and Medicaid Extenders Act of 2010

Code Sec.	Act Sec.
36B(f)(2)(B)	208(a)
36B(f)(2)(B)(ii)	208(b)

¶25,010 Table of Amendments to Other Acts

Tax Relief, Unemployment Insurance Reauthorization, and Job Creation Act of 2010

Amended Act Sec.	H.R. 4853 Sec.	Par. (¶)	Amended Act Sec.	H.R. 4853 Sec.	Par. (¶)
			704(a)	764(b)	¶7075
Economic Growth and Tax Relief Reconciliation Act of 2001			**American Recovery and Reinvestment Act of 2009**		
901(a)	101(a)	¶7010			
			1004(c)(1)	103(a)(2)	¶7017
Jobs Growth Tax Relief Reconciliation Act of 2003			1603(a), Div. B	707(a)	¶7055
			1603(j), Div. B	707(b)	¶7055
303	102(a)	¶7015	**Patient Protection and Affordable Care Act of 2010**		
Tax Relief and Health Care Act of 2006					
119(d), Div. A	756(a)	¶7070	10909(c)-(d)	101(b)(1)-(2)	¶7010
Heartland Disaster Tax Relief Act of 2008					
702(d)(1)	764(b)	¶7075			

¶25,015 Table of Act Sections Not Amending Internal Revenue Code Sections

Tax Relief, Unemployment Insurance Reauthorization, and Job Creation Act of 2010

Paragraph

Sec. 1. Short title; etc. . . . . ¶7005

Sec. 201. Temporary extension of increased alternative minimum tax exemption amount . . . . ¶7020

Sec. 301. Reinstatement of estate tax; repeal of carryover basis . . . . ¶7025

Sec. 302. Modifications to estate, gift, and generation-skipping transfer taxes . . . . ¶7030

Sec. 304. Application of EGTRRA sunset to this title . . . . ¶7035

Sec. 601. Temporary employee payroll tax cut . . . . ¶7040

Paragraph

Sec. 701. Incentives for biodiesel and renewable diesel . . . . ¶7045

Sec. 704. Excise tax credits and outlay payments for alternative fuel and alternative fuel mixtures . . . . ¶7050

Sec. 725. Tax-free distributions from individual retirement plans for charitable purposes . . . . ¶7060

Sec. 753. Empowerment zone tax incentives . . . . ¶7065

¶25,020 Act Sections Amending Code Sections

Tax Relief, Unemployment Insurance Authorization, and Job Creation Act of 2010

Act Sec.	Code Sec.	Act Sec.	Code Sec.
101(b)	24(b)(3)(B)	301(a)	7701(a)(47)
101(b)	25(e)(1)(E)	301(b)	2505(a)(1)
101(b)	25A(i)(5)(B)	302(a)(1)	2010(c)
101(b)	25B(g)(2)	302(a)(2)(A)-(C)	2001(c)(1)-(2)
101(b)	26(a)(1)	302(b)(1)(A)	2505(a)(1)
101(b)	30(c)(2)(B)(ii)	302(b)(2)	2502(a)
101(b)	30B(g)(2)(B)(ii)	302(d)(1)(A)	2001(b)(2)
101(b)	30D(c)(2)(B)(ii)	302(d)(1)(B)	2001(g)
101(b)	36C	302(d)(2)	2505(a)
101(b)	36C(a)(3)	302(e)	2511(c)
101(b)	36C(b)(4)	303(a)	2210
101(b)	36C(h)	303(a)	2010(c)(2)-(6)
101(b)	137(a)(2)	303(b)(1)	2505(a)(1)
101(b)	137(b)(4)	303(b)(2)	2631(c)
101(b)	137(d)-(e)	303(b)(3)	6018(a)(1)
101(b)	137(f)	401(a)(1)-(2)	168(k)(2)
101(b)	904(i)	401(b)	168(k)(5)
101(b)	1016(a)(26)	401(c)(1)	168(k)(4)(D)(iii)
101(b)	1400C(d)[(2)]	401(c)(2)	168(k)(4)(I)
101(b)	6211(b)(4)(A)	401(d)(1)	168(k)
103(a)(1)	25A(i)	401(d)(2)	168(k)(2)(B)(ii)
103(b)(1)-(2)	24(d)(4)	401(d)(3)(A)-(C)	168(k)(4)(D)(ii)-(v)
103(c)(1)-(2)	32(b)(3)	401(d)(4)(A)-(C)	168(l)(5)(A)-(C)
201(a)(1)-(2)	55(d)(1)(A)-(B)	401(d)(5)	168(n)(2)(C)
202(a)(1)-(2)	26(a)(2)	401(d)(6)	1400L(b)(2)(D)
301(a)	121(d)(9)	401(d)(7)	1400N(d)(3)(B)
301(a)	170(e)(1)	402(a)	179(b)(1)(B)-(D)
301(a)	684	402(b)	179(b)(2)(B)-(D)
301(a)	684(a)	402(c)	179(b)(6)
301(a)	684(b)	402(d)	179(d)(1)(A)(ii)
301(a)	1014(f)	402(e)	179(c)(2)
301(a)	1022	503(a)	6402(f)(3)(C)
301(a)	1040	701(a)	40A(g)
301(a)	1221(a)(3)(C)	701(b)(1)	6426(c)(6)
301(a)	1246(e)	701(b)(2)	6427(e)(6)(B)
301(a)	1291(e)	702(a)	45(d)(8)(B)
301(a)	1296(i)	703(a)	45L(g)
301(a)	2664	704(a)	6426(d)(5)
301(a)	4947(a)(2)(A)	704(a)	6426(e)(3)
301(a)	6018	704(a)	6427(e)(6)(C)
301(a)	6019	704(b)	6426(d)(2)
301(a)	6075(a)	705(a)	451(i)(3)
301(a)	6075(b)(3)	706(a)	613A(c)(6)(H)(ii)
301(a)	6716	708(a)(1)(A)-(B)	40(e)(1)(A)-(B)

Act Sec.	Code Sec.	Act Sec.	Code Sec.
708(a)(2)	40(h)	737(b)(2)	168(e)(8)(E)
708(b)(1)	6426(b)(6)	737(b)(3)(A)–(B)	179(f)(2)(B)–(C)
708(c)(1)	6427(e)(6)(A)	738(a)	168(i)(15)(D)
709(a)	45M(b)(1)(A)–(E)	739(a)	168(j)(8)
709(b)	45M(b)(2)(C)–(F)	740(a)	170(e)(3)(C)(iv)
709(c)	45M(b)(3)(C)–(F)	741(a)	170(e)(3)(D)(iv)
709(d)(1)(A)–(B)	45M(e)(1)	742(a)	170(e)(6)(G)
709(d)(2)(A)–(B)	45M(e)(2)	743(a)	179E(g)
709(d)(3)	45M(e)(3)	744(a)	181(f)
710(a)	25C(g)(2)	745(a)	198(h)
710(b)(1)	25C(a)–(b)	746(a)(1)–(2)	199(d)(8)(C)
710(b)(2)(A)	25C(c)(1)	747(a)	512(b)(13)(E)(iv)
710(b)(2)(B)	25C(d)(3)(E)	748(a)	871(k)(1)–(2)
710(b)(2)(C)(i)	25C(d)(4)	749(a)	897(h)(4)(A)(ii)
710(b)(2)(C)(ii)	25C(d)(2)(A)(ii)	750(a)	953(e)(10)
710(b)(2)(D)(i)	25C(c)(4)	750(a)	954(h)(9)
710(b)(2)(D)(ii)	25C(c)(1)	750(b)	953(e)(10)
710(b)(2)(E)	25C(c)(2)(A)	751(a)	954(c)(6)(C)
710(b)(3)	25C(e)(3)	752(a)	1367(a)(2)
711(a)	30C(g)(2)	753(a)(1)	1391(d)(1)(A)(i)
721(a)	62(a)(2)(D)	753(a)(2)	1391(h)(2)
722(a)	164(b)(5)(I)	753(b)(1)–(2)	1202(a)(2)(C)
723(a)	170(b)(1)(E)(vi)	754(a)	1400(f)
723(b)	170(b)(2)(B)(iii)	754(b)	1400A(b)
724(a)	222(e)	754(c)(1)	1400B(b)(2)–(4)
725(a)	408(d)(8)(F)	754(c)(2)(A)(i)–(ii)	1400B(e)(2)
726(a)	2105(d)(3)	754(c)(2)(B)	1400B(g)(2)
727(a)	132(f)(2)	754(d)	1400C(i)
728(a)	6409	755(a)	7652(f)(1)
731(a)	41(h)(1)(B)	757(a)	51(c)(4)(B)
731(b)	45C(b)(1)(D)	758(a)(1)–(2)	54E(c)(1)
732(a)	45A(f)	758(b)	6431(f)(3)(A)(iii)
733(a)(1)–(3)	45D(f)(1)(E)–(G)	759(a)	163(h)(3)(E)(iv)
733(b)	45D(f)(3)	760(a)(1)–(2)	1202(a)(4)
734(a)	45G(f)	761(a)	1400L(d)(2)(D)
735(a)	45N(e)	762(a)	1400N(h)
736(a)	45P(f)	763	1400N(c)(5)
737(a)	168(e)(3)(E)	764(a)	1400N(a)
737(b)(1)	168(e)(7)(A)(i)	765(a)(1)–(2)	1400N(d)(6)

Regulated Investment Company Modernization Act of 2010

Act Sec.	Code Sec.	Act Sec.	Code Sec.
101(a)	1212(a)(3)–(4)	301(c)(1)(A)–(B)	853(c)
101(b)(1)	1212(a)(1)(C)	301(c)(2)(A)–(B)	853(d)
101(b)(2)	1222(10)	301(d)(1)(A)–(B)	853A(c)
201(a)(1)–(2)	851(d)	301(d)(2)(A)–(B)	853A(d)
201(b)	851(i)	301(e)(1)(A)–(D)	854(b)(1)
201(c)	852(b)(2)(G)	301(e)(2)	854(b)(2)–(5)
301(a)(1)	852(b)(3)(C)	301(f)(1)	871(k)(1)(C)
301(a)(2)	860(f)(2)(B)	301(f)(2)	871(k)(2)(C)
301(b)	852(b)(5)(A)	301(g)(1)–(2)	855

Act Sec.	Code Sec.	Act Sec.	Code Sec.
302(a)	852(c)(1)	308(a)	852(b)(8)
302(b)(1)	852(c)(4)	308(b)(1)	852(b)(10)
302(b)(2)	871(k)(1)-(2)	308(b)(2)	852(c)(2)
303(a)	852(g)	308(b)(3)	871(k)(2)(D)
304(a)	855(a)(1)	309(a)	852(b)(4)(E)
304(b)	855(a)(2)	309(b)	852(b)(4)(E)(ii)
304(c)	855(a)	401(a)(1)-(4)	4982(f)(1)-(4)
305(a)	316(b)(4)	402(a)	4982(e)(5)-(7)
306(a)(1)	302(b)(5)-(6)	403(a)	4982(c)(4)
306(a)(2)	302(a)	404(a)	4982(b)(1)(B)
306(b)	267(f)(3)(D)	501(a)	6697
307(a)	562(c)	501(b)	860(j)
307(b)	562(c)	502(a)	852(f)(1)(C)

Airport and Airway Extension Act of 2010, Part IV

Act Sec.	Code Sec.	Act Sec.	Code Sec.
2(a)	4081(d)(2)(B)	3(a)(1)-(2)	9502(d)(1)
2(b)(1)	4261(j)(1)(A)(ii)	3(b)	9502(e)(2)
2(b)(2)	4271(d)(1)(A)(ii)		

Claims Resolution Act of 2010

Act Sec.	Code Sec.
801(a)(1)-(4)	6402(f)

Medicare and Medicaid Extenders Act of 2010

Act Sec.	Code Sec.
208(a)	36B(f)(2)(B)
208(b)	36B(f)(2)(B)(ii)

¶27,001 Client Letters

¶27,005 CLIENT LETTER #1

Re: Tax Relief Act of 2010: General Information

Dear Client:

After weeks of intense negotiations between the White House and Congressional leaders, Congress passed and President Obama signed into law a two-year extension of soon-to-have-expired Bush-era tax cuts, including extension of current individual tax rates and capital gains/dividend tax rates. Called the most sweeping tax law in a decade, the Tax Relief, Unemployment Insurance Reauthorization and Job Creation Act of 2010 (H.R. 4853), was approved by the Senate on December 15, 2010 and by the House on December 16, 2010. The new law is, however, much more than just an extension of existing tax rates. The new law also provides a temporary across-the-board payroll tax cut for wage earners, a retroactive AMT "patch," estate tax relief, education and energy incentives and many valuable incentives for businesses, including 100 percent bonus depreciation and extension of many temporary tax breaks. This letter highlights many of the key incentives in the new law. As always, please call or email our office for more details.

Individuals

Tax rates. Among the most valuable tax breaks for individuals in the new law are a two-year extension of individual income tax rate reductions and a payroll tax cut. Both will deliver immediate tax savings starting in January 2011. The new law keeps in place the current 10, 15, 25, 28, 33, and 35 percent individual tax rates for two years, through December 31, 2012. If Congress had not passed this extension, the individual tax rates would have jumped significantly for all income levels. The new law also extends full repeal of the limitation on itemized deductions and the personal exemption phaseout for two years. Married couples filing jointly will also benefit from extended provisions designed to ameliorate the so-called marriage penalty.

Payroll tax cut. The payroll tax cut is designed to get more money into workers' paychecks and to encourage consumer spending. Effective for calendar year 2011, the employee share of the OASDI portion of Social Security taxes is reduced from 6.2 percent to 4.2 percent up to the taxable wage base of $106,800. Self-employed individuals also benefit. Self-employed individuals will pay 10.4 percent on self-employment income up to the wage base (reduced from the normal 12.4 percent rate). The payroll cut replaces the Making Work Pay credit, which reduced income tax withholding for wage earners in 2009 and 2010. The payroll tax cut, unlike the credit, does not exclude some individuals based on their earnings and has the potential of significantly higher benefits (with a maximum payroll tax reduction of $2,136 on wages at or above the $106,800 level as compared to a maximum available $800 Making Work Pay credit for married couples filing jointly ($400 for single individuals)).

Capital gains/dividends. The new law also extends reduced capital gains and dividend tax rates. Like the individual rate cuts, the extended capital gains and dividend tax rates are temporary and will expire after 2012 unless Congress intervenes. In the meantime, however, for two years (2011 and 2012), individuals in the 10 and 15 percent rate brackets can take advantage of a zero percent capital gains and dividend tax rate. Individuals in higher rate brackets will enjoy a maximum tax rate of 15 percent on capital gains, as opposed to a 20 percent rate that had been scheduled to replace it and with dividends taxed at income tax rates. Only net capital gains and qualified dividends are eligible for this special tax treatment. If you have any questions about your capital gain/dividend income, please contact our office.

AMT patch. More and more individuals are finding themselves falling under the alternative minimum tax (AMT) because of the way the AMT is structured. To prevent the AMT from encroaching on middle income taxpayers, Congress has routinely enacted so-called "AMT patches." The new law continues this trend by providing higher exemption amounts and other targeted relief.

More incentives. Along with all these incentives, the new law extends many popular but temporary tax breaks. Extended for 2011 and 2012 are:

- $1,000 child tax credit
- Enhanced earned income tax credit
- Adoption credit with modifications
- Dependent care credit
- Deduction for certain mortgage insurance premiums

The new law also extends retroactively some other valuable tax incentives for individuals that expired at the end of 2009. These incentives are extended for 2010 and 2011 and include:

- State and local sales tax deduction
- Teacher's classroom expense deduction
- Charitable contributions of IRA proceeds
- Charitable contributions of appreciated property for conservation purposes

Businesses

Bonus depreciation. Bonus depreciation is intended to help businesses depreciate purchases faster against their taxable income, thereby encouraging businesses to invest in more equipment. Bonus depreciation allows businesses to recover the costs of certain capital expenditures more quickly than under ordinary tax depreciation schedules. Businesses can use bonus depreciation to immediately write off a percentage of the cost of depreciable property. The new law makes 100 percent bonus depreciation available for qualified investments made after September 8, 2010 and before January 1, 2012. It also continues bonus depreciation, albeit at 50 percent, on property placed in service after December 31, 2011 and before January 1, 2013. There are special rules for certain longer-lived and transportation property. Additionally, certain taxpayers may claim refundable credits in lieu of bonus depreciation. 100 percent bonus depreciation is a valuable tax break and businesses have only a short window to take advantage of it. Please contact our office so we can help you plan for 100 bonus depreciation.

Code Sec. 179 expensing. Along with bonus depreciation, the new law also provides for enhanced Code Sec. 179 expensing for 2012. Under current law, the Code Sec. 179 dollar and investment limits are $500,000 and $2 million, respectively,

¶27,005

for tax years beginning in 2010 and 2011. The new law provides for a $125,000 dollar limit (indexed for inflation) and a $500,000 investment limit (indexed for inflation) for tax years beginning in 2012 (but not after).

Research credit. Many businesses urged Congress to make the research credit permanent after the credit expired at the end of 2009. While this proposal enjoyed significant support in Congress, its cost was deemed prohibitive. Instead, Congress extended the research tax credit for two years, for 2010 and 2011.

More incentives. Other valuable business incentives in the new law include extensions of:

- 100 percent exclusion of gain from qualified small business stock
- Transit benefits parity
- Work Opportunity Tax Credit (with modifications)
- New Markets Tax Credit (with modifications)
- Differential wage credit
- Brownfields remediation
- Active financing exception/look-through treatment for CFCs
- Tax incentives for empowerment zones
- Special rules for charitable deductions by corporations and other businesses
- And more

Energy

In 2010, Congress had been expected to pass comprehensive energy legislation including new and enhanced tax incentives. For a number of reasons, an energy bill did not pass. However, the new law extends some energy tax breaks for businesses. The new law also extends, but modifies, a popular energy tax break for individuals.

Businesses. For businesses, one of the most valuable energy incentives is the Code Sec. 1603 cash grant in lieu of a tax credit program. This incentive encourages the development of alternative energy sources, such as wind energy. Other business energy incentives extended by the new law include excise tax and other credits for alternative fuels, percentage depletion for oil and gas from marginal wells, and other targeted incentives.

Individuals. Individuals who made energy efficiency improvements to their homes in 2009 or 2010 are likely familiar with the Code Sec. 25C energy tax credit. This credit rewards individuals who install energy efficient furnaces or add insulation, or make other improvements to reduce energy usage. The new law extends the credit through 2011 but reduces some of its benefits. Although 2010 is soon over, there may still be time to take advantage of the more generous credit. Please contact our office.

Education

The Tax Code includes a number of incentives to encourage individuals to save for education expenses. In 2009, Congress enhanced the Hope education credit and renamed it the American Opportunity Tax Credit (AOTC). Like many other incentives, the AOTC was temporary. The new law extends it for two years, through 2012. Along with the AOTC, the new law also extends:

- Higher education tuition deduction
- Student loan interest deduction
- Exclusion for employer-provided educational assistance
- Enhanced Coverdell education savings accounts
- Special rules for certain scholarships

Estate and gift taxes

The federal estate tax, along with federal gift and generation skipping transfer (GST) taxes, was significantly overhauled in 2001. At that time, Congress set in motion a gradual reduction of the estate tax until abolishing it for 2010. Under budget rules, however, those changes could extend for only 10 years; starting in 2011, the estate tax had been scheduled to revert to its pre-2001 levels of 55 percent and a $1 million exclusion.

Estate tax. The new law revives the estate tax, but with a maximum estate tax rate of 35 percent with a $5 million exclusion. The revived estate tax is in place for decedents dying in 2011 and 2012. The new law gives estates the option to elect to apply the estate tax at the 35 percent/$5 million levels for 2010 or to apply carryover basis for 2010. The new law also allows "portability" between spouses of the maximum exclusion and extends some other taxpayer-friendly provisions originally enacted in 2001.

This far-reaching multi-billion dollar tax package affects almost every taxpayer. Keep in mind that many of its provisions are temporary. It is important to plan early to maximize your tax savings. Please contact our office if you have any questions.

Sincerely yours,

¶27,010 CLIENT LETTER #2

Re: Tax Relief Act of 2010: Fifteen-Year Recovery Period Extended

Dear Client:

The Tax Relief, Unemployment Insurance Reauthorization, and Job Creation Act of 2010 (Tax Relief Act of 2010) allows affected taxpayers an additional two years to take advantage of the reduced recovery period for qualified restaurant property, leasehold improvement property, and retail improvement property. The provisions originally enacted by the American Jobs Creation Act of 2004 for restaurant and leasehold improvement property, and expanded to include retail improvement property by the Emergency Economic Stabilization Act of 2008 are further extended by the Tax Relief Act of 2010 for property placed in service before January 1, 2012.

Because your business reported restaurant, retail or leasehold improvement property in prior years, you may want to note this favorable tax development when planning to acquire qualified restaurant, retail or leasehold property. The specific requirements for qualification of the improvement property for 15-year treatment are somewhat detailed and complex, and we would be happy to assist you in ensuring that your tax benefits from use of such property are maximized.

Please call our office at your earliest convenience to arrange an appointment.

Sincerely yours,

¶27,015 CLIENT LETTER #3

Re: Tax Relief Act of 2010: Employee Payroll Tax Reduction

Dear Client:

The Tax Relief, Unemployment Insurance Reauthorization, and Job Creation Act of 2010 (Tax Relief Act of 2010) provides a "payroll tax holiday" that is estimated to inject over $110 billion into the economy in 2011. This is accomplished by reducing the employee-share of the OASDI portion of Social Security taxes from 6.2 percent to 4.2 percent for wages earned up to the taxable wage base of $106,800 in calendar year 2011. The Medicare component is the same (1.45 percent), for a combined "payroll tax holiday" tax rate of 5.65 percent. The employer's combined tax rate remains unchanged at 7.65 percent.

Self-employed individuals also receive a two-percent reduction (from 12.4 percent to 10.4 percent) on the OASDI portion of self-employment taxes. When combined with the Medicare component of 2.9 percent, the total self-employment tax rate is 13.3 percent on self-employment income up to the same threshold amount.

Under the Tax Relief Act of 2010, self-employed individuals calculate the deduction for employment taxes without regard to the temporary rate reduction (that is, one half of 15.3 percent of self-employment income). An enhanced percentage that represents the employer portion of the deduction allows the self-employed individual to deduct the full amount of the employer portion of self-employment taxes. For any tax year that begins in 2011, the self-employment tax deduction equals the sum of 59.6 percent of the applicable OASDI taxes, plus 50 percent of the applicable Medicare taxes.

Unlike the Making Work Pay credit, which expires after 2010, the two-percent OASDI reduction is available to all wage earners irrespective of income level. Because the payroll rate reduction does not phase out, any individual earning at or above the OASDI cap of $106,800 receives a $2,126 tax benefit in 2011. Individuals who do not pay into Social Security, including some public employees, will not benefit from the payroll tax rate reduction, although they did benefit from the Making Work Pay credit.

However, the IRS has cautioned Congress that it needs time to program its computer systems for any late year legislation. Therefore, you may not see the effects of the payroll tax cut until mid-January of 2011.

The payroll tax holiday is only one provision of this multi-billion dollar tax cut package. We would like to discuss other tax relief provisions that may be available to you. Please call our office at your earliest convenience to arrange an appointment.

Sincerely yours,

¶27,020 CLIENT LETTER #4

Re: Tax Relief Act of 2010: Extension of Alternative Minimum Tax Relief

Dear Client:

As you know, the alternative minimum tax (AMT) is trapping more middle income taxpayers every year. To partially alleviate this tax burden, Congress has been enacting annual "patches" to the AMT to increase exemption amounts and provide other relief. The Tax Relief, Unemployment Insurance Reauthorization, and Job Creation Act of 2010 (Tax Relief Act of 2010) increases the AMT exemption amounts for 2010 to $72,450 for married couples filing jointly and surviving spouses, $47,450 for single taxpayers and heads of households, and $36,225 for married individuals filing separately. For 2011, the exemption amounts are increased to $74,450 for married couples filing jointly and surviving spouses, $48,450 for single taxpayers and heads of households, and $37,225 for married individuals filing separately.

The AMT exemption amounts are phased out at certain income levels, and although the exemption amounts have increased for 2010 and 2011, the threshold levels for calculating the phase-out remain unchanged. However, because the phase-out calculation is affected by the amount of the exemption, an increase in the exemption also increases the maximum amount of alternative minimum taxable income a person can have before the exemption is phased out. The rules requiring married individuals filing separately to increase alternative minimum taxable income for purposes of the phase-out continue to apply.

The Tax Relief Act of 2010 also extends the ability to use your nonrefundable personal credits, including the credit for child and dependent care and similar credits, to offset both regular tax (as reduced by the foreign tax credit) and alternative minimum tax liability for 2010 and 2011. Tax planning strategies can be used to reduce the impact of the AMT. As a general rule, taxpayers subject to the AMT should accelerate income into AMT years and postpone deductions into non-AMT years. We believe that a thorough analysis of your current and projected tax situation could minimize or eliminate your exposure to AMT liability. Please contact our office to make an appointment to discuss this important tax planning opportunity.

Sincerely yours,

¶27,025 CLIENT LETTER #5

Re: Tax Relief Act of 2010: Benefits for Businesses

Dear Client:

Business planning for 2011 and beyond just got more certain with passage of the Tax Relief, Unemployment Insurance Reauthorization and Job Creation Act of 2010 (H.R. 4853). The multi-billion dollar new law extends, renews or enhances a large number of business tax incentives. This letter highlights the key business tax incentives in the new law. As always, please contact our office for more details.

Business spending. During past economic slowdowns, Congress has used bonus depreciation and enhanced Code Sec. 179 small business expensing to help jumpstart business spending. The new law provides for 100 bonus depreciation. The 100 percent bonus depreciation rate applies to qualified property acquired after September 8, 2010 and before January 1, 2012 and placed in service before January 1, 2012 (or before January 1, 2013 for certain longer-lived and transportation property). Additionally, 50 percent bonus depreciation is available for qualified property placed in service in 2012. Moreover, certain corporations may be able to elect to accelerate any alternative minimum tax (AMT) credit in lieu of bonus depreciation.

Along with bonus depreciation, the new law extends enhanced Code Sec. 179 expensing for 2012 but not at the 2010 and 2011 dollar and investment limits. For 2010 and 2011, the Code Sec. 179 dollar limit is $500,000 and the investment limit is $2 million. The new law makes no changes to these limits for 2010 and 2011. However, the dollar limit will fall to $125,000 (indexed for inflation) and the investment limit will fall to $500,000 (indexed for inflation) for tax years beginning in 2012 (and sunsetting after December 31, 2012). The 2012 amounts, while reduced from 2010 and 2011, are still above the amounts that would have been in place for 2012 absent the new law ($25,000/$200,000 respectively).

For 2010 and 2011, special rules apply to qualified real property. Taxpayers can elect up to $250,000 of the $500,000 dollar limit for qualified leasehold improvement property, qualified restaurant property and qualified retail improvement property. The new law does not extend these special rules beyond 2011. The new law does renew a 15-year recovery period for qualified leasehold improvement property, qualified restaurant property and qualified retail improvement property for 2010 and 2011.

Payroll tax cut. The new law reduces an employee's share of Social Security taxes (the OASDI portion) from 6.2 percent to 4.2 percent up to the taxable maximum amount of $106,800 for calendar year 2011. The new law does not reduce the employer's share, which remains at 6.2 percent for 2011. Self-employed individuals, including independent contractors with which a business may contract, are also entitled to a 2 percentage point reduction in payroll taxes, from 12.4 percent to 10.4 percent.

The IRS has instructed employers to start using new withholding tables and reducing the amount of Social Security tax withheld as soon as possible in 2011 but no later than January 31, 2011. The IRS also instructed employers to make any offsetting adjustments in an employee's pay for Social Security over-withheld during January as soon as possible but no later than March 31, 2011.

¶27,025

The new law does not extend payroll tax forgiveness for qualified new hires. This incentive was part of the Hiring Incentives to Restore Employment (HIRE) Act of 2010 and will expire, as scheduled, after 2010. Under the HIRE Act, qualified employers do not have to pay their share of OASDI for a covered employee's employment from the day after March 18, 2010 through December 31, 2010. The HIRE Act also provides for a worker retention credit, which qualified employers may be able to claim if the covered employee works a certain number of weeks and meets other requirements. If you have any questions about the interaction between the HIRE Act and the new law, please contact our office.

Tax brackets. Businesses owners, such as sole proprietors, who are taxed at the individual tax rates will benefit from an extension of reduced individual tax rates. The new law extends for two years (2011 and 2012) the current individual tax rates of 10, 15, 25, 28, 33, and 35 percent). Absent the new law, all of the rates would have risen with the top two rates increasing from 33 and 35 percent to 36 and 39.6 percent respectively.

Estate tax. Under the new law, the federal estate tax will again apply to the estates of decedents dying after December 31, 2009 and before January 1, 2013. The new law sets a maximum estate tax rate of 35 percent with a $5 million exclusion ($10 million for married couples). Additionally, executors of estates of individuals who died in 2010 can elect out of the estate tax (and apply modified carryover basis rules) or can elect to have the estate tax apply.

Research tax credit. In recent years, Congress has come close to making the Code Sec. 41 research tax credit permanent but the cost of a permanent credit has been prohibitive. The new law renews the credit, which expired at the end of 2009, for 2010 and 2011.

Work Opportunity Tax Credit. The Work Opportunity Tax Credit (WOTC) rewards employers that hire economically-disadvantaged individuals and individuals from groups with historically high rates of unemployment. The WOTC was scheduled to expire after August 31, 2011. The new law extends the WOTC through the end of 2011. However, the new law does not extend two groups that were added to the credit in 2009 (unemployed veterans and disconnected youth).

Energy. Recent laws have used the Tax Code to encourage the development and production of alternative fuels, such as energy from wind and biomass. Many of these incentives are temporary. The new law extends, renews or enhances some of the incentives, including:

- Grants for certain alternative energy property in lieu of tax credits
- Tax credits for biodiesel and renewable diesel fuel
- Tax credit for refined coal facilities
- Percentage depletion for oil and gas from marginal wells
- Special tax incentives for builders of energy-efficient homes
- And more

Business tax extenders. A package of business tax incentives, known as extenders because they regularly expire and are regularly extended, is renewed by the new law. They include:

¶27,025

- Differential wage credit
- New Markets Tax Credit (with modifications)
- Brownfields remediation
- Tax treatment of certain dividends of RICs and certain investments of RICs
- Active financing exception/look-through treatment for CFCs
- Tax incentives for empowerment zones and the District of Columbia
- Indian employment credit
- Railroad track maintenance credit
- Mine rescue training credit
- Code Sec. 199 deduction for Puerto Rico
- Five-year write-off of farm machinery
- Accelerated depreciation for business property on an Indian reservation
- And more

What's not included. Despite significant support in Congress, the new law does not repeal a controversial expansion of information reporting. The Patient Protection and Affordable Care Act of 2010 requires businesses to report payments for property and payments to corporations aggregating $600 or more in a calendar year made after December 31, 2011. Congress may revisit this requirement before the effective date. The new law also does not lower the corporate tax rate, another proposal that could be addressed in the future.

The new law extends, renews or enhances a large number of tax incentives targeted to businesses. Please contact our office if you have any questions about the provisions we have discussed or any of the measures in the new law. Our office can help you plan a strategy that maximizes your tax savings.

Sincerely yours,

¶27,030 CLIENT LETTER #6

Re: Tax Relief Act of 2010: Benefits for Individuals

Dear Client:

Many individuals entered 2010 uncertain over the fate of federal tax incentives scheduled to expire at year-end. On December 17, President Obama signed the Tax Relief, Unemployment Insurance Reauthorization and Job Creation Act of 2010 (H.R. 4853) after passage by the Senate on December 15 and the House on December 16. The new law extends, renews or enhances a large number of individual tax incentives, among the most far reaching being reduced individual income tax rates and an across-the board payroll tax cut for 2011. This letter highlights the key individual tax incentives in the new law. As always, please contact our office for more details.

Individual tax rates. Reduced individual tax rates put in place in 2001 were scheduled to expire after 2010. The new law extends the reduced rates for two years. The current rate brackets (10, 15, 25, 28, 33 and 35 percent) remain unchanged for 2011 and 2012. The new law also extends full repeal of the itemized deduction limitation and full repeal of the personal exemption phase-out, both scheduled to expire after 2010, for two years.

The extension of the reduced individual tax rates is significant. If the old rates had returned, the top two rates would have jumped from 33 and 35 percent to 36 and 39.6 percent, respectively. The current 10 percent rate would have disappeared. Additionally, marriage penalty relief in the form of an expanded 15 percent rate bracket would also have expired.

AMT relief. Along with extending these rate cuts, the new law targets relief to taxpayers facing the alternative minimum tax (AMT). Because the AMT is not indexed for inflation, and for other reasons, the tax steadily encroaches on middle income taxpayers. The new law stops this encroachment by giving individuals higher exemption amounts and providing other targeted relief. The reach of the AMT often surprises individuals. While the provisions in the new law are helpful, it is also important to plan strategically for the AMT. Unlike the income tax rates, the higher AMT exemption had already expired at the end of 2009 before the new law stepped in to save it. Its two-year extension, therefore, expires earlier, at the end of 2011.

Payroll tax cut. Social Security is financed through a dedicated payroll tax. Employers and employees each pay 6.2 percent of wages up to the taxable maximum of $106,800 (in 2010 and 2011), while self-employed individuals pay 12.4 percent. Effective for calendar year 2010, the new law reduces the employee-share from 6.2 percent to 4.2 percent up to the taxable maximum. The employer-share remains unchanged. Self-employed individuals will pay 10.4 percent on self-employment income up to the taxable maximum. The reduction has no effect on an individual's future Social Security benefits.

Let's look at an example.

Tyler, who is single, earns $106,800 (the maximum taxable wage). For 2011, the new law reduces Tyler's share of Social Security taxes on his earnings to 4.2 percent. Tyler will see $2,136 in savings for 2011.

The payroll tax cut replaces the Making Work Pay credit, which temporarily reduced income tax withholding in 2009 and 2010. The Making Work Pay credit phased-out for higher-income individuals. The payroll tax cut is across-the-board (up to the taxable maximum of $106,800).

Shortly after the new law was passed, the IRS instructed employers to start reducing the amount of Social Security tax withheld as soon as possible in 2011 but no later than January 31, 2011. For any Social Security tax over-withheld in January, employers should make an offsetting adjustment in an individual's pay no later than March 31, 2011.

The payroll tax cut opens up some tax planning opportunities for individuals. The savings could be contributed to an IRA or another retirement savings vehicle, thereby compounding available tax benefits. The savings also could be used to help fund a Coverdell education savings account. Please contact our office for details.

Capital gains/dividends. In 2003, Congress set new maximum tax rates for qualified capital gains and dividends but, like the individual rate cuts, these taxpayer-friendly rates were temporary. For 2010, the maximum tax rate is 15 percent (zero percent for individuals in the 10 and 15 percent tax brackets). The new law extends these rates for two years, through December 31, 2012. In a related development, the new law extends the temporary 100 percent exclusion of gain on certain small business stock.

Child tax credit. Many individuals enjoy the benefit of the $1,000 per child tax credit. Without the new law, the child tax credit would have dropped to $500 for 2011. The new law extends the $1,000 credit and keeps the refundability threshold at $3,000 for 2011 and 2012. In related developments, the new law also extends some enhancements to the earned income tax credit and the adoption credit for two years.

Estate tax. Under the new law, the federal estate tax will again apply to the estates of decedents dying after December 31, 2009 and before January 1, 2013. The new law sets a maximum estate tax rate of 35 percent with a $5 million exclusion ($10 million for married couples). Additionally, executors of estates of individuals who died in 2010 can elect out of the estate tax (and apply modified carryover basis rules) or can elect to have the estate tax apply. This election, and many of the other estate tax provisions in the new law, is very technical. Besides the estate tax, there are provisions in the new law extending and modifying the federal gift tax and the federal generation skipping transfer (GST) tax. Please contact our office so we can discuss how these changes will affect your estate planning.

Education. A variety of tax incentives are available to help save for and finance education costs. Like so many incentives, they are temporary. The new law extends some of the most popular education tax incentives. They include:

- American Opportunity Tax Credit
- Higher education tuition deduction
- Student loan interest deduction
- Exclusion for employer-provided educational assistance
- Enhancements to Coverdell education savings accounts
- Special rules for certain scholarships

The education incentives in the Tax Code are among the most complex. Often, taxpayers will mistakenly believe they cannot claim more than one or they may inadvertently claim ones they should not. Our office can help you sort through the complexity of the federal education tax incentives.

Energy. Individuals who made some energy-efficient improvements in 2009 or 2010 may have benefitted from a special tax break. This tax incentive rewarded individuals who installed energy-efficient windows, doors, furnaces, and other items in their homes. The credit, while very valuable, was also very complex. The new law extends the credit but also adds to the complexity by reinstating rules for the credit in place before 2009. The complexity is certain to confuse taxpayers. Please contact our office if you are planning to install new windows, doors, heating or cooling systems, or other energy-efficient items so you do not miss out on this tax break.

More incentives. The new law extends many valuable but temporary tax incentives for individuals. They include the state and local sales tax deduction, the teacher's classroom expense deduction, and special rules for individuals who contribute IRA proceeds to charity. Keep in mind that not all of the expired temporary individual tax incentives were extended. Among the incentives not extended are the additional standard deduction for real property taxes, the $2,400 exclusion for unemployment benefits, the first-time homebuyer tax credit, COBRA premium assistance, and some others. If you have any questions about which incentives were extended, please contact our office.

The new law provides many options for tax planning for 2011, 2012 and beyond. Please contact our office and we can discuss how you can maximize your tax savings.

Sincerely yours,

¶27,035 CLIENT LETTER #7

Re: Tax Relief Act of 2010: Bonus Depreciation and Code Sec. 179 Expense Deduction

Dear Client:

To encourage economic stimulus and job creation, Congress has enacted the Tax Relief, Unemployment Insurance Reauthorization, and Job Creation Act of 2010 (Tax Relief Act of 2010). The Tax Relief Act of 2010 provides significantly increased incentives for business investment in capital and equipment, including a temporary extension of bonus depreciation, a bonus depreciation allowance of 100 percent of the cost of qualified property placed in service after September 8, 2010 and before January 1, 2012, and temporary increases in the deductible amount and investment limitation under Code Sec. 179 for tax years beginning in 2012.

The Tax Relief Act of 2010 extends the 50-percent first-year bonus depreciation allowance for two years to apply to qualifying property in service in the tax year through 2012 (through 2013 for certain longer-lived and transportation property). In addition, the provision expands the first-year bonus depreciation deduction to 100 percent of the cost of qualified property placed in service after September 8, 2010 and before January 1, 2012 (before January 1, 2013 for certain longer-lived and transportation property).

Under the extension provisions, a corporation also is permitted to increase the minimum tax credit limitation by the bonus depreciation amount with respect to certain property placed in service after December 31, 2010 and before January 1, 2013 (January 1, 2014 in the case of longer-lived and transportation property).

In addition to the bonus depreciation changes, the Tax Relief Act of 2010 increases the deduction and investment limits under Code Sec. 179. Generally, Code Sec. 179 permits a business that satisfies limitations on annual investment to elect to deduct (or "expense") the cost of qualifying property rather than depreciate the cost over time. For tax years beginning in 2010 and 2011, taxpayers are permitted to expense up to $500,000 of the cost of qualifying property under Code Sec. 179, reduced by the amount by which the qualified investment exceeds $2,000,000. Qualifying property includes depreciable tangible personal property purchased for use in the active conduct of a trade or business. However, after 2011, the expense deduction limit of $500,000 was set to drop to $25,000. Similarly, the phase-out amount was scheduled to be reduced to $200,000.

To address this concern, the Tax Relief Act of 2010 increased the maximum amount a taxpayer may expense under Code Sec. 179 for tax years beginning in 2012 to $125,000 of the cost of qualifying property placed in service in the tax year, reduced, but not below zero, by the amount by which the cost of qualifying property placed in service in the tax year exceeds $500,000. These amounts are to be indexed for inflation. However, for tax years beginning in 2013 and thereafter, the maximum expense deduction permitted drops to $25,000 of the cost of qualifying property placed in service for the taxable year, with a maximum phase-out limit of $200,000, not indexed for inflation.

The incentives for investing in business property in 2011 and 2012 are significant. Because these provisions are temporary and generally apply only to tax years

¶27,035

beginning in 2011 and 2012, new purchases should be made and placed in service accordingly.

If you have any questions about how this development applies to you, or about any other aspects of this legislation, please contact our office at your convenience.

Sincerely yours,

¶27,040 CLIENT LETTER #8

Re: Tax Relief Act of 2010: Deduction for Educator Expenses

Dear Client:

The deduction for educator expenses, which was set to expire on December 31, 2009, is extended through December 31, 2011 by the Tax Relief, Unemployment Insurance Reauthorization, and Job Creation Act of 2010 (Tax Relief Act of 2010). This popular deduction recognizes that many education professionals purchase classroom supplies with their own money, and allows them to deduct up to $250 of certain out-of-pocket classroom expenses from gross income. Married taxpayers who file joint returns are entitled to a maximum deduction of $500, if both spouses are eligible educators and incur qualified expenses.

Instructors, counselors, principals, and classroom aides, as well as teachers, who work at least 900 hours during the school year, are eligible to take the deduction. However, qualifying individuals must work in a kindergarten, elementary, or secondary school through grade 12. Consequently, expenses for home-schooling do not qualify for the educator expense deduction.

The $250 deduction can be taken for items purchased at any time during the year. Teachers who have not spent $250 by the end of a year should consider pre-buying supplies for the following year, since any unused portion of the deduction cannot be carried over. Year-end purchases made while school is out for the holidays qualify even if the supplies are not used until the following year.

Classroom supplies, such as paper and pens, glue, and scissors qualify, as well as purchases of books and computer equipment, including software. For courses in health and physical education, the supplies must relate to athletics. The IRS has advised teachers and other educators to save their receipts and keep records of their expenses in a folder or envelope noting the date, amount, and purpose of the purchase.

If you have expenses exceeding $250 or have purchased non-classroom supplies, you may still take an employment-related miscellaneous itemized deduction subject to the two-percent floor.

We would be happy to answer any questions concerning your classroom related expenses, including the requirements for deducting any excess amounts over $250. Please contact us at your earliest convenience to arrange an appointment.

Sincerely yours,

¶27,045 CLIENT LETTER #9

Re: Tax Relief Act of 2010: Extension of Research Credit

Dear Client:

The Tax Relief, Unemployment Insurance Reauthorization, and Job Creation Act of 2010 (Tax Relief Act of 2010) extends the research credit to apply to any amounts paid or incurred for qualified research and experimentation before January 1, 2012. The 2008 Stabilization Act, which previously extended the research credit through December 31, 2009, also increased the rates used to compute the credit using the alternative simplified method from 12 to 14 percent, and repealed the alternative incremental research method for tax years ending after December 31, 2008. These modifications remain intact with the Tax Relief Act of 2010's two-year extension of the research credit.

The research credit was provided to encourage taxpayers to increase their research expenditures. The credit applies to incremental increases in qualified research expenses paid or incurred by a business, to increases in basic research payments made by a business to universities and certain other qualified organizations, and to payments made or incurred by a business to an energy research consortium. The research credit is the sum of the following three components:

1. The incremental research credit, unless an election is made to use the alternative simplified credit method;
2. The basic research payment credit, which is equal to 20 percent of allowable basic research payments made to universities and certain nonprofit scientific organizations; and
3. A credit equal to 20 percent of qualifying energy research consortium payments made or incurred after August 8, 2005.

The incremental research credit is equal to the sum of 20 percent of the excess of qualified research expenses (QREs) for the tax year over the average annual QREs paid in a base year, plus 20 percent of the basic research payments made to qualified organizations to perform basic research.

The alternative simplified research credit equals 14 percent of the amount by which the qualified research expenses exceed 50 percent of the average qualified research expenses for the three preceding tax years. However, if you don't have qualified research expenses in any of the preceding three tax years, then the credit is equal to six percent of the qualified research expenses for the current tax year. The election to use the alternative simplified method remains in effect for all succeeding tax years unless revoked with the consent of the IRS.

In order to claim the credit, the research must be undertaken for the purpose of discovering information that is technological in nature which can be applied to develop a new or improved component for your business. Substantially all of the research activities involved in the experimentation process must be related to the new or improved function, performance, reliability or quality of the business component.

If you are interested in claiming the research credit, we would like to discuss these requirements with you in greater detail. Please contact us at your earliest convenience to arrange an appointment.

Sincerely yours,

Topical Index

References are to paragraph (¶) numbers

A

Accumulated earnings tax
. tax rate . . . 603

Adoption
. credit against tax
. . dollar limitation . . . 370
. employer-provided assistance programs
. . income exclusion . . . 370

Alaska Native Settlement Trusts
. special rules . . . 612

Alcohol fuels credit . . . 546

Alternative fuel vehicle refueling property credit . . . 548

Alternative fuels credit . . . 544

Alternative minimum tax
. bonus depreciation . . . 502
. . accelerated credit in lieu of deduction . . . 504
. capital gains . . . 405
. child tax credit . . . 360
. dividends . . . 420
. earned income credit . . . 355
. exemption amounts . . . 375
. nonrefundable personal credits . . . 376
. prior year minimum credit
. . accelerated credit in lieu of deduction . . . 504
. small business stock, exclusion of gain on sale . . . 415

American opportunity credit
. modification of Hope credit . . . 371

American Samoa economic development credit . . . 536

Automobiles
. bonus depreciation . . . 502

B

Basis
. carryover basis, property acquired from decedent . . . 740; 760

Biodiesel fuels credit . . . 544

Bonds
. DC enterprise zone . . . 445
. empowerment zone . . . 440
. Gulf Opportunity Zone . . . 450
. Hurricane Ike disaster area . . . 450
. Midwestern disaster area . . . 450
. New York Liberty Zone . . . 470
. public educational facilities . . . 460
. small issuer exception, arbitrage rebate . . . 455
. zone academy bonds . . . 465

Bonus depreciation
. alternative minimum tax . . . 502
. Gulf Opportunity Zone . . . 450
. increased allowance . . . 502
. luxury car depreciation cap . . . 502
. prior year minimum credit
. . accelerated credit in lieu of deduction . . . 504

Brownfields remediation costs . . . 518

C

Capital gains
. alternative minimum tax . . . 405
. collapsible corporation stock . . . 609
. DC enterprise zone assets
. . zero-percent rate . . . 445
. nonqualified withdrawals of construction funds
. . Merchant Marine Act . . . 405
. principal residence of decedent
. . exclusion of gain on sale . . . 750
. qualified dividends
. . pass-through treatment . . . 425
. . tax rates . . . 420
. rollover, empowerment zone . . . 440
. tax rates . . . 405
. . five-year holding period . . . 410
. U.S. real property interests
. . disposition, withholding of tax . . . 405

Charitable contributions
. book inventory donations, corporations . . . 563
. computer technology and equipment, corporations . . . 566
. food inventory . . . 560
. IRA distributions . . . 352
. real property, conservation purposes . . . 353
. S corporations, basis adjustment . . . 557

Child care
. child and dependent care credit . . . 365
. employer-provided child care credit . . . 522

Child tax credit
. alternative minimum tax offset . . . 360
. amount of credit . . . 360
. refundability of credit . . . 360

Coal production facilities . . . 550

Code Sec. 306 stock . . . 420

Collapsible corporations . . . 609

Computer software
. expensing election . . . 506

Conservation easements
. contribution date . . . 735
. distance requirements . . . 735

Controlled foreign corporations (CFCs)
. related CFC payments
. . look-through treatment . . . 629
. subpart F income exceptions
. . active financing income . . . 623
. . insurance income . . . 626

Corporations
. accumulated earnings tax . . . 603
. charitable contributions
. . book inventory . . . 563
. . computer technology and equipment . . . 566
. . food inventory . . . 560
. collapsible corporation rules . . . 609

Coverdell education savings accounts . . . 330

Credits against tax
. adoption credit . . . 370
. alcohol fuels credit . . . 546

CRE

Credits against tax—continued
. alternative fuel vehicle refueling property credit . . .
  548
. alternative fuels credit . . . 544
. alternative minimum tax
. . accelerated credit election . . . 504
. American opportunity credit
. . modification of Hope credit . . . 371
. American Samoa economic development credit . . .
  536
. biodiesel fuels credit . . . 544
. child and dependent care credit . . . 365
. child tax credit . . . 360
. DC enterprise zone employment credit . . . 445
. DC first-time homebuyer credit . . . 445
. earned income credit . . . 355; 356
. employer-provided child care credit . . . 522
. empowerment zone employment credit . . . 440
. energy credit
. . grants in lieu of credit . . . 540
. energy efficient appliance credit . . . 542
. Hope credit
. . modification . . . 371
. Indian employment credit . . . 530
. military differential wage payments, employer
  credit . . . 526
. mine rescue team training credit . . . 534
. new markets tax credit . . . 528
. railroad track maintenance credit . . . 532
. renewable diesel fuels credit . . . 544
. renewable electricity production credit
. . grants in lieu of credit . . . 540
. . refined coal facilities . . . 550
. research credit . . . 520
. residential energy property credit . . . 372
. state death tax credit . . . 725
. work opportunity credit . . . 524
. zone academy bonds . . . 465

D

Depletion
. marginal production properties
. . suspension of percentage depletion limitation . . .
  552
Depreciation
. bonus depreciation
. . Gulf Opportunity Zone . . . 450
. . increased allowance . . . 502
. . luxury car depreciation cap . . . 502
. . prior year minimum credit, accelerated credit in lieu
  of deduction . . . 504
. motorsports entertainment complexes . . . 510
. qualified Indian reservation property . . . 512
. qualified leasehold improvement property . . . 508
. qualified restaurant property . . . 508
. qualified retail improvement property . . . 508
Differential military pay, employer credit . . . 526
District of Columbia
. enterprise zone employment credit . . . 445
. first-time homebuyer credit . . . 445
Dividends
. extraordinary dividends . . . 420
. qualified dividends
. . Code Sec. 306 stock . . . 420
. . foreign corporations . . . 420
. . pass-through treatment . . . 425
. . tax rates . . . 420

Dividends—continued
. regulated investment companies
. . allocation requirements . . . 809
. . capital gains dividends . . . 809
. . deficiency dividends . . . 839
. . dividends paid deduction . . . 827
. . exempt-interest dividends . . . 815; 833
. . preferential dividends . . . 827
. . reporting requirements . . . 809
. . spillover dividends . . . 818
. unrecaptured section 1250 gain . . . 420
Domestic production activities deduction
. Puerto Rico . . . 632

E

Earned income credit . . . 355; 356
Education
. American opportunity credit . . . 371
. Coverdell education savings accounts . . . 330
. employer-provided educational assistance plans . . .
  335
. Hope credit . . . 371
. scholarships, federal service requirements . . . 340
. student loans, interest deduction . . . 345
. tax-exempt bonds
. . public school construction, rebate exception . . . 455
. . qualified public educational facilities . . . 460
. teachers' classroom expenses . . . 327
. tuition and fees deduction . . . 350
Electric energy
. renewable electricity production credit
. . grants in lieu of credit . . . 540
Electric utility companies
. electric transmission property, sales or
  dispositions . . . 554
Employers
. adoption assistance programs . . . 370
. child care facilities and services . . . 522
. DC enterprise zone employment credit . . . 445
. educational assistance plans . . . 335
. empowerment zone employment credit . . . 440
. military differential wage payments, credit . . . 526
Empowerment zones . . . 440
Energy credit
. grants in lieu of credit . . . 540
Energy efficient appliance credit . . . 542
Energy incentives
. alternative fuel vehicle refueling property credit . . .
  548
. alternative fuels credit . . . 544
. biodiesel fuels credit . . . 544
. energy credit
. . grants in lieu of credit . . . 540
. energy efficient appliance credit . . . 542
. new energy efficient homes credit . . . 538
. renewable diesel fuels credit . . . 544
. renewable electricity production credit
. . grants in lieu of credit . . . 540
. . refined coal facilities . . . 550
Environmental remediation costs . . . 518
Estate tax
. applicable exclusion amount . . . 715
. . unused portion, predeceased spouse . . . 718

Estate tax—continued
. carryover basis . . . 740; 760
. . reporting requirements . . . 745
. conservation easements
. . contribution date and distance requirements . . . 735
. decedents dying in 2010, special election . . . 705; 740
. five-percent surtax . . . 710
. installment payments
. . closely held business interest . . . 785
. . lending and finance business interest . . . 790
. . nonreadily tradable holding company stock . . . 795
. pecuniary bequests
. . limitation on recognition of gain . . . 755
. qualified family-owned business interest . . . 720
. reinstatement of tax . . . 705
. returns, extension of time to file . . . 705
. sale of principal residence . . . 750
. state death tax credit . . . 725
. state death tax deduction . . . 730
. stepped-up basis . . . 740; 760
. tax rates . . . 710

Excise taxes
. alcohol fuels credit . . . 546
. alternative fuels credit . . . 544
. biodiesel fuels credit . . . 544
. regulated investment companies
. . capital gain net income distribution . . . 836
. . distributed amount determination . . . 836
. . exempt entity ownership exemption . . . 836
. . gain and loss deferral . . . 836
. renewable diesel fuels credit . . . 544
. rum, cover over amount . . . 635

Exempt organizations
. unrelated business income, payments from controlled entities . . . 615

Exemptions
. personal exemptions, phaseout for high-income taxpayers . . . 325

F

Film and television production
. expensing election . . . 514

Foreign corporations
. RIC dividend payments
. . exemption from withholding . . . 430
. stock dividends . . . 420

Foreign investment in U.S. real property (FIRPTA)
. qualified investment entity, regulated investment companies . . . 620

Foreign tax credit
. dividend income, tax rate differential . . . 420

Fringe benefits
. adoption assistance programs . . . 370
. educational assistance plans . . . 335
. van pools and transit passes . . . 380

Fuels
. alcohol fuels credit . . . 546
. alternative fuels credit . . . 544
. biodiesel fuels credit . . . 544
. renewable diesel fuels credit . . . 544

G

Generation-skipping transfer tax
. applicable rate . . . 710

Generation-skipping transfer tax—continued
. exemption
. . allocation, late election . . . 780
. . allocation, substantial compliance . . . 780
. . allocation, unused portion . . . 765
. . increased amount . . . 715
. inclusion ratio, valuation rules . . . 775
. qualified severance of trust . . . 770
. reinstatement of tax . . . 705
. returns, extension of time to file . . . 705

Gift tax
. applicable exclusion amount, increase . . . 715
. five-percent surtax . . . 710
. tax rates . . . 710

Government assistance programs
. eligibility, tax refunds disregarded . . . 384

Gulf Opportunity Zone
. bonus depreciation . . . 450
. low-income housing credit . . . 450
. rehabilitation credit . . . 450
. tax-exempt bonds . . . 450

H

Health and accident plans
. premium assistance credit . . . 373

Hope credit
. modification . . . 371

Hurricane Ike disaster area
. private activity bonds . . . 450

I

Income tax rates—see Tax rates

Indian employment credit . . . 530

Indian reservation property
. MACRS recovery periods . . . 512

Indian trust accounts
. litigation settlement payments . . . 388

Individual retirement accounts (IRAs)
. distributions, charitable contributions . . . 352

Investment tax credit
. energy credit
. . grants in lieu of credit . . . 540

Itemized deductions
. limitation for high-income taxpayers . . . 320
. sales taxes, election to deduct . . . 326

L

Leasehold improvement property
. 15-year MACRS recovery period . . . 508

Losses
. regulated investment companies
. . late-year losses . . . 830
. . loss carryover . . . 803
. . net capital loss treatment . . . 812

Low-income housing credit
. Gulf Opportunity Zone . . . 450

M

Marriage penalty
. joint filers, 15-percent bracket . . . 310
. standard deduction . . . 315

Midwestern disaster area
. private activity bonds . . . 450

Military personnel
. active duty reservists and national guardsmen
. . differential wages, employer credit . . . 526

Mine rescue team training credit . . . 534

Mine safety equipment
. expensing election . . . 516

Modified Accelerated Cost Recovery System (MACRS)
. bonus depreciation
. . Gulf Opportunity Zone . . . 450
. . increased allowance . . . 502
. . prior year minimum credit, accelerated credit in lieu of deduction . . . 504
. motorsports entertainment complexes . . . 510
. qualified Indian reservation property . . . 512
. qualified leasehold improvement property . . . 508
. qualified restaurant property . . . 508
. qualified retail improvement property . . . 508

Mortgage insurance premiums
. deduction . . . 328

Motorsports entertainment complexes
. seven-year MACRS recovery period . . . 510

Mutual funds—see Regulated investment companies (RICs)

N

New energy efficient homes credit . . . 538

New markets tax credit . . . 528

New York Liberty Zone
. bond authorization . . . 470

Nonresident aliens
. RIC dividend payments, withholding . . . 430
. RIC stock, estate tax treatment . . . 386

O

Oil and gas
. marginal production properties
. . suspension of percentage depletion limitation . . . 552

P

Partnerships
. qualified dividend income . . . 425

Payroll tax
. reduction for 2011 . . . 312

Pecuniary bequests
. appreciated property
. . limitation on recognition of gain . . . 755

Percentage depletion
. marginal production properties
. . income limitation suspension . . . 552

Personal exemptions
. phaseout for high-income taxpayers . . . 325

Personal holding companies
. tax rate . . . 606

Possessions of the U.S.
. American Samoa, economic development credit . . . 536
. Virgin Islands, rum excise taxes . . . 635

Premium assistance credit
. advance payments . . . 373

Prior year minimum credit
. accelerated credit election . . . 504

Puerto Rico
. domestic production activities deduction . . . 632
. rum excise taxes, cover over amount . . . 635

Q

Qualified dividends
. capital gains tax rates . . . 420
. pass-through entities . . . 425

Qualified family-owned business interest
. estate tax, deduction . . . 720

Qualified leasehold improvement property
. 15-year MACRS recovery period . . . 508

Qualified restaurant property
. 15-year MACRS recovery period . . . 508

Qualified retail improvement property
. 15-year MACRS recovery period . . . 508

Qualified zone academy bonds . . . 465

R

Railroad Retirement Tax Act
. Tier 1 taxes, reduction for 2011 . . . 312

Railroad track maintenance credit
. qualified expenditures . . . 532

Real estate investment trusts (REITs)
. qualified dividend income . . . 425

Refunds of tax
. disregarded for government assistance eligibility . . . 384

Regulated investment companies (RICs)
. asset test . . . 806
. basis, deferral of sales load . . . 842
. capital gains dividends
. . allocation requirements . . . 809
. . reporting requirements . . . 809
. capital loss, carryover . . . 803
. deficiency dividends
. . deduction penalty, repeal . . . 839
. distributions
. . dividend allocation requirements . . . 809
. . reporting requirements . . . 809
. . return of capital, allocation requirements . . . 821
. . stock redemption . . . 824
. dividends
. . allocation requirements . . . 809
. . capital gains dividends . . . 809
. . deficiency dividend deduction, penalty repeal . . . 839
. . dividends paid deduction . . . 827
. . exempt-interest dividends . . . 815
. . exempt-interest dividends, holding period exception . . . 833
. . foreign persons, withholding . . . 430
. . preferential dividends . . . 827
. . qualified dividends, pass-through treatment . . . 425
. . reporting requirements . . . 809
. . spillover dividends . . . 818
. earnings and profits, capital loss treatment . . . 812
. excise taxes
. . capital gain net income distribution . . . 836

Regulated investment companies (RICs)—continued
. excise taxes—continued
. . distributed amount determination . . . 836
. . exempt entity ownership exemption . . . 836
. . gain and loss deferral . . . 836
. exempt-interest dividends
. . allocation requirements . . . 809
. . holding period exception . . . 833
. . pass-through distributions . . . 815
. . reporting requirements . . . 809
. foreign persons, distributions
. . allocation requirements . . . 809
. . reporting requirements . . . 809
. foreign tax credits
. . allocation requirements . . . 809
. . pass-through distributions . . . 815
. . reporting requirements . . . 809
. gross income test . . . 806
. late-year losses, deferral . . . 830
. losses
. . capital loss carryover . . . 803
. . late-year losses, deferral . . . 830
. . net capital loss treatment . . . 812
. penalties
. . deficiency dividend deduction, repeal . . . 839
. preferential dividends
. . dividends paid deduction . . . 827
. return of capital, allocation requirements . . . 821
. sales load, basis deferral . . . 842
. spillover dividends, distribution requirements . . . 818
. stock
. . nonresident noncitizens, estate tax treatment . . . 386
. . stock redemption . . . 824
. . U.S. real property holding companies . . . 620
Rehabilitation credit
. Gulf Opportunity Zone . . . 450
Renewable diesel fuels credit . . . 544
Renewable electricity production credit
. grants in lieu of credit . . . 540
. refined coal facilities . . . 550
Reporting requirements
. Alaska Native Settlement Trusts . . . 612
. carryover basis . . . 745
. estate tax
. . extension of time to file . . . 705
. generation-skipping transfer tax
. . extension of time to file . . . 705
. regulated investment companies . . . 809
Research credit . . . 520
Residential energy property credit . . . 372
Residential property
. mortgage insurance premiums . . . 328
. new energy efficient homes credit . . . 538
Restaurants
. qualified restaurant property, 15-year MACRS recovery period . . . 508
Retail businesses
. qualified retail improvement property, 15-year MACRS recovery period . . . 508
Rum
. excise taxes, cover over amounts . . . 635

S

S corporations
. charitable contributions, basis adjustment . . . 557

S corporations—continued
. qualified dividend income . . . 425
Sales taxes
. election to deduct . . . 326
Scholarships
. federal service requirements . . . 340
Sec. 179 deduction
. computer software . . . 506
. DC enterprise zone . . . 445
. election . . . 506
. empowerment zone . . . 440
. increased limits . . . 506
Self-employment tax
. reduction for 2011 . . . 312
Small business stock
. exclusion of gain . . . 418
. . alternative minimum tax . . . 415
. . empowerment zone . . . 440
Social security taxes
. withholding, reduction for 2011 . . . 312
Standard deduction
. married taxpayers . . . 315
State and local taxes
. sales taxes, election to deduct . . . 326
State death taxes
. deduction . . . 730
. tax credit . . . 725
Student loans
. interest deduction, phaseout . . . 345
Subpart F income
. active financing income exceptions . . . 623
. insurance income exceptions . . . 626
. related CFC payments, look-through treatment . . . 629
Surviving spouse
. estate tax, unused applicable exclusion amount . . . 718

T

Tax credits—see Credits against tax
Tax rates
. 15-percent bracket . . . 310
. accumulated earnings tax . . . 603
. capital gains . . . 405
. . five-year holding period . . . 410
. estate tax . . . 710
. generation-skipping transfer tax . . . 710
. gift tax . . . 710
. income tax . . . 305
. personal holding companies . . . 606
. qualified dividends . . . 420
Teachers' classroom expense deduction . . . 327
Transit passes, fringe benefit . . . 380
Tuition and fees deduction . . . 350

U

Unemployment compensation
. erroneous payment, refund offsets . . . 382
U.S. real property interests
. disposition, withholding of tax . . . 405
Unrelated business income
. controlled entity payments, exclusion . . . 615

UNR

References are to paragraph (¶) numbers

V

Van pools, fringe benefit . . . 380
Virgin Islands
. rum excise taxes, cover over amount . . . 635

W

Withholding of tax
. payroll taxes
. . reduction for 2011 . . . 312

Withholding of tax—continued
. RIC dividend payments
. . foreign corporations . . . 430
. . nonresident aliens . . . 430

Work opportunity credit . . . 524

Z

Zone academy bonds . . . 465